Success in Accounting is just a click away…

With *WileyPLUS*, students and instructors will experience success in the classroom.

When students succeed—when they stay on-task and make the breakthrough that turns confusion into confidence—they are empowered to realize the possibilities for greatness that lies within each of them. Our goal is to create an environment where students reach their full potential and experience the exhilaration of academic success that will last them a lifetime. *WileyPLUS* can help you reach that goal.

Wiley**PLUS** is an online suite of resources—including the complete text—that will help any student:

- come to class better prepared for lectures
- get immediate feedback and context-sensitive help on assignments and quizzes
- track progress throughout the course

"I just wanted to say how much this program helped me in studying… I was able to actually see my mistakes and correct them. … I really think that other students should have the chance to use *WileyPLUS*."

Ashlee Krisko, *Oakland University*

www.wiley.com/college/wileyplus

80% of students surveyed said it improved their understanding of the material.*

* Based on a spring 2005 survey of 972 student users of *WileyPLUS*

WileyPLUS is built around the activities you perform

Prepare & Present

Create outstanding class presentations using a wealth of resources, such as PowerPoint™ slides, interactive simulations, and more. Plus you can easily upload any materials you have created into your course, and combine them with the resources Wiley provides you with.

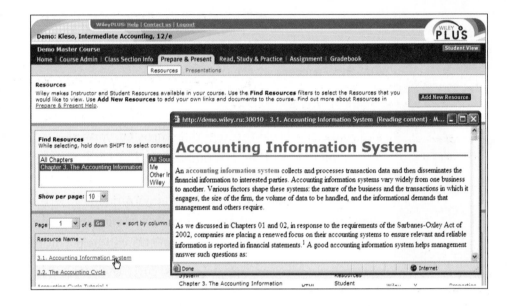

Create Assignments

Automate the assigning and grading of homework or quizzes by using the provided question banks, or by writing your own. Student results will be automatically graded and recorded in your gradebook. *WileyPLUS* also links homework problems to relevant sections of the online text, hints, or solutions—context-sensitive help where students need it most!

Track Student Progress

Keep track of your students' progress via an instructor's gradebook, which allows you to analyze individual and overall class results. This gives you an accurate and realistic assessment of your students' progress and level of understanding.

Now Available with WebCT and Blackboard!

Now you can seamlessly integrate all of the rich content and resources available with *WileyPLUS* with the power and convenience of your WebCT or BlackBoard course. You and your students get the best of both worlds with single sign-on, an integrated gradebook, list of assignments and roster, and more. If your campus is using another course management system, contact your local Wiley Representative.

"I studied more for this class than I would have without *WileyPLUS*."

Melissa Lawler, *Western Washington Univ.*

For more information on what *WileyPLUS* can do to help your students reach their potential, please visit

www.wiley.com/college/wileyplus

76% of students surveyed said it made them better prepared for tests.*

TO THE STUDENT

You have the potential to make a difference!

WileyPLUS is a powerful online system packed with features to help you make the most of your potential, and get the best grade you can!

With Wiley**PLUS** you get:

A complete online version of your text and other study resources

Study more effectively and get instant feedback when you practice on your own. Resources like self-assessment quizzes, tutorials, and animations bring the subject matter to life, and help you master the material.

Problem-solving help, instant grading, and feedback on your homework and quizzes

You can keep all of your assigned work in one location, making it easy for you to stay on task. Plus, many homework problems contain direct links to the relevant portion of your text to help you deal with problem-solving obstacles at the moment they come up.

The ability to track your progress and grades throughout the term.

A personal gradebook allows you to monitor your results from past assignments at any time. You'll always know exactly where you stand.

If your instructor uses *WileyPLUS*, you will receive a URL for your class. If not, your instructor can get more information about *WileyPLUS* by visiting www.wiley.com/college/wileyplus

"It has been a great help, and I believe it has helped me to achieve a better grade."

Michael Morris, *Columbia Basin College*

69% of students surveyed said it helped them get a better grade.*

*Based on a spring 2005 survey of 972 student users of *WileyPLUS*

TWELFTH EDITION

INTERMEDIATE ACCOUNTING

Volume 1

TWELFTH EDITION

INTERMEDIATE ACCOUNTING

Volume 1

DONALD E. KIESO PH.D., C.P.A.
KPMG Peat Marwick Emeritus Professor of Accounting
Northern Illinois University
DeKalb, Illinois

JERRY J. WEYGANDT PH.D., C.P.A.
Arthur Andersen Alumni Professor of Accounting
University of Wisconsin
Madison, Wisconsin

TERRY D. WARFIELD PH.D.
Associate Professor
University of Wisconsin
Madison, Wisconsin

WILEY

John Wiley & Sons

Dedicated to our wives, Donna, Enid, and Mary, for their love, support, and encouragement

PUBLISHER	Susan Elbe
EXECUTIVE EDITOR	Christopher DeJohn
SENIOR ACQUISITIONS EDITOR	Mark Bonadeo
ASSISTANT EDITOR	Brian Kamins
DEVELOPMENT EDITOR	Ann Torbert
PRODUCTION SERVICES MANAGER	Jeanine Furino
SENIOR MARKETING MANAGER	Amy Scholz
CREATIVE DIRECTOR	Harry Nolan
TEXT DESIGNER	Nancy Fields
PRODUCTION SERVICES MANAGEMENT	Ingrao Associates
SENIOR ILLUSTRATION EDITOR	Anna Melhorn
SENIOR MEDIA EDITOR	Allie Morris
PROJECT EDITOR	Ed Brislin
EDITORIAL ASSISTANT	Alison Stanley
MARKETING ASSISTANT	Vanessa Ahrens
PRODUCTION ASSISTANT	Andrea Juda
COVER PHOTO	© Jan Stromme/Lonely Planet Images/Getty Images, Inc.
Cover Design	Howard Grossman

This book was set in Palatino by Techbooks and printed and bound by Von Hoffmann. The cover was printed by Lehigh Press.

This book is printed on acid free paper. ∞

To order books or for customer service, please call 1-800-CALL WILEY (225-5945).

Material from the Uniform CPA Examinations and Unofficial Answers, copyright © 1965, 1966, 1967, 1968, 1969, 1970, 1971, 1972, 1973, 1974, 1975, 1976, 1977, 1978, 1979, 1980, 1981, 1982, 1983, 1984, 1985, 1986, 1987, 1988, 1990, 1991, 1992, and 1993 by the American Institute of Certified Public Accountants, Inc., is adapted with permission.

This book contains quotations from *Accounting Research Bulletins, Accounting Principles Board Opinions, Accounting Principles Board Statements, Accounting Interpretations,* and *Accounting Terminology Bulletins,* copyright © 1953, 1956, 1966, 1968, 1969, 1970, 1971, 1972, 1973, 1974, 1975, 1976, 1977, 1978, 1979, 1980, 1981, 1982 by the American Institute of Certified Public Accountants, Inc., 1211 Avenue of the Americas, New York, NY 10036.

This book contains citations from various FASB pronouncements. Copyright © by Financial Accounting Standards Board, 401 Merritt 7, P.O. Box 5116, Norwalk, CT 06856 U.S.A. Reprinted with permission. Copies of complete documents are available from Financial Accounting Standards Board.

Material from the Certificate in Management Accounting Examinations, copyright © 1975, 1976, 1977, 1978, 1979, 1980, 1981, 1982, 1983, 1984, 1985, 1986, 1987, 1988, 1989, 1990, 1991, 1992, and 1993 by the Institute of Certified Management Accountants, 10 Paragon Drive, Montvale, NJ 07645, is adapted with permission.

Material from the Certified Internal Auditor Examinations, copyright © May 1984, November 1984, May 1986 by The Institute of Internal Auditors, 249 Maitland Ave., Altemonte Springs, FL 32701, is adapted with permission.

The financial statements and accompanying notes reprinted from the 2004 Annual Report of Procter & Gamble Company are courtesy of P&G, copyright © 2004, all rights reserved.

ISBN-13 978-0-471-77192-0
ISBN-10 0-471-77192-9

Printed in the United States of America

10 9 8 7 6 5 4 3 2

ABOUT THE AUTHORS

Donald E. Kieso, Ph.D., C.P.A., received his bachelor's degree from Aurora University and his doctorate in accounting from the University of Illinois. He has served as chairman of the Department of Accountancy and is currently the KPMG Peat Marwick Emeritus Professor of Accounting at Northern Illinois University. He has public accounting experience with Price Waterhouse & Co. (San Francisco and Chicago) and Arthur Andersen & Co. (Chicago) and research experience with the Research Division of the American Institute of Certified Public Accountants (New York). He has done postdoctorate work as a Visiting Scholar at the University of California at Berkeley and is a recipient of NIU's Teaching Excellence Award and four Golden Apple Teaching Awards. Professor Kieso is the author of other accounting and business books and is a member of the American Accounting Association, the American Institute of Certified Public Accountants, and the Illinois CPA Society. He has served as a member of the Board of Directors of the Illinois CPA Society, the AACSB's Accounting Accreditation Committees, the State of Illinois Comptroller's Commission, as Secretary-Treasurer of the Federation of Schools of Accountancy, and as Secretary-Treasurer of the American Accounting Association. Professor Kieso served as a charter member of the national Accounting Education Change Commission. He is the recipient of the Outstanding Accounting Educator Award from the Illinois CPA Society, the FSA's Joseph A. Silvoso Award of Merit, and the NIU Foundation's Humanitarian Award for Service to Higher Education.

Jerry J. Weygandt, Ph.D., C.P.A., is Arthur Andersen Alumni Professor of Accounting at the University of Wisconsin—Madison. He Holds a Ph.D. in accounting from the University of Illinois. Articles by Professor Weygandt have appeared in the *Accounting Review, Journal of Accounting Research, Accounting Horizons, Journal of Accountancy,* and other academic and professional journals. These articles have examined such financial reporting issues as accounting for price-level adjustments, pensions, convertible securities, stock option contracts, and interim reports. Professor Weygandt is author of other accounting and financial reporting books and is a member of the American Accounting Association, the American Institute of Certified Public Accountants, and the Wisconsin Society of Certified Public Accountants. He has served on numerous committees of the American Accounting Association and as a member of the editorial board of the *Accounting Review;* he also has served as President and Secretary-Treasurer of the American Accounting Association. In addition, he has been actively involved with the American Institute of Certified Public Accountants and has been a member of the Accounting Standards Executive Committee (AcSEC) of that organization. He has served on the FASB task force that examined the reporting issues related to accounting for income taxes and as a trustee of the Financial Accounting Foundation. Professor Weygandt has received the Chancellor's Award for Excellence in Teaching and the Beta Gamma Sigma Dean's Teaching Award. He is on the board of directors of M & I Bank of Southern Wisconsin. He is the recipient of the Wisconsin Institute of CPA's Outstanding Educator's Award and the Lifetime Achievement Award. In 2001 he received the American Accounting Association's Outstanding Accounting Educator Award.

Terry D. Warfield, Ph.D., is associate professor of accounting at the University of Wisconsin—Madison. He received a B.S. and M.B.A. from Indiana University and a Ph.D. in accounting from the University of Iowa. Professor Warfield's area of expertise is financial reporting, and prior to his academic career, he worked for five years in the banking industry. He served as the Academic Accounting Fellow in the Office of the Chief Accountant at the U.S. Securities and Exchange Commission in Washington, D.C. from 1995–1996. Professor Warfield's primary research interests concern financial accounting standards and disclosure policies. He has published scholarly articles in *The*

Accounting Review, Journal of Accounting and Economics, Research in Accounting Regulation, and *Accounting Horizons,* and he has served on the editorial boards of *The Accounting Review, Accounting Horizons,* and *Issues in Accounting Education.* He has served as president of the Financial Accounting and Reporting Section, the Financial Accounting Standards Committee of the American Accounting Association (Chair 1995–1996), and on the AAA-FASB Research Conference Committee. Professor Warfield has received teaching awards at both the University of Iowa and the University of Wisconsin, and he was named to the Teaching Academy at the University of Wisconsin in 1995. Professor Warfield has developed and published several case studies based on his research for use in accounting classes. These cases have been selected for the AICPA Professor-Practitioner Case Development Program and have been published in *Issues in Accounting Education.*

PREFACE

THE ACCOUNTING ENVIRONMENT

Since the 11th Edition of *Intermediate Accounting*, much has happened in the financial reporting arena. Given the series of accounting scandals and eroding public confidence in auditing and financial reporting, Congress passed the most important legislation since the Securities Act of 1934, the Sarbanes-Oxley Act of 2002. That legislation and the resulting Public Accounting Oversight Board established as a result of it now compel the profession to reexamine its most fundamental concepts and principles.

With this reexamination come many questions related to financial reporting: How, for example, should we value assets and liabilities? What should be the proper reporting for off-balance-sheet financing transactions? How should we account for the complex hybrid and derivative securities that are increasing in use? What should be the proper reporting for the many restatements that are taking place in corporate America? How quickly should we converge international and U.S. GAAP? What is the proper reporting for defined-benefit pension plans? These are difficult questions, but ones that need serious study and action.

Some judge these questions mundane compared to larger questions faced by society, such as what we should do with Social Security, health-care reform, or international relationships. Yet, the accounting scandals have focused attention on the importance of proper accounting to all of us. Consider, for example, the over 90 million Americans who have investments in stocks either directly, through mutual funds, or through employer-sponsored retirement funds. Consider the numerous retirees who are now suffering hardship because the companies they worked for reported incorrect information in attempts to hype stock prices or compensation. Or think of the many Americans who trusted corporate financial reports and invested in companies like **WorldCom**, **Enron**, and **Fannie Mae**, only to find that the numbers were wrong. What these events tell us is that accounting is essential for our economy to function effectively. Without high-quality accounting standards, capital markets cannot efficiently allocate capital to its best use in building and maintaining our economy and way of life. Thus, we must get the accounting right!

We believe that recent legislation will be helpful, because it puts increased emphasis on proper and high-quality reporting. Companies, and the individuals who run these companies, must adhere to sound reporting practices or face severe sanctions. It is an exciting time for those involved in financial reporting. Interest has never been higher in developing and reporting information that will be useful to interested parties. We therefore believe it imperative that *every student of business understands the fundamentals of accounting and financial reporting to ensure that the system will be continually developed and improved.*

LINKING THE ACCOUNTING ENVIRONMENT WITH ACCOUNTING EDUCATION

In this edition of *Intermediate Accounting*, we continue a tradition, begun over 30 years ago, of helping students understand, prepare, and use financial information by linking accounting education with the "real-world" accounting environment. As indicated above, the importance of students understanding the role of financial information in capital markets has never been more important.

An important feature of *Intermediate Accounting,* therefore, is an enhanced effort to provide more perspective on the information provided by financial reporting. As a result, special boxed insights titled "What Do the Numbers Mean?" illustrate how reporting methods affect the decisions of financial statement users. By means of these boxes, originally introduced in the 11th Edition, we hope to convey the excitement and ever-changing nature of accounting, illuminating its significance and highlighting its importance.

In addition, for the 12th Edition, we have added at the *Gateway to the Profession* portal (the book's companion website) a "B set" of additional exercises online, as well as information about access to additional versions of the Professional Simulations and a new "Accounting in Action" continuing problem. The continuing problem provides students a real-world context in which to apply the concepts they are learning in the textbook. The *Gateway to the Profession* also provides students and instructors access to all the material previously delivered on the *Take Action! CD.*

The 12th Edition of *Intermediate Accounting* introduces a revised element to the "Using Your Judgment" section of the end-of-chapter material. A "Professional Simulation" in each chapter provides students with a new and integrative context for applying the concepts introduced in the chapter. To complement the Professional Simulation, in the 12th Edition we have introduced in each chapter a "Professional Research" case. These cases give students an opportunity to conduct authoritative research using the Financial Accounting Research System (FARS). These new and enhanced elements are patterned after the computerized CPA exam. They expand the focus of many of the elements of the *Gateway to the Professional* portal (writing, working in teams, using the analyst's toolkit) to help students learn how to use accounting facts and procedures in various business contexts.

Another key feature of this edition is the introduction of **WileyPLUS,** an online suite of resources, including access to an online version of the complete text. Within WileyPLUS, the online version of the text will be integrated with the Accounting Research database (FARS). Students will be able to conduct authoritative research in a seamless environment. In addition, WileyPLUS contains all of the elements of the *Gateway to the Profession* portal, plus a homework management system and resources for creating class presentations. (See page xx for a complete description of this content-rich resource.)

Throughout the book, we continue to strive for a balanced discussion of conceptual and procedural presentations so that these elements are mutually reinforcing. In addition, text discussions explain the rationale behind business transactions before addressing the accounting and reporting for those transactions. As in prior editions, we have thoroughly revised and updated the text to include all the latest developments in the accounting profession and practice. For example, we have completely revised the chapter on accounting changes and error corrections to reflect new accounting standards for accounting changes. Benefiting from the comments and recommendations of adopters of the 11th Edition, we have made significant revisions: We have expanded explanations where necessary; simplified complicated discussions and illustrations; integrated realism to heighten interest and relevancy; and added new topics and coverage to maintain currency. Finally, to provide the instructor with flexibility of use and no loss in topic coverage, we have moved discussions of less commonly used methods and more complex or specialized topics to the *Gateway to the Profession* portal.

NEW FEATURES

Based on extensive reviews, focus groups, and interactions with other intermediate accounting instructors and students, we have developed a number of new pedagogical features and content changes, designed both to help students learn more effectively and to answer the changing needs of the course.

Editorial Review

The 12th Edition of *Intermediate Accounting* has undergone an editorial review and line-by-line editing process to improve the readability of the text. The goals of this process were to retain the book's numerous examples and analogies that set the standard in the intermediate accounting course, but to simplify words and reduce sentence and paragraph length wherever possible without sacrificing precision. This review placed emphasis on introducing an active voice and conversational style in the presentation.

Major Chapter Revisions

In response to new FASB standards, we have significantly revised several chapters:

- Chapters 4 and 22 have been revised in response to the new standard on *accounting changes*. They now include comprehensive illustrations with a focus on the presentation of comparative statements when reporting accounting changes and errors.
- Chapter 10 presents a revised section on exchanges of nonmonetary assets and introduces the concept of commercial substance in accounting for exchanges.
- Chapter 16 has been revised in light of the new standard on stock-based compensation, which requires recognition of compensation expense using the fair-value model. A revised chapter-end appendix covers the accounting for restricted stock and stock appreciation rights.

New Appendixes

In addition to the revised appendix for Chapter 16 (see above), we also developed two new appendixes: on the accounting for variable-interest entities (Chapter 17), and on international accounting (Chapter 24). We added Appendix 24B in order to provide additional insight into the issue of convergence of U.S. and international accounting standards. We believe that convergence will continue to gain momentum and that students should be aware of this issue as their careers develop.

FARS Cases

In response to increased demand for accounting research skills and the requirements of the computerized CPA exam, each chapter now has a Professional Research case. These new cases give students an opportunity to conduct authoritative research, using either the Financial Accounting Research System (FARS) CD-ROM or FARS Online. Both of these products are available through John Wiley & Sons Higher Education Division.

Updated Supplements

All supplements are updated. In particular, the Solutions Manual questions are newly classified by textbook learning objective, the PowerPoint presentations are newly designed, and there are more review questions and over 400 new Test bank questions.

Gateway to the Profession Portal

The book companion *website at www.wiley.com/college/kieso* (with separate areas for instructors and for students) has been completely revamped. At this website, now titled *Gateway to the Profession*, students can access the following resources:

- A "B set" of additional exercises, providing additional practice opportunities for students (solutions available to instructors).
- For each chapter, a new "Accounting in Action" continuing problem, which follows the evolution of CM^2 Corporation from a start-up to an initial public offering (IPO). The continuing problem provides students with a real-world context in which to apply the concepts they are learning in the textbook. Instructors can use the continuing problem in its entirety or in parts, as desired.

- Information about access to online and additional versions of the Professional Simulations, which are found in each chapter of the text.
- Financial statements for **The Procter & Gamble Company, The Coca-Cola Company,** and **PepsiCo.**
- Access to the Student, Analyst, and Professional Toolkits previously delivered on the *Take Action! CD*. We describe the content of these three toolkits later in the preface (see pages xxi–xxiv).

ENHANCED FEATURES OF THE 12TH EDITION

We have continued and enhanced many of the features of the 11th Edition of *Intermediate Accounting*, including the following.

Real-World Emphasis

One of the goals of the intermediate accounting course is to orient students to the application of accounting principles and techniques in practice. Accordingly, we have continued our practice of using numerous examples from real companies throughout the text. The names of these real companies are highlighted in red. Illustration and exhibits marked by the icon shown here in the margin, or by company logos, are excerpts from actual financial statements of real firms.

Johnson&Johnson

WHAT DO THE NUMBERS MEAN?

At the start of each chapter, we have updated and introduced new chapter-opening vignettes to provide an even better real-world context that helps motivate student interest in the chapter topic. Also, throughout the chapters, the "What Do the Numbers Mean?" boxed inserts also provide real-world extensions of the material presented in the text.

P&G

The Coca-Cola Company

🌐 **PEPSICO**

In addition, Appendix 5B contains the 2004 annual report of **The Procter & Gamble Company (P&G)**. The book's website contains the 2004 annual reports of **The Coca-Cola Company** and of **PepsiCo, Inc.** Problems in the *Using Your Judgment* section (see description below) involve study of the P&G annual report or comparison of the annual reports of The Coca-Cola Company and PepsiCo. Also, links to many real-company financial reports appear in the company database at the *Gateway to the Profession* portal.

Currency and Accuracy

Accounting continually changes as its environment changes; an up-to-date book is therefore a necessity. As in past editions, we have strived to make this edition the most up-to-date and accurate textbook available.

International Coverage

INTERNATIONAL INSIGHT

Having a basic understanding of international accounting is becoming ever more important as the profession moves toward convergence of GAAP and international standards. Thus, we continue to include marginal *International Insights*, marked with the icon shown here, which we updated throughout to reflect changes in international accounting. These paragraphs describe or compare IASB standards and accounting practices in other countries with U.S. GAAP. This feature helps students understand that other countries sometimes use different recognition and measurement principles to report financial information. In addition, a *new* appendix on international accounting follows Chapter 24.

Streamlined Presentation

We also have continued our efforts to keep the topic coverage of *Intermediate Accounting* in line with the way instructors are *currently* teaching the course. Accordingly, we have moved some optional topics into chapter-end appendixes, and we have omitted altogether some topics that formerly were covered in appendixes. Often, these omitted topics have been moved to the *Gateway to the Profession* portal. Details are noted in the list of specific content changes below and in the list of portal content later in the preface.

Additional Exercises

Our study of the intermediate accounting course indicates the importance of the end-of-chapter Exercises for teaching and practicing important accounting concepts. In the 12th Edition, therefore, we have prepared an additional set of exercises. These new exercises are available at the *Gateway to the Profession* portal. (Solutions are available at the instructor's portion of the website.)

Using Your Judgment Section

We have revised and updated the *Using Your Judgment* section at the end of each chapter. Elements included in this section include the following:

- A Financial Reporting Problem, featuring **The Procter & Gamble Company**.
- A Financial Statement Analysis Case that asks students to use the information in published accounting reports to conduct financial analysis.
- A Comparative Analysis Case, featuring **The Coca-Cola Company** and **PepsiCo, Inc.**, that asks students to compare and contrast the financial reporting for these two companies.
- A Research Case, that asks students to read articles from the popular financial press and apply them to the chapter topic.
- An International Reporting Case that explores differences in reporting by international companies.
- A Professional Research: Financial Accounting and Reporting case that gives students practice conducting authoritative research using the Financial Accounting Research System (FARS).
- A Professional Simulation, newly revised for this edition, which models the computerized CPA exam.

The *Using Your Judgment* assignments are designed to help develop students' critical thinking, analytical, and research skills.

CONTENT CHANGES

The following list outlines the content revisions and improvements made in chapters of the 12th Edition.

Chapter 1
- Enhanced discussion of the hierarchy of generally accepted accounting principles.
- Reduced emphasis on AICPA.
- Updated international discussion.
- Enhanced discussion of the Sarbanes-Oxley Act of 2002.

Chapter 2
- Enhanced discussion of fair values and their use in financial accounting.

Chapter 3
- Enhanced coverage of the accounting cycle, with complete discussion and comprehensive example of Pioneer Advertising from inception to preparation of the financial statements.

- Improved discussion of financial statements in the chapter with illustration of the use of a worksheet in an appendix.

Chapter 4

- Updated illustration in the chapter-opening vignette.
- New chart on irregular items.
- New discussion of income statement reporting of a change in accounting principle.

Chapter 5

- Updated chapter-opening vignette on balance sheet and cash flow quality.
- New "What Do the Numbers Mean?" box on contractual commitments.
- Incorporated "significant non-cash financing and investing activities" into the statement of cash flows.

Chapter 7

- New chapter-opening vignette on abuse of allowance accounts.
- New illustration of the role of credit card operations and bad debts at major retailers.

Chapter 8

- Updated chapter-opening vignette on the importance of inventory information.

Chapter 9

- New "What Do the Numbers Mean?" box on the deficient reporting of lower-of-cost-or-market recoveries.

Chapter 10

- Updated chapter-opening vignette on variation in fixed assets across companies.
- Major rewrite of the discussion of nonmonetary exchanges in response to the recent FASB standard.

Chapter 11

- Updated chapter-opening vignette on recent changes in international accounting for impairments.

Chapter 12

- New "What Do the Numbers Mean?" box on impairment issues at **Krispy Kreme**.
- Rewrite of negative goodwill discussion.

Chapter 13

- New chapter-opening vignette related to international differences in the definition of a liability.
- Enhanced introduction to the discussion of contingencies.

Chapter 14

- New "What Do the Numbers Mean?" box on the economics of bonds.
- Enhanced "What Do the Numbers Mean?" box on bond ratings and default risk.
- Expanded discussion of required disclosures of long-term liabilities, including the recent SEC rule on contractual obligations.

Chapter 15

- New chapter-opening vignette on the importance of dividends in stock yields.
- New illustration on the prevalence of stock buy-backs.
- Updated discussion on responses to the new standard on redeemable preferred stock.

Chapter 16
- New chapter-opening vignette on stock options.
- Enhanced discussion of the distinctions between debt and equity and its relationship to hybrid or dilutive securities.
- Major rewrite of the discussion of stock-based compensation in response to the recent standard, including new illustrations and exhibits.
- New "What Do the Numbers Mean?" box on contingently convertible bonds (CoCos).
- New appendix on restricted stock and stock appreciation rights, based on the accounting guidance in the recent standard.

Chapter 17
- Updated chapter-opening vignette on international accounting for equity investments.
- New "What Do the Numbers Mean?" box on fair value accounting at **Morgan Stanley**.
- New "What Do the Numbers Mean?" box on off-balance-sheet transactions.
- New "What Do the Numbers Mean?" box on impairments.
- Reorganized discussion of fair value hedges in Appendix 17A.
- New appendix (Appendix 17B) on variable-interest entities.

Chapter 18
- New chapter-opening vignette on revenue recognition.
- New "What Do the Numbers Mean?" box on the revenue recognition challenges of gift cards.

Chapter 19
- New chapter-opening vignette on uncertain tax provisions.
- Enhanced discussion of net operating losses (NOLs) and when they can be used.
- New "What Do the Numbers Mean?" box on NOLs.

Chapter 20
- New chapter-opening vignette on changes in pension plan use.
- New "What Do the Numbers Mean?" box on mix of defined-benefit and defined-contribution plans.
- New "What Do the Numbers Mean?" box on pension underfunding.
- New illustration of pension worksheet in Excel format.
- Updated discussion on the **Pension Benefit Guarantee Corporation**.
- Eliminated discussion in appendix of OPEB transition adjustment, given its limited applicability.

Chapter 21
- New discussion of the leasing market, with special emphasis on lessors.
- New chart on equipment leasing growth.
- New "What Do the Numbers Mean?" box on recognition problems related to operating leases.

Chapter 22
- Complete rewrite of first section concerning accounting changes and errors, incorporating the guidance in the recent FASB standard.
- New emphasis on preparation of comparative statements.

Chapter 23
- Updated the treatment of stock options in response to the recent standard.

- Updated "What Do the Numbers Mean?" box on manipulation of operating cash flow.

Chapter 24

- New discussion of expanded disclosure requirements in the wake of the Sarbanes-Oxley Act of 2002.
- New "What Do the Numbers Mean?" box on the importance of disclosure for efficient securities markets.
- New discussion of managements' reporting on and auditor attestation on the effectiveness of internal controls.
- Enhanced discussion of Internet reporting with emphasis on "XBRL."
- New appendix (Appendix 24B) on international accounting.

END-OF-CHAPTER ASSIGNMENT MATERIAL

At the end of each chapter, we have provided a comprehensive set of review and home-work material. This section consists of Questions, Brief Exercises, Exercises, Problems, and short Concepts for Analysis exercises. These materials are followed by the Using Your Judgment section, described earlier (see page xvi). For this edition, we have up-dated many of these end-of-chapter materials. All of the assignment materials have been class-tested and/or double-checked for accuracy and clarity.

The Questions are designed primarily for review, self-testing, and classroom dis-cussion purposes, as well as for homework assignments. Typically a Brief Exercise cov-ers one topic, and an Exercise covers one or two topics. The Problems are designed to develop a professional level of achievement and are more challenging and time-consuming to solve than the Exercises. In the 12th Edition, the Brief Exercises, Exer-cises, and Problems now are classified by learning objective number. All Brief Exercises and Exercises and selected Problems are available in WileyPLUS with automatic grad-ing capability.

The Concepts for Analysis (formerly called Conceptual Cases) generally require discussion, as opposed to quantitative solutions. They are intended to confront the stu-dent with situations calling for conceptual analysis and the exercise of judgment in identifying issues and problems and in evaluating alternatives.

Separate icons next to Exercises, Problems, and Concepts for Analysis indicate home-work materials that offer more than just a quantitative challenge. Homework materials that are especially suited for group assignments, for example, are identified by the red icon shown here in the margin. Homework materials suitable as writing assignments are marked with the pencil icon shown here in the margin. Items that address ethics issues are identified by the scale (balance) icon. Homework materials that can be solved using the Excel Problems supplement are identified by the spreadsheet icon shown at left.

Probably no more than one-fourth of the total exercise, problem, and concepts for analysis material must be used to cover the subject matter adequately. Consequently, problem assignments may be varied from year to year without repetition. As noted ear-lier, a *new* additional set of Exercises is available at the book's website, to provide an even wider assortment of exercises from which to choose.

WileyPLUS

As described earlier, **WileyPLUS** is a suite of resources that contains online homework, with access to an online version of the text, plus all of the elements of the *Gateway to the Profession* portal. WileyPLUS gives you the technology to create an environment where students reach their full potential and experience academic success. Instructor resources include a wealth of presentation and preparation tools, easy-to-navigate as-signment and assessment tools, and a complete system to administer and manage your course exactly as you wish. In addition, a premium version of WileyPLUS is available that will include access to FARS (Financial Accounting Research System) Online, a series of active learning modules titled *Mastering FARS Online: An Active Leaning Approach*, the *Rockford Practice Set* powered by new general ledger software, and Excel Working Papers.

WileyPLUS is built around the activities you regularly perform:

- **Prepare and present class presentations** using relevant Wiley resources such as PowerPoint™ slides, image galleries, animations, and other WileyPLUS materials. You can also upload your own resources or web pages to use in conjunction with Wiley materials.
- **Create assignments** by choosing from end-of-chapter exercises, selected problems, and test bank questions organized by chapter, study objective, level of difficulty, and source—or add your own questions. WileyPLUS automatically grades students' homework and quizzes and records the results in your gradebook.
- **Offer context-sensitive help to students, 24/7.** When you assign homework or quizzes, you decide if and when students get access to hints, solutions, or answers where appropriate. Or they can be linked to relevant sections of their complete, online text for additional help whenever and wherever they need it most.
- **Track student progress.** You can analyze students' results and assess their level of understanding on an individual and class level using the WileyPLUS gradebook, and you can export data to your own personal gradebook.
- Seamlessly integrate all of the rich WileyPLUS content and resources with the power and convenience of your **WebCT** or **Blackboard** course—with a single sign-on.

In addition to the classroom presentation tools, the homework management system, and the online version of the text, **WileyPLUS** offers rich content in the *Gateway to the Profession* portal.

Content of the *Gateway to the Profession* Portal

As noted earlier, the *Gateway to the Profession* portal includes the Analyst's Toolkit, the Professional Toolkit, and the Student Toolkit, whose content is described below.

Analyst's Toolkit

Tools in the Analyst's Toolkit consist of the following items.

Database of Real Companies. Links to more than 20 annual reports of well-known companies, including three international companies, are provided at the *Gateway to the Profession* portal. Classes can use these annual reports in a variety of ways. For example, they can use them to illustrate different presentations of financial information or to compare note disclosures across companies. In addition, classes can use these reports to analyze a company's financial condition and compare its prospects with those of other companies in the same industry. Assignment material provides some examples of different types of analysis that students can perform. Each of the companies in the database of real companies is identified by a Web address to facilitate the gathering of additional information, if desired.

Additional Enrichment Material. An online chapter on Financial Statement Analysis is provided at the portal, along with related assignment material. This chapter can also be used in conjunction with the database of annual reports of real companies.

Spreadsheet Tools. Present value templates are provided. These templates can be used to solve time value of money problems.

Additional Internet Links. A number of useful links related to financial analysis are provided to expand expertise in analyzing real-world reporting.

Professional Toolkit

Consistent with expanding beyond technical accounting knowledge, the *Gateway to the Profession* materials emphasize certain skills necessary to become a successful accountant or financial manager. The following materials will help students develop needed professional skills.

Writing Materials. A primer on professional communications gives students a framework for writing professional materials. This primer discusses issues such as the top-ten writing problems, strategies for rewriting, how to do revisions, and tips on clarity. This primer has been class-tested and is effective in helping students enhance their writing skills.

Group-Work Materials. Recent evaluations of accounting education have identified the need to develop more skills in group problem solving. The *Gateway to the Profession* portal provides a second primer dealing with the role that work-groups play in organizations. Information is included on what makes a successful group, how you can participate effectively in the group, and do's and don'ts of group formation.

Ethics. The Professional Toolkit contains expanded materials on the role of ethics in the profession, including references to speeches and articles on ethics in accounting; codes of ethics for major professional bodies; and examples and additional case studies on ethics.

Career Professional Spotlights. Every student should have a good understanding of the profession he or she is entering. Career vignettes on the *Gateway to the Profession* portal indicate the types of work that accountants do. Other aspects of the spotlights on careers are included at the *Gateway to the Profession* to help students make successful career choices. These include important links to websites that can provide useful career information to facilitate the student's efforts in this area.

Student Toolkit

Also included at the *Gateway to the Profession* are features that help students process and understand the course materials. They are:

Interactive Tutorials. To help students better understand some of the more difficult topics in intermediate accounting, we have developed a number of interactive tutorials that provide expanded discussion and explanation in a visual and narrative context. Topics addressed are:

- the accounting cycle
- accounting for bad debts (recording uncollectible accounts)
- disposition (transfer) of receivables
- inventory methods
- dollar-value LIFO
- interest capitalization
- depreciation methods

These tutorials are for the benefit of the student and should require no use of class time on the part of instructors.

Expanded Discussion and Illustrations. The Expanded Discussion section provides additional topics not covered in depth in the textbook. *The Gateway to the Profession* gives the flexibility to enrich or expand the course by discussion of additional topics such as those listed below. Topics included, with appropriate chapter linkage, are as follows.

Gateway to the Profession Topics

Chapter 1
- Expanded discussion of ethical issues in financial accounting.

Chapter 2
- Discussion of accounting for changing prices.

Chapter 3
- Presentation of worksheet using the periodic inventory method.
- Specialized journals and methods of processing accounting data.
- Tutorial on the accounting cycle.

Chapter 6
- Present-value–based measurements, including an expanded discussion of spreadsheet tools for solving present-value problems.

Chapter 7
- Discussion of how a four-column bank reconciliation (the proof of cash) can be used for control purposes.
- Expanded example, with accounting entries, of transfers of receivables without recourse.
- Tutorial on the accounting for bad debts.
- Tutorial on transfer of receivables.

Chapter 8
- Tutorial on inventory methods (cost flow assumptions).
- Tutorial on LIFO issues, including dollar-value LIFO.

Chapter 10
- Tutorial on interest capitalization.

Chapter 11
- Discussion of lesser-used depreciation methods, such as the retirement and replacement methods.
- Tutorial on depreciation methods.

Chapter 12
- Expanded discussion on valuing goodwill.

Chapter 13
- Expanded discussion on property taxes.

Chapter 15
- Expanded discussion on the par value method for treasury stock.
- Expanded discussion on quasi-reorganizations.

Chapter 16
- Comprehensive earnings per share illustration.

Chapter 17
- Illustration of accounting entries for transfers of investment securities.
- Expanded discussion of special issues related to investments.

Chapter 19
- Discussion of the conceptual aspects of interperiod tax allocation, including the deferred and net of tax methods.
- Discussion, with examples, of accounting for intraperiod tax allocations.

Chapter 21
- Discussion of real estate leases and leveraged leases.

Chapter 23
- Discussion, with a detailed example, of the T-account method for preparing a statement of cash flows.

Chapter 24

- Discussion of accounting for changing prices, both for general and specific price-level changes.
- Financial analysis primer.

In addition to these materials, illustrative disclosures of financial reporting practices are provided.

Self-Study Tests and Additional Self-Tests. Each chapter on the *Gateway to the Profession* portal includes two sets of self-tests, to allow students to check their understanding of key concepts from the chapter. The software automatically grades the tests and points students to material they need to study further.

Glossary. A complete glossary of all the key terms used in the text is provided, in alphabetical order as well as via Wiley's Flash card technology for drill and practice. Page numbers show where these key terms appear in the text.

Learning-Style Survey. Research on left brain/right brain differences and also on learning and personality differences suggests that each person has preferred ways to receive and communicate information. After taking this learning-style quiz, students will be able to identify their particular learning styles and pinpoint the study aids in the textbook that will help them learn the material.

In summary, the *Gateway to the Profession* portal is a comprehensive complement to the 12th Edition of *Intermediate Accounting*, providing new materials as well as a new way to communicate those materials.

SUPPLEMENTARY MATERIALS

Accompanying this textbook is an improved and expanded package of student learning aids and instructor teaching aids. The *Intermediate Accounting,* 12th Edition, *Gateway to the Profession* portal at *www.wiley.com/college/kieso* provides various tools for students and instructors. This portal offers expanded materials in the three toolkits previously described. In addition, as described earlier, WileyPLUS offers resources to help you prepare class presentations, create assignments, offer help to students, and track student progress.

Other teaching and learning aids to supplement the textbook are described below.

Instructor Teaching Aids

The following teaching aids are available to support instructors using the 12th Edition.

Instructor's Resource CD. The *Instructor's Resource CD* contains electronic versions of the Instructor's Manual, Solutions Manual, Test Bank, computerized Test Bank, PowerPoint™ presentations, and other instructor resources.

Solutions Manual, Vols. 1 and 2. The *Solutions Manual* provides answers to all end-of-chapter questions, brief exercises, exercises, problems, and case materials. Classification tables categorize solutions by topic, and the new solutions manual also categorizes solutions by textbook learning objective. The estimated time to complete exercises, problems, and cases is provided.

Test Bank: Vols. 1 and 2. The 12th Edition Test Bank contains *over 400 new testing questions.* Exercises, problems, true/false, multiple choice, and conceptual short-answer questions help instructors test students' knowledge and communication skills.

Computerized Test Bank. This easy-to-use program allows instructors to create multiple versions of the same test. This computerized test bank also has authoring capabilities and randomizing functions.

Instructor's Manual, Vols. 1 and 2. The *Instructor's Manual* contains lecture outlines, chapter reviews, sample syllabi, printed teaching transparency masters, and much more.

Solutions Transparencies, Vols. 1 and 2. These acetate transparencies contain solutions to textbook end-of-chapter material. The transparencies contain large, bold type for classroom presentation.

PowerPoint™ Presentations. The PowerPoint™ presentations are designed to enhance classroom presentation of chapter topics and examples. The 12th Edition templates now have a new design with review questions and many examples illustrating textbook content.

Teaching Transparencies. These four-color acetates provide illustrations of key concepts for classroom viewing.

Solutions to Rockford Practice Set. This supplement provides solutions to the *Rockford Practice Set*, which is available in print form or electronically through the premium version of WileyPLUS.

Solutions to Excel Workbook Templates. Available for download from the KWW website, these are solutions to the *Solving Problems Using Excel Workbook* templates.

Course Management Resources. Course content cartridges are available from both WebCT and Blackboard.

Periodic Newsletters. The textbook is supplemented by the publication of periodic newsletters. These faculty-oriented supplements include the following sections:

- "Update"—Provides the latest information about new accounting standards promulgated since the text was published.

- "Financial Reporting Challenges"—Addresses a contemporary issue being debated by accounting professionals and standard setters, which may result in a new accounting standard.

- "By the Way. . ."—Provides a "heads up" to instructors on topics addressed in the text (usually the subject of a recent change in accounting standards), to increase instructors' awareness of its implications for their courses.

- "CPA Exam Update"—Offers the latest information about the CPA exam. This item is prepared by Debra R. Hopkins (CPA, CIA), CPA Review Director, Northern Illinois University, DeKalb, Illinois.

Student Learning Aids

Student Study Guide, Vols. 1 and 2. Each chapter of the Study Guide contains a chapter review, chapter outline, and a glossary of key terms. Demonstration problems, multiple-choice, true/false, matching, and other exercises are included.

Problem-Solving Survival Guide, Vols. 1 and 2. This study guide contains exercises and problems that help students develop their intermediate accounting problem-solving skills. Explanations assist in the approach, set-up, and completion of accounting problems. Tips alert students to common pitfalls and misconceptions.

Working Papers, Vols. 1 and 2. The working papers are printed templates that can help students correctly format their textbook accounting solutions. Working paper templates are available for all end-of-chapter brief exercises, exercises, problems, and cases.

Excel Working Papers, Vols. 1 and 2. The *Excel Working Papers* are Excel templates that students can use to correctly format their textbook accounting solutions. Working paper templates are available for all end-of-chapter brief exercises, exercises, problems, and cases.

Solving Problems Using Excel Workbook. A useful introduction to Excel, this workbook helps students work with preprogrammed spreadsheets, and it explains how students can design their own spreadsheet. This workbook is packaged with a CD containing Excel templates that allow students to complete the selected end-of-chapter exercises and problems identified by a spreadsheet icon in the margin of the main textbook.

Rockford Corporation: An Accounting Practice Set. This practice set helps students review the accounting cycle and the preparation of financial statements.

Rockford Corporation: A Computerized Accounting Practice Set. The computerized Rockford practice set is a general ledger software version of the printed practice set. Available within WileyPLUS Premium Version.

ACKNOWLEDGMENTS

We thank the many users of our 11th Edition who contributed to the revision through their comments and instructive criticism. Special thanks are extended to the focus group participants and the primary reviewers of and contributors to our 12th Edition manuscript.

Lisa Bostick
University of Tampa

Greg Brookins
Santa Monica College

Laura Delaune
Louisiana State University

Lynda Dennis
University of Central Florida

Claire Eckstein
CUNY—Baruch

Dave Farber
Michigan State University

Clyde Galbraith
West Chester University

Ellen Goldberg
Northern Virginia Community College

Marty Gosman
Quinnipiac College

Julia Higgs
Florida Atlantic University

Geoffrey Horlick
St. Francis College

Marilyn Hunt
University of Central Florida

Cynthia Jeffrey
Iowa State University

Mary Jo Jones
Eastern University

Art Joy
University of South Florida

Celina Jozci
University of South Florida

Lisa Koonce
University of Texas at Austin

Timothy Lindquist
University of Northern Iowa

Barbara Lippincott
University of Tampa

Gary Luoma
University of Southern California

Daphne Main
University of New Orleans

Ed Nathan
University of Houston

Hugo Nurnberg
CUNY – Baruch

Ann O'Brien
University of Wisconsin—Madison

Anne Oppegard
Augustana College, SD

Alee Phillips
University of Kansas

Marlene Plumlee
University of Utah

Wing Poon
Montclair State University

Jay Price
Utah State University

Paul (Jep) Robertson
Henderson State University

Larry Roman
Cuyahoga Community College

Bob Rouse
College of Charleston

Tim Shea
University of Wisconsin – Madison

Jerry Siebel
University of South Florida

Karen Squires
University of Tampa

Douglas Smith
Samford University

Gary Taylor
University of Alabama

Lynn Thomas
Kansas State University

Tom Tierney
University of Wisconsin—Madison

David Weiner
University of San Francisco

Steve Zeff
Rice University

We also thank other colleagues who provided helpful criticism and made valuable suggestions as members of focus groups, survey participants, or as adopters and reviewers of previous editions.

Diana Adcox
University of North Florida

Noel Addy
Mississippi State University

Roberta Allen
Texas Tech University

James Bannister
University of Hartford

Charles Baril
James Madison University

Kathleen Buaer
Midwestern State University

Janice Bell
California State University at Northridge

Larry Bergin
Winona State University

Lynn Bible
University of Nevada, Reno

John C. Borke
University of Wisconsin—Platteville

Tiffany Bortz
University of Texas, Dallas

Phillip Buchanan
George Mason University

Tom Buchman
University of Colorado, Boulder

Suzanne M. Busch
California State University—Hayward

Eric Carlsen
Kean College of New Jersey

Tom Carment
Northeastern State University

Tommy Carnes
Western Carolina University

Robert Cluskey
Tennessee State University

Edwin Cohen
DePaul University

W. Terry Dancer
Arkansas State University

Lee Dexter
Moorhead State University

Judith Doing
University of Arizona

Joanne Duke
San Francisco State University

Richard Dumont
Teikyo Post University

William Dwyer
DeSales University

Dean S. Eiteman
Indiana University—Pennsylvania

Larry R. Falcetto
Emporia State University

Richard Fern
Eastern Kentucky University

Richard Fleischman
John Carroll University

Stephen L. Fogg
Temple University

William Foster
New Mexico State University

Clyde Galbraith
West Chester University

Marshall Geiger
University of Richmond

Susan Gill
Washington State University

Harold Goedde
State University of New York at Oneonta

Lynford E. Graham
Rutgers University

Donald J. Griffin
Cayuga Community College

Marcia I. Halvorsen
University of Cincinnati

Garry Heesacker
Central Washington University

Kenneth Henry
Florida International University

Wayne M. Higley
Buena Vista University

Judy Hora
University of San Diego

Geoffrey R. Horlick
St. Francis College

Kathy Hsu
University of Louisiana, Layfayette

M. Zarar Iqbal
California Polytechnic State University—San Luis Obispo

Daniel Ivancevich
University of North Carolina at Wilmington

Susan Ivancevich
University of North Carolina at Wilmington

Cynthia Jeffrey
Iowa State University

Scott Jeris
San Francisco State University

James Johnston
Louisiana Tech University

Jeff Jones
University of Texas—San Antonio

Celina Jozsi
University of South Florida

Douglas W. Kieso
Aurora University

Paul D. Kimmel
University of Wisconsin—Milwaukee

Martha King
Emporia State University

Florence Kirk
State University of New York at Oswego

Mark Kohlbeck
Florida Atlantic University

Lisa Koonce
University of Texas—Austin

Steve Lafave
Augsburg College

Ellen Landgraf
Loyola University, Chicago

Tom Largay
Thomas College

David B. Law
Youngstown State University

Henry LeClerc
Suffolk Community College—Selden Campus

Patsy Lee
University of Texas—Arlington

Lydia Leporte
Tidewater Community College

Timothy Lindquist
University of Northern Iowa

Tom Linsmeier
Michigan State University

Ellen Lippman
University of Portland

Daphne Main
University of New Orleans

Mostafa Maksy
Northeastern Illinois University

Danny Matthews
Midwestern State University

Noel McKeon
Florida Community College

Robert J. Matthews
New Jersey City University

Robert Milbrath
University of Houston

James Miller
Gannon University

John Mills
University of Nevada—Reno

Joan Monnin-Callahan
University of Cincinnati

Mohamed E. Moustafa
California State University—Long Beach

Siva Nathan
Georgia State University

Kermit Natho
Georgia State University

Joseph Nicassio
Westmoreland County Community College

Patricia Parker
Columbus State Community College

Richard Parker
Olivet College

Obeau S. Persons
Rider University

Ray Pfeiffer
University of Massachusetts—Amherst

Robert Rambo
University of New Orleans

Debbie Rankin
Lincoln University

MaryAnn Reynolds
Western Washington University

Vernon Richardson
University of Arkansas

Richard Riley
West Virginia University

Jeffrey D. Ritter
St. Norbert College

Paul (Jep) Robertson
Henderson State University

Steven Rock
University of Colorado

John Rossi
Moravian College

Tim Ryan
Southern Illinois University

Victoria Rymer
University of Maryland

James Sander
Butler University

John Sander
University of Southern Maine

George Sanders
Western Washington University

Howard Shapiro
Eastern Washington University

Douglas Sharp
Wichita State University

Phil Siegel
Florida Atlantic University

John R. Simon
Northern Illinois University

Keith Smith
George Washington University

Pam Smith
Northern Illinois University

Billy S. Soo
Boston College

Carlton D. Stolle
Texas A&M University

William Stout
University of Louisville

Pamela Stuerke
Case Western Reserve University

Ron Stunda
Birmingham Southern College

Eric Sussman
University of California. Los Angeles

Diane L. Tanner
University of North Florida

Gary Testa
Brooklyn College

Paula B. Thomas
Middle Tennessee State University

Elizabeth Venuti
Hofstra University

James D. Waddington, Jr.,
Hawaii Pacific University

Dick Wasson
Southwestern College

Frank F. Weinberg
Golden Gate University

Jeannie Welsh
LaSalle University

Shari H. Wescott
Houston Baptist University

Michael Willenborg
University of Connecticut

William H. Wilson
Oregon Health University

Kenneth Wooling
Hampton University

Joni Young
University of New Mexico

Paul Zarowin
New York University

Stephen A. Zeff
Rice University

In addition, we thank the following colleagues who contributed to several of the unique features of this edition.

Gateway to the Profession Portal and FARS Cases

Jack Cathey
University of North Carolina—Charlotte

Michelle Ephraim
Worcester Polytechnic Institute

Erik Frederickson
Madison, Wisconsin

Jason Hart
Deloitte & Touche, Milwaukee

Kelly Krieg
E & Y, Milwaukee

Jeremy Kunicki
Walgreens

Andrew Prewitt
KPMG, Chicago

Jeff Seymour
KPMG, Minneapolis

Matt Sullivan
Deloitte & Touche, Milwaukee

Jen Vaughn
PricewaterhouseCoopers, Chicago

Erin Viel
PricewaterhouseCoopers, Milwaukee

Edward Wertheim
Northeastern University

Ancillary Authors, Contributors, Proofers, and Accuracy Checkers

Mary Ann Benson

John C. Borke
University of Wisconsin—Platteville

Jack Cathey
University of North Carolina—Charlotte

Betty Connor
University of Colorado at Denver

Robert Derstine
Villanova University

Gregory Dold
Southwestern College

Jan Duffy
Iowa State University

Jim Emig
Villanova University

Larry Falcetto
Emporia State University

Tom Forehand
State University of New York—New Paltz

Rosemary Fullerton
Utah State University

Clyde Galbraith
West Chester University

Alicia Gmeiner
Elm Street Publishing Services

Edwin Hackleman
Delta Software

Coby Harmon
University of California, Santa Barbara

Wayne Higley
Buena Vista University

Debra R. Hopkins
Northern Illinois University

Judi Hora
University of San Diego

Marilyn F. Hunt

Douglas W. Kieso
Aurora University

Mark Kohlbeck
Florida Atlantic University

Jennifer Laudermilch
PricewaterhouseCoopers

Ann Martin
University of Colorado at Denver

Barbara Muller
Arizona State University

Don Newell
Delta Software

Tom Noland
University of Houston

Paul (Jep) Robertson
Henderson State University

Rex A. Schildhouse
University of Phoenix—San Diego

Alice Sineath
Forsyth Technical Community College

Dick D. Wasson
Southwestern College, San Diego University

WileyPLUS Developers and Reviewers

James Mraz

Jan Mardon

Melanie Yon

Perspectives and "From Classroom to Career" Interviews

Stuart Weiss, *Stuart Weiss Business Writing, Inc., Portland, Oregon*

Practicing Accountants and Business Executives

From the fields of corporate and public accounting, we owe thanks to the following practitioners for their technical advance and for consenting to interviews.

Ron Bernard
NFL Enterprises

Mike Crooch
FASB

Tracy Golden
Deloitte & Touche

John Gribble
PricewaterhouseCoopers

Darien Griffin
S.C. Johnson & Son Wax

Michael Lehman
Sun Microsystems, Inc.

Michele Lippert
Evoke.com

Sue McGrath
Vision Capital Management

David Miniken
Sweeney Conrad

Robert Sack
University of Virginia

Clare Schulte
Deloitte & Touche

Willie Sutton
Mutual Community Savings Bank, Durham, NC

Lynn Turner
Glass, Lewis, LLP

Gary Valenzuela
Yahoo!

Rachel Woods
PricewaterhouseCoopers

Arthur Wyatt
Arthur Anderson & Co., and the University of Illinois—Urbana

In addition, we appreciate the exemplary support and professional commitment given us by the development, marketing, production, and editorial staffs of John Wiley & Sons, including the following: Susan Elbe, Chris DeJohn, Mark Bonadeo, Amy Scholz, Alison Stanley, Ed Brislin, Allie Morris, Vanessa Ahrens, Jeanine Furino, Harry Nolan, Anna Melhorn, and Lenore Belton. Thanks to Terry Ann Kremer for her careful line edit of the book and to Ann Torbert for her editorial assistance in pulling together the various pieces of the manuscript. Thanks, too, to Suzanne Ingrao for her production work, to the management and staff at TechBooks for their work on the textbook, and to Alicia Gmeiner and the management and staff at Elm Street Publishing Services for their work on the solutions manual.

We also appreciate the cooperation of the American Institute of Certified Public Accountants and the Financial Accounting Standards Board in permitting us to quote from their pronouncements. We thank The Procter & Gamble Company for permitting us to use its 2004 annual report for our specimen financial statements. We also acknowledge permission from the American Institute of Certified Public Accountants, the Institute of Management Accountants, and the Institute of Internal Auditors to adapt and use material from the Uniform CPA Examinations, the CMA Examinations, and the CIA Examination, respectively.

If this book helps teachers instill in their students an appreciation for the challenges, worth, and limitations of accounting, if it encourages students to evaluate critically and understand financial accounting theory and practice, and if it prepares students for advanced study, professional examinations, and the successful and ethical pursuit of their careers in accounting or business, then we will have attained our objectives.

Suggestions and comments from users of this book will be appreciated.

Donald E. Kieso
Somonauk, Illinois

Jerry J. Weygandt
Madison, Wisconsin

Terry D. Warfield
Madison, Wisconsin

BRIEF CONTENTS

CHAPTER 1
Financial Accounting and
Accounting Standards, 1

CHAPTER 2
Conceptual Framework Underlying
Financial Accounting, 27

CHAPTER 3
The Accounting Information System, 61

CHAPTER 4
Income Statement and
Related Information, 125

CHAPTER 5
Balance Sheet and Statement of
Cash Flows, 169

CHAPTER 6
Accounting and the Time Value
of Money, 251

CHAPTER 7
Cash and Receivables, 313

CHAPTER 8
Valuation of Inventories: A Cost-
Basis Approach, 367

CHAPTER 9
Inventories: Additional Valuation Issues, 421

CHAPTER 10
Acquisition and Disposition of Property, Plant,
and Equipment, 471

CHAPTER 11
Depreciation, Impairments,
and Depletion, 521

CHAPTER 12
Intangible Assets, 571

CHAPTER 13
Current Liabilities and Contingencies, 617

CHAPTER 14
Long-Term Liabilities, 671

CONTENTS

CHAPTER 1

FINANCIAL ACCOUNTING AND ACCOUNTING STANDARDS   1

The Size of the New York Phone Book, If Necessary, 1

FINANCIAL STATEMENTS AND FINANCIAL REPORTING, 2

Accounting and Capital Allocation, 3

The Challenges Facing Financial Accounting, 4

Objectives of Financial Reporting, 4

The Need to Develop Standards, 5

PARTIES INVOLVED IN STANDARD SETTING, 6

Securities and Exchange Commission (SEC), 6

American Institute of Certified Public Accountants (AICPA), 7

Financial Accounting Standards Board (FASB), 8

Governmental Accounting Standards Board (GASB), 10

Changing Role of the AICPA, 11

GENERALLY ACCEPTED ACCOUNTING PRINCIPLES, 12

ISSUES IN FINANCIAL REPORTING, 13

Standard Setting in a Political Environment, 13

The Expectations Gap, 15

International Accounting Standards, 16

Ethics in the Environment of Financial Accounting, 16

Conclusion, 17

CHAPTER 2

CONCEPTUAL FRAMEWORK UNDERLYING FINANCIAL ACCOUNTING   27

Show Me the Earnings!, 27

CONCEPTUAL FRAMEWORK, 28

The Need for a Conceptual Framework, 28

Development of a Conceptual Framework, 29

FIRST LEVEL: BASIC OBJECTIVES, 31

SECOND LEVEL: FUNDAMENTAL CONCEPTS, 31

Qualitative Characteristics of Accounting Information, 31

Basic Elements, 34

THIRD LEVEL: RECOGNITION AND MEASUREMENT CONCEPTS, 36

Basic Assumptions, 36

Basic Principles of Accounting, 38

Constraints, 43

Summary of the Structure, 46

CHAPTER 3

THE ACCOUNTING INFORMATION SYSTEM   61

Needed: A Reliable Information System, 61

ACCOUNTING INFORMATION SYSTEM, 62

Basic Terminology, 63

Debits and Credits, 64

Basic Equation, 65

Financial Statements and Ownership Structure, 66

THE ACCOUNTING CYCLE, 67

Identifying and Recording Transactions and Other Events, 68

Journalizing, 69

Posting, 70

Trial Balance, 74

Adjusting Entries, 75

Adjusted Trial Balance, 84

Preparing Financial Statements, 85

Closing, 86

Post-Closing Trial Balance, 88

Reversing Entries, 89

The Accounting Cycle Summarized, 89

Financial Statements for a Merchandising Company, 89

***APPENDIX 3A* CASH-BASIS ACCOUNTING VERSUS ACCRUAL-BASIS ACCOUNTING, 94**

CONVERSION FROM CASH BASIS TO ACCRUAL BASIS, 96

Service Revenue Computation, 96

Operating Expense Computation, 97

THEORETICAL WEAKNESSES OF THE CASH BASIS, 98

APPENDIX 3B USING REVERSING ENTRIES, 99

ILLUSTRATION OF REVERSING ENTRIES—ACCRUALS, 99

ILLUSTRATION OF REVERSING ENTRIES—PREPAYMENTS, 100

Summary of Reversing Entries, 101

APPENDIX 3C USING A WORKSHEET: THE ACCOUNTING CYCLE REVISITED, 101

Worksheet Columns, 102

Adjustments Entered on the Worksheet, 102

Preparing Financial Statements from a Work Sheet, 104

CHAPTER 4

INCOME STATEMENT AND RELATED INFORMATION   125

Which Income Number?, 125

INCOME STATEMENT, 126

Usefulness of the Income Statement, 126

Limitations of the Income Statement, 127

Quality of Earnings, 127

FORMAT OF THE INCOME STATEMENT, 129

Elements of the Income Statement, 129

Single-Step Income Statements, 130

Multiple-Step Income Statements, 130

Condensed Income Statements, 133

REPORTING IRREGULAR ITEMS, 134

Discontinued Operations, 136

Extraordinary Items, 137

Unusual Gains and Losses, 139

Changes in Accounting Principle, 140

Changes in Estimates, 141

Summary of Irregular Items, 142

SPECIAL REPORTING ISSUES, 143

Intraperiod Tax Allocation, 143

Earnings per Share, 144

Retained Earnings Statement, 146

Comprehensive Income, 147

CHAPTER 5

BALANCE SHEET AND STATEMENT OF CASH FLOWS   169

"There Ought to Be a Law," 169

SECTION 1 BALANCE SHEET, 170

USEFULNESS OF THE BALANCE SHEET, 170

LIMITATIONS OF THE BALANCE SHEET, 172

CLASSIFICATION IN THE BALANCE SHEET, 172

Current Assets, 173

Noncurrent Assets, 177

Liabilities, 179

Owners' Equity, 182

Balance Sheet Format, 182

ADDITIONAL INFORMATION REPORTED, 184

Contingencies, 185

Accounting Policies, 185

Contractual Situations, 185

Fair Values, 186

TECHNIQUES OF DISCLOSURE, 187

Parenthetical Explanations, 187

Notes, 187

Cross-Reference and Contra Items, 189

Supporting Schedules, 189

Terminology, 190

SECTION 2 STATEMENT OF CASH FLOWS, 190

PURPOSE OF THE STATEMENT OF CASH FLOWS, 190

CONTENT AND FORMAT OF THE STATEMENT OF CASH FLOWS, 191

PREPARATION OF THE STATEMENT OF CASH FLOWS, 193

USEFULNESS OF THE STATEMENT OF CASH FLOWS, 195

Financial Liquidity, 197

Financial Flexibility, 197

Free Cash Flow, 197

APPENDIX 5A RATIO ANALYSIS— A REFERENCE, 200

USING RATIOS TO ANALYZE PERFORMANCE, 200

APPENDIX 5B SPECIMEN FINANCIAL STATEMENT: THE PROCTER & GAMBLE COMPANY, 202

CHAPTER 6

ACCOUNTING AND THE TIME VALUE OF MONEY   251

The Magic of Interest, 251

BASIC TIME VALUE CONCEPTS, 252

Applications of Time Value Concepts, 252

The Nature of Interest, 253

Simple Interest, 254

Compound Interest, 255

Fundamental Variables, 258

SINGLE-SUM PROBLEMS, 259

Future Value of a Single Sum, 259

Present Value of a Single Sum, 261

Solving for Other Unknowns in
Single-Sum Problems, 263

ANNUITIES, 264

Future Value of an Ordinary Annuity, 264

Future Value of an Annuity Due, 267

Examples of Future Value of
Annuity Problems, 268

Present Value of an Ordinary Annuity, 270

Present Value of an Annuity Due, 272

Examples of Present Value of
Annuity Problems, 273

MORE COMPLEX SITUATIONS, 275

Deferred Annuities, 275

Valuation of Long-Term Bonds, 277

Effective-Interest Method of Amortization of Bond
Discount or Premium, 278

PRESENT VALUE MEASUREMENT, 279

Choosing an Appropriate Interest Rate, 280

Example of Expected Cash Flow, 281

APPENDIX 6A **USING
FINANCIAL CALCULATORS, 284**

FUTURE VALUE OF A SINGLE SUM, 284

Plus and Minus, 285

Compounding Periods, 285

Rounding, 285

PRESENT VALUE OF A SINGLE SUM, 285

FUTURE VALUE OF AN ORDINARY ANNUITY, 285

FUTURE VALUE OF AN ANNUITY DUE, 286

PRESENT VALUE OF AN ORDINARY ANNUITY, 286

USEFUL APPLICATIONS OF THE FINANCIAL CALCULATOR, 287

Auto Loan, 287

Mortgage Loan Amount, 287

Individual Retirement Account (IRA), 288

CHAPTER 7
CASH AND RECEIVABLES   **313**

No-Tell Nortel, 313

SECTION 1 **CASH, 314**

WHAT IS CASH?, 314

MANAGEMENT AND CONTROL OF CASH, 315

REPORTING CASH, 316

Restricted Cash, 316

Bank Overdrafts, 317

Cash Equivalents, 317

SUMMARY OF CASH-RELATED ITEMS, 317

SECTION 2 **RECEIVABLES, 318**

RECOGNITION OF ACCOUNTS RECEIVABLE, 320

Trade Discounts, 320

Cash Discounts (Sales Discounts), 320

Nonrecognition of Interest Element, 321

VALUATION OF ACCOUNTS RECEIVABLE, 321

Uncollectible Accounts Receivable, 322

RECOGNITION OF NOTES RECEIVABLE, 326

Note Issued at Face Value, 327

Note Not Issued at Face Value, 328

Choice of Interest Rate, 331

VALUATION OF NOTES RECEIVABLE, 331

DISPOSITION OF ACCOUNTS AND NOTES RECEIVABLE, 332

Secured Borrowing, 332

Sales of Receivables, 333

Secured Borrowing versus Sale, 336

PRESENTATION AND ANALYSIS, 337

Presentation of Receivables, 337

Analysis of Receivables, 338

APPENDIX 7A **CASH CONTROLS, 340**

USING BANK ACCOUNTS, 340

THE IMPREST PETTY CASH SYSTEM, 340

PHYSICAL PROTECTION OF CASH BALANCES, 341

RECONCILIATION OF BANK BALANCES, 342

CHAPTER 8
**VALUATION OF INVENTORIES:
A COST-BASIS APPROACH**   **367**

Inventories in the Crystal Ball, 367

INVENTORY CLASSIFICATION AND CONTROL, 368

Classification, 368

Control, 370

BASIC ISSUES IN INVENTORY VALUATION, 372

PHYSICAL GOODS INCLUDED IN INVENTORY, 372

Goods in Transit, 373

Consigned Goods, 373

Special Sales Agreements, 374

Effect of Inventory Errors, 375

COSTS INCLUDED IN INVENTORY, 377

Product Costs, 377

Period Costs, 378

Treatment of Purchase Discounts, 379

WHAT COST FLOW ASSUMPTION TO ADOPT?, 380

Specific Identification, 381

Average Cost, 382

First-In, First-Out (FIFO), 382

Last-In, First-Out (LIFO), 384

SPECIAL ISSUES RELATED TO LIFO, 384

LIFO Reserve, 384

LIFO Liquidation, 385

Dollar-Value LIFO, 387

Comparison of LIFO Approaches, 392

Major Advantages of LIFO, 392

Major Disadvantages of LIFO, 393

BASIS FOR SELECTION OF INVENTORY METHOD, 395

Inventory Valuation Methods—
Summary Analysis, 396

CHAPTER 9
INVENTORIES: ADDITIONAL
VALUATION ISSUES   421

What Do Inventory Changes Tell Us?, 421

LOWER-OF-COST-OR-MARKET, 422

Lower-of-Cost-or-Market—Ceiling and
Floor, 423

How Lower-of-Cost-or-Market Works, 424

Methods of Applying
Lower-of-Cost-or-Market, 425

Recording "Market" Instead of Cost, 426

Evaluation of the
Lower-of-Cost-or-Market Rule, 429

VALUATION BASES, 429

Valuation at Net Realizable Value, 429

Valuation Using Relative Sales Value, 430

Purchase Commitments—A Special Problem, 431

THE GROSS PROFIT METHOD OF
ESTIMATING INVENTORY, 433

Computation of Gross Profit Percentage, 434

Evaluation of Gross Profit Method, 435

RETAIL INVENTORY METHOD, 436

Retail-Method Concepts, 437

Retail Inventory Method with Markups and
Markdowns—Conventional Method, 438

Special Items Relating to Retail Method, 440

Evaluation of Retail Inventory Method, 441

PRESENTATION AND ANALYSIS, 442

Presentation of Inventories, 442

Analysis of Inventories, 443

***APPENDIX 9A* LIFO RETAIL**
METHODS, 445

STABLE PRICES—LIFO RETAIL METHOD, 445

FLUCTUATING PRICES—DOLLAR-VALUE LIFO
RETAIL METHOD, 446

Subsequent Adjustments under Dollar-Value
LIFO Retail, 448

CHANGING FROM CONVENTIONAL RETAIL TO LIFO, 449

CHAPTER 10
ACQUISITION AND DISPOSITION OF
PROPERTY, PLANT, AND EQUIPMENT   471

Where Have All the Assets Gone?, 471

ACQUISITION AND VALUATION OF PROPERTY, PLANT,
AND EQUIPMENT, 473

Cost of Land, 473

Cost of Buildings, 474

Cost of Equipment, 474

Self-Constructed Assets, 474

Interest Costs During Construction, 475

Observations, 480

VALUATION, 481

Cash Discounts, 481

Deferred-Payment Contracts, 481

Lump-Sum Purchases, 482

Issuance of Stock, 483

Exchanges of Nonmonetary Assets, 484

Accounting for Contributions, 489

Other Asset Valuation Methods, 490

COSTS SUBSEQUENT TO ACQUISITION, 491

Additions, 492

Improvements and Replacements, 492

Rearrangement and Reinstallation, 493

Repairs, 493

Summary of Costs Subsequent to
Acquisition, 494

DISPOSITIONS OF PLANT ASSETS, 495

Sale of Plant Assets, 495

Involuntary Conversion, 496

Miscellaneous Problems, 496

CHAPTER 11
DEPRECIATION, IMPAIRMENTS,
AND DEPLETION 521

Do They Matter?, 521

DEPRECIATION—A METHOD OF COST ALLOCATION, 522
Factors Involved in the Depreciation Process, 523
Methods of Depreciation, 525
Special Depreciation Methods, 528
Hybrid or Combination Methods, 529
Special Depreciation Issues, 530

IMPAIRMENTS, 534
Recognizing Impairments, 534
Measuring Impairments, 535
Restoration of Impairment Loss, 536
Impairment of Assets to Be Disposed of, 536

DEPLETION, 537
Establishing a Depletion Base, 537
Write-Off of Resource Cost, 538
Continuing Controversy, 539
Special Problems in Depletion Accounting, 541

PRESENTATION AND ANALYSIS, 543
Presentation of Property, Plant, Equipment, and
Natural Resources, 543
Analysis of Property, Plant, Equipment, 544

APPENDIX 11A **INCOME TAX**
DEPRECIATION, 547

MODIFIED ACCELERATED COST RECOVERY SYSTEM, 547
Tax Lives (Recovery Periods), 548
Tax Depreciation Methods, 548
Example of MACRS System, 548
Optional Straight-line Method, 550
Tax versus Book Depreciation, 550

CHAPTER 12
INTANGIBLE ASSETS 571

Untouchable, 571

INTANGIBLE ASSET ISSUES, 572
Characteristics, 572
Valuation, 573
Amortization of Intangibles, 573

TYPES OF INTANGIBLE ASSETS, 575
Marketing-Related Intangible Assets, 575
Customer-Related Intangible Assets, 576
Artistic-Related Intangible Assets, 577
Contract-Related Intangible Assets, 577

Technology-Related Intangible Assets, 578
Goodwill, 580

IMPAIRMENT OF INTANGIBLE ASSETS, 584
Impairment of Limited-Life Intangibles, 584
Impairment of Indefinite-Life Intangibles Other
Than Goodwill, 585
Impairment of Goodwill, 586

RESEARCH AND DEVELOPMENT COSTS, 587
Identifying R&D Activities, 588
Accounting for R&D Activities, 588
Other Costs Similar to R&D Costs, 590
Conceptual Questions, 592

PRESENTATION OF INTANGIBLES AND
RELATED ITEMS, 592
Presentation of Intangible Assets, 592
Presentation of Research and
Development Costs, 594

APPENDIX 12A **ACCOUNTING FOR COMPUTER**
SOFTWARE COSTS, 596

DIVERSITY IN PRACTICE, 596

THE PROFESSION'S POSITION, 597

ACCOUNTING FOR CAPITALIZED SOFTWARE COSTS, 597

REPORTING SOFTWARE COSTS, 598

SETTING STANDARDS FOR SOFTWARE ACCOUNTING, 599

CHAPTER 13
CURRENT LIABILITIES
AND CONTINGENCIES 617

Now You See It, Now You Don't, 617

SECTION 1 **CURRENT LIABILITIES, 618**

WHAT IS A LIABILITY?, 618

WHAT IS A CURRENT LIABILITY?, 619
Accounts Payable, 619
Notes Payable, 620
Current Maturities of Long-Term Debt, 621
Short-Term Obligations Expected to
Be Refinanced, 622
Dividends Payable, 624
Customer Advances and Deposits, 624
Unearned Revenues, 624
Sales Taxes Payable, 625
Income Taxes Payable, 626
Employee-Related Liabilities, 626

SECTION 2 CONTINGENCIES, 631

GAIN CONTINGENCIES, 632

LOSS CONTINGENCIES, 632
Litigation, Claims, and Assessments, 634
Guarantee and Warranty Costs, 635
Premiums and Coupons, 637
Environmental Liabilities, 639
Self-Insurance, 641

SECTION 3 PRESENTATION
AND ANALYSIS, 642
Presentation of Current Liabilities, 642
Presentation of Contingencies, 644
Analysis of Current Liabilities, 645

APPENDIX 13A COMPUTATION OF
EMPLOYEES' BONUSES, 647

CHAPTER 14
LONG-TERM LIABILITIES   671
Your Debt Is Killing My Stock, 671

SECTION 1 BONDS PAYABLE, 672

ISSUING BONDS, 673

TYPES AND RATINGS OF BONDS, 673

VALUATION OF BOND PAYABLE—DISCOUNT
AND PREMIUM, 674
Bonds Issued at Par on Interest Date, 677
Bonds Issued at Discount or Premium on
Interest Date, 677
Bonds Issued between Interest Dates, 678

EFFECTIVE-INTEREST METHOD, 679
Bonds Issued at a Discount, 679
Bonds Issued at a Premium, 680
Accruing Interest, 681
Classification of Discount and Premium, 682

COSTS OF ISSUING BONDS, 682

TREASURY BONDS, 683

EXTINGUISHMENT OF DEBT, 683

SECTION 2 LONG-TERM NOTES PAYABLE, 685

NOTES ISSUED AT FACE VALUE, 686

NOTES NOT ISSUED AT FACE VALUE, 686
Zero-Interest-Bearing Notes, 686
Interest-Bearing Notes, 687

SPECIAL NOTES PAYABLE SITUATIONS, 688
Notes Issued for Property, Goods, and Services, 688
Choice of Interest Rate, 689

MORTGAGE NOTES PAYABLE, 691

SECTION 3 REPORTING AND ANALYSIS OF
LONG-TERM DEBT, 691

OFF-BALANCE-SHEET FINANCING, 691
Different Forms, 692
Rationale, 692

PRESENTATION AND ANALYSIS OF LONG-TERM DEBT, 694
Presentation of Long-Term Debt, 694
Analysis of Long-Term Debt, 695

APPENDIX 14A ACCOUNTING FOR
TROUBLED DEBT, 697

IMPAIRMENTS, 698
Example of Loss on Impairment, 698

TROUBLED DEBT RESTRUCTURINGS, 699
Settlement of Debt, 701
Modification of Terms, 702
Concluding Remarks, 706

Logo Credits, LC-1
Index, I-1
Official Accounting Pronouncements, P-1

TWELFTH EDITION

INTERMEDIATE ACCOUNTING

Volume 1

FINANCIAL ACCOUNTING AND ACCOUNTING STANDARDS

The Size of the New York Phone Book, If Necessary

Enron, Global Crossing, Kmart, WorldCom, Williams Cos., and Xerox are all companies that the Securities and Exchange Commission (SEC) recently scrutinized because of accounting issues. Share prices of all these companies have declined substantially. Investors punish any company whose quality of earnings is in doubt.

The unfortunate part of accounting scandals is that we all pay. For example, Enron's market capitalization totaled $80 billion before disclosure of its accounting irregularities. Today, it is bankrupt. Employees lost their pension money and investors their savings. Further, the entire stock market caught "Enronitis," a distrust of accounting that has led to substantial declines in the overall stock market. At one point, at least 10 congressional committees were inquiring into corporate governance issues, and Congress introduced over 30 Enron-related bills that addressed matters such as regulation of derivative securities, auditor–client conflicts, and development of an oversight body to regulate the accounting profession.

Companies have also taken steps to respond to the many investor concerns about the completeness and reliability of the accounting numbers. Many companies now expand the financial disclosures in their annual reports. For example, General Electric's CEO Jeffrey Immelt stated, "I want people to think about GE as we think of GE—as a transparent company." He noted that GE's annual report will be "the size of New York City's phone book, if necessary" to provide the information needed to help investors and creditors make the proper investing decisions.

We believe that meaningful reform will come out of these recent investigations into sloppy or fraudulent accounting. Although many consider the United States to have the finest financial reporting system in the world, we must do better. As former chair of the FASB Ed Jenkins remarked recently, "If anything positive results . . . it may be that [these accounting issues] serve as an indelible reminder to all that transparent financial reporting does matter and that lack of transparency imposes significant costs on all who participate [in our markets]."

Learning Objectives

After studying this chapter, you should be able to:

1 Identify the major financial statements and other means of financial reporting.
2 Explain how accounting assists in the efficient use of scarce resources.
3 Describe some of the challenges facing accounting.
4 Identify the objectives of financial reporting.
5 Explain the need for accounting standards.
6 Identify the major policy-setting bodies and their role in the standard-setting process.
7 Explain the meaning of generally accepted accounting principles.
8 Describe the impact of user groups on the standard-setting process.
9 Understand issues related to ethics and financial accounting.

As our opening story indicates, companies must provide relevant and reliable information so that our capital markets work efficiently. This chapter explains the environment of financial reporting and the many factors affecting it, as follows.

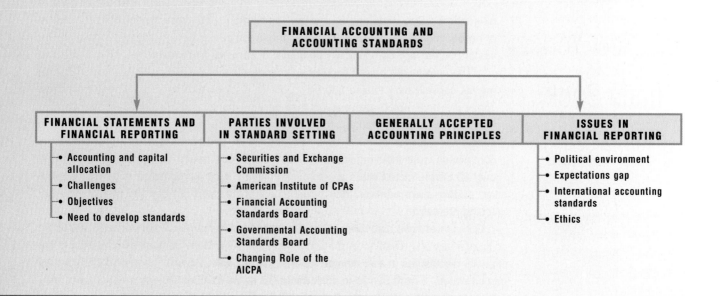

FINANCIAL STATEMENTS AND FINANCIAL REPORTING

The essential characteristics of accounting are: (1) the identification, measurement, and communication of financial information about (2) economic entities to (3) interested parties. **Financial accounting** is the process that culminates in the preparation of financial reports on the enterprise for use by both internal and external parties. Users of these financial reports include investors, creditors, managers, unions, and government agencies. In contrast, **managerial accounting** is the process of identifying, measuring, analyzing, and communicating financial information needed by management to plan, control, and evaluate a company's operations.

Financial statements are the principal means through which a company communicates its financial information to those outside it. These statements provide a company's history quantified in money terms. The **financial statements** most frequently provided are (1) the balance sheet, (2) the income statement, (3) the statement of cash flows, and (4) the statement of owners' or stockholders' equity. Note disclosures are an integral part of each financial statement.

Some financial information is better provided, or can be provided only, by means of **financial reporting** other than formal financial statements. Examples include the president's letter or supplementary schedules in the corporate annual report, prospectuses, reports filed with government agencies, news releases, management's forecasts, and social or environmental impact statements. Companies may need to provide such information because of authoritative pronouncement, regulatory rule, or custom. Or they may supply it because management wishes to disclose it voluntarily.

OBJECTIVE 1
Identify the major financial statements and other means of financial reporting.

In this textbook, we focus on the development of two types of financial information: (1) the basic financial statements and (2) related disclosures.

Accounting and Capital Allocation

Resources are limited. As a result, people try to conserve them and ensure that they are used effectively. Efficient use of resources often determines whether a business thrives. This fact places a substantial burden on the accounting profession.

Accountants must measure performance accurately and fairly on a timely basis, so that the right managers and companies are able to attract investment capital. For example, relevant and reliable financial information allows investors and creditors to compare the income and assets employed by such companies as **IBM**, **McDonald's**, **Microsoft**, and **Ford**. Because these users can assess the relative return and risks associated with investment opportunities, they channel resources more effectively. Illustration 1-1 shows how this process of capital allocation works.

<table>
<tr><td>Financial Reporting</td><td>Users
(present and potential)</td><td>Capital Allocation</td></tr>
<tr><td>The financial information a company provides to help users with capital allocation decisions about the company.</td><td>Investors and creditors use financial reports to make their capital allocation decisions.</td><td>The process of determining how and at what cost money is allocated among competing interests.</td></tr>
</table>

ILLUSTRATION 1-1
Capital Allocation Process

OBJECTIVE 2
Explain how accounting assists in the efficient use of scarce resources.

An effective process of capital allocation is critical to a healthy economy. It promotes productivity, encourages innovation, and provides an efficient and liquid market for buying and selling securities and obtaining and granting credit.[1] As we indicated in our opening story, unreliable and irrelevant information leads to poor capital allocation, which adversely affects the securities markets.

IT's NOT THE ECONOMY, ANYMORE, STUPID

It's not the economy anymore. It's the accounting. That's what many investors seem to be saying these days. As indicated in our opening story, even the slightest hint of any accounting irregularity at a company leads to a subsequent pounding of the company's stock price. For example, recent editions of the *Wall Street Journal* had the following headlines related to accounting and its effects on the economy.

- Stocks take a beating as accounting woes spread beyond **Enron**.
- Once hot **Krispy Kreme** ousts its CEO amid accounting woes.
- **Nortel** unveils new accounting flubs.
- Accounting woes at **AIG** take their toll on insurers' shares.
- Bank stocks fall as investors take issue with **PNC**'s accounting.

It now has become clear that investors must trust the accounting numbers or they will abandon the market and put their resources elsewhere. With investor uncertainty, the cost of capital increases for companies who need additional resources. In short, relevant and reliable financial information is necessary for markets to be efficient.

WHAT DO THE NUMBERS MEAN?

---

[1]AICPA Special Committee on Financial Reporting, "Improving Business Reporting—A Customer Focus," *Journal of Accountancy*, Supplement (October 1994).

The Challenges Facing Financial Accounting

OBJECTIVE 3
Describe some of the challenges facing accounting.

Much is right about financial reporting in the United States. We presently have the most liquid, deep, secure, and efficient public capital markets of any country at any time in history. One reason for this success is that our financial statements and related disclosures capture and organize financial information in a useful and reliable fashion. However, much still needs to be done. For example, if we move to the year 2020 and look back at financial reporting today, we might read the following:

- **Nonfinancial Measurements.** Financial reports failed to provide some key performance measures widely used by management, such as customer satisfaction indexes, backlog information, and reject rates on goods purchased.
- **Forward-looking Information.** Financial reports failed to provide forward-looking information needed by present and potential investors and creditors. One individual noted that financial statements in 2005 should have started with the phrase, "Once upon a time," to signify their use of historical cost and accumulation of past events.
- **Soft Assets.** Financial reports focused on hard assets (inventory, plant assets) but failed to provide much information about a company's soft assets (intangibles). The best assets are often intangible. Consider **Microsoft**'s know-how and market dominance, **Dell**'s unique marketing setup and well-trained employees, and **J. Crew**'s brand image.
- **Timeliness.** Companies only prepared financial statements quarterly, and provided audited financials annually. Little to no real-time financial statement information was available.

We believe each of these challenges must be met for the accounting profession to provide the type of information needed for an efficient capital allocation process. We are confident that changes will occur, based on these positive signs:

INTERNATIONAL INSIGHT

The objectives of financial reporting differ across nations. Traditionally, the primary objective of accounting in many continental European nations and in Japan was conformity with the law. In contrast, Canada, the U.K., the Netherlands, and many other nations share the U.S. view that the primary objective is to provide information for investors.

- Already some companies voluntarily disclose information deemed relevant to investors. Often such information is nonfinancial. For example, regional banking companies, such as **BankOne Corp.**, **Fifth Third Bancorp**, and **Sun Trust Banks**, now include data on loan growth, credit quality, fee income, operating efficiency, capital management, and management strategy.
- Initially, companies used the World Wide Web to provide limited financial data. Now most companies publish their annual reports in several formats on the Web. The most innovative companies offer sections of their annual reports in a format that the user can readily manipulate, such as in an Excel spreadsheet format. Companies also format their financial reports using extensible business reporting language (XBRL), which permits quicker and lower cost access to companies' financial information.
- More accounting standards now require the recording or disclosing of fair value information. For example, companies either record investments in stocks and bonds, debt obligations, and derivatives at fair value or companies show information related to fair values in the notes to the financial statements.

Changes in these directions will enhance the relevance of financial reporting and provide useful information to financial statement readers.

Objectives of Financial Reporting

OBJECTIVE 4
Identify the objectives of financial reporting.

To establish a foundation for financial accounting and reporting, the accounting profession identified a set of **objectives of financial reporting** by **business enterprises**. Financial reporting should provide information that:

1 Is useful to present and potential investors and creditors and other users **in making rational investment, credit, and similar decisions**. The information should be comprehensible to those who have a **reasonable understanding** of business and economic activities and are willing to study the information with reasonable diligence.

2 Helps present and potential investors, creditors, and other users **assess the amounts, timing, and uncertainty of prospective cash receipts** from dividends or interest and the proceeds from the sale, redemption, or maturity of securities or loans. Since investors' and creditors' cash flows are related to enterprise cash flows, financial reporting should provide information to help investors, creditors, and others assess the amounts, timing, and uncertainty of prospective net cash inflows to the related enterprise.

3 **Clearly portrays the economic resources of an enterprise, the claims to those resources** (obligations of the enterprise to transfer resources to other entities and owners' equity), and the effects of transactions, events, and circumstances that change its resources and claims to those resources.[2]

In brief, the objectives of financial reporting are to provide information that is (1) useful in investment and credit decisions, (2) useful in assessing cash flow prospects, and (3) about company resources, claims to those resources, and changes in them.

The emphasis on "assessing cash flow prospects" does not mean that the cash basis is preferred over the accrual basis of accounting. That is not the case. Information based on **accrual accounting generally better indicates a company's present and continuing ability to generate favorable cash flows** than does information limited to the financial effects of cash receipts and payments.[3]

Recall from your first accounting course the objective of **accrual-basis accounting**: It ensures that a company records events that change its financial statements in the periods in which the events occur, rather than only in the periods in which it receives or pays cash. Using the accrual basis to determine net income means that a company recognizes revenues when it earns them rather than when it receives cash. Similarly, it recognizes expenses when it incurs them rather than when it pays them. Under accrual accounting, a company generally recognizes revenues when it makes sales. The company can then relate the revenues to the economic environment of the period in which they occurred. Over the long run, trends in revenues and expenses are generally more meaningful than trends in cash receipts and disbursements.

The Need to Develop Standards

The main controversy in setting accounting standards is, "Whose rules should we play by, and what should they be?" The answer is not immediately clear. Users of financial accounting statements have both coinciding and conflicting needs for information of various types. To meet these needs, and to satisfy the fiduciary[4] reporting responsibility of management, companies prepare a single set of **general-purpose financial statements**. Users expect these statements to present fairly, clearly, and completely the company's financial operations.

The accounting profession has attempted to develop a set of standards that are generally accepted and universally practiced. Otherwise, each enterprise would have to develop its own standards. Further, readers of financial statements would have to familiarize themselves with every company's peculiar accounting and

> **OBJECTIVE 5**
> **Explain the need for accounting standards.**

---

[2]"Objectives of Financial Reporting by Business Enterprises," *Statement of Financial Accounting Concepts No. 1* (Stamford, Conn.: FASB, November 1978), pars. 5–8.

[3]*SFAC No. 1*, p. iv. As used here, *cash flow* means "cash generated and used in operations." The term *cash flows* also frequently means cash obtained by borrowing and used to repay borrowing, cash used for investments in resources and obtained from the disposal of investments, and cash contributed by or distributed to owners.

[4]Management's fiduciary responsibility is to manage assets with care and trust.

reporting practices. It would be almost impossible to prepare statements that could be compared.

This common set of standards and procedures is called **generally accepted accounting principles (GAAP)**. The term "generally accepted" means either that an authoritative accounting rule-making body has established a principle of reporting in a given area or that over time a given practice has been accepted as appropriate because of its universal application.[5] Although principles and practices continue to provoke both debate and criticism, most members of the financial community recognize them as the standards that over time have proven to be most useful. We present a more extensive discussion of what constitutes GAAP later in this chapter.

PARTIES INVOLVED IN STANDARD SETTING

OBJECTIVE 6
Identify the major policy-setting bodies and their role in the standard-setting process.

INTERNATIONAL INSIGHT

The International Organization of Securities Commissions (IOSCO), established in 1987, consists of more than 100 securities regulatory agencies or securities exchanges from all over the world. Collectively, its members represent a substantial proportion of the world's capital markets. The SEC is a member of IOSCO.

Four organizations are instrumental in the development of financial accounting standards (GAAP) in the United States:

1 Securities and Exchange Commission (SEC)
2 American Institute of Certified Public Accountants (AICPA)
3 Financial Accounting Standards Board (FASB)
4 Government Accounting Standards Board (GASB)

Securities and Exchange Commission (SEC)

External financial reporting and auditing developed in tandem with the growth of the industrial economy and its capital markets. However, when the stock market crashed in 1929 and the nation's economy plunged into the Great Depression, there were calls for increased government regulation of business generally, and especially financial institutions and the stock market.

As a result of these events, the federal government established the **Securities and Exchange Commission (SEC)** to help develop and standardize financial information presented to stockholders. The SEC is a federal agency. It administers the Securities Exchange Act of 1934 and several other acts. Most companies that issue securities to the public or are listed on a stock exchange are required to file audited financial statements with the SEC. In addition, the SEC has broad powers to prescribe, in whatever detail it desires, the accounting practices and standards to be employed by companies that fall within its jurisdiction. The SEC currently exercises oversight over 12,000 companies that are listed on the major exchanges (e.g., the New York Stock Exchange and the Nasdaq).

Public/Private Partnership

At the time the SEC was created, no group—public or private—issued accounting standards. The SEC encouraged the creation of a private standard-setting body because it believed that the private sector had the appropriate resources and talent to achieve this daunting task. As a result, accounting standards have developed in the private sector either through the American Institute of Certified Public Accountants (AICPA) or the Financial Accounting Standards Board (FASB).

The SEC has affirmed its support for the FASB by indicating that financial statements conforming to standards set by the FASB are presumed to have substantial authoritative support. In short, the **SEC requires registrants to adhere to GAAP**. In addition, the SEC indicated in its reports to Congress that "it continues to believe that the initiative for establishing and improving accounting standards should remain in the private sector, subject to Commission oversight."

---

[5]The terms *principles* and *standards* are used interchangeably in practice and throughout this textbook.

SEC Oversight

The SEC's partnership with the private sector works well. The SEC acts with remarkable restraint in the area of developing accounting standards. Generally, **the SEC relies on the FASB to develop accounting standards**.

The SEC's involvement in the development of accounting standards varies. In some cases, the SEC rejects a standard proposed by the private sector. In other cases, the SEC prods the private sector into taking quicker action on certain reporting problems, such as accounting for investments in debt and equity securities and the reporting of derivative instruments. In still other situations, the SEC communicates problems to the FASB, responds to FASB exposure drafts, and provides the FASB with counsel and advice upon request.

The SEC's mandate is to establish accounting principles. The private sector, therefore, must listen carefully to the views of the SEC. In some sense the private sector is the formulator and the implementor of the standards.[6] However, when the private sector fails to address accounting problems as quickly as the SEC would like, the partnership between the SEC and the private sector can be strained. This occurred in the recent deliberations on the accounting for business combinations and intangible assets, and concerns over the accounting for off-balance sheet special-purpose entities, highlighted in the failure of **Enron**.

Enforcement

As we indicated earlier, companies listed on a stock exchange must submit their financial statements to the SEC. If the SEC believes that an accounting or disclosure irregularity exists regarding the form or content of the financial statements, it sends a deficiency letter to the company. Companies usually resolve these deficiency letters quickly. However, if disagreement continues, the SEC may issue a "stop order," which prevents the registrant from issuing or trading securities on the exchanges. The Department of Justice may also file criminal charges for violations of certain laws. The SEC process, private sector initiatives, and civil and criminal litigation help to ensure the integrity of financial reporting for public companies.

American Institute of Certified Public Accountants (AICPA)

The **American Institute of Certified Public Accountants (AICPA)**, which is the national professional organization of practicing Certified Public Accountants (CPAs), has been an important contributor to the development of GAAP. Various committees and boards established since the founding of the AICPA have contributed to this effort.

Committee on Accounting Procedure

At the urging of the SEC, the AICPA appointed the Committee on Accounting Procedure in 1939. The **Committee on Accounting Procedure (CAP)**, composed of practicing CPAs, issued 51 **Accounting Research Bulletins** during the years 1939 to 1959. These bulletins dealt with a variety of accounting problems. But this problem-by-problem approach failed to provide the needed structured body of accounting principles. In response, in 1959 the AICPA created the Accounting Principles Board.

INTERNATIONAL INSIGHT

Nations also differ in the degree to which they developed national standards and consistent accounting practices. One indicator of the level of a nation's accounting is the nature of the accounting profession within the country. For example, the Netherlands, the U.K., Canada, and the U.S. established professional accounting bodies in the nineteenth century. In contrast, Hong Kong, Singapore, and Korea established similar bodies only in the last half century.

---

[6]One writer described the relationship of the FASB and SEC and the development of financial reporting standards using the analogy of a pearl. The pearl (a financial reporting standard) "is formed by the reaction of certain oysters (FASB) to an irritant (the SEC)—usually a grain of sand—that becomes embedded inside the shell. The oyster coats this grain with layers of nacre, and ultimately a pearl is formed. The pearl is a joint result of the irritant (SEC) and oyster (FASB); without both, it cannot be created." John C. Burton, "Government Regulation of Accounting and Information," *Journal of Accountancy* (June 1982).

Accounting Principles Board

The major purposes of the **Accounting Principles Board (APB)** were to (1) advance the written expression of accounting principles, (2) determine appropriate practices, and (3) narrow the areas of difference and inconsistency in practice. To achieve these objectives, the APB's mission was twofold: to develop an overall conceptual framework to assist in the resolution of problems as they become evident and to substantively research individual issues before the AICPA issued pronouncements. The Board's 18 to 21 members, selected primarily from public accounting, also included representatives from industry and academia. The Board's official pronouncements, called **APB Opinions**, were intended to be based mainly on research studies and be supported by reasons and analysis. Between its inception in 1959 and its dissolution in 1973, the APB issued 31 opinions.

Unfortunately, the APB came under fire early, charged with lack of productivity and failing to act promptly to correct alleged accounting abuses. Later the APB tackled numerous thorny accounting issues, only to meet a buzz saw of opposition from industry and CPA firms. It also ran into occasional governmental interference. In 1971 the accounting profession's leaders, anxious to avoid governmental rule-making, appointed a Study Group on Establishment of Accounting Principles. Commonly known as the **Wheat Committee** for its chair Francis Wheat, this group examined the organization and operation of the APB and determined the necessary changes to attain better results. The Study Group submitted its recommendations to the AICPA Council in the spring of 1972. The AICPA Council adopted the recommendations in total, and implemented them by early 1973.

Financial Accounting Standards Board (FASB)

The Wheat Committee's recommendations resulted in the demise of the APB and the creation of a new standard-setting structure composed of three organizations—the Financial Accounting Foundation (FAF), the Financial Accounting Standards Board (FASB), and the Financial Accounting Standards Advisory Council (FASAC). The **Financial Accounting Foundation** selects the members of the FASB and the Advisory Council, funds their activities, and generally oversees the FASB's activities.

The major operating organization in this three-part structure is the **Financial Accounting Standards Board (FASB)**. Its mission is to establish and improve standards of financial accounting and reporting for the guidance and education of the public, which includes issuers, auditors, and users of financial information. The expectations of success and support for the new FASB relied on several significant differences between it and its predecessor, the APB:

INTERNATIONAL INSIGHT

The U.S. legal system is based on English common law, whereby the government generally allows professionals to make the rules. The private sector, therefore, develops these rules (standards). Conversely, some countries follow codified law, which leads to government-run accounting systems.

1 **Smaller Membership.** The FASB consists of seven members, replacing the relatively large 18-member APB.

2 **Full-time, Remunerated Membership.** FASB members are well-paid, full-time members appointed for renewable 5-year terms. The APB members volunteered their part-time work.

3 **Greater Autonomy.** The APB was a senior committee of the AICPA. The FASB is not part of any single professional organization. It is appointed by and answerable only to the Financial Accounting Foundation.

4 **Increased Independence.** APB members retained their private positions with firms, companies, or institutions. FASB members must sever all such ties.

5 **Broader Representation.** All APB members were required to be CPAs and members of the AICPA. Currently, it is not necessary to be a CPA to be a member of the FASB.

In addition to research help from its own staff, the FASB relies on the expertise of various task force groups formed for various projects and on the **Financial Accounting Standards Advisory Council (FASAC)**. FASAC consults with the FASB on major policy and technical issues and also helps select task force members.

Due Process

In establishing financial accounting standards, the FASB relies on two basic premises: (1) The FASB should be responsive to the needs and viewpoints of the entire economic community, not just the public accounting profession. (2) It should operate in full view of the public through a "due process" system that gives interested persons ample opportunity to make their views known. To ensure the achievement of these goals, the FASB follows specific steps to develop a typical FASB Statement of Financial Accounting Standards, as Illustration 1-2 shows.

ILLUSTRATION 1-2
The Due Process System of the FASB

The passage of a new FASB **Standards Statement** requires the support of four of the seven Board members. FASB Statements are considered GAAP and thereby binding in practice. All ARBs and APB Opinions implemented by 1973 (when the FASB formed) continue to be effective until amended or superseded by FASB pronouncements. In recognition of possible misconceptions of the term "principles," the FASB uses the term **financial accounting standards** in its pronouncements.

Types of Pronouncements

The FASB issues three major types of pronouncements:

1 Standards, Interpretations, and Staff Positions.

2 Financial Accounting Concepts.

3 Emerging Issues Task Force Statements.

Standards, Interpretation, and Staff Positions. Financial accounting **standards** issued by the FASB are considered generally accepted accounting principles. In addition, the FASB also issues **interpretations** that modify or extend existing standards. Interpretations have the same authority, and require the same votes for passage, as standards. The APB also issued interpretations of APB Opinions. Both types of interpretations are now considered authoritative for purposes of determining GAAP. Finally, the FASB issues staff positions, which provide interpretive guidance and also minor amendments to standards and interpretations. These staff positions have the same authority as standards and interpretations. The Board also has issued FASB Technical Bulletins, which provide timely guidance on selected issues; staff positions are now used in lieu of technical bulletins. Since replacing the APB, the FASB has issued 154 standards, 47 interpretations, and over 30 staff positions. (See list at the back of the book.)

Financial Accounting Concepts. As part of a long-range effort to move away from the problem-by-problem approach, the FASB in November 1978 issued the first in a series of **Statements of Financial Accounting Concepts** as part of its conceptual framework project. (See list at the back of the book.) The series sets forth fundamental objectives and concepts that the Board uses in developing future standards of financial accounting and reporting. The Board intends to form a cohesive set of interrelated concepts—a conceptual framework—that will serve as tools for solving existing and emerging problems in a consistent manner. Unlike a Statement of Financial Accounting Standards, **a Statement of Financial Accounting Concepts does not establish GAAP.** Concepts statements, however, pass through the same due process system (discussion memo, public hearing, exposure draft, etc.) as do standards statements.

Emerging Issues Task Force Statements. In 1984 the FASB created the **Emerging Issues Task Force (EITF).** The EITF is comprised of representatives from CPA firms and financial statement preparers. Observers from the SEC and AICPA also attend EITF meetings. The purpose of the task force is to reach a consensus on how to account for new and unusual financial transactions that may potentially create differing financial reporting practices. Examples include accounting for pension plan terminations, revenue from barter transactions by Internet companies, and excessive amounts paid to takeover specialists. The EITF also provided timely guidance for the reporting of the losses arising from the terrorist attacks on the World Trade Center on September 11, 2001.

We cannot overestimate the importance of the EITF. In one year, for example, the task force examined 61 emerging financial reporting issues and arrived at a consensus on approximately 75 percent of them. The FASB reviews and approves all EITF consensuses. And the SEC indicated that it will view consensus solutions as preferred accounting. Further, it requires persuasive justification for departing from them.

The EITF helps the FASB in many ways. For example, emerging issues often attract public attention. If not resolved quickly, they can lead to financial crises and scandal. They can also undercut public confidence in current reporting practices. The next step, possible governmental intervention, would threaten the continuance of standard setting in the private sector. The EITF identifies controversial accounting problems as they arise. The EITF determines whether it can quickly resolve them, or whether to involve the FASB in solving them. In essence, it becomes a "problem filter" for the FASB. Thus, the FASB will hopefully work on more pervasive long-term problems, while the EITF deals with short-term emerging issues.

Governmental Accounting Standards Board (GASB)

Financial statements prepared by state and local governments are not comparable with financial reports prepared by private business organizations. The lack of comparability was highlighted in the 1970s when a number of large cities such as New York and Cleveland faced potential bankruptcy. As result, the **Governmental Accounting Standards Board (GASB)** came into being.

The operational structure of the GASB is similar to that of the FASB. That is, it has an advisory council called the Governmental Accounting Standards Advisory Council (GASAC), and has its own technical staff and task forces to assist its work.

The creation of the GASB was controversial. Many believe that there should be only one standard-setting body—the FASB. It was hoped that dividing standard-setting between the GASB, which deals with state and local government reporting, and the FASB, which addresses reporting for all other entities, would not lead to conflict. Since we are primarily concerned with financial reports prepared by profit-seeking organizations, this textbook focuses on standards issued by the FASB. Illustration 1-3 shows the current formal organizational structure for the development of financial reporting standards.

ILLUSTRATION 1-3
Organizational Structure
for Setting Accounting
Standards

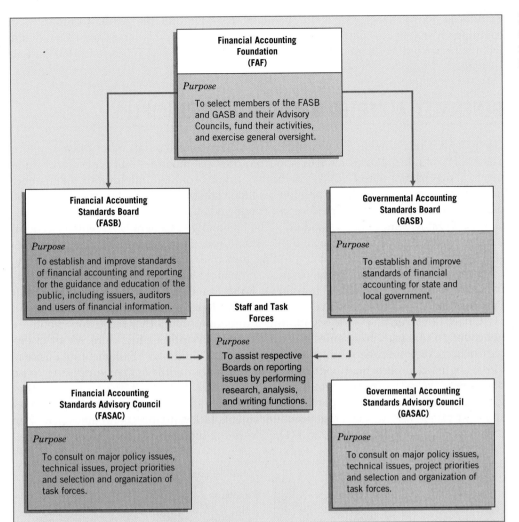

Changing Role of the AICPA

For several decades the AICPA provided leadership in developing accounting principles and rules. More than any other organization, it regulated the accounting profession, and developed and enforced accounting practice. When the FASB replaced the Accounting Principles Board, the AICPA established the **Accounting Standards Executive Committee (AcSEC)** as the committee authorized to speak for the AICPA in the area of financial accounting and reporting. It does so through various written communications:

Audit and Accounting Guides summarize the accounting practices of specific industries and provide specific guidance on matters not addressed by the FASB. Examples are accounting for casinos, airlines, colleges and universities, banks, insurance companies, and many others.

Statements of Position (SOP) provide guidance on financial reporting topics until the FASB sets standards on the issue in question. SOPs may update, revise, and clarify audit and accounting guides or provide free-standing guidance.

Practice Bulletins indicate AcSEC's views on narrow financial reporting issues not considered by the FASB.

Recently, the role of the AICPA in standard-setting has diminished. The FASB and the AICPA agree that, after a transition period, the AICPA and AcSEC no longer will issue authoritative accounting guidance for public companies. Furthermore, while the AICPA has been the leader in developing auditing standards through its **Auditing**

Standards Board, the Sarbanes-Oxley Act of 2002 requires the Public Company Accounting Oversight Board to oversee the development of auditing standards. The AICPA will continue to develop and grade the CPA examination, which is administered in all 50 states.

GENERALLY ACCEPTED ACCOUNTING PRINCIPLES

<table>
<tr><td>

OBJECTIVE 7
Explain the meaning of generally accepted accounting principles.

</td></tr>
</table>

Generally accepted accounting principles (GAAP) have substantial authoritative support. The AICPA's Code of Professional Conduct requires that members prepare financial statements in accordance with GAAP. Specifically, Rule 203 of this Code prohibits a member from expressing an unqualified opinion on financial statements that contain a material departure from generally accepted accounting principles.

The FASB is working on a standard, "The Hierarchy of Generally Accepted Accounting Principles," that defines the meaning of generally accepted accounting principles. This standard identifies the sources of accounting principles and the framework for selecting the principles to be used in the preparation of financial statements. The standard categorizes the major sources of GAAP as follows: **FASB Standards, Interpretations, and Staff Positions; APB Opinions**; and **AICPA Accounting Research Bulletins**.[7]

Often, however, a specific accounting transaction occurs that these documents do not cover. In this case, companies must use other authoritative literature. Major examples include AICPA Industry Auditing and Accounting Guides and Statements of Position. The recognized professional bodies provide substantial authoritative support to these documents. Why? Because these professional bodies vote their issuance only after giving interested and affected parties the opportunity to react to exposure drafts and respond at public hearings. If these pronouncements lack guidance, companies may then consider other sources. Illustration 1-4 presents the hierarchy of these sources.[8] If the

ILLUSTRATION 1-4
The House of GAAP

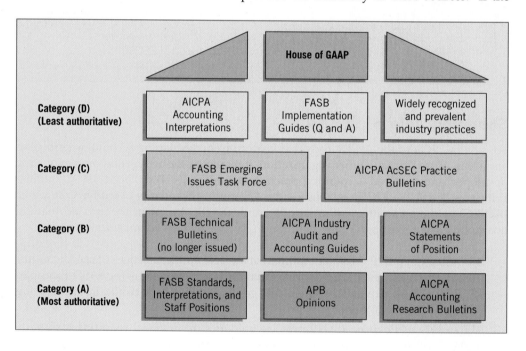

---

[7]The auditing literature presented the GAAP hierarchy prior to the issuance of this standard. The FASB decided that the GAAP hierarchy should be directed specifically to the company because it is the company (not the auditor) that is responsible for selecting the accounting principles for financial statements. As a result, the GAAP hierarchy should reside in the accounting literature, not the auditing literature. "The Hierarchy of Generally Accepted Accounting Principles," *Proposed Statement of Financial Accounting Standards* (Norwalk, Conn.: FASB, April 28, 2005.)

[8]See for example, Douglas Sauter, "Remodeling the House of GAAP," *Journal of Accountancy* (July 1991), pp. 30–37.

accounting treatment of an event is not specified by a Category A pronouncement, then Categories B through D should be investigated. If there is a conflict between pronouncements in B through D, companies should follow the higher category. For example, B is higher than C.

If none of these pronouncements addresses the event, companies seek support from other accounting literature. Examples include FASB Concepts Statements, International Accounting Standards, and accounting articles.[9]

YOU HAVE TO STEP BACK

WHAT DO THE NUMBERS MEAN?

Should the accounting profession have principles-based standards or rules-based standards? Critics of the profession today say that over the past three decades, standard-setters have moved away from broad accounting principles aimed at ensuring that companies' financial statements are fairly presented.

Instead, these critics say, standard-setters have moved toward drafting voluminous rules that, if technically followed in "check-box" fashion, may shield auditors and companies from legal liability. That has resulted in companies creating complex capital structures that comply with GAAP but hide billions of dollars of debt and other obligations. To add fuel to the fire, the chief accountant of the enforcement division of the SEC recently noted, "One can violate SEC laws and still comply with GAAP."

In short, what he is saying is that it is not enough just to check the boxes. You then have to step back and determine whether the *overall impression* created by GAAP financial statements fairly portrays the underlying economics of the company. It is a tough standard, but one that auditors and corporate management should strive to achieve.

Sources: Adapted from S. Liesman, "SEC Accounting Cop's Warning: Playing by the Rules May Not Head Off Fraud Issues," *Wall Street Journal* (February 12, 2002), p. C7. See also "Study Pursuant to Section 108(d) of the Sarbanes-Oxley Act of 2002 on the Adoption by the United States Financial Reporting System of a Principles-Based Accounting System," *SEC* (July 25, 2003).

ISSUES IN FINANCIAL REPORTING

Since the implementation of an accounting standard may affect many interests, much discussion often occurs about who should develop these standards and to whom they should apply. We discuss some of the major issues below.

Standard Setting in a Political Environment

User groups are possibly the most powerful force influencing the development of accounting standards. User groups consist of those most interested in or affected by accounting standards, rules, and procedures. Like lobbyists in our state and national capitals, user groups play a significant role. **Accounting standards are as much a product**

---

[9]A reasonable question to ask is, "Why is one set of documents more authoritative than others?" There are two explanations. First, at the time the AICPA or FASB developed a standard, the SEC recognized these organizations as the appropriate body to establish accounting principles. Second, in most cases, a document is more authoritative if, before the document is issued, its contents are (a) debated in a public forum, (b) exposed in writing to the public for comment, and (c) approved by the Board.

Existing GAAP comprises over 2,000 pronouncements. Recently the FASB has started a project to codify all these pronouncements into one major document. Everything in this document will be considered authoritative. Any material excluded would be considered non-authoritative.

of political action as they are of careful logic or empirical findings. User groups may want particular economic events accounted for or reported in a particular way, and they fight hard to get what they want. They know that the most effective way to influence the standards is to participate in the formulation of these standards or to try to influence or persuade the formulator of them.

These user groups often target the FASB, to pressure it to influence changes in the existing standards and the development of new ones.[10] In fact, these pressures have been multiplying. Some influential groups demand that the accounting profession act more quickly and decisively to solve its problems. Other groups resist such action, preferring to implement change more slowly, if at all. Illustration 1-5 shows the various user groups that apply pressure.

OBJECTIVE 8
Describe the impact of user groups on the standard-setting process.

ILLUSTRATION 1-5
User Groups that
Influence the
Formulation of
Accounting Standards

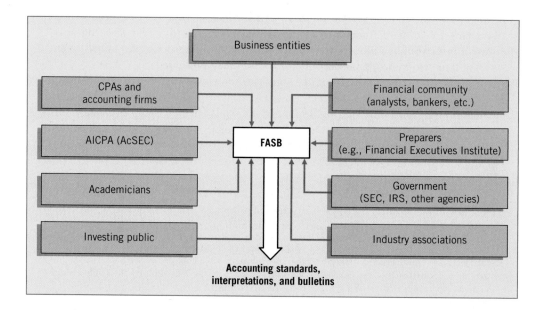

Should there be politics in setting standards for financial accounting and reporting? Why not? We have politics at home; at school; at the fraternity, sorority, and dormitory; at the office; at church, temple, and mosque. Politics is everywhere. Standard setting is part of the real world, and it cannot escape politics and political pressures.

THE ECONOMIC CONSEQUENCES OF GOODWILL

WHAT DO THE NUMBERS MEAN?

Investors generally ignore an accounting change, except when it substantially affects net income. Recently issued goodwill rules are one such change. Under previous GAAP, companies with goodwill charged it to revenues over time. Under new rules, companies no longer have to write off this cost. The effect on the bottom line for some companies is substantial. For example, assuming no goodwill amortization, **International Paper** estimates an income increase of 21 percent, **Johnson Controls** 16 percent, and **Pepsi Bottling Group** 30 percent.

Some believe this change will increase their stock's attractiveness. Others argue that it should have no effect because the write-off is a mere bookkeeping charge. Still others argue that the change has no effect on cash flows, but that investors will perceive the company to be more profitable, and therefore a good buy in the marketplace. In short, the numbers have consequences. What do you think?

---

[10]FASB board members acknowledged that they undertook many of the Board's projects, such as "Accounting for Contingencies," "Accounting for Pensions," "Statement of Cash Flows," and "Accounting for Derivatives," due to political pressure.

That is not to say that politics in standard setting is a negative force. Considering the **economic consequences**[11] of many accounting standards, special interest groups should vocalize their reactions to proposed standards. What the Board should *not* do is issue pronouncements that are primarily politically motivated. While paying attention to its constituencies, the Board should base its standards on sound research and a conceptual framework that has its foundation in economic reality.

The Expectations Gap

Accounting scandals at companies like **Enron, Cendant, Sunbeam, Rite-Aid, Xerox,** and **WorldCom** have attracted the attention of Congress. In 2002, it enacted legislation—the **Sarbanes-Oxley Act.** The new law increases the resources for the SEC to combat fraud and curb poor reporting practices.[12] And the SEC has increased its policing efforts, approving new auditor independence rules and materiality guidelines for financial reporting. In addition, the Sarbanes-Oxley Act introduces sweeping changes to the institutional structure of the accounting profession. The following are some of the key provisions of the legislation.

- Establishes an oversight board, the **Public Company Accounting Oversight Board (PCAOB),** for accounting practices. The PCAOB has oversight and enforcement authority and establishes auditing, quality control, and independence standards and rules.
- Implements stronger independence rules for auditors. Audit partners, for example, are required to rotate every five years and auditors are prohibited from offering certain types of consulting services to corporate clients.
- Requires CEOs and CFOs to personally certify that financial statements and disclosures are accurate and complete and requires CEOs and CFOs to forfeit bonuses and profits when there is an accounting restatement.
- Requires audit committees to be comprised of independent members and members with financial expertise.
- Requires codes of ethics for senior financial officers.

In addition, Section 404 of the Sarbanes-Oxley Act requires public companies to attest to the effectiveness of their internal controls over financial reporting. **Internal controls** are a system of checks and balances designed to prevent and detect fraud and errors. Most companies have these systems in place, but many have never completely documented them. Companies are finding that it is a costly process but perhaps badly needed. Already intense examination of internal controls has found lingering problems in the way companies operate. Recently, 424 companies reported deficiencies in internal control.[13] Many problems involved closing the books, revenue recognition deficiencies, reconciling accounts, or dealing with inventory. **SunTrust Bank,** for example, fired three officers after discovering errors in how the company calculates its allowance for bad debts. And **Visteon,** a car parts supplier, said it found problems recording and managing receivables from its largest customer, **Ford Motor.**

Will these changes be enough? The **expectations gap**—what the public thinks accountants *should* do and what accountants think they *can* do—is difficult to close. Due

---

[11]*Economic consequences* means the impact of accounting reports on the wealth positions of issuers and users of financial information, and the decision-making behavior resulting from that impact. The resulting behavior of these individuals and groups could have detrimental financial effects on the providers of the financial information. See Stephen A. Zeff, "The Rise of 'Economic Consequences'," *Journal of Accountancy* (December 1978), pp. 56–63. We extend appreciation to Professor Zeff for his insights on this chapter.

[12]*Sarbanes-Oxley Act of 2002,* H. R. Rep. No. 107-610 (2002).

[13]Leah Townsend, "Internal Control Deficiency Disclosures—Interim Alert," *Yellow Card—Interim Trend Alert* (April 12, 2005), Glass, Lewis & Co., LLC.

to the number of fraudulent reporting cases, some question whether the profession is doing enough. Although the profession can argue rightfully that accounting cannot be responsible for every financial catastrophe, it must continue to strive to meet the needs of society. However, efforts to meet these needs will become more costly to society. The development of a highly transparent, clear, and reliable system will require considerable resources.

International Accounting Standards

INTERNATIONAL INSIGHT

Foreign accounting firms that provide an audit report for a U.S.-listed company are subject to the authority of the accounting oversight board (mandated by the Sarbanes-Oxley Act).

Former Secretary of the Treasury Lawrence Summers indicated that the single most important innovation shaping the capital markets was the idea of generally accepted accounting principles. He went on to say that we need something similar internationally.

We believe that the Secretary is right. Relevant and reliable financial information is a necessity for viable capital markets. Unfortunately, companies outside the United States often prepare financial statements using standards different from U.S. GAAP. As a result, international companies such as **Coca-Cola**, **Microsoft**, and **IBM** have to develop financial information in different ways. Beyond the additional costs these companies incur, users of the financial statements often must understand at least two sets of GAAP. (Understanding one set is hard enough!) It is not surprising therefore that there is a growing demand for one set of high-quality international standards.

Presently, there are two sets of standards accepted for international use—U.S. GAAP and the International Financial Reporting Standards (IFRS) issued by the London-based **International Accounting Standards Board (IASB)**. As you will learn, there are many similarities between U.S. and IASB standards.

U.S. companies that list overseas are still permitted to use U.S. GAAP. Conversely foreign companies listed on our exchanges are required to reconcile their financial information to U.S. GAAP. The reason for the reconciliation is that U.S. GAAP is more extensive and detailed than the IASB standards.

Already 90 countries use IFRS, and the European Union now requires all listed companies in Europe (over 7,000 companies) to use it. The FASB and the IASB are now working hard to find common ground related to existing and proposed standards. Both parties recognize that global markets will best be served if only one set of GAAP is used. The task will not be easy, but the environment is conducive to convergence of the two systems. As Mary Barth, a member of the IASB noted, "There is still a lot to do, but I would never have dreamed we would be working as closely with the FASB as we do today."

Throughout the textbook, we provide in the margins international insights to help you understand the international reporting environment. In addition, Appendix 24B has an expanded discussion of international accounting.

Ethics in the Environment of Financial Accounting

OBJECTIVE 9
Understand issues related to ethics and financial accounting.

Robert Sack, a noted commentator on the subject of accounting ethics, observed, "Based on my experience, new graduates tend to be idealistic . . . thank goodness for that! Still it is very dangerous to think that your armor is all in place and say to yourself, 'I would have never given in to that.' The pressures don't explode on us; they build, and we often don't recognize them until they have us."

These observations are particularly appropriate for anyone entering the business world. In accounting, as in other areas of business, we frequently encounter ethical dilemmas. Some of these dilemmas are simple and easy to resolve. However, many are not, requiring difficult choices among allowable alternatives.

Companies that concentrate on "maximizing the bottom line," "facing the challenges of competition," and "stressing short-term results" place accountants in an environment of conflict and pressure. Basic questions such as, "Is this way of communicating financial information good or bad?" "Is it right or wrong?" "What should I do in the circumstance?" cannot always be answered by simply adhering to GAAP or following the rules of the profession. Technical competence is not enough when encountering ethical decisions.

Doing the right thing is not always easy or obvious. The pressures "to bend the rules," "to play the game," "to just ignore it" can be considerable. For example, "Will my decision affect my job performance negatively?", "Will my superiors be upset?", "Will my colleagues be unhappy with me?" are often questions business people face in making a tough ethical decision. The decision is more difficult because there is no comprehensive ethical system to provide guidelines.

Time, job, client, personal, and peer pressures can complicate the process of ethical sensitivity and selection among alternatives. Throughout this textbook, **we present ethical considerations to help sensitize you** to the type of situations you may encounter in the performance of your professional responsibility.

Expanded Discussion of Ethical Issues in Financial Reporting

HERE COME THE POLITICS

Given the many recent accounting scandals mentioned so far in the text, it is not surprising that both political parties are working to ensure that corporate management be ethical. President Bush, for example, announced a set of proposals to crack down on unethical behavior by corporate officials, expanding the offenses subject to criminal and civil penalties. And both the SEC and the Justice Department are to get more funding to combat financial fraud. At the same time, Democrats in Congress have pushed for more corporate-reform initiatives. So it is not surprising that both houses in Congress passed the Sarbanes-Oxley Act of 2002 with almost unanimous support and the president quickly signed it into law.

One thing is certain: Recent financial reporting undermined consumer confidence in corporate America and the capital markets. Because these issues hurt the U.S. economy, we can expect politicians to continue to seek solutions.

WHAT DO THE NUMBERS MEAN?

Conclusion

Bob Herz, FASB chairman, believes that there are three fundamental considerations the FASB must keep in mind in its standard-setting activities: (1) improvement in financial reporting, (2) simplification of the accounting literature and the standard-setting process, and (3) international convergence. These are notable objectives, and the Board is making good progress on all three dimensions. Issues such as off-balance-sheet financing, measurement of fair values, enhanced criteria for revenue recognition, and stock option accounting are examples of where the Board has exerted leadership. Improvements in financial reporting should follow.

Also, the Board is making it easier to understand what GAAP is. Presently GAAP is contained in a number of different documents. The lack of a single source makes it difficult to access and understand generally accepted principles. The Board is embarked on a long-term project ("the codification") that will compile GAAP in one document. This codification will organize existing GAAP by accounting topic regardless of its source (FASB Statements, APB Opinions, and so on). The codified standards will then be considered to be GAAP and to be authoritative, and all other literature will be considered non-authoritative.

Finally, international convergence is underway. Some projects already are completed and differences eliminated. Many more are on the drawing board. The crisis caused in the capital markets due to accounting irregularities of companies like **Enron**, **Krispy Kreme, Fannie Mae, Xerox**, and a host of others has caused the profession to reexamine its processes and standards. At present, we believe that the profession is reacting responsibly to remedy identified shortcomings.

SUMMARY OF LEARNING OBJECTIVES

KEY TERMS

Accounting Principles
  Board (APB), 8
Accounting Research
  Bulletins, 7
accrual-basis
  accounting, 5
American Institute of
  Certified Public
  Accountants (AICPA), 7
APB Opinions, 8
Auditing Standards
  Board, 11–12
Committee on
  Accounting Procedure
  (CAP), 7
Emerging Issues Task
  Force (EITF), 10
expectations gap, 15
financial accounting, 2
Financial Accounting
  Standards Board
  (FASB), 8
financial reporting, 2
financial statements, 2
generally accepted
  accounting principles
  (GAAP), 6
Governmental
  Accounting Standards
  Board (GASB), 10
International Accounting
  Standards Board
  (IASB), 16
interpretations, 9
objectives of financial
  reporting, 4
Public Company
  Accounting Oversight
  Board (PCAOB), 15
Sarbanes-Oxley Act of
  2002, 15
Securities and Exchange
  Commission (SEC), 6
Standards Statement, 9
Statement of Financial
  Accounting
  Concepts, 10
Wheat Committee, 8

1. Identify the major financial statements and other means of financial reporting. Companies most frequently provide (1) the balance sheet, (2) the income statement, (3) the statement of cash flows, and (4) the statement of owners' or stockholders' equity. Financial reporting other than financial statements may take various forms. Examples include the president's letter and supplementary schedules in the corporate annual report, prospectuses, reports filed with government agencies, news releases, management's forecasts, and descriptions of a company's social or environmental impact.

2. Explain how accounting assists in the efficient use of scarce resources. Accounting provides reliable, relevant, and timely information to managers, investors, and creditors to allow resource allocation to the most efficient enterprises. Accounting also provides measurements of efficiency (profitability) and financial soundness.

3. Describe some of the challenges facing accounting. Financial reports fail to provide (1) some key performance measures widely used by management, (2) forward-looking information needed by investors and creditors, (3) sufficient information on a company's soft assets (intangibles), and (4) real-time financial information.

4. Identify the objectives of financial reporting. The objectives of financial reporting are to provide information that is (1) useful in investment and credit decisions, (2) useful in assessing cash flow prospects, and (3) about enterprise resources, claims to those resources, and changes in them.

5. Explain the need for accounting standards. The accounting profession has attempted to develop a set of standards that is generally accepted and universally practiced. Without this set of standards, each company would have to develop its own standards. Readers of financial statements would have to familiarize themselves with every company's peculiar accounting and reporting practices. As a result, it would be almost impossible to prepare statements that could be compared.

6. Identify the major policy-setting bodies and their role in the standard-setting process. The *Securities and Exchange Commission (SEC)* is a federal agency that has the broad powers to prescribe, in whatever detail it desires, the accounting standards to be employed by companies that fall within its jurisdiction. The *American Institute of Certified Public Accountants (AICPA)* issued standards through its Committee on Accounting Procedure and Accounting Principles Board. The *Financial Accounting Standards Board (FASB)* establishes and improves standards of financial accounting and reporting for the guidance and education of the public.

7. Explain the meaning of generally accepted accounting principles. Generally accepted accounting principles (GAAP) are those principles that have substantial authoritative support, such as FASB Standards, Interpretations, and Staff Positions, APB Opinions and Interpretations, AICPA Accounting Research Bulletins, and other authoritative pronouncements.

8. Describe the impact of user groups on the standard-setting process. User groups may want particular economic events accounted for or reported in a particular way, and they fight hard to get what they want. They especially target the FASB to influence changes in the existing standards and the development of new ones. Because of the accelerated rate of change and the increased complexity of our economy, these pressures have been multiplying. Accounting standards are as much a product of political action as they are of careful logic or empirical findings. The IASB is working with U.S. standard setters toward international convergence of standards.

9. **Understand issues related to ethics and financial accounting.** Financial accountants are called on for moral discernment and ethical decision making. Decisions sometimes are difficult because a public consensus has not emerged to formulate a comprehensive ethical system that provides guidelines in making ethical judgments.

QUESTIONS

1. Differentiate broadly between financial accounting and managerial accounting.

2. Differentiate between "financial statements" and "financial reporting."

3. How does accounting help the capital allocation process?

4. What are some of the major challenges facing the accounting profession?

5. What are the major objectives of financial reporting?

6. Of what value is a common set of standards in financial accounting and reporting?

7. What is the likely limitation of "general-purpose financial statements"?

8. In what way is the Securities and Exchange Commission concerned about and supportive of accounting principles and standards?

9. What was the Committee on Accounting Procedure, and what were its accomplishments and failings?

10. For what purposes did the AICPA in 1959 create the Accounting Principles Board?

11. Distinguish among Accounting Research Bulletins, Opinions of the Accounting Principles Board, and Statements of the Financial Accounting Standards Board.

12. If you had to explain or define "generally accepted accounting principles or standards," what essential characteristics would you include in your explanation?

13. In what ways was it felt that the statements issued by the Financial Accounting Standards Board would carry greater weight than the opinions issued by the Accounting Principles Board?

14. How are FASB discussion memoranda and FASB exposure drafts related to FASB "statements"?

15. Distinguish between FASB "statements of financial accounting standards" and FASB "statements of financial accounting concepts."

16. What is Rule 203 of the Code of Professional Conduct?

17. Rank from the most authoritative to the least authoritative, the following three items: FASB Technical Bulletins, AICPA Practice Bulletins, and FASB Standards.

18. The chairman of the FASB at one time noted that "the flow of standards can only be slowed if (1) producers focus less on quarterly earnings per share and tax benefits and more on quality products, and (2) accountants and lawyers rely less on rules and law and more on professional judgment and conduct." Explain his comment.

19. What is the purpose of FASB Staff Positions?

20. Explain the role of the Emerging Issues Task Force in establishing generally accepted accounting principles.

21. What is the purpose of the Governmental Accounting Standards Board?

22. What are some possible reasons why another organization, such as the Governmental Accounting Standards Board, should not issue financial reporting standards?

23. What are the sources of pressure that change and influence the development of accounting principles and standards?

24. Some individuals have indicated that the FASB must be cognizant of the economic consequences of its pronouncements. What is meant by "economic consequences"? What dangers exist if politics play too much of a role in the development of financial reporting standards?

25. If you were given complete authority in the matter, how would you propose that accounting principles or standards should be developed and enforced?

26. One writer recently noted that 99.4 percent of all companies prepare statements that are in accordance with GAAP. Why then is there such concern about fraudulent financial reporting?

27. What is the "expectations gap"? What is the profession doing to try to close this gap?

28. The Sarbanes-Oxley Act was enacted to combat fraud and curb poor reporting practices. What are some key provisions of this legislation?

29. A number of foreign countries have reporting standards that differ from those in the United States. What are some of the main reasons why reporting standards are often different among countries?

30. Why would it be advantageous for U.S. GAAP and International GAAP to be the same?

31. How are financial accountants challenged in their work to make ethical decisions? Is technical mastery of GAAP not sufficient to the practice of financial accounting?

CONCEPTS FOR ANALYSIS

CA1-1 (Financial Accounting) Alan Rodriquez has recently completed his first year of studying accounting. His instructor for next semester has indicated that the primary focus will be the area of financial accounting.

Instructions
- **(a)** Differentiate between financial accounting and managerial accounting.
- **(b)** One part of financial accounting involves the preparation of financial statements. What are the financial statements most frequently provided?
- **(c)** What is the difference between financial statements and financial reporting?

CA1-2 (Objectives of Financial Reporting) Celia Cruz, a recent graduate of the local state university, is presently employed by a large manufacturing company. She has been asked by Angeles Ochoa, controller, to prepare the company's response to a current Discussion Memorandum published by the Financial Accounting Standards Board (FASB). Cruz knows that the FASB has issued seven *Statements of Financial Accounting Concepts*, and she believes that these concept statements could be used to support the company's response to the Discussion Memorandum. She has prepared a rough draft of the response citing *Statement of Financial Accounting Concepts No. 1*, "Objectives of Financial Reporting by Business Enterprises."

Instructions
- **(a)** Identify the three objectives of financial reporting as presented in *Statement of Financial Accounting Concepts No. 1 (SFAC No. 1)*.
- **(b)** Describe the level of sophistication expected of the users of financial information by *SFAC No. 1*.

(CMA adapted)

CA1-3 (Accounting Numbers and the Environment) Hardly a day goes by without an article appearing on the crises affecting many of our financial institutions in the United States. It is estimated that the savings and loan (S&L) debacle of the 1980s, for example, ended up costing $500 billion ($2,000 for every man, woman, and child in the United States). Some argue that if the S&Ls had been required to report their investments at market value instead of cost, large losses would have been reported earlier, which would have signaled regulators to close those S&Ls and, therefore, minimize the losses to U.S. taxpayers.

Instructions
Explain how reported accounting numbers might affect an individual's perceptions and actions. Cite two examples.

CA1-4 (Need for Accounting Standards) Some argue that having various organizations establish accounting principles is wasteful and inefficient. Rather than mandating accounting standards, each company could voluntarily disclose the type of information it considered important. In addition, if an investor wants additional information, the investor could contact the company and pay to receive the additional information desired.

Instructions
Comment on the appropriateness of this viewpoint.

CA1-5 (AICPA's Role in Standard Setting) One of the major groups involved in the standard-setting process is the American Institute of Certified Public Accountants. Initially it was the primary organization that established accounting principles in the United States. Subsequently it relinquished most of its power to the FASB.

Instructions
- **(a)** Identify the two committees of the AICPA that established accounting principles prior to the establishment of the FASB.
- **(b)** Speculate as to why these two organizations failed. In your answer, identify steps the FASB has taken to avoid failure.
- **(c)** What is the present role of the AICPA in the standard-setting environment?

CA1-6 (FASB Role in Standard Setting) A press release announcing the appointment of the trustees of the new Financial Accounting Foundation stated that the Financial Accounting Standards Board (to be appointed by the trustees) ". . . will become the established authority for setting accounting principles under which corporations report to the shareholders and others" (AICPA news release July 20, 1972).

Instructions
- **(a)** Identify the sponsoring organization of the FASB and the process by which the FASB arrives at a decision and issues an accounting standard.

(b) Indicate the major types of pronouncements issued by the FASB and the purposes of each of these pronouncements.

CA1-7 (Government Role in Standard Setting) Recently an article stated "the setting of accounting standards in the United States is now about 70 years old. It is a unique process in our society, one that has undergone numerous changes over the years. The standards are established by a private sector entity that has no dominant sponsor and is not part of any professional organization or trade association. The governmental entity that provides oversight, on the other hand, is far more a friend than a competitor or an antagonist."

Instructions

Identify the governmental entity that provides oversight and indicate its role in the standard-setting process.

 CA1-8 (Politicization of Standard Setting) Some accountants have said that politicization in the development and acceptance of generally accepted accounting principles (i.e., standard setting) is taking place. Some use the term "politicization" in a narrow sense to mean the influence by governmental agencies, particularly the Securities and Exchange Commission, on the development of generally accepted accounting principles. Others use it more broadly to mean the compromise that results when the bodies responsible for developing generally accepted accounting principles are pressured by interest groups (SEC, American Accounting Association, businesses through their various organizations, Institute of Management Accountants, financial analysts, bankers, lawyers, and so on).

Instructions

(a) The Committee on Accounting Procedure of the AICPA was established in the mid- to late 1930s and functioned until 1959, at which time the Accounting Principles Board came into existence. In 1973, the Financial Accounting Standards Board was formed and the APB went out of existence. Do the reasons these groups were formed, their methods of operation while in existence, and the reasons for the demise of the first two indicate an increasing politicization (as the term is used in the broad sense) of accounting standard setting? Explain your answer by indicating how the CAP, the APB, and the FASB operated or operate. Cite specific developments that tend to support your answer.

(b) What arguments can be raised to support the "politicization" of accounting standard setting?

(c) What arguments can be raised against the "politicization" of accounting standard setting?

(CMA adapted)

CA1-9 (Models for Setting Accounting Standards) Presented below are three models for setting accounting standards.

1. The purely political approach, where national legislative action decrees accounting standards.

2. The private, professional approach, where financial accounting standards are set and enforced by private professional actions only.

3. The public/private mixed approach, where standards are basically set by private-sector bodies that behave as though they were public agencies and whose standards to a great extent are enforced through governmental agencies.

Instructions

(a) Which of these three models best describes standard setting in the United States? Comment on your answer.

(b) Why do companies, financial analysts, labor unions, industry trade associations, and others take such an active interest in standard setting?

(c) Cite an example of a group other than the FASB that attempts to establish accounting standards. Speculate as to why another group might wish to set its own standards.

CA1-10 (Standard-Setting Terminology) Andrew Wyeth, an administrator at a major university, recently said, "I've got some CDs in my IRA, which I set up to beat the IRS." As elsewhere, in the world of accounting and finance, it often helps to be fluent in abbreviations and acronyms.

Instructions

Presented below is a list of common accounting acronyms. Identify the term for which each acronym stands, and provide a brief definition of each term.

(a)	AICPA	**(e)**	FAF	**(i)**	CPA	**(m)**	GASB
(b)	CAP	**(f)**	FASAC	**(j)**	FASB		
(c)	ARB	**(g)**	SOP	**(k)**	SEC		
(d)	APB	**(h)**	GAAP	**(l)**	IASB		

CA1-11 **(Accounting Organizations and Documents Issued)** Presented below are a number of accounting organizations and types of documents they have issued.

Instructions

Match the appropriate document to the organization involved. Note that more than one document may be issued by the same organization. If no document is provided for an organization, write in "0."

Organization

1. _____ Accounting Standards Executive Committee
2. _____ Accounting Principles Board
3. _____ Committee on Accounting Procedure
4. _____ Financial Accounting Standards Board

Document

(a) Opinions
(b) Practice Bulletins
(c) Accounting Research Bulletins
(d) Financial Accounting Standards
(e) Statements of Position

CA1-12 **(Accounting Pronouncements)** Standard setting bodies have issued a number of authoritative pronouncements. A list is provided on the left, below, with a description of these pronouncements on the right.

Instructions

Match the description to the pronouncements.

1. _____ Staff Positions
2. _____ Interpretations (of the Financial Accounting Standards Board)
3. _____ Statement of Financial Accounting Standards
4. _____ EITF Statements
5. _____ Opinions
6. _____ Statement of Financial Accounting Concepts

(a) Official pronouncements of the APB.
(b) Sets forth fundamental objectives and concepts that will be used in developing future standards.
(c) Primary document of the FASB that establishes GAAP.
(d) Provides additional guidance on implementing or applying FASB Standards or Interpretations.
(e) Provides guidance on how to account for new and unusual financial transactions that have the potential for creating diversity in financial reporting practices.
(f) Represent extensions or modifications of existing standards.

CA1-13 **(Issues Involving Standard Setting)** When the FASB issues new standards, the implementation date is usually 12 months from date of issuance, with early implementation encouraged. Paula Popovich, controller, discusses with her financial vice president the need for early implementation of a standard that would result in a fairer presentation of the company's financial condition and earnings. When the financial vice president determines that early implementation of the standard will adversely affect the reported net income for the year, he discourages Popovich from implementing the standard until it is required.

Instructions

Answer the following questions.
(a) What, if any, is the ethical issue involved in this case?
(b) Is the financial vice president acting improperly or immorally?
(c) What does Popovich have to gain by advocacy of early implementation?
(d) Which stakeholders might be affected by the decision against early implementation?

(CMA adapted)

CA1-14 **(Securities and Exchange Commission)** The U.S. Securities and Exchange Commission (SEC) was created in 1934 and consists of five commissioners and a large professional staff. The SEC professional staff is organized into five divisions and several principal offices. The primary objective of the SEC is to support fair securities markets. The SEC also strives to foster enlightened stockholder participation in corporate decisions of publicly traded companies. The SEC has a significant presence in financial markets, the development of accounting practices, and corporation-shareholder relations, and has the power to exert influence on entities whose actions lie within the scope of its authority.

Instructions

(a) Explain from where the Securities and Exchange Commission receives its authority.
(b) Describe the official role of the Securities and Exchange Commission in the development of financial accounting theory and practices.

(c) Discuss the interrelationship between the Securities and Exchange Commission and the Financial Accounting Standards Board with respect to the development and establishment of financial accounting theory and practices.

(CMA adapted)

CA1-15 (Standard-Setting Process) In 1973, the responsibility for developing and issuing rules on accounting practices was given to the Financial Accounting Foundation and, in particular, to an arm of the foundation called the Financial Accounting Standards Board (FASB). The generally accepted accounting principles established by the FASB are enunciated through a publication series entitled *Statements of Financial Accounting Standards*. These statements are issued periodically, and over 150 have been issued. The statements have a significant influence on the way in which financial statements are prepared by U.S. corporations.

Instructions
(a) Describe the process by which a topic is selected or identified as appropriate for study by the Financial Accounting Standards Board (FASB).
(b) Once a topic is considered appropriate for consideration by the FASB, a series of steps is followed before a *Statement of Financial Accounting Standards* is issued. Describe the major steps in the process leading to the issuance of a standard.
(c) Identify at least three other organizations that influence the setting of generally accepted accounting principles (GAAP).

(CMA adapted)

CA1-16 (Financial Reporting Pressures) Presented below is abbreviated testimony from Troy Normand in the **WorldCom** case. He was a manager in the corporate reporting department and is one of five individuals who pleaded guilty. He is testifying in hopes of receiving no prison time when he is ultimately sentenced.

Q. Mr. Normand, if you could just describe for the jury how the meeting started and what was said during the meeting?

A. I can't recall exactly who initiated the discussion, but right away Scott Sullivan acknowledged that he was aware we had problems with the entries, David Myers had informed him, and we were considering resigning.

He said that he respected our concerns but that we weren't being asked to do anything that he believed was wrong. He mentioned that he acknowledged that the company had lost focus quite a bit due to the preparations for the Sprint merger, and that he was putting plans in place and projects in place to try to determine where the problems were, why the costs were so high.

He did say he believed that the initial statements that we produced, that the line costs in those statements could not have been as high as they were, that he believes something was wrong and there was no way that the costs were that high.

I informed him that I didn't believe the entry we were being asked to do was right, that I was scared, and I didn't want to put myself in a position of going to jail for him or the company. He responded that he didn't believe anything was wrong, nobody was going to be going to jail, but that if it later was found to be wrong, that he would be the person going to jail, not me.

He asked that I stay, don't jump off the plane, let him land it softly, that's basically how he put it. And he mentioned that he had a discussion with Bernie Ebbers asking Bernie to reduce projections going forward and that Bernie had refused.

Q. Mr. Normand, you said that Mr. Sullivan said something about don't jump out of the plane. What did you understand him to mean when he said that?

A. Not to quit.

Q. During this meeting, did Mr. Sullivan say anything about whether you would be asked to make entries like this in the future?

A. Yes, he made a comment that from that point going forward we wouldn't be asked to record any entries, high-level late adjustments, that the numbers would be the numbers.

Q. What did you understand that to be mean, the numbers would be the numbers?

A. That after the preliminary statements were issued, with the exception of any normal transaction, valid transaction, we wouldn't be asked to be recording any more late entries.

Q. I believe you testified that Mr. Sullivan said something about the line cost numbers not being accurate. Did he ask you to conduct any analysis to determine whether the line cost numbers were accurate?

A. No, he did not.

Q. Did anyone ever ask you to do that?

A. No.

Q. Did you ever conduct any such analysis?

A. No, I didn't.

Q. During this meeting, did Mr. Sullivan ever provide any accounting justification for the entry you were asked to make?

A. No, he did not.

Q. Did anything else happen during the meeting?

A. I don't recall anything else.

Q. How did you feel after this meeting?

A. Not much better actually. I left his office not convinced in any way that what we were asked to do was right. However, I did question myself to some degree after talking with him wondering whether I was making something more out of what was really there.

Instructions

Answer the following questions.

- **(a)** What appears to be the ethical issue involved in this case?
- **(b)** Is Troy Normand acting improperly or immorally?
- **(c)** What would you do if you were Troy Normand?
- **(d)** Who are the major stakeholders in this case?

CA1-17 **(Economic Consequences)** Presented below are comments made in the financial press.

Instructions

Prepare responses to the requirements in each item.

- **(a)** Rep. John Dingell, the ranking Democrat on the House Commerce Committee, threw his support behind the FASB's controversial derivatives accounting standard and encouraged the FASB to adopt the rule promptly. Indicate why a member of Congress might feel obligated to comment on this proposed FASB standard.
- **(b)** In a strongly worded letter to Senator Lauch Faircloth (R-NC) and House Banking Committee Chairman Jim Leach (R-IA), the American Institute of Certified Public Accountants (AICPA) cautioned against government intervention in the accounting standard-setting process, warning that it had the potential of jeopardizing U.S. capital markets. Explain how government intervention could possibly affect capital markets adversely.

CA1-18 **(Standard-Setting Process, Economic Consequences)** The following letter was sent to the SEC and the FASB by leaders of the business community.

Dear Sirs:

The FASB has been struggling with accounting for derivatives and hedging for many years. The FASB has now developed, over the last few weeks, a new approach that it proposes to adopt as a final standard. We understand that the Board intends to adopt this new approach as a final standard without exposing it for public comment and debate, despite the evident complexity of the new approach, the speed with which it has been developed and the significant changes to the exposure draft since it was released more than one year ago. Instead, the Board plans to allow only a brief review by selected parties, limited to issues of operationality and clarity, and would exclude questions as to the merits of the proposed approach.

As the FASB itself has said throughout this process, its mission does not permit it to consider matters that go beyond accounting and reporting considerations. Accordingly, the FASB may not have adequately considered the wide range of concerns that have been expressed about the derivatives and hedging proposal, including concerns related to the potential impact on the capital markets, the weakening of companies' ability to manage risk, and the adverse control implications of implementing costly and complex new rules imposed at the same time as other major initiatives, including the Year 2000 issues and a single European currency. We believe that these crucial issues must be considered, if not by the FASB, then by the Securities and Exchange Commission, other regulatory agencies, or Congress.

We believe it is essential that the FASB solicit all comments in order to identify and address all material issues that may exist before issuing a final standard. We understand the desire to bring this process to a prompt conclusion, but the underlying issues are so important to this nation's businesses, the customers they serve and the economy as a whole that expediency cannot be the dominant consideration. As a result, we urge the FASB to expose its new proposal for public comment, following the established due process procedures that are essential to acceptance of its standards, and providing sufficient time to affected parties to understand and assess the new approach.

We also urge the SEC to study the comments received in order to assess the impact that these proposed rules may have on the capital markets, on companies' risk management practices, and on management and financial controls. These vital public policy matters deserve consideration as part of the Commission's oversight responsibilities.

We believe that these steps are essential if the FASB is to produce the best possible accounting standard while minimizing adverse economic effects and maintaining the competitiveness of U.S. businesses in the international marketplace.

Very truly yours,

(This letter was signed by the chairs of 22 of the largest U.S. companies.)

Instructions

Answer the following questions.

(a) Explain the "due process" procedures followed by the FASB in developing a financial reporting standard.

(b) What is meant by the term "economic consequences" in accounting standard setting?

(c) What economic consequences arguments are used in this letter?

(d) What do you believe is the main point of the letter?

(e) Why do you believe a copy of this letter was sent by the business community to influential members of the United States Congress?

USING YOUR JUDGMENT

Financial Reporting Problem

Kate Jackson, a new staff accountant, is confused because of the complexities involving accounting standard setting. Specifically, she is confused by the number of bodies issuing financial reporting standards of one kind or another and the level of authoritative support that can be attached to these reporting standards. Kate decides that she must review the environment in which accounting standards are set, if she is to increase her understanding of the accounting profession.

Kate recalls that during her accounting education there was a chapter or two regarding the environment of financial accounting and the development of accounting standards. However, she remembers that her instructor placed little emphasis on these chapters.

Instructions

(a) Help Kate by identifying key organizations involved in accounting standard setting.

(b) Kate asks for guidance regarding authoritative support. Please assist her by explaining what is meant by authoritative support.

(c) Give Kate a historical overview of how standard setting has evolved so that she will not feel that she is the only one to be confused.

(d) What authority for compliance with GAAP has existed throughout the period of standard setting?

International Reporting Case

Michael Sharpe, former Deputy Chairman of the International Accounting Standards Committee (IASC), made the following comments to the 63rd Annual Conference of the Financial Executives Institute (FEI).

There is an irreversible movement towards the harmonization of financial reporting throughout the world. The international capital markets require an end to:

1 The confusion caused by international companies announcing different results depending on the set of accounting standards applied. Recent announcements by **Daimler-Benz** [now **DaimlerChrysler**] highlight the confusion that this causes.

2 Companies in some countries obtaining unfair commercial advantages from the use of particular national accounting standards.

3 The complications in negotiating commercial arrangements for international joint ventures caused by different accounting requirements.

4 The inefficiency of international companies having to understand and use a myriad of different accounting standards depending on the countries in which they operate and the countries in which they raise capital and debt. Executive talent is wasted on keeping up to date with numerous sets of accounting standards and the never-ending changes to them.

5 The inefficiency of investment managers, bankers, and financial analysts as they seek to compare financial reporting drawn up in accordance with different sets of accounting standards.

6   Failure of many stock exchanges and regulators to require companies subject to their jurisdiction to provide comparable, comprehensive, and transparent financial reporting frameworks giving international comparability.

Instructions

(a) What is the International Accounting Standards Board?

(b) What stakeholders might benefit from the use of International Accounting Standards?

(c) What do you believe are some of the major obstacles to harmonization?

Professional Research: Financial Accounting and Reporting

As a newly enrolled accounting major, you are anxious to better understand accounting institutions and sources of accounting literature. As a first step, you decide to explore the FASB's Statement of Financial Accounting Concepts No. 1 (CON 1).

Instructions

Using the **Financial Accounting Research System (FARS)**, respond to the following items. (Provide text strings used in your search.)

(a) Find *Statement of Financial Accounting Concepts No. 1*. List three ways to access it on FARS.

(b) According to CON 1, "…financial reporting includes not only financial statements but also other means of communicating information." What other means are there of communicating information?

(c) According to CON 1, "…many people base economic decisions on their relationships to and knowledge about business enterprises and thus are potentially interested in the information provided by financial reporting." Indicate some of the users and the information they are most directly concerned with in economic decision making.

Professional Simulation

In this simulation you are asked questions regarding accounting principles. Prepare response to all parts.

KWW_Professional _Simulation

Generally Accepted Accounting Principles | **Time Remaining 4 hours 30 minutes** | copy paste calculator sheet standards help splitter done

Directions | Situation | Explanation | Resources

At the completion of Bloom Company's audit, the president, Judy Bloom, asks about the meaning of the phrase "in conformity with generally accepted accounting principles" that appears in your audit report on the management's financial statements. Judy observes that the meaning of the phrase must include something more and different than what she thinks of as "principles."

Directions | Situation | Explanation | Resources

(a) Explain the meaning of the term "accounting principles" as used in the audit report. (Do not discuss in this part the significance of "generally accepted.")

(b) President Bloom wants to know how you determine whether or not an accounting principle is generally accepted. Discuss the sources of evidence for determining whether an accounting principle has substantial authoritative support. Do not merely list the titles of publications.

Remember to check the book's companion website to find additional resources for this chapter.

CONCEPTUAL FRAMEWORK UNDERLYING FINANCIAL ACCOUNTING

Show Me the Earnings!

The growth of new-economy business on the Internet has led to the development of new measures of performance. When **Priceline.com** splashed on the dot-com scene, it touted steady growth in a measure called "unique offers by users" to explain its heady stock price. To draw investors to its stock, **Drugstore.com** focused on the number of "unique customers" at its website. After all, new businesses call for new performance measures, right?

Not necessarily. In fact, these indicators failed to show any consistent relationship between profits and website visits. Eventually, as the graphs below show, the profits never materialized, and stock prices fell. The lesson here: Although the new economy may require some new measures, investors need to be careful not to forget the reliable traditional ones.[1]

[1]Story and graphs adapted from Gretchen Morgenson, "How Did They Value Stocks? Count the Absurd Ways," *New York Times* (March 18, 2001), section 3, p. 1.

Learning Objectives

After studying this chapter, you should be able to:

1 Describe the usefulness of a conceptual framework.

2 Describe the FASB's efforts to construct a conceptual framework.

3 Understand the objectives of financial reporting.

4 Identify the qualitative characteristics of accounting information.

5 Define the basic elements of financial statements.

6 Describe the basic assumptions of accounting.

7 Explain the application of the basic principles of accounting.

8 Describe the impact that constraints have on reporting accounting information.

As our opening story indicates, users of financial statements need relevant and reliable information. To help develop this type of financial information, financial accounting and reporting relies on a conceptual framework. In this chapter, we discuss the basic concepts underlying the conceptual framework, as follows.

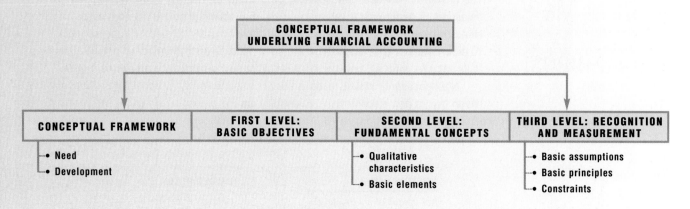

CONCEPTUAL FRAMEWORK

A **conceptual framework** is like a **constitution**: It is "a coherent system of interrelated objectives and fundamentals that can lead to consistent standards and that prescribes the nature, function, and limits of financial accounting and financial statements."[2] Many consider the FASB's real contribution to depend on the quality and utility of the conceptual framework.

The Need for a Conceptual Framework

OBJECTIVE 1
Describe the usefulness of a conceptual framework.

Why do we need a conceptual framework? First, to be useful, standard setting should build on and relate to an established body of concepts and objectives. A soundly developed conceptual framework thus enables the FASB to issue more useful and consistent standards over time. **A coherent set of standards and rules should result.** The framework should increase financial statement users' understanding of and confidence in financial reporting. It should enhance comparability among companies' financial statements.

Second, the profession should be able to more quickly solve new and emerging **practical problems by referring to an existing framework of basic theory.** For example, Sunshine Mining (a silver-mining company) sold two issues of bonds. It can redeem them either with $1,000 in cash or with 50 ounces of silver, whichever is worth

---

[2] "Conceptual Framework for Financial Accounting and Reporting: Elements of Financial Statements and Their Measurement," *FASB Discussion Memorandum* (Stamford, Conn.: FASB, 1976), page 1 of the "Scope and Implications of the Conceptual Framework Project" section. For an excellent discussion of the functions of the conceptual framework, see Reed K. Storey and Sylvia Storey, Special Report, "The Framework of Financial Accounting and Concepts" (Norwalk, Conn.: FASB, 1998), pp. 85–88.

more at maturity. Both bond issues have a stated interest rate of 8.5 percent. At what amounts should Sunshine or the buyers of the bonds record them? What is the amount of the premium or discount on the bonds? And how should Sunshine amortize this amount, if the bond redemption payments are to be made in silver (the future value of which is unknown at the date of issuance?) Consider that Sunshine cannot know, at the date of issuance, the value of future silver bond redemption payments.

It is difficult, if not impossible, for the FASB to prescribe the proper accounting treatment quickly for situations like this. Practicing accountants, however, must resolve such problems on a daily basis. How? Though good judgment and with the help of a universally accepted conceptual framework, practitioners can quickly focus on an acceptable treatment.

WHAT'S YOUR PRINCIPLE?

The need for a conceptual framework is highlighted by recent accounting scandals such as those at **Enron**, **Healthsouth**, and other companies. To restore public confidence in the financial reporting process, Congress passed the Sarbanes-Oxley Act of 2002 ("SOX"). One of the provisions of SOX is a requirement for the Securities and Exchange Commission (SEC) to evaluate the usefulness of "principles-based" accounting standards relative to the current set of accounting standards (which many argue are too "rules-based").

Some have suggested a move toward principles-based standards because they believe that companies exploited the detailed provisions in rules-based standards to manage accounting reports, rather than report the economic substance of transactions. For example, many of the off-balance-sheet arrangements of Enron avoided transparent reporting by barely achieving 3 percent outside equity ownership, a requirement in an obscure accounting standard interpretation. Enron's financial engineers were able to structure transactions to achieve a desired accounting treatment, even if that accounting treatment did not reflect the transaction's true nature.

In 2003 the SEC issued a report recommending that accounting standard setters move away from a rules-based approach toward a more principles-based approach ("Study Pursuant to Section 108(d) . . ."). If the profession adopts this approach, accounting standards will be more conceptual in nature, and the financial reporting objective of each standard will be more clearly stated. Top management's financial reporting responsibility will shift from demonstrating compliance with rules to demonstrating that a company has attained financial reporting objectives.

Source: "Study Pursuant to Section 108(d) of the Sarbanes-Oxley Act of 2002 on the Adoption by the United States Financial Reporting System of a Principles-Based Accounting System," *www.sec.gov/news/studies/principlesbasedstand.htm*.

WHAT DO THE NUMBERS MEAN?

Development of a Conceptual Framework

Over the years, numerous organizations developed and published their own conceptual frameworks, but no single framework was universally accepted and relied on in practice. In 1976 the FASB began to develop a conceptual framework that would be a basis for setting accounting standards and for resolving financial reporting controversies. The FASB has since issued six Statements of Financial Accounting Concepts that relate to financial reporting for business exterprises.[3] They are as follows.

OBJECTIVE 2
Describe the FASB's efforts to construct a conceptual framework.

---

[3]The FASB also issued a Statement of Financial Accounting Concepts that relates to nonbusiness organizations: "Objectives of Financial Reporting by Nonbusiness Organizations," *Statement of Financial Accounting Concepts No. 4* (December 1980).

1 *SFAC No. 1*, "Objectives of Financial Reporting by Business Enterprises," presents the goals and purposes of accounting.

2 *SFAC No. 2*, "Qualitative Characteristics of Accounting Information," examines the characteristics that make accounting information useful.

3 *SFAC No. 3*, "Elements of Financial Statements of Business Enterprises," provides definitions of items in financial statements, such as assets, liabilities, revenues, and expenses.

4 *SFAC No. 5*, "Recognition and Measurement in Financial Statements of Business Enterprises," sets forth fundamental recognition and measurement criteria and guidance on what information should be formally incorporated into financial statements and when.

5 *SFAC No. 6*, "Elements of Financial Statements," replaces *SFAC No. 3* and expands its scope to include not-for-profit organizations.

6 *SFAC No. 7*, "Using Cash Flow Information and Present Value in Accounting Measurements," provides a framework for using expected future cash flows and present values as a basis for measurement.

Illustration 2-1 provides an overview of the conceptual framework.[4] The first level lists the **objectives**—that is, the goals and purposes of accounting. Ideally, accounting standards developed according to a conceptual framework will result in more useful accounting reports.

ILLUSTRATION 2-1
Conceptual Framework for Financial Reporting

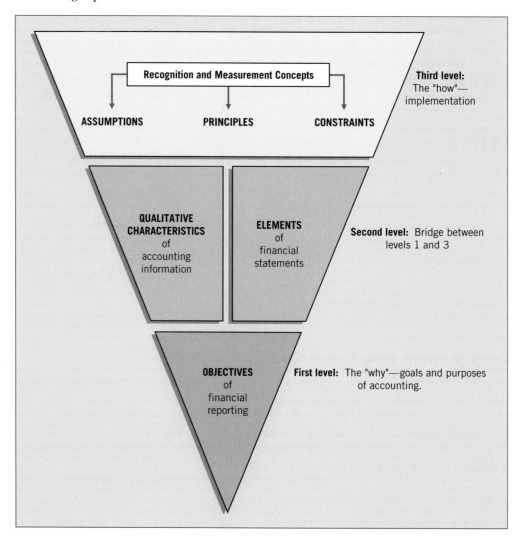

[4]Adapted from William C. Norby, *The Financial Analysts Journal* (March–April 1982), p. 22.

The second level provides the **qualitative characteristics** that make accounting information useful and the **elements** of financial statements (assets, liabilities, and so on). The third level identifies the **recognition and measurement concepts** used in establishing and applying accounting standards. These concepts include assumptions, principles, and constraints that describe the present reporting environment. We examine these three levels of the conceptual framework next.

FIRST LEVEL: BASIC OBJECTIVES

As we discussed in Chapter 1, the **objectives of financial reporting** are to provide information that is: (1) useful to those making investment and credit decisions, who have a reasonable understanding of business and economic activities; (2) helpful to present and potential investors, creditors, and other users in assessing the amounts, timing, and uncertainty of future cash flows; and (3) about economic resources, the claims to those resources, and the changes in them.

The objectives, therefore, broadly concern information that is useful to investor and creditor decisions. That concern narrows to the investors' and creditors' interest in receiving cash from their investments in, or loans to, business enterprises. Finally, the objectives focus on the financial statements, which provide information useful in assessing future cash flows. This approach is referred to as **decision usefulness**.

To provide information to decision makers, companies prepare general-purpose financial statements. These statements provide the most useful information possible at the least cost. However, users do need reasonable knowledge of business and financial accounting matters to understand the information contained in financial statements. This point is important. It means that financial statement preparers assume a level of competence on the part of users. This assumption impacts the way and the extent to which companies report information.

SECOND LEVEL: FUNDAMENTAL CONCEPTS

The objectives (first level) focus on the goals and purposes of accounting. Later, we will discuss the ways these goals and purposes are implemented (third level). What, then, is the purpose of the second level? The second level provides conceptual building blocks that explain the qualitative characteristics of accounting information and define the elements of financial statements. That is, the second level forms a bridge between the **why** of accounting (the objectives) and the **how** of accounting (recognition and measurement).

Qualitative Characteristics of Accounting Information

Should companies like **Walt Disney** or **Kellogg's** provide information in their financial statements on how much it costs them to acquire their assets (historical cost basis) or how much the assets are currently worth (fair-value basis)? Should **PepsiCo** combine and show as one company the four main segments of its business, or should it report PepsiCo Beverages, Frito Lay, Quaker Foods, and PepsiCo International as four separate segments?

How does a company choose an acceptable accounting method, the amount and types of information to disclose, and the format in which to present it? The answer: By determining **which alternative provides the most useful information for decision-making purposes (decision usefulness)**. The FASB identified the **qualitative characteristics** of accounting information that distinguish better (more useful) information from inferior (less useful) information for decision-making purposes.[5] In addition, the

OBJECTIVE 3
Understand the objectives of financial reporting.

INTERNATIONAL INSIGHT

In Switzerland, Germany, Korea, and other nations, the primary providers of capital to companies are large banks. Creditors maintain very close ties to companies and can obtain information directly from them. Creditors do not need to rely on publicly available information, and financial information focuses on creditor protection. This process of capital allocation, however, is changing. It is likely that the need for publicly available information will change as well.

OBJECTIVE 4
Identify the qualitative characteristics of accounting information.

---

[5]"Qualitative Characteristics of Accounting Information," *Statement of Financial Accounting Concepts No. 2* (Stamford, Conn.: FASB, May 1980).

FASB identified certain constraints (cost-benefit and materiality) as part of the conceptual framework (discussed later in the chapter). As Illustration 2-2 shows, the characteristics may be viewed as a hierarchy.

ILLUSTRATION 2-2
Hierarchy of Accounting
Qualities

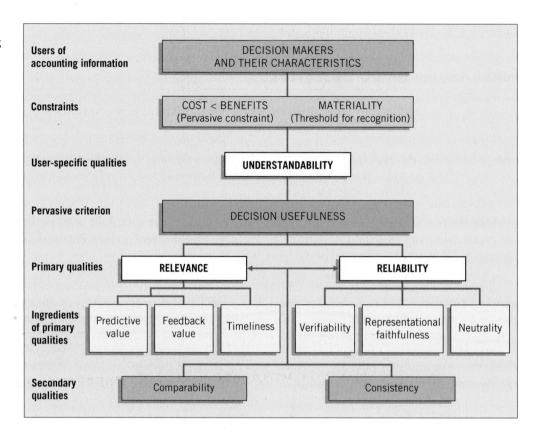

Decision Makers (Users) and Understandability

Decision makers vary widely in the types of decisions they make, how they make decisions, the information they already possess or can obtain from other sources, and their ability to process the information. For information to be useful, there must be a connection (linkage) between these users and the decisions they make. This link, **understandability**, is the quality of information that lets reasonably informed users see its significance.

For example, assume that **IBM Corp**. issues a three-months' report that shows interim earnings way down. This interim report provides relevant and reliable information for decision-making purposes. Now say that some users, upon reading the report, decide to sell their stock. Other users, however, do not understand the report's content and significance. They are surprised when IBM declares a smaller year-end dividend and the value of the stock declines. Thus, although IBM presented highly relevant and reliable information, it was useless to those who did not understand it.

Primary Qualities: Relevance and Reliability

Relevance and reliability are the two primary qualities that make accounting information useful for decision making. As stated in FASB *Concepts Statement No. 2*, "the qualities that distinguish 'better' (more useful) information from 'inferior' (less useful) information are primarily the qualities of relevance and reliability, with some other characteristics that those qualities imply."[6]

---

[6]Ibid., par. 15.

Relevance. To be relevant, accounting information must be capable of making a difference in a decision.[7] Information with no bearing on a decision is irrelevant. Relevant information helps users predict the ultimate outcome of past, present, and future events. That is, it has **predictive value**. Relevant information also helps users confirm or correct prior expectations; it has **feedback value**. For example, when **UPS (United Parcel Service)** issues an interim report, the information in it is relevant because it provides both a basis for forecasting annual earnings and feedback on past performance.

Finally, relevant information is available to decision makers before it loses its capacity to influence their decisions. It has **timeliness**. If UPS waited to report its interim results until six months after the end of the period, the information would be much less useful for decision-making purposes. **For information to be relevant, it needs predictive or feedback value, presented on a timely basis.**

Reliability. Accounting information is reliable to the extent that **it is verifiable, is a faithful representation, and is reasonably free of error and bias**. Reliability is a necessity, because most users have neither the time nor the expertise to evaluate the factual content of the information.

Verifiability occurs when independent measurers, using the same methods, obtain similar results. For example, would several independent auditors reach the same conclusion about a set of financial statements? If not, then the statements are not verifiable. Auditors could not render an opinion on such statements.

Representational faithfulness means that the numbers and descriptions match what really existed or happened. If **General Motors'** income statement reports sales of $225 billion when it had sales of $193.5 billion, then the statement fails to faithfully represent the proper sales amount.

Neutrality means that a company cannot select information to favor one set of interested parties over another. Unbiased information must be the overriding consideration. For example, in the notes to financial statements, tobacco companies such as **R. J. Reynolds** should not suppress information about the numerous lawsuits that have been filed because of tobacco-related health concerns—even though such disclosure is damaging to the company.

Neutrality in standard setting has come under increasing attack. Some argue that the FASB should not issue standards that cause undesirable economic effects on an industry or company. We disagree. Standards must be free from bias, or we will no longer have credible financial statements. Without credible financial statements, individuals will no longer use this information. An analogy demonstrates the point: In the United States, many individuals bet on boxing matches because such contests are assumed not to be fixed. But nobody bets on wrestling matches. Why? Because the public assumes that wrestling matches are rigged. If financial information is biased (rigged), the public will lose confidence and no longer use it.

Secondary Qualities: Comparability and Consistency

Information about a company is more useful if decision makers can compare it with similar information about another company and with similar information about the same company at other points in time. The first of these qualities is **comparability**, and the second is **consistency**.

Comparability. Information that is measured and reported in a similar manner for different companies is considered comparable. Comparability enables users to identify the real similarities and differences in economic events between companies.

For example, the accounting for pensions in the United States differs from that in Japan. In the United States, companies record pension cost as incurred. In Japan, companies record little or no charge to income for these costs. As a result, it is difficult to compare and evaluate the financial results of **General Motors** or **Ford** to Japanese competitors.

---

[7]Ibid., par. 47.

Also, resource allocation decisions involve evaluating alternatives. A valid evaluation can be made only if comparable information is available.

Consistency. When a company applies the same accounting treatment to similar events, from period to period, the company shows consistent use of accounting standards. The idea of consistency does not mean, however, that companies cannot switch from one accounting method to another. A company *can* change methods, but it must first demonstrate that the newly adopted method is preferable to the old. If approved, the company must then disclose the nature and effect of the accounting change, as well as the justification for it, in the financial statements for the period in which it made the change.[8] When a change in accounting principles occurs, the auditor refers to it in an explanatory paragraph of the audit report. This paragraph identifies the nature of the change and refers the reader to the note in the financial statements that discusses the change in detail.[9]

WHAT DO THE NUMBERS MEAN?

YOU MAY NEED A MAP

Beyond touting nonfinancial measures to investors (see opening story), many companies increasingly promote the performance of their companies through the reporting of various "pro-forma" earnings measures. A recent survey of newswire reports found 36 instances of the reporting of pro-forma measures in just a three-day period.

Pro-forma measures are standard measures (such as earnings) that companies adjust, usually for one-time or nonrecurring items. For example, companies usually adjust earnings for the effects of an extraordinary item. Such adjustments make the numbers more comparable to numbers reported in periods without the unusual item.

However, rather than increasing comparability, it appears that some companies use pro-forma reporting to accentuate the positive in their results. Examples include **Yahoo Inc.** and **Cisco**, which define pro-forma income after adding back payroll tax expense. **Level 8 Systems** transformed an operating loss into a pro-forma profit by adding back expenses for depreciation and amortization of intangible assets.

Lynn Turner, former Chief Accountant at the SEC, calls such earnings measures EBS— "Everything but Bad Stuff." To provide investors a more complete picture of company profitability, not the story preferred by management, the SEC issued Regulation G (REG G). REG G requires companies to reconcile non-GAAP financial measures to GAAP, thereby giving investors a roadmap to analyze adjustments companies make to their GAAP numbers to arrive at pro-forma results.

Sources: Adapted from Gretchen Morgenson, "How Did They Value Stocks? Count the Absurd Ways," *New York Times* (March 18, 2001), section 3, p. 1; and Gretchen Morgenson, "Expert Advice: Focus on Profit," *New York Times* (March 18, 2001), section 3, p. 14. See also SEC Regulation G, "Conditions for Use of Non-GAAP Financial Measures, "Release No. 33–8176 (March 28, 2003).

Basic Elements

OBJECTIVE 5
Define the basic elements of financial statements.

An important aspect of developing any theoretical structure is the body of **basic elements** or definitions to be included in it. Accounting uses many terms with distinctive and specific meanings. These terms constitute the language of business or the jargon of accounting.

---

[8]Surveys indicate that users highly value consistency. They note that a change tends to destroy the comparability of data before and after the change. Some companies assist users to understand the pre- and post-change data. Generally, however, users say they lose the ability to analyze over time. It is hoped that the new standard on accounting changes will improve the comparability of the data before and after the change.

[9]"Reports on Audited Financial Statements," *Statement on Auditing Standards No. 58* (New York: AICPA, April 1988), par. 34.

One such term is **asset**. Is it merely something we own? Or is an asset something we have the right to use, as in the case of leased equipment? Or is it anything of value used by a company to generate revenues—in which case, should we also consider the managers of a company as an asset?

As this example illustrates, it seems necessary, therefore, to develop basic definitions for the elements of financial statements. *Concepts Statement No. 6* defines the ten interrelated elements that most directly relate to measuring the performance and financial status of a business enterprise. We list them here for review and information purposes; you need not memorize these definitions at this point. We will explain and examine each of these elements in more detail in subsequent chapters.

ELEMENTS OF FINANCIAL STATEMENTS

ASSETS. Probable future economic benefits obtained or controlled by a particular entity as a result of past transactions or events.

LIABILITIES. Probable future sacrifices of economic benefits arising from present obligations of a particular entity to transfer assets or provide services to other entities in the future as a result of past transactions or events.

EQUITY. Residual interest in the assets of an entity that remains after deducting its liabilities. In a business enterprise, the equity is the ownership interest.

INVESTMENTS BY OWNERS. Increases in net assets of a particular enterprise resulting from transfers to it from other entities of something of value to obtain or increase ownership interests (or equity) in it. Assets are most commonly received as investments by owners, but that which is received may also include services or satisfaction or conversion of liabilities of the enterprise.

DISTRIBUTIONS TO OWNERS. Decreases in net assets of a particular enterprise resulting from transferring assets, rendering services, or incurring liabilities by the enterprise to owners. Distributions to owners decrease ownership interests (or equity) in an enterprise.

COMPREHENSIVE INCOME. Change in equity (net assets) of an entity during a period from transactions and other events and circumstances from nonowner sources. It includes all changes in equity during a period except those resulting from investments by owners and distributions to owners.

REVENUES. Inflows or other enhancements of assets of an entity or settlement of its liabilities (or a combination of both) during a period from delivering or producing goods, rendering services, or other activities that constitute the entity's ongoing major or central operations.

EXPENSES. Outflows or other using up of assets or incurrences of liabilities (or a combination of both) during a period from delivering or producing goods, rendering services, or carrying out other activities that constitute the entity's ongoing major or central operations.

GAINS. Increases in equity (net assets) from peripheral or incidental transactions of an entity and from all other transactions and other events and circumstances affecting the entity during a period except those that result from revenues or investments by owners.

LOSSES. Decreases in equity (net assets) from peripheral or incidental transactions of an entity and from all other transactions and other events and circumstances affecting the entity during a period except those that result from expenses or distributions to owners.[10]

---

[10]"Elements of Financial Statements," *Statement of Financial Accounting Concepts No. 6* (Stamford, Conn.: FASB, December 1985), pp. ix and x.

The FASB classifies the elements into two distinct groups. The first group of three elements—assets, liabilities, and equity—describes amounts of resources and claims to resources at a **moment in time**. The other seven elements describe transactions, events, and circumstances that affect a company during a **period of time**. The first class, affected by elements of the second class, provides at any time the cumulative result of all changes. This interaction is referred to as "articulation." That is, key figures in one financial statement correspond to balances in another.

THIRD LEVEL: RECOGNITION AND MEASUREMENT CONCEPTS

The third level of the framework consists of concepts that implement the basic objectives of level one. These concepts explain how companies should recognize, measure, and report financial elements and events. The FASB sets forth most of these in its *Statement of Financial Accounting Concepts No. 5*, "Recognition and Measurement in Financial Statements of Business Enterprises." According to *SFAC No. 5*, to be recognized, an item (event or transaction) must meet the definition of an "element of financial statements" as defined in *SFAC No. 6* and must be measurable. Most aspects of current practice follow these recognition and measurement concepts.

The accounting profession continues to use the concepts in *SFAC No. 5* as operational guidelines. Here, we identify the concepts as basic assumptions, principles, and constraints. Not everyone uses this classification system, so focus your attention more on **understanding the concepts** than on how we classify and organize them. These concepts serve as guidelines in responding to controversial financial reporting issues.

Basic Assumptions

OBJECTIVE 6
Describe the basic assumptions of accounting.

Four basic **assumptions** underlie the financial accounting structure: (1) **economic entity**, (2) **going concern**, (3) **monetary unit**, and (4) **periodicity**. We'll look at each in turn.

Economic Entity Assumption

The **economic entity assumption means that economic activity can be identified with a particular unit of accountability**. In other words, a company keeps its activity separate and distinct from its owners and any other business unit. At the most basic level, the economic entity assumption dictates that **Panera Bread Company** record the company's financial activities separate from those of its owners and managers. Equally important, financial statement users need to be able to distinguish the activities and elements of different companies, such as **General Motors**, **Ford**, and **DaimlerChrysler**. If users could not distinguish the activities of different companies, how would they know which company financially outperformed the other?

The entity concept does not apply solely to the segregation of activities among competing companies, such as **Best Buy** and **Circuit City**. An individual, department, division, or an entire industry could be considered a separate entity if we choose to define it in this manner. Thus, **the entity concept does not necessarily refer to a legal entity**. A parent and its subsidiaries are separate **legal** entities, but merging their activities for accounting and reporting purposes does not violate the **economic entity** assumption.[11]

---

[11]The concept of the entity is changing. For example, defining the "outer edges" of companies is now harder. Public companies often consist of multiple public subsidiaries, each with joint ventures, licensing arrangements, and other affiliations. Increasingly, companies form and dissolve joint ventures or customer-supplier relationships in a matter of months or weeks. These "virtual companies" raise accounting issues about how to account for the entity. See Steven H. Wallman, "The Future of Accounting and Disclosure in an Evolving World: The Need for Dramatic Change," *Accounting Horizons* (September 1995).

WHAT DO THE NUMBERS MEAN?

The importance of the entity assumption is illustrated by scandals involving **W. R. Grace** and, more recently, **Adelphia**. In both cases, senior company employees entered into transactions that blurred the line between the employee's financial interests and those of the company. At Adelphia, among many other self-dealings, the company guaranteed over $2 billion of loans to the founding family. W. R. Grace used company funds to pay for an apartment and chef for the company chairman. As a result of these transactions, these insiders benefitted at the expense of shareholders. Additionally, the financial statements failed to disclose the transactions. Such disclosure would have allowed shareholders to sort out the impact of the employee transactions on company results.

Going Concern Assumption

Most accounting methods rely on the **going concern assumption—that the company will have a long life**. Despite numerous business failures, most companies have a fairly high continuance rate. As a rule, we expect companies to last long enough to fulfill their objectives and commitments.

This assumption has significant implications. The historical cost principle would be of limited usefulness if we assume eventual liquidation. Under a liquidation approach, for example, a company would better state asset values at net realizable value (sales price less costs of disposal) than at acquisition cost. **Depreciation and amortization policies are justifiable and appropriate only if we assume some permanence to the company.** If a company adopts the liquidation approach, the current/non-current classification of assets and liabilities loses much of its significance. Labeling anything a fixed or long-term asset would be difficult to justify. Indeed, listing liabilities on the basis of priority in liquidation would be more reasonable.

The going concern assumption applies in most business situations. **Only where liquidation appears imminent is the assumption inapplicable.** In these cases a total revaluation of assets and liabilities can provide information that closely approximates the company's net realizable value. You will learn more about accounting problems related to a company in liquidation in advanced accounting courses.

Monetary Unit Assumption

The **monetary unit assumption** means that money is the common denominator of economic activity and provides an appropriate basis for accounting measurement and analysis. That is, the monetary unit is the most effective means of expressing to interested parties changes in capital and exchanges of goods and services. **The monetary unit is relevant, simple, universally available, understandable, and useful.** Application of this assumption depends on the even more basic assumption that quantitative data are useful in communicating economic information and in making rational economic decisions.

In the United States, accounting ignores price-level changes (inflation and deflation) and assumes that the unit of measure—the dollar—remains reasonably stable. We therefore use the monetary unit assumption to justify adding 1980 dollars to 2007 dollars without any adjustment. The FASB in *SFAC No. 5* indicated that it expects the dollar, unadjusted for inflation or deflation, to continue to be used to measure items recognized in financial statements. Only if circumstances change dramatically (such as if the United States experiences high inflation similar to that in many South American countries) will the FASB again consider "inflation accounting."

INTERNATIONAL INSIGHT

Due to their experiences with persistent inflation, several South American countries produce "constant-currency" financial reports. Typically, companies in these countries use a general price-level index to adjust for the effects of inflation.

Accounting for Changing Prices

Periodicity Assumption

To measure the results of a company's activity accurately, we would need to wait until it liquidates. Decision makers, however, cannot wait that long for such information.

Users need to know a company's performance and economic status on a timely basis so that they can evaluate and compare firms, and take appropriate actions. Therefore, companies must report information periodically.

The **periodicity (or time period) assumption** implies that a company can divide its economic activities into artificial time periods. These time periods vary, but the most common are monthly, quarterly, and yearly.

The shorter the time period, the more difficult it is to determine the proper net income for the period. A month's results usually prove less reliable than a quarter's results, and a quarter's results are likely to be less reliable than a year's results. Investors desire and demand that a company quickly process and disseminate information. Yet the quicker a company releases the information, the more likely the information will include errors. **This phenomenon provides an interesting example of the trade-off between relevance and reliability in preparing financial data.**

The problem of defining the time period becomes more serious as product cycles shorten and products become obsolete more quickly. Many believe that, given technology advances, companies need to provide more online, real-time financial information to ensure the availability of relevant information.

Basic Principles of Accounting

OBJECTIVE 7
Explain the application of the basic principles of accounting.

We generally use four basic **principles of accounting** to record transactions: (1) historical cost, (2) revenue recognition, (3) matching, and (4) full disclosure. Again, we look at each in turn.

Historical Cost Principle

GAAP requires that companies account for and report most assets and liabilities on the basis of acquisition price. This is often referred to as the **historical cost principle**. Cost has an important advantage over other valuations: **it is reliable**. To illustrate this advantage, consider the problems if companies select current selling price instead. Companies might have difficulty establishing a value for unsold items. Every member of the accounting department might value the assets differently. Further, how often would it be necessary to establish sales value? All companies close their accounts at least annually. Some compute their net income every month. These companies would have to place a sales value on every asset each time they wished to determine income. Critics raise similar objections against current cost (replacement cost, present value of future cash flows) and any other basis of valuation **except historical cost**.

What about liabilities? Do companies account for them on a cost basis? Yes, they do. Companies issue liabilities, such as bonds, notes, and accounts payable, in exchange for assets, or perhaps services, for an agreed-upon price. **This price, established by the exchange transaction, is the "cost" of the liability.** A company uses this amount to record the liability in the accounts and report it in financial statements.

In general, users prefer historical cost because it provides them with a reliable benchmark for measuring historical trends. However, **fair value information** may be more useful for certain types of assets and liabilities and in certain industries. For example, companies report many financial instruments, including derivatives, at fair value, and inventories at lower of cost or market. Certain industries, such as brokerage houses and mutual funds, prepare their basic financial statements on a fair value basis.

At initial acquisition, historical cost equals fair value. In subsequent periods, as market and economic conditions change, historical cost and fair value often diverge. As a result, fair value measures or estimates often provide more relevant information about the expected future cash flows related to the asset or liability. For example, when long-lived assets decline in value, a fair value measure determines any impairment loss.

The FASB now appears to support greater use of fair value measurements in the financial statements. The Board believes that fair value information is more relevant to users than historical cost. Fair value measurement, it is argued, provides better insight into the value of a company's asset and liabilities (its financial position) and provides a better basis for assessing future cash flow prospects.

The FASB is developing a standard on "Fair Value Measurements," which provides guidance on how to measure fair value. This standard applies to both financial and nonfinancial assets that are measured at fair value. As a result, we should now have increased consistency and comparability when fair value measurements are used in the financial statements and related notes. Such consistency and comparability is very much needed in light of controversies using fair values at companies like **Enron** (valuation of energy contracts) and **J. P. Morgan** (valuation of its bond portfolio). In addition, this new standard clarifies and incorporates the guidance in *Concepts Statement 7*, "Using Cash Flow Information and Present Value in Accounting Measurements," for using present value techniques to estimate future cash flows, and it provides enhanced disclosure of fair value information.[12]

As we indicated above, we presently have a "mixed-attribute" system that permits the use of historical cost, fair value, and other valuation bases. Although the historical cost principle continues to be the primary basis for valuation, recording and reporting of fair value information is increasing.

Revenue Recognition Principle

A crucial question for many companies is when to recognize revenue. Revenue recognition generally occurs (1) when **realized** or **realizable** and (2) when **earned**. This approach has often been referred to as the **revenue recognition principle**.

A company **realizes** revenues when it exchanges products (goods or services), merchandise, or other assets for cash or claims to cash. Revenues are realizable when assets received or held are readily convertible into cash or claims to cash. Assets are readily convertible when they are salable or interchangeable in an active market at readily determinable prices without significant additional cost.

In addition to the first test (realized or realizable), a company delays recognition of revenues until earned. Revenues are considered **earned** when the company substantially accomplishes what it must do to be entitled to the benefits represented by the revenues.[13] Generally, an objective test, such as a sale, indicates the point at which a company recognizes revenue. The sale provides an objective and verifiable measure of revenue—the sales price. Any basis for revenue recognition short of actual sale opens the door to wide variations in practice. **Recognition at the time of sale provides a uniform and reasonable test.**

However, as Illustration 2-3 (page 40) shows, exceptions to the rule exist. We discuss these exceptions in the following sections.

During Production. A company can recognize revenue **before** it completes the job in certain long-term construction contracts. In this method, a company recognizes revenue periodically, based on the percentage of the job it has completed. Although technically a transfer of ownership has not occurred, the earning process is considered substantially completed at various stages of construction. If it is not possible to obtain dependable estimates of cost and progress, then a company delays revenue recognition until it completes the job.

At End of Production. At times, a company may recognize revenue **after completion of the production cycle but before the sale takes place.** This occurs if products or other assets are salable in an active market at readily determinable prices without significant

---

[12]"Fair Value Measurement," *Proposed Statement of Financial Accounting Standards* (Norwalk, Conn.: FASB, October 21, 2005).

[13]"Recognition and Measurement in Financial Statements of Business Enterprises," *Statement of Financial Accounting Concepts No. 5* (Stamford, Conn.: FASB, December 1984), par. 83(a) and (b).

ILLUSTRATION 2-3
Timing of Revenue
Recognition

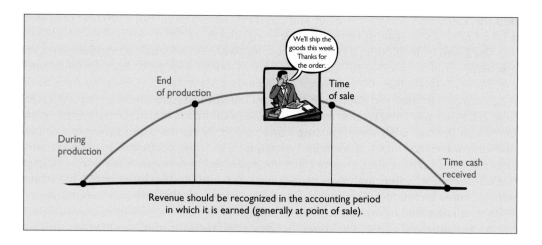

additional cost. An example is the mining of certain minerals. Once a company mines the mineral, a ready market at a quoted price exists. The same holds true for some agricultural products.

Upon Receipt of Cash. **Receipt of cash is another basis for revenue recognition.** Companies use the cash-basis approach only when collection is uncertain at the time of sale.

One form of the cash basis is the **installment-sales method**. Here, a company requires payment in periodic installments over a long period of time. Its most common use is in retail, such as for farm and home equipment and furnishings. Companies frequently justify the installment-sales method based on the high risk of not collecting an account receivable. In some instances, this reasoning may be valid. Generally, though, if a sale has been completed, the company should recognize the sale; if bad debts are expected, the company should record them as separate estimates.

To summarize, a company records revenue in the period when realized or realizable and when earned. Normally, this is the date of sale. But circumstances may dictate application of the percentage-of-completion approach, the end-of-production approach, or the receipt-of-cash approach.

**WHAT DO THE
NUMBERS MEAN?**

No TAKE-BACKS!

Investors in **Lucent Technologies** got an unpleasant surprise when the SEC forced the company to restate its financial results. What happened? Lucent violated one of the fundamental criteria for revenue recognition—the "no take-back" rule. This rule holds that a company should not book revenue on inventory that it shipped if the customer can return it at some point in the future. In this particular case, Lucent agreed to take back shipped inventory from its distributors if they could not sell the items to their customers.

Lucent recorded the sales on the shipped goods, which helped it report continued sales growth. However, Lucent's distributors did indeed return many of those shipped goods. The restatement erased $679 million in revenues, turning an operating profit into a loss. In response, Lucent's stock price declined $1.31 per share or 8.5 percent. Lucent has since changed its policy. It now records inventory as sold only when the final customer buys the equipment, not when Lucent ships the inventory to the distributor.

The lesson for investors: Review a company's revenue recognition policy for indications that revenues may be overstated due to generous return provisions for inventory. And remember, no take-backs!

Source: Adapted from S. Young, "Lucent Slashes First Quarter Outlook, Erases Revenue from Latest Quarter," *Wall Street Journal Online Edition* (December 22, 2000).

Matching Principle

In recognizing expenses, the approach is "Let the expense follow the revenues." Companies recognize expenses not when they pay wages or make a product, but when the work (service) or the product actually contributes to revenue. Thus, companies tie expense recognition to revenue recognition. This practice is referred to as the **matching principle**, because it dictates that **efforts (expenses) be matched with accomplishment (revenues) whenever it is reasonable and practicable to do so.**

Some costs, however, are difficult to associate with revenue. As a result, some other approach must be developed. Often, companies use a "rational and systematic" allocation policy that will approximate the matching principle. This type of expense recognition involves assumptions about the benefits that a company receives as well as the cost associated with those benefits. For example, a company like **Intel** or **Motorola** allocates the cost of a long-lived asset over all of the accounting periods during which it uses the asset because the asset contributes to the generation of revenue throughout its useful life.

HOLLYWOOD ACCOUNTING

WHAT DO THE NUMBERS MEAN?

Hollywood accounting illustrates that the problem of expense recognition is as complex as that of revenue recognition. Following then-existing GAAP standards, major motion picture studios capitalized advertising and marketing costs, and then amortized these costs against revenues over the life of the film. As a result, many investors suggested that the studios overstated their profit numbers. Under a new GAAP standard, the studios must now amortize these costs over no more than three months. In many cases, the studios have to expense them immediately.

Similarly, the studios often allocated the costs related to abandoned projects to overhead, thus spreading them out over the lives of the successful projects. Not anymore. The studios must now expense these costs as incurred.

Here is a rough estimate of the amounts of capitalized advertising costs some major studios charged off in response to the change in GAAP.

Studio (Parent Company)	Capitalized Advertising (in millions)
Columbia Tri-Star (Sony)	$200
Paramount (Viacom)	200
20th Century Fox (News Corp)	150

The more conservative approach results from a stricter application of the definitions of assets and expenses. While many argue that advertising and marketing costs have future service potential, difficulty in reliably measuring these benefits suggests they are not assets. Therefore, a very short amortization period or immediate write-off is justified. Under these new guidelines, investors will have more reliable measures for assessing the performance of companies in this industry.

Companies charge some costs to the current period as expenses (or losses) simply because they cannot determine a connection with revenue. Examples of these types of costs are officers' salaries and other administrative expenses.

Costs are generally classified into two groups: **product costs** and **period costs**. **Product costs**, such as material, labor, and overhead, attach to the product. Companies carry these costs into future periods if they recognize the revenue from the product in subsequent periods. **Period costs**, such as officers' salaries and other administrative expenses, attach to the period. Companies charge off such costs in the immediate period, even though benefits associated with these costs may occur in the future. Why? Because companies cannot determine a direct relationship between period costs and revenue. Illustration 2-4 (page 42) summarizes these expense recognition procedures.

ILLUSTRATION 2-4
Expense Recognition

Type of Cost	Relationship	Recognition
Product costs: • Material • Labor • Overhead	Direct relationship between cost and revenue.	Recognize in period of revenue (matching).
Period costs: • Salaries • Administrative costs	No direct relationship between cost and revenue.	Expense as incurred.

As indicated in the discussion of Hollywood accounting, there is some debate about the conceptual validity of the matching principle. A major concern is that matching permits companies to defer certain costs and treat them as assets on the balance sheet. In fact, these costs may not have future benefits. If abused, this principle permits the balance sheet to become a "dumping ground" for unmatched costs. In addition, there appears to be no objective definition of "systematic and rational."

Full Disclosure Principle

In deciding what information to report, companies follow the general practice of providing information that is of sufficient importance to influence the judgment and decisions of an informed user. Often referred to as the **full disclosure principle**, it recognizes that the nature and amount of information included in financial reports reflects a series of judgmental trade-offs. These trade-offs strive for (1) sufficient detail to disclose matters that **make a difference** to users, yet (2) sufficient condensation to make the **information understandable**, keeping in mind costs of preparing and using it.

Users find information about financial position, income, cash flows, and investments in one of three places: (1) within the main body of financial statements, (2) in the notes to those statements, or (3) as supplementary information.

As discussed in Chapter 1, the **financial statements** are the balance sheet, income statement, statement of cash flows, and statement of owners' equity. They are a structured means of communicating financial information. To be recognized in the main body of financial statements, **an item should meet the definition of a basic element, be measurable with sufficient certainty, and be relevant and reliable.**[14]

Disclosure is not a substitute for proper accounting. As a former chief accountant of the SEC noted, "Good disclosure does not cure bad accounting any more than an adjective or adverb can be used without, or in place of, a noun or verb." Thus, for example, cash-basis accounting for cost of goods sold is misleading, even if a company discloses accrual-basis amounts in the notes to the financial statements.

The **notes to financial statements** generally amplify or explain the items presented in the main body of the statements. If the main body of the financial statements gives an incomplete picture of the performance and position of the company, the notes should provide the additional information needed. Information in the notes does not have to be quantifiable, nor does it need to qualify as an element. Notes can be partially or totally narrative. Examples of notes include descriptions of the accounting policies and methods used in measuring the elements reported in the statements, explanations of uncertainties and contingencies, and statistics and details too voluminous for inclusion in the statements. The notes can be essential to understanding the company's performance and position.

Supplementary information may include details or amounts that present a different perspective from that adopted in the financial statements. It may be quantifiable information that is high in relevance but low in reliability. For example, oil and gas companies typically provide information on proven reserves as well as the related discounted cash flows.

---

[14]*SFAC No. 5*, par. 63.

Supplementary information may also include management's explanation of the financial information and its discussion of the significance of that information. For example, many business combinations have produced financing arrangements that demand new accounting and reporting practices and principles. In each of these situations, the same problem must be faced: making sure the company presents enough information to ensure that the **reasonably prudent investor** will not be misled.

We discuss the content, arrangement, and display of financial statements, along with other facets of full disclosure, in Chapters 4, 5, and 24.

Constraints

In providing information with the qualitative characteristics that make it useful, companies must consider two overriding factors that limit (constrain) the reporting. These constraints are: (1) the **cost-benefit relationship** and (2) **materiality**. We also review two other less-dominant yet important constraints that are part of the reporting environment: **industry practices** and **conservatism**.

OBJECTIVE 8
Describe the impact that constraints have on reporting accounting information.

Cost-Benefit Relationship

Too often, users assume that information is free. But preparers and providers of accounting information know that it is not. Therefore, companies must consider the **cost-benefit relationship**: They must weigh the costs of providing the information against the benefits that can be derived from using it. Standard-setting bodies and governmental agencies use cost-benefit analysis before making final their informational requirements. In order to justify requiring a particular measurement or disclosure, the benefits perceived to be derived from it must exceed the costs perceived to be associated with it.

A corporate executive made the following remark to the FASB about a proposed standard: "In all my years in the financial arena, I have never seen such an absolutely ridiculous proposal. . . . To dignify these 'actuarial' estimates by recording them as assets and liabilities would be virtually unthinkable except for the fact that the FASB has done equally stupid things in the past. . . . For God's sake, use common sense just this once."[15] Although extreme, this remark indicates the frustration expressed by members of the business community about standard setting, and whether the benefits of a given standard exceed the costs.

The difficulty in cost-benefit analysis is that the costs and especially the benefits are not always evident or measurable. The costs are of several kinds: costs of collecting and processing, of disseminating, of auditing, of potential litigation, of disclosure to competitors, and of analysis and interpretation. Benefits to preparers may include greater management control and access to capital at a lower cost. Users may receive better information for allocation of resources, tax assessment, and rate regulation. As noted earlier, benefits are generally more difficult to quantify than are costs.

The recent implementation of the provisions of the Sarbanes-Oxley Act of 2002 illustrates the challenges in assessing costs and benefits of standards. One study estimated the increased costs of complying with the new internal-control standards related to the financial reporting process to be an average of $7.8 million per company. However, the study concluded that ". . .quantifying the benefits of improved more reliable financial reporting is not fully possible."[16]

Despite the difficulty in assessing the costs and benefits of its standards, the FASB attempts to determine that each proposed standard will fill a significant need and that the costs imposed to meet the standard are justified in relation to overall benefits of

---

[15]"Decision-Usefulness: The Overriding Objective," *FASB Viewpoints* (October 19, 1983), p. 4.

[16]Charles Rivers and Associates, "Sarbanes-Oxley Section 404: Costs and Remediation of Deficiencies" letter from Deloitte and Touche, Ernst and Young, KPMG, and Pricewaterhouse-Coopers to the SEC (April 11, 2005).

the resulting information. In addition, the Board seeks input on costs and benefits as part of its due process.[17]

Materiality

The **materiality** constraint concerns an item's impact on a company's overall financial operations. An item is *material* if its inclusion or omission would influence or change the judgment of a reasonable person.[18] It is *immaterial,* and therefore irrelevant, if it would have no impact on a decision maker. In short, **it must make a difference** or a company need not disclose it.

The point involved here is of **relative size and importance**. If the amount involved is significant when compared with the other revenues and expenses, assets and liabilities, or net income of the company, sound and acceptable standards should be followed in reporting it. If the amount is so small that it is unimportant when compared with other items, applying a particular standard may be considered of less importance.

It is difficult to provide firm guidelines in judging when a given item is or is not material. Materiality varies both with relative amount and with relative importance. For example, the two sets of numbers presented below illustrate relative size.

ILLUSTRATION 2-5
Materiality Comparison

	Company A	Company B
Sales	$10,000,000	$100,000
Costs and expenses	9,000,000	90,000
Income from operations	$ 1,000,000	$ 10,000
Unusual gain	$ 20,000	$ 5,000

During the period in question, the revenues and expenses, and therefore the net incomes of Company A and Company B, are proportional. Each reported an unusual gain. In looking at the abbreviated income figures for Company A, it appears insignificant whether the amount of the unusual gain is set out separately or merged with the regular operating income. The gain is only 2 percent of the net income. If merged, it would not seriously distort the net income figure. Company B has had an unusual gain of only $5,000. However, it is relatively much more significant than the larger gain realized by A. For Company B, an item of $5,000 amounts to 50 percent of its income from operations. Obviously, the inclusion of such an item in ordinary operating income would affect the amount of that income materially. Thus we see the importance of the **relative size** of an item in determining its materiality.

Companies and their auditors generally adopt the rule of thumb that anything under 5 percent of net income is considered immaterial. However, the SEC indicates that a company may use this percentage for an initial assessment of materiality, but it must also consider other factors.[19] For example, companies can no longer fail to record items in order to meet consensus analysts' earnings numbers, preserve a positive earnings trend, convert a loss to a profit or vice versa, increase management compensation, or hide an illegal transaction like a bribe. In other words, **companies must consider both quantitative and qualitative factors in determining whether an item is material.**

---

[17]For example, as part of its project on "Share-Based Payment," *SFAS No. 123R,* the Board conducted a field study and surveyed commercial software providers to collect information on the costs of measuring the fair values of share-based compensation arrangements.

[18]*SFAC No. 2,* par. 132, sets forth the essence of materiality: "The omission or misstatement of an item in a financial report is material if, in the light of surrounding circumstances, the magnitude of the item is such that it is probable that the judgment of a reasonable person relying upon the report would have been changed or influenced by the inclusion or correction of the item." The auditing profession also adopted this same concept of materiality. See "Audit Risk and Materiality in Conducting an Audit," *Statement on Auditing Standards No. 47* (New York: AICPA, 1983), par. 6.

[19]"Materiality," *SEC Staff Accounting Bulletin No. 99* (Washington, D.C.: SEC, 1999).

The SEC also indicated that in determining materiality, companies must consider each misstatement separately and the aggregate effect of all misstatements. For example, at one time, **General Dynamics** disclosed that its Resources Group improved its earnings by $5.8 million. At the same time, it disclosed that one of its other subsidiaries had taken write-offs of $6.7 million. Although both numbers exceeded the $2.5 million that General Dynamics as a whole earned for the year, the company disclosed neither as unusual because it considered the net effect on earnings as immaterial. **This practice is prohibited** because each item must be considered separately. In addition, even though an individual item may be immaterial, it may be considered material when added to other immaterial items. Companies must disclose such items.

Materiality factors in a great many internal accounting decisions, too. Examples of such judgments that companies must make include: the amount of classification required in a subsidiary expense ledger, the degree of accuracy required in prorating expenses among the departments of a company, and the extent to which adjustments should be made for accrued and deferred items. Only by **the exercise of good judgment and professional expertise** can reasonable and appropriate answers be found, which is the materiality constraint sensibly applied.

LIVING IN A MATERIAL WORLD

The first line of defense for many companies caught "cooking the books" had been to argue that a questionable accounting item is immaterial. That defense has not been working so well lately, in the wake of recent accounting meltdowns at **Enron** and **Global Crossing** and the tougher rules on materiality issued by the SEC (*SAB 99*).

For example, the SEC alleged in a case against **Sunbeam** that the company racked up so many immaterial adjustments that they added up to a material misstatement that misled investors about the company's financial position. More recently, the SEC called for a number of companies, such as **Jack in the Box**, **McDonalds**, and **AIG**, to restate prior financial statements for the effects of incorrect accounting. In some cases, the restatements did not meet traditional materiality thresholds. Don Nicholaisen, SEC Chief Accountant, observed that whether the amount is material or not-material, some transactions appear to be "flat out intended to mislead investors." In essence he is saying that any wrong accounting for a transaction can represent important information to the users of financial statements.

Responding to new concerns about materiality, blue-chip companies such as **IBM** and **General Electric** are providing expanded disclosures of transactions that used to fall below the materiality radar. As a result, some good may yet come from the recent accounting failures.

Source: Adapted from K. Brown and J. Weil, "A Lot More Information Is 'Material' After Enron," *Wall Street Journal Online Edition* (February 22, 2002); S. D. Jones and R. Gibson, "Restaurants Serve Up Restatements," *Wall Street Journal* (January 26, 2005), p. C3; and R. McTauge, "Nicholaisen Says Restatement Needed When Deal Lacks Business Purpose," *Securities Regulation & Law Reporter* (May 9, 2005).

WHAT DO THE NUMBERS MEAN?

Industry Practices

Another practical consideration is **industry practices**. **The peculiar nature of some industries and business concerns** sometimes requires departure from basic theory. For example, public-utility companies report noncurrent assets first on the balance sheet to highlight the industry's capital-intensive nature. Agricultural companies often report crops at market value because it is costly to develop accurate cost figures on individual crops.

Such variations from basic theory are infrequent, yet they do exist. Whenever we find what appears to be a violation of basic accounting theory, we should determine whether some peculiarity of the industry explains the violation before we criticize the procedures followed.

Conservatism

Few conventions in accounting are as misunderstood as the constraint of conservatism. **Conservatism** means **when in doubt, choose the solution that will be least likely to overstate assets and income**. Note that the conservatism convention does not urge that net assets or net income be *understated.* Unfortunately, some interpret conservatism to mean just that.

All that conservatism does, properly applied, is provide a reasonable guide in difficult situations: Refrain from overstatement of net income and net assets. Examples of conservatism in accounting are the use of the lower-of-cost-or-market approach in valuing inventories, and the rule that companies recognize accrued net losses on firm purchase commitments for goods for inventory. When in doubt, it is better to understate than overstate net income and net assets. Of course, if no doubt exists, there is no need to apply this constraint.

Summary of the Structure

Illustration 2-6 presents the conceptual framework discussed in this chapter. It is similar to Illustration 2-1, except that it provides additional information for each level. We cannot overemphasize the usefulness of this conceptual framework in helping to understand many of the problem areas that we examine in later chapters.

ILLUSTRATION 2-6
Conceptual Framework
for Financial Reporting

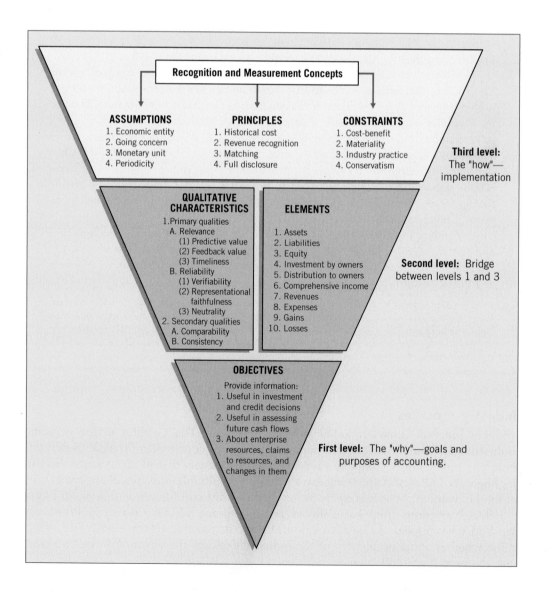

KEY TERMS

assumption, *36*

comparability, *33*

conceptual framework, *28*

conservatism, *46*

consistency, *33*

constraints, *43*

cost-benefit relationship, *43*

decision usefulness, *31*

earned (revenue), *39*

economic entity assumption, *36*

elements, basic, *34*

feedback value, *33*

full disclosure principle, *42*

going concern assumption, *37*

historical cost principle, *38*

industry practices, *45*

matching principle, *41*

materiality, *44*

monetary unit assumption, *37*

neutrality, *33*

notes to financial statements, *42*

objectives of financial reporting, *31*

period costs, *41*

periodicity (time period) assumption, *38*

predictive value, *33*

principles of accounting, *38*

product costs, *41*

qualitative characteristics, *31*

realizable (revenue), *39*

realized (revenue), *39*

relevance, *32*

reliability, *32*

representational faithfulness, *33*

revenue recognition principle, *39*

supplementary information, *42*

timeliness, *33*

understandability, *32*

verifiability, *33*

SUMMARY OF LEARNING OBJECTIVES

1. Describe the usefulness of a conceptual framework. The accounting profession needs a conceptual framework to: (1) build on and relate to an established body of concepts and objectives, (2) provide a framework for solving new and emerging practical problems, (3) increase financial statement users' understanding of and confidence in financial reporting, and (4) enhance comparability among companies' financial statements.

2. Describe the FASB's efforts to construct a conceptual framework. The FASB issued six Statements of Financial Accounting Concepts that relate to financial reporting for business enterprises. These concept statements provide the basis for the conceptual framework. They include objectives, qualitative characteristics, and elements. In addition, measurement and recognition concepts are developed.

3. Understand the objectives of financial reporting. Financial reporting should provide information that is: (1) useful to those making investment and credit decisions who have a reasonable understanding of business activities; (2) helpful to present and potential investors, creditors, and others in assessing future cash flows; and (3) about economic resources and the claims to and changes in them.

4. Identify the qualitative characteristics of accounting information. The overriding criterion by which accounting choices can be judged is decision usefulness—that is, providing information that is most useful for decision making. Relevance and reliability are the two primary qualities. Comparability and consistency are the secondary qualities, that make accounting information useful for decision making.

5. Define the basic elements of financial statements. The basic elements of financial statements are: (1) assets, (2) liabilities, (3) equity, (4) investments by owners, (5) distributions to owners, (6) comprehensive income, (7) revenues, (8) expenses, (9) gains, and (10) losses. We define these ten elements on page 35.

6. Describe the basic assumptions of accounting. Four basic assumptions underlying financial accounting are: (1) *Economic entity:* The activity of a company can be kept separate and distinct from its owners and any other business unit. (2) *Going concern:* The company will have a long life. (3) *Monetary unit:* Money is the common denominator by which economic activity is conducted, and the monetary unit provides an appropriate basis for measurement and analysis. (4) *Periodicity:* The economic activities of a company can be divided into artificial time periods.

7. Explain the application of the basic principles of accounting. (1) *Historical cost principle:* Existing GAAP requires that companies account for and report most assets and liabilities on the basis of acquisition price. (2) *Revenue recognition:* A company generally recognizes revenue when (a) realized or realizable and (b) earned. (3) *Matching principle:* A company recognizes expenses when the work (service) or the product actually makes its contribution to revenue. (4) *Full disclosure principle:* Companies generally provide information that is of sufficient importance to influence the judgment and decisions of an informed user.

8. Describe the impact that constraints have on reporting accounting information. The constraints and their impact are: (1) *Cost-benefit relationship:* The cost of providing the information must be weighed against the benefits that can be derived from using the information. (2) *Materiality:* Sound and acceptable standards should be followed if the amount involved is significant when compared with the other revenues and expenses, assets and liabilities, or net income of the company. (3) *Industry practices:* Follow the general practices in the company's industry, which sometimes requires departure from basic theory. (4) *Conservatism:* When in doubt, choose the solution that will be least likely to overstate net assets and net income.

QUESTIONS

1. What is a conceptual framework? Why is a conceptual framework necessary in financial accounting?

2. What are the primary objectives of financial reporting as indicated in *Statement of Financial Accounting Concepts No. 1?*

3. What is meant by the term "qualitative characteristics of accounting information"?

4. Briefly describe the two primary qualities of useful accounting information.

5. According to the FASB conceptual framework, the objectives of financial reporting for business enterprises are based on the needs of the users of financial statements. Explain the level of sophistication that the Board assumes about the users of financial statements.

6. What is the distinction between comparability and consistency?

7. Why is it necessary to develop a definitional framework for the basic elements of accounting?

8. Expenses, losses, and distributions to owners are all decreases in net assets. What are the distinctions among them?

9. Revenues, gains, and investments by owners are all increases in net assets. What are the distinctions among them?

10. What are the four basic assumptions that underlie the financial accounting structure?

11. The life of a business is divided into specific time periods, usually a year, to measure results of operations for each such time period and to portray financial conditions at the end of each period.

    (a) This practice is based on the accounting assumption that the life of the business consists of a series of time periods and that it is possible to measure accurately the results of operations for each period. Comment on the validity and necessity of this assumption.

    (b) What has been the effect of this practice on accounting? What is its relation to the accrual system? What influence has it had on accounting entries and methodology?

12. What is the basic accounting problem created by the monetary unit assumption when there is significant inflation? What appears to be the FASB position on a stable monetary unit?

13. The chairman of the board of directors of the company for which you are chief accountant has told you that he has little use for accounting figures based on cost. He believes that replacement values are of far more significance to the board of directors than "out-of-date costs." Present some arguments to convince him that accounting data should still be based on cost.

14. When is revenue generally recognized? Why has that date been chosen as the point at which to recognize the revenue resulting from the entire producing and selling process?

15. Magnus Eatery operates a catering service specializing in business luncheons for large corporations. Magnus requires customers to place their orders 2 weeks in advance of the scheduled events. Magnus bills its customers on the tenth day of the month following the date of service and requires that payment be made within 30 days of the billing date. Conceptually, when should Magnus recognize revenue related to its catering service?

16. What is the difference between realized and realizable? Give an example of where the concept of realizable is used to recognize revenue.

17. What is the justification for the following deviations from recognizing revenue at the time of sale?

    (a) Installment sales method of recognizing revenue.

    (b) Recognition of revenue at completion of production for certain agricultural products.

    (c) The percentage-of-completion basis in long-term construction contracts.

18. Jane Hull Company paid $135,000 for a machine in 2007. The Accumulated Depreciation account has a balance of $46,500 at the present time. The company could sell the machine today for $150,000. The company president believes that the company has a "right to this gain." What does the president mean by this statement? Do you agree?

19. Three expense recognition methods (associating cause and effect, systematic and rational allocation, and immediate recognition) were discussed in the text under the matching principle. Indicate the basic nature of each of these types of expenses and give two examples of each.

20. *Statement of Financial Accounting Concepts No. 5* identifies four characteristics that an item must have before it is recognized in the financial statements. What are these four characteristics?

21. Briefly describe the types of information concerning financial position, income, and cash flows that might be provided: (a) within the main body of the financial statements, (b) in the notes to the financial statements, or (c) as supplementary information.

22. In January 2008, Alan Jackson Inc. doubled the amount of its outstanding stock by selling on the market an additional 10,000 shares to finance an expansion of the business. You propose that this information be shown by a footnote on the balance sheet as of December 31, 2007. The president objects, claiming that this sale took place after December 31, 2007, and, therefore, should not be shown. Explain your position.

23. Describe the two major constraints inherent in the presentation of accounting information.

24. What are some of the costs of providing accounting information? What are some of the benefits of accounting information? Describe the cost-benefit factors that should be considered when new accounting standards are being proposed.

25. How are materiality (and immateriality) related to the proper presentation of financial statements? What factors and measures should be considered in assessing the materiality of a misstatement in the presentation of a financial statement?

26. The treasurer of Joan Osborne Co. has heard that conservatism is a doctrine that is followed in accounting and, therefore, proposes that several policies be followed that are conservative in nature. State your opinion with respect to each of the policies listed below.

(a) The company gives a 2-year warranty to its customers on all products sold. The estimated warranty costs incurred from this year's sales should be entered as an expense this year instead of an expense in the period in the future when the warranty is made good.

(b) When sales are made on account, there is always uncertainty about whether the accounts are collectible. Therefore, the treasurer recommends recording the sale when the cash is received from the customers.

(c) A personal liability lawsuit is pending against the company. The treasurer believes there is an even chance that the company will lose the suit and have to pay damages of $200,000 to $300,000. The treasurer recommends that a loss be recorded and a liability created in the amount of $300,000.

(d) The inventory should be valued at "cost or market, whichever is lower" because the losses from price declines should be recognized in the accounts in the period in which the price decline takes place.

BRIEF EXERCISES

(LO 4) **BE2-1** Discuss whether the changes described in each of the cases below require recognition in the CPA's audit report as to consistency. (Assume that the amounts are material.)

(a) The company changed its inventory method to FIFO from weighted-average, which had been used in prior years.

(b) The company disposed of one of the two subsidiaries that had been included in its consolidated statements for prior years.

(c) The estimated remaining useful life of plant property was reduced because of obsolescence.

(d) The company is using an inventory valuation method that is different from those used by all other companies in its industry.

(LO 4) **BE2-2** Identify which qualitative characteristic of accounting information is best described in each item below. (Do not use relevance and reliability.)

(a) The annual reports of **Best Buy Co.** are audited by certified public accountants.

(b) **Black & Decker** and **Cannondale Corporation** both use the FIFO cost flow assumption.

(c) **Starbucks Corporation** has used straight-line depreciation since it began operations.

(d) **Motorola** issues its quarterly reports immediately after each quarter ends.

(LO 5) **BE2-3** For each item below, indicate to which category of elements of financial statements it belongs.

(a) Retained earnings	**(e)** Depreciation	**(h)** Dividends
(b) Sales	**(f)** Loss on sale of equipment	**(i)** Gain on sale of investment
(c) Additional paid-in capital	**(g)** Interest payable	**(j)** Issuance of common stock
(d) Inventory		

(LO 6) **BE2-4** Identify which basic assumption of accounting is best described in each item below.

(a) The economic activities of **FedEx Corporation** are divided into 12-month periods for the purpose of issuing annual reports.

(b) **Solectron Corporation, Inc.** does not adjust amounts in its financial statements for the effects of inflation.

(c) **Walgreen Co.** reports current and noncurrent classifications in its balance sheet.

(d) The economic activities of **General Electric** and its subsidiaries are merged for accounting and reporting purposes.

(LO 7) **BE2-5** Identify which basic principle of accounting is best described in each item below.

    (a) **Norfolk Southern Corporation** reports revenue in its income statement when it is earned instead of when the cash is collected.

    (b) **Yahoo, Inc.** recognizes depreciation expense for a machine over the 2-year period during which that machine helps the company earn revenue.

    (c) **Oracle Corporation** reports information about pending lawsuits in the notes to its financial statements.

    (d) **Eastman Kodak Company** reports land on its balance sheet at the amount paid to acquire it, even though the estimated fair market value is greater.

(LO 8) **BE2-6** What accounting constraints are illustrated by the items below?

    (a) Zip's Farms, Inc. reports agricultural crops on its balance sheet at market value.

    (b) Crimson Tide Corporation does not accrue a contingent lawsuit gain of $650,000.

    (c) Wildcat Company does not disclose any information in the notes to the financial statements unless the value of the information to financial statement users exceeds the expense of gathering it.

    (d) Sun Devil Corporation expenses the cost of wastebaskets in the year they are acquired.

(LO 8) **BE2-7** Presented below are three different transactions related to materiality. Explain whether you would classify these transactions as material.

    (a) Marcus Co. has reported a positive trend in earnings over the last 3 years. In the current year, it reduces its bad debt allowance to ensure another positive earnings year. The impact of this adjustment is equal to 3% of net income.

    (b) Sosa Co. has an extraordinary gain of $3.1 million on the sale of plant assets and a $3.3 million loss on the sale of investments. It decides to net the gain and loss because the net effect is considered immaterial. Sosa Co.'s income for the current year was $10 million.

    (c) Seliz Co. expenses all capital equipment under $25,000 on the basis that it is immaterial. The company has followed this practice for a number of years.

(LO 6) **BE2-8** If the going concern assumption is not made in accounting, discuss the differences in the amounts shown in the financial statements for the following items.

    (a) Land.
    (b) Unamortized bond premium.
    (c) Depreciation expense on equipment.
    (d) Merchandise inventory.
    (e) Prepaid insurance.

(LO 6, 7, 8) **BE2-9** What accounting assumption, principle, or modifying convention does **Target Corporation** use in each of the situations below?

    (a) Target uses the lower of cost or market basis to value inventories.

    (b) Target was involved in litigation over the last year. This litigation is disclosed in the financial statements.

    (c) Target allocates the cost of its depreciable assets over the life it expects to receive revenue from these assets.

    (d) Target records the purchase of a new **Dell** PC at its cash equivalent price.

(LO 5) **BE2-10** Explain how you would decide whether to record each of the following expenditures as an asset or an expense. Assume all items are material.

    (a) Legal fees paid in connection with the purchase of land are $1,500.

    (b) Benjamin Bratt, Inc. paves the driveway leading to the office building at a cost of $21,000.

    (c) A meat market purchases a meat-grinding machine at a cost of $3,500.

    (d) On June 30, Alan and Alda, medical doctors, pay 6 months' office rent to cover the month of July and the next 5 months.

    (e) Tim Taylor's Hardware Company pays $9,000 in wages to laborers for construction on a building to be used in the business.

    (f) Nancy Kwan's Florists pays wages of $2,100 for November to an employee who serves as driver of their delivery truck.

EXERCISES

(LO 4, 8) **E2-1 (Qualitative Characteristics)** *SFAC No. 2* identifies the qualitative characteristics that make accounting information useful. Presented below are a number of questions related to these qualitative characteristics and underlying constraints.

(a) What is the quality of information that enables users to confirm or correct prior expectations?

(b) Identify the two overall or pervasive constraints developed in *SFAC No. 2*.

(c) The chairman of the SEC at one time noted, "If it becomes accepted or expected that accounting principles are determined or modified in order to secure purposes other than economic measurement, we assume a grave risk that confidence in the credibility of our financial information system will be undermined." Which qualitative characteristic of accounting information should ensure that such a situation will not occur? (Do not use reliability.)

(d) Billy Owens Corp. switches from FIFO to average cost to FIFO over a 2-year period. Which qualitative characteristic of accounting information is not followed?

(e) Assume that the profession permits the savings and loan industry to defer losses on investments it sells, because immediate recognition of the loss may have adverse economic consequences on the industry. Which qualitative characteristic of accounting information is not followed? (Do not use relevance or reliability.)

(f) What are the two primary qualities that make accounting information useful for decision making?

(g) Rex Chapman, Inc. does not issue its first-quarter report until after the second quarter's results are reported. Which qualitative characteristic of accounting is not followed? (Do not use relevance.)

(h) Predictive value is an ingredient of which of the two primary qualities that make accounting information useful for decision-making purposes?

(i) Ronald Coles, Inc. is the only company in its industry to depreciate its plant assets on a straight-line basis. Which qualitative characteristic of accounting information may not be followed? (Do not use industry practices.)

(j) Jeff Malone Company has attempted to determine the replacement cost of its inventory. Three different appraisers arrive at substantially different amounts for this value. The president, nevertheless, decides to report the middle value for external reporting purposes. Which qualitative characteristic of information is lacking in these data? (Do not use reliability or representational faithfulness.)

(LO 4) **E2-2 (Qualitative Characteristics)** The qualitative characteristics that make accounting information useful for decision-making purposes are as follows.

Relevance	Timeliness	Representational faithfulness
Reliability	Verifiability	Comparability
Predictive value	Neutrality	Consistency
Feedback value		

Instructions

Identify the appropriate qualitative characteristic(s) to be used given the information provided below.

(a) Qualitative characteristic being employed when companies in the same industry are using the same accounting principles.

(b) Quality of information that confirms users' earlier expectations.

(c) Imperative for providing comparisons of a company from period to period.

(d) Ignores the economic consequences of a standard or rule.

(e) Requires a high degree of consensus among individuals on a given measurement.

(f) Predictive value is an ingredient of this primary quality of information.

(g) Two qualitative characteristics that are related to both relevance and reliability.

(h) Neutrality is an ingredient of this primary quality of accounting information.

(i) Two primary qualities that make accounting information useful for decision-making purposes.

(j) Issuance of interim reports is an example of what primary ingredient of relevance?

(LO 5) **E2-3 (Elements of Financial Statements)** Ten interrelated elements that are most directly related to measuring the performance and financial status of an enterprise are provided below.

Assets	Distributions to owners	Expenses
Liabilities	Comprehensive income	Gains
Equity	Revenues	Losses
Investments by owners		

Instructions

Identify the element or elements from page 51 associated with the 12 items below.

  (a) Arises from peripheral or incidental transactions.
  (b) Obligation to transfer resources arising from a past transaction.
  (c) Increases ownership interest.
  (d) Declares and pays cash dividends to owners.
  (e) Increases in net assets in a period from nonowner sources.
  (f) Items characterized by service potential or future economic benefit.
  (g) Equals increase in assets less liabilities during the year, after adding distributions to owners and subtracting investments by owners.
  (h) Arises from income statement activities that constitute the entity's ongoing major or central operations.
  (i) Residual interest in the assets of the enterprise after deducting its liabilities.
  (j) Increases assets during a period through sale of product.
  (k) Decreases assets during the period by purchasing the company's own stock.
  (l) Includes all changes in equity during the period, except those resulting from investments by owners and distributions to owners.

(LO 6, 7, 8) **E2-4** **(Assumptions, Principles, and Constraints)** Presented below are the assumptions, principles, and constraints used in this chapter.

  1. Economic entity assumption
  2. Going concern assumption
  3. Monetary unit assumption
  4. Periodicity assumption
  5. Historical cost principle
  6. Matching principle
  7. Full disclosure principle
  8. Cost-benefit relationship
  9. Materiality
  10. Industry practices
  11. Conservatism

Instructions

Identify by number the accounting assumption, principle, or constraint that describes each situation below. Do not use a letter more than once.

  (a) Allocates expenses to revenues in the proper period.
  (b) Indicates that market value changes subsequent to purchase are not recorded in the accounts. (Do not use revenue recognition principle.)
  (c) Ensures that all relevant financial information is reported.
  (d) Rationale why plant assets are not reported at liquidation value. (Do not use historical cost principle.)
  (e) Anticipates all losses, but reports no gains.
  (f) Indicates that personal and business record keeping should be separately maintained.
  (g) Separates financial information into time periods for reporting purposes.
  (h) Permits the use of market value valuation in certain specific situations.
  (i) Requires that information significant enough to affect the decision of reasonably informed users should be disclosed. (Do not use full disclosure principle.)
  (j) Assumes that the dollar is the "measuring stick" used to report on financial performance.

(LO 6, 7, 8) **E2-5** **(Assumptions, Principles, and Constraints)** Presented below are a number of operational guidelines and practices that have developed over time.

Instructions

Select the assumption, principle, or constraint that most appropriately justifies these procedures and practices. (Do not use qualitative characteristics.)

  (a) Market value changes are not recognized in the accounting records.
  (b) Lower of cost or market is used to value inventories.
  (c) Financial information is presented so that investors will not be misled.
  (d) Intangible assets are capitalized and amortized over periods benefited.
  (e) Repair tools are expensed when purchased.
  (f) Agricultural companies use market value for purposes of valuing crops.
  (g) Each enterprise is kept as a unit distinct from its owner or owners.
  (h) All significant postbalance sheet events are reported.
  (i) Revenue is recorded at point of sale.
  (j) All important aspects of bond indentures are presented in financial statements.
  (k) Rationale for accrual accounting.
  (l) The use of consolidated statements is justified.
  (m) Reporting must be done at defined time intervals.
  (n) An allowance for doubtful accounts is established.
  (o) All payments out of petty cash are charged to Miscellaneous Expense. (Do not use conservatism.)

(p) Goodwill is recorded only at time of purchase.

(q) No profits are anticipated and all possible losses are recognized.

(r) A company charges its sales commission costs to expense.

(LO 7) **E2-6** **(Full Disclosure Principle)** Presented below are a number of facts related to R. Kelly, Inc. Assume that no mention of these facts was made in the financial statements and the related notes.

Instructions

Assume that you are the auditor of R. Kelly, Inc. and that you have been asked to explain the appropriate accounting and related disclosure necessary for each of these items.

(a) The company decided that, for the sake of conciseness, only net income should be reported on the income statement. Details as to revenues, cost of goods sold, and expenses were omitted.

(b) Equipment purchases of $170,000 were partly financed during the year through the issuance of a $110,000 notes payable. The company offset the equipment against the notes payable and reported plant assets at $60,000.

(c) R. Kelly has reported its ending inventory at $2,100,000 in the financial statements. No other information related to inventories is presented in the financial statements and related notes.

(d) The company changed its method of valuing inventories from weighted-average to FIFO. No mention of this change was made in the financial statements.

(LO 7) **E2-7** **(Accounting Principles—Comprehensive)** Presented below are a number of business transactions that occurred during the current year for Fresh Horses, Inc.

Instructions

In each of the situations, discuss the appropriateness of the journal entries in terms of generally accepted accounting principles.

(a) The president of Fresh Horses, Inc. used his expense account to purchase a new Suburban solely for personal use. The following journal entry was made.

Miscellaneous Expense	29,000	
Cash		29,000

(b) Merchandise inventory that cost $620,000 is reported on the balance sheet at $690,000, the expected selling price less estimated selling costs. The following entry was made to record this increase in value.

Merchandise Inventory	70,000	
Revenue		70,000

(c) The company is being sued for $500,000 by a customer who claims damages for personal injury apparently caused by a defective product. Company attorneys feel extremely confident that the company will have no liability for damages resulting from the situation. Nevertheless, the company decides to make the following entry.

Loss from Lawsuit	500,000	
Liability for Lawsuit		500,000

(d) Because the general level of prices increased during the current year, Fresh Horses, Inc. determined that there was a $16,000 understatement of depreciation expense on its equipment and decided to record it in its accounts. The following entry was made.

Depreciation Expense	16,000	
Accumulated Depreciation		16,000

(e) Fresh Horses, Inc. has been concerned about whether intangible assets could generate cash in case of liquidation. As a consequence, goodwill arising from a purchase transaction during the current year and recorded at $800,000 was written off as follows.

Retained Earnings	800,000	
Goodwill		800,000

(f) Because of a "fire sale," equipment obviously worth $200,000 was acquired at a cost of $155,000. The following entry was made.

Equipment	200,000	
Cash		155,000
Revenue		45,000

(LO 7) **E2-8** **(Accounting Principles—Comprehensive)** Presented on page 54 is information related to Garth Brooks, Inc.

Instructions

Comment on the appropriateness of the accounting procedures followed by Garth Brooks, Inc.

(a) Depreciation expense on the building for the year was $60,000. Because the building was increasing in value during the year, the controller decided to charge the depreciation expense to retained earnings instead of to net income. The following entry is recorded.

Retained Earnings	60,000	
Accumulated Depreciation — Buildings		60,000

(b) Materials were purchased on January 1, 2006, for $120,000 and this amount was entered in the Materials account. On December 31, 2006, the materials would have cost $141,000, so the following entry is made.

Inventory	21,000	
Gain on Inventories		21,000

(c) During the year, the company purchased equipment through the issuance of common stock. The stock had a par value of $135,000 and a fair market value of $450,000. The fair market value of the equipment was not easily determinable. The company recorded this transaction as follows.

Equipment	135,000	
Common Stock		135,000

(d) During the year, the company sold certain equipment for $285,000, recognizing a gain of $69,000. Because the controller believed that new equipment would be needed in the near future, she decided to defer the gain and amortize it over the life of any new equipment purchased.

(e) An order for $61,500 has been received from a customer for products on hand. This order was shipped on January 9, 2007. The company made the following entry in 2006.

Accounts Receivable	61,500	
Sales		61,500

See the book's website, www.wiley.com/college/kieso, for Additional Exercises.

CONCEPTS FOR ANALYSIS

CA2-1 **(Conceptual Framework—General)** Roger Morgan has some questions regarding the theoretical framework in which standards are set. He knows that the FASB and other predecessor organizations have attempted to develop a conceptual framework for accounting theory formulation. Yet, Roger's supervisors have indicated that these theoretical frameworks have little value in the practical sense (i.e., in the real world). Roger did notice that accounting standards seem to be established after the fact rather than before. He thought this indicated a lack of theory structure but never really questioned the process at school because he was too busy doing the homework.

Roger feels that some of his anxiety about accounting theory and accounting semantics could be alleviated by identifying the basic concepts and definitions accepted by the profession and considering them in light of his current work. By doing this, he hopes to develop an appropriate connection between theory and practice.

Instructions

(a) Help Roger recognize the purpose of and benefit of a conceptual framework.

(b) Identify any *Statements of Financial Accounting Concepts* issued by FASB that may be helpful to Roger in developing his theoretical background.

CA2-2 **(Conceptual Framework—General)** The Financial Accounting Standards Board (FASB) has developed a conceptual framework for financial accounting and reporting. The FASB has issued seven *Statements of Financial Accounting Concepts*. These statements are intended to set forth objectives and fundamentals that will be the basis for developing financial accounting and reporting standards. The objectives identify the goals and purposes of financial reporting. The fundamentals are the underlying concepts of financial accounting that guide the selection of transactions, events, and circumstances to be accounted for; their recognition and measurement; and the means of summarizing and communicating them to interested parties.

The purpose of *Statement of Financial Accounting Concepts No. 2,* "Qualitative Characteristics of Accounting Information," is to examine the characteristics that make accounting information useful. The characteristics or qualities of information discussed in SFAC No. 2 are the ingredients that make information useful and the qualities to be sought when accounting choices are made.

Instructions

  (a) Identify and discuss the benefits that can be expected to be derived from the FASB's conceptual framework study.

  (b) What is the most important quality for accounting information as identified in *Statement of Financial Accounting Concepts No. 2*? Explain why it is the most important.

  (c) *Statement of Financial Accounting Concepts No. 2* describes a number of key characteristics or qualities for accounting information. Briefly discuss the importance of any three of these qualities for financial reporting purposes.

(CMA adapted)

CA2-3 (Objectives of Financial Reporting) Regis Gordon and Kathy Medford are discussing various aspects of the FASB's pronouncement *Statement of Financial Accounting Concepts No. 1*, "Objectives of Financial Reporting by Business Enterprises." Regis indicates that this pronouncement provides little, if any, guidance to the practicing professional in resolving accounting controversies. He believes that the statement provides such broad guidelines that it would be impossible to apply the objectives to present-day reporting problems. Kathy concedes this point but indicates that objectives are still needed to provide a starting point for the FASB in helping to improve financial reporting.

Instructions

  (a) Indicate the basic objectives established in *Statement of Financial Accounting Concepts No. 1*.

  (b) What do you think is the meaning of Kathy's statement that the FASB needs a starting point to resolve accounting controversies?

CA2-4 (Qualitative Characteristics) Accounting information provides useful information about business transactions and events. Those who provide and use financial reports must often select and evaluate accounting alternatives. FASB *Statement of Financial Accounting Concepts No. 2*, "Qualitative Characteristics of Accounting Information," examines the characteristics of accounting information that make it useful for decision making. It also points out that various limitations inherent in the measurement and reporting process may necessitate trade-offs or sacrifices among the characteristics of useful information.

Instructions

  (a) Describe briefly the following characteristics of useful accounting information.

    (1) Relevance   **(4)** Comparability

    (2) Reliability   **(5)** Consistency

    (3) Understandability

  (b) For each of the following pairs of information characteristics, give an example of a situation in which one of the characteristics may be sacrificed in return for a gain in the other.

    (1) Relevance and reliability.   **(3)** Comparability and consistency.

    (2) Relevance and consistency.   **(4)** Relevance and understandability.

  (c) What criterion should be used to evaluate trade-offs between information characteristics?

CA2-5 (Revenue Recognition and Matching Principle) After the presentation of your report on the examination of the financial statements to the board of directors of Bones Publishing Company, one of the new directors expresses surprise that the income statement assumes that an equal proportion of the revenue is earned with the publication of every issue of the company's magazine. She feels that the "crucial event" in the process of earning revenue in the magazine business is the cash sale of the subscription. She says that she does not understand why most of the revenue cannot be "recognized" in the period of the sale.

Instructions

  (a) List the various accepted times for recognizing revenue in the accounts and explain when the methods are appropriate.

  (b) Discuss the propriety of timing the recognition of revenue in Bones Publishing Company's accounts with:

    (1) The cash sale of the magazine subscription.

    (2) The publication of the magazine every month.

    (3) Both events, by recognizing a portion of the revenue with the cash sale of the magazine subscription and a portion of the revenue with the publication of the magazine every month.

CA2-6 (Revenue Recognition and Matching Principle) On June 5, 2006, McCoy Corporation signed a contract with Sulu Associates under which Sulu agreed (1) to construct an office building on land owned by McCoy, (2) to accept responsibility for procuring financing for the project and finding tenants, and (3) to manage the property for 35 years. The annual net income from the project, after debt service, was to be divided equally between McCoy Corporation and Sulu Associates. Sulu was to accept its share of future net income as full payment for its services in construction, obtaining finances and tenants, and management of the project.

By May 31, 2007, the project was nearly completed, and tenants had signed leases to occupy 90% of the available space at annual rentals totaling $4,000,000. It is estimated that, after operating expenses and debt service, the annual net income will amount to $1,500,000.

The management of Sulu Associates believed that (a) the economic benefit derived from the contract with McCoy should be reflected on its financial statements for the fiscal year ended May 31, 2007, and directed that revenue be accrued in an amount equal to the commercial value of the services Sulu had rendered during the year, (b) this amount should be carried in contracts receivable, and (c) all related expenditures should be charged against the revenue.

Instructions
  (a) Explain the main difference between the economic concept of business income as reflected by Sulu's management and the measurement of income under generally accepted accounting principles.
  (b) Discuss the factors to be considered in determining when revenue should be recognized for the purpose of accounting measurement of periodic income.
  (c) Is the belief of Sulu's management in accordance with generally accepted accounting principles for the measurement of revenue and expense for the year ended May 31, 2007? Support your opinion by discussing the application to this case of the factors to be considered for asset measurement and revenue and expense recognition.

(AICPA adapted)

CA2-7 (Matching Principle) An accountant must be familiar with the concepts involved in determining earnings of a business entity. The amount of earnings reported for a business entity is dependent on the proper recognition, in general, of revenue and expense for a given time period. In some situations, costs are recognized as expenses at the time of product sale. In other situations, guidelines have been developed for recognizing costs as expenses or losses by other criteria.

Instructions
  (a) Explain the rationale for recognizing costs as expenses at the time of product sale.
  (b) What is the rationale underlying the appropriateness of treating costs as expenses of a period instead of assigning the costs to an asset? Explain.
  (c) In what general circumstances would it be appropriate to treat a cost as an asset instead of as an expense? Explain.
  (d) Some expenses are assigned to specific accounting periods on the basis of systematic and rational allocation of asset cost. Explain the underlying rationale for recognizing expenses on the basis of systematic and rational allocation of asset cost.
  (e) Identify the conditions under which it would be appropriate to treat a cost as a loss.

(AICPA adapted)

CA2-8 (Matching Principle) Accountants try to prepare income statements that are as accurate as possible. A basic requirement in preparing accurate income statements is to match costs against revenues properly. Proper matching of costs against revenues requires that costs resulting from typical business operations be recognized in the period in which they expired.

Instructions
  (a) List three criteria that can be used to determine whether such costs should appear as charges in the income statement for the current period.
  (b) As generally presented in financial statements, the following items or procedures have been criticized as improperly matching costs with revenues. Briefly discuss each item from the viewpoint of matching costs with revenues and suggest corrective or alternative means of presenting the financial information.
    (1) Receiving and handling costs.
    (2) Valuation of inventories at the lower of cost or market.
    (3) Cash discounts on purchases.

CA2-9 (Matching Principle) Carlos Rodriguez sells and erects shell houses, that is, frame structures that are completely finished on the outside but are unfinished on the inside except for flooring, partition studding, and ceiling joists. Shell houses are sold chiefly to customers who are handy with tools and who have time to do the interior wiring, plumbing, wall completion and finishing, and other work necessary to make the shell houses livable dwellings.

Rodriguez buys shell houses from a manufacturer in unassembled packages consisting of all lumber, roofing, doors, windows, and similar materials necessary to complete a shell house. Upon commencing operations in a new area, Rodriguez buys or leases land as a site for its local warehouse, field office, and display houses. Sample display houses are erected at a total cost of $30,000 to $44,000 including the cost of the unassembled packages. The chief element of cost of the display houses is the unassembled packages, inasmuch as erection is a short, low-cost operation. Old sample models are torn down or altered into new models every 3 to 7 years. Sample display houses have little salvage value because dismantling and moving costs amount to nearly as much as the cost of an unassembled package.

Instructions

   (a) A choice must be made between (1) expensing the costs of sample display houses in the periods in which the expenditure is made and (2) spreading the costs over more than one period. Discuss the advantages of each method.

   (b) Would it be preferable to amortize the cost of display houses on the basis of (1) the passage of time or (2) the number of shell houses sold? Explain.

(AICPA adapted)

 CA2-10 (Qualitative Characteristics) Recently, your Uncle Waldo Ralph, who knows that you always have your eye out for a profitable investment, has discussed the possibility of your purchasing some corporate bonds. He suggests that you may wish to get in on the "ground floor" of this deal. The bonds being issued by Cricket Corp. are 10-year debentures which promise a 40% rate of return. Cricket manufactures novelty/party items.

     You have told Waldo that, unless you can take a look at Cricket's financial statements, you would not feel comfortable about such an investment. Believing that this is the chance of a lifetime, Uncle Waldo has procured a copy of Cricket's most recent, unaudited financial statements which are a year old. These statements were prepared by Mrs. John Cricket. You peruse these statements, and they are quite impressive. The balance sheet showed a debt-to-equity ratio of 0.10 and, for the year shown, the company reported net income of $2,424,240.

     The financial statements are not shown in comparison with amounts from other years. In addition, no significant note disclosures about inventory valuation, depreciation methods, loan agreements, etc. are available.

Instructions

Write a letter to Uncle Waldo explaining why it would be unwise to base an investment decision on the financial statements that he has provided to you. Be sure to explain why these financial statements are neither relevant nor reliable.

CA2-11 (Matching) Hinckley Nuclear Power Plant will be "mothballed" at the end of its useful life (approximately 20 years) at great expense. The matching principle requires that expenses be matched to revenue. Accountants Jana Kingston and Pete Henning argue whether it is better to allocate the expense of mothballing over the next 20 years or ignore it until mothballing occurs.

Instructions

Answer the following questions.

   (a) What stakeholders should be considered?
   (b) What ethical issue, if any, underlies the dispute?
   (c) What alternatives should be considered?
   (d) Assess the consequences of the alternatives.
   (e) What decision would you recommend?

CA2-12 (Cost-Benefit) The AICPA Special Committee on Financial Reporting proposed the following constraints related to financial reporting.

   1. Business reporting should exclude information outside of management's expertise or for which management is not the best source, such as information about competitors.

   2. Management should not be required to report information that would significantly harm the company's competitive position.

   3. Management should not be required to provide forecasted financial statements. Rather, management should provide information that helps users forecast for themselves the company's financial future.

   4. Other than for financial statements, management need report only the information it knows. That is, management should be under no obligation to gather information it does not have, or does not need, to manage the business.

   5. Companies should present certain elements of business reporting only if users and management agree they should be reported—a concept of flexible reporting.

   6. Companies should not have to report forward-looking information unless there are effective deterrents to unwarranted litigation that discourages companies from doing so.

Instructions

For each item, briefly discuss how the proposed constraint addresses concerns about the costs and benefits of financial reporting.

USING YOUR JUDGMENT

Financial Reporting Problem

P&G **The Procter & Gamble Company (P&G)**

The financial statements of **P&G** are presented in Appendix 5B or can be accessed on the KWW website.

Instructions

Refer to P&G's financial statements and the accompanying notes to answer the following questions.

(a) Using the notes to the consolidated financial statements, determine P&G's revenue recognition policies. Discuss the impact of trade promotions on P&G's financial statements.

(b) Give two examples of where historical cost information is reported in P&G's financial statements and related notes. Give two examples of the use of fair value information reported in either the financial statements or related notes.

(c) How can we determine that the accounting principles used by P&G are prepared on a basis consistent with those of last year?

(d) What is P&G's accounting policy related to advertising? What accounting principle does P&G follow regarding accounting for advertising? Where are advertising expenses reported in the financial statements?

Financial Statement Analysis Case

Wal-Mart

Wal-Mart Stores provided the following disclosure in a recent annual report.

> *New accounting pronouncement (partial)* . . . the Securities and Exchange Commission issued Staff Accounting Bulletin No. 101—"Revenue Recognition in Financial Statements" (*SAB 101*). This SAB deals with various revenue recognition issues, several of which are common within the retail industry. As a result of the issuance of this SAB . . . the Company is currently evaluating the effects of the SAB on its method of recognizing revenues related to layaway sales and will make any accounting method changes necessary during the first quarter of [next year].

In response to *SAB 101* Wal-Mart changed its revenue recognition policy for layaway transactions, in which Wal-Mart sets aside merchandise for customers who make partial payment. Before the change, Wal-Mart recognized all revenue on the sale at the time of the layaway. After the change, Wal-Mart does not recognize revenue until customers satisfy all payment obligations and take possession of the merchandise.

Instructions

(a) Discuss the expected effect on income (1) in the year that Wal-Mart makes the changes in its revenue recognition policy, and (2) in the years following the change.

(b) Evaluate the extent to which Wal-Mart's previous revenue policy was consistent with the revenue recognition principle.

(c) If all retailers had used a revenue recognition policy similar to Wal-Mart's before the change, are there any concerns with respect to the qualitative characteristic of comparability? Explain.

Comparative Analysis Case

The Coca-Cola Company and PepsiCo, Inc.

Instructions

Go to the KWW website, and use information found there to answer the following questions related to **The Coca-Cola Company** and **PepsiCo, Inc.**

(a) What are the primary lines of business of these two companies as shown in their notes to the financial statements?

(b) Which company has the dominant position in beverage sales?

(c) How are inventories for these two companies valued? What cost allocation method is used to report inventory? How does their accounting for inventories affect comparability between the two companies?

(d) Which company changed its accounting policies during 2004 which affected the consistency of the financial results from the previous year? What were these changes?

Research Case

Retrieval of Information on Public Company

There are several commonly available indexes that enable individuals to locate articles previously included in numerous business publications and periodicals. Articles can generally be searched by company or by subject matter. Four common indexes are the *Wall Street Journal Index*, *Business Abstracts* (formerly the *Business Periodical Index*), *Predicasts F&S Index*, and *ABI/Inform*.

Instructions

Use one of these resources to find an article about a company in which you are interested. Read the article and answer the following questions. (*Note:* Your library may have CD-ROM versions of these indexes.)

(a) What is the article about?

(b) What company-specific information is included in the article?

(c) Identify any accounting-related issues discussed in the article.

International Reporting Case

As discussed in Chapter 1, the **International Accounting Standards Board (IASB)** develops accounting standards for many international companies. The IASB also has developed a conceptual framework to help guide the setting of accounting standards. Following is an Overview of the IASB Framework.

Objective of Financial Statements
> To provide information about the financial position, performance, and changes in financial position of an enterprise that is useful to a wide range of users in making economic decisions.

Underlying Assumptions
> Accrual basis
> Going concern

Qualitative Characteristics of Financial Statements

Understandability	Reliability (continued)
Relevance	Neutrality
Materiality	Prudence
Reliability	Completeness
Faithful representation	Comparability
Substance over form	

Constraints on Relevant and Reliable Information
> Timeliness
> Balance between benefit and cost
> Balance between qualitative characteristics

True and Fair Presentation

Elements of Financial Statements
> *Asset:* A resource controlled by the enterprise as a result of past events and from which future economic benefits are expected to flow to the enterprise.
>
> *Liability:* A present obligation of the enterprise arising from past events, the settlement of which is expected to result in an outflow from the enterprise of resources embodying economic benefits.
>
> *Equity:* The residual interest in the assets of the enterprise after deducting all its liabilities.
>
> *Income:* Increases in economic benefits during the accounting period in the form of inflows or enhancements of assets or decreases of liabilities that result in increases in equity, other than those relating to contributions from equity participants.
>
> *Expenses:* Decreases in economic benefits during the accounting period in the form of outflows or depletions of assets or incurrences of liabilities that result in decreases in equity, other than those relating to distributions to equity participants.

Instructions

Identify at least three similarities and at least three differences between the FASB and IASB conceptual frameworks as revealed in the above Overview.

Professional Research: Financial Accounting and Reporting

Your aunt recently received the annual report for a company in which she has invested. The report notes that the statements have been prepared in accordance with "generally accepted accounting principles." She has also heard that certain terms have special meanings in accounting relative to everyday use. She would like you to explain the meaning of terms she has come across related to accounting.

Instructions

Using the **Financial Accounting Research System (FARS)**, respond to the following items. (Provide text strings used in your search.)

(a) How is "materiality" defined in the conceptual framework?

(b) The concepts statements provide several examples in which specific quantitative materiality guidelines are provided to firms. Identity at least two of these examples. Do you think the materiality guidelines should be quantified? Why or why not?

(c) The concepts statements discuss the concept of "articulation" between financial statement elements. Briefly summarize the meaning of this term and how it relates to an entity's financial statements.

Professional Simulation

In this simulation you are asked to address questions regarding the FASB's conceptual framework. Prepare responses to all parts.

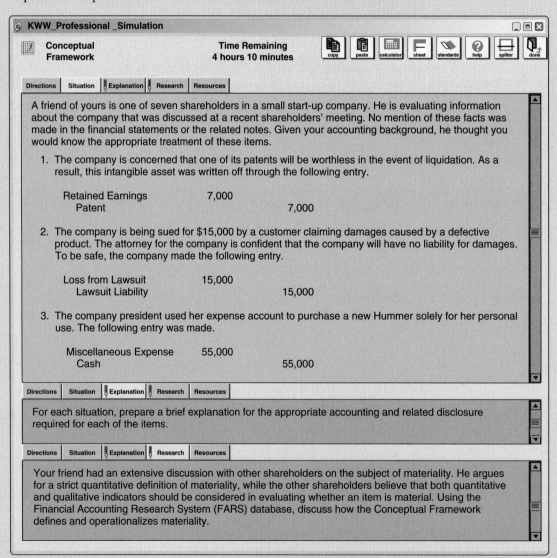

⬜ **KWW_Professional _Simulation**

📋 **Conceptual Framework** **Time Remaining** **4 hours 10 minutes** [copy] [paste] [calculator] [sheet] [standards] [help] [splitter] [done]

| Directions | Situation | Explanation | Research | Resources |

A friend of yours is one of seven shareholders in a small start-up company. He is evaluating information about the company that was discussed at a recent shareholders' meeting. No mention of these facts was made in the financial statements or the related notes. Given your accounting background, he thought you would know the appropriate treatment of these items.

1. The company is concerned that one of its patents will be worthless in the event of liquidation. As a result, this intangible asset was written off through the following entry.

Retained Earnings	7,000	
Patent		7,000

2. The company is being sued for $15,000 by a customer claiming damages caused by a defective product. The attorney for the company is confident that the company will have no liability for damages. To be safe, the company made the following entry.

Loss from Lawsuit	15,000	
Lawsuit Liability		15,000

3. The company president used her expense account to purchase a new Hummer solely for her personal use. The following entry was made.

Miscellaneous Expense	55,000	
Cash		55,000

| Directions | Situation | Explanation | Research | Resources |

For each situation, prepare a brief explanation for the appropriate accounting and related disclosure required for each of the items.

| Directions | Situation | Explanation | Research | Resources |

Your friend had an extensive discussion with other shareholders on the subject of materiality. He argues for a strict quantitative definition of materiality, while the other shareholders believe that both quantitative and qualitative indicators should be considered in evaluating whether an item is material. Using the Financial Accounting Research System (FARS) database, discuss how the Conceptual Framework defines and operationalizes materiality.

Remember to check the book's companion website to find additional resources for this chapter.

THE ACCOUNTING INFORMATION SYSTEM

Needed: A Reliable Information System

Maintaining a set of accounting records is not optional. The Internal Revenue Service (IRS) requires that businesses prepare and retain a set of records and documents that can be audited. The Foreign Corrupt Practices Act (federal legislation) requires public companies to ". . . make and keep books, records, and accounts, which, in reasonable detail, accurately and fairly reflect the transactions and dispositions of the assets. . . ." But beyond these two reasons, a company that fails to keep an accurate record of its business transactions may lose revenue and is more likely to operate inefficiently.

Consider, for example, the Long Island Railroad (LIRR), once one of the nation's busiest commuter lines. The LIRR lost money because of poor recordkeeping. It forgot to bill some customers, mistakenly paid some payables twice, and neglected to record redemptions of bonds. FFP Marketing, which operates convenience stores in 11 states, provides another example. The SEC forced it to restate earnings when an audit uncovered faulty bookkeeping for its credit card accounts and fuel payables.

Inefficient accounting also cost the City of Cleveland, Ohio. An audit discovered over 313 examples of dysfunctional accounting, costing taxpayers over $1.3 million. Its poor accounting system resulted in the Cleveland treasurer's ignorance of available cash, which led to missed investment opportunities. Further, delayed recording of pension payments created the false impression of $13 million in the city coffers.

Even the use of computers is no assurance of accuracy and efficiency. "The conversion to a new system called MasterNet fouled up data processing records to the extent that Bank of America was frequently unable to produce or deliver customer statements on a timely basis," said an executive at one of the country's largest banks.

Although these situations may occur only rarely in large organizations, they illustrate the point: Companies must properly maintain accounts and detailed records or face unnecessary costs. The SEC suspended trading in FFP Marketing's stock until it corrected the errors and re-issued financial statements. The City of Cleveland's municipal bond rating took a hit because of its poor accounting practices.

Learning Objectives

After studying this chapter, you should be able to:

1 Understand basic accounting terminology.

2 Explain double-entry rules.

3 Identify steps in the accounting cycle.

4 Record transactions in journals, post to ledger accounts, and prepare a trial balance.

5 Explain the reasons for preparing adjusting entries.

6 Prepare financial statements from the adjusted trial balance.

7 Prepare closing entries.

8 Explain how to adjust inventory accounts at year-end.

As the opening story indicates, a reliable information system is a necessity for all companies. The purpose of this chapter is to explain and illustrate the features of an accounting information system. The content and organization of this chapter are as follows.

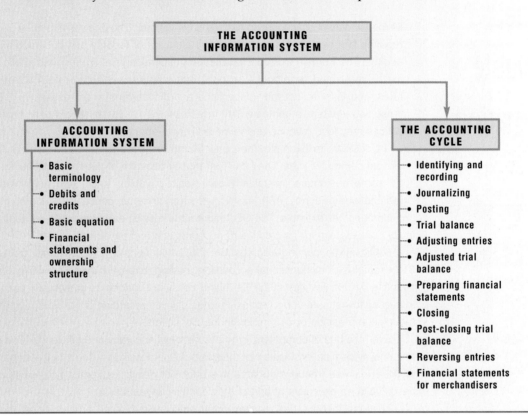

ACCOUNTING INFORMATION SYSTEM

An **accounting information system** collects and processes transaction data and then disseminates the financial information to interested parties. Accounting information systems vary widely from one business to another. Various factors shape these systems: the nature of the business and the transactions in which it engages, the size of the firm, the volume of data to be handled, and the informational demands that management and others require.

As we discussed in Chapters 1 and 2, in response to the requirements of the Sarbanes-Oxley Act of 2002, companies are placing a renewed focus on their accounting systems to ensure relevant and reliable information is reported in financial statements.[1] A good accounting information system helps management answer such questions as:

How much and what kind of debt is outstanding?

Were our sales higher this period than last?

What assets do we have?

What were our cash inflows and outflows?

---

[1]One study of first compliance with the internal-control testing provisions of the Sarbanes-Oxley Act documented material weaknesses for about 13 percent of companies reporting in 2004 and 2005. L. Townsend, "Internal Control Deficiency Disclosures–Interim Alert," *Yellow Card–Interim Trend Alert* (April 12, 2005) Glass, Lewis & Co., LLC.

Did we make a profit last period?

Are any of our product lines or divisions operating at a loss?

Can we safely increase our dividends to stockholders?

Is our rate of return on net assets increasing?

Management can answer many other questions with the data provided by an efficient accounting system. A well-devised accounting information system benefits every type of company.

Basic Terminology

Financial accounting rests on a set of concepts (discussed in Chapters 1 and 2) for identifying, recording, classifying, and interpreting transactions and other events relating to enterprises. You therefore need to understand the **basic terminology employed in collecting accounting data**.

BASIC TERMINOLOGY

EVENT. A happening of consequence. An event generally is the source or cause of changes in assets, liabilities, and equity. Events may be external or internal.

TRANSACTION. An **external event** involving a transfer or exchange between two or more entities.

ACCOUNT. A systematic arrangement that shows the effect of transactions and other events on a specific element (asset, liability, and so on). Companies keep a separate account for each asset, liability, revenue, and expense, and for capital (owners' equity).

REAL AND NOMINAL ACCOUNTS. Real (permanent) **accounts** are asset, liability, and equity accounts; they appear on the balance sheet. **Nominal** (temporary) **accounts** are revenue, expense, and dividend accounts; except for dividends, they appear on the income statement. Companies periodically close nominal accounts; they do not close real accounts.

LEDGER. The book (or computer printouts) containing the accounts. A **general ledger** is a collection of all the asset, liability, owners' equity, revenue, and expense accounts. A **subsidiary ledger** contains the details related to a given general ledger account.

JOURNAL. The "book of original entry" where the company initially records transactions and selected other events. Various amounts are transferred from the book of original entry, the journal, to the ledger.

POSTING. The process of transferring the essential facts and figures from the book of original entry to the ledger accounts.

TRIAL BALANCE. The list of all open accounts in the ledger and their balances. The trial balance taken immediately after all adjustments have been posted is called an **adjusted trial balance**. A trial balance taken immediately after closing entries have been posted is called a **post-closing** or **after-closing trial balance**. Companies may prepare a trial balance at any time.

ADJUSTING ENTRIES. Entries made at the end of an accounting period to bring all accounts up to date on an accrual basis, so that the company can prepare correct financial statements.

FINANCIAL STATEMENTS. Statements that reflect the collection, tabulation, and final summarization of the accounting data. Four statements are involved: (1) The **balance sheet** shows the financial condition of the enterprise at the end of a period.

OBJECTIVE 1
Understand basic accounting terminology.

(2) The **income statement** measures the results of operations during the period. (3) The **statement of cash flows** reports the cash provided and used by operating, investing, and financing activities during the period. (4) The **statement of retained earnings** reconciles the balance of the retained earnings account from the beginning to the end of the period.

CLOSING ENTRIES. The formal process by which the enterprise reduces all nominal accounts to zero and determines and transfers the net income or net loss to an owners' equity account. Also known as "closing the ledger," "closing the books," or merely "closing."

OBJECTIVE 2
Explain double-entry rules.

Debits and Credits

The terms **debit** (Dr.) and **credit** (Cr.) mean left and right, respectively. These terms do not mean increase or decrease, but instead describe *where* a company makes entries in the recording process. That is, when a company enters an amount on the left side of an account, it **debits** the account. When it makes an entry on the right side, it **credits** the account. When comparing the totals of the two sides, an account shows a **debit balance** if the total of the debit amounts exceeds the credits. An account shows a **credit balance** if the credit amounts exceed the debits.

The positioning of debits on the left and credits on the right is simply an accounting custom. We could function just as well if we reversed the sides. However, the United States adopted the custom, now the rule, of having debits on the left side of an account and credits on the right side, similar to the custom of driving on the right-hand side of the road. This rule applies to all accounts.

The equality of debits and credits provides the basis for the double-entry system of recording transactions (sometimes referred to as double-entry bookkeeping). Under the universally used **double-entry accounting** system, a company records the dual (two-sided) effect of each transaction in appropriate accounts. This system provides a logical method for recording transactions. It also offers a means of proving the accuracy of the recorded amounts. If a company records every transaction with equal debits and credits, then the sum of all the debits to the accounts must equal the sum of all the credits.

Illustration 3-1 presents the basic guidelines for an accounting system. Increases to all asset and expense accounts occur on the left (or debit side) and decreases on the

ILLUSTRATION 3-1
Double-entry (Debit and Credit) Accounting System

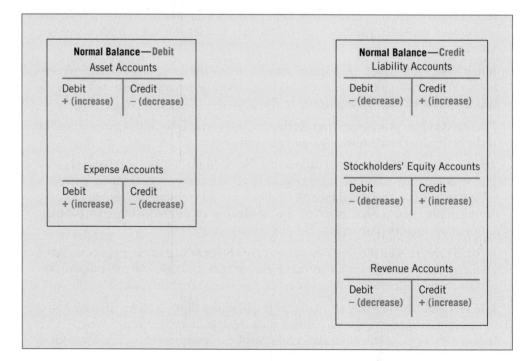

right (or credit side). Conversely, increases to all liability and revenue accounts occur on the right (or credit side) and decreases on the left (or debit side). A company increases stockholders' equity accounts, such as Common Stock and Retained Earnings, on the credit side, but increases Dividends on the debit side.

Basic Equation

In a double-entry system, for every debit there must be a credit, and vice versa. This leads us, then, to the basic equation in accounting (Illustration 3-2).

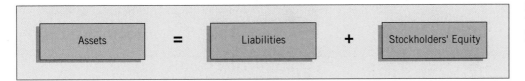

ILLUSTRATION 3-2
The Basic Accounting Equation

Illustration 3-3 expands this equation to show the accounts that make up stockholders' equity. The figure also shows the debit/credit rules and effects on each type of account. Study this diagram carefully. It will help you understand the fundamentals of the double-entry system. Like the basic equation, the expanded basic equation must also balance (total debits equal total credits).

ILLUSTRATION 3-3
Expanded Basic Equation and Debit/Credit Rules and Effects

Every time a transaction occurs, the elements of the equation change. However, the basic equality remains. To illustrate, consider the following eight different transactions for Perez Inc.

1 Owners invest $40,000 in exchange for common stock.

2 Disburse $600 cash for secretarial wages.

3 Purchase office equipment priced at $5,200, giving a 10 percent promissory note in exchange.

<u>**4**</u>   Receive $4,000 cash for services rendered.

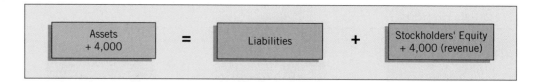

<u>**5**</u>   Pay off a short-term liability of $7,000.

<u>**6**</u>   Declare a cash dividend of $5,000.

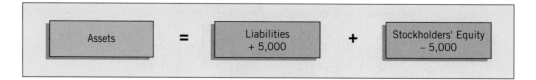

<u>**7**</u>   Convert a long-term liability of $80,000 into common stock.

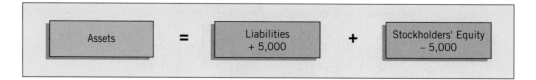

<u>**8**</u>   Pay cash of $16,000 for a delivery van.

Financial Statements and Ownership Structure

The stockholders' equity section of the balance sheet reports common stock and retained earnings. The income statement reports revenues and expenses. The statement of retained earnings reports dividends. Because a company transfers dividends, revenues, and expenses to retained earnings at the end of the period, a change in any one of these three items affects stockholders' equity. Illustration 3-4 shows the stockholders' equity relationships.

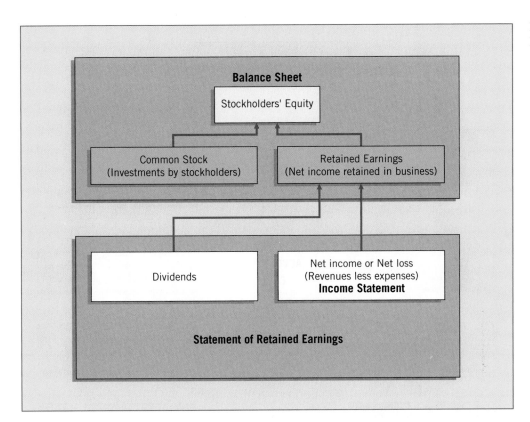

ILLUSTRATION 3-4
Financial Statements and
Ownership Structure

The enterprise's ownership structure dictates the types of accounts that are part of or affect the equity section. A corporation commonly uses Common Stock, Additional Paid-in Capital, Dividends, and Retained Earnings accounts. A proprietorship or a partnership uses a Capital account and a Drawing account: A Capital account indicates the owner's or owners' investment in the company. A Drawing account tracks withdrawals by the owner(s).

Illustration 3-5 summarizes and relates the transactions affecting owners' equity to the nominal (temporary) and real (permanent) classifications and to the types of business ownership.

ILLUSTRATION 3-5
Effects of Transactions on
Owners' Equity Accounts

Transactions Affecting Owners' Equity	Impact on Owners' Equity	Ownership Structure			
		Proprietorships and Partnerships		Corporations	
		Nominal (Temporary) Accounts	Real (Permanent) Accounts	Nominal (Temporary) Accounts	Real (Permanent) Accounts
Investment by owner(s)	Increase		Capital		Common Stock and related accounts
Revenues earned	Increase	Revenue ⎤		Revenue ⎤	Retained Earnings
Expenses incurred	Decrease	Expense ⎬	Capital	Expense ⎬	
Withdrawal by owner(s)	Decrease	Drawing ⎦		Dividends ⎦	

THE ACCOUNTING CYCLE

Illustration 3-6 shows the steps in the **accounting cycle**. An enterprise normally uses these accounting procedures to record transactions and prepare financial statements.

OBJECTIVE 3
Identify steps in the
accounting cycle.

ILLUSTRATION 3-6
The Accounting Cycle

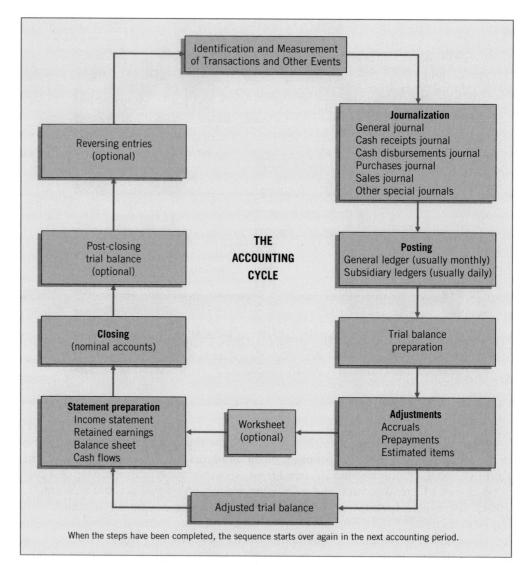

Accounting Cycle Tutorial

Identifying and Recording Transactions and Other Events

The first step in the accounting cycle is analysis of transactions and selected other events. The first problem is to determine what to record. Although GAAP provides guidelines, no simple rules exist that state which events a company should record. Although changes in a company's personnel or managerial policies may be important, the company should not record these items in the accounts. On the other hand, a company should record all cash sales or purchases—no matter how small.

The concepts we presented in Chapter 2 determine what to recognize in the accounts. An item should be recognized in the financial statements if it is an element, is measurable, and is relevant and reliable. Consider human resources. **R. G. Barry & Co.** at one time reported as supplemental data total assets of $14,055,926, including $986,094 for "Net investments in human resources." **AT&T** and **ExxonMobil Company** also experimented with human resource accounting. Should we value employees for balance sheet and income statement purposes? Certainly skilled employees are an important asset (highly relevant), but the problems of determining their value and measuring it reliably have not yet been solved. Consequently, human resources are not recorded. Perhaps when measurement techniques become more sophisticated and accepted, such information will be presented, if only in supplemental form.

The FASB uses the phrase "transactions and other events and circumstances that affect a business enterprise" to describe the sources or causes of changes in an entity's

UNDERLYING CONCEPTS

Assets are probable economic benefits controlled by a particular entity as a result of a past transaction or event. Do human resources of a company meet this definition?

assets, liabilities, and equity.[2] Events are of two types: (1) **External events** involve interaction between an entity and its environment, such as a transaction with another entity, a change in the price of a good or service that an entity buys or sells, a flood or earthquake, or an improvement in technology by a competitor. (2) **Internal events** occur within an entity, such as using buildings and machinery in operations, or transferring or consuming raw materials in production processes.

Many events have both external and internal elements. For example, hiring an employee, which involves an exchange of salary for labor, is an external event. Using the services of labor is part of production, an internal event. Further, an entity may initiate and control events, such as the purchase of merchandise or use of a machine. Or, events may be beyond its control, such as an interest rate change, theft, or a tax hike.

Transactions are types of external events. They may be an exchange between two entities where each receives and sacrifices value, such as purchases and sales of goods or services. Or, transactions may be transfers in one direction only. For example, an entity may incur a liability without directly receiving value in exchange, such as charitable contributions. Other examples include investments by owners, distributions to owners, payment of taxes, gifts, casualty losses, and thefts.

In short, an enterprise records as many events as possible that affect its financial position. As discussed earlier in the case of human resources, it omits some events because of tradition and others because of complicated measurement problems. Recently, however, the accounting profession shows more receptiveness to accepting the challenge of measuring and reporting events previously viewed as too complex and immeasurable.

Journalizing

A company records in **accounts** those transactions and events that affect its assets, liabilities, and equities. The **general ledger** contains all the asset, liability, stockholders' equity, revenue, and expense accounts. A **T-account** (see Illustration 3-3, page 65) shows the effect of transactions on particular asset, liability, equity, revenue, and expense accounts.

In practice, companies do not record transactions and selected other events originally in the ledger. A transaction affects two or more accounts, each of which is on a different page in the ledger. Therefore, in order to have a complete record of each transaction or other event in one place, a company uses a **journal** (also called "the book of original entry"). In its simplest form, a **general journal** chronologically lists transactions and other events, expressed in terms of debits and credits to accounts.

> **OBJECTIVE 4**
> **Record transactions in journals, post to ledger accounts, and prepare a trial balance.**

Illustration 3-7 depicts the technique of journalizing, using the first two transactions for Softbyte, Inc. These transactions were:

September 1   Stockholders invested $15,000 cash in the corporation in exchange for shares of stock.

Purchased computer equipment for $7,000 cash.

The J1 indicates these two entries are on the first page of the general journal.

GENERAL JOURNAL J1

Date	Account Titles and Explanation	Ref.	Debit	Credit
2007 Sept. 1	Cash Common Stock (Issued shares of stock for cash)		15,000	15,000
1	Computer Equipment Cash (Purchased equipment for cash)		7,000	7,000

ILLUSTRATION 3-7
Technique of Journalizing

---

[2]"Elements of Financial Statements of Business Enterprises," *Statement of Financial Accounting Concepts No. 6* (Stamford, Conn.: FASB, 1985), pp. 259–260.

Expanded Discussion of
Special Journals

Each **general journal entry** consists of four parts: (1) the accounts and amounts to be debited (Dr.), (2) the accounts and amounts to be credited (Cr.), (3) a date, and (4) an explanation. A company enters debits first, followed by the credits (slightly indented). The explanation begins below the name of the last account to be credited and may take one or more lines. A company completes the "Ref." column at the time it posts the accounts.

In some cases, a company uses **special journals** in addition to the general journal. Special journals summarize transactions possessing a common characteristic (e.g., cash receipts, sales, purchases, cash payments). As a result, using them reduces bookkeeping time.

Posting

The procedure of transferring journal entries to the ledger accounts is called **posting**. Posting involves the following steps.

1 In the ledger, enter in the appropriate columns of the debited account(s) the date, journal page, and debit amount shown in the journal.

2 In the reference column of the journal, write the account number to which the debit amount was posted.

3 In the ledger, enter in the appropriate columns of the credited account(s) the date, journal page, and credit amount shown in the journal.

4 In the reference column of the journal, write the account number to which the credit amount was posted.

Illustration 3-8 diagrams these four steps, using the first journal entry of Softbyte, Inc. The illustration shows the general ledger accounts in **standard account form**. Some

ILLUSTRATION 3-8
Posting a Journal Entry

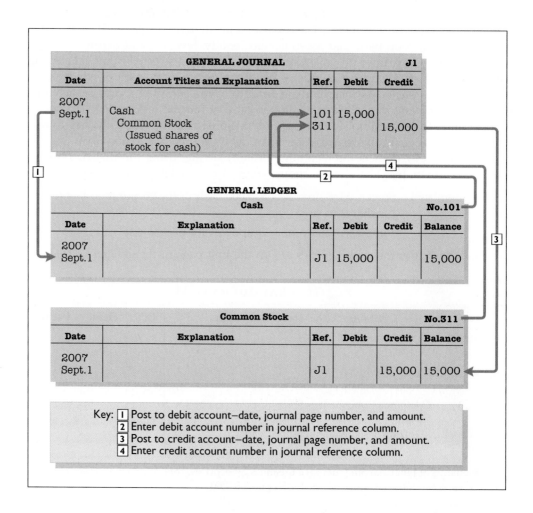

companies call this form the **three-column form of account** because it has three money columns—debit, credit, and balance. The balance in the account is determined after each transaction. The explanation space and reference columns provide special information about the transaction. The boxed numbers indicate the sequence of the steps.

The numbers in the "Ref." column of the general journal refer to the ledger accounts to which a company posts the respective items. For example, the "101" placed in the column to the right of "Cash" indicates that the company posted this $15,000 item to Account No. 101 in the ledger.

The posting of the general journal is completed when a company records all of the posting reference numbers opposite the account titles in the journal. Thus the number in the posting reference column serves two purposes: (1) It indicates the ledger account number of the account involved. (2) It indicates the completion of posting for the particular item. Each company selects its own numbering system for its ledger accounts. Many begin numbering with asset accounts and then follow with liabilities, owners' equity, revenue, and expense accounts, in that order.

The ledger accounts in Illustration 3-8 show the accounts after completion of the posting process. The reference J1 (General Journal, page 1) indicates the source of the data transferred to the ledger account.

Expanded Example. To show an expanded example of the basic steps in the recording process, we use the October transactions of Pioneer Advertising Agency Inc. Pioneer's accounting period is a month. Illustrations 3-9 through 3-18 show the journal entry and posting of each transaction. For simplicity, we use a T-account form instead of the standard account form. Study the transaction analyses carefully.

The purpose of transaction analysis is (1) to identify the type of account involved, and (2) to determine whether a debit or a credit is required. You should always perform this type of analysis before preparing a journal entry. Doing so will help you understand the journal entries discussed in this chapter as well as more complex journal entries in later chapters. Keep in mind that every journal entry affects one or more of the following items: assets, liabilities, stockholders' equity, revenues, or expenses.

1 October 1: Stockholders invest $100,000 cash in an advertising venture to be known as Pioneer Advertising Agency Inc.

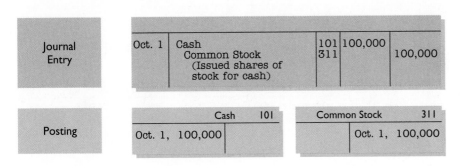

ILLUSTRATION 3-9
Investment of Cash by Stockholders

2 October 1: Pioneer Advertising purchases office equipment costing $50,000 by signing a 3-month, 12%, $50,000 note payable.

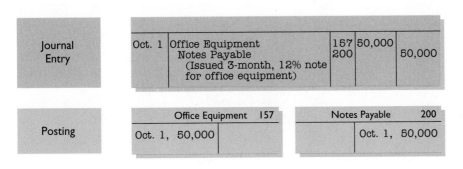

ILLUSTRATION 3-10
Purchase of Office Equipment

3 October 2: Pioneer Advertising receives a $12,000 cash advance from R. Knox, a client, for advertising services that are expected to be completed by December 31.

ILLUSTRATION 3-11
Receipt of Cash for
Future Service

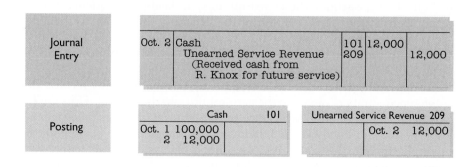

4 October 3: Pioneer Advertising pays $9,000 office rent, in cash, for October.

ILLUSTRATION 3-12
Payment of Monthly Rent

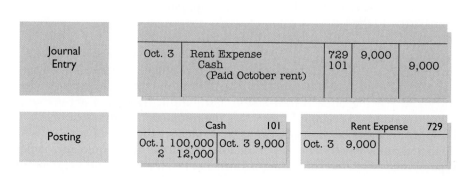

5 October 4: Pioneer Advertising pays $6,000 for a one-year insurance policy that will expire next year on September 30.

ILLUSTRATION 3-13
Payment for Insurance

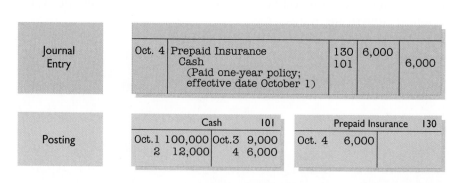

6 October 5: Pioneer Advertising purchases, for $25,000 on account, an estimated 3-month supply of advertising materials from Aero Supply.

ILLUSTRATION 3-14
Purchase of Supplies on
Account

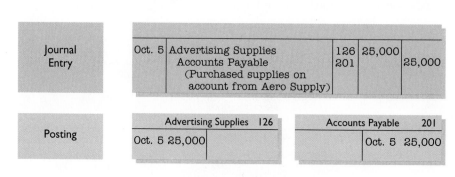

7 October 9: Pioneer Advertising signs a contract with a local newspaper for advertising inserts (flyers) to be distributed starting the last Sunday in November. Pioneer will start work on the content of the flyers in November. Payment of $7,000 is due following delivery of the Sunday papers containing the flyers.

> A business transaction has not occurred. There is only an agreement between Pioneer Advertising and the newspaper for the services to be provided in November. Therefore, no journal entry is necessary in October.

ILLUSTRATION 3-15
Signing a Contract

8 October 20: Pioneer Advertising's board of directors declares and pays a $5,000 cash dividend to stockholders.

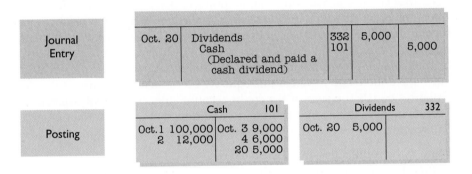

ILLUSTRATION 3-16
Declaration and Payment of Dividend by Corporation

9 October 26: Pioneer Advertising pays employee salaries in cash. Employees are paid once a month, every four weeks. The total payroll is $10,000 per week, or $2,000 per day. In October, the pay period began on Monday, October 1. As a result, the pay period ended on Friday, October 26, with salaries of $40,000 being paid.

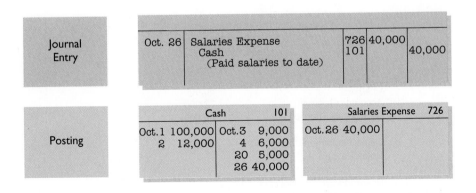

ILLUSTRATION 3-17
Payment of Salaries

10 October 31: Pioneer Advertising receives $28,000 in cash and bills Copa Company $72,000 for advertising services of $100,000 provided in October. (See Illustration 3-18 on the following page.)

Journal Entry	Oct. 31	Cash	101	28,000	
		Accounts Receivable	112	72,000	
		Service Revenue	400		100,000
		(Recognize revenue for services provided)			

	Cash	101		Accounts Receivable	112		Service Revenue	400
Oct.1	100,000	Oct.3 9,000	Oct. 31	72,000			Oct. 31	100,000
2	12,000	4 6,000						
31	28,000	20 5,000						
		26 40,000						

ILLUSTRATION 3-18
Recognize Revenue for
Services Provided

Trial Balance

A **trial balance** lists accounts and their balances at a given time. A company usually prepares a trial balance at the end of an accounting period. The trial balance lists the accounts in the order in which they appear in the ledger, with debit balances listed in the left column and credit balances in the right column. The totals of the two columns must agree.

The trial balance proves the mathematical equality of debits and credits after posting. Under the double-entry system this equality occurs when the sum of the debit account balances equals the sum of the credit account balances. A trial balance also uncovers errors in journalizing and posting. In addition, it is useful in the preparation of financial statements. The procedures for preparing a trial balance consist of:

1 Listing the account titles and their balances.

2 Totaling the debit and credit columns.

3 Proving the equality of the two columns.

For example, Illustration 3-19 presents the trial balance prepared from the ledger of Pioneer Advertising Agency Inc. Note that the total debits ($287,000) equal the total credits ($287,000). A trial balance also often shows account numbers to the left of the account titles.

ILLUSTRATION 3-19
Trial Balance
(Unadjusted)

PIONEER ADVERTISING AGENCY INC.
TRIAL BALANCE
OCTOBER 31, 2007

	Debit	Credit
Cash	$ 80,000	
Accounts Receivable	72,000	
Advertising Supplies	25,000	
Prepaid Insurance	6,000	
Office Equipment	50,000	
Notes Payable		$ 50,000
Accounts Payable		25,000
Unearned Service Revenue		12,000
Common Stock		100,000
Dividends	5,000	
Service Revenue		100,000
Salaries Expense	40,000	
Rent Expense	9,000	
	$287,000	$287,000

A trial balance does not prove that a company recorded all transactions or that the ledger is correct. Numerous errors may exist even though the trial balance columns agree. For example, the trial balance may balance even when a company (1) fails to journalize a transaction, (2) omits posting a correct journal entry, (3) posts a journal entry twice, (4) uses incorrect accounts in journalizing or posting, or (5) makes offsetting errors in recording the amount of a transaction. In other words, as long as a company posts equal debits and credits, even to the wrong account or in the wrong amount, the total debits will equal the total credits.

Adjusting Entries

In order for a company, like **McDonald's**, to record revenues in the period in which it earns them, and to recognize expenses in the period in which it incurs them, McDonald's makes **adjusting entries** at the end of the accounting period. In short, adjustments ensure that McDonald's follows the revenue recognition and matching principles.

> **OBJECTIVE 5**
> **Explain the reasons for preparing adjusting entries.**

The use of adjusting entries makes it possible to report on the balance sheet the appropriate assets, liabilities, and owners' equity at the statement date. Adjusting entries also make it possible to report on the income statement the proper revenues and expenses for the period. However, the trial balance—the first pulling together of the transaction data—may not contain up-to-date and complete data. This occurs for the following reasons.

1 Some events are not journalized daily because it is not expedient. Examples are the consumption of supplies and the earning of wages by employees.

2 Some costs are not journalized during the accounting period because these costs expire with the passage of time rather than as a result of recurring daily transactions. Examples of such costs are building and equipment deterioration and rent and insurance.

3 Some items may be unrecorded. An example is a utility service bill that will not be received until the next accounting period.

Adjusting entries are required every time a company, such as **Coca-Cola**, prepares financial statements. At that time, Coca-Cola must analyze each account in the trial balance to determine whether it is complete and up-to-date for financial statement purposes. The analysis requires a thorough understanding of Coca-Cola's operations and the interrelationship of accounts. Because of this involved process, usually a skilled accountant prepares the adjusting entries. In gathering the adjustment data, Coca-Cola may need to make inventory counts of supplies and repair parts. Further, it may prepare supporting schedules of insurance policies, rental agreements, and other contractual commitments. Companies often prepare adjustments after the balance sheet date. However, they date the entries as of the balance sheet date.

Types of Adjusting Entries

Adjusting entries are classified as either prepayments or accruals. Each of these classes has two subcategories, as Illustration 3-20 shows.

Prepayments	Accruals
1. **Prepaid Expenses.** Expenses paid in cash and recorded as assets before they are used or consumed.	3. **Accrued Revenues.** Revenues earned but not yet received in cash or recorded.
2. **Unearned Revenues.** Revenues received in cash and recorded as liabilities before they are earned.	4. **Accrued Expenses.** Expenses incurred but not yet paid in cash or recorded.

ILLUSTRATION 3-20
Classes of Adjusting Entries

We review specific examples and explanations of each type of adjustment in subsequent sections. We base each example on the October 31 trial balance of Pioneer Advertising Agency Inc. (Illustration 3-19). We assume that Pioneer uses an accounting period of one month. Thus, Pioneer will make monthly adjusting entries, dated October 31.

Adjusting Entries for Prepayments

As we indicated earlier, prepayments are either prepaid expenses or unearned revenues. Adjusting entries for prepayments, required at the statement date, record the portion of the prepayment that represents the **expense incurred or the revenue earned** in the current accounting period.

If a company does not make an adjustment for these prepayments, the asset and liability are overstated, and the related expense and revenue are understated. For example, in Pioneer's trial balance (Illustration 3-19), the balance in the asset Advertising Supplies shows only supplies purchased. This balance is overstated; the related expense account, Supplies Expense, is understated because the cost of supplies used has not been recognized. Thus the adjusting entry for prepayments will decrease a balance sheet account and increase an income statement account. Illustration 3-21 shows the effects of adjusting entries for prepayments.

ILLUSTRATION 3-21
Adjusting Entries for
Prepayments

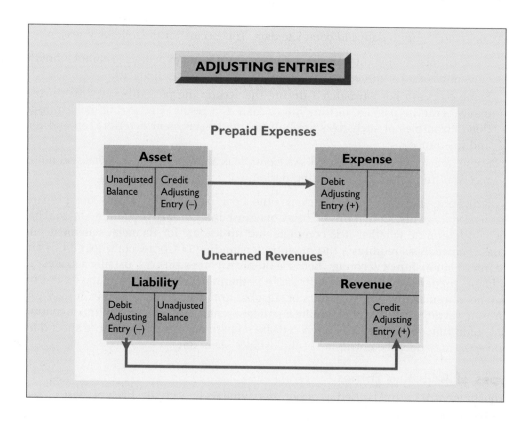

Prepaid Expenses. Assets paid for and recorded before a company, uses them are called **prepaid expenses.** When a company incurs a cost, it debits an asset account to show the service or benefit it will receive in the future. Prepayments often occur in regard to insurance, supplies, advertising, and rent. In addition, companies make prepayments when purchasing buildings and equipment.

Prepaid expenses expire either with the passage of time (e.g., rent and insurance) or **through use and consumption** (e.g., supplies). The expiration of these costs does not require daily recurring entries, an unnecessary and impractical task. Accordingly, a company, like **Walgreens,** usually postpones the recognition of such cost expirations until it prepares financial statements. At each statement date, Walgreens makes adjusting entries to record the expenses that apply to the current accounting period and to show the unexpired costs in the asset accounts.

As was shown above, prior to adjustment, assets are overstated and expenses are understated. Thus, the prepaid expense adjusting entry results in a debit to an expense account and a credit to an asset account.

Supplies. A business enterprise may use several different types of supplies. For example, a CPA firm will use office supplies such as stationery, envelopes, and accounting paper. An advertising firm will stock advertising supplies such as graph paper, video film, and poster paper. Supplies are generally debited to an asset account when they are acquired. Recognition of supplies used is generally deferred until the adjustment process. At that time, a physical inventory (count) of supplies is taken. The difference between the balance in the Supplies (asset) account and the cost of supplies on hand represents the supplies used (expense) for the period.

For example, Pioneer (see Illustration 3-19) purchased advertising supplies costing $25,000 on October 5. Pioneer therefore debited the asset Advertising Supplies. This account shows a balance of $25,000 in the October 31 trial balance. An inventory count at the close of business on October 31 reveals that $10,000 of supplies are still on hand. Thus, the cost of supplies used is $15,000 ($25,000 − $10,000). Pioneer makes the following adjusting entry.

<table>
<tr><td colspan="3" align="center">Oct. 31</td></tr>
<tr><td>Advertising Supplies Expense</td><td>15,000</td><td></td></tr>
<tr><td>   Advertising Supplies</td><td></td><td>15,000</td></tr>
<tr><td colspan="3" align="center">(To record supplies used)</td></tr>
</table>

After Pioneer posts the adjusting entry, the two supplies accounts in T-account form show the following.

Advertising Supplies			Advertising Supplies Expense	
10/ 5	25,000	10/31 Adj. 15,000	10/31 Adj. 15,000	
10/31	Bal. 10,000			

The asset account Advertising Supplies now shows a balance of $10,000, which equals the cost of supplies on hand at the statement date. In addition, Advertising Supplies Expense shows a balance of $15,000, which equals the cost of supplies used in October. **Without an adjusting entry, October expenses are understated and net income overstated by $15,000. Moreover, both assets and owners' equity are overstated by $15,000 on the October 31 balance sheet.**

Insurance. Most companies maintain fire and theft insurance on merchandise and equipment, personal liability insurance for accidents suffered by customers, and automobile insurance on company cars and trucks. The extent of protection against loss determines the cost of the insurance (the amount of the premium to be paid.) The insurance policy specifies the term and coverage. The minimum term usually covers one year, but three- to five-year terms are available and may offer lower annual premiums. A company usually debits insurance premiums to the asset account Prepaid Insurance when paid. At the financial statement date, it then debits Insurance Expense and credits Prepaid Insurance for the cost that expired during the period.

For example, on October 4, Pioneer paid $6,000 for a one-year fire insurance policy, beginning October 1. Pioneer debited the cost of the premium to Prepaid Insurance at that time. This account still shows a balance of $6,000 in the October 31 trial balance. An analysis of the policy reveals that $500 ($6,000 ÷ 12) of insurance expires each month. Thus, Pioneer makes the following adjusting entry.

<table>
<tr><td colspan="3" align="center">Oct. 31</td></tr>
<tr><td>Insurance Expense</td><td>500</td><td></td></tr>
<tr><td>   Prepaid Insurance</td><td></td><td>500</td></tr>
<tr><td colspan="3" align="center">(To record insurance expired)</td></tr>
</table>

Supplies

Oct. 5

Supplies purchased; record asset

Oct. 31

Supplies used; record supplies expense

A	=	L +	SE
			−15,000
−15,000			

Cash Flows
no effect

ILLUSTRATION 3-22
Supplies Accounts after Adjustment

Insurance

Oct. 4

Insurance purchased; record asset

Insurance Policy			
Oct	Nov	Dec	Jan
$500	$500	$500	$500
Feb	March	April	May
$500	$500	$500	$500
June	July	Aug	Sept
$500	$500	$500	$500
1 YEAR $6,000			

Oct. 31
Insurance expired; record insurance expense

A	=	L +	SE
			−500
−500			

Cash Flows
no effect

After Pioneer posts the adjusting entry, the insurance-related accounts show:

ILLUSTRATION 3-23
Insurance Accounts after Adjustment

Prepaid Insurance				Insurance Expense		
10/ 4	6,000	10/31	Adj. 500	10/31	Adj. 500	
10/31	Bal. 5,500					

The asset Prepaid Insurance shows a balance of $5,500, which represents the unexpired cost for the remaining 11 months of coverage. At the same time, the balance in Insurance Expense equals the insurance cost that expired in October. **Without an adjusting entry, October expenses are understated by $500 and net income overstated by $500. Moreover, both assets and owners' equity also are overstated by $500 on the October 31 balance sheet.**

Depreciation. Companies, like **Caterpillar** or **Boeing**, typically own various productive facilities, such as buildings, equipment, and motor vehicles. These assets provide a service for a number of years. The term of service is commonly referred to as the **useful life** of the asset. Because Caterpillar, for example, expects an asset such as a building to provide service for many years, Caterpillar records the building as an asset, rather than an expense, in the year the building is acquired. Caterpillar records such assets at cost, as required by the historical cost principle.

According to the matching principle, Caterpillar should report a portion of the cost of a long-lived asset as an expense during each period of the asset's useful life. The process of **depreciation** allocates the cost of an asset to expense over its useful life in a rational and systematic manner.

Need for depreciation adjustment. Generally accepted accounting principles (GAAP) view the acquisition of productive facilities as a long-term prepayment for services. The need for making periodic adjusting entries for depreciation is, therefore, the same as we described for other prepaid expenses. That is, a company recognizes the expired cost (expense) during the period and reports the unexpired cost (asset) at the end of the period. The primary causes of depreciation of a productive facility are actual use, deterioration due to the elements, and obsolescence. For example, at the time Caterpillar acquires an asset, the effects of these factors cannot be known with certainty. Therefore, Caterpillar must estimate them. **Thus, depreciation is an estimate rather than a factual measurement of the expired cost.**

To estimate depreciation expense, Caterpillar often divides the cost of the asset by its useful life. For example, if Caterpillar purchases equipment for $10,000 and expects its useful life to be 10 years, Caterpillar records annual depreciation of $1,000.

In the case of Pioneer Advertising, it estimates depreciation on its office equipment to be $4,800 a year (cost $50,000 less salvage value $2,000 divided by useful life of 10 years), or $400 per month. Accordingly, Pioneer recognizes depreciation for October by the following adjusting entry.

Depreciation

Oct.1

Office equipment purchased; record asset ($50,000)

Office Equipment			
Oct	Nov	Dec	Jan
$400	$400	$400	$400
Feb	March	April	May
$400	$400	$400	$400
June	July	Aug	Sept
$400	$400	$400	$400
Depreciation = $4,800/year			

Oct. 31
Depreciation recognized; record depreciation expense

A	=	L	+	SE
				−400
−400				

Cash Flows
no effect

Oct. 31

Depreciation Expense	400	
Accumulated Depreciation—Office Equipment		400
(To record monthly depreciation)		

After Pioneer posts the adjusting entry, the accounts show the following.

ILLUSTRATION 3-24
Accounts after Adjustment for Depreciation

Office Equipment		
10/1	50,000	

Accumulated Depreciation—Office Equipment				Depreciation Expense		
		10/31	Adj. 400	10/31	Adj. 400	

The balance in the accumulated depreciation account will increase $400 each month. Therefore, after journalizing and posting the adjusting entry at November 30, the balance will be $800.

Statement presentation. Accumulated Depreciation—Office Equipment is a contra asset account. A **contra asset account** offsets an asset account on the balance sheet. This means that the accumulated depreciation account offsets the Office Equipment account on the balance sheet. Its normal balance is a credit. Pioneer uses this account instead of crediting Office Equipment in order to disclose both the original cost of the equipment and the total expired cost to date. In the balance sheet, Pioneer deducts Accumulated Depreciation—Office Equipment from the related asset account as follows.

Office equipment	$50,000	
Less: Accumulated depreciation—office equipment	400	$49,600

ILLUSTRATION 3-25
Balance Sheet Presentation of Accumulated Depreciation

The **book value** of any depreciable asset is the difference between its cost and its related accumulated depreciation. In Illustration 3-25, the book value of the equipment at the balance sheet date is $49,600. Note that the asset's book value generally differs from its market value because depreciation is not a matter of valuation but rather a means of cost allocation.

Note also that depreciation expense identifies that portion of the asset's cost that expired in October. As in the case of other prepaid adjustments, without this adjusting entry, total assets, total owners' equity, and net income are overstated, and depreciation expense is understated.

A company records depreciation expense for each piece of equipment, such as delivery or store equipment, and for all buildings. A company also establishes related accumulated depreciation accounts for the above, such as Accumulated Depreciation—Delivery Equipment; Accumulated Depreciation—Store Equipment; and Accumulated Depreciation—Buildings.

Unearned Revenues. Revenues received in cash and recorded as liabilities before a company earns them are called **unearned revenues**. Such items as rent, magazine subscriptions, and customer deposits for future service may result in unearned revenues. Airlines, such as **Northwest**, **American**, and **Southwest**, treat receipts from the sale of tickets as unearned revenue until they provide the flight service. Tuition received prior to the start of a semester is another example of unearned revenue. Unearned revenues are the opposite of prepaid expenses. Indeed, unearned revenue on the books of one company is likely to be a prepayment on the books of the company that made the advance payment. For example, if we assume identical accounting periods, a landlord will have unearned rent revenue when a tenant has prepaid rent.

When a company, such as **Intel**, receives payment for services to be provided in a future accounting period, it credits an unearned revenue (a liability) account to recognize the obligation that exists. It subsequently earns the revenues through rendering service to a customer. However, making daily recurring entries to record this revenue is impractical. Therefore, Intel delays recognition of earned revenue until the adjustment process. Then Intel makes an adjusting entry to record the revenue that it earned and to show the liability that remains. In the typical case, liabilities are overstated and revenues are understated prior to adjustment. **Thus, the adjusting entry for unearned revenues results in a debit (decrease) to a liability account and a credit (increase) to a revenue account.**

For example, Pioneer Advertising received $12,000 on October 2 from R. Knox for advertising services expected to be completed by December 31. Pioneer credited the payment to Unearned Service Revenue. This account shows a balance of $12,000 in the October 31 trial balance. Analysis reveals that Pioneer earned $4,000 of these services in October. Thus, Pioneer makes the following adjusting entry.

Unearned Revenues

Oct. 2

Cash is received in advance; liability is recorded

Oct. 31

Service is provided; revenue is recorded

A	=	L	+	SE
−4,000				
				+4,000

Cash Flows
no effect

Oct. 31

Unearned Service Revenue	4,000	
Service Revenue		4,000
(To record revenue for services provided)		

After Pioneer posts the adjusting entry, the accounts show the following.

ILLUSTRATION 3-26
Service Revenue
Accounts after
Prepayments Adjustment

Unearned Service Revenue							Service Revenue					
10/31	Adj.	4,000	10/ 2		12,000					10/31	Bal.	100,000
			10/31	Bal.	8,000					31	Adj.	4,000

The liability Unearned Service Revenue now shows a balance of $8,000, which represents the remaining advertising services expected to be performed in the future. At the same time, Service Revenue shows total revenue earned in October of $104,000. **Without this adjustment, revenues and net income are understated by $4,000 in the income statement. Moreover, liabilities are overstated and owners' equity are understated by $4,000 on the October 31 balance sheet.**

Adjusting Entries for Accruals

The second category of adjusting entries is accruals. Companies make adjusting entries for accruals to record unrecognized revenues earned and expenses incurred in the current accounting period. Without an accrual adjustment, the revenue account (and the related asset account) or the expense account (and the related liability account) are understated. Thus, the adjusting entry for accruals **will increase both a balance sheet and an income statement account**. Illustration 3-27 shows adjusting entries for accruals.

ILLUSTRATION 3-27
Adjusting Entries for
Accruals

Accrued Revenues

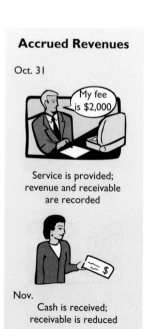

Oct. 31

Service is provided;
revenue and receivable
are recorded

Nov.
Cash is received;
receivable is reduced

Accrued Revenues. Revenues earned but not yet received in cash or recorded at the statement date are **accrued revenues**. A company accrues revenues with the passing of time, as in the case of interest revenue and rent revenue. Because interest and rent do not involve daily transactions, these items are often unrecorded at the statement date. Or accrued revenues may result from unbilled or uncollected services that a company performed, as in the case of commissions and fees. A company does not record commissions or fees daily, because only a portion of the total service has been provided.

An adjusting entry shows the receivable that exists at the balance sheet date and records the revenue that a company earned during the period. Prior to adjustment both assets and revenues are understated. Accordingly, **an adjusting entry** for accrued revenues results in a debit (increase) to an asset account and a credit (increase) to a revenue account.

In October Pioneer earned $2,000 for advertising services that it did not bill to clients before October 31. Pioneer therefore did not yet record these services. Thus, Pioneer makes the following adjusting entry.

	Oct. 31		
Accounts Receivable		2,000	
Service Revenue			2,000
(To record revenue for services provided)			

A	=	L	+	SE
+2,000				
				+2,000

Cash Flows
no effect

After Pioneer posts the adjusting entry, the accounts show the following.

Accounts Receivable		Service Revenue	
10/31　　　72,000			10/31　　　100,000
31　Adj.　2,000			31　　　　4,000
			31　Adj.　2,000
10/31　Bal. 74,000			10/31　Bal. 106,000

ILLUSTRATION 3-28
Receivable and Revenue Accounts after Accrual Adjustment

The asset Accounts Receivable shows that clients owe $74,000 at the balance sheet date. The balance of $106,000 in Service Revenue represents the total revenue earned during the month ($100,000 + $4,000 + $2,000). **Without an adjusting entry, assets and owners' equity on the balance sheet, and revenues and net income on the income statement, are understated.**

Accrued Expenses. Expenses incurred but not yet paid or recorded at the statement date are called **accrued expenses**, such as interest, rent, taxes, and salaries. Accrued expenses result from the same causes as accrued revenues. In fact, an accrued expense on the books of one company is an accrued revenue to another company. For example, the $2,000 accrual of service revenue by Pioneer is an accrued expense to the client that received the service.

Adjustments for accrued expenses record the obligations that exist at the balance sheet date and recognize the expenses that apply to the current accounting period. Prior to adjustment, both liabilities and expenses are understated. Therefore, the adjusting entry for accrued expenses results in a debit (increase) to an expense account and a credit (increase) to a liability account.

Accrued Interest. Pioneer signed a three-month note payable in the amount of $50,000 on October 1. The note requires interest at an annual rate of 12 percent. Three factors determine the amount of the interest accumulation: (1) the face value of the note; (2) the interest rate, which is always expressed as an annual rate; and (3) the length of time the note is outstanding. The total interest due on Pioneer's $50,000 note at its due date three months hence is $1,500 ($50,000 × 12% × 3/12), or $500 for one month. Illustration 3-29 shows the formula for computing interest and its application to Pioneer. Note that the formula expresses the time period as a fraction of a year.

ILLUSTRATION 3-29
Formula for Computing
Interest

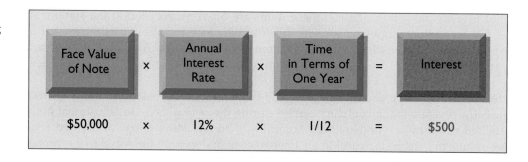

Pioneer makes the accrued expense adjusting entry at October 31 as follows.

$$
\begin{array}{lcc}
& \text{Oct. 31} & \\
\text{Interest Expense} & 500 & \\
\quad \text{Interest Payable} & & 500 \\
\multicolumn{3}{c}{\text{(To record interest on notes payable)}}
\end{array}
$$

A	=	L	+	SE
				−500
		+500		

Cash Flows
no effect

After Pioneer posts this adjusting entry, the accounts show the following.

ILLUSTRATION 3-30
Interest Accounts after
Adjustment

Interest Expense		Interest Payable	
10/31	500	10/31	500

Interest Expense shows the interest charges applicable to the month of October. Interest Payable shows the amount of interest owed at the statement date. Pioneer will not pay this amount until the note comes due at the end of three months. Why does Pioneer use the Interest Payable account instead of crediting Notes Payable? By recording interest payable separately, Pioneer discloses the two types of obligations (interest and principal) in the accounts and statements. **Without this adjusting entry, both liabilities and interest expense are understated, and both net income and owners' equity are overstated.**

Accrued Salaries. Companies pay for some types of expenses, such as employee salaries and commissions, after the services have been performed. For example, Pioneer last paid salaries on October 26. It will not pay salaries again until November 23. However, as shown in the calendar below, three working days remain in October (October 29–31).

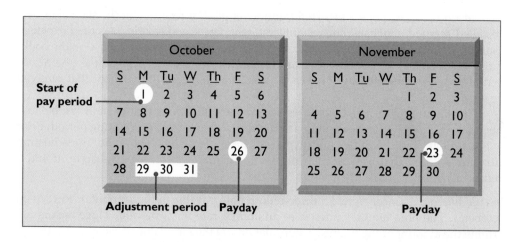

At October 31, the salaries for these days represent an accrued expense and a related liability to Pioneer. The employees receive total salaries of $10,000 for a five-day work week, or $2,000 per day. Thus, accrued salaries at October 31 are $6,000 ($2,000 × 3). Pioneers makes the adjusting entry as follows.

A	=	L	+	SE
				−6,000
		+6,000		

Cash Flows
no effect

Oct. 31

Salaries Expense	6,000	
Salaries Payable		6,000
(To record accrued salaries)		

After Pioneer posts this adjusting entry, the accounts show the following.

Salaries Expense			Salaries Payable		
10/26	40,000			10/31	Adj. 6,000
31	Adj. 6,000				
10/31	Bal. 46,000				

ILLUSTRATION 3-31
Salary Accounts after Adjustment

After this adjustment, the balance in Salaries Expense of $46,000 (23 days × $2,000) is the actual salary expense for October. The balance in Salaries Payable of $6,000 is the amount of the liability for salaries owed as of October 31. **Without the $6,000 adjustment for salaries, both Pioneer's expenses and liabilities are understated by $6,000.**

Pioneer pays salaries every four weeks. Consequently, the next payday is November 23, when it will again pay total salaries of $40,000. The payment consists of $6,000 of salaries payable at October 31 plus $34,000 of salaries expense for November (17 working days as shown in the November calendar × $2,000). Therefore, Pioneer makes the following entry on November 23.

A	=	L	+	SE
		−6,000		
				−34,000
−40,000				

Cash Flows
−40,000

Nov. 23

Salaries Payable	6,000	
Salaries Expense	34,000	
Cash		40,000
(To record November 23 payroll)		

This entry eliminates the liability for Salaries Payable that Pioneer recorded in the October 31 adjusting entry. This entry also records the proper amount of Salaries Expense for the period between November 1 and November 23.

AM I COVERED?

Rather than purchasing insurance to cover casualty losses and other obligations, some companies "self-insure." That is, a company decides to pay for any possible claims, as they arise, out of its own resources. The company also purchases an insurance policy to cover losses that exceed certain amounts.

For example, **Almost Family, Inc.**, a healthcare services company, has a self-insured employee health-benefit program. However, Almost Family ran into accounting problems when it failed to record an accrual of the liability for benefits not covered by its back-up insurance policy. This led to restatement of Almost Family's fiscal results for the accrual of the benefit expense.

WHAT DO THE NUMBERS MEAN?

Bad Debts

Oct. 31
Uncollectible accounts; record bad debt expense

Bad Debts. Proper matching of revenues and expenses dictates recording bad debts as an expense of the period in which a company earned revenue instead of the period in which the company writes off the accounts or notes. The proper valuation of the receivable balance also requires recognition of uncollectible receivables. Proper matching and valuation require an adjusting entry.

At the end of each period, a company, such as **General Mills**, estimates the amount of receivables that will later prove to be uncollectible. General Mills bases the estimate on various factors: the amount of bad debts it experienced in past years, general economic conditions, how long the receivables are past due, and other factors that indicate the extent of uncollectibility. To illustrate, assume that, based on past experience, Pioneer reasonably estimates a bad debt expense for the month of $1,600. It makes the adjusting entry for bad debts as follows.

	Oct. 31		
Bad Debt Expense		1,600	
Allowance for Doubtful Accounts			1,600
(To record monthly bad debt expense)			

A	= L	+	SE
−1,600	−1,600		

After Pioneer posts the adjusting entry, the accounts show the following.

ILLUSTRATION 3-32
Accounts after
Adjustment for Bad
Debt Expense

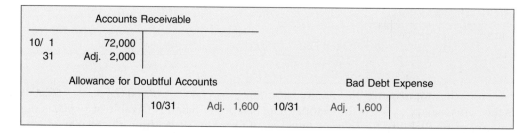

A company often expresses bad debts as a percentage of the revenue on account for the period. Or a company may compute bad debts by adjusting the Allowance for Doubtful Accounts to a certain percentage of the trade accounts receivable and trade notes receivable at the end of the period.

Adjusted Trial Balance

After journalizing and posting all adjusting entries, Pioneer prepares another trial balance from its ledger accounts. This trial balance is called an **adjusted trial balance**. It shows the balance of all accounts, including those adjusted, at the end of the accounting period. The adjusted trial balance thus shows the effects of all financial events that occurred during the accounting period.

ILLUSTRATION 3-33
Adjusted Trial Balance

PIONEER ADVERTISING AGENCY INC.
ADJUSTED TRIAL BALANCE
OCTOBER 31, 2007

	Debit	Credit
Cash	$ 80,000	
Accounts Receivable	74,000	
Allowance for Doubtful Accounts		$ 1,600
Advertising Supplies	10,000	
Prepaid Insurance	5,500	
Office Equipment	50,000	
Accumulated Depreciation—		
Office Equipment		400
Notes Payable		50,000
Accounts Payable		25,000
Interest Payable		500
Unearned Service Revenue		8,000
Salaries Payable		6,000
Common Stock		100,000
Dividends	5,000	
Service Revenue		106,000
Salaries Expense	46,000	
Advertising Supplies Expense	15,000	
Rent Expense	9,000	
Insurance Expense	500	
Interest Expense	500	
Depreciation Expense	400	
Bad Debt Expense	1,600	
	$297,500	$297,500

Preparing Financial Statements

Pioneer can prepare financial statements directly from the adjusted trial balance.
Illustrations 3-34 and 3-35 show the interrelationships of data in the adjusted trial balance and the financial statements.

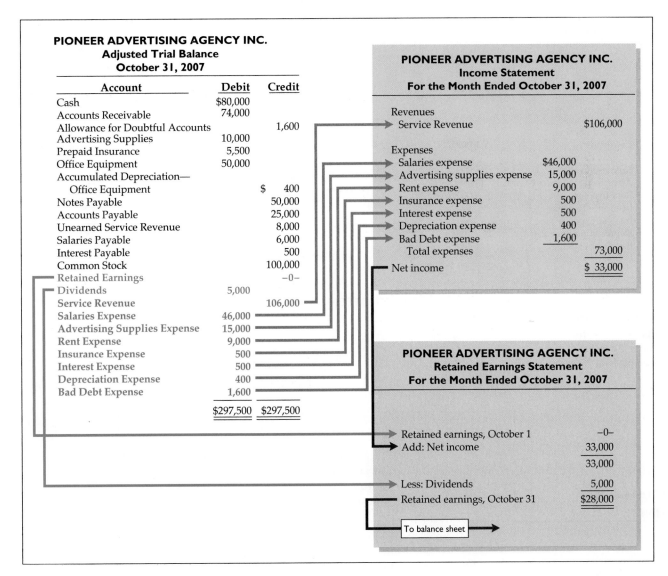

ILLUSTRATION 3-34
Preparation of the Income Statement and Retained Earnings Statement from the Adjusted Trial Balance

As Illustration 3-34 shows, Pioneer begins preparation of the income statement from the revenue and expense accounts. It derives the retained earnings statement from the retained earnings and dividends accounts and the net income (or net loss) shown in the income statement. As Illustration 3-35 shows, Pioneer then prepares the balance sheet from the asset and liability accounts, the common stock account, and the ending retained earnings balance as reported in the retained earnings statement.

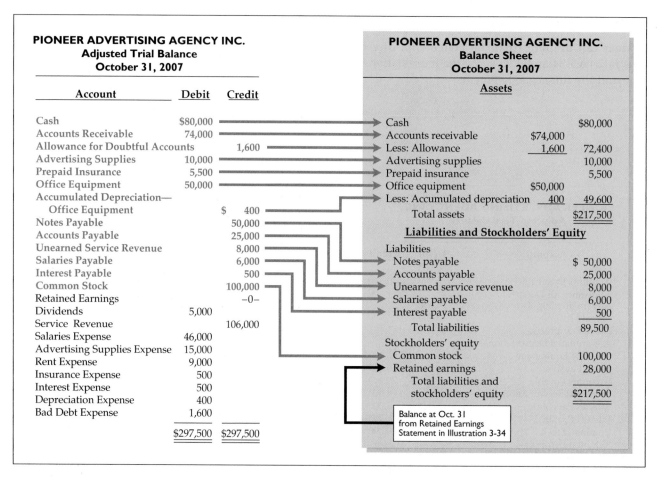

ILLUSTRATION 3-35
Preparation of the
Balance Sheet from the
Adjusted Trial Balance

24/7 ACCOUNTING

WHAT DO THE
NUMBERS MEAN?

To achieve the vision of "24/7 accounting," a company must be able to update revenue, income, and balance sheet numbers every day within the quarter and publish them on the Internet. Such real-time reporting responds to the demand for more timely financial information made available to all investors—not just to analysts with access to company management.

Two obstacles typically stand in the way of 24/7 accounting: having the necessary accounting systems to close the books on a daily basis, and reliability concerns associated with unaudited real-time data. Only a few companies have the necessary accounting capabilties. **Cisco Systems**, which pioneered the concept of the 24-hour close, is one such company.

Closing

Basic Process

OBJECTIVE 7
Prepare closing entries.

The **closing process** reduces the balance of nominal (temporary) accounts to zero in order to prepare the accounts for the next period's transactions. In the closing process Pioneer transfers all of the revenue and expense account balances (income statement items) to a clearing or suspense account called Income Summary. The Income Summary account matches revenues and expenses.

Pioneer uses this clearing account only at the end of each accounting period. The account represents the net income or net loss for the period. It then transfers the net result of this matching (the net income or net loss) to an owners' equity account. (For a corporation, the owners' equity account is retained earnings; for proprietorships and partnerships, it is a capital account.) Companies post all such **closing entries** to the appropriate general ledger accounts.

Closing Entries

In practice, companies generally prepare closing entries only at the end of a company's annual accounting period. However, to illustrate the journalizing and posting of closing entries, we will assume that Pioneer Advertising Agency Inc. closes its books monthly. Illustration 3-36 shows the closing entries at October 31.

	GENERAL JOURNAL		J3
Date	**Account Titles and Explanation**	**Debit**	**Credit**
	Closing Entries		
	(1)		
Oct. 31	Service Revenue	106,000	
	Income Summary		106,000
	(To close revenue account)		
	(2)		
31	Income Summary	73,000	
	Advertising Supplies Expense		15,000
	Depreciation Expense		400
	Insurance Expense		500
	Salaries Expense		46,000
	Rent Expense		9,000
	Interest Expense		500
	Bad Debt Expense		1,600
	(To close expense accounts)		
	(3)		
31	Income Summary	33,000	
	Retained Earnings		33,000
	(To close net income to retained earnings)		
	(4)		
31	Retained Earnings	5,000	
	Dividends		5,000
	(To close dividends to retained earnings)		

ILLUSTRATION 3-36
Closing Entries Journalized

A couple of cautions about preparing closing entries: (1) Avoid unintentionally doubling the revenue and expense balances rather than zeroing them. (2) Do not close Dividends through the Income Summary account. **Dividends are not expenses, and they are not a factor in determining net income.**

Posting Closing Entries

Illustration 3-37 shows the posting of closing entries and the ruling of accounts. All temporary accounts have zero balances after posting the closing entries. In addition, note that the balance in Retained Earnings represents the accumulated undistributed earnings of Pioneer at the end of the accounting period. Pioneer reports this amount in the balance sheet as the ending amount reported on the retained earnings statement. As noted above, **Pioneer uses the Income Summary account only in closing.** It does not journalize and post entries to this account during the year.

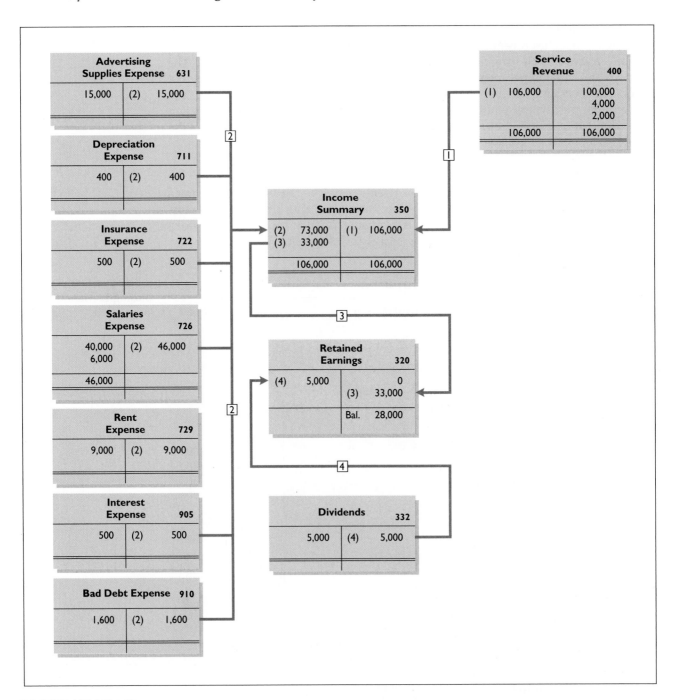

ILLUSTRATION 3-37
Posting of Closing Entries

As part of the closing process, Pioneer totals, balances, and double-rules the **temporary accounts**—revenues, expenses, and dividends—as shown in T-account form in Illustration 3-37. It does not close the **permanent accounts**—assets, liabilities, and stockholders' equity (Common Stock and Retained Earnings). Instead, the preparer draws a single rule beneath the current-period entries, and enters beneath the single rules the account balance to be carried forward to the next period. (For example, see Retained Earnings.)

After the closing process, each income statement account and the dividend account are balanced out to zero and are ready for use in the next accounting period.

Post-Closing Trial Balance

Recall that a trial balance is prepared after entering the regular transactions of the period, and that a second trial balance (the adjusted trial balance) occurs after posting the adjusting entries. A company may take a third trial balance after posting the closing entries.

The trial balance after closing, called the **post-closing trial balance**, consists only of asset, liability, and owners' equity accounts—the real accounts.

Reversing Entries

After preparing the financial statements and closing the books, a company may reverse some of the adjusting entries before recording the regular transactions of the next period. Such entries are called **reversing entries**. A company makes a reversing entry at the beginning of the next accounting period; this entry is the exact opposite of the related adjusting entry made in the previous period. Making reversing entries is an optional step in the accounting cycle that a company may perform at the beginning of the next accounting period. Appendix 3B discusses reversing entries in more detail.

The Accounting Cycle Summarized

A summary of the steps in the accounting cycle shows a logical sequence of the accounting procedures used during a fiscal period:

1 Enter the transactions of the period in appropriate journals.

2 Post from the journals to the ledger (or ledgers).

3 Take an unadjusted trial balance (trial balance).

4 Prepare adjusting journal entries and post to the ledger(s).

5 Take a trial balance after adjusting (adjusted trial balance).

6 Prepare the financial statements from the second trial balance.

7 Prepare closing journal entries and post to the ledger(s).

8 Take a trial balance after closing (post-closing trial balance).

9 Prepare reversing entries (optional) and post to the ledger(s).

A company normally completes all of these steps in every fiscal period.

STATEMENTS, PLEASE

The use of a worksheet at the end of each month or quarter enables a company to prepare interim financial statements even though it closes the books only at the end of each year. For example, assume that Google closes its books on December 31, but it wants monthly financial statements. To do this, at the end of January, Google prepares an adjusted trial balance (using a worksheet as illustrated in Appendix 3C) to supply the information needed for statements for January.

At the end of February, it uses a worksheet again. Note that because Google did not close the accounts at the end of January, the income statement taken from the adjusted trial balance on February 28 will present the net income for two months. If Google wants an income statement for only the month of February, the company obtains it by subtracting the items in the January income statement from the corresponding items in the income statement for the two months of January and February.

If Google executes such a process daily, it can realize "24/7 accounting" (see box on page 86).

WHAT DO THE NUMBERS MEAN?

Financial Statements for a Merchandising Company

Pioneer Advertising Agency Inc. is a service company. A detailed set of financial statements is now shown for a merchandising company, Uptown Cabinet Corp. The financial statements on pages 90 and 91 are prepared from the adjusted trial balance.

Income Statement

The income statement for Uptown is self-explanatory. The income statement classifies amounts into such categories as gross profit on sales, income from operations, income before taxes, and net income. Although earnings per share information is required to be shown on the face of the income statement for a corporation, we omit this item here; it will be discussed more fully later in the text. *(For homework problems, do not present earnings per share information unless required to do so).*

ILLUSTRATION 3-38
An Income Statement

UPTOWN CABINET CORP.			
INCOME STATEMENT			
FOR THE YEAR ENDED DECEMBER 31, 2007			
Net sales			$400,000
Cost of goods sold			316,000
Gross profit on sales			84,000
Selling expenses			
Sales salaries expense		$20,000	
Traveling expense		8,000	
Advertising expense		2,200	
Total selling expenses		30,200	
Administrative expenses			
Salaries, office and general	$19,000		
Depreciation expense—furniture and equipment	6,700		
Property tax expense	5,300		
Rent expense	4,300		
Bad debt expense	1,000		
Telephone and Internet expense	600		
Insurance expense	360		
Total administrative expenses		37,260	
Total selling and administrative expenses			67,460
Income from operations			16,540
Other revenues and gains			
Interest revenue			800
			17,340
Other expenses and losses			
Interest expense			1,700
Income before income taxes			15,640
Income taxes			3,440
Net income			$ 12,200

Statement of Retained Earnings

A corporation may retain the net income earned in the business, or it may distribute it to stockholders by payment of dividends. In the illustration, Uptown added the net income earned during the year to the balance of retained earnings on January 1, thereby increasing the balance of retained earnings. Deducting dividends of $2,000 results in the ending retained earnings balance of $26,400 on December 31.

ILLUSTRATION 3-39
A Statement of Retained Earnings

UPTOWN CABINET CORP.		
STATEMENT OF RETAINED EARNINGS		
FOR THE YEAR ENDED DECEMBER 31, 2007		
Retained earnings, January 1	$16,200	
Add: Net income	12,200	
	28,400	
Less: Dividends	2,000	
Retained earnings, December 31	$26,400	

The Accounting Cycle · 91

Balance Sheet

The balance sheet for Uptown is a classified balance sheet. Interest receivable, prepaid insurance, and prepaid rent expense are included as current assets. Uptown considers these assets current because they will be converted into cash or used by the business within a relatively short period of time. Uptown deducts the amount of Allowance for Doubtful Accounts from the total of accounts, notes, and interest receivable because it estimates that only $54,800 of $57,800 will be collected in cash.

In the property, plant, and equipment section, Uptown deducts the accumulated depreciation from the cost of the furniture and equipment. The difference represents the book or carrying value of the furniture and equipment.

The balance sheet shows property tax payable as a current liability because it is an obligation that is payable within a year. The balance sheet also shows other short-term liabilities such as accounts payable.

The bonds payable, due in 2015, are long-term liabilities. As a result, the balance sheet shows the account in a separate section. (The company paid interest on the bonds on December 31.)

Because Uptown is a corporation, the capital section of the balance sheet, called the stockholders' equity section in the illustration, differs somewhat from the capital section for a proprietorship. Total stockholders' equity consists of the common stock, which is the original investment by stockholders, and the earnings retained in the business. *For homework purposes, unless instructed otherwise, prepare an unclassified balance sheet.*

ILLUSTRATION 3-40
A Balance Sheet

UPTOWN CABINET CORP.			
BALANCE SHEET			
AS OF DECEMBER 31, 2007			
Assets			
Current assets			
Cash			$ 1,200
Notes receivable	$16,000		
Accounts receivable	41,000		
Interest receivable	800	$57,800	
Less: Allowance for doubtful accounts		3,000	54,800
Merchandise inventory			40,000
Prepaid insurance			540
Prepaid rent expense			500
Total current assets			97,040
Property, plant, and equipment			
Furniture and equipment		67,000	
Less: Accumulated depreciation		18,700	
Total property, plant, and equipment			48,300
Total assets			$145,340
Liabilities and Stockholders' Equity			
Current liabilities			
Notes payable			$ 20,000
Accounts payable			13,500
Property tax payable			2,000
Income tax payable			3,440
Total current liabilities			38,940
Long-term liabilities			
Bonds payable, due June 30, 2015			30,000
Total liabilities			68,940
Stockholders' equity			
Common stock, $5.00 par value, issued			
and outstanding, 10,000 shares		$50,000	
Retained earnings		26,400	
Total stockholders' equity			76,400
Total liabilities and stockholders' equity			$145,340

Closing Entries

Uptown makes closing entries as follows.

General Journal
December 31, 2007

Interest Revenue	800	
Sales	400,000	
Income Summary		400,800
(To close revenues to Income Summary)		
Income Summary	388,600	
Cost of Goods Sold		316,000
Sales Salaries Expense		20,000
Traveling Expense		8,000
Advertising Expense		2,200
Salaries, Office and General		19,000
Depreciation Expense—Furniture and Equipment		6,700
Rent Expense		4,300
Property Tax Expense		5,300
Bad Debt Expense		1,000
Telephone and Internet Expense		600
Insurance Expense		360
Interest Expense		1,700
Income Tax Expense		3,440
(To close expenses to Income Summary)		
Income Summary	12,200	
Retained Earnings		12,200
(To close Income Summary to Retained Earnings)		
Retained Earnings	2,000	
Dividends		2,000
(To close Dividends to Retained Earnings)		

Inventory and Cost of Goods Sold

OBJECTIVE 8
Explain how to adjust inventory accounts at year-end.

Because Uptown is a merchandising company, it has inventory. Companies with inventory generally use a **perpetual inventory system**. With such a system, a company records the cost of the inventory purchased and sold directly in the Inventory account as the purchases and sales occur. Therefore, the balance in the Inventory account should represent the ending inventory amount, and no adjusting entries are needed. To ensure this accuracy, a physical count of the items in inventory is performed on an annual basis.

With the perpetual inventory system, because the company debits purchases directly to the Inventory account, it does not use a Purchases account. However, the company does use a Cost of Goods Sold account to accumulate the issuances from inventory. That is, when inventory is sold, the company credits the cost of the sold goods to Inventory and debits Cost of Goods Sold. In closing the accounts, the company credits Cost of Goods Sold and debits Income Summary.

With a **periodic inventory system**, a company uses a Purchases account to record purchases of inventory during the period. Here, the Inventory account remains **unchanged** during the period. The Inventory account represents the beginning inventory amount throughout the period. Then, at the end of the accounting period the company must adjust the inventory account by **closing out the beginning inventory amount** and **recording the ending inventory amount**. A company determines the ending inventory by physically counting the items on hand and valuing them at cost or at the lower-of-cost-or-market. Under the periodic inventory system, a company therefore determines the cost of goods sold by adding the beginning inventory together with net purchases and deducting the ending inventory.

To illustrate how to compute cost of goods sold with a periodic inventory system, assume that Collegiate Apparel Shop begins with an inventory of $30,000. It records purchases of $200,000, transportation-in of $6,000, purchase returns and allowances of $1,000, and purchase discounts of $3,000. The ending inventory is $26,000. Collegiate computes cost of goods sold as shown in Illustration 3-41.

Beginning inventory		$ 30,000
Purchases	$200,000	
Less: Purchase returns and allowances	$1,000	
Purchase discounts	3,000	4,000
Net purchases		196,000
Plus: Transportation-in		6,000
Cost of goods purchased		202,000
Cost of goods available for sale		232,000
Less: Ending inventory		26,000
Cost of goods sold		$206,000

ILLUSTRATION 3-41
Computation of Cost of Goods Sold under Periodic Inventory System

Cost of goods sold will be the same amount whether a company uses the perpetual or periodic method.

SUMMARY OF LEARNING OBJECTIVES

1. **Understand basic accounting terminology.** Understanding the following eleven terms helps in understanding key accounting concepts: (1) Event. (2) Transaction. (3) Account. (4) Real and nominal accounts. (5) Ledger. (6) Journal. (7) Posting. (8) Trial balance. (9) Adjusting entries. (10) Financial statements. (11) Closing entries.

2. **Explain double-entry rules.** The left side of any account is the debit side; the right side is the credit side. All asset and expense accounts are increased on the left or debit side and decreased on the right or credit side. Conversely, all liability and revenue accounts are increased on the right or credit side and decreased on the left or debit side. Stockholders' equity accounts, Common Stock and Retained Earnings, are increased on the credit side. Dividends is increased on the debit side.

3. **Identify steps in the accounting cycle.** The basic steps in the accounting cycle are (1) identifying and measuring transactions and other events; (2) journalizing; (3) posting; (4) preparing an unadjusted trial balance; (5) making adjusting entries; (6) preparing an adjusted trial balance; (7) preparing financial statements; and (8) closing.

4. **Record transactions in journals, post to ledger accounts, and prepare a trial balance.** The simplest journal form chronologically lists transactions and events expressed in terms of debits and credits to particular accounts. The items entered in a general journal must be transferred (posted) to the general ledger. Companies should prepare an unadjusted trial balance at the end of a given period after they have recorded the entries in the journal and posted them to the ledger.

5. **Explain the reasons for preparing adjusting entries.** Adjustments achieve a proper matching of revenues and expenses, so as to determine net income for the current period and to achieve an accurate statement of end-of-the-period balances in assets, liabilities, and owners' equity accounts.

6. **Prepare financial statements from the adjusted trial balance.** Companies can prepare financial statements directly from the adjusted trial balance. The income statement is prepared from the revenue and expense accounts. The statement of retained earnings is prepared from the retained earnings account, dividends, and net income (or net loss). The balance sheet is prepared from the asset, liability, and equity accounts.

7. **Prepare closing entries.** In the closing process, the company transfers all of the revenue and expense account balances (income statement items) to a clearing account called Income Summary, which is used only at the end of the fiscal year. Revenues

KEY TERMS

account, *63*
accounting cycle, *67*
accounting information system, *62*
accrued expenses, *81*
accrued revenues, *80*
adjusted trial balance, *84*
adjusting entry, *63, 75*
balance sheet, *63*
book value, *79*
closing entries, *64, 87*
closing process, *86*
contra asset account, *79*
credit, *64*
debit, *64*
depreciation, *78*
double-entry accounting, *64*
event, *63*
financial statements, *63*
general journal, *69*
general ledger, *69*
income statement, *64*
journal, *63*
ledger, *63*
nominal accounts, *63*
periodic inventory system, *92*
perpetual inventory system, *92*
post-closing trial balance, *89*
posting, *63, 70*
prepaid expenses, *76*

real accounts, *63*

reversing entries, *89*

special journals, *70*

statement of cash flows, *64*

statement of retained earnings, *64*

T-account, *69*

transaction, *63*

trial balance, *63, 74*

unearned revenues, *79*

useful life, *78*

and expenses are matched in the Income Summary account. The net result of this matching represents the net income or net loss for the period. That amount is then transferred to an owners' equity account (Retained Earnings for a corporation and capital accounts for proprietorships and partnerships).

8. **Explain how to adjust inventory accounts at year-end.** Under a perpetual inventory system the balance in the Inventory account represents the ending inventory amount. When companies maintain the inventory records in a periodic inventory system, they use a Purchases account; the Inventory account is unchanged during the period. The Inventory account represents the beginning inventory amount throughout the period. At the end of the accounting period the company must adjust the Inventory account by closing out the beginning inventory amount and recording the ending inventory amount.

APPENDIX
3A Cash-Basis Accounting versus Accrual-Basis Accounting

OBJECTIVE 9
Differentiate the cash basis of accounting from the accrual basis of accounting.

Most companies use **accrual-basis accounting**: They recognize revenue when it is earned and expenses in the period incurred, without regard to the time of receipt or payment of cash.

Some small enterprises and the average individual taxpayer, however, use a strict or modified cash-basis approach. Under the **strict cash basis**, companies record revenue only when they receive cash, and they record expenses only when they disperse cash. Determining income on the cash basis rests upon collecting revenue and paying expenses. The cash basis ignores two principles: the revenue recognition principle and the matching principle. Consequently, cash-basis financial statements are not in conformity with GAAP.

An illustration will help clarify the differences between accrual-basis and cash-basis accounting. Assume that Quality Contractor signs an agreement to construct a garage for $22,000. In January, Quality begins construction, incurs costs of $18,000 on credit, and by the end of January delivers a finished garage to the buyer. In February, Quality collects $22,000 cash from the customer. In March, Quality pays the $18,000 due the creditors. Illustrations 3A-1 and 3A-2 show the net incomes for each month under cash-basis accounting and accrual-basis accounting.

ILLUSTRATION 3A-1
Income Statement—Cash Basis

QUALITY CONTRACTOR				
INCOME STATEMENT—CASH BASIS				
For the Month of				
	January	February	March	Total
Cash receipts	$–0–	$22,000	$ –0–	$22,000
Cash payments	–0–	–0–	18,000	18,000
Net income (loss)	$–0–	$22,000	$(18,000)	$ 4,000

QUALITY CONTRACTOR
INCOME STATEMENT—ACCRUAL BASIS
For the Month of

	January	February	March	Total
Revenues	$22,000	$-0-	$-0-	$22,000
Expenses	18,000	-0-	-0-	18,000
Net income (loss)	$ 4,000	$-0-	$-0-	$ 4,000

For the three months combined, total net income is the same under both cash-basis accounting and accrual-basis accounting. The difference is in the **timing** of revenues and expenses. The basis of accounting also affects the balance sheet. Illustrations 3A-3 and 3A-4 show Quality Contractor's balance sheets at each month-end under the cash basis and the accrual basis.

QUALITY CONTRACTOR
BALANCE SHEETS—CASH BASIS
As of

	January 31	February 28	March 31
Assets			
Cash	$-0-	$22,000	$4,000
Total assets	$-0-	$22,000	$4,000
Liabilities and Owners' Equity			
Owners' equity	$-0-	$22,000	$4,000
Total liabilities and owners' equity	$-0-	$22,000	$4,000

QUALITY CONTRACTOR
BALANCE SHEETS—ACCRUAL BASIS
As of

	January 31	February 28	March 31
Assets			
Cash	$ -0-	$22,000	$4,000
Accounts receivable	22,000	-0-	-0-
Total assets	$22,000	$22,000	$4,000
Liabilities and Owners' Equity			
Accounts payable	$18,000	$18,000	$ -0-
Owners' equity	4,000	4,000	4,000
Total liabilities and owners' equity	$22,000	$22,000	$4,000

Analysis of Quality's income statements and balance sheets shows the ways in which cash-basis accounting is inconsistent with basic accounting theory:

1 The cash basis understates revenues and assets from the construction and delivery of the garage in January. It ignores the $22,000 of accounts receivable, representing a near-term future cash inflow.

2 The cash basis understates expenses incurred with the construction of the garage and the liability outstanding at the end of January. It ignores the $18,000 of accounts payable, representing a near-term future cash outflow.

3 The cash basis understates owners' equity in January by not recognizing the revenues and the asset until February. It also overstates owners' equity in February by not recognizing the expenses and the liability until March.

In short, cash-basis accounting violates the accrual concept underlying financial reporting.

The **modified cash basis** is a mixture of the cash basis and the accrual basis. It is based on the pure cash basis but with modifications that have substantial support, such as capitalizing and depreciating plant assets or recording inventory. This method is often followed by professional services firms (doctors, lawyers, accountants, consultants) and by retail, real estate, and agricultural operations.[1]

CONVERSION FROM CASH BASIS TO ACCRUAL BASIS

Not infrequently companies want to convert a cash basis or a modified cash basis set of financial statements to the accrual basis for presentation to investors and creditors. To illustrate this conversion, assume that Dr. Diane Windsor, like many small business owners, keeps her accounting records on a cash basis. In the year 2007, Dr. Windsor received $300,000 from her patients and paid $170,000 for operating expenses, resulting in an excess of cash receipts over disbursements of $130,000 ($300,000 − $170,000). At January 1 and December 31, 2007, she has accounts receivable, unearned service revenue, accrued liabilities, and prepaid expenses as shown in Illustration 3A-5.

ILLUSTRATION 3A-5
Financial Information Related to Dr. Diane Windsor

	January 1, 2007	December 31, 2007
Accounts receivable	$12,000	$9,000
Unearned service revenue	–0–	4,000
Accrued liabilities	2,000	5,500
Prepaid expenses	1,800	2,700

Service Revenue Computation

To convert the amount of cash received from patients to service revenue on an accrual basis, we must consider changes in accounts receivable and unearned service revenue during the year. Accounts receivable at the beginning of the year represents revenues earned last year that are collected this year. Ending accounts receivable indicates revenues earned this year that are not yet collected. Therefore, to compute revenue on an accrual basis, we subtract beginning accounts receivable and add ending accounts receivable, as the formula in Illustration 3A-6 shows.

ILLUSTRATION 3A-6
Conversion of Cash Receipts to Revenue—Accounts Receivable

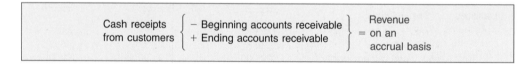

Similarly, beginning unearned service revenue represents cash received last year for revenues earned this year. Ending unearned service revenue results from collections this year that will be recognized as revenue next year. Therefore, to compute revenue

---

[1] Companies in the following situations might use a cash or modified cash basis.

(1) A company that is primarily interested in cash flows (for example, a group of physicians that distributes cash-basis earnings for salaries and bonuses).

(2) A company that has a limited number of financial statement users (small, closely held company with little or no debt).

(3) A company that has operations that are relatively straightforward (small amounts of inventory, long-term assets, or long-term debt).

on an accrual basis, we add beginning unearned service revenue and subtract ending unearned service revenue, as the formula in Illustration 3A-7 shows.

Cash receipts from customers	{	+ Beginning unearned service revenue − Ending unearned service revenue	} Revenue = on an accrual basis

ILLUSTRATION 3A-7
Conversion of Cash Receipts to Revenue—Unearned Service Revenue

Therefore, for Dr. Windsor's dental practice, to convert cash collected from customers to service revenue on an accrual basis, we would make the computations shown in Illustration 3A-8.

Cash receipts from customers		$300,000
− Beginning accounts receivable	$(12,000)	
+ Ending accounts receivable	9,000	
+ Beginning unearned service revenue	–0–	
− Ending unearned service revenue	(4,000)	(7,000)
Service revenue (accrual)		$293,000

ILLUSTRATION 3A-8
Conversion of Cash Receipts to Service Revenue

Operating Expense Computation

To convert cash paid for operating expenses during the year to operating expenses on an accrual basis, we must consider changes in prepaid expenses and accrued liabilities. First, we need to recognize as this year's expenses the amount of beginning prepaid expenses. (The cash payment for these occurred last year.) Therefore, to arrive at operating expense on an accrual basis, we add the beginning prepaid expenses balance to cash paid for operating expenses.

Conversely, ending prepaid expenses result from cash payments made this year for expenses to be reported next year. (Under the accrual basis, Dr. Windsor would have deferred recognizing these payments as expenses until a future period.) To convert these cash payments to operating expenses on an accrual basis, we deduct ending prepaid expenses from cash paid for expenses, as the formula in Illustration 3A-9 shows.

Cash paid for operating expenses	{	+ Beginning prepaid expenses − Ending prepaid expenses	} Expenses = on an accrual basis

ILLUSTRATION 3A-9
Conversion of Cash Payments to Expenses—Prepaid Expenses

Similarly, beginning accrued liabilities result from expenses recognized last year that require cash payments this year. Ending accrued liabilities relate to expenses recognized this year that have not been paid. To arrive at expense on an accrual basis, we deduct beginning accrued liabilities and add ending accrued liabilities to cash paid for expenses, as the formula in Illustration 3A-10 shows.

Cash paid for operating expenses	{	− Beginning accrued liabilities + Ending accrued liabilities	} Expenses = on an accrual basis

ILLUSTRATION 3A-10
Conversion of Cash Payments to Expenses—Accrued Liabilities

Therefore, for Dr. Windsor's dental practice, to convert cash paid for operating expenses to operating expenses on an accrual basis, we would make the computations shown in Illustration 3A-11.

ILLUSTRATION 3A-11
Conversion of Cash Paid
to Operating Expenses

Cash paid for operating expenses		$170,000
+ Beginning prepaid expense	$1,800	
− Ending prepaid expense	(2,700)	
− Beginning accrued liabilities	(2,000)	
+ Ending accrued liabilities	5,500	2,600
Operating expenses (accrual)		$172,600

This entire conversion can be completed in worksheet form as shown in Illustration 3A-12.

ILLUSTRATION 3A-12
Conversion of Statement
of Cash Receipts and
Disbursements to Income
Statement

DIANE WINDSOR, D.D.S.
Conversion of Income Statement Data from Cash Basis to Accrual Basis
For the Year 2007

	A	B Cash Basis	C Adjustments Add	D Adjustments Deduct	E Accrual Basis
2	Collections from customers	$300,000			
3	− Accounts receivable, Jan. 1			$12,000	
4	+ Accounts receivable, Dec. 31		$9,000		
5	+ Unearned service revenue, Jan. 1		—	—	
6	− Unearned service revenue, Dec. 31			4,000	
7	Service revenue				$293,000
8	Disbursement for expenses	170,000			
9	+ Prepaid expenses, Jan. 1		1,800		
10	− Prepaid expenses, Dec. 31			2,700	
11	− Accrued liabilities, Jan. 1			2,000	
12	+ Accrued liabilities, Dec. 31		5,500		
13	Operating expenses				172,600
14	Excess of cash collections over disbursements—cash basis	$130,000			
15	Net income—accrual basis				$120,400

Sheet1 / Sheet2 / Sheet3

Using this approach, we adjust collections and disbursements on a cash basis to revenue and expense on an accrual basis, to arrive at accrual net income. In any conversion from the cash basis to the accrual basis, depreciation or amortization is an additional expense in arriving at net income on an accrual basis.

THEORETICAL WEAKNESSES OF THE CASH BASIS

The cash basis reports exactly when cash is received and when cash is disbursed. To many people that information represents something concrete. Isn't cash what it is all about? Does it make sense to invent something, design it, produce it, market and sell it, if you aren't going to get cash for it in the end? Many frequently say, "Cash is the real bottom line," and also, "Cash is the oil that lubricates the economy." If so, then what is the merit of accrual accounting?

Today's economy is considerably more lubricated by credit than by cash. The accrual basis, not the cash basis, recognizes all aspects of the credit phenomenon. Investors, creditors, and other decision makers seek timely information about an enterprise's *future* cash flows. Accrual-basis accounting provides this information by reporting the cash inflows and outflows associated with earnings activities as soon as these companies can estimate these cash flows with an acceptable degree of certainty. Receivables and payables are forecasters of future cash inflows and outflows. In other words, accrual-basis accounting aids in predicting future cash flows by reporting transactions and other events with cash consequences at the time the transactions and events occur, rather than when the cash is received and paid.

KEY TERMS

accrual basis, *94*
modified cash basis, *96*
strict cash basis, *94*

| **SUMMARY OF LEARNING OBJECTIVE FOR APPENDIX 3A** |

9. Differentiate the cash basis of accounting from the accrual basis of accounting. The cash basis of accounting records revenues when cash is received and expenses when cash is paid. The accrual basis recognizes revenue when earned and expenses in the period incurred, without regard to the time of the receipt or payment of cash. Accrual-basis accounting is theoretically preferable because it provides information about future cash inflows and outflows associated with earnings activities as soon as companies can estimate these cash flows with an acceptable degree of certainty. Cash-basis accounting is not in conformity with GAAP.

APPENDIX 3B

Using Reversing Entries

Use of reversing entries simplifies the recording of transactions in the next accounting period. The use of reversing entries, however, does not change the amounts reported in the financial statements for the previous period.

ILLUSTRATION OF REVERSING ENTRIES—ACCRUALS

A company most often uses reversing entries to reverse two types of adjusting entries: accrued revenues and accrued expenses. To illustrate the optional use of reversing entries for accrued expenses, we use the following transaction and adjustment data.

> **OBJECTIVE 10**
> Identify adjusting entries that may be reversed.

1 October 24 (initial salary entry): Paid $4,000 of salaries incurred between October 10 and October 24.

2 October 31 (adjusting entry): Incurred salaries between October 25 and October 31 of $1,200, to be paid in the November 8 payroll.

3 November 8 (subsequent salary entry): Paid salaries of $2,500. Of this amount, $1,200 applied to accrued wages payable at October 31 and $1,300 to wages payable for November 1 through November 8.

Illustration 3B-1 (page 100) shows the comparative entries.

The comparative entries show that the first three entries are the same whether or not the company uses reversing entries. The last two entries differ. The November 1 reversing entry eliminates the $1,200 balance in Salaries Payable, created by the October 31 adjusting entry. The reversing entry also creates a $1,200 credit balance in the Salaries Expense account. As you know, it is unusual for an expense account to have a credit balance. However, the balance is correct in this instance. Why? Because the company will debit the entire amount of the first salary payment in the new accounting period to Salaries Expense. This debit eliminates the credit balance. The resulting debit balance in the expense account will equal the salaries expense incurred in the new accounting period ($1,300 in this example).

When a company makes reversing entries, it debits all cash payments of expenses to the related expense account. This means that on November 8 (and every payday) the company debits Salaries Expense for the amount paid without regard to the existence of any accrued salaries payable. Repeating the same entry simplifies the recording process in an accounting system.

REVERSING ENTRIES NOT USED			REVERSING ENTRIES USED		
Initial Salary Entry					
Oct. 24	Salaries Expense	4,000	Oct. 24	Salaries Expense	4,000
	Cash	4,000		Cash	4,000
Adjusting Entry					
Oct. 31	Salaries Expense	1,200	Oct. 31	Salaries Expense	1,200
	Salaries Payable	1,200		Salaries Payable	1,200
Closing Entry					
Oct. 31	Income Summary	5,200	Oct. 31	Income Summary	5,200
	Salaries Expense	5,200		Salaries Expense	5,200
Reversing Entry					
Nov. 1	No entry is made.		Nov. 1	Salaries Payable	1,200
				Salaries Expense	1,200
Subsequent Salary Entry					
Nov. 8	Salaries Payable	1,200	Nov. 8	Salaries Expense	2,500
	Salaries Expense	1,300		Cash	2,500
	Cash	2,500			

ILLUSTRATION 3B-1
Comparison of Entries for Accruals, with and without Reversing Entries

ILLUSTRATION OF REVERSING ENTRIES—PREPAYMENTS

Up to this point, we assumed the recording of all prepayments as prepaid expense or unearned revenue. In some cases, though, a company records prepayments directly in expense or revenue accounts. When this occurs, a company may also reverse prepayments.

To illustrate the use of reversing entries for prepaid expenses, we use the following transaction and adjustment data.

1 December 10 (initial entry): Purchased $20,000 of office supplies with cash.

2 December 31 (adjusting entry): Determined that $5,000 of office supplies are on hand.

Illustration 3B-2 shows the comparative entries.

ILLUSTRATION 3B-2
Comparison of Entries for Prepayments, with and without Reversing Entries

REVERSING ENTRIES NOT USED			REVERSING ENTRIES USED		
Initial Purchase of Supplies Entry					
Dec. 10	Office Supplies	20,000	Dec. 10	Office Supplies Expense	20,000
	Cash	20,000		Cash	20,000
Adjusting Entry					
Dec. 31	Office Supplies Expense	15,000	Dec. 31	Office Supplies	5,000
	Office Supplies	15,000		Office Supplies Expense	5,000
Closing Entry					
Dec. 31	Income Summary	15,000	Dec. 31	Income Summary	15,000
	Office Supplies Expense	15,000		Office Supplies Expense	15,000
Reversing Entry					
Jan. 1	No entry		Jan. 1	Office Supplies Expense	5,000
				Office Supplies	5,000

After the adjusting entry on December 31 (regardless of whether using reversing entries), the asset account Office Supplies shows a balance of $5,000, and Office Supplies Expense shows a balance of $15,000. If the company initially debits Office Supplies Expense when it purchases the supplies, it then makes a reversing entry to return to the expense account the cost of unconsumed supplies. The company then continues to debit Office Supplies Expense for additional purchases of office supplies during the next period.

Prepaid items are generally entered in real accounts (assets and liabilities), thus making reversing entries unnecessary. This approach is used because it is advantageous for items that a company needs to apportion over several periods (e.g., supplies and parts inventories). However, for other items that do not follow this regular pattern and that may or may not involve two or more periods, a company ordinarily enters them initially in revenue or expense accounts. The revenue and expense accounts may not require adjusting, and the company thus systematically closes them to Income Summary.

Using the nominal accounts adds consistency to the accounting system. It also makes the recording more efficient, particularly when a large number of such transactions occur during the year. For example, the bookkeeper knows to expense invoice items (except for capital asset acquisitions). He or she need not worry whether an item will result in a prepaid expense at the end of the period, because the company will make adjustments at the end of the period.

Summary of Reversing Entries

We summarize guidelines for reversing entries as follows.

1 All accrued items should be reversed.

2 All prepaid items for which a company debited or credited the original cash transaction to an expense or revenue account should be reversed.

3 Adjusting entries for depreciation and bad debts are not reversed.

Recognize that reversing entries do not have to be used. Therefore, some accountants avoid them entirely.

SUMMARY OF LEARNING OBJECTIVE FOR APPENDIX 3B

10. **Identify adjusting entries that may be reversed.** Reversing entries are most often used to reverse two types of adjusting entries: accrued revenues and accrued expenses. Prepayments may also be reversed if the initial entry to record the transaction is made to an expense or revenue account.

Using a Worksheet: The Accounting Cycle Revisited

In this appendix we provide an additional illustration of the end-of-period steps in the accounting cycle and illustrate the use of a worksheet in this process. Using a **worksheet** often facilitates the end-of-period (monthly, quarterly, or annually) accounting and reporting process. Use of a worksheet helps a company prepare the financial statements on a more timely basis. How? With a worksheet, a company need not wait until it journalizes and posts the adjusting and closing entries.

A company prepares a worksheet either on columnar paper or within an electronic spreadsheet. In either form, a company uses the worksheet to adjust account balances and to prepare financial statements.

The worksheet does not replace the financial statements. Instead, it is an informal device for accumulating and sorting information needed for the financial statements. Completing the worksheet provides considerable assurance that a company properly handled all of the details related to the end-of-period accounting and statement

> **OBJECTIVE 11**
> Prepare a 10-column worksheet.

preparation. The 10-column worksheet in Illustration 3C-1 (page 103) provides columns for the first trial balance, adjustments, adjusted trial balance, income statement, and balance sheet.

Worksheet Columns

Trial Balance Columns

Uptown Cabinet Corp., shown in Illustration 3C-1, obtains data for the trial balance from its ledger balances at December 31. The amount for Merchandise Inventory, $40,000, is the year-end inventory amount, which results from the application of a perpetual inventory system.

Adjustments Columns

After Uptown enters all adjustment data on the worksheet, it establishes the equality of the adjustment columns. It then extends the balances in all accounts to the adjusted trial balance columns.

Adjustments Entered on the Worksheet

Items (a) through (g) below serve as the basis for the adjusting entries made in the worksheet for Uptown shown in Illustration 3C-1.

(a) Depreciation of furniture and equipment at the rate of 10% per year based on original cost of $67,000.

(b) Estimated bad debts of one-quarter of 1 percent of sales ($400,000).

(c) Insurance expired during the year $360.

(d) Interest accrued on notes receivable as of December 31, $800.

(e) The Rent Expense account contains $500 rent paid in advance, which is applicable to next year.

(f) Property taxes accrued December 31, $2,000.

(g) Income tax payable estimated $3,440.

The adjusting entries shown on the December 31, 2007, worksheet are as follows.

	(a)		
Depreciation Expense—Furniture and Equipment		6,700	
Accumulated Depreciation—Furniture and Equipment			6,700
	(b)		
Bad Debt Expense		1,000	
Allowance for Doubtful Accounts			1,000
	(c)		
Insurance Expense		360	
Prepaid Insurance			360
	(d)		
Interest Receivable		800	
Interest Revenue			800
	(e)		
Prepaid Rent Expense		500	
Rent Expense			500
	(f)		
Property Tax Expense		2,000	
Property Tax Payable			2,000
	(g)		
Income Tax Expense		3,440	
Income Tax Payable			3,440

Uptown Cabinet transfers the adjusting entries to the Adjustments columns of the worksheet, often designating each by letter. The trial balance lists any new accounts resulting from the adjusting entries, as illustrated on the worksheet. (For example, see the accounts listed in rows 27 through 35 in Illustration 3C-1.) Uptown then totals and balances the Adjustments columns.

Adjusted Trial Balance

The adjusted trial balance shows the balance of all accounts after adjustment at the end of the accounting period. For example, Uptown adds the $2,000 shown opposite the Allowance for Doubtful Accounts in the Trial Balance Cr. column to the $1,000 in the Adjustments Cr. column. The company then extends the $3,000 total to the Adjusted Trial Balance Cr. column. Similarly, Uptown reduces the $900 debit opposite Prepaid Insurance by the $360 credit in the Adjustments column. The result, $540, is shown in the Adjusted Trial Balance Dr. column.

Income Statement and Balance Sheet Columns

Uptown extends all the debit items in the Adjusted Trial Balance columns into the Income Statement or Balance Sheet columns to the right. It similarly extends all the credit items.

The next step is to total the Income Statement columns. Uptown needs the amount of net income or loss for the period to balance the debit and credit columns. The net income of $12,200 is shown in the Income Statement Dr. column because revenues exceeded expenses by that amount.

UPTOWN CABINET CORP.
Ten-Column Worksheet for The Year Ended December 31, 2007

	Accounts	Trial Balance Dr.	Trial Balance Cr.	Adjustments Dr.	Adjustments Cr.	Adjusted Trial Balance Dr.	Adjusted Trial Balance Cr.	Income Statement Dr.	Income Statement Cr.	Balance Sheet Dr.	Balance Sheet Cr.
2	Cash	1,200				1,200				1,200	
3	Notes receivable	16,000				16,000				16,000	
4	Accounts receivable	41,000				41,000				41,000	
5	Allowance for doubtful accounts		2,000		(b) 1,000		3,000				3,000
6	Merchandise inventory	40,000				40,000				40,000	
7	Prepaid insurance	900			(c) 360	540				540	
8	Furniture and equipment	67,000				67,000				67,000	
9	Accumulated depreciation—furniture and equipment		12,000		(a) 6,700		18,700				18,700
10	Notes payable		20,000				20,000				20,000
11	Accounts payable		13,500				13,500				13,500
12	Bonds payable		30,000				30,000				30,000
13	Common stock		50,000				50,000				50,000
14	Retained earnings, Jan. 1, 2007		16,200				16,200				16,200
15	Dividends	2,000				2,000				2,000	
16	Sales		400,000				400,000		400,000		
17	Cost of goods sold	316,000				316,000		316,000			
18	Sales salaries expense	20,000				20,000		20,000			
19	Advertising expense	2,200				2,200		2,200			
20	Traveling expense	8,000				8,000		8,000			
21	Salaries, office and general	19,000				19,000		19,000			
22	Telephone and Internet expense	600				600		600			
23	Rent expense	4,800			(e) 500	4,300		4,300			
24	Property tax expense	3,300		(f) 2,000		5,300		5,300			
25	Interest expense	1,700				1,700		1,700			
26	Totals	543,700	543,700								
27	Depreciation expense—furniture and equipment			(a) 6,700		6,700		6,700			
28	Bad debt expense			(b) 1,000		1,000		1,000			
29	Insurance expense			(c) 360		360		360			
30	Interest receivable			(d) 800		800				800	
31	Interest revenue				(d) 800		800		800		
32	Prepaid rent expense			(e) 500		500				500	
33	Property tax payable				(f) 2,000		2,000				2,000
34	Income tax expense			(g) 3,440		3,440		3,440			
35	Income tax payable				(g) 3,440		3,440				3,440
36	Totals			14,800	14,800	554,200	554,200	388,600	400,800		
37	Net income							12,200			12,200
38	Totals							400,800	400,800	169,040	169,040

ILLUSTRATION 3C-1
Use of a Worksheet

Uptown then balances the Income Statement columns. The company also enters the net income of $12,200 in the Balance Sheet Cr. column as an increase in retained earnings.

Preparing Financial Statements from a Worksheet

The worksheet provides the information needed for preparation of the financial statements without reference to the ledger or other records. In addition, the worksheet sorts the data into appropriate columns, which facilitates the preparation of the statements. The financial statements for Uptown Cabinet are shown in Chapter 3, pages 90–91.

SUMMARY OF LEARNING OBJECTIVE FOR APPENDIX 3C

KEY TERM

worksheet, *101*

11. Prepare a 10-column worksheet. The 10-column worksheet provides columns for the first trial balance, adjustments, adjusted trial balance, income statement, and balance sheet. The worksheet does not replace the financial statements. Instead, it is an informal device for accumulating and sorting information needed for the financial statements.

Note: All asterisked Questions, Exercises, Problems, and Cases relate to material contained in the appendixes to the chapter.

QUESTIONS

1. Give an example of a transaction that results in:

(a) A decrease in an asset and a decrease in a liability.

(b) A decrease in one asset and an increase in another asset.

(c) A decrease in one liability and an increase in another liability.

2. Do the following events represent business transactions? Explain your answer in each case.

(a) A computer is purchased on account.

(b) A customer returns merchandise and is given credit on account.

(c) A prospective employee is interviewed.

(d) The owner of the business withdraws cash from the business for personal use.

(e) Merchandise is ordered for delivery next month.

3. Name the accounts debited and credited for each of the following transactions.

(a) Billing a customer for work done.

(b) Receipt of cash from customer on account.

(c) Purchase of office supplies on account.

(d) Purchase of 15 gallons of gasoline for the delivery truck.

4. Why are revenue and expense accounts called temporary or nominal accounts?

5. Omar Morena, a fellow student, contends that the double-entry system means that each transaction must be recorded twice. Is Omar correct? Explain.

6. Is it necessary that a trial balance be taken periodically? What purpose does it serve?

7. Indicate whether each of the items below is a real or nominal account and whether it appears in the balance sheet or the income statement.

(a) Prepaid Rent.

(b) Salaries and Wages Payable.

(c) Merchandise Inventory.

(d) Accumulated Depreciation.

(e) Office Equipment.

(f) Service Revenue.

(g) Office Salaries Expense.

(h) Supplies on Hand.

8. Employees are paid every Saturday for the preceding work week. If a balance sheet is prepared on Wednesday, December 31, what does the amount of wages earned during the first three days of the week (12/29, 12/30, 12/31) represent? Explain.

9. (a) How do the components of revenues and expenses differ between a merchandising company and a service enterprise? (b) Explain the income measurement process of a merchandising company.

10. What is the purpose of the Cost of Goods Sold account? (Assume a periodic inventory system.)

11. Under a perpetual system, what is the purpose of the Cost of Goods Sold account?

12. If the $3,900 cost of a new microcomputer and printer purchased for office use were recorded as a debit to Purchases, what would be the effect of the error on the balance sheet and income statement in the period in which the error was made?

13. What differences are there between the trial balance before closing and the trial balance after closing with respect to the following accounts?

(a) Accounts Payable.

(b) Expense accounts.

(c) Revenue accounts.

(d) Retained Earnings account.

(e) Cash.

14. What are adjusting entries and why are they necessary?

15. What are closing entries and why are they necessary?

16. John Damon, maintenance supervisor for Red Sox Insurance Co., has purchased a riding lawnmower and accessories to be used in maintaining the grounds around corporate headquarters. He has sent the following information to the accounting department.

Cost of mower and		Date purchased	7/1/07
accessories	$3,000	Monthly salary of	
Estimated useful life	5 yrs	groundskeeper	$1,100
		Estimated annual	
		fuel cost	$150

Compute the amount of depreciation expense (related to the mower and accessories) that should be reported on Red Sox's December 31, 2007, income statement. Assume straight-line depreciation.

17. Selanne Enterprises made the following entry on December 31, 2007.

Interest Expense	10,000	
Interest Payable		10,000
(To record interest expense due on loan from Anaheim National Bank.)		

What entry would Anaheim National Bank make regarding its outstanding loan to Selanne Enterprises? Explain why this must be the case.

*18. Distinguish between cash-basis accounting and accrual-basis accounting. Why is accrual-basis accounting acceptable for most business enterprises and the cash-basis unacceptable in the preparation of an income statement and a balance sheet?

*19. When wages expense for the year is computed, why are beginning accrued wages subtracted from, and ending accrued wages added to, wages paid during the year?

*20. List two types of transactions that would receive different accounting treatment using (a) strict cash-basis accounting, and (b) a modified cash basis.

*21. What are reversing entries, and why are they used?

*22. "A worksheet is a permanent accounting record, and its use is required in the accounting cycle." Do you agree? Explain.

BRIEF EXERCISES

(LO 4) **BE3-1** Transactions for Argot Company for the month of May are presented below. Prepare journal entries for each of these transactions. (You may omit explanations.)

May	1	B.D. Argot invests $3,000 cash in exchange for common stock in a small welding corporation.
	3	Buys equipment on account for $1,100.
	13	Pays $400 to landlord for May rent.
	21	Bills Noble Corp. $500 for welding work done.

(LO 4) **BE3-2** Brett Favre Repair Shop had the following transactions during the first month of business. Journalize the transactions. (Omit explanations.)

Aug.	2	Invested $12,000 cash and $2,500 of equipment in the business.
	7	Purchased supplies on account for $400. (Debit asset account.)
	12	Performed services for clients, for which $1,300 was collected in cash and $670 was billed to the clients.
	15	Paid August rent $600.
	19	Counted supplies and determined that only $270 of the supplies purchased on August 7 are still on hand.

(LO 4, 5) **BE3-3** On July 1, 2007, Blair Co. pays $18,000 to Hindi Insurance Co. for a 3-year insurance contract. Both companies have fiscal years ending December 31. For Blair Co. journalize the entry on July 1 and the adjusting entry on December 31.

(LO 4, 5) **BE3-4** Using the data in BE3-3, journalize the entry on July 1 and the adjusting entry on December 31 for Hindi Insurance Co. Hindi uses the accounts Unearned Insurance Revenue and Insurance Revenue.

(LO 4, 5) **BE3-5** Assume that on February 1, **Procter & Gamble (P&G)** paid $840,000 in advance for 2 years' insurance coverage. Prepare P&G's February 1 journal entry and the annual adjusting entry on June 30.

(LO 4, 5) **BE3-6** Mogilny Corporation owns a warehouse. On November 1, it rented storage space to a lessee (tenant) for 3 months for a total cash payment of $2,700 received in advance. Prepare Mogilny's November 1 journal entry and the December 31 annual adjusting entry.

(LO 4, 5) **BE3-7** Catherine Janeway Company's weekly payroll, paid on Fridays, totals $6,000. Employees work a 5-day week. Prepare Janeway's adjusting entry on Wednesday, December 31, and the journal entry to record the $6,000 cash payment on Friday, January 2.

(LO 5) **BE3-8** Included in Martinez Company's December 31 trial balance is a note receivable of $10,000. The note is a 4-month, 12% note dated October 1. Prepare Martinez's December 31 adjusting entry to record $300 of accrued interest, and the February 1 journal entry to record receipt of $10,400 from the borrower.

(LO 5) **BE3-9** Prepare the following adjusting entries at August 31 for **Walgreens**.

    (a) Interest on notes payable of $400 is accrued.
    (b) Fees earned but unbilled total $1,400.
    (c) Salaries earned by employees of $700 have not been recorded.
    (d) Bad debt expense for year is $900.

Use the following account titles: Service Revenue, Accounts Receivable, Interest Expense, Interest Payable, Salaries Expense, Salaries Payable, Allowance for Doubtful Accounts, and Bad Debt Expense.

(LO 5) **BE3-10** At the end of its first year of operations, the trial balance of Rafael Company shows Equipment $30,000 and zero balances in Accumulated Depreciation—Equipment and Depreciation Expense. Depreciation for the year is estimated to be $3,000. Prepare the adjusting entry for depreciation at December 31, and indicate the balance sheet presentation for the equipment at December 31.

(LO 8) **BE3-11** Willis Corporation has beginning inventory $81,000; Purchases $540,000; Freight-in $16,200; Purchase Returns $5,800; Purchase Discounts $5,000; and ending inventory $70,200. Compute cost of goods sold.

(LO 7) **BE3-12** Karen Sepaniak has year-end account balances of Sales $828,900; Interest Revenue $13,500; Cost of Goods Sold $556,200; Operating Expenses $189,000; Income Tax Expense $35,100; and Dividends $18,900. Prepare the year-end closing entries.

(LO 9) ***BE3-13** Smith Company had cash receipts from customers in 2007 of $152,000. Cash payments for operating expenses were $97,000. Smith has determined that at January 1, accounts receivable was $13,000, and prepaid expenses were $17,500. At December 31, accounts receivable was $18,600, and prepaid expenses were $23,200. Compute (a) service revenue and (b) operating expenses.

(LO 10) ***BE3-14** Assume that **Best Buy** made a December 31 adjusting entry to debit Salaries Expense and credit Salaries Payable for $3,600 for one of its departments. On January 2, Best Buy paid the weekly payroll of $6,000. Prepare Best Buy's (a) January 1 reversing entry; (b) January 2 entry (assuming the reversing entry was prepared); and (c) January 2 entry (assuming the reversing entry was not prepared).

EXERCISES

(LO 4) **E3-1** **(Transaction Analysis—Service Company)** Beverly Crusher is a licensed CPA. During the first month of operations of her business (a sole proprietorship), the following events and transactions occurred.

April	2	Invested $32,000 cash and equipment valued at $14,000 in the business.
	2	Hired a secretary-receptionist at a salary of $290 per week payable monthly.
	3	Purchased supplies on account $700. (Debit an asset account.)
	7	Paid office rent of $600 for the month.
	11	Completed a tax assignment and billed client $1,100 for services rendered. (Use Service Revenue account.)
	12	Received $3,200 advance on a management consulting engagement.
	17	Received cash of $2,300 for services completed for Ferengi Co.
	21	Paid insurance expense $110.
	30	Paid secretary-receptionist $1,160 for the month.
	30	A count of supplies indicated that $120 of supplies had been used.
	30	Purchased a new computer for $6,100 with personal funds. (The computer will be used exclusively for business purposes.)

Instructions

Journalize the transactions in the general journal. (Omit explanations.)

(LO 4) **E3-2** **(Corrected Trial Balance)** The trial balance of Wanda Landowska Company (shown on the next page) does not balance. Your review of the ledger reveals the following: (a) Each account had a normal balance. (b) The debit footings in Prepaid Insurance, Accounts Payable, and Property Tax Expense were each understated $100. (c) A transposition error was made in Accounts Receivable and Service Revenue; the correct balances for Accounts Receivable and Service Revenue are $2,750 and $6,690, respectively. (d) A debit posting to Advertising Expense of $300 was omitted. (e) A $1,500 cash drawing by the owner was debited to Wanda Landowska, Capital, and credited to Cash.

WANDA LANDOWSKA COMPANY
TRIAL BALANCE
APRIL 30, 2007

	Debit	Credit
Cash	$ 4,800	
Accounts Receivable	2,570	
Prepaid Insurance	700	
Equipment		$ 8,000
Accounts Payable		4,500
Property Tax Payable	560	
Wanda Landowska, Capital		11,200
Service Revenue	6,960	
Salaries Expense	4,200	
Advertising Expense	1,100	
Property Tax Expense		800
	$20,890	$24,500

Instructions

Prepare a correct trial balance.

(LO 4)   **E3-3**   **(Corrected Trial Balance)**   The trial balance of Blues Traveler Corporation does not balance.

BLUES TRAVELER CORPORATION
TRIAL BALANCE
APRIL 30, 2007

	Debit	Credit
Cash	$ 5,912	
Accounts Receivable	5,240	
Supplies on Hand	2,967	
Furniture and Equipment	6,100	
Accounts Payable		$ 7,044
Common Stock		8,000
Retained Earnings		2,000
Service Revenue		5,200
Office Expense	4,320	
	$24,539	$22,244

An examination of the ledger shows these errors.

1. Cash received from a customer on account was recorded (both debit and credit) as $1,380 instead of $1,830.
2. The purchase on account of a computer costing $3,200 was recorded as a debit to Office Expense and a credit to Accounts Payable.
3. Services were performed on account for a client, $2,250, for which Accounts Receivable was debited $2,250 and Service Revenue was credited $225.
4. A payment of $95 for telephone charges was entered as a debit to Office Expenses and a debit to Cash.
5. The Service Revenue account was totaled at $5,200 instead of $5,280.

Instructions

From this information prepare a corrected trial balance.

(LO 4)   **E3-4**   **(Corrected Trial Balance)**   The trial balance of Watteau Co. (shown on the next page) does not balance.

WATTEAU CO.
TRIAL BALANCE
JUNE 30, 2007

	Debit	Credit
Cash		$ 2,870
Accounts Receivable	$ 3,231	
Supplies	800	
Equipment	3,800	
Accounts Payable		2,666
Unearned Service Revenue	1,200	
Common Stock		6,000
Retained Earnings		3,000
Service Revenue		2,380
Wages Expense	3,400	
Office Expense	940	
	$13,371	$16,916

Each of the listed accounts should have a normal balance per the general ledger. An examination of the ledger and journal reveals the following errors.

1. Cash received from a customer on account was debited for $570, and Accounts Receivable was credited for the same amount. The actual collection was for $750.
2. The purchase of a computer printer on account for $500 was recorded as a debit to Supplies for $500 and a credit to Accounts Payable for $500.
3. Services were performed on account for a client for $890. Accounts Receivable was debited for $890 and Service Revenue was credited for $89.
4. A payment of $65 for telephone charges was recorded as a debit to Office Expense for $65 and a debit to Cash for $65.
5. When the Unearned Service Revenue account was reviewed, it was found that $325 of the balance was earned prior to June 30.
6. A debit posting to Wages Expense of $670 was omitted.
7. A payment on account for $206 was credited to Cash for $206 and credited to Accounts Payable for $260.
8. A dividend of $575 was debited to Wages Expense for $575 and credited to Cash for $575.

Instructions
Prepare a correct trial balance. (*Note:* It may be necessary to add one or more accounts to the trial balance.)

(LO 5) **E3-5 (Adjusting Entries)** The ledger of Duggan Rental Agency on March 31 of the current year includes the following selected accounts before adjusting entries have been prepared.

	Debit	Credit
Prepaid Insurance	$ 3,600	
Supplies	2,800	
Equipment	25,000	
Accumulated Depreciation—Equipment		$ 8,400
Notes Payable		20,000
Unearned Rent Revenue		9,300
Rent Revenue		60,000
Interest Expense	–0–	
Wage Expense	14,000	

An analysis of the accounts shows the following.

1. The equipment depreciates $250 per month.
2. One-third of the unearned rent was earned during the quarter.
3. Interest of $500 is accrued on the notes payable.
4. Supplies on hand total $850.
5. Insurance expires at the rate of $300 per month.

Instructions
Prepare the adjusting entries at March 31, assuming that adjusting entries are made quarterly. Additional accounts are: Depreciation Expense; Insurance Expense; Interest Payable; and Supplies Expense. (Omit explanations.)

(LO 5)   **E3-6**   **(Adjusting Entries)**   Karen Weller, D.D.S., opened a dental practice on January 1, 2007. During the first month of operations the following transactions occurred.

1. Performed services for patients who had dental plan insurance. At January 31, $750 of such services was earned but not yet billed to the insurance companies.
2. Utility expenses incurred but not paid prior to January 31 totaled $520.
3. Purchased dental equipment on January 1 for $80,000, paying $20,000 in cash and signing a $60,000, 3-year note payable. The equipment depreciates $400 per month. Interest is $500 per month.
4. Purchased a one-year malpractice insurance policy on January 1 for $12,000.
5. Purchased $1,600 of dental supplies. On January 31, determined that $500 of supplies were on hand.

Instructions

Prepare the adjusting entries on January 31. (Omit explanations.) Account titles are: Accumulated Depreciation—Dental Equipment; Depreciation Expense; Service Revenue; Accounts Receivable; Insurance Expense; Interest Expense; Interest Payable; Prepaid Insurance; Supplies; Supplies Expense; Utilities Expense; and Utilities Payable.

(LO 5)   **E3-7**   **(Analyze Adjusted Data)**   A partial adjusted trial balance of Piper Company at January 31, 2007, shows the following.

PIPER COMPANY ADJUSTED TRIAL BALANCE JANUARY 31, 2007		
	Debit	Credit
Supplies	$ 700	
Prepaid Insurance	2,400	
Salaries Payable		$ 800
Unearned Revenue		750
Supplies Expense	950	
Insurance Expense	400	
Salaries Expense	1,800	
Service Revenue		2,000

Instructions

Answer the following questions, assuming the year begins January 1.

(a) If the amount in Supplies Expense is the January 31 adjusting entry, and $850 of supplies was purchased in January, what was the balance in Supplies on January 1?

(b) If the amount in Insurance Expense is the January 31 adjusting entry, and the original insurance premium was for one year, what was the total premium and when was the policy purchased?

(c) If $2,500 of salaries was paid in January, what was the balance in Salaries Payable at December 31, 2006?

(d) If $1,600 was received in January for services performed in January, what was the balance in Unearned Revenue at December 31, 2006?

(LO 5)   **E3-8**   **(Adjusting Entries)**   Andy Roddick is the new owner of Ace Computer Services. At the end of August 2007, his first month of ownership, Roddick is trying to prepare monthly financial statements. Below is some information related to unrecorded expenses that the business incurred during August.

1. At August 31, Roddick owed his employees $1,900 in wages that will be paid on September 1.
2. At the end of the month he had not yet received the month's utility bill. Based on past experience, he estimated the bill would be approximately $600.
3. On August 1, Roddick borrowed $30,000 from a local bank on a 15-year mortgage. The annual interest rate is 8%.
4. A telephone bill in the amount of $117 covering August charges is unpaid at August 31.

Instructions

Prepare the adjusting journal entries as of August 31, 2007, suggested by the information above.

(LO 5) **E3-9** **(Adjusting Entries)** Selected accounts of Urdu Company are shown below.

Supplies			
Beg. Bal.	800	10/31	470

Accounts Receivable		
10/17	2,400	
10/31	1,650	

Salaries Expense		
10/15	800	
10/31	600	

Salaries Payable		
	10/31	600

Unearned Service Revenue			
10/31	400	10/20	650

Supplies Expense	
10/31	470

Service Revenue		
	10/17	2,400
	10/31	1,650
	10/31	400

Instructions

From an analysis of the T-accounts, reconstruct (a) the October transaction entries, and (b) the adjusting journal entries that were made on October 31, 2007. Prepare explanations for each journal entry.

(LO 5) **E3-10** **(Adjusting Entries)** Greco Resort opened for business on June 1 with eight air-conditioned units. Its trial balance on August 31 is as follows.

GRECO RESORT TRIAL BALANCE AUGUST 31, 2007		
	Debit	Credit
Cash	$ 19,600	
Prepaid Insurance	4,500	
Supplies	2,600	
Land	20,000	
Cottages	120,000	
Furniture	16,000	
Accounts Payable		$ 4,500
Unearned Rent Revenue		4,600
Mortgage Payable		60,000
Common Stock		91,000
Retained Earnings		9,000
Dividends	5,000	
Rent Revenue		76,200
Salaries Expense	44,800	
Utilities Expense	9,200	
Repair Expense	3,600	
	$245,300	$245,300

Other data:

1. The balance in prepaid insurance is a one-year premium paid on June 1, 2007.
2. An inventory count on August 31 shows $450 of supplies on hand.
3. Annual depreciation rates are cottages (4%) and furniture (10%). Salvage value is estimated to be 10% of cost.
4. Unearned Rent Revenue of $3,800 was earned prior to August 31.
5. Salaries of $375 were unpaid at August 31.
6. Rentals of $800 were due from tenants at August 31.
7. The mortgage interest rate is 8% per year.

Instructions

(a) Journalize the adjusting entries on August 31 for the 3-month period June 1–August 31. (Omit explanations.)

(b) Prepare an adjusted trial balance on August 31.

(LO 6) **E3-11 (Prepare Financial Statements)** The adjusted trial balance of Anderson Cooper Co. as of December 31, 2007, contains the following.

ANDERSON COOPER CO.
ADJUSTED TRIAL BALANCE
DECEMBER 31, 2007

Account Titles	Dr.	Cr.
Cash	$19,472	
Accounts Receivable	6,920	
Prepaid Rent	2,280	
Equipment	18,050	
Accumulated Depreciation		$ 4,895
Notes Payable		5,700
Accounts Payable		5,472
Common Stock		20,000
Retained Earnings		11,310
Dividends	3,000	
Service Revenue		11,590
Salaries Expense	6,840	
Rent Expense	2,260	
Depreciation Expense	145	
Interest Expense	83	
Interest Payable		83
	$59,050	$59,050

Instructions

(a) Prepare an income statement.

(b) Prepare a statement of retained earnings.

(c) Prepare a classified balance sheet.

(LO 6) **E3-12 (Prepare Financial Statements)** Santo Design Agency was founded by Thomas Grant in January 2003. Presented below is the adjusted trial balance as of December 31, 2007.

SANTO DESIGN AGENCY
ADJUSTED TRIAL BALANCE
DECEMBER 31, 2007

	Dr.	Cr.
Cash	$ 11,000	
Accounts Receivable	21,500	
Art Supplies	5,000	
Prepaid Insurance	2,500	
Printing Equipment	60,000	
Accumulated Depreciation		$ 35,000
Accounts Payable		5,000
Interest Payable		150
Notes Payable		5,000
Unearned Advertising Revenue		5,600
Salaries Payable		1,300
Common Stock		10,000
Retained Earnings		3,500
Advertising Revenue		61,500
Salaries Expense	11,300	
Insurance Expense	850	
Interest Expense	500	
Depreciation Expense	7,000	
Art Supplies Expense	3,400	
Rent Expense	4,000	
	$127,050	$127,050

Instructions

(a) Prepare an income statement and a statement of retained earnings for the year ending December 31, 2007, and an unclassified balance sheet at December 31.

(b) Answer the following questions.

(1) If the note has been outstanding 6 months, what is the annual interest rate on that note?

(2) If the company paid $17,500 in salaries in 2007, what was the balance in Salaries Payable on December 31, 2006?

(LO 7) **E3-13** **(Closing Entries)** The adjusted trial balance of Lopez Company shows the following data pertaining to sales at the end of its fiscal year, October 31, 2007: Sales $800,000, Freight-out $12,000, Sales Returns and Allowances $24,000, and Sales Discounts $15,000.

Instructions

(a) Prepare the sales revenue section of the income statement.

(b) Prepare separate closing entries for (1) sales and (2) the contra accounts to sales.

(LO 7) **E3-14** **(Closing Entries)** Presented below is information related to Gonzales Corporation for the month of January 2007.

Cost of goods sold	$208,000	Salary expense	$ 61,000
Freight-out	7,000	Sales discounts	8,000
Insurance expense	12,000	Sales returns and allowances	13,000
Rent expense	20,000	Sales	350,000

Instructions

Prepare the necessary closing entries.

(LO 8) **E3-15** **(Missing Amounts)** Presented below is financial information for two different companies.

	Alatorre Company	Eduardo Company
Sales	$90,000	(d)
Sales returns	(a)	$ 5,000
Net sales	81,000	95,000
Cost of goods sold	56,000	(e)
Gross profit	(b)	38,000
Operating expenses	15,000	23,000
Net income	(c)	15,000

Instructions

Compute the missing amounts.

(LO 8) **E3-16** **(Find Missing Amounts—Periodic Inventory)** Financial information is presented below for four different companies.

	Pamela's Cosmetics	Dean's Grocery	Anderson Wholesalers	Baywatch Supply Co.
Sales	$78,000	(c)	$144,000	$100,000
Sales returns	(a)	$ 5,000	12,000	9,000
Net sales	74,000	94,000	132,000	(g)
Beginning inventory	16,000	(d)	44,000	24,000
Purchases	88,000	100,000	(e)	85,000
Purchase returns	6,000	10,000	8,000	(h)
Ending inventory	(b)	48,000	30,000	28,000
Cost of goods sold	64,000	72,000	(f)	72,000
Gross profit	10,000	22,000	18,000	(i)

Instructions

Determine the missing amounts (a–i). Show all computations.

(LO 8) **E3-17** **(Cost of Goods Sold Section—Periodic Inventory)** The trial balance of the Neville Mariner Company at the end of its fiscal year, August 31, 2007, includes the following accounts: Merchandise Inventory $17,500; Purchases $149,400; Sales $200,000; Freight-in $4,000; Sales Returns and Allowances $4,000; Freight-out $1,000; and Purchase Returns and Allowances $2,000. The ending merchandise inventory is $25,000.

Instructions

Prepare a cost of goods sold section for the year ending August 31.

(LO 7) **E3-18** **(Closing Entries for a Corporation)** Presented on the next page are selected account balances for Homer Winslow Co. as of December 31, 2007.

Merchandise Inventory 12/31/07	$ 60,000	Cost of Goods Sold	$225,700
Common Stock	75,000	Selling Expenses	16,000
Retained Earnings	45,000	Administrative Expenses	38,000
Dividends	18,000	Income Tax Expense	30,000
Sales Returns and Allowances	12,000		
Sales Discounts	15,000		
Sales	410,000		

Instructions

Prepare closing entries for Homer Winslow Co. on December 31, 2007. (Omit explanations.)

(LO 4) **E3-19 (Transactions of a Corporation, Including Investment and Dividend)** Scratch Miniature Golf and Driving Range Inc. was opened on March 1 by Scott Verplank. The following selected events and transactions occurred during March.

Mar.	1	Invested $50,000 cash in the business in exchange for common stock.
	3	Purchased Michelle Wie's Golf Land for $38,000 cash. The price consists of land $10,000; building $22,000; and equipment $6,000. (Make one compound entry.)
	5	Advertised the opening of the driving range and miniature golf course, paying advertising expenses of $1,600.
	6	Paid cash $1,480 for a one-year insurance policy.
	10	Purchased golf equipment for $2,500 from Singh Company, payable in 30 days.
	18	Received golf fees of $1,200 in cash.
	25	Declared and paid a $500 cash dividend.
	30	Paid wages of $900.
	30	Paid Singh Company in full.
	31	Received $750 of fees in cash.

Scratch uses the following accounts: Cash; Prepaid Insurance; Land; Buildings; Equipment; Accounts Payable; Common Stock; Dividends; Service Revenue; Advertising Expense; and Wages Expense.

Instructions

Journalize the March transactions. (Provide explanations for the journal entries.)

(LO 9) *E3-20 **(Cash to Accrual Basis)** Jill Accardo, M.D., maintains the accounting records of Accardo Clinic on a cash basis. During 2007, Dr. Accardo collected $142,600 from her patients and paid $55,470 in expenses. At January 1, 2007, and December 31, 2007, she had accounts receivable, unearned service revenue, accrued expenses, and prepaid expenses as follows. (All long-lived assets are rented.)

	January 1, 2007	December 31, 2007
Accounts receivable	$9,250	$15,927
Unearned service revenue	2,840	4,111
Accrued expenses	3,435	2,108
Prepaid expenses	1,917	3,232

Instructions

Prepare a schedule that converts Dr. Accardo's "excess of cash collected over cash disbursed" for the year 2007 to net income on an accrual basis for the year 2007.

(LO 9) *E3-21 **(Cash and Accrual Basis)** Wayne Rogers Corp. maintains its financial records on the cash basis of accounting. Interested in securing a long-term loan from its regular bank, Wayne Rogers Corp. requests you as its independent CPA to convert its cash-basis income statement data to the accrual basis. You are provided with the following summarized data covering 2006, 2007, and 2008.

	2006	2007	2008
Cash receipts from sales:			
On 2006 sales	$295,000	$160,000	$30,000
On 2007 sales	–0–	355,000	90,000
On 2008 sales			408,000
Cash payments for expenses:			
On 2006 expenses	185,000	67,000	25,000
On 2007 expenses	40,000[a]	160,000	55,000
On 2008 expenses		45,000[b]	218,000

[a]Prepayments of 2007 expenses.
[b]Prepayments of 2008 expenses.

Instructions

(a) Using the data above, prepare abbreviated income statements for the years 2006 and 2007 on the cash basis.

(b) Using the data above, prepare abbreviated income statements for the years 2006 and 2007 on the accrual basis.

(LO 5, 10) *E3-22 **(Adjusting and Reversing Entries)** When the accounts of Daniel Barenboim Inc. are examined, the adjusting data listed below are uncovered on December 31, the end of an annual fiscal period.

1. The prepaid insurance account shows a debit of $5,280, representing the cost of a 2-year fire insurance policy dated August 1 of the current year.
2. On November 1, Rental Revenue was credited for $1,800, representing revenue from a subrental for a 3-month period beginning on that date.
3. Purchase of advertising materials for $800 during the year was recorded in the Advertising Expense account. On December 31, advertising materials of $290 are on hand.
4. Interest of $770 has accrued on notes payable.

Instructions
Prepare the following in general journal form.
(a) The adjusting entry for each item.
(b) The reversing entry for each item where appropriate.

(LO 11) *E3-23 **(Worksheet)** Presented below are selected accounts for Alvarez Company as reported in the worksheet at the end of May 2007.

Accounts	Adjusted Trial Balance		Income Statement		Balance Sheet	
	Dr.	Cr.	Dr.	Cr.	Dr.	Cr.
Cash	9,000					
Merchandise Inventory	80,000					
Sales		450,000				
Sales Returns and Allowances	10,000					
Sales Discounts	5,000					
Cost of Goods Sold	250,000					

Instructions
Complete the worksheet by extending amounts reported in the adjusted trial balance to the appropriate columns in the worksheet. Do not total individual columns.

(LO 11) *E3-24 **(Worksheet and Balance Sheet Presentation)** The adjusted trial balance for Ed Bradley Co. is presented in the following worksheet for the month ended April 30, 2007.

ED BRADLEY CO.
WORKSHEET (PARTIAL)
FOR THE MONTH ENDED APRIL 30, 2007

Account Titles	Adjusted Trial Balance		Income Statement		Balance Sheet	
	Dr.	Cr.	Dr.	Cr.	Dr.	Cr.
Cash	$19,472					
Accounts Receivable	6,920					
Prepaid Rent	2,280					
Equipment	18,050					
Accumulated Depreciation		$ 4,895				
Notes Payable		5,700				
Accounts Payable		5,472				
Bradley, Capital		34,960				
Bradley, Drawing	6,650					
Service Revenue		11,590				
Salaries Expense	6,840					
Rent Expense	2,260					
Depreciation Expense	145					
Interest Expense	83					
Interest Payable		83				

Instructions
Complete the worksheet and prepare a classified balance sheet.

(LO 11) *E3-25 (**Partial Worksheet Preparation**) Jurassic Park Co. prepares monthly financial statements from a worksheet. Selected portions of the January worksheet showed the following data.

JURASSIC PARK CO.						
WORKSHEET (PARTIAL)						
FOR THE MONTH ENDED JANUARY 31, 2007						
	Trial Balance		Adjustments		Adjusted Trial Balance	
Account Title	Dr.	Cr.	Dr.	Cr.	Dr.	Cr.
Supplies	3,256			(a) 1,500	1,756	
Accumulated Depreciation		6,682		(b) 257		6,939
Interest Payable		100		(c) 50		150
Supplies Expense			(a) 1,500		1,500	
Depreciation Expense			(b) 257		257	
Interest Expense			(c) 50		50	

During February no events occurred that affected these accounts, but at the end of February the following information was available.

(a) Supplies on hand	$715
(b) Monthly depreciation	$257
(c) Accrued interest	$ 50

Instructions
Reproduce the data that would appear in the February worksheet, and indicate the amounts that would be shown in the February income statement.

See the book's website, www.wiley.com/college/kieso, for Additional Exercises.

PROBLEMS

(LO 4, 6, 7) **P3-1 (Transactions, Financial Statements—Service Company)** Listed below are the transactions of Shigeki Muruyama, D.D.S., for the month of September.

Sept.	1	Muruyama begins practice as a dentist and invests $20,000 cash.
	2	Purchases furniture and dental equipment on account from Green Jacket Co. for $17,280.
	4	Pays rent for office space, $680 for the month.
	4	Employs a receptionist, Michael Bradley.
	5	Purchases dental supplies for cash, $942.
	8	Receives cash of $1,690 from patients for services performed.
	10	Pays miscellaneous office expenses, $430.
	14	Bills patients $5,120 for services performed.
	18	Pays Green Jacket Co. on account, $3,600.
	19	Withdraws $3,000 cash from the business for personal use.
	20	Receives $980 from patients on account.
	25	Bills patients $2,110 for services performed.
	30	Pays the following expenses in cash: office salaries $1,400; miscellaneous office expenses $85.
	30	Dental supplies used during September, $330.

Instructions
(a) Enter the transactions shown above in appropriate general ledger accounts. Use the following ledger accounts: Cash; Accounts Receivable; Supplies on Hand; Furniture and Equipment; Accumulated Depreciation; Accounts Payable; Shigeki Muruyama, Capital; Service Revenue; Rent Expense; Miscellaneous Office Expense; Office Salaries Expense; Supplies Expense; Depreciation Expense; and Income Summary. Allow 10 lines for the Cash and Income Summary accounts, and 5 lines for each of the other accounts needed. Record depreciation using a 5-year life on the furniture and equipment, the straight-line method, and no salvage value. Do not use a drawing account.

(b) Prepare a trial balance.

(c) Prepare an income statement, an unclassified balance sheet, and a statement of owner's equity.

(d) Close the ledger.

(e) Prepare a post-closing trial balance.

(LO 5, 6) **P3-2 (Adjusting Entries and Financial Statements)** Yount Advertising Agency was founded in January 2003. Presented below are adjusted and unadjusted trial balances as of December 31, 2007.

	Unadjusted		Adjusted	
	Dr.	Cr.	Dr.	Cr.
Cash	$ 11,000		$ 11,000	
Accounts Receivable	20,000		21,500	
Art Supplies	8,400		5,000	
Prepaid Insurance	3,350		2,500	
Printing Equipment	60,000		60,000	
Accumulated Depreciation		$ 28,000		$ 35,000
Accounts Payable		5,000		5,000
Interest Payable		–0–		150
Notes Payable		5,000		5,000
Unearned Advertising Revenue		7,000		5,600
Salaries Payable		–0–		1,300
Common Stock		10,000		10,000
Retained Earnings		3,500		3,500
Advertising Revenue		58,600		61,500
Salaries Expense	10,000		11,300	
Insurance Expense			850	
Interest Expense	350		500	
Depreciation Expense			7,000	
Art Supplies Expense			3,400	
Rent Expense	4,000		4,000	
	$117,100	$117,100	$127,050	$127,050

YOUNT ADVERTISING AGENCY
TRIAL BALANCE
DECEMBER 31, 2007

Instructions

(a) Journalize the annual adjusting entries that were made. (Omit explanations.)

(b) Prepare an income statement and a statement of retained earnings for the year ending December 31, 2007, and an unclassified balance sheet at December 31.

(c) Answer the following questions.

(1) If the note has been outstanding 3 months, what is the annual interest rate on that note?

(2) If the company paid $13,500 in salaries in 2007, what was the balance in Salaries Payable on December 31, 2006?

(LO 5) **P3-3 (Adjusting Entries)** A review of the ledger of Oklahoma Company at December 31, 2007, produces the following data pertaining to the preparation of annual adjusting entries.

1. Salaries Payable $0. There are eight salaried employees. Salaries are paid every Friday for the current week. Five employees receive a salary of $700 each per week, and three employees earn $500 each per week. December 31 is a Tuesday. Employees do not work weekends. All employees worked the last 2 days of December.

2. Unearned Rent Revenue $369,000. The company began subleasing office space in its new building on November 1. Each tenant is required to make a $5,000 security deposit that is not refundable until occupancy is terminated. At December 31, the company had the following rental contracts that are paid in full for the entire term of the lease.

Date	Term (in months)	Monthly Rent	Number of Leases
Nov. 1	6	$4,000	5
Dec. 1	6	$8,500	4

3. Prepaid Advertising $13,200. This balance consists of payments on two advertising contracts. The contracts provide for monthly advertising in two trade magazines. The terms of the contracts are as shown at the top of page 117.

Contract	Date	Amount	Number of Magazine Issues
A650	May 1	$6,000	12
B974	Oct. 1	7,200	24

The first advertisement runs in the month in which the contract is signed.

4. Notes Payable $80,000. This balance consists of a note for one year at an annual interest rate of 12%, dated June 1.

Instructions

Prepare the adjusting entries at December 31, 2007. (Show all computations).

(LO 4, 5, 6, 7) **P3-4 (Financial Statements, Adjusting and Closing Entries)** The trial balance of Daphne Main Fashion Center contained the following accounts at November 30, the end of the company's fiscal year.

DAPHNE MAIN FASHION CENTER
TRIAL BALANCE
NOVEMBER 30, 2007

	Debit	Credit
Cash	$ 26,700	
Accounts Receivable	33,700	
Merchandise Inventory	45,000	
Store Supplies	5,500	
Store Equipment	85,000	
Accumulated Depreciation—Store Equipment		$ 18,000
Delivery Equipment	48,000	
Accumulated Depreciation—Delivery Equipment		6,000
Notes Payable		51,000
Accounts Payable		48,500
Common Stock		90,000
Retained Earnings		8,000
Sales		757,200
Sales Returns and Allowances	4,200	
Cost of Goods Sold	497,400	
Salaries Expense	140,000	
Advertising Expense	26,400	
Utilities Expense	14,000	
Repair Expense	12,100	
Delivery Expense	16,700	
Rent Expense	24,000	
	$978,700	$978,700

Adjustment data:

1. Store supplies on hand totaled $3,500.
2. Depreciation is $9,000 on the store equipment and $7,000 on the delivery equipment.
3. Interest of $11,000 is accrued on notes payable at November 30.

Other data:

1. Salaries expense is 70% selling and 30% administrative.
2. Rent expense and utilities expense are 80% selling and 20% administrative.
3. $30,000 of notes payable are due for payment next year.
4. Repair expense is 100% administrative.

Instructions

(a) Journalize the adjusting entries.
(b) Prepare an adjusted trial balance.
(c) Prepare a multiple-step income statement and retained earnings statement for the year and a classified balance sheet as of November 30, 2007.
(d) Journalize the closing entries.
(e) Prepare a post-closing trial balance.

(LO 5) **P3-5 (Adjusting Entries)** The accounts listed on the next page appeared in the December 31 trial balance of the Jane Alexander Theater.

	Debit	Credit
Equipment	$192,000	
Accumulated Depreciation—Equipment		$ 60,000
Notes Payable		90,000
Admissions Revenue		380,000
Advertising Expense	13,680	
Salaries Expense	57,600	
Interest Expense	1,400	

Instructions

(a) From the account balances listed above and the information given below, prepare the annual adjusting entries necessary on December 31. (Omit explanations.)

    (1) The equipment has an estimated life of 16 years and a salvage value of $40,000 at the end of that time. (Use straight-line method.)

    (2) The note payable is a 90-day note given to the bank October 20 and bearing interest at 10%. (Use 360 days for denominator.)

    (3) In December 2,000 coupon admission books were sold at $25 each. They could be used for admission any time after January 1.

    (4) Advertising expense paid in advance and included in Advertising Expense $1,100.

    (5) Salaries accrued but unpaid $4,700.

(b) What amounts should be shown for each of the following on the income statement for the year?

    (1) Interest expense.   (3) Advertising expense.

    (2) Admissions revenue.   (4) Salaries expense.

(LO 5, 6) **P3-6** **(Adjusting Entries and Financial Statements)** Presented below are the trial balance and the other information related to Carlos Beltran, a consulting engineer.

CARLOS BELTRAN, CONSULTING ENGINEER
TRIAL BALANCE
DECEMBER 31, 2007

	Debit	Credit
Cash	$ 31,500	
Accounts Receivable	49,600	
Allowance for Doubtful Accounts		$ 750
Engineering Supplies Inventory	1,960	
Unexpired Insurance	1,100	
Furniture and Equipment	25,000	
Accumulated Depreciation—Furniture and Equipment		6,250
Notes Payable		7,200
Carlos Beltran, Capital		35,010
Service Revenue		100,000
Rent Expense	9,750	
Office Salaries Expense	28,500	
Heat, Light, and Water Expense	1,080	
Miscellaneous Office Expense	720	
	$149,210	$149,210

---

1. Fees received in advance from clients $6,900.
2. Services performed for clients that were not recorded by December 31, $4,900.
3. Bad debt expense for the year is $1,430.
4. Insurance expired during the year $480.
5. Furniture and equipment is being depreciated at $12\frac{1}{2}\%$ per year.
6. Carlos Beltran gave the bank a 90-day, 10% note for $7,200 on December 1, 2007.
7. Rent of the building is $750 per month. The rent for 2007 has been paid, as has that for January 2008.
8. Office salaries earned but unpaid December 31, 2007, $2,510.

Instructions

(a) From the trial balance and other information given, prepare annual adjusting entries as of December 31, 2007. (Omit explanations.)

(b) Prepare an income statement for 2007, a classified balance sheet, and a statement of owner's equity. Carlos Beltran withdrew $17,000 cash for personal use during the year.

(LO 5, 6) **P3-7** **(Adjusting Entries and Financial Statements)** Ana Alicia Advertising Corp. was founded in January 2003. Presented on the next page are the adjusted and unadjusted trial balances as of December 31, 2007.

ANA ALICIA ADVERTISING CORP.
TRIAL BALANCE
DECEMBER 31, 2007

	Unadjusted		Adjusted	
	Dr.	Cr.	Dr.	Cr.
Cash	$ 7,000		$ 7,000	
Accounts Receivable	19,000		22,000	
Art Supplies	8,500		5,500	
Prepaid Insurance	3,250		2,500	
Printing Equipment	60,000		60,000	
Accumulated Depreciation		$ 27,000		$ 33,750
Accounts Payable		5,000		5,000
Interest Payable				150
Notes Payable		5,000		5,000
Unearned Service Revenue		7,000		5,600
Salaries Payable				1,500
Common Stock		10,000		10,000
Retained Earnings		4,500		4,500
Service Revenue		58,600		63,000
Salaries Expense	10,000		11,500	
Insurance Expense			750	
Interest Expense	350		500	
Depreciation Expense			6,750	
Art Supplies Expense	5,000		8,000	
Rent Expense	4,000		4,000	
	$117,100	$117,100	$128,500	$128,500

Instructions

(a) Journalize the annual adjusting entries that were made. (Omit explanations.)

(b) Prepare an income statement and a statement of retained earnings for the year ending December 31, 2007, and an unclassified balance sheet at December 31, 2007.

(c) Answer the following questions.

(1) If the useful life of equipment is 8 years, what is the expected salvage value?

(2) If the note has been outstanding 3 months, what is the annual interest rate on that note?

(3) If the company paid $12,500 in salaries in 2007, what was the balance in Salaries Payable on December 31, 2006?

(LO 4, 5, 6, 7) ***P3-8 (Adjusting and Closing)** Following is the trial balance of the Platteville Golf Club, Inc. as of December 31. The books are closed annually on December 31.

PLATTEVILLE GOLF CLUB, INC.
TRIAL BALANCE
DECEMBER 31

	Debit	Credit
Cash	$ 15,000	
Accounts Receivable	13,000	
Allowance for Doubtful Accounts		$ 1,100
Prepaid Insurance	9,000	
Land	350,000	
Buildings	120,000	
Accumulated Depreciation of Buildings		38,400
Equipment	150,000	
Accumulated Depreciation of Equipment		70,000
Common Stock		400,000
Retained Earnings		82,000
Dues Revenue		200,000
Greens Fee Revenue		8,100
Rental Revenue		15,400
Utilities Expense	54,000	
Salaries Expense	80,000	
Maintenance Expense	24,000	
	$815,000	$815,000

Instructions

(a) Enter the balances in ledger accounts. Allow five lines for each account.

(b) From the trial balance and the information given, prepare annual adjusting entries and post to the ledger accounts. (Omit explanations.)

    (1) The buildings have an estimated life of 25 years with no salvage value (straight-line method).

    (2) The equipment is depreciated at 10% per year.

    (3) Insurance expired during the year $3,500.

    (4) The rental revenue represents the amount received for 11 months for dining facilities. The December rent has not yet been received.

    (5) It is estimated that 15% of the accounts receivable will be uncollectible.

    (6) Salaries earned but not paid by December 31, $3,600.

    (7) Dues paid in advance by members $8,900.

(c) Prepare an adjusted trial balance.

(d) Prepare closing entries and post.

(LO 4, 5, 6, 7) ***P3-9 (Adjusting and Closing)** Presented below is the December 31 trial balance of Nancy Drew Boutique.

NANCY DREW BOUTIQUE
TRIAL BALANCE
DECEMBER 31

	Debit	Credit
Cash	$ 18,500	
Accounts Receivable	42,000	
Allowance for Doubtful Accounts		$ 700
Inventory, December 31	80,000	
Prepaid Insurance	5,100	
Furniture and Equipment	84,000	
Accumulated Depreciation—Furniture and Equipment		35,000
Notes Payable		28,000
Common Stock		80,600
Retained Earnings		10,000
Sales		600,000
Cost of Goods Sold	398,000	
Sales Salaries Expense	50,000	
Advertising Expense	6,700	
Administrative Salaries Expense	65,000	
Office Expense	5,000	
	$754,300	$754,300

Instructions

(a) Construct T-accounts and enter the balances shown.

(b) Prepare adjusting journal entries for the following and post to the T-accounts. (Omit explanations.) Open additional T-accounts as necessary. (The books are closed yearly on December 31.)

    (1) Bad debts are estimated to be $1,400.

    (2) Furniture and equipment is depreciated based on a 6-year life (no salvage value).

    (3) Insurance expired during the year $2,550.

    (4) Interest accrued on notes payable $3,360.

    (5) Sales salaries earned but not paid $2,400.

    (6) Advertising paid in advance $700.

    (7) Office supplies on hand $1,500, charged to Office Expense when purchased.

(c) Prepare closing entries and post to the accounts.

(LO 9) ***P3-10 (Cash and Accrual Basis)** On January 1, 2007, Jill Monroe and Jenni Meno formed a computer sales and service enterprise in Soapsville, Arkansas, by investing $90,000 cash. The new company, Razorback Sales and Service, has the following transactions during January.

    1. Pays $6,000 in advance for 3 months' rent of office, showroom, and repair space.

    2. Purchases 40 personal computers at a cost of $1,500 each, 6 graphics computers at a cost of $3,000 each, and 25 printers at a cost of $450 each, paying cash upon delivery.

3. Sales, repair, and office employees earn $12,600 in salaries during January, of which $3,000 was still payable at the end of January.

4. Sells 30 personal computers at $2,550 each, 4 graphics computers for $4,500 each, and 15 printers for $750 each; $75,000 is received in cash in January, and $30,750 is sold on a deferred payment basis.

5. Other operating expenses of $8,400 are incurred and paid for during January; $2,000 of incurred expenses are payable at January 31.

Instructions

(a) Using the transaction data above, prepare (1) a cash-basis income statement, and (2) an accrual-basis income statement for the month of January.

(b) Using the transaction data above, prepare (1) a cash-basis balance sheet and (2) an accrual-basis balance sheet as of January 31, 2007.

(c) Identify the items in the cash basis financial statements that make cash-basis accounting inconsistent with the theory underlying the elements of financial statements.

(LO 5, 6, 7, 11) *P3-11 **(Worksheet, Balance Sheet, Adjusting and Closing Entries)** Noah's Ark has a fiscal year ending on September 30. Selected data from the September 30 work sheet are presented below.

	NOAH'S ARK **WORKSHEET** **FOR THE YEAR ENDED SEPTEMBER 30, 2007**			
	Trial Balance		Adjusted Trial Balance	
	Dr.	Cr.	Dr.	Cr.
Cash	37,400		37,400	
Supplies	18,600		1,200	
Prepaid Insurance	31,900		3,900	
Land	80,000		80,000	
Equipment	120,000		120,000	
Accumulated Depreciation		36,200		43,000
Accounts Payable		14,600		14,600
Unearned Admissions Revenue		2,700		1,700
Mortgage Payable		50,000		50,000
N. Y. Berge, Capital		109,700		109,700
N. Y. Berge, Drawing	14,000		14,000	
Admissions Revenue		278,500		279,500
Salaries Expense	109,000		109,000	
Repair Expense	30,500		30,500	
Advertising Expense	9,400		9,400	
Utilities Expense	16,900		16,900	
Property Taxes Expense	18,000		21,000	
Interest Expense	6,000		12,000	
Totals	491,700	491,700		
Insurance Expense ✓			28,000	
Supplies Expense ✓			17,400	
Interest Payable ✓				6,000
Depreciation Expense ✓			6,800	
Property Taxes Payable ✓				3,000
Totals			507,500	507,500

Instructions

(a) Prepare a complete worksheet.

(b) Prepare a classified balance sheet. (*Note:* $10,000 of the mortgage payable is due for payment in the next fiscal year.)

(c) Journalize the adjusting entries using the worksheet as a basis.

(d) Journalize the closing entries using the worksheet as a basis.

(e) Prepare a post-closing trial balance.

USING YOUR JUDGMENT

Financial Reporting Problem

P&G **The Procter & Gamble Company (P&G)**

The financial statements of P&G are presented in Appendix 5B or can be accessed on the KWW website.

Instructions

Refer to these financial statements and the accompanying notes to answer the following questions.

(a) What were P&G's total assets at June 30, 2004? At June 30, 2003?

(b) How much cash (and cash equivalents) did P&G have on June 30, 2004?

(c) What were P&G's research and development costs in 2002? In 2004?

(d) What were P&G's revenues in 2002? In 2004?

(e) Using P&G's financial statements and related notes, identify items that may result in adjusting entries for prepayments and accruals.

(f) What were the amounts of P&G's depreciation and amortization expense in 2002, 2003, and 2004?

Financial Statement Analysis Case

Kellogg Company

Kellogg Company has its headquarters in Battle Creek, Michigan. The company manufactures and sells ready-to-eat breakfast cereals and convenience foods including cookies, toaster pastries, and cereal bars. Selected data from Kellogg Company's 2003 annual report follows (dollar amounts in millions).

	2003	2002	2001
Sales	$8,811.50	$8,304.10	$7,548.40
Gross profit %	44.40	45.50	44.20
Operating profit	$1,544.10	$1,508.1	$1,167.9
Net cash flow less capital expenditures	$923.8	$746.4	$855.5
Net earnings	$787.1	$720.9	$473.6

In its 2003 annual report, Kellogg Company disclosed that its financial model is designed to achieve sustainable financial performance. To measure financial performance, Kellogg focuses on realistic targets related to sales, gross profit margin, earnings growth, and cash flow.

Instructions

(a) Compute the percentage change in sales, operating profit, net cash flow, and net earnings from year to year for the years presented.

(b) Evaluate Kellogg's performance. Which trend seems most favorable? Which trend seems least favorable? What are the implications of these trends for Kellogg's sustainable performance objectives? Explain.

Comparative Analysis Case

The Coca-Cola Company

 PEPSICO

The Coca-Cola Company and PepsiCo, Inc.

Instructions

Go to the KWW website and use information found there to answer the following questions related to The Coca-Cola Company and PepsiCo, Inc.

(a) Which company had the greater percentage increase in total assets from 2003 to 2004?

(b) Using the Selected Financial Data section of these two companies, determine their 5-year compound growth rates related to net sales and income from continuing operations.

(c) Which company had more depreciation and amortization expense for 2004? Provide a rationale as to why there is a difference in these amounts between the two companies.

Research Case

The Enterprise Standard Industrial Classification (SIC) coding scheme, a published classification of firms into separate industries, is commonly used in practice. SIC codes permit identification of company activities on three levels of detail. Two-digit codes designate a "major group," three-digit codes designate an "industry group," and four-digit codes identify a specific "industry."

Instructions

Use the *Standard Industrial Classification Manual* (published by the U.S. Government's Office of Management and Budget in 1987) to answer the following questions.

(a) On what basis are SIC codes assigned to companies?

(b) Identify the major group/industry group/industry represented by the following codes.

12	3571	75
271	7033	872

(c) Identify the SIC code for the following industries.

(1) Golfing equipment—manufacturing.
(2) Worm farms.
(3) Felt tip markers—manufacturing.
(4) Household appliance stores, electric or gas—retail.
(5) Advertising agencies.

(d) You are interested in examining several companies in the passenger airline industry. Determine the appropriate two-, three-, and four-digit SIC codes. Use *Wards Business Directory of U.S. Private and Public Companies (Vol. 5)* to compile a list of the five largest parent companies (by total sales) in the industry. *Note:* If Wards is not available, alternative sources include *Standard & Poor's Register of Corporations, Directors, and Executives, Standard & Poor's Industry Surveys,* and the Dun & Bradstreet *Million Dollar Directory.*

Professional Research: Financial Accounting and Reporting

Recording transactions in the accounting system requires knowledge of the important characteristics of the elements of financial statements, such as assets and liabilities. In addition, accountants must understand the inherent uncertainty in accounting measures and distinctions between related accounting concepts that are important in evaluating the effects of transactions on the financial statements.

Instructions

Using the **Financial Accounting Research System (FARS)**, provide explanations for the following items. (Provide text strings used in your search.)

(a) The three essential characteristics of assets.

(b) The three essential characteristics of liabilities.

(c) Uncertainty and its effect on financial statements.

(d) The difference between realization and recognition.

Professional Simulation

In this simulation you are asked to address questions regarding the accounting information system. Prepare responses to all parts.

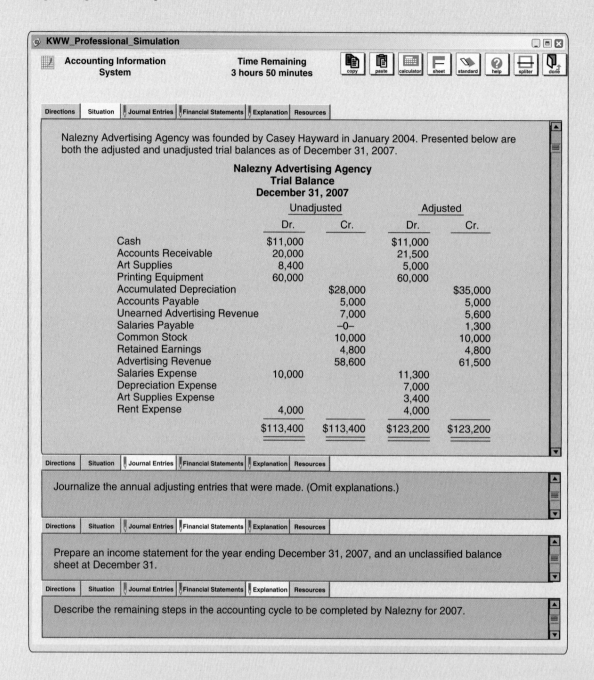

KWW_Professional_Simulation

Accounting Information System

Time Remaining 3 hours 50 minutes

copy | paste | calculator | sheet | standard | help | splitter | done

Directions | Situation | Journal Entries | Financial Statements | Explanation | Resources

Nalezny Advertising Agency was founded by Casey Hayward in January 2004. Presented below are both the adjusted and unadjusted trial balances as of December 31, 2007.

Nalezny Advertising Agency
Trial Balance
December 31, 2007

	Unadjusted Dr.	Unadjusted Cr.	Adjusted Dr.	Adjusted Cr.
Cash	$11,000		$11,000	
Accounts Receivable	20,000		21,500	
Art Supplies	8,400		5,000	
Printing Equipment	60,000		60,000	
Accumulated Depreciation		$28,000		$35,000
Accounts Payable		5,000		5,000
Unearned Advertising Revenue		7,000		5,600
Salaries Payable		–0–		1,300
Common Stock		10,000		10,000
Retained Earnings		4,800		4,800
Advertising Revenue		58,600		61,500
Salaries Expense	10,000		11,300	
Depreciation Expense			7,000	
Art Supplies Expense			3,400	
Rent Expense	4,000		4,000	
	$113,400	$113,400	$123,200	$123,200

Directions | Situation | Journal Entries | Financial Statements | Explanation | Resources

Journalize the annual adjusting entries that were made. (Omit explanations.)

Directions | Situation | Journal Entries | Financial Statements | Explanation | Resources

Prepare an income statement for the year ending December 31, 2007, and an unclassified balance sheet at December 31.

Directions | Situation | Journal Entries | Financial Statements | Explanation | Resources

Describe the remaining steps in the accounting cycle to be completed by Nalezny for 2007.

Remember to check the book's companion website to find additional resources for this chapter.

wiley.com/college/kieso

INCOME STATEMENT AND RELATED INFORMATION

Which Income Number?

Recently, 40 percent of the companies in the Standards and Poor's 500 provided investors a choice in reported income numbers. In addition to income measured according to generally accepted accounting principles (GAAP), companies also reported an income measure that they adjusted for certain items. Companies make these adjustments because they believe the items are not representative of operating results. In some cases these adjustments are quite large. As we show in the following table, in a recent quarter the reporting of such "pro forma" income measures put a very different spin on operating results. In some cases (**JDS-Uniphase**, **PMC-Sierra**, and **Yahoo**), a loss under GAAP measurement rules became an operating profit after pro forma adjustments.

Company	Earnings Per Share Pro Forma	GAAP		Company	Earnings Per Share Pro Forma	GAAP
JDS-Uniphase	$0.14	−$1.13		**PMC-Sierra**	0.02	−0.38
Checkfree	0.04	−1.17		**Qualcomm**	0.29	0.18
Amazon.com	−0.22	−0.66		**Yahoo**	0.01	−0.02

Characteristic of pro forma reporting practices is Amazon.com. It adjusted for items such as stock-based compensation, amortization of goodwill and intangibles, impairment charges, and equity in losses of investees. All of these adjustments make pro forma earnings higher than GAAP income. In its earnings announcement, Amazon defended its pro forma reporting, saying that it gives better insight into the fundamental operations of the business.

So what's wrong with focusing investors on the fundamentals of the business? According to Ed Jenkins, former chair of the FASB, one problem is that there are no standards for the reporting of pro forma numbers. As a result, investors will have a hard time comparing Amazon's pro forma measure with that reported by another company, which has a different idea of what is fundamental to its business. Also, there is concern that companies may use pro forma reporting to deflect investor attention from bad news. In response, the SEC issued Regulation G, which requires companies to reconcile non-GAAP financial measures to GAAP. This regulation provides investors with a roadmap to analyze adjustments companies make to their GAAP numbers to arrive at pro forma results.[1]

---

[1]Story adapted from David Henry, "The Numbers Game," *Business Week* (May 14, 2001), pp. 100–110. See also SEC Regulation G, "Conditions for Use of Non-GAAP Financial Measures," *Release No. 33-8176* (March 28, 2003).

Learning Objectives

After studying this chapter, you should be able to:

1 Understand the uses and limitations of an income statement.

2 Prepare a single-step income statement.

3 Prepare a multiple-step income statement.

4 Explain how to report irregular items.

5 Explain intraperiod tax allocation.

6 Identify where to report earnings per share information.

7 Prepare a retained earnings statement.

8 Explain how to report other comprehensive income.

As we indicate in the opening story, investors need complete and comparable information on income and its components to assess company profitability correctly. In this chapter we examine the many different types of revenues, expenses, gains, and losses that affect the income statement and related information, as follows.

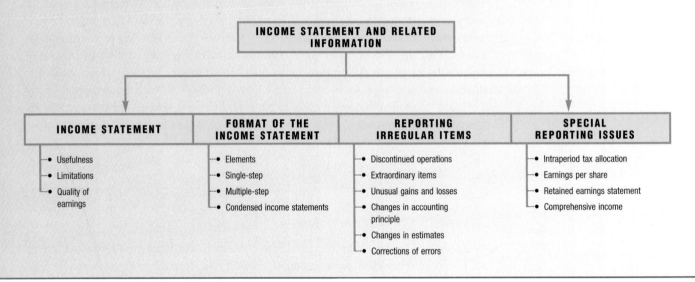

INCOME STATEMENT

The **income statement** is the report that measures the success of company operations for a given period of time. (It is also often called the statement of income or statement of earnings.[2]) The business and investment community uses the income statement to determine profitability, investment value, and creditworthiness. It provides investors and creditors with information that helps them predict the **amounts**, **timing**, **and uncertainty of future cash flows**.

Usefulness of the Income Statement

The income statement helps users of financial statements predict future cash flows in a number of ways. For example, investors and creditors use the income statement information to:

1 **Evaluate the past performance of the company.** Examining revenues and expenses indicates how the company performed and allows comparison of its performance to its competitors. For example, analysts use the income data provided by **Daimler-Chrysler** to compare its performance to that of **Ford**.

2 **Provide a basis for predicting future performance.** Information about past performance helps to determine important trends that, if continued, provide

Which company did better last year?

---

[2]*Accounting Trends and Techniques—2004* (New York: AICPA) indicates that out of 600 companies surveyed, 242 used the term *income* in the title of income statements, 261 used *operations* (many companies had net losses), and 90 used *earnings*.

information about future performance. For example, **General Electric** at one time reported consistent increases in revenues. Obviously past success does not necessarily translate into future success. However, analysts can better predict future revenues, and hence earnings and cash flows, if a reasonable correlation exists between past and future performance.

3 **Help assess the risk or uncertainty of achieving future cash flows.** Information on the various components of income—revenues, expenses, gains, and losses—highlights the relationships among them. It also helps to assess the risk of not achieving a particular level of cash flows in the future. For example, investors and creditors often segregate **IBM**'s operating performance from other nonrecurring sources of income because IBM primarily generates revenues and cash through its operations. Thus, results from continuing operations usually have greater significance for predicting future performance than do results from nonrecurring activities and events.

In summary, information in the income statement—revenues, expenses, gains, and losses—helps users evaluate past performance. It also provides insights into the likelihood of achieving a particular level of cash flows in the future.

Limitations of the Income Statement

Because net income is an estimate and reflects a number of assumptions, income statement users need to be aware of certain limitations associated with its information. Some of these limitations include:

1 **Companies omit items from the income statement that they cannot measure reliably.** Current practice prohibits recognition of certain items from the determination of income even though the effects of these items can arguably affect the company's performance. For example, a company may not record unrealized gains and losses on certain investment securities in income when there is uncertainty that it will ever realize the changes in value. In addition, more and more companies, like **Cisco Systems** and **Microsoft**, experience increases in value due to brand recognition, customer service, and product quality. A common framework for identifying and reporting these types of values is still lacking.

2 **Income numbers are affected by the accounting methods employed.** One company may depreciate its plant assets on an accelerated basis; another chooses straight-line depreciation. Assuming all other factors are equal, the first company will report lower income. In effect, we are comparing apples to oranges.

3 **Income measurement involves judgment.** For example, one company in good faith may estimate the useful life of an asset to be 20 years while another company uses a 15-year estimate for the same type of asset. Similarly, some companies may make optimistic estimates of future warranty returns and bad debt write-offs, which results in lower expense and higher income.

In summary, several limitations of the income statement reduce the usefulness of its information for predicting the amounts, timing, and uncertainty of future cash flows.

Quality of Earnings

So far, our discussion has highlighted the importance of information in the income statement for investment and credit decisions, including the evaluation of the company and its managers.[3] Companies try to meet or beat Wall Street expectations so that the

---

[3]In support of the usefulness of income information, accounting researchers have documented an association between the market prices of companies and reported income. See W. H. Beaver, "Perspectives on Recent Capital Markets Research," *The Accounting Review* (April 2002), pp. 453–474.

market price of their stock and the value of management's stock options increase. As a result, companies have incentives to manage income to meet earnings targets or to make earnings look less risky.

Recently, the SEC has expressed concern that the motivations to meet earnings targets may override good business practices. This erodes the quality of earnings and the quality of financial reporting. As indicated by one SEC chairman, "Managing may be giving way to manipulation; integrity may be losing out to illusion."[4] As a result, the SEC has started to take decisive action to prevent the practice of earnings management.

What is **earnings management**? It is often defined as the planned timing of revenues, expenses, gains, and losses to smooth out bumps in earnings. In most cases, companies use earnings management to increase income in the current year at the expense of income in future years. For example, they prematurely recognize sales (i.e., before earned) in order to boost earnings. As one commentator noted, ". . . it's like popping a cork in [opening] a bottle of wine before it is ready."

Companies also use earnings management to decrease current earnings in order to increase income in the future. The classic case is the use of "cookie jar" reserves. Companies establish these reserves by using unrealistic assumptions to estimate liabilities for such items as loan losses, restructuring charges, and warranty returns. The companies then reduce these reserves in the future to increase reported income in the future.

Such earnings management negatively affects the **quality of earnings** if it distorts the information in a way that is less useful for predicting future earnings and cash flows. Markets rely on trust. The bond between shareholders and the company must remain strong. Investors or others losing faith in the numbers reported in the financial statements will damage U.S. capital markets. As we mentioned in the opening story, we need heightened scrutiny of income measurement and reporting to ensure the quality of earnings and investors' confidence in the income statement.

WHAT DO THE NUMBERS MEAN?

MANAGE UP, MANAGE DOWN

Managing earnings up or down adversely affects the quality of earnings. For example, **W. R. Grace** managed earnings down by taking excess "cookie jar" reserves in good earnings years. During the early 1990s, Grace was growing fast, with profits increasing 30 percent annually. Analysts' targets had Grace growing 24 percent each year. Worried about meeting these growth expectations, Grace began stashing away excess profits in an all-purpose reserve (a "cookie jar"). In 1995, when profits fell below expectations, Grace wanted to reduce this reserve and so increase income. The SEC objected, noting this violated generally accepted accounting principles.

More recently, **MicroStrategy** managed earnings up by booking revenue for future software upgrades, even though it had not yet delivered them. And **Rent-Way, Inc.** managed its earnings up by understating some $65 million in expenses relating to such items as automobile maintenance and insurance payments.

Does the market value accounting quality? Apparently so: The stock of each of these companies took a beating in the marketplace when the earnings management practices came to light. For example, Rent-Way's stock price plummeted from above $25 per share to below $10 per share when it announced restatements for its improper expense accounting. So, whether managing earnings up or down, companies had better be prepared to pay the price for poor accounting quality.

---

[4]A. Levitt, "The Numbers Game." Remarks to NYU Center for Law and Business, September 28, 1998 (Securities and Exchange Commission, 1998).

FORMAT OF THE INCOME STATEMENT

Elements of the Income Statement

Net income results from revenue, expense, gain, and loss transactions. The income statement summarizes these transactions. This method of income measurement, the **transaction approach**, focuses on the income-related activities that have occurred during the period.[5] The statement can further classify income by customer, product line, or function or by operating and nonoperating, continuing and discontinued, and regular and irregular categories.[6] The following lists more formal definitions of income-related items, referred to as the major elements of the income statement.

ELEMENTS OF FINANCIAL STATEMENTS

REVENUES. Inflows or other enhancements of assets of an entity or settlements of its liabilities during a period from delivering or producing goods, rendering services, or other activities that constitute the entity's ongoing major or central operations.

EXPENSES. Outflows or other using-up of assets or incurrences of liabilities during a period from delivering or producing goods, rendering services, or carrying out other activities that constitute the entity's ongoing major or central operations.

GAINS. Increases in equity (net assets) from peripheral or incidental transactions of an entity except those that result from revenues or investments by owners.

LOSSES. Decreases in equity (net assets) from peripheral or incidental transactions of an entity except those that result from expenses or distributions to owners.[7]

Revenues take many forms, such as sales, fees, interest, dividends, and rents. Expenses also take many forms, such as cost of goods sold, depreciation, interest, rent, salaries and wages, and taxes. Gains and losses also are of many types, resulting from the sale of investments or plant assets, settlement of liabilities, write-offs of assets due to impairments or casualty.

The distinction between revenues and gains, and between expenses and losses, depend to a great extent on the typical activities of the company. For example, when **McDonald's** sells a hamburger, it records the selling price as revenue. However, when McDonald's sells land, it records any excess of the selling price over the book value as a gain. This difference in treatment results because the sale of the hamburger is part of McDonald's regular operations. The sale of land is not.

INTERNATIONAL INSIGHT

Companies in some nations prepare financial reporting on the same basis as tax returns. In such cases, companies have incentives to *minimize* reported income.

---

[5]The most common alternative to the transaction approach is the **capital maintenance approach** to income measurement. Under this approach, a company determines income for the period based on the change in equity, after adjusting for capital contributions (e.g., investments by owners) or distributions (e.g., dividends). The main drawback associated with the capital maintenance approach is that the components of income are not evident in its measurement. The Internal Revenue Service uses the capital maintenance approach to identify unreported income and refers to this approach as the "net worth check."

[6]The term "irregular" encompasses transactions and other events that are derived from developments outside the normal operations of the business.

[7]"Elements of Financial Statements," *Statement of Financial Accounting Concepts No. 6* (Stamford, Conn.: FASB, 1985), pars. 78–89.

We cannot overemphasize the importance of reporting these elements. Most decision makers find the *parts* of a financial statement to be more useful than the whole. As we indicated earlier, investors and creditors are interested in predicting the amounts, timing, and uncertainty of future income and cash flows. Having income statement elements shown in some detail and in comparison with prior years' data allows decision makers to better assess future income and cash flows.

Single-Step Income Statements

OBJECTIVE 2
Prepare a single-step income statement.

In reporting revenues, gains, expenses, and losses, companies often use a format known as the **single-step income statement**. The single-step statement consists of just two groupings: revenues and expenses. Expenses are deducted from revenues to arrive at net income or loss, hence the expression "single-step." Frequently companies report income tax separately as the last item before net income to indicate its relationship to income before income tax. Illustration 4-1 shows the single-step income statement of Dan Deines Company.

ILLUSTRATION 4-1
Single-Step Income
Statement

DAN DEINES COMPANY		
INCOME STATEMENT		
FOR THE YEAR ENDED DECEMBER 31, 2007		
Revenues		
Net sales	$2,972,413	
Dividend revenue	98,500	
Rental revenue	72,910	
Total revenues		3,143,823
Expenses		
Cost of goods sold	1,982,541	
Selling expenses	453,028	
Administrative expenses	350,771	
Interest expense	126,060	
Income tax expense	66,934	
Total expenses		2,979,334
Net income		$ 164,489
Earnings per common share		$1.74

Companies that use the single-step income statement in financial reporting typically do so because of its simplicity. In recent years, though, the multiple-step form has gained popularity.[8]

The primary advantage of the single-step format lies in its simple presentation and the absence of any implication that one type of revenue or expense item has priority over another. This format thus eliminates potential classification problems.

Multiple-Step Income Statements

OBJECTIVE 3
Prepare a multiple-step income statement.

Some contend that including other important revenue and expense classifications makes the income statement more useful. These further classifications include:

1 A separation of operating and nonoperating activities of the company. For example, companies often present income from operations followed by sections entitled "Other revenues and gains" and "Other expenses and losses." These other categories include such transactions as interest revenue and expense, gains or losses from sales of long-term assets, and dividends received.

---

[8]*Accounting Trends and Techniques—2004* (New York: AICPA). Of the 600 companies surveyed by the AICPA, 467 employed the multiple-step form, and 133 employed the single-step income statement format. This is a reversal from 1983, when 314 used the single-step form and 286 used the multiple-step form.

2 A classification of expenses by functions, such as merchandising (cost of goods sold), selling, and administration. This permits immediate comparison with costs of previous years and with other departments in the same year.

Companies use a **multiple-step income statement** to recognize these additional relationships. This statement separates operating transactions from nonoperating transactions, and matches costs and expenses with related revenues. It highlights certain intermediate components of income that analysts use to compute ratios for assessing the performance of the company.

Intermediate Components of the Income Statement

When a company uses a multiple-step income statement, it may prepare some or all of the following sections or subsections.

INCOME STATEMENT SECTIONS

1 OPERATING SECTION. A report of the revenues and expenses of the company's principal operations.
  (a) Sales or Revenue Section. A subsection presenting sales, discounts, allowances, returns, and other related information. Its purpose is to arrive at the net amount of sales revenue.
  (b) Cost of Goods Sold Section. A subsection that shows the cost of goods that were sold to produce the sales.
  (c) Selling Expenses. A subsection that lists expenses resulting from the company's efforts to make sales.
  (d) Administrative or General Expenses. A subsection reporting expenses of general administration.

2 NONOPERATING SECTION. A report of revenues and expenses resulting from secondary or auxiliary activities of the company. In addition, special gains and losses that are infrequent or unusual, but not both, are normally reported in this section. Generally these items break down into two main subsections:
  (a) Other Revenues and Gains. A list of the revenues earned or gains incurred, generally net of related expenses, from nonoperating transactions.
  (b) Other Expenses and Losses. A list of the expenses or losses incurred, generally net of any related incomes, from nonoperating transactions.

3 INCOME TAX. A short section reporting federal and state taxes levied on income from continuing operations.

4 DISCONTINUED OPERATIONS. Material gains or losses resulting from the disposition of a segment of the business.

5 EXTRAORDINARY ITEMS. Unusual and infrequent material gains and losses.

6 EARNINGS PER SHARE.

Although the content of the operating section is always the same, the organization of the material can differ. The breakdown above uses a **natural expense classification**. Manufacturing concerns and merchandising companies in the wholesale trade commonly use this. Another classification of operating expenses, recommended for retail stores, uses a **functional expense classification** of administrative, occupancy, publicity, buying, and selling expenses.

Usually, financial statements provided to external users have less detail than internal management reports. Internal reports include more expense categories—usually grouped along lines of responsibility. This detail allows top management to judge staff performance. Irregular transactions such as discontinued operations and extraordinary items are reported separately, following income from continuing operations.

Dan Deines Company's statement of income illustrates the multiple-step income statement. This statement, shown in Illustration 4-2, includes items 1, 2, 3, and 6

ILLUSTRATION 4-2
Multiple-Step Income
Statement

*Income Statements
for Real Companies*

DAN DEINES COMPANY			
INCOME STATEMENT			
FOR THE YEAR ENDED DECEMBER 31, 2007			
Sales Revenue			
Sales			$3,053,081
Less: Sales discounts		$ 24,241	
Sales returns and allowances		56,427	80,668
Net sales revenue			2,972,413
Cost of Goods Sold			
Merchandise inventory, Jan. 1, 2007		461,219	
Purchases	$1,989,693		
Less: Purchase discounts	19,270		
Net purchases	1,970,423		
Freight and transportation-in	40,612	2,011,035	
Total merchandise available for sale		2,472,254	
Less: Merchandise inventory, Dec. 31, 2007		489,713	
Cost of goods sold			1,982,541
Gross profit on sales			989,872
Operating Expenses			
Selling expenses			
Sales salaries and commissions	202,644		
Sales office salaries	59,200		
Travel and entertainment	48,940		
Advertising expense	38,315		
Freight and transportation-out	41,209		
Shipping supplies and expense	24,712		
Postage and stationery	16,788		
Depreciation of sales equipment	9,005		
Telephone and Internet expense	12,215	453,028	
Administrative expenses			
Officers' salaries	186,000		
Office salaries	61,200		
Legal and professional services	23,721		
Utilities expense	23,275		
Insurance expense	17,029		
Depreciation of building	18,059		
Depreciation of office equipment	16,000		
Stationery, supplies, and postage	2,875		
Miscellaneous office expenses	2,612	350,771	803,799
Income from operations			186,073
Other Revenues and Gains			
Dividend revenue		98,500	
Rental revenue		72,910	171,410
			357,483
Other Expenses and Losses			
Interest on bonds and notes			126,060
Income before income tax			231,423
Income tax			66,934
Net income for the year			$ 164,489
Earnings per common share			$1.74

from the list on page 131.[9] Note that in arriving at net income, the statement presents three subtotals of note:

1 Net sales revenue
2 Gross profit on sales
3 Income from operations

The disclosure of net sales revenue is useful because Deines reports regular revenues as a separate item. It discloses irregular or incidental revenues elsewhere in the income statement. As a result, analysts can more easily understand and assess trends in revenue from continuing operations.

Similarly, the reporting of gross profit provides a useful number for evaluating performance and predicting future earnings. Statement readers may study the trend in gross profits to determine how successfully a company uses its resources. They also may use that information to understand how competitive pressure affected profit margins.

Finally, disclosing income from operations highlights the difference between regular and irregular or incidental activities. This disclosure helps users recognize that incidental or irregular activities are unlikely to continue at the same level. Furthermore, disclosure of operating earnings may assist in comparing different companies and assessing operating efficiencies.

Condensed Income Statements

In some cases a single income statement cannot possibly present all the desired expense detail. To solve this problem, a company includes only the totals of expense groups in the statement of income. It then also prepares supplementary schedules to support the totals. This format may thus reduce the income statement itself to a few lines on a single sheet. For this reason, readers who wish to study all the reported data on operations must give their attention to the supporting schedules. For example, consider the income statement shown in Illustration 4-3 for Dan Deines Company. This statement is a condensed version of the more detailed multiple-step statement presented earlier. It is more representative of the type found in practice.

DAN DEINES COMPANY INCOME STATEMENT FOR THE YEAR ENDED DECEMBER 31, 2007		
Net sales		$2,972,413
Cost of goods sold		1,982,541
Gross profit		989,872
Selling expenses (see Note D)	$453,028	
Administrative expenses	350,771	803,799
Income from operations		186,073
Other revenues and gains		171,410
		357,483
Other expenses and losses		126,060
Income before income tax		231,423
Income tax		66,934
Net income for the year		$ 164,489
Earnings per share		$1.74

ILLUSTRATION 4-3
Condensed Income Statement

Illustration 4-4 shows an example of a supporting schedule, cross-referenced as Note D and detailing the selling expenses.

[9]Companies must include *earnings per share* or *net loss per share* on the face of the income statement.

ILLUSTRATION 4-4
Sample Supporting
Schedule

Note D: Selling expenses	
Sales salaries and commissions	$202,644
Sales office salaries	59,200
Travel and entertainment	48,940
Advertising expense	38,315
Freight and transportation-out	41,209
Shipping supplies and expense	24,712
Postage and stationery	16,788
Depreciation of sales equipment	9,005
Telephone and Internet expense	12,215
Total selling expenses	$453,028

How much detail should a company include in the income statement? On the one hand, a company wants to present a simple, summarized statement so that readers can readily discover important factors. On the other hand, it wants to disclose the results of all activities and to provide more than just a skeleton report. As we showed above, the income statement always includes certain basic elements, but companies can present them in various formats.

REPORTING IRREGULAR ITEMS

OBJECTIVE 4
Explain how to report irregular items.

As the use of a multiple-step or condensed income statement illustrates, GAAP allows flexibility in the presentation of the components of income. However, the FASB developed specific guidelines in two important areas: what to include in income and how to report certain unusual or irregular items.

What should be included in net income has been a controversy for many years. For example, should companies report irregular gains and losses, and corrections of revenues and expenses of prior years, as part of retained earnings? Or should companies first present them in the income statement and then carry them to retained earnings?

This issue is extremely important because the number and magnitude of irregular items are substantial. For example, Illustration 4-5 identifies the most common types and number of irregular items reported in a survey of 600 large companies. Notice that more than one-third of the surveyed firms reported restructuring charges, which often contain write-offs and other one-time items. About 20 percent of the surveyed firms reported either an extraordinary item or a discontinued operation charge. And many companies had two or more accounting changes in 2003.[10]

ILLUSTRATION 4-5
Number of Irregular
Items Reported in a
Recent Year by 600
Large Companies

_____
[10]*Accounting Trends and Techniques—2004* (New York: AICPA).

As our opening story discusses, we need consistent and comparable income reporting practices to avoid "promotional" information reported by companies. Developing a framework for reporting irregular items is important to ensure reliable income information.[11]

Some users advocate a **current operating performance approach** to income reporting. These analysts argue that the most useful income measure reflects only regular and recurring revenue and expense elements. Irregular items do not reflect a company's future earning power.

In contrast, others warn that a focus on operating income potentially misses important information about a company's performance. Any gain or loss experienced by the company, whether directly or indirectly related to operations, contributes to its long-run profitability. As one analyst notes, "write-offs matter. . . . They speak to the volatility of (past) earnings."[12] As a result, analysts can use some nonoperating items to assess the riskiness of future earnings. Furthermore, determining which items are operating and which are irregular requires judgment. This might lead to differences in the treatment of irregular items and to possible manipulation of income measures.

ARE ONE-TIME CHARGES BUGGING YOU?

WHAT DO THE NUMBERS MEAN?

Which number—net income or income from operations—should an analyst use in evaluating companies that have unusual items? Some argue that operating income better represents what will happen in the future. Others note that special items are often no longer special. For example, one study noted that in 2001, companies in the Standard & Poor's 500 index wrote off items totaling $165 billion—more than in the prior five years combined.

A study by Multex.com and the *Wall Street Journal* indicated that analysts should not ignore these charges. Based on data for companies taking unusual charges from 1996–2001, the study documented that companies reporting the largest unusual charges had more negative stock price performance following the charge, compared to companies with smaller charges. Thus, rather than signaling the end of bad times, these unusual charges indicated poorer future earnings.

In fact, some analysts use these charges to weed out stocks that may be headed for a fall. Following the "cockroach theory," any charge indicating a problem raises the probability of more problems. Thus, investors should be wary of the increasing use of restructuring and other one-time charges, which may bury expenses that signal future performance declines.

Source: Adapted from J. Weil and S. Liesman, "Stock Gurus Disregard Most Big Write-offs, But They Often Hold Vital Clues to Outlook," *Wall Street Journal Online* (December 31, 2001).

So, what to do? The accounting profession has **adopted a modified all-inclusive concept and requires application of this approach in practice**. This approach indicates that companies record most items, including irregular ones, as part of net income.[13] In addition, companies are required to highlight irregular items in the financial statements so that users can better determine the long-run earning power of the company.

INTERNATIONAL INSIGHT

In many countries the "modified all-inclusive" income statement approach does not parallel that of the U.S. For example, companies in these countries take some gains and losses directly to owners' equity accounts instead of reporting them on the income statement.

---

[11]The FASB and other international accounting standard setters continue to study the best way to report income. See *Reporting Financial Performance: A Proposed Approach* (Norwalk, Conn.: FASB, September 1999).

[12]D. McDermott, "Latest Profit Data Stir Old Debate Between Net and Operating Income," *Wall Street Journal* (May 3, 1999).

[13]The FASB issued a statement of concepts that offers some guidance on this topic— "Recognition and Measurement in Financial Statements of Business Enterprises," *Statement of Financial Accounting Concepts No. 5* (Stamford, Conn.: FASB, 1984).

Irregular items fall into six general categories, which we discuss in the following sections:

1 Discontinued operations.

2 Extraordinary items.

3 Unusual gains and losses.

4 Changes in accounting principle.

5 Changes in estimates.

6 Corrections of errors.

Discontinued Operations

As Illustration 4-5 shows, one of **the most common types of irregular items is discontinued operations**. **A discontinued operation** occurs when two things happen: (a) a company eliminates the results of operations and cash flows of a *component* from its ongoing operations, and (b) there is no significant continuing involvement in that component after the disposal transaction.

To illustrate a **component**, **S. C. Johnson** manufactures and sells consumer products. It has several product groups, each with different product lines and brands. For S. C. Johnson, a product group is the lowest level at which it can clearly distinguish the operations and cash flows from the rest of the company's operations. Therefore each product group is a component of the company. If a component were disposed of, S. C. Johnson would classify it as a discontinued operation.

Here is another example. Assume that Softso Inc. has experienced losses with certain brands in its beauty-care products group. As a result, Softso decides to sell that part of its business. It will discontinue any continuing involvement in the product group after the sale. In this case, Softso eliminates the operations and the cash flows of the product group from its ongoing operations, and reports it as a discontinued operation.

On the other hand, assume Softso decides to remain in the beauty-care business but will discontinue the brands that experienced losses. Because Softso cannot differentiate the cash flows from the brands from the cash flows of the product group as a whole, it cannot consider the brands a component. Softso does not classify any gain or loss on the sale of the brands as a discontinued operation.

Companies report as discontinued operations (in a separate income statement category) the gain or loss from **disposal of a component of a business**. In addition, companies report the **results of operations of a component that has been or will be disposed of** separately from continuing operations. Companies show the effects of discontinued operations net of tax as a separate category, after continuing operations but before extraordinary items.[14]

To illustrate, Multiplex Products, Inc., a highly diversified company, decides to discontinue its electronics division. During the current year, the electronics division lost $300,000 (net of tax). Multiplex sold the division at the end of the year at a loss of $500,000 (net of tax). Multiplex shows the information on the current year's income statement as follows.

ILLUSTRATION 4-6
Income Statement
Presentation of
Discontinued Operations

Income from continuing operations		$20,000,000
Discontinued operations		
Loss from operation of discontinued electronics		
division (net of tax)	$300,000	
Loss from disposal of electronics division (net of tax)	500,000	800,000
Net income		$19,200,000

[14]"Accounting for the Impairment or Disposal of Long-Lived Assets," *Statement of Financial Accounting Standards No. 144* (Norwalk, Conn.: FASB, 2001), par. 4. This standard requires discontinued-operation reporting, even though the assets disposed of (i.e., component of the business) do not meet the definition of a business segment.

Companies use the phrase **"Income from continuing operations"** only when gains or losses on discontinued operations occur.

Extraordinary Items

Extraordinary items are nonrecurring **material** items that differ significantly from a company's typical business activities. The criteria for extraordinary items are as follows.

> Extraordinary items are events and transactions that are distinguished by their unusual nature **and** by the infrequency of their occurrence. Classifying an event or transaction as an extraordinary item requires meeting **both** of the following criteria:
>
> **(a) Unusual Nature.** The underlying event or transaction should possess a high degree of abnormality and be of a type clearly unrelated to, or only incidentally related to, the ordinary and typical activities of the company, taking into account the environment in which it operates.
>
> **(b) Infrequency of Occurrence.** The underlying event or transaction should be of a type that the company does not reasonably expect to recur in the foreseeable future, taking into account the environment in which the company operates.[15]

For further clarification, the following gains and losses are **not extraordinary items**.

(a) Write-down or write-off of receivables, inventories, equipment leased to others, deferred research and development costs, or other intangible assets.

(b) Gains or losses from exchange or translation of foreign currencies, including those relating to major devaluations and revaluations.

(c) Gains or losses on disposal of a component of an entity (reported as a discontinued operation).

(d) Other gains or losses from sale or abandonment of property, plant, or equipment used in the business.

(e) Effects of a strike, including those against competitors and major suppliers.

(f) Adjustment of accruals on long-term contracts.[16]

The above items are not considered extraordinary "because they are usual in nature and may be expected to recur as a consequence of customary and continuing business activities."

Only rarely does an event or transaction clearly meet the criteria for an extraordinary item.[17] For example, a company classifies gains or losses such as (a) and (d) above as extraordinary if they **resulted directly from a major casualty** (such as an earthquake), **an expropriation**, or a **prohibition under a newly enacted law or regulation**. Such circumstances clearly meet the criteria of unusual and infrequent. For example, **Weyerhaeuser Company** (forest and lumber) incurred an extraordinary item (an approximate $36 million loss) as a result of volcanic activity at Mount St. Helens. The eruption destroyed standing timber, logs, buildings, equipment, and transportation systems covering 68,000 acres.

In determining whether an item is extraordinary, **a company must consider the environment in which it operates**. The environment includes such factors as industry characteristics, geographic location, and the nature and extent of governmental regulations. Thus, the FASB accords extraordinary item treatment to the loss from hail damages to a tobacco grower's crops if hailstorm damage in its locality is rare. On the other hand, frost damage to a citrus grower's crop in Florida does not qualify as extraordinary because frost damage normally occurs there every three or four years.

INTERNATIONAL INSIGHT

Classification of items as extraordinary differs across nations. Even in countries with similar criteria for identifying extraordinary items, they are not interpreted identically. Thus, what is extraordinary in the U.S. is not necessarily extraordinary elsewhere.

---

[15]"Reporting the Results of Operations," *Opinions of the Accounting Principles Board No. 30* (New York: AICPA, 1973), par. 20.

[16]Ibid., par. 23, as amended by "Accounting for the Impairment or Disposal of Long-lived Assets," *Statement of Financial Accounting Standards No. 144* (Norwalk, Conn.: FASB, 2001).

[17]*Accounting Trends and Techniques—2004* (New York: AICPA) indicates that just 12 of the 600 companies surveyed reported an extraordinary item.

Similarly, when a company sells the only significant security investment it has ever owned, the gain or loss meets the criteria of an extraordinary item. Another company, however, that has a portfolio of securities acquired for investment purposes would not report such a sales as an extraordinary item. Sale of such securities is part of its ordinary and typical activities.[18]

In addition, considerable judgment must be exercised in determining whether to report an item as extraordinary. For example, the government condemned the forest-lands of some paper companies to preserve state or national parks or forests. Is such an event extraordinary, or is it part of a paper company's normal operations? Such determination is not easy. Much depends on the frequency of previous condemnations, the expectation of future condemnations, materiality, and the like.[19]

WHAT DO THE NUMBERS MEAN?

EXTRAORDINARY TIMES

No recent event better illustrates the difficulties of determining whether a transaction meets the definition of extraordinary than the financial impacts of the terrorist attack on the World Trade Center on September 11, 2001.

To many, this event, which resulted in the tragic loss of lives, jobs, and in some cases, entire businesses, clearly meets the criteria for unusual and infrequent. For example, in the wake of the terrorist attack that destroyed the World Trade Center and turned much of lower Manhattan including Wall Street into a war zone, airlines, insurance companies, and other businesses recorded major losses due to property damage, business disruption, and suspension of airline travel and of securities trading.

But, to the surprise of many, the FASB did not permit extraordinary item reporting for losses arising from the terrorist attacks. The reason? After much deliberation, the Emerging Issues Task Force (EITF) of the FASB decided that measurement of the possible loss was too difficult. Take the airline industry as an example: What portion of the airlines' losses after September 11 was related to the terrorist attack, and what portion was due to the ongoing recession? Also, the FASB did not want companies to use the attack as a reason for reporting as extraordinary some losses that had little direct relationship to the attack. Indeed, energy company **AES** and shoe retailer **Footstar**, who both were experiencing profit pressure before 9/11, put some of the blame for their poor performance on the attack.

Source: Julie Creswell, "Bad News Bearers Shift the Blame," *Fortune* (October 15, 2001), p. 44.

Companies must show extraordinary items net of taxes in a separate section in the income statement, usually just before net income. After listing the usual revenues, expenses, and income taxes, the remainder of the statement shows the following.

ILLUSTRATION 4-7
Income Statement
Placement of
Extraordinary Items

Income before extraordinary items
Extraordinary items (less applicable income tax of $_____)
Net income

---

[18]Debt extinguishments had been the most common reason for companies reporting extraordinary items. The FASB has now eliminated extraordinary item treatment for these gains and losses, unless they are both unusual and infrequent in nature ("Rescission of FASB Statements No. 4, 44, and 64 and Technical Corrections," *Statement of Financial Accounting Standards No. 145* (Norwalk, Conn.: FASB, 2002). Thus, reporting an extraordinary item is likely to become a rare event in the future.

[19]Because assessing the materiality of individual items requires judgment, determining what is extraordinary is difficult. However, in making materiality judgments, companies should consider extraordinary items individually, and not in the aggregate. "Reporting the Results of Operations," op. cit., par. 24.

For example, Illustration 4-8 shows how **Keystone Consolidated Industries** reported an extraordinary loss.

Keystone Consolidated Industries, Inc.

Income before extraordinary item	$11,638,000
Extraordinary item—flood loss (Note E)	1,216,000
Net income	$10,422,000

Note E: Extraordinary Item. The Keystone Steel and Wire Division's Steel Works experienced a flash flood on June 22. The extraordinary item represents the estimated cost, net of related income taxes of $1,279,000, to restore the steel works to full operation.

ILLUSTRATION 4-8
Income Statement
Presentation of
Extraordinary Items

Unusual Gains and Losses

Because of the restrictive criteria for extraordinary items, financial statement users must carefully examine the financial statements for items that are **unusual or infrequent but not both**. Recall that companies cannot consider items such as write-downs of inventories and transaction gains and losses from fluctuation of foreign exchange as extraordinary items. Thus, companies sometimes show these items with their normal recurring revenues and expenses. If not material in amount, companies combine these with other items in the income statement. If material, companies must disclose them separately, and report them **above** "Income (loss) before extraordinary items."

For example, **PepsiCo, Inc.** presented an unusual charge in its income statement, as Illustration 4-9 shows.

PEPSICO
PepsiCo, Inc.
(in millions)

Net sales	$20,917
Costs and expenses, net	
Cost of sales	8,525
Selling, general, and administrative expenses	9,241
Amortization of intangible assets	199
Unusual items (Note 2)	290
Operating income	$ 2,662

Note 2 (Restructuring Charge)

Dispose and write down assets	$183
Improve productivity	94
Strengthen the international bottler structure	13
Net loss	$290

The net charge to strengthen the international bottler structure includes proceeds of $87 million associated with a settlement related to a previous Venezuelan bottler agreement, which were partially offset by related costs.

ILLUSTRATION 4-9
Income Statement
Presentation of
Unusual Charges

Restructuring charges, like the one PepsiCo reported, have been common in recent years (see also Illustration 4-5). A **restructuring charge** relates to a major reorganization of company affairs, such as costs associated with employee layoffs, plant closing costs, write-offs of assets, and so on. A company should not report a restructuring charge as an extraordinary item, because these write-offs are part of a company's ordinary and typical activities.

Companies tend to **report unusual items in a separate section just above "Income from operations before income taxes" and "Extraordinary items,"** especially when there are multiple unusual items. For example, when **General Electric Company** experienced multiple unusual items in one year, it reported them in a separate "Unusual items" section of the income statement below "Income before unusual items and income taxes." When preparing a multiple-step income statement for homework purposes, you should report unusual gains and losses in the "Other revenues and gains" or "Other expenses and losses" section unless you are instructed to prepare a separate unusual items section.[20]

In dealing with events that are either unusual or nonrecurring but not both, the profession attempted to prevent a practice that many believed was misleading. Companies often reported such transactions on a net-of-tax basis and prominently displayed the earnings per share effect of these items. Although not captioned "Extraordinary items," companies presented them in the same manner. Some had referred to these as "first cousins" to extraordinary items.

As a consequence, the Board specifically **prohibited a net-of-tax treatment for such items,** to ensure that users of financial statements can easily differentiate extraordinary items—reported net of tax—from material items that are unusual or infrequent, but not both.

Changes in Accounting Principle

Changes in accounting occur frequently in practice, because important events or conditions may be in dispute or uncertain at the statement date. One type of accounting change results when a company adopts a different accounting principle. Changes in accounting principle include a change in the method of inventory pricing from FIFO to average cost, or a change in accounting for construction contracts from the percentage-of-completion to the completed-contract method.[21]

A company recognizes a change in accounting principle by making a **retrospective adjustment** to the financial statements. Such an adjustment recasts the prior years' statements on a basis consistent with the newly adopted principle. The company records the cumulative effect of the change for prior periods as an adjustment to beginning retained earnings of the earliest year presented.

To illustrate, Gaubert Inc. decided in March 2007 to change from FIFO to weighted-average inventory pricing. Gaubert's income before taxes, using the new weighted-average method in 2007, is $30,000. Illustration 4-10 presents the pretax income data for 2005 and 2006 for this example.

ILLUSTRATION 4-10
Calculation of a Change in Accounting Principle

Year	FIFO	Weighted-Average Method	Excess of FIFO over Weighted-Average Method
2005	$40,000	$35,000	$5,000
2006	30,000	27,000	3,000
Total			$8,000

---

[20]Many companies report "one-time items." However, some companies take restructuring charges practically every year. **Citicorp** (now **Citigroup**) took restructuring charges six years in a row, between 1988 and 1993; **Eastman Kodak Co.** did so five out of six years in 1989 to 1994. Research indicates that the market discounts the earnings of companies that report a series of "nonrecurring" items. Such evidence supports the contention that these elements reduce the quality of earnings. J. Elliott and D. Hanna, "Repeated Accounting Write-offs and the Information Content of Earnings," *Journal of Accounting Research* (Supplement, 1996).

[21]"Accounting Changes and Error Corrections," *Statement of Financial Accounting Standards No. 154* (Norwalk, Conn.: FASB, 2005). In Chapter 22, we examine in greater detail the problems related to accounting changes.

Illustration 4-11 shows the information Gaubert presented in its comparative income statements, based on a 30 percent tax rate.

	2007	2006	2005
Income before taxes	$30,000	$27,000	$35,000
Income tax	9,000	8,100	10,500
Net income	$21,000	$18,900	$24,500

ILLUSTRATION 4-11
Income Statement
Presentation of a Change
in Accounting Principle

Thus, under the retrospective approach, the company recasts the prior years' income numbers under the newly adopted method. This approach thus preserves comparability across years.

Changes in Estimates

Estimates are inherent in the accounting process. For example, companies estimate useful lives and salvage values of depreciable assets, uncollectible receivables, inventory obsolescence, and the number of periods expected to benefit from a particular expenditure. Not infrequently, due to time, circumstances, or new information, even estimates originally made in good faith must be changed. A company accounts for such **changes in estimates** in the period of change if they affect only that period, or in the period of change and future periods if the change affects both.

To illustrate a change in estimate that affects only the period of change, assume that DuPage Materials Corp. consistently estimated its bad debt expense at 1 percent of credit sales. In 2006 however, DuPage determines that it must revise upward the estimate of bad debts for the current year's credit sales to 2 percent, or double the prior years' percentage. The 2 percent rate is necessary to reduce accounts receivable to net realizable value. Using 2 percent results in a bad debt charge of $240,000, or double the amount using the 1 percent estimate for prior years, DuPage records the provision at December 31, 2006, as follows.

Bad Debt Expense	240,000	
Allowance for Doubtful Accounts		240,000

DuPage includes the entire change in estimate in 2006 income because the change does not affect future periods. **Companies do not handle changes in estimate retrospectively.** That is, such changes are not carried back to adjust prior years. (We examine changes in estimate that affect both the current and future periods in greater detail in Chapter 22.) **Changes in estimate are not considered errors or extraordinary items.**

Corrections of Errors

Errors occur as a result of mathematical mistakes, mistakes in the application of accounting principles, or oversight or misuse of facts that existed at the time financial statements were prepared. In recent years, many companies have corrected for errors in their financial statements. For example, one consulting group noted that error-driven restatements were up 28 percent (to 414 restatements) in 2004.[22] The most common errors involved improper reporting of revenue, accounting for stock options, allowances for receivables, inventories, restructurings, and loss contingencies.

Companies must correct errors by making proper entries in the accounts and reporting the corrections in the financial statements. Corrections of errors are treated as **prior period adjustments**, similar to changes in accounting principles. Companies record a correction of an error in the year in which it is discovered. They report the

---

[22]Carrie Johnson, "Restatements Up 28% in 2004," *Washingtonpost.com* (January 20, 2005), p. E 04.

error in the financial statements as an adjustment to the beginning balance of retained earnings. If a company prepares comparative financial statements, it should restate the prior statements for the effects of the error.

To illustrate, in 2008, Hillsboro Co. determined that it incorrectly overstated its accounts receivable and sales revenue by $100,000 in 2007. In 2008, Hillboro makes the following entry to correct for this error (ignore income taxes).

Retained Earnings	100,000	
Accounts Receivable		100,000

Retained Earnings is debited because sales revenue, and therefore net income, was overstated in a prior period. Accounts Receivable is credited to reduce this overstated balance to the correct amount.

Summary of Irregular Items

The public accounting profession now tends to accept a modified all-inclusive income concept instead of the current operating performance concept. Except for changes in accounting principle and error corrections, which are charged or credited directly to retained earnings, companies close all other irregular gains or losses or nonrecurring items to Income Summary and include them in the income statement.

Of these irregular items, companies classify **discontinued operations of a component** of a business as a separate item in the income statement, after "Income from continuing operations." Companies show the **unusual, material, nonrecurring items** that significantly differ from the typical or customary business activities in a separate

ILLUSTRATION 4-12
Summary of Irregular Items in the Income Statement

Type of Situation[a]	Criteria	Examples	Placement on Income Statement
Discontinued operations	Disposal of a component of a business for which the company can clearly distinguish operations and cash flows from the rest of the company's operations.	Sale by diversified company of major division that represents only activities in electronics industry. Food distributor that sells wholesale to supermarket chains and through fast-food restaurants decides to discontinue the division that sells to one of two classes of customers.	Show in separate section after continuing operations but before extraordinary items. (Shown net of tax.)
Extraordinary items	Material, and both unusual and infrequent (nonrecurring).	Gains or losses resulting from casualties, an expropriation, or a prohibition under a new law.	Show in separate section entitled "Extraordinary items." (Shown net of tax.)
Unusual gains or losses, not considered extraordinary	Material; character typical of the customary business activities; unusual or infrequent but not both.	Write-downs of receivables, inventories; adjustments of accrued contract prices; gains or losses from fluctuations of foreign exchange; gains or losses from sales of assets used in business.	Show in separate section above income before extraordinary items. Often reported in "Other revenues and gains" or "Other expenses and losses" section. (Not shown net of tax.)
Changes in principle	Change from one generally accepted principle to another.	Change in the basis of inventory pricing from FIFO to average cost.	Recast prior years' income statements on the same basis as the newly adopted principle.
Changes in estimates	Normal, recurring corrections and adjustments.	Changes in the realizability of receivables and inventories; changes in estimated lives of equipment, intangible assets; changes in estimated liability for warranty costs, income taxes, and salary payments.	Show change only in the affected accounts. (Not shown net of tax.)
Corrections of errors	Mistake, misuse of facts.	Error in reporting revenue.	Restate prior years' income statements to correct for error.

[a]This summary provides only the general rules to be followed in accounting for the various situations described above. Exceptions do exist in some of these situations.

"Extraordinary items" section below "Discontinued operations." They separately disclose other items of a material amount that are of an **unusual or nonrecurring** nature and are **not considered extraordinary**.

Because of the numerous intermediate income figures created by the reporting of these irregular items, readers must carefully evaluate earnings information reported by the financial press. Illustration 4-12 (page 142) summarizes the basic concepts that we previously discussed. Although simplified, the chart provides a useful framework for determining the treatment of special items affecting the income statement.

SPECIAL REPORTING ISSUES

Intraperiod Tax Allocation

Companies report irregular items (except for unusual gains and losses) on the income statement or statement of retained earnings net of tax. This procedure is called **intraperiod tax allocation**, that is, allocation within a period. It relates the income tax expense (sometimes referred to as the income tax provision) of the fiscal period to the **specific items** that give rise to the amount of the tax provision.

> **OBJECTIVE 5**
> **Explain intraperiod tax allocation.**

Intraperiod tax allocation helps financial statement users better understand the impact of income taxes on the various components of net income. For example, readers of financial statements will understand how much income tax expense relates to "income from continuing operations" and how much relates to certain irregular transactions and events. This approach should help users to better predict the amount, timing, and uncertainty of future cash flows. In addition, intraperiod tax allocation discourages statement readers from using pretax measures of performance when evaluating financial results, and thereby recognizes that income tax expense is a real cost.

Companies use intraperiod tax allocation on the income statement for the following items: (1) income from continuing operations, (2) discontinued operations, and (3) extraordinary items. The general concept is "**let the tax follow the income.**"

To compute the income tax expense attributable to "Income from continuing operations," a company would find the income tax expense related to both the revenue and expense transactions used in determining this income. (In this computation, the company does not consider the tax consequences of items excluded from the determination of "Income from continuing operations.") Companies then associate a separate tax effect with each irregular item (e.g., discontinued operations and extraordinary items). Here we look in more detail at calculation of intraperiod tax allocation for extraordinary gains and losses.

Extraordinary Gains

In applying the concept of intraperiod tax allocation, assume that Schindler Co. has income before income tax and extraordinary item of $250,000. It has an extraordinary gain of $100,000 from a condemnation settlement received on one its properties. Assuming a 30 percent income tax rate, Schindler presents the following information on the income statement.

Income before income tax and extraordinary item		$250,000
Income tax		75,000
Income before extraordinary item		175,000
Extraordinary gain—condemnation settlement	$100,000	
Less: Applicable income tax	30,000	70,000
Net income		$245,000

ILLUSTRATION 4-13
Intraperiod Tax Allocation, Extraordinary Gain

Schindler determines the income tax of $75,000 ($250,000 × 30%) attributable to "Income before income tax and extraordinary item" from revenue and expense transactions related to this income. Schindler omits the tax consequences of items excluded from the determination of "Income before income tax and extraordinary item." The company shows a separate tax effect of $30,000 as "Extraordinary gain—condemnation settlement."

Extraordinary Losses

To illustrate the reporting of an extraordinary loss, assume that Schindler Co. has income before income tax and extraordinary item of $250,000. It suffers an extraordinary loss from a major casualty of $100,000. Assuming a 30 percent tax rate, Schindler presents the income tax on the income statement as shown in Illustration 4-14. In this case, the loss provides a positive tax benefit of $30,000. Schindler, therefore, subtracts it from the $100,000 loss.

ILLUSTRATION 4-14
Intraperiod Tax
Allocation, Extraordinary
Loss

Income before income tax and extraordinary item		$250,000
Income tax		75,000
Income before extraordinary item		175,000
Extraordinary item—loss from casualty	$100,000	
Less: Applicable income tax reduction	30,000	70,000
Net income		$105,000

Companies may also report the tax effect of an extraordinary item by means of a note disclosure, as illustrated below.

ILLUSTRATION 4-15
Note Disclosure of
Intraperiod Tax Allocation

Income before income tax and extraordinary item	$250,000
Income tax	75,000
Income before extraordinary item	175,000
Extraordinary item, less applicable income tax reduction (Note 1)	70,000
Net income	$105,000

Note 1: During the year the Company suffered a major casualty loss of $70,000, net of applicable income tax reduction of $30,000.

Earnings per Share

A company customarily sums up the results of its operations in one important figure: net income. However, the financial world has widely accepted an even more distilled and compact figure as the most significant business indicator—**earnings per share** (EPS).

The computation of earnings per share is usually straightforward. **Earnings per share is net income minus preferred dividends (income available to common stockholders), divided by the weighted average of common shares outstanding.**[23]

To illustrate, assume that Lancer, Inc. reports net income of $350,000. It declares and pays preferred dividends of $50,000 for the year. The weighted average number of common shares outstanding during the year is 100,000 shares. Lancer computes earnings per share of $3, as shown in Illustration 4-16.

ILLUSTRATION 4-16
Equation Illustrating
Computation of Earnings
per Share

$$\frac{\text{Net Income} - \text{Preferred Dividends}}{\text{Weighted Average of Common Shares Outstanding}} = \text{Earnings per Share}$$

$$\frac{\$350,000 - \$50,000}{100,000} = \$3$$

---

[23]In calculating earnings per share, companies deduct preferred dividends from net income if the dividends are declared or if they are cumulative though not declared.

Note that EPS measures the number of dollars earned by each share of common stock. It does not represent the dollar amount paid to stockholders in the form of dividends.

Prospectuses, proxy material, and annual reports to stockholders commonly use the "net income per share" or "earnings per share" ratio. The financial press, statistical services like Standard & Poor's, and Wall Street securities analysts also highlight EPS. Because of its importance, **companies must disclose earnings per share on the face of the income statement**. A company that reports a discontinued operation or an extraordinary item must report per share amounts for these line items either on the face of the income statement or in the notes to the financial statements.[24]

To illustrate, consider the income statement for Poquito Industries Inc. shown in Illustration 4-17. Notice the order in which Poquito shows the data, with per share information at the bottom. Assume that the company had 100,000 shares outstanding for the entire year. The Poquito income statement, as Illustration 4-17 shows, is highly condensed. Poquito would need to describe items such as "Unusual charge," "Discontinued operations," and "Extraordinary item" fully and appropriately in the statement or related notes.

ILLUSTRATION 4-17
Income Statement

POQUITO INDUSTRIES INC. **INCOME STATEMENT** **FOR THE YEAR ENDED DECEMBER 31, 2007**		
Sales revenue		$1,420,000
Cost of goods sold		600,000
Gross profit		820,000
Selling and administrative expenses		320,000
Income from operations		500,000
Other revenues and gains		
Interest revenue		10,000
Other expenses and losses		
Loss on disposal of part of Textile Division	$ (5,000)	
Unusual charge—loss on sale of investments	(45,000)	(50,000)
Income from continuing operations before income tax		460,000
Income tax		184,000
Income from continuing operations		276,000
Discontinued operations		
Income from operations of Pizza Division, less applicable income tax of $24,800	54,000	
Loss on disposal of Pizza Division, less applicable income tax of $41,000	(90,000)	(36,000)
Income before extraordinary item		240,000
Extraordinary item—loss from earthquake, less applicable income tax of $23,000		(45,000)
Net income		$ 195,000
Per share of common stock		
Income from continuing operations		$2.76
Income from operations of discontinued division, net of tax		0.54
Loss on disposal of discontinued operation, net of tax		(0.90)
Income before extraordinary item		2.40
Extraordinary loss, net of tax		(0.45)
Net income		$1.95

Many corporations have simple capital structures that include only common stock. For these companies, a presentation such as "Earnings per common share" is appropriate on the income statement. In many instances, however, companies' earnings per

---

[24]"Earnings Per Share," *Statement of Financial Accounting Standards No. 128* (Norwalk, Conn.: FASB, 1996).

share are subject to dilution (reduction) in the future because existing contingencies permit the issuance of additional common shares.[25]

In summary, the simplicity and availability of EPS figures lead to their widespread use. Because of the importance that the public, even the well-informed public, attaches to earnings per share, companies must make the EPS figure as meaningful as possible.

Retained Earnings Statement

<table>
<tr><td>**OBJECTIVE 7**
Prepare a retained
earnings statement.</td></tr>
</table>

Net income increases retained earnings. A net loss decreases retained earnings. Both cash and stock dividends decrease retained earnings. Changes in accounting principles (generally) and prior period adjustments may increase or decrease retained earnings. Companies charge or credit these adjustments (net of tax) to the opening balance of retained earnings. This excludes the adjustments from the determination of net income for the current period.

Companies may show retained earnings information in different ways. For example, some companies prepare a separate retained earnings statement, as Illustration 4-18 shows.

ILLUSTRATION 4-18
Retained Earnings
Statement

TIGER WOODS INC. RETAINED EARNINGS STATEMENT FOR THE YEAR ENDED DECEMBER 31, 2007		
Retained earnings, January 1, as reported		$1,050,000
Correction for understatement of net income in prior period (inventory error)		50,000
Retained earnings, January 1, as adjusted		1,100,000
Add: Net income		360,000
		1,460,000
Less: Cash dividends	$100,000	
Stock dividends	200,000	300,000
Retained earnings, December 31		$1,160,000

The reconciliation of the beginning to the ending balance in retained earnings provides information about why net assets increased or decreased during the year. The association of dividend distributions with net income for the period indicates what management is doing with earnings: It may be "plowing back" into the business part or all of the earnings, distributing all current income, or distributing current income plus the accumulated earnings of prior years.[26]

Restrictions of Retained Earnings

Companies often restrict retained earnings to comply with contractual requirements, board of directors' policy, or current necessity. Generally, companies disclose in the notes to the financial statements the amounts of restricted retained earnings. In some cases, companies transfer the amount of retained earnings restricted to an account titled **Appropriated Retained Earnings**. The retained earnings section may therefore report two separate amounts—(1) retained earnings free (unrestricted) and (2) retained earnings appropriated (restricted). The total of these two amounts equals the total retained earnings.

---

[25]Ibid. We discuss the computational problems involved in accounting for these dilutive securities in earnings per share computations in Chapter 16.

[26]*Accounting Trends and Techniques—2004* (New York: AICPA) indicates that most companies (593 of 600 surveyed) present changes in retained earnings either within the statement of stockholders' equity (586 firms) or in a separate statement of retained earnings. Only 2 of the 600 companies prepare a combined statement of income and retained earnings.

Comprehensive Income

Companies generally include in income all revenues, expenses, and gains and losses recognized during the period. These items are classified within the income statement so that financial statement readers can better understand the significance of various components of net income. Changes in accounting principles and corrections of errors are excluded from the calculation of net income because their effects relate to prior periods.

In recent years, there is increased use of fair values for measuring assets and liabilities. Furthermore, possible reporting of gains and losses related to changes in fair value have placed a strain on income reporting. Because fair values are continually changing, some argue that recognizing these gains and losses in net income is misleading. The FASB agrees and has identified a limited number of transactions that should be recorded directly to stockholders equity. One example is unrealized gains and losses on available-for-sale securities.[27] These gains and losses are excluded from net income, thereby reducing volatility in net income due to fluctuations in fair value. At the same time disclosure of the potential gain or loss is provided.

Companies include these items that bypass the income statement in a measure called comprehensive income. **Comprehensive income** includes all changes in equity during a period *except* those resulting from investments by owners and distributions to owners. Comprehensive income, therefore, includes the following: all revenues and gains, expenses and losses reported in net income, and all gains and losses that bypass net income but affect stockholders' equity. These items—non-owner changes in equity that bypass the income statement—are referred to as **other comprehensive income**.

The FASB decided that companies must display the components of other comprehensive income in one of three ways: **(1) a second income statement; (2) a combined statement of comprehensive income; or (3) as a part of the statement of stockholders' equity.** [28] Regardless of the format used, companies must add net income to other comprehensive income to arrive at comprehensive income. Companies are not required to report earnings per share information related to comprehensive income.[29]

To illustrate, assume that V. Gill Inc. reports the following information for 2007: sales revenue $800,000; cost of goods sold $600,000; operating expenses $90,000; and an unrealized holding gain on available-for-sale securities of $30,000, net of tax.

OBJECTIVE 8
Explain how to report other comprehensive income.

Second Income Statement

Illustration 4-19 (page 148) shows the two-income statement format based on the above information for V. Gill. Reporting comprehensive income in a separate statement indicates that the gains and losses identified as other comprehensive income have the same status as traditional gains and losses. Placing net income as the starting point in the comprehensive income statement highlights the relationship of the statement to the traditional income statement.

---

[27]We further discuss available-for-sale securities in Chapter 17. Additional examples of other comprehensive items are translation gains and losses on foreign currency, excess of additional pension liability over unrecognized prior service cost, and unrealized gains and losses on certain hedging transactions.

[28]"Reporting Comprehensive Income," *Statement of Financial Accounting Standards No. 130* (Norwalk, Conn.: FASB, June 1997). *Accounting Trends and Techniques—2004* (New York: AICPA) indicates that for the 600 companies surveyed, 580 report comprehensive income. Most companies (488 of 580) include comprehensive income as part of the statement of stockholders' equity.

[29]A company must display the components of other comprehensive income either (1) net of related tax effects, or (2) before related tax effects, with one amount shown for the aggregate amount of tax related to the total amount of other comprehensive income. Both alternatives must show each component of other comprehensive income, net of related taxes either in the face of the statement or in the notes.

ILLUSTRATION 4-19
Two-Statement Format:
Comprehensive Income

V. GILL INC. INCOME STATEMENT FOR THE YEAR ENDED DECEMBER 31, 2007	
Sales revenue	$800,000
Cost of goods sold	600,000
Gross profit	200,000
Operating expenses	90,000
Net income	$110,000

V. GILL INC. COMPREHENSIVE INCOME STATEMENT FOR THE YEAR ENDED DECEMBER 31, 2007	
Net income	$110,000
Other comprehensive income	
Unrealized holding gain, net of tax	30,000
Comprehensive income	$140,000

Combined Statement of Comprehensive Income

The second approach to reporting other comprehensive income provides a **combined statement** of comprehensive income. In this approach, the traditional net income is a subtotal, with total comprehensive income shown as a final total. The combined statement has the advantage of not requiring the creation of a new financial statement. However, burying net income as a subtotal on the statement is a disadvantage.

Statement of Stockholders' Equity

A third approach reports other comprehensive income items in a **statement of stockholders' equity** (often referred to as statement of changes in stockholders' equity). This statement reports the changes in each stockholder's equity account and in total stockholders' equity during the year. Companies often prepare **in columnar form** the statement of stockholders' equity. In this format, they use columns for each account and for total stockholders' equity.

To illustrate, assume the same information for V. Gill. The company had the following stockholder equity account balances at the beginning of 2007: Common Stock $300,000; Retained Earnings $50,000; and Accumulated Other Comprehensive Income $60,000. No changes in the Common Stock account occurred during the year. Illustration 4-20 shows a statement of stockholders' equity for V. Gill.

V. GILL INC. STATEMENT OF STOCKHOLDERS' EQUITY FOR THE YEAR ENDED DECEMBER 31, 2007					
	Total	Comprehensive Income	Retained Earnings	Accumulated Other Comprehensive Income	Common Stock
Beginning balance	$410,000		$ 50,000	$60,000	$300,000
Comprehensive income					
Net income	110,000	$110,000	110,000		
Other comprehensive income					
Unrealized holding gain, net of tax	30,000	30,000		30,000	
Comprehensive income		$140,000			
Ending balance	$550,000		$160,000	$90,000	$300,000

Most companies use the statement of stockholders' equity approach to provide information related to other comprehensive income. Because many companies already provide a statement of stockholders' equity, adding additional columns to display information related to comprehensive income is not costly.

Examples of Comprehensive Income Reporting

Balance Sheet Presentation

Regardless of the display format used, V. Gill reports the **accumulated other comprehensive income** of $90,000 in the stockholders' equity section of the balance sheet as follows.

V. GILL INC.
BALANCE SHEET
AS OF DECEMBER 31, 2007
(STOCKHOLDERS' EQUITY SECTION)

Stockholders' equity	
Common stock	$300,000
Retained earnings	160,000
Accumulated other comprehensive income	90,000
Total stockholders' equity	$550,000

ILLUSTRATION 4-21
Presentation of Accumulated Other Comprehensive Income in the Balance Sheet

By providing information on the components of comprehensive income, as well as accumulated other comprehensive income, the company communicates information about all changes in net assets.[30] With this information, users will better understand the quality of the company's earnings.

SUMMARY OF LEARNING OBJECTIVES

1. **Understand the uses and limitations of an income statement.** The income statement provides investors and creditors with information that helps them predict the amounts, timing, and uncertainty of future cash flows. Also, the income statement helps users determine the risk (level of uncertainty) of not achieving particular cash flows. The limitations of an income statement are: (1) The statement does not include many items that contribute to general growth and well-being of a company. (2) Income numbers are often affected by the accounting methods used. (3) Income measures are subject to estimates.

The *transaction approach* focuses on the activities that occurred during a given period. Instead of presenting only a net change in net assets, it discloses the components of the change. The transaction approach to income measurement requires the use of revenue, expense, loss, and gain accounts.

2. **Prepare a single-step income statement.** In a single-step income statement, just two groupings exist: revenues and expenses. Expenses are deducted from revenues to arrive at net income or loss—a single subtraction. Frequently, companies report income tax separately as the last item before net income.

3. **Prepare a multiple-step income statement.** A multiple-step income statement shows two further classifications: (1) a separation of operating results from those obtained through the subordinate or nonoperating activities of the company; and (2) a classification of expenses by functions, such as merchandising or manufacturing, selling, and administration.

KEY TERMS

accumulated other comprehensive income, 149
appropriated retained earnings, 146
capital maintenance approach, 129 (ftn)
changes in estimates, 141
comprehensive income, 147
current operating performance approach, 135
discontinued operation, 136
earnings management, 128
earnings per share, 144
extraordinary items, 137
income statement, 126
intraperiod tax allocation, 143
irregular items, 136

---

[30]Corrections of errors and changes in accounting principles are not considered other comprehensive income items.

modified all-inclusive
concept, *135*

multiple-step income
statement, *131*

other comprehensive
income, *147*

prior period adjustments,
141

quality of earnings, *128*

single-step income
statement, *130*

statement of
stockholders' equity,
148

transaction approach, *129*

4. Explain how to report irregular items. Companies generally close irregular gains or losses or nonrecurring items to Income Summary and include them in the income statement as follows: (1) Discontinued operations of a component of a business are classified as a separate item, after continuing operations. (2) The unusual, material, nonrecurring items that are significantly different from the customary business activities are shown in a separate section for extraordinary items, below discontinued operations. (3) Other items of a material amount that are of an unusual or nonrecurring nature and are not considered extraordinary are separately disclosed as a component of continuing operations. Changes in accounting principle and corrections of errors are adjusted through retained earnings.

5. Explain intraperiod tax allocation. Companies should relate the tax expense for the year to specific items on the income statement to provide a more informative disclosure to statement users. This procedure, intraperiod tax allocation, relates the income tax expense for the fiscal period to the following items that affect the amount of the tax provisions: (1) income from continuing operations, (2) discontinued operations, and (3) extraordinary items.

6. Identify where to report earnings per share information. Because of the inherent dangers of focusing attention solely on earnings per share, the profession concluded that companies must disclose earnings per share on the face of the income statement. A company that reports a discontinued operation or an extraordinary item must report per share amounts for these line items either on the face of the income statement or in the notes to the financial statements.

7. Prepare a retained earnings statement. The retained earnings statement should disclose net income (loss), dividends, adjustments due to changes in accounting principles, error corrections, and restrictions of retained earnings.

8. Explain how to report other comprehensive income. Companies report the components of other comprehensive income in a second statement, a combined statement of comprehensive income, or in a statement of stockholders' equity.

QUESTIONS

1. What kinds of questions about future cash flows do investors and creditors attempt to answer with information in the income statement?

2. How can information based on past transactions be used to predict future cash flows?

3. Identify at least two situations in which important changes in value are not reported in the income statement.

4. Identify at least two situations in which application of different accounting methods or accounting estimates results in difficulties in comparing companies.

5. Explain the transaction approach to measuring income. Why is the transaction approach to income measurement preferable to other ways of measuring income?

6. What is earnings management?

7. How can earnings management affect the quality of earnings?

8. Why should caution be exercised in the use of the income figure derived in an income statement? What are the objectives of generally accepted accounting principles in their application to the income statement?

9. A *Wall Street Journal* article noted that **MicroStrategy** reported higher income than its competitors by using a more aggressive policy for recognizing revenue on future upgrades to its products. Some contend that MicroStrategy's quality of earnings is low. What does the term "quality of earnings" mean?

10. What is the major distinction (a) between revenues and gains and (b) between expenses and losses?

11. What are the advantages and disadvantages of the single-step income statement?

12. What is the basis for distinguishing between operating and nonoperating items?

13. Distinguish between the modified all-inclusive income statement and the current operating performance income statement. According to present generally accepted accounting principles, which is recommended? Explain.

14. How should correction of errors be reported in the financial statements?

15. Discuss the appropriate treatment in the financial statements of each of the following.

   (a) An amount of $113,000 realized in excess of the cash surrender value of an insurance policy on the life of one of the founders of the company who died during the year.

   (b) A profit-sharing bonus to employees computed as a percentage of net income.

   (c) Additional depreciation on factory machinery because of an error in computing depreciation for the previous year.

   (d) Rent received from subletting a portion of the office space.

   (e) A patent infringement suit, brought 2 years ago against the company by another company, was settled this year by a cash payment of $725,000.

   (f) A reduction in the Allowance for Doubtful Accounts balance, because the account appears to be considerably in excess of the probable loss from uncollectible receivables.

16. Indicate where the following items would ordinarily appear on the financial statements of Allepo, Inc. for the year 2007.

   (a) The service life of certain equipment was changed from 8 to 5 years. If a 5-year life had been used previously, additional depreciation of $425,000 would have been charged.

   (b) In 2007 a flood destroyed a warehouse that had a book value of $1,600,000. Floods are rare in this locality.

   (c) In 2007 the company wrote off $1,000,000 of inventory that was considered obsolete.

   (d) An income tax refund related to the 2004 tax year was received.

   (e) In 2004, a supply warehouse with an expected useful life of 7 years was erroneously expensed.

   (f) Allepo, Inc. changed from weighted-average to FIFO inventory pricing.

17. Give the section of a multiple-step income statement in which each of the following is shown.

   (a) Loss on inventory write-down.

   (b) Loss from strike.

   (c) Bad debt expense.

   (d) Loss on disposal of a component of the business.

   (e) Gain on sale of machinery.

   (f) Interest revenue.

   (g) Depreciation expense.

   (h) Material write-offs of notes receivable.

18. Barry Bonds Land Development, Inc. purchased land for $70,000 and spent $30,000 developing it. It then sold the land for $160,000. Tom Glavine Manufacturing purchased land for a future plant site for $100,000. Due to a change in plans, Glavine later sold the land for $160,000. Should these two companies report the land sales, both at gains of $60,000, in a similar manner?

19. You run into Rex Grossman at a party and begin discussing financial statements. Rex says, "I prefer the single-step income statement because the multiple-step format generally overstates income." How should you respond to Rex?

20. Federov Corporation has eight expense accounts in its general ledger which could be classified as selling expenses. Should Federov report these eight expenses separately in its income statement or simply report one total amount for selling expenses?

21. Jose DeLeon Investments reported an unusual gain from the sale of certain assets in its 2007 income statement. How does intraperiod tax allocation affect the reporting of this unusual gain?

22. What effect does intraperiod tax allocation have on reported net income?

23. Letterman Company computed earnings per share as follows.

$$\frac{\text{Net income}}{\text{Common shares outstanding at year-end}}$$

Letterman has a simple capital structure. What possible errors might the company have made in the computation? Explain.

24. Maria Shriver Corporation reported 2007 earnings per share of $7.21. In 2008, Maria Shriver reported earnings per share as follows.

On income before extraordinary item	$6.40
On extraordinary item	1.88
On net income	$8.28

Is the increase in earnings per share from $7.21 to $8.28 a favorable trend?

25. What is meant by "tax allocation within a period"? What is the justification for such practice?

26. When does tax allocation within a period become necessary? How should this allocation be handled?

27. During 2007, Natsume Sozeki Company earned income of $1,000,000 before income taxes and realized a gain of $450,000 on a government-forced condemnation sale of a division plant facility. The income is subject to income taxation at the rate of 34%. The gain on the sale of the plant is taxed at 30%. Proper accounting suggests that the unusual gain be reported as an extraordinary item. Illustrate an appropriate presentation of these items in the income statement.

28. On January 30, 2006, a suit was filed against Pierogi Corporation under the Environmental Protection Act. On August 6, 2007, Pierogi Corporation agreed to settle the action and pay $920,000 in damages to certain current and former employees. How should this settlement be reported in the 2007 financial statements? Discuss.

29. Tiger Paper Company decided to close two small pulp mills in Conway, New Hampshire, and Corvallis, Oregon. Would these closings be reported in a separate section entitled "Discontinued operations after income from continuing operations"? Discuss.

30. What major types of items are reported in the retained earnings statement?

31. Generally accepted accounting principles usually require the use of accrual accounting to "fairly present" income. If the cash receipts and disbursements method of accounting will "clearly reflect" taxable income, why does this method not usually also "fairly present" income?

32. State some of the more serious problems encountered in seeking to achieve the ideal measurement of periodic net income. Explain what accountants do as a practical alternative.

33. What is meant by the terms *elements* and *items* as they relate to the income statement? Why might items have to be disclosed in the income statement?

34. What are the three ways that other comprehensive income may be displayed (reported)?

35. How should the disposal of a component of a business be disclosed in the income statement?

BRIEF EXERCISES

(LO 2) **BE4-1** Tim Allen Co. had sales revenue of $540,000 in 2007. Other items recorded during the year were:

Cost of goods sold	$320,000
Wage expense	120,000
Income tax expense	25,000
Increase in value of company reputation	15,000
Other operating expenses	10,000
Unrealized gain on value of patents	20,000

Prepare a single-step income statement for Allen for 2007. Allen has 100,000 shares of stock outstanding.

(LO 2) **BE4-2** Turner Corporation had net sales of $2,400,000 and interest revenue of $31,000 during 2007. Expenses for 2007 were: cost of goods sold $1,250,000; administrative expenses $212,000; selling expenses $280,000; interest expense $45,000. Turner's tax rate is 30%. The corporation had 100,000 shares of common stock authorized and 70,000 shares issued and outstanding during 2007. Prepare a single-step income statement for the year ended December 31, 2007.

(LO 3) **BE4-3** Using the information provided in BE4-2, prepare a condensed multiple-step income statement for Turner Corporation.

(LO 3, 4) **BE4-4** Green Day Corporation had income from continuing operations of $12,600,000 in 2007. During 2007, it disposed of its restaurant division at an after-tax loss of $189,000. Prior to disposal, the division operated at a loss of $315,000 (net of tax) in 2007. Green Day had 10,000,000 shares of common stock outstanding during 2007. Prepare a partial income statement for Green Day beginning with income from continuing operations.

(LO 4, 5) **BE4-5** J. Depp Corporation had income before income taxes for 2007 of $7,300,000. In addition, it suffered an unusual and infrequent pretax loss of $770,000 from a volcano eruption. The corporation's tax rate is 30%. Prepare a partial income statement for J. Depp beginning with income before income taxes. The corporation had 5,000,000 shares of common stock outstanding during 2007.

(LO 4) **BE4-6** During 2007 Lebron James Company changed from FIFO to weighted-average inventory pricing. Pretax income in 2006 and 2005 (James's first year of operations) under FIFO was $160,000 and $180,000, respectively. Pretax income using weighted-average pricing in the prior years would have been $145,000 in 2006 and $170,000 in 2005. In 2007, Lebron James Company reported pretax income (using weighted-average pricing) of $190,000. Show comparative income statements for Lebron James Company, beginning with "Income before income tax," as presented on the 2007 income statement. (The tax rate in all years is 30%.)

(LO 4) **BE4-7** Jana Kingston Company has recorded bad debt expense in the past at a rate of 1½% of net sales. In 2007, Kingston decides to increase its estimate to 2%. If the new rate had been used in prior years, cumulative bad debt expense would have been $380,000 instead of $285,000. In 2007, bad debt expense will be $120,000 instead of $90,000. If Kingston's tax rate is 30%, what amount should it report as the cumulative effect of changing the estimated bad debt rate?

(LO 6) **BE4-8** In 2007, Kirby Puckett Corporation reported net income of $1,200,000. It declared and paid preferred stock dividends of $250,000. During 2007, Puckett had a weighted average of 190,000 common shares outstanding. Compute Puckett's 2007 earnings per share.

(LO 7) **BE4-9** Lincoln Corporation has retained earnings of $675,000 at January 1, 2007. Net income during 2007 was $2,400,000, and cash dividends declared and paid during 2007 totaled $75,000. Prepare a retained earnings statement for the year ended December 31, 2007.

(LO 4, 7) **BE4-10** Using the information from BE4-9, prepare a retained earnings statement for the year ended December 31, 2007. Assume an error was discovered: land costing $80,000 (net of tax) was charged to repairs expense in 2004.

(LO 8) **BE4-11** On January 1, 2007, Creative Works Inc. had cash and common stock of $60,000. At that date the company had no other asset, liability or equity balances. On January 2, 2007, it purchased for cash $20,000 of equity securities that it classified as available-for-sale. It received cash dividends of $3,000 during the year on these securities. In addition, it has an unrealized holding gain on these securities of $5,000 net of tax. Determine the following amounts for 2007: (a) net income; (b) comprehensive income; (c) other comprehensive income; and (d) accumulated other comprehensive income (end of 2007).

EXERCISES

(LO 2) **E4-1** **(Computation of Net Income)** Presented below are changes in all the account balances of Fritz Reiner Furniture Co. during the current year, except for retained earnings.

	Increase (Decrease)		Increase (Decrease)
Cash	$ 79,000	Accounts Payable	$(51,000)
Accounts Receivable (net)	45,000	Bonds Payable	82,000
Inventory	127,000	Common Stock	125,000
Investments	(47,000)	Additional Paid-in Capital	13,000

Instructions
Compute the net income for the current year, assuming that there were no entries in the Retained Earnings account except for net income and a dividend declaration of $19,000 which was paid in the current year.

(LO 2) **E4-2** **(Income Statement Items)** Presented below are certain account balances of Paczki Products Co.

Rental revenue	$ 6,500	Sales discounts	$ 7,800
Interest expense	12,700	Selling expenses	99,400
Beginning retained earnings	114,400	Sales	390,000
Ending retained earnings	134,000	Income tax	31,000
Dividend revenue	71,000	Cost of goods sold	184,400
Sales returns	12,400	Administrative expenses	82,500

Instructions
From the foregoing, compute the following: (a) total net revenue, (b) net income, (c) dividends declared during the current year.

(LO 2) **E4-3** **(Single-step Income Statement)** The financial records of LeRoi Jones Inc. were destroyed by fire at the end of 2007. Fortunately the controller had kept certain statistical data related to the income statement as presented below.

1. The beginning merchandise inventory was $92,000 and decreased 20% during the current year.
2. Sales discounts amount to $17,000.
3. 20,000 shares of common stock were outstanding for the entire year.
4. Interest expense was $20,000.
5. The income tax rate is 30%.
6. Cost of goods sold amounts to $500,000.

7. Administrative expenses are 20% of cost of goods sold but only 8% of gross sales.
8. Four-fifths of the operating expenses relate to sales activities.

Instructions

From the foregoing information prepare an income statement for the year 2007 in single-step form.

(LO 2, 3)

E4-4 **(Multiple-step and Single-step)** Two accountants for the firm of Elwes and Wright are arguing about the merits of presenting an income statement in a multiple-step versus a single-step format. The discussion involves the following 2007 information related to P. Bride Company ($000 omitted).

Administrative expense	
Officers' salaries	$ 4,900
Depreciation of office furniture and equipment	3,960
Cost of goods sold	60,570
Rental revenue	17,230
Selling expense	
Transportation-out	2,690
Sales commissions	7,980
Depreciation of sales equipment	6,480
Sales	96,500
Income tax	9,070
Interest expense	1,860

Instructions

(a) Prepare an income statement for the year 2007 using the multiple-step form. Common shares outstanding for 2007 total 40,550 (000 omitted).

(b) Prepare an income statement for the year 2007 using the single-step form.

(c) Which one do you prefer? Discuss.

(LO 3, 4)

E4-5 **(Multiple-step and Extraordinary Items)** The following balances were taken from the books of Maria Conchita Alonzo Corp. on December 31, 2007.

Interest revenue	$ 86,000		Accumulated depreciation—equipment	$ 40,000
Cash	51,000		Accumulated depreciation—building	28,000
Sales	1,380,000		Notes receivable	155,000
Accounts receivable	150,000		Selling expenses	194,000
Prepaid insurance	20,000		Accounts payable	170,000
Sales returns and allowances	150,000		Bonds payable	100,000
Allowance for doubtful			Administrative and general	
accounts	7,000		expenses	97,000
Sales discounts	45,000		Accrued liabilities	32,000
Land	100,000		Interest expense	60,000
Equipment	200,000		Notes payable	100,000
Building	140,000		Loss from earthquake damage	
Cost of goods sold	621,000		(extraordinary item)	150,000
			Common stock	500,000
			Retained earnings	21,000

Assume the total effective tax rate on all items is 34%.

Instructions

Prepare a multiple-step income statement; 100,000 shares of common stock were outstanding during the year.

(LO 2, 3)

E4-6 **(Multiple-step and Single-step)** The accountant of Whitney Houston Shoe Co. has compiled the following information from the company's records as a basis for an income statement for the year ended December 31, 2007.

Rental revenue	$ 29,000
Interest on notes payable	(18,000)
Market appreciation on land above cost	31,000
Wages and salaries—sales	(114,800)
Materials and supplies—sales	(17,600)
Income tax	(37,400)
Wages and salaries—administrative	(135,900)
Other administrative expenses	(51,700)
Cost of goods sold	(496,000)
Net sales	980,000
Depreciation on plant assets (70% selling, 30% administrative)	(65,000)
Cash dividends declared	16,000

There were 20,000 shares of common stock outstanding during the year.

Instructions

(a) Prepare a multiple-step income statement.

(b) Prepare a single-step income statement.

(c) Which format do you prefer? Discuss.

(LO 2, 4, 6) **E4-7 (Income Statement, EPS)** Presented below are selected ledger accounts of Tucker Corporation as of December 31, 2007.

Cash	$ 50,000
Administrative expenses	100,000
Selling expenses	80,000
Net sales	540,000
Cost of goods sold	210,000
Cash dividends declared (2007)	20,000
Cash dividends paid (2007)	15,000
Discontinued operations (loss before income taxes)	40,000
Depreciation expense, not recorded in 2006	30,000
Retained earnings, December 31, 2006	90,000
Effective tax rate 30%	

Instructions

(a) Compute net income for 2007.

(b) Prepare a partial income statement beginning with income from continuing operations before income tax, and including appropriate earnings per share information. Assume 10,000 shares of common stock were outstanding during 2007.

(LO 3, 4, 5, 6, 7) **E4-8 (Multiple-step Statement with Retained Earnings)** Presented below is information related to Ivan Calderon Corp. for the year 2007.

Net sales	$1,300,000	Write-off of inventory due to obsolescence	$ 80,000
Cost of goods sold	780,000	Depreciation expense omitted by accident in 2006	55,000
Selling expenses	65,000	Casualty loss (extraordinary item) before taxes	50,000
Administrative expenses	48,000	Cash dividends declared	45,000
Dividend revenue	20,000	Retained earnings at December 31, 2006	980,000
Interest revenue	7,000	Effective tax rate of 34% on all items	

Instructions

(a) Prepare a multiple-step income statement for 2007. Assume that 60,000 shares of common stock are outstanding.

(b) Prepare a separate retained earnings statement for 2007.

(LO 6) **E4-9 (Earnings Per Share)** The stockholders' equity section of Tkachuk Corporation appears below as of December 31, 2007.

8% preferred stock, $50 par value, authorized		
100,000 shares, outstanding 90,000 shares		$ 4,500,000
Common stock, $1.00 par, authorized and issued 10 million shares		10,000,000
Additional paid-in capital		20,500,000
Retained earnings	$134,000,000	
Net income	33,000,000	167,000,000
		$202,000,000

Net income for 2007 reflects a total effective tax rate of 34%. Included in the net income figure is a loss of $18,000,000 (before tax) as a result of a major casualty, which should be classified as an extraordinary item. Preferred stock dividends of $360,000 were declared and paid in 2007. Dividends of $1,000,000 were declared and paid to common stockholders in 2007.

Instructions

Compute earnings per share data as it should appear on the income statement of Tkachuk Corporation.

(LO 3, 4, 5, 6) **E4-10 (Condensed Income Statement—Periodic Inventory Method)** Presented below are selected ledger accounts of Spock Corporation at December 31, 2007.

Cash	$ 185,000	Sales salaries	$284,000
Merchandise inventory	535,000	Office salaries	346,000
Sales	4,275,000	Purchase returns	15,000
Advances from customers	117,000	Sales returns	79,000
Purchases	2,786,000	Transportation-in	72,000
Sales discounts	34,000	Accounts receivable	142,500
Purchase discounts	27,000	Sales commissions	83,000

Travel and entertainment—sales	$ 69,000	Telephone—sales	$ 17,000
Accounting and legal services	33,000	Utilities—office	32,000
Insurance expense—office	24,000	Miscellaneous office expenses	8,000
Advertising	54,000	Rental revenue	240,000
Transportation-out	93,000	Extraordinary loss (before tax)	70,000
Depreciation of office equipment	48,000	Interest expense	176,000
Depreciation of sales equipment	36,000	Common stock ($10 par)	900,000

Spock's effective tax rate on all items is 34%. A physical inventory indicates that the ending inventory is $686,000.

Instructions

Prepare a condensed 2007 income statement for Spock Corporation.

(LO 7) **E4-11** **(Retained Earnings Statement)** Eddie Zambrano Corporation began operations on January 1, 2004. During its first 3 years of operations, Zambrano reported net income and declared dividends as follows.

	Net income	Dividends declared
2004	$ 40,000	$ –0–
2005	125,000	50,000
2006	160,000	50,000

The following information relates to 2007.

Income before income tax	$240,000
Prior period adjustment: understatement of 2005 depreciation expense (before taxes)	$ 25,000
Cumulative decrease in income from change in inventory methods (before taxes)	$ 35,000
Dividends declared (of this amount, $25,000 will be paid on Jan. 15, 2008)	$100,000
Effective tax rate	40%

Instructions

(a) Prepare a 2007 retained earnings statement for Eddie Zambrano Corporation.
(b) Assume Eddie Zambrano Corp. restricted retained earnings in the amount of $70,000 on December 31, 2007. After this action, what would Zambrano report as total retained earnings in its December 31, 2007, balance sheet?

(LO 4, 5, 6) **E4-12** **(Earnings per Share)** At December 31, 2006, Shiga Naoya Corporation had the following stock outstanding.

10% cumulative preferred stock, $100 par, 107,500 shares	$10,750,000
Common stock, $5 par, 4,000,000 shares	20,000,000

During 2007, Shiga Naoya did not issue any additional common stock. The following also occurred during 2007.

Income from continuing operations before taxes	$23,650,000
Discontinued operations (loss before taxes)	$ 3,225,000
Preferred dividends declared	$ 1,075,000
Common dividends declared	$ 2,200,000
Effective tax rate	35%

Instructions

Compute earnings per share data as it should appear in the 2007 income statement of Shiga Naoya Corporation. (Round to two decimal places.)

(LO 4, 5, 6) **E4-13** **(Change in Accounting Principle)** Tim Mattke Company began operations in 2005 and for simplicity reasons, adopted weighted-average pricing for inventory. In 2007, in accordance with other companies in its industry, Mattke changed its inventory pricing to FIFO. The pretax income data is reported below.

Year	Weighted-Average	FIFO
2005	$370,000	$395,000
2006	390,000	430,000
2007	410,000	450,000

Instructions

(a) What is Mattke's net income in 2007? Assume a 35% tax rate in all years.
(b) Compute the cumulative effect of the change in accounting principle from weighted-average to FIFO inventory pricing.
(c) Show comparative income statements for Tim Mattke Company, beginning with income before income tax, as presented on the 2007 income statement.

(LO 3, 8)   **E4-14**   **(Comprehensive Income)**   Roxanne Carter Corporation reported the following for 2007: net sales $1,200,000; cost of goods sold $750,000; selling and administrative expenses $320,000; and an unrealized holding gain on available-for-sale securities $18,000.

Instructions

Prepare a statement of comprehensive income, using the two-income statement format. Ignore income taxes and earnings per share.

(LO 7, 8)   **E4-15**   **(Comprehensive Income)**   C. Reither Co. reports the following information for 2007: sales revenue $700,000; cost of goods sold $500,000; operating expenses $80,000; and an unrealized holding loss on available-for-sale securities for 2007 of $60,000. It declared and paid a cash dividend of $10,000 in 2007.

     C. Reither Co. has January 1, 2007, balances in common stock $350,000; accumulated other comprehensive income $80,000; and retained earnings $90,000. It issued no stock during 2007.

Instructions

Prepare a statement of stockholders' equity.

(LO 2, 4, 5, 6, 7, 8)   **E4-16**   **(Various Reporting Formats)**   The following information was taken from the records of Roland Carlson Inc. for the year 2007. Income tax applicable to income from continuing operations $187,000; income tax applicable to loss on discontinued operations $25,500; income tax applicable to extraordinary gain $32,300; income tax applicable to extraordinary loss $20,400; and unrealized holding gain on available-for-sale securities $15,000.

Extraordinary gain	$ 95,000	Cash dividends declared	$ 150,000
Loss on discontinued operations	75,000	Retained earnings January 1, 2007	600,000
Administrative expenses	240,000	Cost of goods sold	850,000
Rent revenue	40,000	Selling expenses	300,000
Extraordinary loss	60,000	Sales	1,900,000

Shares outstanding during 2007 were 100,000.

Instructions

(a) Prepare a single-step income statement for 2007.
(b) Prepare a retained earnings statement for 2007.
(c) Show how comprehensive income is reported using the second income statement format.

See the book's website, www.wiley.com/college/kieso, for Additional Exercises.

PROBLEMS

(LO 3, 4, 5, 6, 7)   **P4-1**   **(Multiple-step Income, Retained Earnings)**   Presented below is information related to American Horse Company for 2007.

Retained earnings balance, January 1, 2007	$ 980,000
Sales for the year	25,000,000
Cost of goods sold	17,000,000
Interest revenue	70,000
Selling and administrative expenses	4,700,000
Write-off of goodwill (not tax deductible)	820,000
Income taxes for 2007	905,000
Gain on the sale of investments (normal recurring)	110,000
Loss due to flood damage—extraordinary item (net of tax)	390,000
Loss on the disposition of the wholesale division (net of tax)	440,000
Loss on operations of the wholesale division (net of tax)	90,000
Dividends declared on common stock	250,000
Dividends declared on preferred stock	70,000

Instructions

Prepare a multiple-step income statement and a retained earnings statement. American Horse Company decided to discontinue its entire wholesale operations and to retain its manufacturing operations. On September 15, American Horse sold the wholesale operations to Rogers Company. During 2007, there were 300,000 shares of common stock outstanding all year.

(LO 2, 6, 7)   **P4-2**   **(Single-step Income, Retained Earnings, Periodic Inventory)**   Presented on page 158 is the trial balance of Mary J. Blige Corporation at December 31, 2007.

MARY J. BLIGE CORPORATION
TRIAL BALANCE
YEAR ENDED DECEMBER 31, 2007

	Debits	Credits
Purchase Discounts		$ 10,000
Cash	$ 205,100	
Accounts Receivable	105,000	
Rent Revenue		18,000
Retained Earnings		260,000
Salaries Payable		18,000
Sales		1,000,000
Notes Receivable	110,000	
Accounts Payable		49,000
Accumulated Depreciation—Equipment		28,000
Sales Discounts	14,500	
Sales Returns	17,500	
Notes Payable		70,000
Selling Expenses	232,000	
Administrative Expenses	99,000	
Common Stock		300,000
Income Tax Expense	38,500	
Cash Dividends	45,000	
Allowance for Doubtful Accounts		5,000
Supplies	14,000	
Freight-in	20,000	
Land	70,000	
Equipment	140,000	
Bonds Payable		100,000
Gain on Sale of Land		30,000
Accumulated Depreciation—Building		19,600
Merchandise Inventory	89,000	
Building	98,000	
Purchases	610,000	
Totals	$1,907,600	$1,907,600

A physical count of inventory on December 31 resulted in an inventory amount of $124,000.

Instructions

Prepare a single-step income statement and a retained earnings statement. Assume that the only changes in retained earnings during the current year were from net income and dividends. Thirty thousand shares of common stock were outstanding the entire year.

(LO 4, 5, 6) **P4-3** **(Irregular Items)** Tony Rich Inc. reported income from continuing operations before taxes during 2007 of $790,000. Additional transactions occurring in 2007 but not considered in the $790,000 are as follows.

1. The corporation experienced an uninsured flood loss (extraordinary) in the amount of $80,000 during the year. The tax rate on this item is 46%.
2. At the beginning of 2005, the corporation purchased a machine for $54,000 (salvage value of $9,000) that had a useful life of 6 years. The bookkeeper used straight-line depreciation for 2005, 2006, and 2007 but failed to deduct the salvage value in computing the depreciation base.
3. Sale of securities held as a part of its portfolio resulted in a loss of $57,000 (pretax).
4. When its president died, the corporation realized $110,000 from an insurance policy. The cash surrender value of this policy had been carried on the books as an investment in the amount of $46,000 (the gain is nontaxable).
5. The corporation disposed of its recreational division at a loss of $115,000 before taxes. Assume that this transaction meets the criteria for discontinued operations.
6. The corporation decided to change its method of inventory pricing from average cost to the FIFO method. The effect of this change on prior years is to increase 2005 income by $60,000 and decrease 2006 income by $20,000 before taxes. The FIFO method has been used for 2007. The tax rate on these items is 40%.

Instructions

Prepare an income statement for the year 2007 starting with income from continuing operations before taxes. Compute earnings per share as it should be shown on the face of the income statement. Common shares outstanding for the year are 80,000 shares. (Assume a tax rate of 30% on all items, unless indicated otherwise.)

(LO 3, 4, 6, 7)

P4-4 **(Multiple- and Single-step Income, Retained Earnings)** The following account balances were included in the trial balance of J.R. Reid Corporation at June 30, 2007.

Sales	$1,678,500	Depreciation of office furniture	
Sales discounts	31,150	and equipment	$ 7,250
Cost of goods sold	896,770	Real estate and other local taxes	7,320
Sales salaries	56,260	Bad debt expense—selling	4,850
Sales commissions	97,600	Building expense—prorated	
Travel expense—salespersons	28,930	to administration	9,130
Freight-out	21,400	Miscellaneous office expenses	6,000
Entertainment expense	14,820	Sales returns	62,300
Telephone and Internet expense—sales	9,030	Dividends received	38,000
Depreciation of sales equipment	4,980	Bond interest expense	18,000
Building expense—prorated to sales	6,200	Income taxes	133,000
Miscellaneous selling expenses	4,715	Depreciation understatement due	
Office supplies used	3,450	to error—2004 (net of tax)	17,700
Telephone and Internet expense—		Dividends declared on	
administration	2,820	preferred stock	9,000
		Dividends declared on common	
		stock	32,000

The Retained Earnings account had a balance of $337,000 at July 1, 2006. There are 80,000 shares of common stock outstanding.

Instructions

(a) Using the multiple-step form, prepare an income statement and a retained earnings statement for the year ended June 30, 2007.

(b) Using the single-step form, prepare an income statement and a retained earnings statement for the year ended June 30, 2007.

(LO 4, 5, 6, 7)

P4-5 **(Irregular Items)** Presented below is a combined single-step income and retained earnings statement for Sandy Freewalt Company for 2007.

		(000 omitted)
Net sales		$640,000
Costs and expenses		
Cost of goods sold		500,000
Selling, general, and administrative expenses		66,000
Other, net		17,000
		583,000
Income before income tax		57,000
Income tax		19,400
Net income		37,600
Retained earnings at beginning of period, as previously reported	$141,000	
Adjustment required for correction of error	(7,000)	
Retained earnings at beginning of period, as restated		134,000
Dividends on common stock		(12,200)
Retained earnings at end of period		$159,400

Additional facts are as follows.

1. "Selling, general, and administrative expenses" for 2007 included a usual but infrequently occurring charge of $10,500,000.

2. "Other, net" for 2007 included an extraordinary item (charge) of $9,000,000. If the extraordinary item (charge) had not occurred, income taxes for 2007 would have been $22,400,000 instead of $19,400,000.

3. "Adjustment required for correction of an error" was a result of a change in estimate (useful life of certain assets reduced to 8 years and a catch-up adjustment made).

4. Sandy Freewalt Company disclosed earnings per common share for net income in the notes to the financial statements.

Instructions

Determine from these additional facts whether the presentation of the facts in the Sandy Freewalt Company income and retained earnings statement is appropriate. If the presentation is not appropriate, describe the appropriate presentation and discuss its theoretical rationale. (Do not prepare a revised statement.)

(LO 4, 5, 7) **P4-6   (Retained Earnings Statement, Prior Period Adjustment)**   Below is the retained earnings account for the year 2007 for LeClair Corp.

Retained earnings, January 1, 2007		$257,600
Add:		
Gain on sale of investments (net of tax)	$41,200	
Net income	84,500	
Refund on litigation with government, related to the year 2004		
(net of tax)	21,600	
Recognition of income earned in 2006, but omitted from income		
statement in that year (net of tax)	25,400	172,700
		430,300
Deduct:		
Loss on discontinued operations (net of tax)	25,000	
Write-off of goodwill (net of tax)	60,000	
Cumulative effect on income of prior years in changing from		
LIFO to FIFO inventory valuation in 2007 (net of tax)	18,200	
Cash dividends declared	32,000	135,200
Retained earnings, December 31, 2007		$295,100

Instructions

(a)   Prepare a corrected retained earnings statement. LeClair Corp. normally sells investments of the type mentioned above. FIFO inventory was used in 2007 to compute net income.

(b)   State where the items that do not appear in the corrected retained earnings statement should be shown.

(LO 4, 5, 6) **P4-7   (Income Statement, Irregular Items)**   Rap Corp. has 100,000 shares of common stock outstanding. In 2007, the company reports income from continuing operations before income tax of $1,210,000. Additional transactions not considered in the $1,210,000 are as follows.

1.   In 2007, Rap Corp. sold equipment for $40,000. The machine had originally cost $80,000 and had accumulated depreciation of $36,000. The gain or loss is considered ordinary.

2.   The company discontinued operations of one of its subsidiaries during the current year at a loss of $190,000 before taxes. Assume that this transaction meets the criteria for discontinued operations. The loss on operations of the discontinued subsidiary was $90,000 before taxes; the loss from disposal of the subsidiary was $100,000 before taxes.

3.   An internal audit discovered that amortization of intangible assets was understated by $35,000 (net of tax) in a prior period. The amount was charged against retained earnings.

4.   The company had a gain of $145,000 on the condemnation of much of its property. The gain is taxed at a total effective rate of 40%. Assume that the transaction meets the requirements of an extraordinary item.

Instructions

Analyze the above information and prepare an income statement for the year 2007, starting with income from continuing operations before income tax. Compute earnings per share as it should be shown on the face of the income statement. (Assume a total effective tax rate of 38% on all items, unless otherwise indicated.)

CONCEPTS FOR ANALYSIS

CA4-1   (Identification of Income Statement Deficiencies)   John Amos Corporation was incorporated and began business on January 1, 2007. It has been successful and now requires a bank loan for additional working capital to finance expansion. The bank has requested an audited income statement for the year 2007. The accountant for John Amos Corporation provides you with the following income statement (page 161) which John Amos plans to submit to the bank.

JOHN AMOS CORPORATION
INCOME STATEMENT

Sales		$850,000
Dividends		32,300
Gain on recovery of insurance proceeds from		
earthquake loss (extraordinary)		38,500
		920,800
Less:		
Selling expenses	$101,100	
Cost of goods sold	510,000	
Advertising expense	13,700	
Loss on obsolescence of inventories	34,000	
Loss on discontinued operations	48,600	
Administrative expense	73,400	780,800
Income before income tax		140,000
Income tax		56,000
Net income		$ 84,000

Instructions

Indicate the deficiencies in the income statement presented above. Assume that the corporation desires a single-step income statement.

CA4-2 (Income Reporting Deficiencies) The following represents a recent income statement for **Boeing Company**.

	($ in millions)
Sales	$21,924
Costs and expenses	20,773
Income from operations	1,151
Other income	122
Interest and debt expense	(130)
Earnings before income taxes	1,143
Income taxes	(287)
Net income	$ 856

It includes only *five* separate numbers (two of which are in billions of dollars), *two* subtotals, and the net earnings figure.

Instructions

(a) Indicate the deficiencies in the income statement.

(b) What recommendations would you make to Boeing to improve the usefulness of its income statement?

CA4-3 (Extraordinary Items) Jeff Foxworthy, vice-president of finance for Red Neck Company, has recently been asked to discuss with the company's division controllers the proper accounting for extraordinary items. Jeff Foxworthy prepared the factual situations presented below as a basis for discussion.

1. An earthquake destroys one of the oil refineries owned by a large multinational oil company. Earthquakes are rare in this geographical location.
2. A publicly held company has incurred a substantial loss in the unsuccessful registration of a bond issue.
3. A large portion of a cigarette manufacturer's tobacco crops are destroyed by a hailstorm. Severe damage from hailstorms is rare in this locality.
4. A large diversified company sells a block of shares from its portfolio of securities acquired for investment purposes.
5. A company that operates a chain of warehouses sells the excess land surrounding one of its warehouses. When the company buys property to establish a new warehouse, it usually buys more land than it expects to use for the warehouse with the expectation that the land will appreciate in value. Twice during the past 5 years the company sold excess land.
6. A company experiences a material loss in the repurchase of a large bond issue that has been outstanding for 3 years. The company regularly repurchases bonds of this nature.
7. A railroad experiences an unusual flood loss to part of its track system. Flood losses normally occur every 3 or 4 years.

8. A machine tool company sells the only land it owns. The land was acquired 10 years ago for future expansion, but shortly thereafter the company abandoned all plans for expansion but decided to hold the land for appreciation.

Instructions

Determine whether the foregoing items should be classified as extraordinary items. Present a rationale for your position.

CA4-4 (Earnings Management) Grace Inc. has recently reported steadily increasing income. The company reported income of $20,000 in 2004, $25,000 in 2005, and $30,000 in 2006. A number of market analysts have recommended that investors buy the stock because they expect the steady growth in income to continue. Grace is approaching the end of its fiscal year in 2007, and it again appears to be a good year. However, it has not yet recorded warranty expense.

Based on prior experience, this year's warranty expense should be around $5,000, but some managers have approached the controller to suggest a larger, more conservative warranty expense should be recorded this year. Income before warranty expense is $43,000. Specifically, by recording an $8,000 warranty accrual this year, Grace could report an increase in income for this year and still be in a position to cover its warranty costs in future years.

Instructions

(a) What is earnings management?

(b) Assume income before warranty expense is $43,000 for both 2007 and 2008 and that total warranty expense over the 2-year period is $10,000. What is the effect of the proposed accounting in 2007? In 2008?

(c) What is the appropriate accounting in this situation?

CA4-5 (Earnings Management) Arthur Miller, controller for the Salem Corporation, is preparing the company's income statement at year-end. He notes that the company lost a considerable sum on the sale of some equipment it had decided to replace. Since the company has sold equipment routinely in the past, Miller knows the losses cannot be reported as extraordinary. He also does not want to highlight it as a material loss since he feels that will reflect poorly on him and the company. He reasons that if the company had recorded more depreciation during the assets' lives, the losses would not be so great. Since depreciation is included among the company's operating expenses, he wants to report the losses along with the company's expenses, where he hopes it will not be noticed.

Instructions

(a) What are the ethical issues involved?

(b) What should Miller do?

CA4-6 (Income Reporting Items) Woody Allen Corp. is an entertainment firm that derives approximately 30% of its income from the Casino Royale Division, which manages gambling facilities. As auditor for Woody Allen Corp., you have recently overheard the following discussion between the controller and financial vice-president.

VICE-PRESIDENT: If we sell the Casino Royale Division, it seems ridiculous to segregate the results of the sale in the income statement. Separate categories tend to be absurd and confusing to the stockholders. I believe that we should simply report the gain on the sale as other income or expense without detail.

CONTROLLER: Professional pronouncements would require that we disclose this information separately in the income statement. If a sale of this type is considered unusual and infrequent, it must be reported as an extraordinary item.

VICE-PRESIDENT: What about the walkout we had last month when employees were upset about their commission income? Would this situation not also be an extraordinary item?

CONTROLLER: I am not sure whether this item would be reported as extraordinary or not.

VICE-PRESIDENT: Oh well, it doesn't make any difference because the net effect of all these items is immaterial, so no disclosure is necessary.

Instructions

(a) On the basis of the foregoing discussion, answer the following questions: Who is correct about handling the sale? What would be the correct income statement presentation for the sale of the Casino Royale Division?

(b) How should the walkout by the employees be reported?

(c) What do you think about the vice-president's observation on materiality?

(d) What are the earnings per share implications of these topics?

CA4-7 **(Identification of Income Statement Weaknesses)** The following financial statement was prepared by employees of Cynthia Taylor Corporation.

CYNTHIA TAYLOR CORPORATION
INCOME STATEMENT
YEAR ENDED DECEMBER 31, 2007

Revenues		
Gross sales, including sales taxes		$1,044,300
Less: Returns, allowances, and cash discounts		56,200
Net sales		988,100
Dividends, interest, and purchase discounts		30,250
Recoveries of accounts written off in prior years		13,850
Total revenues		1,032,200
Costs and expenses		
Cost of goods sold, including sales taxes		465,900
Salaries and related payroll expenses		60,500
Rent		19,100
Freight-in and freight-out		3,400
Bad debt expense		27,800
Total costs and expenses		576,700
Income before extraordinary items		455,500
Extraordinary items		
Loss on discontinued styles (Note 1)		71,500
Loss on sale of marketable securities (Note 2)		39,050
Loss on sale of warehouse (Note 3)		86,350
Total extraordinary items		196,900
Net income		$ 258,600
Net income per share of common stock		$2.30

Note 1: New styles and rapidly changing consumer preferences resulted in a $71,500 loss on the disposal of discontinued styles and related accessories.

Note 2: The corporation sold an investment in marketable securities at a loss of $39,050. The corporation normally sells securities of this nature.

Note 3: The corporation sold one of its warehouses at an $86,350 loss.

Instructions

Identify and discuss the weaknesses in classification and disclosure in the single-step income statement above. You should explain why these treatments are weaknesses and what the proper presentation of the items would be in accordance with GAAP.

CA4-8 **(Classification of Income Statement Items)** As audit partner for Noriyuki and Morita, you are in charge of reviewing the classification of unusual items that have occurred during the current year. The following material items have come to your attention.

1. A merchandising company incorrectly overstated its ending inventory 2 years ago. Inventory for all other periods is correctly computed.
2. An automobile dealer sells for $137,000 an extremely rare 1930 S type Invicta which it purchased for $21,000 10 years ago. The Invicta is the only such display item the dealer owns.
3. A drilling company during the current year extended the estimated useful life of certain drilling equipment from 9 to 15 years. As a result, depreciation for the current year was materially lowered.
4. A retail outlet changed its computation for bad debt expense from 1% to ½ of 1% of sales because of changes in its customer clientele.
5. A mining concern sells a foreign subsidiary engaged in uranium mining, although it (the seller) continues to engage in uranium mining in other countries.
6. A steel company changes from the average-cost method to the FIFO method for inventory costing purposes.
7. A construction company, at great expense, prepared a major proposal for a government loan. The loan is not approved.
8. A water pump manufacturer has had large losses resulting from a strike by its employees early in the year.

9. Depreciation for a prior period was incorrectly understated by $950,000. The error was discovered in the current year.

10. A large sheep rancher suffered a major loss because the state required that all sheep in the state be killed to halt the spread of a rare disease. Such a situation has not occurred in the state for 20 years.

11. A food distributor that sells wholesale to supermarket chains and to fast-food restaurants (two distinguishable classes of customers) decides to discontinue the division that sells to one of the two classes of customers.

Instructions

From the foregoing information, indicate in what section of the income statement or retained earnings statement these items should be classified. Provide a brief rationale for your position.

CA4-9 (Comprehensive Income) Ferguson Arthur, Jr., controller for Jenkins Corporation, is preparing the company's financial statements at year-end. Currently, he is focusing on the income statement and determining the format for reporting comprehensive income. During the year, the company earned net income of $400,000 and had unrealized gains on available-for-sale securities of $20,000. In the previous year net income was $410,000, and the company had no unrealized gains or losses.

Instructions
(a) Show how income and comprehensive income will be reported on a comparative basis for the current and prior years, using the separate income statement format.
(b) Show how income and comprehensive income will be reported on a comparative basis for the current and prior years, using the combined income statement format.
(c) Which format should Arthur recommend?

USING YOUR JUDGMENT

Financial Reporting Problem

  The Procter & Gamble Company (P&G)
The financial statements of **P&G** are presented in Appendix 5B or can be accessed on the KWW website.

Instructions
Refer to P&G's financial statements and the accompanying notes to answer the following questions.
(a) What type of income statement format does P&G use? Indicate why this format might be used to present income statement information.
(b) What are P&G's primary revenue sources?
(c) Compute P&G's gross profit for each of the years 2002–2004. Explain why gross profit increased in 2004.
(d) Why does P&G make a distinction between operating and nonoperating revenue?
(e) What financial ratios did P&G choose to report in its "Financial Summary" section covering the years 1994–2004?

Financial Statement Analysis Cases

Case 1 Bankruptcy Prediction

The Z-score bankruptcy prediction model uses balance sheet and income information to arrive at a Z-Score, which can be used to predict financial distress:

$$Z = \frac{\text{Working capital}}{\text{Total assets}} \times 1.2 + \frac{\text{Retained earnings}}{\text{Total assets}} \times 1.4 + \frac{\text{EBIT}}{\text{Total assets}} \times 3.3 + \frac{\text{Sales}}{\text{Total assets}} \times .99$$
$$+ \frac{\text{MV equity}}{\text{Total liabilities}} \times 0.6$$

EBIT is earnings before interest and taxes. MV Equity is the market value of common equity, which can be determined by multiplying stock price by shares outstanding.

Following extensive testing, it has been shown that companies with Z-scores above 3.0 are unlikely to fail; those with Z-scores below 1.81 are very likely to fail. While the original model was developed for publicly held manufacturing companies, the model has been modified to apply to companies in various industries, emerging companies, and companies not traded in public markets.

Instructions

(a) Use information in the financial statements of a company like Walgreens or Deere & Co. to compute the Z-score for the past 2 years.

(b) Interpret your result. Where does the company fall in the financial distress range?

(c) The Z-score uses EBIT as one of its elements. Why do you think this income measure is used?

Case 2 Dresser Industries

Dresser Industries provides products and services to oil and natural gas exploration, production, transmission and processing companies. A recent income statement is reproduced below. Dollar amounts are in millions.

Sales	$2,697.0
Service revenues	1,933.9
Share of earnings of unconsolidated affiliates	92.4
Total revenues	4,723.3
Cost of sales	1,722.7
Cost of services	1,799.9
Total costs of sales and services	3,522.6
Gross earnings	1,200.7
Selling, engineering, administrative and general expenses	(919.8)
Special charges	(70.0)
Other income (deductions)	
Interest expense	(47.4)
Interest earned	19.1
Other, net	4.8
Earnings before income taxes and other items below	187.4
Income taxes	(79.4)
Minority interest	(10.3)
Earnings from continuing operations	97.7
Discontinued operations	(35.3)
Earnings before extraordinary items	62.4
Extraordinary items	(6.3)
Net earnings	$56.1

Instructions

Assume that 177,636,000 shares of stock were issued and outstanding. Prepare the per-share portion of the income statement. Remember to begin with "Income from continuing operations."

Case 3 P/E Ratios

One of the more closely watched ratios by investors is the price/earnings or P/E ratio. By dividing price per share by earnings per share, analysts get insight into the value the market attaches to a company's earnings. More specifically, a high P/E ratio (in comparison to companies in the same industry) may suggest the stock is overpriced. Also, there is some evidence that companies with low P/E ratios are underpriced and tend to outperform the market. However, the ratio can be misleading.

P/E ratios are sometime misleading because the E (earnings) is subject to a number of assumptions and estimates that could result in overstated earnings and a lower P/E. Some analysts conduct "revenue analysis" to evaluate the quality of an earnings number. Revenues are less subject to management estimates and all earnings must begin with revenues. These analysts also compute the price-to-sales ratio (PSR = price per share ÷ sales per share) to assess whether a company is performing well compared to similar companies. If a company has a price-to-sales ratio significantly higher than its competitors, investors may be betting on a stock that has yet to prove itself. [*Source*: Janice Revell, "Beyond P/E," *Fortune* (May 28, 2001), p. 174.]

Instructions
(a) Identify some of the estimates or assumptions that could result in overstated earnings.
(b) Compute the P/E ratio and the PSR for **Tootsie Roll** and **Hershey's** for 2004.
(c) Use these data to compare the quality of each company's earnings.

Comparative Analysis Case

The Coca-Cola Company and PepsiCo, Inc.

Instructions
Go to the KWW website and use information found there to answer the following questions related to **The Coca-Cola Company** and **PepsiCo, Inc.**

(a) What type of income format(s) is used by these two companies? Identify any differences in income statement format between these two companies.

(b) What are the gross profits, operating profits, and net incomes for these two companies over the 3-year period 2002–2004? Which company has had better financial results over this period of time?

(c) Identify the irregular items reported by these two companies in their income statements over the 3-year period 2002–2004. Do these irregular items appear to be significant?

(d) Refer to Coca-Cola's Management Analysis section under "Reconciliation of Non-GAAP Financial Measures". What adjustments does Coca-Cola make to arrive at "adjusted net income"? Why does Coca-Cola make these adjustments?

Research Cases

Case 1

Most libraries maintain the annual reports of large companies on file or on microfiche.

Instructions
Obtain the 2004 annual reports for **Goodyear Tire and Rubber Co.** and **Northrop Grumman Corp.**, and answer the following questions concerning their income statements. (*Note:* Larger libraries may have CD-ROM products such as *Laser Disclosure* or *Compact Disclosure*. Goodyear Tire and Rubber Co. and Northrop Grumman Corp. can be found online in the SEC EDGAR database.)

(a) Describe the major differences between the income statement formats.

(b) Identify any irregular items on either of the income statements.

(c) Neither company includes a separate line for depreciation expense. Does depreciation expense appear on another financial statement?

(d) Northrop Grumman's income statement includes significantly more detail than Goodyear's. Which presentation do you prefer? Why?

Case 2

The April 1996 issue of the *Journal of Accountancy* includes an article by Dennis R. Beresford, L. Todd Johnson, and Cheri L. Reither, entitled "Is a Second Income Statement Needed?"

Instructions
Read the article and answer the following questions.

(a) On what basis would the "second income statement" be prepared? Briefly describe this basis.

(b) Why is there a perceived need for a second income statement?

(c) Identify three alternatives for reporting the proposed measure of income.

International Reporting Case

Presented below is the income statement for a British company, **Avon Rubber PLC**.

Avon Rubber PLC

Consolidated Profit and Loss Account
for the year ended 30 September

	Before exceptional items £'000	Exceptional items £'000	Total £'000
Turnover	250,509	–	250,509
Cost of sales	(209,739)	–	(209,739)
Gross profit	40,770	–	40,770
Net operating expenses (including £681,000 (2002; £626,000) goodwill amortisation)	(30,349)	(6,701)	(37,050)
Operating profit	10,421	(6,701)	3,720
Share of profits of joint venture and associate	21	–	21
Total operating profit including joint venture and associate	10,442	(6,701)	3,741
Loss on disposal of fixed assets	—	(1,205)	(1,205)
Loss on disposal of operations	—	(568)	(568)
Profit on ordinary activities before interest	10,442	(8,474)	1,968
Interest receivable	609	–	609
Interest payable	(4,032)	–	(4,032)
Profit/(loss) on ordinary activities before taxation	7,019	(8,474)	(1,455)
Taxation	(2,810)	2,500	(310)
Profit/(loss) on ordinary activities after taxation	4,209	(5,974)	(1,765)
Minority interests	194	–	194
Profit/(loss) for the financial year	4,403	(5,974)	(1,571)
Dividends	(2,031)	–	(2,031)
Retained profit/(loss) for the financial year	2,372	(5,974)	(3,602)
Earnings/(loss) per ordinary share			
Basic			(5.7)p

Instructions

(a) Review the Avon Rubber income statement and identify at least three differences between the British income statement and an income statement of a U.S. company as presented in the chapter.

(b) Identify any irregular items reported by Avon Rubber. Is the reporting of these irregular items in Avon's income statement similar to reporting of these items in U.S. companies' income statements? Explain.

Professional Research: Financial Accounting and Reporting

Your client took accounting a number of years ago and was unaware of comprehensive income reporting. He is not convinced that any accounting standards exist for comprehensive income.

Instructions

Using the **Financial Accounting Research System (FARS)**, respond to the following items. (Provide text strings used in your search.)

(a) What statement addresses comprehensive income directly? When was it issued?

(b) Provide the definition of comprehensive income.

(c) Define classifications within net income; give examples.

(d) Define classifications within other comprehensive income; give examples.

(e) What are reclassification adjustments?

Professional Simulation

In this simulation you are asked to compute various income amounts. Assume a tax rate of 30% and 100,000 shares of common stock outstanding during the year. Prepare responses to all parts.

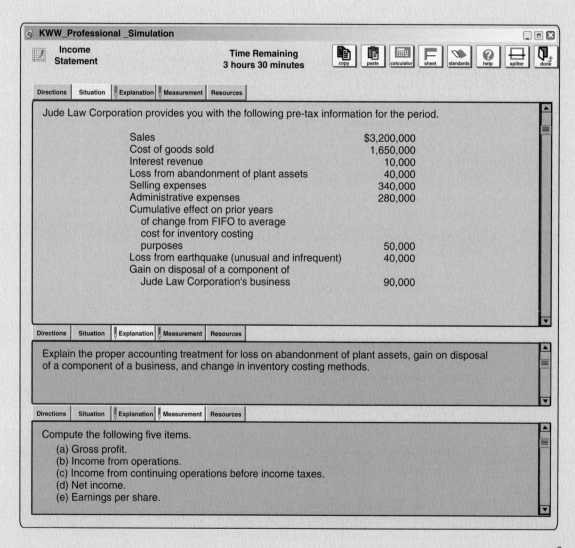

KWW_Professional _Simulation

Income Statement — Time Remaining 3 hours 30 minutes

copy · paste · calculator · sheet · standards · help · splitter · done

Directions | Situation | Explanation | Measurement | Resources

Jude Law Corporation provides you with the following pre-tax information for the period.

Sales	$3,200,000
Cost of goods sold	1,650,000
Interest revenue	10,000
Loss from abandonment of plant assets	40,000
Selling expenses	340,000
Administrative expenses	280,000
Cumulative effect on prior years of change from FIFO to average cost for inventory costing purposes	50,000
Loss from earthquake (unusual and infrequent)	40,000
Gain on disposal of a component of Jude Law Corporation's business	90,000

Directions | Situation | Explanation | Measurement | Resources

Explain the proper accounting treatment for loss on abandonment of plant assets, gain on disposal of a component of a business, and change in inventory costing methods.

Directions | Situation | Explanation | Measurement | Resources

Compute the following five items.

(a) Gross profit.
(b) Income from operations.
(c) Income from continuing operations before income taxes.
(d) Net income.
(e) Earnings per share.

Remember to check the book's companion website to find additional resources for this chapter.

BALANCE SHEET AND STATEMENT OF CASH FLOWS

"There Ought to Be a Law"

As one manager noted, "There ought to be a law that before you can buy a stock, you must be able to read a balance sheet." We agree, and the same can be said for a statement of cash flows.

Krispy Kreme Doughnuts provides an example of how stunning earnings growth can hide real problems. Not long ago the doughnut maker was a glamour stock with a 60 percent earnings per share growth rate and a price-earnings ratio around 70. Seven months later its stock price had dropped 72 percent. What happened? Stockholders alleged that Krispy Kreme may have been inflating its revenues and not taking enough bad debt expense (which inflated both assets and income). In addition, Krispy Kreme's operating cash flow was negative. Most financially sound companies throw off positive cash flow.

Here are additional examples of how one rating agency rated the earnings quality of some companies, using some key balance sheet and statement of cash flow measurements.

Earnings-Quality

Winners	Company	Earnings-Quality Indicators
	Avon Products	Strong cash flow
	Capital One Financial	Conservatively capitalized
	Ecolab	Good management of working capital
	Timberland	Minimal off-balance-sheet commitments

Earnings-Quality

Losers	Company	Earnings-Quality Indicators
	Ford Motor	High debt and underfunded pension plan
	Kroger	High goodwill and debt
	Ryder System	Negative free cash flow
	Teco Energy	Selling assets to meet liquidity needs

Just as a deteriorating balance sheet and statement of cash flows warn of earnings declines (and falling stock prices), improving balance sheet and cash flow information is a leading indicator of improved earnings.[1]

---

[1]Adapted from Gretchen Morgenson, "How Did They Value Stocks? Count the Absurd Ways," *New York Times on the Web* (March 18, 2001), and from K. Badanhausen, J. Gage, C. Hall, and M. Ozanian, "Beyond Balance Sheet: Earnings Quality," *Forbes.com* (January 28, 2005).

Learning Objectives

After studying this chapter, you should be able to:

1 Explain the uses and limitations of a balance sheet.

2 Identify the major classifications of the balance sheet.

3 Prepare a classified balance sheet using the report and account formats.

4 Determine which balance sheet information requires supplemental disclosure.

5 Describe the major disclosure techniques for the balance sheet.

6 Indicate the purpose of the statement of cash flows.

7 Identify the content of the statement of cash flows.

8 Prepare a statement of cash flows.

9 Understand the usefulness of the statement of cash flows.

Readers of the financial statements sometimes ignore important information in the balance sheet and statement of cash flows. As our opening story shows, analyzing these financial statements helps investors avoid surprises in earnings. In this chapter we examine the many different types of assets, liabilities, and stockholders' equity items that affect the balance sheet and the statement of cash flows. The content and organization of the chapter are as follows.

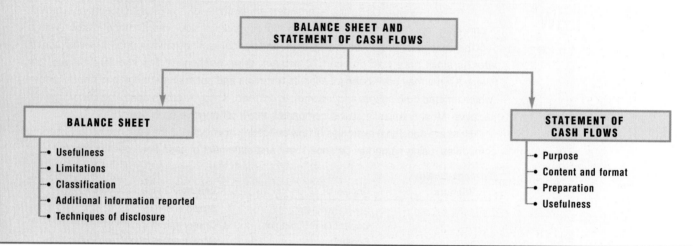

SECTION 1	BALANCE SHEET

The **balance sheet**, sometimes referred to as the **statement of financial position**, reports the assets, liabilities, and stockholders' equity of a business enterprise at a specific date. This financial statement provides information about the nature and amounts of investments in enterprise resources, obligations to creditors, and the owners' equity in net resources.[2] It therefore helps in predicting the amounts, timing, and uncertainty of future cash flows.

USEFULNESS OF THE BALANCE SHEET

By providing information on assets, liabilities, and stockholders' equity, the balance sheet provides a basis for computing rates of return and evaluating the capital structure of the enterprise. As our opening story indicates, analysts also use information in the balance sheet to assess a company's risk[3] and future cash flows. In this regard,

---

[2]*Accounting Trends and Techniques—2004* (New York: AICPA) indicates that approximately 96 percent of the companies surveyed used the term "balance sheet." The term "statement of financial position" is used infrequently, although it is conceptually appealing.

[3]Risk conveys the unpredictability of future events, transactions, circumstances, and results of the company.

analysts use the balance sheet to assess a company's liquidity, solvency, and financial flexibility.

Liquidity describes "the amount of time that is expected to elapse until an asset is realized or otherwise converted into cash or until a liability has to be paid."[4] Creditors are interested in short-term liquidity ratios, such as the ratio of cash (or near cash) to short-term liabilities. These ratios indicate whether a company, like **Amazon**, will have the resources to pay its current and maturing obligations. Similarly, stockholders assess liquidity to evaluate the possibility of future cash dividends or the buyback of shares. In general, the greater Amazon's liquidity, the lower its risk of failure.

Solvency refers to the ability of a company to pay its debts as they mature. For example, when a company carries a high level of long-term debt relative to assets, it has lower solvency than a similar company with a low level of long-term debt. Companies with higher debt are relatively more risky because they will need more of their assets to meet their fixed obligations (interest and principal payments).

Liquidity and solvency affect a company's **financial flexibility,** which measures the "ability of an enterprise to take effective actions to alter the amounts and timing of cash flows so it can respond to unexpected needs and opportunities."[5] For example, a company may become so loaded with debt—so financially inflexible—that it has little or no sources of cash to finance expansion or to pay off maturing debt. A company with a high degree of financial flexibility is better able to survive bad times, to recover from unexpected setbacks, and to take advantage of profitable and unexpected investment opportunities. Generally, the greater an enterprise's financial flexibility, the lower its risk of failure.

How quickly will my assets convert to cash?

Obligation Ocean

We are drowning in a sea of debt!

GROUNDED

WHAT DO THE NUMBERS MEAN?

The terrorist attacks of September 11, 2001, showed how vulnerable the major airlines are to falling demand for their services. Since that infamous date, major airlines have reduced capacity and slashed jobs to avoid bankruptcy. **United Airlines**, the second largest U.S. air carrier, **Northwest Airlines**, the fourth largest U.S. carrier, **US Airways**, the seventh largest U.S. carrier, and several smaller competitors have filed for bankruptcy.

Here are some statements made in a recent annual report of **Delta Airlines**, whose auditors have noted that there is substantial doubt about the company's ability to continue as a going concern.

> "If we are unsuccessful in further reducing our operating costs...we will need to restructure our costs under Chapter 11 of the U.S. Bankruptcy Code.... We have substantial liquidity needs and there is no assurance that we will be able to obtain the necessary financing to meet those needs on acceptable terms, if at all."

The financial distress related to the airline industry was not an insider's secret. The airlines' balance sheets clearly revealed their financial inflexibility and low liquidity even before September 11. For example, major airlines such as **Braniff**, **Continental**, **Eastern**, **Midway**, and **America West** declared bankruptcy before September 11.

Conversely, some airlines have done well. In 2004, **Southwest Airlines** recorded its 32nd consecutive year of profitability.

---

[4]"Reporting Income, Cash Flows, and Financial Position of Business Enterprises," *Proposed Statement of Financial Accounting Concepts* (Stamford, Conn.: FASB, 1981), par. 29.

[5]"Reporting Income, Cash Flows, and Financial Position of Business Enterprises," *Proposed Statement of Financial Accounting Concepts* (Stamford, Conn.: FASB, 1981), par. 25.

Hmm... I wonder if they will pay me back?

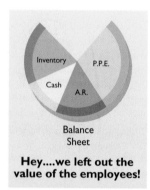

Hey....we left out the value of the employees!

LIMITATIONS OF THE BALANCE SHEET

Some of the major limitations of the balance sheet are:

1 Most assets and liabilities are reported at **historical cost**. As a result, the information provided in the balance sheet has high reliability. But it is often criticized for not reporting a more relevant fair value. For example, **Georgia-Pacific** owns timber and other assets that may appreciate in value after purchase. Yet, Georgia-Pacific reports any increase only if and when it sells the assets.

2 Companies use **judgments and estimates** to determine many of the items reported in the balance sheet. For example, in its balance sheet, **Dell** estimates the amount of receivables that it will collect, the useful life of its warehouses, and the number of computers that will be returned under warranty.

3 The balance sheet necessarily **omits many items that are of financial value** but that a company cannot record objectively. For example, the knowledge and skill of **Intel** employees in developing new computer chips are arguably the company's most significant asset. However, because Intel cannot reliably measure the value of its employees and other intangible assets (such as customer base, research superiority, and reputation), it does not recognize these items in the balance sheet. Similarly, many other liabilities are reported in an "off-balance-sheet" manner, if at all.

The recent bankruptcy of the seventh-largest U.S. company, **Enron**, highlights the omission of important items in the balance sheet. In Enron's case, it failed to disclose certain off-balance-sheet financing obligations in its main financial statements.[6]

CLASSIFICATION IN THE BALANCE SHEET

OBJECTIVE 2
Identify the major classifications of the balance sheet.

Balance sheet accounts are **classified**. That is, balance sheets group together similar items to arrive at significant subtotals. Furthermore, the material is arranged so that important relationships are shown.

The FASB has often noted that the parts and subsections of financial statements can be more informative than the whole. Therefore, the FASB discourages the reporting of summary accounts alone (total assets, net assets, total liabilities, etc.). Instead, companies should report and classify individual items in sufficient detail to permit users to assess the amounts, timing, and uncertainty of future cash flows. Such classification also makes it easier for users to evaluate the company's liquidity and financial flexibility, profitability, and risk.

To classify items in financial statements, companies group those items with similar characteristics and separate items with different characteristics.[7] For example, companies should report separately:

1 Assets that differ in their **type or expected function** in the company's central operations or other activities. For example, **IBM** reports merchandise inventories separately from property, plant, and equipment.

2 Assets and liabilities with **different implications for the company's financial flexibility**. For example, a company that uses assets in its operations, like **Walgreens**, should report those assets separately from assets held for investment and assets subject to restrictions, such as leased equipment.

3 Assets and liabilities with **different general liquidity characteristics**. For example, **Boeing Company** reports cash separately from inventories.

---

[6]We discuss several of these omitted items (such as leases and other off-balance-sheet arrangements) in later chapters. See Wayne Upton, Jr., Special Report: *Business and Financial Reporting, Challenges from the New Economy* (Norwalk, Conn.: FASB, 2001).

[7]"Reporting Income, Cash Flows, and Financial Positions of Business Enterprises," *Proposed Statement of Financial Accounting Concepts* (Stamford, Conn.: FASB, 1981), par. 51.

The three general classes of items included in the balance sheet are assets, liabilities, and equity. We defined them in Chapter 2 as follows.

ELEMENTS OF THE BALANCE SHEET

1 *ASSETS*. Probable future economic benefits obtained or controlled by a particular entity as a result of past transactions or events.

2 *LIABILITIES*. Probable future sacrifices of economic benefits arising from present obligations of a particular entity to transfer assets or provide services to other entities in the future as a result of past transactions or events.

3 *EQUITY*. Residual interest in the assets of an entity that remains after deducting its liabilities. In a business enterprise, the equity is the ownership interest.[8]

Companies then further divide these items into several subclassifications. Illustration 5-1 indicates the general format of balance sheet presentation.

Assets	Liabilities and Owners' Equity
Current assets	Current liabilities
Long-term investments	Long-term debt
Property, plant, and equipment	Owners' equity
Intangible assets	Capital stock
Other assets	Additional paid-in capital
	Retained earnings

ILLUSTRATION 5-1
Balance Sheet
Classifications

A company may classify the balance sheet in some other manner, but you usually see little departure from these major subdivisions in practice. A proprietorship or partnership does present the classifications within the owners' equity section a little differently, as we will show later in the chapter.

Current Assets

Current assets are cash and other assets a company expects to convert into cash, sell, or consume either in one year or in the operating cycle, whichever is longer. The operating cycle is the average time between when a company acquires materials and supplies and when it receives cash for sales of the product (for which it acquired the materials and supplies). The cycle operates from cash through inventory, production, receivables, and back to cash. When several operating cycles occur within one year, a company uses the one-year period. If the operating cycle is more than one year, a company uses the longer period.

Current assets are presented in the balance sheet in order of liquidity. The five major items found in the current assets section, and their bases of valuation, are shown in Illustration 5-2.

Item	Basis of Valuation
Cash and cash equivalents	Fair value
Short-term investments	Generally, fair value
Receivables	Estimated amount collectible
Inventories	Lower of cost or market
Prepaid expenses	Cost

ILLUSTRATION 5-2
Current Assets and Basis
of Valuation

---

[8]"Elements of Financial Statements of Business Enterprises," *Statement of Financial Accounting Concepts No. 6* (Stamford, Conn.: FASB, 1985), paras. 25, 35 and 49.

A company does not report these five items as current assets if it does not expect to realize them in one year or in the operating cycle, whichever is longer. For example, a company excludes cash restricted for purposes other than payment of current obligations or for use in current operations from the current assets section. **Generally, if a company expects to convert an asset into cash or to use it to pay a current liability within a year or the operating cycle, whichever is longer, it classifies the asset as current.**

This rule, however, is subject to interpretation. A company classifies an investment in common stock as either a current asset or a noncurrent asset depending on management's intent. When it has small holdings of common stocks or bonds that it will hold long-term, it should not classify them as current.

Although a current asset is well defined, certain theoretical problems also develop. For example, how is including prepaid expenses in the current assets section justified? The rationale is that if a company did not pay these items in advance, it would instead need to use other current assets during the operating cycle. If we follow this logic to its ultimate conclusion, however, any asset previously purchased saves the use of current assets during the operating cycle and would be considered current.

Another problem occurs in the current-asset definition when a company consumes plant assets during the operating cycle. Conceptually, it seems that a company should place an amount equal to the current depreciation charge on the plant assets in the current assets section, because it will consume them in the next operating cycle. However, this conceptual problem is ignored. This example illustrates that the formal distinction made between some current and noncurrent assets is somewhat arbitrary.

Cash

Cash is generally considered to consist of currency and demand deposits (monies available on demand at a financial institution.) **Cash equivalents** are short-term highly liquid investments that will mature within three months or less. Most companies use the caption "Cash and cash equivalents," and they indicate that this amount approximates fair value.

A company must disclose any restrictions or commitments related to the availability of cash. As an example, see the excerpt from the annual report of **Alterra Healthcare Corp.** in Illustration 5-3.

ILLUSTRATION 5-3
Balance Sheet
Presentation of
Restricted Cash

Alterra
AGING WITH CHOICE

Alterra Healthcare Corp.

Current assets

Cash	$18,728,000
Restricted cash and investments (Note 7)	7,191,000

Note 7: Restricted Cash and Investments. Restricted cash and investments consist of certificates of deposit restricted as collateral for lease arrangements and debt service with interest rates ranging from 4.0% to 5.5%.

Alterra Healthcare restricted cash to meet an obligation due currently. Therefore, Alterra included this restricted cash under current assets.

If a company restricts cash for purposes other than current obligations, it excludes the cash from current assets. Illustration 5-4 shows an example of this, excerpted from the annual report of **Owens Corning, Inc.**

Owens Corning, Inc.
(in millions)

Current assets	
Cash and cash equivalents	$ 70
Restricted securities—Fibreboard—current portion (Note 23)	900
Other assets	
Restricted securities—Fibreboard (Note 23)	938

Note 23 (in part). The Insurance Settlement funds are held in and invested by the Fibreboard Settlement Trust (the "Trust") and are available to satisfy Fibreboard's pending and future asbestos related liabilities. . . . The assets of the Trust are comprised of cash and marketable securities (collectively, the "Trust Assets") and are reflected on Owens Corning's consolidated balance sheet as restricted assets. These assets are reflected as current assets or other assets, with each category denoted "Restricted securities—Fibreboard."

ILLUSTRATION 5-4
Balance Sheet Presentation of Current and Noncurrent Restricted Cash

Short-Term Investments

Companies group investments in debt and equity securities into three separate portfolios for valuation and reporting purposes:

Held-to-maturity: Debt securities that a company has the positive intent and ability to hold to maturity.

Trading: Debt and equity securities bought and held primarily for sale in the near term to generate income on short-term price differences.

Available-for-sale: Debt and equity securities not classified as held-to-maturity or trading securities.

A company should report trading securities (whether debt or equity) as current assets. It classifies individual held-to-maturity and available-for-sale securities as current or noncurrent depending on the circumstances. It should report held-to-maturity securities at amortized cost. All trading and available-for-sale securities are reported at fair value.[9]

For example, see Illustration 5-5, which is an excerpt from the annual report of **Intuit Inc.** with respect to its available-for-sale investments.

Intuit Inc.
(in thousands)

Assets	
Cash and cash equivalents	$ 170,043
Short-term investments (Note 2)	1,036,758

Note 2 (in part). The following schedule summarizes the estimated fair value of our short-term investments (all available-for-sale):

Corporate notes	$ 50,471
Municipal bonds	931,374
U.S. government securities	54,913

ILLUSTRATION 5-5
Balance Sheet Presentation of Investments in Securities

[9]"Accounting for Certain Investments in Debt and Equity Securities," *Statement of Financial Accounting Standards No. 115* (Norwalk, Conn.: FASB, 1993).

Receivables

A company should clearly identify any anticipated loss due to uncollectibles, the amount and nature of any nontrade receivables, and any receivables used as collateral. Major categories of receivables should be shown in the balance sheet or the related notes. For receivables arising from unusual transactions (such as sale of property, or a loan to affiliates or employees), companies should separately classify these as long-term, unless collection is expected within one year. **Mack Trucks, Inc.** reported its receivables as shown in Illustration 5-6.

ILLUSTRATION 5-6
Balance Sheet
Presentation of
Receivables

Mack Trucks, Inc.

Current assets

Trade receivables	
Accounts receivable	$102,212,000
Affiliated companies	1,157,000
Installment notes and contracts	625,000
Total	103,994,000
Less: Allowance for uncollectible accounts	8,194,000
Trade receivables—net	95,800,000
Receivables from unconsolidated financial subsidiaries	22,106,000

UNDERLYING CONCEPTS

The lower-of-cost-or-market valuation reflects the use of *conservatism* in accounting.

Inventories

To present inventories properly, a company discloses the basis of valuation (e.g., lower-of-cost-or-market) and the method of pricing (e.g., FIFO or LIFO). A manufacturing concern (like **Abbott Laboratories**, shown in Illustration 5-7) also indicates the stage of completion of the inventories.

ILLUSTRATION 5-7
Balance Sheet
Presentation of
Inventories, Showing
Stage of Completion

Abbott Laboratories
(in thousands)

Current assets

Inventories	
Finished products	$ 772,478
Work in process	338,818
Materials	384,148
Total inventories	1,495,444

Note 1 (in part): Inventories. Inventories are stated at the lower of cost (first-in, first-out basis) or market.

Weyerhaeuser Company, a forestry company and lumber manufacturer with several finished-goods product lines, reported its inventory as shown in Illustration 5-8.

Weyerhaeuser Company

Current assets

Inventories—at FIFO lower of cost or market

Logs and chips	$ 68,471,000
Lumber, plywood and panels	86,741,000
Pulp, newsprint and paper	47,377,000
Containerboard, paperboard, containers and cartons	59,682,000
Other products	161,717,000
Total product inventories	423,988,000
Materials and supplies	175,540,000

ILLUSTRATION 5-8
Balance Sheet
Presentation of
Inventories, Showing
Product Lines

Prepaid Expenses

A company includes prepaid expenses in current assets if it will receive benefits (usually services) within one year or the operating cycle, whichever is longer.[10] As we discussed earlier, these items are current assets because if they had not already been paid, they would require the use of cash during the next year or the operating cycle. A company reports prepaid expenses at the amount of the unexpired or unconsumed cost.

A common example is the prepayment for an insurance policy. A company classifies it as a prepaid expense because the payment precedes the receipt of the benefit of coverage. Other common prepaid expenses include prepaid rent, advertising, taxes, and office or operating supplies. **Knight Ridder, Inc.**, for example, listed its prepaid expenses in current assets as shown in Illustration 5-9.

Knight Ridder, Inc.

(in thousands)

Current assets

Cash, including short-term cash investments of $7,001	$ 41,661
Accounts receivable, net of allowances of $20,238	416,498
Inventories	52,786
Prepaids	30,767
Other current assets	34,382

ILLUSTRATION 5-9
Balance Sheet
Presentation of Prepaid
Expenses

Noncurrent Assets

Noncurrent assets are those not meeting the definition of current assets. They include a variety of items, as we discuss in the following sections.

Long-Term Investments

Long-term investments, often referred to simply as investments, normally consist of one of four types:

1 Investments in securities, such as bonds, common stock, or long-term notes.

2 Investments in tangible fixed assets not currently used in operations, such as land held for speculation.

---

[10]*Accounting Trends and Techniques—2004* (New York: AICPA) in its survey of 600 annual reports identified 351 companies that reported prepaid expenses.

3 Investments set aside in special funds such as a sinking fund, pension fund, or plant expansion fund. This includes the cash surrender value of life insurance.

4 Investments in nonconsolidated subsidiaries or affiliated companies.

Companies expect to hold long-term investments for many years. They usually present them on the balance sheet just below "Current assets," in a separate section called "Investments." Realize that many securities classified as long-term investments are, in fact, readily marketable. But a company does not include them as current assets unless it intends to convert them to cash in the short-term—that is, within a year or in the operating cycle, whichever is longer. As indicated earlier, securities classified as available-for-sale are reported at fair value, and held-to-maturity securities are reported at amortized cost.

Motorola, Inc. reported its investments section, located between "Property, plant, and equipment" and "Other assets," as shown in Illustration 5-10.

ILLUSTRATION 5-10
Balance Sheet
Presentation of Long-
Term Investments

Motorola, Inc.

(in millions)

Investments	
Equity investments	$ 872
Other investments	2,567
Fair value adjustment to available-for-sale securities	2,487
Total	$5,926

Property, Plant, and Equipment

Property, plant, and equipment are tangible long-lived assets used in the regular operations of the business. These assets consist of physical property such as land, buildings, machinery, furniture, tools, and wasting resources (timberland, minerals). With the exception of land, a company either depreciates (e.g., buildings) or depletes (e.g., timberlands or oil reserves) these assets.

Mattel, Inc. presented its property, plant, and equipment in its balance sheet as shown in Illustration 5-11.

ILLUSTRATION 5-11
Balance Sheet
Presentation of
Property, Plant, and
Equipment

Mattel, Inc.

Property, plant, and equipment	
Land	$ 32,793,000
Buildings	257,430,000
Machinery and equipment	564,244,000
Capitalized leases	23,271,000
Leasehold improvements	74,988,000
	952,726,000
Less: Accumulated depreciation	472,986,000
	479,740,000
Tools, dies and molds, net	168,092,000
Property, plant, and equipment, net	647,832,000

A company discloses the basis it uses to value property, plant, and equipment; any liens against the properties; and accumulated depreciation–usually in the notes to the statements.

Intangible Assets

Intangible assets lack physical substance and are not financial instruments (see definition on page 186). They include patents, copyrights, franchises, goodwill, trademarks, trade names, and customer lists. A company writes off (amortizes) limited-life intangible assets over their useful lives. It periodically assesses indefinite-life intangibles (such as goodwill) for impairment. Intangibles can represent significant economic resources, yet financial analysts often ignore them, because valuation is difficult.

PepsiCo, Inc. reported intangible assets in its balance sheet as shown in Illustration 5-12.

PEPSICO

PepsiCo, Inc.
(in millions)

Intangible assets	
Goodwill	$3,374
Trademarks	1,320
Other identifiable intangibles	147
Total intangibles	$4,841

ILLUSTRATION 5-12
Balance Sheet
Presentation of Intangible
Assets

Other Assets

The items included in the section "Other assets" vary widely in practice. Some include items such as long-term prepaid expenses, prepaid pension cost, and noncurrent receivables. Other items that might be included are assets in special funds, deferred income taxes, property held for sale, and restricted cash or securities. A company should limit this section to include only unusual items sufficiently different from assets included in specific categories.

Liabilities

Similar to assets, companies classify liabilities as current or long-term.

Current Liabilities

Current liabilities are the obligations that a company reasonably expects to liquidate either through the use of current assets or the creation of other current liabilities. This concept includes:

1 Payables resulting from the acquisition of goods and services: accounts payable, wages payable, taxes payable, and so on.

2 Collections received in advance for the delivery of goods or performance of services, such as unearned rent revenue or unearned subscriptions revenue.

3 Other liabilities whose liquidation will take place within the operating cycle, such as the portion of long-term bonds to be paid in the current period or short-term obligations arising from purchase of equipment.

At times, a liability that is payable within the next year is not included in the current liabilities section. This occurs either when the company expects to refinance the debt through another long-term issue[11] or to retire the debt out of noncurrent assets. This approach is used because liquidation does not result from the use of current assets or the creation of other current liabilities.

Companies do not report current liabilities in any consistent order. In general, though, companies most commonly list notes payable, accounts payable, or short-term

---

[11]"Classification of Short-term Obligations Expected to Be Refinanced," *Statement of Financial Accounting Standards No. 6* (Stamford, Conn.: FASB, 1975).

debt as the first item. Income taxes payable, current maturities of long-term debt, or other current liabilities are commonly listed last. For example, see **Halliburton Company**'s current liabilities section in Illustration 5-13.

ILLUSTRATION 5-13
Balance Sheet
Presentation of
Current Liabilities

Halliburton Company
(in millions)

Current liabilities	
Short-term notes payable	$1,570
Accounts payable	782
Accrued employee compensation and benefits	267
Unearned revenues	386
Income taxes payable	113
Accrued special charges	6
Current maturities of long-term debt	8
Other current liabilities	694
Total current liabilities	3,826

Current liabilities include such items as trade and nontrade notes and accounts payable, advances received from customers, and current maturities of long-term debt. If the amounts are material, companies classify income taxes and other accrued items separately. A company should fully describe in the notes any information about a secured liability—for example, stock held as collateral on notes payable—to identify the assets providing the security.

The excess of total current assets over total current liabilities is referred to as **working capital** (sometimes called **net working capital**). Working capital represents the net amount of a company's relatively liquid resources. That is, it is the liquidity buffer available to meet the financial demands of the operating cycle.

Companies seldom disclose an amount for working capital on the balance sheet. But bankers and other creditors compute it as an indicator of the short-run liquidity of a company. To determine the actual liquidity and availability of working capital to meet current obligations, however, requires analysis of the composition of the current assets and their nearness to cash.

WHAT DO THE
NUMBERS MEAN?

"SHOW ME THE ASSETS!"

Recently, concerned about the liquidity and solvency of many dot-com companies, creditors have demanded more assurance that these companies can pay their bills when due. A key indicator for creditors is the amount of working capital. For example, when a report predicted that **Amazon.com**'s working capital would turn negative, the company's vendors began to explore steps that would ensure that Amazon would pay them.

Some vendors have demanded that their dot-com customers sign notes stating that the goods shipped to them serve as collateral for the transaction. Other vendors began shipping goods on consignment—an arrangement whereby the vendor retains ownership of the goods until a third party buys and pays for them.

Such creditor protection measures arise from creditors' concerns about dot-coms' lack of tangible assets that they can convert to cash to meet short-term obligations. For example, the primary asset for many dot-coms is its customer list. However, these lists have little resale value because privacy agreements prohibit sharing the customer information.

With fewer hard assets that they can convert to cash, a dot-com can experience a severe credit squeeze as vendors curtail shipments or take other measures to limit their financial risk. Such actions can further erode the company's liquidity and financial flexibility.

Long-Term Liabilities

Long-term liabilities are obligations that a company does not reasonably expect to liquidate within the normal operating cycle. Instead, it expects to pay them at some date beyond that time. Bonds payable, notes payable, some deferred income tax amounts, lease obligations, and pension obligations are the most common examples. **Companies classify long-term liabilities that mature within the current operating cycle as current liabilities if payment of the obligation requires the use of current assets.**

Generally, long-term liabilities are of three types:

1 Obligations arising from specific financing situations, such as the issuance of bonds, long-term lease obligations, and long-term notes payable.

2 Obligations arising from the ordinary operations of the company, such as pension obligations and deferred income tax liabilities.

3 Obligations that depend on the occurrence or non-occurrence of one or more future events to confirm the amount payable, or the payee, or the date payable, such as service or product warranties and other contingencies.

Companies generally provide a great deal of supplementary disclosure for long-term liabilities, because most long-term debt is subject to various covenants and restrictions for the protection of lenders.[12]

It is desirable to report any premium or discount separately as an addition to or subtraction from the bonds payable. Companies frequently describe the terms of all long-term liability agreements (including maturity date or dates, rates of interest, nature of obligation, and any security pledged to support the debt) in notes to the financial statements. Illustration 5-14 provides an example of this, taken from an excerpt from **The Great Atlantic & Pacific Tea Company**'s financials.

The Great Atlantic & Pacific Tea Company, Inc.

Total current liabilities	$978,109,000
Long-term debt (See note)	254,312,000
Obligations under capital leases	252,618,000
Deferred income taxes	57,167,000
Other non-current liabilities	127,321,000
Note: Indebtedness. Debt consists of:	
9.5% senior notes, due in annual installments of $10,000,000	$ 40,000,000
Mortgages and other notes due through 2011 (average interest rate of 9.9%)	107,604,000
Bank borrowings at 9.7%	67,225,000
Commercial paper at 9.4%	100,102,000
	314,931,000
Less: Current portion	(60,619,000)
Total long-term debt	$254,312,000

ILLUSTRATION 5-14
Balance Sheet Presentation of Long-Term Debt

---

[12]Companies usually explain the pertinent rights and privileges of the various securities (both debt and equity) outstanding in the notes to the financial statements. Examples of information that companies should disclose are dividend and liquidation preferences, participation rights, call prices and dates, conversion or exercise prices or rates and pertinent dates, sinking fund requirements, unusual voting rights, and significant terms of contracts to issue additional shares. "Disclosure of Information about Capital Structure," *Statement of Financial Accounting Standards No. 129* (Norwalk: FASB, 1997), par. 4.

Owners' Equity

The **owners' equity** (**stockholders' equity**) section is one of the most difficult sections to prepare and understand. This is due to the complexity of capital stock agreements and the various restrictions on stockholders' equity imposed by state corporation laws, liability agreements, and boards of directors. Companies usually divide the section into three parts:

STOCKHOLDERS' EQUITY SECTION

1 *CAPITAL STOCK.* The par or stated value of the shares issued.

2 *ADDITIONAL PAID-IN CAPITAL.* The excess of amounts paid in over the par or stated value.

3 *RETAINED EARNINGS.* The corporation's undistributed earnings.

For capital stock, companies must disclose the par value and the authorized, issued, and outstanding share amounts. A company usually presents the additional paid-in capital in one amount, although subtotals are informative if the sources of additional capital are varied and material. The retained earnings amount may be divided between the **unappropriated** (the amount that is usually available for dividend distribution) and **restricted** (e.g., by bond indentures or other loan agreements) amounts. In addition, companies show any capital stock reacquired (treasury stock) as a reduction of stockholders' equity.

Illustration 5-15 presents an example of the stockholders' equity section from **Quanex Corporation**.

ILLUSTRATION 5-15
Balance Sheet
Presentation of
Stockholders' Equity

Quanex Corporation
(in thousands)

Stockholders' equity (Note 12):	
Preferred stock, no par value, 1,000,000 shares authorized;	
345,000 issued and outstanding	$ 86,250
Common stock, $0.50 par value, 25,000,000 shares authorized;	
13,638,005 shares issued and outstanding	6,819
Additional paid-in capital	87,260
Retained earnings	57,263
	$237,592

The ownership or stockholders' equity accounts in a corporation differ considerably from those in a partnership or proprietorship. Partners show separately their permanent capital accounts and the balance in their temporary accounts (drawing accounts). Proprietorships ordinarily use a single capital account that handles all of the owner's equity transactions.

Balance Sheet Format

OBJECTIVE 3
Prepare a classified balance sheet using the report and account formats.

One common arrangement that companies use in presenting a classified balance sheet is the **account form**. It lists assets, by sections, on the left side, and liabilities and stockholders' equity, by sections, on the right side. The main disadvantage is the need for a sufficiently wide space in which to present the items side by side. Often, the account form requires two facing pages.

To avoid this disadvantage, the **report form** lists the sections one above the other, on the same page. See, for example, Illustration 5-16, which lists assets, followed by liabilities and stockholders' equity directly below, on the same page.[13]

ILLUSTRATION 5-16
Classified Report Form
Balance Sheet

SCIENTIFIC PRODUCTS, INC.
BALANCE SHEET
DECEMBER 31, 2006

Assets

Current assets			
Cash		$ 42,485	
Available-for-sale securities—at fair value		28,250	
Accounts receivable	$165,824		
Less: Allowance for doubtful accounts	1,850	163,974	
Notes receivable		23,000	
Inventories—at average cost		489,713	
Supplies on hand		9,780	
Prepaid expenses		16,252	
Total current assets			$ 773,454
Long-term investments			
Investments in Warren Co.			87,500
Property, plant, and equipment			
Land—at cost		125,000	
Buildings—at cost	975,800		
Less: Accumulated depreciation	341,200	634,600	
Total property, plant, and equipment			759,600
Intangible assets			
Goodwill			100,000
Total assets			$1,720,554

Liabilities and Stockholders' Equity

Current liabilities			
Notes payable to banks		$ 50,000	
Accounts payable		197,532	
Accrued interest on notes payable		500	
Income taxes payable		62,520	
Accrued salaries, wages, and other liabilities		9,500	
Deposits received from customers		420	
Total current liabilities			$ 320,472
Long-term debt			
Twenty-year 12% debentures, due January 1, 2016			500,000
Total liabilities			820,472
Stockholders' equity			
Paid in on capital stock			
Preferred, 7%, cumulative			
Authorized, issued, and outstanding,			
30,000 shares of $10 par value	$300,000		
Common—			
Authorized, 500,000 shares of			
$1 par value; issued and			
outstanding, 400,000 shares	400,000		
Additional paid-in capital	37,500	737,500	
Retained earnings		162,582	
Total stockholders' equity			900,082
Total liabilities and stockholders' equity			$1,720,554

UNDERLYING CONCEPTS

The presentation of balance sheet information meets one of the objectives of financial reporting—to provide information about enterprise resources, claims to resources, and changes in them.

---

[13]*Accounting Trends and Techniques—2004* (New York: AICPA) indicates that all of the 600 companies surveyed use either the "report form" (506) or the "account form" (94), sometimes collectively referred to as the "customary form."

Infrequently, companies use other balance sheet formats. For example, companies sometimes deduct current liabilities from current assets to arrive at working capital. Or, they deduct all liabilities from all assets.

WARNING SIGNALS

WHAT DO THE NUMBERS MEAN?

Analysts use balance sheet information in models designed to predict financial distress. Researcher E. I. Altman pioneered a bankruptcy-prediction model that derives a "Z-score" by combining balance sheet and income measures in the following equation.

$$Z = \frac{\text{Working capital}}{\text{Total assets}} \times 1.2 + \frac{\text{Retained earnings}}{\text{Total assets}} \times 1.4 + \frac{\text{EBIT}}{\text{Total assets}} \times 3.3$$
$$+ \frac{\text{Sales}}{\text{Total assets}} \times 0.99 + \frac{\text{MV equity}}{\text{Total liabilities}} \times 0.6$$

Following extensive testing, Altman found that companies with Z-scores above 3.0 are unlikely to fail. Those with Z-scores below 1.81 are very likely to fail.

Altman developed the original model for publicly held manufacturing companies. He and others have modified the model to apply to companies in various industries, emerging companies, and companies not traded in public markets.

At one time, the use of Z-scores was virtually unheard of among practicing accountants. Today, auditors, management consultants, and courts of law use this measure to help evaluate the overall financial position and trends of a firm. In addition, banks use Z-scores for loan evaluation. While a low score does not guarantee bankruptcy, the model has been proven accurate in many situations.

Source: Adapted from E. I. Altman and E. Hotchkiss, *Corporate Financial Distress and Bankruptcy,* 3rd edition (New York: John Wiley and Sons, 2005).

Presentation of Balance Sheet Formats for Various Real Companies

---

ADDITIONAL INFORMATION REPORTED

OBJECTIVE 4
Determine which balance sheet information requires supplemental disclosure.

The balance sheet is not complete if a company simply lists the assets, liabilities, and owners' equity accounts. It still needs to provide important supplemental information. This may be information not presented elsewhere in the statement, or it may elaborate on items in the balance sheet. There are normally four types of information that are supplemental to account titles and amounts presented in the balance sheet. They are listed below.

SUPPLEMENTAL BALANCE SHEET INFORMATION

1 *CONTINGENCIES.* Material events that have an uncertain outcome.
2 *ACCOUNTING POLICIES.* Explanations of the valuation methods used or the basic assumptions made concerning inventory valuations, depreciation methods, investments in subsidiaries, etc.
3 *CONTRACTUAL SITUATIONS.* Explanations of certain restrictions or covenants attached to specific assets or, more likely, to liabilities.
4 *FAIR VALUES.* Disclosures of fair values, particularly for financial instruments.

Contingencies

A **contingency** is an existing situation involving uncertainty as to possible gain (gain contingency) or loss (loss contingency) that will ultimately be resolved when one or more future events occur or fail to occur. In short, contingencies are material events with an uncertain future. Examples of gain contingencies are tax operating-loss carry-forwards or company litigation against another party. Typical loss contingencies relate to litigation, environmental issues, possible tax assessments, or government investigations. We examine the accounting and reporting requirements involving contingencies more fully in Chapter 13.

Accounting Policies

APB Opinion No. 22 recommends disclosure for all significant accounting principles and methods that involve selection from among alternatives or those that are peculiar to a given industry.[14] For instance, companies can compute inventories under several cost flow assumptions (e.g., LIFO and FIFO), depreciate plant and equipment under several accepted methods (e.g., double-declining balance and straight-line), and carry investments at different valuations (e.g., cost, equity, and fair value). Sophisticated users of financial statements know of these possibilities and examine the statements closely to determine the methods used.

Companies must also disclose information about the nature of their operations, the use of estimates in preparing financial statements, certain significant estimates, and vulnerabilities due to certain concentrations.[15] Illustration 5-17 shows an example of such a disclosure.

Chesapeake Corporation

Risks and Uncertainties. Chesapeake operates in three business segments which offer a diversity of products over a broad geographic base. The Company is not dependent on any single customer, group of customers, market, geographic area or supplier of materials, labor or services. Financial statements include, where necessary, amounts based on the judgments and estimates of management. These estimates include allowances for bad debts, accruals for landfill closing costs, environmental remediation costs, loss contingencies for litigation, self-insured medical and workers' compensation insurance and determinations of discount and other rate assumptions for pensions and postretirement benefit expenses.

ILLUSTRATION 5-17
Balance Sheet Disclosure of Significant Risks and Uncertainties

Disclosure of significant accounting principles and methods and of risks and uncertainties is particularly useful if given in a separate **Summary of Significant Accounting Policies** preceding the notes to the financial statements or as the initial note.

Contractual Situations

Companies should disclose contractual situations, if significant, in the notes to the financial statements. For example, they must clearly state the essential provisions of lease contracts, pension obligations, and stock option plans in the notes. Analysts want to know not only the amount of the liabilities, but also how the different contractual provisions affect the company at present and in the future.

---

[14]"Disclosure of Accounting Policies," *Opinions of the Accounting Principles Board No. 22* (New York: AICPA, 1972).

[15]"Disclosure of Certain Significant Risks and Uncertainties," *Statement of Position 94-6* (New York: AICPA, 1994).

Companies must disclose the following commitments if the amounts are material: commitments related to obligations to maintain working capital, to limit the payment of dividends, to restrict the use of assets, and to require the maintenance of certain financial ratios. Management must exercise considerable judgment to determine whether omission of such information is misleading. The rule in this situation is, "When in doubt, disclose." It is better to disclose a little too much information than not enough.

WHAT ABOUT YOUR COMMITMENTS?

**WHAT DO THE
NUMBERS MEAN?**

Many of the recent accounting scandals related to the nondisclosure of significant contractual obligations. In response, the SEC has mandated that companies disclose contractual obligations in a tabular summary in the management discussion and analysis section of the company's annual report.

Presented below, as an example, is a disclosure from **The Procter & Gamble Company**.

Contractual Commitments, as of June 30, 2004 ($ in millions)

	Total	Less Than 1 Year	1–3 Years	3–5 Years	After 5 Years
Recorded liabilities					
Total debt	$20,399	$ 8,229	$3,954	$1,935	$ 6,281
Capital leases	252	30	46	169	7
Wella domination and profit transfer agreement	1,106	1,106	–	–	–
Other					
Interest payments relating to long-term debt	7,587	715	1,202	874	4,796
Operating leases	920	186	284	185	265
Minimum pension funding[1]	702	237	465	–	–
Purchase obligations[2]	5,471	1,640	1,334	955	1,542
Total contractual commitments	$36,437	$12,143	$7,285	$4,118	$12,891

[1]Represents future pension payments to comply with local funding requirements. The projected payments beyond fiscal year 2007 are not currently determinable.

[2]The amounts indicated in this line primarily reflect future contractual payments under various take-or-pay arrangements entered into as part of the normal course of business.

Fair Values

As we discussed in Chapter 2, companies use historical cost as the primary valuation basis in financial statements. However, fair value information may be more useful for certain types of assets and liabilities. This is particularly so in the case of financial instruments.

Financial instruments are defined as cash, an ownership interest, or a contractual right to receive or obligation to deliver cash or another financial instrument. Such contractual rights to receive cash or other financial instruments are assets. Contractual obligations to pay are liabilities. Cash, investments, accounts receivable, and payables are examples of financial instruments.

Financial instruments are increasing both in use and variety. As a consequence of the increasing use, companies must disclose both the carrying value and the estimated fair values of their financial instruments. For example, **YUM! Brands Inc.**, a franchiser of restaurants such as Pizza Hut and Taco Bell, provides extensive disclosures of the fair value of its financial instrument assets and liabilities, as shown in Illustration 5-18. We provide more extensive discussion of financial instrument accounting and reporting in Chapters 7, 14, 16, and 17.

YUM! Brands Inc.

The carrying amounts and fair values of our other financial instruments subject to fair value disclosures are as follows:

	Carrying Amount	Fair Value
Debt		
Short-term borrowings and long-term debt, excluding capital leases and the derivative instrument adjustments	$ 1,925	$ 2,181
Debt-related derivative instruments		
Open contracts in a net asset position	31	31
Lease guarantees	8	37
Guarantees of supporting financial arrangements of certain franchisees, unconsolidated affiliates and other third parties	8	10
Letters of credit	–	3

We estimated the fair value of debt, debt-related derivative instruments, foreign currency-related derivative instruments, guarantees and letters of credit using market quotes and calculations based on market rates.

ILLUSTRATION 5-18
Disclosure of Financial Instrument Fair Values

TECHNIQUES OF DISCLOSURE

Companies should disclose as completely as possible the effect of various contingencies on financial condition, the methods of valuing assets and liabilities, and the company's contracts and agreements. To disclose this pertinent information, companies may use parenthetical explanations, notes, cross reference and contra items, and supporting schedules.

OBJECTIVE 5
Describe the major disclosure techniques for the balance sheet.

Parenthetical Explanations

Companies often provide additional information by parenthetical explanations following the item. For example, Illustration 5-19 shows a parenthetical explanation of the number of shares issued by **Ford Motor Company** on the balance sheet under Stockholders' Equity.

Ford Motor Company

Stockholders' Equity (in millions)

Common stock, par value $0.01 per share (1,837 million shares issued) $18

ILLUSTRATION 5-19
Parenthetical Disclosure of Shares Issued—Ford Motor Company

This additional pertinent balance sheet information adds clarity and completeness. It has an advantage over a note because it brings the additional information into the body of the statement where readers will less likely overlook it. Companies, however, should avoid lengthy parenthetical explanations, which might be distracting.

UNDERLYING CONCEPTS

The user-specific quality of *understandability* requires accountants to be careful in describing transactions and events.

Notes

Companies use notes if they cannot conveniently show additional explanations as parenthetical explanations. Illustration 5-20 (page 188) shows how **International Paper Company** reported its inventory costing methods in its accompanying notes.

ILLUSTRATION 5-20
Note Disclosure

International Paper Company

(Note 11)

Inventories by major category were (millions):

Raw materials	$ 371
Finished pulp, paper and packaging products	1,796
Finished lumber and panel products	184
Operating supplies	351
Other	16
Total inventories	$2,718

The last-in, first-out inventory method is used to value most of International Paper's U.S. inventories. Approximately 70% of total raw materials and finished products inventories were valued using this method. If the first-in, first-out method had been used, it would have increased total inventories balances by approximately $170 million.

Companies commonly use notes to disclose the following: the existence and amount of any preferred stock dividends in arrears, the terms of or obligations imposed by purchase commitments, special financial arrangements and instruments, depreciation policies, any changes in the application of accounting principles, and the existence of contingencies.

Notes therefore must present all essential facts as completely and succinctly as possible. Careless wording may mislead rather than aid readers. Notes should add to the total information made available in the financial statements, not raise unanswered questions or contradict other portions of the statements. The following notes illustrate the presentation of such information.

ILLUSTRATION 5-21
More Note
Disclosures

Alberto-Culver Company

Note 3: Long-Term Debt. Various borrowing arrangements impose restrictions on such items as total debt, working capital, dividend payments, treasury stock purchases and interest expense. The company was in compliance with these arrangements and $68 million of consolidated retained earnings was not restricted as to the payment of dividends and purchases of treasury stock.

Consolidated Papers, Inc.

Note 7: Commitments. The company had capital expenditure purchase commitments outstanding of approximately $17 million.

Willamette Industries, Inc.

Note 4: Property, Plant, and Equipment (partial): The company changed its accounting estimates relating to depreciation. The estimated service lives for most machinery and equipment were extended five years. The change was based upon a study performed by the company's engineering department, comparisons to typical industry practices, and the effect of the company's extensive capital investments which have resulted in a mix of assets with longer productive lives due to technological advances. As a result of the change, net income was increased $51,900, or $0.46 per diluted share.

Cross-Reference and Contra Items

Companies "cross-reference" a direct relationship between an asset and a liability on the balance sheet. For example, as shown in Illustration 5-22, on December 31, 2006, a company might show the following entries—one listed among the current assets, and the other listed among the current liabilities.

Current Assets (in part)	
Cash on deposit with sinking fund trustee for redemption of bonds payable—see Current liabilities	$800,000

Current Liabilities (in part)	
Bonds payable to be redeemed in 2007—see Current assets	$2,300,000

ILLUSTRATION 5-22
Cross-Referencing and Contra Items

This cross-reference points out that the company will redeem $2,300,000 of bonds payable currently, for which it has only set aside $800,000. Therefore, it needs additional cash from unrestricted cash, from sales of investments, from profits, or from some other source. Alternatively, the company can show the same information parenthetically.

Another common procedure is to establish contra or adjunct accounts. A **contra account** on a balance sheet reduces either an asset, liability, or owners' equity account. Examples include Accumulated Depreciation and Discount on Bonds Payable. Contra accounts provide some flexibility in presenting the financial information. With the use of the Accumulated Depreciation account, for example, a reader of the statement can see the original cost of the asset as well as the depreciation to date.

An **adjunct account**, on the other hand, increases either an asset, liability, or owners' equity account. An example is Premium on Bonds Payable, which, when added to the Bonds Payable account, describes the total bond liability of the company.

Supporting Schedules

Often a company needs a separate schedule to present more detailed information about certain assets or liabilities, as follows.

Property, plant, and equipment	
Land, buildings, equipment, and other fixed assets—net (see Schedule 3)	$643,300

ILLUSTRATION 5-23
Disclosure through Use of Supporting Schedules

SCHEDULE 3
LAND, BUILDINGS, EQUIPMENT, AND OTHER FIXED ASSETS

	Total	Land	Buildings	Equip.	Other Fixed Assets
Balance January 1, 2007	$740,000	$46,000	$358,000	$260,000	$76,000
Additions in 2007	161,200		120,000	38,000	3,200
	901,200	46,000	478,000	298,000	79,200
Assets retired or sold in 2007	31,700			27,000	4,700
Balance December 31, 2007	869,500	46,000	478,000	271,000	74,500
Depreciation taken to January 1, 2007	196,000		102,000	78,000	16,000
Depreciation taken in 2007	56,000		28,000	24,000	4,000
	252,000		130,000	102,000	20,000
Depreciation on assets retired in 2007	25,800			22,000	3,800
Depreciation accumulated December 31, 2007	226,200		130,000	80,000	16,200
Book value of assets	$643,300	$46,000	$348,000	$191,000	$58,300

Terminology

The account titles in the general ledger do not necessarily represent the best terminology for balance sheet purposes. Companies often use brief account titles and include technical terms that only accountants understand. But many persons unacquainted with accounting terminology examine balance sheets. Thus, balance sheets should contain descriptions that readers will generally understand and clearly interpret.

For example, companies have used the term "reserve" in differing ways: to describe amounts deducted from assets (contra accounts such as accumulated depreciation and allowance for doubtful accounts), as a part of the title of contingent or estimated liabilities, and to describe an appropriation of retained earnings. Because of the different meanings attached to this term, misinterpretation often resulted from its use. Therefore, the profession has recommended that companies use the word **reserve** only to describe an appropriation of retained earnings. The use of the term in this narrower sense—to describe appropriated retained earnings—has resulted in a better understanding of its significance when it appears in a balance sheet. However, the term "appropriated" appears more logical, and we encourage its use.

For years the profession has recommended that the use of the word **surplus** be discontinued in balance sheet presentations of owners' equity. The use of the terms *capital surplus*, *paid-in surplus*, and *earned surplus* is confusing. Although condemned by the profession, these terms appear all too frequently in current financial statements.

SECTION 2	*STATEMENT OF CASH FLOWS*

Chapter 2 indicated that one of the three basic objectives of financial reporting is "assessing the amounts, timing, and uncertainty of cash flows." The three financial statements we have looked at so far—the income statement, the statement of stockholders' equity, and the balance sheet—each present some information about the cash flows of an enterprise during a period. But they do so to a limited extent. For instance, the income statement provides information about resources provided by operations, but not exactly cash. The statement of stockholders' equity shows the amount of cash used to pay dividends or purchase treasury stock. Comparative balance sheets might show what assets the company has acquired or disposed of and what liabilities it has incurred or liquidated.

However, none of these statements presents a detailed summary of all the cash inflows and outflows, or the sources and uses of cash during the period. To fill this need, the FASB requires the **statement of cash flows** (also called the **cash flow statement**).[16]

PURPOSE OF THE STATEMENT OF CASH FLOWS

The primary purpose of a statement of cash flows is to provide relevant information about the cash receipts and cash payments of an enterprise during a period. To achieve this purpose, the statement of cash flows reports the following: (1) the cash effects of operations during a period, (2) investing transactions, (3) financing transactions, and (4) the net increase or decrease in cash during the period.[17]

Reporting the sources, uses, and net increase or decrease in cash helps investors, creditors, and others know what is happening to a company's most liquid resource. Be-

---

[16]"Statement of Cash Flows," *Statement of Financial Accounting Standards No. 95* (Stamford, Conn.: FASB, 1987).

[17]The FASB recommends the basis as "cash and cash equivalents." **Cash equivalents** are liquid investments that mature within three months or less.

cause most individuals maintain a checkbook and prepare a tax return on a cash basis, they can comprehend the information reported in the statement of cash flows, such as causes and effects of cash inflows and outflows and the net change in cash.

The statement of cash flows provides answers to the following simple but important questions:

1 Where did the cash come from during the period?

2 What was the cash used for during the period?

3 What was the change in the cash balance during the period?

WATCH THAT CASH FLOW

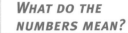
WHAT DO THE NUMBERS MEAN?

Investors usually focus on net income measured on an accrual basis. However, information on cash flows can be important for assessing a company's liquidity, financial flexibility, and overall financial performance. The graph below shows **W. T. Grant's** financial performance over 7 years.

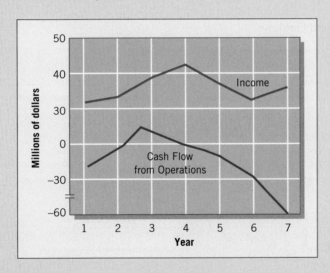

Although W. T. Grant showed consistent profits and even some periods of earnings growth, its cash flow began to "go south" starting in about year 3. The company filed for bankruptcy shortly after year 7. Financial statement readers who studied the company's cash flows would have found an early-warning signal of W. T. Grant's problems.

CONTENT AND FORMAT OF THE STATEMENT OF CASH FLOWS

Companies classify cash receipts and cash payments during a period into three different activities in the statement of cash flows—operating, investing, and financing activities, defined as follows.

OBJECTIVE 7
Identify the content of the statement of cash flows.

1 **Operating activities** involve the cash effects of transactions that enter into the determination of net income.

2 **Investing activities** include making and collecting loans and acquiring and disposing of investments (both debt and equity) and property, plant, and equipment.

3 **Financing activities** involve liability and owners' equity items. They include (a) obtaining resources from owners and providing them with a return on their investment, and (b) borrowing money from creditors and repaying the amounts borrowed.

Illustration 5-24 shows the basic format of the statement of cash flows.

Statement of Cash Flows	
Cash flows from operating activities	$XXX
Cash flows from investing activities	XXX
Cash flows from financing activities	XXX
Net increase (decrease) in cash	XXX
Cash at beginning of year	XXX
Cash at end of year	$XXX

Illustration 5-25 graphs the inflows and outflows of cash classified by activity.

ILLUSTRATION 5-25 Cash Inflows and Outflows

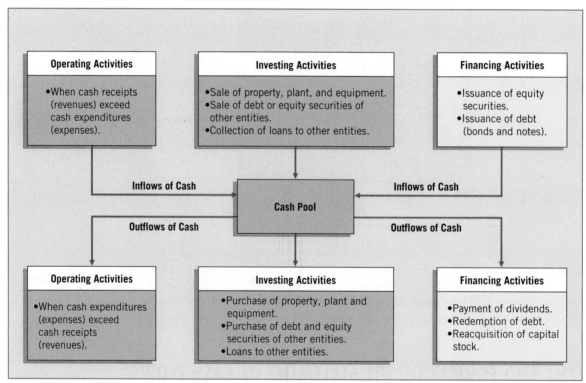

The statement's value is that it helps users evaluate liquidity, solvency, and financial flexibility. As we indicated earlier in the chapter, **liquidity** refers to the "nearness to cash" of assets and liabilities. **Solvency** is the firm's ability to pay its debts as they mature. **Financial flexibility** is a company's ability to respond and adapt to financial adversity and unexpected needs and opportunities.

We have devoted Chapter 23 entirely to the preparation and content of the statement of cash flows. The intervening chapters will cover several elements and complex topics that affect the content of a typical statement of cash flows. The presentation in this chapter is introductory—a reminder of the existence of the statement of cash flows and its usefulness.

PREPARATION OF THE STATEMENT OF CASH FLOWS

Companies obtain the information to prepare the statement of cash flows from several sources: (1) comparative balance sheets, (2) the current income statement, and (3) selected transaction data. Preparing the statement of cash flows from these sources involves four steps:

1 Determine the cash provided by or used in operating activities.

2 Determine the cash provided by or used in investing and financing activities.

3 Determine the change (increase or decrease) in cash during the period.

4 Reconcile the change in cash with the beginning and the ending cash balances.

The following simple example demonstrates how companies apply these steps in preparing a statement of cash flows.

On January 1, 2007, in its first year of operations, Telemarketing Inc. issued 50,000 shares of $1 par value common stock for $50,000 cash. The company rented its office space, furniture, and telecommunications equipment and performed marketing services throughout the first year. In June 2007 the company purchased land for $15,000. Illustration 5-26 shows the company's comparative balance sheets at the beginning and end of 2007.

> **OBJECTIVE 8**
> Prepare a statement of cash flows.

INTERNATIONAL INSIGHT

Not all countries require statements of cash flows. Some countries require a statement reporting sources and applications of "funds" (often defined as working capital). Others have no requirement for either cash or funds flow statements.

ILLUSTRATION 5-26 Comparative Balance Sheets

TELEMARKETING INC. BALANCE SHEETS			
Assets	Dec. 31, 2007	Jan. 1, 2007	Increase/Decrease
Cash	$31,000	$–0–	$31,000 Increase
Accounts receivable	41,000	–0–	41,000 Increase
Land	15,000	–0–	15,000 Increase
Total	$87,000	$–0–	
Liabilities and Stockholders' Equity			
Accounts payable	$12,000	$–0–	12,000 Increase
Common stock	50,000	–0–	50,000 Increase
Retained earnings	25,000	–0–	25,000 Increase
Total	$87,000	$–0–	

Illustration 5-27 presents the income statement and additional information.

TELEMARKETING INC. INCOME STATEMENT FOR THE YEAR ENDED DECEMBER 31, 2007	
Revenues	$172,000
Operating expenses	120,000
Income before income tax	52,000
Income tax	13,000
Net income	$ 39,000

Additional information:
Dividends of $14,000 were paid during the year.

ILLUSTRATION 5-27
Income Statement Data

Cash provided by operating activities is the excess of cash receipts over cash payments from operating activities. Companies determine this amount by converting net income on an accrual basis to a cash basis. To do so, they add to or deduct from net income those items in the income statement that do not affect cash. This procedure requires that a company analyze not only the current year's income statement but also the comparative balance sheets and selected transaction data.

Analysis of Telemarketing's comparative balance sheets reveals two items that will affect the computation of net cash provided by operating activities:

1   The increase in accounts receivable reflects a noncash increase of $41,000 in revenues.

2   The increase in accounts payable reflects a noncash increase of $12,000 in expenses.

Therefore, to arrive at cash provided by operations, Telemarketing Inc. deducts from net income the increase in accounts receivable ($41,000), and it adds back to net income the increase in accounts payable ($12,000). As a result of these adjustments, the company determines cash provided by operations to be $10,000, computed as shown in Illustration 5-28.

ILLUSTRATION 5-28
Computation of Net Cash
Provided by Operations

Net income		$39,000
Adjustments to reconcile net income		
to net cash provided by operating activities:		
Increase in accounts receivable	$(41,000)	
Increase in accounts payable	12,000	(29,000)
Net cash provided by operating activities		$10,000

INTERNATIONAL INSIGHT

International Accounting Standard 7 requires a statement of cash flows. Both international standards and U.S. GAAP specify that the cash flows must be classified as operating, investing, or financing.

Telemarketing Inc.'s only investing activity was the land purchase. It had two financing activities: (1) the increase of $50,000 in common stock resulting from the issuance of 50,000 shares for cash, and (2) the payment of $14,000 cash in dividends. Illustration 5-29 presents Telemarketing Inc.'s statement of cash flows for 2007.

ILLUSTRATION 5-29   Statement of Cash Flows

TELEMARKETING INC.		
STATEMENT OF CASH FLOWS		
FOR THE YEAR ENDED DECEMBER 31, 2007		
Cash flows from operating activities		
Net income		$39,000
Adjustments to reconcile net income to		
net cash provided by operating activities:		
Increase in accounts receivable	$(41,000)	
Increase in accounts payable	12,000	(29,000)
Net cash provided by operating activities		10,000
Cash flows from investing activities		
Purchase of land	(15,000)	
Net cash used by investing activities		(15,000)
Cash flows from financing activities		
Issuance of common stock	50,000	
Payment of cash dividends	(14,000)	
Net cash provided by financing activities		36,000
Net increase in cash		31,000
Cash at beginning of year		–0–
Cash at end of year		$31,000

The increase in cash of $31,000 reported in the statement of cash flows agrees with the increase of $31,000 in cash calculated from the comparative balance sheets.

Not all of a company's significant activities involve cash. Examples of significant noncash activities are:

1 Issuance of common stock to purchase assets.

2 Conversion of bonds into common stock.

3 Issuance of debt to purchase assets.

4 Exchanges of long-lived assets.

Significant financing and investing activities that do not affect cash are not reported in the body of the statement of cash flows. Rather, these activities are reported in either a separate schedule at the bottom of the statement of cash flows or in separate notes to the financial statements. Such reporting of these noncash activities satisfies the full disclosure principle. *In solving homework assignments, you should present significant noncash activities in a separate schedule at the bottom of the statement of cash flows.*

Illustration 5-30 shows an example of a comprehensive statement of cash flows. Note that the company purchased equipment through the issuance of $50,000 of bonds, which is a significant noncash transaction.

Indirect method

ILLUSTRATION 5-30
Comprehensive
Statement of Cash Flows

NESTOR COMPANY STATEMENT OF CASH FLOWS FOR THE YEAR ENDED DECEMBER 31, 2007		
Cash flows from operating activities		
Net income		$320,750
Adjustments to reconcile net income to net cash provided by operating activities:		
Depreciation expense	$88,400	
Amortization of intangibles	16,300	
Gain on sale of plant assets	(8,700)	
Increase in accounts receivable (net)	(11,000)	
Decrease in inventory	15,500	
Decrease in accounts payable	(9,500)	91,000
Net cash provided by operating activities		411,750
Cash flows from investing activities		
Sale of plant assets	90,500	
Purchase of equipment	(182,500)	
Purchase of land	(70,000)	
Net cash used by investing activities		(162,000)
Cash flows from financing activities		
Payment of cash dividend	(19,800)	
Issuance of common stock	100,000	
Redemption of bonds	(50,000)	
Net cash provided by financing activities		30,200
Net increase in cash		279,950
Cash at beginning of year		135,000
Cash at end of year		$414,950
Noncash investing and financing activities		
Purchase of equipment through issuance of $50,000 of bonds		

add back b/c non cash

*Additional Disclosures
of Cash Flow Reporting*

USEFULNESS OF THE STATEMENT OF CASH FLOWS

OBJECTIVE 9
**Understand the
usefulness of the
statement of cash
flows.**

"Happiness is a positive cash flow" is certainly true. Although net income provides a long-term measure of a company's success or failure, cash is the lifeblood of a company. Without cash, a company will not survive. For small and newly developing companies, cash flow is the single most important element for survival. Even medium and large companies must control cash flow.

Creditors examine the cash flow statement carefully because they are concerned about being paid. They begin their examination by finding net cash provided by operating activities. A high amount indicates that a company is able to generate sufficient cash from operations to pay its bills without further borrowing. Conversely, a low or negative amount of net cash provided by operating activities indicates that a company may have to borrow or issue equity securities to acquire sufficient cash to pay its bills. Consequently, creditors look for answers to the following questions in the company's cash flow statements.

1 How successful is the company in generating net cash provided by operating activities?

2 What are the trends in net cash flow provided by operating activities over time?

3 What are the major reasons for the positive or negative net cash provided by operating activities?

You should recognize that companies can fail even though they report net income. The difference between net income and net cash provided by operating activities can be substantial. Companies such as **W. T. Grant Company** and **Prime Motor Inn**, for example, reported high net income numbers but negative net cash provided by operating activities. Eventually both companies filed for bankruptcy.

In addition, substantial increases in receivables and/or inventory can explain the difference between positive net income and negative net cash provided by operating activities. For example, in its first year of operations Hu Inc. reported a net income of $80,000. Its net cash provided by operating activities, however, was a negative $95,000, as shown in Illustration 5-31.

ILLUSTRATION 5-31
Negative Net Cash Provided by Operating Activities

HU INC.		
NET CASH FLOW FROM OPERATING ACTIVITIES		
Cash flows from operating activities		
Net income		$ 80,000
Adjustments to reconcile net income to net cash provided by operating activities:		
Increase in receivables	$ (75,000)	
Increase in inventories	(100,000)	(175,000)
Net cash provided by operating activities		$(95,000)

Hu could easily experience a "cash crunch" because it has its cash tied up in receivables and inventory. If Hu encounters problems in collecting receivables, or if inventory moves slowly or becomes obsolete, its creditors may have difficulty collecting on their loans.

CASH IS KING?

WHAT DO THE NUMBERS MEAN?

Analysts increasingly use cash-flow-based measures of income, such as cash flow provided by operations, instead of or in addition to net income. The reason for the change is that they have been losing faith in accrual-accounting-based net income numbers.

Sadly, these days even cash flow from operations isn't always what it seems to be. For example, in 2002 **WorldCom, Inc.** disclosed that it had improperly capitalized expenses: It moved $3.8 billion of cash outflows from the "Cash from operating activities" section of the cash flow statement to the "Investing activities" section, thereby greatly enhancing cash provided by operating activities.

Similarly, in 2002 **Dynegy, Inc.** restated its cash flow statement for 2001. In doing so, the company removed $300 million tied to its complex natural gas trading operation from operating cash flow and instead put that amount into the financing section—a drop of 37 percent in cash flow from operations.

Source: Henny Sender, "Sadly, These Days Even Cash Flow Isn't Always What It Seems To Be," *Wall Street Journal Online* (May 8, 2002).

Financial Liquidity

Readers of financial statements often assess liquidity by using the **current cash debt coverage ratio**. It indicates whether the company can pay off its current liabilities from its operations in a given year. Illustration 5-32 shows the formula for this ratio.

$$\frac{\text{Net Cash Provided by Operating Activities}}{\text{Average Current Liabilities}} = \begin{array}{c}\text{Current Cash}\\\text{Debt Coverage Ratio}\end{array}$$

ILLUSTRATION 5-32
Formula for Current Cash
Debt Coverage Ratio

The higher the current cash debt coverage ratio, the less likely a company will have liquidity problems. For example, a ratio near 1:1 is good: It indicates that the company can meet all of its current obligations from internally generated cash flow.

Financial Flexibility

The **cash debt coverage ratio** provides information on financial flexibility. It indicates a company's ability to repay its liabilities from net cash provided by operating activities, without having to liquidate the assets employed in its operations. Illustration 5-33 shows the formula for this ratio. (Notice its similarity to the current cash debt coverage ratio. However, because it uses average total liabilities in place of average current liabilities, it takes a somewhat longer-range view.)

$$\frac{\text{Net Cash Provided by Operating Activities}}{\text{Average Total Liabilities}} = \begin{array}{c}\text{Cash Debt}\\\text{Coverage Ratio}\end{array}$$

ILLUSTRATION 5-33
Formula for Cash Debt
Coverage Ratio

The higher this ratio, the less likely the company will experience difficulty in meeting its obligations as they come due. It signals whether the company can pay its debts and survive if external sources of funds become limited or too expensive.

Free Cash Flow

A more sophisticated way to examine a company's financial flexibility is to develop a free cash flow analysis. **Free cash flow** is the amount of discretionary cash flow a company has for purchasing additional investments, retiring its debt, purchasing treasury stock, or simply adding to its liquidity. Financial statement users calculate free cash flow as net cash provided by operating activities less capital expenditures and dividends. Obviously, the greater the amount of free cash flow, the greater the company's amount of financial flexibility.

Questions that a free cash flow analysis answers are:

1 Is the company able to pay its dividends without resorting to external financing?

2 If business operations decline, will the company be able to maintain its needed capital investment?

3 What is the amount of discretionary cash flow that can be used for additional investment, retirement of debt, purchase of treasury stock, or addition to liquidity?

Illustration 5-34 (on page 198) is a free cash flow analysis using the cash flow statement for Nestor Company (shown in Illustration 5-30).

ILLUSTRATION 5-34
Free Cash Flow
Computation

NESTOR COMPANY	
FREE CASH FLOW ANALYSIS	
Net cash provided by operating activities	$411,750
Less: Capital expenditures	(252,500)
Dividends	(19,800)
Free cash flow	$139,450

This analysis shows that Nestor has a positive, and substantial, net cash provided by operating activities of $411,750. Nestor's statement of cash flows reports that the company purchased equipment of $182,500 and land of $70,000 for total capital spending of $252,500.

In a free cash flow analysis, we first deduct capital spending, to indicate it is the least discretionary expenditure a company generally makes. (Without continued efforts to maintain and expand facilities, it is unlikely that Nestor can continue to maintain its competitive position.) We then deduct dividends. Although a company *can* cut its dividend, it usually will do so only in **a financial emergency**. The amount resulting after these deductions is the company's free cash flow. Nestor has more than sufficient cash flow to meet its dividend payment and therefore has satisfactory financial flexibility.

As you can see from looking back at Illustration 5-30, Nestor used its free cash flow to redeem bonds and add to its liquidity. If it finds additional investments that are profitable, it can increase its spending without putting its dividend or basic capital spending in jeopardy. Companies that have strong financial flexibility can take advantage of profitable investments even in tough times. In addition, strong financial flexibility frees companies from worry about survival in poor economic times. In fact, those with strong financial flexibility often fare better in a poor economy because they can take advantage of opportunities that other companies cannot.

KEY TERMS

account form, *182*

adjunct account, *189*

available-for-sale
  securities, *175*

balance sheet, *170*

cash debt coverage ratio,
  197

contingency, *185*

contra account, *189*

current assets, *173*

current cash debt
  coverage ratio, *197*

current liabilities, *179*

financial flexibility, *171*

financial instruments, *186*

financing activities, *191*

free cash flow, *197*

held-to-maturity
  securities, *175*

intangible assets, *179*

SUMMARY OF LEARNING OBJECTIVES

1. **Explain the uses and limitations of a balance sheet.** The balance sheet provides information about the nature and amounts of investments in enterprise resources, obligations to creditors, and the owners' equity. The balance sheet contributes to financial reporting by providing a basis for (1) computing rates of return, (2) evaluating the capital structure of the enterprise, and (3) assessing the liquidity, solvency, and financial flexibility of the enterprise.

Three limitations of a balance sheet are: (1) The balance sheet does not reflect fair value because accountants use a historical cost basis in valuing and reporting most assets and liabilities. (2) Companies must use judgments and estimates to determine certain amounts, such as the collectibility of receivables and the useful life of long-term tangible and intangible assets. (3) The balance sheet omits many items that are of financial value to the business but cannot be recorded objectively, such as human resources, customer base, and reputation.

2. **Identify the major classifications of the balance sheet.** The general elements of the balance sheet are assets, liabilities, and equity. The major classifications of assets are current assets; long-term investments; property, plant, and equipment; intangible assets; and other assets. The major classifications of liabilities are current and long-term liabilities. The balance sheet of a corporation generally classifies owners' equity as capital stock, additional paid-in capital, and retained earnings.

3. Prepare a classified balance sheet using the report and account formats. The report form lists liabilities and stockholders' equity directly below assets on the same page. The account form lists assets, by sections, on the left side, and liabilities and stockholders' equity, by sections, on the right side.

4. Determine which balance sheet information requires supplemental disclosure. Four types of information normally are supplemental to account titles and amounts presented in the balance sheet: (1) *Contingencies:* Material events that have an uncertain outcome. (2) *Accounting policies:* Explanations of the valuation methods used or the basic assumptions made concerning inventory valuation, depreciation methods, investments in subsidiaries, etc. (3) *Contractual situations:* Explanations of certain restrictions or covenants attached to specific assets or, more likely, to liabilities. (4) *Fair values:* Disclosures related to fair values, particularly related to financial instruments.

5. Describe the major disclosure techniques for the balance sheet. Companies use four methods to disclose pertinent information in the balance sheet: (1) *Parenthetical explanations:* Parenthetical information provides additional information or description following the item. (2) *Notes:* A company uses notes if it cannot conveniently show additional explanations or descriptions as parenthetical explanations. (3) *Cross-reference and contra items:* Companies "cross-reference" a direct relationship between an asset and a liability on the balance sheet. (4) *Supporting schedules:* Often a company needs a separate schedule to present more detailed information about certain assets or liabilities, because the balance sheet provides just a single summary item.

6. Indicate the purpose of the statement of cash flows. The primary purpose of a statement of cash flows is to provide relevant information about the cash receipts and cash payments of an enterprise during a period. Reporting the sources, uses, and net change in cash enables financial statement readers to know what is happening to a company's most liquid resource.

7. Identify the content of the statement of cash flows. In the statement of cash flows, companies classify their cash receipts and cash payments during a period into three different activities: (1) *Operating activities:* Involve the cash effects of transactions that enter into the determination of net income. (2) *Investing activities:* Include making and collecting loans, and acquiring and disposing of investments (both debt and equity) and of property, plant, and equipment. (3) *Financing activities:* Involve liability and owners' equity items. Financing activities include (a) obtaining capital from owners and providing them with a return on their investment, and (b) borrowing money from creditors and repaying the amounts borrowed.

8. Prepare a statement of cash flows. The information to prepare the statement of cash flows usually comes from (1) comparative balance sheets, (2) the current income statement, and (3) selected transaction data. Companies follow these steps to prepare the statement of cash flows from these sources: (1) Determine the cash provided by operating activities. (2) Determine the cash provided by or used in investing and financing activities. (3) Determine the change (increase or decrease) in cash during the period. (4) Reconcile the change in cash with the beginning and ending cash balances.

9. Understand the usefulness of the statement of cash flows. Creditors examine the cash flow statement carefully because they are concerned about being paid. The net cash flow provided by operating activities in relation to the company's liabilities is helpful in making this assessment. Two ratios used in this regard are the current cash debt ratio and the cash debt ratio. In addition, the amount of free cash flow provides creditors and stockholders with a picture of the company's financial flexibility.

investing activities, *191*

liquidity, *171*

long-term investments, *177*

long-term liabilities, *181*

operating activities, *191*

owners' (stockholders') equity, *182*

property, plant, and equipment, *178*

report form, *183*

reserve, *190*

solvency, *171*

statement of cash flows, *190*

trading securities, *175*

working capital, *180*

APPENDIX
5A Ratio Analysis—A Reference

USING RATIOS TO ANALYZE PERFORMANCE

> **OBJECTIVE 10**
> Identify the major types of financial ratios and what they measure.

Analysts and other interested parties can gather qualitative information from financial statements by examining relationships between items on the statements and identifying trends in these relationships. A useful starting point in developing this information is ratio analysis.

A **ratio** expresses the mathematical relationship between one quantity and another. **Ratio analysis** expresses the relationship among pieces of selected financial statement data, in a **percentage**, a **rate**, or a simple **proportion**.

To illustrate, **IBM Corporation** recently had current assets of $46,970 million and current liabilities of $39,798 million. We find the ratio between these two amounts by dividing current assets by current liabilities. The alternative means of expression are:

Percentage: Current assets are 118% of current liabilities.

Rate: Current assets are 1.18 times as great as current liabilities.

Proportion: The relationship of current assets to current liabilities is 1.18:1.

To analyze financial statements, we classify ratios into four types, as follows:

Expanded Discussion of Financial Statement Analysis

MAJOR TYPES OF RATIOS

LIQUIDITY RATIOS. Measures of the company's short-term ability to pay its maturing obligations.

ACTIVITY RATIOS. Measures of how effectively the company uses its assets.

PROFITABILITY RATIOS. Measures of the degree of success or failure of a given company or division for a given period of time.

COVERAGE RATIOS. Measures of the degree of protection for long-term creditors and investors.

In Chapter 5 we discussed two ratios related to the statement of cash flows (current cash debt coverage and cash debt coverage). Throughout the remainder of the textbook, we provide ratios to help you understand and interpret the information presented in financial statements. Illustration 5A-1 presents the ratios that we will use throughout the text. You should find this chart helpful as you examine these ratios in more detail in the following chapters. An appendix to Chapter 24 further discusses financial statement analysis.

ILLUSTRATION 5A-1   A Summary of Financial Ratios

Ratio	Formula	Purpose or Use
I. Liquidity		
1. Current ratio	$\dfrac{\text{Current assets}}{\text{Current liabilities}}$	Measures short-term debt-paying ability
2. Quick or acid-test ratio	$\dfrac{\text{Cash, marketable securities, and receivables (net)}}{\text{Current liabilities}}$	Measures immediate short-term liquidity
3. Current cash debt coverage ratio	$\dfrac{\text{Net cash provided by operating activities}}{\text{Average current liabilities}}$	Measures a company's ability to pay off its current liabilities in a given year from its operations
II. Activity		
4. Receivables turnover	$\dfrac{\text{Net sales}}{\text{Average trade receivables (net)}}$	Measures liquidity of receivables
5. Inventory turnover	$\dfrac{\text{Cost of goods sold}}{\text{Average inventory}}$	Measures liquidity of inventory
6. Asset turnover	$\dfrac{\text{Net sales}}{\text{Average total assets}}$	Measures how efficiently assets are used to generate sales
III. Profitability		
7. Profit margin on sales	$\dfrac{\text{Net income}}{\text{Net sales}}$	Measures net income generated by each dollar of sales
8. Rate of return on assets	$\dfrac{\text{Net income}}{\text{Average total assets}}$	Measures overall profitability of assets
9. Rate of return on common stock equity	$\dfrac{\text{Net income minus preferred dividends}}{\text{Average common stockholders' equity}}$	Measures profitability of owners' investment
10. Earnings per share	$\dfrac{\text{Net income minus preferred dividends}}{\text{Weighted shares outstanding}}$	Measures net income earned on each share of common stock
11. Price-earnings ratio	$\dfrac{\text{Market price of stock}}{\text{Earnings per share}}$	Measures the ratio of the market price per share to earnings per share
12. Payout ratio	$\dfrac{\text{Cash dividends}}{\text{Net income}}$	Measures percentage of earnings distributed in the form of cash dividends
IV. Coverage		
13. Debt to total assets	$\dfrac{\text{Total debt}}{\text{Total assets}}$	Measures the percentage of total assets provided by creditors
14. Times interest earned	$\dfrac{\text{Income before interest expense and taxes}}{\text{Interest expense}}$	Measures ability to meet interest payments as they come due
15. Cash debt coverage ratio	$\dfrac{\text{Net cash provided by operating activities}}{\text{Average total liabilities}}$	Measures a company's ability to repay its total liabilities in a given year from its operations
16. Book value per share	$\dfrac{\text{Common stockholders' equity}}{\text{Outstanding shares}}$	Measures the amount each share would receive if the company were liquidated at the amounts reported on the balance sheet

---

SUMMARY OF LEARNING OBJECTIVE FOR APPENDIX 5A

10. Identify the major types of financial ratios and what they measure. Ratios express the mathematical relationship between one quantity and another, expressed as a percentage, a rate, or a proportion. *Liquidity* ratios measure the short-term ability to pay maturing obligations. *Activity* ratios measure the effectiveness of asset usage. *Profitability* ratios measure the success or failure of an enterprise. *Coverage* ratios measure the degree of protection for long-term creditors and investors.

KEY TERMS

activity ratios, *200*

coverage ratios, *200*

liquidity ratios, *200*

profitability ratios, *200*

ratio analysis, *200*

APPENDIX
5B

Specimen Financial Statements: The Procter & Gamble Company

The following pages contain the financial statements, accompanying notes, and other information from the 2004 annual report of **The Procter & Gamble Company (P&G)**. The Procter & Gamble Company manufactures and markets a range of consumer products in various countries throughout the world. The Company markets over 300 branded products in more than 160 countries. It manages its business in five product segments: Fabric and Home Care, Baby and Family Care, Beauty Care, Health Care, and Snacks and Beverages.

We do not expect that you will comprehend P&G's financial statements and the accompanying notes in their entirety at your first reading. But we expect that by the time you complete the material in this textbook, your level of understanding and interpretive ability will have grown enormously.

At this point we recommend that you take 20 to 30 minutes to scan the following statements and notes. Your goal should be to familiarize yourself with the contents and accounting elements. Throughout the following 19 chapters, when you are asked to refer to specific parts of P&G's financial statements, do so! Then, when you have completed reading this book, we challenge you to reread P&G's financials to see how much greater and more sophisticated your understanding of them has become.

P&G

Consumers around the world trust P&G brands – such as Pampers, Tide, Ariel, Pantene, Wella, Always, Crest, Bounty, Charmin, Olay, Pringles, Iams, Downy, Actonel, Folgers and Head & Shoulders – to make everyday life a little bit better. Almost 110,000 P&G people in over 80 countries worldwide work hard to earn that trust.

Touching lives, improving life. P&G.

Financial Highlights

Amounts in millions except per share amounts	Years Ended June 30		
	2004	2003	% Change
Net Sales	**$51,407**	$43,377	19%
Operating Income	**9,827**	7,853	25%
Net Earnings	**6,481**	5,186	25%
Per Common Share[1]			
Diluted Net Earnings	**2.32**	1.85	25%
Dividends	**0.93**	0.82	13%

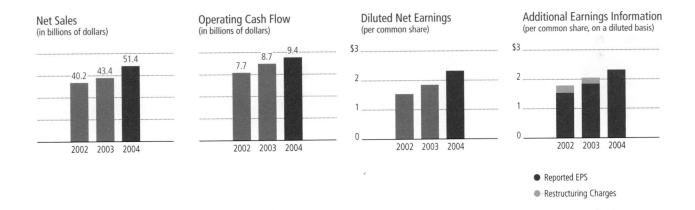

Net Sales
(in billions of dollars)

Operating Cash Flow
(in billions of dollars)

Diluted Net Earnings
(per common share)

Additional Earnings Information
(per common share, on a diluted basis)

● Reported EPS
● Restructuring Charges

Fellow Shareholders,

P&G is delivering broad-based, organic growth driven by clear strategies and a unique combination of P&G strengths. P&G's performance has accelerated over the past three years, and we are confident double-digit earnings-per-share growth is sustainable for the foreseeable future.

Sustaining P&G's Growth

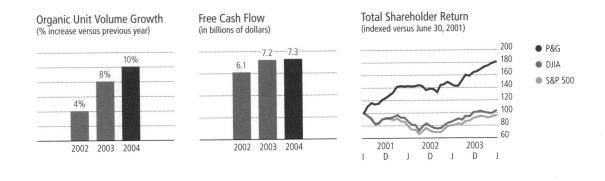

Organic Unit Volume Growth
(% increase versus previous year)

Free Cash Flow
(in billions of dollars)

Total Shareholder Return
(indexed versus June 30, 2001)

● P&G
● DJIA
● S&P 500

Three years of strong performance is a good start, but it's long-term performance that counts. Consistent performance is not easy. Growing P&G sales 4%–6% per year is roughly the equivalent of adding a brand the size of Tide – every year.

We're confident P&G can reliably deliver the future growth to which we've committed. Our strategies are working. There still is room to grow. Our strengths enable us to respond to external trends and challenges. Major changes are improving the consistency of P&G performance.

Build existing core businesses into strong global leaders.

Grow leading brands in big countries with winning customers. Accelerate growth in Western Europe.

Accelerate faster-growing, higher-margin health and beauty businesses.

Accelerate growth in developing markets and with lower-income consumers.

P&G strategies, strengths, and the systemic and structural changes we've made to improve the reliability of our performance should give shareholders confidence that P&G can sustain double-digit earnings-per-share growth for the foreseeable future.

A.G. Lafley
Chairman of the Board, President and Chief Executive

August 6, 2004

Management's Responsibility for Financial Reporting

Procter & Gamble has been built through the generations by the character of its people. That character is reflected in our Purpose, Values and Principles and in how well we live them as individuals and as a Company. High quality financial reporting is one of our responsibilities – one that we execute with integrity.

High quality financial reporting is characterized by accuracy, objectivity and transparency. Management is responsible for maintaining an effective system of internal controls over financial reporting to deliver those characteristics in all material respects. The Board of Directors, through its Audit Committee, provides oversight. They have engaged Deloitte & Touche LLP to audit our consolidated financial statements, on which they have issued an unqualified opinion.

Our commitment to providing timely, accurate and understandable information to investors encompasses:

Communicating expectations to employees. Key employee responsibilities are reinforced through the Company's "Worldwide Business Conduct Manual," which sets forth the Company's commitment to conduct its business affairs with high ethical standards. Every one of P&G's employees – from senior management on down – is held personally accountable for compliance. The Worldwide Business Conduct Manual is available on our website at www.pg.com.

Maintaining a strong internal control environment. Our system of internal controls includes written policies and procedures, segregation of duties and the careful selection and development of employees. The system is designed to provide reasonable assurance that transactions are executed as authorized and appropriately recorded, that assets are safeguarded and that accounting records are sufficiently reliable to permit the preparation of financial statements that conform in all material respects with accounting principles generally accepted in the United States of America. We monitor these internal controls through control self-assessments by business unit management and an ongoing program of internal audits around the world.

Executing financial stewardship. We maintain specific programs and activities to ensure that employees understand their fiduciary responsibilities to shareholders. This ongoing effort encompasses financial discipline in our strategic and daily business decisions and brings particular focus to maintaining accurate financial reporting and effective controls through process improvement, skill development and oversight.

Exerting rigorous oversight of the business. We continuously review our business results and strategic choices. Our Global Leadership Council is actively involved – from understanding strategies to reviewing key initiatives, financial performance and control assessments. The intent is to ensure we remain objective in our assessments, constructively challenge the approach to business opportunities, identify potential issues and ensure reward and recognition systems are appropriately aligned with results.

Engaging our Disclosure Committee. We maintain disclosure controls and procedures designed to ensure that information required to be disclosed is recorded, processed, summarized and reported timely and accurately. Our Disclosure Committee is a group of senior-level executives responsible for evaluating disclosure implications of significant business activities and events. The Committee reports its findings to the CEO and CFO, providing an effective process to evaluate our external disclosure obligations.

Encouraging strong and effective corporate governance from our Board of Directors. We have an active, capable and diligent Board that meets the required standards for independence, and we welcome the Board's oversight as a representative of the shareholders. Our Audit Committee comprises independent directors with the financial knowledge and experience to provide appropriate oversight. We review significant accounting policies, financial reporting and internal control matters with them and encourage their independent discussions with our external auditors. Our corporate governance guidelines, as well as the charter of the Audit Committee and certain other committees of our Board, are available on our website at www.pg.com.

P&G has a strong history of doing what's right. We know great companies are built on strong ethical standards and principles. Our financial results are delivered from that culture of accountability, and we take responsibility for the quality and accuracy of our financial reporting. We present this information proudly, with the expectation that those who use it will understand our Company, recognize our commitment to performance with integrity and share our confidence in P&G's future.

A. G. Lafley

Chairman of the Board,
President and Chief Executive

Clayton C. Daley, Jr.

Chief Financial Officer

Report of Independent Registered Public Accounting Firm

Deloitte.

To the Board of Directors and Shareholders of
The Procter & Gamble Company:

We have audited the accompanying consolidated balance sheets of The Procter & Gamble Company and subsidiaries (the "Company") as of June 30, 2004 and 2003 and the related consolidated statements of earnings, shareholders' equity and cash flows for each of the three years in the period ended June 30, 2004. These financial statements are the responsibility of the Company's management. Our responsibility is to express an opinion on these financial statements based on our audits.

We conducted our audits in accordance with standards of the Public Company Accounting Oversight Board (United States). Those standards require that we plan and perform the audits to obtain reasonable assurance about whether the financial statements are free of material misstatement. An audit includes examining, on a test basis, evidence supporting the amounts and disclosures in the nancial statements. An audit also includes assessing the accounting principles used and signi cant estimates made by management, as well as evaluating the overall financial statement presentation. We believe that our audits provide a reasonable basis for our opinion.

In our opinion, such consolidated financial statements present fairly, in all material respects, the nancial position of the Company at June 30, 2004 and 2003 and the results of its operations and cash flows for each of the three years in the period ended June 30, 2004, in conformity with accounting principles generally accepted in the United States of America.

Deloitte + Touche LLP

Deloitte & Touche LLP
Cincinnati, Ohio

August 6, 2004

Consolidated Statements of Earnings

	Years Ended June 30		
Amounts in millions except per share amounts	**2004**	2003	2002
Net Sales	**$51,407**	$43,377	$40,238
Cost of products sold	**25,076**	22,141	20,989
Selling, general and administrative expense	**16,504**	13,383	12,571
Operating Income	**9,827**	7,853	6,678
Interest expense	**629**	561	603
Other non-operating income, net	**152**	238	308
Earnings Before Income Taxes	**9,350**	7,530	6,383
Income taxes	**2,869**	2,344	2,031
Net Earnings	**$6,481**	$5,186	$4,352
Basic Net Earnings Per Common Share[1]	**$2.46**	$1.95	$1.63
Diluted Net Earnings Per Common Share[1]	**$2.32**	$1.85	$1.54
Dividends Per Common Share[1]	**$0.93**	$0.82	$0.76

[1] Restated for two-for-one stock split effective May 21, 2004.

See accompanying Notes to Consolidated Financial Statements

Consolidated Statements of Cash Flows

		Years ended June 30	
Amounts in millions	**2004**	2003	2002
Cash and Cash Equivalents, Beginning of Year	**$5,912**	$3,427	$2,306
Operating Activities			
Net earnings	**6,481**	5,186	4,352
Depreciation and amortization	**1,733**	1,703	1,693
Deferred income taxes	**415**	63	389
Change in accounts receivable	**(159)**	163	96
Change in inventories	**56**	(56)	159
Change in accounts payable, accrued and other liabilities	**625**	936	684
Change in other operating assets and liabilities	**(88)**	178	(98)
Other	**299**	527	467
Total Operating Activities	**9,362**	8,700	7,742
Investing Activities			
Capital expenditures	**(2,024)**	(1,482)	(1,679)
Proceeds from asset sales	**230**	143	227
Acquisitions	**(7,476)**	(61)	(5,471)
Change in investment securities	**(121)**	(107)	88
Total Investing Activities	**(9,391)**	(1,507)	(6,835)
Financing Activities			
Dividends to shareholders	**(2,539)**	(2,246)	(2,095)
Change in short-term debt	**4,911**	(2,052)	1,394
Additions to long-term debt	**1,963**	1,230	1,690
Reductions of long-term debt	**(1,188)**	(1,060)	(461)
Proceeds from the exercise of stock options	**555**	269	237
Treasury purchases	**(4,070)**	(1,236)	(568)
Total Financing Activities	**(368)**	(5,095)	197
Effect of Exchange Rate Changes on Cash and Cash Equivalents	**(46)**	387	17
Change in Cash and Cash Equivalents	**(443)**	2,485	1,121
Cash and Cash Equivalents, End of Year	**$5,469**	$5,912	$3,427
Supplemental Disclosure			
Cash payments for:			
Interest	**$630**	$538	$629
Income taxes	**1,634**	1,703	941
Non-cash spin-off of Jif and Crisco businesses	-	-	150
Acquisition of Businesses			
Fair value of assets acquired, excluding cash	**$11,954**	$61	$6,042
Fair value of liabilities assumed	**(4,478)**	-	(571)
Acquisitions	**7,476**	61	5,471

See accompanying Notes to Consolidated Financial Statements

Consolidated Balance Sheets
Assets

Amounts in millions	June 30 2004	2003
Current Assets		
Cash and cash equivalents	$5,469	$5,912
Investment securities	423	300
Accounts receivable	4,062	3,038
Inventories		
Materials and supplies	1,191	1,095
Work in process	340	291
Finished goods	2,869	2,254
Total Inventories	4,400	3,640
Deferred income taxes	958	843
Prepaid expenses and other receivables	1,803	1,487
Total Current Assets	**17,115**	15,220
Property, Plant and Equipment		
Buildings	5,206	4,729
Machinery and equipment	19,456	18,222
Land	642	591
	25,304	23,542
Accumulated depreciation	(11,196)	(10,438)
Net Property, Plant and Equipment	**14,108**	13,104
Goodwill and Other Intangible Assets		
Goodwill	19,610	11,132
Trademarks and other intangible assets, net	4,290	2,375
Net Goodwill and Other Intangible Assets	**23,900**	13,507
Other Non-Current Assets	1,925	1,875
Total Assets	**$57,048**	$43,706

See accompanying Notes to Consolidated Financial Statements

Consolidated Balance Sheets
Liabilities and Shareholders' Equity

Amounts in millions	June 30 2004	2003
Current Liabilities		
Accounts payable	$3,617	$2,795
Accrued and other liabilities	7,689	5,512
Taxes payable	2,554	1,879
Debt due within one year	8,287	2,172
Total Current Liabilities	22,147	12,358
Long-Term Debt	12,554	11,475
Deferred Income Taxes	2,261	1,396
Other Non-Current Liabilities	2,808	2,291
Total Liabilities	39,770	27,520
Shareholders' Equity[1]		
Convertible Class A preferred stock, stated value $1 per share (600 shares authorized)	1,526	1,580
Non-Voting Class B preferred stock, stated value $1 per share (200 shares authorized)	-	-
Common stock, stated value $1 per share (5,000 shares authorized; shares outstanding: 2004 - 2,543.8, 2003 - 2,594.4)	2,544	2,594
Additional paid-in capital	2,425	1,634
Reserve for ESOP debt retirement	(1,283)	(1,308)
Accumulated other comprehensive income	(1,545)	(2,006)
Retained earnings	13,611	13,692
Total Shareholders' Equity	17,278	16,186
Total Liabilities and Shareholders' Equity	$57,048	$43,706

[1] Restated for two-for-one stock split effective May 21, 2004.

See accompanying Notes to Consolidated Financial Statements

Consolidated Statements of Shareholders' Equity

(Restated for two-for-one stock split effective May 21, 2004)

Dollars in millions/ Shares in thousands	Common Shares Outstanding	Common Stock	Preferred Stock	Additional Paid-In Capital	Reserve for ESOP Debt Retirement	Accumulated Other Comprehensive Income	Retained Earnings	Total	Total Comprehensive Income
Balance June 30, 2001	2,591,476	$2,591	$1,701	$762	$(1,375)	$(2,120)	$10,451	$12,010	
Net earnings							4,352	4,352	$4,352
Other comprehensive income:									
Financial statement translation						263		263	263
Net investment hedges, net of $238 tax						(397)		(397)	(397)
Other, net of tax benefits						(106)		(106)	(106)
Total comprehensive income									$4,112
Dividends to shareholders:									
Common							(1,971)	(1,971)	
Preferred, net of tax benefits							(124)	(124)	
Spin-off of Jif and Crisco							(150)	(150)	
Treasury purchases	(15,363)	(15)		25[1,2]			(578)	(568)	
Employee plan issuances	16,646	17		344				361	
Preferred stock conversions	8,781	9	(67)	58				-	
ESOP debt guarantee reduction					36			36	
Balance June 30, 2002	2,601,540	2,602	1,634	1,189	(1,339)	(2,360)	11,980	13,706	
Net earnings							5,186	5,186	$5,186
Other comprehensive income:									
Financial statement translation						804		804	804
Net investment hedges, net of $251 tax						(418)		(418)	(418)
Other, net of tax benefits						(32)		(32)	(32)
Total comprehensive income									$5,540
Dividends to shareholders:									
Common							(2,121)	(2,121)	
Preferred, net of tax benefits							(125)	(125)	
Treasury purchases	(28,276)	(28)		20[1,2]			(1,228)	(1,236)	
Employee plan issuances	14,312	14		377				391	
Preferred stock conversions	6,819	6	(54)	48				-	
ESOP debt guarantee reduction					31			31	
Balance June 30, 2003	2,594,395	2,594	1,580	1,634	(1,308)	(2,006)	13,692	16,186	
Net earnings							6,481	6,481	$6,481
Other comprehensive income:									
Financial statement translation						750		750	750
Net investment hedges, net of $207 tax						(348)		(348)	(348)
Other, net of tax benefits						59		59	59
Total comprehensive income									$6,942
Dividends to shareholders:									
Common							(2,408)	(2,408)	
Preferred, net of tax benefits							(131)	(131)	
Treasury purchases	(79,893)	(80)		33[2]			(4,023)	(4,070)	
Employee plan issuances	22,678	23		711				734	
Preferred stock conversions	6,658	7	(54)	47				-	
ESOP debt guarantee reduction					25			25	
Balance June 30, 2004	2,543,838	$2,544	$1,526	$2,425	$(1,283)	$(1,545)	$13,611	$17,278	

[1] Premium on equity put options totaled $6 and $18 for 2003 and 2002, respectively.
[2] Includes impacts arising from stock split.

See accompanying Notes to Consolidated Financial Statements

Notes to Consolidated Financial Statements

Note 1 Summary of Significant Accounting Policies

Nature of Operations

The Procter & Gamble Company's (the Company) business is focused on providing consumer branded products of superior quality and value. The Company markets approximately 300 consumer products in more than 160 countries around the world. Our products are sold primarily through retail operations including mass merchandisers, grocery stores, membership club stores and drug stores.

Basis of Presentation

The Consolidated Financial Statements include The Procter & Gamble Company and its controlled subsidiaries. Intercompany transactions are eliminated in consolidation. Investments in certain companies over which the Company exerts significant influence, but does not control the financial and operating decisions, are accounted for as equity method investments.

Use of Estimates

Preparation of financial statements in conformity with accounting principles generally accepted in the United States of America (U.S. GAAP) requires management to make estimates and assumptions that affect the amounts reported in the Consolidated Financial Statements and accompanying disclosures. These estimates are based on management's best knowledge of current events and actions the Company may undertake in the future. Estimates are used in accounting for, among other items, consumer and trade promotion accruals, pensions, post-employment benefits, stock options, useful lives for depreciation and amortization, future cash flows associated with impairment testing for goodwill and long-lived assets, deferred tax assets, potential income tax assessments and contingencies. Actual results may ultimately differ from estimates, although management does not believe such changes would materially affect the financial statements in any individual year.

Revenue Recognition

Sales are recognized when revenue is realized or realizable and has been earned. Most revenue transactions represent sales of inventory, and the revenue recorded includes shipping and handling costs, which generally are included in the list price to the customer. The Company's policy is to recognize revenue when title to the product, ownership and risk of loss transfer to the customer, which generally is on the date of shipment. A provision for payment discounts and product return allowances is recorded as a reduction of sales in the same period that the revenue is recognized.

Trade promotions, consisting primarily of customer pricing allowances, merchandising funds and consumer coupons, are offered through various programs to customers and consumers. Sales are recorded net of trade promotion spending, which is recognized as incurred, generally at the time of the sale. Most of these arrangements have terms of approximately one year. Accruals for expected payouts under these programs are included as accrued marketing and promotion in the accrued and other current liabilities line in the Consolidated Balance Sheets.

Cost of Products Sold

Cost of products sold primarily comprises direct materials and supplies consumed in the manufacture of product, as well as manufacturing labor and direct overhead expense necessary to acquire and convert the purchased materials and supplies into finished product. Cost of products sold also includes the cost to distribute products to customers, inbound freight costs, internal transfer costs, warehousing costs and other shipping and handling activity. Shipping and handling costs invoiced to customers are included in net sales.

Selling, General and Administrative

Selling, general and administrative expense primarily includes marketing expenses, including the cost of media, advertising and related costs; selling expenses; research and development costs; administrative and other indirect overhead costs; and other miscellaneous operating items.

Other Non-Operating Income, Net

Other non-operating income, net primarily includes interest and investment income and gains and losses from divestitures.

Currency Translation

Financial statements of operating subsidiaries outside the United States of America (U.S.) generally are measured using the local currency as the functional currency. Adjustments to translate those statements into U.S. dollars are recorded in other comprehensive income (OCI). For subsidiaries operating in highly inflationary economies, the U.S. dollar is the functional currency. Remeasurement adjustments for financial statements in highly inflationary economies and other transactional exchange gains and losses are reflected in earnings.

Cash Flow Presentation

The Statement of Cash Flows is prepared using the indirect method, which reconciles net earnings to cash flow from operating activities. These adjustments include the removal of timing differences between the occurrence of operating receipts and payments and their recognition in net earnings. The adjustments also remove from operating activities cash flows arising from investing and financing activities, which are

Millions of dollars except per share amounts

presented separately from operating activities. Cash flows from foreign currency transactions and operations are translated at an average exchange rate for the period. Cash flows from hedging activities are included in the same category as the items being hedged. Cash flows from derivative instruments designated as net investment hedges are classified as financing activities. Cash flows from other derivative instruments used to manage interest, commodity or currency exposures are classified as operating activities. Cash paid for acquisitions is classified as investing activities.

Cash Equivalents
Highly liquid investments with maturities of three months or less when purchased are considered cash equivalents and recorded at cost.

Investments
Investment securities consist of readily-marketable debt and equity securities. These securities are reported at fair value. Unrealized gains or losses on securities classified as trading are charged to earnings. Unrealized gains or losses on securities classified as available for sale are recorded net of tax in OCI.

Other investments that are not controlled and over which the Company does not have the ability to exercise significant influence are accounted under the cost method.

Inventory Valuation
Inventories are valued at cost, which is not in excess of current market prices. Product-related inventories are primarily maintained on the first-in, first-out method. Minor amounts of product inventories, including certain cosmetics and commodities are maintained on the last-in, first-out method. The cost of spare part inventories is maintained using the average cost method.

Goodwill and Other Intangible Assets
The cost of intangible assets with determinable useful lives is amortized to reflect the pattern of economic benefits consumed, principally on a straight-line basis over the estimated periods benefited. Goodwill and indefinite-lived intangibles are not amortized, but are evaluated annually for impairment. The Company evaluates a number of factors to determine whether an indefinite life is appropriate, including the competitive environment, market share, brand history, operating plan and the macroeconomic environment of the country in which the brand is sold. Due to the nature of the Company's business, there are a number of brand intangibles that have been determined to have

indefinite lives. If it is determined that a brand intangible does not have an indefinite life, the Company's policy is to amortize such assets over the expected useful life, which generally ranges from 5 to 20 years. Patents, technology and other intangibles with contractual terms are amortized over their respective contractual lives. Other non-contractual intangible assets with determinable lives are amortized over periods ranging from 5 to 20 years.

Where certain events or changes in operating conditions occur, lives on intangible assets with determinable lives may be adjusted and an impairment assessment may be performed on the recoverability of the carrying amounts. The annual evaluation for impairment of goodwill and indefinite-lived intangibles is based on valuation models that incorporate internal projections of expected future cash flows and operating plans.

Property, Plant and Equipment
Property, plant and equipment are recorded at cost reduced by accumulated depreciation. Depreciation expense is recognized over the assets' estimated useful lives using the straight-line method. Machinery and equipment includes office furniture and equipment (15-year life), computer equipment and capitalized software (3 to 5-year lives) and manufacturing equipment (3 to 20-year lives). Buildings are depreciated over an estimated useful life of 40 years. Estimated useful lives are periodically reviewed and, where appropriate, changes are made prospectively. Where certain events or changes in operating conditions occur, asset lives may be adjusted and an impairment assessment may be performed on the recoverability of the carrying amounts.

Fair Values of Financial Instruments
Certain financial instruments are required to be recorded at fair value. The estimated fair values of such financial instruments, including certain debt instruments, investment securities and derivatives, have been determined using market information and valuation methodologies, primarily discounted cash flow analysis. These estimates require considerable judgment in interpreting market data and changes in assumptions or estimation methods could significantly affect the fair value estimates. However, the Company does not believe any such changes would have a material impact on its financial condition or results of operations. Other financial instruments, including cash equivalents, other investments and short-term debt, are recorded at cost, which approximates fair value. The fair valve of long-term debt is disclosed in Note 6.

Stock-Based Compensation

The Company has employee stock option plans, which are described more fully in Note 8. The Company accounts for its employee stock option plans under the intrinsic value recognition and measurement provisions of Accounting Principles Board (APB) Opinion No. 25, "Accounting for Stock Issued to Employees," and related interpretations. As stock options have been issued with exercise prices equal to the market value of the underlying shares on the grant date, no compensation expense has resulted.

Had compensation expense for the plans been determined based on the fair value of the options on the grant date, consistent with SFAS No. 123, "Accounting for Stock-Based Compensation," the Company's net earnings and earnings per common share would have been as follows:

	Years ended June 30		
	2004[1]	2003	2002
Net Earnings			
As reported	**$6,481**	$5,186	$4,352
Pro forma adjustments	**(325)**	(398)	(442)
Pro forma	**6,156**	4,788	3,910
Net Earnings Per Common Share			
Basic			
As reported	**$2.46**	$1.95	$1.63
Pro forma adjustments	**(0.12)**	(0.15)	(0.17)
Pro forma	**2.34**	1.80	1.46
Diluted			
As reported	**2.32**	1.85	1.54
Pro forma adjustments	**(0.12)**	(0.15)	(0.15)
Pro forma	**2.20**	1.70	1.39

[1] During the current year, the timing of the annual grant was moved from September to February resulting in lower expense, as the associated pro forma expense is amortized over the three-year vesting period.

Stock Split

In March 2004, the Company's Board of Directors approved a two-for-one stock split effective for common and preferred shareholders of record as of May 21, 2004. The financial statements, notes and other references to share and per share data have been restated to reflect the stock split for all periods presented.

New Pronouncements and Reclassifications

No new accounting pronouncements issued or effective during the fiscal year have had or are expected to have a material impact on the financial statements. Certain reclassifications of prior years' amounts have been made to conform to the current year presentation.

Note 2 Restructuring Program

In 1999, concurrent with a reorganization of its operations into product-based Global Business Units, the Company initiated a multi-year restructuring program. Costs included enrollment reductions, manufacturing consolidations and portfolio choices to scale back or discontinue under-performing businesses and initiatives. Total restructuring program charges were $751 in 2003, including $351 in separations related to approximately 5,000 people, $190 in asset write-downs and $87 in accelerated depreciation related to long-lived assets that were taken out of service prior to the end of their normal service period. Total restructuring program charges were $958 in 2002, including $393 in separations related to approximately 7,400 people, $208 in asset write-downs and $135 in accelerated depreciation.

At June 30, 2003, the program was substantially complete with a remaining reserve of $335. Substantially all of this liability was settled through cash payments by the end of 2004.

The Company continues to undertake projects to maintain a competitive cost structure, including manufacturing streamlining and work force rationalization, as part of its normal operations.

Note 3 Acquisitions and Spin-Off

Wella Acquisition

On September 2, 2003, the Company acquired a controlling interest in Wella AG (Wella). Through a stock purchase agreement with the majority shareholders of Wella and a tender offer made on the remaining shares, the Company acquired a total of 81% of Wella's outstanding shares, including 99% of Wella's outstanding voting class shares. In June 2004, the Company and Wella entered into a Domination and Profit Transfer Agreement (the Domination Agreement) pursuant to which the Company is entitled to exercise full operating control and receive 100% of the future earnings of Wella. As consideration for the Domination Agreement, the Company will pay the holders of the remaining outstanding shares of Wella a guaranteed perpetual annual dividend payment. Alternatively, the remaining Wella shareholders may elect to tender their shares to the Company for an agreed price. The fair value of the total guaranteed annual dividend payments is $1.11 billion, which approximates the cost if all remaining shares were tendered. Because the Domination Agreement transfers operational and economic control of the remaining outstanding shares to the Company, it has been accounted for as an acquisition of the remaining shares, with a liability recorded equal to the fair value of the guaranteed payments. Because of the tender feature, the liability is recorded as a current liability in the accrued and other liabilities

Millions of dollars except per share amounts

line of the Consolidated Balance Sheets. Payments made under the guaranteed annual dividend provisions will be allocated between interest expense and a reduction of the liability, as appropriate. The total purchase price for Wella, including acquisition costs, was $6.27 billion based on exchange rates at the acquisition dates. It was funded with a combination of cash, debt and the liability recorded under the Domination Agreement

The acquisition of Wella, with over $3 billion in annual net sales, gives the Company access to the professional hair care category plus greater scale and scope in hair care, hair colorants, cosmetics and fragrance products, while providing potential for significant synergies. The operating results of the Wella business are reported in the Company's Beauty Care business segment beginning September 2, 2003.

The following table provides pro forma results of operations for the years ended June 30, 2004, 2003 and 2002, as if Wella had been acquired as of the beginning of each fiscal year presented. The pro forma results include certain adjustments, including adjustments to convert Wella's historical financial information from International Accounting Standards (IAS) into U.S. GAAP, estimated interest impacts from funding of the acquisition and estimated amortization of definite-lived intangible assets. However, pro forma results do not include any anticipated cost savings or other effects of the integration of Wella. Accordingly, such amounts are not necessarily indicative of the results that would have occurred if the acquisition had occurred on the dates indicated or that may result in the future.

Pro forma results	Years ended June 30		
	2004	2003	2002
Net Sales	**$51,958**	$46,751	$43,070
Net Earnings	**6,402**	5,222	4,345
Diluted Net Earnings per Common Share	**$2.29**	$1.86	$1.54

The Company is in the process of finalizing independent appraisals for certain assets to assist management in allocating the purchase price to the individual assets acquired and liabilities assumed. This may result in adjustments to the carrying values of Wella's recorded assets and liabilities, including the amount of any residual value allocated to goodwill. The Company is also completing its analysis of collaboration plans that may result in additional purchase price allocation adjustments. The preliminary allocation of the purchase price included in the current period balance sheet is based on the current best estimates of man-

agement and is subject to revision based on final determination of fair values and collaboration plans. The Company anticipates the valuations and other studies will be completed prior to the anniversary date of the acquisition. The preliminary allocation of the total purchase price of Wella resulted in the following condensed balance sheet of assets acquired and liabilities assumed.

Current assets	$1,825
Property, plant and equipment	443
Goodwill	5,864
Intangible assets	1,709
Other non-current assets	225
Total assets acquired	10,066
Current liabilities	2,114
Non-current liabilities	1,679
Total liabilities assumed	3,793
Net assets acquired	6,273

The Wella acquisition resulted in $5.86 billion in goodwill, all of which was allocated to the Beauty Care segment, and $1.71 billion in total intangible assets acquired with $1.15 billion allocated to trademarks with indefinite lives. The remaining $556 of acquired intangibles have determinable useful lives and were assigned to trademarks of $267, patents and technology of $10, professional customer relationships of $214 and license and other intangible assets of $65. Total intangible assets acquired with determinable lives have a weighted-average life of 11 years (8 years for trademarks, 5 years for patents and technology, 15 years for professional customer relationships and 23 years for license and other intangible assets).

China Venture

On June 18, 2004, the Company purchased the remaining 20% stake in its China venture from its partner, Hutchison Whampoa China Ltd. (Hutchison), giving the Company full ownership in its operations in China. The net purchase price was $1.85 billion, which is the purchase price of $2.00 billion net of minority interest and related obligations that were eliminated as a result of the transaction. The acquisition was funded by debt. The fair value of the incremental individual assets and liabilities acquired approximates current book value. Accordingly, the purchase price was recorded as goodwill, which was allocated to multiple business segments.

Millions of dollars except per share amounts

Clairol Acquisition

On November 16, 2001, the Company completed the acquisition of the Clairol business from The Bristol-Myers Squibb Company for approximately $5.03 billion in cash, financed primarily with debt. The operating results of the Clairol business are reported in the Company's Beauty Care segment beginning November 16, 2001.

The following table provides pro forma results of operations for the year ended June 30, 2002 as if Clairol had been acquired as of the beginning of the fiscal year. Pro forma information for 2004 and 2003 is not presented as the results of Clairol are included with those of the Company for the entire year. The pro forma results include adjustments for estimated interest expense on acquisition funding and amortization of definite-lived intangible assets. However, pro forma results do not include any anticipated cost savings or other effects of the integration of Clairol. Accordingly, such amounts are not necessarily indicative of the results that would have occurred if the acquisition had closed on the dates indicated or that may result in the future.

	Year ended June 30
Pro forma results	2002
Net Sales	$40,780
Net Earnings	4,406
Diluted Net Earnings per Common Share	$1.56

Jif and Crisco Spin-off

On May 31, 2002, the Jif peanut butter and Crisco shortening brands were spun off to the Company's shareholders and subsequently merged into The J.M. Smucker Company (Smucker). The Company's shareholders received one new common Smucker share for every 50 shares held in the Company, totaling 26 million shares, or approximately $900 in market value. This transaction was not included in the results of operations, since a spin-off to the Company's shareholders is recorded at net book value, or $150, in a manner similar to dividends.

Other minor business purchases and intangible asset acquisitions totaled $384, $61 and $446 in 2004, 2003 and 2002, respectively.

Note 4 Goodwill and Intangible Assets

The change in net carrying amount of goodwill for the years ended June 30, 2004 and 2003 was allocated by reportable business segment as follows:

	2004	2003
Fabric and Home Care, beginning of year	$460	$451
Acquisitions	148	-
Translation and other	6	9
End of year	614	460
Baby and Family Care, beginning of year	884	830
Acquisitions	19	-
Translation and other	38	54
End of year	941	884
Beauty Care, beginning of year	6,600	6,542
Acquisitions	7,277	-
Translation and other	580	58
End of year	14,457	6,600
Health Care, beginning of year	2,908	2,866
Acquisitions	386	-
Translation and other	21	42
End of year	3,315	2,908
Snacks and Beverages, beginning of year	280	277
Translation and other	3	3
End of year	283	280
Goodwill, Net, beginning of year	11,132	10,966
Acquisitions	7,830	-
Translation and other	648	166
End of year	19,610	11,132

For the year ended June 30, 2004, goodwill increased primarily due to the acquisition of Wella and the purchase of the remaining stake in the China venture.

Identifiable intangible assets as of June 30, 2004 and 2003 were comprised of:

	June 30, 2004		June 30, 2003	
	Gross Carrying Amount	Accumulated Amortization	Gross Carrying Amount	Accumulated Amortization
Intangible Assets with Determinable Lives				
Trademarks	$1,012	$155	$499	$85
Patents and technology	518	250	492	204
Other	554	165	316	140
	2,084	570	1,307	429
Trademarks with Indefinite Lives	2,945	169	1,666	169
	5,029	739	2,973	598

Millions of dollars except per share amounts

The amortization of intangible assets for the years ended June 30, 2004, 2003 and 2002 was $165, $100 and $97, respectively. Estimated amortization expense over the next five years is as follows: 2005 - $171; 2006 - $169; 2007 - $119; 2008 - $106; and 2009 - $104. Such estimates do not reflect the impact of future foreign exchange rate changes.

Note 5 Supplemental Financial Information

Selected components of current and non-current liabilities were as follows:

	June 30	
	2004	2003
Accrued and Other Current Liabilities		
Marketing and promotion	$1,876	$1,802
Liability under Wella Domination Agreement	1,106	-
Compensation expenses	1,049	804
Other	3,658	2,906
	7,689	5,512
Other Non-Current Liabilities		
Pension benefits	$1,798	$1,301
Other postretirement benefits	142	181
Other	868	809
	2,808	2,291

Selected Operating Expenses

Research and development costs are charged to earnings as incurred and were $1,802 in 2004, $1,665 in 2003 and $1,601 in 2002. Advertising costs are charged to earnings as incurred and were $5,504 in 2004, $4,373 in 2003 and $3,773 in 2002. Both of these are components of selling, general and administrative expense.

Note 6 Short-Term and Long-Term Debt

	June 30	
	2004	2003
Short-Term Debt		
USD commercial paper	$6,059	$717
Non-USD commercial paper	149	147
Current portion of long-term debt	1,518	1,093
Other	561	215
	8,287	2,172

The weighted average short-term interest rates were 1.5% and 3.6% as of June 30, 2004 and 2003, respectively. The rate decrease reflected an increase in commercial paper within short-term debt.

	June 30	
	2004	2003
Long-Term Debt		
6.60% USD note due December, 2004	$1,000	$1,000
4.00% USD note due April, 2005	400	400
5.75% EUR note due September, 2005	1,827	1,725
1.50% JPY note due December, 2005	503	459
3.50% CHF note due February, 2006	240	222
5.40% EUR note due August, 2006	365	-
4.75% USD note due June, 2007	1,000	1,000
6.13% USD note due May, 2008	500	500
4.30% USD note due August, 2008	500	500
3.50% USD note due December, 2008	650	-
6.88% USD note due September, 2009	1,000	1,000
2.00% JPY note due June, 2010	458	417
9.36% ESOP debentures due 2007-2021[1]	1,000	1,000
4.85% USD note due December, 2015	700	-
8.00% USD note due September, 2024	200	200
6.45% USD note due January, 2026	300	300
6.25% GBP note due January, 2030	906	827
5.25% GBP note due January, 2033	363	331
5.50% USD note due February, 2034	500	-
Debt assumed by acquiring non-cash capital leases	252	146
All other long-term debt	1,408	2,541
Current portion of long-term debt	(1,518)	(1,093)
	12,554	11,475

[1] Debt issued by the ESOP is guaranteed by the Company and must be recorded as debt of the Company as discussed in Note 9.

Long-term weighted average interest rates were 4.0% and 3.7% as of June 30, 2004 and 2003, respectively, and included the effects of related interest rate swaps discussed in Note 7.

The fair value of the long-term debt was $13,168 and $12,396 at June 30, 2004 and 2003, respectively. Long-term debt maturities during the next five fiscal years are as follows: 2005 - $1,518; 2006 - $2,625; 2007 - $1,433; 2008 - $972; and 2009 - $1,150. The Company has no material obligations that are secured.

Millions of dollars except per share amounts

Note 7 Risk Management Activities

As a multinational company with diverse product offerings, the Company is exposed to market risks, such as changes in interest rates, currency exchange rates and commodity pricing. To manage the volatility related to these exposures, the Company evaluates exposures on a consolidated basis to take advantage of logical exposure netting. For the remaining exposures, the Company enters into various derivative transactions. Such derivative transactions, which are executed in accordance with the Company's policies in areas such as counterparty exposure and hedging practices, are accounted for under SFAS No. 133, "Accounting for Derivative Instruments and Hedging Activities," as amended and interpreted. The Company does not hold or issue derivative financial instruments for speculative trading purposes.

At inception, the Company formally designates and documents the financial instrument as a hedge of a specific underlying exposure. The Company formally assesses, both at inception and at least quarterly on an ongoing basis, whether the financial instruments used in hedging transactions are effective at offsetting changes in either the fair value or cash flows of the related underlying exposure. Fluctuations in the derivative value generally are offset by changes in the fair value or cash flows of the exposures being hedged. This offset is driven by the high degree of effectiveness between the exposure being hedged and the hedging instrument. Any ineffective portion of an instrument's change in fair value is immediately recognized in earnings.

Credit Risk

The Company has established strict counterparty credit guidelines and normally enters into transactions with investment grade financial institutions. Counterparty exposures are monitored daily and downgrades in credit rating are reviewed on a timely basis. Credit risk arising from the inability of a counterparty to meet the terms of the Company's financial instrument contracts generally is limited to the amounts, if any, by which the counterparty's obligations exceed the obligations of the Company. The Company does not expect to incur material credit losses on its risk management or other financial instruments.

Interest Rate Management

The Company's policy is to manage interest cost using a mixture of fixed-rate and variable-rate debt. To manage this risk in a cost efficient manner, the Company enters into interest rate swaps in which the Company agrees to exchange, at specified intervals, the difference between fixed and variable interest amounts calculated by reference to an agreed-upon notional principal amount.

Interest rate swaps that meet specific conditions under SFAS No. 133 are accounted for as fair value hedges. Changes in the fair value of both the hedging instruments and the underlying debt obligations are immediately recognized in earnings as equal and offsetting gains and losses in the interest expense component of the income statement. The fair value of the Company's interest rate swap agreements was a net asset of $45 and $322 at June 30, 2004 and 2003, respectively. All existing fair value hedges are 100% effective. As a result, there is no impact to earnings due to hedge ineffectiveness.

Foreign Currency Management

The Company manufactures and sells its products in a number of countries throughout the world and, as a result, is exposed to movements in foreign currency exchange rates. The purpose of the Company's foreign currency hedging program is to reduce the risk caused by short-term changes in exchange rates.

The Company primarily utilizes forward exchange contracts and purchased options with maturities of less than 18 months and currency swaps with maturities up to 5 years. These instruments are intended to offset the effect of exchange rate fluctuations on forecasted sales, inventory purchases, intercompany royalties and intercompany loans denominated in foreign currencies and are therefore accounted for as cash flow hedges. The fair value of these instruments at June 30, 2004 and June 30, 2003 was $47 and $27 in assets and $140 and $92 in liabilities, respectively. The effective portion of the changes in fair value for these instruments are reported in OCI and reclassified into earnings in the same financial statement line item and in the same period or periods during which the hedged transactions affect earnings. The ineffective portion, which is not material for any year presented, is immediately recognized in earnings.

Certain instruments used by the Company for foreign exchange risk do not meet the requirements for hedge accounting treatment. In these cases, the change in value of the instruments is designed to offset the foreign currency impact of intercompany financing transactions, income from international operations and other balance sheet revaluations. The fair value of these instruments at June 30, 2004 and 2003 was $71 and $113 in assets and $26 and $26 in liabilities, respectively. The gain or loss on these instruments is immediately recognized in earnings. The net impact of such instruments, included in selling, general and administrative expense, was $80, $264 and $50 of gains in 2004, 2003 and 2002, respectively, which substantially offset foreign currency transaction losses of the items being hedged.

Net Investment Hedging

The Company hedges certain net investment positions in major currencies. To accomplish this, the Company borrows directly in foreign currency and designates a portion of foreign currency debt as a hedge of net investments in foreign subsidiaries. In addition, certain foreign currency swaps are designated as hedges of the Company's related foreign net investments. Under SFAS No. 133, changes in the fair value of these instruments are immediately recognized in OCI, to offset the change in the value of the net investment being hedged. Currency effects of these hedges reflected in OCI were a $348 and $418 after-tax loss in 2004 and 2003, respectively. Accumulated net balances were a $586 after-tax loss in 2004 and a $238 after-tax loss in 2003.

Commodity Price Management

Raw materials used by the Company are subject to price volatility caused by weather, supply conditions, political and economic variables and other unpredictable factors. To manage the volatility related to certain anticipated inventory purchases, the Company uses futures and options with maturities generally less than one year and swap contracts with maturities up to five years. These market instruments are designated as cash flow hedges under SFAS No. 133. Accordingly, the mark-to-market gain or loss on qualifying hedges is reported in OCI and reclassified into cost of products sold in the same period or periods during which the hedged transaction affects earnings. Qualifying cash flow hedges currently recorded in OCI are not considered material. The mark-to-market gain or loss on non-qualifying, excluded and ineffective portions of hedges is immediately recognized in cost of products sold. Commodity hedging activity was not material to the Company's financial statements for any of the years presented.

Note 8 Earnings Per Share and Stock Options

Net Earnings Per Common Share

Net earnings less preferred dividends (net of related tax benefits) are divided by the weighted average number of common shares outstanding during the year to calculate basic net earnings per common share. Diluted net earnings per common share are calculated to give effect to stock options and assuming conversion of preferred stock (see Note 9).

Net earnings and common share balances used to calculate basic and diluted net earnings per share were as follows:

	Years ended June 30		
	2004	2003	2002
Net Earnings	**$6,481**	$5,186	$4,352
Preferred dividends, net of tax benefit	**(131)**	(125)	(124)
Net earnings available to common shareholders	**6,350**	5,061	4,228
Preferred dividends, net of tax benefit	**131**	125	124
Preferred dividend impact on funding of ESOP	**(4)**	(9)	(12)
Diluted net earnings	**6,477**	5,177	4,340

	Years ended June 30		
Shares in millions	**2004**	2003	2002
Basic weighted average common shares outstanding	**2,580.1**	2,593.2	2,594.8
Effect of dilutive securities			
Conversion of preferred shares[1]	**164.0**	170.2	177.6
Exercise of stock options[2]	**46.0**	39.2	37.5
Diluted weighted average common shares outstanding	**2,790.1**	2,802.6	2,809.9

[1] Despite being included currently in diluted net earnings per common share, the actual conversion to common stock occurs pursuant to the repayment of the ESOP debt through 2021.

[2] Approximately 38 million in 2004, 66 million in 2003 and 72 million in 2002 of the Company's outstanding stock options were not included in the diluted net earnings per share calculation because to do so would have been antidilutive (i.e., the exercise price exceeded market value).

Stock-Based Compensation

The Company has a primary stock-based compensation plan under which stock options are granted annually to key managers and directors with exercise prices equal to the market price of the underlying shares on the date of grant. Grants were made under plans approved by shareholders in 1992, 2001 and 2003. Grants issued since September 2002 are vested after three years and have a ten-year life. Grants issued from July 1998 through August 2002 are vested after three years and have a fifteen-year life, while grants issued prior to July 1998 are vested after one year and have a ten-year life. The Company also makes other minor grants to employees, for which vesting terms and option lives are not substantially different.

Millions of dollars except per share amounts

Had the provision of SFAS No. 123 expensing been applied, the Company's net earnings and earnings per common share would have been impacted as summarized in the discussion of the Company's stock-based compensation accounting policy in Note 1. In calculating the impact for options granted, the Company has estimated the fair value of each grant using the Black-Scholes option-pricing model. Assumptions are evaluated and revised, as necessary, to reflect market conditions and experience. The following assumptions were used:

Options Granted	Years ended June 30		
	2004	2003	2002
Interest rate	**3.8%**	3.9%	5.4%
Dividend yield	**1.8%**	1.8%	2.2%
Expected volatility	**20%**	20%	20%
Expected life in years	**8**	8	12

The following table summarizes stock option activity during 2004, 2003 and 2002:

Options in Thousands	June 30		
	2004	2003	2002
Outstanding, beginning of year	**259,598**	240,326	208,392
Granted	**40,866**	35,759	50,080
Jif and Crisco spin-off adjustment	**-**	-	1,622
Exercised	**(22,307)**	(13,904)	(16,297)
Canceled	**(1,864)**	(2,583)	(3,471)
Outstanding, end of year	**276,293**	259,598	240,326
Exercisable	**151,828**	118,202	92,664
Available for grant	**165,399**	203,593	229,071
Average price			
Outstanding, beginning of year	**$35.75**	$33.34	$31.82
Granted	**51.06**	45.68	35.09
Exercised	**24.88**	19.35	14.53
Outstanding, end of year	**38.85**	35.75	33.34
Exercisable, end of year	**35.39**	35.44	28.50
Weighted average fair value of options granted during the year	**12.50**	10.99	10.57

Stock options outstanding at June 30, 2004 were in the following exercise price ranges:

	Outstanding Options		
Range of Prices	Number Outstanding (Thousands)	Weighted Avg. Exercise Price	Weighted Avg. Remaining Contractual Life in Years
$16.43 to 30.11	**36,863**	**$24.07**	**2.6**
31.01 to 34.84	**95,260**	**32.72**	**11.5**
35.10 to 46.24	**82,825**	**43.70**	**6.9**
48.73 to 52.98	**61,345**	**50.69**	**9.9**

Stock options exercisable at June 30, 2004 were in the following exercise price ranges:

	Exercisable Options	
Range of Prices	Number Exercisable (Thousands)	Weighted Average Exercise Price
$16.43 to 30.11	**36,863**	**$24.07**
31.01 to 34.84	**48,426**	**31.06**
35.10 to 46.24	**43,624**	**42.36**
48.73 to 52.98	**22,915**	**49.49**

The Company repurchases common shares to mitigate the dilutive impact of options. Beyond that, the Company may make additional discretionary purchases based on cash availability, market trends and other factors.

In limited cases, the Company also issues stock appreciation rights, generally in countries where stock options are not permitted by local governments. The obligations and associated compensation expense are adjusted for changes in intrinsic value. The impact of these adjustments is not material.

Note 9 Postretirement Benefits and Employee Stock Ownership Plan

The Company offers various postretirement benefits to its employees.

Defined Contribution Retirement Plans
The most prevalent employee benefit plans offered are defined contribution plans, which cover substantially all employees in the U.S., as well as employees in certain other countries. These plans are fully funded.

Millions of dollars except per share amounts

Under the defined contribution plans, the Company generally makes contributions to participants based on individual base salaries and years of service. In the U.S., the contribution is set annually. Historically, the Company has contributed approximately 15% of total participants' annual wages and salaries.

The Company maintains The Procter & Gamble Profit Sharing Trust (Trust) and Employee Stock Ownership Plan (ESOP) to provide a portion of the funding for the U.S. defined contribution plan, as well as other retiree benefits. Operating details of the ESOP are provided at the end of this Note. The fair value of the ESOP Series A shares reduces the Company's cash contribution required to fund the U.S. defined contribution plan. Defined contribution expense, which approximates the Company's cash contribution to the plan that is funded in the subsequent year, was $274, $286 and $279 in 2004, 2003 and 2002, respectively.

Defined Benefit Retirement Plans and Other Retiree Benefits
Certain other employees, primarily outside the U.S., are covered by local defined benefit pension plans as well as other retiree benefit plans.

The Company also provides certain other retiree benefits, primarily health care and life insurance, for substantially all U.S. employees who become eligible for these benefits when they meet minimum age and service requirements. Generally, the health care plans require cost sharing with retirees and pay a stated percentage of expenses, reduced by deductibles and other coverages. These benefits primarily are funded by ESOP Series B shares, as well as certain other assets contributed by the Company.

The Medicare Prescription Drug, Improvement and Modernization Act of 2003 was signed into law on December 8, 2003. This Act introduces a Medicare prescription-drug benefit beginning in 2006 as well as a federal subsidy to sponsors of retiree health care plans that provide a benefit at least "actuarially equivalent" to the Medicare benefit. Management has concluded that the Company's plans are at least "actuarially equivalent" to the Medicare benefit and, accordingly, has included the federal subsidy from the Act in the normal year-end measurement process for other retiree benefit plans. The impact is a reduction to the benefit obligation of $195 as of June 30, 2004. The impact to net periodic pension cost and to benefits paid in future years is not expected to be material.

Obligation and Funded Status. The Company uses a June 30 measurement date for its defined benefit retirement plans and other retiree benefit plans. The following provides a reconciliation of benefit obligations, plan assets and funded status of these plans:

	Years ended June 30			
	Pension Benefits		Other Retiree Benefits	
	2004	2003	**2004**	2003
Change in benefit obligation				
Benefit obligation at				
beginning of year[1]	**$3,543**	$2,970	**$2,914**	$2,135
Service cost	**157**	124	**89**	62
Interest cost	**204**	173	**172**	150
Participants'				
contributions	**14**	7	**31**	27
Amendments	**50**	(33)	**(258)**	(2)
Actuarial loss (gain)	**5**	138	**(460)**	645
Acquisitions	**590**	42	**7**	-
Curtailments				
and settlements	**(39)**	(29)	**(8)**	-
Special termination				
benefits	**12**	1	**41**	7
Currency translation	**288**	305	**5**	13
Benefit payments	**(208)**	(155)	**(133)**	(123)
Benefit obligation				
at end of year[1]	**4,616**	3,543	**2,400**	2,914
Change in plan assets				
Fair value of plan				
assets at				
beginning of year	**$1,558**	$1,332	**$2,277**	$2,347
Actual return on				
plan assets	**194**	(36)	**651**	1
Acquisitions	**185**	1	**-**	-
Employer				
contributions	**412**	337	**18**	25
Participants'				
contributions	**14**	7	**31**	27
Settlements	**(21)**	(27)	**-**	-
Currency translation	**129**	99	**(1)**	-
Benefit payments	**(208)**	(155)	**(133)**	(123)
Fair value of plan assets				
at end of year	**2,263**	1,558	**2,843**	2,277
Funded status	**(2,353)**	(1,985)	**443**	**(637)**

[1] For the pension benefit plans, the benefit obligation is the projected benefit obligation. For other retiree benefit plans, the benefit obligation is the accumulated postretirement benefit obligation.

Millions of dollars except per share amounts

	Years ended June 30			
	Pension Benefits		Other Retiree Benefits	
	2004	2003	**2004**	2003
Calculation of net amount recognized				
Funded status at end of year	**$(2,353)**	$(1,985)	**$443**	$(637)
Unrecognized net actuarial loss (gain)	**902**	930	**(344)**	435
Unrecognized transition amount	**12**	13	**-**	-
Unrecognized prior service cost	**38**	(9)	**(259)**	(2)
Net amount recognized	**(1,401)**	(1,051)	**(160)**	(204)
Classification of net amount recognized				
Prepaid benefit cost	**$253**	$173	**$1**	$2
Accrued benefit cost	**(1,872)**	(1,407)	**(161)**	(206)
Intangible asset	**75**	31	**-**	-
Accumulated other comprehensive income	**143**	152	**-**	-
Net amount recognized	**(1,401)**	(1,051)	**(160)**	(204)

The underfunding of pension benefits is primarily a function of the different funding incentives that exist outside of the U.S. In certain countries where the Company has major operations, there are no legal requirements or financial incentives provided to companies to pre-fund pension obligations. In these instances, benefit payments are typically paid directly from the Company's cash as they become due, rather than through the creation of a separate pension fund.

The accumulated benefit obligation for all defined benefit retirement plans was $3,822 and $2,850 at June 30, 2004 and June 30, 2003, respectively. Plans with accumulated benefit obligations in excess of plan assets and plans with projected benefit obligations in excess of plan assets as of June 30, consist of the following:

	Years ended June 30			
	Accumulated Benefit Obligation Exceeds Fair Value of Plan Assets		Projected Benefit Obligation Exceeds Fair Value of Plan Assets	
	2004	2003	**2004**	2003
Projected benefit obligation	**$2,809**	$2,945	**$4,059**	$3,179
Accumulated benefit obligation	**2,396**	2,310	**3,320**	2,492
Fair value of plan assets	**638**	979	**1,676**	1,186

Net Periodic Benefit Cost. Components of the net periodic benefit cost were as follows:

	Years ended June 30					
	Pension Benefits			Other Retiree Benefits		
	2004	2003	2002	**2004**	2003	2002
Service cost	**$157**	$124	$114	**$89**	$62	$49
Interest cost	**204**	173	153	**172**	150	116
Expected return on plan assets	**(153)**	(127)	(133)	**(329)**	(333)	(320)
Amortization of deferred amounts	**3**	4	7	**(1)**	(1)	(1)
Curtailment and settlement loss (gain)	**-**	5	1	**-**	-	(1)
Recognized net actuarial loss (gain)	**28**	13	9	**1**	(27)	(64)
Gross benefit cost	**239**	192	151	**(68)**	(149)	(221)
Dividends on ESOP preferred stock	**-**	-	-	**(73)**	(74)	(76)
Net periodic benefit cost	**239**	192	151	**(141)**	(223)	(297)

Millions of dollars except per share amounts

Assumptions. The Company determines its actuarial assumptions on an annual basis. These assumptions are weighted to reflect each country that may have an impact on the cost of providing retirement benefits. The weighted-average assumptions for the defined benefit and other retiree benefit calculations, as well as assumed health care cost trend rates, for the years ended June 30, are as follows:

	Years ended June 30			
	Pension Benefits		Other Retiree Benefits	
Actuarial assumptions	**2004**	2003	**2004**	2003
Assumptions used to determine benefit obligations[1]				
Discount rate	**5.2%**	5.1%	**6.1%**	5.8%
Rate of compensation increase	**3.1%**	3.1%	-	-
Assumptions used to determine net periodic pension cost[2]				
Discount rate	**5.1%**	5.6%	**5.8%**	7.0%
Expected return on plan assets	**7.4%**	7.7%	**9.5%**	9.5%
Rate of compensation increase	**3.0%**	3.5%	-	-
Assumed health care cost trend rates				
Health care cost trend rates assumed for next year[3]	-	-	**9.7%**	11.4%
Rate that the health care cost trend rate is assumed to decline to (ultimate trend rate)	-	-	**5.1%**	5.0%
Year that the rate reaches the ultimate trend rate	-	-	**2010**	2010

[1] Determined as of end of year.
[2] Determined as of beginning of year.
[3] Rate is applied to current plan costs net of Medicare; estimated initial rate for "gross eligible charges" (charges inclusive of Medicare) is 7.7% for 2004 and 8.8% for 2003.

Several factors are considered in developing the estimate for the long-term expected rate of return on plan assets. For the defined benefit plans, these include historical rates of return of broad equity and bond indices and projected long-term rates of return from pension investment consultants. The expected long-term rates of return for plan assets are 8%-9% for equities and 5%-6% bonds. The rate of return on other retiree benefit plan assets, comprised primarily of Company stock, is based on the long-term projected return of 9.5% and reflects the historical pattern of favorable returns on the Company's stock relative to broader market indices (e.g., S&P 500).

Assumed health care cost trend rates could have a significant effect on the amounts reported for the other retiree benefit plans. A one-percentage point change in assumed health care cost trend rates would have the following effects:

	One-Percentage Point Increase	One-Percentage Point Decrease
Effect on total service and interest cost components	**$51**	**$(46)**
Effect on postretirement benefit obligation	**323**	**(268)**

Plan Assets. The Company's target asset allocation for the year ending June 30, 2005 and actual asset allocation by asset category as of June 30, 2004, and 2003, are as follows:

	Target Allocation	
	Pension Benefits	Other Retiree Benefits
Asset Category	2005	2005
Equity securities[1]	64%	99%
Debt securities	32%	1%
Real estate	4%	-%
Total	100%	100%

	Plan Asset Allocation at June 30			
	Pension Benefits		Other Retiree Benefits	
Asset Category	**2004**	2003	**2004**	2003
Equity securities[1]	**64%**	62%	**99%**	99%
Debt securities	**32%**	35%	**1%**	1%
Real estate	**4%**	3%	**-%**	-%
Total	**100%**	100%	**100%**	100%

[1] Equity securities for other retiree plan assets include Company stock, net of Series B ESOP debt (see Note 6), of $2,744 and $2,182, as of June 30, 2004 and 2003, respectively.

The Company's investment objective for defined benefit plan assets is to meet the plans' benefit obligations, while minimizing the potential for future required Company plan contributions. The investment strategies focus on asset class diversification, liquidity to meet benefit payments and an appropriate balance of long-term investment return and risk. Target ranges for asset allocations are determined by matching the actuarial projections of the plans' future liabilities and benefit payments with expected long-term rates of return on the assets, taking into account investment return volatility and correlations across asset classes. Plan assets are diversified across several investment managers and are generally invested in liquid funds that are selected to track broad market equity and bond indices. Investment risk is carefully controlled with plan assets rebalanced to target allocations on a periodic basis and continual monitoring of investment managers performance relative to the investment guidelines established with each investment manager.

Cash Flows. Management's best estimate of its cash requirements for the defined benefit plans and other retiree benefit plans for the year ending June 30, 2005 is $237 and $20, respectively. For the defined benefit plans, this is comprised of expected benefit payments of $71, which are paid directly to participants of unfunded plans from employer assets, as well as expected contributions to funded plans of $166. For other retiree benefit plans, this is comprised of expected contributions that will be used directly for benefit payments. Expected contributions are dependent on many variables, including the variability of the market value of the assets as compared to the obligation and other market or regulatory conditions. In addition, the Company takes into consideration its business investment opportunities and resulting cash requirements. Accordingly, actual funding may differ greatly from current estimates.

Total benefit payments expected to be paid to participants, which include payments funded from the Company's assets, as discussed above, as well as payments paid from the plans are as follows:

| | Years ended June 30 | |
	Pension Benefits	Other Retiree Benefits
Expected benefit payments		
2005	$191	$144
2006	177	152
2007	193	166
2008	207	176
2009	207	185
2010 – 2014	1,180	1,058

Employee Stock Ownership Plan

The Company maintains the ESOP to provide funding for certain employee benefits discussed in the preceding paragraphs.

The ESOP borrowed $1.00 billion in 1989 and the proceeds were used to purchase Series A ESOP Convertible Class A Preferred Stock to fund a portion of the defined contribution retirement plan in the U.S. Principal and interest requirements were paid by the Trust from dividends on the preferred shares and from advances from the Company. The final payment for the original borrowing of $1.00 billion was made in 2004 and the remaining debt of the ESOP consists of amounts owed to the Company. Each share is convertible at the option of the holder into one share of the Company's common stock. The dividend for the current year was $0.93 per share. The liquidation value is $6.82 per share.

In 1991, the ESOP borrowed an additional $1.00 billion. The proceeds were used to purchase Series B ESOP Convertible Class A Preferred Stock to fund a portion of retiree health care benefits. These shares are considered plan assets, net of the associated debt, of the Other Retiree Benefits plan discussed above. Debt service requirements are funded by preferred stock dividends and cash contributions from the Company. Each share is convertible at the option of the holder into one share of the Company's common stock. The dividend for the current year was $1.02 per share. The liquidation value is $12.96 per share.

As permitted by Statement of Position (SOP) 93-6, "Employers Accounting for Employee Stock Ownership Plans," the Company has elected, where applicable, to continue its practices, which are based on SOP 76-3, "Accounting Practices for Certain Employee Stock Ownership Plans." ESOP debt, which is guaranteed by the Company, is recorded as debt (see Note 6). Preferred shares issued to the ESOP are offset by the reserve for ESOP debt retirement in the Consolidated Balance Sheets and the Consolidated Statements of Shareholders' Equity. Interest incurred on the ESOP debt is recorded as interest expense. Dividends on all preferred shares, net of related tax benefits, are charged to retained earnings.

Millions of dollars except per share amounts

As required by SOP 76-3, the preferred shares of the ESOP are allocated based on debt service requirements, net of advances made by the Company to the Trust. The number of preferred shares outstanding at June 30, was as follows:

Shares in Thousands	June 30		
	2004	2003	2002
Allocated	**62,511**	64,492	66,191
Unallocated	**28,296**	31,534	35,374
Total Series A	**90,807**	96,026	101,565
Allocated	**21,399**	20,648	19,738
Unallocated	**48,528**	50,718	52,908
Total Series B	**69,927**	71,366	72,646

For purposes of calculating diluted net earnings per common share, the preferred shares held by the ESOP are considered converted from inception. Diluted net earnings are calculated assuming that all preferred shares are converted to common, and therefore are adjusted to reflect the incremental ESOP funding that would be required due to the difference in dividend rate between preferred and common shares (see Note 8).

Note 10 Income Taxes

Under SFAS No. 109, "Accounting for Income Taxes," income taxes are recognized for the amount of taxes payable for the current year and for the impact of deferred tax liabilities and assets, which represent future tax consequences of events that have been recognized differently in the financial statements than for tax purposes. Deferred tax assets and liabilities are established using the enacted statutory tax rates and are adjusted for changes in such rates in the period of change. Earnings before income taxes consisted of the following:

	Years ended June 30		
	2004	2003	2002
United States	**$6,023**	$4,920	$4,411
International	**3,327**	2,610	1,972
	9,350	7,530	6,383

The income tax provision consisted of the following:

	Years ended June 30		
	2004	2003	2002
Current Tax Expense			
U.S. Federal	**$1,508**	$1,595	$975
International	**830**	588	551
U.S. State and Local	**116**	98	116
	2,454	2,281	1,642
Deferred Tax Expense			
U.S. Federal	**348**	125	571
International and other	**67**	(62)	(182)
	415	63	389
	2,869	2,344	2,031

The Company's effective income tax rate was 30.7%, 31.1% and 31.8% in 2004, 2003 and 2002, respectively, compared to the U.S. statutory rate of 35.0%. The country mix impacts of foreign operations reduced the Company's effective tax rate to a larger degree in 2004 than the previous fiscal years: 4.1% in 2004, 3.8% in 2003 and 3.1% in 2002. The Company's higher effective tax rate in 2002 also reflected the impact of restructuring costs. Taxes impacted shareholders' equity with credits of $351 and $361 for the years ended June 30, 2004 and 2003, respectively. These primarily relate to the tax effects of net investment hedges and tax benefits from the exercise of stock options.

The Company has undistributed earnings of foreign subsidiaries of $16.75 billion at June 30, 2004, for which deferred taxes have not been provided. Such earnings are considered indefinitely invested in the foreign subsidiaries. If such earnings were repatriated, additional tax expense may result, although the calculation of such additional taxes is not practicable.

Millions of dollars except per share amounts

Deferred income tax assets and liabilities were comprised of the following:

	June 30	
	2004	2003
Deferred Tax Assets		
Unrealized loss on financial instruments	**$381**	$287
Loss and other carryforwards	**365**	311
Advance payments	**226**	182
Other postretirement benefits	**95**	93
Other	**1,169**	820
Valuation allowances	**(342)**	(158)
	1,894	1,535
Deferred Tax Liabilities		
Fixed assets	**(1,350)**	(1,175)
Goodwill and other intangible assets	**(1,281)**	(410)
Other	**(352)**	(287)
	(2,983)	(1,872)

Net operating loss carryforwards were $1,398 and $1,222 at June 30, 2004 and June 30, 2003, respectively. If unused, $299 will expire between 2005 and 2014. The remainder, totaling $1,099 at June 30, 2004, may be carried forward indefinitely.

Note 11 Commitments and Contingencies

Guarantees

In conjunction with certain transactions, primarily divestitures, the Company may provide routine indemnifications (e.g., retention of previously existing environmental, tax and employee liabilities) whose terms range in duration and often are not explicitly defined. Generally, the maximum obligation under such indemnifications is not explicitly stated and, as a result, the overall amount of these obligations cannot be reasonably estimated. Other than obligations recorded as liabilities at the time of divestiture, historically the Company has not made significant payments for these indemnifications. The Company believes that if it were to incur a loss in any of these matters, the loss would not have a material effect on the Company's financial condition or results of operations.

In certain situations, the Company guarantees loans for suppliers and customers. The total amount of guarantees issued under such arrangements is not material.

Off-Balance Sheet Arrangements

The Company does not have off-balance sheet financing arrangements, including variable interest entities, under FASB Interpretation No. 46, "Consolidation of Variable Interest Entities," that have a material impact on the financial statements.

Purchase Commitments

The Company has purchase commitments for materials, supplies, services and property, plant and equipment as part of the normal course of business. Due to the proprietary nature of many of the Company's materials and processes, certain supply contracts contain penalty provisions for early termination. The Company does not expect potential payments under these provisions to materially affect results of operations or its financial condition in any individual year.

Operating Leases

The Company leases certain property and equipment for varying periods under operating leases. Future minimum rental commitments under noncancellable operating leases are as follows: 2005 - $186; 2006 - $150; 2007 - $134; 2008 - $99; 2009 - $86; and $265 thereafter.

Litigation

The Company is subject to various lawsuits and claims with respect to matters such as governmental regulations, income taxes and other actions arising out of the normal course of business. The Company is also subject to contingencies pursuant to environmental laws and regulations that in the future may require the Company to take action to correct the effects on the environment of prior manufacturing and waste disposal practices. Accrued environmental liabilities for remediation and closure costs were $36 and $34 at June 30, 2004 and 2003, respectively. Current year expenditures were not material.

While considerable uncertainty exists, in the opinion of management and Company counsel, the ultimate liabilities resulting from such lawsuits and claims will not materially affect the Company's financial condition.

Millions of dollars except per share amounts

Note 12 Segment Information

The Company is organized into five product-based Global Business Units. The segments, which are generally determined by the product type and end-point user benefits offered, manufacture and market products as follows:

- Fabric and Home Care includes laundry detergents, dish care, fabric enhancers and surface cleaners.
- Beauty Care includes retail and professional hair care, skin care, feminine care, cosmetics, fine fragrances and personal cleansing.
- Baby and Family Care includes diapers, baby wipes, bath tissue and kitchen towels.
- Health Care includes oral care, personal health care, pharmaceuticals and pet health and nutrition.
- Snacks and Beverages includes coffee, snacks, commercial services and juice. In August 2004, the Company divested the juice business.

Effective July 1, 2004, the Company realigned its businesses and associated management responsibilities to three business units: Beauty Care; Health, Baby and Family Care; and Household Care, which will include the current Fabric and Home Care business as well as the Snacks and Beverages business.

The accounting policies of the operating segments are generally the same as those described in Note 1, Summary of Significant Accounting Policies. Differences from these policies and U.S. GAAP primarily reflect: income taxes, which are reflected in the business segments using estimated local statutory rates; the recording of fixed assets at historical exchange rates in certain high inflation economies; and the treatment of unconsolidated investees. Unconsolidated investees are managed as integral parts of the Company's business units for management and segment reporting purposes. Accordingly, these partially owned operations are reflected as consolidated subsidiaries in segment results, with 100% recognition of the individual income statement line items through before-tax earnings, while after-tax earnings are adjusted to reflect only the Company's ownership percentage. Entries to eliminate the individual revenues and expenses, adjusting the method of accounting to the equity method as required by U.S. GAAP, are included in Corporate.

Corporate includes certain operating and non-operating activities that are not reflected in the operating results used internally to measure and evaluate the operating segments, as well as eliminations to adjust management reporting principles to U.S. GAAP. Operating activities in Corporate include the results of incidental businesses managed at the corporate level along with the elimination of individual revenues and expenses generated by companies over which the Company exerts significant influence, but does not control. Operating elements also comprise intangible asset amortization, certain employee benefit costs and other general corporate items. The non-operating elements include financing and investing activities. In addition, Corporate includes the historical results of certain divested businesses of the former Food and Beverage segment. Corporate assets primarily include cash, investment securities, goodwill and other non-current intangible assets.

The Company had net sales in the U.S. of $23,688, $21,853 and $21,198 for the years ended June 30, 2004, 2003 and 2002, respectively. Assets in the U.S. totaled $23,687 and $23,424 as of June 30, 2004 and 2003, respectively.

The Company's largest customer, Wal-Mart Stores, Inc. and its affiliates, accounted for 17%, 18% and 17% of consolidated net sales in 2004, 2003 and 2002, respectively. These sales occurred primarily in the U.S.

Millions of dollars except per share amounts

		Fabric and Home Care	Beauty Care	Baby and Family Care	Health Care	Snacks and Beverages	Corporate	Total
Net Sales	**2004**	**$13,868**	**$17,122**	**$10,718**	**$6,991**	**$3,482**	**$(774)**	**$51,407**
	2003	12,560	12,221	9,933	5,796	3,238	(371)	43,377
	2002	11,618	10,723	9,233	4,979	3,249	436	40,238
Before-Tax Earnings	**2004**	**3,287**	**3,662**	**1,623**	**1,448**	**557**	**(1,227)**	**9,350**
	2003	3,080	2,899	1,448	1,034	460	(1,391)	7,530
	2002	2,728	2,354	1,272	795	476	(1,242)	6,383
Net Earnings	**2004**	**2,203**	**2,422**	**996**	**962**	**363**	**(465)**	**6,481**
	2003	2,059	1,984	882	706	306	(751)	5,186
	2002	1,831	1,610	738	521	303	(651)	4,352
Depreciation and Amortization	**2004**	**331**	**393**	**550**	**153**	**119**	**187**	**1,733**
	2003	332	345	558	156	125	187	1,703
	2002	326	339	503	163	121	241	1,693
Total Assets	**2004**	**5,512**	**7,869**	**7,229**	**2,639**	**1,831**	**31,968**	**57,048**
	2003	5,174	5,389	6,974	2,642	2,040	21,487	43,706
Capital Expenditures	**2004**	**538**	**433**	**714**	**164**	**134**	**41**	**2,024**
	2003	357	343	548	144	125	(35)	1,482
	2002	368	354	702	158	125	(28)	1,679

Note 13 Quarterly Results (Unaudited)

		Quarters Ended				
		Sept 30	Dec 31	Mar 31	Jun 30	Total Year
Net Sales	**2003–2004**	**$12,195**	**$13,221**	**$13,029**	**$12,962**	**$51,407**
	2002–2003	10,796	11,005	10,656	10,920	43,377
Operating Income	**2003–2004**	**2,643**	**2,742**	**2,303**	**2,139**	**9,827**
	2002–2003	2,179	2,248	1,957	1,469	7,853
Net Earnings	**2003–2004**	**1,761**	**1,818**	**1,528**	**1,374**	**6,481**
	2002–2003	1,464	1,494	1,273	955	5,186
Diluted Net Earnings Per Common Share[1]	**2003–2004**	**$0.63**	**$0.65**	**$0.55**	**$0.50**	**$2.32**
	2002–2003	0.52	0.53	0.46	0.34	1.85

[1] Restated for two-for-one stock split effective May 21, 2004.

Millions of dollars except per share amounts

Financial Summary (Unaudited)

	2004	2003	2002	2001	2000	1999	1998	1997	1996
Net Sales	$51,407	$43,377	$40,238	$ 39,244	$39,951	$38,125	$37,154	$35,764	$35,284
Operating Income	9,827	7,853	6,678	4,736	5,954	6,253	6,055	5,488	4,815
Net Earnings	6,481	5,186	4,352	2,922	3,542	3,763	3,780	3,415	3,046
Net Earnings Margin	12.6%	12.0%	10.8%	7.4%	8.9%	9.9%	10.2%	9.5%	8.6%
Basic Net Earnings Per Common Share[1]	$2.46	$1.95	$1.63	$1.08	$1.30	$1.38	$1.37	$1.22	$1.07
Diluted Net Earnings Per Common Share[1]	2.32	1.85	1.54	1.03	1.23	1.29	1.28	1.14	1.00
Dividends Per Common Share[1]	0.93	0.82	0.76	0.70	0.64	0.57	0.51	0.45	0.40
Restructuring Program Charges[2]	$-	$751	$958	$1,850	$814	$481	$-	$-	$-
Research and Development Expense	1,802	1,665	1,601	1,769	1,899	1,726	1,546	1,469	1,399
Advertising Expense	5,504	4,373	3,773	3,612	3,793	3,639	3,801	3,574	3,374
Total Assets	57,048	43,706	40,776	34,387	34,366	32,192	31,042	27,598	27,762
Capital Expenditures	2,024	1,482	1,679	2,486	3,018	2,828	2,559	2,129	2,179
Long-Term Debt	12,554	11,475	11,201	9,792	9,012	6,265	5,774	4,159	4,678
Shareholders' Equity	17,278	16,186	13,706	12,010	12,287	12,058	12,236	12,046	11,722

[1] Restated for two-for-one stock split effective May 21, 2004.
[2] Restructuring program charges, on an after-tax basis, totaled $538, $706, $1,475, $688 and $385 for 2003, 2002, 2001, 2000 and 1999 respectively.

QUESTIONS

1. How does information from the balance sheet help users of the financial statements?

2. What is meant by solvency? What information in the balance sheet can be used to assess a company's solvency?

3. A recent financial magazine indicated that the airline industry has poor financial flexibility. What is meant by financial flexibility, and why is it important?

4. Discuss at least two situations in which estimates could affect the usefulness of information in the balance sheet.

5. Safin Company reported an increase in inventories in the past year. Discuss the effect of this change on the current ratio (current assets ÷ current liabilities). What does this tell a statement user about Safin Company's liquidity?

6. What is meant by liquidity? Rank the following assets from one to five in order of liquidity.

    (a) Goodwill.

    (b) Inventories.

    (c) Buildings.

    (d) Short-term investments.

    (e) Accounts receivable.

7. What are the major limitations of the balance sheet as a source of information?

8. Discuss at least two items that are important to the value of companies like **Intel** or **IBM** but that are not recorded in their balance sheets. What are some reasons why these items are not recorded in the balance sheet?

9. How does separating current assets from property, plant, and equipment in the balance sheet help analysts?

10. In its December 31, 2007, balance sheet Oakley Corporation reported as an asset, "Net notes and accounts receivable, $7,100,000." What other disclosures are necessary?

11. Should available-for-sale securities always be reported as a current asset? Explain.

12. What is the relationship between current assets and current liabilities?

13. The New York Knicks, Inc. sold 10,000 season tickets at $2,000 each. By December 31, 2007, 18 of the 40 home games had been played. What amount should be reported as a current liability at December 31, 2007?

14. What is working capital? How does working capital relate to the operating cycle?

15. In what section of the balance sheet should the following items appear, and what balance sheet terminology would you use?

    (a) Treasury stock (recorded at cost).

    (b) Checking account at bank.

    (c) Land (held as an investment).

    (d) Sinking fund.

    (e) Unamortized premium on bonds payable.

    (f) Copyrights.

    (g) Pension fund assets.

    (h) Premium on capital stock.

    (i) Long-term investments (pledged against bank loans payable).

16. Where should the following items be shown on the balance sheet, if shown at all?

    (a) Allowance for doubtful accounts receivable.

    (b) Merchandise held on consignment.

    (c) Advances received on sales contract.

    (d) Cash surrender value of life insurance.

    (e) Land.

    (f) Merchandise out on consignment.

    (g) Franchises.

    (h) Accumulated depreciation of plant and equipment.

    (i) Materials in transit—purchased f.o.b. destination.

17. State the generally accepted accounting principle applicable to the balance sheet valuation of each of the following assets.

    (a) Trade accounts receivable.

    (b) Land.

    (c) Inventories.

    (d) Trading securities (common stock of other companies).

    (e) Prepaid expenses.

18. Refer to the definition of assets on page 173. Discuss how a leased building might qualify as an asset of the lessee (tenant) under this definition.

19. Christine Agazzi says, "Retained earnings should be reported as an asset, since it is earnings which are reinvested in the business." How would you respond to Agazzi?

20. The creditors of Nick Anderson Company agree to accept promissory notes for the amount of its indebtedness with a proviso that two-thirds of the annual profits must be applied to their liquidation. How should these notes be reported on the balance sheet of the issuing company? Give a reason for your answer.

21. What are some of the techniques of disclosure for the balance sheet?

22. What is a "Summary of Significant Accounting Policies"?

23. What types of contractual obligations must be disclosed in great detail in the notes to the balance sheet? Why do you think these detailed provisions should be disclosed?

24. What is the profession's recommendation in regard to the use of the term "surplus"? Explain.

25. What is the purpose of a statement of cash flows? How does it differ from a balance sheet and an income statement?

26. The net income for the year for Won Long, Inc. is $750,000, but the statement of cash flows reports that the cash provided by operating activities is $640,000. What might account for the difference?

27. Net income for the year for Jenkins, Inc. was $750,000, but the statement of cash flows reports that cash provided by operating activities was $860,000. What might account for the difference?

28. Differentiate between operating activities, investing activities, and financing activities.

29. Each of the following items must be considered in preparing a statement of cash flows. Indicate where each item is to be reported in the statement, if at all. Assume that net income is reported as $90,000.

   (a) Accounts receivable increased from $32,000 to $39,000 from the beginning to the end of the year.

(b) During the year, 10,000 shares of preferred stock with a par value of $100 a share were issued at $115 per share.

(c) Depreciation expense amounted to $14,000, and bond premium amortization amounted to $5,000.

(d) Land increased from $10,000 to $30,000.

30. Marker Co. has net cash provided by operating activities of $900,000. Its average current liabilities for the period are $1,000,000, and its average total liabilities are $1,500,000. Comment on the company's liquidity and financial flexibility, given this information.

31. Net income for the year for Hatfield, Inc. was $750,000, but the statement of cash flows reports that cash provided by operating activities was $860,000. Hatfield also reported capital expenditures of $75,000 and paid dividends in the amount of $20,000. Compute Hatfield's free cash flow.

32. What is the purpose of a free cash flow analysis?

 BRIEF EXERCISES

(LO 3) **BE5-1** La Bouche Corporation has the following accounts included in its December 31, 2007, trial balance: Accounts Receivable $110,000; Inventories $290,000; Allowance for Doubtful Accounts $8,000; Patents $72,000; Prepaid Insurance $9,500; Accounts Payable $77,000; Cash $27,000. Prepare the current assets section of the balance sheet listing the accounts in proper sequence.

(LO 3) **BE5-2** Jodi Corporation's adjusted trial balance contained the following asset accounts at December 31, 2007: Cash $7,000; Land $40,000; Patents $12,500; Accounts Receivable $90,000; Prepaid Insurance $5,200; Inventory $34,000; Allowance for Doubtful Accounts $4,000; Trading Securities $11,000. Prepare the current assets section of the balance sheet, listing the accounts in proper sequence.

(LO 3) **BE5-3** Included in Goo Goo Dolls Company's December 31, 2007, trial balance are the following accounts: Prepaid Rent $5,200; Held-to-Maturity Securities $61,000; Unearned Fees $17,000; Land Held for Investment $39,000; Long-term Receivables $42,000. Prepare the long-term investments section of the balance sheet.

(LO 3) **BE5-4** Adam Ant Company's December 31, 2007, trial balance includes the following accounts: Inventories $120,000; Buildings $207,000; Accumulated Depreciation–Equipment $19,000; Equipment $190,000; Land Held for Investment $46,000; Accumulated Depreciation–Buildings $45,000; Land $61,000; Timberland $70,000. Prepare the property, plant, and equipment section of the balance sheet.

(LO 3) **BE5-5** Mason Corporation has the following accounts included in its December 31, 2007, trial balance: Trading Securities $21,000; Goodwill $150,000; Prepaid Insurance $12,000; Patents $220,000; Franchises $110,000. Prepare the intangible assets section of the balance sheet.

(LO 3) **BE5-6** Mickey Snyder Corporation's adjusted trial balance contained the following asset accounts at December 31, 2007: Prepaid Rent $12,000; Goodwill $40,000; Franchise Fees Receivable $2,000; Franchises $47,000; Patents $33,000; Trademarks $10,000. Prepare the intangible assets section of the balance sheet.

(LO 3) **BE5-7** John Hawk Corporation's adjusted trial balance contained the following liability accounts at December 31, 2007. Bonds Payable (due in 3 years) $100,000; Accounts Payable $72,000; Notes Payable (due in 90 days) $12,500; Accrued Salaries $4,000; Income Taxes Payable $7,000. Prepare the current liabilities section of the balance sheet.

(LO 3) **BE5-8** Included in Ewing Company's December 31, 2007, trial balance are the following accounts: Accounts Payable $240,000; Pension Liability $375,000; Discount on Bonds Payable $24,000; Advances from Customers $41,000; Bonds Payable $400,000; Wages Payable $27,000; Interest Payable $12,000; Income Taxes Payable $29,000. Prepare the current liabilities section of the balance sheet.

(LO 3) **BE5-9** Use the information presented in BE5–8 for Ewing Company to prepare the long-term liabilities section of the balance sheet.

(LO 3) **BE5-10** Kevin Flynn Corporation's adjusted trial balance contained the following accounts at December 31, 2007: Retained Earnings $120,000; Common Stock $700,000; Bonds Payable $100,000; Additional Paid-in Capital $200,000; Goodwill $55,000; Accumulated Other Comprehensive Loss $150,000. Prepare the stockholders' equity section of the balance sheet.

(LO 3) **BE5-11** Young Company's December 31, 2007, trial balance includes the following accounts: Investment in Common Stock $70,000; Retained Earnings $114,000; Trademarks $31,000; Preferred Stock $172,000; Common Stock $55,000; Deferred Income Taxes $88,000; Additional Paid-in Capital $174,000. Prepare the stockholders' equity section of the balance sheet.

(LO 8) **BE5-12** Midwest Beverage Company reported the following items in the most recent year.

Net income	$40,000
Dividends paid	5,000
Increase in accounts receivable	10,000
Increase in accounts payable	5,000
Purchase of equipment (capital expenditure)	8,000
Depreciation expense	4,000
Issue of notes payable	20,000

Compute net cash provided by operating activities, the net change in cash during the year, and free cash flow.

(LO 8) **BE5-13** Kes Company reported 2007 net income of $151,000. During 2007, accounts receivable increased by $13,000 and accounts payable increased by $9,500. Depreciation expense was $39,000. Prepare the cash flows from operating activities section of the statement of cash flows.

(LO 8) **BE5-14** Yorkis Perez Corporation engaged in the following cash transactions during 2007.

Sale of land and building	$181,000
Purchase of treasury stock	40,000
Purchase of land	37,000
Payment of cash dividend	85,000
Purchase of equipment	53,000
Issuance of common stock	147,000
Retirement of bonds	100,000

Compute the net cash provided (used) by investing activities.

(LO 8) **BE5-15** Use the information presented in BE5-14 for Yorkis Perez Corporation to compute the net cash used (provided) by financing activities.

(LO 9) **BE5-16** Using the information in BE5-14, determine Yorkis Perez's free cash flow, assuming that it reported net cash provided by operating activities of $400,000.

EXERCISES

(LO 2, 3) **E5-1** **(Balance Sheet Classifications)** Presented below are a number of balance sheet accounts of Deep Blue Something, Inc.

(a)	Investment in Preferred Stock.	**(h)**	Accrued Interest on Notes Payable.
(b)	Treasury Stock.	**(i)**	Deficit.
(c)	Common Stock.	**(j)**	Trading Securities.
(d)	Cash Dividends Payable.	**(k)**	Income Taxes Payable.
(e)	Accumulated Depreciation.	**(l)**	Unearned Subscription Revenue.
(f)	Warehouse in Process of Construction.	**(m)**	Work in Process.
(g)	Petty Cash.	**(n)**	Accrued Vacation Pay.

Instructions

For each of the accounts above, indicate the proper balance sheet classification. In the case of borderline items, indicate the additional information that would be required to determine the proper classification.

(LO 2, 3) **E5-2** **(Classification of Balance Sheet Accounts)** Presented on the next page are the captions of Faulk Company's balance sheet.

(a)	Current assets.	**(f)**	Current liabilities.
(b)	Investments.	**(g)**	Non-current liabilities.
(c)	Property, plant, and equipment.	**(h)**	Capital stock.
(d)	Intangible assets.	**(i)**	Additional paid-in capital.
(e)	Other assets.	**(j)**	Retained earnings.

Instructions

Indicate by letter where each of the following items would be classified.

1.	Preferred stock.	**11.**	Cash surrender value of life insurance.
2.	Goodwill.	**12.**	Notes payable (due next year).
3.	Wages payable.	**13.**	Office supplies.
4.	Trade accounts payable.	**14.**	Common stock.
5.	Buildings.	**15.**	Land.
6.	Trading securities.	**16.**	Bond sinking fund.
7.	Current portion of long-term debt.	**17.**	Merchandise inventory.
8.	Premium on bonds payable.	**18.**	Prepaid insurance.
9.	Allowance for doubtful accounts.	**19.**	Bonds payable.
10.	Accounts receivable.	**20.**	Taxes payable.

(LO 2, 3) **E5-3** **(Classification of Balance Sheet Accounts)** Assume that Fielder Enterprises uses the following headings on its balance sheet.

(a)	Current assets.	**(f)**	Current liabilities.
(b)	Investments.	**(g)**	Long-term liabilities.
(c)	Property, plant, and equipment.	**(h)**	Capital stock.
(d)	Intangible assets.	**(i)**	Paid-in capital in excess of par.
(e)	Other assets.	**(j)**	Retained earnings.

Instructions

Indicate by letter how each of the following usually should be classified. If an item should appear in a note to the financial statements, use the letter "N" to indicate this fact. If an item need not be reported at all on the balance sheet, use the letter "X."

1.	Unexpired insurance.	**12.**	Twenty-year issue of bonds payable that will mature within the next year. (No sinking fund exists, and refunding is not planned.)
2.	Stock owned in affiliated companies.		
3.	Unearned subscriptions revenue.		
4.	Advances to suppliers.	**13.**	Machinery retired from use and held for sale.
5.	Unearned rent revenue.	**14.**	Fully depreciated machine still in use.
6.	Preferred stock.	**15.**	Accrued interest on bonds payable.
7.	Premium on preferred stock.	**16.**	Salaries that company budget shows will be paid to employees within the next year.
8.	Copyrights.		
9.	Petty cash fund.	**17.**	Discount on bonds payable. (Assume related to bonds payable in No. 12.)
10.	Sales tax payable.		
11.	Accrued interest on notes receivable.	**18.**	Accumulated depreciation.

(LO 2, 3) **E5-4** **(Preparation of a Classified Balance Sheet)** Assume that Denis Savard Inc. has the following accounts at the end of the current year.

1.	Common Stock.	**14.**	Accumulated Depreciation—Buildings.
2.	Discount on Bonds Payable.	**15.**	Cash Restricted for Plant Expansion.
3.	Treasury Stock (at cost).	**16.**	Land Held for Future Plant Site.
4.	Note Payable, short-term.	**17.**	Allowance for Doubtful Accounts— Accounts Receivable.
5.	Raw Materials.		
6.	Preferred Stock Investments—Long-term.	**18.**	Retained Earnings.
7.	Unearned Rent Revenue.	**19.**	Premium on Common Stock.
8.	Work in Process.	**20.**	Unearned Subscriptions Revenue.
9.	Copyrights.	**21.**	Receivables—Officers (due in one year).
10.	Buildings.	**22.**	Finished Goods.
11.	Notes Receivable (short-term).	**23.**	Accounts Receivable.
12.	Cash.	**24.**	Bonds Payable (due in 4 years).
13.	Accrued Salaries Payable.		

Instructions

Prepare a classified balance sheet in good form. (No monetary amounts are necessary.)

(LO 3)   **E5-5**   **(Preparation of a Corrected Balance Sheet)**   Uhura Company has decided to expand its operations. The bookkeeper recently completed the balance sheet presented below in order to obtain additional funds for expansion.

UHURA COMPANY
BALANCE SHEET
FOR THE YEAR ENDED 2007

Current assets	
Cash	$230,000
Accounts receivable (net)	340,000
Inventories at lower of average cost or market	401,000
Trading securities—at cost (fair value $120,000)	140,000
Property, plant, and equipment	
Building (net)	570,000
Office equipment (net)	160,000
Land held for future use	175,000
Intangible assets	
Goodwill	80,000
Cash surrender value of life insurance	90,000
Prepaid expenses	12,000
Current liabilities	
Accounts payable	135,000
Notes payable (due next year)	125,000
Pension obligation	82,000
Rent payable	49,000
Premium on bonds payable	53,000
Long-term liabilities	
Bonds payable	500,000
Stockholders' equity	
Common stock, $1.00 par, authorized	
400,000 shares, issued 290,000	290,000
Additional paid-in capital	160,000
Retained earnings	?

Instructions

Prepare a revised balance sheet given the available information. Assume that the accumulated depreciation balance for the buildings is $160,000 and for the office equipment, $105,000. The allowance for doubtful accounts has a balance of $17,000. The pension obligation is considered a long-term liability.

(LO 2, 3)   **E5-6**   **(Corrections of a Balance Sheet)**   The bookkeeper for Geronimo Company has prepared the following balance sheet as of July 31, 2007.

GERONIMO COMPANY
BALANCE SHEET
AS OF JULY 31, 2007

Cash	$ 69,000	Notes and accounts payable	$ 44,000
Accounts receivable (net)	40,500	Long-term liabilities	75,000
Inventories	60,000	Stockholders' equity	155,500
Equipment (net)	84,000		$274,500
Patents	21,000		
	$274,500		

The following additional information is provided.

1. Cash includes $1,200 in a petty cash fund and $15,000 in a bond sinking fund.
2. The net accounts receivable balance is comprised of the following three items: (a) accounts receivable—debit balances $52,000; (b) accounts receivable—credit balances $8,000; (c) allowance for doubtful accounts $3,500.
3. Merchandise inventory costing $5,300 was shipped out on consignment on July 31, 2007. The ending inventory balance does not include the consigned goods. Receivables in the amount of $5,300 were recognized on these consigned goods.

4. Equipment had a cost of $112,000 and an accumulated depreciation balance of $28,000.
5. Taxes payable of $6,000 were accrued on July 31. Geronimo Company, however, had set up a cash fund to meet this obligation. This cash fund was not included in the cash balance, but was offset against the taxes payable amount.

Instructions

Prepare a corrected classified balance sheet as of July 31, 2007, from the available information, adjusting the account balances using the additional information.

(LO 3) **E5-7** **(Current Assets Section of the Balance Sheet)** Presented below are selected accounts of Yasunari Kawabata Company at December 31, 2007.

Finished Goods	$ 52,000	Cost of Goods Sold	$2,100,000
Revenue Received in Advance	90,000	Notes Receivable	40,000
Equipment	253,000	Accounts Receivable	161,000
Work-in-Process	34,000	Raw Materials	207,000
Cash	37,000	Supplies Expense	60,000
Short-term Investments in Stock	31,000	Allowance for Doubtful Accounts	12,000
Customer Advances	36,000	Licenses	18,000
Cash Restricted for Plant Expansion	50,000	Additional Paid-in Capital	88,000
		Treasury Stock	22,000

The following additional information is available.

1. Inventories are valued at lower of cost or market using LIFO.
2. Equipment is recorded at cost. Accumulated depreciation, computed on a straight-line basis, is $50,600.
3. The short-term investments have a fair value of $29,000. (Assume they are trading securities.)
4. The notes receivable are due April 30, 2009, with interest receivable every April 30. The notes bear interest at 6%. (*Hint:* Accrue interest due on December 31, 2007.)
5. The allowance for doubtful accounts applies to the accounts receivable. Accounts receivable of $50,000 are pledged as collateral on a bank loan.
6. Licenses are recorded net of accumulated amortization of $14,000.
7. Treasury stock is recorded at cost.

Instructions

Prepare the current assets section of Yasunari Kawabata Company's December 31, 2007, balance sheet, with appropriate disclosures.

(LO 2) **E5-8** **(Current vs. Long-term Liabilities)** Frederic Chopin Corporation is preparing its December 31, 2007, balance sheet. The following items may be reported as either a current or long-term liability.

1. On December 15, 2007, Chopin declared a cash dividend of $2.50 per share to stockholders of record on December 31. The dividend is payable on January 15, 2008. Chopin has issued 1,000,000 shares of common stock, of which 50,000 shares are held in treasury.
2. At December 31, bonds payable of $100,000,000 are outstanding. The bonds pay 12% interest every September 30 and mature in installments of $25,000,000 every September 30, beginning September 30, 2008.
3. At December 31, 2006, customer advances were $12,000,000. During 2007, Chopin collected $30,000,000 of customer advances, and advances of $25,000,000 were earned.

Instructions

For each item above indicate the dollar amounts to be reported as a current liability and as a long-term liability, if any.

(LO 2, 3) **E5-9** **(Current Assets and Current Liabilities)** The current assets and current liabilities sections of the balance sheet of Allessandro Scarlatti Company appear as follows.

ALLESSANDRO SCARLATTI COMPANY
BALANCE SHEET (PARTIAL)
DECEMBER 31, 2007

Cash		$ 40,000	Accounts payable	$ 61,000
Accounts receivable	$89,000		Notes payable	67,000
Less: Allowance for				$128,000
doubtful accounts	7,000	82,000		
Inventories		171,000		
Prepaid expenses		9,000		
		$302,000		

The following errors in the corporation's accounting have been discovered:

1. January 2008 cash disbursements entered as of December 2007 included payments of accounts payable in the amount of $39,000, on which a cash discount of 2% was taken.
2. The inventory included $27,000 of merchandise that had been received at December 31 but for which no purchase invoices had been received or entered. Of this amount, $12,000 had been received on consignment; the remainder was purchased f.o.b. destination, terms 2/10, n/30.
3. Sales for the first four days in January 2008 in the amount of $30,000 were entered in the sales book as of December 31, 2007. Of these, $21,500 were sales on account and the remainder were cash sales.
4. Cash, not including cash sales, collected in January 2008 and entered as of December 31, 2007, totaled $35,324. Of this amount, $23,324 was received on account after cash discounts of 2% had been deducted; the remainder represented the proceeds of a bank loan.

Instructions

(a) Restate the current assets and current liabilities sections of the balance sheet in accordance with good accounting practice. (Assume that both accounts receivable and accounts payable are recorded gross.)

(b) State the net effect of your adjustments on Allesandro Scarlatti Company's retained earnings balance.

(LO 3, 4) **E5-10 (Current Liabilities)** Norma Smith is the controller of Baylor Corporation and is responsible for the preparation of the year-end financial statements. The following transactions occurred during the year.

(a) On December 20, 2007, an employee filed a legal action against Baylor for $100,000 for wrongful dismissal. Management believes the action to be frivolous and without merit. The likelihood of payment to the employee is remote.

(b) Bonuses to key employees based on net income for 2007 are estimated to be $150,000.

(c) On December 1, 2007, the company borrowed $600,000 at 8% per year. Interest is paid quarterly.

(d) Credit sales for the year amounted to $10,000,000. Baylor's expense provision for doubtful accounts is estimated to be 3% of credit sales.

(e) On December 15, 2007, the company declared a $2.00 per share dividend on the 40,000 shares of common stock outstanding, to be paid on January 5, 2008.

(f) During the year, customer advances of $160,000 were received; $50,000 of this amount was earned by December 31, 2007.

Instructions

For each item above, indicate the dollar amount to be reported as a current liability. If a liability is not reported, explain why.

(LO 3) **E5-11 (Balance Sheet Preparation)** Presented below is the adjusted trial balance of Kelly Corporation at December 31, 2007.

	Debits	Credits
Cash	$?	
Office Supplies	1,200	
Prepaid Insurance	1,000	
Equipment	48,000	
Accumulated Depreciation—Equipment		$ 4,000
Trademarks	950	
Accounts Payable		10,000
Wages Payable		500
Unearned Service Revenue		2,000
Bonds Payable, due 2014		9,000
Common Stock		10,000
Retained Earnings		25,000
Service Revenue		10,000
Wages Expense	9,000	
Insurance Expense	1,400	
Rent Expense	1,200	
Interest Expense	900	
Total	$?	$?

Additional information:

1. Net loss for the year was $2,500.
2. No dividends were declared during 2007.

Instructions

Prepare a classified balance sheet as of December 31, 2007.

(LO 3)   **E5-12   (Preparation of a Balance Sheet)**   Presented below is the trial balance of John Nalezny Corporation at December 31, 2007.

	Debits	Credits
Cash	$ 197,000	
Sales		$ 8,100,000
Trading Securities (at cost, $145,000)	153,000	
Cost of Goods Sold	4,800,000	
Long-term Investments in Bonds	299,000	
Long-term Investments in Stocks	277,000	
Short-term Notes Payable		90,000
Accounts Payable		455,000
Selling Expenses	2,000,000	
Investment Revenue		63,000
Land	260,000	
Buildings	1,040,000	
Dividends Payable		136,000
Accrued Liabilities		96,000
Accounts Receivable	435,000	
Accumulated Depreciation—Buildings		152,000
Allowance for Doubtful Accounts		25,000
Administrative Expenses	900,000	
Interest Expense	211,000	
Inventories	597,000	
Extraordinary Gain		80,000
Long-term Notes Payable		900,000
Equipment	600,000	
Bonds Payable		1,000,000
Accumulated Depreciation—Equipment		60,000
Franchise	160,000	
Common Stock ($5 par)		1,000,000
Treasury Stock	191,000	
Patent	195,000	
Retained Earnings		78,000
Additional Paid-in Capital		80,000
Totals	$12,315,000	$12,315,000

Instructions

Prepare a balance sheet at December 31, 2007, for John Nalezny Corporation. Ignore income taxes.

(LO 7)   **E5-13   (Statement of Cash Flows—Classifications)**   The major classifications of activities reported in the statement of cash flows are operating, investing, and financing. Classify each of the transactions listed below as:

1. Operating activity—add to net income.
2. Operating activity—deduct from net income.
3. Investing activity.
4. Financing activity.
5. Reported as significant noncash activity.

The transactions are as follows.

(a) Issuance of capital stock.   (h) Payment of cash dividends.
(b) Purchase of land and building.   (i) Exchange of furniture for office equipment.
(c) Redemption of bonds.   (j) Purchase of treasury stock.
(d) Sale of equipment.   (k) Loss on sale of equipment.
(e) Depreciation of machinery.   (l) Increase in accounts receivable during the year.
(f) Amortization of patent.   (m) Decrease in accounts payable during the year.
(g) Issuance of bonds for plant assets.

(LO 8)   **E5-14   (Preparation of a Statement of Cash Flows)**   The comparative balance sheets of Constantine Cavamanlis Inc. at the beginning and the end of the year 2007 appear on the next page.

CONSTANTINE CAVAMANLIS INC.
BALANCE SHEETS

Assets	Dec. 31, 2007	Jan. 1, 2007	Inc./Dec.
Cash	$ 45,000	$ 13,000	$32,000 Inc.
Accounts receivable	91,000	88,000	3,000 Inc.
Equipment	39,000	22,000	17,000 Inc.
Less: Accumulated depreciation	(17,000)	(11,000)	6,000 Inc.
Total	$158,000	$112,000	
Liabilities and Stockholders' Equity			
Accounts payable	$ 20,000	$ 15,000	5,000 Inc.
Common stock	100,000	80,000	20,000 Inc.
Retained earnings	38,000	17,000	21,000 Inc.
Total	$158,000	$112,000	

Net income of $44,000 was reported, and dividends of $23,000 were paid in 2007. New equipment was purchased and none was sold.

Instructions
Prepare a statement of cash flows for the year 2007.

(LO 8, 9) **E5-15 (Preparation of a Statement of Cash Flows)** Presented below is a condensed version of the comparative balance sheets for Zubin Mehta Corporation for the last two years at December 31.

	2007	2006
Cash	$177,000	$ 78,000
Accounts receivable	180,000	185,000
Investments	52,000	74,000
Equipment	298,000	240,000
Less: Accumulated depreciation	(106,000)	(89,000)
Current liabilities	134,000	151,000
Capital stock	160,000	160,000
Retained earnings	307,000	177,000

Additional information:
Investments were sold at a loss (not extraordinary) of $10,000; no equipment was sold; cash dividends paid were $30,000; and net income was $160,000.

Instructions
(a) Prepare a statement of cash flows for 2007 for Zubin Mehta Corporation.
(b) Determine Zubin Mehta Corporation's free cash flow.

(LO 8, 9) **E5-16 (Preparation of a Statement of Cash Flows)** A comparative balance sheet for Shabbona Corporation is presented below.

	December 31	
Assets	2007	2006
Cash	$ 73,000	$ 22,000
Accounts receivable	82,000	66,000
Inventories	180,000	189,000
Land	71,000	110,000
Equipment	260,000	200,000
Accumulated depreciation—equipment	(69,000)	(42,000)
Total	$597,000	$545,000
Liabilities and Stockholders' Equity		
Accounts payable	$ 34,000	$ 47,000
Bonds payable	150,000	200,000
Common stock ($1 par)	214,000	164,000
Retained earnings	199,000	134,000
Total	$597,000	$545,000

Additional information:

1. Net income for 2007 was $125,000.
2. Cash dividends of $60,000 were declared and paid.
3. Bonds payable amounting to $50,000 were retired through issuance of common stock.

Instructions

(a) Prepare a statement of cash flows for 2007 for Shabbona Corporation.
(b) Determine Shabbona Corporation's current cash debt coverage ratio, cash debt coverage ratio, and free cash flow. Comment on its liquidity and financial flexibility.

(LO 3, 8) **E5-17** **(Preparation of a Statement of Cash Flows and a Balance Sheet)** Grant Wood Corporation's balance sheet at the end of 2006 included the following items.

Current assets	$235,000	Current liabilities	$150,000
Land	30,000	Bonds payable	100,000
Building	120,000	Common stock	180,000
Equipment	90,000	Retained earnings	44,000
Accum. depr.—building	(30,000)	Total	$474,000
Accum. depr.—equipment	(11,000)		
Patents	40,000		
Total	$474,000		

The following information is available for 2007.

1. Net income was $55,000.
2. Equipment (cost $20,000 and accumulated depreciation $8,000) was sold for $10,000.
3. Depreciation expense was $4,000 on the building and $9,000 on equipment.
4. Patent amortization was $2,500.
5. Current assets other than cash increased by $29,000. Current liabilities increased by $13,000.
6. An addition to the building was completed at a cost of $27,000.
7. A long-term investment in stock was purchased for $16,000.
8. Bonds payable of $50,000 were issued.
9. Cash dividends of $30,000 were declared and paid.
10. Treasury stock was purchased at a cost of $11,000.

Instructions

(Show only totals for current assets and current liabilities.)
(a) Prepare a statement of cash flows for 2007.
(b) Prepare a balance sheet at December 31, 2007.

(LO 8, 9) **E5-18** **(Preparation of a Statement of Cash Flows, Analysis)** The comparative balance sheets of Madrasah Corporation at the beginning and end of the year 2007 appear below.

MADRASAH CORPORATION BALANCE SHEETS			
Assets	Dec. 31, 2007	Jan. 1, 2007	Inc./Dec.
Cash	$ 20,000	$ 13,000	$ 7,000 Inc.
Accounts receivable	106,000	88,000	18,000 Inc.
Equipment	39,000	22,000	17,000 Inc.
Less: Accumulated depreciation	(17,000)	(11,000)	6,000 Inc.
Total	$148,000	$112,000	
Liabilities and Stockholders' Equity			
Accounts payable	$ 20,000	$ 15,000	5,000 Inc.
Common stock	100,000	80,000	20,000 Inc.
Retained earnings	28,000	17,000	11,000 Inc.
Total	$148,000	$112,000	

Net income of $44,000 was reported, and dividends of $33,000 were paid in 2007. New equipment was purchased and none was sold.

Instructions

(a) Prepare a statement of cash flows for the year 2007.

(b) Compute the current ratio (current assets ÷ current liabilities) as of January 1, 2007, and December 31, 2007, and compute free cash flow for the year 2007.

(c) In light of the analysis in (b), comment on Madrasah's liquidity and financial flexibility.

See the book's website, www.wiley.com/college/kieso, for Additional Exercises.

PROBLEMS

(LO 3) **P5-1** **(Preparation of a Classified Balance Sheet, Periodic Inventory)** Presented below is a list of accounts in alphabetical order.

Accounts Receivable	Land
Accrued Wages	Land for Future Plant Site
Accumulated Depreciation—Buildings	Loss from Flood
Accumulated Depreciation—Equipment	Notes Payable (due next year)
Advances to Employees	Patent
Advertising Expense	Payroll Taxes Payable
Allowance for Doubtful Accounts	Pension Obligations
Bond Sinking Fund	Petty Cash
Bonds Payable	Preferred Stock
Building	Premium on Bonds Payable
Cash in Bank	Premium on Preferred Stock
Cash on Hand	Prepaid Rent
Cash Surrender Value of Life Insurance	Purchases
Commission Expense	Purchase Returns and Allowances
Common Stock	Retained Earnings
Copyright	Sales
Dividends Payable	Sales Discounts
Equipment	Sales Salaries
Gain on Sale of Equipment	Trading Securities
Interest Receivable	Transportation-in
Inventory—Beginning	Treasury Stock (at cost)
Inventory—Ending	Unearned Subscriptions Revenue

Instructions

Prepare a classified balance sheet in good form. (No monetary amounts are to be shown.)

(LO 3) **P5-2** **(Balance Sheet Preparation)** Presented below are a number of balance sheet items for Letterman, Inc., for the current year, 2007.

Goodwill	$ 125,000	Accumulated depreciation—	
Payroll taxes payable	177,591	equipment	$ 292,000
Bonds payable	300,000	Inventories	239,800
Discount on bonds payable	15,000	Rent payable—short-term	45,000
Cash	360,000	Taxes payable	98,362
Land	480,000	Long-term rental obligations	480,000
Notes receivable	545,700	Common stock, $1 par value	200,000
Notes payable to banks	265,000	Preferred stock, $10 par value	150,000
Accounts payable	590,000	Prepaid expenses	87,920
Retained earnings	?	Equipment	1,470,000
Income taxes receivable	97,630	Trading securities	121,000
Unsecured notes payable		Accumulated depreciation—	
(long-term)	1,600,000	building	170,200
		Building	1,640,000

Instructions

Prepare a classified balance sheet in good form. Common stock authorized was 400,000 shares, and preferred stock authorized was 20,000 shares. Assume that notes receivable and notes payable are short-term, unless stated otherwise. Cost and fair value of trading securities are the same.

(LO 3) **P5–3** **(Balance Sheet Adjustment and Preparation)** The adjusted trial balance of Side Kicks Company and other related information for the year 2007 are presented on the next page.

SIDE KICKS COMPANY
ADJUSTED TRIAL BALANCE
DECEMBER 31, 2007

	Debits	Credits
Cash	$ 41,000	
Accounts Receivable	163,500	
Allowance for Doubtful Accounts		$ 8,700
Prepaid Insurance	5,900	
Inventory	308,500	
Long-term Investments	339,000	
Land	85,000	
Construction Work in Progress	124,000	
Patents	36,000	
Equipment	400,000	
Accumulated Depreciation of Equipment		140,000
Unamortized Discount on Bonds Payable	20,000	
Accounts Payable		148,000
Accrued Expenses		49,200
Notes Payable		94,000
Bonds Payable		400,000
Common Stock		500,000
Premium on Common Stock		45,000
Retained Earnings		138,000
	$1,522,900	$1,522,900

Additional information:

1. The LIFO method of inventory value is used.
2. The cost and fair value of the long-term investments that consist of stocks and bonds is the same.
3. The amount of the Construction Work in Progress account represents the costs expended to date on a building in the process of construction. (The company rents factory space at the present time.) The land on which the building is being constructed cost $85,000, as shown in the trial balance.
4. The patents were purchased by the company at a cost of $40,000 and are being amortized on a straight-line basis.
5. Of the unamortized discount on bonds payable, $2,000 will be amortized in 2008.
6. The notes payable represent bank loans that are secured by long-term investments carried at $120,000. These bank loans are due in 2008.
7. The bonds payable bear interest at 8% payable every December 31, and are due January 1, 2018.
8. 600,000 shares of common stock of a par value of $1 were authorized, of which 500,000 shares were issued and outstanding.

Instructions

Prepare a balance sheet as of December 31, 2007, so that all important information is fully disclosed.

(LO 3, 4) **P5-4** **(Preparation of a Corrected Balance Sheet)** Presented below and on the next page is the balance sheet of Russell Crowe Corporation as of December 31, 2007.

RUSSELL CROWE CORPORATION
BALANCE SHEET
DECEMBER 31, 2007

Assets	
Goodwill (Note 2)	$ 120,000
Buildings (Note 1)	1,640,000
Inventories	312,100
Land	750,000
Accounts receivable	170,000
Treasury stock (50,000 shares)	87,000
Cash on hand	175,900
Assets allocated to trustee for plant expansion	
Cash in bank	70,000
U.S. Treasury notes, at cost and fair value	138,000
	$3,463,000

Equities

Notes payable (Note 3)	$ 600,000
Common stock, authorized and issued, 1,000,000 shares, no par	1,150,000
Retained earnings	658,000
Appreciation capital (Note 1)	570,000
Federal income taxes payable	75,000
Reserve for depreciation recorded to date on the building	410,000
	$3,463,000

Note 1: Buildings are stated at cost, except for one building that was recorded at appraised value. The excess of appraisal value over cost was $570,000. Depreciation has been recorded based on cost.

Note 2: Goodwill in the amount of $120,000 was recognized because the company believed that book value was not an accurate representation of the fair market value of the company. The gain of $120,000 was credited to Retained Earnings.

Note 3: Notes payable are long-term except for the current installment due of $100,000.

Instructions

Prepare a corrected classified balance sheet in good form. The notes above are for information only.

(LO 3) **P5-5 (Balance Sheet Adjustment and Preparation)** Presented below is the balance sheet of Stephen King Corporation for the current year, 2007.

STEPHEN KING CORPORATION
BALANCE SHEET
DECEMBER 31, 2007

Current assets	$ 449,000	Current liabilities	$ 344,000
Investments	640,000	Long-term liabilities	1,000,000
Property, plant, and equipment	1,720,000	Stockholders' equity	1,770,000
Intangible assets	305,000		$3,114,000
	$3,114,000		

The following information is presented.

1. The current assets section includes: cash $114,000, accounts receivable $170,000 less $10,000 for allowance for doubtful accounts, inventories $180,000, and unearned revenue $5,000. Inventories are stated on the lower of FIFO cost or market.
2. The investments section includes: the cash surrender value of a life insurance contract $40,000; investments in common stock, short-term (trading) $80,000 and long-term (available-for-sale) $270,000, and bond sinking fund $250,000. The cost and fair value of investments in common stock are the same.
3. Property, plant, and equipment includes: buildings $1,040,000 less accumulated depreciation $360,000; equipment $450,000 less accumulated depreciation $180,000; land $500,000; and land held for future use $270,000.
4. Intangible assets include: a franchise $165,000; goodwill $100,000; and discount on bonds payable $40,000.
5. Current liabilities include: accounts payable $104,000; notes payable—short-term $80,000 and long-term $120,000; and taxes payable $40,000.
6. Long-term liabilities are composed solely of 7% bonds payable due 2015.
7. Stockholders' equity has: preferred stock, no par value, authorized 200,000 shares, issued 70,000 shares for $450,000; and common stock, $1.00 par value, authorized 400,000 shares, issued 100,000 shares at an average price of $10. In addition, the corporation has retained earnings of $320,000.

Instructions

Prepare a balance sheet in good form, adjusting the amounts in each balance sheet classification as affected by the information given above.

(LO 3, 8, 9) **P5-6 (Preparation of a Statement of Cash Flows and a Balance Sheet)** Alistair Cooke Inc. had the balance sheet shown on the following page at December 31, 2006.

ALISTAIR COOKE INC.
BALANCE SHEET
DECEMBER 31, 2006

Cash	$ 20,000	Accounts payable	$ 30,000
Accounts receivable	21,200	Long-term notes payable	41,000
Investments	32,000	Common stock	100,000
Plant assets (net)	81,000	Retained earnings	23,200
Land	40,000		$194,200
	$194,200		

During 2007 the following occurred.

1. Alistair Cooke Inc. sold part of its investment portfolio for $17,000. This transaction resulted in a gain of $3,400 for the firm. The company classifies its investments as available-for-sale.
2. A tract of land was purchased for $18,000 cash.
3. Long-term notes payable in the amount of $16,000 were retired before maturity by paying $16,000 cash.
4. An additional $24,000 in common stock was issued at par.
5. Dividends totaling $8,200 were declared and paid to stockholders.
6. Net income for 2007 was $32,000 after allowing for depreciation of $12,000.
7. Land was purchased through the issuance of $30,000 in bonds.
8. At December 31, 2007, Cash was $39,000, Accounts Receivable was $41,600, and Accounts Payable remained at $30,000.

Instructions
(a) Prepare a statement of cash flows for 2007.
(b) Prepare an unclassified balance sheet as it would appear at December 31, 2007.
(c) How might the statement of cash flows help the user of the financial statements? Compute two cash flow ratios.

(LO 1, 3, 8, 9) **P5-7 (Preparation of a Statement of Cash Flows and Balance Sheet)** Jay Leno Inc. had the following balance sheet at December 31, 2006.

JAY LENO INC.
BALANCE SHEET
DECEMBER 31, 2006

Cash	$ 20,000	Accounts payable	$ 30,000
Accounts receivable	21,200	Bonds payable	41,000
Investments	32,000	Common stock	100,000
Plant assets (net)	81,000	Retained earnings	23,200
Land	40,000		$194,200
	$194,200		

During 2007 the following occurred.

1. Leno liquidated its available-for-sale investment portfolio at a loss of $3,000.
2. A tract of land was purchased for $38,000.
3. An additional $26,000 in common stock was issued at par.
4. Dividends totaling $10,000 were declared and paid to stockholders.
5. Net income for 2007 was $35,000, including $12,000 in depreciation expense.
6. Land was purchased through the issuance of $30,000 in additional bonds.
7. At December 31, 2007, Cash was $66,200, Accounts Receivable was $42,000, and Accounts Payable was $40,000.

Instructions
(a) Prepare a statement of cash flows for the year 2007 for Leno.
(b) Prepare the balance sheet as it would appear at December 31, 2007.
(c) Compute Leno's free cash flow and the current cash debt coverage ratio for 2007.
(d) Use the analysis of Leno to illustrate how information in the balance sheet and statement of cash flows helps the user of the financial statements.

CONCEPTS FOR ANALYSIS

CA5-1 (Reporting the Financial Effects of Varied Transactions) In an examination of Juan Acevedo Corporation as of December 31, 2007, you have learned that the following situations exist. No entries have been made in the accounting records for these items.

1. The corporation erected its present factory building in 1992. Depreciation was calculated by the straight-line method, using an estimated life of 35 years. Early in 2007, the board of directors conducted a careful survey and estimated that the factory building had a remaining useful life of 25 years as of January 1, 2007.
2. An additional assessment of 2006 income taxes was levied and paid in 2007.
3. When calculating the accrual for officers' salaries at December 31, 2007, it was discovered that the accrual for officers' salaries for December 31, 2006, had been overstated.
4. On December 15, 2007, Acevedo Corporation declared a cash dividend on its common stock outstanding, payable February 1, 2008, to the common stockholders of record December 31, 2007.

Instructions

Describe fully how each of the items above should be reported in the financial statements of Acevedo Corporation for the year 2007.

CA5-2 (Current Asset and Liability Classification) Below are the titles of a number of debit and credit accounts as they might appear on the balance sheet of Ethan Allen Corporation as of October 31, 2007.

Debits	Credits
Interest Accrued on U.S. Government Securities	Capital Stock—Preferred — *Equity*
Notes Receivable	11% First Mortgage Bonds, due in 2014 - *long term L*
Petty Cash Fund	Preferred Cash Dividend, payable Nov. 1, 2007 —
U.S. Government Securities	Allowance for Doubtful Accounts Receivable
Treasury Stock — *Equity*	Federal Income Taxes Payable
Unamortized Bond Discount *long term L*	Customers' Advances (on contracts to be completed next year)
Cash in Bank	Premium on Bonds Redeemable in 2007
Land — *PPE*	Officers' 2007 Bonus Accrued
Inventory of Operating Parts and Supplies	Accrued Payroll
Inventory of Raw Materials	Notes Payable
Patents *Intangible*	Accrued Interest on Bonds
Cash and U.S. Government Bonds Set Aside for Property Additions *long term*	Accumulated Depreciation — *PPE contra asset*
Investment in Subsidiary *long term Invest*	Accounts Payable
Accounts Receivable:	Capital in Excess of Par — *Equity*
U.S. Government Contracts	Accrued Interest on Notes Payable
Regular	8% First Mortgage Bonds, to be redeemed in 2007 out of current assets
Installments—Due Next Year	
Installments—Due After Next year *other assets*	
Goodwill — *Intangible*	
Inventory of Finished Goods —	
Inventory of Work in Process —	
Deficit — *Equity contra account*	

Instructions

Select the current asset and current liability items from among these debits and credits. If there appear to be certain borderline cases that you are unable to classify without further information, mention them and explain your difficulty, or give your reasons for making questionable classifications, if any.

(AICPA adapted)

CA5-3 (Identifying Balance Sheet Deficiencies) The assets of Annika Sorenstam Corporation are presented on the next page (000s omitted).

ANNIKA SORENSTAM CORPORATION
BALANCE SHEET (PARTIAL)
DECEMBER 31, 2007

Assets

Current assets		
Cash		$ 100,000
Unclaimed payroll checks		27,500
Trading securities (fair value $30,000) at cost		37,000
Accounts receivable (less bad debt reserve)		75,000
Inventories—at lower of cost (determined by the next-in,		
first-out method) or market		240,000
Total current assets		479,500
Tangible assets		
Land (less accumulated depreciation)		80,000
Buildings and equipment	$800,000	
Less: Accumulated depreciation	250,000	550,000
Net tangible assets		630,000
Long-term investments		
Stocks and bonds		100,000
Treasury stock		70,000
Total long-term investments		170,000
Other assets		
Discount on bonds payable		19,400
Sinking fund		975,000
Total other assets		994,400
Total assets		$2,273,900

Instructions
Indicate the deficiencies, if any, in the foregoing presentation of Annika Sorenstam Corporation's assets.

CA5-4 (Critique of Balance Sheet Format and Content) Presented below and on the next page is the balance sheet of Bellemy Brothers Corporation (000s omitted).

BELLEMY BROTHERS CORPORATION
BALANCE SHEET
DECEMBER 31, 2007

Assets

Current assets		
Cash	$26,000	
Marketable securities	18,000	
Accounts receivable	25,000	
Merchandise inventory	20,000	
Supplies inventory	4,000	
Stock investment in Subsidiary Company	20,000	$113,000
Investments		
Treasury stock		25,000
Property, plant, and equipment		
Buildings and land	91,000	
Less: Reserve for depreciation	31,000	60,000
Other assets		
Cash surrender value of life insurance		19,000
Total assets		$217,000

Liabilities and Stockholders' Equity

Current liabilities		
Accounts payable	$22,000	
Reserve for income taxes	15,000	
Customers' accounts with credit balances	1	$ 37,001
Deferred credits		
Unamortized premium on bonds payable		2,000
Long-term liabilities		
Bonds payable		60,000
Total liabilities		99,001

Common stock		
Common stock, par $5	85,000	
Earned surplus	24,999	
Cash dividends declared	8,000	117,999
Total liabilities and stockholders' equity		$217,000

Instructions

Evaluate the balance sheet presented. State briefly the proper treatment of any item criticized.

CA5-5 (Presentation of Property, Plant, and Equipment) Andrea Pafko, corporate comptroller for Nicholson Industries, is trying to decide how to present "Property, plant, and equipment" in the balance sheet. She realizes that the statement of cash flows will show that the company made a significant investment in purchasing new equipment this year, but overall she knows the company's plant assets are rather old. She feels that she can disclose one figure titled "Property, plant, and equipment, net of depreciation," and the result will be a low figure. However, it will not disclose the age of the assets. If she chooses to show the cost less accumulated depreciation, the age of the assets will be apparent. She proposes the following.

Property, plant, and equipment, net of depreciation	$10,000,000
rather than	
Property, plant, and equipment	$50,000,000
Less: Accumulated depreciation	(40,000,000)
Net book value	$10,000,000

Instructions

Answer the following questions.

(a) What are the ethical issues involved?

(b) What should Pafko do?

CA5-6 (Cash Flow Analysis) The partner in charge of the James Spencer Corporation audit comes by your desk and leaves a letter he has started to the CEO and a copy of the cash flow statement for the year ended December 31, 2007. Because he must leave on an emergency, he asks you to finish the letter by explaining: (1) the disparity between net income and cash flow; (2) the importance of operating cash flow; (3) the renewable source(s) of cash flow; and (4) possible suggestions to improve the cash position.

JAMES SPENCER CORPORATION
STATEMENT OF CASH FLOWS
FOR THE YEAR ENDED DECEMBER 31, 2007

Cash flows from operating activities		
Net income		$100,000
Adjustments to reconcile net income to net cash provided by operating activities:		
Depreciation expense	$ 10,000	
Amortization expense	1,000	
Loss on sale of fixed assets	5,000	
Increase in accounts receivable (net)	(40,000)	
Increase in inventory	(35,000)	
Decrease in accounts payable	(41,000)	(100,000)
Net cash provided by operating activities		–0–
Cash flows from investing activities		
Sale of plant assets	25,000	
Purchase of equipment	(100,000)	
Purchase of land	(200,000)	
Net cash used by investing activities		(275,000)
Cash flows from financing activities		
Payment of dividends	(10,000)	
Redemption of bonds	(100,000)	
Net cash used by financing activities		(110,000)
Net decrease in cash		(385,000)
Cash balance, January 1, 2007		400,000
Cash balance, December 31, 2007		$ 15,000

Date

James Spencer, III, CEO
James Spencer Corporation
125 Wall Street
Middleton, Kansas 67458

Dear Mr. Spencer:

I have good news and bad news about the financial statements for the year ended December 31, 2007. The good news is that net income of $100,000 is close to what we predicted in the strategic plan last year, indicating strong performance this year. The bad news is that the cash balance is seriously low. Enclosed is the Statement of Cash Flows, which best illustrates how both of these situations occurred simultaneously . . .

Instructions
Complete the letter to the CEO, including the four components requested by your boss.

USING YOUR JUDGMENT

Financial Reporting Problem

The Procter & Gamble Company (P&G)
The financial statements of P&G are presented in Appendix 5B or can be accessed on the KWW website.

Instructions
Refer to P&G's financial statements and the accompanying notes to answer the following questions.

(a) What alternative formats could P&G have adopted for its balance sheet? Which format did it adopt?

(b) Identify the various techniques of disclosure P&G might have used to disclose additional pertinent financial information. Which technique does it use in its financials?

(c) In what classifications are P&G's investments reported? What valuation basis does P&G use to report its investments? How much working capital did P&G have on June 30, 2004? On June 30, 2003?

(d) What were P&G's cash flows from its operating, investing, and financing activities for 2004? What were its trends in net cash provided by operating activities over the period 2002 to 2004? Explain why the change in accounts payable and in accrued and other liabilities is added to net income to arrive at net cash provided by operating activities.

(e) Compute P&G's (1) current cash debt coverage ratio, (2) cash debt coverage ratio, and (3) free cash flow for 2004. What do these ratios indicate about P&G's financial condition?

Financial Statement Analysis Cases

Case 1   Uniroyal Technology Corporation
Uniroyal Technology Corporation (UTC), with corporate offices in Sarasota, Florida, is organized into three operating segments. The high-performance plastics segment is responsible for research, development, and manufacture of a wide variety of products, including orthopedic braces, graffiti-resistant seats for buses and airplanes, and a static-resistant plastic used in the central processing units of microcomputers. The coated fabrics segment manufactures products such as automobile seating, door and instrument panels, and specialty items such as waterproof seats for personal watercraft and stain-resistant, easy-cleaning upholstery fabrics. The foams and adhesives segment develops and manufactures products used in commercial roofing applications.

The following items relate to operations in a recent year.

1   Serious pressure was placed on profitability by sharply increasing raw material prices. Some raw materials increased in price 50% during the past year. Cost containment programs were instituted and product prices were increased whenever possible, which resulted in profit margins actually improving over the course of the year.

2   The company entered into a revolving credit agreement, under which UTC may borrow the lesser of $15,000,000 or 80% of eligible accounts receivable. At the end of the year, approximately $4,000,000

was outstanding under this agreement. The company plans to use this line of credit in the upcoming year to finance operations and expansion.

Instructions

(a) Should investors be informed of raw materials price increases, such as described in item 1? Does the fact that the company successfully met the challenge of higher prices affect the answer? Explain.

(b) How should the information in item 2 be presented in the financial statements of UTC?

Case 2   Sherwin-Williams Company

Sherwin-Williams, based in Cleveland, Ohio, manufactures a wide variety of paint and other coatings, which are marketed through its specialty stores and in other retail outlets. The company also manufactures paint for automobiles. The Automotive Division has had financial difficulty. During a recent year, five branch locations of the Automotive Division were closed, and new management was put in place for the branches remaining. The following titles were shown on Sherwin-Williams's balance sheet for that year.

Accounts payable	Machinery and equipment
Accounts receivable, less allowance	Other accruals
Accrued taxes	Other capital
Buildings	Other current assets
Cash and cash equivalents	Other long-term liabilities
Common stock	Postretirement obligations other than pensions
Employee compensation payable	Retained earnings
Finished goods inventories	Short-term investments
Intangibles and other assets	Taxes payable
Land	Work in process and raw materials inventories
Long-term debt	

Instructions

(a) Organize the accounts in the general order in which they would have been presented in a classified balance sheet.

(b) When several of the branch locations of the Automotive Division were closed, what balance sheet accounts were most likely affected? Did the balance in those accounts decrease or increase?

Case 3   Deere and Company

Below is the SEC-mandated disclosure of contractual obligations provided by Deere & Company in its 2004 annual report. Deere & Company reported current assets of $17,855 and total current liabilities of $7,888 at October 31, 2004. All dollars are in millions.

Aggregate Contractual Obligations

Most of the company's contractual obligations to make payments to third parties are debt obligations. In addition, the company has off-balance sheet obligations for the purchases of raw materials and services along with agreements for future lease payments. The payment schedule for these contractual obligations in millions of dollars is as follows:

	Total	Less than 1 year	1–3 years	3–5 years	More than 5 years
Total debt					
Equipment Operations	$ 2,958	$ 312	$ 281	$ 8	$2,357
Financial Services	11,265	3,146	4,393	1,541	2,185
Total	14,223	3,458	4,674	1,549	4,542
Purchase obligations	2,306	2,274	32		
Operating leases	367	75	130	59	103
Capital leases	12	2	3	2	5
Contractual obligations	$16,908	$5,809	$4,839	$1,610	$4,650

Instructions

(a) Compute Deere & Company's working capital and current ratio (current assets ÷ current liabilities) with and without the contractual obligations reported in the schedule.

(b) Briefly discuss how the information provided in the contractual obligation disclosure would be useful in evaluating Deere & Company for loans: (1) due in one year, (2) due in five years.

Case 4   Amazon.com

The incredible growth of Amazon.com has put fear into the hearts of traditional retailers. Amazon's stock price has soared to amazing levels. However, it is often pointed out in the financial press that the company did not report its first profit until 2003. The following financial information is taken from Amazon's 2003 financial statements.

($ in millions)	2003	2002
Current assets	$1,821	$1,616
Total assets	2,162	1,990
Current liabilities	1,253	1,066
Total liabilities	3,198	3,343
Cash provided by operations	392	174
Capital expenditures	46	39
Dividends paid	0	0
Net income(loss)	35	(149)
Sales	5,264	3,933

Instructions

(a) Calculate free cash flow for Amazon for 2003 and 2002 and discuss its ability to finance expansion from internally generated cash. Thus far Amazon has avoided purchasing large warehouses. Instead, it has used those of others. It is possible, however, that in order to increase customer satisfaction the company may have to build its own warehouses. If this happens, how might your impression of its ability to finance expansion change?

(b) Discuss any potential implications of the change in Amazon's cash provided by operations from 2002 to 2003.

(c) Based on your findings in parts (a) and (b), can you conclude whether or not Amazon's amazing stock price is justified?

Comparative Analysis Case

The Coca-Cola Company and PepsiCo, Inc.

Instructions

Go to the KWW website and use information found there to answer the following questions related to **The Coca-Cola Company** and **PepsiCo, Inc.**

(a) What format(s) did these companies use to present their balance sheets?

(b) How much working capital did each of these companies have at the end of 2004? Speculate as to their rationale for the amount of working capital they maintain.

(c) What is the most significant difference in the asset structure of the two companies? What causes this difference?

(d) What are the companies' annual and 4-year (2000–2004) growth rates in total assets and long-term debt?

(e) What were these two companies' trends in net cash provided by operating activities over the period 2002 to 2004?

(f) Compute both companies' (1) current cash debt coverage ratio, (2) cash debt coverage ratio, and (3) free cash flow. What do these ratios indicate about the financial condition of the two companies?

(g) What ratios do each of these companies use in the Management's Discussion and Analysis section of the annual report to explain their financial condition related to debt financing?

Research Case

Publicly-owned companies registered with the Securities and Exchange Commission electronically file required reports via the EDGAR (Electronic Data Gathering, Analysis, and Retrieval) system.

EDGAR can easily be accessed via the Internet (**www.sec.gov**) using the following steps.

1 Select "Filings and Forms (EDGAR)" from the home page.

2 Select "Search for company filings."

3 Select "CIK Lookup" and enter the name(s) of the company(ies) you are investigating. Write down the CIK number(s) and return to the previous page.

4 To examine filings, click on "Historical EDGAR Archives" and enter the appropriate CIK number (including all zeroes). When the list of filings appears, click on the desired filing under the "Company name" column.

Instructions

(a) Determine the CIK numbers for the following companies: **Ford Motor Co.** and **Wisconsin Electric.**

(b) Examine the balance sheet formats included in the following filings.
  (1) Ford Motor Co. Form 10-K (html version) filed March 10, 2005.
  (2) Wisconsin Electric annual report to shareholders (10-K, html version) filed March 11, 2005.

Do you notice anything "unusual" about the balance sheet formats? Why do you think the balance sheets are presented in this manner?

International Reporting Case

Presented below is the balance sheet for **Tomkins PLC**, a British company.

Instructions

(a) Identify at least three differences in balance sheet reporting between British and U.S. firms, as shown in Tomkins's balance sheet.

(b) Review Tomkins's balance sheet and identify how the format of this financial statement provides useful information, as illustrated in the chapter.

✦OMKINS

TOMKINS PLC Consolidated Balance Sheet at January 3, 2004		
CAPITAL EMPLOYED		
Fixed assets		
Intangible assets		216.7
Tangible assets		793.7
Investments		7.4
		1,017.8
Current assets		
Stock		373.9
Debtors		624.2
Cash		175.6
		1,173.7
Current liabilities		
Creditors: amounts falling due within one year		(502.3)
Net current assets		671.4
Total assets less current liabilities		1,689.2
Creditors: amounts falling due after more than one year		(488.4)
Provisions for liabilities and charges		(423.5)
Net assets		777.3
CAPITAL AND RESERVES		
Called up share capital		
Ordinary shares		38.7
Convertible cumulative preference shares		337.2
Redeemable convertible cumulative preference shares		—
		375.9
Share premium account		92.8
Capital redemption reserve		461.9
Own shares		(6.4)
Profit and loss account		(180.2)
Shareholders' funds		
Equity shareholders' funds	406.8	
Non-equity shareholders' funds	337.2	744.0
Equity minority interest		33.3
		777.3

Professional Research: Financial Accounting and Reporting

In light of the full disclosure principle, investors and creditors need to know the balances for assets, liabilities, and equity as well as the accounting policies adopted by management to measure the items reported in the balance sheet.

Instructions

Using the **Financial Accounting Research System (FARS)**, respond to the following items. (Provide text strings used in your search.)

(a) Identify the statement that addresses the disclosure of accounting policies.

(b) How are "Accounting Policies" defined in the standard?

(c) What are the three scenarios that would result in detailed disclosure of the accounting methods used?

(d) What are some examples of common disclosures that are required under this statement?

Professional Simulation

In this simulation you are asked to address questions related to the balance sheet. Prepare responses to all parts.

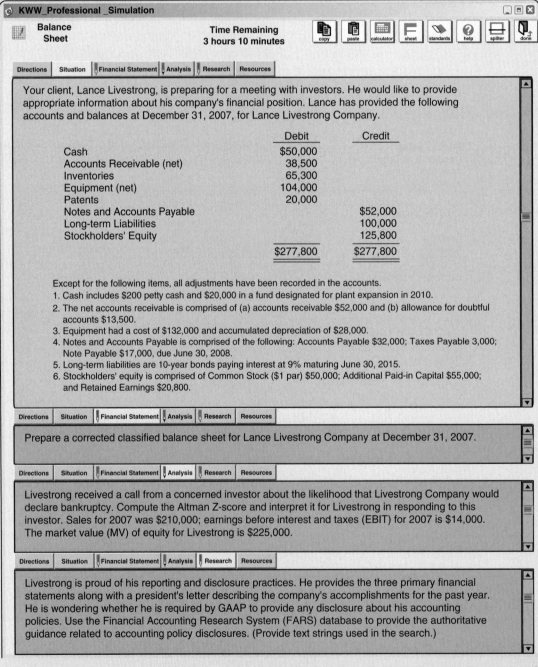

KWW_Professional _Simulation

Balance Sheet

Time Remaining 3 hours 10 minutes

copy | paste | calculator | sheet | standards | help | splitter | done

Directions | Situation | Financial Statement | Analysis | Research | Resources

Your client, Lance Livestrong, is preparing for a meeting with investors. He would like to provide appropriate information about his company's financial position. Lance has provided the following accounts and balances at December 31, 2007, for Lance Livestrong Company.

	Debit	Credit
Cash	$50,000	
Accounts Receivable (net)	38,500	
Inventories	65,300	
Equipment (net)	104,000	
Patents	20,000	
Notes and Accounts Payable		$52,000
Long-term Liabilities		100,000
Stockholders' Equity		125,800
	$277,800	$277,800

Except for the following items, all adjustments have been recorded in the accounts.
1. Cash includes $200 petty cash and $20,000 in a fund designated for plant expansion in 2010.
2. The net accounts receivable is comprised of (a) accounts receivable $52,000 and (b) allowance for doubtful accounts $13,500.
3. Equipment had a cost of $132,000 and accumulated depreciation of $28,000.
4. Notes and Accounts Payable is comprised of the following: Accounts Payable $32,000; Taxes Payable 3,000; Note Payable $17,000, due June 30, 2008.
5. Long-term liabilities are 10-year bonds paying interest at 9% maturing June 30, 2015.
6. Stockholders' equity is comprised of Common Stock ($1 par) $50,000; Additional Paid-in Capital $55,000; and Retained Earnings $20,800.

Directions | Situation | Financial Statement | Analysis | Research | Resources

Prepare a corrected classified balance sheet for Lance Livestrong Company at December 31, 2007.

Directions | Situation | Financial Statement | Analysis | Research | Resources

Livestrong received a call from a concerned investor about the likelihood that Livestrong Company would declare bankruptcy. Compute the Altman Z-score and interpret it for Livestrong in responding to this investor. Sales for 2007 was $210,000; earnings before interest and taxes (EBIT) for 2007 is $14,000. The market value (MV) of equity for Livestrong is $225,000.

Directions | Situation | Financial Statement | Analysis | Research | Resources

Livestrong is proud of his reporting and disclosure practices. He provides the three primary financial statements along with a president's letter describing the company's accomplishments for the past year. He is wondering whether he is required by GAAP to provide any disclosure about his accounting policies. Use the Financial Accounting Research System (FARS) database to provide the authoritative guidance related to accounting policy disclosures. (Provide text strings used in the search.)

Remember to check the book's companion website to find additional resources for this chapter.

ACCOUNTING AND THE TIME VALUE OF MONEY

The Magic of Interest

Sidney Homer, author of *A History of Interest Rates*, wrote, "$1,000 invested at a mere 8 percent for 400 years would grow to $23 quadrillion—$5 million for every human on earth. But the first 100 years are the hardest." This startling quote highlights the power of time and compounding interest on money. Equally significant, although Homer did not mention it, is the fact that a small difference in the interest rate makes a big difference in the amount of monies accumulated over time.

Taking an example more realistic than Homer's 400-year investment, assume that you had $20,000 in a tax-free retirement account. Half the money is in stocks returning 12 percent, and the other half is in bonds earning 8 percent. Assuming reinvested profits and quarterly compounding, your bonds would be worth $22,080 after 10 years, a doubling of their value. But your stocks, returning 4 percent more, would be worth $32,620, or triple your initial value. The following chart shows this impact.

Because of interest paid on investments, money received a week from today is not the same as money received today. Business people are acutely aware of this timing factor, and they invest and borrow only after carefully analyzing the relative amounts of cash flows over time.

Learning Objectives

After studying this chapter, you should be able to:

1 Identify accounting topics where the time value of money is relevant.
2 Distinguish between simple and compound interest.
3 Use appropriate compound interest tables.
4 Identify variables fundamental to solving interest problems.
5 Solve future and present value of 1 problems.
6 Solve future value of ordinary and annuity due problems.
7 Solve present value of ordinary and annuity due problems.
8 Solve present value problems related to deferred annuities and bonds.
9 Apply expected cash flows to present value measurement.

As we indicated in the opening story, the timing of the returns on an investment has an important effect on the worth of the investment (asset). Similarly, the timing of debt repayment has an important effect on the value of the debt commitment (liability). As a financial expert, you will be expected to make present and future value measurements and to understand their implications. The purpose of this chapter is to present the tools and techniques that will help you measure the present value of future cash inflows and outflows. The content and organization of the chapter are as follows.

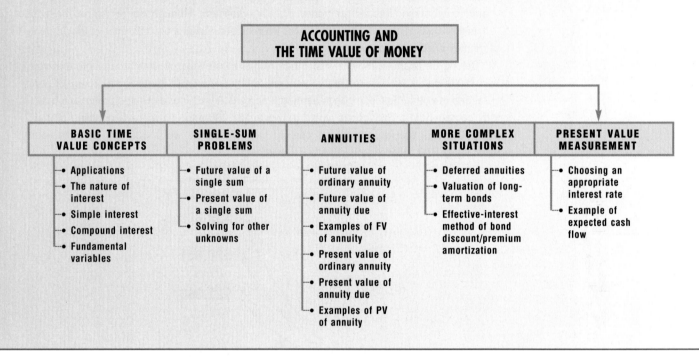

BASIC TIME VALUE CONCEPTS

OBJECTIVE 1
Identify accounting topics where the time value of money is relevant.

In accounting (and finance), the phrase **time value of money** indicates a relationship between time and money—that a dollar received today is worth more than a dollar promised at some time in the future. Why? Because of the opportunity to invest today's dollar and receive interest on the investment. Yet, when deciding among investment or borrowing alternatives, it is essential to be able to compare today's dollar and tomorrow's dollar on the same footing—to "compare apples to apples." Investors do that by using the concept of **present value**, which has many applications in accounting.

Applications of Time Value Concepts

Financial reporting uses different measurements in different situations—historical cost for equipment, net realizable value for some inventories, fair value for investments. As we discussed in Chapter 2, the FASB increasingly is requiring the use of fair values in the measurement of assets and liabilities. According to the FASB's recent standard on fair value measurements, the most useful fair value measures are based on prices established in active markets. However, for many assets and liabilities, market-based fair value information is not readily available. In these cases, fair value can be estimated based on the expected future cash flows related to the asset or liability.

Using present value techniques, these future cash flows then can be converted into present values.[1]

Because of the increased use of present values in this and other contexts, it is important to understand present value techniques.[2] We list some of the applications of present value-based measurements to accounting topics below; we discuss many of these in the following chapters.

PRESENT VALUE-BASED ACCOUNTING MEASUREMENTS

1 *NOTES.* Valuing noncurrent receivables and payables that carry no stated interest rate or a lower than market interest rate.

2 *LEASES.* Valuing assets and obligations to be capitalized under long-term leases and measuring the amount of the lease payments and annual leasehold amortization.

3 *PENSIONS AND OTHER POSTRETIREMENT BENEFITS.* Measuring service cost components of employers' postretirement benefits expense and postretirement benefits obligation.

4 *LONG-TERM ASSETS.* Evaluating alternative long-term investments by discounting future cash flows. Determining the value of assets acquired under deferred payment contracts. Measuring impairments of assets.

5 *SINKING FUNDS.* Determining the contributions necessary to accumulate a fund for debt retirements.

6 *BUSINESS COMBINATIONS.* Determining the value of receivables, payables, liabilities, accruals, and commitments acquired or assumed in a "purchase."

7 *DISCLOSURES.* Measuring the value of future cash flows from oil and gas reserves for disclosure in supplementary information.

8 *INSTALLMENT CONTRACTS.* Measuring periodic payments on long-term purchase contracts.

In addition to accounting and business applications, compound interest, annuity, and present value concepts apply to personal finance and investment decisions. In purchasing a home or car, planning for retirement, and evaluating alternative investments, you will need to understand time value of money concepts.

The Nature of Interest

Interest is payment for the use of money. It is the excess cash received or repaid over and above the amount lent or borrowed (**principal**). For example, Corner Bank lends Hillfarm Company $10,000 with the understanding that it will repay $11,500. The excess over $10,000, or $1,500, represents interest expense.

The lender generally states the amount of interest as a rate over a specific period of time. For example, if Hillfarm borrowed $10,000 for one year before repaying $11,500, the rate of interest is 15 percent per year ($1,500 ÷ $10,000). The custom of

---

[1]"Fair Value Measurement," Proposed *Statement of Financial Accounting Standards* (Norwalk, Conn.: FASB, October 21, 2005).

[2]Many recent standards, such as *FASB Statements No. 106, 107, 109, 113, 114, 116, 141, 142,* and *144,* have addressed the issue of present value in the pronouncement or related basis for conclusions.

expressing interest as a percentage rate is an established business practice.[3] In fact, business managers make investing and borrowing decisions on the basis of the rate of interest involved, rather than on the actual dollar amount of interest to be received or paid.

How is the interest rate determined? One important factor is the level of credit risk (risk of nonpayment) involved. Other factors being equal, the higher the credit risk, the higher the interest rate. Low-risk borrowers like **Microsoft** or **Intel** can probably obtain a loan at or slightly below the going market rate of interest. However, a bank would probably charge the neighborhood delicatessen several percentage points above the market rate, if granting the loan at all.

The amount of interest involved in any financing transaction is a function of three variables:

VARIABLES IN INTEREST COMPUTATION

1 *PRINCIPAL.* The amount borrowed or invested.
2 *INTEREST RATE.* A percentage of the outstanding principal.
3 *TIME.* The number of years or fractional portion of a year that the principal is outstanding.

Thus, the following three relationships apply:

- The larger the principal amount, the larger the dollar amount of interest.
- The higher the interest rate, the larger the dollar amount of interest.
- The longer the time period, the larger the dollar amount of interest.

Simple Interest

OBJECTIVE 2
Distinguish between simple and compound interest.

Companies compute **simple interest** on the amount of the principal only. It is the return on (or growth of) the principal for one time period. The following equation expresses simple interest.[4]

$$\text{Interest} = p \times i \times n$$

where

$$p = \text{principal}$$
$$i = \text{rate of interest for a single period}$$
$$n = \text{number of periods}$$

To illustrate, Barstow Electric Inc. borrows $10,000 for 3 years with a simple interest rate of 8% per year. It computes the total interest it will pay as follows.

$$\text{Interest} = p \times i \times n$$
$$= \$10,000 \times .08 \times 3$$
$$= \$2,400$$

---

[3]Federal law requires the disclosure of interest rates on an **annual basis** in all contracts. That is, instead of stating the rate as "1% per month," contracts must state the rate as "12% per year" if it is simple interest or "12.68% per year" if it is compounded monthly.

[4]Business mathematics and business finance textbooks traditionally state simple interest as: I(interest) $= P$(principal) $\times R$(rate) $\times T$(time).

If Barstow borrows $10,000 for 3 months at 8%, the interest is $200, computed as follows.

$$\text{Interest} = \$10,000 \times .08 \times 3/12$$
$$= \$200$$

Compound Interest

John Maynard Keynes, the legendary English economist, supposedly called it magic. Mayer Rothschild, the founder of the famous European banking firm, proclaimed it the eighth wonder of the world. Today, people continue to extol its wonder and its power. The object of their affection? Compound interest.

We compute **compound interest** on principal **and** on any interest earned that has not been paid or withdrawn. It is the return on (or growth of) the principal for two or more time periods. Compounding computes interest not only on the principal but also on the interest earned to date on that principal, assuming the interest is left on deposit.

To illustrate the difference between simple and compound interest, assume that Vasquez Company deposits $10,000 in the Last National Bank, where it will earn simple interest of 9% per year. It deposits another $10,000 in the First State Bank, where it will earn compound interest of 9% per year compounded annually. In both cases, Vasquez will not withdraw any interest until 3 years from the date of deposit. Illustration 6-1 shows the computation of interest Vasquez will receive, as well as its accumulated year-end balance.

ILLUSTRATION 6-1
Simple vs. Compound Interest

Last National Bank					First State Bank		
Simple Interest Calculation	Simple Interest	Accumulated Year-end Balance			Compound Interest Calculation	Compound Interest	Accumulated Year-end Balance
Year 1 $10,000.00 × 9%	$ 900.00	$10,900.00			Year 1 $10,000.00 × 9%	$ 900.00	$10,900.00
Year 2 $10,000.00 × 9%	900.00	$11,800.00			Year 2 $10,900.00 × 9%	981.00	$11,881.00
Year 3 $10,000.00 × 9%	900.00	$12,700.00			Year 3 $11,881.00 × 9%	1,069.29	$12,950.29
	$2,700		→ $250.29 ← Difference			$2,950.29	

Note in the illustration above that simple interest uses the initial principal of $10,000 to compute the interest in all 3 years. **Compound interest uses the accumulated balance (principal plus interest to date) at each year-end to compute interest in the succeeding year.** This explains the larger balance in the compound interest account.

Obviously, any rational investor would choose compound interest, if available, over simple interest. In the example above, compounding provides $250.29 of additional interest revenue. For practical purposes, compounding assumes that unpaid interest earned becomes a part of the principal. Furthermore, the accumulated balance at the end of each year becomes the new principal sum on which interest is earned during the next year.

Compound interest is the typical interest computation applied in business situations. This occurs particularly in our economy, where companies use and finance large amounts of long-lived assets over long periods of time. Financial managers view and evaluate their investment opportunities in terms of a series of periodic returns, each of which they can reinvest to yield additional returns. Simple interest usually applies only to short-term investments and debts that involve a time span of one year or less.

WHAT DO THE NUMBERS MEAN?

The current debate on Social Security reform provides a great context to illustrate the power of compounding. One proposed idea is for the government to give $1,000 to every citizen at birth. This gift would be deposited in an account that would earn interest tax-free until the citizen retires. Assuming the account earns a modest 5% annual return until retirement at age 65, the $1,000 would grow to $23,839. With monthly compounding, the $1,000 deposited at birth would grow to $25,617.

Why start so early? If the government waited until age 18 to deposit the money, it would grow to only $9,906 with annual compounding. That is, reducing the time invested by a third results in more than a 50% reduction in retirement money. The example illustrates the importance of starting early when the power of compounding is involved.

Compound Interest Tables (see pages 302–311)

OBJECTIVE 3
Use appropriate compound interest tables.

We present five different types of compound interest tables at the end of this chapter. These tables should help you study this chapter as well as solve other problems involving interest.

INTEREST TABLES AND THEIR CONTENTS

1 *FUTURE VALUE OF 1* TABLE. Contains the amounts to which 1 will accumulate if deposited now at a specified rate and left for a specified number of periods. (Table 1)

2 *PRESENT VALUE OF 1* TABLE. Contains the amounts that must be deposited now at a specified rate of interest to equal 1 at the end of a specified number of periods. (Table 2)

3 *FUTURE VALUE OF AN ORDINARY ANNUITY OF 1* TABLE. Contains the amounts to which periodic rents of 1 will accumulate if the payments (rents) are invested at the **end** of each period at a specified rate of interest for a specified number of periods. (Table 3)

4 *PRESENT VALUE OF AN ORDINARY ANNUITY OF 1* TABLE. Contains the amounts that must be deposited now at a specified rate of interest to permit withdrawals of 1 at the **end** of regular periodic intervals for the specified number of periods. (Table 4)

5 *PRESENT VALUE OF AN ANNUITY DUE OF 1* TABLE. Contains the amounts that must be deposited now at a specified rate of interest to permit withdrawals of 1 at the **beginning** of regular periodic intervals for the specified number of periods. (Table 5)

Illustration 6-2 lists the general format and content of these tables. It shows how much principal plus interest a dollar accumulates to at the end of each of five periods, at three different rates of compound interest.

ILLUSTRATION 6-2
Excerpt from Table 6-1

	FUTURE VALUE OF 1 AT COMPOUND INTEREST (EXCERPT FROM TABLE 6-1, PAGE 303)		
Period	9%	10%	11%
1	1.09000	1.10000	1.11000
2	1.18810	1.21000	1.23210
3	1.29503	1.33100	1.36763
4	1.41158	1.46410	1.51807
5	1.53862	1.61051	1.68506

The compound tables rely on basic formulas. For example, the formula to determine the future value factor (*FVF*) for 1 is:

$$FVF_{n,i} = (1 + i)^n$$

where

$FVF_{n,i}$ = future value factor for *n* periods at *i* interest

  n = number of periods

  i = rate of interest for a single period

Financial calculators include preprogrammed $FVF_{n,i}$ and other time value of money formulas. We illustrate the use of these tools to solve time value of money problems in Appendix 6A.

To illustrate the use of interest tables to calculate compound amounts, assume an interest rate of 9%. Illustration 6-3 shows the future value to which 1 accumulates (the future value factor).

Period	Beginning-of-Period Amount	× Multiplier (1 + *i*) =	End-of-Period Amount*	Formula (1 + *i*)^n
1	1.00000	1.09	1.09000	$(1.09)^1$
2	1.09000	1.09	1.18810	$(1.09)^2$
3	1.18810	1.09	1.29503	$(1.09)^3$

*Note that these amounts appear in Table 6-1 in the 9% column.

ILLUSTRATION 6-3
Accumulation of Compound Amounts

Throughout our discussion of compound interest tables, note the intentional use of the term **periods** instead of **years**. Interest is generally expressed in terms of an annual rate. However, many business circumstances dictate a compounding period of less than one year. In such circumstances, a company must convert the annual interest rate to correspond to the length of the period. To convert the "annual interest rate" into the "compounding period interest rate," a company **divides the annual rate by the number of compounding periods per year**.

In addition, companies determine the number of periods by **multiplying the number of years involved by the number of compounding periods per year**. To illustrate, assume an investment of $1 for 6 years at 8% annual interest compounded **quarterly**. Using Table 6-1, page 302, read the factor that appears in the 2% column on the 24th row—6 years × 4 compounding periods per year, namely 1.60844, or approximately $1.61. Thus, all compound interest tables use the term **periods**, not **years**, to express the quantity of *n*. Illustration 6-4 shows how to determine (1) the interest rate per compounding period and (2) the number of compounding periods in four situations of differing compounding frequency.[5]

12% Annual Interest Rate over 5 Years Compounded	Interest Rate per Compounding Period	Number of Compounding Periods
Annually (1)	.12 ÷ 1 = .12	5 years × 1 compounding per year = 5 periods
Semiannually (2)	.12 ÷ 2 = .06	5 years × 2 compoundings per year = 10 periods
Quarterly (4)	.12 ÷ 4 = .03	5 years × 4 compoundings per year = 20 periods
Monthly (12)	.12 ÷ 12 = .01	5 years × 12 compoundings per year = 60 periods

ILLUSTRATION 6-4
Frequency of Compounding

[5]Because interest is theoretically earned (accruing) every second of every day, it is possible to calculate interest that is **compounded continuously**. Using the natural, or Napierian, system of logarithms facilitates computations involving continuous compounding. As a practical matter, however, most business transactions assume interest to be compounded no more frequently than daily.

How often interest is compounded can substantially affect the rate of return. For example, a 9% annual interest compounded **daily** provides a 9.42% yield, or a difference of 0.42%. The 9.42% is the **effective yield**.[6] The annual interest rate (9%) is the **stated, nominal,** or **face rate**. When the compounding frequency is greater than once a year, the effective interest rate will always exceed the stated rate.

Illustration 6-5 shows how compounding for five different time periods affects the effective yield and the amount earned by an investment of $10,000 for one year.

ILLUSTRATION 6-5
Comparison of Different
Compounding Periods

Interest Rate	Compounding Periods				
	Annually	Semiannually	Quarterly	Monthly	Daily
8%	8.00%	8.16%	8.24%	8.30%	8.33%
	$800	$816	$824	$830	$833
9%	9.00%	9.20%	9.31%	9.38%	9.42%
	$900	$920	$931	$938	$942
10%	10.00%	10.25%	10.38%	10.47%	10.52%
	$1,000	$1,025	$1,038	$1,047	$1,052

Fundamental Variables

OBJECTIVE 4
Identify variables
fundamental to solving
interest problems.

The following four variables are fundamental to all compound interest problems.

FUNDAMENTAL VARIABLES

1 *RATE OF INTEREST.* This rate, unless otherwise stated, is an annual rate that must be adjusted to reflect the length of the compounding period if less than a year.

2 *NUMBER OF TIME PERIODS.* This is the number of compounding periods. (A period may be equal to or less than a year.)

3 *FUTURE VALUE.* The value at a future date of a given sum or sums invested assuming compound interest.

4 *PRESENT VALUE.* The value now (present time) of a future sum or sums discounted assuming compound interest.

Illustration 6-6 depicts the relationship of these four fundamental variables in a **time diagram**.

---

[6]The formula for calculating the **effective rate**, in situations where the compounding frequency (*n*) is greater than once a year, is as follows.

$$\text{Effective rate} = (1 + i)^n - 1$$

To illustrate, if the stated annual rate is 8% compounded quarterly (or 2% per quarter), the effective annual rate is:

$$
\begin{aligned}
\text{Effective rate} &= (1 + .02)^4 - 1 \\
&= (1.02)^4 - 1 \\
&= 1.0824 - 1 \\
&= .0824 \\
&= 8.24\%
\end{aligned}
$$

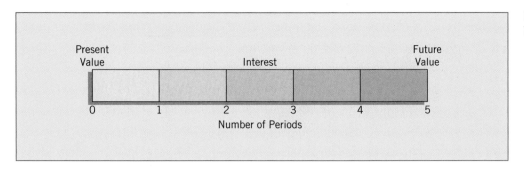

ILLUSTRATION 6-6
Basic Time Diagram

In some cases, all four of these variables are known. However, at least one variable is unknown in many business situations. To better understand and solve the problems in this chapter, we encourage you to sketch compound interest problems in the form of the preceding time diagram.

SINGLE-SUM PROBLEMS

Many business and investment decisions involve a single amount of money that either exists now or will in the future. Single-sum problems are generally classified into one of the following two categories.

OBJECTIVE 5
Solve future and present value of 1 problems.

1 Computing the **unknown** future value of a known single sum of money that is invested now for a certain number of periods at a certain interest rate.

2 Computing the **unknown** present value of a known single sum of money in the future that is discounted for a certain number of periods at a certain interest rate.

When analyzing the information provided, determine first whether the problem involves a future value or a present value. Then apply the following general rules, depending on the situation:

- **If solving for a future value**, *accumulate* all cash flows to a future point. In this instance, interest increases the amounts or values over time so that the future value exceeds the present value.

- **If solving for a present value**, *discount* all cash flows from the future to the present. In this case, **discounting** reduces the amounts or values, so that the present value is less than the future amount.

Preparation of time diagrams aids in identifying the unknown as an item in the future or the present. Sometimes the problem involves neither a future value nor a present value. Instead, the unknown is the interest or discount rate, or the number of compounding or discounting periods.

Future Value of a Single Sum

To determine the **future value** of a single sum, multiply the future value factor by its present value (principal), as follows.

$$FV = PV\ (FVF_{n,i})$$

where

$$FV = \text{future value}$$
$$PV = \text{present value (principal or single sum)}$$
$$FVF_{n,i} = \text{future value factor for } n \text{ periods at } i \text{ interest}$$

To illustrate, Bruegger Co. wants to determine the future value of $50,000 invested for 5 years compounded annually at an interest rate of 11%. Illustration 6-7 (on page 260) shows this investment situation in time-diagram form.

ILLUSTRATION 6-7
Future Value
Time Diagram
$(n = 5, i = 11\%)$

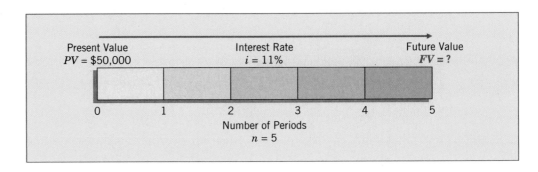

Using the future value formula, Bruegger solves this investment problem as follows.

$$\text{Future value} = PV \ (FVF_{n,i})$$
$$= \$50,000 \ (FVF_{5,11\%})$$
$$= \$50,000 \ (1 + .11)^5$$
$$= \$50,000 \ (1.68506)$$
$$= \$84,253$$

To determine the future value factor of 1.68506 in the formula above, Bruegger uses a financial calculator or reads the appropriate table, in this case Table 6-1 (11% column and the 5-period row).

Companies can apply this time diagram and formula approach to routine business situations. To illustrate, assume that **Commonwealth Edison Company** deposited $250 million in an escrow account with **Northern Trust Company** at the beginning of 2007 as a commitment toward a power plant to be completed December 31, 2010. How much will the company have on deposit at the end of 4 years if interest is 10%, compounded semiannually?

With a known present value of $250 million, a total of 8 compounding periods (4 × 2), and an interest rate of 5% per compounding period (.10 ÷ 2), the company can time-diagram this problem and determine the future value as shown in Illustration 6-8.

ILLUSTRATION 6-8
Future Value
Time Diagram
$(n = 8, i = 5\%)$

$$\text{Future value} = \$250,000,000 \ (FVF_{8,5\%})$$
$$= \$250,000,000 \ (1 + .05)^8$$
$$= \$250,000,000 \ (1.47746)$$
$$= \$369,365,000$$

Using a future value factor found in Table 1 (5% column, 8-period row), we find that the deposit of $250 million will accumulate to $369,365,000 by December 31, 2010.

Present Value of a Single Sum

The Bruegger example on page 260 showed that $50,000 invested at an annually compounded interest rate of 11% will equal $84,253 at the end of 5 years. It follows, then, that $84,253, 5 years in the future, is worth $50,000 now. That is, $50,000 is the present value of $84,253. The **present value** is the amount needed to invest now, to produce a known future value.

The present value is always a smaller amount than the known future value, due to earned and accumulated interest. In determining the future value, a company moves forward in time using a process of **accumulation**. In determining present value, it moves backward in time using a process of **discounting**.

As indicated earlier, a "present value of 1 table" appears at the end of this chapter as Table 6-2. Illustration 6-9 demonstrates the nature of such a table. It shows the present value of 1 for five different periods at three different rates of interest.

<table>
<tr><td colspan="4" align="center">**PRESENT VALUE OF 1 AT COMPOUND INTEREST**
(EXCERPT FROM TABLE 6-2, PAGE 305)</td></tr>
<tr><td>Period</td><td>9%</td><td>10%</td><td>11%</td></tr>
<tr><td>1</td><td>0.91743</td><td>0.90909</td><td>0.90090</td></tr>
<tr><td>2</td><td>0.84168</td><td>0.82645</td><td>0.81162</td></tr>
<tr><td>3</td><td>0.77218</td><td>0.75132</td><td>0.73119</td></tr>
<tr><td>4</td><td>0.70843</td><td>0.68301</td><td>0.65873</td></tr>
<tr><td>5</td><td>0.64993</td><td>0.62092</td><td>0.59345</td></tr>
</table>

ILLUSTRATION 6-9
Excerpt from Table 6-2

The following formula is used to determine the present value of 1 (present value factor):

$$PVF_{n,i} = \frac{1}{(1 + i)^n}$$

where

$PVF_{n,i}$ = present value factor for n periods at i interest

To illustrate, assuming an interest rate of 9%, the present value of 1 discounted for three different periods is as shown in Illustration 6-10.

<table>
<tr><td>Discount
Periods</td><td>1</td><td>÷ $(1 + i)^n$</td><td>= Present Value*</td><td>Formula
$1/(1 + i)^n$</td></tr>
<tr><td>1</td><td>1.00000</td><td>1.09</td><td>.91743</td><td>$1/(1.09)^1$</td></tr>
<tr><td>2</td><td>1.00000</td><td>$(1.09)^2$</td><td>.84168</td><td>$1/(1.09)^2$</td></tr>
<tr><td>3</td><td>1.00000</td><td>$(1.09)^3$</td><td>.77218</td><td>$1/(1.09)^3$</td></tr>
<tr><td colspan="5">*Note that these amounts appear in Table 6-2 in the 9% column.</td></tr>
</table>

ILLUSTRATION 6-10
Present Value of $1
Discounted at 9% for
Three Periods

The present value of any single sum (future value), then, is as follows.

$$PV = FV\ (PVF_{n,i})$$

where

PV = present value

FV = future value

$PVF_{n,i}$ = present value factor for n periods at i interest

To illustrate, what is the present value of $84,253 to be received or paid in 5 years discounted at 11% compounded annually? Illustration 6-11 (on page 262) shows this problem as a time diagram.

ILLUSTRATION 6-11
Present Value
Time Diagram
($n = 5$, $i = 11\%$)

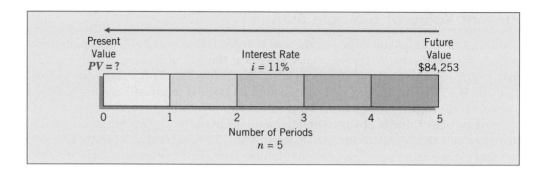

Using the formula, we solve this problem as follows.

$$\text{Present value} = FV\ (PVF_{n,i})$$
$$= \$84{,}253\ (PVF_{5,11\%})$$
$$= \$84{,}253 \left(\frac{1}{(1 + .11)^5} \right)$$
$$= \$84{,}253\ (.59345)$$
$$= \$50{,}000$$

To determine the present value factor of 0.59345, use a financial calculator or read the present value of a single sum in Table 6-2 (11% column, 5-period row).

The time diagram and formula approach can be applied in a variety of situations. For example, assume that your rich uncle decides to give you $2,000 for a trip to Europe when you graduate from college 3 years from now. He proposes to finance the trip by investing a sum of money now at 8% compound interest that will provide you with $2,000 upon your graduation. The only conditions are that you graduate and that you tell him how much to invest now.

To impress your uncle, you set up the time diagram in Illustration 6-12 and solve this problem as follows.

ILLUSTRATION 6-12
Present Value
Time Diagram
($n = 3$, $i = 8\%$)

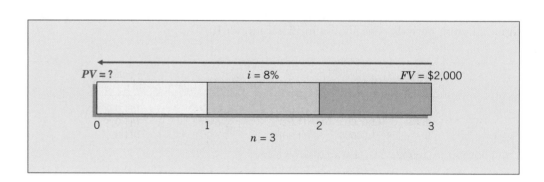

$$\text{Present value} = \$2{,}000\ (PVF_{3,8\%})$$
$$= \$2{,}000 \left(\frac{1}{(1 + .08)^3} \right)$$
$$= \$2{,}000\ (.79383)$$
$$= \$1{,}587.66$$

Advise your uncle to invest $1,587.66 now to provide you with $2,000 upon graduation. To satisfy your uncle's other condition, you must pass this course (and many more).

Solving for Other Unknowns in Single-Sum Problems

In computing either the future value or the present value in the previous single-sum illustrations, both the number of periods and the interest rate were known. In many business situations, both the future value and the present value are known, but the number of periods or the interest rate is unknown. The following two examples are single-sum problems (future value and present value) with either an unknown number of periods (n) or an unknown interest rate (i). These examples, and the accompanying solutions, demonstrate that knowing any three of the four values (future value, FV; present value, PV; number of periods, n; interest rate, i) allows you to derive the remaining unknown variable.

Example—Computation of the Number of Periods

The Village of Somonauk wants to accumulate $70,000 for the construction of a veterans monument in the town square. At the beginning of the current year, the Village deposited $47,811 in a memorial fund that earns 10% interest compounded annually. How many years will it take to accumulate $70,000 in the memorial fund?

In this illustration, the Village knows both the present value ($47,811) and the future value ($70,000), along with the interest rate of 10%. Illustration 6-13 depicts this investment problem as a time diagram.

ILLUSTRATION 6-13
Time Diagram to Solve for Unknown Number of Periods

Knowing both the present value and the future value allows the Village to solve for the unknown number of periods. It may use either the future value or the present value formulas, as shown in Illustration 6-14.

Future Value Approach	Present Value Approach
$FV = PV\,(FVF_{n,10\%})$	$PV = FV\,(PVF_{n,10\%})$
$\$70{,}000 = \$47{,}811\,(FVF_{n,10\%})$	$\$47{,}811 = \$70{,}000\,(PVF_{n,10\%})$
$FVF_{n,10\%} = \dfrac{\$70{,}000}{\$47{,}811} = 1.46410$	$PVF_{n,10\%} = \dfrac{\$47{,}811}{\$70{,}000} = .68301$

ILLUSTRATION 6-14
Solving for Unknown Number of Periods

Using the future value factor of 1.46410, refer to Table 6-1 and read down the 10% column to find that factor in the 4-period row. Thus, it will take 4 years for the $47,811 to accumulate to $70,000 if invested at 10% interest compounded annually. Or, using the present value factor of 0.68301, refer to Table 6-2 and read down the 10% column to find that factor in the 4-period row.

Example—Computation of the Interest Rate

Advanced Design, Inc. needs $1,409,870 for basic research 5 years from now. The company currently has $800,000 to invest for that purpose. At what rate of interest must it invest the $800,000 to fund basic research projects of $1,409,870, 5 years from now?

The time diagram in Illustration 6-15 depicts this investment situation.

ILLUSTRATION 6-15
Time Diagram to Solve
for Unknown Interest
Rate

Advanced Design may determine the unknown interest rate from either the future value approach or the present value approach, as Illustration 6-16 shows.

ILLUSTRATION 6-16
Solving for Unknown
Interest Rate

Future Value Approach	Present Value Approach
$FV = PV (FVF_{5,i})$	$PV = FV (PVF_{5,i})$
$\$1,409,870 = \$800,000 (FVF_{5,i})$	$\$800,000 = \$1,409,870 (PVF_{5,i})$
$FVF_{5,i} = \dfrac{\$1,409,870}{\$800,000} = 1.76234$	$PVF_{5,i} = \dfrac{\$800,000}{\$1,409,870} = .56743$

Using the future value factor of 1.76234, refer to Table 6-1 and read across the 5-period row to find that factor in the 12% column. Thus, the company must invest the $800,000 at 12% to accumulate to $1,409,870 in 5 years. Or, using the present value factor of .56743 and Table 6-2, again find that factor at the juncture of the 5-period row and the 12% column.

ANNUITIES

The preceding discussion involved only the accumulation or discounting of a single principal sum. However, many situations arise in which a series of dollar amounts are paid or received periodically, such as installment loans or sales; regular, partially recovered invested funds; or a series of realized cost savings.

For example, a life insurance contract involves a series of equal payments made at equal intervals of time. Such a process of periodic payment represents the accumulation of a sum of money through an annuity. An **annuity**, by definition, requires the following: (1) periodic payments or receipts (called **rents**) of the same amount, (2) the same-length interval between such rents, and (3) compounding of **interest** once each interval. The **future value of an annuity** is the sum of all the rents plus the accumulated compound interest on them.

Note that the rents may occur at either the beginning or the end of the periods. If the rents occur at the end of each period, an annuity is classified as an **ordinary annuity**. If the rents occur at the beginning of each period, an annuity is classified as an **annuity due**.

OBJECTIVE 6
Solve future value of
ordinary and annuity
due problems.

Future Value of an Ordinary Annuity

One approach to determining the future value of an annuity computes the value to which **each** of the rents in the series will accumulate, and then totals their individual future values.

For example, assume that $1 is deposited at the **end** of each of 5 years (an ordinary annuity) and earns 12% interest compounded annually. Illustration 6-17 shows the computation of the future value, using the "future value of 1" table (Table 6-1) for each of the five $1 rents.

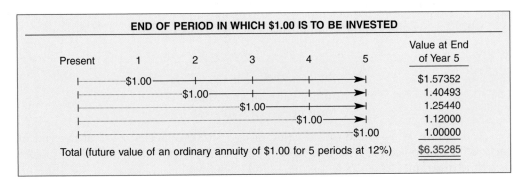

ILLUSTRATION 6-17
Solving for the Future Value of an Ordinary Annuity

Because an ordinary annuity consists of rents deposited at the end of the period, those rents earn no interest during the period. For example, the third rent earns interest for only two periods (periods four and five). It earns no interest for the third period since it is not deposited until the end of the third period. When computing the future value of an ordinary annuity, the number of compounding periods will always be **one less than the number of rents**.

The foregoing procedure for computing the future value of an ordinary annuity always produces the correct answer. However, it can become cumbersome if the number of rents is large. A formula provides a more efficient way of expressing the future value of an ordinary annuity of 1. This formula sums the individual rents plus the compound interest, as follows:

$$FVF\text{-}OA_{n,i} = \frac{(1 + i)^n - 1}{i}$$

where

$$FVF\text{-}OA_{n,i} = \text{future value factor of an ordinary annuity}$$
$$i = \text{rate of interest per period}$$
$$n = \text{number of compounding periods}$$

For example, $FVF\text{-}OA_{5,12\%}$ refers to the value to which an ordinary annuity of 1 will accumulate in 5 periods at 12% interest.

Using the formula above has resulted in the development of tables, similar to those used for the "future value of 1" and the "present value of 1" for both an ordinary annuity and an annuity due. Illustration 6-18 provides an excerpt from the "future value of an ordinary annuity of 1" table.

ILLUSTRATION 6-18
Excerpt from Table 6-3

	FUTURE VALUE OF AN ORDINARY ANNUITY OF 1 (EXCERPT FROM TABLE 6-3, PAGE 307)		
Period	10%	11%	12%
1	1.00000	1.00000	1.00000
2	2.10000	2.11000	2.12000
3	3.31000	3.34210	3.37440
4	4.64100	4.70973	4.77933
5	6.10510	6.22780	6.35285*

*Note that this annuity table factor is the same as the sum of the future values of 1 factors shown in Illustration 6-17.

Interpreting the table, if $1 is invested at the end of each year for 4 years at 11% interest compounded annually, the value of the annuity at the end of the fourth year is $4.71 (4.70973 × $1.00). Now, multiply the factor from the appropriate line and column of the table by the dollar amount of **one rent** involved in an ordinary annuity. The result: the accumulated sum of the rents and the compound interest to the date of the last rent.

The following formula computes the future value of an ordinary annuity.

$$\text{Future value of an ordinary annuity} = R \, (FVF\text{-}OA_{n,i})$$

where

$$R = \text{periodic rent}$$
$$FVF\text{-}OA_{n,i} = \text{future value of an ordinary annuity factor}$$
$$\text{for } n \text{ periods at } i \text{ interest}$$

To illustrate, what is the future value of five $5,000 deposits made at the end of each of the next 5 years, earning interest of 12%? Illustration 6-19 depicts this problem as a time diagram.

ILLUSTRATION 6-19
Time Diagram for Future Value of Ordinary Annuity ($n = 5$, $i = 12\%$)

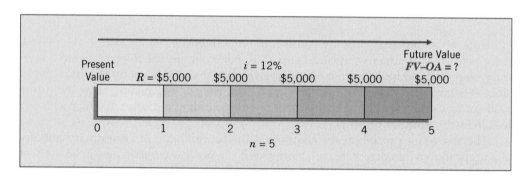

Use of the formula solves this investment problem as follows.

$$\text{Future value of an ordinary annuity} = R \, (FVF\text{-}OA_{n,i})$$
$$= \$5,000 \, (FVF\text{-}OA_{5,12\%})$$
$$= \$5,000 \left(\frac{(1 + .12)^5 - 1}{.12} \right)$$
$$= \$5,000 \, (6.35285)$$
$$= \$31,764.25$$

To determine the future value of an ordinary annuity factor of 6.35285 in the formula above, use a financial calculator or read the appropriate table, in this case, Table 6-3 (12% column and the 5-period row).

To illustrate these computations in a business situation, assume that Hightown Electronics deposits $75,000 at the end of each 6-month period for the next 3 years, to accumulate enough money to meet debts that mature in 3 years. What is the future value that the company will have on deposit at the end of 3 years if the annual interest rate is 10%? The time diagram in Illustration 6-20 depicts this situation.

ILLUSTRATION 6-20
Time Diagram for Future Value of Ordinary Annuity ($n = 6$, $i = 5\%$)

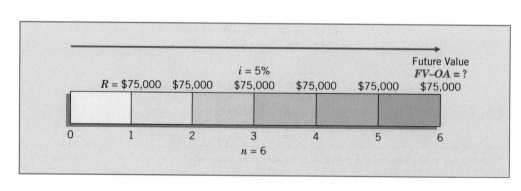

The formula solution for the Hightown Electronics situation is as follows.

$$\text{Future value of an ordinary annuity} = R \, (FVF\text{-}OA_{n,i})$$
$$= \$75,000 \, (FVF\text{-}OA_{6,5\%})$$
$$= \$75,000 \left(\frac{(1 + .05)^6 - 1}{.05} \right)$$
$$= \$75,000 \, (6.80191)$$
$$= \$510,143.25$$

Thus, six 6-month deposits of $75,000 earning 5% per period will grow to $510,143.25.

Future Value of an Annuity Due

The preceding analysis of an ordinary annuity assumed that the periodic rents occur at the **end** of each period. Recall that an **annuity due** assumes periodic rents occur at the **beginning** of each period. This means an annuity due will accumulate interest during the first period (in contrast to an ordinary annuity rent, which will not). In other words, the two types of annuities differ in the number of interest accumulation periods involved.

If rents occur at the end of a period (ordinary annuity), in determining the **future value of an annuity** there will be one less interest period than if the rents occur at the beginning of the period (annuity due). Illustration 6-21 shows this distinction.

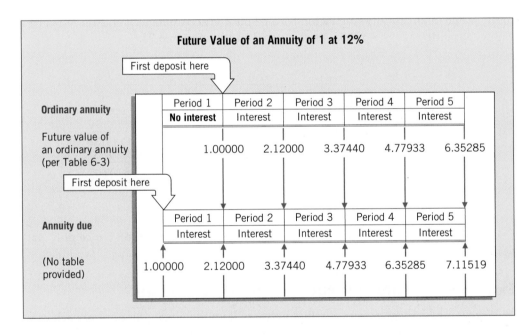

ILLUSTRATION 6-21
Comparison of the Future Value of an Ordinary Annuity with an Annuity Due

In this example, the cash flows from the annuity due come exactly one period earlier than for an ordinary annuity. As a result, the future value of the annuity due factor is exactly 12% higher than the ordinary annuity factor. For example, the value of an ordinary annuity factor at the end of period one at 12% is 1.00000, whereas for an annuity due it is 1.12000.

To find the future value of an annuity due factor, multiply the future value of an ordinary annuity factor by 1 plus the interest rate. For example, to determine the future value of an annuity due interest factor for 5 periods at 12% compound interest, simply multiply the future value of an ordinary annuity interest factor for 5 periods (6.35285), by one plus the interest rate (1 + .12), to arrive at 7.11519 (6.35285 × 1.12).

To illustrate the use of the ordinary annuity tables in converting to an annuity due, assume that Sue Lotadough plans to deposit $800 a year on each birthday of her son

Howard. She makes the first deposit on his tenth birthday, at 6% interest compounded annually. Sue wants to know the amount she will have accumulated for college expenses by her son's eighteenth birthday.

If the first deposit occurs on Howard's tenth birthday, Sue will make a total of 8 deposits over the life of the annuity (assume no deposit on the eighteenth birthday), as shown in Illustration 6-22. Because all the deposits are made at the beginning of the periods, they represent an annuity due.

ILLUSTRATION 6-22
Annuity Due
Time Diagram

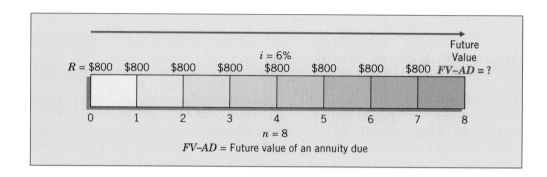

Referring to the "future value of an ordinary annuity of 1" table for 8 periods at 6%, Sue finds a factor of 9.89747. She then multiplies this factor by $(1 + .06)$ to arrive at the future value of an annuity due factor. As a result, the accumulated value on Howard's eighteenth birthday is $8,393.05, as calculated in Illustration 6-23.

ILLUSTRATION 6-23
Computation of
Accumulated Value of
Annuity Due

1. Future value of an ordinary annuity of 1 for 8 periods at 6% (Table 6-3)	9.89747
2. Factor $(1 + .06)$	$\times$ 1.06
3. Future value of an annuity due of 1 for 8 periods at 6%	10.49132
4. Periodic deposit (rent)	$\times$ $800
5. Accumulated value on son's eighteenth birthday	$8,393.05

Depending on the college he chooses, Howard may have enough to finance only part of his first year of school.

Examples of Future Value of Annuity Problems

The foregoing annuity examples relied on three known values—amount of each rent, interest rate, and number of periods. Using these values enables us to determine the unknown fourth value, future value.

The first two future value problems we present illustrate the computations of (1) the amount of the rents and (2) the number of rents. The third problem illustrates the computation of the future value of an annuity due.

Computation of Rent

Assume that you plan to accumulate $14,000 for a down payment on a condominium apartment 5 years from now. For the next 5 years, you earn an annual return of 8% compounded semiannually. How much should you deposit at the end of each 6-month period?

The $14,000 is the future value of 10 (5×2) semiannual end-of-period payments of an unknown amount, at an interest rate of 4% $(8\% \div 2)$. Illustration 6-24 depicts this problem as a time diagram.

ILLUSTRATION 6-24
Future Value of Ordinary
Annuity Time Diagram
($n = 10$, $i = 4\%$)

Using the formula for the future value of an ordinary annuity, you determine the amount of each rent as follows.

$$\text{Future value of an ordinary annuity} = R\ (FVF\text{-}OA_{n,i})$$

$$\$14,000 = R\ (FVF\text{-}OA_{10,4\%})$$

$$\$14,000 = R(12.00611)$$

$$R = \$1,166.07$$

Thus, you must make 10 semiannual deposits of $1,166.07 each in order to accumulate $14,000 for your down payment.

Computation of the Number of Periodic Rents

Suppose that a company's goal is to accumulate $117,332 by making periodic deposits of $20,000 at the end of each year, which will earn 8% compounded annually while accumulating. How many deposits must it make?

The $117,332 represents the future value of $n(?)$ $20,000 deposits, at an 8% annual rate of interest. Illustration 6-25 depicts this problem in a time diagram.

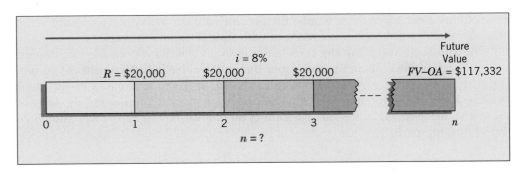

ILLUSTRATION 6-25
Future Value of Ordinary
Annuity Time Diagram,
to Solve for Unknown
Number of Periods

Using the future value of an ordinary annuity formula, the company obtains the following factor.

$$\text{Future value of an ordinary annuity} = R\ (FVF\text{-}OA_{n,i})$$

$$\$117,332 = \$20,000\ (FVF\text{-}OA_{n,8\%})$$

$$FVF\text{-}OA_{n,8\%} = \frac{\$117,332}{\$20,000} = 5.86660$$

Use Table 6-3 and read down the 8% column to find 5.86660 in the 5-period row. Thus, the company must make five deposits of $20,000 each.

Computation of the Future Value

To create his retirement fund, Walter Goodwrench, a mechanic, now works weekends. Mr. Goodwrench deposits $2,500 today in a savings account that earns 9% interest. He plans to deposit $2,500 every year for a total of 30 years. How much cash will Mr. Good-wrench accumulate in his retirement savings account, when he retires in 30 years? Illustration 6-26 depicts this problem in a time diagram.

ILLUSTRATION 6-26
Future Value
Annuity Due
Time Diagram
($n = 30$, $i = 9\%$)

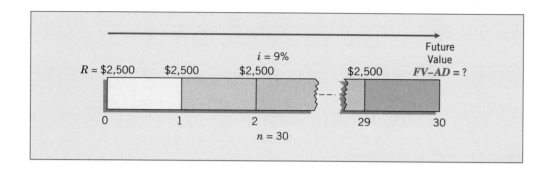

Using the "future value of an ordinary annuity of 1" table, Mr. Goodwrench computes the solution as shown in Illustration 6-27.

ILLUSTRATION 6-27
Computation of
Accumulated Value of an
Annuity Due

1. Future value of an ordinary annuity of 1 for 30 periods at 9%	136.30754
2. Factor (1 + .09)	× 1.09
3. Future value of an annuity due of 1 for 30 periods at 9%	148.57522
4. Periodic rent	× $2,500
5. Accumulated value at end of 30 years	$371,438

Present Value of an Ordinary Annuity

OBJECTIVE 7
Solve present value of
ordinary and annuity
due problems.

The present value of an annuity is **the single sum** that, if invested at compound interest now, would provide for an annuity (a series of withdrawals) for a certain number of future periods. In other words, the present value of an ordinary annuity is the present value of a series of equal rents, to withdraw at equal intervals.

One approach to finding the present value of an annuity determines the present value of each of the rents in the series and then totals their individual present values. For example, we may view an annuity of $1, to be received at the **end** of each of 5 periods, as separate amounts. We then compute each present value using the table of present values (see pages 303–304), assuming an interest rate of 12%. Illustration 6-28 shows this approach.

ILLUSTRATION 6-28
Solving for the Present
Value of an Ordinary
Annuity

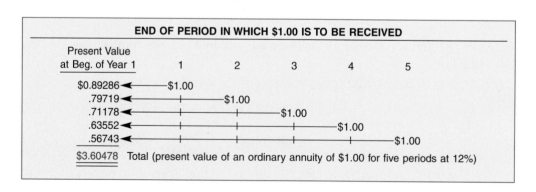

This computation tells us that if we invest the single sum of $3.60 today at 12% interest for 5 periods, we will be able to withdraw $1 at the end of each period for 5 periods. We can summarize this cumbersome procedure by the following formula.

$$PVF\text{-}OA_{n,i} = \frac{1 - \dfrac{1}{(1 + i)^n}}{i}$$

The expression $PVF\text{-}OA_{n,i}$ refers to the present value of an ordinary annuity of 1 factor for n periods at i interest. Ordinary annuity tables base present values on this formula. Illustration 6-29 shows an excerpt from such a table.

ILLUSTRATION 6-29
Excerpt from Table 6-4

PRESENT VALUE OF AN ORDINARY ANNUITY OF 1			
(EXCERPT FROM TABLE 6-4, PAGE 309)			
Period	10%	11%	12%
1	0.90909	0.90090	0.89286
2	1.73554	1.71252	1.69005
3	2.48685	2.44371	2.40183
4	3.16986	3.10245	3.03735
5	3.79079	3.69590	3.60478*

*Note that this annuity table factor is equal to the sum of the present value of 1 factors shown in Illustration 6-28.

The general formula for the present value of any ordinary annuity is as follows.

Present value of an ordinary annuity $= R\,(PVF\text{-}OA_{n,i})$

where

R = periodic rent (ordinary annuity)

$PVF\text{-}OA_{n,i}$ = present value of an ordinary annuity of 1 for n periods at i interest

To illustrate with an example, what is the present value of rental receipts of $6,000 each, to be received at the end of each of the next 5 years when discounted at 12%? This problem may be time-diagrammed and solved as shown in Illustration 6-30.

ILLUSTRATION 6-30
Present Value of Ordinary
Annuity Time Diagram

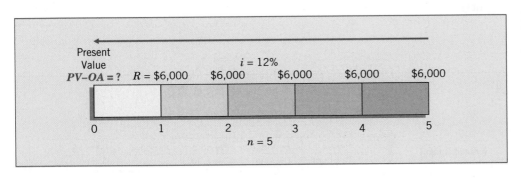

The formula for this calculation is as shown below.

Present value of an ordinary annuity $= R\,(PVF\text{-}OA_{n,i})$

$= \$6,000\,(PVF\text{-}OA_{5,12\%})$

$= \$6,000\,(3.60478)$

$= \$21,628.68$

The present value of the 5 ordinary annuity rental receipts of $6,000 each is $21,628.68. To determine the present value of the ordinary annuity factor 3.60478, use a financial calculator or read the appropriate table, in this case Table 6-4 (12% column and 5-period row).

UP IN SMOKE

Time value of money concepts also can be relevant to public policy debates. For example, several states had to determine how to receive the payments from tobacco companies as settlement for a national lawsuit against the companies for the healthcare costs of smoking.

The **State of Wisconsin** was due to collect 25 years of payments totaling $5.6 billion. The state could wait to collect the payments, or it could sell the payments to an investment bank (a process called *securitization*). If it were to sell the payments, it would receive a lump-sum payment today of $1.26 billion. Is this a good deal for the state? Assuming a discount rate of 8% and that the payments will be received in equal amounts (e.g., an annuity), the present value of the tobacco payment is:

$5.6 billion ÷ 25 = $224 million × 10.67478* = $2.39 billion

*PV-OA(i = 8%, n = 25)

Why would some in the state be willing to take just $1.26 billion today for an annuity whose present value is almost twice that amount? One reason is that Wisconsin was facing a hole in its budget that could be plugged in part by the lump-sum payment. Also, some believed that the risk of not getting paid by the tobacco companies in the future makes it prudent to get the money earlier.

If this latter reason has merit, then the present value computation above should have been based on a higher interest rate. Assuming a discount rate of 15%, the present value of the annuity is $1.448 billion ($5.6 billion ÷ 25 = $224 million; $224 million × 6.46415), which is much closer to the lump-sum payment offered to the State of Wisconsin.

Present Value of an Annuity Due

In our discussion of the present value of an ordinary annuity, we discounted the final rent based on the number of rent periods. In determining the present value of an annuity due, there is always one fewer discount period. Illustration 6-31 shows this distinction.

ILLUSTRATION 6-31
Comparison of Present
Value of an Ordinary
Annuity with an Annuity
Due

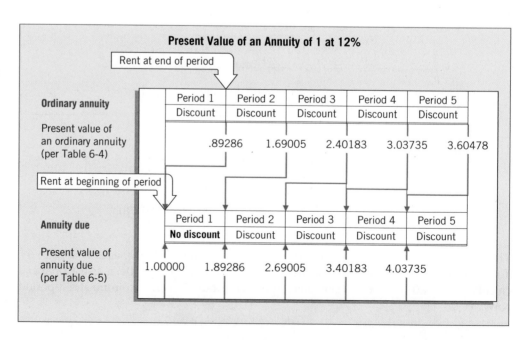

Because each cash flow comes exactly one period sooner in the present value of the annuity due, the present value of the cash flows is exactly 12% higher than the present value of an ordinary annuity. Thus, **to find the present value of an annuity due factor, multiply the present value of an ordinary annuity factor by 1 plus the interest rate** (that is, $1 + i$).

To determine the present value of an annuity due interest factor for 5 periods at 12% interest, take the present value of an ordinary annuity for 5 periods at 12% interest (3.60478) and multiply it by 1.12 to arrive at the present value of an annuity due, 4.03735 (3.60478 × 1.12). We provide present value of annuity due factors in Table 6-5.

To illustrate, Space Odyssey, Inc., rents a communications satellite for 4 years with annual rental payments of $4.8 million to be made at the beginning of each year. If the relevant annual interest rate is 11%, what is the present value of the rental obligations? Illustration 6-32 shows the company's time diagram for this problem.

ILLUSTRATION 6-32
Present Value
of Annuity Due
Time Diagram
($n = 4, i = 11\%$)

Illustration 6-33 shows the computations to solve this problem.

1. Present value of an ordinary annuity of 1 for 4 periods at 11% (Table 6-4)	3.10245
2. Factor (1 + .11)	× 1.11
3. Present value of an annuity due of 1 for 4 periods at 11%	3.44372
4. Periodic deposit (rent)	× $4,800,000
5. Present value of payments	$16,529,856

ILLUSTRATION 6-33
Computation of Present
Value of an Annuity Due

Using Table 6-5 also locates the desired factor 3.44371 and computes the present value of the lease payments to be $16,529,808. (The difference in computations is due to rounding.)

Examples of Present Value of Annuity Problems

In the following three examples, we demonstrate the computation of (1) the present value, (2) the interest rate, and (3) the amount of each rent.

Computation of the Present Value of an Ordinary Annuity

You have just won a lottery totaling $4,000,000. You learn that you will receive a check in the amount of $200,000 at the end of each of the next 20 years. What amount have you really won? That is, what is the present value of the $200,000 checks you will receive over the next 20 years? Illustration 6-34 (on page 274) shows a time diagram of this enviable situation (assuming an appropriate interest rate of 10%).

You calculate the present value as follows:

$$\text{Present value of an ordinary annuity} = R \, (PVF\text{-}OA_{n,i})$$
$$= \$200,000 \, (PVF\text{-}OA_{20,10\%})$$
$$= \$200,000 \, (8.51356)$$
$$= \$1,702,712$$

ILLUSTRATION 6-34
Time Diagram to Solve
for Present Value of
Lottery Payments

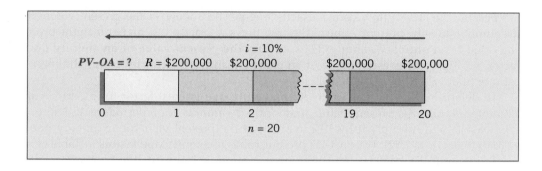

As a result, if the state deposits $1,702,712 now and earns 10% interest, it can withdraw $200,000 a year for 20 years to pay you the $4,000,000.

Computation of the Interest Rate

Many shoppers use credit cards to make purchases. When you receive the invoice for payment, you may pay the total amount due or you may pay the balance in a certain number of payments. For example, assume you receive an invoice from MasterCard with a balance due of $528.77. You may pay it off in 12 equal monthly payments of $50 each, with the first payment due one month from now. What rate of interest would you be paying?

The $528.77 represents the present value of the 12 payments of $50 each at an unknown rate of interest. The time diagram in Illustration 6-35 depicts this situation.

ILLUSTRATION 6-35
Time Diagram to Solve
for Effective Interest Rate
on Loan

You calculate the rate as follows.

$$\text{Present value of an ordinary annuity} = R\,(PVF\text{-}OA_{n,i})$$
$$\$528.77 = \$50\,(PVF\text{-}OA_{12,i})$$
$$(PVF\text{-}OA_{12,i}) = \frac{\$528.77}{\$50} = 10.57540$$

Referring to Table 6-4 and reading across the 12-period row, you find 10.57534 in the 2% column. Since 2% is a monthly rate, the nominal annual rate of interest is 24% (12 × 2%). The effective annual rate is 26.82413% [$(1 + .02)^{12} - 1$]. Obviously, you are better off paying the entire bill now if possible.

Computation of a Periodic Rent

Norm and Jackie Remmers have saved $36,000 to finance their daughter Dawna's college education. They deposited the money in the Bloomington Savings and Loan Association, where it earns 4% interest compounded semiannually. What equal amounts can their daughter withdraw at the end of every 6 months during her 4 college years, without exhausting the fund? Illustration 6-36 shows a time diagram of this situation.

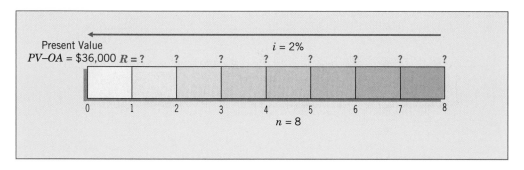

ILLUSTRATION 6-36
Time Diagram for
Ordinary Annuity for a
College Fund

Determining the answer by simply dividing $36,000 by 8 withdrawals is wrong. Why? Because that ignores the interest earned on the money remaining on deposit. Dawna must consider that interest is compounded semiannually at 2% (4% ÷ 2) for 8 periods (4 years × 2). Thus, using the same present value of an ordinary annuity formula, she determines the amount of each withdrawal that she can make as follows.

$$\text{Present value of an ordinary annuity} = R\,(PVF\text{-}OA_{n,i})$$

$$\$36,000 = R\,(PVF\text{-}OA_{8,2\%})$$

$$\$36,000 = R\,(7.32548)$$

$$R = \$4,914.35$$

MORE COMPLEX SITUATIONS

Solving time value problems often requires using more than one table. For example, a business problem may need computations of both present value of a single sum and present value of an annuity. Two such common situations are:

1 Deferred annuities.
2 Bond problems.

> **OBJECTIVE 8**
> Solve present value problems related to deferred annuities and bonds.

Deferred Annuities

A **deferred annuity** is an annuity in which the rents begin after a specified number of periods. A deferred annuity does not begin to produce rents until two or more periods have expired. For example, "an **ordinary annuity** of six annual rents deferred 4 years" means that no rents will occur during the first 4 years, and that the first of the six rents will occur at the end of the fifth year. "An **annuity due** of six annual rents deferred 4 years" means that no rents will occur during the first 4 years, and that the first of six rents will occur at the beginning of the fifth year.

Future Value of a Deferred Annuity

Computing the future value of a deferred annuity is relatively straightforward. Because there is no accumulation or investment on which interest may accrue, the future value of a deferred annuity is the same as the future value of an annuity not deferred. That is, computing the future value simply ignores the deferred period.

To illustrate, assume that Sutton Corporation plans to purchase a land site in 6 years for the construction of its new corporate headquarters. Because of cash flow problems, Sutton budgets deposits of $80,000, on which it expects to earn 5% annually, only at the end of the fourth, fifth, and sixth periods. What future value will Sutton have accumulated at the end of the sixth year? Illustration 6-37 shows a time diagram of this situation.

ILLUSTRATION 6-37
Time Diagram for Future
Value of Deferred
Annuity

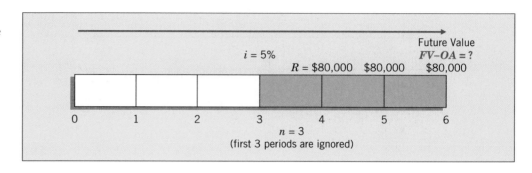

Sutton determines the value accumulated by using the standard formula for the future value of an ordinary annuity:

$$\text{Future value of an ordinary annuity} = R\,(FVF\text{-}OA_{n,i})$$

$$= \$80,000\,(FVF\text{-}OA_{3,5\%})$$

$$= \$80,000\,(3.15250)$$

$$= \$252,200$$

Present Value of a Deferred Annuity

Computing the present value of a deferred annuity must recognize the interest that accrues on the original investment during the deferral period.

To compute the present value of a deferred annuity, we compute the present value of an ordinary annuity of 1 as if the rents had occurred for the entire period. We then subtract the present value of rents that were not received during the deferral period. We are left with the present value of the rents actually received subsequent to the deferral period.

To illustrate, Tom Bytehead has developed and copyrighted tutorial software for students in advanced accounting. He agrees to sell the copyright to Campus Micro Systems for six annual payments of $5,000 each. The payments will begin 5 years from today. Given an annual interest rate of 8%, what is the present value of the six payments?

This situation is an ordinary annuity of 6 payments deferred 4 periods. The time diagram in Illustration 6-38 depicts this sales agreement.

ILLUSTRATION 6-38
Time Diagram for Present
Value of Deferred
Annuity

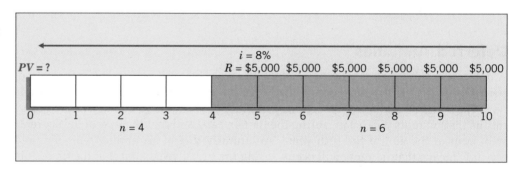

Two options are available to solve this problem. The first is to use only Table 6-4, as shown in Illustration 6-39.

ILLUSTRATION 6-39
Computation of the
Present Value of a
Deferred Annuity

1. Each periodic rent		$5,000
2. Present value of an ordinary annuity of 1 for total periods (10) [number of rents (6) plus number of deferred periods (4)] at 8%	6.71008	
3. Less: Present value of an ordinary annuity of 1 for the number of deferred periods (4) at 8%	−3.31213	
4. Difference		× 3.39795
5. Present value of six rents of $5,000 deferred 4 periods		$16,989.75

The subtraction of the present value of an annuity of 1 for the deferred periods eliminates the nonexistent rents during the deferral period. It converts the present value of an ordinary annuity of $1.00 for 10 periods to the present value of 6 rents of $1.00, deferred 4 periods.

Alternatively, Bytehead can use both Table 6-2 and Table 6-4 to compute the present value of the 6 rents. He can first discount the annuity 6 periods. However, because the annuity is deferred 4 periods, he must treat the present value of the annuity as a future amount to be discounted another 4 periods. The time diagram in Illustration 6-40 depicts this two-step process.

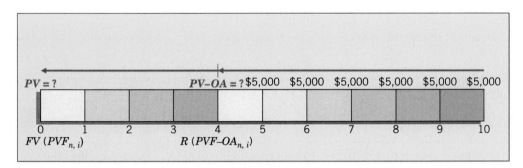

ILLUSTRATION 6-40
Time Diagram for Present Value of Deferred Annuity (2-Step Process)

Calculation using formulas would be done in two steps, as follows.

Step 1: Present value of
an ordinary annuity = R $(PVF\text{-}OA_{n,i})$

= $5,000 $(PVF\text{-}OA_{6,8\%})$

= $5,000 (4.62288)
(Table 6-4, Present value of an ordinary annuity)

= $23,114.40

Step 2: Present value of
a single sum = FV $(PVF_{n,i})$

= $23,114.40 $(PVF_{4,8\%})$

= $23,114.40 (.73503)
(Table 6-2, Present value of a single sum)

= $16,989.78

The present value of $16,989.78 computed above is the same as in Illustration 6-39, although computed differently. (The $0.03 difference is due to rounding.)

Valuation of Long-Term Bonds

A long-term bond produces two cash flows: (1) periodic interest payments during the life of the bond, and (2) the principal (face value) paid at maturity. At the date of issue, bond buyers determine the present value of these two cash flows using the market rate of interest.

The periodic interest payments represent an annuity. The principal represents a single-sum problem. The current market value of the bonds is the combined present values of the interest annuity and the principal amount.

To illustrate, Alltech Corporation on January 1, 2007 issues $100,000 of 9% bonds due in 5 years with interest payable annually at year-end. The current market rate of interest for bonds of similar risk is 11%. What will the buyers pay for this bond issue?

The time diagram in Illustration 6-41 depicts both cash flows.

ILLUSTRATION 6-41
Time Diagram to Solve
for Bond Valuation

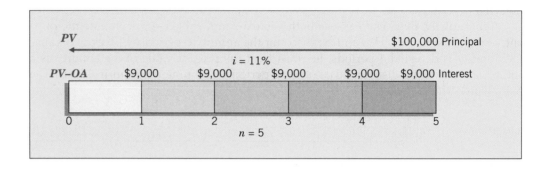

Alltech computes the present value of the two cash flows by discounting at 11% as follows.

ILLUSTRATION 6-42
Computation of the
Present Value of an
Interest-Bearing Bond

1. Present value of the principal: FV ($PVF_{5,11\%}$) = \$100,000 (.59345)	\$59,345.00
2. Present value of the interest payments: R ($PVF\text{-}OA_{5,11\%}$) = \$9,000 (3.69590)	33,263.10
3. Combined present value (market price)—carrying value of bonds	\$92,608.10

By paying \$92,608.10 at date of issue, the buyers of the bonds will realize an effective yield of 11% over the 5-year term of the bonds. This is true because Alltech discounted the cash flows at 11%.

Effective-Interest Method of Amortization of Bond Discount or Premium

In the previous example (Illustration 6-42), Alltech Corporation issued bonds at a discount, computed as follows.

ILLUSTRATION 6-43
Computation of Bond
Discount

Maturity value (face amount) of bonds		\$100,000.00
Present value of the principal	\$59,345.00	
Present value of the interest	33,263.10	
Proceeds (present value and cash received)		92,608.10
Discount on bonds issued		\$ 7,391.90

Alltech amortizes (writes off to interest expense) the amount of this discount over the life of the bond issue.

The preferred procedure for amortization of a discount or premium is the **effective-interest method.** Under the effective-interest method:

1 The company issuing the bond first computes bond interest expense by multiplying the carrying value of the bonds at the beginning of the period by the effective interest rate.

2 The company then determines the bond discount or premium amortization by comparing the bond interest expense with the interest to be paid.

Illustration 6-44 depicts the computation of bond amortization.

*Use of Spreadsheets
to Calculate Bond
Amortization*

Bond Interest Expense		Bond Interest Paid		
$\begin{pmatrix} \text{Carrying Value} \\ \text{of Bonds at} \\ \text{Beginning of Period} \end{pmatrix} \times \begin{matrix} \text{Effective} \\ \text{Interest} \\ \text{Rate} \end{matrix}$	$-$	$\begin{pmatrix} \text{Face Amount} \\ \text{of Bonds} \end{pmatrix} \times \begin{matrix} \text{Stated} \\ \text{Interest} \\ \text{Rate} \end{matrix}$	$=$	$\begin{matrix} \text{Amortization} \\ \text{Amount} \end{matrix}$

ILLUSTRATION 6-44
Amortization
Computation

The effective-interest method produces a periodic interest expense equal to **a constant percentage of the carrying value of the bonds**. Since the percentage used is the effective rate of interest incurred by the borrower at the time of issuance, the effective-interest method results in matching expenses with revenues.

We can use the data from the Alltech Corporation example to illustrate the effective-interest method of amortization. Alltech issued $100,000 face value of bonds at a discount of $7,391.90, resulting in a carrying value of $92,608.10. Illustration 6-45 shows the effective-interest amortization schedule for Alltech's bonds.

SCHEDULE OF BOND DISCOUNT AMORTIZATION
5-YEAR, 9% BONDS SOLD TO YIELD 11%

Date	Cash Interest Paid	Interest Expense	Bond Discount Amortization	Carrying Value of Bonds
1/1/07				$92,608.10
12/31/07	$9,000[a]	$10,186.89[b]	$1,186.89[c]	93,794.99[d]
12/31/08	9,000	10,317.45	1,317.45	95,112.44
12/31/09	9,000	10,462.37	1,462.37	96,574.81
12/31/10	9,000	10,623.23	1,623.23	98,198.04
12/31/11	9,000	10,801.96	1,801.96	100,000.00
	$45,000	$52,391.90	$7,391.90	

[a]$100,000 ×.09 = $9,000   [c]$10,186.89 − $9,000 = $1,186.89
[b]$92,608.10 ×.11 = $10,186.89   [d]$92,608.10 + $1,186.89 = $93,794.99

ILLUSTRATION 6-45
Effective-Interest
Amortization Schedule

We use the amortization schedule illustrated above for note and bond transactions in Chapters 7 and 14.

PRESENT VALUE MEASUREMENT

In the past, most accounting calculations of present value relied on the most likely cash flow amount. *Concepts Statement No. 7* introduces an **expected cash flow approach**.[7] It uses a range of cash flows and incorporates the probabilities of those cash flows to provide a more relevant measurement of present value.

To illustrate the expected cash flow model, assume that there is a 30% probability that future cash flows will be $100, a 50% probability that they will be $200, and a 20% probability that they will be $300. In this case, the expected cash flow would be $190 [($100 × 0.3) + ($200 × 0.5) + ($300 × 0.2)]. Traditional present value approaches would use the most likely estimate ($200). However, that estimate fails to consider the different probabilities of the possible cash flows.

OBJECTIVE 9
Apply expected cash
flows to present value
measurement.

---

[7]"Using Cash Flow Information and Present Value in Accounting Measurements," *Statement of Financial Accounting Concepts No. 7* (Norwalk, Conn.: FASB, 2000).

FED WATCHING

A popular pastime in today's financial markets is "Fed watching." Why is the practice of following the policy decisions of the Federal Reserve Bank and its chair, Alan Greenspan (now Ben Bernanke), of interest? Through a number of policy options, the Fed has the ability to move interest rates up or down—and these rate changes can affect the wealth of all market participants. For example, if the Fed wants to raise rates (because the overall economy is getting overheated), it can raise the discount rate, which is the rate banks pay to borrow money from the Fed. This rate increase will factor into the rates banks and other creditors use to lend money. As a result, companies will think twice about borrowing money to expand their businesses. The result will be a slowing economy. A rate cut does just the opposite: It makes borrowing cheaper, and can help the economy expand as more companies borrow to expand their operations.

But what is good for the borrowers may not be so good for lenders. Banks earn interest on loans and investments and pay interest to depositors, and recently, with long-term rates remaining at nearly all-time lows, some banks are now at risk if interest rates rise. This is because the banks get squeezed when they make long-term loans at fixed rates (e.g., 30-year mortgage loans) but pay depositors variable rates on shorter-term deposits (e.g., 6-month certificates of deposit). The banks lose if the Fed raises rates because they will continue to earn lower returns on their long-term loans but pay higher interest on deposits.

Some banks–**Fifth-Third Bank** and **New York Community Bancorp**—recently incurred significant charges to change the balance of their assets and liabilities to guard against higher interest rates. So it is not surprising that all companies, whether borrowers or lenders, are Fed watchers.

Source: Adapted from David Franecki, "Thanks, Alan: These Stock Groups Stand to Gain from Fed Rate Cuts," *Barrons Online* (January 22, 2001); and A. C. Puwaslki; "Banks Exposed to a Flattening Yield Curve and Rising Interest Rates," *Industry Analysis: Regional Banks and Thrifts,* Center for Financial Research and Analysis (February 23, 2005).

Choosing an Appropriate Interest Rate

After determining expected cash flows, a company must then use the proper interest rate to discount the cash flows. The interest rate used for this purpose has three components:

THREE COMPONENTS OF INTEREST

1 *PURE RATE OF INTEREST (2%–4%).* This would be the amount a lender would charge if there were no possibilities of default and no expectation of inflation.

2 *EXPECTED INFLATION RATE OF INTEREST (0%–?).* Lenders recognize that in an inflationary economy, they are being paid back with less valuable dollars. As a result, they increase their interest rate to compensate for this loss in purchasing power. When inflationary expectations are high, interest rates are high.

3 *CREDIT RISK RATE OF INTEREST (0%–5%).* The government has little or no credit risk (i.e., risk of nonpayment) when it issues bonds. A business enterprise, however, depending upon its financial stability, profitability, etc., can have a low or a high credit risk.

The FASB takes the position that after computing the expected cash flows, a company should discount those cash flows by the **risk-free rate of return**. That rate is defined as **the pure rate of return plus the expected inflation rate**. The Board notes that the expected cash flow framework adjusts for credit risk because it incorporates the probability of receipt or payment into the computation of expected cash flows. Therefore, the rate used to discount the expected cash flows should consider only the pure rate of interest and the inflation rate.

Example of Expected Cash Flow

To illustrate, assume that Al's Appliance Outlet offers a 2-year warranty on all products sold. In 2007 Al's Appliance sold $250,000 of a particular type of clothes dryer. Al's Appliance entered into an agreement with Ralph's Repair to provide all warranty service on the dryers sold in 2007. To determine the warranty expense to record in 2007 and the amount of warranty liability to record on the December 31, 2007, balance sheet, Al's Appliance must measure the fair value of the agreement. Since there is not a ready market for these warranty contracts, Al's Appliance uses expected cash flow techniques to value the warranty obligation.

Based on prior warranty experience, Al's Appliance estimates the expected cash outflows associated with the dryers sold in 2007, as shown in Illustration 6-46.

	Cash Flow Estimate	×	Probability Assessment	=	Expected Cash Flow
2007	$3,800		20%		$ 760
	6,300		50%		3,150
	7,500		30%		2,250
			Total		$6,160
2008	$5,400		30%		$1,620
	7,200		50%		3,600
	8,400		20%		1,680
			Total		$6,900

ILLUSTRATION 6-46
Expected Cash
Outflows—Warranties

Applying expected cash flow concepts to these data, Al's Appliance estimates warranty cash outflows of $6,160 in 2008 and $6,900 in 2009.

Illustration 6-47 shows the present value of these cash flows, assuming a risk-free rate of 5 percent and cash flows occurring at the end of the year.

Year	Expected Cash Flow	×	PV Factor, $i = 5\%$	=	Present Value
2007	$6,160		0.95238		$ 5,866.66
2008	6,900		0.90703		6,258.51
			Total		$12,125.17

ILLUSTRATION 6-47
Present Value of Cash
Flows

KEY TERMS

annuity, *264*

annuity due, *264*

compound interest, *255*

deferred annuity, *275*

discounting, *259*

effective yield, *258*

effective-interest
    method, *278*

expected cash flow
    approach, *279*

face rate, *258*

future value, *259*

future value of an
    annuity, *264*

interest, *253*

nominal rate, *258*

ordinary annuity, *264*

present value, *259*

principal, *253*

risk-free rate of
    return, *281*

simple interest, *254*

stated rate, *258*

time value of money, *252*

SUMMARY OF LEARNING OBJECTIVES

1. Identify accounting topics where the time value of money is relevant. Some of the applications of present value–based measurements to accounting topics are: (1) notes, (2) leases, (3) pensions and other postretirement benefits, (4) long-term assets, (5) sinking funds, (6) business combinations, (7) disclosures, and (8) installment contracts.

2. Distinguish between simple and compound interest. See items 1 and 2 in the Fundamental Concepts on page 283.

3. Use appropriate compound interest tables. In order to identify which of the five compound interest tables to use, determine whether you are solving for (1) the future value of a single sum, (2) the present value of a single sum, (3) the future value of a series of sums (an annuity), or (4) the present value of a series of sums (an annuity). In addition, when a series of sums (an annuity) is involved, identify whether these sums are received or paid (1) at the beginning of each period (annuity due) or (2) at the end of each period (ordinary annuity).

4. Identify variables fundamental to solving interest problems. The following four variables are fundamental to all compound interest problems: (1) *Rate of interest:* unless otherwise stated, an annual rate, adjusted to reflect the length of the compounding period if less than a year. (2) *Number of time periods:* the number of compounding periods (a period may be equal to or less than a year). (3) *Future value:* the value at a future date of a given sum or sums invested assuming compound interest. (4) *Present value:* the value now (present time) of a future sum or sums discounted assuming compound interest.

5. Solve future and present value of 1 problems. See items 5(a) and 6(a) in the Fundamental Concepts on page 283.

6. Solve future value of ordinary and annuity due problems. See item 5(b) in the Fundamental Concepts on page 283.

7. Solve present value of ordinary and annuity due problems. See item 6(b) in the Fundamental Concepts on page 283.

8. Solve present value problems related to deferred annuities and bonds. Deferred annuities are annuities in which rents begin after a specified number of periods. The future value of a deferred annuity is computed the same as the future value of an annuity not deferred. To find the present value of a deferred annuity, compute the present value of an ordinary annuity of 1 as if the rents had occurred for the entire period, and then subtract the present value of rents not received during the deferral period. The current market value of bonds combines the present values of the interest annuity and the principal amount.

9. Apply expected cash flows to present value measurement. The expected cash flow approach uses a range of cash flows and the probabilities of those cash flows to provide the most likely estimate of expected cash flows. The proper interest rate used to discount the cash flows is the risk-free rate of return.

FUNDAMENTAL CONCEPTS

1 *SIMPLE INTEREST.* Interest on principal only, regardless of interest that may have accrued in the past.

2 *COMPOUND INTEREST.* Interest accrues on the unpaid interest of past periods as well as on the principal.

3 *RATE OF INTEREST.* Interest is usually expressed as an annual rate, but when the compounding period is shorter than one year, the interest rate for the shorter period must be determined.

4 *ANNUITY.* A series of payments or receipts (called rents) that occur at equal intervals of time. Types of annuities:

  (a) *Ordinary Annuity.* Each rent is payable (receivable) at the end of the period.

  (b) *Annuity Due.* Each rent is payable (receivable) at the beginning of the period.

5 *FUTURE VALUE.* Value at a later date of a single sum that is invested at compound interest.

  (a) *Future Value of 1* (or value of a single sum). The future value of $1 (or a single given sum), *FV*, at the end of *n* periods at *i* compound interest rate (Table 6-1).

  (b) *Future Value of an Annuity.* The future value of a series of rents invested at compound interest. In other words, the accumulated total that results from a series of equal deposits at regular intervals invested at compound interest. Both deposits and interest increase the accumulation.

    (1) *Future Value of an Ordinary Annuity.* The future value on the date of the last rent (Table 6-3).

    (2) *Future Value of an Annuity Due.* The future value one period after the date of the last rent. When an annuity due table is not available, use Table 6-3 with the following formula.

$$\text{Value of annuity due of 1 for } n \text{ rents} = \text{(Value of ordinary annuity for } n \text{ rents)} \times (1 + \text{interest rate})$$

6 *PRESENT VALUE.* The value at an earlier date (usually now) of a given future sum discounted at compound interest.

  (a) *Present Value of 1* (or present value of a single sum). The present value (worth) of $1 (or a given sum), due *n* periods hence, discounted at *i* compound interest (Table 6-2).

  (b) *Present Value of an Annuity.* The present value (worth) of a series of rents discounted at compound interest. In other words, it is the sum when invested at compound interest that will permit a series of equal withdrawals at regular intervals.

    (1) *Present Value of an Ordinary Annuity.* The value now of $1 to be received or paid at the end of each period (rents) for *n* periods, discounted at *i* compound interest (Table 6-4).

    (2) *Present Value of an Annuity Due.* The value now of $1 to be received or paid at the beginning of each period (rents) for *n* periods, discounted at *i* compound interest (Table 6-5). To use Table 4 for an annuity due, apply this formula.

$$\text{Present value of annuity due of 1 for } n \text{ rents} = \text{(Present value of an ordinary annuity of } n \text{ rents} \times (1 + \text{interest rate})$$

APPENDIX 6A

Using Financial Calculators

OBJECTIVE 10
Use a financial
calculator to solve
time value of money
problems.

Business professionals, once they have mastered the underlying concepts in Chapter 6, will often use a financial (business) calculator to solve time value of money problems. In many cases, they must use calculators if interest rates or time periods do not correspond with the information provided in the compound interest tables.

To use financial calculators, you enter the time value of money variables into the calculator. Illustration 6A-1 shows the five most common keys used to solve time value of money problems.[1]

ILLUSTRATION 6A-1
Financial Calculator Keys

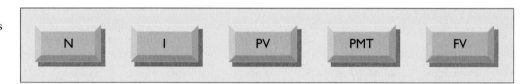

where

$$
\begin{aligned}
&\text{N} &&= \text{number of periods} \\
&\text{I} &&= \text{interest rate per period (some calculators use I/YR or i)} \\
&\text{PV} &&= \text{present value (occurs at the beginning of the first period)} \\
&\text{PMT} &&= \text{payment (all payments are equal, and none are skipped)} \\
&\text{FV} &&= \text{future value (occurs at the end of the last period)}
\end{aligned}
$$

In solving time value of money problems in this appendix, you will generally be given three of four variables and will have to solve for the remaining variable. The fifth key (the key not used) is given a value of zero to ensure that this variable is not used in the computation.

Use of Spreadsheets to Solve Time Value of Money Problems

FUTURE VALUE OF A SINGLE SUM

To illustrate the use of a financial calculator, let's assume that you want to know the future value of $50,000 invested to earn 11%, compounded annually for 5 years, as pictured in Illustration 6A-2.

ILLUSTRATION 6A-2
Calculator Solution for Future Value of a Single Sum

---

[1]On many calculators, these keys are actual buttons on the face of the calculator; on others, they appear on the display after the user accesses a present value menu.

The diagram shows you the information (inputs) to enter into the calculator: N = 5, I = 11, PV = −50,000, and PMT = 0. You then press FV for the answer: $84,253. This is the same answer as shown on page 260, when we used compound interest tables to compute the future value of a single sum. As indicated, the PMT key was given a value of zero because a series of payments did not occur in this problem.

Plus and Minus

The use of plus and minus signs in time value of money problems with a financial calculator can be confusing. Most financial calculators are programmed so that the positive and negative cash flows in any problem offset each other. In the future value problem above, we identified the 50,000 initial investment as a negative (outflow); the answer 84,253 was shown as a positive, reflecting a cash inflow. If the 50,000 were entered as a positive, then the final answer would have been reported as a negative (−84,253).

Hopefully, the sign convention will not cause confusion. If you understand what is required in a problem, you should be able to interpret a positive or negative amount in determining the solution to a problem.

Compounding Periods

In the problem above, we assumed that compounding occurs once a year. Some financial calculators have a default setting, which assumes that compounding occurs 12 times a year. You must determine what default period has been programmed into your calculator and change it as necessary to arrive at the proper compounding period.

Rounding

Most financial calculators store and calculate using 12 decimal places. As a result, because compound interest tables generally have factors only up to 5 decimal places, a slight difference in the final answer can result. In most time value of money problems, the final answer will not include more than two decimal points.

PRESENT VALUE OF A SINGLE SUM

To illustrate how a present value problem is solved using a financial calculator, assume that you want to know the present value of $84,253 to be received in 5 years, discounted at 11% compounded annually. Illustration 6A-3 pictures this problem.

ILLUSTRATION 6A-3
Calculator Solution for Present Value of a Single Sum

In this case, you enter N = 5, I = 11, PMT = 0, FV = 84,253, and then press the PV key to find the present value of $50,000.

FUTURE VALUE OF AN ORDINARY ANNUITY

To illustrate the future value of an ordinary annuity, assume that you are asked to determine the future value of five $5,000 deposits made at the end of each of the next 5 years, each of which earns interest at 12%, compounded annually, as pictured in Illustration 6A-4 (on page 286).

ILLUSTRATION 6A-4
Calculator Solution for
Future Value of an
Ordinary Annuity

In this case, you enter N = 5, I = 12, PV = 0, PMT = −5,000, and then press FV to arrive at the answer $31,764.24.[2] The $5,000 payments are shown as negatives because the deposits represent cash outflows that will accumulate with interest to the amount to be received (cash inflow) at the end of 5 years.

FUTURE VALUE OF AN ANNUITY DUE

Recall from the discussion in Chapter 6 that in any annuity problem you must determine whether the periodic payments occur at the *beginning* or the *end* of the period. If the first payment occurs at the beginning of the period, most financial calculators have a key marked "Begin" (or "Due") that you press to switch from the end-of-period payment mode (for an ordinary annuity) to beginning-of-period payment mode (for an annuity due). For most calculators, the word BEGIN is displayed to indicate that the calculator is set for an annuity due problem. (Some calculators use DUE.)

To illustrate a future value of an annuity due problem, let's revisit a problem from Chapter 6: Sue Lotadough plans to deposit $800 per year in a fund on each of her son's birthdays, starting today (his tenth birthday). All amounts on deposit in the fund will earn 6% compounded annually. Sue wants to know the amount she will have accumulated for college expenses on her son's eighteenth birthday. She will make 8 deposits into the fund. (Assume no deposit will be made on the eighteenth birthday.) This problem is pictured in Illustration 6A-5.

ILLUSTRATION 6A-5
Calculator Solution for
Future Value of an
Annuity Due

In this case, you enter N = 8, I = 6, PV = 0, PMT = −800, and then press FV to arrive at the answer of $8,393.05. You must be in the BEGIN or DUE mode to solve this problem correctly. Before starting to solve any annuity problem, make sure that your calculator is switched to the proper mode.

PRESENT VALUE OF AN ORDINARY ANNUITY

To illustrate how to solve a present value of an ordinary annuity problem using a financial calculator, assume that you are asked to determine the present value of rental receipts of $6,000 each to be received at the end of each of the next 5 years, when discounted at 12%, as pictured in Illustration 6A-6.

---

[2]Note that on page 266 the answer using the compound interest tables is $31,764.25—a difference of 1 cent due to rounding.

ILLUSTRATION 6A-6
Calculator Solution for
Present Value of an
Ordinary Annuity

In this case, you enter N = 5, I = 12, PMT = 6,000, FV = 0, and then press PV to arrive at the answer of $21,628.66.[3]

USEFUL APPLICATIONS OF THE FINANCIAL CALCULATOR

With a financial calculator you can solve for any interest rate or for any number of periods in a time value of money problem. Here are some examples of these applications.

Auto Loan

Assume you are financing a car with a 3-year loan. The loan has a 9.5% nominal annual interest rate, compounded monthly. The price of the car is $6,000, and you want to determine the monthly payments, assuming that the payments start one month after the purchase. This problem is pictured in Illustration 6A-7.

ILLUSTRATION 6A-7
Calculator Solution for
Auto Loan Payments

By entering N = 36 (12 × 3), I = 9.5, PV = 6,000, FV = 0, and then pressing PMT, you can determine that the monthly payments will be $192.20. Note that the payment key is usually programmed for 12 payments per year. Thus, you must change the default (compounding period) if the payments are different than monthly.

Mortgage Loan Amount

Let's say you are evaluating financing options for a loan on your house. You decide that the maximum mortgage payment you can afford is $700 per month. The annual interest rate is 8.4%. If you get a mortgage that requires you to make monthly payments over a 15-year period, what is the maximum purchase price you can afford? Illustration 6A-8 depicts this problem.

ILLUSTRATION 6A-8
Calculator Solution for
Mortgage Amount

---

[3]If the rental payments were received at the beginning of the year, then it would be necessary to switch to the BEGIN or DUE mode. In this case, the present value of the payments would be $24,224.10.

Entering N = 180 (12 × 15 years), I = 8.4, PMT = −700, FV = 0, and pressing PV, you find a present value of $71,509.81—the maximum house price you can afford, given that you want to keep your mortgage payments at $700. Note that by changing any of the variables, you can quickly conduct "what-if" analyses for different factual situations.

Individual Retirement Account (IRA)

Assume you opened an IRA on April 15, 1997, with a deposit of $2,000. Since then you have deposited $100 in the account every 2 weeks (26 deposits per year, with the first $100 deposit made on April 29, 1997). The account pays 7.6% annual interest compounded semi-monthly (with each deposit). How much will be in the account on April 15, 2007? Illustration 6A-9 depicts this problem.

ILLUSTRATION 6A-9
Calculator Solution for
IRA Balance

By entering N = 260 (26 × 10 years), I = 7.6, PV = −2,000, PMT = −100, and pressing FV, you determine the future value of $43,131.79. This is the amount that the IRA will grow to over the 10-year period. Note that in this problem we use four of the keys and solve for the fifth. Thus, we combine the future value of a single sum and of an annuity. Other problems similar to this are illustrated in Chapters 7 and 14.

SUMMARY OF LEARNING OBJECTIVE FOR APPENDIX 6A

10. Use a financial calculator to solve time value of money problems. Financial calculators can be used to solve the same and additional problems as those solved with time value of money tables. One enters into the financial calculator the amounts for all but one of the unknown elements of a time value of money problem (periods, interest rate, payments, future or present value). Particularly useful situations involve interest rates and compounding periods not presented in the tables.

Note: All **asterisked** Exercises and Problems relate to material contained in the chapter appendix. You will need a calculator for these assignments.

QUESTIONS

1. What is the time value of money? Why should accountants have an understanding of compound interest, annuities, and present value concepts?

2. Identify three situations in which accounting measures are based on present values. Do these present value applications involve single sums or annuities, or both single sums and annuities? Explain.

3. What is the nature of interest? Distinguish between "simple interest" and "compound interest."

4. What are the components of an interest rate? Why is it important for accountants to understand these components?

5. Presented are a number of values taken from compound interest tables involving the same number of periods and the same rate of interest. Indicate what each of these four values represents.

(a) 6.71008   **(c)** .46319
(b) 2.15892   **(d)** 14.48656

6. Bill Jones is considering two investment options for a $1,000 gift he received for graduation. Both investments have 8% annual interest rates. One offers quarterly compounding; the other compounds on a semiannual basis. Which investment should he choose? Why?

7. Brenda Starr deposited $18,000 in a money market certificate that provides interest of 10% compounded quarterly if the amount is maintained for 3 years. How much will Brenda Starr have at the end of 3 years?

8. Charlie Brown will receive $50,000 on December 31, 2012 (5 years from now) from a trust fund established by his father. Assuming the appropriate interest rate for discounting is 12% (compounded semiannually), what is the present value of this amount today?

9. What are the primary characteristics of an annuity? Differentiate between an "ordinary annuity" and an "annuity due."

10. Linus, Inc. owes $30,000 to Peanuts Company. How much would Linus have to pay each year if the debt is retired through four equal payments (made at the end of the year), given an interest rate on the debt of 12%? (Round to two decimal places.)

11. The Forths are planning for a retirement home. They estimate they will need $160,000, 4 years from now to purchase this home. Assuming an interest rate of 10%, what amount must be deposited at the end of each of the 4 years to fund the home price? (Round to two decimal places.)

12. Assume the same situation as in Question 11, except that the four equal amounts are deposited at the beginning of the period rather than at the end. In this case, what amount must be deposited at the beginning of each period? (Round to two decimals.)

13. Explain how the future value of an ordinary annuity interest table is converted to the future value of an annuity due interest table.

14. Explain how the present value of an ordinary annuity interest table is converted to the present value of an annuity due interest table.

15. In a book named *Treasure,* the reader has to figure out where a 2.2 pound, 24 kt gold horse has been buried. If the horse is found, a prize of $25,000 a year for 20 years is provided. The actual cost of the publisher to purchase an annuity to pay for the prize is $210,000. What

interest rate (to the nearest percent) was used to determine the amount of the annuity? (Assume end-of-year payments.)

16. Greg Norman Enterprises leases property to Tiger Woods, Inc. Because Tiger Woods, Inc. is experiencing financial difficulty, Norman agrees to receive five rents of $10,000 at the end of each year, with the rents deferred 3 years. What is the present value of the five rents discounted at 12%?

17. Answer the following questions.

(a) On May 1, 2007, Liselotte Neumann Company sold some machinery to Tee-off Company on an installment contract basis. The contract required five equal annual payments, with the first payment due on May 1, 2007. What present value concept is appropriate for this situation?

(b) On June 1, 2007, Mike Brisky Inc. purchased a new machine that it does not have to pay for until May 1, 2009. The total payment on May 1, 2009, will include both principal and interest. Assuming interest at a 12% rate, the cost of the machine would be the total payment multiplied by what time value of money concept?

(c) Kelly Gibson Inc. wishes to know how much money it will have available in 5 years if five equal amounts of $35,000 are invested, with the first amount invested immediately. What interest table is appropriate for this situation?

(d) Patty Sheehan invests in a "jumbo" $200,000, 3-year certificate of deposit at First Wisconsin Bank. What table would be used to determine the amount accumulated at the end of 3 years?

18. Recently Vickie Maher was interested in purchasing a Honda Acura. The salesperson indicated that the price of the car was either $27,000 cash or $6,900 at the end of each of 5 years. Compute the effective interest rate to the nearest percent that Vickie would pay if she chooses to make the five annual payments.

19. Recently, property/casualty insurance companies have been criticized because they reserve for the total loss as much as 5 years before it may happen. The IRS has joined the debate because they say the full reserve is unfair from a taxation viewpoint. What do you believe is the IRS position?

BRIEF EXERCISES

(LO 5)   **BE6-1**   Steve Allen invested $10,000 today in a fund that earns 8% compounded annually. To what amount will the investment grow in 3 years? To what amount would the investment grow in 3 years if the fund earns 8% annual interest compounded semiannually?

(LO 5)   **BE6-2**   Itzak Perlman needs $20,000 in 4 years. What amount must he invest today if his investment earns 12% compounded annually? What amount must he invest if his investment earns 12% annual interest compounded quarterly?

(LO 5)   **BE6-3**   Natalie Portman will invest $30,000 today. She needs $222,000 in 21 years. What annual interest rate must she earn?

(LO 5)   **BE6-4**   Dan Webster will invest $10,000 today in a fund that earns 5% annual interest. How many years will it take for the fund to grow to $13,400?

(LO 6)   **BE6-5**   Anne Boleyn will invest $5,000 a year for 20 years in a fund that will earn 12% annual interest. If the first payment into the fund occurs today, what amount will be in the fund in 20 years? If the first payment occurs at year-end, what amount will be in the fund in 20 years?

(LO 6)   **BE6-6**   William Cullen Bryant needs $200,000 in 10 years. How much must he invest at the end of each year, at 11% interest, to meet his needs?

(LO 5)   **BE6-7**   Jack Thompson's lifelong dream is to own his own fishing boat to use in his retirement. Jack has recently come into an inheritance of $400,000. He estimates that the boat he wants will cost $350,000 when he retires in 5 years. How much of his inheritance must he invest at an annual rate of 12% (compounded annually) to buy the boat at retirement?

(LO 5)   **BE6-8**   Refer to the data in BE6-7. Assuming quarterly compounding of amounts invested at 12%, how much of Jack Thompson's inheritance must be invested to have enough at retirement to buy the boat?

(LO 6)   **BE6-9**   Luther Vandross is investing $12,961 at the end of each year in a fund that earns 10% interest. In how many years will the fund be at $100,000?

(LO 7)   **BE6-10**   Grupo Rana wants to withdraw $20,000 each year for 10 years from a fund that earns 8% interest. How much must he invest today if the first withdrawal is at year-end? How much must he invest today if the first withdrawal takes place immediately?

(LO 7)   **BE6-11**   Mark Twain's VISA balance is $1,124.40. He may pay it off in 18 equal end-of-month payments of $75 each. What interest rate is Mark paying?

(LO 7)   **BE6-12**   Corinne Dunbar is investing $200,000 in a fund that earns 8% interest compounded annually. What equal amounts can Corinne withdraw at the end of each of the next 20 years?

(LO 6)   **BE6-13**   Bayou Inc. will deposit $20,000 in a 12% fund at the end of each year for 8 years beginning December 31, 2007. What amount will be in the fund immediately after the last deposit?

(LO 7)   **BE6-14**   Hollis Stacy wants to create a fund today that will enable her to withdraw $20,000 per year for 8 years, with the first withdrawal to take place 5 years from today. If the fund earns 8% interest, how much must Hollis invest today?

(LO 8)   **BE6-15**   Acadian Inc. issues $1,000,000 of 7% bonds due in 10 years with interest payable at year-end. The current market rate of interest for bonds of similar risk is 8%. What amount will Acadian receive when it issues the bonds?

(LO 7)   **BE6-16**   Walt Frazier is settling a $20,000 loan due today by making 6 equal annual payments of $4,864.51. Determine the interest rate on this loan, if the payments begin one year after the loan is signed.

(LO 7)   **BE6-17**   Consider the loan in BE6-16. What payments must Walt Frazier make to settle the loan at the same interest rate but with the 6 payments beginning on the day the loan is signed?

EXERCISES

(Interest rates are per annum unless otherwise indicated.)

(LO 3)   **E6-1   (Using Interest Tables)**   For each of the following cases, indicate (a) to what rate columns, and (b) to what number of periods you would refer in looking up the interest factor.

   1.   In a future value of 1 table

Annual Rate	Number of Years Invested	Compounded
a. 9%	9	Annually
b. 12%	5	Quarterly
c. 10%	15	Semiannually

2. In a present value of an annuity of 1 table

Annual Rate	Number of Years Involved	Number of Rents Involved	Frequency of Rents
a. 9%	25	25	Annually
b. 10%	15	30	Semiannually
c. 12%	7	28	Quarterly

(LO 2, 5)
E6-2 **(Simple and Compound Interest Computations)** Alan Jackson invests $20,000 at 8% annual interest, leaving the money invested without withdrawing any of the interest for 8 years. At the end of the 8 years, Alan withdrew the accumulated amount of money.

▶ **Instructions**
    (a) Compute the amount Alan would withdraw assuming the investment earns simple interest.
    (b) Compute the amount Alan would withdraw assuming the investment earns interest compounded annually.
    (c) Compute the amount Alan would withdraw assuming the investment earns interest compounded semiannually.

(LO 5, 6, 7)
E6-3 **(Computation of Future Values and Present Values)** Using the appropriate interest table, answer each of the following questions. (Each case is independent of the others.)

    (a) What is the future value of $7,000 at the end of 5 periods at 8% compounded interest?
    (b) What is the present value of $7,000 due 8 periods hence, discounted at 11%?
    (c) What is the future value of 15 periodic payments of $7,000 each made at the end of each period and compounded at 10%?
    (d) What is the present value of $7,000 to be received at the end of each of 20 periods, discounted at 5% compound interest?

(LO 6, 7)
E6-4 **(Computation of Future Values and Present Values)** Using the appropriate interest table, answer the following questions. (Each case is independent of the others).

    (a) What is the future value of 20 periodic payments of $4,000 each made at the beginning of each period and compounded at 8%?
    (b) What is the present value of $2,500 to be received at the beginning of each of 30 periods, discounted at 10% compound interest?
    (c) What is the future value of 15 deposits of $2,000 each made at the beginning of each period and compounded at 10%? (Future value as of the end of the fifteenth period.)
    (d) What is the present value of six receipts of $1,000 each received at the beginning of each period, discounted at 9% compounded interest?

(LO 6, 7)
E6-5 **(Computation of Present Value)** Using the appropriate interest table, compute the present values of the following periodic amounts due at the end of the designated periods.

    (a) $30,000 receivable at the end of each period for 8 periods compounded at 12%.
    (b) $30,000 payments to be made at the end of each period for 16 periods at 9%.
    (c) $30,000 payable at the end of the seventh, eighth, ninth, and tenth periods at 12%.

(LO 5, 6, 7)
E6-6 **(Future Value and Present Value Problems)** Presented below are three unrelated situations.

    (a) Dwayne Wade Company recently signed a lease for a new office building, for a lease period of 10 years. Under the lease agreement, a security deposit of $12,000 is made, with the deposit to be returned at the expiration of the lease, with interest compounded at 10% per year. What amount will the company receive at the time the lease expires?
    (b) Serena Williams Corporation, having recently issued a $20 million, 15-year bond issue, is committed to make annual sinking fund deposits of $600,000. The deposits are made on the last day of each year and yield a return of 10%. Will the fund at the end of 15 years be sufficient to retire the bonds? If not, what will the deficiency be?
    (c) Under the terms of his salary agreement, president Rex Walters has an option of receiving either an immediate bonus of $40,000, or a deferred bonus of $70,000 payable in 10 years. Ignoring tax considerations, and assuming a relevant interest rate of 8%, which form of settlement should Walters accept?

(LO 8)
E6-7 **(Computation of Bond Prices)** What would you pay for a $50,000 debenture bond that matures in 15 years and pays $5,000 a year in interest if you wanted to earn a yield of:

    (a) 8%?   **(b)** 10%?   **(c)** 12%?

(LO 8)
E6-8 **(Computations for a Retirement Fund)** Clarence Weatherspoon, a super salesman contemplating retirement on his fifty-fifth birthday, decides to create a fund on an 8% basis that will enable him to

withdraw $20,000 per year on June 30, beginning in 2014 and continuing through 2017. To develop this fund, Clarence intends to make equal contributions on June 30 of each of the years 2010–2013.

Instructions

(a) How much must the balance of the fund equal on June 30, 2013, in order for Clarence Weatherspoon to satisfy his objective?

(b) What are each of Clarence's contributions to the fund?

(L0 5) **E6-9 (Unknown Rate)** LEW Company purchased a machine at a price of $100,000 by signing a note payable, which requires a single payment of $123,210 in 2 years. Assuming annual compounding of interest, what rate of interest is being paid on the loan?

(L0 5) **E6-10 (Unknown Periods and Unknown Interest Rate)** Consider the following independent situations.

(a) Mike Finley wishes to become a millionaire. His money market fund has a balance of $92,296 and has a guaranteed interest rate of 10%. How many years must Mike leave that balance in the fund in order to get his desired $1,000,000?

(b) Assume that Serena Williams desires to accumulate $1 million in 15 years using her money market fund balance of $182,696. At what interest rate must Serena's investment compound annually?

(L0 7) **E6-11 (Evaluation of Purchase Options)** Sosa Excavating Inc. is purchasing a bulldozer. The equipment has a price of $100,000. The manufacturer has offered a payment plan that would allow Sosa to make 10 equal annual payments of $16,274.53, with the first payment due one year after the purchase.

Instructions

(a) How much total interest will Sosa pay on this payment plan?

(b) Sosa could borrow $100,000 from its bank to finance the purchase at an annual rate of 9%. Should Sosa borrow from the bank or use the manufacturer's payment plan to pay for the equipment?

(L0 5, 6, 7) **E6-12 (Analysis of Alternatives)** The Black Knights Inc., a manufacturer of high-sugar, low-sodium, low-cholesterol TV dinners, would like to increase its market share in the Sunbelt. In order to do so, Black Knights has decided to locate a new factory in the Panama City area. Black Knights will either buy or lease a site depending upon which is more advantageous. The site location committee has narrowed down the available sites to the following three buildings.

Building A: Purchase for a cash price of $600,000, useful life 25 years.

Building B: Lease for 25 years with annual lease payments of $69,000 being made at the beginning of the year.

Building C: Purchase for $650,000 cash. This building is larger than needed; however, the excess space can be sublet for 25 years at a net annual rental of $7,000. Rental payments will be received at the end of each year. The Black Knights Inc. has no aversion to being a landlord.

Instructions

In which building would you recommend that The Black Knights Inc. locate, assuming a 12% cost of funds?

(L0 8) **E6-13 (Computation of Bond Liability)** Lance Armstrong Inc. manufactures cycling equipment. Recently the vice president of operations of the company has requested construction of a new plant to meet the increasing demand for the company's bikes. After a careful evaluation of the request, the board of directors has decided to raise funds for the new plant by issuing $2,000,000 of 11% term corporate bonds on March 1, 2007, due on March 1, 2022, with interest payable each March 1 and September 1. At the time of issuance, the market interest rate for similar financial instruments is 10%.

Instructions

As the controller of the company, determine the selling price of the bonds.

(L0 8) **E6-14 (Computation of Pension Liability)** Nerwin, Inc. is a furniture manufacturing company with 50 employees. Recently, after a long negotiation with the local labor union, the company decided to initiate a pension plan as a part of its compensation plan. The plan will start on January 1, 2007. Each employee covered by the plan is entitled to a pension payment each year after retirement. As required by accounting standards, the controller of the company needs to report the pension obligation (liability). On the basis of a discussion with the supervisor of the Personnel Department and an actuary from an insurance company, the controller develops the following information related to the pension plan.

Average length of time to retirement	15 years
Expected life duration after retirement	10 years
Total pension payment expected each year after retirement for all employees. Payment made at the end of the year.	$700,000 per year

The interest rate to be used is 8%.

Instructions

On the basis of the information above, determine the present value of the pension obligation (liability).

(LO 5, 6) **E6-15** **(Investment Decision)** Andrew Bogut just received a signing bonus of $1,000,000. His plan is to invest this payment in a fund that will earn 8%, compounded annually.

Instructions

(a) If Bogut plans to establish the AB Foundation once the fund grows to $1,999,000, how many years until he can establish the foundation?

(b) Instead of investing the entire $1,000,000, Bogut invests $300,000 today and plans to make 9 equal annual investments into the fund beginning one year from today. What amount should the payments be if Bogut plans to establish the $1,999,000 foundation at the end of 9 years?

(LO 6, 7) **E6-16** **(Retirement of Debt)** Jesper Parnevik borrowed $70,000 on March 1, 2005. This amount plus accrued interest at 12% compounded semiannually is to be repaid March 1, 2015. To retire this debt, Jesper plans to contribute to a debt retirement fund five equal amounts starting on March 1, 2010, and for the next 4 years. The fund is expected to earn 10% per annum.

Instructions

How much must be contributed each year by Jesper Parnevik to provide a fund sufficient to retire the debt on March 1, 2015?

(LO 7) **E6-17** **(Computation of Amount of Rentals)** Your client, Ron Santo Leasing Company, is preparing a contract to lease a machine to Souvenirs Corporation for a period of 25 years. Santo has an investment cost of $365,755 in the machine, which has a useful life of 25 years and no salvage value at the end of that time. Your client is interested in earning an 11% return on its investment and has agreed to accept 25 equal rental payments at the end of each of the next 25 years.

Instructions

You are requested to provide Santo with the amount of each of the 25 rental payments that will yield an 11% return on investment.

(LO 5, 7) **E6-18** **(Least Costly Payoff)** Assume that **Sonic Foundry Corporation** has a contractual debt outstanding. Sonic has available two means of settlement: It can either make immediate payment of $2,600,000, or it can make annual payments of $300,000 for 15 years, each payment due on the last day of the year.

Instructions

Which method of payment do you recommend, assuming an expected effective interest rate of 8% during the future period?

(LO 5, 7) **E6-19** **(Least Costly Payoff)** Assuming the same facts as those in E6-18 except that the payments must begin now and be made on the first day of each of the 15 years, what payment method would you recommend?

(LO 9) **E6-20** **(Expected Cash Flows)** For each of the following, determine the expected cash flows.

	Cash Flow Estimate	Probability Assessment
(a)	$ 3,800	20%
	6,300	50%
	7,500	30%
(b)	$ 5,400	30%
	7,200	50%
	8,400	20%
(c)	$(1,000)	10%
	2,000	80%
	5,000	10%

(LO 9) **E6-21** **(Expected Cash Flows and Present Value)** Andrew Kelly is trying to determine the amount to set aside so that he will have enough money on hand in 2 years to overhaul the engine on his vintage used car. While there is some uncertainty about the cost of engine overhauls in 2 years, by conducting some research online, Andrew has developed the following estimates.

Engine Overhaul Estimated Cash Outflow	Probability Assessment
$200	10%
450	30%
550	50%
750	10%

Instructions

How much should Andrew Kelly deposit today in an account earning 6%, compounded annually, so that he will have enough money on hand in 2 years to pay for the overhaul?

(LO 10) ***E6-22 (Determine Interest Rate)** Reba McEntire wishes to invest $19,000 on July 1, 2007, and have it accumulate to $49,000 by July 1, 2017.

Instructions

Use a financial calculator to determine at what exact annual rate of interest Reba must invest the $19,000.

(LO 10) ***E6-23 (Determine Interest Rate)** On July 17, 2006, Tim McGraw borrowed $42,000 from his grandfather to open a clothing store. Starting July 17, 2007, Tim has to make ten equal annual payments of $6,500 each to repay the loan.

Instructions

Use a financial calculator to determine what interest rate Tim is paying.

(LO 10) ***E6-24 (Determine Interest Rate)** As the purchaser of a new house, Patty Loveless has signed a mortgage note to pay the Memphis National Bank and Trust Co. $14,000 every 6 months for 20 years, at the end of which time she will own the house. At the date the mortgage is signed the purchase price was $198,000, and a down payment of $20,000 was made. The first payment will be made 6 months after the date the mortgage is signed.

Instructions

Using a financial calculator, compute the exact rate of interest earned on the mortgage by the bank.

See the book's website, www.wiley.com/college/kieso, for Additional Exercises.

PROBLEMS

(Interest rates are per annum unless otherwise indicated.)

(LO 5, 6, 7) **P6-1 (Various Time Value Situations)** Answer each of these unrelated questions.

   (a) On January 1, 2007, Aaron Brown Corporation sold a building that cost $250,000 and that had accumulated depreciation of $100,000 on the date of sale. Brown received as consideration a $275,000 noninterest-bearing note due on January 1, 2010. There was no established exchange price for the building, and the note had no ready market. The prevailing rate of interest for a note of this type on January 1, 2007, was 9%. At what amount should the gain from the sale of the building be reported?

   (b) On January 1, 2007, Aaron Brown Corporation purchased 200 of the $1,000 face value, 9%, 10-year bonds of Walters Inc. The bonds mature on January 1, 2017, and pay interest annually beginning January 1, 2008. Brown purchased the bonds to yield 11%. How much did Brown pay for the bonds?

   (c) Aaron Brown Corporation bought a new machine and agreed to pay for it in equal annual installments of $4,000 at the end of each of the next 10 years. Assuming that a prevailing interest rate of 8% applies to this contract, how much should Brown record as the cost of the machine?

   (d) Aaron Brown Corporation purchased a special tractor on December 31, 2007. The purchase agreement stipulated that Brown should pay $20,000 at the time of purchase and $5,000 at the end of each of the next 8 years. The tractor should be recorded on December 31, 2007, at what amount, assuming an appropriate interest rate of 12%?

   (e) Aaron Brown Corporation wants to withdraw $100,000 (including principal) from an investment fund at the end of each year for 9 years. What should be the required initial investment at the beginning of the first year if the fund earns 11%?

(LO 5, 6, 7) **P6-2 (Various Time Value Situations)** Using the appropriate interest table, provide the solution to each of the following four questions by computing the unknowns.

   (a) What is the amount of the payments that Tom Brokaw must make at the end of each of 8 years to accumulate a fund of $70,000 by the end of the eighth year, if the fund earns 8% interest, compounded annually?

   (b) Anderson Cooper is 40 years old today and he wishes to accumulate $500,000 by his sixty-fifth birthday so he can retire to his summer place on Lake Hopatcong. He wishes to accumulate this amount by making equal deposits on his fortieth through his sixty-fourth birthdays. What annual deposit must Anderson make if the fund will earn 12% interest compounded annually?

(c) Jane Pauley has $20,000 to invest today at 9% to pay a debt of $56,253. How many years will it take her to accumulate enough to liquidate the debt?

(d) Maria Shriver has a $27,600 debt that she wishes to repay 4 years from today; she has $18,181 that she intends to invest for the 4 years. What rate of interest will she need to earn annually in order to accumulate enough to pay the debt?

(LO 5, 6, 7) **P6-3** **(Analysis of Alternatives)** Assume that **Wal-Mart, Inc.** has decided to surface and maintain for 10 years a vacant lot next to one of its discount-retail outlets to serve as a parking lot for customers. Management is considering the following bids involving two different qualities of surfacing for a parking area of 12,000 square yards.

Bid A: A surface that costs $5.25 per square yard to install. This surface will have to be replaced at the end of 5 years. The annual maintenance cost on this surface is estimated at 20 cents per square yard for each year except the last year of its service. The replacement surface will be similar to the initial surface.

Bid B: A surface that costs $9.50 per square yard to install. This surface has a probable useful life of 10 years and will require annual maintenance in each year except the last year, at an estimated cost of 9 cents per square yard.

Instructions

Prepare computations showing which bid should be accepted by Wal-Mart, Inc. You may assume that the cost of capital is 9%, that the annual maintenance expenditures are incurred at the end of each year, and that prices are not expected to change during the next 10 years.

(LO 6, 7) **P6-4** **(Evaluating Payment Alternatives)** Terry O'Malley has just learned he has won a $900,000 prize in the lottery. The lottery has given him two options for receiving the payments: (1) If Terry takes all the money today, the state and federal governments will deduct taxes at a rate of 46% immediately. (2) Alternatively, the lottery offers Terry a payout of 20 equal payments of $62,000 with the first payment occurring when Terry turns in the winning ticket. Terry will be taxed on each of these payments at a rate of 25%.

Instructions

Assuming Terry can earn an 8% rate of return (compounded annually) on any money invested during this period, which pay-out option should he choose?

(LO 5, 6, 7) **P6-5** **(Analysis of Alternatives)** Sally Brown died, leaving to her husband Linus an insurance policy contract that provides that the beneficiary (Linus) can choose any one of the following four options.

(a) $55,000 immediate cash.

(b) $3,700 every 3 months payable at the end of each quarter for 5 years.

(c) $18,000 immediate cash and $1,600 every 3 months for 10 years, payable at the beginning of each 3-month period.

(d) $4,000 every 3 months for 3 years and $1,200 each quarter for the following 25 quarters, all payments payable at the end of each quarter.

Instructions

If money is worth 2½% per quarter, compounded quarterly, which option would you recommend that Linus exercise?

(LO 8) **P6-6** **(Purchase Price of a Business)** During the past year, Nicole Bobek planted a new vineyard on 150 acres of land that she leases for $27,000 a year. She has asked you as her accountant to assist her in determining the value of her vineyard operation.

The vineyard will bear no grapes for the first 5 years (1–5). In the next 5 years (6–10), Nicole estimates that the vines will bear grapes that can be sold for $60,000 each year. For the next 20 years (11–30) she expects the harvest will provide annual revenues of $100,000. But during the last 10 years (31–40) of the vineyard's life, she estimates that revenues will decline to $80,000 per year.

During the first 5 years the annual cost of pruning, fertilizing, and caring for the vineyard is estimated at $9,000; during the years of production, 6–40, these costs will rise to $10,000 per year. The relevant market rate of interest for the entire period is 12%. Assume that all receipts and payments are made at the end of each year.

Instructions

Dick Button has offered to buy Nicole's vineyard business by assuming the 40-year lease. On the basis of the current value of the business, what is the minimum price Nicole should accept?

(LO 5, 6, 7) **P6-7** **(Time Value Concepts Applied to Solve Business Problems)** Answer the following questions related to Derek Lee Inc.

(a) Derek Lee Inc. has $572,000 to invest. The company is trying to decide between two alternative uses of the funds. One alternative provides $80,000 at the end of each year for 12 years, and the other is to receive a single lump sum payment of $1,900,000 at the end of the 12 years. Which alternative should Lee select? Assume the interest rate is constant over the entire investment.

(b) Derek Lee Inc. has completed the purchase of new Dell computers. The fair market value of the equipment is $824,150. The purchase agreement specifies an immediate down payment of $200,000 and semiannual payments of $76,952 beginning at the end of 6 months for 5 years. What is the interest rate, to the nearest percent, used in discounting this purchase transaction?

(c) Derek Lee Inc. loans money to John Kruk Corporation in the amount of $600,000. Lee accepts an 8% note due in 7 years with interest payable semiannually. After 2 years (and receipt of interest for 2 years), Lee needs money and therefore sells the note to Chicago National Bank, which demands interest on the note of 10% compounded semiannually. What is the amount Lee will receive on the sale of the note?

(d) Derek Lee Inc. wishes to accumulate $1,300,000 by December 31, 2017, to retire bonds outstanding. The company deposits $300,000 on December 31, 2007, which will earn interest at 10% compounded quarterly, to help in the retirement of this debt. In addition, the company wants to know how much should be deposited at the end of each quarter for 10 years to ensure that $1,300,000 is available at the end of 2017. (The quarterly deposits will also earn at a rate of 10%, compounded quarterly.) (Round to even dollars.)

(LO 6, 7) **P6-8** **(Analysis of Alternatives)** Homer Simpson Inc., a manufacturer of steel school lockers, plans to purchase a new punch press for use in its manufacturing process. After contacting the appropriate vendors, the purchasing department received differing terms and options from each vendor. The Engineering Department has determined that each vendor's punch press is substantially identical and each has a useful life of 20 years. In addition, Engineering has estimated that required year-end maintenance costs will be $1,000 per year for the first 5 years, $2,000 per year for the next 10 years, and $3,000 per year for the last 5 years. Following is each vendor's sale package.

Vendor A: $45,000 cash at time of delivery and 10 year-end payments of $15,000 each. Vendor A offers all its customers the right to purchase at the time of sale a separate 20-year maintenance service contract, under which Vendor A will perform all year-end maintenance at a one-time initial cost of $10,000.

Vendor B: Forty seminannual payments of $8,000 each, with the first installment due upon delivery. Vendor B will perform all year-end maintenance for the next 20 years at no extra charge.

Vendor C: Full cash price of $125,000 will be due upon delivery.

Instructions
Assuming that both Vendor A and B will be able to perform the required year-end maintenance, that Simpson's cost of funds is 10%, and the machine will be purchased on January 1, from which vendor should the press be purchased?

(LO 5, 6, 7) **P6-9** **(Analysis of Business Problems)** Jean-Luc is a financial executive with Starship Enterprises. Although Jean-Luc has not had any formal training in finance or accounting, he has a "good sense" for numbers and has helped the company grow from a very small company ($500,000 sales) to a large operation ($45 million in sales). With the business growing steadily, however, the company needs to make a number of difficult financial decisions in which Jean-Luc feels a little "over his head." He therefore has decided to hire a new employee with "numbers" expertise to help him. As a basis for determining whom to employ, he has decided to ask each prospective employee to prepare answers to questions relating to the following situations he has encountered recently. Here are the questions.

(a) In 2005, Starship Enterprises negotiated and closed a long-term lease contract for newly constructed truck terminals and freight storage facilities. The buildings were constructed on land owned by the company. On January 1, 2006, Starship took possession of the leased property. The 20-year lease is effective for the period January 1, 2006, through December 31, 2025. Advance rental payments of $800,000 are payable to the lessor (owner of facilities) on January 1 of each of the first 10 years of the lease term. Advance payments of $300,000 are due on January 1 for each of the last 10 years of the lease term. Starship has an option to purchase all the leased facilities for $1 on December 31, 2025. At the time the lease was negotiated, the fair market value of the truck terminals and freight storage facilities was approximately $7,200,000. If the company had borrowed the money to purchase the facilities, it would have had to pay 10% interest. Should the company have purchased rather than leased the facilities?

(b) Last year the company exchanged a piece of land for a non-interest-bearing note. The note is to be paid at the rate of $12,000 per year for 9 years, beginning one year from the date of disposal of the land. An appropriate rate of interest for the note was 11%. At the time the land was originally purchased, it cost $90,000. What is the fair value of the note?

(c) The company has always followed the policy to take any cash discounts on goods purchased. Recently the company purchased a large amount of raw materials at a price of $800,000 with terms 2/10, n/30 on which it took the discount. Starship has recently estimated its cost of funds at 10%. Should Starship continue this policy of always taking the cash discount?

(LO 5, 6, 7) **P6-10** **(Analysis of Lease vs. Purchase)** Jose Rijo Inc. owns and operates a number of hardware stores in the New England region. Recently the company has decided to locate another store in a rapidly growing area of Maryland. The company is trying to decide whether to purchase or lease the building and related facilities.

Purchase: The company can purchase the site, construct the building, and purchase all store fixtures. The cost would be $1,650,000. An immediate down payment of $400,000 is required, and the remaining $1,250,000 would be paid off over 5 years at $300,000 per year (including interest). The property is expected to have a useful life of 12 years, and then it will be sold for $500,000. As the owner of the property, the company will have the following out-of-pocket expenses each period.

Property taxes (to be paid at the end of each year)	$40,000
Insurance (to be paid at the beginning of each year)	27,000
Other (primarily maintenance which occurs at the end of each year)	16,000
	$83,000

Lease: First National Bank has agreed to purchase the site, construct the building, and install the appropriate fixtures for Rijo Inc. if Rijo will lease the completed facility for 12 years. The annual costs for the lease would be $240,000. Rijo would have no responsibility related to the facility over the 12 years. The terms of the lease are that Rijo would be required to make 12 annual payments (the first payment to be made at the time the store opens and then each following year). In addition, a deposit of $100,000 is required when the store is opened. This deposit will be returned at the end of the twelfth year, assuming no unusual damage to the building structure or fixtures.

Currently the cost of funds for Rijo Inc. is 10%.

Instructions
Which of the two approaches should Rijo Inc. follow?

(LO 8) **P6-11** **(Pension Funding)** You have been hired as a benefit consultant by Maugarite Alomar, the owner of Attic Angels. She wants to establish a retirement plan for herself and her three employees. Maugarite has provided the following information: The retirement plan is to be based upon annual salary for the last year before retirement and is to provide 50% of Maugarite's last-year annual salary and 40% of the last-year annual salary for each employee. The plan will make annual payments at the beginning of each year for 20 years from the date of retirement. Maugarite wishes to fund the plan by making 15 annual deposits beginning January 1, 2007. Invested funds will earn 12% compounded annually. Information about plan participants as of January 1, 2007, is as follows.

Maugarite Alomar, owner: Current annual salary of $40,000; estimated retirement date January 1, 2032.

Kenny Rogers, flower arranger: Current annual salary of $30,000; estimated retirement date January 1, 2037.

Anita Baker, sales clerk: Current annual salary of $15,000; estimated retirement date January 1, 2027.

Willie Nelson, part-time bookkeeper: Current annual salary of $15,000; estimated retirement date January 1, 2022.

In the past, Maugarite has given herself and each employee a year-end salary increase of 4%. Maugarite plans to continue this policy in the future.

Instructions
(a) Based upon the above information, what will be the annual retirement benefit for each plan participant? (Round to the nearest dollar.) (*Hint:* Maugarite will receive raises for 24 years.)
(b) What amount must be on deposit at the end of 15 years to ensure that all benefits will be paid? (Round to the nearest dollar.)
(c) What is the amount of each annual deposit Maugarite must make to the retirement plan?

(LO 8) **P6-12** **(Pension Funding)** James Qualls, newly appointed controller of KBS, is considering ways to reduce his company's expenditures on annual pension costs. One way to do this is to switch KBS's pension fund assets from First Security to NET Life. KBS is a very well-respected computer manufacturer that recently has experienced a sharp decline in its financial performance for the first time in its 25-year history. Despite financial problems, KBS still is committed to providing its employees with good pension and postretirement health benefits.

Under its present plan with First Security, KBS is obligated to pay $43 million to meet the expected value of future pension benefits that are payable to employees as an annuity upon their retirement from the company. On the other hand, NET Life requires KBS to pay only $35 million for identical future pension benefits. First Security is one of the oldest and most reputable insurance companies in North America. NET Life has a much weaker reputation in the insurance industry. In pondering the significant difference in annual pension costs, Qualls asks himself, "Is this too good to be true?"

Instructions

Answer the following questions.

(a) Why might NET Life's pension cost requirement be $8 million less than First Security's requirement for the same future value?

(b) What ethical issues should James Qualls consider before switching KBS's pension fund assets?

(c) Who are the stakeholders that could be affected by Qualls's decision?

(LO 7, 9) **P6-13 (Expected Cash Flows and Present Value)** Larry's Lawn Equipment sells high-quality lawn mowers and offers a 3-year warranty on all new lawn mowers sold. In 2007, Larry sold $300,000 of new specialty mowers for golf greens for which Larry's service department does not have the equipment to do the service. Larry has entered into an agreement with Mower Mavens to provide all warranty service on the special mowers sold in 2007. Larry wishes to measure the fair value of the agreement to determine the warranty liability for sales made in 2007. The controller for Larry's Lawn Equipment estimates the following expected warranty cash outflows associated with the mowers sold in 2007.

Year	Cash Flow Estimate	Probability Assessment
2008	$2,000	20%
	4,000	60%
	5,000	20%
2009	$2,500	30%
	5,000	50%
	6,000	20%
2010	$3,000	30%
	6,000	40%
	7,000	30%

Instructions

Using expected cash flow and present value techniques, determine the value of the warranty liability for the 2007 sales. Use an annual discount rate of 5%. Assume all cash flows occur at the end of the year.

(LO 7, 9) **P6-14 (Expected Cash Flows and Present Value)** At the end of 2007, Richards Company is conducting an impairment test and needs to develop a fair value estimate for machinery used in its manufacturing operations. Given the nature of Richard's production process, the equipment is for special use. (No second-hand market values are available.) The equipment will be obsolete in 2 years, and Richard's accountants have developed the following cash flow information for the equipment.

Year	Net Cash Flow Estimate	Probability Assessment
2008	$6,000	40%
	8,000	60%
2009	$ (500)	20%
	2,000	60%
	3,000	20%
Scrap value		
2009	$ 500	50%
	700	50%

Instructions

Using expected cash flow and present value techniques, determine the fair value of the machinery at the end of 2007. Use a 6% discount rate. Assume all cash flows occur at the end of the year.

(LO 10) ***P6-15 (Various Time Value of Money Situations)** Using a financial calculator, provide a solution to each of the following questions.

(a) What is the amount of the payments that Karla Zehms must make at the end of each of 8 years to accumulate a fund of $70,000 by the end of the eighth year, if the fund earns 7.25% interest, compounded annually?

(b) Bill Yawn is 40 years old today, and he wishes to accumulate $500,000 by his sixty-fifth birthday so he can retire to his summer place on Lake Winnebago. He wishes to accumulate this amount by making equal deposits on his fortieth through sixty-fourth birthdays. What annual deposit must Bill make if the fund will earn 9.65% interest compounded annually?

(c) Jane Mayer has a $26,000 debt that she wishes to repay 4 years from today. She has $17,000 that she intends to invest for the 4 years. What rate of interest will she need to earn annually in order to accumulate enough to pay the debt?

(LO 10) *P6-16 (Various Time Value of Money Situations) Using a financial calculator, solve for the unknowns in each of the following situations.

(a) Wayne Eski wishes to invest $150,000 today to ensure payments of $20,000 to his son at the end of each year for the next 15 years. At what interest rate must the $150,000 be invested? (Round the answer to two decimal points.)

(b) On June 1, 2007, Shelley Long purchases lakefront property from her neighbor, Joey Brenner, and agrees to pay the purchase price in seven payments of $16,000 each, the first payment to be payable June 1, 2008. (Assume that interest compounded at an annual rate of 7.35% is implicit in the payments.) What is the purchase price of the property?

(c) On January 1, 2007, Cooke Corporation purchased 200 of the $1,000 face value, 8% coupon, 10-year bonds of Howe Inc. The bonds mature on January 1, 2017, and pay interest annually beginning January 1, 2008. Cooke purchased the bonds to yield 10.65%. How much did Cooke pay for the bonds?

(LO 10) *P6-17 (Various Time Value of Money Situations) Using a financial calculator, provide a solution to each of the following situations.

(a) On March 12, 2007, William Scott invests in a $180,000 insurance policy that earns 5.25% compounded annually. The annuity policy allows William to receive annual payments, the first of which is payable to William on March 12, 2008. What will be the amount of each of the 20 equal annual receipts?

(b) Bill Schroeder owes a debt of $35,000 from the purchase of his new sport utility vehicle. The debt bears annual interest of 9.1% compounded monthly. Bill wishes to pay the debt and interest in equal monthly payments over 8 years, beginning one month hence. What equal monthly payments will pay off the debt and interest?

(c) On January 1, 2007, Sammy Sosa offers to buy Mark Grace's used snowmobile for $8,000, payable in five equal installments, which are to include 8.25% interest on the unpaid balance and a portion of the principal. If the first payment is to be made on January 1, 2007, how much will each payment be?

(d) Repeat the requirements in part (c), assuming Sosa makes the first payment on December 31, 2007.

USING YOUR JUDGMENT

Financial Reporting Problem

 The Procter & Gamble Company (P&G)

The financial statements and accompanying notes of **P&G** are presented in Appendix 5B or can be accessed on the KWW website.

 Instructions

(a) Examining each item in P&G's balance sheet, identify those items that require present value, discounting, or interest computations in establishing the amount reported. (The accompanying notes are an additional source for this information.)

(b) (1) What interest rates are disclosed by P&G as being used to compute interest and present values?
(2) Why are there so many different interest rates applied to P&G's financial statement elements (assets, liabilities, revenues, and expenses)?

Financial Statement Analysis Case

Consolidated Natural Gas Company

Consolidated Natural Gas Company (CNG), with corporate headquarters in Pittsburgh, Pennsylvania, is one of the largest producers, transporters, distributors, and marketers of natural gas in North America.

Periodically, the company experiences a decrease in the value of its gas and oil producing properties, and a special charge to income was recorded in order to reduce the carrying value of those assets.

Assume the following information: In 2005, CNG estimated the cash inflows from its oil and gas producing properties to be $350,000 per year. During 2006, the write-downs described above caused the estimate to be decreased to $275,000 per year. Production costs (cash outflows) associated with all these properties were estimated to be $125,000 per year in 2005, but this amount was revised to $175,000 per year in 2006.

Instructions

(Assume that all cash flows occur at the end of the year.)

(a) Calculate the present value of net cash flows for 2005–2007 (three years), using the 2005 estimates and a 10% discount factor.

(b) Calculate the present value of net cash flows for 2006–2008 (three years), using the 2006 estimates and a 10% discount factor.

(c) Compare the results using the two estimates. Is information on future cash flows from oil and gas producing properties useful, considering that the estimates must be revised each year? Explain.

Research Cases

Case 1

To access the Internet and EDGAR, follow the steps outlined in the Research Case on page 248.

Firms registered with the U.S. Securities and Exchange Commission (SEC) are required to file an annual report on Form 10-K within 60 days of their fiscal year end. The Form 10-K includes certain information not provided in a firm's annual report to shareholders.

Instructions

Examine the most recent Form 10-K of a company of your choice and answer the following questions.

(a) Each 10-K is required to include information regarding several aspects of a firm, referenced by item numbers. Identify the 14 items included in the 10-K.

(b) Each 10-K must include the firm's financial statements. Does the 10-K you examined include the firm's financial statements? If not, how did the firm comply with the financial statement requirement?

(c) What financial statement schedules are included with the 10-K you examined?

Case 2

In May 2001 the FASB published the first of a series of articles entitled *Understanding the Issues*, which are designed to enhance FASB constituents' understanding of various accounting issues. In the first installment, "Expected Cash Flows," Ed Trott and Wayne Upton explained issues related to *FASB Concepts Statement No. 7*.

Instructions

The article can be accessed at the FASB website (**www.fasb.org**). Read the article and answer the following questions.

(a) What are the three areas in which the FASB received objections to its exposure draft for *Concepts Statement No. 7*?

(b) What has been the traditional approach to estimating cash flows and present values? What were some of the problems with the "traditional approach to present value"?

(c) What are the principles the Board identified in application of present value to accounting measurements?

(d) How do present values computed using the model in *Concepts Statement No. 7* include the effects of inflation?

Professional Research: Financial Accounting and Reporting

At a recent meeting of the accounting staff in your company, the controller raised the issue of using present value techniques to conduct impairment tests for some of the company's fixed assets. Some of the more senior members of the staff admitted having little knowledge of present value concepts in this context, but they had heard about a recent FASB Concepts Statement that may be relevant. As the junior staff in the department, you have been asked to conduct some research of the authoritative literature on this topic and report back at the staff meeting next week.

Instructions

Using the **Financial Accounting Research System (FARS)**, respond to the following items. (Provide text strings used in your search.)

(a) Identify the recent concept statement that addresses present value measurement in accounting.

(b) What are some of the contexts in which present value concepts are applied in accounting measurement?

(c) Provide definitions for the following terms:
- **(1)** Best estimate.
- **(2)** Estimated cash flow (contrasted to expected cash flow).
- **(3)** Fresh-start measurement.
- **(4)** Interest methods of allocation.

Professional Simulation

In this simulation you are asked to address questions concerning the application of time value of money concepts to accounting problems. Prepare responses to all parts.

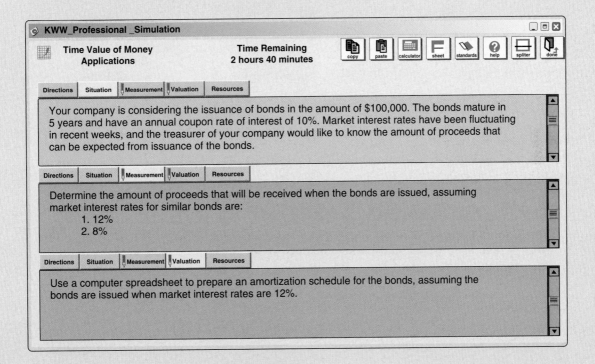

KWW_Professional _Simulation

Time Value of Money Applications

Time Remaining 2 hours 40 minutes

copy · paste · calculator · sheet · standards · help · splitter · done

Directions | Situation | Measurement | Valuation | Resources

Your company is considering the issuance of bonds in the amount of $100,000. The bonds mature in 5 years and have an annual coupon rate of interest of 10%. Market interest rates have been fluctuating in recent weeks, and the treasurer of your company would like to know the amount of proceeds that can be expected from issuance of the bonds.

Directions | Situation | Measurement | Valuation | Resources

Determine the amount of proceeds that will be received when the bonds are issued, assuming market interest rates for similar bonds are:
1. 12%
2. 8%

Directions | Situation | Measurement | Valuation | Resources

Use a computer spreadsheet to prepare an amortization schedule for the bonds, assuming the bonds are issued when market interest rates are 12%.

Remember to check the book's companion website to find additional resources for this chapter.

TABLE 6-1 FUTURE VALUE OF 1 (FUTURE VALUE OF A SINGLE SUM)

$$FVF_{n,i} = (1 + i)^n$$

(n) Periods	2%	2½%	3%	4%	5%	6%
1	1.02000	1.02500	1.03000	1.04000	1.05000	1.06000
2	1.04040	1.05063	1.06090	1.08160	1.10250	1.12360
3	1.06121	1.07689	1.09273	1.12486	1.15763	1.19102
4	1.08243	1.10381	1.12551	1.16986	1.21551	1.26248
5	1.10408	1.13141	1.15927	1.21665	1.27628	1.33823
6	1.12616	1.15969	1.19405	1.26532	1.34010	1.41852
7	1.14869	1.18869	1.22987	1.31593	1.40710	1.50363
8	1.17166	1.21840	1.26677	1.36857	1.47746	1.59385
9	1.19509	1.24886	1.30477	1.42331	1.55133	1.68948
10	1.21899	1.28008	1.34392	1.48024	1.62889	1.79085
11	1.24337	1.31209	1.38423	1.53945	1.71034	1.89830
12	1.26824	1.34489	1.42576	1.60103	1.79586	2.01220
13	1.29361	1.37851	1.46853	1.66507	1.88565	2.13293
14	1.31948	1.41297	1.51259	1.73168	1.97993	2.26090
15	1.34587	1.44830	1.55797	1.80094	2.07893	2.39656
16	1.37279	1.48451	1.60471	1.87298	2.18287	2.54035
17	1.40024	1.52162	1.65285	1.94790	2.29202	2.69277
18	1.42825	1.55966	1.70243	2.02582	2.40662	2.85434
19	1.45681	1.59865	1.75351	2.10685	2.52695	3.02560
20	1.48595	1.63862	1.80611	2.19112	2.65330	3.20714
21	1.51567	1.67958	1.86029	2.27877	2.78596	3.39956
22	1.54598	1.72157	1.91610	2.36992	2.92526	3.60354
23	1.57690	1.76461	1.97359	2.46472	3.07152	3.81975
24	1.60844	1.80873	2.03279	2.56330	3.22510	4.04893
25	1.64061	1.85394	2.09378	2.66584	3.38635	4.29187
26	1.67342	1.90029	2.15659	2.77247	3.55567	4.54938
27	1.70689	1.94780	2.22129	2.88337	3.73346	4.82235
28	1.74102	1.99650	2.28793	2.99870	3.92013	5.11169
29	1.77584	2.04641	2.35657	3.11865	4.11614	5.41839
30	1.81136	2.09757	2.42726	3.24340	4.32194	5.74349
31	1.84759	2.15001	2.50008	3.37313	4.53804	6.08810
32	1.88454	2.20376	2.57508	3.50806	4.76494	6.45339
33	1.92223	2.25885	2.65234	3.64838	5.00319	6.84059
34	1.96068	2.31532	2.73191	3.79432	5.25335	7.25103
35	1.99989	2.37321	2.81386	3.94609	5.51602	7.68609
36	2.03989	2.43254	2.89828	4.10393	5.79182	8.14725
37	2.08069	2.49335	2.98523	4.26809	6.08141	8.63609
38	2.12230	2.55568	3.07478	4.43881	6.38548	9.15425
39	2.16474	2.61957	3.16703	4.61637	6.70475	9.70351
40	2.20804	2.68506	3.26204	4.80102	7.03999	10.28572

TABLE 6-1   FUTURE VALUE OF 1

8%	9%	10%	11%	12%	15%	(n) Periods
1.08000	1.09000	1.10000	1.11000	1.12000	1.15000	1
1.16640	1.18810	1.21000	1.23210	1.25440	1.32250	2
1.25971	1.29503	1.33100	1.36763	1.40493	1.52088	3
1.36049	1.41158	1.46410	1.51807	1.57352	1.74901	4
1.46933	1.53862	1.61051	1.68506	1.76234	2.01136	5
1.58687	1.67710	1.77156	1.87041	1.97382	2.31306	6
1.71382	1.82804	1.94872	2.07616	2.21068	2.66002	7
1.85093	1.99256	2.14359	2.30454	2.47596	3.05902	8
1.99900	2.17189	2.35795	2.55803	2.77308	3.51788	9
2.15892	2.36736	2.59374	2.83942	3.10585	4.04556	10
2.33164	2.58043	2.85312	3.15176	3.47855	4.65239	11
2.51817	2.81267	3.13843	3.49845	3.89598	5.35025	12
2.71962	3.06581	3.45227	3.88328	4.36349	6.15279	13
2.93719	3.34173	3.79750	4.31044	4.88711	7.07571	14
3.17217	3.64248	4.17725	4.78459	5.47357	8.13706	15
3.42594	3.97031	4.59497	5.31089	6.13039	9.35762	16
3.70002	4.32763	5.05447	5.89509	6.86604	10.76126	17
3.99602	4.71712	5.55992	6.54355	7.68997	12.37545	18
4.31570	5.14166	6.11591	7.26334	8.61276	14.23177	19
4.66096	5.60441	6.72750	8.06231	9.64629	16.36654	20
5.03383	6.10881	7.40025	8.94917	10.80385	18.82152	21
5.43654	6.65860	8.14028	9.93357	12.10031	21.64475	22
5.87146	7.25787	8.95430	11.02627	13.55235	24.89146	23
6.34118	7.91108	9.84973	12.23916	15.17863	28.62518	24
6.84847	8.62308	10.83471	13.58546	17.00000	32.91895	25
7.39635	9.39916	11.91818	15.07986	19.04007	37.85680	26
7.98806	10.24508	13.10999	16.73865	21.32488	43.53532	27
8.62711	11.16714	14.42099	18.57990	23.88387	50.06561	28
9.31727	12.17218	15.86309	20.62369	26.74993	57.57545	29
10.06266	13.26768	17.44940	22.89230	29.95992	66.21177	30
10.86767	14.46177	19.19434	25.41045	33.55511	76.14354	31
11.73708	15.76333	21.11378	28.20560	37.58173	87.56507	32
12.67605	17.18203	23.22515	31.30821	42.09153	100.69983	33
13.69013	18.72841	25.54767	34.75212	47.14252	115.80480	34
14.78534	20.41397	28.10244	38.57485	52.79962	133.17552	35
15.96817	22.25123	30.91268	42.81808	59.13557	153.15185	36
17.24563	24.25384	34.00395	47.52807	66.23184	176.12463	37
18.62528	26.43668	37.40434	52.75616	74.17966	202.54332	38
20.11530	28.81598	41.14479	58.55934	83.08122	232.92482	39
21.72452	31.40942	45.25926	65.00087	93.05097	267.86355	40

TABLE 6-2   PRESENT VALUE OF 1 (PRESENT VALUE OF A SINGLE SUM)

$$PVF_{n,i} = \frac{1}{(1 + i)^n} = (1 + i)^{-n}$$

(n) Periods	2%	2½%	3%	4%	5%	6%
1	.98039	.97561	.97087	.96154	.95238	.94340
2	.96117	.95181	.94260	.92456	.90703	.89000
3	.94232	.92860	.91514	.88900	.86384	.83962
4	.92385	.90595	.88849	.85480	.82270	.79209
5	.90573	.88385	.86261	.82193	.78353	.74726
6	.88797	.86230	.83748	.79031	.74622	.70496
7	.87056	.84127	.81309	.75992	.71068	.66506
8	.85349	.82075	.78941	.73069	.67684	.62741
9	.83676	.80073	.76642	.70259	.64461	.59190
10	.82035	.78120	.74409	.67556	.61391	.55839
11	.80426	.76214	.72242	.64958	.58468	.52679
12	.78849	.74356	.70138	.62460	.55684	.49697
13	.77303	.72542	.68095	.60057	.53032	.46884
14	.75788	.70773	.66112	.57748	.50507	.44230
15	.74301	.69047	.64186	.55526	.48102	.41727
16	.72845	.67362	.62317	.53391	.45811	.39365
17	.71416	.65720	.60502	.51337	.43630	.37136
18	.70016	.64117	.58739	.49363	.41552	.35034
19	.68643	.62553	.57029	.47464	.39573	.33051
20	.67297	.61027	.55368	.45639	.37689	.31180
21	.65978	.59539	.53755	.43883	.35894	.29416
22	.64684	.58086	.52189	.42196	.34185	.22751
23	.63416	.56670	.50669	.40573	.32557	.26180
24	.62172	.55288	.49193	.39012	.31007	.24698
25	.60953	.53939	.47761	.37512	.29530	.23300
26	.59758	.52623	.46369	.36069	.28124	.21981
27	.58586	.51340	.45019	.34682	.26785	.20737
28	.57437	.50088	.43708	.33348	.25509	.19563
29	.56311	.48866	.42435	.32065	.24295	.18456
30	.55207	.47674	.41199	.30832	.23138	.17411
31	.54125	.46511	.39999	.29646	.22036	.16425
32	.53063	.45377	.38834	.28506	.20987	.15496
33	.52023	.44270	.37703	.27409	.19987	.14619
34	.51003	.43191	.36604	.26355	.19035	.13791
35	.50003	.42137	.35538	.25342	.18129	.13011
36	.49022	.41109	.34503	.24367	.17266	.12274
37	.48061	.40107	.33498	.23430	.16444	.11579
38	.47119	.39128	.32523	.22529	.15661	.10924
39	.46195	.38174	.31575	.21662	.14915	.10306
40	.45289	.37243	.30656	.20829	.14205	.09722

TABLE 6-2   PRESENT VALUE OF 1

8%	9%	10%	11%	12%	15%	(n) Periods
.92593	.91743	.90909	.90090	.89286	.86957	1
.85734	.84168	.82645	.81162	.79719	.75614	2
.79383	.77218	.75132	.73119	.71178	.65752	3
.73503	.70843	.68301	.65873	.63552	.57175	4
.68058	.64993	.62092	.59345	.56743	.49718	5
.63017	.59627	.56447	.53464	.50663	.43233	6
.58349	.54703	.51316	.48166	.45235	.37594	7
.54027	.50187	.46651	.43393	.40388	.32690	8
.50025	.46043	.42410	.39092	.36061	.28426	9
.46319	.42241	.38554	.35218	.32197	.24719	10
.42888	.38753	.35049	.31728	.28748	.21494	11
.39711	.35554	.31863	.28584	.25668	.18691	12
.36770	.32618	.28966	.25751	.22917	.16253	13
.34046	.29925	.26333	.23199	.20462	.14133	14
.31524	.27454	.23939	.20900	.18270	.12289	15
.29189	.25187	.21763	.18829	.16312	.10687	16
.27027	.23107	.19785	.16963	.14564	.09293	17
.25025	.21199	.17986	.15282	.13004	.08081	18
.23171	.19449	.16351	.13768	.11611	.07027	19
.21455	.17843	.14864	.12403	.10367	.06110	20
.19866	.16370	.13513	.11174	.09256	.05313	21
.18394	.15018	.12285	.10067	.08264	.04620	22
.17032	.13778	.11168	.09069	.07379	.04017	23
.15770	.12641	.10153	.08170	.06588	.03493	24
.14602	.11597	.09230	.07361	.05882	.03038	25
.13520	.10639	.08391	.06631	.05252	.02642	26
.12519	.09761	.07628	.05974	.04689	.02297	27
.11591	.08955	.06934	.05382	.04187	.01997	28
.10733	.08216	.06304	.04849	.03738	.01737	29
.09938	.07537	.05731	.04368	.03338	.01510	30
.09202	.06915	.05210	.03935	.02980	.01313	31
.08520	.06344	.04736	.03545	.02661	.01142	32
.07889	.05820	.04306	.03194	.02376	.00993	33
.07305	.05340	.03914	.02878	.02121	.00864	34
.06763	.04899	.03558	.02592	.01894	.00751	35
.06262	.04494	.03235	.02335	.01691	.00653	36
.05799	.04123	.02941	.02104	.01510	.00568	37
.05369	.03783	.02674	.01896	.01348	.00494	38
.04971	.03470	.02430	.01708	.01204	.00429	39
.04603	.03184	.02210	.01538	.01075	.00373	40

TABLE 6-3 FUTURE VALUE OF AN ORDINARY ANNUITY OF 1

$$\text{FVF-OA}_{n,i} = \frac{(1 + i)^n - 1}{i}$$

(n) Periods	2%	2½%	3%	4%	5%	6%
1	1.00000	1.00000	1.00000	1.00000	1.00000	1.00000
2	2.02000	2.02500	2.03000	2.04000	2.05000	2.06000
3	3.06040	3.07563	3.09090	3.12160	3.15250	3.18360
4	4.12161	4.15252	4.18363	4.24646	4.31013	4.37462
5	5.20404	5.25633	5.30914	5.41632	5.52563	5.63709
6	6.30812	6.38774	6.46841	6.63298	6.80191	6.97532
7	7.43428	7.54743	7.66246	7.89829	8.14201	8.39384
8	8.58297	8.73612	8.89234	9.21423	9.54911	9.89747
9	9.75463	9.95452	10.15911	10.58280	11.02656	11.49132
10	10.94972	11.20338	11.46338	12.00611	12.57789	13.18079
11	12.16872	12.48347	12.80780	13.48635	14.20679	14.97164
12	13.41209	13.79555	14.19203	15.02581	15.91713	16.86994
13	14.68033	15.14044	15.61779	16.62684	17.71298	18.88214
14	15.97394	16.51895	17.08632	18.29191	19.59863	21.01507
15	17.29342	17.93193	18.59891	20.02359	21.57856	23.27597
16	18.63929	19.38022	20.15688	21.82453	23.65749	25.67253
17	20.01207	20.86473	21.76159	23.69751	25.84037	28.21288
18	21.41231	22.38635	23.41444	25.64541	28.13238	30.90565
19	22.84056	23.94601	25.11687	27.67123	30.53900	33.75999
20	24.29737	25.54466	26.87037	29.77808	33.06595	36.78559
21	25.78332	27.18327	28.67649	31.96920	35.71925	39.99273
22	27.29898	28.86286	30.53678	34.24797	38.50521	43.39229
23	28.84496	30.58443	32.45288	36.61789	41.43048	46.99583
24	30.42186	32.34904	34.42647	39.08260	44.50200	50.81558
25	32.03030	34.15776	36.45926	41.64591	47.72710	54.86451
26	33.67091	36.01171	38.55304	44.31174	51.11345	59.15638
27	35.34432	37.91200	40.70963	47.08421	54.66913	63.70577
28	37.05121	39.85980	42.93092	49.96758	58.40258	68.52811
29	38.79223	41.85630	45.21885	52.96629	62.32271	73.63980
30	40.56808	43.90270	47.57542	56.08494	66.43885	79.05819
31	42.37944	46.00027	50.00268	59.32834	70.76079	84.80168
32	44.22703	48.15028	52.50276	62.70147	75.29883	90.88978
33	46.11157	50.35403	55.07784	66.20953	80.06377	97.34316
34	48.03380	52.61289	57.73018	69.85791	85.06696	104.18376
35	49.99448	54.92821	60.46208	73.65222	90.32031	111.43478
36	51.99437	57.30141	63.27594	77.59831	95.83632	119.12087
37	54.03425	59.73395	66.17422	81.70225	101.62814	127.26812
38	56.11494	62.22730	69.15945	85.97034	107.70955	135.90421
39	58.23724	64.78298	72.23423	90.40915	114.09502	145.05846
40	60.40198	67.40255	75.40126	95.02552	120.79977	154.76197

TABLE 6-3   FUTURE VALUE OF AN ORDINARY ANNUITY OF 1

8%	9%	10%	11%	12%	15%	(n) Periods
1.00000	1.00000	1.00000	1.00000	1.00000	1.00000	1
2.08000	2.09000	2.10000	2.11000	2.12000	2.15000	2
3.24640	3.27810	3.31000	3.34210	3.37440	3.47250	3
4.50611	4.57313	4.64100	4.70973	4.77933	4.99338	4
5.86660	5.98471	6.10510	6.22780	6.35285	6.74238	5
7.33592	7.52334	7.71561	7.91286	8.11519	8.75374	6
8.92280	9.20044	9.48717	9.78327	10.08901	11.06680	7
10.63663	11.02847	11.43589	11.85943	12.29969	13.72682	8
12.48756	13.02104	13.57948	14.16397	14.77566	16.78584	9
14.48656	15.19293	15.93743	16.72201	17.54874	20.30372	10
16.64549	17.56029	18.53117	19.56143	20.65458	24.34928	11
18.97713	20.14072	21.38428	22.71319	24.13313	29.00167	12
21.49530	22.95339	24.52271	26.21164	28.02911	34.35192	13
24.21492	26.01919	27.97498	30.09492	32.39260	40.50471	14
27.15211	29.36092	31.77248	34.40536	37.27972	47.58041	15
30.32428	33.00340	35.94973	39.18995	42.75328	55.71747	16
33.75023	36.97371	40.54470	44.50084	48.88367	65.07509	17
37.45024	41.30134	45.59917	50.39593	55.74972	75.83636	18
41.44626	46.01846	51.15909	56.93949	63.43968	88.21181	19
45.76196	51.16012	57.27500	64.20283	72.05244	102.44358	20
50.42292	56.76453	64.00250	72.26514	81.69874	118.81012	21
55.45676	62.87334	71.40275	81.21431	92.50258	137.63164	22
60.89330	69.53194	79.54302	91.14788	104.60289	159.27638	23
66.76476	76.78981	88.49733	102.17415	118.15524	184.16784	24
73.10594	84.70090	98.34706	114.41331	133.33387	212.79302	25
79.95442	93.32398	109.18177	127.99877	150.33393	245.71197	26
87.35077	102.72314	121.09994	143.07864	169.37401	283.56877	27
95.33883	112.96822	134.20994	159.81729	190.69889	327.10408	28
103.96594	124.13536	148.63093	178.39719	214.58275	377.16969	29
113.28321	136.30754	164.49402	199.02088	241.33268	434.74515	30
123.34587	149.57522	181.94343	221.91317	271.29261	500.95692	31
134.21354	164.03699	201.13777	247.32362	304.84772	577.10046	32
145.95062	179.80032	222.25154	275.52922	342.42945	644.66553	33
158.62667	196.98234	245.47670	306.83744	384.52098	765.36535	34
172.31680	215.71076	271.02437	341.58955	431.66350	881.17016	35
187.10215	236.12472	299.12681	380.16441	484.46312	1014.34568	36
203.07032	258.37595	330.03949	422.98249	543.59869	1167.49753	37
220.31595	282.62978	364.04343	470.51056	609.83053	1343.62216	38
238.94122	309.06646	401.44778	523.26673	684.01020	1546.16549	39
259.05652	337.88245	442.59256	581.82607	767.09142	1779.09031	40

TABLE 6-4 PRESENT VALUE OF AN ORDINARY ANNUITY OF 1

$$PVF\text{-}OA_{n,i} = \frac{1 - \dfrac{1}{(1+i)^n}}{i}$$

(n) Periods	2%	2½%	3%	4%	5%	6%
1	.98039	.97561	.97087	.96154	.95238	.94340
2	1.94156	1.92742	1.91347	1.88609	1.85941	1.83339
3	2.88388	2.85602	2.82861	2.77509	2.72325	2.67301
4	3.80773	3.76197	3.71710	3.62990	3.54595	3.46511
5	4.71346	4.64583	4.57971	4.45182	4.32948	4.21236
6	5.60143	5.50813	5.41719	5.24214	5.07569	4.91732
7	6.47199	6.34939	6.23028	6.00205	5.78637	5.58238
8	7.32548	7.17014	7.01969	6.73274	6.46321	6.20979
9	8.16224	7.97087	7.78611	7.43533	7.10782	6.80169
10	8.98259	8.75206	8.53020	8.11090	7.72173	7.36009
11	9.78685	9.51421	9.25262	8.76048	8.30641	7.88687
12	10.57534	10.25776	9.95400	9.38507	8.86325	8.38384
13	11.34837	10.98319	10.63496	9.98565	9.39357	8.85268
14	12.10625	11.69091	11.29607	10.56312	9.89864	9.29498
15	12.84926	12.38138	11.93794	11.11839	10.37966	9.71225
16	13.57771	13.05500	12.56110	11.65230	10.83777	10.10590
17	14.29187	13.71220	13.16612	12.16567	11.27407	10.47726
18	14.99203	14.35336	13.75351	12.65930	11.68959	10.82760
19	15.67846	14.97889	14.32380	13.13394	12.08532	11.15812
20	16.35143	15.58916	14.87747	13.59033	12.46221	11.46992
21	17.01121	16.18455	15.41502	14.02916	12.82115	11.76408
22	17.65805	16.76541	15.93692	14.45112	13.16300	12.04158
23	18.29220	17.33211	16.44361	14.85684	13.48857	12.30338
24	18.91393	17.88499	16.93554	15.24696	13.79864	12.55036
25	19.52346	18.42438	17.41315	15.62208	14.09394	12.78336
26	20.12104	18.95061	17.87684	15.98277	14.37519	13.00317
27	20.70690	19.46401	18.32703	16.32959	14.64303	13.21053
28	21.28127	19.96489	18.76411	16.66306	14.89813	13.40616
29	21.84438	20.45355	19.18845	16.98371	15.14107	13.59072
30	22.39646	20.93029	19.60044	17.29203	15.37245	13.76483
31	22.93770	21.39541	20.00043	17.58849	15.59281	13.92909
32	23.46833	21.84918	20.38877	17.87355	15.80268	14.08404
33	23.98856	22.29188	20.76579	18.14765	16.00255	14.23023
34	24.49859	22.72379	21.13184	18.41120	16.19290	14.36814
35	24.99862	23.14516	21.48722	18.66461	16.37419	14.49825
36	25.48884	23.55625	21.83225	18.90828	16.54685	14.62099
37	25.96945	23.95732	22.16724	19.14258	16.71129	14.73678
38	26.44064	24.34860	22.49246	19.36786	16.86789	14.84602
39	26.90259	24.73034	22.80822	19.58448	17.01704	14.94907
40	27.35548	25.10278	23.11477	19.79277	17.15909	15.04630

TABLE 6-4   PRESENT VALUE OF AN ORDINARY ANNUITY OF 1

8%	9%	10%	11%	12%	15%	(n) Periods
.92593	.91743	.90909	.90090	.89286	.86957	1
1.78326	1.75911	1.73554	1.71252	1.69005	1.62571	2
2.57710	2.53130	2.48685	2.44371	2.40183	2.28323	3
3.31213	3.23972	3.16986	3.10245	3.03735	2.85498	4
3.99271	3.88965	3.79079	3.69590	3.60478	3.35216	5
4.62288	4.48592	4.35526	4.23054	4.11141	3.78448	6
5.20637	5.03295	4.86842	4.71220	4.56376	4.16042	7
5.74664	5.53482	5.33493	5.14612	4.96764	4.48732	8
6.24689	5.99525	5.75902	5.53705	5.32825	4.77158	9
6.71008	6.41766	6.14457	5.88923	5.65022	5.01877	10
7.13896	6.80519	6.49506	6.20652	5.93770	5.23371	11
7.53608	7.16073	6.81369	6.49236	6.19437	5.42062	12
7.90378	7.48690	7.10336	6.74987	6.42355	5.58315	13
8.24424	7.78615	7.36669	6.98187	6.62817	5.72448	14
8.55948	8.06069	7.60608	7.19087	6.81086	5.84737	15
8.85137	8.31256	7.82371	7.37916	6.97399	5.95424	16
9.12164	8.54363	8.02155	7.54879	7.11963	6.04716	17
9.37189	8.75563	8.20141	7.70162	7.24967	6.12797	18
9.60360	8.95012	8.36492	7.83929	7.36578	6.19823	19
9.81815	9.12855	8.51356	7.96333	7.46944	6.25933	20
10.01680	9.29224	8.64869	8.07507	7.56200	6.31246	21
10.20074	9.44243	8.77154	8.17574	7.64465	6.35866	22
10.37106	9.58021	8.88322	8.26643	7.71843	6.39884	23
10.52876	9.70661	8.98474	8.34814	7.78432	6.43377	24
10.67478	9.82258	9.07704	8.42174	7.84314	6.46415	25
10.80998	9.92897	9.16095	8.48806	7.89566	6.49056	26
10.93516	10.02658	9.23722	8.54780	7.94255	6.51353	27
11.05108	10.11613	9.30657	8.60162	7.98442	6.53351	28
11.15841	10.19828	9.36961	8.65011	8.02181	6.55088	29
11.25778	10.27365	9.42691	8.69379	8.05518	6.56598	30
11.34980	10.34280	9.47901	8.73315	8.08499	6.57911	31
11.43500	10.40624	9.52638	8.76860	8.11159	6.59053	32
11.51389	10.46444	9.56943	8.80054	8.13535	6.60046	33
11.58693	10.51784	9.60858	8.82932	8.15656	6.60910	34
11.65457	10.56682	9.64416	8.85524	8.17550	6.61661	35
11.71719	10.61176	9.67651	8.87859	8.19241	6.62314	36
11.77518	10.65299	9.70592	8.89963	8.20751	6.62882	37
11.82887	10.69082	9.73265	8.91859	8.22099	6.63375	38
11.87858	10.72552	9.75697	8.93567	8.23303	6.63805	39
11.92461	10.75736	9.77905	8.95105	8.24378	6.64178	40

TABLE 6-5   PRESENT VALUE OF AN ANNUITY DUE OF 1

$$PVF\text{-}AD_{n,i} = 1 + \frac{1 - \dfrac{1}{(1+i)^{n-1}}}{i}$$

(n) Periods	2%	2½%	3%	4%	5%	6%
1	1.00000	1.00000	1.00000	1.00000	1.00000	1.00000
2	1.98039	1.97561	1.97087	1.96154	1.95238	1.94340
3	2.94156	2.92742	2.91347	2.88609	2.85941	2.83339
4	3.88388	3.85602	3.82861	3.77509	3.72325	3.67301
5	4.80773	4.76197	4.71710	4.62990	4.54595	4.46511
6	5.71346	5.64583	5.57971	5.45182	5.32948	5.21236
7	6.60143	6.50813	6.41719	6.24214	6.07569	5.91732
8	7.47199	7.34939	7.23028	7.00205	6.78637	6.58238
9	8.32548	8.17014	8.01969	7.73274	7.46321	7.20979
10	9.16224	8.97087	8.78611	8.43533	8.10782	7.80169
11	9.98259	9.75206	9.53020	9.11090	8.72173	8.36009
12	10.78685	10.51421	10.25262	9.76048	9.30641	8.88687
13	11.57534	11.25776	10.95400	10.38507	9.86325	9.38384
14	12.34837	11.98319	11.63496	10.98565	10.39357	9.85268
15	13.10625	12.69091	12.29607	11.56312	10.89864	10.29498
16	13.84926	13.38138	12.93794	12.11839	11.37966	10.71225
17	14.57771	14.05500	13.56110	12.65230	11.83777	11.10590
18	15.29187	14.71220	14.16612	13.16567	12.27407	11.47726
19	15.99203	15.35336	14.75351	13.65930	12.68959	11.82760
20	16.67846	15.97889	15.32380	14.13394	13.08532	12.15812
21	17.35143	16.58916	15.87747	14.59033	13.46221	12.46992
22	18.01121	17.18455	16.41502	15.02916	13.82115	12.76408
23	18.65805	17.76541	16.93692	15.45112	14.16300	13.04158
24	19.29220	18.33211	17.44361	15.85684	14.48857	13.30338
25	19.91393	18.88499	17.93554	16.24696	14.79864	13.55036
26	20.52346	19.42438	18.41315	16.62208	15.09394	13.78336
27	21.12104	19.95061	18.87684	16.98277	15.37519	14.00317
28	21.70690	20.46401	19.32703	17.32959	15.64303	14.21053
29	22.28127	20.96489	19.76411	17.66306	15.89813	14.40616
30	22.84438	21.45355	20.18845	17.98371	16.14107	14.59072
31	23.39646	21.93029	20.60044	18.29203	16.37245	14.76483
32	23.93770	22.39541	21.00043	18.58849	16.59281	14.92909
33	24.46833	22.84918	21.38877	18.87355	16.80268	15.08404
34	24.98856	23.29188	21.76579	19.14765	17.00255	15.23023
35	25.49859	23.72379	22.13184	19.41120	17.19290	15.36814
36	25.99862	24.14516	22.48722	19.66461	17.37419	15.49825
37	26.48884	24.55625	22.83225	19.90828	17.54685	15.62099
38	26.96945	24.95732	23.16724	20.14258	17.71129	15.73678
39	27.44064	25.34860	23.49246	20.36786	17.86789	15.84602
40	27.90259	25.73034	23.80822	20.58448	18.01704	15.94907

TABLE 6-5   PRESENT VALUE OF AN ANNUITY DUE OF 1

8%	9%	10%	11%	12%	15%	(n) Periods
1.00000	1.00000	1.00000	1.00000	1.00000	1.00000	1
1.92593	1.91743	1.90909	1.90090	1.89286	1.86957	2
2.78326	2.75911	2.73554	2.71252	2.69005	2.62571	3
3.57710	3.53130	3.48685	3.44371	3.40183	3.28323	4
4.31213	4.23972	4.16986	4.10245	4.03735	3.85498	5
4.99271	4.88965	4.79079	4.69590	4.60478	4.35216	6
5.62288	5.48592	5.35526	5.23054	5.11141	4.78448	7
6.20637	6.03295	5.86842	5.71220	5.56376	5.16042	8
6.74664	6.53482	6.33493	6.14612	5.96764	5.48732	9
7.24689	6.99525	6.75902	6.53705	6.32825	5.77158	10
7.71008	7.41766	7.14457	6.88923	6.65022	6.01877	11
8.13896	7.80519	7.49506	7.20652	6.93770	6.23371	12
8.53608	8.16073	7.81369	7.49236	7.19437	6.42062	13
8.90378	8.48690	8.10336	7.74987	7.42355	6.58315	14
9.24424	8.78615	8.36669	7.98187	7.62817	6.72448	15
9.55948	9.06069	8.60608	8.19087	7.81086	6.84737	16
9.85137	9.31256	8.82371	8.37916	7.97399	6.95424	17
10.12164	9.54363	9.02155	8.54879	8.11963	7.04716	18
10.37189	9.75563	9.20141	8.70162	8.24967	7.12797	19
10.60360	9.95012	9.36492	8.83929	8.36578	7.19823	20
10.81815	10.12855	9.51356	8.96333	8.46944	7.25933	21
11.01680	10.29224	9.64869	9.07507	8.56200	7.31246	22
11.20074	10.44243	9.77154	9.17574	8.64465	7.35866	23
11.37106.	10.58021	9.88322	9.26643	8.71843	7.39884	24
11.52876	10.70661	9.98474	9.34814	8.78432	7.43377	25
11.67478	10.82258	10.07704	9.42174	8.84314	7.46415	26
11.80998	10.92897	10.16095	9.48806	8.89566	7.49056	27
11.93518	11.02658	10.23722	9.54780	8.94255	7.51353	28
12.05108	11.11613	10.30657	9.60162	8.98442	7.53351	29
12.15841	11.19828	10.36961	9.65011	9.02181	7.55088	30
12.25778	11.27365	10.42691	9.69379	9.05518	7.56598	31
12.34980	11.34280	10.47901	9.73315	9.08499	7.57911	32
12.43500	11.40624	10.52638	9.76860	9.11159	7.59053	33
12.51389	11.46444	10.56943	9.80054	9.13535	7.60046	34
12.58693	11.51784	10.60858	9.82932	9.15656	7.60910	35
12.65457	11.56682	10.64416	9.85524	9.17550	7.61661	36
12.71719	11.61176	10.67651	9.87859	9.19241	7.62314	37
12.77518	11.65299	10.70592	9.89963	9.20751	7.62882	38
12.82887	11.69082	10.73265	9.91859	9.22099	7.63375	39
12.87858	11.72552	10.75697	9.93567	9.23303	7.63805	40

CASH AND RECEIVABLES

No-Tell Nortel

Recently, **Nortel** announced that its net income for 2003 was really half what it originally reported. In addition, the company had understated net income for 2002. How could this happen? One reason: It appears that Nortel set up "cookie jar" reserves, using the allowance for doubtful accounts as the cookie jar. As the following chart shows, in 2002 Nortel overestimated the amount of bad debt expense (with a sizable allowance for doubtful accounts). Then, in 2003 Nortel slashed the amount of bad debt expense, even though the total money owed by customers remained nearly unchanged. In 2002, its allowance was 19 percent of receivables compared to 10 percent in 2003—quite a difference.

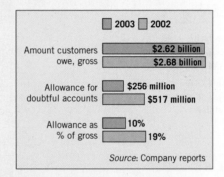

It is difficult to determine if the allowance was too high in 2002 or too low in 2003, or both. Whatever the case, the use of the allowance cookie jar permitted Nortel to report higher operating margins and net income in 2003.

This analysis suggests the importance of looking carefully at the amount of bad debt expense reported in annual reports. Sometimes companies use it to artificially *decrease* income. Others understate bad debt expense to *increase* income. For example, analysts have noted that many large hospitals, such as **Tenet Healthcare** and **HCA**, may be facing increasing uncollectible accounts that are presently not fully reflected in their balance sheets.

Adapted from J. Weil, "At Nortel, Warning Signs Existed Months Ago, *Wall Street Journal* (May 18, 2004), p. C3; and B. McLean, "Reality Checkup," *Fortune* (January 12, 2004), p. 140.

Learning Objectives

After studying this chapter, you should be able to:

1 Identify items considered as cash.

2 Indicate how to report cash and related items.

3 Define receivables and identify the different types of receivables.

4 Explain accounting issues related to recognition of accounts receivable.

5 Explain accounting issues related to valuation of accounts receivable.

6 Explain accounting issues related to recognition of notes receivable.

7 Explain accounting issues related to valuation of notes receivable.

8 Explain accounting issues related to disposition of accounts and notes receivable.

9 Describe how to report and analyze receivables.

As our opening story indicates, estimating the collectibility of accounts receivable has important implications for accurate reporting of operating profits, net income, and assets. In this chapter we discuss cash and receivables—two assets that are important to companies as diverse as **Nortel** and **Tenet Healthcare**. The content and organization of the chapter are as follows.

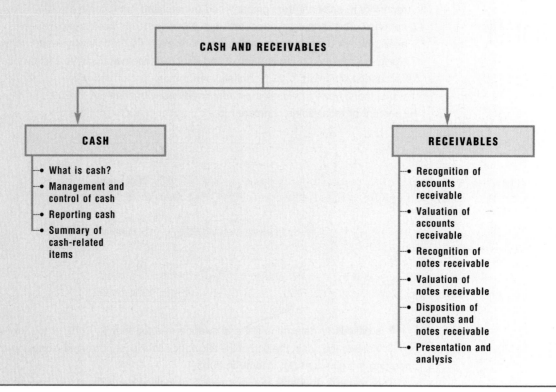

SECTION 1	*CASH*

WHAT IS CASH?

Cash, the most liquid of assets, is the standard medium of exchange and the basis for measuring and accounting for all other items. Companies generally classify cash as a current asset. Cash consists of coin, currency, and available funds on deposit at the bank. Negotiable instruments such as money orders, certified checks, cashier's checks, personal checks, and bank drafts are also viewed as cash. What about savings accounts? Banks do have the legal right to demand notice before withdrawal. But, because banks rarely demand prior notice, savings accounts nevertheless are considered cash.

Some negotiable instruments provide small investors with an opportunity to earn interest. These items, more appropriately classified as temporary investments than as cash, include money market funds, money market savings certificates, certificates of deposit (CDs), and similar types of deposits and "short-term paper."[1] These securities usually contain restrictions or penalties on their conversion to cash. Money market funds that provide checking account privileges, however, are usually classified as cash.

Certain items present classification problems: Companies treat **postdated checks and I.O.U.s** as receivables. They also treat **travel advances** as receivables if collected from employees or deducted from their salaries. Otherwise, companies classify the travel advance as a prepaid expense. **Postage stamps on hand** are classified as part of office supplies inventory or as a prepaid expense. Because **petty cash funds and change funds are used** to meet current operating expenses and liquidate current liabilities, companies include these funds in current assets as cash.

MANAGEMENT AND CONTROL OF CASH

Cash is the asset most susceptible to improper diversion and use. Management faces two problems in accounting for cash transactions: (1) to establish proper controls to prevent any unauthorized transactions by officers or employees, and (2) to provide information necessary to properly manage cash on hand and cash transactions. Yet even with sophisticated control devices, errors can and do happen. For example, the *Wall Street Journal* ran a story entitled "A $7.8 Million Error Has a Happy Ending for a Horrified Bank." The story described how **Manufacturers Hanover Trust Co.** mistakenly overpaid about $7.8 million in cash dividends to its stockholders. (As implied in the headline, most stockholders returned the monies.)

To safeguard cash and to ensure the accuracy of the accounting records for cash, companies need effective **internal control** over cash. Provisions of the Sarbanes-Oxley Act of 2002 call for enhanced efforts to increase the quality of internal control (for cash and other assets). Such efforts are expected to result in improved financial reporting.

However, the increasing volume of transactions conducted with the swipe of a debit or credit card presents new challenges to the effort to maintain control over liquid assets. As one writer noted, "In 5,000 years there have been only four times that we have changed the way we pay—there was barter to coinage; coins to paper; paper to checks; and then cards. Just since 1995, the amount of stuff that American consumers buy using plastic has increased 430 percent."[2] In 2003, for the first time, Americans bought more using cards than cash.[3] In addition, electronic commerce conducted over the Internet continues to grow.

---

[1]A variety of "short-term paper" is available for investment. For example, **certificates of deposit** (CDs) represent formal evidence of indebtedness, issued by a bank, subject to withdrawal under the specific terms of the instrument. Issued in $1,000 to $100,000 denominations, they have maturities anywhere from 7 days to 10 years and generally pay interest at the short-term interest rate in effect at the date of issuance.

Banks and savings and loan associations issue **money-market savings certificates** in denominations of $10,000 or more for 6-month periods (6 to 48 months). The interest rate is tied to the 26-week Treasury bill rate.

In **money-market funds**, a variation of the mutual fund, the mix of Treasury bills and commercial paper making up the fund's portfolio determines the yield. Most money-market funds require an initial minimum investment of $1,000; many allow withdrawal by check or wire transfer.

Treasury bills are U.S. government obligations generally issued with 4-, 13-, and 26-week maturities; they are sold in $10,000 denominations at weekly government auctions.

Commercial paper is a short-term note issued by corporations with good credit ratings. Often issued in $5,000 and $10,000 denominations, these notes generally yield a higher rate than Treasury bills.

[2]K. Brooker, "Just One Word: Plastic," *Fortune* (February 23, 2004), p. 130.

[3]Ibid, p. 132. Non-U.S. consumers are even bigger users of digital cash than U.S. consumers. For example, non-check payments in Japan and Europe comprise over 70 percent of all payment transactions. U.S. consumers' continued use of checks and cash for payment raises fraud concerns, though, as duplication technology makes it easier to forge checks and currency.

Each of these trends contributes to the shift from cold cash to digital cash, and poses new challenges for the control of cash. In the appendix to this chapter, we discuss some of the basic control procedures used to ensure the correct reporting of cash.

REPORTING CASH

OBJECTIVE 2
Indicate how to report cash and related items.

Although the reporting of cash is relatively straightforward, a number of issues merit special attention. These issues relate to the reporting of:

1 Restricted cash.
2 Bank overdrafts.
3 Cash equivalents.

Restricted Cash

Petty cash, payroll, and dividend funds are examples of cash set aside for a particular purpose. In most situations, these fund balances are not material. Therefore, companies do not segregate them from cash in the financial statements. When material in amount, companies segregate **restricted cash** from "regular" cash for reporting purposes. Companies classify restricted cash either in the current assets or in the long-term assets section, depending on the date of availability or disbursement. Classification in the current section is appropriate if using the cash for payment of existing or maturing obligations (within a year or the operating cycle, whichever is longer). On the other hand, companies show the restricted cash in the long-term section of the balance sheet if holding the cash for a longer period of time.

Cash classified in the long-term section is frequently set aside for plant expansion, retirement of long-term debt or, in the case of **International Thoroughbred Breeders**, for entry fee deposits.

ILLUSTRATION 7-1
Disclosure of
Restricted Cash

International Thoroughbred Breeders

Restricted cash and investments (See Note) $3,730,000

Note: Restricted Cash. At year-end, the Company had approximately $3,730,000, which was classified as restricted cash and investments. These funds are primarily cash received from horsemen for nomination and entry fees to be applied to upcoming racing meets, purse winnings held in trust for horsemen, and amounts held for unclaimed ticketholder winnings.

Banks and other lending institutions often require customers to maintain minimum cash balances in checking or savings accounts. The SEC defines these minimum balances, called **compensating balances**, as "that portion of any demand deposit (or any time deposit or certificate of deposit) maintained by a corporation which constitutes support for existing borrowing arrangements of the corporation with a lending institution. Such arrangements would include both outstanding borrowings and the assurance of future credit availability."[4]

---

[4]*Accounting Series Release No. 148*, "Amendments to Regulations S-X and Related Interpretations and Guidelines Regarding the Disclosure of Compensating Balances and Short-Term Borrowing Arrangements," Securities and Exchange Commission (November 13, 1973). The SEC defines 15 percent of liquid assets (current cash balances, whether restricted or not, plus marketable securities) as being material, thereby requiring additional reporting.

To avoid misleading investors about the amount of cash available to meet recurring obligations, the SEC recommends that companies state separately **legally restricted deposits** held as compensating balances against **short-term** borrowing arrangements among the "Cash and cash equivalent items" in current assets. Companies should classify separately restricted deposits held as compensating balances against **long-term** borrowing arrangements as noncurrent assets in either the investments or other assets sections, using a caption such as "Cash on deposit maintained as compensating balance." In cases where compensating balance arrangements exist without agreements that restrict the use of cash amounts shown on the balance sheet, companies should describe the arrangements and the amounts involved in the notes.

Bank Overdrafts

Bank overdrafts occur when a company writes a check for more than the amount in its cash account. Companies should report bank overdrafts in the current liabilities section, adding them to the amount reported as accounts payable. If material, companies should disclose these items separately, either on the face of the balance sheet or in the related notes.[5]

Bank overdrafts are generally not offset against the cash account. A major exception is when available cash is present in another account in the same bank on which the overdraft occurred. Offsetting in this case is required.

Cash Equivalents

A current classification that has become popular is "Cash and cash equivalents."[6] **Cash equivalents** are short-term, highly liquid investments that are both (a) readily convertible to known amounts of cash, and (b) so near their maturity that they present insignificant risk of changes in interest rates. Generally, only investments with original maturities of three months or less qualify under these definitions. Examples of cash equivalents are Treasury bills, commercial paper, and money market funds. Some companies combine cash with temporary investments on the balance sheet. In these cases, they describe the amount of the temporary investments either parenthetically or in the notes.

Additional Disclosures of Restricted Cash

SUMMARY OF CASH-RELATED ITEMS

Cash and cash equivalents include the medium of exchange and most negotiable instruments. If the item cannot be quickly converted to coin or currency, a company separately classifies it as an investment, receivable, or prepaid expense. Companies segregate and classify cash that is unavailable for payment of currently maturing liabilities in the long-term assets section. Illustration 7-2 (page 318) summarizes the classification of cash-related items.

---

[5]Bank overdrafts usually occur because of a simple oversight by the company writing the check. Banks often expect companies to have overdrafts from time to time and therefore negotiate a fee as payment for this possible occurrence. However, at one time, E. F. Hutton (a large brokerage firm) began intentionally overdrawing its accounts by astronomical amounts—on some days exceeding $1 billion—thus obtaining interest-free loans that it could invest. Because the amounts were so large and fees were not negotiated in advance, E. F. Hutton came under criminal investigation for its actions.

[6]*Accounting Trends and Techniques—2004,* indicates that approximately 6 percent of the companies surveyed use the caption "Cash," 83 percent use "Cash and cash equivalents," and 4 percent use a caption such as "Cash and marketable securities" or similar terminology.

ILLUSTRATION 7-2
Classification of Cash-
Related Items

Classification of Cash, Cash Equivalents, and Noncash Items		
Item	Classification	Comment
Cash	Cash	If unrestricted, report as cash. If restricted, identify and classify as current and noncurrent assets.
Petty cash and change funds	Cash	Report as cash.
Short-term paper	Cash equivalents	Investments with maturity of less than 3 months, often combined with cash.
Short-term paper	Temporary investments	Investments with maturity of 3 to 12 months.
Postdated checks and IOU's	Receivables	Assumed to be collectible.
Travel advances	Receivables	Assumed to be collected from employees or deducted from their salaries.
Postage on hand (as stamps or in postage meters)	Prepaid expenses	May also be classified as office supplies inventory.
Bank overdrafts	Current liability	If right of offset exists, reduce cash.
Compensating balances	Cash separately classified as a deposit maintained as compensating balance	Classify as current or noncurrent in the balance sheet. Disclose separately in notes details of the arrangement.

WHAT DO THE NUMBERS MEAN?

TOO MUCH OF A GOOD THING?

Can it ever be a bad thing to have too much cash on hand? Maybe so. As the data in the following table indicate, **General Motors** and some other major companies have been stockpiling cash at levels not recently seen.

Company	Total Cash (in billions)
General Motors	$54.8
Berkshire Hathaway	$36.0
Ford Motor Company	$33.6
Hewlett-Packard	$13.9
Intel	$13.5

Given the low returns on cash, investors may ask why companies maintain such large cash balances. Some companies with good growth prospects plan to use these resources to fuel growth. They intend to step up spending on property, plant, and equipment or on research and development. Or they may hold cash in order to acquire other companies that have growth prospects. However, without good use for stockpiled cash, stockholders would be better served by a payout in the form of a cash dividend.

SECTION 2	*RECEIVABLES*

Receivables are claims held against customers and others for money, goods, or services. For financial statement purposes, companies classify receivables as either **current** (short-term) or **noncurrent** (long-term). Companies expect to collect **current receivables** within a year or during the current operating cycle, whichever is longer. They classify all other receivables as **noncurrent**. Receivables are further classified in the balance sheet as either trade or nontrade receivables.

OBJECTIVE 3
Define receivables and identify the different types of receivables.

Customers often owe a company amounts for goods bought or services rendered. A company may subclassify these **trade receivables**, usually the most significant item it possesses, into accounts receivable and notes receivable. **Accounts receivable** are oral promises of the purchaser to pay for goods and services sold. They represent "open accounts" resulting from short-term extensions of credit. A company normally collects them within 30 to 60 days. **Notes receivable** are written promises to pay a certain sum of money on a specified future date. They may arise from sales, financing, or other transactions. Notes may be short-term or long-term.

Nontrade receivables arise from a variety of transactions. Some examples of nontrade receivables are:

1   Advances to officers and employees.

2   Advances to subsidiaries.

3   Deposits paid to cover potential damages or losses.

4   Deposits paid as a guarantee of performance or payment.

5   Dividends and interest receivable.

6   Claims against:

    (a) Insurance companies for casualties sustained.

    (b) Defendants under suit.

    (c) Governmental bodies for tax refunds.

    (d) Common carriers for damaged or lost goods.

    (e) Creditors for returned, damaged, or lost goods.

    (f) Customers for returnable items (crates, containers, etc.).

Because of the peculiar nature of nontrade receivables, companies generally report them as separate items in the balance sheet. Illustration 7-3 shows the reporting of trade and non-trade receivables in the balance sheets of **Adolph Coors Company** and **Seaboard Corporation**.

ILLUSTRATION 7-3
Receivables Balance Sheet Presentations

Adolph Coors Company
(in thousands)

Current assets	
Cash and cash equivalents	$160,038
Short-term investments	96,190
Accounts and notes receivable	
Trade, less allowance for doubtful accounts of $299	106,962
Subsidiaries	11,896
Other, less allowance for certain claims of $584	7,751
Inventories	102,660
Other supplies, less allowance for obsolete supplies of $3,968	27,729
Prepaid expenses and other assets	12,848
Deferred tax asset	22,917
Total current assets	$548,991

Seaboard Corporation
(in thousands)

Current assets		
Cash and cash equivalents		$ 19,760
Short-term investments		91,375
Receivables		
Trade	$194,966	
Due from foreign affiliates	36,662	
Other	41,816	
		273,444
Allowance for doubtful receivables		(29,801)
Net receivables		243,643
Inventories		218,030
Deferred income taxes		14,132
Prepaid expenses and deposits		23,760
Total current assets		$610,700

The basic issues in accounting for accounts and notes receivable are the same: **recognition**, **valuation**, and **disposition**. We discuss these basic issues for accounts and notes receivable next.

RECOGNITION OF ACCOUNTS RECEIVABLE

OBJECTIVE 4
Explain accounting issues related to recognition of accounts receivable.

In most receivables transactions, the amount to be recognized is the exchange price between the two parties. **The exchange price is the amount due from the debtor** (a customer or a borrower). Some type of business document, often an invoice, serves as evidence of the exchange price. Two factors may complicate the measurement of the exchange price: (1) the availability of discounts (trade and cash discounts), and (2) the length of time between the sale and the due date of payments (the interest element).

Trade Discounts

Prices may be subject to a trade or quantity discount. Companies use such **trade discounts** to avoid frequent changes in catalogs, to alter prices for different quantities purchased, or to hide the true invoice price from competitors.

Trade discounts are commonly quoted in percentages. For example, say your textbook has a list price of $90, and the publisher sells it to college bookstores for list less a 30 percent trade discount. The publisher then records the receivable at $63 per textbook. The publisher, per normal practice, simply deducts the trade discount from the list price and bills the customer net.

As another example, **Maxwell House** at one time sold a 10-ounce jar of its instant coffee listing at $5.85 to supermarkets for $5.05, a trade discount of approximately 14 percent. The supermarkets in turn sold the instant coffee for $5.20 per jar. Maxwell House records the receivable and related sales revenue at $5.05 per jar, not $5.85.

Cash Discounts (Sales Discounts)

Companies offer **cash discounts (sales discounts)** to induce prompt payment. Cash discounts generally read in terms such as 2/10, n/30 (2 percent if paid within 10 days, gross amount due in 30 days), or 2/10, E.O.M., net 30, E.O.M. (2 percent if paid any time before the tenth day of the following month, with full payment received by the thirtieth of the following month).

Companies usually take sales discounts unless their cash is severely limited. Why? A company that receives a 1 percent reduction in the sales price for payment within 10 days, total payment due within 30 days, effectively earns 18.25 percent (.01 ÷ [20/365]), or at least avoids that rate of interest cost.

Companies usually record sales and related sales discount transactions by entering the receivable and sale at the gross amount. Under this method, companies recognize sales discounts only when they receive payment within the discount period. The income statement shows sales discounts as a deduction from sales to arrive at net sales.

Some contend that sales discounts not taken reflect penalties added to an established price to encourage prompt payment. That is, the seller offers sales on account at a slightly higher price than if selling for cash. The cash discount offered offsets the increase. Thus, customers who pay within the discount period actually purchase at the cash price. Those who pay after expiration of the discount period pay a penalty for the delay—an amount in excess of the cash price. Per this reasoning, companies record sales and receivables net. They subsequently debit any discounts not taken to Accounts Receivable and credit to Sales Discounts Forfeited. The entries in Illustration 7-4 show the difference between the gross and net methods.

Gross Method			Net Method		
Sales of $10,000, terms 2/10, n/30					
Accounts Receivable	10,000		Accounts Receivable	9,800	
Sales		10,000	Sales		9,800
Payment of $4,000 received within discount period					
Cash	3,920		Cash	3,920	
Sales Discounts	80		Accounts Receivable		3,920
Accounts Receivable		4,000			
Payment of $6,000 received after discount period					
Cash	6,000		Accounts Receivable	120	
Accounts Receivable		6,000	Sales Discounts		
			Forfeited		120
			Cash	6,000	
			Accounts Receivable		6,000

ILLUSTRATION 7-4
Entries under Gross and Net Methods of Recording Cash (Sales) Discounts

If using the gross method, a company reports sales discounts as a deduction from sales in the income statement. Proper matching dictates that the company also reasonably estimates the expected discounts to be taken and charge that amount against sales. If using the net method, a company considers Sales Discounts Forfeited as an "Other revenue" item.[7]

Theoretically, the recognition of Sales Discounts Forfeited is correct. The receivable is stated closer to its realizable value, and the net sales figure measures the revenue earned from the sale. As a practical matter, however, companies seldom use the net method because it requires additional analysis and bookkeeping. For example, the net method requires adjusting entries to record sales discounts forfeited on accounts receivable that have passed the discount period.

Nonrecognition of Interest Element

Ideally, a company should measure receivables in terms of their present value, that is, the discounted value of the cash to be received in the future. When expected cash receipts require a waiting period, the receivable face amount is not worth the amount that the company ultimately receives.

To illustrate, assume that **Best Buy** makes a sale on account for $1,000 with payment due in four months. The applicable annual rate of interest is 12 percent, and payment is made at the end of four months. The present value of that receivable is not $1,000 but $961.54 ($1,000 × .96154). In other words, the $1,000 Best Buy receives four months from now is not the same as the $1,000 received today.

Theoretically, any revenue after the period of sale is interest revenue. In practice, companies ignore interest revenue related to accounts receivable because the amount of the discount is not usually material in relation to the net income for the period. The profession specifically excludes from present value considerations "receivables arising from transactions with customers in the normal course of business which are due in customary trade terms not exceeding approximately one year."[8]

UNDERLYING CONCEPTS

Materiality means it must make a difference to a decision maker. The FASB believes that present value concepts can be ignored for short-term receivables.

VALUATION OF ACCOUNTS RECEIVABLE

Reporting of receivables involves (1) classification and (2) valuation on the balance sheet. Classification involves determining the length of time each receivable will be outstanding. Companies classify receivables intended to be collected within a year or the operating cycle, whichever is longer, as current. All other receivables are classified as long-term.

[7]To the extent that discounts not taken reflect a short-term financing, some argue that companies could use an interest revenue account to record these amounts.

[8]"Interest on Receivables and Payables," *Opinions of the Accounting Principles Board No. 21* (New York: AICPA, 1971), par. 3(a).

OBJECTIVE 5
Explain accounting
issues related to
valuation of accounts
receivable.

Companies value and report short-term receivables at net realizable value—the net amount they expect to receive in cash. Determining net realizable value requires estimating both uncollectible receivables and any returns or allowances to be granted.

Uncollectible Accounts Receivable

As one revered accountant aptly noted, the credit manager's idea of heaven probably would be a place where everyone (eventually) paid his or her debts.[9] The recent experiences of **Circuit City**, **Sears** (now **Sears Holdings**), **Target**, and **Kohls**, as shown in Illustration 7-5, indicate the importance of credit sales for many companies. Note that for Sears, increased bad debt expense led to a lower stock price, which prompted Sears to sell its credit card portfolio to **Citigroup** in 2003.

ILLUSTRATION 7-5
Credit and Its Costs

Sales on any basis other than cash make uncertain the possibility of collecting the account. An uncollectible account receivable is a loss of revenue that requires, through proper entry in the accounts, a decrease in the asset accounts receivable and a related decrease in income and stockholders' equity. Companies recognize the loss in revenue and the decrease in income by recording bad debt expense.

Companies use two procedures to record uncollectible accounts:

METHODS FOR RECORDING UNCOLLECTIBLES

1 *DIRECT WRITE-OFF METHOD.* No entry is made until a specific account has definitely been established as uncollectible. Then the loss is recorded by crediting Accounts Receivable and debiting Bad Debt Expense.

2 *ALLOWANCE METHOD.* An estimate is made of the expected uncollectible accounts from all sales made on account or from the total of outstanding receivables. This estimate is entered as an expense and an indirect reduction in accounts receivable (via an increase in the allowance account) in the period in which the sale is recorded.

---

[9]William J. Vatter, *Managerial Accounting* (Englewood Cliffs, N.J.: Prentice-Hall, 1950), p. 60.

The **direct write-off method** records the bad debt in the period in which a company determines that it cannot collect a specific receivable. In contrast, the **allowance method** enters the expense on an estimated basis in the accounting period in which the sales on account occur.

Supporters of the **direct write-off method** (which is used for tax purposes) contend that it records facts, not estimates. It assumes that a good account receivable resulted from each sale, and that later events revealed certain accounts to be uncollectible and worthless. From a practical standpoint this method is simple and convenient to apply. But the direct write-off method is theoretically deficient: It usually fails to match costs with revenues of the period. Nor does it result in receivables being stated at estimated realizable value on the balance sheet. **As a result, using the direct write-off method is not considered appropriate, except when the amount uncollectible is immaterial.**

Advocates of the **allowance method** believe that companies should record bad debt expense in the same period as the sale, to properly match expenses and revenues and to achieve a proper carrying value for accounts receivable. They contend that although estimates are involved, companies can predict the percentage of uncollectible receivables from past experiences, present market conditions, and an analysis of the outstanding balances. Many companies set their credit policies to provide for a certain percentage of uncollectible accounts. (In fact, many feel that failure to reach that percentage means that they are losing sales due to overly restrictive credit policies.)

The FASB considers the collectibility of receivables a loss contingency. Thus, the allowance method is appropriate in situations where it is probable that an asset has been impaired and that the amount of the loss can be reasonably estimated.[10]

A receivable is a prospective cash inflow. The probability of its collection must be considered in valuing cash flows. These estimates normally are based either on (1) percentage of sales or (2) outstanding receivables.

Percentage-of-Sales (Income Statement) Approach

If there is a fairly stable relationship between previous years' credit sales and bad debts, then a company can convert that relationship into a percentage and use it to determine this year's bad debt expense.

The **percentage-of-sales approach** matches costs with revenues because it relates the charge to the period in which a company records the sale. To illustrate, assume that Chad Shumway Corp. estimates from past experience that about 2 percent of credit sales become uncollectible. If Chad Shumway has credit sales of $400,000 in 2007, it records bad debt expense using the percentage-of-sales method as follows.

Bad Debt Expense	8,000	
Allowance for Doubtful Accounts		8,000

The Allowance for Doubtful Accounts is a valuation account (i.e., a contra asset), subtracted from trade receivables on the balance sheet.[11] The amount of bad debt expense and the related credit to the allowance account are unaffected by any balance currently existing in the allowance account. Because the bad debt expense estimate is related to a nominal account (Sales), any balance in the allowance is ignored. Therefore, the percentage of sales method achieves a proper matching of cost and revenues. This method is frequently referred to as the **income statement approach**.

Percentage-of-Receivables (Balance Sheet) Approach

Using past experience, a company can estimate the percentage of its outstanding receivables that will become uncollectible, without identifying specific accounts. This procedure provides a reasonably accurate estimate of the receivables' realizable value. But,

UNDERLYING CONCEPTS

The percentage-of-sales method illustrates the matching principle, which relates expenses to revenues earned.

---

[10]"Accounting for Contingencies," *Statement of Financial Accounting Standards No. 5* (Stamford, Conn.: FASB, 1975), par. 8.

[11]The account description employed for the allowance account is usually Allowance for Doubtful Accounts or simply Allowance. *Accounting Trends and Techniques—2004*, for example, indicates that approximately 86 percent of the companies surveyed used "allowance" in their description.

it does not fit the concept of matching cost and revenues. Rather, it simply reports receivables in the balance sheet at net realizable value. Hence it is referred to as the **percentage-of-receivables** (or **balance sheet**) **approach.**

Companies may apply this method using one **composite rate** that reflects an estimate of the uncollectible receivables. Or, companies may set up an **aging schedule** of accounts receivable, which applies a different percentage based on past experience to the various age categories. An aging schedule also identifies which accounts require special attention by indicating the extent to which certain accounts are past due. The following schedule of Wilson & Co. is an example.

ILLUSTRATION 7-6
Accounts Receivable
Aging Schedule

WILSON & CO.
AGING SCHEDULE

Name of Customer	Balance Dec. 31	Under 60 days	61–90 days	91–120 days	Over 120 days
Western Stainless Steel Corp.	$ 98,000	$ 80,000	$18,000		
Brockway Steel Company	320,000	320,000			
Freeport Sheet & Tube Co.	55,000				$55,000
Allegheny Iron Works	74,000	60,000		$14,000	
	$547,000	$460,000	$18,000	$14,000	$55,000

Summary

Age	Amount	Percentage Estimated to be Uncollectible	Required Balance in Allowance
Under 60 days old	$460,000	4%	$18,400
61–90 days old	18,000	15%	2,700
91–120 days old	14,000	20%	2,800
Over 120 days	55,000	25%	13,750
Year-end balance of allowance for doubtful accounts			$37,650

Wilson reports bad debt expense of $37,650 for this year, assuming that no balance existed in the allowance account.

To change the illustration slightly, **assume that the allowance account had a credit balance of $800 before adjustment**. In this case, Wilson adds $36,850 ($37,650 − $800) to the allowance account, and makes the following entry.

Bad Debt Expense	36,850	
Allowance for Doubtful Accounts		36,850

Wilson therefore states the balance in the Allowance account at $37,650. **If the Allowance balance before adjustment had a debit balance of $200,** then Wilson records bad debt expense of $37,850 ($37,650 desired balance + $200 debit balance). In the percentage-of-receivables method, Wilson **cannot ignore** the balance in the allowance account, because the percentage is related to a real account (Accounts Receivable).

Companies usually do not prepare an aging schedule to determine bad debt expense. Rather, they prepare it as a control device to determine the composition of receivables and to identify delinquent accounts. Companies base the estimated loss percentage developed for each category on previous loss experience and the advice of credit department personnel.

Tutorial on Recording Uncollectible Accounts

Whether using a composite rate or an aging schedule, the primary objective of the percentage of outstanding receivables method for financial statement purposes is to report receivables in the balance sheet at net realizable value. However, it is deficient in that it may not match the bad debt expense to the period in which the sale takes place.

The allowance for doubtful accounts as a percentage of receivables will vary, depending on the industry and the economic climate. Companies such as **Eastman Kodak, General Electric,** and **Monsanto** have recorded allowances ranging from $3 to $6 per

$100 of accounts receivable. Other large companies, such as **CPC International** ($1.48), **Texaco** ($1.23), and **USX Corp.** ($0.78), have had bad debt allowances of less than $1.50 per $100. At the other extreme are hospitals that allow for $15 to $20 per $100 of accounts receivable.[12]

GOING FOR BROKE

The start of the new millennium has been a tough one for companies and their investors, creditors, and employees. **Enron, Kmart,** and **WorldCom** all declared bankruptcy—with WorldCom representing the largest bankruptcy ever. The trend seems to be continuing.

It is not surprising that banks and other creditors are raising their lending standards to guard against future loan defaults. Even so, some question whether creditors have set up reasonable bad debt allowances to ensure that financial performance is reported accurately. Indeed, one recent analysis for hospitals (mentioned in our opening story) indicates that additional bad debt expense needed to properly reflect future write-offs could result in an earnings hit of as much as 18 percent for some hospitals. That will be tough medicine for these companies to swallow.

Source: Adapted from: Julie Creswell, "First Going for Broke," *Fortune* (February 18, 2002), pp. 24–25; Bethany McLean, "Reality Check-up," *Fortune* (January 12, 2004), pp. 140.

WHAT DO THE NUMBERS MEAN?

In summary, the percentage-of-receivables method results in a more accurate valuation of receivables on the balance sheet. From a matching viewpoint, the percentage-of-sales approach provides the better results. Illustration 7-7 relates these methods to the basic theory.

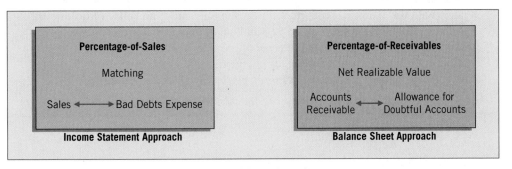

ILLUSTRATION 7-7
Comparison of Methods for Estimating Uncollectibles

The account title employed for the allowance account is usually Allowance for Doubtful Accounts or simply Allowance.

---

[12]A U.S. Department of Commerce study indicated, as a general rule, the following relationships between the age of accounts receivable and their uncollectibility.

30 days or less	4% uncollectible
31–60 days	10% uncollectible
61–90 days	17% uncollectible
91–120 days	26% uncollectible

After 120 days, an approximate 3–4 percent increase in uncollectibles for every 30 days outstanding occurs for the remainder of the first year.

Regardless of the method chosen, determining the expense associated with uncollectible accounts requires a large degree of judgment. Recent concern exists that, similar to **Nortel** in our opening story, some banks use this judgment to manage earnings. By overestimating the amounts of uncollectible loans in a good earnings year, the bank can "save for a rainy day" in a future period. In future (less-profitable) periods, banks can reduce the overly conservative allowance for loan loss account to increase earnings. In this regard, the SEC brought action against **Suntrust Banks**, requiring a reversal of $100 million of bad debt expense. This reversal increased aftertax profit by $61 million.[13]

Collection of Accounts Receivable Written Off

When a company determines a particular account receivable to be uncollectible, it removes the balance from the books by debiting Allowance for Doubtful Accounts and crediting Accounts Receivable. If it eventually collects on a receivable that it previously wrote off, it first reestablishes the receivable by debiting Accounts Receivable and crediting Allowance for Doubtful Accounts. The company then debits Cash and credits the customer's account for the amount received.

If using the direct write-off approach, the company debits the amount collected to Cash and credits a revenue account entitled Uncollectible Amounts Recovered, with proper notation in the customer's account.

WHAT DO THE NUMBERS MEAN?

COLLECTION IS A CLICK AWAY

What do lenders do with uncollectible receivables? After they record bad debts on their books, they next to try to collect what they can from the deadbeat customers. Some lenders auction their bad loans in the market for distressed debt, usually paying a fee of 5–15 percent to a distressed debt broker, who arranges the sale.

Recently, several Web sites have sprung up to provide a meeting place between lenders with bad loans and collectors. These sites are sort of an "eBay of deadbeats." For example, **Bank One Corp.** listed $211 million of unpaid credit card receivables on **DebtforSale.com**. While the lendors generally recover less than 10 percent of the face value of the receivables in an auction, by going online they can reduce the costs of their bad debts. Online services charge just 0.5–1 percent for their auction services.

Source: Adapted from P. Gogoi, "An eBay of Deadbeats," *Business Week* (September 18, 2000), p. 124.

RECOGNITION OF NOTES RECEIVABLE

A note receivable is supported by a formal **promissory note**, a written promise to pay a certain sum of money at a specific future date. Such a note is a negotiable instrument that a **maker** signs in favor of a designated **payee** who may legally and readily sell or otherwise transfer the note to others. Although notes contain an interest element because of the time value of money, companies classify them as interest-bearing or noninterest-bearing. **Interest-bearing notes** have a stated rate of interest. **Zero-interest-bearing notes** (noninterest-bearing) include interest as part of their face amount. Notes receivable are considered fairly liquid, even if long-term, because companies may easily convert them to cash (although they might pay a fee to do so).

---

[13]Recall from our earnings management discussion in Chapter 4 that increasing or decreasing income through management manipulation can reduce the quality of financial reports.

Companies frequently accept notes receivable from customers who need to extend the payment period of an outstanding receivable. Or they require notes from high-risk or new customers. In addition, companies often use notes in loans to employees and subsidiaries, and in the sales of property, plant, and equipment. In some industries (e.g., the pleasure and sport boat industry) notes support all credit sales. The majority of notes, however, originate from lending transactions. The basic issues in accounting for notes receivable are the same as those for accounts receivable: **recognition, valuation, and disposition**.

Companies generally record short-term notes at face value (less allowances) because the interest implicit in the maturity value is immaterial. A general rule is that notes treated as cash equivalents (maturities of three months or less and easily converted to cash) are not subject to premium or discount amortization.

However, companies should record and report long-term notes receivable at the **present value of the cash they expect to collect**. When the interest stated on an interest-bearing note equals the effective (market) rate of interest, the note sells at face value.[14] When the stated rate differs from the market rate, the cash exchanged (present value) differs from the face value of the note. Companies then record this difference, either a discount or a premium, and amortize it over the life of a note to approximate the effective (market) interest rate. This illustrates one of the many situations in which time value of money concepts are applied to accounting measurement.

OBJECTIVE 6
Explain accounting issues related to recognition of notes receivable.

Note Issued at Face Value

To illustrate the discounting of a note issued at face value, assume that Bigelow Corp. lends Scandinavian Imports $10,000 in exchange for a $10,000, three-year note bearing interest at 10 percent annually. The market rate of interest for a note of similar risk is also 10 percent. We show the time diagram depicting both cash flows in Illustration 7-8.

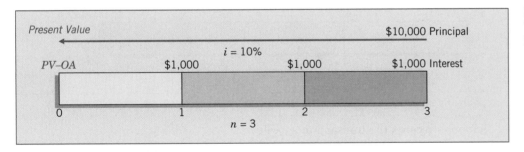

ILLUSTRATION 7-8
Time Diagram for Note Issued at Face Value

Bigelow computes the present value or exchange price of the note as follows.

Face value of the note		$10,000
Present value of the principal:		
$10,000 (PVF$_{3,10\%}$) = $10,000 × .75132	$7,513	
Present value of the interest:		
$1,000 (PVF-OA$_{3,10\%}$) = $1,000 × 2.48685	2,487	
Present value of the note		10,000
Difference		$ –0–

ILLUSTRATION 7-9
Present Value of Note—Stated and Market Rates the Same

---

[14]The **stated interest rate**, also referred to as the face rate or the coupon rate, is the rate contracted as part of the note. The **effective-interest rate**, also referred to as the *market rate* or the *effective yield*, is the rate used in the market to determine the value of the note —that is, the discount rate used to determine present value.

In this case, the present value of the note equals its face value, because the effective and stated rates of interest are also the same. Bigelow records the receipt of the note as follows.

Notes Receivable	10,000	
Cash		10,000

Bigelow recognizes the interest earned each year as follows.

Cash	1,000	
Interest Revenue		1,000

Note Not Issued at Face Value

Zero-Interest-Bearing Notes

If a company receives a zero-interest-bearing note, its present value is the cash paid to the issuer. Because the company knows both the future amount and the present value of the note, it can compute the interest rate. This rate is often referred to as the **implicit interest rate**. Companies record the difference between the future (face) amount and the present value (cash paid) as a discount and amortize it to interest revenue over the life of the note.

To illustrate, Jeremiah Company receives a three-year, $10,000 zero-interest-bearing note, the present value of which is $7,721.80. The implicit rate that equates the total cash to be received ($10,000 at maturity) to the present value of the future cash flows ($7,721.80) is 9 percent (the present value of 1 for three periods at 9 percent is .77218). We show the time diagram depicting the one cash flow in Illustration 7-10.

ILLUSTRATION 7-10
Time Diagram for Zero-Interest-Bearing Note

Jeremiah records the transaction as follows:

Notes Receivable	10,000.00	
Discount on Notes Receivable ($10,000 − $7,721.80)		2,278.20
Cash		7,721.80

The Discount on Notes Receivable is a valuation account. Companies report it on the balance sheet as a contra-asset account to notes receivable. They then amortize the discount, and recognize interest revenue annually using the **effective-interest method**. Illustration 7-11 (page 329) shows the three-year discount amortization and interest revenue schedule.

Jeremiah records interest revenue at the end of the first year using the effective-interest method as follows.

Discount on Notes Receivable	694.96	
Interest Revenue ($7,721.80 × 9%)		694.96

The amount of the discount, $2,278.20 in this case, represents the interest revenue Jeremiah will receive from the note over the three years.

Interest-Bearing Notes

Often the stated rate and the effective rate differ. The zero-interest-bearing note is one example.

As indicated in Appendix 6A, you can use a financial calculator to solve this problem.

Calculator Solution for Present Value of Note Receivable

	Inputs	Answer
N	3	
I	10	
PV	?	−10,000
PMT	1,000	
FV	10,000	

Calculator Solution for Effective-Interest Rate on Note

	Inputs	Answer
N	3	
I	?	9
PV	−7,721.80	
PMT	0	
FV	10,000	

ILLUSTRATION 7-11
Discount Amortization
Schedule—Effective-
Interest Method

SCHEDULE OF NOTE DISCOUNT AMORTIZATION
EFFECTIVE-INTEREST METHOD
0% NOTE DISCOUNTED AT 9%

	Cash Received	Interest Revenue	Discount Amortized	Carrying Amount of Note
Date of issue				$7,721.80
End of year 1	$ –0–	$ 694.96[a]	$ 694.96[b]	8,416.76[c]
End of year 2	–0–	757.51	757.51	9,174.27
End of year 3	–0–	825.73[d]	825.73	10,000.00
	$ –0–	$2,278.20	$2,278.20	

[a]$7,721.80 × .09 = $694.96   [c]$7,721.80 + $694.96 = $8,416.76
[b]$694.96 − 0 = $694.96   [d]5¢ adjustment to compensate for rounding

To illustrate a more common situation, assume that Morgan Corp. makes a loan to Marie Co. and receives in exchange a three-year, $10,000 note bearing interest at 10 percent annually. The market rate of interest for a note of similar risk is 12 percent. We show the time diagram depicting both cash flows in Illustration 7-12.

ILLUSTRATION 7-12
Time Diagram for
Interest-Bearing Note

Morgan computes the present value of the two cash flows as follows.

Face value of the note		$10,000
Present value of the principal:		
$10,000 ($PVF_{3,12\%}$) = $10,000 × .71178	$7,118	
Present value of the interest:		
$1,000 ($PVF\text{-}OA_{3,12\%}$) = $1,000 × 2.40183	2,402	
Present value of the note		9,520
Difference (Discount)		$ 480

In this case, because the effective rate of interest (12 percent) exceeds the stated rate (10 percent), the present value of the note is less than the face value. That is, Morgan exchanged the note at a **discount**. Morgan records the receipt of the note at a discount as follows.

Notes Receivable	10,000	
Discount on Notes Receivable		480
Cash		9,520

Morgan then amortizes the discount and recognizes interest revenue annually using the **effective-interest method**. Illustration 7-14 (page 330) shows the three-year discount amortization and interest revenue schedule.

ILLUSTRATION 7-14
Discount Amortization
Schedule—Effective-
Interest Method

	Cash Received	Interest Revenue	Discount Amortized	Carrying Amount of Note

SCHEDULE OF NOTE DISCOUNT AMORTIZATION
EFFECTIVE-INTEREST METHOD
10% NOTE DISCOUNTED AT 12%

	Cash Received	Interest Revenue	Discount Amortized	Carrying Amount of Note
Date of issue				$ 9,520
End of year 1	$1,000ª	$1,142ᵇ	$142ᶜ	9,662ᵈ
End of year 2	1,000	1,159	159	9,821
End of year 3	1,000	1,179	179	10,000
	$3,000	$3,480	$480	

ª$10,000 × 10% = $1,000 ᶜ$1,142 − $1,000 = $142
ᵇ$9,520 × 12% = $1,142 ᵈ$9,520 + $142 = $9,662

On the date of issue, the note has a present value of $9,520. Its unamortized discount—additional interest revenue spread over the three-year life of the note—is $480.

At the end of year 1, Morgan receives $1,000 in cash. But its interest revenue is $1,142 ($9,520 × 12%). The difference between $1,000 and $1,142 is the amortized discount, $142. Morgan records receipt of the annual interest and amortization of the discount for the first year as follows (amounts per amortization schedule).

Cash	1,000	
Discount on Notes Receivable	142	
Interest Revenue		1,142

The carrying amount of the note is now $9,662 ($9,520 + $142). Morgan repeats this process until the end of year 3.

When the present value exceeds the face value, the note is exchanged at a premium. Companies record the premium on a note receivable as a debit and amortize it using the effective-interest method over the life of the note as annual reductions in the amount of interest revenue recognized.

Notes Received for Property, Goods, or Services

When a **note is received in exchange for property, goods, or services** in a bargained transaction entered into at arm's length, the stated interest rate is presumed to be fair unless:

1 No interest rate is stated, or

2 The stated interest rate is unreasonable, or

3 The face amount of the note is materially different from the current cash sales price for the same or similar items or from the current market value of the debt instrument.[15]

In these circumstances, the company measures the present value of the note by the fair value of the property, goods, or services or by an amount that reasonably approximates the market value of the note.

To illustrate, Oasis Development Co. sold a corner lot to Rusty Pelican as a restaurant site. Oasis accepted in exchange a five-year note having a maturity value of $35,247 and no stated interest rate. The land originally cost Oasis $14,000. At the date of sale the land had a fair market value of $20,000. Given the criterion above, Oasis uses the fair market value of the land, $20,000, as the present value of the note. Oasis therefore records the sale as:

Notes Receivable	35,247	
Discount on Notes Receivable ($35,247 − $20,000)		15,247
Land		14,000
Gain on Sale of Land ($20,000 − $14,000)		6,000

Calculator Solution for
Effective-Interest
Rate on Note

	Inputs	Answer
N	5	
I	?	12
PV	−20,000	
PMT	0	
FV	35,247	

---

[15]"Interest on Receivables and Payables," *Opinions of the Accounting Principles Board No. 21* (New York: AICPA, 1971), par. 12.

Oasis amortizes the discount to interest revenue over the five-year life of the note using the effective-interest method.

Choice of Interest Rate

In note transactions, other factors involved in the exchange, such as the fair market value of the property, goods, or services, determine the effective or real interest rate. But, if a company cannot determine that fair value, and if the note has no ready market, determining the present value of the note is more difficult. To estimate the present value of a note under such circumstances, the company must approximate an applicable interest rate that may differ from the stated interest rate. This process of interest-rate approximation is called **imputation**. The resulting interest rate is called an **imputed interest rate**.

The prevailing rates for similar instruments, from issuers with similar credit ratings, affect the choice of a rate. Restrictive covenants, collateral, payment schedule, and the existing prime interest rate also impact the choice. A company determines the imputed interest rate when it receives the note. It ignores any subsequent changes in prevailing interest rates.

VALUATION OF NOTES RECEIVABLE

Like accounts receivable, companies record and report short-term notes receivable at their net realizable value—that is, at their face amount less all necessary allowances. The primary notes receivable allowance account is Allowance for Doubtful Accounts. The computations and estimations involved in valuing short-term notes receivable and in recording bad debt expense and the related allowance **exactly parallel that for trade accounts receivable**. Companies estimate the amount of uncollectibles by using either a percentage of sales revenue or an analysis of the receivables.

> **OBJECTIVE 7**
> Explain accounting issues related to valuation of notes receivable.

Long-term notes receivable, however, pose additional estimation problems. For evidence, we need only look at the problems that financial institutions, most notably money-center banks, have had in collecting receivables from energy loans, real estate loans, and loans to less-developed countries.[16]

A company considers a note receivable **impaired** when collecting all amounts due (both principal and interest) will likely not occur. We discuss impairments, as well as restructurings, of receivables and debts in detail in Appendix 14A.

PUTTING THE SQUEEZE ON

When the economy slows, lenders such as **J.P. Morgan** and **First Chicago** get stingier in granting new loans or renewing loans to existing customers. This tightening of loans is referred to as a "credit squeeze."

However, it is sometimes difficult for banks to cut back on lending when the economy goes from good times to bad. When times are good and banks are competing for lending business, lenders often grant business customers "lines of credit" as a sweetener to close a loan. In contrast to a term loan that is supported by a note, a line of credit allows borrowing on a day-to-day basis.

When times turn bad, the bank can cut back on loans via notes receivable, but it still must honor the lines of credit, even to weak customers. For example, **Xerox Inc.** got a $7 billion line of credit before it hit the skids. Although denied by the traditional loan markets, Xerox has been able to draw on its line of credit to make ends meet. Thus, what seemed like of good competitive tool in good times has put the squeeze on *lenders* when times have turned bad.

Source: Adapted from H. Timmons and D. Sparks, "Feeling a Credit Squeeze," *Business Week* (December 4, 2000), pp. 148–149.

WHAT DO THE NUMBERS MEAN?

---

[16]A wise person once said that a bank lending money to a Third World country is like lending money to one's children: You should never expect to get the interest, let alone the principal.

DISPOSITION OF ACCOUNTS AND NOTES RECEIVABLE

OBJECTIVE 8
Explain accounting issues related to disposition of accounts and notes receivable.

In the normal course of events, companies collect accounts and notes receivable when due and then remove them from the books. However, the growing size and significance of credit sales and receivables has led to changes in this "normal course of events." **In order to accelerate the receipt of cash from receivables, the owner may transfer accounts or notes receivables to another company for cash.**

There are various reasons for this early transfer. First, for competitive reasons, providing sales financing for customers is virtually mandatory in many industries. In the sale of durable goods, such as automobiles, trucks, industrial and farm equipment, computers, and appliances, most sales are on an installment contract basis. Many major companies in these industries have created wholly-owned subsidiaries specializing in receivables financing. For example, **General Motors Corp.** has **General Motors Acceptance Corp. (GMAC)**, and **John Deere** has **John Deere Credit.**

Second, the **holder** may sell receivables because money is tight and access to normal credit is unavailable or too expensive. Also, a firm may sell its receivables, instead of borrowing, to avoid violating existing lending agreements.

Finally, billing and collection of receivables are often time-consuming and costly. Credit card companies such as **MasterCard, VISA, American Express, Diners Club, Discover**, and others take over the collection process and provide merchants with immediate cash.

Conversely, some **purchasers** of receivables buy them to obtain the legal protection of ownership rights afforded a purchaser of assets versus the lesser rights afforded a secured creditor. In addition, banks and other lending institutions may need to purchase receivables because of legal lending limits. That is, they cannot make any additional loans but they can buy receivables and charge a fee for this service.

The transfer of receivables to a third party for cash happens in one of two ways:

1 Secured borrowing.
2 Sales of receivables.

Secured Borrowing

A company often uses receivables as collateral in a borrowing transaction. In fact, a creditor often requires that the debtor designate (assign) or pledge[17] receivables as security for the loan. If the loan is not paid when due, the creditor can convert the collateral to cash —that is, to collect the receivables.

To illustrate, on March 1, 2007, Howat Mills, Inc. provides (assigns) $700,000 of its accounts receivable to Citizens Bank as collateral for a $500,000 note. Howat Mills continues to collect the accounts receivable; the account debtors are not notified of the arrangement. Citizens Bank assesses a finance charge of 1 percent of the accounts receivable and interest on the note of 12 percent. Howat Mills makes monthly payments to the bank for all cash it collects on the receivables. Illustration 7-15 (page 333) shows the entries for the secured borrowing for Howatt Mills and Citizens Bank.

In addition to recording the collection of receivables, Howat Mills must recognize all discounts, returns and allowances, and bad debts. Each month Howat Mills uses the proceeds from the collection of the accounts receivable to retire the note obligation. In addition, it pays interest on the note.[18]

---

[17]If a company transfers the receivables for custodial purposes, the custodial arrangement is often referred to as a **pledge**.

[18]What happens if Citizens Bank collected the transferred accounts receivable rather than Howat Mills? Citizens Bank would simply remit the cash proceeds to Howat Mills, and Howat Mills would make the same entries shown in Illustration 7-15. As a result, Howat Mills reports these "collaterized" receivables as an asset on the balance sheet.

Howat Mills, Inc.			Citizens Bank		
Transfer of accounts receivable and issuance of note on March 1, 2007					
Cash	493,000		Notes Receivable	500,000	
Finance Charge	7,000*		Finance Revenue		7,000*
Notes Payable		500,000	Cash		493,000
*(1% × $700,000)					
Collection in March of $440,000 of accounts less cash discounts of $6,000 plus receipt of $14,000 sales returns					
Cash	434,000				
Sales Discounts	6,000				
Sales Returns	14,000		(No entry)		
Accounts Receivable		454,000			
($440,000 + $14,000 = $454,000)					
Remitted March collections plus accrued interest to the bank on April 1					
Interest Expense	5,000*		Cash	439,000	
Notes Payable	434,000		Interest Revenue		5,000*
Cash		439,000	Notes Receivable		434,000
*($500,000 × .12 × 1/12)					
Collection in April of the balance of accounts less $2,000 written off as uncollectible					
Cash	244,000				
Allowance for Doubtful Accounts	2,000		(No entry)		
Accounts Receivable		246,000*			
*($700,000 − $454,000)					
Remitted the balance due of $66,000 ($500,000 − $434,000) on the note plus interest on May 1					
Interest Expense	660*		Cash	66,660	
Notes Payable	66,000		Interest Revenue		660*
Cash		66,660	Notes Receivable		66,000
*($66,000 × .12 × 1/12)					

ILLUSTRATION 7-15
Entries for Transfer of Receivables—Secured Borrowing

Sales of Receivables

Sales of receivables have increased substantially in recent years. A common type is a sale to a factor. **Factors** are finance companies or banks that buy receivables from businesses for a fee and then collect the remittances directly from the customers. **Factoring receivables** is traditionally associated with the textile, apparel, footwear, furniture, and home furnishing industries.[19] Illustration 7-16 shows a typical factoring arrangement.

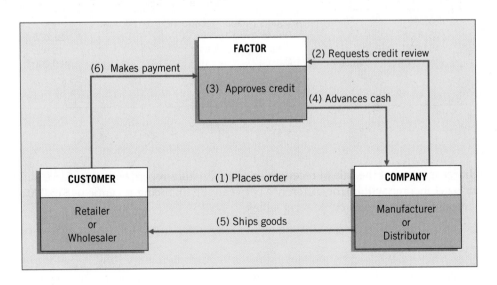

ILLUSTRATION 7-16
Basic Procedures in Factoring

---

[19]Credit cards like **MasterCard** and **VISA** are a type of factoring arrangement. Typically the purchaser of the receivable charges a ¾–1½ percent commission of the receivables purchased (the commission is 4–5 percent for credit card factoring).

A recent phenomenon in the sale (transfer) of receivables is securitization. **Securitization** takes a pool of assets such as credit card receivables, mortgage receivables, or car loan receivables, and sells shares in these pools of interest and principal payments. This, in effect, creates securities backed by these pools of assets. Virtually every asset with a payment stream and a long-term payment history is a candidate for securitization.

What are the differences between factoring and securitization? Factoring usually involves sale to only one company, fees are high, the quality of the receivables is low, and the seller afterward does not service the receivables. In a securitization, many investors are involved, margins are tight, the receivables are of higher quality, and the seller usually continues to service the receivables.

In either a factoring or a securitization transaction, a company sells receivables on either a **without recourse** or a **with recourse** basis.[20]

Sale without Recourse

Comprehensive Illustration of Sale Without Recourse

When buying receivables **without recourse**, the purchaser assumes the risk of collectibility and absorbs any credit losses. The transfer of accounts receivable in a nonrecourse transaction is an outright sale of the receivables both in form (transfer of title) and substance (transfer of control). In nonrecourse transactions, as in any sale of assets, the seller debits Cash for the proceeds and credits Accounts Receivable for the face value of the receivables. The seller recognizes the difference, reduced by any provision for probable adjustments (discounts, returns, allowances, etc.), as a Loss on the Sale of Receivables. The seller uses a Due from Factor account (reported as a receivable) to account for the proceeds retained by the factor to cover probable sales discounts, sales returns, and sales allowances.

To illustrate, Crest Textiles, Inc. factors $500,000 of accounts receivable with Commercial Factors, Inc., on a **without recourse** basis. Crest Textiles transfers the receivable records to Commercial Factors, which will receive the collections. Commercial Factors assesses a finance charge of 3 percent of the amount of accounts receivable and retains an amount equal to 5 percent of the accounts receivable (for probable adjustments). Crest Textiles and Commercial Factors make the following journal entries for the receivables transferred without recourse.

ILLUSTRATION 7-17
Entries for Sale of
Receivables Without
Recourse

Crest Textiles, Inc.				Commercial Factors, Inc.		
Cash	460,000			Accounts (Notes) Receivable	500,000	
Due from Factor	25,000*			Due to Crest Textiles		25,000
Loss on Sale of Receivables	15,000**			Financing Revenue		15,000
Accounts (Notes) Receivable		500,000		Cash		460,000
*(5% × $500,000)						
**(3% × $500,000)						

In recognition of the sale of receivables, Crest Textiles records a loss of $15,000. The factor's net income will be the difference between the financing revenue of $15,000 and the amount of any uncollectible receivables.

---

[20]**Recourse** is the right of a transferee of receivables to receive payment from the transferor of those receivables for (1) failure of the debtors to pay when due, (2) the effects of prepayments, or (3) adjustments resulting from defects in the eligibility of the transferred receivables. See "Accounting for Transfers and Servicing of Financial Assets and Extinguishments of Liabilities," *Statement of Financial Accounting Standards No. 140* (Stamford, Conn.: FASB, 2000), p. 155.

Sale with Recourse

For receivables sold **with recourse**, the seller guarantees payment to the purchaser in the event the debtor fails to pay. To record this type of transaction, the seller uses a **financial components approach**, because the seller has a continuing involvement with the receivable.[21] In this approach, each party to the sale only recognizes the assets and liabilities that it controls after the sale.

To illustrate, assume the same information as in Illustration 7-17 for Crest Textiles and for Commercial Factors, except that Crest Textiles sold the receivables on a with-recourse basis. Crest Textiles determines that this recourse obligation has a fair value of $6,000. To determine the loss on the sale of the receivables, Crest Textiles computes the net proceeds from the sale as follows.

Cash received	$460,000	
Due from factor	25,000	$485,000
Less: Recourse obligation		6,000
Net proceeds		$479,000

ILLUSTRATION 7-18
Net Proceeds Computation

Net proceeds are cash or other assets received in a sale less any liabilities incurred. Crest Textiles then computes the loss as follows.

Carrying (book) value	$500,000
Net proceeds	479,000
Loss on sale of receivables	$ 21,000

ILLUSTRATION 7-19
Loss on Sale Computation

Illustration 7-20 shows the journal entries for both Crest Textiles and Commercial Factors for the receivables sold with recourse.

Crest Textiles, Inc.				Commercial Factors, Inc.			
Cash	460,000			Accounts Receivable	500,000	
Due from Factor	25,000			Due to Crest Textiles		25,000
Loss on Sale of				Financing Revenue		15,000
Receivables	21,000			Cash		460,000
Accounts (Notes)						
Receivable		500,000				
Recourse Liability		6,000				

ILLUSTRATION 7-20
Entries for Sale of Receivables with Recourse

---

[21]Accounting standards before *SFAS No. 140* generally required that the transferor account for financial assets transferred as an inseparable unit that had been entirely sold or entirely retained. Those standards were difficult to apply and produced inconsistent and arbitrary results. Values are now assigned to such components as the recourse provision, servicing rights, and agreement to reacquire.

In this case, Crest Textiles recognizes a loss of $21,000. In addition, it records a liability of $6,000 to indicate the probable payment to Commercial Factors for uncollectible receivables. If Commercial Factors collects all the receivables, Crest Textiles eliminates its recourse liability and increases income. Commercial Factors' net income is the financing revenue of $15,000. It will have no bad debts related to these receivables.

UGLY DUCKLINGS

WHAT DO THE NUMBERS MEAN?

Ugly Duckling is a used-car dealer that has carved out a niche by selling cars to customers with questionable credit histories. Ugly Duckling and other "sub-prime lenders" earn a profit by loaning money to riskier borrowers so they can purchase automobiles or homes. To compensate for the higher probability of default of these customers, sub-prime lenders charge higher rates of interest on these high-risk loans. In many instances these companies package their sub-prime loans and sell them as securities. However, recognition of gains on these transfers of receivables is appropriate only if Ugly Duckling can reasonably estimate the proportion of the loans that borrowers will not repay (the receivables are sold with recourse).

However, estimating loan defaults is difficult. If sub-prime lenders fail to set rates high enough to cover unexpected higher rates of default, a severe cash squeeze will result. In addition, if too many of the loans that it sells then default, Ugly Duckling will have to take them back, thereby eliminating any gain it recorded on the original sale. Indeed, in one year alone, **ContiFinancial** had to write off over $654 million in sub-prime loans. Similarly, bank regulators had to step in and take over **Superior Bank FSB**, which specialized in sub-prime loans, because it overestimated the value of its sub-prime loans.

Thus, the sub-prime lending business is a risky one. Depending on default and interest rate assumptions on these receivables, companies like Ugly Duckling may not survive to grow into lending swans.

Secured Borrowing versus Sale

The FASB concluded that a sale occurs only if the seller surrenders control of the receivables to the buyer. The following three conditions must be met before a company can record a sale:

1 The transferred asset has been isolated from the transferor (put beyond reach of the transferor and its creditors).

2 The transferees have obtained the right to pledge or exchange either the transferred assets or beneficial interests in the transferred assets.

3 The transferor does not maintain effective control over the transferred assets through an agreement to repurchase or redeem them before their maturity.

If the three conditions are met, a sale occurs. Otherwise, the transferor should record the transfer as a secured borrowing. If sale accounting is appropriate, a company must still consider assets obtained and liabilities incurred in the transaction. Illustration 7-21 (page 337) shows the rules of accounting for transfers of receivables. As it shows, if there is continuing involvement in a sale transaction, a company must record the assets obtained and liabilities incurred.

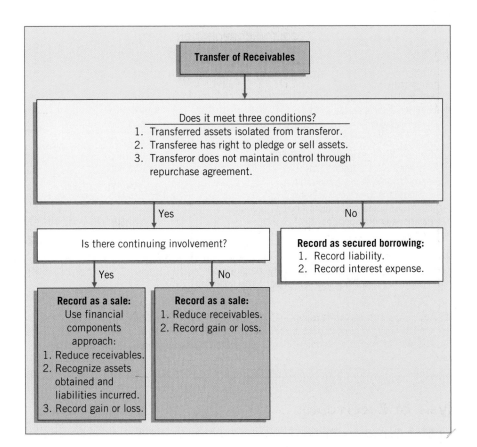

ILLUSTRATION 7-21
Accounting for Transfers
of Receivables

PRESENTATION AND ANALYSIS

Presentation of Receivables

The general rules in classifying receivables are:

1 Segregate the different types of receivables that a company possesses, if material.

2 Appropriately offset the valuation accounts against the proper receivable accounts.

3 Determine that receivables classified in the current assets section will be converted into cash within the year or the operating cycle, whichever is longer.

4 Disclose any loss contingencies that exist on the receivables.

5 Disclose any receivables designated or pledged as collateral.

6 Disclose all significant concentrations of credit risk arising from receivables.[22]

The assets sections of Colton Corporation's balance sheet in Illustration 7-22 (page 338) show many of the disclosures required for receivables.

> **OBJECTIVE 9**
> **Describe how to report and analyze receivables.**

---

[22]Concentrations of credit risk exist when receivables have common characteristics that may affect their collection. These common characteristics might be companies in the same industry or same region of the country. For example, **Quantum Corporation** reported that sales of its disk drives to its top five customers (including **Hewlett-Packard**) represented nearly 40 percent of its revenues in 2003. Financial statements users want to know if a substantial amount of receivables from such sales are to customers facing uncertain economic conditions. No numerical guidelines are provided as to what is meant by a "concentration of credit risk."

Three items should be disclosed with an identified concentration: (1) information on the characteristic that determines the concentration, (2) the amount of loss that could occur upon nonperformance, and (3) information on any collateral related to the receivable. "Disclosures about Fair Value of Financial Instruments," *Statement of Financial Accounting Standards No. 107* (Norwalk, Conn.: FASB, 1991), par. 15.

ILLUSTRATION 7-22
Disclosure of Receivables

*Additional Disclosures
of Receivables*

**INTERNATIONAL
INSIGHT**

Holding receivables that it will
pay in a foreign currency represents risk that the exchange
rate may move against the
company. This results in a decrease in the amount collected
in terms of U.S. dollars.
Companies engaged in cross-
border transactions often
"hedge" these receivables by
buying contracts to exchange
currencies at specified amounts
at future dates.

COLTON CORPORATION BALANCE SHEET (PARTIAL) AS OF DECEMBER 31, 2007		
Current assets		
Cash and cash equivalents		$ 1,870,250
Accounts receivable (Note 2)	$8,977,673	
Less: Allowance for doubtful accounts	500,226	
	8,477,447	
Advances to subsidiaries due 9/30/08	2,090,000	
Notes receivable—trade (Note 2)	1,532,000	
Federal income taxes refundable	146,704	
Dividends and interest receivable	75,500	
Other receivables and claims (including debit balances in accounts payable)	174,620	12,496,271
Total current assets		14,366,521
Noncurrent receivables		
Notes receivable from officers and key employees		376,090
Claims receivable (litigation settlement to be collected over four years)		585,000

Note 2: Accounts and Notes Receivable. In November 2007, the Company arranged with a finance company to refinance a part of its indebtedness. The loan is evidenced by a 12% note payable. The note is payable on demand and is secured by substantially all the accounts receivable.

Analysis of Receivables

Receivables Turnover Ratio

Analysts frequently compute financial ratios to evaluate the liquidity of a company's ac-counts receivable. To assess the liquidity of the receivables, they use the **receivables turnover ratio**. This ratio measures the number of times, on average, a company collects receivables during the period. The ratio is computed by dividing net sales by average (net) receivables outstanding during the year. Theoretically, the numerator should include only net credit sales, but this information is frequently unavailable. However, if the relative amounts of credit and cash sales remain fairly constant, the trend indicated by the ratio will still be valid. Barring significant seasonal factors, average receivables outstanding can be computed from the beginning and ending balances of net trade receivables.

To illustrate, **Circuit City** reported 2004 net sales of $9,745 million, its beginning and ending accounts receivable balances were $380 million and $580 million, respectively. Illustration 7-23 shows the computation of its accounts receivables turnover ratio.

ILLUSTRATION 7-23
Computation of Accounts
Receivable Turnover

$$\frac{\text{Net Sales}}{\text{Average Trade Receivables (net)}} = \frac{\text{Accounts Receivable}}{\text{Turnover}}$$

$$\frac{\$9,745}{(\$580 + \$380)/2} = 20.3 \text{ times, or every 18 days } (365 \div 20.3)$$

UNDERLYING CONCEPTS

Providing information that will
help users assess a company's
current liquidity and prospective cash flows is a primary
objective of accounting.

This information[23] shows how successful the company is in collecting its outstand-ing receivables. If possible, an aging schedule should also be prepared to help determine how long receivables have been outstanding. A satisfactory receivables turnover may have resulted because certain receivables were collected quickly though others have been outstanding for a relatively long period. An aging schedule would reveal such patterns.

---

[23]Often the receivables turnover is transformed to **days to collect accounts receivable** or **days outstanding**—an average collection period. In this case, 20.3 is divided into 365 days, resulting in 18 days. Several figures other than 365 could be used. A common alternative is 360 days because it is divisible by 30 (days) and 12 (months). *Use 365 days in any homework computations.*

KEY TERMS

accounts receivable, *319*

aging schedule, *324*

allowance method, *323*

bank overdrafts, *317*

cash, *314*

cash discounts, *320*

cash equivalents, *317*

compensating balances, *316*

direct write-off method, *323*

factoring receivables, *333*

financial components approach, *335*

imputed interest rate, *331*

net realizable value, *322*

nontrade receivables, *319*

notes receivable, *319*

percentage-of-receivables approach, *324*

percentage-of-sales approach, *323*

promissory note, *326*

receivables, *318*

receivables turnover ratio, *338*

restricted cash, *316*

sales discounts, *320*

securitization, *334*

trade discounts, *320*

trade receivables, *319*

with recourse, *335*

without recourse, *334*

zero-interest-bearing notes, *326*

SUMMARY OF LEARNING OBJECTIVES

1. **Identify items considered cash.** To be reported as "cash," an asset must be readily available for the payment of current obligations and free from contractual restrictions that limit its use in satisfying debts. Cash consists of coin, currency, and available funds on deposit at the bank. Negotiable instruments such as money orders, certified checks, cashier's checks, personal checks, and bank drafts are also viewed as cash. Savings accounts are usually classified as cash.

2. **Indicate how to report cash and related items.** Companies report cash as a current asset in the balance sheet. The reporting of other related items are: (1) *Restricted cash:* The SEC recommends that companies state separately legally restricted deposits held as compensating balances against short-term borrowing among the "Cash and cash equivalent items" in current assets. Restricted deposits held against long-term borrowing arrangements should be separately classified as noncurrent assets in either the investments or other assets sections. (2) *Bank overdrafts:* Companies should report overdrafts in the current liabilities section and usually add them to the amount reported as accounts payable. If material, these items should be separately disclosed either on the face of the balance sheet or in the related notes. (3) *Cash equivalents:* Companies often report this item together with cash as "Cash and cash equivalents."

3. **Define receivables and identify the different types of receivables.** Receivables are claims held against customers and others for money, goods, or services. The receivables are classified into three types: (1) current or noncurrent, (2) trade or nontrade, (3) accounts receivable or notes receivable.

4. **Explain accounting issues related to recognition of accounts receivable.** Two issues that may complicate the measurement of accounts receivable are: (1) The availability of discounts (trade and cash discounts), and (2) the length of time between the sale and the payment due dates (the interest element).

   Ideally, companies should measure receivables in terms of their present value—that is, the discounted value of the cash to be received in the future. The profession specifically excludes from the present-value considerations receivables arising from normal business transactions that are due in customary trade terms within approximately one year.

5. **Explain accounting issues related to valuation of accounts receivable.** Companies value and report short-term receivables at net realizable value—the net amount expected to be received in cash, which is not necessarily the amount legally receivable. Determining net realizable value requires estimating uncollectible receivables.

6. **Explain accounting issues related to recognition of notes receivable.** Companies record short-term notes at face value and long-term notes receivable at the present value of the cash they expect to collect. When the interest stated on an interest-bearing note equals the effective (market) rate of interest, the note sells at face value. When the stated rate differs from the effective rate, a company records either a discount or premium.

7. **Explain accounting issues related to valuation of notes receivable.** Like accounts receivable, companies record and report short-term notes receivable at their net realizable value. The same is also true of long-term receivables. Special issues relate to uncollectibles and impairments.

8. **Explain accounting issues related to disposition of accounts and notes receivable.** To accelerate the receipt of cash from receivables, the owner may transfer the receivables to another company for cash in one of two ways: (1) *Secured borrowing:* A creditor often requires that the debtor designate or pledge receivables as security for the loan. (2) *Sales (factoring) of receivables:* Factors are finance companies or banks that buy receivables from businesses and then collect the remittances directly from the customers. In many cases, transferors may have some continuing involvement with the receivable sold. Companies use a financial components approach to record this type of transaction.

9. **Describe how to report and analyze receivables.** Companies should report receivables with appropriate offset of valuation accounts against receivables, classify receivables as current or noncurrent, identify pledged or designated receivables, and identify concentrations of risks arising from receivables. Analysts assess receivables based on turnover and the days outstanding.

APPENDIX 7A

Cash Controls

As we indicated in Chapter 7, cash creates many management and control problems. In this appendix, we discuss some of the basic control issues related to cash.

USING BANK ACCOUNTS

OBJECTIVE 10
Explain common techniques employed to control cash.

INTERNATIONAL INSIGHT

Multinational corporations often have cash accounts in more than one currency. For financial statement purposes, these corporations typically translate these currencies into U.S. dollars, using the exchange rate in effect at the balance sheet date.

To obtain desired control objectives, a company can vary the number and location of banks and the types of bank accounts. For large companies operating in multiple locations, the location of bank accounts can be important. Establishing collection accounts in strategic locations can accelerate the flow of cash into the company by shortening the time between a customer's mailing of a payment and the company's use of the cash. Multiple collection centers generally reduce the size of a company's **collection float**. This is the difference between the amount on deposit according to the company's records and the amount of collected cash according to the bank record.

Large, multilocation companies frequently use **lockbox accounts** to collect in cities with heavy customer billing. The company rents a local post office box and authorizes a local bank to pick up the remittances mailed to that box number. The bank empties the box at least once a day and immediately credits the company's account for collections. The greatest advantage of a lockbox is that it accelerates the availability of collected cash. Generally, in a lockbox arrangement the bank microfilms the checks for record purposes and provides the company with a deposit slip, a list of collections, and any customer correspondence. Thus, a lockbox system improves the control over cash and accelerates collection of cash. If the income generated from accelerating the receipt of funds exceeds the cost of the lockbox system, then it is a worthwhile undertaking.

The **general checking account** is the principal bank account in most companies and frequently the only bank account in small businesses. A company deposits in and disburses cash from this account. A company cycles all transactions through it. For example, a company deposits from and disburses to all other bank accounts through the general checking account.

Companies use **imprest bank accounts** to make a specific amount of cash available for a limited purpose. The account acts as a clearing account for a large volume of checks or for a specific type of check. To clear a specific and intended amount through the imprest account, a company transfers that amount from the general checking account or other source. Companies often use imprest bank accounts for disbursing payroll checks, dividends, commissions, bonuses, confidential expenses (e.g., officers' salaries), and travel expenses.

THE IMPREST PETTY CASH SYSTEM

Almost every company finds it necessary to pay small amounts for miscellaneous expenses such as taxi fares, minor office supplies, and employee's lunches. Disbursements by check for such items is often impractical, yet some control over them is important.

A simple method of obtaining reasonable control, while adhering to the rule of disbursement by check, is the **imprest system for petty cash** disbursements. This is how the system works:

1 The company designates a petty cash custodian, and gives the custodian a small amount of currency from which to make payments. It records transfer of funds to petty cash as:

Petty Cash	300	
Cash		300

2 The petty cash custodian obtains signed receipts from each individual to whom he or she pays cash, attaching evidence of the disbursement to the petty cash receipt. Petty cash transactions are not recorded until the fund is reimbursed; someone other than the petty cash custodian records those entries.

3 When the supply of cash runs low, the custodian presents to the general cashier a request for reimbursement supported by the petty cash receipts and other disbursement evidence. The custodian receives a company check to replenish the fund. At this point, the company records transactions based on petty cash receipts.

Office Supplies Expense	42	
Postage Expense	53	
Entertainment Expense	76	
Cash Over and Short	2	
Cash		173

4 If the company decides that the amount of cash in the petty cash fund is excessive, it lowers the fund balance as follows.

Cash	50	
Petty Cash		50

A company makes entries to the Petty Cash account only to increase or decrease the size of the fund.

A company uses a **Cash Over and Short** account when the petty cash fund fails to prove out. That is, an error occurs such as incorrect change, overpayment of expense, or lost receipt. If cash proves out **short** (i.e., the sum of the receipts and cash in the fund is less than the imprest amount), the company debits the shortage to the Cash Over and Short account. If cash proves out **over**, it credits the overage to Cash Over and Short. The company closes Cash Over and Short only at the end of the year. It generally shows Cash Over and Short on the income statement as an "Other expense or revenue."

There are usually expense items in the fund except immediately after reimbursement. Therefore, to maintain accurate financial statements, a company must reimburse the funds at the end of each accounting period and also when nearly depleted.

Under the imprest system the petty cash custodian is responsible at all times for the amount of the fund on hand either as cash or in the form of signed receipts. These receipts provide the evidence required by the disbursing officer to issue a reimbursement check. Further, a company follows two additional procedures to obtain more complete control over the petty cash fund:

1 A superior of the petty cash custodian makes surprise counts of the fund from time to time to determine that a satisfactory accounting of the fund has occurred.

2 The company cancels or mutilates petty cash receipts after they have been submitted for reimbursement, so that they cannot be used to secure a second reimbursement.

PHYSICAL PROTECTION OF CASH BALANCES

Not only must a company safeguard cash receipts and cash disbursements through internal control measures, but it must also protect the cash on hand and in banks. Because receipts become cash on hand and disbursements are made from cash in banks, adequate control of receipts and disbursements is part of the protection of cash balances, along with certain other procedures.

Physical protection of cash is so elementary a necessity that it requires little discussion. A company should make every effort to minimize the cash on hand in the office. It should only have on hand a petty cash fund, the current day's receipts, and perhaps funds for making change. Insofar as possible, it should keep these funds in a vault, safe, or locked cash drawer. The company should transmit intact each day's receipts to the bank as soon as practicable. Accurately stating the amount of available cash both in internal management reports and in external financial statements is also extremely important.

Every company has a record of cash received, disbursed, and the balance. Because of the many cash transactions, however, errors or omissions may occur in keeping this record. Therefore, a company must periodically prove the balance shown in the general ledger. It can count cash actually present in the office—petty cash, change funds, and undeposited receipts—for comparison with the company records. For cash on deposit, a company prepares a bank reconciliation—a reconciliation of the company's record and the bank's record of the company's cash.

RECONCILIATION OF BANK BALANCES

At the end of each calendar month the bank supplies each customer with a **bank statement** (a copy of the bank's account with the customer) together with the customer's checks that the bank paid during the month.[1] If neither the bank nor the customer made any errors, if all deposits made and all checks drawn by the customer reached the bank within the same month, and if no unusual transactions occurred that affected either the company's or the bank's record of cash, the balance of cash reported by the bank to the customer equals that shown in the customer's own records. This condition seldom occurs for one or more of the reconciling items presented below. Hence, a company expects differences between its record of cash and the bank's record. Therefore, it must reconcile the two to determine the nature of the differences between the two amounts.

RECONCILING ITEMS

1 *DEPOSITS IN TRANSIT.* End-of-month deposits of cash recorded on the depositor's books in one month are received and recorded by the bank in the following month.

2 *OUTSTANDING CHECKS.* Checks written by the depositor are recorded when written but may not be recorded by (may not "clear") the bank until the next month.

3 *BANK CHARGES.* Charges recorded by the bank against the depositor's balance for such items as bank services, printing checks, **not-sufficient-funds (NSF) checks**, and safe-deposit box rentals. The depositor may not be aware of these charges until the receipt of the bank statement.

4 *BANK CREDITS.* Collections or deposits by the bank for the benefit of the depositor that may be unknown to the depositor until receipt of the bank statement. Examples are note collection for the depositor and interest earned on interest-bearing checking accounts.

5 *BANK OR DEPOSITOR ERRORS.* Errors on either the part of the bank or the part of the depositor cause the bank balance to disagree with the depositor's book balance.

---

[1]As we mentioned in Chapter 7, paper checks continue to be used as a means of payment. However, ready availability of desktop publishing software and hardware has created new opportunities for check fraud in the form of duplicate, altered, and forged checks. At the same time, new fraud-fighting technologies, such as ultraviolet imaging, high-capacity barcodes, and biometrics, are being developed. These technologies convert paper documents into electronically processed document files, thereby reducing the risk of fraud.

A **bank reconciliation** is a schedule explaining any differences between the bank's and the company's records of cash. If the difference results only from transactions not yet recorded by the bank, the company's record of cash is considered correct. But, if some part of the difference arises from other items, either the bank or the company must adjust its records.

A company may prepare two forms of a bank reconciliation. One form reconciles from the bank statement balance to the book balance or vice versa. The other form reconciles both the bank balance and the book balance to a correct cash balance. Most companies use this latter form. Illustration 7A-1 shows a sample of that form and its common reconciling items.

Balance per bank statement (end of period)		$$$
Add: Deposits in transit	$$	
Undeposited receipts (cash on hand)	$$	
Bank errors that understate the bank statement balance	$$	$$
		$$$
Deduct: Outstanding checks	$$	
Bank errors that overstate the bank statement balance	$$	$$
Correct cash balance		$$$
Balance per depositor's books		$$$
Add: Bank credits and collections not yet recorded in the books	$$	
Book errors that understate the book balance	$$	$$
		$$$
Deduct: Bank charges not yet recorded in the books	$$	
Book errors that overstate the book balance	$$	$$
Correct cash balance		$$$

ILLUSTRATION 7A-1
Bank Reconciliation Form and Content

This form of reconciliation consists of two sections: (1) "Balance per bank statement" and (2) "Balance per depositor's books." Both sections end with the same "Correct cash balance." The correct cash balance is the amount to which the books must be adjusted and is the amount reported on the balance sheet. **Companies prepare adjusting journal entries for all the addition and deduction items appearing in the "Balance per depositor's books" section.** Companies should immediately call to the bank's attention any errors attributable to it.

To illustrate, Nugget Mining Company's books show a cash balance at the Denver National Bank on November 30, 2007, of $20,502. The bank statement covering the month of November shows an ending balance of $22,190. An examination of Nugget's accounting records and November bank statement identified the following reconciling items.

1 A deposit of $3,680 that Nugget mailed November 30 does not appear on the bank statement.

2 Checks written in November but not charged to the November bank statement are:

Check #7327	$ 150
#7348	4,820
#7349	31

3 Nugget has not yet recorded the $600 of interest collected by the bank November 20 on Sequoia Co. bonds held by the bank for Nugget.

4 Bank service charges of $18 are not yet recorded on Nugget's books.

5 The bank returned one of Nugget's customer's checks for $220 with the bank statement, marked "NSF." The bank treated this bad check as a disbursement.

6 Nugget discovered that it incorrectly recorded check #7322, written in November for $131 in payment of an account payable, as $311.

7 A check for Nugent Oil Co. in the amount of $175 that the bank incorrectly charged to Nugget accompanied the statement.

Nugget reconciled the bank and book balances to the correct cash balance of $21,044 as shown in Illustration 7A-2 (page 344).

ILLUSTRATION 7A-2
Sample Bank
Reconciliation

NUGGET MINING COMPANY			
BANK RECONCILIATION			
DENVER NATIONAL BANK, NOVEMBER 30, 2007			
Balance per bank statement (end of period)			$22,190
Add: Deposit in transit	(1)	$3,680	
Bank error—incorrect check charged to account by bank	(7)	175	3,855
			26,045
Deduct: Outstanding checks	(2)		5,001
Correct cash balance			$21,044
Balance per books			$20,502
Add: Interest collected by the bank	(3)	$ 600	
Error in recording check #7322	(6)	180	780
			21,282
Deduct: Bank service charges	(4)	18	
NSF check returned	(5)	220	238
Correct cash balance			$21,044

The journal entries required to adjust and correct Nugget's books in early December 2007 are taken from the items in the "Balance per books" section and are as follows.

Cash	600	
Interest Revenue		600
(To record interest on Sequoia Co. bonds, collected by bank)		
Cash	180	
Accounts Payable		180
(To correct error in recording amount of check #7322)		
Office Expense—Bank Charges	18	
Cash		18
(To record bank service charges for November)		
Accounts Receivable	220	
Cash		220
(To record customer's check returned NSF)		

After posting the entries, Nugget's cash account will have a balance of $21,044. Nugget should return the Nugent Oil Co. check to Denver National Bank, informing the bank of the error.

Expanded Discussion of a Four-Column Bank Reconciliation

WHAT DO THE NUMBERS MEAN?

BOUNCE A CHECK, GET BANNED

Rebecca Cobos overdrew her checking account at a **Bank of America** branch in Los Angeles. When she could not immediately repay the bank, it not only closed her account but also had her, in effect, banned for five years from opening a checking account at most other banks.

Bank of America did so by reporting the 23-year-old university secretary to **Chex-Systems**, a national database to which 80 percent of banks in the country subscribe. Once lodged in ChexSystems, your name automatically stays there for five years, whether your offense was bouncing a check or two or committing serious fraud. The large majority of banks using ChexSystems reject any checking-account applicant they find in the database.

Maintained by a unit of the check-printing company **Deluxe Corp.**, ChexSystems currently has about seven million names on file. Bank officials and executives of the unit, called eFund, defend the database as a valuable weapon in the battle against fraud and high-risk customers. And there is no denying that many of those who end up in the database have been financially careless, or worse.

Source: Paul Beckett, "It's Not in the Mail," *Wall Street Journal* (August 1, 2000), p. A1.

SUMMARY OF LEARNING OBJECTIVE FOR APPENDIX 7A

10. Explain common techniques employed to control cash. The common techniques employed to control cash are: (1) *Using bank accounts:* A company can vary the number and location of banks and the types of accounts to obtain desired control objectives. (2) *The imprest petty cash system:* It may be impractical to require small amounts of various expenses be paid by check, yet some control over them is important. (3) *Physical protection of cash balances:* Adequate control of receipts and disbursements is a part of the protection of cash balances. Every effort should be made to minimize the cash on hand in the office. (4) *Reconciliation of bank balances:* Cash on deposit is not available for count and is proved by preparing a bank reconciliation.

Note: All **asterisked** Questions, Brief Exercises, Exercises, Problems, and Concepts for Analysis relate to material covered in the appendix to the chapter.

QUESTIONS

1. What may be included under the heading of "cash"?

2. In what accounts should the following items be classified?

  (a) Coins and currency.

  (b) U.S. Treasury (government) bonds.

  (c) Certificate of deposit.

  (d) Cash in a bank that is in receivership.

  (e) NSF check (returned with bank statement).

  (f) Deposit in foreign bank (exchangeability limited).

  (g) Postdated checks.

  (h) Cash to be used for retirement of long-term bonds.

  (i) Deposits in transit.

  (j) 100 shares of **Dell** stock (intention is to sell in one year or less).

  (k) Savings and checking accounts.

  (l) Petty cash.

  (m) Stamps.

  (n) Travel advances.

3. Define a "compensating balance." How should a compensating balance be reported?

4. Michael Tilsen Thomas Inc. reported in a recent annual report "Restricted cash for debt redemption." What section of the balance sheet would report this item?

5. What are the reasons that a company gives trade discounts? Why are trade discounts not recorded in the accounts like cash discounts?

6. What are two methods of recording accounts receivable transactions when a cash discount situation is involved? Which is more theoretically correct? Which is used in practice more of the time? Why?

7. What are the basic problems that occur in the valuation of accounts receivable?

8. What is the theoretical justification of the allowance method as contrasted with the direct write-off method of accounting for bad debts?

9. Indicate how well the percentage-of-sales method and the aging method accomplish the objectives of the allowance method of accounting for bad debts.

10. Of what merit is the contention that the allowance method lacks the objectivity of the direct write-off method? Discuss in terms of accounting's measurement function.

11. Explain how the accounting for bad debts can be used for earnings management.

12. Because of calamitous earthquake losses, Kishwaukee Company, one of your client's oldest and largest customers, suddenly and unexpectedly became bankrupt. Approximately 30% of your client's total sales have been made to Kishwaukee Company during each of the past several years. The amount due from Kishwaukee Company—none of which is collectible—equals 22% of total accounts receivable, an amount that is considerably in excess of what was determined to be an adequate provision for doubtful accounts at the close of the preceding year. How would your client record the write-off of the Kishwaukee Company receivable if it is using the allowance method of accounting for bad debts? Justify your suggested treatment.

13. What is the normal procedure for handling the collection of accounts receivable previously written off using the direct write-off method? The allowance method?

14. On January 1, 2007, John Singer Co. sells property for which it had paid $690,000 to Sargent Company, receiving in return Sargent's zero-interest-bearing note for $1,000,000 payable in 5 years. What entry would John Singer make to record the sale, assuming that John Singer frequently sells similar items of property for a cash sales price of $620,000?

15. What is "imputed interest"? In what situations is it necessary to impute an interest rate for notes receivable? What are the considerations in imputing an appropriate interest rate?

16. Indicate three reasons why a company might sell its receivables to another company.

17. When is the financial components approach to recording the transfers of receivables used? When should a transfer of receivables be recorded as a sale?

18. Hale Hardware is planning to factor some of its receivables. The cash received will be used to pay for inventory purchases. The factor has indicated that it will require "recourse" on the sold receivables. Explain to the controller of Hale Hardware what "recourse" is and how the recourse will be reflected in Hale's financial statements after the sale of the receivables.

19. Outkast Outfitters Company includes in its trial balance for December 31 an item for Accounts Receivable $769,000. This balance consists of the following items:

Due from regular customers	$523,000
Refund receivable on prior year's income taxes (an established claim)	15,500

Travel advance to employees	22,000
Loan to wholly owned subsidiary	45,500
Advances to creditors for goods ordered	61,000
Accounts receivable assigned as security for loans payable	75,000
Notes receivable past due plus interest on these notes	27,000
Total	$769,000

Illustrate how these items should be shown in the balance sheet as of December 31.

20. What is the accounts receivable turnover ratio, and what type of information does it provide?

21. You are evaluating Hawthorn Downs Racetrack for a potential loan. An examination of the notes to the financial statements indicates restricted cash at year-end amounts to $100,000. Explain how you would use this information in evaluating Hawthorn's liquidity.

*22. Distinguish among the following: (1) a general checking account, (2) an imprest bank account, and (3) a lockbox account.

BRIEF EXERCISES

(LO 1) **BE7-1** Stowe Enterprises owns the following assets at December 31, 2007.

Cash in bank—savings account	63,000	Checking account balance	17,000
Cash on hand	9,300	Postdated checks	750
Cash refund due from IRS	31,400	Certificates of deposit (180-day)	90,000

What amount should be reported as cash?

(LO 4) **BE7-2** Montoya Co. uses the gross method to record sales made on credit. On June 1, 2007, it made sales of $40,000 with terms 3/15, n/45. On June 12, 2007, Montoya received full payment for the June 1 sale. Prepare the required journal entries for Montoya Co.

(LO 4) **BE7-3** Use the information from BE7-2, assuming Montoya Co. uses the net method to account for cash discounts. Prepare the required journal entries for Montoya Co.

(LO 5) **BE7-4** Battle Tank, Inc. had net sales in 2007 of $1,200,000. At December 31, 2007, before adjusting entries, the balances in selected accounts were: Accounts Receivable $250,000 debit, and Allowance for Doubtful Accounts $2,100 credit. If Battle Tank estimates that 2% of its net sales will prove to be uncollectible, prepare the December 31, 2007, journal entry to record bad debt expense.

(LO 5) **BE7-5** Use the information presented in BE7-4 for Battle Tank, Inc.

    (a) Instead of estimating the uncollectibles at 2% of net sales, assume that 10% of accounts receivable will prove to be uncollectible. Prepare the entry to record bad debts expense.

    (b) Instead of estimating uncollectibles at 2% of net sales, assume Battle Tank prepares an aging schedule that estimates total uncollectible accounts at $24,600. Prepare the entry to record bad debts expense.

(LO 6) **BE7-6** Addams Family Importers sold goods to Acme Decorators for $20,000 on November 1, 2007, accepting Acme's $20,000, 6-month, 6% note. Prepare Addams's November 1 entry, December 31 annual adjusting entry, and May 1 entry for the collection of the note and interest.

(LO 6) **BE7-7** Aero Acrobats lent $15,944 to Afterburner, Inc., accepting Afterburner's 2-year, $20,000, zero-interest-bearing note. The implied interest rate is 12%. Prepare Aero's journal entries for the initial transaction, recognition of interest each year, and the collection of $20,000 at maturity.

(LO 8) **BE7-8** On October 1, 2007, Akira, Inc. assigns $1,000,000 of its accounts receivable to Alisia National Bank as collateral for a $700,000 note. The bank assesses a finance charge of 2% of the receivables assigned and interest on the note of 9%. Prepare the October 1 journal entries for both Akira and Alisia.

(LO 8)   **BE7-9**   CRC Incorporated factored $100,000 of accounts receivable with Fredrick Factors Inc. on a without recourse basis. Fredrick assesses a 2% finance charge of the amount of accounts receivable and retains an amount equal to 6% of accounts receivable for possible adjustments. Prepare the journal entry for CRC Incorporated and Fredrick Factors to record the factoring of the accounts receivable to Fredrick.

(LO 8)   **BE7-10**   Use the information in BE7-9 for CRC. Assume that the receivables are sold with recourse. Prepare the journal entry for CRC to record the sale, assuming that the recourse obligation has a fair value of $7,500.

(LO 8)   **BE7-11**   Keyser Woodcrafters sells $200,000 of receivables to Commercial Factors, Inc. on a with recourse basis. Commercial assesses a finance charge of 5% and retains an amount equal to 4% of accounts receivable. Keyser estimates the fair value of the recourse obligation to be $8,000. Prepare the journal entry for Keyser to record the sale.

(LO 8)   **BE7-12**   Use the information presented in BE7-11 for Keyser Woodcrafters but assume that the recourse obligation has a fair value of $4,000, instead of $8,000. Prepare the journal entry and discuss the effects of this change in the value of the recourse obligation on Keyser's financial statements.

(LO 9)   **BE7-13**   The financial statements of **General Mills, Inc.** report net sales of $5,416,000,000. Accounts receivable are $277,300,000 at the beginning of the year and $337,800,000 at the end of the year. Compute General Mills's accounts receivable turnover ratio. Compute General Mills's average collection period for accounts receivable in days.

(LO 10)   *****BE7-14**   Genesis Company designated Alex Kidd as petty cash custodian and established a petty cash fund of $200. The fund is reimbursed when the cash in the fund is at $17. Petty cash receipts indicate funds were disbursed for office supplies $94 and miscellaneous expense $87. Prepare journal entries for the establishment of the fund and the reimbursement.

(LO 10)   *****BE7-15**   Jaguar Corporation is preparing a bank reconciliation and has identified the following potential reconciling items. For each item, indicate if it is (1) added to balance per bank statement, (2) deducted from balance per bank statement, (3) added to balance per books, or (4) deducted from balance per books.

    (a) Deposit in transit $5,500.   **(d)** Outstanding checks $7,422.
    (b) Interest credited to Jaguar's account $31.   **(e)** NSF check returned $377.
    (c) Bank service charges $25.

(LO 10)   *****BE7-16**   Use the information presented in BE7-15 for Jaguar Corporation. Prepare any entries necessary to make Jaguar's accounting records correct and complete.

EXERCISES

(LO 1)   **E7-1**   **(Determining Cash Balance)**   The controller for Clint Eastwood Co. is attempting to determine the amount of cash to be reported on its December 31, 2007, balance sheet. The following information is provided.

    1. Commercial savings account of $600,000 and a commercial checking account balance of $900,000 are held at First National Bank of Yojimbo. *cash*

    2. Money market fund account held at Volonte Co. (a mutual fund organization) permits Eastwood to write checks on this balance, $5,000,000. *temporary investment*

    3. Travel advances of $180,000 for executive travel for the first quarter of next year (employee to reimburse through salary reduction). *receivable*

    4. A separate cash fund in the amount of $1,500,000 is restricted for the retirement of long-term debt. *another asset*

    5. Petty cash fund of $1,000. *cash*

    6. An I.O.U. from Marianne Koch, a company customer, in the amount of $190,000. *receivable*

    7. A bank overdraft of $110,000 has occurred at one of the banks the company uses to deposit its cash receipts. At the present time, the company has no deposits at this bank. *current liability*

    8. The company has two certificates of deposit, each totaling $500,000. These CDs have a maturity of 120 days. *temporary investments*

    9. Eastwood has received a check that is dated January 12, 2008, in the amount of $125,000. *cash*

    10. Eastwood has agreed to maintain a cash balance of $500,000 at all times at First National Bank of Yojimbo to ensure future credit availability. *cash*

    11. Eastwood has purchased $2,100,000 of commercial paper of Sergio Leone Co. which is due in 60 days. *cash equivilant*

    12. Currency and coin on hand amounted to $7,700. *cash*

Instructions

    (a) Compute the amount of cash to be reported on Eastwood Co.'s balance sheet at December 31, 2007.

    (b) Indicate the proper reporting for items that are not reported as cash on the December 31, 2007, balance sheet.

(LO 1)   **E7-2**   **(Determine Cash Balance)**   Presented below are a number of independent situations.

Instructions

For each individual situation, determine the amount that should be reported as cash. If the item(s) is not reported as cash, explain the rationale.

    1. Checking account balance $925,000; certificate of deposit $1,400,000; cash advance to subsidiary of $980,000; utility deposit paid to gas company $180.

    2. Checking account balance $600,000; an overdraft in special checking account at same bank as normal checking account of $17,000; cash held in a bond sinking fund $200,000; petty cash fund $300; coins and currency on hand $1,350.

    3. Checking account balance $590,000; postdated check from customer $11,000; cash restricted due to maintaining compensating balance requirement of $100,000; certified check from customer $9,800; postage stamps on hand $620.

    4. Checking account balance at bank $37,000; money market balance at mutual fund (has checking privileges) $48,000; NSF check received from customer $800.

    5. Checking account balance $700,000; cash restricted for future plant expansion $500,000; short-term Treasury bills $180,000; cash advance received from customer $900 (not included in checking account balance); cash advance of $7,000 to company executive, payable on demand; refundable deposit of $26,000 paid to federal government to guarantee performance on construction contract.

(LO 3, 4)   **E7-3**   **(Financial Statement Presentation of Receivables)**   Jim Carrie Company shows a balance of $181,140 in the Accounts Receivable account on December 31, 2006. The balance consists of the following.

Installment accounts due in 2007	$23,000
Installment accounts due after 2007	34,000
Overpayments to creditors	2,640
Due from regular customers, of which $40,000 represents	
accounts pledged as security for a bank loan	79,000
Advances to employees	1,500
Advance to subsidiary company (made in 2002)	81,000

Instructions

Illustrate how the information above should be shown on the balance sheet of Jim Carrie Company on December 31, 2006.

(LO 3, 4)   **E7-4**   **(Determine Ending Accounts Receivable)**   Your accounts receivable clerk, Mitra Adams, to whom you pay a salary of $1,500 per month, has just purchased a new Buick. You decided to test the accuracy of the accounts receivable balance of $82,000 as shown in the ledger.

    The following information is available for your *first year* in business.

(1) Collections from customers	$198,000
(2) Merchandise purchased	320,000
(3) Ending merchandise inventory	90,000
(4) Goods are marked to sell at 40% above cost	

Instructions

Compute an estimate of the ending balance of accounts receivable from customers that should appear in the ledger and any apparent shortages. Assume that all sales are made on account.

(LO 4)   **E7-5**   **(Record Sales Gross and Net)**   On June 3, Arnold Company sold to Chester Company merchandise having a sale price of $3,000 with terms of 2/10, n/60, f.o.b. shipping point. An invoice totaling $90, terms n/30, was received by Chester on June 8 from John Booth Transport Service for the freight cost. On June 12, the company received a check for the balance due from Chester Company.

Instructions

    (a) Prepare journal entries on the Arnold Company books to record all the events noted above under each of the following bases.

        (1) Sales and receivables are entered at gross selling price.

        (2) Sales and receivables are entered at net of cash discounts.

    (b) Prepare the journal entry under basis 2, assuming that Chester Company did not remit payment until July 29.

(LO 4) **E7-6** **(Recording Sales Transactions)** Presented below is information from Perez Computers Incorporated.

July 1 Sold $20,000 of computers to Robertson Company with terms 3/15, n/60. Perez uses the gross method to record cash discounts.

10 Perez received payment from Robertson for the full amount owed from the July transactions.

17 Sold $200,000 in computers and peripherals to The Clark Store with terms of 2/10, n/30.

30 The Clark Store paid Perez for its purchase of July 17.

Instructions

Prepare the necessary journal entries for Perez Computers.

(LO 5) **E7-7** **(Recording Bad Debts)** Duncan Company reports the following financial information before adjustments.

	Dr.	Cr.
Accounts Receivable	$100,000	
Allowance for Doubtful Accounts		$ 2,000
Sales (all on credit)		900,000
Sales Returns and Allowances	50,000	

Instructions

Prepare the journal entry to record Bad Debt Expense assuming Duncan Company estimates bad debts at (a) 1% of net sales and (b) 5% of accounts receivable.

(LO 5) **E7-8** **(Recording Bad Debts)** At the end of 2007 Aramis Company has accounts receivable of $800,000 and an allowance for doubtful accounts of $40,000. On January 16, 2008, Aramis Company determined that its receivable from Ramirez Company of $6,000 will not be collected, and management authorized its write-off.

Instructions

(a) Prepare the journal entry for Aramis Company to write off the Ramirez receivable.

(b) What is the net realizable value of Aramis Company's accounts receivable before the write-off of the Ramirez receivable?

(c) What is the net realizable value of Aramis Company's accounts receivable after the write-off of the Ramirez receivable? AR- Allowance

(LO 5) **E7-9** **(Computing Bad Debts and Preparing Journal Entries)** The trial balance before adjustment of Reba McIntyre Inc. shows the following balances.

	Dr.	Cr.
Accounts Receivable	$90,000	
Allowance for Doubtful Accounts	1,750	
Sales (all on credit)		$680,000

Instructions

Give the entry for estimated bad debts assuming that the allowance is to provide for doubtful accounts on the basis of (a) 4% of gross accounts receivable and (b) 1% of net sales.

(LO 5) **E7-10** **(Bad-Debt Reporting)** The chief accountant for Emily Dickinson Corporation provides you with the following list of accounts receivable written off in the current year.

Date	Customer	Amount
March 31	E. L. Masters Company	$7,800
June 30	Stephen Crane Associates	6,700
September 30	Amy Lowell's Dress Shop	7,000
December 31	R. Frost, Inc.	9,830

Emily Dickinson Corporation follows the policy of debiting Bad Debt Expense as accounts are written off. The chief accountant maintains that this procedure is appropriate for financial statement purposes because the Internal Revenue Service will not accept other methods for recognizing bad debts.

All of Emily Dickinson Corporation's sales are on a 30-day credit basis. Sales for the current year total $2,200,000, and research has determined that bad debt losses approximate 2% of sales.

Instructions

(a) Do you agree or disagree with Dickinson's policy concerning recognition of bad debt expense? Why or why not?

(b) By what amount would net income differ if bad debt expense was computed using the percentage-of-sales approach?

(LO 5) **E7-11 (Bad Debts—Aging)** Danica Patrick, Inc. includes the following account among its trade receivables.

Hopkins Co.

1/1	Balance forward	700	1/28	Cash (#1710)	1,100
1/20	Invoice #1710	1,100	4/2	Cash (#2116)	1,350
3/14	Invoice #2116	1,350	4/10	Cash (1/1 Balance)	155
4/12	Invoice #2412	1,710	4/30	Cash (#2412)	1,000
9/5	Invoice #3614	490	9/20	Cash (#3614 and	
10/17	Invoice #4912	860		part of #2412)	790
11/18	Invoice #5681	2,000	10/31	Cash (#4912)	860
12/20	Invoice #6347	800	12/1	Cash (#5681)	1,250
			12/29	Cash (#6347)	800

Instructions

Age the balance and specify any items that apparently require particular attention at year-end.

(LO 4, 5, 8) **E7-12 (Journalizing Various Receivable Transactions)** Presented below is information related to James Garfield Corp.

July 1 James Garfield Corp. sold to Warren Harding Co. merchandise having a sales price of $8,000 with terms 2/10, net/60. Garfield records its sales and receivables net.

5 Accounts receivable of $9,000 (gross) are factored with Andrew Jackson Credit Corp. without recourse at a financing charge of 9%. Cash is received for the proceeds; collections are handled by the finance company. (These accounts were all past the discount period.)

9 Specific accounts receivable of $9,000 (gross) are pledged to Alf Landon Credit Corp. as security for a loan of $6,000 at a finance charge of 6% of the amount of the loan. The finance company will make the collections. (All the accounts receivable are past the discount period.)

Dec. 29 Warren Harding Co. notifies Garfield that it is bankrupt and will pay only 10% of its account. Give the entry to write off the uncollectible balance using the allowance method. (*Note*: First record the increase in the receivable on July 11 when the discount period passed.)

Instructions

Prepare all necessary entries in general journal form for Garfield Corp.

(LO 8) **E7-13 (Assigning Accounts Receivable)** On April 1, 2007, Rasheed Company assigns $400,000 of its accounts receivable to the Third National Bank as collateral for a $200,000 loan due July 1, 2007. The assignment agreement calls for Rasheed Company to continue to collect the receivables. Third National Bank assesses a finance charge of 2% of the accounts receivable, and interest on the loan is 10% (a realistic rate of interest for a note of this type).

Instructions

(a) Prepare the April 1, 2007, journal entry for Rasheed Company.

(b) Prepare the journal entry for Rasheed's collection of $350,000 of the accounts receivable during the period from April 1, 2007, through June 30, 2007.

(c) On July 1, 2007, Rasheed paid Third National all that was due from the loan it secured on April 1, 2007. Prepare the journal entry to record this payment.

(LO 5, 8) **E7-14 (Journalizing Various Receivable Transactions)** The trial balance before adjustment for Phil Collins Company shows the following balances.

	Dr.	Cr.
Accounts Receivable	$82,000	
Allowance for Doubtful Accounts	2,120	
Sales		$430,000

Instructions

Using the data above, give the journal entries required to record each of the following cases. (Each situation is independent.)

1. To obtain additional cash, Collins factors without recourse $25,000 of accounts receivable with Stills Finance. The finance charge is 10% of the amount factored.

2. To obtain a one-year loan of $55,000, Collins assigns $65,000 of specific receivable accounts to Crosby Financial. The finance charge is 8% of the loan; the cash is received and the accounts turned over to Crosby Financial.

3. The company wants to maintain the Allowance for Doubtful Accounts at 5% of gross accounts receivable.

4. The company wishes to increase the allowance account by 1½% of net sales.

(LO 8) **E7-15 (Transfer of Receivables with Recourse)** Ames Quartet Inc. factors receivables with a carrying amount of $200,000 to Joffrey Company for $160,000 on a with recourse basis.

Instructions

The recourse provision has a fair value of $1,000. This transaction should be recorded as a sale. Prepare the appropriate journal entry to record this transaction on the books of Ames Quartet Inc.

(LO 8) **E7-16 (Transfer of Receivables with Recourse)** Beyoncé Corporation factors $175,000 of accounts receivable with Kathleen Battle Financing, Inc. on a with recourse basis. Kathleen Battle Financing will collect the receivables. The receivables records are transferred to Kathleen Battle Financing on August 15, 2007. Kathleen Battle Financing assesses a finance charge of 2% of the amount of accounts receivable and also reserves an amount equal to 4% of accounts receivable to cover probable adjustments.

Instructions

    (a) What conditions must be met for a transfer of receivables with recourse to be accounted for as a sale?

    (b) Assume the conditions from part (a) are met. Prepare the journal entry on August 15, 2007, for Beyoncé to record the sale of receivables, assuming the recourse obligation has a fair value of $2,000.

(LO 8) **E7-17 (Transfer of Receivables without Recourse)** JFK Corp. factors $300,000 of accounts receivable with LBJ Finance Corporation on a without recourse basis on July 1, 2007. The receivables records are transferred to LBJ Finance, which will receive the collections. LBJ Finance assesses a finance charge of 1½% of the amount of accounts receivable and retains an amount equal to 4% of accounts receivable to cover sales discounts, returns, and allowances. The transaction is to be recorded as a sale.

Instructions

    (a) Prepare the journal entry on July 1, 2007, for JFK Corp. to record the sale of receivables without recourse.

    (b) Prepare the journal entry on July 1, 2007, for LBJ Finance Corporation to record the purchase of receivables without recourse.

(LO 6, 7) **E7-18 (Note Transactions at Unrealistic Interest Rates)** On July 1, 2007, Agincourt Inc. made two sales.

    1. It sold land having a fair market value of $700,000 in exchange for a 4-year zero-interest-bearing promissory note in the face amount of $1,101,460. The land is carried on Agincourt's books at a cost of $590,000.

    2. It rendered services in exchange for a 3%, 8-year promissory note having a face value of $400,000 (interest payable annually).

Agincourt Inc. recently had to pay 8% interest for money that it borrowed from British National Bank. The customers in these two transactions have credit ratings that require them to borrow money at 12% interest.

Instructions

Record the two journal entries that should be recorded by Agincourt Inc. for the sales transactions above that took place on July 1, 2007.

(LO 6, 7) **E7-19 (Notes Receivable with Unrealistic Interest Rate)** On December 31, 2005, Ed Abbey Co. performed environmental consulting services for Hayduke Co. Hayduke was short of cash, and Abbey Co. agreed to accept a $200,000 zero-interest-bearing note due December 31, 2007, as payment in full. Hayduke is somewhat of a credit risk and typically borrows funds at a rate of 10%. Abbey is much more credit-worthy and has various lines of credit at 6%.

Instructions

    (a) Prepare the journal entry to record the transaction of December 31, 2005, for the Ed Abbey Co.

    (b) Assuming Ed Abbey Co.'s fiscal year-end is December 31, prepare the journal entry for December 31, 2006.

    (c) Assuming Ed Abbey Co.'s fiscal year-end is December 31, prepare the journal entry for December 31, 2007.

(LO 9) **E7-20 (Analysis of Receivables)** Presented below is information for Jones Company.

    1. Beginning-of-the-year Accounts Receivable balance was $15,000.

    2. Net sales (all on account) for the year were $100,000. Jones does not offer cash discounts.

    3. Collections on accounts receivable during the year were $70,000.

Instructions

    (a) Prepare (summary) journal entries to record the items noted above.

    (b) Compute Jones's accounts receivable turnover ratio for the year. The company does not believe it will have any bad debts.

    (c) Use the turnover ratio computed in (b) to analyze Jones's liquidity. The turnover ratio last year was 6.0.

(L0 8) **E7-21** **(Transfer of Receivables)**   Use the information for Jones Company as presented in E7-20. Jones is planning to factor some accounts receivable at the end of the year. Accounts totaling $25,000 will be transferred to Credit Factors, Inc. with recourse. Credit Factors will retain 5% of the balances for probable adjustments and assesses a finance charge of 4%. The fair value of the recourse obligation is $1,200.

Instructions

(a) Prepare the journal entry to record the sale of the receivables.

(b) Compute Jones's accounts receivables turnover ratio for the year, assuming the receivables are sold, and discuss how factoring of receivables affects the turnover ratio.

(L0 10) ***E7-22** **(Petty Cash)**   Carolyn Keene, Inc. decided to establish a petty cash fund to help ensure internal control over its small cash expenditures. The following information is available for the month of April.

1. On April 1, it established a petty cash fund in the amount of $200.
2. A summary of the petty cash expenditures made by the petty cash custodian as of April 10 is as follows.

Delivery charges paid on merchandise purchased	$60.00
Supplies purchased and used	25.00
Postage expense	33.00
I.O.U. from employees	17.00
Miscellaneous expense	36.00

The petty cash fund was replenished on April 10. The balance in the fund was $27.
3. The petty cash fund balance was increased $100 to $300 on April 20.

Instructions

Prepare the journal entries to record transactions related to petty cash for the month of April.

(L0 10) ***E7-23** **(Petty Cash)**   The petty cash fund of Fonzarelli's Auto Repair Service, a sole proprietorship, contains the following.

1. Coins and currency		$ 15.20
2. Postage stamps		2.90
3. An I.O.U. from Richie Cunningham, an employee, for cash advance		40.00
4. Check payable to Fonzarelli's Auto Repair from Pottsie Weber, an employee, marked NSF		34.00
5. Vouchers for the following:		
Stamps	$ 20.00	
Two Rose Bowl tickets for Nick Fonzarelli	170.00	
Printer cartridge	14.35	204.35
		$296.45

The general ledger account Petty Cash has a balance of $300.

Instructions

Prepare the journal entry to record the reimbursement of the petty cash fund.

(L0 10) ***E7-24** **(Bank Reconciliation and Adjusting Entries)**   Angela Lansbury Company deposits all receipts and makes all payments by check. The following information is available from the cash records.

June 30 Bank Reconciliation

Balance per bank	$ 7,000
Add: Deposits in transit	1,540
Deduct: Outstanding checks	(2,000)
Balance per books	$ 6,540

Month of July Results

	Per Bank	Per Books
Balance July 31	$8,650	$9,250
July deposits	5,000	5,810
July checks	4,000	3,100
July note collected (not included in July deposits)	1,000	—
July bank service charge	15	—
July NSF check from a customer, returned by the bank (recorded by bank as a charge)	335	—

Instructions

    (a) Prepare a bank reconciliation going from balance per bank and balance per book to correct cash balance.

    (b) Prepare the general journal entry or entries to correct the Cash account.

(LO 10) ***E7-25** (Bank Reconciliation and Adjusting Entries)** Logan Bruno Company has just received the August 31, 2007, bank statement, which is summarized below.

County National Bank	Disbursements	Receipts	Balance
Balance, August 1			$ 9,369
Deposits during August		$32,200	41,569
Note collected for depositor, including $40 interest		1,040	42,609
Checks cleared during August	$34,500		8,109
Bank service charges	20		8,089
Balance, August 31			8,089

The general ledger Cash account contained the following entries for the month of August.

Cash			
Balance, August 1	10,050	Disbursements in August	34,903
Receipts during August	35,000		

Deposits in transit at August 31 are $3,800, and checks outstanding at August 31 total $1,050. Cash on hand at August 31 is $310. The bookkeeper improperly entered one check in the books at $146.50 which was written for $164.50 for supplies (expense); it cleared the bank during the month of August.

Instructions

    (a) Prepare a bank reconciliation dated August 31, 2007, proceeding to a correct balance.

    (b) Prepare any entries necessary to make the books correct and complete.

    (c) What amount of cash should be reported in the August 31 balance sheet?

> **See the book's website, www.wiley.com/college/kieso, for Additional Exercises.**

PROBLEMS

(LO 2) **P7-1 (Determine Proper Cash Balance)** Dumaine Equipment Co. closes its books regularly on December 31, but at the end of 2007 it held its cash book open so that a more favorable balance sheet could be prepared for credit purposes. Cash receipts and disbursements for the first 10 days of January were recorded as December transactions. The following information is given.

    1. January cash receipts recorded in the December cash book totaled $39,640, of which $22,000 represents cash sales, and $17,640 represents collections on account for which cash discounts of $360 were given.

    2. January cash disbursements recorded in the December check register liquidated accounts payable of $26,450 on which discounts of $250 were taken.

    3. The ledger has not been closed for 2007.

    4. The amount shown as inventory was determined by physical count on December 31, 2007.

The company uses the periodic method of inventory.

Instructions

    (a) Prepare any entries you consider necessary to correct Dumaine's accounts at December 31.

    (b) To what extent was Dumaine Equipment Co. able to show a more favorable balance sheet at December 31 by holding its cash book open? (Compute working capital and the current ratio.) Assume that the balance sheet that was prepared by the company showed the following amounts:

	Dr.	Cr.
Cash	$39,000	
Receivables	42,000	
Inventories	67,000	
Accounts payable		$45,000
Other current liabilities		14,200

(LO 5)   **P7-2   (Bad-Debt Reporting)**   Presented below are a series of unrelated situations.

1. Spock Company's unadjusted trial balance at December 31, 2007, included the following accounts.

	Debit	Credit
Allowance for doubtful accounts	$4,000	
Net sales		$1,500,000

Spock Company estimates its bad debt expense to be 1½% of net sales. Determine its bad debt expense for 2007.

2. An analysis and aging of Scotty Corp. accounts receivable at December 31, 2007, disclosed the following.

Amounts estimated to be uncollectible	$ 180,000
Accounts receivable	1,750,000
Allowance for doubtful accounts (per books)	125,000

What is the net realizable value of Scotty's receivables at December 31, 2007?

3. Uhura Co. provides for doubtful accounts based on 3% of credit sales. The following data are available for 2007.

Credit sales during 2007	$2,100,000
Allowance for doubtful accounts 1/1/07	17,000
Collection of accounts written off in prior years	
(customer credit was reestablished)	8,000
Customer accounts written off as uncollectible during 2007	30,000

What is the balance in the Allowance for Doubtful Accounts at December 31, 2007?

4. At the end of its first year of operations, December 31, 2007, Chekov Inc. reported the following information.

Accounts receivable, net of allowance for doubtful accounts	$950,000
Customer accounts written off as uncollectible during 2007	24,000
Bad debt expense for 2007	84,000

What should be the balance in accounts receivable at December 31, 2007, before subtracting the allowance for doubtful accounts?

5. The following accounts were taken from Chappel Inc.'s trial balance at December 31, 2007.

	Debit	Credit
Net credit sales		$750,000
Allowance for doubtful accounts	$ 14,000	
Accounts receivable	410,000	

If doubtful accounts are 3% of accounts receivable, determine the bad debt expense to be reported for 2007.

Instructions

Answer the questions relating to each of the five independent situations as requested.

(LO 5)   **P7-3   (Bad-Debt Reporting—Aging)**   Mary Pierce Corporation operates in an industry that has a high rate of bad debts. Before any year-end adjustments, the balance in Pierce's Accounts Receivable account was $555,000 and the Allowance for Doubtful Accounts had a credit balance of $35,000. The year-end balance reported in the balance sheet for the Allowance for Doubtful Accounts will be based on the aging schedule shown below.

Days Account Outstanding	Amount	Probability of Collection
Less than 16 days	$300,000	.98
Between 16 and 30 days	100,000	.90
Between 31 and 45 days	80,000	.85
Between 46 and 60 days	40,000	.75
Between 61 and 75 days	20,000	.40
Over 75 days	15,000	.00

Instructions

(a)   What is the appropriate balance for the Allowance for Doubtful Accounts at year-end?
(b)   Show how accounts receivable would be presented on the balance sheet.
(c)   What is the dollar effect of the year-end bad debt adjustment on the before-tax income?

(CMA adapted)

(LO 5)   **P7-4   (Bad-Debt Reporting)**   From inception of operations to December 31, 2007, Blaise Pascal Corporation provided for uncollectible accounts receivable under the allowance method: provisions were made monthly at 2% of credit sales; bad debts written off were charged to the allowance account; recoveries of bad debts previously written off were credited to the allowance account; and no year-end adjustments to the allowance account were made. Pascal's usual credit terms are net 30 days.

The balance in the Allowance for Doubtful Accounts was $154,000 at January 1, 2007. During 2007 credit sales totaled $9,000,000, interim provisions for doubtful accounts were made at 2% of credit sales, $95,000 of bad debts were written off, and recoveries of accounts previously written off amounted to $15,000. Pascal installed a computer facility in November 2007, and an aging of accounts receivable was prepared for the first time as of December 31, 2007. A summary of the aging is as follows.

Classification by Month of Sale	Balance in Each Category	Estimated % Uncollectible
November–December 2007	$1,080,000	2%
July–October	650,000	10%
January–June	420,000	25%
Prior to 1/1/07	150,000	70%
	$2,300,000	

Based on the review of collectibility of the account balances in the "prior to 1/1/07" aging category, additional receivables totaling $60,000 were written off as of December 31, 2007. The 70% uncollectible estimate applies to the remaining $90,000 in the category. Effective with the year ended December 31, 2007, Pascal adopted a new accounting method for estimating the allowance for doubtful accounts at the amount indicated by the year-end aging analysis of accounts receivable.

Instructions

(a) Prepare a schedule analyzing the changes in the Allowance for Doubtful Accounts for the year ended December 31, 2007. Show supporting computations in good form. (*Hint*: In computing the 12/31/07 allowance, subtract the $60,000 write-off).

(b) Prepare the journal entry for the year-end adjustment to the Allowance for Doubtful Accounts balance as of December 31, 2007.

(AICPA adapted)

(LO 5) **P7-5** **(Bad-Debt Reporting)** Presented below is information related to the Accounts Receivable accounts of Gulistan Inc. during the current year 2007.

1. An aging schedule of the accounts receivable as of December 31, 2007, is as follows.

Age	Net Debit Balance	% to Be Applied after Correction Is Made
Under 60 days	$172,342	1%
61–90 days	136,490	3%
91–120 days	39,924*	6%
Over 120 days	23,644	$4,200 definitely uncollectible; estimated remainder uncollectible is 25%
	$372,400	

*The $2,740 write-off of receivables is related to the 91-to-120 day category.

2. The Accounts Receivable control account has a debit balance of $372,400 on December 31, 2007.
3. Two entries were made in the Bad Debt Expense account during the year: (1) a debit on December 31 for the amount credited to Allowance for Doubtful Accounts, and (2) a credit for $2,740 on November 3, 2007, and a debit to Allowance for Doubtful Accounts because of a bankruptcy.
4. The Allowance for Doubtful Accounts is as follows for 2007.

Allowance for Doubtful Accounts				
Nov. 3	Uncollectible accounts written off	2,740	Jan. 1 Beginning balance	8,750
			Dec. 31 5% of $372,400	18,620

5. A credit balance exists in the Accounts Receivable (61–90 days) of $4,840, which represents an advance on a sales contract.

Instructions

Assuming that the books have not been closed for 2007, make the necessary correcting entries.

(LO 3, 4, 5) **P7-6** **(Journalize Various Accounts Receivable Transactions)** The balance sheet of Antonio Vivaldi Company at December 31, 2007, includes the following.

Notes receivable	$ 36,000	
Accounts receivable	182,100	
Less: Allowance for doubtful accounts	17,300	200,800

Transactions in 2007 include the following.

1. Accounts receivable of $138,000 were collected including accounts of $40,000 on which 2% sales discounts were allowed.
2. $6,300 was received in payment of an account which was written off the books as worthless in 2007. (*Hint:* Reestablish the receivable account.)
3. Customer accounts of $17,500 were written off during the year.
4. At year-end the Allowance for Doubtful Accounts was estimated to need a balance of $20,000. This estimate is based on an analysis of aged accounts receivable.

Instructions

Prepare all journal entries necessary to reflect the transactions above.

(LO 8) **P7-7** **(Assigned Accounts Receivable—Journal Entries)** Nikos Company finances some of its current operations by assigning accounts receivable to a finance company. On July 1, 2007, it assigned, under guarantee, specific accounts amounting to $100,000. The finance company advanced to Nikos 80% of the accounts assigned (20% of the total to be withheld until the finance company has made its full recovery), less a finance charge of ½% of the total accounts assigned.

On July 31 Nikos Company received a statement that the finance company had collected $55,000 of these accounts and had made an additional charge of ½% of the total accounts outstanding as of July 31. This charge is to be deducted at the time of the first remittance due Nikos Company from the finance company. (*Hint*: Make entries at this time.) On August 31, 2007, Nikos Company received a second statement from the finance company, together with a check for the amount due. The statement indicated that the finance company had collected an additional $30,000 and had made a further charge of ½% of the balance outstanding as of August 31.

Instructions

Make all entries on the books of Nikos Company that are involved in the transactions above.

(AICPA adapted)

(LO 6) **P7-8** **(Notes Receivable with Realistic Interest Rate)** On October 1, 2007, Jeppo Farm Equipment Company sold a pecan-harvesting machine to Lujan Brothers Farm, Inc. In lieu of a cash payment Lujan Brothers Farm gave Jeppo a 2-year, $100,000, 8% note (a realistic rate of interest for a note of this type). The note required interest to be paid annually on October 1. Jeppo's financial statements are prepared on a calendar-year basis.

Instructions

Assuming Lujan Brothers Farm fulfills all the terms of the note, prepare the necessary journal entries for Jeppo Farm Equipment Company for the entire term of the note.

(LO 6) **P7-9** **(Notes Receivable Journal Entries)** On December 31, 2007, Menachem Inc. rendered services to Begin Corporation at an agreed price of $91,844.10, accepting $36,000 down and agreeing to accept the balance in four equal installments of $18,000 receivable each December 31. An assumed interest rate of 11% is imputed.

Instructions

Prepare the entries that would be recorded by Menachem Inc. for the sale and for the receipts and interest on the following dates. (Assume that the effective interest method is used for amortization purposes.)

(a) December 31, 2007.	**(c)** December 31, 2009.	**(e)** December 31, 2011.
(b) December 31, 2008.	**(d)** December 31, 2010.	

(LO 6, 7) **P7-10** **(Comprehensive Receivables Problem)** Connecticut Inc. had the following long-term receivable account balances at December 31, 2006.

Note receivable from sale of division	$1,800,000
Note receivable from officer	400,000

Transactions during 2007 and other information relating to Connecticut's long-term receivables were as follows.

1. The $1,800,000 note receivable is dated May 1, 2006, bears interest at 9%, and represents the balance of the consideration received from the sale of Connecticut's electronics division to New York Company. Principal payments of $600,000 plus appropriate interest are due on May 1, 2007, 2008, and 2009. The first principal and interest payment was made on May 1, 2007. Collection of the note installments is reasonably assured.

2. The $400,000 note receivable is dated December 31, 2006, bears interest at 8%, and is due on December 31, 2009. The note is due from Sean May, president of Connecticut Inc. and is collateralized by 10,000 shares of Connecticut's common stock. Interest is payable annually on December 31, and all interest payments were paid on their due dates through December 31, 2007. The quoted market price of Connecticut's common stock was $45 per share on December 31, 2007.

3. On April 1, 2007, Connecticut sold a patent to Pennsylvania Company in exchange for a $200,000 zero-interest-bearing note due on April 1, 2009. There was no established exchange price for the patent, and the note had no ready market. The prevailing rate of interest for a note of this type at April 1, 2007, was 12%. The present value of $1 for two periods at 12% is 0.797 (use this factor). The patent had a carrying value of $40,000 at January 1, 2007, and the amortization for the year ended December 31, 2007, would have been $8,000. The collection of the note receivable from Pennsylvania is reasonably assured.

4. On July 1, 2007, Connecticut sold a parcel of land to Harrisburg Company for $200,000 under an installment sale contract. Harrisburg made a $60,000 cash down payment on July 1, 2007, and signed a 4-year 11% note for the $140,000 balance. The equal annual payments of principal and interest on the note will be $45,125 payable on July 1, 2008, through July 1, 2011. The land could have been sold at an established cash price of $200,000. The cost of the land to Connecticut was $150,000. Circumstances are such that the collection of the installments on the note is reasonably assured.

Instructions

(a) Prepare the long-term receivables section of Connecticut's balance sheet at December 31, 2007.

(b) Prepare a schedule showing the current portion of the long-term receivables and accrued interest receivable that would appear in Connecticut's balance sheet at December 31, 2007.

(c) Prepare a schedule showing interest revenue from the long-term receivables that would appear on Connecticut's income statement for the year ended December 31, 2007.

(LO 8, 9)
P7-11 (Income Effects of Receivables Transactions) Radisson Company requires additional cash for its business. Radisson has decided to use its accounts receivable to raise the additional cash and has asked you to determine the income statement effects of the following contemplated transactions.

1. On July 1, 2007, Radisson assigned $400,000 of accounts receivable to Stickum Finance Company. Radisson received an advance from Stickum of 85% of the assigned accounts receivable less a commission of 3% on the advance. Prior to December 31, 2007, Radisson collected $220,000 on the assigned accounts receivable, and remitted $232,720 to Stickum, $12,720 of which represented interest on the advance from Stickum.

2. On December 1, 2007, Radisson sold $300,000 of net accounts receivable to Wunsch Company for $250,000. The receivables were sold outright on a without recourse basis.

3. On December 31, 2007, an advance of $120,000 was received from First Bank by pledging $160,000 of Radisson's accounts receivable. Radisson's first payment to First Bank is due on January 30, 2008.

Instructions

Prepare a schedule showing the income statement effects for the year ended December 31, 2007, as a result of the above facts.

(LO 10) ***P7-12 (Petty Cash, Bank Reconciliation)** Bill Howe is reviewing the cash accounting for Kappeler, Inc., a local mailing service. Howe's review will focus on the petty cash account and the bank reconciliation for the month ended May 31, 2007. He has collected the following information from Kappeler's bookkeeper for this task.

Petty Cash

1. The petty cash fund was established on May 10, 2007, in the amount of $250.
2. Expenditures from the fund by the custodian as of May 31, 2007, were evidenced by approved receipts for the following.

Postage expense	$33.00
Mailing labels and other supplies	75.00
I.O.U. from employees	30.00
Shipping charges	57.45
Newspaper advertising	22.80
Miscellaneous expense	15.35

On May 31, 2007, the petty cash fund was replenished and increased to $300; currency and coin in the fund at that time totaled $16.40.

Bank Reconciliation

<table>
<tr><td colspan="4" align="center">**THIRD NATIONAL BANK**
BANK STATEMENT</td></tr>
<tr><td></td><td>Disbursements</td><td>Receipts</td><td>Balance</td></tr>
<tr><td>Balance, May 1, 2007</td><td></td><td></td><td>$8,769</td></tr>
<tr><td>Deposits</td><td></td><td>$28,000</td><td></td></tr>
<tr><td>Note payment direct from customer (interest of $30)</td><td></td><td>930</td><td></td></tr>
<tr><td>Checks cleared during May</td><td>$31,150</td><td></td><td></td></tr>
<tr><td>Bank service charges</td><td>27</td><td></td><td></td></tr>
<tr><td>Balance, May 31, 2007</td><td></td><td></td><td>6,522</td></tr>
</table>

Kappeler's Cash Account

Balance, May 1, 2007	$ 9,150
Deposits during May 2007	31,000
Checks written during May 2007	(31,835)

Deposits in transit are determined to be $3,000, and checks outstanding at May 31 total $550. Cash on hand (besides petty cash) at May 31, 2007, is $246.

Instructions

(a) Prepare the journal entries to record the transactions related to the petty cash fund for May.

(b) Prepare a bank reconciliation dated May 31, 2007, proceeding to a correct cash balance, and prepare the journal entries necessary to make the books correct and complete.

(c) What amount of cash should be reported in the May 31, 2007, balance sheet?

(LO 10) *P7-13 **(Bank Reconciliation and Adjusting Entries)** The cash account of Jose Orozco Co. showed a ledger balance of $3,969.85 on June 30, 2007. The bank statement as of that date showed a balance of $4,150. Upon comparing the statement with the cash records, the following facts were determined.

1. There were bank service charges for June of $25.

2. A bank memo stated that Bao Dai's note for $900 and interest of $36 had been collected on June 29, and the bank had made a charge of $5.50 on the collection. (No entry had been made on Orozco's books when Bao Dai's note was sent to the bank for collection.)

3. Receipts for June 30 for $2,890 were not deposited until July 2.

4. Checks outstanding on June 30 totaled $2,136.05.

5. The bank had charged the Orozco Co.'s account for a customer's uncollectible check amounting to $453.20 on June 29.

6. A customer's check for $90 had been entered as $60 in the cash receipts journal by Orozco on June 15.

7. Check no. 742 in the amount of $491 had been entered in the cash journal as $419, and check no. 747 in the amount of $58.20 had been entered as $582. Both checks had been issued to pay for purchases of equipment.

Instructions

(a) Prepare a bank reconciliation dated June 30, 2007, proceeding to a correct cash balance.

(b) Prepare any entries necessary to make the books correct and complete.

(LO 10) *P7-14 **(Bank Reconciliation and Adjusting Entries)** Presented below is information related to Tanizaki Inc.

Balance per books at October 31, $41,847.85; receipts $173,523.91; disbursements $166,193.54. Balance per bank statement November 30, $56,274.20.

The following checks were outstanding at November 30.

1224	$1,635.29
1230	2,468.30
1232	3,625.15
1233	482.17

Included with the November bank statement and not recorded by the company were a bank debit memo for $27.40 covering bank charges for the month, a debit memo for $572.13 for a customer's check returned and marked NSF, and a credit memo for $1,400 representing bond interest collected by the bank in the name of Tanizaki Inc. Cash on hand at November 30 recorded and awaiting deposit amounted to $1,915.40.

Instructions

(a) Prepare a bank reconciliation (to the correct balance) at November 30, for Tanizaki Inc. from the information above.

(b) Prepare any journal entries required to adjust the cash account at November 30.

CONCEPTS FOR ANALYSIS

CA7-1 (Bad-Debt Accounting) Ariel Company has significant amounts of trade accounts receivable. Ariel uses the allowance method to estimate bad debts instead of the direct write-off method. During the year, some specific accounts were written off as uncollectible, and some that were previously written off as uncollectible were collected.

Instructions

(a) What are the deficiencies of the direct write-off method?

(b) What are the two basic allowance methods used to estimate bad debts, and what is the theoretical justification for each?

(c) How should Ariel account for the collection of the specific accounts previously written off as uncollectible?

CA7-2 (Various Receivable Accounting Issues) Anne Archer Company uses the net method of accounting for sales discounts. Anne Archer also offers trade discounts to various groups of buyers.

On August 1, 2007, Archer sold some accounts receivable on a without recourse basis. Archer incurred a finance charge.

Archer also has some notes receivable bearing an appropriate rate of interest. The principal and total interest are due at maturity. The notes were received on October 1, 2007, and mature on September 30, 2009. Archer's operating cycle is less than one year.

Instructions

(a) (1) Using the net method, how should Archer account for the sales discounts at the date of sale? What is the rationale for the amount recorded as sales under the net method?

(2) Using the net method, what is the effect on Archer's sales revenues and net income when customers do not take the sales discounts?

(b) What is the effect of trade discounts on sales revenues and accounts receivable? Why?

(c) How should Archer account for the accounts receivable factored on August 1, 2007? Why?

(d) How should Archer account for the note receivable and the related interest on December 31, 2007? Why?

CA7-3 (Bad-Debt Reporting Issues) Orlando Bloom conducts a wholesale merchandising business that sells approximately 5,000 items per month with a total monthly average sales value of $250,000. Its annual bad debt ratio has been approximately $1\frac{1}{2}\%$ of sales. In recent discussions with his bookkeeper, Mr. Bloom has become confused by all the alternatives apparently available in handling the Allowance for Doubtful Accounts balance. The following information has been shown.

1. An allowance can be set up (a) on the basis of a percentage of sales or (b) on the basis of a valuation of all past due or otherwise questionable accounts receivable. Those considered uncollectible can be charged to such allowance at the close of the accounting period, or specific items can be charged off directly against (1) Gross Sales or to (2) Bad Debt Expense in the year in which they are determined to be uncollectible.

2. Collection agency and legal fees, and so on, incurred in connection with the attempted recovery of bad debts can be charged to (a) Bad Debt Expense, (b) Allowance for Doubtful Accounts, (c) Legal Expense, or (d) General Expense.

3. Debts previously written off in whole or in part but currently recovered can be credited to (a) Other Revenue, (b) Bad Debt Expense, or (c) Allowance for Doubtful Accounts.

Instructions

Which of the foregoing methods would you recommend to Mr. Bloom in regard to (1) allowances and charge-offs, (2) collection expenses, and (3) recoveries? State briefly and clearly the reasons supporting your recommendations.

CA7-4 (Basic Note and Accounts Receivable Transactions)

Part 1

On July 1, 2007, John Depp Company, a calendar-year company, sold special-order merchandise on credit and received in return an interest-bearing note receivable from the customer. John Depp Company will receive interest at the prevailing rate for a note of this type. Both the principal and interest are due in one lump sum on June 30, 2008.

Instructions

When should John Depp Company report interest revenue from the note receivable? Discuss the rationale for your answer.

Part 2

On December 31, 2007, John Depp Company had significant amounts of accounts receivable as a result of credit sales to its customers. Depp uses the allowance method based on credit sales to estimate bad debts. Past experience indicates that 2% of credit sales normally will not be collected. This pattern is expected to continue.

Instructions

   (a) Discuss the rationale for using the allowance method based on credit sales to estimate bad debts. Contrast this method with the allowance method based on the balance in the trade receivables accounts.

   (b) How should John Depp Company report the allowance for doubtful accounts on its balance sheet at December 31, 2007? Also, describe the alternatives, if any, for presentation of bad debt expense in John Depp Company's 2007 income statement.

(AICPA adapted)

CA7-5 **(Bad-Debt Reporting Issues)** Rosita Arenas Company sells office equipment and supplies to many organizations in the city and surrounding area on contract terms of 2/10, n/30. In the past, over 75% of the credit customers have taken advantage of the discount by paying within 10 days of the invoice date.

The number of customers taking the full 30 days to pay has increased within the last year. Current indications are that less than 60% of the customers are now taking the discount. Bad debts as a percentage of gross credit sales have risen from the 1.5% provided in past years to about 4% in the current year.

The controller has responded to a request for more information on the deterioration in collections of accounts receivable with the report reproduced below.

ROSITA ARENAS COMPANY
FINANCE COMMITTEE REPORT—ACCOUNTS RECEIVABLE COLLECTIONS
MAY 31, 2007

The fact that some credit accounts will prove uncollectible is normal. Annual bad debt write-offs have been 1.5% of gross credit sales over the past five years. During the last fiscal year, this percentage increased to slightly less than 4%. The current Accounts Receivable balance is $1,600,000. The condition of this balance in terms of age and probability of collection is as follows.

Proportion of Total	Age Categories	Probability of Collection
68%	not yet due	99%
15%	less than 30 days past due	96½%
8%	30 to 60 days past due	95%
5%	61 to 120 days past due	91%
2½%	121 to 180 days past due	70%
1½%	over 180 days past due	20%

The Allowance for Doubtful Accounts had a credit balance of $43,300 on June 1, 2006. Rosita Arenas Company has provided for a monthly bad debts expense accrual during the current fiscal year based on the assumption that 4% of gross credit sales will be uncollectible. Total gross credit sales for the 2006–2007 fiscal year amounted to $4,000,000. Write-offs of bad accounts during the year totaled $145,000.

Instructions

   (a) Prepare an accounts receivable aging schedule for Rosita Arenas Company using the age categories identified in the controller's report to the finance committee showing:
      (1) The amount of accounts receivable outstanding for each age category and in total.
      (2) The estimated amount that is uncollectible for each category and in total.

   (b) Compute the amount of the year-end adjustment necessary to bring Allowance for Doubtful Accounts to the balance indicated by the age analysis. Then prepare the necessary journal entry to adjust the accounting records.

   (c) In a recessionary environment with tight credit and high interest rates:
      (1) Identify steps Rosita Arenas Company might consider to improve the accounts receivable situation.
      (2) Then evaluate each step identified in terms of the risks and costs involved.

(CMA adapted)

CA7-6 (Sale of Notes Receivable) Sergey Luzov Wholesalers Co. sells industrial equipment for a standard 3-year note receivable. Revenue is recognized at time of sale. Each note is secured by a lien on the equipment and has a face amount equal to the equipment's list price. Each note's stated interest rate is below the customer's market rate at date of sale. All notes are to be collected in three equal annual installments beginning one year after sale. Some of the notes are subsequently sold to a bank with recourse, some are subsequently sold without recourse, and some are retained by Luzov. At year end, Luzov evaluates all outstanding notes receivable and provides for estimated losses arising from defaults.

Instructions
- **(a)** What is the appropriate valuation basis for Luzov's notes receivable at the date it sells equipment?
- **(b)** How should Luzov account for the sale, without recourse, of a February 1, 2007, note receivable sold on May 1, 2007? Why is it appropriate to account for it in this way?
- **(c)** At December 31, 2007, how should Luzov measure and account for the impact of estimated losses resulting from notes receivable that it
    - **(1)** Retained and did **not** sell?
    - **(2)** Sold to bank with recourse?

(AICPA adapted)

CA7-7 (Zero-Interest-Bearing Note Receivable) On September 30, 2006, Tiger Machinery Co. sold a machine and accepted the customer's zero-interest-bearing note. Tiger normally makes sales on a cash basis. Since the machine was unique, its sales price was not determinable using Tiger's normal pricing practices.

After receiving the first of two equal annual installments on September 30, 2007, Tiger immediately sold the note with recourse. On October 9, 2008, Tiger received notice that the note was dishonored, and it paid all amounts due. At all times prior to default, the note was reasonably expected to be paid in full.

Instructions
- **(a)** **(1)** How should Tiger determine the sales price of the machine?
    - **(2)** How should Tiger report the effects of the zero-interest-bearing note on its income statement for the year ended December 31, 2006? Why is this accounting presentation appropriate?
- **(b)** What are the effects of the sale of the note receivable with recourse on Tiger's income statement for the year ended December 31, 2007, and its balance sheet at December 31, 2007?
- **(c)** How should Tiger account for the effects of the note being dishonored?

CA7-8 (Reporting of Notes Receivable, Interest, and Sale of Receivables) On July 1, 2007, Gale Sondergaard Company sold special-order merchandise on credit and received in return an interest-bearing note receivable from the customer. Sondergaard will receive interest at the prevailing rate for a note of this type. Both the principal and interest are due in one lump sum on June 30, 2008.

On September 1, 2007, Sondergaard sold special-order merchandise on credit and received in return a zero-interest-bearing note receivable from the customer. The prevailing rate of interest for a note of this type is determinable. The note receivable is due in one lump sum on August 31, 2009.

Sondergaard also has significant amounts of trade accounts receivable as a result of credit sales to its customers. On October 1, 2007, some trade accounts receivable were assigned to Irene Dunne Finance Company on a non-notification (Sondergaard handles collections) basis for an advance of 75% of their amount at an interest charge of 8% on the balance outstanding.

On November 1, 2007, other trade accounts receivable were sold on a without recourse basis. The factor withheld 5% of the trade accounts receivable factored as protection against sales returns and allowances and charged a finance charge of 3%.

Instructions
- **(a)** How should Sondergaard determine the interest revenue for 2007 on the:
    - **(1)** Interest-bearing note receivable? Why?
    - **(2)** Zero-interest-bearing note receivable? Why?
- **(b)** How should Sondergaard report the interest-bearing note receivable and the zero-interest-bearing note receivable on its balance sheet at December 31, 2007?
- **(c)** How should Sondergaard account for subsequent collections on the trade accounts receivable assigned on October 1, 2007, and the payments to Irene Dunne Finance? Why?
- **(d)** How should Sondergaard account for the trade accounts receivable factored on November 1, 2007? Why?

(AICPA adapted)

CA7-9 (Accounting for Zero-Interest-Bearing Note) Soon after beginning the year-end audit work on March 10 at Engone Company, the auditor has the following conversation with the controller.

CONTROLLER: The year ended March 31st should be our most profitable in history and, as a consequence, the board of directors has just awarded the officers generous bonuses.

AUDITOR: I thought profits were down this year in the industry, according to your latest interim report.

CONTROLLER: Well, they were down, but 10 days ago we closed a deal that will give us a substantial increase for the year.

AUDITOR: Oh, what was it?

CONTROLLER: Well, you remember a few years ago our former president bought stock in Rocketeer Enterprises because he had those grandiose ideas about becoming a conglomerate. For 6 years we have not been able to sell this stock, which cost us $3,000,000 and has not paid a nickel in dividends. Thursday we sold this stock to Campbell Inc. for $4,000,000. So, we will have a gain of $700,000 ($1,000,000 pretax) which will increase our net income for the year to $4,000,000, compared with last year's $3,800,000. As far as I know, we'll be the only company in the industry to register an increase in net income this year. That should help the market value of the stock!

AUDITOR: Do you expect to receive the $4,000,000 in cash by March 31st, your fiscal year-end?

CONTROLLER: No. Although Campbell Inc. is an excellent company, they are a little tight for cash because of their rapid growth. Consequently, they are going to give us a $4,000,000 zero-interest-bearing note with payments of $400,000 per year for the next 10 years. The first payment is due on March 31 of next year.

AUDITOR: Why is the note zero-interest-bearing?

CONTROLLER: Because that's what everybody agreed to. Since we don't have any interest-bearing debt, the funds invested in the note do not cost us anything and besides, we were not getting any dividends on the Rocketeer Enterprises stock.

Instructions

Do you agree with the way the controller has accounted for the transaction? If not, how should the transaction be accounted for?

CA7-10 (Receivables Management) As the manager of the accounts receivable department for Vicki Maher Leather Goods, Ltd., you recently noticed that Percy Shelley, your accounts receivable clerk who is paid $1,200 per month, has been wearing unusually tasteful and expensive clothing. (This is Vicki Maher's first year in business.) This morning, Shelley drove up to work in a brand new Lexus.

Naturally suspicious by nature, you decide to test the accuracy of the accounts receivable balance of $132,000 as shown in the ledger. The following information is available for your first year (precisely 9 months ended September 30, 2007) in business.

(1) Collections from customers	$198,000
(2) Merchandise purchased	360,000
(3) Ending merchandise inventory	90,000
(4) Goods are marked to sell at 40% above cost.	

Instructions

Assuming all sales were made on account, compute the ending accounts receivable balance that should appear in the ledger, noting any apparent shortage. Then, draft a memo dated October 3, 2007, to John Castle, the branch manager, explaining the facts in this situation. Remember that this problem is serious, and you do not want to make hasty accusations.

CA7-11 (Bad-Debt Reporting) Santo Company is a subsidiary of Hughes Corp. The controller believes that the yearly allowance for doubtful accounts for Santo should be 2% of net credit sales. The president, nervous that the parent company might expect the subsidiary to sustain its 10% growth rate, suggests that the controller increase the allowance for doubtful accounts to 3% yearly. The supervisor thinks that the lower net income, which reflects a 6% growth rate, will be a more sustainable rate for Santo Company.

Instructions

(a) Should the controller be concerned with Santo Company's growth rate in estimating the allowance? Explain your answer.

(b) Does the president's request pose an ethical dilemma for the controller? Give your reasons.

USING YOUR JUDGMENT

Financial Reporting Problem

P&G The Procter & Gamble Company (P&G)

The financial statements of **P&G** are presented in Appendix 5B or can be accessed on the KWW website.

Instructions

Refer to P&G's financial statements and the accompanying notes to answer the following questions.

(a) What criteria does P&G use to classify "Cash and cash equivalents" as reported in its balance sheet?

(b) As of June 30, 2004, what balances did P&G have in cash and cash equivalents? What were the major uses of cash during the year?

(c) P&G reports no allowance for doubtful accounts, suggesting that bad debt expense is not material for this company. Is it reasonable that a company like P&G would not have material bad debt expense? Explain.

Financial Statement Analysis Cases

Case I Occidental Petroleum Corporation

Occidental Petroleum Corporation reported the following information in its 2003 Annual Report.

Occidental Petroleum Corporation
Consolidated Balance Sheets
(in millions)

Assets at December 31,	2003	2002
Current assets		
Cash and cash equivalents	$ 683	$ 146
Trade receivables, net of allowances	804	608
Receivables from joint ventures, partnerships, and other	330	321
Inventories	510	491
Prepaid expenses and other	147	307
Total current assets	2,474	1,873
Long-term receivables, net	264	275

Notes to Consolidated Financial Statements
Cash and Cash Equivalents.   Cash equivalents consist of highly liquid investments. Cash equivalents totaled approximately $661 million and $116 million at December 31, 2003 and 2002, respectively.

Trade Receivables.   Occidental has agreement to sell, under a revolving sale program, an undivided percentage ownership interest in a designated pool of non-interest-bearing receivables. Under this program, Occidental serves as the collection agent with respect to the receivables sold. An interest in new receivables is sold as collections are made from customers. The balance sold at December 31, 2003, was $360 million.

Instructions

(a) What items other than coin and currency may be included in "cash"?

(b) What items may be included in "cash equivalents"?

(c) What are compensating balance arrangements, and how should they be reported in financial statements?

(d) What are the possible differences between cash equivalents and short-term (temporary) investments?

(e) Assuming that the sale agreement meets the criteria for sale accounting, cash proceeds were $345 million, the carrying value of the receivables sold was $360 million, and the fair value of the recourse obligation was $15 million, what was the effect on income from the sale of receivables?

(f) Briefly discuss the impact of the transaction in (e) on Occidental's liquidity.

Case 2 Microsoft Corporation

Microsoft is the leading developer of software in the world. To continue to be successful Microsoft must generate new products, which requires significant amounts of cash. Shown on page 364 is the current asset and current liability information from Microsoft's June 30, 2004, balance sheet (in millions). Following the Microsoft data is the current asset and current liability information for **Oracle** (in millions), another major software developer.

MICROSOFT CORPORATION
BALANCE SHEETS (PARTIAL)
As of June 30
(in millions)

Current assets	2004	2003
Cash and equivalents	$15,982	$ 6,438
Short-term investments	44,610	42,610
Accounts receivable	5,890	5,196
Other	4,084	4,729
Total current assets	$70,566	$58,973
Total current liabilities	$14,969	$13,974

ORACLE
BALANCE SHEETS (PARTIAL)
As of May 31
(in millions)

Current assets	2004	2003
Cash and equivalents	$ 4,138	$ 4,737
Short-term investments	4,449	1,782
Receivables	2,012	1,920
Other current assets	737	788
Total current assets	$11,336	$9,227
Current liabilities	$ 4,272	$4,158

Part 1 (Cash and Cash Equivalents)

Instructions

(a) What is the definition of a cash equivalent? Give some examples of cash equivalents. How do cash equivalents differ from other types of short-term investments?

(b) Calculate (1) the current ratio and (2) working capital for each company for 2004 and discuss your results.

(c) Is it possible to have too many liquid assets?

Part 2 (Accounts Receivables)

Microsoft provided the following disclosure related to its accounts receivable.

Allowance for Doubtful Accounts. The allowance for doubtful accounts reflects our best estimate of probable losses inherent in the accounts receivable balance. We determine the allowance based on known troubled accounts, historical experience, and other currently available evidence. Activity in the allowance for doubtful accounts is as follows:

(in millions)

Year Ended June 30	Balance at beginning of period	Charged to costs and expenses	Write-offs and other	Balance at end of period
2002	$174	$192	$(157)	$209
2003	209	118	(85)	242
2004	242	44	(120)	166

Instructions

(a) Compute Microsoft's receivables turnover ratio for 2004 and discuss your results. Microsoft had sales revenue of $36,835 million in 2004.

(b) Reconstruct the summary journal entries for 2004 based on the information in the disclosure.

(c) Briefly discuss how the accounting for bad debts affects the analysis in Part 2 (a).

Comparative Analysis Case

The Coca-Cola Company and PepsiCo, Inc.

Instructions

Go to the KWW website and use the information found there to answer the following questions related to The Coca-Cola Company and PepsiCo, Inc.

(a) What were the cash and cash equivalents reported by Coca-Cola and PepsiCo at the end of 2004? What does each company classify as cash equivalents?

(b) What were the accounts receivable (net) for Coca-Cola and PepsiCo at the end of 2004? Which company reports the greater allowance for doubtful accounts receivable (amount and percentage of gross receivable) at the end of 2004?

(c) Assuming that all "net operating revenues" (Coca-Cola) and all "net sales" (PepsiCo) were net *credit* sales, compute the receivables turnover ratio for 2004 for Coca-Cola and PepsiCo; also compute the days outstanding for receivables. What is your evaluation of the difference?

Research Cases

Case 1

Accounting Trends and Techniques, published annually by the American Institute of Certified Public Accountants, is a survey of 600 annual reports to stockholders. The survey covers selected industrial, merchandising, and service companies.

Instructions

Examine the section regarding the use of receivables for financing and answer the following questions.

(a) For the most recent year, how many of the companies surveyed disclosed (1) receivables sold, and (2) receivables used as collateral?

(b) Examine the disclosure provided by a company that sold receivables and a company that used its receivables as collateral. Summarize the major terms of the transactions.

Case 2

The January 20, 1999, edition of the *Wall Street Journal* contained an article by Jonathan Weil titled "Americredit Accounting Practices Are Criticized by Research Firm."

Instructions

Read the article and answer the following questions.

(a) Why is Americredit's accounting for receivables criticized?

(b) How does the "cash-out" method of accounting for loan sales respond to the criticisms from part (a)?

(c) What are warning signs that investors can use to identify problems at sub-prime lenders?

Professional Research: Financial Accounting and Reporting

As the new staff person in your company's treasury department, you have been asked to conduct research related to a proposed transfer of receivables. Your supervisor wants the authoritative sources for the following items that are discussed in the securitization agreement.

Instructions

Using the **Financial Accounting Research System (FARS)**, respond to the following items. (Provide text strings used in your search.)

(a) List the current statement and the previous statement that addressed transfers of receivables.

(b) Provide definitions for the following:

    (1) Transfer.

    (2) Recourse.

    (3) Collateral.

(c) Provide other examples (besides recourse and collateral) that qualify as continuing involvement.

Professional Simulation

In this simulation you are asked to address various requirements regarding the accounting for receivables. Prepare responses to all parts.

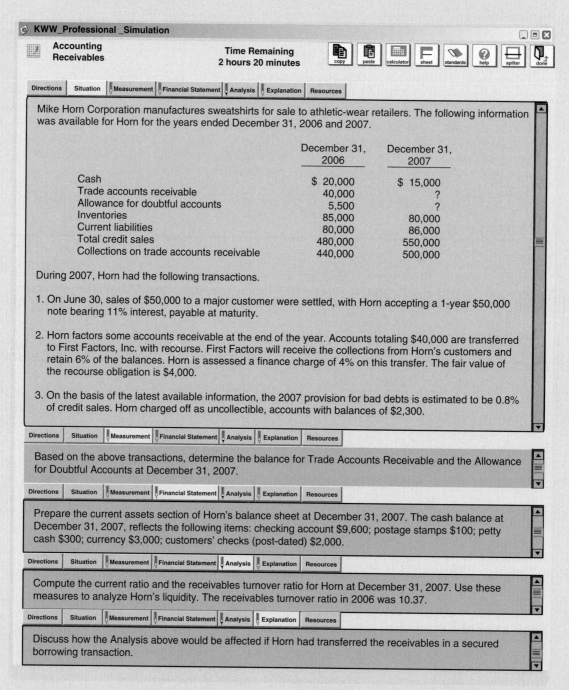

		December 31, 2006	December 31, 2007
Cash		$ 20,000	$ 15,000
Trade accounts receivable		40,000	?
Allowance for doubtful accounts		5,500	?
Inventories		85,000	80,000
Current liabilities		80,000	86,000
Total credit sales		480,000	550,000
Collections on trade accounts receivable		440,000	500,000

During 2007, Horn had the following transactions.

1. On June 30, sales of $50,000 to a major customer were settled, with Horn accepting a 1-year $50,000 note bearing 11% interest, payable at maturity.

2. Horn factors some accounts receivable at the end of the year. Accounts totaling $40,000 are transferred to First Factors, Inc. with recourse. First Factors will receive the collections from Horn's customers and retain 6% of the balances. Horn is assessed a finance charge of 4% on this transfer. The fair value of the recourse obligation is $4,000.

3. On the basis of the latest available information, the 2007 provision for bad debts is estimated to be 0.8% of credit sales. Horn charged off as uncollectible, accounts with balances of $2,300.

Based on the above transactions, determine the balance for Trade Accounts Receivable and the Allowance for Doubtful Accounts at December 31, 2007.

Prepare the current assets section of Horn's balance sheet at December 31, 2007. The cash balance at December 31, 2007, reflects the following items: checking account $9,600; postage stamps $100; petty cash $300; currency $3,000; customers' checks (post-dated) $2,000.

Compute the current ratio and the receivables turnover ratio for Horn at December 31, 2007. Use these measures to analyze Horn's liquidity. The receivables turnover ratio in 2006 was 10.37.

Discuss how the Analysis above would be affected if Horn had transferred the receivables in a secured borrowing transaction.

VALUATION OF INVENTORIES: A COST-BASIS APPROACH

Inventories in the Crystal Ball

A substantial increase in inventory may be a leading indicator of an upcoming decline in profit margins. Take the auto industry as an example. Detroit's inventories have been growing for several years because the domestic manufacturers like to run the factories at full capacity, even if they are not selling cars as fast as they can make them. The current arrangement is particularly tough for **General Motors**. It overproduces and then tries to push the sales with incentives and month-long "blow-out" sales. GM is hoping that the ever-growing market will cover the problem until customer demand grows to the point where the cars are purchased without so many incentives.

But recently, all that was growing was GM inventories. Not too long ago, the average sticker on a Cadillac DeVille was $54,193, but the net price after incentives was $42,211. This meant that the factory was giving up a substantial amount of profit through rebates, dealer cash, or lease or interest rate subsidies. A similar deal could be had at **Ford**, which was selling Explorers for $25,745 net, a 24 percent reduction for various factory incentives. But inventories at GM and Ford continued to grow, even with these significant incentives.[1]

These data concern investors. As one analyst remarked, "When inventory grows faster than sales, profits drop." That is, when companies face slowing sales and growing inventory, then markdowns in prices usually result. These markdowns, in turn, lead to lower sales revenue and income, thereby squeezing profit margins on sales.[2]

Research supporting these observations indicates that increases in retailers' inventory translate into lower prices and lower net income.[3] Interestingly, the same research found that for manufacturers, only increases in finished goods inventory lead to future profit declines. Increases in raw materials and work-in-process inventories signal that the company is building its inventory to meet increased demand. Therefore, future sales and income will be higher. These research results reinforce the usefulness of the GAAP requirement for manufacturers to disclose their inventory components on the balance sheet or in related notes.

---

[1]J. Flint, "Inventories: Too Much of a Good Thing," *Forbes.com* (September 21, 2004).

[2]S. Pulliam, "Heard on the Street," *Wall Street Journal* (May 21, 1997), p. C1.

[3]Victor Bernard and J. Noel, "Do Inventory Disclosures Predict Sales and Earnings?" *Journal of Accounting, Auditing, and Finance* (March 1991), pp. 145–182.

Learning Objectives

After studying this chapter, you should be able to:

1 Identify major classifications of inventory.

2 Distinguish between perpetual and periodic inventory systems.

3 Identify the effects of inventory errors on the financial statements.

4 Understand the items to include as inventory cost.

5 Describe and compare the cost flow assumptions used to account for inventories.

6 Explain the significance and use of a LIFO reserve.

7 Understand the effect of LIFO liquidations.

8 Explain the dollar-value LIFO method.

9 Identify the major advantages and disadvantages of LIFO.

10 Understand why companies select given inventory methods.

As our opening story indicates, information on inventories and changes in inventory helps to predict financial performance. In this chapter we discuss the basic issues related to accounting and reporting for inventory. The content and organization of the chapter are as follows.

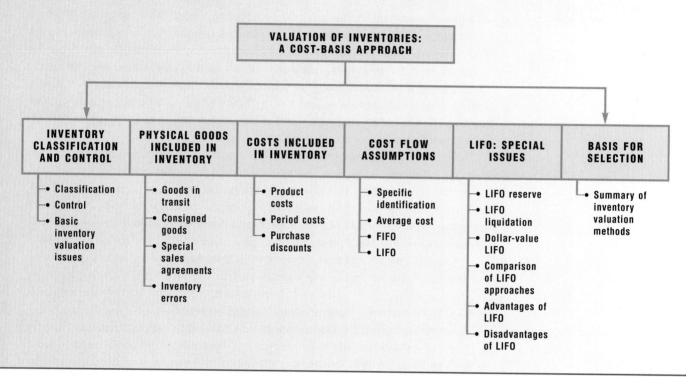

INVENTORY CLASSIFICATION AND CONTROL

Classification

Inventories are asset items that a company holds for sale in the ordinary course of business, or goods that it will use or consume in the production of goods to be sold. The description and measurement of inventory require careful attention. The investment in inventories is frequently the largest current asset of merchandising (retail) and manufacturing businesses.

A **merchandising concern,** such as **Wal-Mart,** usually purchases its merchandise in a form ready for sale. It reports the cost assigned to unsold units left on hand as **merchandise inventory.** Only one inventory account, Merchandise Inventory, appears in the financial statements.

Manufacturing concerns, on the other hand, produce goods to sell to merchandising firms. Many of the largest U.S. businesses are manufacturers, such as **Boeing, IBM, ExxonMobil, Procter & Gamble, Ford,** and **Motorola.** Although the products they produce may differ, manufacturers normally have three inventory accounts—Raw Materials, Work in Process, and Finished Goods.

A company reports the cost assigned to goods and materials on hand but not yet placed into production as **raw materials inventory.** Raw materials include the wood to make a baseball bat or the steel to make a car. These materials can be traced directly to the end product.

At any point in a continuous production process some units are only partially processed. The cost of the raw material for these unfinished units, plus the direct labor cost applied specifically to this material and a ratable share of manufacturing overhead costs, constitute the **work in process inventory**.

Companies report the costs identified with the completed but unsold units on hand at the end of the fiscal period as **finished goods inventory**. Illustration 8-1 contrasts the financial statement presentation of inventories of **Wal-Mart** (a merchandising company) with those of **Caterpillar** (a manufacturing company.) The remainder of the balance sheet is essentially similar for the two types of companies.

ILLUSTRATION 8-1
Comparison of Presentation of Current Assets for Merchandising and Manufacturing Companies

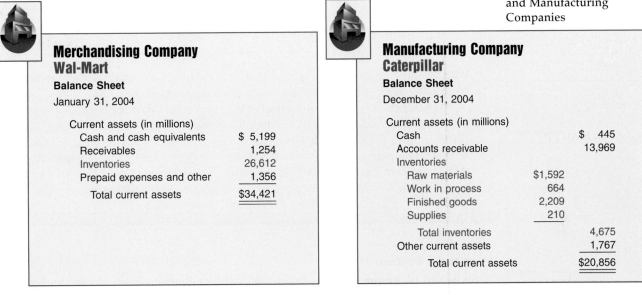

Merchandising Company
Wal-Mart

Balance Sheet

January 31, 2004

Current assets (in millions)	
Cash and cash equivalents	$ 5,199
Receivables	1,254
Inventories	26,612
Prepaid expenses and other	1,356
Total current assets	$34,421

Manufacturing Company
Caterpillar

Balance Sheet

December 31, 2004

Current assets (in millions)		
Cash		$ 445
Accounts receivable		13,969
Inventories		
Raw materials	$1,592	
Work in process	664	
Finished goods	2,209	
Supplies	210	
Total inventories		4,675
Other current assets		1,767
Total current assets		$20,856

As indicated above, a manufacturing company, like **Caterpillar**, also might include a Manufacturing or Factory **Supplies Inventory** account. In it, Caterpillar would include such items as machine oils, nails, cleaning material, and the like—supplies that are used in production but are not the primary materials being processed.

Illustration 8-2 shows the differences in the flow of costs through a merchandising company and a manufacturing company.

Additional Inventory Disclosures

ILLUSTRATION 8-2
Flow of Costs through Manufacturing and Merchandising Companies

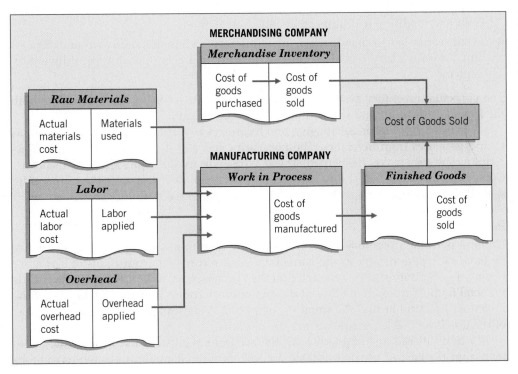

Control

For various reasons, management is vitally interested in inventory planning and control. Whether a company manufactures or merchandises goods, it needs an accurate accounting system with up-to-date records. It may lose sales and customers if it does not stock products in the desired style, quality, and quantity. Further, companies must monitor inventory levels carefully to limit the financing costs of carrying large amounts of inventory.

Companies use one of two types of systems for maintaining accurate inventory records—the perpetual system or the periodic system.

Perpetual System

OBJECTIVE 2
Distinguish between perpetual and periodic inventory systems.

A **perpetual inventory system** continuously tracks changes in the Inventory account. That is, a company records all purchases and sales (issues) of goods directly in the Inventory account **as they occur**. The accounting features of a perpetual inventory system are as follows.

1 Purchases of merchandise for resale or raw materials for production are debited to Inventory rather than to Purchases.

2 Freight-in, purchase returns and allowances, and purchase discounts are debited to Inventory rather than in separate accounts.

3 Cost of goods sold is recorded at the time of each sale by debiting Cost of Goods Sold and crediting Inventory.

4 A subsidiary ledger of individual inventory records is maintained as a control measure. The subsidiary records show the quantity and cost of each type of inventory on hand.

The perpetual inventory system provides a continuous record of the balances in both the Inventory account and the Cost of Goods Sold account.

A computerized recordkeeping system records nearly instantaneously any additions to and issuances from inventory. The popularity and affordability of computerized accounting software makes the perpetual system cost-effective for many kinds of businesses. Companies like **Target**, **Best Buy**, and **Sears Holdings** now incorporate the recording of sales with optical scanners at the cash register into perpetual inventory systems.

Periodic System

Under a **periodic inventory system**, a company determines the quantity of inventory on hand only periodically, as the name implies. It records all acquisitions of inventory during the accounting period by debiting the Purchases account. A company then adds the total in the Purchases account at the end of the accounting period to the cost of the inventory on hand at the beginning of the period. This sum determines the total cost of the goods available for sale during the period.

To compute the cost of goods sold, the company then subtracts the ending inventory from the cost of goods available for sale. Note that under a periodic inventory system, the cost of goods sold is a residual amount that depends on a physically counted ending inventory.

Once a year, companies take the **physical inventory count** required by a periodic system.[4] However, most companies need more current information regarding their inventory levels to protect against stockouts or overpurchasing and to aid in preparation of monthly or quarterly financial data. As a consequence, many companies use a **modified perpetual inventory system**. This system provides detailed inventory records of increases and decreases in quantities only—not dollar amounts. It is merely a memorandum device outside the double-entry system, which helps in determining the level of inventory at any point in time.

Whether a company maintains a perpetual inventory in quantities and dollars or in quantities only, or has no perpetual inventory record at all, it probably takes a physical inventory once a year. No matter what type of inventory records companies use, they all face the danger of loss and error. Waste, breakage, theft, improper entry, failure to prepare or record requisitions, and other similar possibilities may cause the inventory records to differ from the actual inventory on hand. Thus all companies need periodic verification of the inventory records by actual count, weight, or measurement, with the counts compared with the detailed inventory records. A company corrects the records to agree with the quantities actually on hand.

Insofar as possible, companies should take the physical inventory near the end of their fiscal year, to properly report inventory quantities in their annual accounting reports. Because this is not always possible, however, physical inventories taken within two or three months of the year's end are satisfactory, if a company maintains detailed inventory records with a fair degree of accuracy.

To illustrate the difference between a perpetual and a periodic system, assume that Fesmire Company had the following transactions during the current year.

Beginning inventory	100 units at $ 6 = $ 600
Purchases	900 units at $ 6 = $5,400
Sales	600 units at $12 = $7,200
Ending inventory	400 units at $ 6 = $2,400

Fesmire records these transactions during the current year as shown in Illustration 8-3.

Perpetual Inventory System		Periodic Inventory System	
1. Beginning inventory, 100 units at $6:			
The inventory account shows the inventory on hand at $600.		The inventory account shows the inventory on hand at $600.	
2. Purchase 900 units at $6:			
Inventory 5,400		Purchases 5,400	
Accounts Payable	5,400	Accounts Payable	5,400
3. Sale of 600 units at $12:			
Accounts Receivable 7,200		Accounts Receivable 7,200	
Sales	7,200	Sales	7,200
Cost of Goods Sold 3,600		(No entry)	
(600 at $6)			
Inventory	3,600		
4. End-of-period entries for inventory accounts, 400 units at $6:			
No entry necessary.		Inventory (ending, by count) 2,400	
The account, Inventory, shows the ending		Cost of Goods Sold 3,600	
balance of $2,400		Purchases	5,400
($600 + $5,400 − $3,600).		Inventory (beginning)	600

ILLUSTRATION 8-3
Comparative Entries—
Perpetual vs. Periodic

---

[4]In recent years, some companies have developed methods of determining inventories, including statistical sampling, that are sufficiently reliable to make unnecessary an annual physical count of each item of inventory.

When a company uses a perpetual inventory system and a difference exists between the perpetual inventory balance and the physical inventory count, it needs a separate entry to adjust the perpetual inventory account. To illustrate, assume that at the end of the reporting period, the perpetual inventory account reported an inventory balance of $4,000. However, a physical count indicates $3,800 is actually on hand. The entry to record the necessary write-down is as follows.

Inventory Over and Short	200	
Inventory		200

Perpetual inventory overages and shortages generally represent a misstatement of cost of goods sold. The difference results from normal and expected shrinkage, breakage, shoplifting, incorrect recordkeeping, and the like. Inventory Over and Short therefore adjusts Cost of Goods Sold. In practice, companies sometimes report Inventory Over and Short in the "Other revenues and gains" or "Other expenses and losses" section of the income statement, depending on its balance. Note that a company using the periodic inventory system does not report the account Inventory Over and Short. The reason: The periodic method does not have accounting records against which to compare the physical count. Instead, a company buries inventory overages and shortages in cost of goods sold.

BASIC ISSUES IN INVENTORY VALUATION

Goods sold (or used) during an accounting period seldom correspond exactly to the goods bought (or produced) during that period. As a result, inventories either increase or decrease during the period. Companies must then allocate the cost of all the goods available for sale (or use) between the goods that were sold or used and those that are still on hand. The **cost of goods available for sale or use** is the *sum* of (1) the cost of the goods on hand at the beginning of the period, and (2) the cost of the goods acquired or produced during the period. The **cost of goods sold** is the *difference* between (1) the cost of goods available for sale during the period and (2) the cost of goods on hand at the end of the period. Illustration 8-4 shows these calculations.

ILLUSTRATION 8-4
Computation of Cost of Goods Sold

Beginning inventory, Jan. 1	$100,000
Cost of goods acquired or produced during the year	800,000
Total cost of goods available for sale	900,000
Ending inventory, Dec. 31	200,000
Cost of goods sold during the year	$700,000

Valuing inventories can be complex. It requires determining the following.

1 **The physical goods to include in inventory** (who owns the goods?—goods in transit, consigned goods, special sales agreements).

2 **The costs to include in inventory** (product vs. period costs).

3 **The cost flow assumption to adopt** (specific identification, average cost, FIFO, LIFO, retail, etc.).

We explore these basic issues in the next three sections.

PHYSICAL GOODS INCLUDED IN INVENTORY

Technically, a company should record purchases when it obtains legal title to the goods. In practice, however, a company records acquisitions when it receives the goods. Why? Because it is difficult to determine the exact time of legal passage of title for every purchase. In addition, no material error likely results from such a practice if consistently applied. Illustration 8-5 indicates the general guidelines companies use in evaluating whether the seller or buyer reports an item as inventory. Exceptions to the general guidelines can arise for goods in transit and consigned goods.

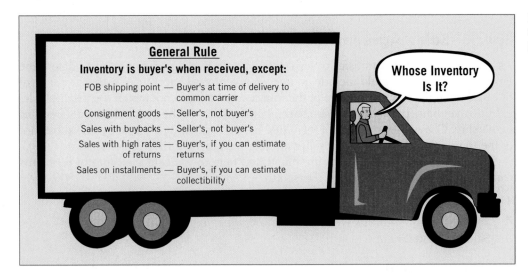

General Rule

Inventory is buyer's when received, except:

FOB shipping point — Buyer's at time of delivery to common carrier

Consignment goods — Seller's, not buyer's

Sales with buybacks — Seller's, not buyer's

Sales with high rates — Buyer's, if you can estimate of returns   returns

Sales on installments — Buyer's, if you can estimate collectibility

Whose Inventory Is It?

ILLUSTRATION 8-5
Guidelines for Determining Ownership

Goods in Transit

Sometimes purchased merchandise remains in transit—not yet received—at the end of a fiscal period. The accounting for these shipped goods depends on who owns them. For example, a company like **Walgreens** determines ownership by applying the "passage of title" rule. If a supplier ships goods to Walgreens **f.o.b. shipping point**, title passes to Walgreens when the supplier delivers the goods to the common carrier, who acts as an agent for Walgreens. (The abbreviation f.o.b. stands for free on board.) If the supplier ships the goods **f.o.b. destination**, title passes to Walgreens only when it receives the goods from the common carrier. "Shipping point" and "destination" are often designated by a particular location, for example, f.o.b. Denver.

When Walgreens obtains legal title to goods, it must record them as purchases in that fiscal period, assuming a periodic inventory system. Thus, goods shipped to Walgreens f.o.b. shipping point, but in transit at the end of the period, belong to Walgreens. It should show the purchase in its records, because legal title to these goods passed to Walgreens upon shipment of the goods. To disregard such purchases results in understating inventories and accounts payable in the balance sheet, and understating purchases and ending inventories in the income statement.

Consigned Goods

Companies market certain products through a **consignment** shipment. Under this arrangement, a company like Williams' Art Gallery (the consignor) ships various art merchandise to **Sotheby's Holdings** (the consignee), who acts as Williams' agent in selling the **consigned goods**. Sotheby's agrees to accept the goods without any liability, except to exercise due care and reasonable protection from loss or damage, until it sells the goods to a third party. When Sotheby's sells the goods, it remits the revenue, less a selling commission and expenses incurred in accomplishing the sale, to Williams.

Goods out on consignment remain the property of the consignor (Williams in the example above). Williams thus includes the goods in its inventory at purchase price or production cost. Occasionally, and only for a significant amount, the consignor shows the inventory out on consignment as a separate item. Sometimes a consignor reports the inventory on consignment in the notes to the financial statements. For example, **Eagle Clothes, Inc.** reported the following related to consigned goods: "Inventories consist of finished goods shipped on consignment to customers of the Company's subsidiary **April-Marcus, Inc.**"

The consignee makes no entry to the inventory account for goods received. Remember, these goods remain the property of the consignor until sold. In fact, the consignee should be extremely careful *not* to include any of the goods consigned as a part of inventory.

Special Sales Agreements

As we indicated earlier, transfer of legal title is the general guideline used to determine whether a company should include an item in inventory. Unfortunately, transfer of legal title and the underlying substance of the transaction often do not match. For example, legal title may have passed to the purchaser, but the seller of the goods retains the risks of ownership. Conversely, transfer of legal title may not occur, but the economic substance of the transaction is such that the seller no longer retains the risks of ownership.

Three special sales situations are illustrated here to indicate the types of problems companies encounter in practice. These are:

1 Sales with buyback agreement.

2 Sales with high rates of return.

3 Sales on installment.

Sales with Buyback Agreement

Sometimes an enterprise finances its inventory without reporting either the liability or the inventory on its balance sheet. This approach, often referred to as a **product financing arrangement**, usually involves a "sale" with either an implicit or explicit "buyback" agreement.

To illustrate, Hill Enterprises transfers ("sells") inventory to Chase, Inc. and simultaneously agrees to repurchase this merchandise at a specified price over a specified period of time. Chase then uses the inventory as collateral and borrows against it. Chase uses the loan proceeds to pay Hill, which repurchases the inventory in the future. Chase employs the proceeds from repayment to meet its loan obligation.

The essence of this transaction is that Hill Enterprises is financing its inventory—and retaining risk of ownership—even though it transferred to Chase technical legal title to the merchandise. By structuring a transaction in this manner, Hill avoids personal property taxes in certain states. Other advantages of this transaction for Hill are the removal of the current liability from its balance sheet and the ability to manipulate income. For Chase, the purchase of the goods may solve a LIFO liquidation problem (discussed later), or Chase may enter into a similar reciprocal agreement at a later date.

These arrangements are often described in practice as "**parking transactions.** " In this situation, Hill simply parks the inventory on Chase's balance sheet for a short period of time. When a repurchase agreement exists at a set price and this price covers all costs of the inventory plus related holding costs, Hill should report the inventory and related liability on its books.[5]

> **UNDERLYING CONCEPTS**
>
> Recognizing revenue at the time the inventory is "parked" violates the revenue recognition principle. This principle requires that the earning process be substantially completed. In this case, the economic benefits remain under the control of the seller.

Sales with High Rates of Return

In industries such as publishing, music, toys, and sporting goods, formal or informal agreements often exist that permit purchasers to return inventory for a full or partial refund.

To illustrate, Quality Publishing Company sells textbooks to Campus Bookstores with an agreement that Campus may return for full credit any books not sold. Historically, Campus Bookstores returned approximately 25 percent of the textbooks from Quality Publishing. How should Quality Publishing report its sales transactions?

One alternative is to record the sale at the full amount and establish an estimated sales returns and allowances account. A second possibility is to not record any sale until circumstances indicate the amount of inventory the buyer will return. The key question

---

[5]"Accounting for Product Financing Arrangements," *Statement of Financial Accounting Standards No. 49* (Stamford, Conn.: FASB, 1981).

is: Under what circumstances should Quality Publishing consider the inventory sold? The answer is that **when Quality Publishing can reasonably estimate the amount of returns**, it should consider the goods sold. Conversely, if returns are unpredictable, Quality Publishing should not consider the goods sold and it should not remove the goods from its inventory.[6]

Sales on Installment

"Goods sold on installment" describes any type of sale in which the sale agreement requires payment in periodic installments over an extended period of time. Because the risk of loss from uncollectibles is higher in installment-sale situations than in other sales transactions, the seller sometimes withholds legal title to the merchandise until the buyer has made all the payments.

The question is whether the seller should consider the inventory sold, even though legal title has not passed. The answer is that **the seller should exclude the goods from its inventory if it can reasonably estimate the percentage of bad debts**.

UNDERLYING CONCEPTS

For goods sold on installment, companies should recognize revenues because they have been substantially earned and are reasonably estimable. Collection is not the most critical event if bad debts can be reasonably estimated.

NO PARKING!

In one of the more elaborate accounting frauds, employees at **Kurzweil Applied Intelligence Inc.** booked millions of dollars in phony inventory sales during a two-year period that straddled two audits and an initial public stock offering. They dummied up phony shipping documents and logbooks to support bogus sales transactions. Then they shipped high-tech equipment, not to customers, but to a public warehouse for "temporary" storage, where some of it sat for 17 months. (Kurzweil still had ownership.)

To foil auditors' attempts to verify the existence of the inventory, Kurzweil employees moved the goods from warehouse to warehouse. To cover the fraudulently recorded sales transactions as auditors closed in, the employees brought back the still-hidden goods, under the pretense that the goods were returned by customers. When auditors uncovered the fraud, the bottom dropped out of Kurzweil's stock.

Source: Adapted from "Anatomy of a Fraud," *Business Week* (September 16, 1996), pp. 90–94.

WHAT DO THE NUMBERS MEAN?

Effect of Inventory Errors

Items incorrectly included or excluded in determining cost of goods sold through inventory misstatements will result in errors in the financial statements. Let's look at two cases, assuming a periodic inventory system.

Ending Inventory Misstated

What would happen if **IBM** correctly records its beginning inventory and purchases, but fails to include some items in ending inventory? In this situation, we would have the following effects on the financial statements at the end of the period.

OBJECTIVE 3
Identify the effects of inventory errors on the financial statements.

Balance Sheet		Income Statement	
Inventory	Understated	Cost of goods sold	Overstated
Retained earnings	Understated		
Working capital	Understated	Net income	Understated
(current assets less current liabilities)			
Current ratio	Understated		
(current assets divided by current liabilities)			

ILLUSTRATION 8-6
Financial Statement Effects of Misstated Ending Inventory

---

[6]"Revenue Recognition When Right of Return Exists," *Statement of Financial Accounting Standards No. 48* (Stamford, Conn.: FASB, 1981).

If ending inventory is understated, working capital and the current ratio are understated. If cost of goods sold is overstated, then net income is understated.

To illustrate the effect on net income over a two-year period (2006–2007), assume that Jay Weiseman Corp. understates its ending inventory by $10,000 in 2006; all other items are correctly stated. The effect of this error is to decrease net income in 2006 and to increase net income in 2007. The error is counterbalanced (offset) in 2007 because beginning inventory is understated and net income is overstated. As Illustration 8-7 shows, the income statement misstates the net income figures for both 2006 and 2007, although the *total* for the two years is correct.

ILLUSTRATION 8-7
Effect of Ending
Inventory Error on Two
Periods

	Incorrect Recording		Correct Recording	
JAY WEISEMAN CORP. (All figures assumed)				
	2006	2007	2006	2007
Revenues	$100,000	$100,000	$100,000	$100,000
Cost of goods sold				
Beginning inventory	25,000	→ 20,000	25,000	→ 30,000
Purchased or produced	45,000	60,000	45,000	60,000
Goods available for sale	70,000	80,000	70,000	90,000
Less: Ending inventory	20,000* ←	40,000	30,000 ←	40,000
Cost of goods sold	50,000	40,000	40,000	50,000
Gross profit	50,000	60,000	60,000	50,000
Administrative and selling expenses	40,000	40,000	40,000	40,000
Net income	$ 10,000	$ 20,000	$ 20,000	$ 10,000

Total income for two years = $30,000   Total income for two years = $30,000

*Ending inventory understated by $10,000 in 2006.

If Weiseman *overstates* ending inventory in 2006, the reverse effect occurs: Inventory, working capital, current ratio, and net income are overstated and cost of goods sold is understated. The effect of the error on net income will be counterbalanced in 2007, but the income statement misstates both years' net income figures.

Purchases and Inventory Misstated

Suppose that Bishop Company does not record as a purchase certain goods that it owns and does not count them in ending inventory. The effect on the financial statements (assuming this is a purchase on account) is as follows.

ILLUSTRATION 8-8
Financial Statement
Effects of Misstated
Purchases and Inventory

Balance Sheet		Income Statement	
Inventory	Understated	Purchases	Understated
Retained earnings	No effect	Cost of goods sold	No effect
Accounts payable	Understated	Net income	No effect
Working capital	No effect	Inventory (ending)	Understated
Current ratio	Overstated		

Omission of goods from purchases and inventory results in an understatement of inventory and accounts payable in the balance sheet; it also results in an understatement of purchases and ending inventory in the income statement. However, the omission of such goods does not affect net income for the period. Why not? Because Bishop understates both purchases and ending inventory by the same amount—the error is thereby offset in cost of goods sold. Total working capital is unchanged, but the current ratio is overstated because of the omission of equal amounts from inventory and accounts payable.

To illustrate the effect on the current ratio, assume that Bishop *understated* accounts payable and ending inventory by $40,000. Illustration 8-9 shows the understated and correct data.

Purchases and Ending Inventory Understated		Purchases and Ending Inventory Correct	
Current assets	$120,000	Current assets	$160,000
Current liabilities	$ 40,000	Current liabilities	$ 80,000
Current ratio	3 to 1	Current ratio	2 to 1

ILLUSTRATION 8-9
Effects of Purchases and Ending Inventory Errors

The understated data indicate a current ratio of 3 to 1, whereas the correct ratio is 2 to 1. Thus, understatement of accounts payable and ending inventory can lead to a "window dressing" of the current ratio. That is, Bishop can make the current ratio appear better than it is.

If Bishop *overstates* both purchases (on account) and ending inventory, then the effects on the balance sheet are exactly the reverse: The financial statements overstate inventory and accounts payable, and understate the current ratio. The overstatement does not affect cost of goods sold and net income because the errors offset one another. Similarly, working capital is not affected.

We cannot overemphasize the importance of proper inventory measurement in presenting accurate financial statements. For example, **Leslie Fay**, a women's apparel maker, had accounting irregularities that wiped out one year's net income and caused a restatement of the prior year's earnings. One reason: It inflated inventory and deflated cost of goods sold. **Anixter Bros. Inc.** had to restate its income by $1.7 million because an accountant in the antenna manufacturing division overstated the ending inventory, thereby reducing its cost of sales. Similarly, **AM International** allegedly recorded as sold products that were only being rented. As a result, inaccurate inventory and sales figures inappropriately added $7.9 million to pretax income.

COSTS INCLUDED IN INVENTORY

One of the most important problems in dealing with inventories concerns the dollar amount at which to carry the inventory in the accounts. **Companies generally account for the acquisition of inventories, like other assets, on a cost basis.**

OBJECTIVE 4
Understand the items to include as inventory cost.

Product Costs

Product costs are those costs that "attach" to the inventory. As a result, a company records product costs in the inventory account. These costs are directly connected with bringing the goods to the buyer's place of business and converting such goods to a salable condition. Such charges include freight charges on goods purchased, other direct costs of acquisition, and labor and other production costs incurred in processing the goods up to the time of sale.

It seems proper also to allocate to inventories a share of any buying costs or expenses of a purchasing department, storage costs, and other costs incurred in storing or handling the goods before their sale. However, because of the practical difficulties involved in allocating such costs and expenses, companies usually exclude these items in valuing inventories.

A manufacturing company's costs include direct materials, direct labor, and manufacturing overhead costs. Manufacturing overhead costs include indirect materials, indirect labor, and various costs, such as depreciation, taxes, insurance, and heat and electricity.

IT WAS THE WILD WEST

The practice of promotional payments, also known as vendor allowances, is widespread in the retail world. Eager to meet sales targets or promote their products through shelf placements and in store advertisements, vendors have been happy to grease the palms of retailers with rebates, allowances, and price breaks.

The question is, "How should retailers account for these payments?" Until recently some retailers recorded the payments as a reduction of selling expense. Unfortunately, in some of these cases the retailers had not actually sold the goods. Others accounted for them as a reduction of cost of goods sold.

Recently the SEC sued three executives of **Kmart Holding** and some Kmart vendors for their role in a $24 million accounting fraud that booked vendor allowances early. The scheme apparently allowed some Kmart managers to meet internal profit-margin targets. Similarly, **Royal Ahold** (a large Dutch supermarket operator) discovered that its U.S. Foodservice unit had improperly accounted for vendor payments, resulting in overstated earnings of at least $500 million. In addition, it found inflated profits at two of its other subsidiaries, also caused by improper accounting for vendor payments.

One analyst noted that it was like "the Wild West out there" because the lack of rules about when to recognize these payments and how to classify them allowed a certain amount of lawlessness. As a result, the FASB recently ruled that unless certain conditions are met, these payments must reduce cost of goods sold on the income statement. The accounting now appears right, but it took some frauds to close the accounting gap in this area.

Source: C. Schneider, "Retailers and Vendor Allowances," *CFO.com* (August 13, 2003).

Period Costs

Period costs are those costs that are indirectly related to the acquisition or production of goods. Period costs such as selling expenses and, under ordinary circumstances, general and administrative expenses are therefore not included as part as part of inventory cost.

Yet, conceptually, these expenses are as much a cost of the product as the initial purchase price and related freight charges attached to the product. Why then do companies exclude these costs from inventoriable items? Because companies generally consider selling expenses as more directly related to the cost of goods sold than to the unsold inventory. In addition, period costs, especially administrative expenses, are so unrelated or indirectly related to the immediate production process that any allocation is purely arbitrary.[7]

Interest is another period cost. Companies usually expense **interest costs** associated with getting inventories ready for sale. Supporters of this approach argue that interest costs are really a **cost of financing**. Others contend that interest costs incurred to finance activities associated with readying inventories for sale are as much a **cost**

---

[7]Companies should not record abnormal freight, handling costs, and amounts of wasted materials (spoilage) as inventory costs. If the costs associated with the actual level of spoilage or product defects are greater than the costs associated with normal spoilage or defects, the company should charge the excess as an expense in the current period. "Inventory Costs: An Amendment of ARB No. 43, Chapter 4," *Statement of Financial Accounting Standards No. 151* (Norwalk, Conn.: FASB 2004.)

of the asset as materials, labor, and overhead. Therefore, they reason, companies should capitalize interest costs.

The FASB ruled that companies should capitalize interest costs related to assets constructed for internal use or assets produced as discrete projects (such as ships or real estate projects) for sale or lease.[8] The FASB emphasized that these discrete projects should take considerable time, entail substantial expenditures, and be likely to involve significant amounts of interest cost. A company should not capitalize interest costs for inventories that it routinely manufactures or otherwise produces in large quantities on a repetitive basis. In this case, the informational benefit does not justify the cost.

Treatment of Purchase Discounts

The use of a **Purchase Discounts** account in a periodic inventory system indicates that the company is reporting its purchases and accounts payable at the gross amount. If a company uses this **gross method**, it reports purchase discounts as a deduction from purchases on the income statement.

Another approach is to record the purchases and accounts payable at an amount **net of the cash discounts**. In this approach, the company records failure to take a purchase discount within the discount period in a Purchase Discounts Lost account. If a company uses this **net method**, it considers purchase discounts lost as a financial expense and reports it in the "Other expenses and losses" section of the income statement. This treatment is considered better for two reasons: (1) It provides a correct reporting of the cost of the asset and related liability. (2) It can measure management inefficiency by holding management responsible for discounts not taken.

To illustrate the difference between the gross and net methods, assume the following transactions.

Gross Method			Net Method		
Purchase cost $10,000, terms 2/10, net 30:					
Purchases	10,000		Purchases	9,800	
Accounts Payable		10,000	Accounts Payable		9,800
Invoices of $4,000 are paid within discount period:					
Accounts Payable	4,000		Accounts Payable	3,920	
Purchase Discounts		80	Cash		3,920
Cash		3,920			
Invoices of $6,000 are paid after discount period:					
Accounts Payable	6,000		Accounts Payable	5,880	
Cash		6,000	Purchase Discounts Lost	120	
			Cash		6,000

ILLUSTRATION 8-10
Entries under Gross and Net Methods

UNDERLYING CONCEPTS

Not using the net method because of resultant difficulties is an example of the application of the cost/benefit constraint.

Many believe that the somewhat more complicated net method is not justified by the resulting benefits. This could account for the widespread use of the less logical but simpler gross method. In addition, some contend that management is reluctant to report in the financial statements the amount of purchase discounts lost.

---

[8]"Capitalization of Interest Cost," *Statement of Financial Accounting Standards No. 34* (Stamford, Conn.: FASB, 1979). The reporting rules related to interest cost capitalization have their greatest impact in accounting for long-term assets. We therefore discuss them in Chapter 10.

**WHAT DO THE
NUMBERS MEAN?**

Does it really matter *where* a company reports certain costs in its income statement, as long as it includes them all as expenses in computing income?

For e-tailers, such as **Amazon.com** or **Drugstore.com**, *where* they report certain selling costs does appear to be important. Contrary to well-established retailer practices, these companies insist on reporting some selling costs—fulfillment costs related to inventory shipping and warehousing—as part of administrative expenses, instead of as cost of goods sold. This practice is allowable within GAAP, *if* applied consistently and adequately disclosed. Although the practice doesn't affect the bottom line, it does make the e-tailers' gross margins look better. For example, at one time Amazon.com reported $265 million of these costs in one quarter. Some experts thought Amazon.com should include those charges in costs of goods sold, which would substantially lower its gross profit, as shown below.

(in millions)

	E-tailer Reporting	Traditional Reporting
Sales	$2,795	$2,795
Cost of goods sold	2,132	2,397
Gross profit	$ 663	$ 398
Gross margin %	24%	14%

Similarly, if **Drugstore.com** and **eToys.com** made similar adjustments, their gross margins would go from positive to negative.

Thus, if you want to be able to compare the operating results of e-tailers to other traditional retailers, it might be a good idea to have a good accounting map in order to navigate their income statements and how they report certain selling costs.

Source: Adapted from P. Elstrom, "The End of Fuzzy Math?" *Business Week*, e.Biz—Net Worth (December 11, 2000). See also *EITF No. 00–10*, "Accounting for Shipping and Handling Fees and Costs." Under this standard, companies must disclose the accounting policy for classifying these selling costs in income.

WHICH COST FLOW ASSUMPTION TO ADOPT?

OBJECTIVE 5
Describe and compare the cost flow assumptions used to account for inventories.

During any given fiscal period, companies typically purchase merchandise at several different prices. If a company prices inventories at cost and it made numerous purchases at different unit costs, which cost price should it use? Conceptually, a specific identification of the given items sold and unsold seems optimal. But this measure often proves both expensive and impossible to achieve. Consequently, companies use one of several systematic inventory **cost flow assumptions**.

Indeed, the actual physical flow of goods and the cost flow assumption often greatly differ. **There is no requirement that the cost flow assumption adopted be consistent with the physical movement of goods.** A company's major objective in selecting a method should be to choose the one that, under the circumstances, most clearly reflects periodic income.[9]

To illustrate, assume that Call-Mart Inc. had the following transactions in its first month of operations.

Date	Purchases	Sold or Issued	Balance
March 2	2,000 @ $4.00		2,000 units
March 15	6,000 @ $4.40		8,000 units
March 19		4,000 units	4,000 units
March 30	2,000 @ $4.75		6,000 units

[9]"Restatement and Revision of Accounting Research Bulletins," *Accounting Research Bulletin No. 43* (New York: AICPA, 1953), Ch. 4, Statement 4.

From this information, Call-Mart computes the ending inventory of 6,000 units and the cost of goods available for sale (beginning inventory + purchases) of $43,900 [(2,000 @ $4.00) + (6,000 @ $4.40) + (2,000 @ $4.75)]. The question is, which price or prices should it assign to the 6,000 units of ending inventory? The answer depends on which cost flow assumption it uses.

Specific Identification

Specific identification calls for identifying each item sold and each item in inventory. A company includes in cost of goods sold the costs of the specific items sold. It includes in inventory the costs of the specific items on hand. This method may be used only in instances where it is practical to separate physically the different purchases made. As a result, most companies only use this method when handling a relatively small number of costly, easily distinguishable items. In the retail trade this includes some types of jewelry, fur coats, automobiles, and some furniture. In manufacturing it includes special orders and many products manufactured under a job cost system.

To illustrate, assume that Call-Mart Inc.'s 6,000 units of inventory consists of 1,000 units from the March 2 purchase, 3,000 from the March 15 purchase, and 2,000 from the March 30 purchase. Illustration 8-11 shows how Call-Mart computes the ending inventory and cost of goods sold.

Date	No. of Units	Unit Cost	Total Cost
March 2	1,000	$4.00	$ 4,000
March 15	3,000	4.40	13,200
March 30	2,000	4.75	9,500
Ending inventory	6,000		$26,700

Cost of goods available for sale (computed in previous section)	$43,900
Deduct: Ending inventory	26,700
Cost of goods sold	$17,200

ILLUSTRATION 8-11
Specific Identification Method

This method appears ideal. Specific identification matches actual costs against actual revenue. Thus, a company reports ending inventory at actual cost. In other words, **under specific identification the cost flow matches the physical flow of the goods**. On closer observation, however, this method has certain deficiencies.

Some argue that specific identification allows a company to manipulate net income. For example, assume that a wholesaler purchases identical plywood early in the year at three different prices. When it sells the plywood, the wholesaler can select either the lowest or the highest price to charge to expense. It simply selects the plywood from a specific lot for delivery to the customer. A business manager, therefore, can manipulate net income by delivering to the customer the higher- or lower-priced item, depending on whether the company seeks lower or higher reported earnings for the period.

Another problem relates to the arbitrary allocation of costs that sometimes occurs with specific inventory items. For example, a company often faces difficulty in relating shipping charges, storage costs, and discounts directly to a given inventory item. This results in allocating these costs somewhat arbitrarily, leading to a "breakdown" in the precision of the specific identification method.[10]

---

[10]The motion picture industry provides a good illustration of the cost allocation problem. Often actors receive a percentage of net income for a given movie or television program. Some actors, however, have alleged that their programs have been extremely profitable to the motion picture studios but they have received little in the way of profit sharing. Actors contend that the studios allocate additional costs to successful projects to avoid sharing profits.

Average Cost

As the name implies, the **average cost method** prices items in the inventory on the basis of the average cost of all similar goods available during the period. To illustrate use of the periodic inventory method (amount of inventory computed at the end of the period), Call-Mart computes the ending inventory and cost of goods sold using a **weighted-average method** as follows.

ILLUSTRATION 8-12
Weighted-Average Method—Periodic Inventory

Date of Invoice	No. Units	Unit Cost	Total Cost
March 2	2,000	$4.00	$ 8,000
March 15	6,000	4.40	26,400
March 30	2,000	4.75	9,500
Total goods available	10,000		$43,900

Weighted-average cost per unit $\frac{\$43,900}{10,000} = \$4.39$

Inventory in units   6,000 units
Ending inventory   6,000 × $4.39 = $26,340

Cost of goods available for sale	$43,900
Deduct: Ending inventory	26,340
Cost of goods sold	$17,560

In computing the average cost per unit, Call-Mart includes the beginning inventory, if any, both in the total units available and in the total cost of goods available.

Companies use the **moving-average method** with perpetual inventory records. Illustration 8-13 shows the application of the average cost method for perpetual records.

ILLUSTRATION 8-13
Moving-Average Method—Perpetual Inventory

Date	Purchased		Sold or Issued		Balance	
March 2	(2,000 @ $4.00)	$ 8,000			(2,000 @ $4.00)	$ 8,000
March 15	(6,000 @ 4.40)	26,400			(8,000 @ 4.30)	34,400
March 19			(4,000 @ $4.30)	$17,200	(4,000 @ 4.30)	17,200
March 30	(2,000 @ 4.75)	9,500			(6,000 @ 4.45)	26,700

In this method, Call-Mart computes a **new average unit cost** each time it makes a purchase. For example, on March 15, after purchasing 6,000 units for $26,400, Call-Mart has 8,000 units costing $34,400 ($8,000 plus $26,400) on hand. The average unit cost is $34,400 divided by 8,000, or $4.30. Call-Mart uses this unit cost in costing withdrawals until it makes another purchase. At that point, Call-Mart computes a new average unit cost. Accordingly, the company shows the cost of the 4,000 units withdrawn on March 19 at $4.30, for a total cost of goods sold of $17,200. On March 30, following the purchase of 2,000 units for $9,500, Call-Mart determines a new unit cost of $4.45, for an ending inventory of $26,700.

Companies often use average cost methods for practical rather than conceptual reasons. These methods are simple to apply and objective. They are not as subject to income manipulation as some of the other inventory pricing methods. In addition, proponents of the average cost methods reason that measuring a specific physical flow of inventory is often impossible. Therefore, it is better to cost items on an average-price basis. This argument is particularly persuasive when dealing with similar inventory items.

First-In, First-Out (FIFO)

The **FIFO (first-in, first-out) method** assumes that a company uses goods in the order in which it purchases them. In other words, the FIFO method assumes that **the first goods purchased are the first used** (in a manufacturing concern) **or the first sold** (in a merchandising concern). The inventory remaining must therefore represent the most recent purchases.

To illustrate, assume that Call-Mart uses the periodic inventory system. It determines its cost of the ending inventory by taking the cost of the most recent purchase and working back until it accounts for all units in the inventory. Call-Mart determines its ending inventory and cost of goods sold as shown in Illustration 8-14.

Date	No. Units	Unit Cost	Total Cost
March 30	2,000	$4.75	$ 9,500
March 15	4,000	4.40	17,600
Ending inventory	6,000		$27,100

Cost of goods available for sale		$43,900
Deduct: Ending inventory		27,100
Cost of goods sold		$16,800

ILLUSTRATION 8-14
FIFO Method—Periodic Inventory

If Call-Mart instead uses a perpetual inventory system in quantities and dollars, it attaches a cost figure to each withdrawal. Then the cost of the 4,000 units removed on March 19 consists of the cost of the items purchased on March 2 and March 15. Illustration 8-15 shows the inventory on a FIFO basis perpetual system for Call-Mart.

Date	Purchased		Sold or Issued	Balance	
March 2	(2,000 @ $4.00)	$ 8,000		2,000 @ $4.00	$ 8,000
March 15	(6,000 @ 4.40)	26,400		2,000 @ 4.00 } 6,000 @ 4.40	34,400
March 19			2,000 @ $4.00 } 2,000 @ 4.40 ($16,800)	4,000 @ 4.40	17,600
March 30	(2,000 @ 4.75)	9,500		4,000 @ 4.40 } 2,000 @ 4.75	27,100

ILLUSTRATION 8-15
FIFO Method—Perpetual Inventory

Here, the ending inventory is $27,100, and the cost of goods sold is $16,800 [(2,000 @ 4.00) + (2,000 @ $4.40)].

Notice that in these two FIFO examples, the cost of goods sold ($16,800) and ending inventory ($27,100) are the same. **In all cases where FIFO is used, the inventory and cost of goods sold would be the same at the end of the month whether a perpetual or periodic system is used.** Why? Because the same costs will always be first in and, therefore, first out. This is true whether a company computes cost of goods sold as it sells goods throughout the accounting period (the perpetual system) or as a residual at the end of the accounting period (the periodic system).

One objective of FIFO is to approximate the physical flow of goods. When the physical flow of goods is actually first-in, first-out, the FIFO method closely approximates specific identification. At the same time, it prevents manipulation of income. With FIFO, a company cannot pick a certain cost item to charge to expense.

Another advantage of the FIFO method is that the ending inventory is close to current cost. Because the first goods in are the first goods out, the ending inventory amount consists of the most recent purchases. This is particularly true with rapid inventory turnover. This approach generally approximates replacement cost on the balance sheet when price changes have not occurred since the most recent purchases.

However, the FIFO method fails to match current costs against current revenues on the income statement. A company charges the oldest costs against the more current revenue, possibly distorting gross profit and net income.

Last-In, First-Out (LIFO)

The **LIFO (last-in, first-out) method** matches the cost of the last goods purchased against revenue. If Call-Mart Inc. uses a periodic inventory system, it assumes that **the cost of the total quantity sold or issued during the month comes from the most recent purchases.** Call Mart prices the ending inventory by using the total units as a basis of computation and disregards the exact dates of sales or issuances. For example, assume that the cost of the 4,000 units withdrawn absorbed the 2,000 units purchased on March 30 and 2,000 of the 6,000 units purchased on March 15. Illustration 8-16 shows how Call-Mart computes the inventory and related cost of goods sold, using the periodic inventory method.

ILLUSTRATION 8-16
LIFO Method—Periodic
Inventory

Date of Invoice	No. Units	Unit Cost	Total Cost
March 2	2,000	$4.00	$ 8,000
March 15	4,000	4.40	17,600
Ending inventory	6,000		$25,600

Goods available for sale	$43,900
Deduct: Ending inventory	25,600
Cost of goods sold	$18,300

If Call-Mart keeps a perpetual inventory record in quantities and dollars, use of the LIFO method results in **different ending inventory and cost of goods sold amounts than the amounts calculated under the periodic method**. Illustration 8-17 shows these differences under the perpetual method.

ILLUSTRATION 8-17
LIFO Method—Perpetual
Inventory

Date	Purchased		Sold or Issued		Balance	
March 2	(2,000 @ $4.00)	$ 8,000			2,000 @ $4.00	$ 8,000
March 15	(6,000 @ 4.40)	26,400			2,000 @ 4.00	34,400
					6,000 @ 4.40	
March 19			(4,000 @ $4.40)		2,000 @ 4.00	16,800
			$17,600		2,000 @ 4.40	
March 30	(2,000 @ 4.75)	9,500			2,000 @ 4.00	
					2,000 @ 4.40	26,300
					2,000 @ 4.75	

*Tutorial on Inventory
Methods*

The month-end periodic inventory computation presented in Illustration 8-16 (inventory $25,600 and cost of goods sold $18,300) shows a different amount from the perpetual inventory computation (inventory $26,300 and cost of goods sold $17,600). The periodic system matches the total withdrawals for the month with the total purchases for the month in applying the last-in, first-out method. In contrast, the perpetual system matches each withdrawal with the immediately preceding purchases. In effect, the periodic computation assumed that Call Mart included the cost of the goods that it purchased on March 30 in the sale or issue on March 19.

SPECIAL ISSUES RELATED TO LIFO

LIFO Reserve

OBJECTIVE 6
Explain the significance and use of a LIFO reserve.

Many companies use LIFO for tax and external reporting purposes. However, they maintain a FIFO, average cost, or standard cost system for internal reporting purposes. There are several reasons to do so: (1) Companies often base their pricing decisions on a FIFO, average, or standard cost assumption, rather than on a LIFO basis. (2) Record-keeping on some other basis is easier because the LIFO assumption usually does not approximate the physical flow of the product. (3) Profit-sharing and other bonus arrangements often depend on a non-LIFO inventory assumption. Finally, (4) the use of a pure LIFO system is troublesome for interim periods, which require estimates of year-end quantities and prices.

The difference between the inventory method used for internal reporting purposes and LIFO is the Allowance to Reduce Inventory to LIFO or the **LIFO reserve**. The change in the allowance balance from one period to the next is the **LIFO effect**. The LIFO effect is the adjustment that companies must make to the accounting records in a given year.

To illustrate, assume that Acme Boot Company uses the FIFO method for internal reporting purposes and LIFO for external reporting purposes. At January 1, 2007, the Allowance to Reduce Inventory to LIFO balance is $20,000. At December 31, 2007, the balance should be $50,000. As a result, Acme Boot realizes a LIFO effect of $30,000 and makes the following entry at year-end.

| Cost of Goods Sold | 30,000 | |
| Allowance to Reduce Inventory to LIFO | | 30,000 |

Acme Boot deducts the Allowance to Reduce Inventory to LIFO from inventory to ensure that it states the inventory on a LIFO basis at year-end.

Companies should disclose either the LIFO reserve or the replacement cost of the inventory, as shown in Illustration 8-18.[11]

American Maize-Products Company

Inventories (Note 3) $80,320,000

Note 3: Inventories. At December 31, $31,516,000 of inventories were valued using the LIFO method. This amount is less than the corresponding replacement value by $3,765,000.

ILLUSTRATION 8-18
Note Disclosures of
LIFO Reserve

Brown Shoe Company, Inc.
(in thousands)

	Current Year	Previous Year
Inventories, (Note 1)	$365,989	$362,274

Note 1 (partial): Inventories. Inventories are valued at the lower of cost or market determined principally by the last-in, first-out (LIFO) method. If the first-in, first-out (FIFO) cost method had been used, inventories would have been $11,709 higher in the current year and $13,424 higher in the previous year.

Additional LIFO Reserve Disclosures

LIFO Liquidation

Up to this point, we have emphasized a **specific-goods approach** to costing LIFO inventories (also called **traditional LIFO** or **unit LIFO**). This approach is often unrealistic for two reasons:

OBJECTIVE 7
Understand the effect of LIFO liquidations.

1 When a company has many different inventory items, the accounting cost of tracking each inventory item is expensive.

2 Erosion of the LIFO inventory can easily occur. Referred to as **LIFO liquidation**, this often distorts net income and leads to substantial tax payments.

---

[11] The AICPA Task Force on LIFO Inventory Problems, *Issues Paper* (New York: AICPA, November 30, 1984), pars. 2–24. The SEC has endorsed this issues paper, and therefore the paper has authoritative status for GAAP purposes.

**WHAT DO THE
NUMBERS MEAN?**

Investors commonly use the current ratio to evaluate a company's liquidity. They compute the current ratio as current assets divided by current liabilities. A higher current ratio indicates that a company is better able to meet its current obligations when they come due. However, it is not meaningful to compare the current ratio for a company using LIFO to one for a company using FIFO. It would be like comparing apples to oranges, since the two companies measure inventory (and cost of goods sold) differently.

To make the current ratio comparable on an apples-to-apples basis, analysts use the LIFO reserve. The following adjustments should do the trick:

> Inventory Adjustment: LIFO inventory + LIFO reserve = FIFO inventory

(For cost of goods sold, add the *change* in the LIFO reserve to LIFO cost of goods sold to yield the comparable FIFO amount.)

For **Brown Shoe, Inc.** (see Illustration 8-18), with current assets of $487.8 million and current liabilities of $217.8 million, the current ratio using LIFO is: $487.8 ÷ $217.8 = 2.2. After adjusting for the LIFO effect, Brown's current ratio under FIFO would be: ($487.8 + $11.7) ÷ $217.8 = 2.3.

Thus, without the LIFO adjustment, the Brown Shoe current ratio is understated.

To understand the LIFO liquidation problem, assume that Basler Co. has 30,000 pounds of steel in its inventory on December 31, 2007, with cost determined on a specific-goods LIFO approach.

	Ending Inventory (2007)		
	Pounds	Unit Cost	LIFO Cost
2004	8,000	$ 4	$ 32,000
2005	10,000	6	60,000
2006	7,000	9	63,000
2007	5,000	10	50,000
	30,000		$205,000

As indicated, the ending 2007 inventory for Basler comprises costs from past periods. These costs are called **layers** (increases from period to period). The first layer is identified as the base layer. Illustration 8-19 shows the layers for Basler.

ILLUSTRATION 8-19
Layers of LIFO Inventory

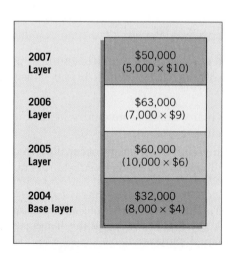

2007 Layer	$50,000 (5,000 × $10)
2006 Layer	$63,000 (7,000 × $9)
2005 Layer	$60,000 (10,000 × $6)
2004 Base layer	$32,000 (8,000 × $4)

Note the increased price of steel over the 4-year period. In 2008, due to metal shortages, Basler had to liquidate much of its inventory (a LIFO liquidation). At the end of 2008, only 6,000 pounds of steel remained in inventory. Because the company uses LIFO, Basler liquidates the most recent layer, 2007, first, followed by the 2006 layer, and so on. The result: Basler matches costs from preceding periods against sales revenues reported in current dollars. As Illustration 8-20 shows, this leads to a distortion in net income and increased taxable income in the current period. Unfortunately **LIFO liquidations can occur frequently when using a specific-goods LIFO approach.**

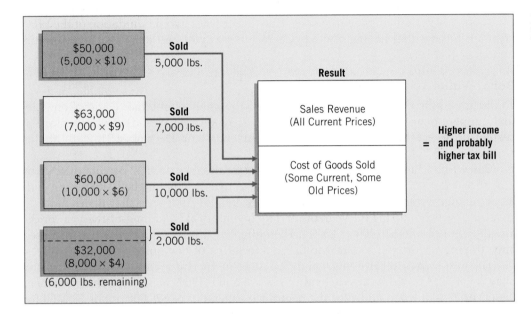

ILLUSTRATION 8-20
LIFO Liquidation

To alleviate the LIFO liquidation problems and to simplify the accounting, companies can combine goods into pools. A **pool** groups items of a similar nature. Thus, instead of only identical units, a company combines, and counts as a group, a number of similar units or products. This method, the **specific-goods pooled LIFO approach,** usually results in fewer LIFO liquidations. Why? Because the reduction of one quantity in the pool may be offset by an increase in another.

The specific-goods pooled LIFO approach eliminates some of the disadvantages of the specific-goods (traditional) accounting for LIFO inventories. This pooled approach, using quantities as its measurement basis, however, creates other problems.

First, most companies continually change the mix of their products, materials, and production methods. As a result, in employing a pooled approach using quantities, companies must continually redefine the pools. This can be time consuming and costly. Second, even when practical, the approach often results in an erosion ("LIFO liquidation") of the layers, thereby losing much of the LIFO costing benefit. An erosion of the layers results due to replacement of a specific good or material in the pool with another good or material. The new item may not be similar enough to be treated as part of the old pool. Therefore a company may need to recognize any inflationary profit deferred on the old goods as it replaces them.

Dollar-Value LIFO

The dollar-value LIFO method overcomes the problems of redefining pools and eroding layers. **The dollar-value LIFO method determines and measures any increases and decreases in a pool in terms of total dollar value, not the physical quantity of the goods in the inventory pool.**

Such an approach has two important advantages over the specific-goods pooled approach. First, companies may include a broader range of goods in a dollar-value

OBJECTIVE 8
Explain the dollar-value LIFO method.

Tutorial on Dollar-Value LIFO

LIFO pool. Second, a dollar-value LIFO pool permits replacement of goods that are similar items, similar in use, or interchangeable. (In contrast, a specific-goods LIFO pool only allows replacement of items that are substantially identical.)

Thus, dollar-value LIFO techniques help protect LIFO layers from erosion. Because of this advantage, companies frequently use the dollar-value LIFO method in practice.[12] Companies use the more traditional LIFO approaches only when dealing with few goods and expecting little change in product mix.

Under the dollar-value LIFO method, one pool may contain the entire inventory. However, companies generally use several pools.[13] In general, the more goods included in a pool, the more likely that increases in the quantities of some goods will offset decreases in other goods in the same pool. Thus, companies avoid liquidation of the LIFO layers. It follows that having fewer pools means less cost and less chance of a reduction of a LIFO layer.[14]

Dollar-Value LIFO Example

To illustrate how the dollar-value LIFO method works, assume that Enrico Company first adopts dollar-value LIFO on December 31, 2006 (base period). The inventory at current prices on that date was $20,000. The inventory on December 31, 2007, at current prices is $26,400.

Can we conclude that Enrico's inventory quantities increased 32 percent during the year ($26,400 ÷ $20,000 = 132%)? First, we need to ask: What is the value of the ending inventory in terms of beginning-of-the-year prices? Assuming that prices have increased 20 percent during the year, the ending inventory at beginning-of-the-year prices amounts to $22,000 ($26,400 ÷ 120%). Therefore, the inventory quantity has increased only 10 percent, or from $20,000 to $22,000 in terms of beginning-of-the-year prices.

The next step is to price this real-dollar quantity increase. This real-dollar quantity increase of $2,000 valued at year-end prices is $2,400 (120% × $2,000). This increment (layer) of $2,400, when added to the beginning inventory of $20,000, totals $22,400 for the December 31, 2007, inventory, as shown below.

First layer—(beginning inventory) in terms of 100	$20,000
Second layer—(2007 increase) in terms of 120	2,400
Dollar-value LIFO inventory, December 31, 2007	$22,400

Note that a layer forms only when the ending inventory at base-year prices exceeds the beginning inventory at base-year prices. And only when a new layer forms must Enrico compute a new index.

---

[12]A study by James M. Reeve and Keith G. Stanga disclosed that the vast majority of respondent companies applying LIFO use the dollar-value method or the dollar-value retail method to apply LIFO. Only a small minority of companies use the specific-goods (unit LIFO) approach or the specific-goods pooling approach. See J.M. Reeve and K.G. Stanga, "The LIFO Pooling Decision," *Accounting Horizons* (June 1987), p. 27.

[13]The Reeve and Stanga study (ibid.) reports that most companies have only a few pools—the median is six for retailers and three for nonretailers. But the distributions are highly skewed; some companies have 100 or more pools. Retailers that use LIFO have significantly more pools than nonretailers. About a third of the nonretailers (mostly manufacturers) use a single pool for their entire LIFO inventory.

[14]A later study shows that when quantities are increasing, multiple pools over a period of time may produce (under rather general conditions) significantly higher cost of goods sold deductions than a single-pool approach. When a stock-out occurs, a single-pool approach may lessen the layer liquidation for that year, but it may not erase the cumulative cost of goods sold advantage accruing to the use of multiple pools built up over the preceding years. See William R. Coon and Randall B. Hayes, "The Dollar Value LIFO Pooling Decision: The Conventional Wisdom Is Too General," *Accounting Horizons* (December 1989), pp. 57–70.

Comprehensive Dollar-Value LIFO Example

To illustrate the use of the dollar-value LIFO method in a more complex situation, assume that Bismark Company develops the following information.

December 31	Inventory at End-of-Year Prices	÷ Price Index (percentage)	= End-of-Year Inventory at Base-Year Prices
(Base year) 2004	$200,000	100	$200,000
2005	299,000	115	260,000
2006	300,000	120	250,000
2007	351,000	130	270,000

At December 31, 2004, Bismark computes the ending inventory under dollar-value LIFO as $200,000, as Illustration 8-21 shows.

Ending Inventory at Base-Year Prices	Layer at Base-Year Prices	Price Index (percentage)	Ending Inventory at LIFO Cost
$200,000	$200,000 ×	100 =	$200,000

ILLUSTRATION 8-21
Computation of 2004
Inventory at LIFO Cost

At December 31, 2005, a comparison of the ending inventory at base-year prices ($260,000) with the beginning inventory at base-year prices ($200,000) indicates that the quantity of goods (in base-year prices) increased $60,000 ($260,000 − $200,000). Bismark prices this increment (layer) at the 2005 index of 115 percent to arrive at a new layer of $69,000. Ending inventory for 2005 is $269,000, composed of the beginning inventory of $200,000 and the new layer of $69,000. Illustration 8-22 shows the computations.

Ending Inventory at Base-Year Prices	Layers at Base-Year Prices	Price Index (percentage)	Ending Inventory at LIFO Cost
$260,000	2004 $200,000 ×	100 =	$200,000
	2005 60,000 ×	115 =	69,000
	$260,000		$269,000

ILLUSTRATION 8-22
Computation of 2005
Inventory at LIFO Cost

At December 31, 2006, a comparison of the ending inventory at base-year prices ($250,000) with the beginning inventory at base-year prices ($260,000) indicates a decrease in the quantity of goods of $10,000 ($250,000 − $260,000). If the ending inventory at base-year prices is less than the beginning inventory at base-year prices, **a company must subtract the decrease from the most recently added layer. When a decrease occurs, the company "peels off" previous layers at the prices in existence when it added the layers.** In Bismark's situation, this means that it removes $10,000 in base-year prices from the 2005 layer of $60,000 at base-year prices. It values the balance of $50,000 ($60,000 − $10,000) at base-year prices at the 2005 price index of 115 percent. As a result, it now values this 2005 layer at $57,500 ($50,000 × 115%). Therefore, Bismark computes the ending inventory at $257,500, consisting of the beginning inventory of $200,000 and the second layer of $57,500. Illustration 8-23 (on page 390) shows the computations for 2006.

ILLUSTRATION 8-23
Computation of 2006
Inventory at LIFO Cost

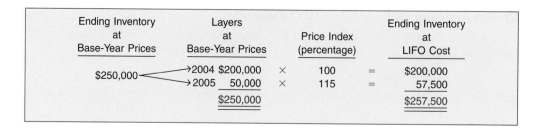

Note that if Bismark eliminates a layer or base (or portion thereof), it cannot rebuild it in future periods. That is, the layer is gone forever.

At December 31, 2007, a comparison of the ending inventory at base-year prices ($270,000) with the beginning inventory at base-year prices ($250,000) indicates an increase in the quantity of goods (in base-year prices) of $20,000 ($270,000 − $250,000). After converting the $20,000 increase to the 2007 price index, the ending inventory is $283,500, composed of the beginning layer of $200,000, a 2005 layer of $57,500, and a 2007 layer of $26,000 ($20,000 × 130%). Illustration 8-24 shows this computation.

ILLUSTRATION 8-24
Computation of 2007
Inventory at LIFO Cost

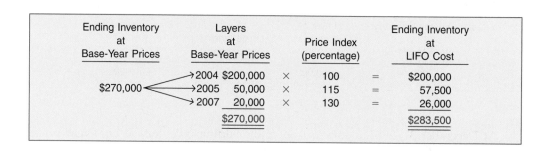

The ending inventory at base-year prices must always equal the total of the layers at base-year prices. Checking that this situation exists will help to ensure correct dollar-value computations.

Selecting a Price Index

Obviously, price changes are critical in dollar-value LIFO. How do companies determine the price indexes? Many companies use the general price-level index that the federal government prepares and publishes each month. The most popular general external price-level index is the **Consumer Price Index for Urban Consumers** (CPI-U).[15] Companies also use more-specific external price indexes. For instance, various organizations compute and publish daily indexes for most commodities (gold, silver, other metals, corn, wheat, and other farm products). Many trade associations prepare indexes for specific product lines or industries. Any of these indexes may be used for dollar-value LIFO purposes.

When a relevant specific external price index is not readily available, a company may compute its own specific internal price index. The desired approach is to price ending inventory at the most current cost. Therefore, a company that chose to compute its own specific internal price index would ordinarily determine current cost by referring to the actual cost of the goods it most recently had purchased. The price index provides a measure of the change in price or cost levels between the base year and the current year. The company then computes the index for each year after the base year. The general formula for computing the index is as follows.

---

[15]Indexes may be **general** (composed of several commodities, goods, or services) or **specific** (for one commodity, good, or service). Additionally, they may be **external** (computed by an outside party, such as the government, commodity exchange, or trade association) or **internal** (computed by the enterprise for its own product or service).

ILLUSTRATION 8-25
Formula for Computing a
Price Index

$$\frac{\text{Ending Inventory for the Period at Current Cost}}{\text{Ending Inventory for the Period at Base-Year Cost}} = \text{Price Index for Current Year}$$

This approach is generally referred to as the **double-extension method**. As its name implies, the value of the units in inventory is extended at *both* base-year prices and current-year prices.

To illustrate this computation, assume that Toledo Company's base-year inventory (January 1, 2007) consisted of the following.

Items	Quantity	Cost per Unit	Total Cost
A	1,000	$ 6	$ 6,000
B	2,000	20	40,000
January 1, 2007, inventory at base-year costs			$46,000

Examination of the ending inventory indicates that the company holds 3,000 units of Item A and 6,000 units of Item B on December 31, 2007. The most recent actual purchases related to these items were as follows.

Items	Purchase Date	Quantity Purchased	Cost per Unit
A	December 1, 2007	4,000	$ 7
B	December 15, 2007	5,000	25
B	November 16, 2007	1,000	22

Toledo double-extends the inventory as shown in Illustration 8-26.

ILLUSTRATION 8-26
Double-Extension
Method of Determining a
Price Index

		12/31/07 Inventory at Base-Year Costs			12/31/07 Inventory at Current-Year Costs	
Items	Units	Base-Year Cost per Unit	Total	Units	Current-Year Cost per Unit	Total
A	3,000	$ 6	$ 18,000	3,000	$ 7	$ 21,000
B	6,000	20	120,000	5,000	25	125,000
B				1,000	22	22,000
			$138,000			$168,000

After the inventories are double-extended, Toledo uses the formula in Illustration 8-25 to develop the index for the current year (2007), as follows.

ILLUSTRATION 8-27
Computation of 2007
Index

$$\frac{\text{Ending Inventory for the Period at Current Cost}}{\text{Ending Inventory for the Period at Base-Year Cost}} = \frac{\$168,000}{\$138,000} = 121.74\%$$

Toledo then applies this index (121.74%) to the layer added in 2007. Note in this illustration that Toledo used the most recent actual purchases to determine current cost; alternatively, it could have used other approaches such as FIFO and average cost. Whichever flow assumption is adopted, a company must use it consistently from one period to another.

Use of the double-extension method is time consuming and difficult where substantial technological change has occurred or where many items are involved. That is, as time passes, the company must determine a new base-year cost for new products, and must keep a base-year cost for each inventory item.[16]

Comparison of LIFO Approaches

We present three different approaches to computing LIFO inventories in this chapter—specific-goods LIFO, specific-goods pooled LIFO, and dollar-value LIFO. As we indicated earlier, the use of the specific-goods LIFO is unrealistic. Most companies have numerous goods in inventory at the end of a period. Costing (pricing) them on a unit basis is extremely expensive and time consuming.

The specific-goods pooled LIFO approach reduces recordkeeping and clerical costs. In addition, it is more difficult to erode the layers because the reduction of one quantity in the pool may be offset by an increase in another. Nonetheless, the pooled approach using quantities as its measurement basis can lead to untimely LIFO liquidations.

As a result, **most companies using a LIFO system employ dollar-value LIFO.** Although the approach appears complex, the logic and the computations are actually quite simple, after determining an appropriate index.

However, problems do exist with the dollar-value LIFO method. The selection of the items to be put in a pool can be subjective.[17] Such a determination, however, is extremely important because manipulation of the items in a pool without conceptual justification can affect reported net income. For example, the SEC noted that some companies have set up pools that are easy to liquidate. As a result, to increase income, a company simply decreases inventory, thereby matching low-cost inventory items to current revenues.

To curb this practice, the SEC has taken a much harder line on the number of pools that companies may establish. In a well-publicized case, **Stauffer Chemical Company** increased the number of LIFO pools from 8 to 280, boosting its net income by $16,515,000 or approximately 13 percent.[18] Stauffer justified the change in its Annual Report on the basis of "achieving a better matching of cost and revenue." The SEC required Stauffer to reduce the number of its inventory pools, contending that some pools were inappropriate and alleging income manipulation.

Major Advantages of LIFO

OBJECTIVE 9
Explain the major advantages and disadvantages of LIFO.

One obvious advantage of LIFO approaches is that the LIFO cost flow often approximates the physical flow of the goods in and out of inventory. For instance, in a coal pile, the last coal in is the first coal out because it is on the top of the pile. The coal remover is not going to take the coal from the bottom of the pile! The coal taken first is the coal placed on the pile last.

However, this is one of only a few situations where the actual physical flow corresponds to LIFO. Therefore most adherents of LIFO use other arguments for its widespread use, as follows.

---

[16]To simplify the analysis, companies may use another approach, initially sanctioned by the Internal Revenue Service for tax purposes. Under this method, a company obtains an index from an outside source or by double-extending only a sample portion of the inventory. For example, the IRS allows all companies to use as their inflation rate for a LIFO pool 80% of the inflation rate reported by the appropriate consumer or producer price indexes prepared by the Bureau of Labor Statistics (BLS). Once the company obtains the index, it divides the ending inventory at current cost by the index to find the base-year cost. Using generally available external indexes greatly simplifies LIFO computations, and frees companies from having to compute internal indexes.

[17]It is suggested that companies analyze how inventory purchases are affected by price changes, how goods are stocked, how goods are used, and if future liquidations are likely. See William R. Cron and Randall Hayes, ibid., p. 57.

[18]Commerce Clearing House, *SEC Accounting Rules* (Chicago: CCH, 1983), par. 4035.

Matching

LIFO matches the more recent costs against current revenues to provide a better measure of current earnings. During periods of inflation, many challenge the quality of non-LIFO earnings, noting that failing to match current costs against current revenues **creates transitory or "paper" profits ("inventory profits")**. Inventory profits occur when the inventory costs matched against sales are less than the inventory replacement cost. This results in understating the cost of goods sold and overstating profit. Using LIFO (rather than a method such as FIFO) matches current costs against revenues, thereby reducing inventory profits.

Tax Benefits/Improved Cash Flow

LIFO's popularity mainly stems from its tax benefits. As long as the price level increases and inventory quantities do not decrease, a deferral of income tax occurs. Why? Because a company matches the items it most recently purchased (at the higher price level) against revenues. For example, when **Fuqua Industries** switched to LIFO, it realized a tax savings of about $4 million. Even if the price level decreases later, the company still temporarily deferred its income taxes. Thus, use of LIFO in such situations improves a company's cash flow.[19]

The tax law requires that if a company uses LIFO for tax purposes, it must also use LIFO for financial accounting purposes[20] (although neither tax law nor GAAP requires a company to pool its inventories in the same manner for book and tax purposes). This requirement is often referred to as the **LIFO conformity rule**. Other inventory valuation methods do not have this requirement.

Future Earnings Hedge

With LIFO, future price declines will not substantially affect a company's future reported earnings. The reason: Since the company records the most recent inventory as sold first, there is not much ending inventory at high prices vulnerable to a price decline. Thus LIFO eliminates or substantially minimizes write-downs to market as a result of price decreases. In contrast, inventory costed under FIFO is more vulnerable to price declines, which can reduce net income substantially.

Major Disadvantages of LIFO

Despite its advantages, LIFO has the following drawbacks.

Reduced Earnings

Many corporate managers view the lower profits reported under the LIFO method in inflationary times as a distinct disadvantage. They would rather have higher reported profits than lower taxes. Some fear that investors may misunderstand an accounting change to LIFO, and that the lower profits may cause the price of the company's stock to fall.

Inventory Understated

LIFO may have a distorting effect on a company's balance sheet. The inventory valuation is normally outdated because the oldest costs remain in inventory. This understatement makes the working capital position of the company appear worse than it

---

[19]In periods of rising prices, the use of fewer pools will translate into greater income tax benefits through the use of LIFO. The use of fewer pools allows companies to offer inventory reductions on some items and inventory increases in others. In contrast, the use of more pools increases the likelihood of liquidating old, low-cost inventory layers and incurring negative tax consequences. See Reeve and Stanga, ibid., pp. 28–29.

[20]Management often selects an accounting procedure because a lower tax results from its use, instead of an accounting method that is conceptually more appealing. Throughout this textbook, we identify accounting procedures that provide income tax benefits to the user.

really is. A good example is **Caterpillar**, which uses LIFO costing for most of its inventory, valued at $4.7 billion at year-end 2004. Under FIFO costing, Caterpillar's inventories have a value of $6.8 billion—almost 50 percent higher than the LIFO amount.

The magnitude and direction of this variation between the carrying amount of inventory and its current price depend on the degree and direction of the price changes and the amount of inventory turnover. The combined effect of rising product prices and avoidance of inventory liquidations increases the difference between the inventory carrying value at LIFO and current prices of that inventory. This magnifies the balance sheet distortion attributed to the use of LIFO.

Physical Flow

LIFO does not approximate the physical flow of the items except in specific situations (such as the coal pile discussed earlier). Originally companies could use LIFO only in certain circumstances. This situation has changed over the years. Now, physical flow characteristics no longer determine whether a company may employ LIFO.

Involuntary Liquidation/Poor Buying Habits

If a company eliminates the base or layers of old costs, it may match old, irrelevant costs against current revenues. A distortion in reported income for a given period may result, as well as detrimental income tax consequences.[21]

Because of the liquidation problem, LIFO may cause poor buying habits. A company may simply purchase more goods and match these goods against revenue to avoid charging the old costs to expense. Furthermore, recall that with LIFO, a company may attempt to manipulate its net income at the end of the year simply by altering its pattern of purchases.[22]

One survey uncovered the following reasons why companies reject LIFO.[23]

ILLUSTRATION 8-28
Why Do Companies
Reject LIFO? Summary of
Responses

Reasons to Reject LIFO	Number	% of Total*
No expected tax benefits		
No required tax payment	34	16%
Declining prices	31	15
Rapid inventory turnover	30	14
Immaterial inventory	26	12
Miscellaneous tax related	38	17
	159	74%
Regulatory or other restrictions	26	12%
Excessive cost		
High administrative costs	29	14%
LIFO liquidation–related costs	12	6
	41	20%
Other adverse consequences		
Lower reported earnings	18	8%
Bad accounting	7	3
	25	11%

*Percentage totals more than 100% as some companies offered more than one explanation.

---

[21]The AICPA Task Force on LIFO Inventory Problems recommends that companies disclose the effects on income of LIFO inventory liquidations in the notes to the financial statements, but that they do not afford special treatment to the effects in the income statement. *Issues Paper* (New York: AICPA, 1984), pp. 36–37.

[22]For example, **General Tire and Rubber** accelerated raw material purchases at the end of the year to minimize the book profit from a liquidation of LIFO inventories and to minimize income taxes for the year.

[23]Michael H. Granof and Daniel Short, "Why Do Companies Reject LIFO?" *Journal of Accounting, Auditing, and Finance* (Summer 1984), pp. 323–333, Table 1, p. 327.

BASIS FOR SELECTION OF INVENTORY METHOD

How does a company choose among the various inventory methods? Although no absolute rules can be stated, preferability for LIFO usually occurs in either of the following circumstances: (1) if selling prices and revenues have been increasing faster than costs, thereby distorting income, and (2) in situations where LIFO has been traditional, such as department stores and industries where a fairly constant "base stock" is present (such as refining, chemicals, and glass).[24]

Conversely, LIFO is probably inappropriate in the following circumstances: (1) where prices tend to lag behind costs; (2) in situations where specific identification is traditional, such as in the sale of automobiles, farm equipment, art, and antique jewelry; or (3) where unit costs tend to decrease as production increases, thereby nullifying the tax benefit that LIFO might provide.[25]

Tax consequences are another consideration. Switching from FIFO to LIFO usually results in an immediate tax benefit. However, switching from LIFO to FIFO can result in a substantial tax burden. For example, when **Chrysler** (now **DaimlerChrysler**) changed from LIFO to FIFO, it became responsible for an additional $53 million in taxes that the company had deferred over 14 years of LIFO inventory valuation. Why, then, would Chrysler, and other companies, change to FIFO? The major reason was the profit crunch of that era. Although Chrysler showed a loss of $7.6 million after the switch, the loss would have been $20 million *more* if the company had not changed its inventory valuation from LIFO to FIFO.

It is questionable whether companies should switch from LIFO to FIFO for the sole purpose of increasing reported earnings. Intuitively one would assume that companies with higher reported earnings would have a higher share valuation (common stock price). However, some studies have indicated that the users of financial data exhibit a much higher sophistication than might be expected. Share prices are the same and, in some cases, even higher under LIFO in spite of lower reported earnings.[26]

The concern about reduced income resulting from adoption of LIFO has even less substance now because the IRS has relaxed the LIFO conformity rule which requires a company employing LIFO for tax purposes to use it for book purposes as well. The IRS has relaxed restrictions against providing non-LIFO income numbers as supplementary information. As a result, companies now provide supplemental non-LIFO disclosures. While not intended to override the basic LIFO method adopted for financial reporting, these disclosures may be useful in comparing operating income and working capital with companies not on LIFO.

For example, **JCPenney, Inc.** a LIFO user, presented the information in its annual report as shown in Illustration 8-29 (on page 396).

---

[24]*Accounting Trends and Techniques—2004* reports that of 833 inventory method disclosures, 251 used LIFO, 384 used FIFO, 167 used average cost, and 31 used other methods. Because of steady or falling raw materials costs and costs savings from electronic data interchange and just-in-time technologies in recent years, many businesses using LIFO no longer experience substantial tax benefits. Even some companies for which LIFO is creating a benefit are finding that the administrative costs associated with LIFO are higher than the LIFO benefit obtained. As a result, some companies are moving to FIFO or average cost.

[25]See Barry E. Cushing and Marc J. LeClere, "Evidence on the Determinants of Inventory Accounting Policy Choice," *The Accounting Review* (April 1992), pp. 355–366, Table 4, p. 363, for a list of factors hypothesized to affect FIFO–LIFO choices.

[26]See, for example, Shyam Sunder, "Relationship Between Accounting Changes and Stock Prices: Problems of Measurement and Some Empirical Evidence," *Empirical Research in Accounting: Selected Studies, 1973* (Chicago: University of Chicago), pp. 1–40. But see Robert Moren Brown, "Short-Range Market Reaction to Changes to LIFO Accounting Using Preliminary Earnings Announcement Dates," *The Journal of Accounting Research* (Spring 1980), which found that companies that do change to LIFO suffer a short-run decline in the price of their stock.

ILLUSTRATION 8-29
Supplemental
Non-LIFO Disclosure

INTERNATIONAL INSIGHT

Many U.S. companies that have international operations use LIFO for U.S. purposes but use FIFO for their foreign subsidiaries.

JCPenney, Inc.

Some companies in the retail industry use the FIFO method in valuing part or all of their inventories. Had JCPenney used the FIFO method and made no other assumptions with respect to changes in income resulting therefrom, income and income per share from continuing operations would have been:

Income from continuing operations (in millions)	$325
Income from continuing operations per share	$4.63

Relaxation of the LIFO conformity rule has led some companies to select LIFO as their inventory valuation method because they will be able to disclose FIFO income numbers in the financial reports if they so desire.[27]

Companies often combine inventory methods. For example, **John Deere** uses LIFO for most of its inventories, and prices the remainder using FIFO. **Hershey Foods** follows the same practice. One reason for these practices is that certain product lines can be highly susceptible to deflation instead of inflation. In addition, if the level of inventory is unstable, unwanted involuntary liquidations may result in certain product lines if using LIFO. Finally, for high inventory turnover in certain product lines, a company cannot justify LIFO's additional recordkeeping and expense. In such cases, a company often uses average cost because it is easy to compute.[28]

Although a company may use a variety of inventory methods to assist in accurate computation of net income, once it selects a pricing method, it must apply it consistently thereafter. If conditions indicate that the inventory pricing method in use is unsuitable, the company must seriously consider all other possibilities before selecting another method. It should clearly explain any change and disclose its effect in the financial statements.

Inventory Valuation Methods—Summary Analysis

The preceding sections of this chapter described a number of inventory valuation methods. Here we present a brief summary of the three major inventory methods to show the effects these valuation methods have on the financial statements. This comparison assumes periodic inventory procedures and the following selected data.

Selected Data		
Beginning cash balance		$ 7,000
Beginning retained earnings		$10,000
Beginning inventory:	4,000 units @ $3	$12,000
Purchases:	6,000 units @ $4	$24,000
Sales:	5,000 units @ $12	$60,000
Operating expenses		$10,000
Income tax rate		40%

[27]Note that a company can use one variation of LIFO for financial reporting purposes and another for tax without violating the LIFO conformity rule. Such a relaxation has caused many problems because the general approach to accounting for LIFO has been "whatever is good for tax is good for financial reporting."

[28]For an interesting discussion of the reasons for and against the use of FIFO and average cost, see Michael H. Granof and Daniel G. Short "For Some Companies, FIFO Accounting Makes Sense," *Wall Street Journal* (August 30, 1982), and the subsequent rebuttal by Gary C. Biddle "Taking Stock of Inventory Accounting Choices," *Wall Street Journal* (September 15, 1982).

Illustration 8-30 shows the comparative results on net income of the use of average cost, FIFO, and LIFO.

	Average Cost	FIFO	LIFO
Sales	$60,000	$60,000	$60,000
Cost of goods sold	18,000[a]	16,000[b]	20,000[c]
Gross profit	42,000	44,000	40,000
Operating expenses	10,000	10,000	10,000
Income before taxes	32,000	34,000	30,000
Income taxes (40%)	12,800	13,600	12,000
Net income	$19,200	$20,400	$18,000

[a] 4,000 @ $3 = $12,000
6,000 @ $4 = 24,000
  $36,000

$36,000 ÷ 10,000 = $3.60
$3.60 × 5,000 = $18,000

[b] 4,000 @ $3 = $12,000
1,000 @ $4 =   4,000
  $16,000

[c] 5,000 @ $4 = $20,000

Notice that gross profit and net income are lowest under LIFO, highest under FIFO, and somewhere in the middle under average cost.

Illustration 8-31 shows the final balances of selected items at the end of the period.

	Inventory	Gross Profit	Taxes	Net Income	Retained Earnings	Cash
Average Cost	$18,000 (5,000 × $3.60)	$42,000	$12,800	$19,200	$29,200 ($10,000 + $19,200)	$20,200[a]
FIFO	$20,000 (5,000 × $4)	$44,000	$13,600	$20,400	$30,400 ($10,000 + $20,400)	$19,400[a]
LIFO	$16,000 (4,000 × $3) (1,000 × $4)	$40,000	$12,000	$18,000	$28,000 ($10,000 + $18,000)	$21,000[a]

[a]Cash at year-end	=	Beg. Balance	+	Sales	−	Purchases	−	Operating expenses	−	Taxes
Average cost—$20,200	=	$7,000	+	$60,000	−	$24,000	−	$10,000	−	$12,800
FIFO—$19,400	=	$7,000	+	$60,000	−	$24,000	−	$10,000	−	$13,600
LIFO—$21,000	=	$7,000	+	$60,000	−	$24,000	−	$10,000	−	$12,000

LIFO results in the highest cash balance at year-end (because taxes are lower). This example assumes that prices are rising. The opposite result occurs if prices are declining.

SUMMARY OF LEARNING OBJECTIVES

KEY TERMS

average cost method, *382*
consigned goods, *373*
cost flow assumptions, *380*
dollar-value LIFO, *387*
double-extension method, *391*

1. **Identify major classifications of inventory.** Only one inventory account, Merchandise Inventory, appears in the financial statements of a merchandising concern. A manufacturer normally has three inventory accounts: Raw Materials, Work in Process, and Finished Goods. Companies report the cost assigned to goods and materials on hand but not yet placed into production as raw materials inventory. They report the cost of the raw materials on which production has been started but not completed, plus the direct labor cost applied specifically to this material and a ratable share of manufacturing overhead costs, as work in process inventory. Finally, they report the costs

finished goods
   inventory, 369

first-in, first-out (FIFO)
   method, 382

f.o.b. destination, 373

f.o.b. shipping point, 373

gross method, 379

inventories, 368

last-in, first-out (LIFO)
   method, 384

LIFO effect, 385

LIFO liquidation, 385

LIFO reserve, 385

merchandise
   inventory, 368

modified perpetual
   inventory system, 371

moving-average
   method, 382

net method, 379

period costs, 378

periodic inventory
   system, 370

perpetual inventory
   system, 370

product costs, 377

Purchase Discounts, 379

raw materials
   inventory, 368

specific-goods pooled
   LIFO approach, 387

specific identification, 381

weighted-average
   method, 382

work in process
   inventory, 369

identified with the completed but unsold units on hand at the end of the fiscal period as finished goods inventory.

2. Distinguish between perpetual and periodic inventory systems. A perpetual inventory system maintains a continuous record of inventory changes in the Inventory account. That is, a company records all purchases and sales (issues) of goods directly in the Inventory account as they occur. Under a periodic inventory system, companies determine the quantity of inventory on hand only periodically. A company debits a Purchases account, but the Inventory account remains the same. It determines cost of goods sold at the end of the period by subtracting ending inventory from cost of goods available for sale. A company ascertains ending inventory by physical count.

3. Identify the effects of inventory errors on the financial statements. *If the company misstates ending inventory*: (1) In the balance sheet, the inventory and retained earnings will be misstated, which will lead to miscalculation of the working capital and current ratio, and (2) in the income statement the cost of goods sold and net income will be misstated. If the company misstates purchases (and related accounts payable) and inventory: (1) In the balance sheet, the inventory and accounts payable will be misstated, which will lead to miscalculation of the current ratio, and (2) in the income statement, purchases and ending inventory will be misstated.

4. Understand the items to include as inventory cost. Product costs are those costs that attach to the inventory and are recorded in the inventory account. Such charges include freight charges on goods purchased, other direct costs of acquisition, and labor and other production costs incurred in processing the goods up to the time of sale. Period costs are those costs that are indirectly related the acquisition or production of the goods. These changes, such as selling expense and general and administrative expenses, are therefore not included as part of inventory cost.

5. Describe and compare the cost flow assumptions used to account for inventories. (1) *Average cost* prices items in the inventory on the basis of the average cost of all similar goods available during the period. (2) *First-in, first-out (FIFO)* assumes that a company uses goods in the order in which it purchases them. The inventory remaining must therefore represent the most recent purchases. (3) *Last-in, first-out (LIFO)* matches the cost of the last goods purchased against revenue.

6. Explain the significance and use of a LIFO reserve. The difference between the inventory method used for internal reporting purposes and LIFO is referred to as the Allowance to Reduce Inventory to LIFO, or the LIFO reserve. The change in LIFO reserve is referred to as the LIFO effect. Companies should disclose either the LIFO reserve or the replacement cost of the inventory in the financial statements.

7. Understand the effect of LIFO liquidations. LIFO liquidations match costs from preceding periods against sales revenues reported in current dollars. This distorts net income and results in increased taxable income in the current period. LIFO liquidations can occur frequently when using a specific-goods LIFO approach.

8. Explain the dollar-value LIFO method. For the dollar-value LIFO method, companies determine and measure increases and decreases in a pool in terms of total dollar value, not the physical quantity of the goods in the inventory pool.

9. Identify the major advantages and disadvantages of LIFO. The major advantages of LIFO are the following: (1) It matches recent costs against current revenues to provide a better measure of current earnings. (2) As long as the price level increases and inventory quantities do not decrease, a deferral of income tax occurs in LIFO. (3) Because of the deferral of income tax, cash flow improves. Major disadvantages are: (1) reduced earnings, (2) understated inventory, (3) does not approximate physical flow of the items except in peculiar situations, and (4) involuntary liquidation issues.

10. **Understand why companies select given inventory methods.** Companies ordinarily prefer LIFO in the following circumstances: (1) if selling prices and revenues have been increasing faster than costs and (2) if a company has a fairly constant "base stock." Conversely, LIFO would probably not be appropriate in the following circumstances: (1) if sale prices tend to lag behind costs, (2) if specific identification is traditional, and (3) when unit costs tend to decrease as production increases, thereby nullifying the tax benefit that LIFO might provide.

QUESTIONS

1. In what ways are the inventory accounts of a retailing company different from those of a manufacturing company?

2. Why should inventories be included in (a) a statement of financial position and (b) the computation of net income?

3. What is the difference between a perpetual inventory and a physical inventory? If a company maintains a perpetual inventory, should its physical inventory at any date be equal to the amount indicated by the perpetual inventory records? Why?

4. Mariah Carey, Inc. indicated in a recent annual report that approximately $19 million of merchandise was received on consignment. Should Mariah Carey, Inc. report this amount on its balance sheet? Explain.

5. What is a product financing arrangement? How should product financing arrangements be reported in the financial statements?

6. Where, if at all, should the following items be classified on a balance sheet?

(a) Goods out on approval to customers.

(b) Goods in transit that were recently purchased f.o.b. destination.

(c) Land held by a realty firm for sale.

(d) Raw materials.

(e) Goods received on consignment.

(f) Manufacturing supplies.

7. At the balance sheet date Paula Abdul Company held title to goods in transit amounting to $214,000. This amount was omitted from the purchases figure for the year and also from the ending inventory. What is the effect of this omission on the net income for the year as calculated when the books are closed? What is the effect on the company's financial position as shown in its balance sheet? Is materiality a factor in determining whether an adjustment for this item should be made?

8. Define "cost" as applied to the valuation of inventories.

9. Distinguish between product costs and period costs as they relate to inventory.

10. **Ford Motor Co.** is considering alternate methods of accounting for the cash discounts it takes when paying suppliers promptly. One method suggested was to report these discounts as financial income when payments are made. Comment on the propriety of this approach.

11. Konerko Inc. purchases 300 units of an item at an invoice cost of $30,000. What is the cost per unit? If the goods are shipped f.o.b. shipping point and the freight bill was $1,500, what is the cost per unit if Konerko Inc. pays the freight charges? If these items were bought on 2/10, n/30 terms and the invoice and the freight bill were paid within the 10-day period, what would be the cost per unit?

12. Specific identification is sometimes said to be the ideal method of assigning cost to inventory and to cost of goods sold. Briefly indicate the arguments for and against this method of inventory valuation.

13. FIFO, weighted average, and LIFO methods are often used instead of specific identification for inventory valuation purposes. Compare these methods with the specific identification method, discussing the theoretical propriety of each method in the determination of income and asset valuation.

14. How might a company obtain a price index in order to apply dollar-value LIFO?

15. Describe the LIFO double-extension method. Using the following information, compute the index at December 31, 2007, applying the double-extension method to a LIFO pool consisting of 25,500 units of product A and 10,350 units of product B. The base-year cost of product A is $10.20 and of product B is $37.00. The price at December 31, 2007, for product A is $19.00 and for product B is $45.60.

16. As compared with the FIFO method of costing inventories, does the LIFO method result in a larger or smaller net income in a period of rising prices? What is the comparative effect on net income in a period of falling prices?

17. What is the dollar-value method of LIFO inventory valuation? What advantage does the dollar-value method have over the specific goods approach of LIFO inventory valuation? Why will the traditional LIFO inventory costing method and the dollar-value LIFO inventory costing method produce different inventory valuations if the composition of the inventory base changes?

18. Explain the following terms.

(a) LIFO layer. (b) LIFO reserve. (c) LIFO effect.

19. On December 31, 2006, the inventory of Mario Lemieux Company amounts to $800,000. During 2007, the company decides to use the dollar-value LIFO method of costing inventories. On December 31, 2007, the inventory is $1,026,000 at December 31, 2007, prices. Using the De-

cember 31, 2006, price level of 100 and the December 31, 2007, price level of 108, compute the inventory value at December 31, 2007, under the dollar-value LIFO method.

20. In an article that appeared in the *Wall Street Journal*, the phrases "phantom (paper) profits" and "high LIFO profits" through involuntary liquidation were used. Explain these phrases.

BRIEF EXERCISES

(LO 1) **BE8-1**   Included in the December 31 trial balance of Billie Joel Company are the following assets.

Cash	$ 190,000	Work in process	$200,000
Equipment (net)	1,100,000	Receivables (net)	400,000
Prepaid insurance	41,000	Patents	110,000
Raw materials	335,000	Finished goods	150,000

Prepare the current assets section of the December 31 balance sheet.

(LO 2) **BE8-2**   Alanis Morrissette Company uses a perpetual inventory system. Its beginning inventory consists of 50 units that cost $30 each. During June, the company purchased 150 units at $30 each, returned 6 units for credit, and sold 125 units at $50 each. Journalize the June transactions.

(LO 4) **BE8-3**   Mayberry Company took a physical inventory on December 31 and determined that goods costing $200,000 were on hand. Not included in the physical count were $15,000 of goods purchased from Taylor Corporation, f.o.b. shipping point, and $22,000 of goods sold to Mount Pilot Company for $30,000, f.o.b. destination. Both the Taylor purchase and the Mount Pilot sale were in transit at year-end. What amount should Mayberry report as its December 31 inventory?

(LO 3) **BE8-4**   Gavin Bryars Enterprises reported cost of goods sold for 2007 of $1,400,000 and retained earnings of $5,200,000 at December 31, 2007. Gavin Bryars later discovered that its ending inventories at December 31, 2006 and 2007, were overstated by $110,000 and $45,000, respectively. Determine the corrected amounts for 2007 cost of goods sold and December 31, 2007, retained earnings.

(LO 5) **BE8-5**   Jose Zorilla Company uses a periodic inventory system. For April, when the company sold 700 units, the following information is available.

	Units	Unit Cost	Total Cost
April 1 inventory	250	$10	$ 2,500
April 15 purchase	400	12	4,800
April 23 purchase	350	13	4,550
	1,000		$11,850

Compute the April 30 inventory and the April cost of goods sold using the average cost method.

(LO 5) **BE8-6**   Data for Jose Zorilla Company are presented in BE8-5. Compute the April 30 inventory and the April cost of goods sold using the FIFO method.

(LO 5) **BE8-7**   Data for Jose Zorilla Company are presented in BE8-5. Compute the April 30 inventory and the April cost of goods sold using the LIFO method.

(LO 8) **BE8-8**   Easy-E Company had ending inventory at end-of-year prices of $100,000 at December 31, 2005; $123,200 at December 31, 2006; and $134,560 at December 31, 2007. The year-end price indexes were 100 at 12/31/05, 110 at 12/31/06, and 116 at 12/31/07. Compute the ending inventory for Easy-E Company for 2005 through 2007 using the dollar-value LIFO method.

(LO 8) **BE8-9**   Wingers uses the dollar-value LIFO method of computing its inventory. Data for the past 3 years follow.

Year Ended December 31	Inventory at Current-year Cost	Price Index
2005	$19,750	100
2006	21,708	108
2007	25,935	114

Instructions

Compute the value of the 2006 and 2007 inventories using the dollar-value LIFO method.

EXERCISES

(LO 4) **E8-1** **(Inventoriable Costs)** Presented below is a list of items that may or may not be reported as inventory in a company's December 31 balance sheet.

1. Goods out on consignment at another company's store.
2. Goods sold on an installment basis (bad debts can be reasonably estimated).
3. Goods purchased f.o.b. shipping point that are in transit at December 31.
4. Goods purchased f.o.b. destination that are in transit at December 31.
5. Goods sold to another company, for which our company has signed an agreement to repurchase at a set price that covers all costs related to the inventory.
6. Goods sold where large returns are predictable.
7. Goods sold f.o.b. shipping point that are in transit at December 31.
8. Freight charges on goods purchased.
9. Interest costs incurred for inventories that are routinely manufactured.
10. Costs incurred to advertise goods held for resale.
11. Materials on hand not yet placed into production by a manufacturing firm.
12. Office supplies.
13. Raw materials on which a manufacturing firm has started production, but which are not completely processed.
14. Factory supplies.
15. Goods held on consignment from another company.
16. Costs identified with units completed by a manufacturing firm, but not yet sold.
17. Goods sold f.o.b. destination that are in transit at December 31.
18. Short-term investments in stocks and bonds that will be resold in the near future.

Instructions

Indicate which of these items would typically be reported as inventory in the financial statements. If an item should **not** be reported as inventory, indicate how it should be reported in the financial statements.

(LO 4) **E8-2** **(Inventoriable Costs)** In your audit of Jose Oliva Company, you find that a physical inventory on December 31, 2007, showed merchandise with a cost of $441,000 was on hand at that date. You also discover the following items were all excluded from the $441,000.

1. Merchandise of $61,000 which is held by Oliva on consignment. The consignor is the Max Suzuki Company.
2. Merchandise costing $38,000 which was shipped by Oliva f.o.b. destination to a customer on December 31, 2007. The customer was expected to receive the merchandise on January 6, 2008.
3. Merchandise costing $46,000 which was shipped by Oliva f.o.b. shipping point to a customer on December 29, 2007. The customer was scheduled to receive the merchandise on January 2, 2008.
4. Merchandise costing $83,000 shipped by a vendor f.o.b. destination on December 30, 2007, and received by Oliva on January 4, 2008.
5. Merchandise costing $51,000 shipped by a vendor f.o.b. seller on December 31, 2007, and received by Oliva on January 5, 2008.

Instructions

Based on the above information, calculate the amount that should appear on Oliva's balance sheet at December 31, 2007, for inventory.

(LO 4) **E8-3** **(Inventoriable Costs)** Assume that in an annual audit of **Harlowe Inc.** at December 31, 2007, you find the following transactions near the closing date.

1. A special machine, fabricated to order for a customer, was finished and specifically segregated in the back part of the shipping room on December 31, 2007. The customer was billed on that date and the machine excluded from inventory although it was shipped on January 4, 2008.
2. Merchandise costing $2,800 was received on January 3, 2008, and the related purchase invoice recorded January 5. The invoice showed the shipment was made on December 29, 2007, f.o.b. destination.
3. A packing case containing a product costing $3,400 was standing in the shipping room when the physical inventory was taken. It was not included in the inventory because it was marked "Hold for shipping instructions." Your investigation revealed that the customer's order was dated December 18, 2007, but that the case was shipped and the customer billed on January 10, 2008. The product was a stock item of your client.

4. Merchandise received on January 6, 2008, costing $680 was entered in the purchase journal on January 7, 2008. The invoice showed shipment was made f.o.b. supplier's warehouse on December 31, 2007. Because it was not on hand at December 31, it was not included in inventory.
5. Merchandise costing $720 was received on December 28, 2007, and the invoice was not recorded. You located it in the hands of the purchasing agent; it was marked "on consignment."

Instructions

Assuming that each of the amounts is material, state whether the merchandise should be included in the client's inventory, and give your reason for your decision on each item.

(LO 2, 4)   **E8-4 (Inventoriable Costs—Perpetual)** Colin Davis Machine Company maintains a general ledger account for each class of inventory, debiting such accounts for increases during the period and crediting them for decreases. The transactions below relate to the Raw Materials inventory account, which is debited for materials purchased and credited for materials requisitioned for use.

1. An invoice for $8,100, terms f.o.b. destination, was received and entered January 2, 2007. The receiving report shows that the materials were received December 28, 2006.
2. Materials costing $28,000, shipped f.o.b. destination, were not entered by December 31, 2006, "because they were in a railroad car on the company's siding on that date and had not been unloaded."
3. Materials costing $7,300 were returned to the supplier on December 29, 2006, and were shipped f.o.b. shipping point. The return was entered on that date, even though the materials are not expected to reach the supplier's place of business until January 6, 2007.
4. An invoice for $7,500, terms f.o.b. shipping point, was received and entered December 30, 2006. The receiving report shows that the materials were received January 4, 2007, and the bill of lading shows that they were shipped January 2, 2007.
5. Materials costing $19,800 were received December 30, 2006, but no entry was made for them because "they were ordered with a specified delivery of no earlier than January 10, 2007."

Instructions

Prepare correcting general journal entries required at December 31, 2006, assuming that the books have not been closed.

(LO 3, 4)   **E8-5 (Inventoriable Costs—Error Adjustments)** Craig Company asks you to review its December 31, 2007, inventory values and prepare the necessary adjustments to the books. The following information is given to you.

1. Craig uses the periodic method of recording inventory. A physical count reveals $234,890 of inventory on hand at December 31, 2007.
2. Not included in the physical count of inventory is $13,420 of merchandise purchased on December 15 from Browser. This merchandise was shipped f.o.b. shipping point on December 29 and arrived in January. The invoice arrived and was recorded on December 31.
3. Included in inventory is merchandise sold to Champy on December 30, f.o.b. destination. This merchandise was shipped after it was counted. The invoice was prepared and recorded as a sale on account for $12,800 on December 31. The merchandise cost $7,350, and Champy received it on January 3.
4. Included in inventory was merchandise received from Dudley on December 31 with an invoice price of $15,630. The merchandise was shipped f.o.b. destination. The invoice, which has not yet arrived, has not been recorded.
5. Not included in inventory is $8,540 of merchandise purchased from Glowser Industries. This merchandise was received on December 31 after the inventory had been counted. The invoice was received and recorded on December 30.
6. Included in inventory was $10,438 of inventory held by Craig on consignment from Jackel Industries.
7. Included in inventory is merchandise sold to Kemp f.o.b. shipping point. This merchandise was shipped after it was counted. The invoice was prepared and recorded as a sale for $18,900 on December 31. The cost of this merchandise was $10,520, and Kemp received the merchandise on January 5.
8. Excluded from inventory was a carton labeled "Please accept for credit." This carton contains merchandise costing $1,500 which had been sold to a customer for $2,600. No entry had been made to the books to reflect the return, but none of the returned merchandise seemed damaged.

Instructions

(a) Determine the proper inventory balance for Craig Company at December 31, 2007.
(b) Prepare any correcting entries to adjust inventory to its proper amount at December 31, 2007. Assume the books have not been closed.

(LO 4) **E8-6** **(Determining Merchandise Amounts—Periodic)** Two or more items are omitted in each of the following tabulations of income statement data. Fill in the amounts that are missing.

	2005	2006	2007
Sales	$290,000	$?	$410,000
Sales returns	11,000	13,000	?
Net sales	?	347,000	?
Beginning inventory	20,000	32,000	?
Ending inventory	?	?	?
Purchases	?	260,000	298,000
Purchase returns and allowances	5,000	8,000	10,000
Transportation-in	8,000	9,000	12,000
Cost of goods sold	233,000	?	293,000
Gross profit on sales	46,000	91,000	97,000

(LO 4) **E8-7** **(Purchases Recorded Net)** Presented below are transactions related to Tom Brokaw, Inc.

> May 10 Purchased goods billed at $15,000 subject to cash discount terms of 2/10, n/60.
> 11 Purchased goods billed at $13,200 subject to terms of 1/15, n/30.
> 19 Paid invoice of May 10.
> 24 Purchased goods billed at $11,500 subject to cash discount terms of 2/10, n/30.

Instructions

(a) Prepare general journal entries for the transactions above under the assumption that purchases are to be recorded at net amounts after cash discounts and that discounts lost are to be treated as financial expense.

(b) Assuming no purchase or payment transactions other than those given above, prepare the adjusting entry required on May 31 if financial statements are to be prepared as of that date.

(LO 4) **E8-8** **(Purchases Recorded, Gross Method)** Cruise Industries purchased $10,800 of merchandise on February 1, 2007, subject to a trade discount of 10% and with credit terms of 3/15, n/60. It returned $2,500 (gross price before trade or cash discount) on February 4. The invoice was paid on February 13.

Instructions

(a) Assuming that Cruise uses the perpetual method for recording merchandise transactions, record the purchase, return, and payment using the gross method.

(b) Assuming that Cruise uses the periodic method for recording merchandise transactions, record the purchase, return, and payment using the gross method.

(c) At what amount would the purchase on February 1 be recorded if the net method were used?

(LO 2) **E8-9** **(Periodic versus Perpetual Entries)** Fong Sai-Yuk Company sells one product. Presented below is information for January for Fong Sai-Yuk Company.

> Jan. 1 Inventory 100 units at $5 each
> 4 Sale 80 units at $8 each
> 11 Purchase 150 units at $6 each
> 13 Sale 120 units at $8.75 each
> 20 Purchase 160 units at $7 each
> 27 Sale 100 units at $9 each

Fong Sai-Yuk uses the FIFO cost flow assumption. All purchases and sales are on account.

Instructions

(a) Assume Fong Sai-Yuk uses a periodic system. Prepare all necessary journal entries, including the end-of-month closing entry to record cost of goods sold. A physical count indicates that the ending inventory for January is 110 units.

(b) Compute gross profit using the periodic system.

(c) Assume Fong Sai-Yuk uses a perpetual system. Prepare all necessary journal entries.

(d) Compute gross profit using the perpetual system.

(LO 3) **E8-10** **(Inventory Errors—Periodic)** Ann M. Martin Company makes the following errors during the current year. (In all cases, assume ending inventory in the following year is correctly stated.)

1. Ending inventory is overstated, but purchases and related accounts payable are recorded correctly.
2. Both ending inventory and purchases and related accounts payable are understated. (Assume this purchase was recorded and paid for in the following year.)
3. Ending inventory is correct, but a purchase on account was not recorded. (Assume this purchase was recorded and paid for in the following year.)

Instructions

Indicate the effect of each of these errors on working capital, current ratio (assume that the current ratio is greater than 1), retained earnings, and net income for the current year and the subsequent year.

(LO 3) **E8-11 (Inventory Errors)** At December 31, 2006, Stacy McGill Corporation reported current assets of $370,000 and current liabilities of $200,000. The following items may have been recorded incorrectly.

1. Goods purchased costing $22,000 were shipped f.o.b. shipping point by a supplier on December 28. McGill received and recorded the invoice on December 29, 2006, but the goods were not included in McGill's physical count of inventory because they were not received until January 4, 2004.
2. Goods purchased costing $15,000 were shipped f.o.b. destination by a supplier on December 26. McGill received and recorded the invoice on December 31, but the goods were not included in McGill's 2006 physical count of inventory because they were not received until January 2, 2007.
3. Goods held on consignment from Claudia Kishi Company were included in McGill's December 31, 2006, physical count of inventory at $13,000.
4. Freight-in of $3,000 was debited to advertising expense on December 28, 2006.

Instructions

(a) Compute the current ratio based on McGill's balance sheet.
(b) Recompute the current ratio after corrections are made.
(c) By what amount will income (before taxes) be adjusted up or down as a result of the corrections?

(LO 3) **E8-12 (Inventory Errors)** The net income per books of Linda Patrick Company was determined without knowledge of the errors indicated.

Year	Net Income per Books	Error in Ending Inventory	
2002	$50,000	Overstated	$ 3,000
2003	52,000	Overstated	9,000
2004	54,000	Understated	11,000
2005	56,000	No error	
2006	58,000	Understated	2,000
2007	60,000	Overstated	8,000

Instructions

Prepare a work sheet to show the adjusted net income figure for each of the 6 years after taking into account the inventory errors.

(LO 2, 5) **E8-13 (FIFO and LIFO—Periodic and Perpetual)** Inventory information for Part 311 of Monique Aaron Corp. discloses the following information for the month of June.

June 1	Balance	300 units @ $10	June 10	Sold	200 units @ $24
11	Purchased	800 units @ $12	15	Sold	500 units @ $25
20	Purchased	500 units @ $13	27	Sold	300 units @ $27

Instructions

(a) Assuming that the periodic inventory method is used, compute the cost of goods sold and ending inventory under (1) LIFO and (2) FIFO.
(b) Assuming that the perpetual inventory method is used and costs are computed at the time of each withdrawal, what is the value of the ending inventory at LIFO?
(c) Assuming that the perpetual inventory method is used and costs are computed at the time of each withdrawal, what is the gross profit if the inventory is valued at FIFO?
(d) Why is it stated that LIFO usually produces a lower gross profit than FIFO?

(LO 5) **E8-14 (FIFO, LIFO and Average Cost Determination)** John Adams Company's record of transactions for the month of April was as follows.

Purchases			Sales		
April 1 (balance on hand)	600 @	$6.00	April 3	500 @	$10.00
4	1,500 @	6.08	9	1,400 @	10.00
8	800 @	6.40	11	600 @	11.00
13	1,200 @	6.50	23	1,200 @	11.00
21	700 @	6.60	27	900 @	12.00
29	500 @	6.79		4,600	
	5,300				

Instructions

  (a) Assuming that periodic inventory records are kept in units only, compute the inventory at April 30 using (1) LIFO and (2) average cost.

  (b) Assuming that perpetual inventory records are kept in dollars, determine the inventory using (1) FIFO and (2) LIFO.

  (c) Compute cost of goods sold assuming periodic inventory procedures and inventory priced at FIFO.

  (d) In an inflationary period, which inventory method—FIFO, LIFO, average cost—will show the highest net income?

(LO 5)   **E8-15 (FIFO, LIFO, Average Cost Inventory)** Shania Twain Company was formed on December 1, 2006. The following information is available from Twain's inventory records for Product BAP.

	Units	Unit Cost
January 1, 2007 (beginning inventory)	600	$ 8.00
Purchases:		
January 5, 2007	1,200	9.00
January 25, 2007	1,300	10.00
February 16, 2007	800	11.00
March 26, 2007	600	12.00

A physical inventory on March 31, 2007, shows 1,600 units on hand.

Instructions

Prepare schedules to compute the ending inventory at March 31, 2007, under each of the following inventory methods.

  (a) FIFO.   **(b)** LIFO.   **(c)** Weighted average.

(LO 2, 5)   **E8-16 (Compute FIFO, LIFO, Average Cost—Periodic)** Presented below is information related to Blowfish radios for the Hootie Company for the month of July.

Date	Transaction	Units In	Unit Cost	Total	Units Sold	Selling Price	Total
July 1	Balance	100	$4.10	$ 410			
6	Purchase	800	4.20	3,360			
7	Sale				300	$7.00	$ 2,100
10	Sale				300	7.30	2,190
12	Purchase	400	4.50	1,800			
15	Sale				200	7.40	1,480
18	Purchase	300	4.60	1,380			
22	Sale				400	7.40	2,960
25	Purchase	500	4.58	2,290			
30	Sale				200	7.50	1,500
	Totals	2,100		$9,240	1,400		$10,230

Instructions

  (a) Assuming that the periodic inventory method is used, compute the inventory cost at July 31 under each of the following cost flow assumptions.

    (1) FIFO.

    (2) LIFO.

    (3) Weighted-average.

  (b) Answer the following questions.

    (1) Which of the methods used above will yield the lowest figure for gross profit for the income statement? Explain why.

    (2) Which of the methods used above will yield the lowest figure for ending inventory for the balance sheet? Explain why.

(LO 2, 5)   **E8-17 (FIFO and LIFO—Periodic and Perpetual)** The following is a record of Pervis Ellison Company's transactions for Boston Teapots for the month of May 2007.

May 1	Balance 400 units @ $20	May 10	Sale 300 units @ $38
12	Purchase 600 units @ $25	20	Sale 540 units @ $38
28	Purchase 400 units @ $30		

Instructions

(a) Assuming that perpetual inventories are **not** maintained and that a physical count at the end of the month shows 560 units on hand, what is the cost of the ending inventory using (1) FIFO and (2) LIFO?

(b) Assuming that perpetual records are maintained and they tie into the general ledger, calculate the ending inventory using (1) FIFO and (2) LIFO.

(LO 2, 5) **E8-18 (FIFO and LIFO; Income Statement Presentation)** The board of directors of Ichiro Corporation is considering whether or not it should instruct the accounting department to shift from a first-in, first-out (FIFO) basis of pricing inventories to a last-in, first-out (LIFO) basis. The following information is available.

Sales	21,000 units @ $50
Inventory, January 1	6,000 units @ 20
Purchases	6,000 units @ 22
	10,000 units @ 25
	7,000 units @ 30
Inventory, December 31	8,000 units @ ?
Operating expenses	$200,000

Instructions

Prepare a condensed income statement for the year on both bases for comparative purposes.

(LO 5) **E8-19 (FIFO and LIFO Effects)** You are the vice-president of finance of Sandy Alomar Corporation, a retail company that prepared two different schedules of gross margin for the first quarter ended March 31, 2007. These schedules appear below.

	Sales ($5 per unit)	Cost of Goods Sold	Gross Margin
Schedule 1	$150,000	$124,900	$25,100
Schedule 2	150,000	129,400	20,600

The computation of cost of goods sold in each schedule is based on the following data.

	Units	Cost per Unit	Total Cost
Beginning inventory, January 1	10,000	$4.00	$40,000
Purchase, January 10	8,000	4.20	33,600
Purchase, January 30	6,000	4.25	25,500
Purchase, February 11	9,000	4.30	38,700
Purchase, March 17	11,000	4.40	48,400

Jane Torville, the president of the corporation, cannot understand how two different gross margins can be computed from the same set of data. As the vice-president of finance you have explained to Ms. Torville that the two schedules are based on different assumptions concerning the flow of inventory costs, i.e., FIFO and LIFO. Schedules 1 and 2 were not necessarily prepared in this sequence of cost flow assumptions.

Instructions

Prepare two separate schedules computing cost of goods sold and supporting schedules showing the composition of the ending inventory under both cost flow assumptions.

(LO 2, 5) **E8-20 (FIFO and LIFO—Periodic)** Howie Long Shop began operations on January 2, 2007. The following stock record card for footballs was taken from the records at the end of the year.

Date	Voucher	Terms	Units Received	Unit Invoice Cost	Gross Invoice Amount
1/15	10624	Net 30	50	$20	$1,000
3/15	11437	1/5, net 30	65	16	1,040
6/20	21332	1/10, net 30	90	15	1,350
9/12	27644	1/10, net 30	84	12	1,008
11/24	31269	1/10, net 30	76	11	836
	Totals		365		$5,234

A physical inventory on December 31, 2007, reveals that 100 footballs were in stock. The bookkeeper informs you that all the discounts were taken. Assume that Howie Long Shop uses the invoice price less discount for recording purchases.

Instructions

(a) Compute the December 31, 2007, inventory using the FIFO method.

(b) Compute the 2007 cost of goods sold using the LIFO method.

(c) What method would you recommend to the owner to minimize income taxes in 2007, using the inventory information for footballs as a guide?

(LO 6) **E8-21 (LIFO Effect)** The following example was provided to encourage the use of the LIFO method.

In a nutshell, LIFO subtracts inflation from inventory costs, deducts it from taxable income, and records it in a LIFO reserve account on the books. The LIFO benefit grows as inflation widens the gap between current-year and past-year (minus inflation) inventory costs. This gap is:

	With LIFO	Without LIFO
Revenues	$3,200,000	$3,200,000
Cost of goods sold	2,800,000	2,800,000
Operating expenses	150,000	150,000
Operating income	250,000	250,000
LIFO adjustment	40,000	0
Taxable income	$210,000	$250,000
Income taxes @ 36%	$ 75,600	$ 90,000
Cash flow	$174,400	$160,000
Extra cash	$14,400	0
Increased cash flow	9%	0%

Instructions

(a) Explain what is meant by the LIFO reserve account.

(b) How does LIFO subtract inflation from inventory costs?

(c) Explain how the cash flow of $174,400 in this example was computed. Explain why this amount may not be correct.

(d) Why does a company that uses LIFO have extra cash? Explain whether this situation will always exist.

(LO 5, 8) **E8-22 (Alternative Inventory Methods—Comprehensive)** Tori Amos Corporation began operations on December 1, 2006. The only inventory transaction in 2006 was the purchase of inventory on December 10, 2006, at a cost of $20 per unit. None of this inventory was sold in 2006. Relevant information is as follows.

Ending inventory units		
December 31, 2006		100
December 31, 2007, by purchase date		
December 2, 2007	100	
July 20, 2007	50	150

During the year the following purchases and sales were made.

Purchases		Sales	
March 15	300 units at $24	April 10	200
July 20	300 units at 25	August 20	300
September 4	200 units at 28	November 18	150
December 2	100 units at 30	December 12	200

The company uses the periodic inventory method.

Instructions

(a) Determine ending inventory under (1) specific identification, (2) FIFO, (3) LIFO and (4) average cost.

(b) Determine ending inventory using dollar-value LIFO. Assume that the December 2, 2007, purchase cost is the current cost of inventory. (*Hint:* The beginning inventory is the base layer priced at $20 per unit.)

(LO 8) **E8-23 (Dollar-Value LIFO)** Oasis Company has used the dollar-value LIFO method for inventory cost determination for many years. The following data were extracted from Oasis' records.

Date	Price Index	Ending Inventory at Base Prices	Ending Inventory at Dollar-Value LIFO
December 31, 2005	105	$92,000	$92,600
December 31, 2006	?	97,000	98,350

Instructions
Calculate the index used for 2006 that yielded the above results.

(LO 8) **E8-24 (Dollar-Value LIFO)** The dollar-value LIFO method was adopted by Enya Corp. on January 1, 2007. Its inventory on that date was $160,000. On December 31, 2007, the inventory at prices existing on that date amounted to $140,000. The price level at January 1, 2007, was 100, and the price level at December 31, 2007, was 112.

Instructions
(a) Compute the amount of the inventory at December 31, 2007, under the dollar-value LIFO method.
(b) On December 31, 2008, the inventory at prices existing on that date was $172,500, and the price level was 115. Compute the inventory on that date under the dollar-value LIFO method.

(LO 8) **E8-25 (Dollar-Value LIFO)** Presented below is information related to Dino Radja Company.

Date	Ending Inventory (End-of-Year Prices)	Price Index
December 31, 2004	$ 80,000	100
December 31, 2005	115,500	105
December 31, 2006	108,000	120
December 31, 2007	122,200	130
December 31, 2008	154,000	140
December 31, 2009	176,900	145

Instructions
Compute the ending inventory for Dino Radja Company for 2004 through 2009 using the dollar-value LIFO method.

(LO 8) **E8-26 (Dollar-Value LIFO)** The following information relates to the Jimmy Johnson Company.

Date	Ending Inventory (End-of-Year Prices)	Price Index
December 31, 2003	$ 70,000	100
December 31, 2004	90,300	105
December 31, 2005	95,120	116
December 31, 2006	105,600	120
December 31, 2007	100,000	125

Instructions
Use the dollar-value LIFO method to compute the ending inventory for Johnson Company for 2003 through 2007.

See the book's website, www.wiley.com/college/kieso, for Additional Exercises.

PROBLEMS

(LO 4, 5, 8) **P8-1 (Various Inventory Issues)** The following independent situations relate to inventory accounting.

1. Jag Co. purchased goods with a list price of $150,000, subject to trade discounts of 20% and 10%, with no cash discounts allowable. How much should Jag Co. record as the cost of these goods?

2. Francis Company's inventory of $1,100,000 at December 31, 2006, was based on a physical count of goods priced at cost and before any year-end adjustments relating to the following items.
   a. Goods shipped from a vendor f.o.b. shipping point on December 24, 2006, at an invoice cost of $69,000 to Francis Company were received on January 4, 2007.
   b. The physical count included $29,000 of goods billed to Sakic Corp. f.o.b. shipping point on December 31, 2006. The carrier picked up these goods on January 3, 2007.
   What amount should Francis report as inventory on its balance sheet?

3. Mark Messier Corp. had 1,500 units of part M.O. on hand May 1, 2006, costing $21 each. Purchases of part M.O. during May were as follows.

	Units	Unit Cost
May 9	2,000	$22.00
17	3,500	23.00
26	1,000	24.00

A physical count on May 31, 2006, shows 2,100 units of part M.O. on hand. Using the FIFO method, what is the cost of part M.O. inventory at May 31, 2006? Using the LIFO method, what is the inventory cost? Using the average cost method, what is the inventory cost?

4. Forsberg Company adopted the dollar-value LIFO method on January 1, 2006 (using internal price indexes and multiple pools). The following data are available for inventory pool A for the 2 years following adoption of LIFO.

Inventory	At Base-Year Cost	At Current-Year Cost
1/1/06	$200,000	$200,000
12/31/06	240,000	252,000
12/31/07	256,000	286,720

Computing an internal price index and using the dollar-value LIFO method, at what amount should the inventory be reported at December 31, 2007?

5. Eric Lindros Inc., a retail store chain, had the following information in its general ledger for the year 2007.

Merchandise purchased for resale	$909,400
Interest on notes payable to vendors	8,700
Purchase returns	16,500
Freight-in	22,000
Freight-out	17,100
Cash discounts on purchases	6,800

What is Lindros' inventoriable cost for 2007?

Instructions
Answer each of the preceding questions about inventories, and explain your answers.

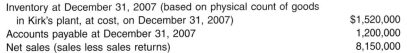

(LO 4) **P8-2** **(Inventory Adjustments)** James T. Kirk Company, a manufacturer of small tools, provided the following information from its accounting records for the year ended December 31, 2007.

Inventory at December 31, 2007 (based on physical count of goods in Kirk's plant, at cost, on December 31, 2007)	$1,520,000
Accounts payable at December 31, 2007	1,200,000
Net sales (sales less sales returns)	8,150,000

Additional information is as follows.

1. Included in the physical count were tools billed to a customer f.o.b. shipping point on December 31, 2007. These tools had a cost of $31,000 and were billed at $40,000. The shipment was on Kirk's loading dock waiting to be picked up by the common carrier.
2. Goods were in transit from a vendor to Kirk on December 31, 2007. The invoice cost was $71,000, and the goods were shipped f.o.b. shipping point on December 29, 2007.
3. Work in process inventory costing $30,000 was sent to an outside processor for plating on December 30, 2007.
4. Tools returned by customers and held pending inspection in the returned goods area on December 31, 2007, were not included in the physical count. On January 8, 2008, the tools costing $32,000 were inspected and returned to inventory. Credit memos totaling $47,000 were issued to the customers on the same date.
5. Tools shipped to a customer f.o.b. destination on December 26, 2007, were in transit at December 31, 2007, and had a cost of $21,000. Upon notification of receipt by the customer on January 2, 2008, Kirk issued a sales invoice for $42,000.
6. Goods, with an invoice cost of $27,000, received from a vendor at 5:00 p.m. on December 31, 2007, were recorded on a receiving report dated January 2, 2008. The goods were not included in the physical count, but the invoice was included in accounts payable at December 31, 2007.
7. Goods received from a vendor on December 26, 2007, were included in the physical count. However, the related $56,000 vendor invoice was not included in accounts payable at December 31, 2007, because the accounts payable copy of the receiving report was lost.

8. On January 3, 2008, a monthly freight bill in the amount of $6,000 was received. The bill specifically related to merchandise purchased in December 2007, one-half of which was still in the inventory at December 31, 2007. The freight charges were not included in either the inventory or in accounts payable at December 31, 2007.

Instructions

Using the format shown below, prepare a schedule of adjustments as of December 31, 2007, to the initial amounts per Kirk's accounting records. Show separately the effect, if any, of each of the eight transactions on the December 31, 2007, amounts. If the transactions would have no effect on the initial amount shown, enter NONE.

	Inventory	Accounts Payable	Net Sales
Initial amounts	$1,520,000	$1,200,000	$8,150,000
Adjustments—increase (decrease)			
1			
2			
3			
4			
5			
6			
7			
8			
Total adjustments			
Adjusted amounts	$	$	$

(AICPA adapted)

(LO 4) **P8-3 (Purchases Recorded Gross and Net)** Some of the transactions of William Dubois Company during August are listed below. Dubois uses the periodic inventory method.

August 10 Purchased merchandise on account, $9,000, terms 2/10, n/30.
    13 Returned part of the purchase of August 10, $1,200, and received credit on account.
    15 Purchased merchandise on account, $12,000, terms 1/10, n/60.
    25 Purchased merchandise on account, $15,000, terms 2/10, n/30.
    28 Paid invoice of August 15 in full.

Instructions

(a) Assuming that purchases are recorded at gross amounts and that discounts are to be recorded when taken:
  (1) Prepare general journal entries to record the transactions.
  (2) Describe how the various items would be shown in the financial statements.
(b) Assuming that purchases are recorded at net amounts and that discounts lost are treated as financial expenses:
  (1) Prepare general journal entries to enter the transactions.
  (2) Prepare the adjusting entry necessary on August 31 if financial statements are to be prepared at that time.
  (3) Describe how the various items would be shown in the financial statements.
(c) Which of the two methods do you prefer and why?

(LO 2, 5) **P8-4 (Compute FIFO, LIFO, and Average Cost—Periodic and Perpetual)** Taos Company's record of transactions concerning part X for the month of April was as follows.

Purchases		Sales	
April 1 (balance on hand)	100 @ $5.00	April 5	300
4	400 @ 5.10	12	200
11	300 @ 5.30	27	800
18	200 @ 5.35	28	100
26	500 @ 5.60		
30	200 @ 5.80		

Instructions

(a) Compute the inventory at April 30 on each of the following bases. Assume that perpetual inventory records are kept in units only. Carry unit costs to the nearest cent.
  (1) First-in, first-out (FIFO).

(2) Last-in, first-out (LIFO).

(3) Average cost.

(b) If the perpetual inventory record is kept in dollars, and costs are computed at the time of each withdrawal, what amount would be shown as ending inventory in 1, 2, and 3 above? Carry average unit costs to four decimal places.

(LO 2, 5) **P8-5** **(Compute FIFO, LIFO and Average Cost—Periodic and Perpetual)** Some of the information found on a detail inventory card for David Letterman Inc. for the first month of operations is as follows.

Date	Received No. of Units	Received Unit Cost	Issued, No. of Units	Balance, No. of Units
January 2	1,200	$3.00		1,200
7			700	500
10	600	3.20		1,100
13			500	600
18	1,000	3.30	300	1,300
20			1,100	200
23	1,300	3.40		1,500
26			800	700
28	1,500	3.60		2,200
31			1,300	900

[handwritten: Total 5600 unita / 900 units FI / 4700 units cost]

Instructions

(a) From these data compute the ending inventory on each of the following bases. Assume that perpetual inventory records are kept in units only. Carry unit costs to the nearest cent and ending inventory to the nearest dollar.

(1) First-in, first-out (FIFO).

(2) Last-in, first-out (LIFO).

(3) Average cost.

(b) If the perpetual inventory record is kept in dollars, and costs are computed at the time of each withdrawal, would the amounts shown as ending inventory in 1, 2, and 3 above be the same? Explain and compute.

(LO 2, 5) **P8-6** **(Compute FIFO, LIFO, Average Cost—Periodic and Perpetual)** Iowa Company is a multiproduct firm. Presented below is information concerning one of its products, the Hawkeye.

Date	Transaction	Quantity	Price/Cost
1/1	Beginning inventory	1,000	$12
2/4	Purchase	2,000	18
2/20	Sale	2,500	30
4/2	Purchase	3,000	23
11/4	Sale	2,000	33

Instructions

Compute cost of goods sold, assuming Iowa uses:

(a) Periodic system, FIFO cost flow.

(b) Perpetual system, FIFO cost flow.

(c) Periodic system, LIFO cost flow.

(d) Perpetual system, LIFO cost flow.

(e) Periodic system, weighted-average cost flow.

(f) Perpetual system, moving-average cost flow.

(LO 5) **P8-7** **(Financial Statement Effects of FIFO and LIFO)** The management of Maine Company has asked its accounting department to describe the effect upon the company's financial position and its income statements of accounting for inventories on the LIFO rather than the FIFO basis during 2007 and 2008. The accounting department is to assume that the change to LIFO would have been effective on January 1, 2007, and that the initial LIFO base would have been the inventory value on December 31, 2006. Presented below are the company's financial statements and other data for the years 2007 and 2008 when the FIFO method was employed.

	Financial Position as of		
	12/31/06	12/31/07	12/31/08
Cash	$ 90,000	$130,000	$ 141,600
Accounts receivable	80,000	100,000	120,000
Inventory	120,000	140,000	180,000
Other assets	160,000	170,000	200,000
Total assets	$450,000	$540,000	$ 641,600

[handwritten: FIFO   FIFO]

Accounts payable	$ 40,000	$ 60,000	$ 80,000
Other liabilities	70,000	80,000	110,000
Common stock	200,000	200,000	200,000
Retained earnings	140,000	200,000	251,600
Total liabilities and equity	$450,000	$540,000	$ 641,600

215,600

	Income for Years Ended	
	12/31/07	12/31/08
Sales	$900,000	$1,350,000
Less: Cost of goods sold	505,000	770,000
Other expenses	205,000	304,000
	710,000	1,074,000
Income before income taxes	190,000	276,000
Income taxes (40%)	76,000	110,400
Net income	$114,000	$ 165,600

FIFO   FIFO

Other data:

1. Inventory on hand at December 31, 2006, consisted of 40,000 units valued at $3.00 each.
2. Sales (all units sold at the same price in a given year):

    2007—150,000 units @ $6.00 each   2008—180,000 units @ $7.50 each

3. Purchases (all units purchased at the same price in given year):

    2007—150,000 units @ $3.50 each   2008—180,000 units @ $4.50 each

4. Income taxes at the effective rate of 40% are paid on December 31 each year.

Instructions

Name the account(s) presented in the financial statements that would have different amounts for 2008 if LIFO rather than FIFO had been used, and state the new amount for each account that is named. Show computations.

(CMA adapted)

(LO 8) **P8-8 (Dollar-Value LIFO)** Falcon's Televisions produces television sets in three categories: portable, midsize, and flat-screen. On January 1, 2006, Falcon adopted dollar-value LIFO and decided to use a single inventory pool. The company's January 1 inventory consists of:

Category	Quantity	Cost per Unit	Total Cost
Portable	6,000	$100	$ 600,000
Midsize	8,000	250	2,000,000
Flat-screen	3,000	400	1,200,000
	17,000		$3,800,000

During 2006, the company had the following purchases and sales.

current price index

Category	Quantity Purchased	Cost per Unit	Quantity Sold	Selling Price per Unit
Portable	15,000	$120	14,000	$150
Midsize	20,000	300	24,000	405
Flat-screen	10,000	460	6,000	600
	45,000		44,000	

Instructions

(Round to four decimals.)

(a) Compute ending inventory, cost of goods sold, and gross profit.
(b) Assume the company uses three inventory pools instead of one. Repeat instruction (a).

(LO 8) **P8-9 (Internal Indexes—Dollar-Value LIFO)** On January 1, 2006, Adis Abeba Wholesalers Inc. adopted the dollar-value LIFO inventory method for income tax and external financial reporting purposes. However, Abeba continued to use the FIFO inventory method for internal accounting and management purposes. In applying the LIFO method, Abeba uses internal conversion price indexes and the multiple pools approach under which substantially identical inventory items are grouped into LIFO inventory pools. The following data were available for inventory pool no. 1, which comprises products A and B, for the 2 years following the adoption of LIFO.

	FIFO Basis per Records		
	Units	Unit Cost	Total Cost
Inventory, 1/1/06			
Product A	10,000	$30	$300,000
Product B	9,000	25	225,000
			$525,000
Inventory, 12/31/06			
Product A	17,000	35	$595,000
Product B	9,000	26	234,000
			$829,000
Inventory, 12/31/07			
Product A	13,000	40	$520,000
Product B	10,000	32	320,000
			$840,000

Instructions

(a) Prepare a schedule to compute the internal conversion price indexes for 2006 and 2007. Round indexes to two decimal places.

(b) Prepare a schedule to compute the inventory amounts at December 31, 2006 and 2007, using the dollar-value LIFO inventory method.

(AICPA adapted)

(LO 8) **P8-10 (Internal Indexes—Dollar-Value LIFO)** Presented below is information related to Mellon Collie Corporation for the last 3 years.

Item	Quantities in Ending Inventories	**Base-Year Cost**		**Current-Year Cost**	
		Unit Cost	Amount	Unit Cost	Amount
December 31, 2005					
A	9,000	$2.00	$18,000	$2.40	$21,600
B	6,000	3.00	18,000	3.55	21,300
C	4,000	5.00	20,000	5.40	21,600
		Totals	$56,000		$64,500
December 31, 2006					
A	9,000	$2.00	$18,000	$2.60	$23,400
B	6,800	3.00	20,400	3.75	25,500
C	6,000	5.00	30,000	6.40	38,400
		Totals	$68,400		$87,300
December 31, 2007					
A	8,000	$2.00	$16,000	$2.70	$21,600
B	8,000	3.00	24,000	4.00	32,000
C	6,000	5.00	30,000	6.20	37,200
		Totals	$70,000		$90,800

Instructions

Compute the ending inventories under the dollar-value LIFO method for 2005, 2006, and 2007. The base period is January 1, 2005, and the beginning inventory cost at that date was $45,000. Compute indexes to two decimal places.

(LO 8) **P8-11 (Dollar-Value LIFO)** Warren Dunn Company cans a variety of vegetable-type soups. Recently, the company decided to value its inventories using dollar-value LIFO pools. The clerk who accounts for inventories does not understand how to value the inventory pools using this new method, so, as a private consultant, you have been asked to teach him how this new method works.

He has provided you with the following information about purchases made over a 6-year period.

Date	Ending Inventory (End-of-Year Prices)	Price Index
Dec. 31, 2003	$ 80,000	100
Dec. 31, 2004	115,500	105
Dec. 31, 2005	108,000	120
Dec. 31, 2006	131,300	130
Dec. 31, 2007	154,000	140
Dec. 31, 2008	174,000	145

You have already explained to him how this inventory method is maintained, but he would feel better about it if you were to leave him detailed instructions explaining how these calculations are done and why he needs to put all inventories at a base-year value.

Instructions

(a) Compute the ending inventory for Warren Dunn Company for 2003 through 2008 using dollar-value LIFO.

(b) Using your computation schedules as your illustration, write a step-by-step set of instructions explaining how the calculations are done. Begin your explanation by briefly explaining the theory behind this inventory method, including the purpose of putting all amounts into base-year price levels.

CONCEPTS FOR ANALYSIS

CA8-1 (Inventoriable Costs) You are asked to travel to Milwaukee to observe and verify the inventory of the Milwaukee branch of one of your clients. You arrive on Thursday, December 30, and find that the inventory procedures have just been started. You spot a railway car on the sidetrack at the unloading door and ask the warehouse superintendent, Predrag Danilovic, how he plans to inventory the contents of the car. He responds, "We are not going to include the contents in the inventory."

Later in the day, you ask the bookkeeper for the invoice on the carload and the related freight bill. The invoice lists the various items, prices, and extensions of the goods in the car. You note that the carload was shipped December 24 from Albuquerque, f.o.b. Albuquerque, and that the total invoice price of the goods in the car was $35,300. The freight bill called for a payment of $1,500. Terms were net 30 days. The bookkeeper affirms the fact that this invoice is to be held for recording in January.

Instructions

(a) Does your client have a liability that should be recorded at December 31? Discuss.

(b) Prepare a journal entry(ies), if required, to reflect any accounting adjustment required. Assume a perpetual inventory system is used by your client.

(c) For what possible reason(s) might your client wish to postpone recording the transaction?

CA8-2 (Inventoriable Costs) Brian Erlacher, an inventory control specialist, is interested in better understanding the accounting for inventories. Although Brian understands the more sophisticated computer inventory control systems, he has little knowledge of how inventory cost is determined. In studying the records of Sherman Enterprises, which sells normal brand-name goods from its own store and on consignment through Lovey Smith Inc., he asks you to answer the following questions.

Instructions

(a) Should Sherman Enterprises include in its inventory normal brand-name goods purchased from its suppliers but not yet received if the terms of purchase are f.o.b. shipping point (manufacturer's plant)? Why?

(b) Should Sherman Enterprises include freight-in expenditures as an inventory cost? Why?

(c) If Sherman Enterprises purchases its goods on terms 2/10, net 30, should the purchases be recorded gross or net? Why?

(d) What are products on consignment? How should they be reported in the financial statements?

(AICPA adapted)

CA8-3 (Inventoriable Costs) Jack McDowell, the controller for McDowell Lumber Company, has recently hired you as assistant controller. He wishes to determine your expertise in the area of inventory accounting and therefore asks you to answer the following unrelated questions.

(a) A company is involved in the wholesaling and retailing of automobile tires for foreign cars. Most of the inventory is imported, and it is valued on the company's records at the actual inventory cost plus freight-in. At year-end, the warehousing costs are prorated over cost of goods sold and ending inventory. Are warehousing costs considered a product cost or a period cost?

(b) A certain portion of a company's "inventory" is composed of obsolete items. Should obsolete items that are not currently consumed in the production of "goods or services to be available for sale" be classified as part of inventory?

(c) A company purchases airplanes for sale to others. However, until they are sold, the company charters and services the planes. What is the proper way to report these airplanes in the company's financial statements?

(d) A company wants to buy coal deposits but does not want the financing for the purchase to be reported on its financial statements. The company therefore establishes a trust to acquire the coal deposits. The company agrees to buy the coal over a certain period of time at specified prices. The trust is able to finance the coal purchase and pay off the loan as it is paid by the company for the minerals. How should this transaction be reported?

CA8-4 **(Accounting Treatment of Purchase Discounts)** Wayne Gretzky Corp., a household appliances dealer, purchases its inventories from various suppliers. Gretzky has consistently stated its inventories at the lower of cost (FIFO) or market.

Instructions

Gretzky is considering alternate methods of accounting for the cash discounts it takes when paying its suppliers promptly. From a theoretical standpoint, discuss the acceptability of each of the following methods.

(a) Financial income when payments are made.
(b) Reduction of cost of goods sold for the period when payments are made.
(c) Direct reduction of purchase cost.

(AICPA adapted)

CA8-5 **(General Inventory Issues)** In January 2007, Wesley Crusher Inc. requested and secured permission from the commissioner of the Internal Revenue Service to compute inventories under the last-in, first-out (LIFO) method and elected to determine inventory cost under the dollar-value LIFO method. Crusher Inc. satisfied the commissioner that cost could be accurately determined by use of an index number computed from a representative sample selected from the company's single inventory pool.

Instructions

(a) Why should inventories be included in (1) a balance sheet and (2) the computation of net income?
(b) The Internal Revenue Code allows some accountable events to be considered differently for income tax reporting purposes and financial accounting purposes, while other accountable events must be reported the same for both purposes. Discuss why it might be desirable to report some accountable events differently for financial accounting purposes than for income tax reporting purposes.
(c) Discuss the ways and conditions under which the FIFO and LIFO inventory costing methods produce different inventory valuations. Do not discuss procedures for computing inventory cost.

(AICPA adapted)

CA8-6 **(LIFO Inventory Advantages)** Jean Honore, president of Fragonard Co., recently read an article that claimed that at least 100 of the country's largest 500 companies were either adopting or considering adopting the last-in, first-out (LIFO) method for valuing inventories. The article stated that the firms were switching to LIFO to (1) neutralize the effect of inflation in their financial statements, (2) eliminate inventory profits, and (3) reduce income taxes. Ms. Honore wonders if the switch would benefit her company.

Fragonard currently uses the first-in, first-out (FIFO) method of inventory valuation in its periodic inventory system. The company has a high inventory turnover rate, and inventories represent a significant proportion of the assets.

Ms. Honore has been told that the LIFO system is more costly to operate and will provide little benefit to companies with high turnover. She intends to use the inventory method that is best for the company in the long run rather than selecting a method just because it is the current fad.

Instructions

(a) Explain to Ms. Honore what "inventory profits" are and how the LIFO method of inventory valuation could reduce them.
(b) Explain to Ms. Honore the conditions that must exist for Fragonard Co. to receive tax benefits from a switch to the LIFO method.

CA8-7 **(Average Cost, FIFO, and LIFO)** Prepare a memorandum containing responses to the following items.

(a) Describe the cost flow assumptions used in average cost, FIFO, and LIFO methods of inventory valuation.
(b) Distinguish between weighted-average cost and moving-average cost for inventory costing purposes.
(c) Identify the effects on both the balance sheet and the income statement of using the LIFO method instead of the FIFO method for inventory costing purposes over a substantial time period when purchase prices of inventoriable items are rising. State why these effects take place.

CA8-8 (LIFO Application and Advantages) Neshki Corporation is a medium-sized manufacturing company with two divisions and three subsidiaries, all located in the United States. The Metallic Division manufactures metal castings for the automotive industry, and the Plastic Division produces small plastic items for electrical products and other uses. The three subsidiaries manufacture various products for other industrial users.

Neshki Corporation plans to change from the lower of first-in, first-out (FIFO) cost or market method of inventory valuation to the last-in, first-out (LIFO) method of inventory valuation to obtain tax benefits. To make the method acceptable for tax purposes, the change also will be made for its annual financial statements.

Instructions
   (a) Describe the establishment of and subsequent pricing procedures for each of the following LIFO inventory methods.
      (1) LIFO applied to units of product when the periodic inventory system is used.
      (2) Application of the dollar-value method to LIFO units of product.
   (b) Discuss the specific advantages and disadvantages of using the dollar-value LIFO application as compared to specific goods LIFO (unit LIFO). Ignore income tax considerations.
   (c) Discuss the general advantages and disadvantages claimed for LIFO methods.

CA8-9 (Dollar-Value LIFO Issues) Maria Callas Co. is considering switching from the specific goods LIFO approach to the dollar-value LIFO approach. Because the financial personnel at Callas know very little about dollar-value LIFO, they ask you to answer the following questions.

   (a) What is a LIFO pool?
   (b) Is it possible to use a LIFO pool concept and not use dollar-value LIFO? Explain.
   (c) What is a LIFO liquidation?
   (d) How are price indexes used in the dollar-value LIFO method?
   (e) What are the advantages of dollar-value LIFO over specific goods LIFO?

CA8-10 (FIFO and LIFO) Günter Grass Company is considering changing its inventory valuation method from FIFO to LIFO because of the potential tax savings. However, the management wishes to consider all of the effects on the company, including its reported performance, before making the final decision.

The inventory account, currently valued on the FIFO basis, consists of 1,000,000 units at $7 per unit on January 1, 2007. There are 1,000,000 shares of common stock outstanding as of January 1, 2007, and the cash balance is $400,000.

The company has made the following forecasts for the period 2007–2009.

	2007	2008	2009
Unit sales (in millions of units)	1.1	1.0	1.3
Sales price per unit	$10	$10	$12
Unit purchases (in millions of units)	1.0	1.1	1.2
Purchase price per unit	$7	$8	$9
Annual depreciation (in thousands of dollars)	$300	$300	$300
Cash dividends per share	$0.15	$0.15	$0.15
Cash payments for additions to and replacement of plant and equipment (in thousands of dollars)	$350	$350	$350
Income tax rate	40%	40%	40%
Operating expenses (exclusive of depreciation) as a percent of sales	15%	15%	15%
Common shares outstanding (in millions)	1	1	1

Instructions
   (a) Prepare a schedule that illustrates and compares the following data for Günter Grass Company under the FIFO and the LIFO inventory method for 2007–2009. Assume the company would begin LIFO at the beginning of 2007.
      (1) Year-end inventory balances.   **(3)** Earnings per share.
      (2) Annual net income after taxes.   **(4)** Cash balance.
      Assume all sales are collected in the year of sale and all purchases, operating expenses, and taxes are paid during the year incurred.
   (b) Using the data above, your answer to (a), and any additional issues you believe need to be considered, prepare a report that recommends whether or not Günter Grass Company should change to the LIFO inventory method. Support your conclusions with appropriate arguments.

(CMA adapted)

CA8-11 (LIFO Choices) Gamble Company uses the LIFO method for inventory costing. In an effort to lower net income, company president Oscar Gamble tells the plant accountant to take the unusual step of recommending to the purchasing department a large purchase of inventory at year-end. The price of the item to be purchased has nearly doubled during the year, and the item represents a major portion of inventory value.

Instructions
Answer the following questions.

(a) Identify the major stakeholders. If the plant accountant recommends the purchase, what are the consequences?

(b) If Gamble Company were using the FIFO method of inventory costing, would Oscar Gamble give the same order? Why or why not?

USING YOUR JUDGMENT

Financial Statement Analysis Cases

Case 1 T J International

T J International was founded in 1969 as Trus Joist International. The firm, a manufacturer of specialty building products, has its headquarters in Boise, Idaho. The company, through its partnership in the Trus Joist MacMillan joint venture, develops and manufactures engineered lumber. This product is a high-quality substitute for structural lumber, and uses lower-grade wood and materials formerly considered waste. The company also is majority owner of the Outlook Window Partnership, which is a consortium of three wood and vinyl window manufacturers.

Following is T J International's adapted income statement and information concerning inventories from its annual report.

T J International

Sales	$618,876,000
Cost of goods sold	475,476,000
Gross profit	143,400,000
Selling and administrative expenses	102,112,000
Income from operations	41,288,000
Other expense	24,712,000
Income before income tax	16,576,000
Income taxes	7,728,000
Net income	$ 8,848,000

Inventories. Inventories are valued at the lower of cost or market and include material, labor, and production overhead costs. Inventories consisted of the following:

	Current Year	Prior Year
Finished goods	$27,512,000	$23,830,000
Raw materials and work-in-progress	34,363,000	33,244,000
	61,875,000	57,074,000
Reduction to LIFO cost	(5,263,000)	(3,993,000)
	$56,612,000	$53,081,000

The last-in, first-out (LIFO) method is used for determining the cost of lumber, veneer, Microllam lumber, TJI joists, and open web joists. Approximately 35 percent of total inventories at the end of the current year were valued using the LIFO method. The first-in, first-out (FIFO) method is used to determine the cost of all other inventories.

Instructions

(a) How much would income before taxes have been if FIFO costing had been used to value all inventories?

(b) If the income tax rate is 46.6%, what would income tax have been if FIFO costing had been used to value all inventories? In your opinion, is this difference in net income between the two methods material? Explain.

(c) Does the use of a different costing system for different types of inventory mean that there is a different physical flow of goods among the different types of inventory? Explain.

Case 2 Noven Pharmaceuticals, Inc.

Noven Pharmaceuticals, Inc., headquartered in Miami, Florida, describes itself in a recent annual report as follows.

Noven Pharmaceuticals, Inc.

Noven is a place of ideas—a company where scientific excellence and state-of-the-art manufacturing combine to create new answers to human needs. Our transdermal delivery systems speed drugs painlessly and effortlessly into the bloodstream by means of a simple skin patch. This technology has proven applications in estrogen replacement, but at Noven we are developing a variety of systems incorporating bestselling drugs that fight everything from asthma, anxiety and dental pain to cancer, heart disease and neurological illness. Our research portfolio also includes new technologies, such as iontophoresis, in which drugs are delivered through the skin by means of electrical currents, as well as products that could satisfy broad consumer needs, such as our anti-microbial mouthrinse.

Noven also reported in its annual report that its activities to date have consisted of product development efforts, some of which have been independent and some of which have been completed in conjunction with **Rhone-Poulenc Rorer (RPR)** and **Ciba-Geigy**. The revenues so far have consisted of money received from licensing fees, "milestone" payments (payments made under licensing agreements when certain stages of the development of a certain product have been completed), and interest on its investments. The company expects that it will have significant revenue in the upcoming fiscal year from the launch of its first product, a transdermal estrogen delivery system.

The current assets portion of Noven's balance sheet follows.

Cash and cash equivalents	$12,070,272
Securities held to maturity	23,445,070
Inventory of supplies	1,264,553
Prepaid and other current assets	825,159
Total current assets	$37,605,054

Inventory of supplies is recorded at the lower of cost (first-in, first-out) or net realizable value and consists mainly of supplies for research and development.

Instructions

(a) What would you expect the physical flow of goods for a pharmaceutical manufacturer to be most like: FIFO, LIFO, or random (flow of goods does not follow a set pattern)? Explain.

(b) What are some of the factors that Noven should consider as it selects an inventory measurement method?

(c) Suppose that Noven had $49,000 in an inventory of transdermal estrogen delivery patches. These patches are from an initial production run, and will be sold during the coming year. Why do you think that this amount is not shown in a separate inventory account? In which of the accounts shown is the inventory likely to be? At what point will the inventory be transferred to a separate inventory account?

Case 3 Albertson's

Albertson's reported that its inventory turnover ratio increased from 8.2 times in 2003 to 8.4 times in 2004. The following data appear in Albertson's annual report.

	Jan. 31, 2002	Jan. 30, 2003	Jan. 29, 2004
Total revenues	$36,605	$35,626	$35,436
Cost of sales	26,179	25,248	25,306
Year-end inventories of FIFO	3,793	3,256	3,611
Year-end inventories of LIFO	3,196	2,973	3,035

(a) Compute Albertson's inventory turnover ratios for 2003 and 2004, using:
   (1) Cost of sales and LIFO inventory.
   (2) Cost of sales and FIFO inventory.
(b) Some firms calculate inventory turnover using sales rather than cost of goods sold in the numerator. Calculate Albertson's 2003 and 2004 turnover, using:
   (1) Sales and LIFO inventory.
   (2) Sales and FIFO inventory.
(c) Describe the method that Albertson's appears to use.
(d) State which method you would choose to evaluate Albertson's performance. Justify your choice.

Research Cases

Case 1

As indicated in the chapter, the FIFO and LIFO inventory methods can result in significantly different income statement and balance sheet figures. However, it is possible to convert income for a LIFO firm to its FIFO-based equivalent. To assist financial statement users in this task, firms using LIFO are required to disclose in their footnotes the "LIFO reserve" (LR)—i.e., the difference between the inventory balance shown on the balance sheet and the amount that would have been reported had the firm used current cost (or FIFO), as illustrated for **Brown Shoe Company** on page 385.

The following equation can be used to convert LIFO cost of goods sold (COGS) to FIFO COGS.

$$COGS_{FIFO} = COGS_{LIFO} - LIFO \text{ effect}$$

where

$$LIFO \text{ effect} = [LR_{ending} - LR_{beginning}]$$

The following equation can be used to convert LIFO net income (NI) to FIFO net income.

$$NI_{FIFO} = NI_{LIFO} + (LIFO \text{ effect}) (1 - \text{tax rate})$$

Instructions

Obtain the annual report of a firm that reports a LIFO reserve in its footnotes.

(a) Identify the LIFO reserve at the two most recent balance sheet dates.
(b) Determine the LIFO effect during the most recent year.
(c) By how much would cost of goods sold during the most recent year change if the firm used FIFO?
(d) By how much would net income during the most recent year change if the firm used FIFO? (*Hint:* To estimate the tax rate, divide income tax expense by income before taxes.)

Case 2

The "Fortune 500" issue of *Fortune* magazine can serve as a useful reference. This annual issue, generally appearing in late April or early May, contains a great deal of information regarding the largest U.S. industrial and service companies.

Instructions

Examine the most recent edition and answer the following questions.

(a) Identify the three largest U.S. corporations in terms of revenue, profit, assets, market value, and employees.
(b) Identify the largest corporation in your state (by total revenue).

Professional Research: Financial Accounting and Reporting

In conducting year-end inventory counts, your audit team is debating the impact of the client's right of return policy both on inventory valuation and revenue recognition. The assistant controller argues that there is no need to worry about the return policies since they have not changed in a while. The audit senior wants a more authoritative answer and has asked you to conduct some research of the authoritative literature, before she presses the point with the client.

Instructions

Using the **Financial Accounting Research System (FARS)**, respond to the following items. (Provide text strings used in your search.)

(a) Which statement addresses revenue recognition when right of return exists?
(b) When is this statement important for a company?

(c) Sales with high rates of return can ultimately cause inventory to be misstated. Why are returns allowed? Should different industries be able to make different types of return policies?

(d) In what situations would a reasonable estimate of returns be difficult to make?

Professional Simulation

In this simulation you are asked to address questions regarding inventory valuation and measurement. Prepare responses to all parts.

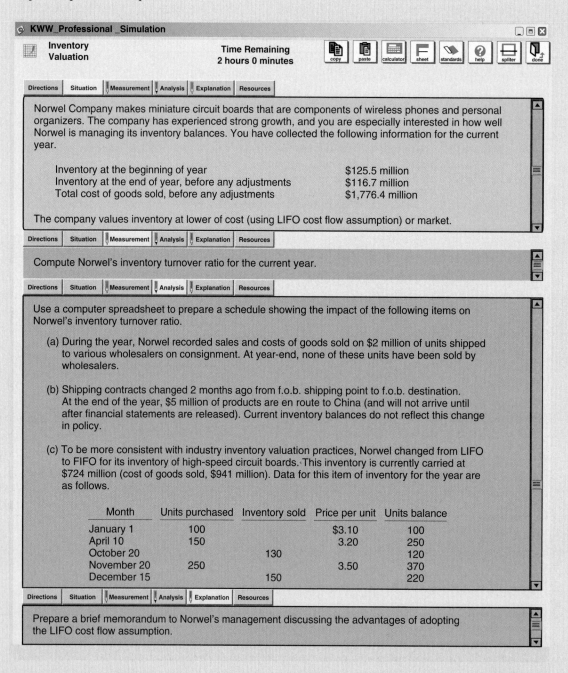

KWW_Professional _Simulation

Inventory Valuation

Time Remaining
2 hours 0 minutes

copy · paste · calculator · sheet · standards · help · splitter · done

Directions · Situation · Measurement · Analysis · Explanation · Resources

Norwel Company makes miniature circuit boards that are components of wireless phones and personal organizers. The company has experienced strong growth, and you are especially interested in how well Norwel is managing its inventory balances. You have collected the following information for the current year.

Inventory at the beginning of year	$125.5 million
Inventory at the end of year, before any adjustments	$116.7 million
Total cost of goods sold, before any adjustments	$1,776.4 million

The company values inventory at lower of cost (using LIFO cost flow assumption) or market.

Compute Norwel's inventory turnover ratio for the current year.

Use a computer spreadsheet to prepare a schedule showing the impact of the following items on Norwel's inventory turnover ratio.

(a) During the year, Norwel recorded sales and costs of goods sold on $2 million of units shipped to various wholesalers on consignment. At year-end, none of these units have been sold by wholesalers.

(b) Shipping contracts changed 2 months ago from f.o.b. shipping point to f.o.b. destination. At the end of the year, $5 million of products are en route to China (and will not arrive until after financial statements are released). Current inventory balances do not reflect this change in policy.

(c) To be more consistent with industry inventory valuation practices, Norwel changed from LIFO to FIFO for its inventory of high-speed circuit boards. This inventory is currently carried at $724 million (cost of goods sold, $941 million). Data for this item of inventory for the year are as follows.

Month	Units purchased	Inventory sold	Price per unit	Units balance
January 1	100		$3.10	100
April 10	150		3.20	250
October 20		130		120
November 20	250		3.50	370
December 15		150		220

Directions · Situation · Measurement · Analysis · Explanation · Resources

Prepare a brief memorandum to Norwel's management discussing the advantages of adopting the LIFO cost flow assumption.

Remember to check the book's companion website to find additional resources for this chapter.

wiley.com/college/kieso

INVENTORIES: ADDITIONAL VALUATION ISSUES

What Do Inventory Changes Tell Us?

Department stores face an ongoing challenge: They need to keep enough inventory to meet customer demand, but not to accumulate too much inventory. If demand falls short of expectations, the department store may be forced to reduce prices on its existing inventory, thus losing sales revenue.

For example, the following table shows recent annual sales and inventory trends for major retailers, compared to the prior year.

Company	Sales	Inventory
Nordstrom	+10.59%	+ 1.73%
Federated Department Stores	+ 2.40%	− 2.95%
JCPenney	+ 3.59%	+ 0.41%
Wal-Mart	+11.63%	+ 9.06%
May Department Stores	+ 8.23%	+13.34%
Target	+11.62%	+18.83%
Best Buy	+17.21%	+25.52%
Circuit City	− 1.97%	+ 7.63%
Sears	−12.22%	+ 4.01%

Source: Company reports, fiscal years 2003 and 2004.

For over half of these retailers, inventories grew faster than sales from one year to the next—a trend that should raise warning flags for investors. Rising levels of inventories indicate that fewer shoppers are turning out to buy merchandise compared to activity in the prior period. As one analyst remarked, ". . . when inventory grows faster than sales, profits drop." That is, when retailers face slower sales and growing inventory, markdowns in prices are usually not far behind. These markdowns, in turn, lead to lower sales revenue and income.

Bankruptcies of retailers like **Ames Department Stores**, **Montgomery Ward**, and **Bradlees Stores** indicate the consequences of poor inventory management. And more recently, **Kmart**, which filed for bankruptcy in January 2002 and has since been acquired by **Sears Holdings**, was in an inventory "Catch-22." In order to work out of bankruptcy, Kmart needed to keep its shelves stocked so that customers would continue to shop in its remaining stores. However, vendors who were worried about Kmart's ability to manage its inventory were reluctant to ship goods without assurances that they would get paid. Thus, investors, creditors, and vendors keep an eye on information about inventories in the retail industry.

Learning Objectives

After studying this chapter, you should be able to:

1 Describe and apply the lower-of-cost-or-market rule.

2 Explain when companies value inventories at net realizable value.

3 Explain when companies use the relative sales value method to value inventories.

4 Discuss accounting issues related to purchase commitments.

5 Determine ending inventory by applying the gross profit method.

6 Determine ending inventory by applying the retail inventory method.

7 Explain how to report and analyze inventory.

As our opening story indicates, information on inventories and changes in inventory helps to predict financial performance—in particular, profits. In this chapter we discuss some of the valuation and estimation concepts that companies use to develop relevant inventory information. The content and organization of the chapter are as follows.

LOWER-OF-COST-OR-MARKET

OBJECTIVE 1
Describe and apply the lower-of-cost-or-market rule.

Inventories are recorded at their cost. However, if inventory declines in value below its original cost, a major departure from the historical cost principle occurs. Whatever the reason for a decline—obsolescence, price-level changes, or damaged goods—a company should write down the inventory to market to report this loss. **A company abandons the historical cost principle when the future utility (revenue-producing ability) of the asset drops below its original cost.** Companies therefore **report inventories at the lower-of-cost-or-market** at each reporting period.

Illustration 9-1 shows how **Eastman Kodak** and **Best Buy** reported this information.

ILLUSTRATION 9-1
Lower-of-Cost-or-Market Disclosures

EASTMAN KODAK

Notes to Financial Statements

The company reduces the carrying value to a lower-of-cost-or-market basis for those items that are excess, obsolete, or slow moving based on management's analysis of inventory levels and future sales forecasts.

BEST BUY

Notes to Financial Statements

Merchandise inventories are recorded at the lower of average cost or market.

Recall that **cost** is the acquisition price of inventory computed using one of the historical cost-based methods—specific identification, average cost, FIFO, or LIFO. The term **market** in the phrase "the lower-of-cost-or-market" (LCM) generally means the cost to replace the item by purchase or reproduction. For a retailer like **Nordstrom**, the term "market" refers to the market in which it purchases goods, not the market in which it sells them. For a manufacturer like **William Wrigley Jr.**, the term "market" refers to the cost to reproduce. Thus the rule really means that **companies value goods at cost or cost to replace, whichever is lower**.

For example, say **Target** purchased a **Timex** calculator wristwatch for $30 for resale. Target can sell the wristwatch for $48.95 and replace it for $25. It should therefore value the wristwatch at $25 for inventory purposes under the lower-of-cost-or-market rule. Target can use the lower-of-cost-or-market rule of valuation after applying any of the cost flow methods discussed above to determine the inventory cost.

A departure from cost is justified because **a company should charge a loss of utility against revenues in the period in which the loss occurs**, not in the period of sale. Note also that the lower-of-cost-or-market method is **a conservative approach to inventory valuation**. That is, when doubt exists about the value of an asset, a company should use the lower value for the asset, which also reduces net income.

Lower-of-Cost-or-Market—Ceiling and Floor

Why use replacement cost to represent market value? Because a decline in the replacement cost of an item usually reflects or predicts a decline in selling price. Using replacement cost allows a company to maintain a consistent rate of gross profit on sales (normal profit margin). Sometimes, however, a reduction in the replacement cost of an item fails to indicate a corresponding reduction in its utility. This requires using two additional valuation limitations to value ending inventory—net realizable value and net realizable value less a normal profit margin.

Net realizable value (NRV) is the estimated selling price in the ordinary course of business, less reasonably predictable costs of completion and disposal (often referred to as net selling price). A normal profit margin is subtracted from that amount to arrive at **net realizable value less a normal profit margin**.

To illustrate, assume that Jerry Mander Corp. has unfinished inventory with a sales value of $1,000, estimated cost of completion of $300, and a normal profit margin of 10 percent of sales. Jerry Mander determines the following net realizable value.

Inventory—sales value	$1,000
Less: Estimated cost of completion and disposal	300
Net realizable value	700
Less: Allowance for normal profit margin (10% of sales)	100
Net realizable value less a normal profit margin	$ 600

ILLUSTRATION 9-2
Computation of Net Realizable Value

The general lower-of-cost-or-market rule is: A company values inventory at the lower-of-cost-or-market, with market limited to an amount that is not more than net realizable value or less than net realizable value less a normal profit margin.[1]

The **upper (ceiling)** is the net realizable value of inventory. The **lower (floor)** is the the net realizable value less a normal profit margin. What is the rationale for these two limitations? Establishing these limits for the value of the inventory prevents companies from over- or understating inventory.

---

[1]"Restatement and Revision of Accounting Research Bulletins," *Accounting Research Bulletin No. 43* (New York: AICPA, 1953), Ch. 4, par. 8.

The maximum limitation, **not to exceed the net realizable value (ceiling),** prevents overstatement of the value of obsolete, damaged, or shopworn inventories. That is, if the replacement cost of an item exceeds its net realizable value, a company should not report inventory at replacement cost. The company can receive only the selling price less cost of disposal. To report the inventory at replacement cost would result in an overstatement of inventory and understatement of the loss in the current period.

To illustrate, assume that **Staples** paid $1,000 for a color laser printer that it can now replace for $900. The printer's net realizable value is $700. At what amount should Staples report the laser printer in the financial statements? To report the replacement cost of $900 overstates the ending inventory and understates the loss for the period. Therefore, Staples should report the printer at $700.

The minimum limitation (floor) is **not to be less than net realizable value reduced by an allowance for an approximately normal profit margin.** The floor establishes a value below which a company should not price inventory, regardless of replacement cost. It makes no sense to price inventory below net realizable value less a normal margin. This minimum amount (floor) measures what the company can receive for the inventory and still earn a normal profit. Use of a floor deters understatement of inventory and overstatement of the loss in the current period.

Illustration 9-3 graphically presents the guidelines for valuing inventory at the lower-of-cost-or-market.

ILLUSTRATION 9-3
Inventory Valuation—
Lower of Cost or Market

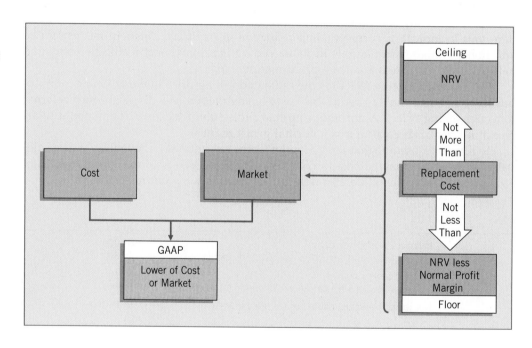

How Lower-of-Cost-or-Market Works

The **designated market value** is the amount that a company compares to cost. It is **always the middle value of three amounts**: replacement cost, net realizable value, and net realizable value less a normal profit margin. To illustrate how to compute designated market value, assume the information relative to the inventory of Regner Foods, Inc., as shown in Illustration 9-4 (on page 425).

Regner Foods then compares designated market value to cost to determine the lower-of-cost-or-market. It determines the final inventory value as shown in Illustration 9-5 (on page 425).

ILLUSTRATION 9-4
Computation of
Designated Market Value

Food	Replacement Cost	Net Realizable Value (Ceiling)	Net Realizable Value Less a Normal Profit Margin (Floor)	Designated Market Value
Spinach	$ 88,000	$120,000	$104,000	$104,000
Carrots	90,000	100,000	70,000	90,000
Cut beans	45,000	40,000	27,500	40,000
Peas	36,000	72,000	48,000	48,000
Mixed vegetables	105,000	92,000	80,000	92,000

Designated Market Value Decision:

Spinach	Net realizable value less a normal profit margin is selected because it is the middle value.
Carrots	Replacement cost is selected because it is the middle value.
Cut beans	Net realizable value is selected because it is the middle value.
Peas	Net realizable value less a normal profit margin is selected because it is the middle value.
Mixed vegetables	Net realizable value is selected because it is the middle value.

ILLUSTRATION 9-5
Determining Final
Inventory Value

Food	Cost	Replacement Cost	Net Realizable Value (Ceiling)	Net Realizable Value Less a Normal Profit Margin (Floor)	Designated Market Value	Final Inventory Value
Spinach	$ 80,000	$ 88,000	$120,000	$104,000	$104,000	$ 80,000
Carrots	100,000	90,000	100,000	70,000	90,000	90,000
Cut beans	50,000	45,000	40,000	27,500	40,000	40,000
Peas	90,000	36,000	72,000	48,000	48,000	48,000
Mixed vegetables	95,000	105,000	92,000	80,000	92,000	92,000
						$350,000

Final Inventory Value:

Spinach	Cost ($80,000) is selected because it is lower than designated market value (net realizable value less a normal profit margin).
Carrots	Designated market value (replacement cost, $90,000) is selected because it is lower than cost.
Cut beans	Designated market value (net realizable value, $40,000) is selected because it is lower than cost.
Peas	Designated market value (net realizable value less a normal profit margin, $48,000) is selected because it is lower than cost.
Mixed vegetables	Designated market value (net realizable value, $92,000) is selected because it is lower than cost.

The application of the lower-of-cost-or-market rule incorporates only losses in value that occur in the normal course of business from such causes as style changes, shift in demand, or regular shop wear. A company reduces damaged or deteriorated goods to net realizable value. When material, it may carry such goods in separate inventory accounts.

Methods of Applying Lower-of-Cost-or-Market

In the Regner Foods illustration, we assumed that the company applied the lower-of-cost-or-market rule to each individual type of food. However, companies may apply the lower-of-cost-or-market rule either directly to each item, to each category, or to the total of the inventory. If a company follows a major category or total inventory approach in applying the lower-of-cost-or-market rule, increases in market prices tend to offset decreases in market prices. To illustrate, assume that Regner Foods separates its food products into two major categories, frozen and canned, as shown in Illustration 9-6.

ILLUSTRATION 9-6
Alternative Applications of Lower-of-Cost-or-Market

	Cost	Designated Market	Lower-of-Cost-or-Market By:		
			Individual Items	Major Categories	Total Inventory
Frozen					
Spinach	$ 80,000	$104,000	$ 80,000		
Carrots	100,000	90,000	90,000		
Cut beans	50,000	40,000	40,000		
Total frozen	230,000	234,000		$230,000	
Canned					
Peas	90,000	48,000	48,000		
Mixed vegetables	95,000	92,000	92,000		
Total canned	185,000	140,000		140,000	
Total	$415,000	$374,000	$350,000	$370,000	$374,000

If Regner Foods applied the lower-of-cost-or-market rule to individual items, the amount of inventory is $350,000. If applying the rule to major categories, it jumps to $370,000. If applying LCM to the total inventory, it totals $374,000. Why this difference? When a company uses a major categories or total inventory approach, market values higher than cost offset market values lower than cost. For Regner Foods, using the major categories approach partially offsets the high market value for spinach. Using the total inventory approach totally offsets it.

Companies usually price inventory on an item-by-item basis. In fact, tax rules require that companies use an individual-item basis barring practical difficulties. In addition, the individual-item approach gives the most conservative valuation for balance sheet purposes.[2] Often, a company prices inventory on a total-inventory basis when it offers only one end product (comprised of many different raw materials). If it produces several end products, a company might use a category approach instead. The method selected should be the one that most clearly reflects income. **Whichever method a company selects, it should apply the method consistently from one period to another.**[3]

Recording "Market" Instead of Cost

One of two methods is used for recording inventory at market. One method, referred to as the **direct method**, substitutes the (lower) market value figure for cost when valuing the inventory. As a result, the company does not report a loss in the income statement because the cost of goods sold already includes the amount of the loss. The second method, referred to as the **indirect method** or **allowance method**, does not change the cost amount. Rather, it establishes a separate contra asset account and a loss account to record the write-off.

We use the following inventory data to illustrate entries under both methods.

Cost of goods sold (before adjustment to market)	$108,000
Ending inventory (cost)	82,000
Ending inventory (at market)	70,000

---

[2] If a company uses dollar-value LIFO, determining the LIFO cost of an individual item may be more difficult. The company might decide that it is more appropriate to apply the lower-of-cost-or-market rule to the total amount of each pool. The AICPA Task Force on LIFO Inventory Problems concluded that the most reasonable approach to applying the lower-of-cost-or-market provisions to LIFO inventories is to base the determination on reasonable groupings of items. A pool constitutes a reasonable grouping.

[3] Inventory accounting for financial statement purposes can be different from income tax purposes. For example, companies cannot use the lower-of-cost-or-market rule with LIFO for tax purposes. However, companies may use the lower-of-cost-or-market and LIFO for financial accounting purposes.

Illustration 9-7 shows the entries for both the direct and indirect methods, assuming the use of a **perpetual** inventory system.

Direct Method		Indirect or Allowance Method		
To reduce inventory from cost to market:				
Cost of Goods Sold	12,000	Loss Due to Market		
Inventory	12,000	Decline of Inventory	12,000	
		Allowance to Reduce		
		Inventory to Market		12,000

ILLUSTRATION 9-7
Accounting for the
Reduction of Inventory to
Market—Perpetual
Inventory System

Identifying the loss due to market decline shows the loss separate from cost of goods sold in the income statement (but not as an extraordinary item). The advantage of this approach is that it does not distort the cost of goods sold.

Illustration 9-8 contrasts the differing amounts reported in the income statements under the two methods, using data from the preceding illustration.

Direct Method	
Revenue from sales	$200,000
Cost of goods sold (after adjustment to market*)	120,000
Gross profit on sales	$ 80,000
Indirect or Allowance Method	
Revenue from sales	$200,000
Cost of goods sold	108,000
Gross profit on sales	92,000
Loss due to market decline of inventory	12,000
	$ 80,000
*Cost of goods sold (before adjustment to market)	$ 108,000
Difference between inventory at cost and market ($82,000–$70,000)	12,000
Cost of goods sold (after adjustment to market)	$ 120,000

ILLUSTRATION 9-8
Income Statement
Presentation—Direct and
Indirect Methods of
Reducing Inventory to
Market

The direct-method presentation buries the loss in the cost of goods sold. The indirect-method presentation is preferable, because it clearly discloses the loss resulting from the market decline of inventory prices.

Using the indirect method, the company would report the Allowance to Reduce Inventory to Market on the balance sheet as a $12,000 deduction from the inventory. This deduction permits both the income statement and the balance sheet to show the ending inventory of $82,000, although the balance sheet shows a net amount of $70,000. It also keeps subsidiary inventory ledgers and records in correspondence with the control account without changing unit prices.

Use of an allowance account permits balance sheet disclosure of the inventory at cost and at the lower of cost or market. However, it raises the problem of how to dispose of the balance of the allowance account in the following period. If the company still has on hand the merchandise in question, it should retain the allowance account. If it does not keep that account, the company will overstate beginning inventory and cost of goods. However, **if the company has sold the goods**, then it should close the account. It then establishes a "new allowance account" for any decline in inventory value that takes place in the current year.[4]

UNDERLYING CONCEPTS

The income statement under the direct method presentation lacks *representational faithfulness*. The cost of goods sold does not represent what it purports to represent. However, allowing this presentation illustrates the concept of materiality. That is, the presentation does not affect net income and would not "change the judgment of a reasonable person."

---

[4]The AICPA Task Force on LIFO Inventory Problems concluded that for LIFO inventories, companies should close the allowance from the prior year and should base the allowance at the end of the year on a new lower-of-cost-or-market computation. *Issues Paper* (New York: AICPA, November 30, 1984), pp. 50–55.

Some accountants leave the allowance account on the books. They merely adjust the balance at the next year-end to agree with the discrepancy between cost and the lower-of-cost-or-market at that balance sheet date. Thus, if prices are falling, the company records a loss. If prices are rising, the company recovers a loss recorded in prior years, and it records a "gain," as shown in Illustration 9-9. Note that this "gain" is not really a gain, but a recovery of a previously recognized loss.

ILLUSTRATION 9-9
Effect on Net Income of Reducing Inventory to Market

Date	Inventory at Cost	Inventory at Market	Amount Required in Valuation Account	Adjustment of Valuation Account Balance	Effect on Net Income
Dec. 31, 2006	$188,000	$176,000	$12,000	$12,000 inc.	Loss
Dec. 31, 2007	194,000	187,000	7,000	5,000 dec.	Gain
Dec. 31, 2008	173,000	174,000	0	7,000 dec.	Gain
Dec. 31, 2009	182,000	180,000	2,000	2,000 inc.	Loss

UNDERLYING CONCEPTS

The inconsistency in the presentation of inventory is an example of the trade-off between *relevancy and reliability.* Market is more relevant than cost, and cost is more reliable than market. Apparently, relevance takes precedence in a down market, and reliability is more important in an up market.

We can think of this net "gain" under the indirect method as the excess of the credit effect of closing the beginning allowance balance over the debit effect of setting up the current year-end allowance account. Recognizing a gain or loss has the same effect on net income as closing the allowance balance to beginning inventory or to cost of goods sold.

WHAT DO THE NUMBERS MEAN?

"PUT IT IN REVERSE"

The lower-of-cost-or-market rule is designed to provide timely information about the decline in the value of inventory. When the value of inventory declines, income takes a hit in the period of the write-down.

What happens in the periods after the write-down? For some companies, gross margins and bottom lines get a boost when they sell inventory that had been written down in a previous period. For example, as the following table shows, **Vishay Technologies, Transwitch,** and **Cisco Systems** reported gains from selling inventory that had previously been written down. The table also evaluates how clearly these companies disclosed the effects of the reversal of inventory write-downs.

Company	Gain from reversal	Disclosure
Vishay Inter-Technology	Not available	Poor—The semi-conductor company did not mention the gain in its earnings announcement. Two weeks later in an SEC filing, Vishay disclosed the gain on the inventory that it had written down.
Transwitch	$600,000	Poor—The company did not mention the gain in its earnings announcement. Three weeks later in an SEC filing, the company disclosed the gain on the inventory that it had written down.
Cisco Systems	$525 million	Full—The networking giant detailed in its earnings release and in SEC filings the gains from selling inventory it had previously written off.

For Transwitch, the reversal of fortunes amounted to 23 percent of net income. The problem is that the $600,000 credit had little to do with the company's ongoing operations, and the company did not do a good job disclosing the effect of the reversal on current-year profitability.

Even when companies do disclose a reversal, it is sometimes hard to determine the impact on income. For example, **Intel** disclosed that is had sold inventory that had been written down in prior periods but did not specify how much reserved inventory was sold.

After the recent accounting scandals, transparency of financial reporting has become a top priority. With better disclosure of the reversals that boost profits in the current period, financial transparency would also get a boost.

Source: S. E. Ante, "The Secret Behind Those Profit Jumps," *Business Week Online* (December 8, 2003).

Evaluation of the Lower-of-Cost-or-Market Rule

The lower-of-cost-or-market rule suffers some conceptual deficiencies:

1 A company recognizes decreases in the value of the the asset and the charge to expense in the period in which the loss in utility occurs—not in the period of sale. On the other hand, it recognizes increases in the value of the asset only at the point of sale. This inconsistent treatment can distort income data.

2 Application of the rule results in inconsistency because a company may value the inventory at cost in one year and at market in the next year.

3 Lower-of-cost-or-market values the inventory in the balance sheet conservatively, but its effect on the income statement may or may not be conservative. Net income for the year in which a company takes the loss is definitely lower. Net income of the subsequent period may be higher than normal if the expected reductions in sales price do not materialize.

4 Application of the lower-of-cost-or-market rule uses a "normal profit" in determining inventory values. Since companies estimate "normal profit" based on past experience (which they may not attain in the future), this subjective measure presents an opportunity for income manipulation.

Many financial statement users appreciate the lower-of-cost-or-market rule because they at least know that it prevents overstatement of inventory. In addition, recognizing all losses but anticipating no gains generally results in lower income.

VALUATION BASES

Valuation at Net Realizable Value

For the most part, companies record inventory at cost or at the lower-of-cost-or-market.[5] However, many believe that for purposes of applying the lower-of-cost-or-market rule, companies should define "market" as **net realizable value** (selling price less estimated costs to complete and sell), rather than as replacement cost. This argument is based on the fact that the amount that companies will collect from this inventory in the future is the net realizable value.[6]

Under limited circumstances, support exists for **recording inventory at net realizable value**, even if that amount is above cost. GAAP permits this exception to the normal recognition rule under the following conditions: (1) when there is a controlled market with a quoted price applicable to all quantities, and (2) when no significant costs of disposal

> **OBJECTIVE 2**
> Explain when companies value inventories at net realizable value.

---

[5]Manufacturing companies frequently employ a **standardized cost system** that predetermines the unit costs for material, labor, and manufacturing overhead and that values raw materials, work in process, and finished goods inventories at their standard costs. For financial reporting purposes, it is acceptable to price inventories at standard costs if there is no significant difference between the actual costs and standard costs. If there is a significant difference, companies should adjust the inventory amounts to actual cost. In *Accounting Research and Terminology Bulletin, Final Edition*, the profession notes that "**standard costs are acceptable if adjusted at reasonable intervals to reflect current conditions**." **Burlington Industries** and **Hewlett-Packard** use standard costs for valuing at least a portion of their inventories.

[6]"The Accounting Basis of Inventories," *Accounting Research Study No. 13* (New York: AICPA, 1973) recommends that companies adopt net realizable value. We also should note that companies frequently fail to apply the rules of lower-of-cost-or-market in practice. For example, companies rarely compute and apply the lower limit—net realizable value less a normal markup—because it is a fairly subjective computation. In addition, companies often do not reduce inventory to market unless its disposition is expected to result in a loss. Furthermore, if the net realizable value of finished goods exceeds cost, companies usually assume that both work in process and raw materials do also. In practice, therefore, *ARB No. 43* is considered a guide, and accountants often exercise professional judgment in lieu of following this pronouncement literally.

are involved. For example, mining companies ordinarily report inventories of certain minerals (rare metals, especially) at selling prices because there is often a controlled market without significant costs of disposal. Similar treatment is given agricultural products that are immediately marketable at quoted prices.

A third reason for allowing valuation at net realizable value is that sometimes it is too difficult to obtain the cost figures. Cost figures are not difficult to determine in, say, a manufacturing plant, where the company combines various raw materials and purchased parts to create a finished product. The manufacturer can use the cost basis to account for various items in inventory, because it knows the cost of each individual component part. The situation is different in a meat-packing plant, however. The "raw material" consists of, say, cattle, each unit of which the company purchases as a whole and then divides into parts that are the products. Instead of one product out of many raw materials or parts, the meat-packing company makes many products from one "unit" of raw material. To allocate the cost of the animal "on the hoof" into the cost of, say, ribs, chuck, and shoulders, is a practical impossibility. It is much easier and more useful for the company to determine the market price of the various products and value them in the inventory at selling price less the various costs necessary to get them to market (costs such as shipping and handling). Hence, because of a peculiarity of the industry, meat-packing companies sometimes carry **inventories at sales price less distribution costs**.

Valuation Using Relative Sales Value

OBJECTIVE 3
Explain when companies use the relative sales value method to value inventories.

A special problem arises when a company buys a group of varying units in a single **lump-sum purchase**, also called a **basket purchase**.

To illustrate, assume that Woodland Developers purchases land for $1 million that it will subdivide into 400 lots. These lots are of different sizes and shapes but can be roughly sorted into three groups graded A, B, and C. As woodland sells the lots, it apportions the purchase cost of $1 million among the lots sold and the lots remaining on hand.

You might wonder why Woodland would not simply divide the total cost of $1 million by 400 lots, to get a cost of $2,500 for each lot. This approach would not recognize that the lots vary in size, shape, and attractiveness. Therefore, to accurately value each unit, the common and most logical practice is to allocate the total among the various units on the basis of their **relative sales value**.

Illustration 9-10 shows the allocation of relative sales value for the Woodland Developers example.

ILLUSTRATION 9-10
Allocation of Costs, Using Relative Sales Value

Lots	Number of Lots	Sales Price Per Lot	Total Sales Price	Relative Sales Price	Total Cost	Cost Allocated to Lots	Cost Per Lot
A	100	$10,000	$1,000,000	100/250	$1,000,000	$ 400,000	$4,000
B	100	6,000	600,000	60/250	1,000,000	240,000	2,400
C	200	4,500	900,000	90/250	1,000,000	360,000	1,800
			$2,500,000			$1,000,000	

Using the amounts given in the "Cost Per Lot" column, Woodland can determine the cost of lots sold and the gross profit as follows.

ILLUSTRATION 9-11
Determination of Gross Profit, Using Relative Sales Value

Lots	Number of Lots Sold	Cost Per Lot	Cost of Lots Sold	Sales	Gross Profit
A	77	$4,000	$308,000	$ 770,000	$ 462,000
B	80	2,400	192,000	480,000	288,000
C	100	1,800	180,000	450,000	270,000
			$680,000	$1,700,000	$1,020,000

The ending inventory is therefore $320,000 ($1,000,000 − $680,000).

Woodland also can compute this inventory amount another way. The ratio of cost to selling price for all the lots is $1 million divided by $2,500,000, or 40 percent. Accordingly, if the total sales price of lots sold is, say $1,700,000, then the cost of the lots sold is 40 percent of $1,700,000, or $680,000. The inventory of lots on hand is then $1 million less $680,000, or $320,000.

The petroleum industry widely uses the relative sales value method to value (at cost) the many products and by-products obtained from a barrel of crude oil.

Purchase Commitments—A Special Problem

In many lines of business, a company's survival and continued profitability depends on its having a sufficient stock of merchandise to meet customer demand. Consequently, it is quite common for a company to make **purchase commitments**, which are agreements to buy inventory weeks, months, or even years in advance. Generally, the seller retains title to the merchandise or materials covered in the purchase commitments. Indeed, the goods may exist only as natural resources as unplanted seed (in the case of agricultural commodities), or as work in process (in the case of a product).[7]

Usually it is neither necessary nor proper for the buyer to make any entries to reflect commitments for purchases of goods that the seller has not shipped. Ordinary orders, for which the buyer and seller will determine prices at the time of shipment and **which are subject to cancellation**, do not represent either an asset or a liability to the buyer. Therefore the buyer need not record such purchase commitments or report them in the financial statements.

What happens, though, if a buyer enters into a formal, noncancelable purchase contract? Even then, the buyer recognizes no asset or liability at the date of inception, **because the contract is "executory" in nature**: Neither party has fulfilled its part of the contract. However, if material, the buyer should disclose such contract details in a note to its financial statements. Illustration 9-12 shows an example of a purchase commitment disclosure.

OBJECTIVE 4
Discuss accounting issues related to purchase commitments.

Note 1: Contracts for the purchase of raw materials in 2007 have been executed in the amount of $600,000. The market price of such raw materials on December 31, 2006, is $640,000.

ILLUSTRATION 9-12
Disclosure of Purchase Commitment

In the disclosure in Illustration 9-12, the contract price was less than the market price at the balance sheet date. **If the contract price is greater than the market price, and the buyer expects that losses will occur when the purchase is effected, the buyer should recognize losses in the period during which such declines in market prices take place.**[8]

As an example, in the early 1980s many Northwest forest-product companies such as **Boise Cascade, Georgia-Pacific,** and **Weyerhaeuser** signed long-term timber-cutting contracts with the **U.S. Forest Service**. These contracts required that the companies pay $310 per thousand board feet for timber-cutting rights. Unfortunately, the market price for timber-cutting rights in late 1984 dropped to $80 per thousand board feet. As a result, a number of these companies had long-term contracts that, if fulfilled, would result in substantial future losses.

---

[7]A recent study noted that about 30 percent of public companies have purchase commitments outstanding, with an estimated value of $725 billion ("SEC Staff Report on Off-Balance Sheet Arrangements, Special Purpose Entities, and Related Issues,") http://www.sec.gov/news/studies/soxoffbalancerpt.pdf, June 2005). Purchase commitments are popular because the buyer can secure a supply of inventory at a known price. The seller also benefits in these arrangements by knowing how much to produce.

[8]*Accounting Research Bulletin No. 43*, op. cit., par. 16.

UNDERLYING CONCEPTS

Reporting the loss is *conservative*. However, reporting the decline in market price is debatable because no asset is recorded. This area demonstrates the need for good definitions of assets and liabilities.

To illustrate the accounting problem, assume that St. Regis Paper Co. signed timber-cutting contracts to be executed in 2007 at a price of $10,000,000. Assume further that the market price of the timber cutting rights on December 31, 2008, dropped to $7,000,000. St. Regis would make the following entry on December 31, 2008.

Unrealized Holding Gain or Loss—Income		
(Purchase Commitments)	3,000,000	
Estimated Liability on Purchase Commitments		3,000,000

St. Regis would report this unrealized holding loss in the income statement under "Other expenses and losses." And because the contract is to be executed within the next fiscal year, St. Regis would report the Estimated Liability on Purchase Commitments in the current liabilities section on the balance sheet. When St. Regis cuts the timber at a cost of $10 million, it would make the following entry.

Purchases (Inventory)	7,000,000	
Estimated Liability on Purchase Commitments	3,000,000	
Cash		10,000,000

The result of the purchase commitment was that St. Regis paid $10 million for a contract worth only $7 million. It recorded the loss in the previous period—when the price actually declined.

If St. Regis can partially or fully recover the contract price before it cuts the timber, it reduces the Estimated Liability on Purchase Commitments. In that case, it then reports in the period of the price increase a resulting gain for the amount of the partial or full recovery. For example, Congress permitted some of the forest-products companies to buy out of their contracts at reduced prices in order to avoid potential bankruptcies. To illustrate, assume that Congress permitted St. Regis to reduce its contract price and therefore its commitment by $1,000,000. The entry to record this transaction is as follows.

Estimated Liability on Purchase Commitments	1,000,000	
Unrealized Holding Gain or Loss—Income		
(Purchase Commitments)		1,000,000

If the market price at the time St. Regis cuts the timber is more than $2,000,000 below the contract price, St. Regis will have to recognize an additional loss in the period of cutting and record the purchase at the lower-of-cost-or-market.

Are purchasers at the mercy of market price declines? Not totally. Purchasers can protect themselves against the possibility of market price declines of goods under contract by hedging. In **hedging**, the purchaser in the purchase commitment simultaneously enters into a contract in which it agrees to sell in the future the same quantity of the same (or similar) goods at a fixed price. Thus the company holds a *buy position* in a purchase commitment and a *sell position* in a futures contract in the same commodity. The purpose of the hedge is to offset the price risk of the buy and sell positions: The company will be better off under one contract by approximately (maybe exactly) the same amount by which it is worse off under the other contract.

For example, St. Regis Paper Co. could have hedged its purchase commitment contract with a futures contract for timber rights of the same amount. In that case, its loss of $3,000,000 on the purchase commitment could have been offset by a $3,000,000 gain on the futures contract.[9]

As easy as this makes it sound, accounting for purchase commitments is still unsettled and controversial. Some argue that companies should report purchase commitments

---

[9]Appendix 17A provides a complete discussion of hedging and the use of derivatives such as futures.

as assets and liabilities at the time they sign the contract.[10] Others believe that the present recognition at the delivery date is more appropriate. *FASB Concepts Statement No. 6* states, "a purchase commitment involves both an item that might be recorded as an asset and an item that might be recorded as a liability. That is, it involves both a right to receive assets and an obligation to pay. . . . If both the right to receive assets and the obligation to pay were recorded at the time of the purchase commitment, the nature of the loss and the valuation account that records it when the price falls would be clearly seen." Although the discussion in *Concepts Statement No. 6* does not exclude the possibility of recording assets and liabilities for purchase commitments, it contains no conclusions or implications about whether companies should record them.[11]

THE GROSS PROFIT METHOD OF ESTIMATING INVENTORY

Companies take a physical inventory to verify the accuracy of the perpetual inventory records or, if no records exist, to arrive at an inventory amount. Sometimes, however, taking a physical inventory is impractical. In such cases, companies use substitute measures to approximate inventory on hand.

> **OBJECTIVE 5**
> Determine ending inventory by applying the gross profit method.

One substitute method of verifying or determining the inventory amount is the **gross profit method** (also called the **gross margin method)**. Auditors widely use this method in situations where they need only an estimate of the company's inventory (e.g., interim reports). Companies also use this method when fire or other catastrophe destroys either inventory or inventory records. The gross profit method relies on three assumptions:

1 The beginning inventory plus purchases equal total goods to be accounted for.

2 Goods not sold must be on hand.

3 The sales, reduced to cost, deducted from the sum of the opening inventory plus purchases, equal ending inventory.

To illustrate, assume that Cetus Corp. has a beginning inventory of $60,000 and purchases of $200,000, both at cost. Sales at selling price amount to $280,000. The gross profit on selling price is 30 percent. Cetus applies the gross margin method as follows.

Beginning inventory (at cost)		$ 60,000
Purchases (at cost)		200,000
Goods available (at cost)		260,000
Sales (at selling price)	$280,000	
Less: Gross profit (30% of $280,000)	84,000	
Sales (at cost)		196,000
Approximate inventory (at cost)		$ 64,000

ILLUSTRATION 9-13
Application of Gross Profit Method

---

[10]See, for example, Yuji Ijiri, *Recognition of Contractual Rights and Obligations, Research Report* (Stamford, Conn.: FASB, 1980), who argues that companies should capitalize firm purchase commitments. "Firm" means that it is unlikely that companies can avoid performance under the contract without a severe penalty.

Also, see Mahendra R. Gujarathi and Stanley F. Biggs, "Accounting for Purchase Commitments: Some Issues and Recommendations," *Accounting Horizons* (September 1988), pp. 75–78. They conclude, "Recording an asset and liability on the date of inception for the noncancelable purchase commitments is suggested as the first significant step towards alleviating the accounting problems associated with the issue. At year-end, the potential gains and losses should be treated as contingencies under *FASB 5* which provides a coherent structure for the accounting and informative disclosure for such gains and losses."

[11]"Elements of Financial Statements," *Statement of Financial Accounting Concepts No. 6* (Stamford, Conn.: FASB, 1985), pars. 251–253.

The current period's records contain all the information Cetus needs to compute inventory at cost, except for the gross profit percentage. Cetus determines the gross profit percentage by reviewing company policies or prior period records. In some cases, companies must adjust this percentage if they consider prior periods unrepresentative of the current period.[12]

Computation of Gross Profit Percentage

In most situations, the **gross profit percentage** is stated as a percentage of selling price. The previous illustration, for example, used a 30 percent gross profit on sales. Gross profit on selling price is the common method for quoting the profit for several reasons: (1) Most companies state goods on a retail basis, not a cost basis. (2) A profit quoted on selling price is lower than one based on cost. This lower rate gives a favorable impression to the consumer. (3) The gross profit based on selling price can never exceed 100 percent.[13]

In Illustration 9-13, the gross profit was a given. But how did Cetus derive that figure? To see how to compute a gross profit percentage, assume that an article cost $15 and sells for $20, a gross profit of $5. As shown in the computations in Illustration 9-14, this markup is $\frac{1}{4}$ or 25 percent of retail, and $\frac{1}{3}$ or, $33\frac{1}{3}$ percent of cost.

ILLUSTRATION 9-14
Computation of Gross Profit Percentage

$$\frac{\text{Markup}}{\text{Retail}} = \frac{\$5}{\$20} = 25\% \text{ at retail} \qquad \frac{\text{Markup}}{\text{Cost}} = \frac{\$5}{\$15} = 33\frac{1}{3}\% \text{ on cost}$$

Although companies normally compute the gross profit on the basis of selling price, you should understand the basic relationship between markup on cost and markup on selling price. For example, assume that a company marks up a given item by 25 percent. What, then, is the **gross profit on selling price**? To find the answer, assume that the item sells for $1. In this case, the following formula applies.

$$\text{Cost} + \text{Gross profit} = \text{Selling price}$$

$$C + .25C = SP$$

$$(1 + .25)C = SP$$

$$1.25C = \$1.00$$

$$C = \$0.80$$

---

[12]An alternative method of estimating inventory using the gross profit percentage is considered by some to be less complicated than the traditional method. This alternative method uses the standard income statement format as follows. (Assume the same data as in the Cetus example above.)

Sales		$280,000		$280,000
Cost of sales				
Beginning inventory	$ 60,000		$ 60,000	
Purchases	200,000		200,000	
Goods available for sale	260,000		260,000	
Ending inventory	(3) ?		(3) 64,000 Est.	
Cost of goods sold		(2) ?		(2)196,000 Est.
Gross profit on sales (30%)		(1) ?		(1) 84,000 Est.

Compute the unknowns as follows: first the gross profit amount, then cost of goods sold, and finally the ending inventory, as shown below.
  (1) $280,000 × 30% = $84,000 (gross profit on sales).
  (2) $280,000 − $84,000 = $196,000 (cost of goods sold).
  (3) $260,000 − $196,000 = $64,000 (ending inventory).

[13]The terms *gross margin percentage*, *rate of gross profit*, and *percentage markup* are synonymous, although companies more commonly use *markup* in reference to cost and *gross profit* in reference to sales.

The gross profit equals $0.20 ($1.00 − $0.80). The rate of gross profit on selling price is therefore 20 percent ($0.20/$1.00).

Conversely, assume that the gross profit on selling price is 20 percent. What is the **markup on cost**? To find the answer, again assume that the item sells for $1. Again, the same formula holds:

$$\text{Cost} + \text{Gross profit} = \text{Selling price}$$

$$C + .20SP = SP$$

$$C = (1 - .20)SP$$

$$C = .80SP$$

$$C = .80(\$1.00)$$

$$C = \$0.80$$

As in the previous example, the markup equals $0.20 ($1.00 − $0.80). The markup on cost is 25 percent ($0.20/$0.80).

Retailers use the following formulas to express these relationships:

1. Gross profit on selling price = $\dfrac{\text{Percentage markup on cost}}{100\% + \text{Percentage markup on cost}}$

2. Percentage markup on cost = $\dfrac{\text{Gross profit on selling price}}{100\% - \text{Gross profit on selling price}}$

ILLUSTRATION 9-15
Formulas Relating to Gross Profit

To understand how to use these formulas, consider their application in the following calculations.

Gross Profit on Selling Price	Percentage Markup on Cost
Given: 20% ⟶	$\dfrac{.20}{1.00 - .20} = 25\%$
Given: 25% ⟶	$\dfrac{.25}{1.00 - .25} = 33\tfrac{1}{3}\%$
$\dfrac{.25}{1.00 + .25} = 20\%$ ⟵	Given: 25%
$\dfrac{.50}{1.00 + .50} = 33\tfrac{1}{3}\%$ ⟵	Given: 50%

ILLUSTRATION 9-16
Application of Gross Profit Formulas

Because selling price exceeds cost, and with the gross profit amount the same for both, **gross profit on selling price will always be less than the related percentage based on cost**. Note that companies do not multiply sales by a cost-based markup percentage. Instead, they must convert the gross profit percentage to a percentage based on selling price.

Evaluation of Gross Profit Method

What are the major disadvantages of the gross profit method? One disadvantage is that **it provides an estimate**. As a result, companies must take a physical inventory once a year to verify the inventory. Second, the gross profit method **uses past percentages** in determining the markup. Although the past often provides answers to the future, a current rate is more appropriate. Note that whenever significant fluctuations occur, companies should adjust the percentage as appropriate. Third, companies must be **careful in applying a blanket gross profit rate**. Frequently, a store or department handles merchandise with widely varying rates of gross profit. In these situations, the company may need to apply the gross profit method by subsections, lines of merchandise, or a similar basis that classifies merchandise according to their respective rates of gross profit. The gross profit method is normally unacceptable for financial reporting purposes because it provides only an estimate. GAAP requires a physical inventory as additional verification of the inventory indicated in the records. Nevertheless, GAAP permits the gross profit method to determine ending inventory for interim (generally quarterly) reporting purposes, provided a company discloses the use of this method. Note that the gross profit method will follow closely the inventory method used (FIFO, LIFO, average cost) because it relies on historical records.

THE SQUEEZE

Managers and analysts closely follow gross profits. A small change in the gross profit rate can significantly affect the bottom line. In 1993, **Apple Computer** suffered a textbook case of shrinking gross profits. In response to pricing wars in the personal computer market, Apple had to quickly reduce the price of its signature Macintosh computers—reducing prices more quickly than it could reduce its costs. As a result its gross profit rate fell from 44 percent in 1992 to 40 percent in 1993. Though the drop of 4 percent seems small, its impact on the bottom line caused Apple's stock price to drop from $57 per share on June 1, 1993, to $27.50 by mid-July 1993.

As another example, **Debenham**, the second largest department store in the United Kingdom, experienced a 14 percentage share price decline. The cause? Mark-downs on slow moving inventory reduced its gross margin.

Source: Alison Smith, "Debenham's Shares Hit by Warning," *Financial Times* (July 24, 2002), p. 21.

WHAT DO THE NUMBERS MEAN?

RETAIL INVENTORY METHOD

OBJECTIVE 6
Determine ending inventory by applying the retail inventory method.

Accounting for inventory in a retail operation presents several challenges. Retailers with certain types of inventory may use the specific identification method to value their inventories. Such an approach makes sense when a retailer holds significant individual inventory units, such as automobiles, pianos, or fur coats. However, imagine attempting to use such an approach at **Target**, **True-Value Hardware**, **Sears Holdings**, or **Bloomingdale's**—high-volume retailers that have many different types of merchandise. It would be extremely difficult to determine the cost of each sale, to enter cost codes on the tickets, to change the codes to reflect declines in value of the merchandise, to allocate costs such as transportation, and so on.

An alternative is to compile the inventories at retail prices. For most retailers, an observable pattern between cost and price exists. The retailer can then use a formula to convert retail prices to cost. This method is called the **retail inventory method**. **It requires that the retailer keep a record of (1) the total cost and retail value of goods purchased, (2) the total cost and retail value of the goods available for sale, and (3) the sales for the period.** Use of the retail inventory method is very common. For example, **Safeway** supermarkets uses the retail inventory method, as does **Target Corp.**, **Wal-Mart**, and **Best Buy**.

Here is how it works at a company like **Best Buy**: Beginning with the retail value of the goods available for sale, Best Buy deducts the sales for the period. This calculation determines an estimated inventory (goods on hand) at retail. It next computes the **cost-to-retail ratio** for all goods. The formula for this computation is to divide the cost of total goods available for sale at cost by the total goods available at retail price. Finally, to obtain ending inventory at cost, Best Buy applies the cost-to-retail ratio to the ending inventory valued at retail. Illustration 9-17 shows the retail inventory method calculations for Best Buy (assumed data).

ILLUSTRATION 9-17
Retail Inventory Method

BEST BUY
(current period)

	Cost	Retail
Beginning inventory	$14,000	$ 20,000
Purchases	63,000	90,000
Goods available for sale	$77,000	110,000
Deduct: Sales		85,000
Ending inventory, at retail		$ 25,000

Ratio of cost to retail ($77,000 ÷ $110,000) = 70%
Ending inventory at cost (70% of $25,000) = $ 17,500

There are different versions of the retail inventory method. These include the **conventional** method (based on lower-of-average-cost-or-market), the **cost** method, the **LIFO retail** method, and the **dollar-value LIFO** retail method. Regardless of which version a company uses, the IRS, various retail associations, and the accounting profession all sanction use of the retail inventory method. One of its advantages is that a company like Target can approximate the inventory balance **without a physical count**. However, to avoid a potential overstatement of the inventory, Target makes periodic inventory counts. Such counts are especially important in retail operations where loss due to shoplifting or breakage is common.

The retail inventory method is particularly useful for any type of interim report, because such reports usually need a fairly quick and reliable measure of the inventory. Also, insurance adjusters often use this method to estimate losses from fire, flood, or other type of casualty. This method also acts as a **control device** because a company will have to explain any deviations from a physical count at the end of the year. Finally, the retail method **expedites the physical inventory count** at the end of the year. The crew taking the physical inventory need record only the retail price of each item. The crew does not need to look up each item's invoice cost, thereby saving time and expense.

Retail-Method Concepts

The amounts shown in the "Retail" column of Illustration 9-17 represent the original retail prices, assuming no price changes. In practice, though, retailers frequently mark up or mark down the prices they charge buyers.

For retailers, the term **markup** means an additional markup of the original retail price. (In another context, such as the gross profit discussion on page 435, we often think of markup on the basis of cost.) **Markup cancellations** are decreases in prices of merchandise that the retailer had marked up above the original retail price.

In a competitive market, retailers often need to use **markdowns**, which are decreases in the original sales prices. Such cuts in sales prices may be necessary because of a decrease in the general level of prices, special sales, soiled or damaged goods, overstocking, and market competition. Markdowns are common in retailing these days. **Markdown cancellations** occur when the markdowns are later offset by increases in the prices of goods that the retailer had marked down—such as after a one-day sale, for example. Neither a markup cancellation nor a markdown cancellation can exceed the original markup or markdown.

To illustrate these concepts, assume that Designer Clothing Store recently purchased 100 dress shirts from Marroway, Inc. The cost for these shirts was $1,500, or $15 a shirt. Designer Clothing established the selling price on these shirts at $30 a shirt. The shirts were selling quickly in anticipation of Father's Day, so the manager added a markup of $5 per shirt. This markup made the price too high for customers, and sales slowed. The manager then reduced the price to $32. At this point we would say that the shirts at Designer Clothing have had a markup of $5 and a markup cancellation of $3.

Right after Father's Day, the manager marked down the remaining shirts to a sale price of $23. At this point, an additional markup cancellation of $2 has taken place, and a $7 markdown has occurred. If the manager later increases the price of the shirts to $24, a markdown cancellation of $1 would occur.

Retail Inventory Method with Markups and Markdowns— Conventional Method

Retailers use markup and markdown concepts in developing the proper inventory valuation at the end of the accounting period. To obtain the appropriate inventory figures, companies must give proper treatment to markups, markup cancellations, markdowns, and markdown cancellations.

To illustrate the different possibilities, consider the data for In-Fusion Inc., shown in Illustration 9-18. In-Fusion can calculate its ending inventory at cost under two assumptions, A and B. (We'll explain the reasons for the two later.)

Assumption A: Computes a cost ratio after markups (and markup cancellations) but before markdowns.

Assumption B: Computes a cost ratio after both markups and markdowns (and cancellations).

ILLUSTRATION 9-18
Retail Inventory Method with Markups and Markdowns

	Cost	Retail
Beginning inventory	$ 500	$ 1,000
Purchases (net)	20,000	35,000
Markups		3,000
Markup cancellations		1,000
Markdowns		2,500
Markdown cancellations		2,000
Sales (net)		25,000

IN-FUSION INC.

	Cost		Retail
Beginning inventory	$ 500		$ 1,000
Purchases (net)	20,000		35,000
Merchandise available for sale	20,500		36,000
Add: Markups		$3,000	
Less: Markup cancellations		(1,000)	
Net markups			2,000
	20,500		38,000
(A) Cost-to-retail ratio $\dfrac{\$20,500}{\$38,000} = 53.9\%$			
Deduct:			
Markdowns		2,500	
Less: Markdown cancellations		(2,000)	
Net markdowns			500
	$20,500		37,500
(B) Cost-to-retail ratio $\dfrac{\$20,500}{\$37,500} = 54.7\%$			
Deduct: Sales (net)			25,000
Ending inventory at retail			$12,500

The computations for In-Fusion are:

Ending inventory at retail × Cost ratio = Value of ending inventory
Assumption A: $12,500 × 53.9% = $6,737.50
Assumption B: $12,500 × 54.7% = $6,837.50

The question becomes: Which assumption and which percentage should In-Fusion use to compute the ending inventory valuation? The answer depends on which retail inventory method In-Fusion chooses.

One approach uses only assumption A (a cost ratio using markups but not markdowns). It approximates the lower-of-average-cost-or-market. We will refer to this approach as the **conventional retail inventory method** or the **lower-of-cost-or-market approach**.

To understand why this method considers only the markups, not the markdowns, in the cost percentage, you must understand how a retail business operates. A markup normally indicates an increase in the market value of the item. On the other hand, a markdown means a decline in the utility of that item. Therefore, to approximate the lower-of-cost-or-market, we would consider markdowns a current loss and so would not include them in calculating the cost-to-retail ratio. Omitting the markdowns would make the cost-to-retail ratio lower, which leads to an approximate lower-of-cost-or-market.

An example will make the distinction between the two methods clear: In-Fusion purchased two items for $5 apiece; the original sales price was $10 each. One item was subsequently written down to $2. Assuming no sales for the period, **if markdowns are considered** in the cost-to-retail ratio (assumption B—the **cost method**), we compute the ending inventory in the following way.

Markdowns Included in Cost-to-Retail Ratio		
	Cost	Retail
Purchases	$10	$20
Deduct: Markdowns		8
Ending inventory, at retail		$12

Cost-to-retail ratio $\dfrac{\$10}{\$12} = 83.3\%$

Ending inventory at cost ($12 × .833) = $10

ILLUSTRATION 9-19
Retail Inventory Method Including Markdowns— Cost Method

This approach (the cost method) reflects an **average cost** of the two items of the commodity without considering the loss on the one item. It values ending inventory at $10.

If markdowns are not considered in the cost-to-retail ratio (assumption A—the **conventional retail method**), we compute the ending inventory as follows.

Markdowns Not Included in Cost-to-Retail Ratio		
	Cost	Retail
Purchases	$10	$20

Cost-to-retail ratio $\dfrac{\$10}{\$20} = 50\%$

Deduct: Markdowns		8
Ending inventory, at retail		$12

Ending inventory, at cost ($12 × .50) = $6

ILLUSTRATION 9-20
Retail Inventory Method Excluding Markdowns— Conventional Method (LCM)

Under this approach (the conventional retail method, in which markdowns are **not considered**), ending inventory would be $6. The inventory valuation of $6 reflects two inventory items, one inventoried at $5 and the other at $1. It reflects the fact that In-Fusion reduced the sales price from $10 to $2, and reduced the cost from $5 to $1.[14]

---

[14]This figure is not really market (replacement cost), but it is net realizable value less the normal margin that is allowed. In other words, the sale price of the goods written down is $2, but subtracting a normal margin of 50 percent ($5 cost, $10 price), the figure becomes $1.

To approximate the lower-of-cost-or-market, In-Fusion must establish the **cost-to-retail ratio**. It does this by dividing the cost of goods available for sale by the sum of the original retail price of these goods plus the net markups. This calculation excludes markdowns and markdown cancellations. Illustration 9-21 shows the basic format for the retail inventory method using the lower-of-cost-or-market approach along with the In-Fusion Inc. information.

ILLUSTRATION 9-21
Comprehensive
Conventional Retail
Inventory Method Format

IN-FUSION INC.		
	Cost	Retail
Beginning inventory	$ 500.00	$ 1,000.00
Purchases (net)	20,000.00	35,000.00
Totals	20,500.00	36,000.00
Add: Net markups		
Markups	$3,000.00	
Markup cancellations	1,000.00	2,000.00
Totals	$20,500.00 ←	→ 38,000.00
Deduct: Net markdowns		
Markdowns	2,500.00	
Markdown cancellations	2,000.00	500.00
Sales price of goods available		37,500.00
Deduct: Sales (net)		25,000.00
Ending inventory, at retail		$12,500.00

$$\text{Cost-to-retail ratio} = \frac{\text{Cost of goods available}}{\text{Original retail price of goods available, plus net markups}}$$

$$= \frac{\$20,500}{\$38,000} = 53.9\%$$

Ending inventory at lower of cost or market (53.9% × $12,500.00) = $ 6,737.50

Because an averaging effect occurs, an exact lower-of-cost-or-market inventory valuation is ordinarily not obtained, but an adequate approximation can be achieved. In contrast, adding net markups **and** deducting net markdowns yields **approximate cost**.

Special Items Relating to Retail Method

The retail inventory method becomes more complicated when we consider such items as freight-in, purchase returns and allowances, and purchase discounts. In the retail method, we treat such items as follows.

- **Freight costs** are part of the purchase cost.
- **Purchase returns** are ordinarily considered as a reduction of the price at both cost and retail.
- **Purchase discounts and allowances** usually are considered as a reduction of the cost of purchases.

In short, the treatment for the items affecting the cost column of the retail inventory approach follows the computation for cost of goods available for sale.[15]

Note also that **sales returns and allowances** are considered as proper adjustments to gross sales. However, when sales are recorded gross, companies do not recognize **sales discounts**. To adjust for the sales discount account in such a situation would provide an ending inventory figure at retail that would be overvalued.

---

[15]When the purchase allowance is not reflected by a reduction in the selling price, no adjustment is made to the retail column.

In addition, a number of special items require careful analysis:

- **Transfers-in** from another department are reported in the same way as purchases from an outside enterprise.
- **Normal shortages** (breakage, damage, theft, shrinkage) should reduce the retail column because these goods are no longer available for sale. Such costs are reflected in the selling price because a certain amount of shortage is considered normal in a retail enterprise. As a result, companies do not consider this amount in computing the cost-to-retail percentage. Rather, to arrive at ending inventory at retail, they show normal shortages as a deduction similar to sales.
- **Abnormal shortages**, on the other hand, are deducted from both the cost and retail columns and reported as a special inventory amount or as a loss. To do otherwise distorts the cost-to-retail ratio and overstates ending inventory.
- **Employee discounts** (given to employees to encourage loyalty, better performance, and so on) are deducted from the retail column in the same way as sales. These discounts should not be considered in the cost-to-retail percentage because they do not reflect an overall change in the selling price.

Illustration 9-22 shows some of these concepts. The company, Extreme Sport Apparel, determines its inventory using the conventional retail inventory method.

ILLUSTRATION 9-22
Conventional Retail Inventory Method—Special Items Included

EXTREME SPORT APPAREL

	Cost		Retail
Beginning inventory	$ 1,000		$ 1,800
Purchases	30,000		60,000
Freight-in	600		—
Purchase returns	(1,500)		(3,000)
Totals	30,100		58,800
Net markups			9,000
Abnormal shortage	(1,200)		(2,000)
Totals	$28,900 ⟵	⟶	65,800
Deduct:			
Net markdowns			1,400
Sales		$36,000	
Sales returns		(900)	35,100
Employee discounts			800
Normal shortage			1,300
			$27,200

Cost-to-retail ratio $= \dfrac{\$28,900}{\$65,800} = 43.9\%$

Ending inventory at lower of cost or market (43.9% × $27,200) = **$11,940.80**

Evaluation of Retail Inventory Method

Companies like **Gap Inc.**, **Circuit City**, or your local department store use the retail inventory method of computing inventory for the following reasons: (1) to permit the computation of net income without a physical count of inventory, (2) as a control measure in determining inventory shortages, (3) in regulating quantities of merchandise on hand, and (4) for insurance information.

One characteristic of the retail inventory method is that it **has an averaging effect on varying rates of gross profit**. This can be problematic when companies apply the method to an entire business, where rates of gross profit vary among departments. There is no allowance for possible distortion of results because of such differences.

Companies refine the retail method under such conditions by computing inventory separately by departments or by classes of merchandise with similar gross profits. In addition, the reliability of this method assumes that the distribution of items in inventory is similar to the "mix" in the total goods available for sale.

PRESENTATION AND ANALYSIS

Presentation of Inventories

OBJECTIVE 7
Explain how to report and analyze inventory.

Additional Inventory Disclosures

Accounting standards require financial statement disclosure of the composition of the inventory, inventory financing arrangements, and the inventory costing methods employed. The standards also require the consistent application of costing methods from one period to another.

Manufacturers should report the inventory composition either in the balance sheet or in a separate schedule in the notes. The relative mix of raw materials, work in process, and finished goods helps in assessing liquidity and in computing the stage of inventory completion.

Significant or unusual financing arrangements relating to inventories may require note disclosure. Examples include transactions with related parties, product financing arrangements, firm purchase commitments, involuntary liquidation of LIFO inventories, and pledging of inventories as collateral. Companies should present inventories pledged as collateral for a loan in the current assets section rather than as an offset to the liability.

A company should also report the basis on which it states inventory amounts (lower-of-cost-or-market) and the method used in determining cost (LIFO, FIFO, average cost, etc.). For example, the annual report of **Mumford of Wyoming** contains the following disclosures.

ILLUSTRATION 9-23
Disclosure of
Inventory Methods

Mumford of Wyoming

Note A: Significant Accounting Policies

Live feeder cattle and feed—last-in, first-out (LIFO) cost, which is below approximate market	$854,800
Live range cattle—lower of principally identified cost or market	$1,240,500
Live sheep and supplies—lower of first-in, first-out (FIFO) cost or market	$674,000
Dressed meat and by-products—principally at market less allowances for distribution and selling expenses	$362,630

The preceding illustration shows that a company can use different pricing methods for different elements of its inventory. If Mumford changes the method of pricing any of its inventory elements, it must report a change in accounting principle. For example, if Mumford changes its method of accounting for live sheep from FIFO to average cost, it should separately report this change, along with the effect on income, in the current and prior periods. Changes in accounting principle require an explanatory paragraph in the auditor's report describing the change in method.

Fortune Brands, Inc. reported its inventories in its annual report as follows (note the "trade practice" followed in classifying inventories among the current assets).

Fortune Brands, Inc.

Current assets

Inventories (Note 2)

Leaf tobacco	$ 563,424,000
Bulk whiskey	232,759,000
Other raw materials, supplies and work in process	238,906,000
Finished products	658,326,000
	$1,693,415,000

Note 2: Inventories

Inventories are priced at the lower of cost (average; first-in, first-out; and minor amounts at last-in, first-out) or market. In accordance with generally recognized trade practice, the leaf tobacco and bulk whiskey inventories are classified as current assets, although part of such inventories due to the duration of the aging process, ordinarily will not be sold within one year.

ILLUSTRATION 9-24
Disclosure of Trade Practice in Valuing Inventories

The following inventory disclosures by **Newmont Gold Company** reveal the use of different bases of valuation, including market value, for different classifications of inventory.

Newmont Gold Company

Current assets	
Inventories (Note 2)	$44,303,000
Noncurrent assets	
Inventories—ore in stockpiles (Note 2)	$5,250,000

Note 2: Inventories

Inventories included in current assets at December 31 were:

Ore and in-process inventory	$11,303,000
Gold bullion and gold precipitates	24,209,000
Materials and supplies	8,791,000
	$44,303,000

Ore and in-process inventory and materials and supplies are stated at the lower of average cost or net realizable value. Gold bullion and gold precipitates are stated at market value, less a provision for estimated refining and delivery charges. Expenditures capitalized as ore and in-process inventory include labor, material and other production costs.

Noncurrent inventories are stated at the lower of average cost or net realizable value and represent ore in stockpiles anticipated to be processed in future years.

ILLUSTRATION 9-25
Disclosure of Different Bases of Valuation

Analysis of Inventories

As our opening story illustrates, the amount of inventory that a company carries can have significant economic consequences. As a result, companies must manage inventories. But, inventory management is a double-edged sword. It requires constant attention. On the one hand, management wants to stock a great variety and quantity of items. Doing so will provide customers with the greatest selection. However, such an inventory policy may incur excessive carrying costs (e.g., investment, storage, insurance, taxes, obsolescence, and damage). On the other hand, low inventory levels lead to stockouts, lost sales, and disgruntled customers.

Using financial ratios helps companies to chart a middle course between these two dangers. Common ratios used in the management and evaluation of inventory levels are inventory turnover and a related measure, average days to sell the inventory.

Inventory Turnover Ratio

The **inventory turnover ratio** measures the number of times on average a company sells the inventory during the period. It measures the liquidity of the inventory. To compute inventory turnover, divide the cost of goods sold by the average inventory on hand during the period.

Barring seasonal factors, analysts compute average inventory from beginning and ending inventory balances. For example, in its 2004 annual report **Kellogg Company** reported a beginning inventory of $649.8 million, an ending inventory of $681 million, and cost of goods sold of $5,299 million for the year. Illustration 9-26 shows the inventory turnover formula and Kellogg Company's 2004 ratio computation below.

ILLUSTRATION 9-26
Inventory Turnover Ratio

$$\text{Inventory Turnover} = \frac{\text{Cost of Goods Sold}}{\text{Average Inventory}}$$

$$= \frac{\$5,299}{(\$681 + \$649.8)/2} = 8 \text{ times}$$

Average Days to Sell Inventory

A variant of the inventory turnover ratio is the **average days to sell inventory**. This measure represents the average number of days' sales for which a company has inventory on hand. For example, the inventory turnover for Kellogg Company of 8 times divided into 365 is approximately 45.6 days.

There are typical levels of inventory in every industry. However, companies that keep their inventory at lower levels with higher turnovers than those of their competitors, and that still can satisfy customer needs, are the most successful.

SUMMARY OF LEARNING OBJECTIVES

KEY TERMS

average days to sell inventory, *444*

conventional retail inventory method, *439*

cost-to-retail ratio, *436*

designated market value, *424*

gross profit method, *433*

gross profit percentage, *434*

hedging, *432*

inventory turnover ratio, *444*

lower limit (floor), *423*

lower-of-cost-or-market (LCM), *423*

lump-sum (basket) purchase, *430*

markdown, *437*

markdown cancellations, *437*

market (for LCM), *423*

markup, *437*

markup cancellations, *437*

1. **Describe and apply the lower-of-cost-or-market rule.** If inventory declines in value below its original cost, for whatever reason, a company should write down the inventory to reflect this loss. The general rule is to abandon the historical cost principle when the future utility (revenue-producing ability) of the asset drops below its original cost.

2. **Explain when companies value inventories at net realizable value.** Companies value inventory at net realizable value when: (1) there is a controlled market with a quoted price applicable to all quantities, (2) no significant costs of disposal are involved, and (3) the cost figures are too difficult to obtain.

3. **Explain when companies use the relative sales value method to value inventories.** When a company purchases a group of varying units at a single lump-sum price—a so-called basket purchase—the company may allocate the total purchase price to the individual items on the basis of relative sales value.

4. **Discuss accounting issues related to purchase commitments.** Accounting for purchase commitments is controversial. Some argue that companies should report purchase commitment contracts as assets and liabilities at the time the contract is signed. Others believe that recognition at the delivery date is most appropriate. The FASB neither excludes nor recommends the recording of assets and liabilities for purchase commitments, but it notes that if companies recorded such contracts at the time of commitment, the nature of the loss and the valuation account should be reported when the price falls.

5. **Determine ending inventory by applying the gross profit method.** Companies follow these steps to determine ending inventory by the gross profit method: (1) Compute

the gross profit percentage on selling price. (2) Compute gross profit by multiplying net sales by the gross profit percentage. (3) Compute cost of goods sold by subtracting gross profit from net sales. (4) Compute ending inventory by subtracting cost of goods sold from total goods available for sale.

6. **Determine ending inventory by applying the retail inventory method.** Companies follow these steps to determine ending inventory by the conventional retail method: (1) To estimate inventory at retail, deduct the sales for the period from the retail value of the goods available for sale. (2) To find the cost-to-retail ratio for all goods passing through a department or firm, divide the total goods available for sale at cost by the total goods available at retail. (3) Convert the inventory valued at retail to approximate cost by applying the cost-to-retail ratio.

7. **Explain how to report and analyze inventory.** Accounting standards require financial statement disclosure of: (1) the composition of the inventory (in the balance sheet or a separate schedule in the notes); (2) significant or unusual inventory financing arrangements; and (3) inventory costing methods employed (which may differ for different elements of inventory). Accounting standards also require the consistent application of costing methods from one period to another. Common ratios used in the management and evaluation of inventory levels are inventory turnover and average days to sell the inventory.

net realizable value (NRV), 423

net realizable value less a normal profit margin, 423

purchase commitments, 431

retail inventory method, 436

upper limit (ceiling), 423

APPENDIX 9A

LIFO Retail Methods

OBJECTIVE 8
Determine ending inventory by applying the LIFO retail methods.

A number of retail establishments have changed from the more conventional treatment to a **LIFO retail method**. For example, the world's largest retailer, **Wal-Mart** uses the LIFO retail method. The primary reason to do so is for the tax advantages associated with valuing inventories on a LIFO basis. In addition, adoption of LIFO results in a better matching of costs and revenues.

The use of LIFO retail is made under two assumptions: (1) stable prices and (2) fluctuating prices.

STABLE PRICES—LIFO RETAIL METHOD

It is much more complex to compute the final inventory balance using a LIFO flow than using the conventional retail method. Under the LIFO retail method, companies like **Wal-Mart** or **Target** consider **both markups and markdowns** in obtaining the proper cost-to-retail percentage. Furthermore, since the LIFO method is concerned only with the additional layer, or the amount that should be subtracted from the previous layer, the beginning inventory is excluded from the cost-to-retail percentage.

A major assumption of the LIFO retail method is that the markups and markdowns apply only to the goods purchased during the current period and not to the beginning inventory. This assumption is debatable and may explain why some companies do not adopt this method.

Illustration 9A-1 (page 446) presents the major concepts involved in the LIFO retail method applied to the Hernandez Company. Note that, to simplify the accounting, we have assumed that the price level has remained unchanged.

ILLUSTRATION 9A-1
LIFO Retail Method—
Stable Prices

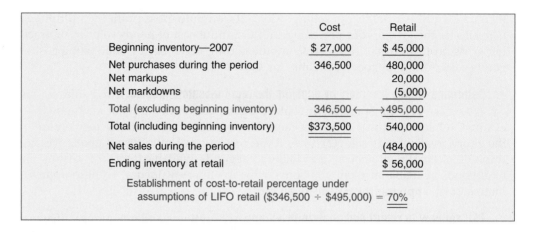

	Cost	Retail
Beginning inventory—2007	$ 27,000	$ 45,000
Net purchases during the period	346,500	480,000
Net markups		20,000
Net markdowns		(5,000)
Total (excluding beginning inventory)	346,500 ←——→	495,000
Total (including beginning inventory)	$373,500	540,000
Net sales during the period		(484,000)
Ending inventory at retail		$ 56,000

Establishment of cost-to-retail percentage under
assumptions of LIFO retail ($346,500 ÷ $495,000) = <u>70%</u>

Illustration 9A-2 indicates that the inventory is composed of two layers: the beginning inventory and the additional increase that occurred in the inventory this period (2007). When we start the next period (2008), the beginning inventory will be composed of those two layers. If an increase in inventory occurs again, an additional layer will be added.

ILLUSTRATION 9A-2
Ending Inventory at LIFO
Cost, 2007—Stable Prices

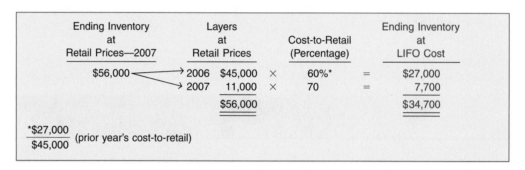

Ending Inventory at Retail Prices—2007	Layers at Retail Prices		Cost-to-Retail (Percentage)		Ending Inventory at LIFO Cost
$56,000 ——→	2006	$45,000 ×	60%*	=	$27,000
——→	2007	11,000 ×	70	=	7,700
		$56,000			$34,700

$\frac{*\$27,000}{\$45,000}$ (prior year's cost-to-retail)

However, if the final inventory figure is below the beginning inventory, Hernandez must reduce the beginning inventory starting with the most recent layer. For example, assume that the ending inventory for 2008 at retail is $50,000. Illustration 9A-3 shows the computation of the ending inventory at cost. Notice that the 2007 layer is reduced from $11,000 to $5,000.

ILLUSTRATION 9A-3
Ending Inventory at LIFO
Cost, 2008—Stable Prices

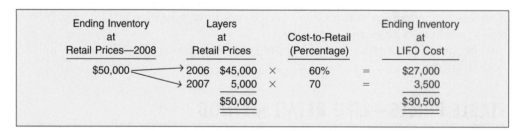

Ending Inventory at Retail Prices—2008	Layers at Retail Prices		Cost-to-Retail (Percentage)		Ending Inventory at LIFO Cost
$50,000 ——→	2006	$45,000 ×	60%	=	$27,000
——→	2007	5,000 ×	70	=	3,500
		$50,000			$30,500

FLUCTUATING PRICES—DOLLAR-VALUE LIFO RETAIL METHOD

The previous example simplified the LIFO retail method by ignoring changes in the selling price of the inventory. Let us now assume that a change in the price level of the inventories occurs (as is usual). If the price level does change, the company must **eliminate the price change** so as to measure the real increase in inventory, not the dollar increase. This approach is referred to as the **dollar-value LIFO retail method**.

To illustrate, assume that the beginning inventory had a retail market value of $10,000 and the ending inventory had a retail market value of $15,000. Assume further that the price level has risen from 100 to 125. It is inappropriate to suggest that a real increase in inventory of $5,000 has occurred. Instead, the company must deflate the ending inventory at retail, as the computation in Illustration 9A-4 shows.

Ending inventory at retail (deflated) $15,000 ÷ 1.25*	$12,000	
Beginning inventory at retail	10,000	
Real increase in inventory at retail	$ 2,000	
Ending inventory at retail on LIFO basis:		
First layer	$10,000	
Second layer ($2,000 × 1.25)	2,500	$12,500
*1.25 = 125 ÷ 100		

ILLUSTRATION 9A-4
Ending Inventory at Retail—Deflated and Restated

This approach is essentially the dollar-value LIFO method discussed in Chapter 8. In computing the LIFO inventory under a dollar-value LIFO approach, the company finds the dollar increase in inventory and deflates it to beginning-of-the-year prices. This indicates whether actual increases or decreases in quantity have occurred. If an increase in quantities occurs, the company prices this increase at the new index, in order to compute the value of the new layer. If a decrease in quantities happens, the company subtracts the increase from the most recent layers to the extent necessary.

The following computations, based on those in Illustration 9A-1 for Hernandez Company, illustrate the differences between the dollar-value LIFO retail method and the regular LIFO retail approach. Assume that the current 2007 price index is 112 (prior year = 100) and that the inventory ($56,000) has remained unchanged. In comparing Illustrations 9A-1 and 9A-5, note that the computations involved in finding the cost-to-retail percentage are exactly the same. However, the dollar-value method determines the increase that has occurred in the inventory in terms of base-year prices.

	Cost	Retail
Beginning inventory—2007	$ 27,000	$ 45,000
Net purchases during the period	346,500	480,000
Net markups		20,000
Net markdowns		(5,000)
Total (excluding beginning inventory)	346,500 ⟷	495,000
Total (including beginning inventory)	$373,500	540,000
Net sales during the period at retail		(484,000)
Ending inventory at retail		$ 56,000
Establishment of cost-to-retail percentage under assumptions of LIFO retail ($346,500 ÷ $495,000) =		70%
A. Ending inventory at retail prices deflated to base-year prices $56,000 ÷ 112 =		$50,000
B. Beginning inventory (retail) at base-year prices		45,000
C. Inventory increase (retail) from beginning of period		$ 5,000

ILLUSTRATION 9A-5
Dollar-Value LIFO Retail Method—Fluctuating Prices

From this information, we compute the inventory amount at cost:

Ending Inventory at Base-Year Retail Prices—2007	Layers at Base-Year Retail Prices		Price Index (percentage)		Cost-to-Retail (percentage)		Ending Inventory at LIFO Cost
$50,000 ⟶ 2006	$45,000	×	100%	×	60%	=	$27,000
⟶ 2007	5,000	×	112	×	70	=	3,920
	$50,000						$30,920

ILLUSTRATION 9A-6
Ending Inventory at LIFO Cost, 2007—Fluctuating Prices

As Illustration 9A-6 shows, before the conversion to cost takes place, Hernandez must restate layers of a particular year to the prices in effect in the year when the layer was added.

Note the difference between the LIFO approach (stable prices) and the dollar-value LIFO method as indicated below.

ILLUSTRATION 9A-7
Comparison of Effect of
Price Assumptions

	LIFO (stable prices)	LIFO (fluctuating prices)
Beginning inventory	$27,000	$27,000
Increment	7,700	3,920
Ending inventory	$34,700	$30,920

The difference of $3,780 ($34,700 − $30,920) results from an increase in the **price** of goods, not from an increase in the **quantity** of goods.

Subsequent Adjustments under Dollar-Value LIFO Retail

The dollar-value LIFO retail method follows the same procedures in subsequent periods as the traditional dollar-value method discussed in Chapter 8. That is, when a real increase in inventory occurs, Hernandez adds a new layer.

To illustrate, using the data from the previous example, assume that the retail value of the 2008 ending inventory at current prices is $64,800, the 2008 price index is 120 percent of base-year, and the cost-to-retail percentage is 75 percent. In base-year dollars, the ending inventory is therefore $54,000 ($64,800/120%). Illustration 9A-8 shows the computation of the ending inventory at LIFO cost.

ILLUSTRATION 9A-8
Ending Inventory at LIFO
Cost, 2008—Fluctuating
Prices

Ending Inventory at Base-Year Retail Prices—2008	Layers at Base-Year Retail Prices		Price Index (percentage)		Cost-to-Retail (percentage)		Ending Inventory at LIFO Cost
$54,000	2006	$45,000 ×	100%	×	60%	=	$27,000
	2007	5,000 ×	112	×	70	=	3,920
	2008	4,000 ×	120	×	75	=	3,600
		$54,000					$34,520

Conversely, when a real decrease in inventory develops, Hernandez "peels off" previous layers at prices in existence when the layers were added. To illustrate, assume that in 2008 the ending inventory in base-year prices is $48,000. The computation of the LIFO inventory is as follows.

ILLUSTRATION 9A-9
Ending Inventory at LIFO
Cost, 2008—Fluctuating
Prices

Ending Inventory at Base-Year Retail Prices—2008	Layers at Base-Year Retail Prices		Price Index (percentage)		Cost-to-Retail (percentage)		Ending Inventory at LIFO Cost
$48,000	2006	$45,000 ×	100%	×	60%	=	$27,000
	2007	3,000 ×	112	×	70	=	2,352
		$48,000					$29,352

The advantages and disadvantages of the lower-of-cost-or-market method (conventional retail) versus LIFO retail are the same for retail operations as for non-retail operations. As a practical matter, a company's selection of which retail inventory method to use often involves determining which method provides a lower taxable income. It might appear that retail LIFO will provide the lower taxable income in a period of rising prices. But this is not always the case. LIFO will provide an approximate current cost matching, but it states ending inventory at cost. The conventional retail method may have a large write-off because of the use of the lower-of-cost-or-market approach, which may offset the LIFO current cost matching.

CHANGING FROM CONVENTIONAL RETAIL TO LIFO

Because conventional retail is a lower-of-cost-or-market approach, the company must restate beginning inventory to a cost basis when changing from the conventional retail to the LIFO method.[1] The usual approach is to compute the cost basis from the purchases of the prior year, adjusted for both markups and markdowns.[2]

To illustrate, assume that Clark Clothing Store employs the conventional retail method but wishes to change to the LIFO retail method beginning in 2007. The amounts shown by the firm's books are as follows.

	At Cost	At Retail
Inventory, January 1, 2007	$ 5,120	$ 15,000
Net purchases in 2007	47,250	100,000
Net markups in 2007		7,000
Net markdowns in 2007		2,000
Sales in 2007		95,000

Illustration 9A-10 shows computation of ending inventory under the **conventional retail method** for 2007.

	Cost	Retail
Inventory January 1, 2007	$ 5,210	$ 15,000
Net purchases	47,250	100,000
Net additional markups		7,000
	$52,460	122,000
Net markdowns		(2,000)
Sales		(95,000)
Ending inventory at retail		$ 25,000
Establishment of cost-to-retail percentage ($52,460 ÷ $122,000) =		43%
December 31, 2007, inventory at cost		
Inventory at retail		$ 25,000
Cost-to-retail ratio		× 43%
Inventory at cost under conventional retail		$ 10,750

ILLUSTRATION 9A-10
Conventional Retail
Inventory Method

Clark Clothing can then quickly approximate the ending inventory for 2007 under the **LIFO retail method** as shown in Illustration 9A-11 (page 450).

---

[1]Changing from the conventional retail method to LIFO retail represents a change in accounting principle. We provide an expanded discussion of accounting principle changes in Chapter 22.

[2]A logical question to ask is, "Why are only the purchases from the prior period considered and not also the beginning inventory?" Apparently the IRS believes that "the purchases-only approach" provides a more reasonable cost basis. The IRS position is debatable. However, for our purposes, it seems appropriate to use the purchases-only approach.

ILLUSTRATION 9A-11
Conversion to LIFO
Retail Inventory Method

December 31, 2007, Inventory at LIFO Cost			

Ending inventory $\dfrac{\text{Retail}}{\$25,000} \times \dfrac{\text{Ratio}}{45\%^*} = \dfrac{\text{LIFO}}{\$11,250}$

*The cost-to-retail ratio was computed as follows:

$\dfrac{\text{Net purchases at cost}}{\substack{\text{Net purchases at retail plus} \\ \text{markups less markdowns}}} = \dfrac{\$47,250}{\$100,000 + \$7,000 - \$2,000} = 45\%$

The difference of $500 ($11,250 − $10,750) between the LIFO retail method and the conventional retail method in the ending inventory for 2007 is the amount by which the company must adjust beginning inventory for 2008. The entry to adjust the inventory to a cost basis is as follows.

Inventory	500	
Adjustment to Record Inventory at Cost		500

KEY TERMS

dollar-value LIFO retail
method, *446*
LIFO retail method, *445*

SUMMARY OF LEARNING OBJECTIVE FOR APPENDIX 9A

8. **Determine ending inventory by applying the LIFO retail methods.** The application of LIFO retail is made under two assumptions: stable prices and fluctuating prices.

Procedures under stable prices: (a) Because the LIFO method is a cost method, both markups and markdowns must be considered in obtaining the proper cost-to-retail percentage. (b) Since the LIFO method is concerned only with the additional layer, or the amount that should be subtracted from the previous layer, the beginning inventory is excluded from the cost-to-retail percentage. (c) The markups and markdowns apply only to the goods purchased during the current period and not to the beginning inventory.

Procedures under fluctuating prices: The steps are the same as for stable prices except that in computing the LIFO inventory under a dollar-value LIFO approach, the dollar increase in inventory is found and deflated to beginning-of-the-year prices. Doing so will determine whether actual increases or decreases in quantity have occurred. If quantities increase, this increase is priced at the new index to compute the new layer. If quantities decrease, the decrease is subtracted from the most recent layers to the extent necessary.

Note: All **asterisked** Questions, Brief Exercises, Exercises, Problems, and Concepts for Analysis relate to material contained in the appendix to the chapter.

QUESTIONS

1. Where there is evidence that the utility of inventory goods, as part of their disposal in the ordinary course of business, will be less than cost, what is the proper accounting treatment?

2. Explain the rationale for the ceiling and floor in the lower-of-cost-or-market method of valuing inventories.

3. Why are inventories valued at the lower-of-cost-or-market? What are the arguments against the use of the LCM method of valuing inventories?

4. What approaches may be employed in applying the lower-of-cost-or-market procedure? Which approach is normally used and why?

5. In some instances accounting principles require a departure from valuing inventories at cost alone. Determine the proper unit inventory price in the following cases.

	Cases				
	1	2	3	4	5
Cost	$15.90	$16.10	$15.90	$15.90	$15.90
Net realizable value	14.30	19.20	15.20	10.40	16.40
Net realizable value less normal profit	12.80	17.60	13.75	8.80	14.80
Market (replacement cost)	14.80	17.20	12.80	9.70	16.80

6. What method(s) might be used in the accounts to record a loss due to a price decline in the inventories? Discuss.

7. What factors might call for inventory valuation at sales prices (net realizable value or market price)?

8. Under what circumstances is relative sales value an appropriate basis for determining the price assigned to inventory?

9. At December 31, 2008, Kidman Co. has outstanding purchase commitments for purchase of 150,000 gallons, at $6.40 per gallon, of a raw material to be used in its manufacturing process. The company prices its raw material inventory at cost or market, whichever is lower. Assuming that the market price as of December 31, 2008, is $5.90, how would you treat this situation in the accounts?

10. What are the major uses of the gross profit method?

11. Distinguish between gross profit as a percentage of cost and gross profit as a percentage of sales price. Convert the following gross profit percentages based on cost to gross profit percentages based on sales price: 20% and 33⅓%. Convert the following gross profit percentages based on sales price to gross profit percentages based on cost: 33⅓% and 60%.

12. Carole Lombard Co. with annual net sales of $6 million maintains a markup of 25% based on cost. Lombard's expenses average 15% of net sales. What is Lombard's gross profit and net profit in dollars?

13. A fire destroys all of the merchandise of Rosanna Arquette Company on February 10, 2008. Presented below is information compiled up to the date of the fire.

Inventory, January 1, 2008	$ 400,000
Sales to February 10, 2008	1,750,000
Purchases to February 10, 2008	1,140,000
Freight-in to February 10, 2008	60,000
Rate of gross profit on selling price	40%

What is the approximate inventory on February 10, 2008?

14. What conditions must exist for the retail inventory method to provide valid results?

15. The conventional retail inventory method yields results that are essentially the same as those yielded by the lower-of-cost-or-market method. Explain. Prepare an illustration of how the retail inventory method reduces inventory to market.

16. (a) Determine the ending inventory under the conventional retail method for the furniture department of Gin Blossoms Department Stores from the following data.

	Cost	Retail
Inventory, Jan. 1	$ 149,000	$ 283,500
Purchases	1,400,000	2,160,000
Freight-in	70,000	
Markups, net		92,000
Markdowns, net		48,000
Sales		2,235,000

(b) If the results of a physical inventory indicated an inventory at retail of $240,000, what inferences would you draw?

17. Deere and Company reported inventory in its balance sheet as follows:

Inventories $1,999,100,000

What additional disclosures might be necessary to present the inventory fairly?

18. Of what significance is inventory turnover to a retail store?

*19. What modifications to the conventional retail method are necessary to approximate a LIFO retail flow?

BRIEF EXERCISES

(LO 1, 2) **BE9-1** Presented below is information related to Alstott Inc.'s inventory.

(per unit)	Skis	Boots	Parkas
Historical cost	$190.00	$106.00	$53.00
Selling price	217.00	145.00	73.75
Cost to distribute	19.00	8.00	2.50
Current replacement cost	203.00	105.00	51.00
Normal profit margin	32.00	29.00	21.25

Determine the following: (a) the two limits to market value (i.e., the ceiling and the floor) that should be used in the lower-of-cost-or-market computation for skis; (b) the cost amount that should be used in the lower-of-cost-or-market comparison of boots; and (c) the market amount that should be used to value parkas on the basis of the lower-of-cost-or-market.

(LO 1, 2) **BE9-2** Robin Corporation has the following four items in its ending inventory.

Item	Cost	Replacement Cost	Net Realizable Value (NRV)	NRV Less Normal Profit Margin
Jokers	$2,000	$1,900	$2,100	$1,600
Penguins	5,000	5,100	4,950	4,100
Riddlers	4,400	4,550	4,625	3,700
Scarecrows	3,200	2,990	3,830	3,070

Determine the final lower-of-cost-or-market inventory value for each item.

(LO 1, 2) **BE9-3** Battletoads Inc. uses a perpetual inventory system. At January 1, 2008, inventory was $214,000 at both cost and market value. At December 31, 2008, the inventory was $286,000 at cost and $269,000 at market value. Prepare the necessary December 31 entry under (a) the direct method and (b) the indirect method.

(LO 3) **BE9-4** PC Plus buys 1,000 computer game CDs from a distributor who is discontinuing those games. The purchase price for the lot is $6,000. PC Plus will group the CDs into three price categories for resale, as indicated below.

Group	No. of CDs	Price per CD
1	100	$ 5.00
2	800	10.00
3	100	15.00

Determine the cost per CD for each group, using the relative sales value method.

(LO 4) **BE9-5** Beavis Company signed a long-term noncancelable purchase commitment with a major supplier to purchase raw materials in 2008 at a cost of $1,000,000. At December 31, 2007, the raw materials to be purchased have a market value of $930,000. Prepare any necessary December 31 entry.

(LO 4) **BE9-6** Use the information for Beavis Company from BE9-5. In 2008, Beavis paid $1,000,000 to obtain the raw materials which were worth $930,000. Prepare the entry to record the purchase.

(LO 5) **BE9-7** Big Hurt Corporation's April 30 inventory was destroyed by fire. January 1 inventory was $150,000, and purchases for January through April totaled $500,000. Sales for the same period were $700,000. Big Hurt's normal gross profit percentage is 31% on sales. Using the gross profit method, estimate Big Hurt's April 30 inventory that was destroyed by fire.

(LO 6) **BE9-8** Bimini Inc. had beginning inventory of $12,000 at cost and $20,000 at retail. Net purchases were $120,000 at cost and $170,000 at retail. Net markups were $10,000; net markdowns were $7,000; and sales were $157,000. Compute ending inventory at cost using the conventional retail method.

(LO 7) **BE9-9** In its 2004 annual report, **Wal-Mart** reported inventory of $26,612 million on January 31, 2004, and $24,401 million on January 31, 2003, cost of sales of $198,747 million for fiscal year 2004, and net sales of $256,329 million. Compute Wal-Mart's inventory turnover and the average days to sell inventory for the fiscal year 2004.

(LO 8) ****BE9-10** Use the information for Bimini Inc. from BE9-8. Compute ending inventory at cost using the LIFO retail method.

(LO 8) ****BE9-11** Use the information for Bimini Inc. from BE9-8, and assume the price level increased from 100 at the beginning of the year to 120 at year-end. Compute ending inventory at cost using the dollar-value LIFO retail method.

EXERCISES

(LO 1, 2) **E9-1 (Lower-of-Cost-or-Market)** The inventory of 3T Company on December 31, 2008, consists of the following items.

Part No.	Quantity	Cost per Unit	Cost to Replace per Unit
110	600	$90	$100
111	1,000	60	52
112	500	80	76
113	200	170	180
120	400	205	208
121[a]	1,600	16	14
122	300	240	235

[a]Part No. 121 is obsolete and has a realizable value of $0.20 each as scrap.

Instructions

(a) Determine the inventory as of December 31, 2008, by the lower-of-cost-or-market method, applying this method directly to each item.

(b) Determine the inventory by the lower-of-cost-or-market method, applying the method to the total of the inventory.

(LO 1, 2) **E9-2 (Lower-of-Cost-or-Market)** Smashing Pumpkins Company uses the lower-of-cost-or-market method, on an individual-item basis, in pricing its inventory items. The inventory at December 31, 2008, consists of products D, E, F, G, H, and I. Relevant per-unit data for these products appear below.

	Item D	Item E	Item F	Item G	Item H	Item I
Estimated selling price	$120	$110	$95	$90	$110	$90
Cost	75	80	80	80	50	36
Replacement cost	120	72	70	30	70	30
Estimated selling expense *disposal*	30	30	30	25	30	30
Normal profit	20	20	20	20	20	20

Instructions

Using the lower-of-cost-or-market rule, determine the proper unit value for balance sheet reporting purposes at December 31, 2008, for each of the inventory items above.

(LO 1, 2) **E9-3 (Lower-of-Cost-or-Market)** Michael Bolton Company follows the practice of pricing its inventory at the lower-of-cost-or-market, on an individual-item basis.

Item No.	Quantity	Cost per Unit	Cost to Replace	Estimated Selling Price	Cost of Completion and Disposal	Normal Profit
1320	1,200	$3.20	$3.00	$4.50	$0.35	$1.25
1333	900	2.70	2.30	3.50	0.50	0.50
1426	800	4.50	3.70	5.00	0.40	1.00
1437	1,000	3.60	3.10	3.20	0.25	0.90
1510	700	2.25	2.00	3.25	0.80	0.60
1522	500	3.00	2.70	3.80	0.40	0.50
1573	3,000	1.80	1.60	2.50	0.75	0.50
1626	1,000	4.70	5.20	6.00	0.50	1.00

Instructions

From the information above, determine the amount of Bolton Company inventory.

(LO 1, 2) **E9-4 (Lower-of-Cost-or-Market—Journal Entries)** Corrs Company began operations in 2007 and determined its ending inventory at cost and at lower-of-cost-or-market at December 31, 2007, and December 31, 2008. This information is presented below.

	Cost	Lower-of-Cost-or-Market
12/31/07	$346,000	$327,000
12/31/08	410,000	395,000

Instructions

(a) Prepare the journal entries required at December 31, 2007, and December 31, 2008, assuming that the inventory is recorded at market, and a perpetual inventory system (direct method) is used.

(b) Prepare journal entries required at December 31, 2007, and December 31, 2008, assuming that the inventory is recorded at cost and an allowance account is adjusted at each year-end under a perpetual system.

(c) Which of the two methods above provides the higher net income in each year?

(LO 1, 2) **E9-5 (Lower-of-Cost-or-Market—Valuation Account)** Presented below is information related to Candlebox Enterprises.

	Jan. 31	Feb. 28	Mar. 31	Apr. 30
Inventory at cost	$15,000	$15,100	$17,000	$13,000
Inventory at the lower-of-cost-or-market	14,500	12,600	15,600	12,300
Purchases for the month		20,000	24,000	26,500
Sales for the month		29,000	35,000	40,000

Instructions

(a) From the information, prepare (as far as the data permit) monthly income statements in columnar form for February, March, and April. The inventory is to be shown in the statement at cost, the gain or loss due to market fluctuations is to be shown separately, and a valuation account is to be set up for the difference between cost and the lower of cost or market.

(b) Prepare the journal entry required to establish the valuation account at January 31 and entries to adjust it monthly thereafter.

(LO 1, 2) **E9-6 (Lower-of-Cost-or-Market—Error Effect)** Winans Company uses the lower-of-cost-or-market method, on an individual-item basis, in pricing its inventory items. The inventory at December 31, 2007, included product X. Relevant per-unit data for product X appear below.

Estimated selling price	$45
Cost	40
Replacement cost	35
Estimated selling expense	14
Normal profit	9

There were 1,000 units of product X on hand at December 31, 2007. Product X was incorrectly valued at $35 per unit for reporting purposes. All 1,000 units were sold in 2008.

Instructions

Compute the effect of this error on net income for 2007 and the effect on net income for 2008, and indicate the direction of the misstatement for each year.

(LO 3) **E9-7 (Relative Sales Value Method)** Phil Collins Realty Corporation purchased a tract of unimproved land for $55,000. This land was improved and subdivided into building lots at an additional cost of $34,460. These building lots were all of the same size but owing to differences in location were offered for sale at different prices as follows.

Group	No. of Lots	Price per Lot
1	9	$3,000
2	15	4,000
3	17	2,400

Operating expenses for the year allocated to this project total $18,200. Lots unsold at the year-end were as follows.

Group 1	5 lots
Group 2	7 lots
Group 3	2 lots

Instructions

At the end of the fiscal year Phil Collins Realty Corporation instructs you to arrive at the net income realized on this operation to date.

(LO 3) **E9-8 (Relative Sales Value Method)** During 2008, Pretenders Furniture Company purchases a carload of wicker chairs. The manufacturer sells the chairs to Pretenders for a lump sum of $59,850, because it is discontinuing manufacturing operations and wishes to dispose of its entire stock. Three types of chairs are included in the carload. The three types and the estimated selling price for each are listed below.

Type	No. of Chairs	Estimated Selling Price Each
Lounge chairs	400	$90
Armchairs	300	80
Straight chairs	700	50

During 2008, Pretenders sells 200 lounge chairs, 100 armchairs, and 120 straight chairs.

Instructions

What is the amount of gross profit realized during 2008? What is the amount of inventory of unsold straight chairs on December 31, 2008?

(LO 4) **E9-9 (Purchase Commitments)** Marvin Gaye Company has been having difficulty obtaining key raw materials for its manufacturing process. The company therefore signed a long-term noncancelable purchase commitment with its largest supplier of this raw material on November 30, 2008, at an agreed price of $400,000. At December 31, 2008, the raw material had declined in price to $365,000.

Instructions

What entry would you make on December 31, 2008, to recognize these facts?

(LO 4) **E9-10 (Purchase Commitments)** At December 31, 2008, Indigo Girls Company has outstanding noncancelable purchase commitments for 36,000 gallons, at $3.00 per gallon, of raw material to be used in its manufacturing process. The company prices its raw material inventory at cost or market, whichever is lower.

Instructions

(a) Assuming that the market price as of December 31, 2008, is $3.30, how would this matter be treated in the accounts and statements? Explain.

(b) Assuming that the market price as of December 31, 2008, is $2.70, instead of $3.30, how would you treat this situation in the accounts and statements?

(c) Give the entry in January 2009, when the 36,000-gallon shipment is received, assuming that the situation given in (b) above existed at December 31, 2008, and that the market price in January 2009 was $2.70 per gallon. Give an explanation of your treatment.

(LO 5) **E9-11** **(Gross Profit Method)** Each of the following gross profit percentages is expressed in terms of cost.

1. 20%.   3. 33⅓%.
2. 25%.   4. 50%.

Instructions

Indicate the gross profit percentage in terms of sales for each of the above.

(LO 5) **E9-12** **(Gross Profit Method)** Mark Price Company uses the gross profit method to estimate inventory for monthly reporting purposes. Presented below is information for the month of May.

Inventory, May 1	$ 160,000
Purchases (gross)	640,000
Freight-in	30,000
Sales	1,000,000
Sales returns	70,000
Purchase discounts	12,000

Instructions

(a) Compute the estimated inventory at May 31, assuming that the gross profit is 30% of sales.

(b) Compute the estimated inventory at May 31, assuming that the gross profit is 30% of cost.

(LO 5) **E9-13** **(Gross Profit Method)** Tim Legler requires an estimate of the cost of goods lost by fire on March 9. Merchandise on hand on January 1 was $38,000. Purchases since January 1 were $72,000; freight-in, $3,400; purchase returns and allowances, $2,400. Sales are made at 33⅓% above cost and totaled $100,000 to March 9. Goods costing $10,900 were left undamaged by the fire; remaining goods were destroyed.

Instructions

(a) Compute the cost of goods destroyed.

(b) Compute the cost of goods destroyed, assuming that the gross profit is 33⅓% of sales.

(LO 5) **E9-14** **(Gross Profit Method)** Rasheed Wallace Company lost most of its inventory in a fire in December just before the year-end physical inventory was taken. The corporation's books disclosed the following.

Beginning inventory	$170,000	Sales	$650,000
Purchases for the year	390,000	Sales returns	24,000
Purchase returns	30,000	Rate of gross margin on net sales	40%

Merchandise with a selling price of $21,000 remained undamaged after the fire. Damaged merchandise with an original selling price of $15,000 had a net realizable value of $5,300.

Instructions

Compute the amount of the loss as a result of the fire, assuming that the corporation had no insurance coverage.

(LO 5) **E9-15** **(Gross Profit Method)** You are called by Tim Duncan of Spurs Co. on July 16 and asked to prepare a claim for insurance as a result of a theft that took place the night before. You suggest that an inventory be taken immediately. The following data are available.

Inventory, July 1	$ 38,000
Purchases—goods placed in stock July 1–15	85,000
Sales—goods delivered to customers (gross)	116,000
Sales returns—goods returned to stock	4,000

Your client reports that the goods on hand on July 16 cost $30,500, but you determine that this figure includes goods of $6,000 received on a consignment basis. Your past records show that sales are made at approximately 40% over cost. Duncan's insurance covers only goods owned.

Instructions

Compute the claim against the insurance company.

(LO 5) **E9-16 (Gross Profit Method)** Gheorghe Moresan Lumber Company handles three principal lines of merchandise with these varying rates of gross profit on cost.

Lumber	25%
Millwork	30%
Hardware and fittings	40%

On August 18, a fire destroyed the office, lumber shed, and a considerable portion of the lumber stacked in the yard. To file a report of loss for insurance purposes, the company must know what the inventories were immediately preceding the fire. No detail or perpetual inventory records of any kind were maintained. The only pertinent information you are able to obtain are the following facts from the general ledger, which was kept in a fireproof vault and thus escaped destruction.

	Lumber	Millwork	Hardware
Inventory, Jan. 1, 2008	$ 250,000	$ 90,000	$ 45,000
Purchases to Aug. 18, 2008	1,500,000	375,000	160,000
Sales to Aug. 18, 2008	2,080,000	533,000	210,000

Instructions
Submit your estimate of the inventory amounts immediately preceding the fire.

(LO 5) **E9-17 (Gross Profit Method)** Presented below is information related to Warren Moon Corporation for the current year.

Beginning inventory	$ 600,000	
Purchases	1,500,000	
Total goods available for sale		$2,100,000
Sales		2,500,000

Instructions
Compute the ending inventory, assuming that **(a)** gross profit is 45% of sales; **(b)** gross profit is 60% of cost; **(c)** gross profit is 35% of sales; and **(d)** gross profit is 25% of cost.

(LO 6) **E9-18 (Retail Inventory Method)** Presented below is information related to Bobby Engram Company.

	Cost	Retail
Beginning inventory	$ 58,000	$100,000
Purchases (net)	122,000	200,000
Net markups		10,345
Net markdowns		26,135
Sales		186,000

Instructions
    (a) Compute the ending inventory at retail.
    (b) Compute a cost-to-retail percentage (round to two decimals) under the following conditions.
        (1) Excluding both markups and markdowns.
        (2) Excluding markups but including markdowns.
        (3) Excluding markdowns but including markups.
        (4) Including both markdowns and markups.
    (c) Which of the methods in (b) above (1, 2, 3, or 4) does the following?
        (1) Provides the most conservative estimate of ending inventory.
        (2) Provides an approximation of lower-of-cost-or-market.
        (3) Is used in the conventional retail method.
    (d) Compute ending inventory at lower-of-cost-or-market (round to nearest dollar).
    (e) Compute cost of goods sold based on (d).
    (f) Compute gross margin based on (d).

(LO 6) **E9-19 (Retail Inventory Method)** Presented below is information related to Ricky Henderson Company.

	Cost	Retail
Beginning inventory	$ 200,000	$ 280,000
Purchases	1,375,000	2,140,000
Markups		95,000
Markup cancellations		15,000
Markdowns		35,000
Markdown cancellations		5,000
Sales		2,200,000

Instructions

Compute the inventory by the conventional retail inventory method.

(LO 6) **E9-20** **(Retail Inventory Method)** The records of Ellen's Boutique report the following data for the month of April.

Sales	$99,000	Purchases (at cost)	$48,000
Sales returns	2,000	Purchases (at sales price)	88,000
Markups	10,000	Purchase returns (at cost)	2,000
Markup cancellations	1,500	Purchase returns (at sales price)	3,000
Markdowns	9,300	Beginning inventory (at cost)	30,000
Markdown cancellations	2,800	Beginning inventory (at sales price)	46,500
Freight on purchases	2,400		

Instructions

Compute the ending inventory by the conventional retail inventory method.

(LO 7) **E9-21** **(Analysis of Inventories)** The financial statements of **General Mills, Inc's.** 2004 annual report disclose the following information.

(in millions)	May 30, 2004	May 25, 2003	May 26, 2002
Inventories	$1,063	$1,082	$1,055

	Fiscal Year	
	2004	2003
Sales	$11,070	$10,506
Cost of goods sold	6,584	6,109
Net income	1,055	917

Instructions

Compute General Mills's **(a)** inventory turnover and **(b)** the average days to sell inventory for 2004 and 2003.

(LO 8) ***E9-22** **(Retail Inventory Method—Conventional and LIFO)** Helen Keller Company began operations on January 1, 2006, adopting the conventional retail inventory system. None of the company's merchandise was marked down in 2006 and, because there was no beginning inventory, its ending inventory for 2006 of $38,100 would have been the same under either the conventional retail system or the LIFO retail system.

On December 31, 2007, the store management considers adopting the LIFO retail system and desires to know how the December 31, 2007, inventory would appear under both systems. All pertinent data regarding purchases, sales, markups, and markdowns are shown below. There has been no change in the price level.

	Cost	Retail
Inventory, Jan. 1, 2007	$ 38,100	$ 60,000
Markdowns (net)		13,000
Markups (net)		22,000
Purchases (net)	130,900	178,000
Sales (net)		167,000

Instructions

Determine the cost of the 2007 ending inventory under both **(a)** the conventional retail method and **(b)** the LIFO retail method.

(LO 8) ***E9-23** **(Retail Inventory Method—Conventional and LIFO)** Leonard Bernstein Company began operations late in 2006 and adopted the conventional retail inventory method. Because there was no beginning inventory for 2006 and no markdowns during 2006, the ending inventory for 2006 was $14,000 under both the conventional retail method and the LIFO retail method. At the end of 2007, management wants to compare the results of applying the conventional and LIFO retail methods. There was no change in the price level during 2007. The following data are available for computations.

	Cost	Retail
Inventory, January 1, 2007	$14,000	$20,000
Sales		80,000
Net markups		9,000
Net markdowns		1,600
Purchases	58,800	81,000
Freight-in	7,500	
Estimated theft		2,000

Instructions

Compute the cost of the 2007 ending inventory under both **(a)** the conventional retail method and **(b)** the LIFO retail method.

(LO 8) ***E9-24 (Dollar-Value LIFO Retail)** You assemble the following information for Seneca Department Store, which computes its inventory under the dollar-value LIFO method.

	Cost	Retail
Inventory on January 1, 2007	$216,000	$300,000
Purchases	364,800	480,000
Increase in price level for year		9%

Instructions

Compute the cost of the inventory on December 31, 2007, assuming that the inventory at retail is **(a)** $294,300 and **(b)** $365,150.

(LO 8) ***E9-25 (Dollar-Value LIFO Retail)** Presented below is information related to Langston Hughes Corporation.

	Price Index	LIFO Cost	Retail
Inventory on December 31, 2008, when dollar-value LIFO is adopted	100	$36,000	$ 74,500
Inventory, December 31, 2009	110	?	100,100

Instructions

Compute the ending inventory under the dollar-value LIFO method at December 31, 2009. The cost-to-retail ratio for 2009 was 60%.

(LO 8) ***E9-26 (Conventional Retail and Dollar-Value LIFO Retail)** Amiras Corporation began operations on January 1, 2007, with a beginning inventory of $30,100 at cost and $50,000 at retail. The following information relates to 2007.

	Retail
Net purchases ($108,500 at cost)	$150,000
Net markups	10,000
Net markdowns	5,000
Sales	126,900

Instructions

  (a) Assume Amiras decided to adopt the conventional retail method. Compute the ending inventory to be reported in the balance sheet.

  (b) Assume instead that Amiras decides to adopt the dollar-value LIFO retail method. The appropriate price indexes are 100 at January 1 and 110 at December 31. Compute the ending inventory to be reported in the balance sheet.

  (c) On the basis of the information in part (b), compute cost of goods sold.

(LO 8) ***E9-27 (Dollar-Value LIFO Retail)** Connie Chung Corporation adopted the dollar-value LIFO retail inventory method on January 1, 2006. At that time the inventory had a cost of $54,000 and a retail price of $100,000. The following information is available.

	Year-End Inventory at Retail	Current Year Cost—Retail %	Year-End Price Index
2006	$118,720	57%	106
2007	138,750	60%	111
2008	125,350	61%	115
2009	162,500	58%	125

The price index at January 1, 2006, is 100.

Instructions

Compute the ending inventory at December 31 of the years 2006–2009. Round to the nearest dollar.

(LO 8) ***E9-28 (Change to LIFO Retail)** John Olerud Ltd., a local retailing concern in the Bronx, N.Y., has decided to change from the conventional retail inventory method to the LIFO retail method starting on January 1, 2008. The company recomputed its ending inventory for 2007 in accordance with the procedures necessary to switch to LIFO retail. The inventory computed was $212,600.

Instructions

Assuming that John Olerud Ltd.'s ending inventory for 2007 under the conventional retail inventory method was $205,000, prepare the appropriate journal entry on January 1, 2008.

See the book's website, www.wiley.com/college/kieso, for Additional Exercises.

PROBLEMS

(LO 1, 2) **P9-1 (Lower-of-Cost-or-Market)** Grant Wood Company manufactures desks. Most of the company's desks are standard models and are sold on the basis of catalog prices. At December 31, 2008, the following finished desks appear in the company's inventory.

Finished Desks	A	B	C	D
2008 catalog selling price	$450	$480	$900	$1,050
FIFO cost per inventory list 12/31/08	470	450	830	960
Estimated current cost to manufacture (at December 31, 2008, and early 2009)	460	440	610	1,000
Sales commissions and estimated other costs of disposal	45	60	90	130
2009 catalog selling price	500	540	900	1,200

The 2008 catalog was in effect through November 2008 and the 2009 catalog is effective as of December 1, 2008. All catalog prices are net of the usual discounts. Generally, the company attempts to obtain a 20% gross margin on selling price and has usually been successful in doing so.

Instructions

At what amount should each of the four desks appear in the company's December 31, 2008, inventory, assuming that the company has adopted a lower-of-FIFO-cost-or-market approach for valuation of inventories on an individual-item basis?

(LO 1, 2) **P9-2 (Lower-of-Cost-or-Market)** T. Allen Home Improvement Company installs replacement siding, windows, and louvered glass doors for single family homes and condominium complexes in northern New Jersey and southern New York. The company is in the process of preparing its annual financial statements for the fiscal year ended May 31, 2007, and Tim Taylor, controller for T. Allen, has gathered the following data concerning inventory.

At May 31, 2007, the balance in T. Allen's Raw Material Inventory account was $408,000, and the Allowance to Reduce Inventory to Market had a credit balance of $29,500. Taylor summarized the relevant inventory cost and market data at May 31, 2007, in the schedule below.

Taylor assigned Patricia Richardson, an intern from a local college, the task of calculating the amount that should appear on T. Allen's May 31, 2007, financial statements for inventory under the lower-of-cost-or-market rule as applied to each item in inventory. Richardson expressed concern over departing from the cost principle.

	Cost	Replacement Cost	Sales Price	Net Realizable Value	Normal Profit
Aluminum siding	$ 70,000	$ 62,500	$ 64,000	$ 56,000	$ 5,100
Cedar shake siding	86,000	79,400	94,000	84,800	7,400
Louvered glass doors	112,000	124,000	186,400	168,300	18,500
Thermal windows	140,000	122,000	154,800	140,000	15,400
Total	$408,000	$387,900	$499,200	$449,100	$46,400

Instructions

(a) **(1)** Determine the proper balance in the Allowance to Reduce Inventory to Market at May 31, 2007.

(2) For the fiscal year ended May 31, 2007, determine the amount of the gain or loss that would be recorded due to the change in the Allowance to Reduce Inventory to Market.

(b) Explain the rationale for the use of the lower-of-cost-or-market rule as it applies to inventories.

(CMA adapted)

(LO 1, 2) **P9-3 (Entries for Lower-of-Cost-or-Market—Direct and Allowance)** Mary Stuart Company determined its ending inventory at cost and at lower of cost or market at December 31, 2006, December 31, 2007, and December 31, 2008, as shown on page 460.

	Cost	Lower-of-Cost-or-Market
12/31/06	$650,000	$650,000
12/31/07	780,000	722,000
12/31/08	900,000	830,000

Instructions

(a) Prepare the journal entries required at December 31, 2007, and at December 31, 2008, assuming that a perpetual inventory system and the direct method of adjusting to market is used.

(b) Prepare the journal entries required at December 31, 2007, and at December 31, 2008, assuming that a perpetual inventory is recorded at cost and reduced to market through the use of an allowance account (indirect method).

(LO 5) **P9-4 (Gross Profit Method)** David Hasselholf Company lost most of its inventory in a fire in December just before the year-end physical inventory was taken. Corporate records disclose the following.

Inventory (beginning)	$ 80,000	Sales	$415,000
Purchases	280,000	Sales returns	21,000
Purchase returns	28,000	Gross profit % based on	
		net selling price	34%

Merchandise with a selling price of $30,000 remained undamaged after the fire, and damaged merchandise has a salvage value of $7,150. The company does not carry fire insurance on its inventory.

Instructions

Prepare a formal labeled schedule computing the fire loss incurred. (Do not use the retail inventory method.)

(LO 5) **P9-5 (Gross Profit Method)** On April 15, 2008, fire damaged the office and warehouse of John Kimmel Corporation. The only accounting record saved was the general ledger, from which the trial balance below was prepared.

JOHN KIMMEL CORPORATION
Trial Balance
March 31, 2008

Cash	$ 20,000	
Accounts receivable	40,000	
Inventory, December 31, 2007	75,000	
Land	35,000	
Building and equipment	110,000	
Accumulated depreciation		$ 41,300
Other assets	3,600	
Accounts payable		23,700
Other expense accruals		10,200
Capital stock		100,000
Retained earnings		52,000
Sales		135,000
Purchases	52,000	
Other expenses	26,600	
	$362,200	$362,200

The following data and information have been gathered.

1. The fiscal year of the corporation ends on December 31.
2. An examination of the April bank statement and canceled checks revealed that checks written during the period April 1–15 totaled $13,000: $5,700 paid to accounts payable as of March 31, $3,400 for April merchandise shipments, and $3,900 paid for other expenses. Deposits during the same period amounted to $12,950, which consisted of receipts on account from customers with the exception of a $950 refund from a vendor for merchandise returned in April.
3. Correspondence with suppliers revealed unrecorded obligations at April 15 of $10,600 for April merchandise shipments, including $2,300 for shipments in transit (f.o.b. shipping point) on that date.
4. Customers acknowledged indebtedness of $36,000 at April 15, 2008. It was also estimated that customers owed another $8,000 that will never be acknowledged or recovered. Of the acknowledged indebtedness, $600 will probably be uncollectible.

5. The companies insuring the inventory agreed that the corporation's fire-loss claim should be based on the assumption that the overall gross profit ratio for the past 2 years was in effect during the current year. The corporation's audited financial statements disclosed this information:

	Year Ended December 31	
	2007	2006
Net sales	$530,000	$390,000
Net purchases	280,000	235,000
Beginning inventory	50,000	75,200
Ending inventory	75,000	50,000

6. Inventory with a cost of $7,000 was salvaged and sold for $3,500. The balance of the inventory was a total loss.

[handwritten: Sales 3,000]

Instructions
Prepare a schedule computing the amount of inventory fire loss. The supporting schedule of the computation of the gross profit should be in good form.

(AICPA adapted)

(LO 6) **P9-6 (Retail Inventory Method)** The records for the Clothing Department of Magdalena Aguilar's Discount Store are summarized below for the month of January.

Inventory, January 1: at retail $25,000; at cost $17,000
Purchases in January: at retail $137,000; at cost $86,500
Freight-in: $7,000
Purchase returns: at retail $3,000; at cost $2,300
Transfers in from suburban branch: at retail $13,000; at cost $9,200
Net markups: $8,000
Net markdowns: $4,000
Inventory losses due to normal breakage, etc.: at retail $400
Sales at retail: $85,000
Sales returns: $2,400

Instructions
(a) Compute the inventory for this department as of January 31, at retail prices.
(b) Compute the ending inventory using lower-of-average-cost-or-market.

(LO 6) **P9-7 (Retail Inventory Method)** Presented below is information related to Edward Braddock Inc.

	Cost	Retail
Inventory, 12/31/07	$250,000	$ 390,000
Purchases	914,500	1,460,000
Purchase returns	60,000	80,000
Purchase discounts	18,000	—
Gross sales (after employee discounts)	—	1,460,000
Sales returns	—	97,500
Markups	—	120,000
Markup cancellations	—	40,000
Markdowns	—	45,000
Markdown cancellations	—	20,000
Freight-in	79,000	—
Employee discounts granted	—	8,000
Loss from breakage (normal)	—	2,500

Instructions
Assuming that Edward Braddock Inc. uses the conventional retail inventory method, compute the cost of its ending inventory at December 31, 2008.

(LO 6) **P9-8 (Retail Inventory Method)** Jared Jones Inc. uses the retail inventory method to estimate ending inventory for its monthly financial statements. The following data pertain to a single department for the month of October 2008.

Inventory, October 1, 2008	
At cost	$ 52,000
At retail	78,000
Purchases (exclusive of freight and returns)	
At cost	262,000
At retail	423,000
Freight-in	16,600
Purchase returns	
At cost	5,600
At retail	8,000
Additional markups	9,000
Markup cancellations	2,000
Markdowns (net)	3,600
Normal spoilage and breakage	10,000
Sales	380,000

Instructions

(a) Using the conventional retail method, prepare a schedule computing estimated lower-of-cost-or-market inventory for October 31, 2008.

(b) A department store using the conventional retail inventory method estimates the cost of its ending inventory as $60,000. An accurate physical count reveals only $47,000 of inventory at lower-of-cost-or-market. List the factors that may have caused the difference between the computed inventory and the physical count.

(LO 1, 2, 4, 7) **P9-9 (Statement and Note Disclosure, LCM, and Purchase Commitment)** Garth Brooks Specialty Company, a division of Fresh Horses Inc., manufactures three models of gear shift components for bicycles that are sold to bicycle manufacturers, retailers, and catalog outlets. Since beginning operations in 1975, Brooks has used normal absorption costing and has assumed a first-in, first-out cost flow in its perpetual inventory system. The balances of the inventory accounts at the end of Brooks's fiscal year, November 30, 2007, are shown below. The inventories are stated at cost before any year-end adjustments.

Finished goods	$647,000
Work-in-process	112,500
Raw materials	240,000
Factory supplies	69,000

The following information relates to Brooks's inventory and operations.

1. The finished goods inventory consists of the items analyzed below.

	Cost	Market
Down tube shifter		
Standard model	$ 67,500	$ 67,000
Click adjustment model	94,500	87,000
Deluxe model	108,000	110,000
Total down tube shifters	270,000	264,000
Bar end shifter		
Standard model	83,000	90,050
Click adjustment model	99,000	97,550
Total bar end shifters	182,000	187,600
Head tube shifter		
Standard model	78,000	77,650
Click adjustment model	117,000	119,300
Total head tube shifters	195,000	196,950
Total finished goods	$647,000	$648,550

2. One-half of the head tube shifter finished goods inventory is held by catalog outlets on consignment.
3. Three-quarters of the bar end shifter finished goods inventory has been pledged as collateral for a bank loan.
4. One-half of the raw materials balance represents derailleurs acquired at a contracted price 20 percent above the current market price. The market value of the rest of the raw materials is $127,400.
5. The total market value of the work-in-process inventory is $108,700.
6. Included in the cost of factory supplies are obsolete items with an historical cost of $4,200. The market value of the remaining factory supplies is $65,900.

7. Brooks applies the lower-of-cost-or-market method to each of the three types of shifters in finished goods inventory. For each of the other three inventory accounts, Brooks applies the lower-of-cost-or-market method to the total of each inventory account.

8. Consider all amounts presented above to be material in relation to Brooks' financial statements taken as a whole.

Instructions

(a) Prepare the inventory section of Brooks's balance sheet as of November 30, 2007, including any required note(s).

(b) Without prejudice to your answer to (a), assume that the market value of Brooks' inventories is less than cost. Explain how this decline would be presented in Brooks' income statement for the fiscal year ended November 30, 2007.

(c) Assume that Brooks has a firm purchase commitment for the same type of derailleur included in the raw materials inventory as of November 30, 2007, and that the purchase commitment is at a contracted price 15% greater than the current market price. These derailleurs are to be delivered to Brooks after November 30, 2007. Discuss the impact, if any, that this purchase commitment would have on Brooks's financial statements prepared for the fiscal year ended November 30, 2007.

(CMA adapted)

(LO 1, 2) **P9-10 (Lower-of-Cost-or-Market)** Fortner Co. follows the practice of valuing its inventory at the lower-of-cost-or-market. The following information is available from the company's inventory records as of December 31, 2006.

Item	Quantity	Unit Cost	Replacement Cost/Unit	Estimated Selling Price/Unit	Completion & Disposal Cost/Unit	Normal Profit Margin/Unit
A	1,100	$7.50	$8.40	$10.50	$1.50	$1.80
B	800	8.20	8.00	9.40	0.90	1.20
C	1,000	5.60	5.40	7.20	1.10	0.60
D	1,000	3.80	4.20	6.30	0.80	1.50
E	1,400	6.40	6.30	6.80	0.70	1.00

Instructions

Finn Berge is an accounting clerk in the accounting department of Fortner Co., and he cannot understand why the market value keeps changing from replacement cost to net realizable value to something that he cannot even figure out. Finn is very confused, and he is the one who records inventory purchases and calculates ending inventory. You are the manager of the department and an accountant.

(a) Calculate the lower-of-cost-or-market using the "individual item" approach.

(b) Show the journal entry he will need to make in order to write down the ending inventory from cost to market.

(c) Then write a memo to Finn explaining what designated market value is as well as how it is computed. Use your calculations to aid in your explanation.

(LO 8) ***P9-11 (Conventional and Dollar-Value LIFO Retail)** As of January 1, 2008, Carl Sandburg Inc. installed the retail method of accounting for its merchandise inventory.

To prepare the store's financial statements at June 30, 2008, you obtain the following data.

	Cost	Selling Price
Inventory, January 1	$ 30,000	$ 43,000
Markdowns		10,500
Markups		9,200
Markdown cancellations		6,500
Markup cancellations		3,200
Purchases	108,800	155,000
Sales		159,000
Purchase returns	2,800	4,000
Sales returns and allowances		8,000

Instructions

(a) Prepare a schedule to compute Sandburg's June 30, 2008, inventory under the conventional retail method of accounting for inventories.

(b) Without prejudice to your solution to part (a), assume that you computed the June 30, 2008, inventory to be $54,000 at retail and the ratio of cost to retail to be 70%. The general price level has increased from 100 at January 1, 2008, to 108 at June 30, 2008. Prepare a schedule to compute the June 30, 2008, inventory at the June 30 price level under the dollar-value LIFO retail method.

(AICPA adapted)

(LO 8) ***P9-12** **(Retail, LIFO Retail, and Inventory Shortage)** Late in 2004, Sara Teasdale and four other investors took the chain of Sprint Department Stores private, and the company has just completed its third year of operations under the ownership of the investment group. Elinor Wylie, controller of Sprint Department Stores, is in the process of preparing the year-end financial statements. Based on the preliminary financial statements, Teasdale has expressed concern over inventory shortages, and she has asked Wylie to determine whether an abnormal amount of theft and breakage has occurred. The accounting records of Sprint Department Stores contain the following amounts on November 30, 2007, the end of the fiscal year.

	Cost	Retail
Beginning inventory	$ 68,000	$100,000
Purchases	248,200	400,000
Net markups		50,000
Net markdowns		110,000
Sales		330,000

According to the November 30, 2007, physical inventory, the actual inventory at retail is $107,000.

Instructions

(a) Describe the circumstances under which the retail inventory method would be applied and the advantages of using the retail inventory method.

(b) Assuming that prices have been stable, calculate the value, at cost, of Sprint Department Stores' ending inventory using the last-in, first-out (LIFO) retail method. Be sure to furnish supporting calculations.

(c) Estimate the amount of shortage, at retail, that has occurred at Sprint Department Stores during the year ended November 30, 2007.

(d) Complications in the retail method can be caused by such items as (1) freight-in costs, (2) purchase returns and allowances, (3) sales returns and allowances, and (4) employee discounts. Explain how each of these four special items is handled in the retail inventory method.

(CMA adapted)

(LO 8) ***P9-13** **(Change to LIFO Retail)** Ulysses Grant Stores Inc., which uses the conventional retail inventory method, wishes to change to the LIFO retail method beginning with the accounting year ending December 31, 2007.

Amounts as shown below appear on the store's books before adjustment.

	At Cost	At Retail
Inventory, January 1, 2007	$ 13,600	$ 24,000
Purchases in 2007	116,200	184,000
Markups in 2007		12,000
Markdowns in 2007		5,500
Sales in 2007		170,000

You are to assume that all markups and markdowns apply to 2007 purchases, and that it is appropriate to treat the entire inventory as a single department.

Instructions

Compute the inventory at December 31, 2007, under the following methods.

(a) The conventional retail method.

(b) The last-in, first-out retail method, effecting the change in method as of January 1, 2007. Assume that the cost-to-retail percentage for 2006 was recomputed correctly in accordance with procedures necessary to change to LIFO. This ratio was 57%.

(AICPA adapted)

(LO 8) ***P9-14** **(Change to LIFO Retail; Dollar-Value LIFO Retail)** Rudyard Kipling Department Store converted from the conventional retail method to the LIFO retail method on January 1, 2006, and is now considering converting to the dollar-value LIFO inventory method. During your examination of the financial statements for the year ended December 31, 2007, management requested that you furnish a summary showing certain computations of inventory cost for the past 3 years.

Here is the available information.

1. The inventory at January 1, 2005, had a retail value of $56,000 and cost of $26,700 based on the conventional retail method.

2. Transactions during 2005 were as follows.

	Cost	Retail
Gross purchases	$311,000	$554,000
Purchase returns	5,200	10,000
Purchase discounts	6,000	
Gross sales (after employee discounts)		551,000
Sales returns		9,000
Employee discounts		3,000
Freight-in	17,600	
Net markups		20,000
Net markdowns		12,000

3. The retail value of the December 31, 2006, inventory was $73,500, the cost ratio for 2006 under the LIFO retail method was 61%, and the regional price index was 105% of the January 1, 2006, price level.

4. The retail value of the December 31, 2007, inventory was $65,880, the cost ratio for 2007 under the LIFO retail method was 60%, and the regional price index was 108% of the January 1, 2006, price level.

Instructions

(a) Prepare a schedule showing the computation of the cost of inventory on hand at December 31, 2005, based on the conventional retail method.

(b) Prepare a schedule showing the recomputation of the inventory to be reported on December 31, 2005, in accordance with procedures necessary to convert from the conventional retail method to the LIFO retail method beginning January 1, 2006. Assume that the retail value of the December 31, 2005, inventory was $63,000.

(c) Without prejudice to your solution to part (b), assume that you computed the December 31, 2005, inventory (retail value $63,000) under the LIFO retail method at a cost of $34,965. Prepare a schedule showing the computations of the cost of the store's 2006 and 2007 year-end inventories under the dollar-value LIFO method.

(AICPA adapted)

CONCEPTS FOR ANALYSIS

CA9-1 (Lower-of-Cost-or-Market) You have been asked by the financial vice-president to develop a short presentation on the lower-of-cost-or-market method for inventory purposes. The financial VP needs to explain this method to the president, because it appears that a portion of the company's inventory has declined in value.

Instructions

The financial VP asks you to answer the following questions.

(a) What is the purpose of the lower-of-cost-or-market method?

(b) What is meant by "market"? (*Hint*: Discuss the ceiling and floor constraints.)

(c) Do you apply the lower-of-cost-or-market method to each individual item, to a category, or to the total of the inventory? Explain.

(d) What are the potential disadvantages of the lower-of-cost-or-market method?

CA9-2 (Lower-of-Cost-or-Market) The market value of Lake Corporation's inventory has declined below its cost. Vickie Maher, the controller, wants to use the allowance method to write down inventory because it more clearly discloses the decline in market value and does not distort the cost of goods sold. Her supervisor, financial vice-president Doug Brucki, prefers the direct method to write down inventory because it does not call attention to the decline in market value.

Instructions

Answer the following questions.

(a) What, if any, is the ethical issue involved?

(b) Is any stakeholder harmed if Brucki's preference is used?

(c) What should Vickie Maher do?

CA9-3 (Lower-of-Cost-or-Market) Lena Horne Corporation purchased a significant amount of raw materials inventory for a new product that it is manufacturing.

Horne uses the lower-of-cost-or-market rule for these raw materials. The replacement cost of the raw materials is above the net realizable value, and both are below the original cost.

Horne uses the average cost inventory method for these raw materials. In the last 2 years, each purchase has been at a lower price than the previous purchase, and the ending inventory quantity for each period has been higher than the beginning inventory quantity for that period.

Instructions
- (a) (1) At which amount should Horne's raw materials inventory be reported on the balance sheet? Why?
  - (2) In general, why is the lower-of-cost-or-market rule used to report inventory?
- (b) What would have been the effect on ending inventory and cost of goods sold had Horne used the LIFO inventory method instead of the average-cost inventory method for the raw materials? Why?

 CA9-4 (Retail Inventory Method) Aragon Company, your client, manufactures paint. The company's president, Catherine Aragon, has decided to open a retail store to sell Aragon paint as well as wallpaper and other supplies that would be purchased from other suppliers. She has asked you for information about the conventional retail method of pricing inventories at the retail store.

Instructions
Prepare a report to the president explaining the retail method of pricing inventories. Your report should include the following points.

- (a) Description and accounting features of the method.
- (b) The conditions that may distort the results under the method.
- (c) A comparison of the advantages of using the retail method with those of using cost methods of inventory pricing.
- (d) The accounting theory underlying the treatment of net markdowns and net markups under the method.

(AICPA adapted)

CA9-5 (Cost Determination, LCM, Retail Method) E. A. Poe Corporation, a retailer and wholesaler of national brand-name household lighting fixtures, purchases its inventories from various suppliers.

Instructions
- (a) (1) What criteria should be used to determine which of Poe's costs are inventoriable?
  - (2) Are Poe's administrative costs inventoriable? Defend your answer.
- (b) (1) Poe uses the lower-of-cost-or-market rule for its wholesale inventories. What are the theoretical arguments for that rule?
  - (2) The replacement cost of the inventories is below the net realizable value less a normal profit margin, which, in turn, is below the original cost. What amount should be used to value the inventories? Why?
- (c) Poe calculates the estimated cost of its ending inventories held for sale at retail using the conventional retail inventory method. How would Poe treat the beginning inventories and net markdowns in calculating the cost ratio used to determine its ending inventories? Why?

(AICPA adapted)

 CA9-6 (Purchase Commitments) Vineland Company signed a long-term purchase contract to buy timber from the U.S. Forest Service at $300 per thousand board feet. Under these terms, Vineland must cut and pay $6,000,000 for this timber during the next year. Currently the market value is $250 per thousand board feet. At this rate, the market price is $5,000,000. Ruben Walker, the controller, wants to recognize the loss in value on the year-end financial statements, but the financial vice-president, Billie Hands, argues that the loss is temporary and should be ignored. Walker notes that market value has remained near $250 for many months, and he sees no sign of significant change.

Instructions
- (a) What are the ethical issues, if any?
- (b) Is any particular stakeholder harmed by the financial vice-president's decision?
- (c) What should the controller do?

*CA9-7 (Retail Inventory Method and LIFO Retail) Presented below are a number of items that may be encountered in computing the cost to retail percentage when using the conventional retail method or the LIFO retail method.

1. Markdowns.
2. Markdown cancellations.

3. Cost of items transferred in from other departments.

4. Retail value of items transferred in from other departments.
5. Sales discounts.
6. Purchases discounts (purchases recorded gross).
7. Estimated retail value of goods broken or stolen.
8. Cost of beginning inventory.
9. Retail value of beginning inventory.
10. Cost of purchases.
11. Retail value of purchases.
12. Markups.
13. Markup cancellations.
14. Employee discounts (sales recorded net).

Instructions

For each of the items listed above, indicate whether this item would be considered in the cost to retail percentage under **(a)** conventional retail and **(b)** LIFO retail.

USING YOUR JUDGMENT

Financial Reporting Problem

 The Procter & Gamble Company (P&G)

The financial statements of P&G are presented in Appendix 5B or can be accessed at the book's website.

Instructions

Refer to P&G's financial statements and the accompanying notes to answer the following questions.

(a) How does P&G value its inventories? Which inventory costing method does P&G use as a basis for reporting its inventories?

(b) How does P&G report its inventories in the balance sheet? In the notes to its financial statements, what three descriptions are used to classify its inventories?

(c) What costs does P&G include in inventory?

(d) What was P&G's inventory turnover ratio in 2004? What is its gross profit percentage? Evaluate P&G's inventory turnover ratio and its gross profit percentage.

Financial Statement Analysis Cases

Case 1 Sonic, Inc.

Sonic, Inc., reported the following information regarding 2006–2007 inventory.

Sonic, Inc.

	2007	2006
Current assets		
Cash	$ 153,010	$ 538,489
Accounts receivable, net of allowance for doubtful accounts of $46,000 in 2007 and $160,000 in 2006	1,627,980	2,596,291
Inventories (Note 2)	1,340,494	1,734,873
Other current assets	123,388	90,592
Assets of discontinued operations	—	32,815
Total current assets	3,244,872	4,993,060

Notes to Consolidated Financial Statements

Note 1 (in part): Nature of Business and Significant Accounting Policies

Inventories—Inventories are stated at the lower-of-cost-or-market. Cost is determined by the last-in, first-out (LIFO) method by the parent company and by the first-in, first-out (FIFO) method by its subsidiaries.

Note 2: Inventories

Inventories consist of the following.

	2007	2006
Raw materials	$1,264,646	$2,321,178
Work in process	240,988	171,222
Finished goods and display units	129,406	711,252
Total inventories	1,635,040	3,203,652
Less: Amount classified as long-term	294,546	1,468,779
Current portion	$1,340,494	$1,734,873

Inventories are stated at the lower of cost determined by the LIFO method or market for Sonic, Inc. Inventories for the two wholly-owned subsidiaries, Sonic Command, Inc. (U.S.) and Sonic Limited (U.K.) are stated on the FIFO method which amounted to $566,000 at October 31, 2006. No inventory is stated on the FIFO method at October 31, 2007. Included in inventory stated at FIFO cost was $32,815 at October 31, 2006, of Sonic Command inventory classified as an asset from discontinued operations (see Note 14). If the FIFO method had been used for the entire consolidated group, inventories after an adjustment to the lower-of-cost-or-market, would have been approximately $2,000,000 and $3,800,000 at October 31, 2007 and 2006, respectively.

Inventory has been written down to estimated net realizable value, and results of operations for 2007, 2006, and 2005 include a corresponding charge of approximately $868,000, $960,000, and $273,000, respectively, which represents the excess of LIFO cost over market.

Inventory of $294,546 and $1,468,779 at October 31, 2007 and 2006, respectively, shown on the balance sheet as a noncurrent asset represents that portion of the inventory that is not expected to be sold currently.

Reduction in inventory quantities during the years ended October 31, 2007, 2006, and 2005 resulted in liquidation of LIFO inventory quantities carried at a lower cost prevailing in prior years as compared with the cost of fiscal 2004 purchases. The effect of these reductions was to decrease the net loss by approximately $24,000, $157,000 and $90,000 at October 31, 2007, 2006, and 2005, respectively.

Instructions

(a) Why might Sonic, Inc., use two different methods for valuing inventory?

(b) Comment on why Sonic, Inc. might disclose how its LIFO inventories would be valued under FIFO.

(c) Why does the LIFO liquidation reduce operating costs?

(d) Comment on whether Sonic would report more or less income if it had been on a FIFO basis for all its inventory.

Case 2 Barrick Gold Corporation

Barrick Gold Corporation, with headquarters in Toronto, Canada, is the world's most profitable and largest gold mining company outside South Africa. Part of the key to Barrick's success has been due to its ability to maintain cash flow while improving production and increasing its reserves of gold-containing property. During 2004, Barrick achieved record growth in cash flow, production, and reserves.

The company maintains an aggressive policy of developing previously identified target areas that have the possibility of a large amount of gold ore, and that have not been previously developed. Barrick limits the riskiness of this development by choosing only properties that are located in politically stable regions, and by the company's use of internally generated funds, rather than debt, to finance growth.

Barrick's inventories are as follows:

Inventories (in millions, US dollars)	
Current	
Gold in process	$133
Mine operating supplies	82
	$215
Non-current (included in Other assets)	
Ore in stockpiles	$65

Instructions

(a) Why do you think that there are no finished goods inventories? Why do you think the raw material, ore in stockpiles, is considered to be a non-current asset?

(b) Consider that Barrick has no finished goods inventories. What journal entries are made to record a sale?

(c) Suppose that gold bullion that cost $1.8 million to produce was sold for $2.4 million. The journal entry was made to record the sale, but no entry was made to remove the gold from the gold in process inventory. How would this error affect the following?

Balance Sheet		Income Statement	
Inventory	?	Cost of goods sold	?
Retained earnings	?	Net income	?
Accounts payable	?		
Working capital	?		
Current ratio	?		

Comparative Analysis Case

The Coca-Cola Company and PepsiCo, Inc.

Instructions

Go to the book's website and use information found there to answer the following questions related to **The Coca-Cola Company** and **PepsiCo, Inc.**

(a) What is the amount of inventory reported by Coca-Cola at December 31, 2004, and by PepsiCo at December 25, 2004? What percent of total assets is invested in inventory by each company?

(b) What inventory costing methods are used by Coca-Cola and PepsiCo? How does each company value its inventories?

(c) In the notes, what classifications (description) are used by Coca-Cola and PepsiCo to categorize their inventories?

(d) Compute and compare the inventory turnover ratios and days to sell inventory for Coca-Cola and PepsiCo for 2004. Indicate why there might be a significant difference between the two companies.

Research Cases

Case 1

Numerous companies have established home pages on the Internet, for example, **Boston Beer Company** (www.samadams.com), **Ford Motor Company** (www.ford.com), and **Kodak** (www.kodak.com). You undoubtedly have noticed company Internet addresses in television commercials or magazine advertisements.

Instructions

Examine the home pages of any two companies and answer the following questions.

(a) What type of information is available?

(b) Is any accounting-related information presented?

(c) Would you describe the home page as informative, promotional, or both? Why?

Case 2

The September 23, 1994, edition of the *Wall Street Journal* includes an article titled "CompUSA Auctions Notebook Computers Through Bulk Sale."

Instructions

Read the article and answer the following questions.

(a) At what amount did CompUSA estimate the retail value of the computers? What was the estimate made by one of the bidders?

(b) What was wrong with the computers?

(c) What were the rules of the auction as specified by CompUSA?

(d) CompUSA had just recorded a $3 million inventory write-down in the preceding quarter. Based on the information in the article, does it appear that additional write-downs were called for?

Professional Research: Financial Accounting and Reporting

Jones Co. is in a technology-intensive industry. Recently, one of its competitors introduced a new product with technology that might render obsolete some of Jones's inventory. The accounting staff wants to follow the appropriate authoritative literature in determining the accounting for this significant market event.

Instructions

Using the **Financial Accounting Research System (FARS)**, respond to the following items. (Provide text strings used in your search.)

(a) Identify the authoritative literature addressing inventory pricing. (*Hint:* Do not ignore the literature issued by predecessors to the FASB.)

(b) List three types of goods that are classified as inventory. What characteristic will automatically exclude an item from being classified as inventory?

(c) Define "market" as used in the phrase "lower-of-cost-or-market."

(d) Explain when it is acceptable to state inventory above cost and which industries allow this practice.

Professional Simulation

In this simulation you are asked to address questions relating to inventory valuation and measurement. Prepare responses to all parts.

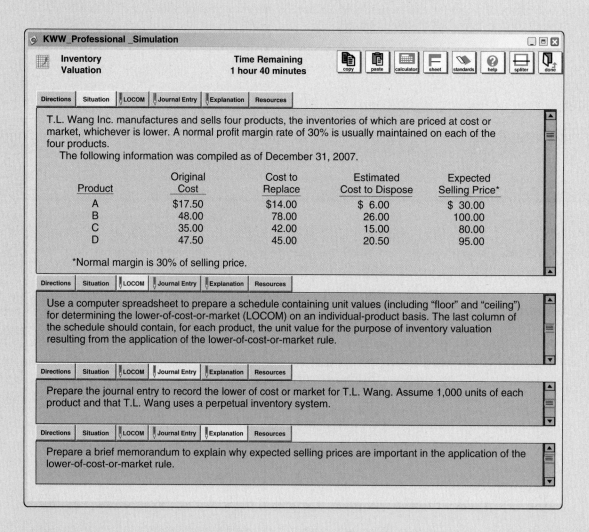

KWW_Professional _Simulation

| Inventory Valuation | Time Remaining 1 hour 40 minutes |

Directions | Situation | LOCOM | Journal Entry | Explanation | Resources

T.L. Wang Inc. manufactures and sells four products, the inventories of which are priced at cost or market, whichever is lower. A normal profit margin rate of 30% is usually maintained on each of the four products.

The following information was compiled as of December 31, 2007.

Product	Original Cost	Cost to Replace	Estimated Cost to Dispose	Expected Selling Price*
A	$17.50	$14.00	$ 6.00	$ 30.00
B	48.00	78.00	26.00	100.00
C	35.00	42.00	15.00	80.00
D	47.50	45.00	20.50	95.00

*Normal margin is 30% of selling price.

Directions | Situation | LOCOM | Journal Entry | Explanation | Resources

Use a computer spreadsheet to prepare a schedule containing unit values (including "floor" and "ceiling") for determining the lower-of-cost-or-market (LOCOM) on an individual-product basis. The last column of the schedule should contain, for each product, the unit value for the purpose of inventory valuation resulting from the application of the lower-of-cost-or-market rule.

Directions | Situation | LOCOM | Journal Entry | Explanation | Resources

Prepare the journal entry to record the lower of cost or market for T.L. Wang. Assume 1,000 units of each product and that T.L. Wang uses a perpetual inventory system.

Directions | Situation | LOCOM | Journal Entry | Explanation | Resources

Prepare a brief memorandum to explain why expected selling prices are important in the application of the lower-of-cost-or-market rule.

Remember to check the book's companion website to find additional resources for this chapter.

ACQUISITION AND DISPOSITION OF PROPERTY, PLANT, AND EQUIPMENT

Where Have All the Assets Gone?

Investments in long-lived assets, such as property, plant, and equipment, are important elements in many companies' balance sheets. As the chart below indicates, major companies, such as **Southwest Airlines** and **Wal-Mart**, recently reported property, plant, and equipment (PP&E) as a percent of total assets ranging from 54 percent up to nearly 77 percent.

However, for various strategic reasons, many companies are now shedding property, plant, and equipment. Instead, they are paying others to manufacture and assemble products—functions they previously performed in their own facilities. Companies are also reducing fixed assets by outsourcing warehousing and distribution. Such logistics outsourcing can cut companies' own costs for keeping and managing inventories, and spare them the need to invest in advanced tracking technologies increasingly required by retailers. In a recent year more than 80 percent of the country's 100 biggest companies used third-party logistics providers.[1] As a result, some companies such as **Nortel** and **Lucent** are decreasing their investment in long-lived assets, as the following chart shows.

Nortel is a good example of these strategies. It has sold and outsourced certain facilities in order to reduce its direct manufacturing activities and costs. Nortel also sold its training and headset businesses. Further, it has aggressively outsourced other operations to reduce costs. Reductions in these areas will enable Nortel and other outsourcing companies to concentrate on their core operations and better manage investments in property, plant and equipment.

---

[1]Adapted from Chapter 1 in Grady Means and David Schneider, *MetaCapitalism: The e-Business Revolution and the Design of 21st-Century Companies and Markets* (New York: John Wiley and Sons, 2000); and Kris Maher, "Global Goods Jugglers," *Wall Street Journal Online* (July 5, 2005).

Learning Objectives

After studying this chapter, you should be able to:

1 Describe property, plant, and equipment.

2 Identify the costs to include in initial valuation of property, plant, and equipment.

3 Describe the accounting problems associated with self-constructed assets.

4 Describe the accounting problems associated with interest capitalization.

5 Understand accounting issues related to acquiring and valuing plant assets.

6 Describe the accounting treatment for costs subsequent to acquisition.

7 Describe the accounting treatment for the disposal of property, plant, and equipment.

As we indicate in the opening story, a company like **Southwest Airlines** has a substantial investment in property, plant, and equipment. Conversely, other companies, such as **Nortel**, have a minor investment in these types of assets. In this chapter, we discuss the proper accounting for the acquisition, use, and disposition of property, plant, and equipment. The content and organization of the chapter are as follows.

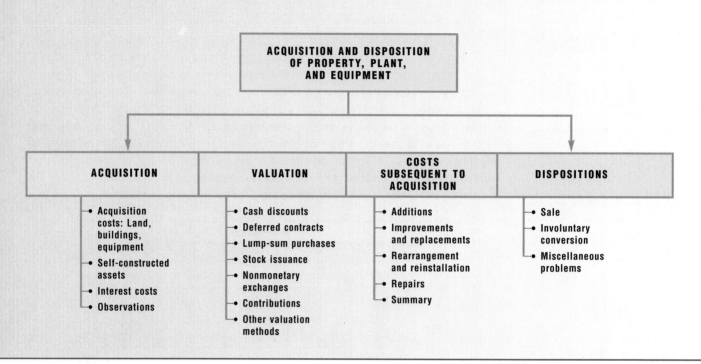

<table>
<tr><td colspan="4" align="center">**ACQUISITION AND DISPOSITION OF PROPERTY, PLANT, AND EQUIPMENT**</td></tr>
<tr><td>**ACQUISITION**</td><td>**VALUATION**</td><td>**COSTS SUBSEQUENT TO ACQUISITION**</td><td>**DISPOSITIONS**</td></tr>
<tr>
<td>
• Acquisition costs: Land, buildings, equipment
• Self-constructed assets
• Interest costs
• Observations
</td>
<td>
• Cash discounts
• Deferred contracts
• Lump-sum purchases
• Stock issuance
• Nonmonetary exchanges
• Contributions
• Other valuation methods
</td>
<td>
• Additions
• Improvements and replacements
• Rearrangement and reinstallation
• Repairs
• Summary
</td>
<td>
• Sale
• Involuntary conversion
• Miscellaneous problems
</td>
</tr>
</table>

OBJECTIVE 1
Describe property, plant, and equipment.

Companies like **Boeing**, **Target**, and **Starbucks** use assets of a durable nature. Such assets are called **property, plant, and equipment**. Other terms commonly used are **plant assets** and **fixed assets**. We use these terms interchangeably throughout this textbook.

Property, plant, and equipment include land, building structures (offices, factories, warehouses), and equipment (machinery, furniture, tools). The major characteristics of property, plant, and equipment are as follows.

1 They are acquired for use in operations and not for resale. Only assets used in normal business operations are classified as property, plant, and equipment. For example, an idle building is more appropriately classified separately as an investment. Land developers or subdividers classify land as inventory.

2 They are long-term in nature and usually depreciated. Property, plant, and equipment yield services over a number of years. Companies allocate the cost of the investment in these assets to future periods through periodic depreciation charges. The exception is land, which is depreciated only if a material decrease in value occurs, such as a loss in fertility of agricultural land because of poor crop rotation, drought, or soil erosion.

3 They possess physical substance. Property, plant, and equipment are tangible assets characterized by physical existence or substance. This differentiates them from intangible assets, such as patents or goodwill. Unlike raw material, however, property, plant, and equipment do not physically become part of a product held for resale.

UNDERLYING CONCEPTS

Market value is relevant to inventory but less so for property, plant, and equipment which, consistent with the going concern assumption, are held for use in the business, not for sale like inventory.

ACQUISITION AND VALUATION OF PROPERTY, PLANT, AND EQUIPMENT

OBJECTIVE 2
Identify the costs to include in initial valuation of property, plant, and equipment.

Most companies use historical cost as the basis for valuing property, plant, and equipment. **Historical cost measures the cash or cash equivalent price of obtaining the asset and bringing it to the location and condition necessary for its intended use.** For example, companies like **Kellogg Co.** consider the purchase price, freight costs, sales taxes, and installation costs of a productive asset as part of the asset's cost. It then allocates these costs to future periods through depreciation. Further, Kellogg **adds to the asset's cost** any related costs incurred **after the asset's acquisition,** such as additions, improvements, or replacements, **if they provide future service potential.** Otherwise, Kellogg expenses these costs immediately.

Disagreement does exist concerning differences between historical cost and other valuation methods (such as replacement cost or fair market value) **arising after acquisition.** *APB Opinion No. 6* states, "property, plant, and equipment should not be written up to reflect appraisal, market, or current values which are above cost." Although the opinion notes minor exceptions, current standards indicate that departures from historical cost are rare. The main reasons for this position are as follows:

1 At the date of acquisition, cost reflects fair value.

2 Historical cost involves actual, not hypothetical, transactions and so is the most reliable.

3 Companies should not anticipate gains and losses but should recognize gains and losses only when the asset is sold.

INTERNATIONAL INSIGHT

In many nations, such as Great Britain and Brazil, companies may revalue their fixed assets at amounts above historical cost. These revaluations may be at appraisal values or at amounts linked to a specified index.

Cost of Land

All expenditures made to acquire land and ready it for use are considered part of the land cost. Thus, when **Wal-Mart** or **Home Depot** purchases land on which to build a new store, its land costs typically include (1) the purchase price; (2) closing costs, such as title to the land, attorney's fees, and recording fees; (3) costs incurred in getting the land in condition for its intended use, such as grading, filling, draining, and clearing; (4) assumption of any liens, mortgages, or encumbrances on the property; and (5) any additional land improvements that have an indefinite life.

Expanded Discussion of Alternative Valuation Methods

For example, when Home Depot purchases land for the purpose of constructing a building, it considers all costs incurred up to the excavation for the new building as land costs. **Removal of old buildings—clearing, grading, and filling—is a land cost because this activity is necessary to get the land in condition for its intended purpose.** Home Depot treats any proceeds from getting the land ready for its intended use, such as salvage receipts on the demolition of an old building or the sale of cleared timber, as **reductions in the price of the land.**

In some cases, when Home Depot purchases land, it may assume certain obligations on the land such as back taxes or liens. In such situations, the cost of the land is the cash paid for it, plus the encumbrances. In other words, if the purchase price of the land is $50,000 cash, but Home Depot assumes accrued property taxes of $5,000 and liens of $10,000, its land cost is $65,000.

Home Depot also might incur **special assessments** for local improvements, such as pavements, street lights, sewers, and drainage systems. It should charge these costs to the Land account because they are relatively permanent in nature. That is, after installation, they are maintained by the local government. In addition, Home Depot should charge any permanent improvements it makes, such as landscaping, to the Land account. It records separately any **improvements with limited lives,** such as private driveways, walks, fences, and parking lots, as Land Improvements. These costs are depreciated over their estimated lives.

Generally, land is part of property, plant, and equipment. However, if the major purpose of acquiring and holding land is speculative, a company more appropriately classifies the land as an **investment**. If a real estate concern holds the land for resale, it should classify the land as **inventory**.

In cases where land is held as an investment, what accounting treatment should be given for taxes, insurance, and other direct costs incurred while holding the land? Many believe these costs should be capitalized. The reason: They are not generating revenue from the investment at this time. Companies generally use this approach except when the asset is currently producing revenue (such as rental property).

Cost of Buildings

The cost of buildings should include all expenditures related directly to their acquisition or construction. These costs include (1) materials, labor, and overhead costs incurred during construction and (2) professional fees and building permits. Generally, companies contract others to construct their buildings. Companies consider all costs incurred, from excavation to completion, as part of the building costs.

But how should companies account for an old building that is on the site of a newly proposed building? Is the cost of removal of the old building a cost of the land or a cost of the new building? Recall that **if a company purchases land with an old building on it, then the cost of demolition less its salvage value is a cost of getting the land ready for its intended use and relates to the land rather than to the new building.** In other words, all costs of getting an asset ready for its intended use are costs of that asset.

Cost of Equipment

The term "equipment" in accounting includes delivery equipment, office equipment, machinery, furniture and fixtures, furnishings, factory equipment, and similar fixed assets. The cost of such assets includes the purchase price, freight and handling charges incurred, insurance on the equipment while in transit, cost of special foundations if required, assembling and installation costs, and costs of conducting trial runs. Costs thus include all expenditures incurred in acquiring the equipment and preparing it for use.

Self-Constructed Assets

OBJECTIVE 3
Describe the accounting problems associated with self-constructed assets.

Occasionally companies construct their own assets. Determining the cost of such machinery and other fixed assets can be a problem. Without a purchase price or contract price, the company must allocate costs and expenses to arrive at the cost of the **self-constructed asset**. Materials and direct labor used in construction pose no problem. A company can trace these costs directly to work and material orders related to the fixed assets constructed.

However, the assignment of indirect costs of manufacturing creates special problems. These indirect costs, called **overhead** or **burden**, include power, heat, light, insurance, property taxes on factory buildings and equipment, factory supervisory labor, depreciation of fixed assets, and supplies.

Companies can handle indirect costs in one of two ways:

1 *Assign no fixed overhead to the cost of the constructed asset.* The major argument for this treatment is that indirect overhead is generally fixed in nature; it does not increase as a result of constructing one's own plant or equipment. This approach assumes that the company will have the same costs regardless of whether it constructs the asset or not. Therefore, to charge a portion of the overhead costs to the equipment will normally reduce current expenses and consequently overstate income of the current period. However, the company would assign to the cost of the constructed asset variable overhead costs that increase as a result of the construction.

2 *Assign a portion of all overhead to the construction process.* This approach, called a **full-costing approach**, is appropriate if one believes that costs attach to all products and assets manufactured or constructed. Under this approach, a company assigns a portion of all overhead to the construction process, as it would to normal production. Advocates say that failure to allocate overhead costs understates the initial cost of the asset and results in an inaccurate future allocation.

Companies should assign to the asset **a pro rata portion** of the fixed overhead to determine its cost. Companies use this treatment extensively because many believe that it results in a better matching of costs with revenues.

If the allocated overhead results in recording construction costs in excess of the costs that an outside independent producer would charge, the company should record the excess overhead as a period loss rather than capitalize it. This avoids capitalizing the asset at more than its probable market value.[2]

Interest Costs During Construction

The proper accounting for interest costs has been a long-standing controversy. Three approaches have been suggested to account for the interest incurred in financing the construction of property, plant, and equipment:

OBJECTIVE 4
Describe the accounting problems associated with interest capitalization.

1 *Capitalize no interest charges during construction.* Under this approach, interest is considered a cost of financing and not a cost of construction. Some contend that if a company had used stock (equity) financing rather than debt, it would not incur this cost. The major argument against this approach is that the use of cash, whatever its source, has an associated implicit interest cost, which should not be ignored.

2 *Charge construction with all costs of funds employed, whether identifiable or not.* This method maintains that the cost of construction should include the cost of financing, whether by cash, debt, or stock. Its advocates say that all costs necessary to get an asset ready for its intended use, including interest, are part of the asset's cost. Interest, whether actual or imputed, is a cost, just as are labor and materials. A major criticism of this approach is that imputing the cost of equity capital (stock) is subjective and outside the framework of a historical cost system.

3 *Capitalize only the actual interest costs incurred during construction.* This approach agrees in part with the logic of the second approach—that interest is just as much a cost as are labor and materials. But this approach capitalizes only interest costs incurred through debt financing. (That is, it does not try to determine the cost of equity financing.) Under this approach, a company that uses debt financing will have an asset of higher cost than a company that uses stock financing. Some consider this approach unsatisfactory because they believe the cost of an asset should be the same whether it is financed with cash, debt, or equity.

Illustration 10-1 (page 476) shows how a company might add interest costs (if any) to the cost of the asset under the three capitalization approaches.

---

[2] The Accounting Standards Executive Committee (AcSEC) of the AICPA has issued an exposure draft related to property, plant, and equipment. In this exposure draft, AcSEC argues against allocation of overhead. Instead, it basically supports capitalization of only direct costs (costs directly related to the specific activities involved in the construction process). AcSEC was concerned that the allocation of overhead costs may lead to overly aggressive allocations and therefore misstatements of income. In addition, not reporting these costs as period costs during the construction period may affect comparisons of period costs and resulting net income from one period to the next. See Accounting Standards Executive Committee, "Accounting for Certain Costs and Activities Related to Property, Plant, and Equipment," Exposure Draft (New York: AICPA, June 29, 2001).

ILLUSTRATION 10-1
Capitalization of Interest Costs

GAAP requires the third approach—capitalizing actual interest (with modification). This method follows the concept that the **historical cost of acquiring an asset includes all costs (including interest) incurred to bring the asset to the condition and location necessary for its intended use**. The rationale for this approach is that during construction, the asset is not generating revenues. Therefore, a company should defer (capitalize) interest costs.[3] Once construction is complete, the asset is ready for its intended use and a company can earn revenues. At this point the company should report interest as an expense and match it to these revenues. It follows that the company should expense any interest cost incurred in purchasing an asset that is ready for its intended use.

To implement this general approach, companies consider three items:

1 Qualifying assets.
2 Capitalization period.
3 Amount to capitalize.

Qualifying Assets

To qualify for interest capitalization, assets must require a period of time to get them ready for their intended use. A company capitalizes interest costs starting with the first expenditure related to the asset. Capitalization continues until the company substantially readies the asset for its intended use.

Assets that qualify for interest cost capitalization include assets under construction for a company's own use (including buildings, plants, and large machinery) and assets intended for sale or lease that are constructed or otherwise produced as discrete projects (e.g., ships or real estate developments).

Examples of assets that do not qualify for interest capitalization are (1) assets that are in use or ready for their intended use, and (2) assets that the company does not use in its earnings activities and that are not undergoing the activities necessary to get them ready for use. Examples of this second type include land remaining undeveloped and assets not used because of obsolescence, excess capacity, or need for repair.

Capitalization Period

The **capitalization period** is the period of time during which a company must capitalize interest. It begins with the presence of three conditions:

1 Expenditures for the asset have been made.
2 Activities that are necessary to get the asset ready for its intended use are in progress.
3 Interest cost is being incurred.

Interest capitalization **continues as long as these three conditions are present**. The capitalization period ends when the asset is substantially complete and ready for its intended use.

INTERNATIONAL INSIGHT

Under international accounting standards, companies may capitalize interest, but it is not the preferred treatment. The benchmark treatment is to expense interest in the period incurred.

---

[3]"Capitalization of Interest Cost," *Statement of Financial Accounting Standards No. 34* (Stamford, Conn.: FASB, 1979).

Amount to Capitalize

The amount of interest to capitalize is limited to the lower of actual interest cost incurred during the period or avoidable interest. **Avoidable interest** is the amount of interest cost during the period that a company could theoretically avoid if it had not made expenditures for the asset. If the actual interest cost for the period is $90,000 and the avoidable interest is $80,000, the company capitalizes only $80,000. Or, if the actual interest cost is $80,000 and the avoidable interest is $90,000, it still capitalizes only $80,000. In no situation should interest cost include a cost of capital charge for stockholders' equity. Furthermore, GAAP requires interest capitalization for a qualifying asset only if its effect, compared with the effect of expensing interest, is material.[4]

To apply the avoidable interest concept, a company determines the potential amount of interest that it may capitalize during an accounting period by multiplying the interest rate(s) by the **weighted-average accumulated expenditures** for qualifying assets during the period.

Weighted-Average Accumulated Expenditures. In computing the weighted-average accumulated expenditures, a company weights the construction expenditures by the amount of time (fraction of a year or accounting period) that it can incur interest cost on the expenditure.

To illustrate, assume a 17-month bridge construction project with current-year payments to the contractor of $240,000 on March 1, $480,000 on July 1, and $360,000 on November 1. The company computes the weighted-average accumulated expenditures for the year ended December 31 as follows.

Expenditures			Capitalization	Weighted-Average
Date	Amount	×	Period* =	Accumulated Expenditures
March 1	$ 240,000		10/12	$200,000
July 1	480,000		6/12	240,000
November 1	360,000		2/12	60,000
	$1,080,000			$500,000

*Months between date of expenditure and date interest capitalization stops or end of year, whichever comes first (in this case December 31).

ILLUSTRATION 10-2
Computation of
Weighted-Average
Accumulated
Expenditures

To compute the weighted-average accumulated expenditures, a company weights the expenditures by the amount of time that it can incur interest cost on each one. For the March 1 expenditure, the company associates 10 months' interest cost with the expenditure. For the expenditure on July 1, it incurs only 6 months' interest costs. For the expenditure made on November 1, the company incurs only 2 months of interest cost.

Interest Rates. Companies follow these principles in selecting the appropriate interest rates to be applied to the weighted-average accumulated expenditures:

1 For the portion of weighted-average accumulated expenditures that is less than or equal to any amounts borrowed specifically to finance construction of the assets, **use the interest rate incurred on the specific borrowings**.

---

[4]Ibid., summary paragraph.

2 For the portion of weighted-average accumulated expenditures that is greater than any debt incurred specifically to finance construction of the assets, **use a weighted average of interest rates incurred on all other outstanding debt during the period.**[5]

Illustration 10-3 shows the computation of a weighted-average interest rate for debt greater than the amount incurred specifically to finance construction of the assets.

ILLUSTRATION 10-3
Computation of
Weighted-Average
Interest Rate

	Principal	Interest
12%, 2-year note	$ 600,000	$ 72,000
9%, 10-year bonds	2,000,000	180,000
7.5%, 20-year bonds	5,000,000	375,000
	$7,600,000	$627,000

$$\text{Weighted-average interest rate} = \frac{\text{Total interest}}{\text{Total principal}} = \frac{\$627,000}{\$7,600,000} = 8.25\%$$

Comprehensive Example of Interest Capitalization

To illustrate the issues related to interest capitalization, assume that on November 1, 2006, Shalla Company contracted Pfeifer Construction Co. to construct a building for $1,400,000 on land costing $100,000 (purchased from the contractor and included in the first payment). Shalla made the following payments to the construction company during 2007.

January 1	March 1	May 1	December 31	Total
$210,000	$300,000	$540,000	$450,000	$1,500,000

Pfeifer Construction completed the building, ready for occupancy, on December 31, 2007. Shalla had the following debt outstanding at December 31, 2007.

Specific Construction Debt

1. 15%, 3-year note to finance purchase of land and construction of the building, dated December 31, 2006, with interest payable annually on December 31 $750,000

Other Debt

2. 10%, 5-year note payable, dated December 31, 2003, with interest payable annually on December 31 $550,000
3. 12%, 10-year bonds issued December 31, 2002, with interest payable annually on December 31 $600,000

Shalla computed the weighted-average accumulated expenditures during 2003 as shown in Illustration 10-4.

ILLUSTRATION 10-4
Computation of
Weighted-Average
Accumulated
Expenditures

Expenditures		Current Year Capitalization	Weighted-Average
Date	Amount ×	Period =	Accumulated Expenditures
January 1	$ 210,000	12/12	$210,000
March 1	300,000	10/12	250,000
May 1	540,000	8/12	360,000
December 31	450,000	0	0
	$1,500,000		$820,000

---

[5]The interest rate to be used may rely exclusively on an average rate of all the borrowings, if desired. For our purposes, we use the specific borrowing rate followed by the average interest rate because we believe it to be more conceptually consistent. Either method can be used; *FASB Statement No. 34* does not provide explicit guidance on this measurement. For a discussion of this issue and others related to interest capitalization, see Kathryn M. Means and Paul M. Kazenski, "SFAS 34: Recipe for Diversity," *Accounting Horizons* (September 1988); and Wendy A. Duffy, "A Graphical Analysis of Interest Capitalization," *Journal of Accounting Education* (Fall 1990).

Note that the expenditure made on December 31, the last day of the year, does not have any interest cost.

Shalla computes the avoidable interest as shown in Illustration 10-5.

ILLUSTRATION 10-5
Computation of
Avoidable Interest

Weighted-Average Accumulated Expenditures	×	Interest Rate	=	Avoidable Interest
$750,000		.15 (construction note)		$112,500
70,000[a]		.1104 (weighted average of other debt)[b]		7,728
$820,000				$120,228

[a]The amount by which the weighted-average accumulated expenditures exceeds the specific construction loan.

[b]Weighted-average interest rate computation:

	Principal	Interest
10%, 5-year note	$ 550,000	$ 55,000
12%, 10-year bonds	600,000	72,000
	$1,150,000	$127,000

$$\text{Weighted-average interest rate} = \frac{\text{Total interest}}{\text{Total principal}} = \frac{\$127,000}{\$1,150,000} = 11.04\%$$

The company determines the actual interest cost, which represents the maximum amount of interest that it may capitalize during 2007, as shown in Illustration 10-6.

ILLUSTRATION 10-6
Computation of Actual
Interest Cost

Construction note	$750,000 ×.15	=	$112,500
5-year note	$550,000 ×.10	=	55,000
10-year bonds	$600,000 ×.12	=	72,000
Actual interest			$239,500

The interest cost that Shalla capitalizes is the lesser of $120,228 (avoidable interest) and $239,500 (actual interest), or $120,228.

Shalla records the following journal entries during 2007:

January 1

Land	100,000	
Building (or Construction in Process)	110,000	
Cash		210,000

March 1

Building	300,000	
Cash		300,000

May 1

Building	540,000	
Cash		540,000

December 31

Building	450,000	
Cash		450,000
Building (Capitalized Interest)	120,228	
Interest Expense ($239,500 − $120,228)	119,272	
Cash ($112,500 + $55,000 + $72,000)		239,500

*Tutorial on Interest
Capitalization*

Shalla should write off capitalized interest cost as part of depreciation over the useful life of the assets involved and not over the term of the debt. It should disclose the total interest cost incurred during the period, with the portion charged to expense and the portion capitalized indicated.

At December 31, 2007, Shalla discloses the amount of interest capitalized either as part of the nonoperating section of the income statement or in the notes accompanying the financial statements. We illustrate both forms of disclosure, in Illustrations 10-7 and 10-8.

ILLUSTRATION 10-7
Capitalized Interest
Reported in the Income
Statement

Income from operations		XXXX
Other expenses and losses:		
Interest expense	$239,500	
Less: Capitalized interest	120,228	119,272
Income before taxes on income		XXXX
Income taxes		XXX
Net income		XXXX

ILLUSTRATION 10-8
Capitalized Interest
Disclosed in a Note

Note 1: Accounting Policies. *Capitalized Interest.* During 2007 total interest cost was $239,500, of which $120,228 was capitalized and $119,272 was charged to expense.

Special Issues Related to Interest Capitalization

Two issues related to interest capitalization merit special attention:

1 Expenditures for land.
2 Interest revenue.

Expenditures for Land. When a company purchases land with the intention of developing it for a particular use, interest costs associated with those expenditures qualify for interest capitalization. If it purchases land as a site for a structure (such as a plant site), **interest costs capitalized during the period of construction are part of the cost of the plant, not the land.** Conversely, if the company develops land for lot sales, it includes any capitalized interest cost as part of the acquisition cost of the developed land. However, it should **not** capitalize interest costs involved in purchasing land held **for speculation** because the asset is ready for its intended use.

Interest Revenue. Companies frequently borrow money to finance construction of assets. They temporarily invest the excess borrowed funds in interest-bearing securities until they need the funds to pay for construction. During the early stages of construction, interest revenue earned may exceed the interest cost incurred on the borrowed funds.

Should companies offset interest revenue against interest cost when determining the amount of interest to capitalize as part of the construction cost of assets? In general, **companies should not net or offset interest revenue against interest cost**. Temporary or short-term investment decisions are not related to the interest incurred as part of the acquisition cost of assets. Therefore, companies should capitalize the interest incurred on qualifying assets whether or not they temporarily invest excess funds in short-term securities. Some criticize this approach because a company can defer the interest cost but report the interest revenue in the current period.

Observations

The interest capitalization requirement, while now universally adopted, is still debated. From a conceptual viewpoint, many believe that, for the reasons mentioned earlier, companies should either capitalize **no interest cost** or **all interest costs**, actual or imputed.

INTERNATIONAL INSIGHT

Under international accounting standards *(IAS No. 23)*, companies may capitalize interest, but it is not the preferred treatment. Thus, the financial statements of U.S. and IAS companies may not be comparable if capitalized interest costs are significant and the IAS company uses the preferred treatment. However, an analyst can convert the U.S. GAAP numbers to be comparable to the IAS company.

The requirement to capitalize interest can significantly impact financial statements. For example, when earnings of building manufacturer **Jim Walter's Corporation** dropped from $1.51 to $1.17 per share, the company offset 11 cents per share of the decline by capitalizing the interest on coal mining projects and several plants under construction.

How do statement users determine the impact of interest capitalization on a company's bottom line? They examine the notes to the financial statements. Companies with material interest capitalization must disclose the amounts of capitalized interest relative to total interest costs. For example, **Anadarko Petroleum Corporation** capitalized nearly 30 percent of its total interest costs in a recent year and provided the following footnote related to capitalized interest.

WHAT DO THE NUMBERS MEAN?

Financial Footnotes

Total interest costs incurred during the year were $82,415,000. Of this amount, the Company capitalized $24,716,000. Capitalized interest is included as part of the cost of oil and gas properties. The capitalization rates are based on the Company's weighted-average cost of borrowings used to finance the expenditures.

VALUATION

Like other assets, **companies should record property, plant, and equipment at the fair market value of what they give up or at the fair value of the asset received**, whichever is more clearly evident. However, the process of asset acquisition sometimes obscures fair market value. For example, if a company buys land and buildings together for one price, how does it determine separate values for the land and buildings? We examine these types of accounting problems in the following sections.

Cash Discounts

When a company purchases plant assets subject to cash discounts for prompt payment, how should it report the discount? If it takes the discount, the company should consider the discount as a reduction in the purchase price of the asset. But should the company reduce the asset cost even if it does not take the discount?

> **OBJECTIVE 5**
> Understand accounting issues related to acquiring and valuing plant assets.

Two points of view exist on this question. One approach considers the discount—whether taken or not—as a reduction in the cost of the asset. The rationale for this approach is that the real cost of the asset is the cash or cash equivalent price of the asset. In addition, some argue that the terms of cash discounts are so attractive that failure to take them indicates management error or inefficiency.

Proponents of the other approach argue that failure to take the discount should not always be considered a loss. The terms may be unfavorable, or it might not be prudent for the company to take the discount. At present, companies use both methods, though most prefer the former method.

Deferred-Payment Contracts

Companies frequently purchase plant assets on long-term credit contracts, using notes, mortgages, bonds, or equipment obligations. **To properly reflect cost, companies account for assets purchased on long-term credit contracts at the present value of the consideration exchanged between the contracting parties at the date of the transaction.**

For example, Greathouse Company purchases an asset today in exchange for a $10,000 zero-interest-bearing note payable four years from now. The company would not record the asset at $10,000. Instead, the present value of the $10,000 note establishes the exchange price of the transaction (the purchase price of the asset). Assuming an appropriate interest rate of 9 percent at which to discount this single payment of $10,000 due four years from now, Greathouse records this asset at $7,084.30 ($10,000 × .70843). [See Table 6-2 for the present value of a single sum, $PV = \$10,000 (PVF_{4,9\%})$.]

When no interest rate is stated, or if the specified rate is unreasonable, the company imputes an appropriate interest rate. The objective is to approximate the interest rate that the buyer and seller would negotiate at arm's length in a similar borrowing transaction. In imputing an interest rate, companies consider such factors as the borrower's credit rating, the amount and maturity date of the note, and prevailing interest rates. **The company uses the cash exchange price of the asset acquired (if determinable) as the basis for recording the asset and measuring the interest element.**

To illustrate, Sutter Company purchases a specially built robot spray painter for its production line. The company issues a $100,000, five-year, zero-interest-bearing note to Wrigley Robotics, Inc. for the new equipment. The prevailing market rate of interest for obligations of this nature is 10 percent. Sutter is to pay off the note in five $20,000 installments, made at the end of each year. Sutter cannot readily determine the fair market value of this specially built robot. Therefore Sutter approximates the robot's value by establishing the market value (present value) of the note. Entries for the date of purchase and dates of payments, plus computation of the present value of the note, are as follows.

Date of Purchase

Equipment	75,816*	
Discount on Notes Payable	24,184	
Notes Payable		100,000

*Present value of note = $20,000 ($PVF\text{-}OA_{5,10\%}$)
= $20,000 (3.79079); Table 6-4
= $75,816

End of First Year

Interest Expense	7,582	
Notes Payable	20,000	
Cash		20,000
Discount on Notes Payable		7,582

Interest expense in the first year under the effective-interest approach is $7,582 [($100,000 − $24,184) × 10%]. The entry at the end of the second year to record interest and principal payment is as follows.

End of Second Year

Interest Expense	6,340	
Notes Payable	20,000	
Cash		20,000
Discount on Notes Payable		6,340

Interest expense in the second year under the effective-interest approach is $6,340 [($100,000 − $24,184) − ($20,000 − $7,582)] × 10%.

If Sutter did not impute an interest rate for deferred-payment contracts, it would record the asset at an amount greater than its fair value. In addition, Sutter would understate interest expense in the income statement for all periods involved.

Lump-Sum Purchases

A special problem of pricing fixed assets arises when a company purchases a group of plant assets at a single **lump-sum price**. When this common situation occurs, the company allocates the total cost among the various assets on the basis of their relative fair market values. The assumption is that costs will vary in direct proportion to fair value. This is the same principle that companies apply to allocate a lump-sum cost among different inventory items.

To determine fair market value, a company should use valuation techniques that are appropriate in the circumstances. In some cases, a single valuation technique will be appropriate. In other cases, multiple valuation approaches might have to be used.

To illustrate, Norduct Homes, Inc. decides to purchase several assets of a small heating concern, Comfort Heating, for $80,000. Comfort Heating is in the process of liquidation. Its assets sold are:

	Book Value	Fair Market Value
Inventory	$30,000	$ 25,000
Land	20,000	25,000
Building	35,000	50,000
	$85,000	$100,000

Norduct Homes allocates the $80,000 purchase price on the basis of the relative fair market values (assuming specific identification of costs is impracticable) in the following manner.

Inventory $\dfrac{\$25,000}{\$100,000} \times \$80,000 = \$20,000$

Land $\dfrac{\$25,000}{\$100,000} \times \$80,000 = \$20,000$

Building $\dfrac{\$50,000}{\$100,000} \times \$80,000 = \$40,000$

ILLUSTRATION 10-9
Allocation of Purchase Price—Relative Fair Market Value Basis

Issuance of Stock

When companies acquire property by issuing securities, such as common stock, the par or stated value of such stock fails to properly measure the property cost. If trading of the stock is active, **the market value of the stock issued is a fair indication of the cost of the property acquired. The stock is a good measure of the current cash equivalent price.**

For example, Upgrade Living Co. decides to purchase some adjacent land for expansion of its carpeting and cabinet operation. In lieu of paying cash for the land, the company issues to Deedland Company 5,000 shares of common stock (par value $10) that have a fair market value of $12 per share. Upgrade Living Co. records the following entry.

Land (5,000 × $12)	60,000	
Common Stock		50,000
Additional Paid-In Capital		10,000

If the company cannot determine the market value of the common stock exchanged, it establishes the market value of the property. It then uses the value of the property as the basis for recording the asset and issuance of the common stock.[6]

---

[6]The valuation approaches that should be used are the market, income, or cost approach, or a combination of these approaches. The *market approach* uses observable prices and other relevant information generated by market transactions involving comparable assets. The *income approach* uses valuation techniques to convert future amounts (for example, cash flows or earnings) to a single present value amount (discounted). The *cost approach* is based on the amount that currently would be required to replace the service capacity of an asset (often referred to as current replacement cost). In determining the fair value, the company should assume the highest and best use of the asset ("Fair Value Measurement," Proposed *Statement of Financial Accounting Standard* (Norwalk, Conn.: FASB, October 21, 2005).

Exchanges of Nonmonetary Assets

The proper accounting for exchanges of nonmonetary assets, such as property, plant, and equipment, is controversial.[7] Some argue that companies should account for these types of exchanges based on the fair value of the asset given up or the fair value of the asset received, with a gain or loss recognized. Others believe that they should account for exchanges based on the recorded amount (book value) of the asset given up, with no gain or loss recognized. Still others favor an approach that recognizes losses in all cases, but defers gains in special situations.

Ordinarily companies account for the exchange of **nonmonetary assets** on the basis of **the fair value of the asset given up or the fair value of the asset received, whichever is clearly more evident.**[8] Thus, companies **should recognize immediately** any gains or losses on the exchange. The rationale for immediate recognition is that most transactions have **commercial substance**, and therefore gains and losses should be recognized.

Meaning of Commercial Substance

As indicated above, fair value is the basis for measuring an asset acquired in a nonmonetary exchange if the transaction has commercial substance. An exchange has commercial substance if the future cash flows change as a result of the transaction. That is, if the two parties' economic positions change, the transaction has commercial substance.

For example, Andrew Co. exchanges some if its equipment for land held by Roddick Inc. It is likely that the timing and amount of the cash flows arising for the land will differ significantly from the cash flows arising from the equipment. As a result, both Andrew Co. and Roddick Inc. are in different economic positions. Therefore, the exchange has commercial substance, and the companies recognize a gain or loss on the exchange.

What if companies exchange similar assets, such as one truck for another truck?[9] Even in an exchange of similar assets, a change in the economic position of the company can result. For example, let's say the useful life of the truck received is significantly longer than that of the truck given up. The cash flows for the trucks can differ significantly. As a result, the transaction has commercial substance, and the company should use fair value as a basis for measuring the asset received in the exchange.

However, it is possible to exchange similar assets but not have a significant difference in cash flows. That is, the company is in the same economic position as before the exchange. In that case, the company recognizes a loss but generally defers a gain.

As we will see in the examples below, use of fair value generally results in recognizing a gain or loss at the time of the exchange. Consequently companies must

---

[7]Nonmonetary assets are items whose price in terms of the monetary unit may change over time. Monetary assets—cash and short- or long-term accounts and notes receivable—are fixed in terms of units of currency by contract or otherwise.

[8]"Accounting for Nonmonetary Transactions," *Opinions of the Accounting Principles Board No. 29* (New York: AICPA, 1973), par 18, and "Exchanges of Nonmonetary Assets, an Amendment of *APB Opinion No. 29*," *Statement of Financial Accounting Standards No. 153* (Norwalk, Conn: FASB, 2004).

[9]In previous accounting standards, the primary factor in determining whether to recognize gains on exchanges was whether the assets were "similar" in nature. This approach was problematic due to the subjectivity of determining similarity in the assets being exchanged. The new commercial-substance condition addresses this concern and contributes to international accounting convergence. The FASB and the IASB have agreed to resolve differences between the U.S. GAAP and International Financial Reporting Standards (IFRS). With the commercial-substance approach, U.S. GAAP and IFRS are now in agreement.

determine if the transaction has commercial substance. To make this determination, they must carefully evaluate the cash flow characteristics of the assets exchanged.[10]

Illustration 10-10 summarizes asset exchange situations and the related accounting.

	Type of Exchange	Accounting Guidance
	Exchange has commercial substance.	Recognize gains and losses immediately.
	Exchange lacks commercial substance—no cash received.	Defer gains; recognize losses immediately.
	Exchange lacks commercial substance—cash received.	Recognize partial gain; recognize losses immediately.*

*If cash is 25% or more of the fair value of the exchange, recognize entire gain because earnings process is complete.

ILLUSTRATION 10-10
Accounting for
Exchanges

As Illustration 10-10 indicates, companies immediately recognize losses they incur on all exchanges. The accounting for gains depends on whether the exchange has commercial substance. If the exchange has commercial substance, the company recognizes the gain immediately. However, the profession modifies the rule for immediate recognition of a gain when an exchange lacks commercial substance: If the company receives no cash in such an exchange, it defers recognition of a gain. If the company receives cash in such an exchange, it recognizes part of the gain immediately.

To illustrate the accounting for these different types of transactions, we examine various loss and gain exchange situations.

Exchanges—Loss Situation

When a company exchanges nonmonetary assets and a loss results, the company recognizes the loss immediately. The rationale: Companies should not value assets at more than their cash equivalent price; if the loss were deferred, assets would be overstated. Therefore, companies recognize a loss immediately whether the exchange has commercial substance or not.

For example, Information Processing, Inc. trades its used machine for a new model at Jerrod Business Solutions Inc. The exchange has commercial substance. The used machine has a book value of $8,000 (original cost $12,000 less $4,000 accumulated depreciation) and a fair value of $6,000. The new model lists for $16,000. Jerrod gives Information Processing a trade-in allowance of $9,000 for the used machine. Information Processing computes the cost of the new asset as follows.

List price of new machine	$16,000
Less: Trade-in allowance for used machine	9,000
Cash payment due	7,000
Fair value of used machine	6,000
Cost of new machine	$13,000

ILLUSTRATION 10-11
Computation of Cost of
New Machine

[10]The determination of the commercial substance of a transaction requires significant judgment. In determining whether future cash flows change, it is necessary to do one of two things: (1) Determine whether the risk, timing, and amount of cash flows arising for the asset received differ from the cash flows associated with the outbound asset. Or, (2) evaluate whether cash flows are affected with the exchange versus without the exchange. Also note that if companies cannot determine fair values of the assets exchanged, then they should use recorded book values in accounting for the exchange.

Information Processing records this transaction as follows:

Equipment	13,000	
Accumulated Depreciation—Equipment	4,000	
Loss on Disposal of Equipment	2,000	
Equipment		12,000
Cash		7,000

We verify the loss on the disposal of the used machine as follows:

ILLUSTRATION 10-12
Computation of Loss on
Disposal of Used
Machine

Fair value of used machine	$6,000
Book value of used machine	8,000
Loss on disposal of used machine	$2,000

Why did Information Processing not use the trade-in allowance or the book value of the old asset as a basis for the new equipment? The company did not use the trade-in allowance because it included a price concession (similar to a price discount). Few individuals pay list price for a new car. Dealers such as Jerrod often inflate trade-in allowances on the used car so that actual selling prices fall below list prices. To record the car at list price would state it at an amount in excess of its cash equivalent price because of the new car's inflated list price. Similarly, use of book value in this situation would overstate the value of the new machine by $2,000.[11]

Exchanges—Gain Situation

Has Commercial Substance. Now let's consider the situation in which a nonmonetary exchange has commercial substance and a gain is realized. In such a case, a company usually records the cost of a nonmonetary asset acquired in exchange for another nonmonetary asset at the **fair value of the asset given up**, and immediately recognizes a gain. The company should use the **fair value of the asset received** only if it is more clearly evident than the fair value of the asset given up.

To illustrate, Interstate Transportation Company exchanged a number of used trucks plus cash for a semi-truck. The used trucks have a combined book value of $42,000 (cost $64,000 less $22,000 accumulated depreciation). Interstate's purchasing agent, experienced in the second-hand market, indicates that the used trucks have a fair market value of $49,000. In addition to the trucks, Interstate must pay $17,000 cash for the semi-truck. Interstate computes the cost of the semi-truck as follows.

ILLUSTRATION 10-13
Computation of Semi-
Truck Cost

Fair value of trucks exchanged	$49,000
Cash paid	17,000
Cost of semi-truck	$66,000

Interstate records the exchange transaction as follows:

Semi-truck	66,000	
Accumulated Depreciation—Trucks	22,000	
Trucks		64,000
Gain on Disposal of Used Trucks		7,000
Cash		17,000

The gain is the difference between the fair value of the used trucks and their book value. We verify the computation as follows.

---

[11]Recognize that for Jerrod (the dealer), the asset given up in the exchange is considered inventory. As a result, Jerrod records a sale and related cost of goods sold. The used machine received by Jerrod is recorded at fair value.

Fair value of used trucks		$49,000
Cost of used trucks	$64,000	
Less: Accumulated depreciation	22,000	
Book value of used trucks		42,000
Gain on disposal of used trucks		$ 7,000

ILLUSTRATION 10-14
Computation of Gain on Disposal of Used Trucks

In this case, Interstate is in a different economic position, and therefore the transaction has commercial substance. Thus, it **recognizes a gain**.

Lacks Commercial Substance—No Cash Received. We now assume that the Interstate Transportation Company exchange lacks commercial substance. That is, the economic position of Interstate did not change significantly as a result of this exchange. In this case, Interstate defers the gain of $7,000 and reduces the basis of the semi-truck. Illustration 10-15 shows two different but acceptable computations to illustrate this reduction.

Fair value of semi-truck	$66,000		Book value of used trucks	$42,000
Less: Gain deferred	7,000	OR	Plus: Cash paid	17,000
Basis of semi-truck	$59,000		Basis of semi-truck	$59,000

ILLUSTRATION 10-15
Basis of Semi-Truck—Fair Value vs. Book Value

Interstate records this transaction as follows:

Semi-truck	59,000	
Accumulated Depreciation—Trucks	22,000	
Trucks		64,000
Cash		17,000

If the exchange lacks commercial substance, the company recognizes the gain (reflected in the basis of the semi-truck) when it later sells the semi-truck, not at the time of the exchange.

Lacks Commercial Substance—Some Cash Received. When a company receives cash (sometimes referred to as "boot") in an exchange that lacks commercial substance, it may immediately recognize a portion of the gain.[12] Illustration 10-16 shows the general formula for gain recognition when an exchange includes some cash.

$$\frac{\text{Cash Received (Boot)}}{\text{Cash Received (Boot)} + \text{Fair Value of Other Assets Received}} \times \text{Total Gain} = \frac{\text{Recognized}}{\text{Gain}}$$

ILLUSTRATION 10-16
Formula for Gain Recognition, Some Cash Received

To illustrate, assume that Queenan Corporation traded in used machinery with a book value of $60,000 (cost $110,000 less accumulated depreciation $50,000) and a fair value of $100,000. It receives in exchange a machine with a fair value of $90,000 plus cash of $10,000. Illustration 10-17 shows calculation of the total gain on the exchange.

Fair value of machine exchanged	$100,000
Book value of machine exchanged	60,000
Total gain	$ 40,000

ILLUSTRATION 10-17
Computation of Total Gain

---

[12]When the monetary consideration is significant, i.e., **25 percent or more** of the fair value of the exchange, both parties consider the transaction a **monetary exchange**. Such "monetary" exchanges rely on the fair values to measure the gains or losses that are recognized in their entirety. *EITF Issue No. 86-29*, "Nonmonetary Transactions: Magnitude of Boot and the Exception to the Use of Fair Value," *Emerging Issues Task Force Abstracts* (October 1, 1987).

Generally, when a transaction lacks commercial substance, a company defers any gain. But because Queenan received $10,000 in cash, it recognizes a partial gain. The portion of the gain a company recognizes is the ratio of monetary assets (cash in this case) to the total consideration received. Queenan computes the partial gain as follows:

ILLUSTRATION 10-18
Computation of Gain Based on Ratio of Cash Received

$$\frac{\$10,000}{\$10,000 + \$90,000} \times \$40,000 = \$4,000$$

Because Queenan recognizes only a gain of $4,000 on this transaction, it defers the remaining $36,000 ($40,000 − $4,000) and reduces the basis (recorded cost) of the new machine. Illustration 10-19 shows the computation of the basis.

ILLUSTRATION 10-19
Computation of Gain Based on Ratio of Cost Received

Fair value of new machine	$90,000		Book value of old machine	$60,000
Less: Gain deferred	36,000	OR	Portion of book value presumed sold	6,000*
Basis of new machine	$54,000		Basis of new machine	$54,000

$$^*\frac{\$10,000}{\$100,000} \times \$60,000 = \$6,000$$

Queenan records the transaction with the following entry.

Cash	10,000	
Machine	54,000	
Accumulated Depreciation—Machine	50,000	
Machine		110,000
Gain on Disposal of Machine		4,000

The rationale for the treatment of a partial gain is as follows: Before a nonmonetary exchange that includes some cash, a company has an unrecognized gain, which is the difference between the book value and the fair value of the old asset. When the exchange occurs, a portion of the fair value is converted to a more liquid asset. The ratio of this liquid asset to the total consideration received is the portion of the total gain that the company realizes. Thus, the company recognizes and records that amount.

Illustration 10-20 presents in summary form the accounting requirements for recognizing gains and losses on exchanges of nonmonetary assets.[13]

ILLUSTRATION 10-20
Summary of Gain and Loss Recognition on Exchanges of Nonmonetary Assets

1. Compute the total gain or loss on the transaction. This amount is equal to the difference between the fair value of the asset given up and the book value of the asset given up.
2. If a loss is computed in step 1, always recognize the entire loss.
3. If a gain is computed in step 1,
   (a) and the exchange has commercial substance, recognize the entire gain.
   (b) and the exchange lacks commercial substance,
      (1) and no cash is involved, no gain is recognized.
      (2) and some cash is given, no gain is recognized.
      (3) and some cash is received, the following portion of the gain is recognized:

$$\frac{\text{Cash Received (Boot)}}{\text{Cash Received (Boot)} + \text{Fair Value of Other Assets Received}} \times \text{Total Gain}^*$$

*If the amount of cash exchanged is 25% or more, recognize entire gain.

---

[13]Adapted from an article by Robert Capettini and Thomas E. King, "Exchanges of Nonmonetary Assets: Some Changes," *The Accounting Review* (January 1976).

Companies disclose in their financial statements nonmonetary exchanges during a period. Such disclosure indicates the nature of the transaction(s), the method of accounting for the assets exchanged, and gains or losses recognized on the exchanges.[14]

ABOUT THOSE SWAPS

WHAT DO THE NUMBERS MEAN?

In a press release, Roy Olofson, former vice president of finance for Global Crossing, accused company executives of improperly describing the company's revenue to the public. He said the company had improperly recorded long-term sales immediately rather than over the term of the contract, had improperly booked as cash transactions swaps of capacity with other carriers, and had fired him when he blew the whistle.

The accounting for the swaps involves exchanges of similar network capacity. Companies have said they engage in such deals because swapping is quicker and less costly than building segments of their own networks, or because such pacts provide redundancies to make their own networks more reliable. In one expert's view, an exchange of similar network capacity is the equivalent of trading a blue truck for a red truck—it shouldn't boost a company's revenue.

But Global Crossing and Qwest, among others, counted as revenue the money received from the other company in the swap. (In general, in transactions involving leased capacity, the companies booked the revenue over the life of the contract.) Some of these companies then treated their own purchases as capital expenditures, which were not run through the income statement. Instead, the spending led to the addition of assets on the balance sheet (and an inflated bottom line.)

The SEC questioned some of these capacity exchanges, because it appeared they were a device to pad revenue. This reaction was not surprising, since revenue growth was a key factor in the valuation of companies such as Global Crossing and Qwest during the craze for tech stocks in the late 1990s and 2000.

Source: Adapted from Henny Sender, "Telecoms Draw Focus for Moves in Accounting," *Wall Street Journal* (March 26, 2002), p. C7.

Accounting for Contributions

Companies sometimes receive or make contributions (donations or gifts). Such contributions, **nonreciprocal transfers**, transfer assets in one direction. A contribution is often some type of asset (such as cash, securities, land, buildings, or use of facilities), but it also could be the forgiveness of a debt.

When companies acquire assets as donations, a strict cost concept dictates that the valuation of the asset should be zero. However, a departure from the cost principle seems justified; the only costs incurred (legal fees and other relatively minor expenditures) are not a reasonable basis of accounting for the assets acquired. To record nothing is to ignore the economic realities of an increase in wealth and assets. Therefore, companies use the **fair value of the asset** to establish its value on the books.

What then is the proper accounting for the credit in this transaction? Some believe the credit should be made to Donated Capital (an additional paid-in capital account). This approach views the increase in assets from a donation as contributed capital, rather than as earned revenue.

Others argue that companies should report donations as revenues from contributions. Their reasoning is that only the owners of a business contribute capital. At issue in this approach is whether the company should report revenue immediately or over the period that the asset is employed. For example, to attract new industry a city may

---

[14]"Accounting for Nonmonetary Transactions," op. cit., par. 28.

offer land, but the receiving enterprise may incur additional costs in the future (e.g., transportation or higher state income taxes) because the location is not the most desirable. As a consequence, some argue that company should defer the revenue and recognize it as the costs are incurred.

The FASB's position is that **in general, companies should recognize contributions received as revenues in the period received.**[15] Companies measure contributions at the fair value of the assets received.[16] To illustrate, Max Wayer Meat Packing, Inc. has recently accepted a donation of land with a fair value of $150,000 from the Memphis Industrial Development Corp. In return Max Wayer Meat Packing promises to build a packing plant in Memphis. Max Wayer's entry is:

Land	150,000	
Contribution Revenue		150,000

When a company contributes a nonmonetary asset, it should record the amount of the donation as an expense at the fair value of the donated asset. If a difference exists between the fair value of the asset and its book value, the company should recognize a gain or loss. To illustrate, Kline Industries donates land to the city of Los Angeles for a city park. The land cost $80,000 and has a fair market value of $110,000. Kline Industries records this donation as follows:

Contribution Expense	110,000	
Land		80,000
Gain on Disposal of Land		30,000

In some cases, companies promise to give (pledge) some type of asset in the future. Should companies record this promise immediately or when they give the assets? If the promise is **unconditional** (depends only on the passage of time or on demand by the recipient for performance), the company should report the contribution expense and related payable immediately. If the promise is **conditional**, the company recognizes expense in the period benefited by the contribution, generally when it transfers the asset.

Other Asset Valuation Methods

The exception to the historical cost principle for assets acquired through donation is based on fair value. Another exception is the **prudent cost** concept. This concept states that if for some reason a company ignorantly paid too much for an asset originally, it is theoretically preferable to charge a loss immediately.

For example, assume that a company constructs an asset at a cost much greater than its present economic usefulness. It would be appropriate to charge these excess costs as a loss to the current period, rather than capitalize them as part of the cost of the asset. In practice, the need to use the prudent cost approach seldom develops. Companies typically either use good reasoning in paying a given price or fail to recognize that they have overpaid.

What happens, on the other hand, if a company makes a bargain purchase or internally constructs a piece of equipment at a cost savings? Such savings should not result in immediate recognition of a gain under any circumstances.

---

[15]"Accounting for Contributions Received and Contributions Made," *Statement of Financial Accounting Standards No. 116* (Norwalk, Conn.: FASB, 1993). The scope of this standard excludes transfers of assets from governmental units to business enterprises. However, we believe that the basic requirements should hold also for these types of contributions. Therefore, companies should record all assets at fair value and all credits as revenue.

[16]"Accounting for Nonmonetary Transactions," op. cit., par. 18. Also, *FASB No. 116* indicates that companies should record expenses on contributions made at the fair value of the assets given up.

COSTS SUBSEQUENT TO ACQUISITION

After installing plant assets and readying them for use, a company incurs additional costs that range from ordinary repairs to significant additions. The major problem is allocating these costs to the proper time periods. **In general, costs incurred to achieve greater future benefits should be capitalized, whereas expenditures that simply maintain a given level of services should be expensed.** In order to capitalize costs, one of three conditions must be present:

1 The useful life of the asset must be increased.

2 The quantity of units produced from the asset must be increased.

3 The quality of the units produced must be enhanced.

For example, a company like **Boeing** should expense expenditures that do not increase an asset's future benefits. That is, it expenses immediately ordinary repairs that maintain the existing condition of the asset or restore it to normal operating efficiency.

Companies expense most expenditures below an established arbitrary minimum amount, say, $100 or $500. Although conceptually this treatment may be incorrect, expediency demands it. Otherwise, companies would set up depreciation schedules for such items as wastepaper baskets and ashtrays.

OBJECTIVE 6
Describe the accounting treatment for costs subsequent to acquisition.

UNDERLYING CONCEPTS

Expensing long-lived ashtrays and waste baskets is an application of the materiality constraint.

DISCONNECTED

It all started with a check of the books by an internal auditor for WorldCom Inc. The telecom giant's newly installed chief executive had asked for a financial review, and the auditor was spot-checking records of capital expenditures. She found the company was using an unorthodox technique to account for one of its biggest expenses: charges paid to local telephone networks to complete long-distance calls.

Instead of recording these charges as operating expenses, WorldCom recorded a significant portion as capital expenditures. The maneuver was worth hundreds of millions of dollars to WorldCom's bottom line. It effectively turned a loss for all of 2001 and the first quarter of 2002 into a profit. The graph below compares WorldCom's accounting to that under GAAP. Soon after this discovery, WorldCom filed for bankruptcy.

WHAT DO THE NUMBERS MEAN?

WorldCom's accounting

❶ Accounted for $3.1 billion in "line costs," including telecom access and transport charges, as capital expenditures.

❷ Planned to amortize $3.1 billion over a period of time, possibly as much as 10 years.

❸ Reported net income of $1.38 billion for 2001.

Expense → Capital Expense / Operating Expense
Capital Expense → Amortization → Higher Net Income
Operating Expense → Cost of Business → Lower Net Income

Generally accepted accounting principles

❶ The $3.1 billion "line-cost" expense would be booked as an operating expense.

❷ The entire $3.1 billion would have been counted as a cost of business for that quarter.

❸ Net income for 2001 would have been a loss, amount to be determined.

Source: Adapted from Jared Sandberg, Deborah Solomon, and Rebecca Blumenstein, "Inside World-Com's Unearthing of a Vast Accounting Scandal," *Wall Street Journal* (June 27, 2002,), p. A1.

The distinction between a **capital (asset) expenditure** and a **revenue (expense) expenditure** is not always clear-cut. Yet, in most cases, **consistent application of a capital/expense policy** is more important than attempting to provide general theoretical guidelines for each transaction. Generally, companies incur four major types of expenditures relative to existing assets.

MAJOR TYPES OF EXPENDITURES

ADDITIONS. Increase or extension of existing assets.

IMPROVEMENTS AND REPLACEMENTS. Substitution of an improved asset for an existing one.

REARRANGEMENT AND REINSTALLATION. Movement of assets from one location to another.

REPAIRS. Expenditures that maintain assets in condition for operation.

Additions

Additions should present no major accounting problems. By definition, **companies capitalize any addition to plant assets because a new asset is created**. For example, the addition of a wing to a hospital, or of an air conditioning system to an office, increases the service potential of that facility. Companies should capitalize such expenditures and match them against the revenues that will result in future periods.

One problem that arises in this area is the accounting for any changes related to the existing structure as a result of the addition. Is the cost incurred to tear down an old wall to make room for the addition, a cost of the addition or an expense or loss of the period? The answer is that it depends on the original intent. If the company had anticipated building an addition later, then this cost of removal is a proper cost of the addition. But if the company had not anticipated this development, it should properly report the removal as a loss in the current period on the basis of inefficient planning. Normally, the company retains the carrying amount of the old wall in the accounts, although theoretically the company should remove it.

Improvements and Replacements

Companies substitute one asset for another through **improvements** and **replacements**. What is the difference between an improvement and a replacement? An **improvement (betterment)** is the substitution of a **better asset** for the one currently used (say, a concrete floor for a wooden floor). A **replacement**, on the other hand, is the substitution of a **similar asset** (a wooden floor for a wooden floor).

Many times improvements and replacements result from a general policy to modernize or rehabilitate an older building or piece of equipment. The problem is differentiating these types of expenditures from normal repairs. Does the expenditure increase the **future service potential** of the asset? Or does it merely **maintain the existing level** of service? Frequently, the answer is not clear-cut. Good judgment is required to correctly classify these expenditures.

If the expenditure increases the future service potential of the asset, a company should capitalize it. The accounting is therefore handled in one of three ways, depending on the circumstances:

1 *Use the substitution approach.* Conceptually, the **substitution approach** is correct if the carrying amount of the old asset is available. It is then a simple matter to remove the cost of the old asset and replace it with the cost of the new asset.

To illustrate, Instinct Enterprises decides to replace the pipes in its plumbing system. A plumber suggests that the company use plastic tubing in place of the cast iron pipes and copper tubing. The old pipe and tubing have a book value of $15,000 (cost of $150,000 less accumulated depreciation of $135,000), and a scrap value of $1,000. The plastic tubing system costs $125,000. If Instinct pays $124,000 for the new tubing after exchanging the old tubing, it makes the following entry:

Plumbing System	125,000	
Accumulated Depreciation	135,000	
Loss on Disposal of Plant Assets	14,000	
Plumbing System		150,000
Cash ($125,000 − $1,000)		124,000

The problem is determining the book value of the old asset. Generally, the components of a given asset depreciate at different rates. However, generally no separate accounting is made. For example, the tires, motor, and body of a truck depreciate at different rates, but most companies use one rate for the entire truck. Companies can set separate depreciation rates, but it is often impractical. If a company cannot determine the carrying amount of the old asset, it adopts one of two other approaches.

2 *Capitalize the new cost.* Another approach capitalizes the improvement and keeps the carrying amount of the old asset on the books. The justification for this approach is that the item is sufficiently depreciated to reduce its carrying amount almost to zero. Although this assumption may not always be true, the differences are often insignificant. Companies usually handle improvements in this manner.

3 *Charge to accumulated depreciation.* In cases when a company does not improve the quantity or quality of the asset itself, but instead extends its useful life, the company debits the expenditure to Accumulated Depreciation rather than to an asset account. The theory behind this approach is that the replacement extends the useful life of the asset and thereby recaptures some or all of the past depreciation. The net carrying amount of the asset is the same whether debiting the asset or accumulated depreciation.

Rearrangement and Reinstallation

Companies incur **rearrangement and reinstallation costs** to benefit future periods. An example is the rearrangement and reinstallation of machines to facilitate future production.

If a company like **Eastman Kodak** can determine or estimate the original installation cost and the accumulated depreciation to date, it handles the rearrangement and reinstallation cost as a replacement. If not, which is generally the case, Eastman Kodak should capitalize the new costs (if material in amount) as an asset to be amortized over future periods expected to benefit. If these costs are immaterial, if they cannot be separated from other operating expenses, or if their future benefit is questionable, the company should immediately expense them.

Repairs

A company makes **ordinary repairs** to maintain plant assets in operating condition. It charges ordinary repairs to an expense account in the period incurred, on the basis that **it is the primary period benefited**. Maintenance charges that occur regularly include replacing minor parts, lubricating and adjusting equipment, repainting, and cleaning. A company treats these as ordinary operating expenses.

It is often difficult to distinguish a repair from an improvement or replacement. The major consideration is whether the expenditure benefits more than one year or one operating cycle, whichever is longer. If a **major repair** (such as an overhaul) occurs, several periods will benefit. A company should handle the cost as an addition, improvement, or replacement.[17]

If companies prepare income statements for short periods of time, say, monthly or quarterly, the same principles apply. Ordinary repairs and other regular maintenance charges for an annual period may benefit several quarters, and companies may need to allocate the cost among those periods. A company will often find it advantageous to concentrate its repair program at a certain time of the year, perhaps during the period of least activity or when the plant is shut down for vacation. Short-term comparative statements might be misleading if the company shows such expenditures as expenses of the quarter in which they were incurred. To give comparability to monthly or quarterly income statements, a company might use an account such as Allowance for Repairs so that it can better assign repair costs to the periods benefited.

To illustrate, Cricket Tractor Company estimated that its total repair expense for the year would be $720,000. It decided to charge each quarter for a portion of the repair cost even though the total cost for the year would occur in only two quarters.

End of First Quarter (zero repair costs incurred)

Repair Expense	180,000	
Allowance for Repairs (¼ × $720,000)		180,000

End of Second Quarter ($344,000 repair costs incurred)

Allowance for Repairs	344,000	
Cash, Wages Payable, Inventory, etc.		344,000
Repair Expense	180,000	
Allowance for Repairs (¼ × $720,000)		180,000

End of Third Quarter (zero repair costs incurred)

Repair Expense	180,000	
Allowance for Repairs (¼ × $720,000)		180,000

End of Fourth Quarter ($380,800 repair costs incurred)

Allowance for Repairs	380,800	
Cash, Wages Payable, Inventory, etc.		380,800
Repair Expense	184,800	
Allowance for Repairs		184,800
($344,000 + $380,800 − $180,000 − $180,000 − $180,000)		

Companies should not carry over a balance in the Allowance for Repairs account to the following year. The fourth quarter would normally absorb the variation from estimates. If a company prepares balance sheets during the year, it will add or subtract the Allowance account from the property, plant, and equipment section to determine a proper valuation.[18]

Summary of Costs Subsequent to Acquisition

Illustration 10-21 summarizes the accounting treatment for various costs incurred subsequent to the acquisition of capitalized assets.

---

[17]AcSEC has proposed (see footnote 2) that companies expense as incurred costs involved for planned major expenditures unless they represent an *additional* component or the *replacement* of an existing component. The "expense as incurred" approach is justified on the basis that these costs are relatively consistent from period to period, that they are not separately identifiable assets or property units in and of themselves, and that they serve only to restore assets to their original operating condition.

[18]Some might argue that the Allowance for Repairs account should be reported as a liability, because it has a credit balance. However, reporting a liability is inappropriate: To whom do you owe the amount? Placement in the stockholders' equity section is also illogical because no addition to the stockholders' investment has taken place.

ILLUSTRATION 10-21
Summary of Costs
Subsequent to
Acquisition of Property,
Plant, and Equipment

Type of Expenditure	Normal Accounting Treatment
Additions	Capitalize cost of addition to asset account.

Improvements and replacements	(a) **Carrying value known:** Remove cost of and accumulated depreciation on old asset, recognizing any gain or loss. Capitalize cost of improvement/replacement.
	(b) **Carrying value unknown:**
	  1. If the asset's useful life is extended, debit accumulated depreciation for cost of improvement/replacement.
	  2. If the quantity or quality of the asset's productivity is increased, capitalize cost of improvement/replacement to asset account.

Rearrangement and reinstallation	(a) If original installation cost is **known**, account for cost of rearrangement/reinstallation as a replacement (carrying value known). (b) If original installation cost is **unknown** and rearrangement/reinstallation cost is **material** in amount and benefits future periods, capitalize as an asset. (c) If original installation cost is **unknown** and rearrangement/reinstallation cost is **not material or future benefit is questionable**, expense the cost when incurred.
Repairs	(a) **Ordinary:** Expense cost of repairs when incurred. (b) **Major:** As appropriate, treat as an addition, improvement, or replacement.

DISPOSITIONS OF PLANT ASSETS

A company, like **Intel**, may retire plant assets voluntarily or dispose of them by sale, exchange, involuntary conversion, or abandonment. Regardless of the type of disposal, depreciation must be taken up to the date of disposition. Then, Intel should remove all accounts related to the retired asset. Generally, the book value of the specific plant asset does not equal its disposal value. As a result, a gain or loss develops. The reason: Depreciation is an estimate of cost allocation and not a process of valuation. **The gain or loss is really a correction of net income** for the years during which Intel used the fixed asset.

    Intel should show gains or losses on the disposal of plant assets in the income statement along with other items from customary business activities. However, if it sold, abandoned, spun off, or otherwise disposed of the "operations of a component of a business," then it should report the results separately in the discontinued operations section of the income statement. That is, Intel should report any gain or loss from disposal of a business component with the related results of discontinued operations.

> **OBJECTIVE 7**
> Describe the accounting treatment for the disposal of property, plant, and equipment.

Sale of Plant Assets

Companies record depreciation for the period of time between the date of the last depreciation entry and the date of sale. To illustrate, assume that Barret Company recorded depreciation on a machine costing $18,000 for 9 years at the rate of $1,200 per year. If it sells the machine in the middle of the tenth year for $7,000, Barret records depreciation to the date of sale as:

Depreciation Expense	600	
Accumulated Depreciation—Machinery		600

The entry for the sale of the asset then is:

Cash	7,000	
Accumulated Depreciation—Machinery	11,400	
[($1,200 × 9)+ $600]		
Machinery		18,000
Gain on Disposal of Machinery		400

The book value of the machinery at the time of the sale is $6,600 ($18,000 − $11,400). Because the machinery sold for $7,000, the amount of the gain on the sale is $400.

Involuntary Conversion

Sometimes an asset's service is terminated through some type of **involuntary conversion** such as fire, flood, theft, or condemnation. Companies report the difference between the amount recovered (e.g., from a condemnation award or insurance recovery), if any, and the asset's book value as a gain or loss. They treat these gains or losses like any other type of disposition. In some cases, these gains or losses may be reported as extraordinary items in the income statement, **if the conditions of the disposition are unusual and infrequent in nature**.

To illustrate, Camel Transport Corp. had to sell a plant located on company property that stood directly in the path of an interstate highway. For a number of years the state had sought to purchase the land on which the plant stood, but the company resisted. The state ultimately exercised its right of eminent domain, which the courts upheld. In settlement, Camel received $500,000, which substantially exceeded the $200,000 book value of the plant and land (cost of $400,000 less accumulated depreciation of $200,000). Camel made the following entry.

Cash	500,000	
Accumulated Depreciation—Plant Assets	200,000	
Plant Assets		400,000
Gain on Disposal of Plant Assets		300,000

If the conditions surrounding the condemnation are judged to be unusual and infrequent, Camel's gain of $300,000 is reported as an extraordinary item.

Some object to the recognition of a gain or loss in certain *involuntary* conversions. For example, the federal government often condemns forests for national parks. The paper companies that owned these forests must report a gain or loss on the condemnation. However, companies such as **Georgia-Pacific** contend that no gain or loss should be reported because they must replace the condemned forest land immediately and so are in the same economic position as they were before. The issue is whether condemnation and subsequent purchase should be viewed as one or two transactions. *FASB Interpretation No. 30* rules against the companies by requiring "that gain or loss be recognized when a nonmonetary asset is involuntarily converted to monetary assets even though an enterprise reinvests or is obligated to reinvest the monetary assets in replacement nonmonetary assets."[19]

Miscellaneous Problems

If a company scraps or abandons an asset without any cash recovery, it recognizes a loss equal to the asset's book value. If scrap value exists, the gain or loss that occurs is the difference between the asset's scrap value and its book value. If an asset still can be used even though it is fully depreciated, it may be kept on the books at historical cost less depreciation.

Companies must disclose in notes to the financial statements the amount of fully depreciated assets in service. For example, **Petroleum Equipment Tools Inc.** in its annual report disclosed, "The amount of fully depreciated assets included in property, plant, and equipment at December 31 amounted to approximately $98,900,000."

---

[19]"Accounting for Involuntary Conversions of Nonmonetary Assets to Monetary Assets," *FASB Interpretation No. 30* (Stamford, Conn.: FASB, 1979), summary paragraph.

SUMMARY OF LEARNING OBJECTIVES

1. Describe property, plant, and equipment. The major characteristics of property, plant, and equipment are: (1) They are acquired for use in operations and not for resale. (2) They are long-term in nature and usually subject to depreciation. And (3) they possess physical substance.

2. Identify the costs to include in initial valuation of property, plant, and equipment. The costs included in initial valuation of property, plant, and equipment are as follows:

Cost of land: Includes all expenditures made to acquire land and to ready it for use. Land costs typically include (1) the purchase price; (2) closing costs, such as title to the land, attorney's fees, and recording fees; (3) costs incurred in getting the land in condition for its intended use, such as grading, filling, draining, and clearing; (4) assumption of any liens, mortgages, or encumbrances on the property; and (5) any additional land improvements that have an indefinite life.

Cost of buildings: Includes all expenditures related directly to their acquisition or construction. These costs include (1) materials, labor, and overhead costs incurred during construction, and (2) professional fees and building permits.

Cost of equipment: Includes the purchase price, freight and handling charges incurred, insurance on the equipment while in transit, cost of special foundations if required, assembling and installation costs, and costs of conducting trial runs.

3. Describe the accounting problems associated with self-constructed assets. Indirect costs of manufacturing create special problems because companies cannot easily trace these costs directly to work and material orders related to the constructed assets. Companies might handle these costs in one of two ways: (1) Assign no fixed overhead to the cost of the constructed asset. Or (2) assign a portion of all overhead to the construction process. Companies use the second method extensively.

4. Describe the accounting problems associated with interest capitalization. Only actual interest (with modifications) should be capitalized. The rationale for this approach is that during construction, the asset is not generating revenue and therefore companies should defer (capitalize) interest cost. Once construction is completed, the asset is ready for its intended use and revenues can be earned. Any interest cost incurred in purchasing an asset that is ready for its intended use should be expensed.

5. Understand accounting issues related to acquiring and valuing plant assets. The following issues relate to acquiring and valuing plant assets: (1) *Cash discounts:* Whether taken or not, they are generally considered a reduction in the cost of the asset; the real cost of the asset is the cash or cash equivalent price of the asset. (2) *Deferred-payment contracts:* Companies account for assets purchased on long-term credit contracts at the present value of the consideration exchanged between the contracting parties. (3) *Lump-sum purchase:* Allocate the total cost among the various assets on the basis of their relative fair market values. (4) *Issuance of stock:* If the stock is actively traded, the market value of the stock issued is a fair indication of the cost of the property acquired. If the market value of the common stock exchanged is not determinable, establish the value of the property and use it as the basis for recording the asset and issuance of the common stock. (5) *Exchanges of nonmonetary assets.* The accounting for exchanges of nonmonetary assets depends on whether the exchange has commercial substance. See Illustrations 10-10 (page 485) and 10-20 (page 488) for summaries of how to account for exchanges. (6) *Contributions:* Record at the fair value of the asset received, and credit revenue for the same amount.

6. Describe the accounting treatment for costs subsequent to acquisition. Illustration 10-21 (page 495) summarizes how to account for costs subsequent to acquisition.

KEY TERMS

additions, *492*

avoidable interest, *477*

capital expenditure, *492*

capitalization period, *476*

commercial substance, *484*

fixed assets, *472*

historical cost, *473*

improvements (betterments), *492*

involuntary conversion, *496*

lump-sum price, *482*

major repairs, *493*

nonmonetary assets, *484*

nonreciprocal transfers, *489*

ordinary repairs, *493*

plant assets, *472*

property, plant, and equipment, *472*

prudent cost, *490*

rearrangement and reinstallation costs, *493*

replacements, *492*

revenue expenditure, *492*

self-constructed asset, *474*

weighted-average accumulated expenditures, *477*

7. Describe the accounting treatment for the disposal of property, plant, and equipment. Regardless of the time of disposal, companies take depreciation up to the date of disposition, and then remove all accounts related to the retired asset. Gains or losses on the retirement of plant assets are shown in the income statement along with other items that arise from customary business activities. Gains or losses on involuntary conversions may be reported as extraordinary items.

QUESTIONS

1. What are the major characteristics of plant assets?

2. Esplanade Inc. owns land that it purchased on January 1, 2000, for $420,000. At December 31, 2007, its current value is $770,000 as determined by appraisal. At what amount should Esplanade report this asset on its December 31, 2007, balance sheet? Explain.

3. Name the items, in addition to the amount paid to the former owner or contractor, that may properly be included as part of the acquisition cost of the following plant assets.

(a) Land.

(b) Machinery and equipment.

(c) Buildings.

4. Indicate where the following items would be shown on a balance sheet.

(a) A lien that was attached to the land when purchased.

(b) Landscaping costs.

(c) Attorney's fees and recording fees related to purchasing land.

(d) Variable overhead related to construction of machinery.

(e) A parking lot servicing employees in the building.

(f) Cost of temporary building for workers during construction of building.

(g) Interest expense on bonds payable incurred during construction of a building.

(h) Assessments for sidewalks that are maintained by the city.

(i) The cost of demolishing an old building that was on the land when purchased.

5. Two positions have normally been taken with respect to the recording of fixed manufacturing overhead as an element of the cost of plant assets constructed by a company for its own use:

(a) It should be excluded completely.

(b) It should be included at the same rate as is charged to normal operations.

What are the circumstances or rationale that support or deny the application of these methods?

6. The Buildings account of Diego Rivera Inc. includes the following items that were used in determining the basis for depreciating the cost of a building.

(a) Organization and promotion expenses.

(b) Architect's fees.

(c) Interest and taxes during construction.

(d) Interest revenue on investments held to fund construction of a building.

Do you agree with these charges? If not, how would you deal with each of the items above in the corporation's books and in its annual financial statements?

7. Jones Company has purchased two tracts of land. One tract will be the site of its new manufacturing plant, while the other is being purchased with the hope that it will be sold in the next year at a profit. How should these two tracts of land be reported in the balance sheet?

8. One financial accounting issue encountered when a company constructs its own plant is whether the interest cost on funds borrowed to finance construction should be capitalized and then amortized over the life of the assets constructed. What is the justification for capitalizing such interest?

9. Provide examples of assets that do not qualify for interest capitalization.

10. What interest rates should be used in determining the amount of interest to be capitalized? How should the amount of interest to be capitalized be determined?

11. How should the amount of interest capitalized be disclosed in the notes to the financial statements? How should interest revenue from temporarily invested excess funds borrowed to finance the construction of assets be accounted for?

12. Discuss the basic accounting problem that arises in handling each of the following situations.

(a) Assets purchased by issuance of capital stock.

(b) Acquisition of plant assets by gift or donation.

(c) Purchase of a plant asset subject to a cash discount.

(d) Assets purchased on a long-term credit basis.

(e) A group of assets acquired for a lump sum.

(f) An asset traded in or exchanged for another asset.

13. Yukio Mishima Industries acquired equipment this year to be used in its operations. The equipment was delivered by the suppliers, installed by Mishima, and placed into operation. Some of it was purchased for cash with discounts available for prompt payment. Some of it was purchased under long-term payment plans for which the interest charges approximated prevailing rates. What costs should Mishima capitalize for the new equipment purchased this year? Explain.

14. Adam Mickiewicz Co. purchased for $2,200,000 property that included both land and a building to be used in operations. The seller's book value was $300,000 for the land and $900,000 for the building. By appraisal, the fair market value was estimated to be $500,000 for the land and $2,000,000 for the building. At what amount should Mickiewicz report the land and the building at the end of the year?

15. Richardson Co. acquires machinery by paying $10,000 cash and signing a $5,000, 2-year, zero-interest-bearing note payable. The note has a present value of $4,058, and Richardson purchased a similar machine last month for $13,500. At what cost should the new equipment be recorded?

16. Sean May is evaluating two recent transactions involving exchanges of equipment. In one case, the exchange has commercial substance. In the second situation, the exchange lacks commercial substance. Explain to Sean the differences in accounting for these two situations.

17. Saadi Company purchased a heavy-duty truck on July 1, 2004, for $30,000. It was estimated that it would have a useful life of 10 years and then would have a trade-in value of $6,000. It was traded on August 1, 2008, for a similar truck costing $39,000; $13,000 was allowed as trade-in value (also fair value) on the old truck and $26,000 was paid in cash. A comparison of expected cash flows for the trucks indicates the exchange lacks commercial substance. What is the entry to record the trade-in? The company uses the straight-line method.

18. Once equipment has been installed and placed in operation, subsequent expenditures relating to this equipment are frequently thought of as repairs or general maintenance and, hence, chargeable to operations in the period in which the expenditure is made. Actually, determination of whether such an expenditure should be charged to operations or capitalized involves a much more careful analysis of the character of the expenditure.

What are the factors that should be considered in making such a decision? Discuss fully.

19. What accounting treatment is normally given to the following items in accounting for plant assets?

(a) Additions.

(b) Major repairs.

(c) Improvements and replacements.

20. New machinery, which replaced a number of employees, was installed and put in operation in the last month of the fiscal year. The employees had been dismissed after payment of an extra month's wages, and this amount was added to the cost of the machinery. Discuss the propriety of the charge. If it was improper, describe the proper treatment.

21. To what extent do you consider the following items to be proper costs of the fixed asset? Give reasons for your opinions.

(a) Overhead of a business that builds its own equipment.

(b) Cash discounts on purchases of equipment.

(c) Interest paid during construction of a building.

(d) Cost of a safety device installed on a machine.

(e) Freight on equipment returned before installation, for replacement by other equipment of greater capacity.

(f) Cost of moving machinery to a new location.

(g) Cost of plywood partitions erected as part of the remodeling of the office.

(h) Replastering of a section of the building.

(i) Cost of a new motor for one of the trucks.

22. Recently, Michelangelo Manufacturing Co. presented the account "Allowance for Repairs" in the long-term liabilities section. Evaluate this procedure.

23. Dimitri Enterprises has a number of fully depreciated assets that are still being used in the main operations of the business. Because the assets are fully depreciated, the president of the company decides not to show them on the balance sheet or disclose this information in the notes. Evaluate this procedure.

24. What are the general rules for how gains or losses on retirement of plant assets should be reported in income?

BRIEF EXERCISES

(LO 2) **BE10-1** Bonanza Brothers Inc. purchased land at a price of $27,000. Closing costs were $1,400. An old building was removed at a cost of $12,200. What amount should be recorded as the cost of the land?

(LO 4) **BE10-2** Brett Hull Company is constructing a building. Construction began on February 1 and was completed on December 31. Expenditures were $1,500,000 on March 1, $1,200,000 on June 1, and $3,000,000 on December 31. Compute Hull's weighted-average accumulated expenditures for interest capitalization purposes.

(LO 4) **BE10-3** Brett Hull Company (see BE10-2) borrowed $1,000,000 on March 1 on a 5-year, 12% note to help finance construction of the building. In addition, the company had outstanding all year a 13%, 5-year, $2,000,000 note payable and a 15%, 4-year, $3,500,000 note payable. Compute the weighted-average interest rate used for interest capitalization purposes.

(LO 4) **BE10-4** Use the information for Brett Hull Company from BE10-2 and BE10-3. Compute avoidable interest for Brett Hull Company.

(LO 5) **BE10-5** Chavez Corporation purchased a truck by issuing an $80,000, 4-year, zero-interest-bearing note to Equinox Inc. The market rate of interest for obligations of this nature is 12%. Prepare the journal entry to record the purchase of this truck.

(LO 5) **BE10-6** Cool Spot Inc. purchased land, building, and equipment from Pinball Wizard Corporation for a cash payment of $306,000. The estimated fair values of the assets are land $60,000, building $220,000, and equipment $80,000. At what amounts should each of the three assets be recorded?

(LO 5) **BE10-7** Dark Wizard Company obtained land by issuing 2,000 shares of its $10 par value common stock. The land was recently appraised at $85,000. The common stock is actively traded at $41 per share. Prepare the journal entry to record the acquisition of the land.

(LO 5) **BE10-8** Strider Corporation traded a used truck (cost $20,000, accumulated depreciation $18,000) for a small computer worth $3,700. Strider also paid $1,000 in the transaction. Prepare the journal entry to record the exchange. (The exchange has commercial substance.)

(LO 5) **BE10-9** Use the information for Strider Corporation from BE10-8. Prepare the journal entry to record the exchange, assuming the exchange lacks commercial substance.

(LO 5) **BE10-10** Sloan Company traded a used welding machine (cost $9,000, accumulated depreciation $3,000) for office equipment with an estimated fair value of $5,000. Sloan also paid $2,000 cash in the transaction. Prepare the journal entry to record the exchange. (The exchange has commercial substance.)

(LO 5) **BE10-11** Bubey Company traded a used truck for a new truck. The used truck cost $30,000 and has accumulated depreciation of $27,000. The new truck is worth $35,000. Bubey also made a cash payment of $33,000. Prepare Bubey's entry to record the exchange. (The exchange lacks commercial substance.)

(LO 5) **BE10-12** Buck Rogers Corporation traded a used truck for a new truck. The used truck cost $20,000 and has accumulated depreciation of $17,000. The new truck is worth $35,000. Rogers also made a cash payment of $33,000. Prepare Rogers' entry to record the exchange. (The exchange has commercial substance.)

(LO 6) **BE10-13** Indicate which of the following costs should be expensed when incurred.

  (a) $13,000 paid to rearrange and reinstall machinery.
  (b) $200 paid for tune-up and oil change on delivery truck.
  (c) $200,000 paid for addition to building.
  (d) $7,000 paid to replace a wooden floor with a concrete floor.
  (e) $2,000 paid for a major overhaul on a truck, which extends the useful life.

(LO 7) **BE10-14** Sim City Corporation owns machinery that cost $20,000 when purchased on January 1, 2004. Depreciation has been recorded at a rate of $3,000 per year, resulting in a balance in accumulated depreciation of $9,000 at December 31, 2006. The machinery is sold on September 1, 2007, for $10,500. Prepare journal entries to (a) update depreciation for 2007 and (b) record the sale.

(LO 7) **BE10-15** Use the information presented for Sim City Corporation in BE10-14, but assume the machinery is sold for $5,200 instead of $10,500. Prepare journal entries to (a) update depreciation for 2007 and (b) record the sale.

EXERCISES

(LO 2) **E10-1** **(Acquisition Costs of Realty)** The following expenditures and receipts are related to land, land improvements, and buildings acquired for use in a business enterprise. The receipts are enclosed in parentheses.

(a)	Money borrowed to pay building contractor (signed a note)	$(275,000)
(b)	Payment for construction from note proceeds	275,000
(c)	Cost of land fill and clearing	8,000
(d)	Delinquent real estate taxes on property assumed by purchaser	7,000
(e)	Premium on 6-month insurance policy during construction	6,000
(f)	Refund of 1-month insurance premium because construction completed early	(1,000)
(g)	Architect's fee on building	22,000
(h)	Cost of real estate purchased as a plant site (land $200,000 and building $50,000)	250,000
(i)	Commission fee paid to real estate agency	9,000
(j)	Installation of fences around property	4,000

(k) Cost of razing and removing building	11,000
(l) Proceeds from salvage of demolished building	(5,000)
(m) Interest paid during construction on money borrowed for construction	13,000
(n) Cost of parking lots and driveways	19,000
(o) Cost of trees and shrubbery planted (permanent in nature)	14,000
(p) Excavation costs for new building	3,000

Instructions

Identify each item by letter and list the items in columnar form, using the headings shown below. All receipt amounts should be reported in parentheses. For any amounts entered in the Other Accounts column also indicate the account title.

Item	Land	Land Improvements	Building	Other Accounts

(LO 2) **E10-2 (Acquisition Costs of Realty)** Martin Buber Co. purchased land as a factory site for $400,000. The process of tearing down two old buildings on the site and constructing the factory required 6 months. The company paid $42,000 to raze the old buildings and sold salvaged lumber and brick for $6,300. Legal fees of $1,850 were paid for title investigation and drawing the purchase contract. Martin Buber paid $2,200 to an engineering firm for a land survey, and $68,000 for drawing the factory plans. The land survey had to be made before definitive plans could be drawn. Title insurance on the property cost $1,500, and a liability insurance premium paid during construction was $900. The contractor's charge for construction was $2,740,000. The company paid the contractor in two installments: $1,200,000 at the end of 3 months and $1,540,000 upon completion. Interest costs of $170,000 were incurred to finance the construction.

Instructions

Determine the cost of the land and the cost of the building as they should be recorded on the books of Martin Buber Co. Assume that the land survey was for the building.

(LO 2) **E10-3 (Acquisition Costs of Trucks)** Kelly Clarkson Corporation operates a retail computer store. To improve delivery services to customers, the company purchases four new trucks on April 1, 2007. The terms of acquisition for each truck are described below.

1. Truck #1 has a list price of $15,000 and is acquired for a cash payment of $13,900.
2. Truck #2 has a list price of $16,000 and is acquired for a down payment of $2,000 cash and a zero-interest-bearing note with a face amount of $14,000. The note is due April 1, 2008. Clarkson would normally have to pay interest at a rate of 10% for such a borrowing, and the dealership has an incremental borrowing rate of 8%.
3. Truck #3 has a list price of $16,000. It is acquired in exchange for a computer system that Clarkson carries in inventory. The computer system cost $12,000 and is normally sold by Clarkson for $15,200. Clarkson uses a perpetual inventory system.
4. Truck #4 has a list price of $14,000. It is acquired in exchange for 1,000 shares of common stock in Clarkson Corporation. The stock has a par value per share of $10 and a market value of $13 per share.

Instructions

Prepare the appropriate journal entries for the foregoing transactions for Clarkson Corporation.

(LO 2, 3) **E10-4 (Purchase and Self-Constructed Cost of Assets)** Worf Co. both purchases and constructs various equipment it uses in its operations. The following items for two different types of equipment were recorded in random order during the calendar year 2008.

Purchase

Cash paid for equipment, including sales tax of $5,000	$105,000
Freight and insurance cost while in transit	2,000
Cost of moving equipment into place at factory	3,100
Wage cost for technicians to test equipment	4,000
Insurance premium paid during first year of operation on this equipment	1,500
Special plumbing fixtures required for new equipment	8,000
Repair cost incurred in first year of operations related to this equipment	1,300

Construction

Material and purchased parts (gross cost $200,000; failed to take 2% cash discount)	$200,000
Imputed interest on funds used during construction (stock financing)	14,000
Labor costs	190,000
Allocated overhead costs (fixed—$20,000; variable—$30,000)	50,000
Profit on self-construction	30,000
Cost of installing equipment	4,400

Instructions

Compute the total cost for each of these two pieces of equipment. If an item is not capitalized as a cost of the equipment, indicate how it should be reported.

(LO 2, 3, 4) **E10-5** **(Treatment of Various Costs)** Ben Sisko Supply Company, a newly formed corporation, incurred the following expenditures related to Land, to Buildings, and to Machinery and Equipment.

Abstract company's fee for title search		$ 520
Architect's fees		3,170
Cash paid for land and dilapidated building thereon		87,000
Removal of old building	$20,000	
Less: Salvage	5,500	14,500
Interest on short-term loans during construction		7,400
Excavation before construction for basement		19,000
Machinery purchased (subject to 2% cash discount, which was not taken)		55,000
Freight on machinery purchased		1,340
Storage charges on machinery, necessitated by noncompletion of building when machinery was delivered		2,180
New building constructed (building construction took 6 months from date of purchase of land and old building)		485,000
Assessment by city for drainage project		1,600
Hauling charges for delivery of machinery from storage to new building		620
Installation of machinery		2,000
Trees, shrubs, and other landscaping after completion of building (permanent in nature)		5,400

Instructions

Determine the amounts that should be debited to Land, to Buildings, and to Machinery and Equipment. Assume the benefits of capitalizing interest during construction exceed the cost of implementation. Indicate how any costs not debited to these accounts should be recorded.

(LO 3, 4) **E10-6** **(Correction of Improper Cost Entries)** Plant acquisitions for selected companies are as follows.

1. Belanna Industries Inc. acquired land, buildings, and equipment from a bankrupt company, Torres Co., for a lump-sum price of $700,000. At the time of purchase, Torres's assets had the following book and appraisal values.

	Book Values	Appraisal Values
Land	$200,000	$150,000
Buildings	250,000	350,000
Equipment	300,000	300,000

To be conservative, the company decided to take the lower of the two values for each asset acquired. The following entry was made.

Land	150,000	
Buildings	250,000	
Equipment	300,000	
Cash		700,000

2. Harry Enterprises purchased store equipment by making a $2,000 cash down payment and signing a 1-year, $23,000, 10% note payable. The purchase was recorded as follows.

Store Equipment	27,300	
Cash		2,000
Note Payable		23,000
Interest Payable		2,300

3. Kim Company purchased office equipment for $20,000, terms 2/10, n/30. Because the company intended to take the discount, it made no entry until it paid for the acquisition. The entry was:

Office Equipment	20,000	
Cash		19,600
Purchase Discounts		400

4. Kaisson Inc. recently received at zero cost land from the Village of Cardassia as an inducement to locate its business in the Village. The appraised value of the land is $27,000. The company made no entry to record the land because it had no cost basis.

5. Zimmerman Company built a warehouse for $600,000. It could have purchased the building for $740,000. The controller made the following entry.

Warehouse	740,000	
Cash		600,000
Profit on Construction		140,000

Instructions

Prepare the entry that should have been made at the date of each acquisition.

(LO 4) **E10-7** **(Capitalization of Interest)** Harrisburg Furniture Company started construction of a combination office and warehouse building for its own use at an estimated cost of $5,000,000 on January 1, 2007. Harrisburg expected to complete the building by December 31, 2007. Harrisburg has the following debt obligations outstanding during the construction period.

Construction loan—12% interest, payable semiannually, issued December 31, 2006	$2,000,000
Short-term loan—10% interest, payable monthly, and principal payable at maturity on May 30, 2008	1,400,000
Long-term loan—11% interest, payable on January 1 of each year. Principal payable on January 1, 2011	1,000,000

Instructions

(Carry all computations to two decimal places.)

   (a) Assume that Harrisburg completed the office and warehouse building on December 31, 2007, as planned at a total cost of $5,200,000, and the weighted average of accumulated expenditures was $3,600,000. Compute the avoidable interest on this project.

   (b) Compute the depreciation expense for the year ended December 31, 2008. Harrisburg elected to depreciate the building on a straight-line basis and determined that the asset has a useful life of 30 years and a salvage value of $300,000.

(LO 4) **E10-8** **(Capitalization of Interest)** On December 31, 2006, Alma-Ata Inc. borrowed $3,000,000 at 12% payable annually to finance the construction of a new building. In 2007, the company made the following expenditures related to this building: March 1, $360,000; June 1, $600,000; July 1, $1,500,000; December 1, $1,500,000. Additional information is provided as follows.

   1. Other debt outstanding

10-year, 13% bond, December 31, 2000, interest payable annually	$4,000,000
6-year, 10% note, dated December 31, 2004, interest payable annually	$1,600,000

   2. March 1, 2007, expenditure included land costs of $150,000

   3. Interest revenue earned in 2007 $49,000

Instructions

   (a) Determine the amount of interest to be capitalized in 2007 in relation to the construction of the building.

   (b) Prepare the journal entry to record the capitalization of interest and the recognition of interest expense, if any, at December 31, 2007.

(LO 4) **E10-9** **(Capitalization of Interest)** On July 31, 2007, Amsterdam Company engaged Minsk Tooling Company to construct a special-purpose piece of factory machinery. Construction was begun immediately and was completed on November 1, 2007. To help finance construction, on July 31 Amsterdam issued a $300,000, 3-year, 12% note payable at Netherlands National Bank, on which interest is payable each July 31. $200,000 of the proceeds of the note was paid to Minsk on July 31. The remainder of the proceeds was temporarily invested in short-term marketable securities (trading securities) at 10% until November 1. On November 1, Amsterdam made a final $100,000 payment to Minsk. Other than the note to Netherlands, Amsterdam's only outstanding liability at December 31, 2007, is a $30,000, 8%, 6-year note payable, dated January 1, 2004, on which interest is payable each December 31.

Instructions

   (a) Calculate the interest revenue, weighted-average accumulated expenditures, avoidable interest, and total interest cost to be capitalized during 2007. Round all computations to the nearest dollar.

   (b) Prepare the journal entries needed on the books of Amsterdam Company at each of the following dates.

      (1) July 31, 2007.

      (2) November 1, 2007.

      (3) December 31, 2007.

(LO 4) **E10-10** **(Capitalization of Interest)** The following three situations involve the capitalization of interest.

Situation I

On January 1, 2007, Oksana Baiul, Inc. signed a fixed-price contract to have Builder Associates construct a major plant facility at a cost of $4,000,000. It was estimated that it would take 3 years to complete the project. Also on January 1, 2007, to finance the construction cost, Oksana Baiul borrowed $4,000,000 payable in 10 annual installments of $400,000, plus interest at the rate of 10%. During 2007, Oksana Baiul made deposit and progress payments totaling $1,500,000 under the contract; the weighted-average amount of accumulated expenditures was $800,000 for the year. The excess borrowed funds were invested in short-term securities, from which Oksana Baiul realized investment income of $250,000.

Instructions

What amount should Oksana Baiul report as capitalized interest at December 31, 2007?

Situation II

During 2007, Midori Ito Corporation constructed and manufactured certain assets and incurred the following interest costs in connection with those activities.

	Interest Costs Incurred
Warehouse constructed for Ito's own use	$30,000
Special-order machine for sale to unrelated customer, produced according to customer's specifications	9,000
Inventories routinely manufactured, produced on a repetitive basis	8,000

All of these assets required an extended period of time for completion.

Instructions

Assuming the effect of interest capitalization is material, what is the total amount of interest costs to be capitalized?

Situation III

Peggy Fleming, Inc. has a fiscal year ending April 30. On May 1, 2007, Peggy Fleming borrowed $10,000,000 at 11% to finance construction of its own building. Repayments of the loan are to commence the month following completion of the building. During the year ended April 30, 2008, expenditures for the partially completed structure totaled $7,000,000. These expenditures were incurred evenly throughout the year. Interest earned on the unexpended portion of the loan amounted to $650,000 for the year.

Instructions

How much should be shown as capitalized interest on Peggy Fleming's financial statements at April 30, 2008?

(CPA adapted)

(LO 2, 3, 5) **E10-11** **(Entries for Equipment Acquisitions)** Jane Geddes Engineering Corporation purchased conveyor equipment with a list price of $10,000. Presented below are three independent cases related to the equipment. (Round to nearest dollar.)

(a) Geddes paid cash for the equipment 8 days after the purchase. The vendor's credit terms are 2/10, n/30. Assume that equipment purchases are recorded gross.

(b) Geddes traded in equipment with a book value of $2,000 (initial cost $8,000), and paid $9,500 in cash one month after the purchase. The old equipment could have been sold for $400 at the date of trade. (The exchange has commercial substance.)

(c) Geddes gave the vendor a $10,800 zero-interest-bearing note for the equipment on the date of purchase. The note was due in one year and was paid on time. Assume that the effective interest rate in the market was 9%.

Instructions

Prepare the general journal entries required to record the acquisition and payment in each of the independent cases above. Round to the nearest dollar.

(LO 2, 3, 5) **E10-12** **(Entries for Asset Acquisition, Including Self-Construction)** Below are transactions related to Fred Couples Company.

(a) The City of Pebble Beach gives the company 5 acres of land as a plant site. The market value of this land is determined to be $81,000.

(b) 13,000 shares of common stock with a par value of $50 per share are issued in exchange for land and buildings. The property has been appraised at a fair market value of $810,000, of which $180,000 has been allocated to land and $630,000 to buildings. The stock of Fred Couples Company is not listed on any exchange, but a block of 100 shares was sold by a stockholder 12 months ago at $65 per share, and a block of 200 shares was sold by another stockholder 18 months ago at $58 per share.

(c) No entry has been made to remove from the accounts for Materials, Direct Labor, and Overhead the amounts properly chargeable to plant asset accounts for machinery constructed during the year. The following information is given relative to costs of the machinery constructed.

Materials used	$12,500
Factory supplies used	900
Direct labor incurred	15,000
Additional overhead (over regular) caused by construction of machinery, excluding factory supplies used	2,700
Fixed overhead rate applied to regular manufacturing operations	60% of direct labor cost
Cost of similar machinery if it had been purchased from outside suppliers	44,000

Instructions

Prepare journal entries on the books of Fred Couples Company to record these transactions.

(LO 2, 5) **E10-13** **(Entries for Acquisition of Assets)** Presented below is information related to Zonker Company.

1. On July 6 Zonker Company acquired the plant assets of Doonesbury Company, which had discontinued operations. The appraised value of the property is:

Land	$ 400,000
Building	1,200,000
Machinery and equipment	800,000
Total	$2,400,000

Zonker Company gave 12,500 shares of its $100 par value common stock in exchange. The stock had a market value of $168 per share on the date of the purchase of the property.

2. Zonker Company expended the following amounts in cash between July 6 and December 15, the date when it first occupied the building.

Repairs to building	$105,000
Construction of bases for machinery to be installed later	135,000
Driveways and parking lots	122,000
Remodeling of office space in building, including new partitions and walls	161,000
Special assessment by city on land	18,000

3. On December 20, the company paid cash for machinery, $260,000, subject to a 2% cash discount, and freight on machinery of $10,500.

Instructions

Prepare entries on the books of Zonker Company for these transactions.

(LO 5) **E10-14** **(Purchase of Equipment with Zero-Interest-Bearing Debt)** Chippewas Inc. has decided to purchase equipment from Central Michigan Industries on January 2, 2007, to expand its production capacity to meet customers' demand for its product. Chippewas issues an $800,000, 5-year, zero-interest-bearing note to Central Michigan for the new equipment when the prevailing market rate of interest for obligations of this nature is 12%. The company will pay off the note in five $160,000 installments due at the end of each year over the life of the note.

Instructions

(a) Prepare the journal entry(ies) at the date of purchase. (Round to nearest dollar in all computations.)

(b) Prepare the journal entry(ies) at the end of the first year to record the payment and interest, assuming that the company employs the effective-interest method.

(c) Prepare the journal entry(ies) at the end of the second year to record the payment and interest.

(d) Assuming that the equipment had a 10-year life and no salvage value, prepare the journal entry necessary to record depreciation in the first year. (Straight-line depreciation is employed.)

(LO 5) **E10-15** **(Purchase of Computer with Zero-Interest-Bearing Debt)** Cardinals Corporation purchased a computer on December 31, 2006, for $105,000, paying $30,000 down and agreeing to pay the balance in five equal installments of $15,000 payable each December 31 beginning in 2007. An assumed interest rate of 10% is implicit in the purchase price.

Instructions

(a) Prepare the journal entry(ies) at the date of purchase. (Round to two decimal places.)

(b) Prepare the journal entry(ies) at December 31, 2007, to record the payment and interest (effective-interest method employed).

(c) Prepare the journal entry(ies) at December 31, 2008, to record the payment and interest (effective-interest method employed).

(LO 5) **E10-16 (Asset Acquisition)** Hayes Industries purchased the following assets and constructed a building as well. All this was done during the current year.

Assets 1 and 2

These assets were purchased as a lump sum for $100,000 cash. The following information was gathered.

Description	Initial Cost on Seller's Books	Depreciation to Date on Seller's Books	Book Value on Seller's Books	Appraised Value
Machinery	$100,000	$50,000	$50,000	$90,000
Office equipment	60,000	10,000	50,000	30,000

Asset 3

This machine was acquired by making a $10,000 down payment and issuing a $30,000, 2-year, zero-interest-bearing note. The note is to be paid off in two $15,000 installments made at the end of the first and second years. It was estimated that the asset could have been purchased outright for $35,900.

Asset 4

This machinery was acquired by trading in used machinery. (The exchange lacks commercial substance.) Facts concerning the trade-in are as follows.

Cost of machinery traded	$100,000
Accumulated depreciation to date of sale	40,000
Fair market value of machinery traded	80,000
Cash received	10,000
Fair market value of machinery acquired	70,000

Asset 5

Office equipment was acquired by issuing 100 shares of $8 par value common stock. The stock had a market value of $11 per share.

Construction of Building

A building was constructed on land purchased last year at a cost of $150,000. Construction began on February 1 and was completed on November 1. The payments to the contractor were as follows.

Date	Payment
2/1	$120,000
6/1	360,000
9/1	480,000
11/1	100,000

To finance construction of the building, a $600,000, 12% construction loan was taken out on February 1. The loan was repaid on November 1. The firm had $200,000 of other outstanding debt during the year at a borrowing rate of 8%.

Instructions

Record the acquisition of each of these assets.

(LO 5) **E10-17 (Nonmonetary Exchange)** Busytown Corporation, which manufactures shoes, hired a recent college graduate to work in its accounting department. On the first day of work, the accountant was assigned to total a batch of invoices with the use of an adding machine. Before long, the accountant, who had never before seen such a machine, managed to break the machine. Busytown Corporation gave the machine plus $340 to Dick Tracy Business Machine Company (dealer) in exchange for a new machine. Assume the following information about the machines.

	Busytown Corp. (Old Machine)	Dick Tracy Co. (New Machine)
Machine cost	$290	$270
Accumulated depreciation	140	–0–
Fair value	85	425

Instructions

For each company, prepare the necessary journal entry to record the exchange. (The exchange has commercial substance.)

(LO 5) **E10-18 (Nonmonetary Exchange)** Cannondale Company purchased an electric wax melter on April 30, 2008, by trading in its old gas model and paying the balance in cash. The following data relate to the purchase.

List price of new melter	$15,800
Cash paid	10,000
Cost of old melter (5-year life, $700 residual value)	11,200
Accumulated depreciation—old melter (straight-line)	6,300
Second-hand market value of old melter	5,200

Instructions

Prepare the journal entry(ies) necessary to record this exchange, assuming that the exchange **(a)** has commercial substance, and **(b)** lacks commercial substance. Cannondale's fiscal year ends on December 31, and depreciation has been recorded through December 31, 2007.

(LO 5) **E10-19 (Nonmonetary Exchange)** Carlos Arruza Company exchanged equipment used in its manufacturing operations plus $3,000 in cash for similar equipment used in the operations of Tony LoBianco Company. The following information pertains to the exchange.

	Carlos Arruza Co.	Tony LoBianco Co.
Equipment (cost)	$28,000	$28,000
Accumulated depreciation	19,000	10,000
Fair value of equipment	12,500	15,500
Cash given up	3,000	

Instructions

(a) Prepare the journal entries to record the exchange on the books of both companies. Assume that the exchange lacks commercial substance.
(b) Prepare the journal entries to record the exchange on the books of both companies. Assume that the exchange has commercial substance.

(LO 5) **E10-20 (Nonmonetary Exchange)** Dana Ashbrook Inc. has negotiated the purchase of a new piece of automatic equipment at a price of $8,000 plus trade-in, f.o.b. factory. Dana Ashbrook Inc. paid $8,000 cash and traded in used equipment. The used equipment had originally cost $62,000; it had a book value of $42,000 and a secondhand market value of $47,800, as indicated by recent transactions involving similar equipment. Freight and installation charges for the new equipment required a cash payment of $1,100.

Instructions

(a) Prepare the general journal entry to record this transaction, assuming that the exchange has commercial substance.
(b) Assuming the same facts as in (a) except that fair value information for the assets exchanged is not determinable. Prepare the general journal entry to record this transaction.

(LO 6) **E10-21 (Analysis of Subsequent Expenditures)** King Donovan Resources Group has been in its plant facility for 15 years. Although the plant is quite functional, numerous repair costs are incurred to maintain it in sound working order. The company's plant asset book value is currently $800,000, as indicated below.

Original cost	$1,200,000
Accumulated depreciation	400,000
Book value	$ 800,000

During the current year, the following expenditures were made to the plant facility.

(a) Because of increased demands for its product, the company increased its plant capacity by building a new addition at a cost of $270,000.
(b) The entire plant was repainted at a cost of $23,000.
(c) The roof was an asbestos cement slate. For safety purposes it was removed and replaced with a wood shingle roof at a cost of $61,000. Book value of the old roof was $41,000.
(d) The electrical system was completely updated at a cost of $22,000. The cost of the old electrical system was not known. It is estimated that the useful life of the building will not change as a result of this updating.
(e) A series of major repairs were made at a cost of $47,000, because parts of the wood structure were rotting. The cost of the old wood structure was not known. These extensive repairs are estimated to increase the useful life of the building.

Instructions

Indicate how each of these transactions would be recorded in the accounting records.

(LO 6) **E10-22 (Analysis of Subsequent Expenditures)** The following transactions occurred during 2008. Assume that depreciation of 10% per year is charged on all machinery and 5% per year on buildings, on a straight-line basis, with no estimated salvage value. Depreciation is charged for a full year on all fixed assets acquired during the year, and no depreciation is charged on fixed assets disposed of during the year.

Jan. 30 A building that cost $132,000 in 1991 is torn down to make room for a new building. The wrecking contractor was paid $5,100 and was permitted to keep all materials salvaged.

Mar. 10 Machinery that was purchased in 2001 for $16,000 is sold for $2,900 cash, f.o.b. purchaser's plant. Freight of $300 is paid on the sale of this machinery.

Mar. 20 A gear breaks on a machine that cost $9,000 in 2003. The gear is replaced at a cost of $8,000. The replacement does not extend the useful life of the machine.

May 18 A special base installed for a machine in 2002 when the machine was purchased has to be replaced at a cost of $5,500 because of defective workmanship on the original base. The cost of the machinery was $14,200 in 2002. The cost of the base was $3,500, and this amount was charged to the Machinery account in 2002.

June 23 One of the buildings is repainted at a cost of $6,900. It had not been painted since it was constructed in 2004.

Instructions

Prepare general journal entries for the transactions. (Round to the nearest dollar.)

(LO 6) **E10-23 (Analysis of Subsequent Expenditures)** Plant assets often require expenditures subsequent to acquisition. It is important that they be accounted for properly. Any errors will affect both the balance sheets and income statements for a number of years.

Instructions

For each of the following items, indicate whether the expenditure should be capitalized (C) or expensed (E) in the period incurred.

(a) _____ Improvement.

(b) _____ Replacement of a minor broken part on a machine.

(c) _____ Expenditure that increases the useful life of an existing asset.

(d) _____ Expenditure that increases the efficiency and effectiveness of a productive asset but does not increase its salvage value.

(e) _____ Expenditure that increases the efficiency and effectiveness of a productive asset and increases the asset's salvage value.

(f) _____ Expenditure that increases the quality of the output of the productive asset.

(g) _____ Improvement to a machine that increased its fair market value and its production capacity by 30% without extending the machine's useful life.

(h) _____ Ordinary repairs.

(LO 6) **E10-24 (Entries for Disposition of Assets)** On December 31, 2007, Travis Tritt Inc. has a machine with a book value of $940,000. The original cost and related accumulated depreciation at this date are as follows.

Machine	$1,300,000
Accumulated depreciation	360,000
Book value	$ 940,000

Depreciation is computed at $60,000 per year on a straight-line basis.

Instructions

Presented below is a set of independent situations. For each independent situation, indicate the journal entry to be made to record the transaction. Make sure that depreciation entries are made to update the book value of the machine prior to its disposal.

(a) A fire completely destroys the machine on August 31, 2008. An insurance settlement of $430,000 was received for this casualty. Assume the settlement was received immediately.

(b) On April 1, 2008, Tritt sold the machine for $1,040,000 to Dwight Yoakam Company.

(c) On July 31, 2008, the company donated this machine to the Mountain King City Council. The fair market value of the machine at the time of the donation was estimated to be $1,100,000.

(LO 7) **E10-25 (Disposition of Assets)** On April 1, 2007, Gloria Estefan Company received a condemnation award of $430,000 cash as compensation for the forced sale of the company's land and building, which stood in the path of a new state highway. The land and building cost $60,000 and $280,000, respectively, when they were acquired. At April 1, 2007, the accumulated depreciation relating to the building amounted to $160,000. On August 1, 2007, Estafan purchased a piece of replacement property for cash. The new land cost $90,000, and the new building cost $400,000.

Instructions
Prepare the journal entries to record the transactions on April 1 and August 1, 2007.

See the book's website, www.wiley.com/college/kieso, for Additional Exercises.

PROBLEMS

(LO 2) **P10-1 (Classification of Acquisition and Other Asset Costs)** At December 31, 2006, certain accounts included in the property, plant, and equipment section of Craig Ehlo Company's balance sheet had the following balances.

Land	$230,000
Buildings	890,000
Leasehold improvements	660,000
Machinery and equipment	875,000

During 2007 the following transactions occurred.

1. Land site number 621 was acquired for $850,000. In addition, to acquire the land Ehlo paid a $51,000 commission to a real estate agent. Costs of $35,000 were incurred to clear the land. During the course of clearing the land, timber and gravel were recovered and sold for $13,000.
2. A second tract of land (site number 622) with a building was acquired for $420,000. The closing statement indicated that the land value was $300,000 and the building value was $120,000. Shortly after acquisition, the building was demolished at a cost of $41,000. A new building was constructed for $330,000 plus the following costs.

Excavation fees	$38,000
Architectural design fees	11,000
Building permit fee	2,500
Imputed interest on funds used	
during construction (stock financing)	8,500

The building was completed and occupied on September 30, 2007.
3. A third tract of land (site number 623) was acquired for $650,000 and was put on the market for resale.
4. During December 2007 costs of $89,000 were incurred to improve leased office space. The related lease will terminate on December 31, 2009, and is not expected to be renewed. (*Hint:* Leasehold improvements should be handled in the same manner as land improvements.)
5. A group of new machines was purchased under a royalty agreement that provides for payment of royalties based on units of production for the machines. The invoice price of the machines was $87,000, freight costs were $3,300, installation costs were $2,400, and royalty payments for 2007 were $17,500.

Instructions
(a) Prepare a detailed analysis of the changes in each of the following balance sheet accounts for 2007.

Land	Leasehold improvements
Buildings	Machinery and equipment

Disregard the related accumulated depreciation accounts.
(b) List the items in the situation that were not used to determine the answer to (a) above, and indicate where, or if, these items should be included in Ehlo's financial statements.

(AICPA adapted)

**(LO 2,
7)** **P10-2 (Classification of Acquisition Costs)** Selected accounts included in the property, plant, and equipment section of Spud Webb Corporation's balance sheet at December 31, 2006, had the following balances.

Land	$ 300,000
Land improvements	140,000
Buildings	1,100,000
Machinery and equipment	960,000

During 2007 the following transactions occurred.

1. A tract of land was acquired for $150,000 as a potential future building site.
2. A plant facility consisting of land and building was acquired from Ken Norman Company in exchange for 20,000 shares of Webb's common stock. On the acquisition date, Webb's stock had a closing market price of $37 per share on a national stock exchange. The plant facility was carried on Norman's books at $110,000 for land and $320,000 for the building at the exchange date. Current appraised values for the land and building, respectively, are $230,000 and $690,000.
3. Items of machinery and equipment were purchased at a total cost of $400,000. Additional costs were incurred as follows.

Freight and unloading	$13,000
Sales taxes	20,000
Installation	26,000

4. Expenditures totaling $95,000 were made for new parking lots, streets, and sidewalks at the corporation's various plant locations. These expenditures had an estimated useful life of 15 years.
5. A machine costing $80,000 on January 1, 1999, was scrapped on June 30, 2007. Double-declining-balance depreciation has been recorded on the basis of a 10-year life.
6. A machine was sold for $20,000 on July 1, 2007. Original cost of the machine was $44,000 on January 1, 2004, and it was depreciated on the straight-line basis over an estimated useful life of 7 years and a salvage value of $2,000.

Instructions

(a) Prepare a detailed analysis of the changes in each of the following balance sheet accounts for 2007.

    Land
    Land improvements
    Buildings
    Machinery and equipment

(*Hint:* Disregard the related accumulated depreciation accounts.)

(b) List the items in the fact situation that were not used to determine the answer to (a), showing the pertinent amounts and supporting computations in good form for each item. In addition, indicate where, or if, these items should be included in Spud Webb's financial statements.

(AICPA adapted)

(LO 2, 3, 5)   **P10-3**   **(Classification of Land and Building Costs)**   Lenny Wilkins Company was incorporated on January 2, 2008, but was unable to begin manufacturing activities until July 1, 2008, because new factory facilities were not completed until that date.

The Land and Building account reported the following items during 2008.

January 31	Land and building	$160,000
February 28	Cost of removal of building	9,800
May 1	Partial payment of new construction	60,000
May 1	Legal fees paid	3,770
June 1	Second payment on new construction	40,000
June 1	Insurance premium	2,280
June 1	Special tax assessment	4,000
June 30	General expenses	36,300
July 1	Final payment on new construction	40,000
December 31	Asset write-up	43,800
		399,950
December 31	Depreciation—2008 at 1%	4,000
December 31, 2008	Account balance	$395,950

The following additional information is to be considered.

1. To acquire land and building the company paid $80,000 cash and 800 shares of its 8% cumulative preferred stock, par value $100 per share. Fair market value of the stock is $107 per share.
2. Cost of removal of old buildings amounted to $9,800, and the demolition company retained all materials of the building.
3. Legal fees covered the following.

Cost of organization	$ 610
Examination of title covering purchase of land	1,300
Legal work in connection with construction contract	1,860
	$3,770

4. Insurance premium covered the building for a 2-year term beginning May 1, 2008.
5. The special tax assessment covered street improvements that are permanent in nature.
6. General expenses covered the following for the period from January 2, 2008, to June 30, 2008.

President's salary	$32,100
Plant superintendent covering supervision of new building	4,200
	$36,300

7. Because of a general increase in construction costs after entering into the building contract, the board of directors increased the value of the building $43,800, believing that such an increase was justified to reflect the current market at the time the building was completed. Retained earnings was credited for this amount.
8. Estimated life of building—50 years.
   Depreciation for 2008—1% of asset value (1% of $400,000, or $4,000).

Instructions

(a) Prepare entries to reflect correct land, building, and depreciation accounts at December 31, 2008.
(b) Show the proper presentation of land, building, and depreciation on the balance sheet at December 31, 2008.

(AICPA adapted)

(LO 2, 5, 7) **P10-4 (Dispositions, Including Condemnation, Demolition, and Trade-in)** Presented below is a schedule of property dispositions for Frank Thomas Co.

Schedule of Property Dispositions					
	Cost	Accumulated Depreciation	Cash Proceeds	Fair Market Value	Nature of Disposition
Land	$40,000	—	$31,000	$31,000	Condemnation
Building	15,000	—	3,600	—	Demolition
▸ Warehouse	70,000	$11,000	74,000	74,000	Destruction by fire
▪ Machine	8,000	3,200	900	7,200	Trade-in
Furniture	10,000	7,850	—	3,100	Contribution
Automobile	8,000	3,460	2,960	2,960	Sale

The following additional information is available.

Land
On February 15, a condemnation award was received as consideration for unimproved land held primarily as an investment, and on March 31, another parcel of unimproved land to be held as an investment was purchased at a cost of $35,000.

Building
On April 2, land and building were purchased at a total cost of $75,000, of which 20% was allocated to the building on the corporate books. The real estate was acquired with the intention of demolishing the building, and this was accomplished during the month of November. Cash proceeds received in November represent the net proceeds from demolition of the building.

Warehouse
On June 30, the warehouse was destroyed by fire. The warehouse was purchased January 2, 2004, and had depreciated $11,000. On December 27, the insurance proceeds and other funds were used to purchase a replacement warehouse at a cost of $90,000.

Machine
On December 26, the machine was exchanged for another machine having a fair market value of $6,300 and cash of $900 was received. (The exchange lacks commercial substance.)

Furniture
On August 15, furniture was contributed to a qualified charitable organization. No other contributions were made or pledged during the year.

Automobile
On November 3, the automobile was sold to Ozzie Guillen, a stockholder.

Instructions
Indicate how these items would be reported on the income statement of Frank Thomas Co.

(AICPA adapted)

(LO 2, 4) **P10-5** **(Classification of Costs and Interest Capitalization)** On January 1, 2007, George Solti Corporation purchased for $600,000 a tract of land (site number 101) with a building. Solti paid a real estate broker's commission of $36,000, legal fees of $6,000, and title guarantee insurance of $18,000. The closing statement indicated that the land value was $500,000 and the building value was $100,000. Shortly after acquisition, the building was razed at a cost of $54,000.

Solti entered into a $3,000,000 fixed-price contract with Slatkin Builders, Inc. on March 1, 2007, for the construction of an office building on land site number 101. The building was completed and occupied on September 30, 2008. Additional construction costs were incurred as follows.

Plans, specifications, and blueprints	$21,000
Architects' fees for design and supervision	82,000

The building is estimated to have a 40-year life from date of completion and will be depreciated using the 150% declining balance method.

To finance construction costs, Solti borrowed $3,000,000 on March 1, 2007. The loan is payable in 10 annual installments of $300,000 plus interest at the rate of 10%. Solti's weighted-average amounts of accumulated building construction expenditures were as follows.

For the period March 1 to December 31, 2007	$1,200,000
For the period January 1 to September 30, 2008	1,900,000

Instructions

(a) Prepare a schedule that discloses the individual costs making up the balance in the land account in respect of land site number 101 as of September 30, 2008.

(b) Prepare a schedule that discloses the individual costs that should be capitalized in the office building account as of September 30, 2008. Show supporting computations in good form.

3,413,000 cost of building

(AICPA adapted)

(LO 2, 4) **P10-6** **(Interest During Construction)** Jerry Landscaping began construction of a new plant on December 1, 2005. On this date the company purchased a parcel of land for $142,000 in cash. In addition, it paid $2,000 in surveying costs and $4,000 for a title insurance policy. An old dwelling on the premises was demolished at a cost of $3,000, with $1,000 being received from the sale of materials.

Architectural plans were also formalized on December 1, 2005, when the architect was paid $30,000. The necessary building permits costing $3,000 were obtained from the city and paid for on December 1 as well. The excavation work began during the first week in December with payments made to the contractor as follows.

Date of Payment	Amount of Payment
March 1	$240,000
May 1	360,000
July 1	60,000

The building was completed on July 1, 2006.

To finance construction of this plant, Jerry borrowed $600,000 from the bank on December 1, 2005. Jerry had no other borrowings. The $600,000 was a 10-year loan bearing interest at 8%.

Instructions

Compute the balance in each of the following accounts at December 31, 2005, and December 31, 2006.

(a) Land.

(b) Buildings.

(c) Interest Expense.

(LO 4) **P10-7** **(Capitalization of Interest)** Wordcrafters Inc. is a book distributor that had been operating in its original facility since 1982. The increase in certification programs and continuing education requirements in several professions has contributed to an annual growth rate of 15% for Wordcrafters since 2002. Wordcrafters' original facility became obsolete by early 2007 because of the increased sales volume and the fact that Wordcrafters now carries tapes and disks in addition to books.

On June 1, 2007, Wordcrafters contracted with Favre Construction to have a new building constructed for $4,000,000 on land owned by Wordcrafters. The payments made by Wordcrafters to Favre Construction are shown in the schedule below.

Date	Amount
July 30, 2007	$1,200,000
January 30, 2008	1,500,000
May 30, 2008	1,300,000
Total payments	$4,000,000

Construction was completed and the building was ready for occupancy on May 27, 2008. Wordcrafters had no new borrowings directly associated with the new building but had the following debt outstanding at May 31, 2008, the end of its fiscal year.

14½%, 5-year note payable of $2,000,000, dated April 1, 2004, with interest payable annually on April 1.

12%, 10-year bond issue of $3,000,000 sold at par on June 30, 2000, with interest payable annually on June 30.

The new building qualifies for interest capitalization. The effect of capitalizing the interest on the new building, compared with the effect of expensing the interest, is material.

Instructions
(a) Compute the weighted average accumulated expenditures on Wordcrafters' new building during the capitalization period.
(b) Compute the avoidable interest on Wordcrafters' new building.
(c) Some interest cost of Wordcrafters Inc. is capitalized for the year ended May 31, 2008.
   (1) Identify the items relating to interest costs that must be disclosed in Wordcrafters' financial statements.
   (2) Compute the amount of each of the items that must be disclosed.

(CMA adapted)

(LO 4) **P10-8** **(Nonmonetary Exchanges)** Susquehanna Corporation wishes to exchange a machine used in its operations. Susquehanna has received the following offers from other companies in the industry.

1. Choctaw Company offered to exchange a similar machine plus $23,000. (The exchange has commercial substance for both parties.)
2. Powhatan Company offered to exchange a similar machine. (The exchange lacks commercial substance for both parties.)
3. Shawnee Company offered to exchange a similar machine, but wanted $8,000 in addition to Susquehanna's machine. (The exchange has commercial substance for both parties.)

In addition, Susquehanna contacted Seminole Corporation, a dealer in machines. To obtain a new machine, Susquehanna must pay $93,000 in addition to trading in its old machine.

	Susquehanna	Choctaw	Powhatan	Shawnee	Seminole
Machine cost	$160,000	$120,000	$147,000	$160,000	$130,000
Accumulated depreciation	50,000	45,000	71,000	75,000	–0–
Fair value	92,000	69,000	92,000	100,000	185,000

Instructions
For each of the four independent situations, prepare the journal entries to record the exchange on the books of each company. (Round to nearest dollar.)

(LO 4) **P10-9** **(Nonmonetary Exchanges)** On August 1, Arna, Inc. exchanged productive assets with Bontemps, Inc. Arna's asset is referred to below as "Asset A," and Bontemps' is referred to as "Asset B." The following facts pertain to these assets.

	Asset A	Asset B
Original cost	$96,000	$110,000
Accumulated depreciation (to date of exchange)	45,000	52,000
Fair market value at date of exchange	60,000	75,000
Cash paid by Arna, Inc.	15,000	
Cash received by Bontemps, Inc.		15,000

Instructions
(a) Assuming that the exchange of Assets A and B has commercial substance, record the exchange for both Arna, Inc. and Bontemps, Inc. in accordance with generally accepted accounting principles.
(b) Assuming that the exchange of Assets A and B lacks commercial substance, record the exchange for both Arna, Inc. and Bontemps, Inc. in accordance with generally accepted accounting principles.

(LO 4) **P10-10** **(Nonmonetary Exchanges)** During the current year, Garrison Construction trades an old crane that has a book value of $80,000 (original cost $140,000 less accumulated depreciation $60,000) for a new crane from Keillor Manufacturing Co. The new crane cost Keillor $165,000 to manufacture and is classified as inventory. The following information is also available.

	Garrison Const.	Keillor Mfg. Co.
Fair market value of old crane	$ 72,000	
Fair market value of new crane		$190,000
Cash paid	118,000	
Cash received		118,000

Instructions

   (a) Assuming that this exchange is considered to have commercial substance, prepare the journal entries on the books of (1) Garrison Construction and (2) Keillor Manufacturing.

   (b) Assuming that this exchange lacks commercial substance for Garrison, prepare the journal entries on the books of Garrison Construction.

   (c) Assuming the same facts as those in (a), except that the fair market value of the old crane is $98,000 and the cash paid is $92,000, prepare the journal entries on the books of (1) Garrison Construction and (2) Keillor Manufacturing.

   (d) Assuming the same facts as those in (b), except that the fair market value of the old crane is $87,000 and the cash paid $103,000, prepare the journal entries on the books of (1) Garrison Construction and (2) Keillor Manufacturing.

(LO 2, 4, 7) **P10-11 (Purchases by Deferred Payment, Lump-sum, and Nonmonetary Exchanges)** Kent Adamson Company, a manufacturer of ballet shoes, is experiencing a period of sustained growth. In an effort to expand its production capacity to meet the increased demand for its product, the company recently made several acquisitions of plant and equipment. Tod Mullinger, newly hired in the position of fixed-asset accountant, requested that Watt Kaster, Adamson's controller, review the following transactions.

Transaction 1

On June 1, 2007, Adamson Company purchased equipment from Venghaus Corporation. Adamson issued a $20,000, 4-year, zero-interest-bearing note to Venghaus for the new equipment. Adamson will pay off the note in four equal installments due at the end of each of the next 4 years. At the date of the transaction, the prevailing market rate of interest for obligations of this nature was 10%. Freight costs of $425 and installation costs of $500 were incurred in completing this transaction. The appropriate factors for the time value of money at a 10% rate of interest are given below.

Future value of $1 for 4 periods	1.46
Future value of an ordinary annuity for 4 periods	4.64
Present value of $1 for 4 periods	0.68
Present value of an ordinary annuity for 4 periods	3.17

Transaction 2

On December 1, 2007, Adamson Company purchased several assets of Haukap Shoes Inc., a small shoe manufacturer whose owner was retiring. The purchase amounted to $210,000 and included the assets listed below. Adamson Company engaged the services of Tennyson Appraisal Inc., an independent appraiser, to determine the fair market values of the assets which are also presented below.

	Haukap Book Value	Fair Market Value
Inventory	$ 60,000	$ 50,000
Land	40,000	80,000
Building	70,000	120,000
	$170,000	$250,000

During its fiscal year ended May 31, 2008, Adamson incurred $8,000 for interest expense in connection with the financing of these assets.

Transaction 3

On March 1, 2005, Adamson Company exchanged a number of used trucks plus cash for vacant land adjacent to its plant site. (The exchange has commercial substance.) Adamson intends to use the land for a parking lot. The trucks had a combined book value of $35,000, as Adamson had recorded $20,000 of accumulated depreciation against these assets. Adamson's purchasing agent, who has had previous dealings in the second-hand market, indicated that the trucks had a fair market value of $46,000 at the time of the transaction. In addition to the trucks, Adamson Company paid $19,000 cash for the land.

Instructions

   (a) Plant assets such as land, buildings, and equipment receive special accounting treatment. Describe the major characteristics of these assets that differentiate them from other types of assets.

   (b) For each of the three transactions described above, determine the value at which Adamson Company should record the acquired assets. Support your calculations with an explanation of the underlying rationale.

   (c) The books of Adamson Company show the following additional transactions for the fiscal year ended May 31, 2008.

      (1) Acquisition of a building for speculative purposes.

      (2) Purchase of a 2-year insurance policy covering plant equipment.

      (3) Purchase of the rights for the exclusive use of a process used in the manufacture of ballet shoes.

For each of these transactions, indicate whether the asset should be classified as a plant asset. If it is a plant asset, explain why it is. If it is not a plant asset, explain why not, and identify the proper classification.

(CMA adapted)

CONCEPTS FOR ANALYSIS

CA10-1 (Acquisition, Improvements, and Sale of Realty) William Bradford Company purchased land for use as its corporate headquarters. A small factory that was on the land when it was purchased was torn down before construction of the office building began. Furthermore, a substantial amount of rock blasting and removal had to be done to the site before construction of the building foundation began. Because the office building was set back on the land far from the public road, Bradford Company had the contractor construct a paved road that led from the public road to the parking lot of the office building.

Three years after the office building was occupied, Bradford Company added four stories to the office building. The four stories had an estimated useful life of 5 years more than the remaining estimated useful life of the original office building.

Ten years later the land and building were sold at an amount more than their net book value, and Bradford Company had a new office building constructed in another state for use as its new corporate headquarters.

Instructions
 (a) Which of the expenditures above should be capitalized? How should each be depreciated or amortized? Discuss the rationale for your answers.
 (b) How would the sale of the land and building be accounted for? Include in your answer an explanation of how to determine the net book value at the date of sale. Discuss the rationale for your answer.

CA10-2 (Accounting for Self-Constructed Assets) Shanette Medical Labs, Inc., began operations 5 years ago producing stetrics, a new type of instrument it hoped to sell to doctors, dentists, and hospitals. The demand for stetrics far exceeded initial expectations, and the company was unable to produce enough stetrics to meet demand.

The company was manufacturing its product on equipment that it built at the start of its operations. To meet demand, more efficient equipment was needed. The company decided to design and build the equipment, because the equipment currently available on the market was unsuitable for producing stetrics.

In 2007, a section of the plant was devoted to development of the new equipment and a special staff was hired. Within 6 months a machine developed at a cost of $714,000 increased production dramatically and reduced labor costs substantially. Elated by the success of the new machine, the company built three more machines of the same type at a cost of $441,000 each.

Instructions
 (a) In general, what costs should be capitalized for self-constructed equipment?
 (b) Discuss the propriety of including in the capitalized cost of self-constructed assets:
  (1) The increase in overhead caused by the self-construction of fixed assets.
  (2) A proportionate share of overhead on the same basis as that applied to goods manufactured for sale.
 (c) Discuss the proper accounting treatment of the $273,000 ($714,000 − $441,000) by which the cost of the first machine exceeded the cost of the subsequent machines. This additional cost should not be considered research and development costs.

CA10-3 (Capitalization of Interest) Zucker Airline is converting from piston-type planes to jets. Delivery time for the jets is 3 years, during which substantial progress payments must be made. The multimillion-dollar cost of the planes cannot be financed from working capital; Zucker must borrow funds for the payments.

Because of high interest rates and the large sum to be borrowed, management estimates that interest costs in the second year of the period will be equal to one-third of income before interest and taxes, and one-half of such income in the third year.

After conversion, Zucker's passenger-carrying capacity will be doubled with no increase in the number of planes, although the investment in planes would be substantially increased. The jet planes have a 7-year service life.

Instructions

Give your recommendation concerning the proper accounting for interest during the conversion period. Support your recommendation with reasons and suggested accounting treatment. (Disregard income tax implications.)

(AICPA adapted)

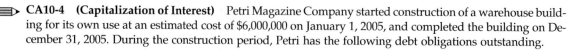

CA10-4 (Capitalization of Interest) Petri Magazine Company started construction of a warehouse building for its own use at an estimated cost of $6,000,000 on January 1, 2005, and completed the building on December 31, 2005. During the construction period, Petri has the following debt obligations outstanding.

Construction loan—12% interest, payable semiannually, issued December 31, 2004	$2,000,000
Short-term loan—10% interest, payable monthly, and principal payable at maturity, on May 30, 2006	1,400,000
Long-term loan—11% interest, payable on January 1 of each year. Principal payable on January 1, 2008	2,000,000

Total cost amounted to $6,200,000, and the weighted average of accumulated expenditures was $4,000,000.

Dee Pettepiece, the president of the company, has been shown the costs associated with this construction project and capitalized on the balance sheet. She is bothered by the "avoidable interest" included in the cost. She argues that, first, all the interest is unavoidable—no one lends money without expecting to be compensated for it. Second, why can't the company use all the interest on all the loans when computing this avoidable interest? Finally, why can't her company capitalize all the annual interest that accrued over the period of construction?

Instructions

You are the manager of accounting for the company. In a memo, explain what avoidable interest is, how you computed it (being especially careful to explain why you used the interest rates that you did), and why the company cannot capitalize all its interest for the year. Attach a schedule supporting any computations that you use.

CA10-5 (Nonmonetary Exchanges) You have two clients that are considering trading machinery with each other. Although the machines are different from each other, you believe that an assessment of expected cash flows on the exchanged assets will indicate the exchange lacks commercial substance. Your clients would prefer that the exchange be deemed to have commercial substance, to allow them to record gains. Here are the facts:

	Client A	Client B
Original cost	$100,000	$150,000
Accumulated depreciation	40,000	80,000
Market value	95,000	125,000
Cash received (paid)	(30,000)	30,000

Instructions

  (a) Record the trade-in on Client A's books assuming the exchange has commercial substance.
  (b) Record the trade-in on Client A's books assuming the exchange lacks commercial substance.
  (c) Write a memo to the controller of Company A indicating and explaining the dollar impact on current and future statements of treating the exchange as having versus lacking commercial substance.
  (d) Record the entry on Client B's books assuming the exchange has commercial substance.
  (e) Record the entry on Client B's books assuming the exchange lacks commercial substance.
  (f) Write a memo to the controller of Company B indicating and explaining the dollar impact on current and future statements of treating the exchange as having versus lacking commercial substance.

CA10-6 (Costs of Acquisition) The invoice price of a machine is $40,000. Various other costs relating to the acquisition and installation of the machine including transportation, electrical wiring, special base, and so on amount to $7,500. The machine has an estimated life of 10 years, with no residual value at the end of that period.

The owner of the business suggests that the incidental costs of $7,500 be charged to expense immediately for the following reasons.

  1. If the machine should be sold, these costs cannot be recovered in the sales price.
  2. The inclusion of the $7,500 in the machinery account on the books will not necessarily result in a closer approximation of the market price of this asset over the years, because of the possibility of changing demand and supply levels.
  3. Charging the $7,500 to expense immediately will reduce federal income taxes.

Instructions
Discuss each of the points raised by the owner of the business.

(AICPA adapted)

CA10-7 (Cost of Land vs. Building) Field Company purchased a warehouse in a downtown district where land values are rapidly increasing. Adolph Phillips, controller, and Wilma Smith, financial vice-president, are trying to allocate the cost of the purchase between the land and the building. Noting that depreciation can be taken only on the building, Phillips favors placing a very high proportion of the cost on the warehouse itself, thus reducing taxable income and income taxes. Smith, his supervisor, argues that the allocation should recognize the increasing value of the land, regardless of the depreciation potential of the warehouse. Besides, she says, net income is negatively impacted by additional depreciation and will cause the company's stock price to go down.

Instructions
Answer the following questions.

(a) What stakeholder interests are in conflict?
(b) What ethical issues does Phillips face?
(c) How should these costs be allocated?

USING YOUR JUDGMENT

Financial Statement Analysis Case

Johnson & Johnson

Johnson & Johnson, the world's leading and most diversified health-care corporation, serves its customers through specialized worldwide franchises. Each of its franchises consists of a number of companies throughout the world that focus on a particular health care market, such as surgical sutures, consumer pharmaceuticals, or contact lenses. Information related to its property, plant, and equipment in its 2004 annual report is shown in the notes to the financial statements as follows.

Johnson & Johnson

Note 1: Property, Plant, and Equipment and Depreciation
Property, plant, and equipment are stated at cost. The Company utilizes the straight-line method of depreciation over the estimated useful lives of the assets:

Building and building equipment	20–40 years
Land and leasehold improvements	10–20 years
Machinery and equipment	2–13 years

Note 3: Property, Plant, and Equipment
At the end of 2004 and 2003, property, plant, and equipment at cost and accumulated depreciation were:

(dollars in millions)	2004	2003
Land and land improvements	$ 515	$ 491
Buildings and building equipment	5,907	5,242
Machinery and equipment	10,155	9,638
Construction in progress	1,787	1,681
	18,664	17,052
Less: Accumulated depreciation	8,228	7,206
	$10,436	$ 9,846

The Company capitalizes interest expense as part of the cost of construction of facilities and equipment. Interest expense capitalized in 2004, 2003, and 2002 was $136 million, $108 million, and $98 million, respectively.

Upon retirement or other disposal of fixed assets, the cost and related amount of accumulated depreciation or amortization are eliminated from the asset and accumulated depreciation accounts, respectively. The difference, if any, between the net asset value and the proceeds is recorded in earnings.

Johnson & Johnson's provided the following selected information in its 2004 cash flow statement.

Johnson & Johnson

Johnson & Johnson
2004 Annual Report
Consolidated Financial Statements (excerpts)

Net cash flows from operating activities	$11,131
Cash flows from investing activities	
Additions to property, plant and equipment	(2,175)
Proceeds from the disposal of assets	237
Acquisition of businesses, net of cash acquired (Note 17)	(580)
Purchases of investments	(11,617)
Sales of investments	12,061
Other	(273)
Net cash used by investing activities	(2,347)
Cash flows from financing activities	
Dividends to shareowners	(3,251)
Repurchase of common stock	(1,384)
Proceeds from short-term debt	514
Retirement of short-term debt	(1,291)
Proceeds from long-term debt	17
Retirement of long-term debt	(395)
Proceeds from the exercise of stock options	642
Net cash used by financing activities	(5,148)
Effect of exchange rate changes on cash and cash equivalents	190
(Decrease)/increase in cash and cash equivalents	3,826
Cash and cash equivalents, beginning of year (Note 1)	5,377
Cash and cash equivalents, end of year (Note 1)	$ 9,203
Supplemental cash flow data	
Cash paid during the year for:	
Interest	$ 222
Income taxes	3,880

Instructions

(a) What was the cost of buildings and building equipment at the end of 2004?

(b) Does Johnson & Johnson use a conservative or liberal method to depreciate its property, plant, and equipment?

(c) What was the actual interest expense incurred by the company in 2004?

(d) What is Johnson & Johnson's free cash flow? From the information provided, comment on Johnson & Johnson's financial flexibility.

Research Case

The March 26, 2002, *Wall Street Journal* includes an article by Henny Sender titled "Telecoms Draw Focus for Moves in Accounting."

Instructions

Read the article and answer the following questions.

(a) What is the EITF referred to in this article?

(b) Explain the accounting issue related to the exchange of similar network capacity.

(c) Why did the EITF not address the issues related to swaps that occurred at companies such as Global Crossing and Qwest Communications?

Professional Research: Financial Accounting and Reporting

Your client is in the planning phase for a major plant expansion, which will involve the construction of a new warehouse. The assistant controller does not believe that interest cost can be included in the cost of the warehouse, because it is a financing expense. Others on the planning team believe that some interest cost can be included in the cost of the warehouse, but no one could identify the specific authoritative guidance for this issue. Your supervisor asks you to research this issue.

Instructions

Using the **Financial Accounting Research System (FARS)**, respond to the following items. (Provide text strings used in your search.)

(a) It is permissible to capitalize interest into the cost of assets? What standard addresses this issue?

(b) What are the objectives for capitalizing interest?

(c) Discuss which assets qualify for interest capitalization.

(d) Is there a limit to the amount of interest that may be capitalized in a period?

(e) What disclosures are required, if interest capitalization is allowed?

Professional Simulation

In this simulation you are asked to address questions regarding the accounting for property, plant, and equipment. Prepare responses to all parts.

DEPRECIATION, IMPAIRMENTS, AND DEPLETION

Do They Matter?

The axiom on Wall Street has been that huge one-time charges don't really count. These highly unusual events don't truly reflect how a company is faring, so Wall Street ignores them. In the last few years write-offs have approached all-time highs. For example, over one-third of the companies surveyed by *Accounting Trends and Techniques* in 2004 reported asset impairments.

However, some companies have taken write-offs so regularly that they really are a reflection of ongoing business. When you adjust for the write-offs, earnings turn out to be far worse—and the companies' shares of stock turn out to be far more expensive. Presented below are data from three companies that recently had charges every year for five consecutive years.

Company	Net Income Before Write-Offs ($ mil)	Net Income After Write-Offs ($ mil)	Percentage Difference	EPS	EPS Adjusted	P/E	P/E Adjusted
International Paper	$591	$ 95	84%	$2.82	$0.46	15	90
Waste Management	755	130	83	1.43	0.25	18	102
Fortune Brands	322	61	81	3.30	0.63	13	67

For example, the data show that International Paper's adjusted earnings come in closer to $0.46 per share than $2.82. This means that its price-to-earnings ratio is closer to 90 than to 15. In short, these companies may be overpriced and are likely set for stock price declines.

One reason for more write-offs may be the tougher U.S. guidelines to determine when companies should consider property, plant, and equipment as impaired. These impairment rules are catching on internationally. Twenty-six Japanese companies adopted impairment standards similar to the U.S. standards, resulting in a combined loss of ¥814.1 billion (yen) in fiscal 2004. Adoption of the impairment standard both signals that the recent economic downturn was behind these companies and introduces more transparent accounting. Thus, while impairments are on the rise in the United States and elsewhere, investors are now receiving better information about fixed-asset values in financial statements.[1]

---

[1] Adapted from "Were Profits Inflated?" *Business Week* (March 4, 2002), p. 14, and from Michael K. Ozanian, "The Secret Charges, *Forbes* (March 4, 2002), p. 102. See also "Losses Pile Up under Stricter Accounting," *International Herald Tribune* (June 2, 2004).

Learning Objectives

After studying this chapter, you should be able to:

1 Explain the concept of depreciation.

2 Identify the factors involved in the depreciation process.

3 Compare activity, straight-line, and decreasing-charge methods of depreciation.

4 Explain special depreciation methods.

5 Explain the accounting issues related to asset impairment.

6 Explain the accounting procedures for depletion of natural resources.

7 Explain how to report and analyze property, plant, equipment, and natural resources.

As noted in the opening story, both U.S. and foreign companies are affected by impairment rules. These rules recognize that when economic conditions deteriorate, companies may need to write off an asset's cost to indicate the decline in its usefulness. The purpose of this chapter is to examine the depreciation process and the methods of writing off the cost of tangible assets and natural resources. The content and organization of the chapter are as follows.

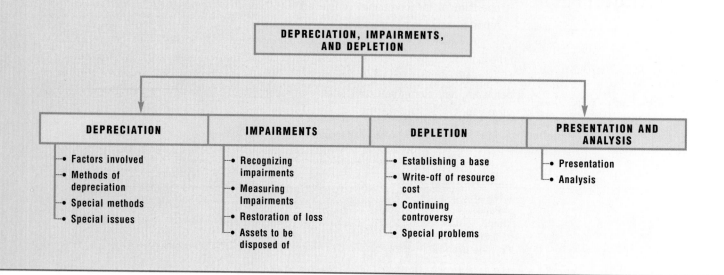

DEPRECIATION—A METHOD OF COST ALLOCATION

Most individuals at one time or another purchase and trade in an automobile. The automobile dealer and the buyer typically discuss what the trade-in value of the old car is. Also, they may talk about what the trade-in value of the new car will be in several years. In both cases a decline in value is considered to be an example of depreciation.

To accountants, however, depreciation is not a matter of valuation. Rather, **depreciation is a means of cost allocation. Depreciation is the accounting process of allocating the cost of tangible assets to expense in a systematic and rational manner to those periods expected to benefit from the use of the asset.** For example, a company like **Goodyear** (one of the world's largest tire manufacturers) does not depreciate assets on the basis of a decline in their fair market value. Instead, it depreciates through systematic charges to expense.

This approach is employed because the value of the asset may fluctuate between the time the asset is purchased and the time it is sold or junked. Attempts to measure these interim value changes have not been well received because values are difficult to measure objectively. Therefore, Goodyear charges the asset's cost to depreciation expense over its estimated life. It makes no attempt to value the asset at fair market value between acquisition and disposition. Companies use the cost allocation approach because it matches costs with revenues and because fluctuations in market value are uncertain and difficult to measure.

When companies write off the cost of long-lived assets over a number of periods, they typically use the term **depreciation**. They use the term **depletion** to describe the reduction in the cost of natural resources (such as timber, gravel, oil, and coal) over a period of time. The expiration of intangible assets, such as patents or copyrights, is called **amortization**.

Factors Involved in the Depreciation Process

Before establishing a pattern of charges to revenue, a company must answer three basic questions:

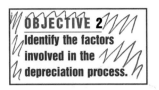

OBJECTIVE 2
Identify the factors involved in the depreciation process.

1 What depreciable base is to be used for the asset?
2 What is the asset's useful life?
3 What method of cost apportionment is best for this asset?

The answers to these questions involve combining several estimates into one single figure. Note the calculations assume perfect knowledge of the future, which is never attainable.

Depreciable Base for the Asset

The base established for depreciation is a function of two factors: the original cost, and salvage or disposal value. We discussed historical cost in Chapter 10. **Salvage value** is the estimated amount that a company will receive when it sells the asset or removes it from service. It is the amount to which a company writes down or depreciates the asset during its useful life. If an asset has a cost of $10,000 and a salvage value of $1,000, its **depreciation base** is $9,000.

Tutorial on Depreciation Methods

Original cost	$10,000
Less: Salvage value	1,000
Depreciation base	$ 9,000

ILLUSTRATION 11-1
Computation of Depreciation Base

From a practical standpoint, companies often assign a zero salvage value. Some long-lived assets, however, have substantial salvage values.

Estimation of Service Lives

The service life of an asset often differs from its physical life. A piece of machinery may be physically capable of producing a given product for many years beyond its service life. But a company may not use the equipment for all that time because the cost of producing the product in later years may be too high. For example, the old Slater cotton mill in Pawtucket, Rhode Island, is preserved in remarkable physical condition as an historic landmark in U.S. industrial development, although its service life was terminated many years ago.[2]

Companies retire assets for two reasons: **physical factors** (such as casualty or expiration of physical life) and **economic factors** (obsolescence). Physical factors are the wear and tear, decay, and casualties that make it difficult for the asset to perform indefinitely. These physical factors set the outside limit for the service life of an asset.

We can classify the economic or functional factors into three categories:

1 **Inadequacy** results when an asset ceases to be useful to a company because the demands of the firm have changed. An example would be the need for a larger building to handle increased production. Although the old building may still be sound, it may have become inadequate for the company's purpose.

2 **Supersession** is the replacement of one asset with another more efficient and economical asset. Examples would be the replacement of the mainframe computer with a PC network, or the replacement of the Boeing 767 with the Boeing 787.

3 **Obsolescence** is the catchall for situations not involving inadequacy and supersession.

---

[2]Taken from J. D. Coughlan and W. K. Strand, *Depreciation Accounting, Taxes and Business Decisions* (New York: The Ronald Press, 1969), pp. 10–12.

Because the distinction between these categories appears artificial, it is probably best to consider economic factors collectively instead of trying to make distinctions that are not clear-cut.

To illustrate the concepts of physical and economic factors, consider a new nuclear power plant. Which is more important in determining the useful life of a nuclear power plant—physical factors or economic factors? The limiting factors seem to be (1) ecological considerations, (2) competition from other power sources, and (3) safety concerns. Physical life does not appear to be the primary factor affecting useful life. Although the plant's physical life may be far from over, the plant may become obsolete in 10 years.

For a house, physical factors undoubtedly are more important than the economic or functional factors relative to useful life. Whenever the physical nature of the asset primarily determines useful life, maintenance plays an extremely vital role. The better the maintenance, the longer the life of the asset.[3]

In most cases, a company estimates the useful life of an asset based on its past experience with the same or similar assets. Others use sophisticated statistical methods to establish a useful life for accounting purposes. And in some cases, companies select arbitrary service lives. In a highly industrial economy such as that of the United States, where research and innovation are so prominent, technological factors have as much effect, if not more, on service lives of tangible plant assets as physical factors do.

ALPHABET DUPE

WHAT DO THE NUMBERS MEAN?

Some companies try to imply that depreciation is not a cost. For example, in their press releases they will often make a bigger deal over earnings before interest, taxes, depreciation, and amortization (often referred to as EBITDA) than net income under GAAP. They like it because it "dresses up" their earnings numbers. Some on Wall Street buy this hype because they don't like the allocations that are required to determine net income. Some banks, without batting an eyelash, even let companies base their loan covenants on EBITDA.

For example, look at Premier Parks, which operates the Six Flags chain of amusement parks. Premier touts its EBITDA performance. But that number masks a big part of how the company operates—and how it spends its money. Premier argues that analysts should ignore depreciation for big-ticket items like roller coasters because the rides have a long life. Critics, however, say that the amusement industry has to spend as much as 50 percent of its EBITDA just to keep its rides and attractions current. Those expenses are not optional—let the rides get a little rusty, and ticket sales start to tail off. That means analysts really should view depreciation associated with the costs of maintaining the rides (or buying new ones) as an everyday expense. It also means investors in those companies should have strong stomachs.

What's the risk of trusting a fad accounting measure? Just look at a recent year's bankruptcy numbers. Of the 147 companies tracked by Moody's that defaulted on their debt, most borrowed money based on EBITDA performance. The bankers in those deals probably wish they had looked at a few other factors. Maybe it's time more investors did so too.

Source: Adapted from Herb Greenberg, Alphabet Dupe: Why EBITDA Falls Short," *Fortune* (July 10, 2000), p. 240.

---

[3]The airline industry also illustrates the type of problem involved in estimation. In the past, aircraft were assumed not to wear out—they just became obsolete. However, some jets have been in service as long as 20 years, and maintenance of these aircraft has become increasingly expensive. In addition, some recent air disasters have heightened the public's concern about worn-out aircraft. As a result, some airlines now replace aircraft not because of obsolescence but because of physical deterioration.

Methods of Depreciation

The third factor involved in the depreciation process is the **method** of cost apportionment. The profession requires that the depreciation method employed be "systematic and rational." Companies may use a number of depreciation methods, as follows.

1 Activity method (units of use or production).

2 Straight-line method.

3 Decreasing charge methods (accelerated):
  (a) Sum-of-the-years'-digits.
  (b) Declining-balance method.

4 Special depreciation methods:
  (a) Group and composite methods.
  (b) Hybrid or combination methods.[4]

To illustrate these depreciation methods, assume that Stanley Coal Mines recently purchased an additional crane for digging purposes. Illustration 11-2 contains the pertinent data concerning this purchase.

UNDERLYING CONCEPTS

Depreciation attempts to match the cost of an asset to the periods that benefit from the use of that asset.

Cost of crane	$500,000
Estimated useful life	5 years
Estimated salvage value	$ 50,000
Productive life in hours	30,000 hours

ILLUSTRATION 11-2
Data Used to Illustrate
Depreciation Methods

Activity Method *machines*

The **activity method** (also called the **variable-charge** or **units-of-production approach**) assumes that depreciation is **a function of use or productivity, instead of the passage of time.** A company considers the life of the asset in terms of either the **output** it provides (units it produces), or an **input** measure such as the number of hours it works. Conceptually, the proper cost association relies on output instead of hours used, but often the output is not easily measurable. In such cases, an input measure such as machine hours is a more appropriate method of measuring the dollar amount of depreciation charges for a given accounting period.

The crane poses no particular depreciation problem. Stanley can measure the usage (hours) relatively easily. If Stanley uses the crane for 4,000 hours the first year, the depreciation charge is:

OBJECTIVE 3
Compare activity, straight-line, and decreasing-charge methods of depreciation.

$$\frac{(\text{Cost less salvage}) \times \text{Hours this year}}{\text{Total estimated hours}} = \text{Depreciation charge}$$

$$\frac{(\$500,000 - \$50,000) \times 4,000}{30,000} = \$60,000$$

ILLUSTRATION 11-3
Depreciation Calculation,
Activity Method—Crane
Example

The major limitation of this method is that it is inappropriate in situations in which depreciation is a function of time instead of activity. For example, a building steadily deteriorates due to the elements (time) regardless of its use. In addition, where economic or functional factors affect an asset, independent of its use, the activity method loses much of its significance. For example, if a company is expanding rapidly, a particular building may soon become obsolete for its intended purposes. In both cases, activity is irrelevant. Another problem in using an activity method is the difficulty of estimating units of output or service hours received.

---

[4]*Accounting Trends and Techniques—2004* reports that of its 600 surveyed companies, for reporting purposes, 580 used straight-line, 22 used declining-balance, 5 used sum-of-the-years'-digits, 41 used an accelerated method (not specified), and 30 used units of production.

In cases where loss of services results from activity or productivity, the activity method matches costs and revenues the best. Companies that desire low depreciation during periods of low productivity, and high depreciation during high productivity, either adopt or switch to an activity method. In this way, a plant running at 40 percent of capacity generates 60 percent lower depreciation charges. **Inland Steel**, for example, switched to units-of-production depreciation at one time and reduced its losses by $43 million, or $1.20 per share.[5]

Straight-Line Method *Easiest*

The **straight-line method** considers depreciation a **function of time rather than a function of usage**. Companies widely use this method because of its simplicity. The straight-line procedure is often the most conceptually appropriate, too. When creeping obsolescence is the primary reason for a limited service life, the decline in usefulness may be constant from period to period. Stanley computes the depreciation charge for the crane as follows.

ILLUSTRATION 11-4
Depreciation Calculation,
Straight-Line Method—
Crane Example

$$\frac{\text{Cost less salvage}}{\text{Estimated service life}} = \text{Depreciation charge}$$

$$\frac{\$500,000 - \$50,000}{5} = \$90,000$$

The major objection to the straight-line method is that it rests on two tenuous assumptions: (1) The asset's economic usefulness is the same each year, and (2) the repair and maintenance expense is essentially the same each period.

One additional problem that occurs in using straight-line—as well as some others—is that distortions in the rate of return analysis (income/assets) develop. Illustration 11-5 indicates how the rate of return increases, given constant revenue flows, because the asset's book value decreases.

ILLUSTRATION 11-5
Depreciation and Rate of
Return Analysis—Crane
Example

Year	Depreciation Expense	Undepreciated Asset Balance (book value)	Income (after depreciation expense)	Rate of Return (Income ÷ Assets)
0		$500,000		
1	$90,000	410,000	$100,000	24.4%
2	90,000	320,000	100,000	31.2%
3	90,000	230,000	100,000	43.5%
4	90,000	140,000	100,000	71.4%
5	90,000	50,000	100,000	200.0%

Decreasing-Charge Methods

The **decreasing-charge methods** provide for a higher depreciation cost in the earlier years and lower charges in later periods. Because these methods allow for higher early-year charges than in the straight-line method, they are often called **accelerated depreciation methods**.

What is the main justification for this approach? The rationale is that companies should charge more depreciation in earlier years because the asset is most productive in its earlier years. Furthermore, the accelerated methods provide a constant cost because the depreciation charge is lower in the later periods, at the time when the repair and maintenance costs are often higher. Generally, companies use one of two decreasing-charge methods: the sum-of-the-years'-digits method, or the declining-balance method.

---

[5]"Double Standard," *Forbes* (November 22, 1982), p. 178.

Sum-of-the-Years'-Digits. The **sum-of-the-years'-digits method** results in a decreasing depreciation charge based on a decreasing fraction of depreciable cost (original cost less salvage value). Each fraction uses the sum of the years as a denominator ($5 + 4 + 3 + 2 + 1 = 15$). The numerator is the number of years of estimated life remaining as of the beginning of the year. In this method, the numerator decreases year by year, and the denominator remains constant (5/15, 4/15, 3/15, 2/15, and 1/15). At the end of the asset's useful life, the balance remaining should equal the salvage value. Illustration 11-6 shows this method of computation.[6]

Year	Depreciation Base	Remaining Life in Years	Depreciation Fraction	Depreciation Expense	Book Value, End of Year
1	$450,000	5	5/15	$150,000	$350,000
2	450,000	4	4/15	120,000	230,000
3	450,000	3	3/15	90,000	140,000
4	450,000	2	2/15	60,000	80,000
5	450,000	1	1/15	30,000	50,000[a]
		15	15/15	$450,000	

[a]Salvage value.

ILLUSTRATION 11-6
Sum-of-the-Years'-Digits
Depreciation Schedule—
Crane Example

Declining-Balance Method. The **declining-balance method** utilizes a depreciation rate (expressed as a percentage) that is some multiple of the straight-line method. For example, the double-declining rate for a 10-year asset is 20 percent (double the straight-line rate, which is 1/10 or 10 percent). Companies apply the constant rate to the declining book value each year.

Unlike other methods, the declining-balance method **does not deduct the salvage value** in computing the depreciation base. The declining-balance rate is multiplied by the book value of the asset at the beginning of each period. Since the depreciation charge reduces the book value of the asset each period, applying the constant-declining-balance rate to a successively lower book value results in lower depreciation charges each year. This process continues until the book value of the asset equals its estimated salvage value. At that time the company discontinues depreciation.

Companies use various multiples in practice. For example, the **double-declining-balance method** depreciates assets at twice (200 percent) the straight-line rate. Illustration 11-7 shows Stanley's depreciation charges if using the double-declining approach.

Year	Book Value of Asset First of Year	Rate on Declining Balance[a]	Depreciation Expense	Balance Accumulated Depreciation	Book Value, End of Year
1	$500,000	40%	$200,000	$200,000	$300,000
2	300,000	40%	120,000	320,000	180,000
3	180,000	40%	72,000	392,000	108,000
4	108,000	40%	43,200	435,200	64,800
5	64,800	40%	14,800[b]	450,000	50,000

[a]Based on twice the straight-line rate of 20% ($90,000/$450,000 = 20%; 20% × 2 = 40%).
[b]Limited to $14,800 because book value should not be less than salvage value.

ILLUSTRATION 11-7
Double-Declining
Depreciation Schedule—
Crane Example

---

[6]What happens if the estimated service life of the asset is, let us say, 51 years? How would we calculate the sum-of-the-years'-digits? Fortunately mathematicians have developed the following formula that permits easy computation:

$$\frac{n(n+1)}{2} = \frac{51(51+1)}{2} = 1,326$$

Companies often switch from the declining-balance method to the straight-line method near the end of the asset's useful life to ensure that they depreciate the asset only to its salvage value.[7]

Special Depreciation Methods

Sometimes companies adopt special depreciation methods. Reasons for doing so might be that a company's assets have unique characteristics, or the nature of the industry. Two of these special methods are:

1 Group and composite methods.
2 Hybrid or combination methods.

Group and Composite Methods

Companies often depreciate multiple-asset accounts using one rate. For example, **AT&T** might depreciate telephone poles, microwave systems, or switchboards by groups.

Two methods of depreciating multiple-asset accounts exist: the group method and the composite method. The choice of method depends on the nature of the assets involved. Companies frequently use the **group method** when the assets are similar in nature and have approximately the same useful lives. They use the **composite approach** when the assets are dissimilar and have different lives. The group method more closely approximates a single-unit cost procedure because the dispersion from the average is not as great. The computation for group or composite methods is essentially the same: find an average and depreciate on that basis.

Companies determine the **composite depreciation rate** by dividing the depreciation per year by the total cost of the assets. To illustrate, Mooney Motors establishes the composite depreciation rate for its fleet of cars, trucks, and campers as shown in Illustration 11-8.

ILLUSTRATION 11-8
Depreciation Calculation, Composite Basis

Asset	Original Cost	Residual Value	Depreciable Cost	Estimated Life (yrs.)	Depreciation per Year (straight-line)
Cars	$145,000	$25,000	$120,000	3	$40,000
Trucks	44,000	4,000	40,000	4	10,000
Campers	35,000	5,000	30,000	5	6,000
	$224,000	$34,000	$190,000		$56,000

Composite depreciation rate = $\dfrac{\$56,000}{\$224,000}$ = 25%

Composite life = 3.39 years ($190,000 ÷ $56,000)

If there are no changes in the asset account, Mooney will depreciate the group of assets to the residual or salvage value at the rate of $56,000 ($224,000 × 25%) a

---

[7]A pure form of the declining-balance method (sometimes appropriately called the "fixed percentage of book value method") has also been suggested as a possibility. This approach finds a rate that depreciates the asset exactly to salvage value at the end of its expected useful life. The formula for determination of this rate is as follows:

$$\text{Depreciation rate} = 1 - \sqrt[n]{\frac{\text{Salvage value}}{\text{Acquisition cost}}}$$

The life in years is n. After computing the depreciation rate, a company applies it on the declining book value of the asset from period to period, which means that depreciation expense will be successively lower. This method is not used extensively in practice due to cumbersome computations. Further, it is not permitted for tax purposes.

year. As a result, it will take Mooney 3.39 years to depreciate these assets. The length of time it takes a company to depreciate it assets on a composite basis is called the **composite life**.

We can highlight the differences between the group or composite method and the single-unit depreciation method by looking at asset retirements. If Mooney retires an asset before, or after, the average service life of the group is reached, it buries the resulting gain or loss in the Accumulated Depreciation account. This practice is justified because Mooney will retire some assets before the average service life and others after the average life. For this reason, the debit to Accumulated Depreciation is the difference between original cost and cash received. Mooney does not record a gain or loss on disposition.

To illustrate, suppose that Mooney Motors sold one of the campers with a cost of $5,000 for $2,600 at the end of the third year. The entry is:

Accumulated Depreciation	2,400	
Cash	2,600	
Cars, Trucks, and Campers		5,000

If Mooney purchases a new type of asset (mopeds, for example), it must compute a new depreciation rate and apply this rate in subsequent periods.

Illustration 11-9 presents a typical financial statement disclosure of the group depreciation method for **Ampco-Pittsburgh Corporation**.

Ampco-Pittsburgh Corporation

Depreciation rates are based on estimated useful lives of the asset groups. Gains or losses on normal retirements or replacements of depreciable assets, subject to composite depreciation methods, are not recognized; the difference between the cost of the assets retired or replaced and the related salvage value is charged or credited to the accumulated depreciation.

ILLUSTRATION 11-9
Disclosure of Group Depreciation Method

The group or composite method simplifies the bookkeeping process and tends to average out errors caused by over- or under-depreciation. As a result, gains or losses on disposals of assets do not distort periodic income.

On the other hand, the unit method has several advantages over the group or composite methods: (1) It simplifies the computation mathematically. (2) It identifies gains and losses on disposal. (3) It isolates depreciation on idle equipment. (4) It represents the best estimate of the depreciation of each asset, not the result of averaging the cost over a longer period of time. As a consequence, companies generally use the unit method. Unless stated otherwise, you should use the unit method in homework problems.[8]

Hybrid or Combination Methods

In addition to the depreciation methods already discussed, companies are free to develop their own special or tailor-made depreciation methods. GAAP requires only that the method result in the allocation of an asset's cost over the asset's life in a **systematic and rational manner**.

---

[8]AcSEC has indicated in an exposure draft that companies should use the unit approach whenever feasible. In fact, it indicates that an even better way to depreciate property, plant, and equipment is to use *component depreciation*. Under component depreciation, a company should depreciate over its expected useful life any part or portion of property, plant, and equipment that can be separately identified as an asset. For example, a company could separate the various components of a building (e.g., roof, heating and cooling system, elevator, leasehold improvements) and depreciate each component over its useful life.

For example, the steel industry widely uses a hybrid depreciation method, called the **production variable method** that is a combination straight-line/activity approach. The following note from **WHX Corporation**'s annual report explains one variation of this method.

ILLUSTRATION 11-10
Disclosure of Hybrid
Depreciation Method

*Expanded Discussion—
Special Depreciation
Methods*

WHX Corporation

The Company utilizes the modified units of production method of depreciation which recognizes that the depreciation of steelmaking machinery is related to the physical wear of the equipment as well as a time factor. The modified units of production method provides for straight-line depreciation charges modified (adjusted) by the level of raw steel production. In the prior year, depreciation under the modified units of production method was $21.6 million or 40% less than straight-line depreciation, and in the current year it was $1.1 million or 2% more than straight-line depreciation.

**WHAT DO THE
NUMBERS MEAN?**

DECELERATING DEPRECIATION

Which depreciation method should management select? Many believe that the method that best matches revenues with expenses should be used. For example, if revenues generated by the asset are constant over its useful life, select straight-line depreciation. On the other hand, if revenues are higher (or lower) at the beginning of the asset's life, then use a decreasing (or increasing) method. Thus, if a company can reliably estimate revenues from the asset, selecting a depreciation method that best matches costs with those revenues would seem to provide the most useful information to investors and creditors for assessing the future cash flows from the asset.

Managers in the real estate industry face a different challenge when considering depreciation choices. Real estate managers object to traditional depreciation methods because in their view, real estate often does not decline in value. In addition, because real estate is highly debt-financed, most real estate concerns report losses in earlier years of operations when the sum of depreciation and interest exceeds the revenue from the real estate project. As a result, real estate companies, like **Kimco Realty**, argue for some form of **increasing-charge** method of depreciation (lower depreciation at the beginning and higher depreciation at the end). With such a method, companies would report higher total assets and net income in the earlier years of the project.[9]

Special Depreciation Issues

We still need to discuss several special issues related to depreciation:

1 How should companies compute depreciation for partial periods?

2 Does depreciation provide for the replacement of assets?

3 How should companies handle revisions in depreciation rates?

---

[9]In this regard, real estate investment trusts (REITs) often report (in addition to net income) an earnings measure, funds from operations (FFO), that adjusts income for depreciation expense and other noncash expenses. This method is not GAAP. There is mixed empirical evidence about whether FFO or GAAP income is more useful to real estate investment trust investors. See, for example, Richard Gore and David Stott, "Toward a More Informative Measure of Operating Performance in the REIT Industry: Net Income vs. FFO," *Accounting Horizons* (December 1998); and Linda Vincent, "The Information Content of FFO for REITs," *Journal of Accounting and Economics* (January 1999).

Depreciation and Partial Periods

Companies seldom purchase plant assets on the first day of a fiscal period or dispose of them on the last day of a fiscal period. A practical question is: How much depreciation should a company charge for the partial periods involved?

In computing depreciation expense for partial periods, companies must determine the depreciation expense for the full year and then prorate this depreciation expense between the two periods involved. This process should continue throughout the useful life of the asset.

Assume, for example, that Steeltex Company purchases an automated drill machine with a 5-year life for $45,000 (no salvage value) on June 10, 2006. The company's fiscal year ends December 31. Steeltex therefore charges depreciation for only $6\frac{2}{3}$ months during that year. The total depreciation for a full year (assuming straight-line depreciation) is $9,000 ($45,000/5). The depreciation for the first, partial year is therefore:

$$\frac{6\frac{2}{3}}{12} \times \$9,000 = \$5,000$$

The partial-period calculation is relatively simple when Steeltex uses straight-line depreciation. But how is partial-period depreciation handled when it uses an accelerated method such as sum-of-the-years'-digits or double-declining balance? As an illustration, assume that Steeltex purchased another machine for $10,000 on July 1, 2006, with an estimated useful life of five years and no salvage value. Illustration 11-11 shows the depreciation figures for 2006, 2007, and 2008.

	Sum-of-the-Years'-Digits	Double-Declining Balance
1st full year	(5/15 × $10,000) = $3,333.33	(40% × $10,000) = $4,000
2nd full year	(4/15 × 10,000) = 2,666.67	(40% × 6,000) = 2,400
3rd full year	(3/15 × 10,000) = 2,000.00	(40% × 3,600) = 1,440

Depreciation from July 1, 2006, to December 31, 2006

6/12 × $3,333.33 = $1,666.67	6/12 × $4,000 = $2,000

Depreciation for 2007

6/12 × $3,333.33 = $1,666.67	6/12 × $4,000 = $2,000
6/12 × 2,666.67 = 1,333.33	6/12 × 2,400 = 1,200
$3,000.00	$3,200

or ($10,000 − $2,000) × 40% = $3,200

Depreciation for 2008

6/12 × $2,666.67 = $1,333.33	6/12 × $2,400 = $1,200
6/12 × 2,000.00 = 1,000.00	6/12 × 1,440 = 720
$2,333.33	$1,920

or ($10,000 − $5,200) × 40% = $1,920

ILLUSTRATION 11-11
Calculation of Partial-Period Depreciation, Two Methods

Sometimes a company like Steeltex modifies the process of allocating costs to a partial period to handle acquisitions and disposals of plant assets more simply. It may compute depreciation for the full period on the opening balance in the asset account and not charge depreciation on acquisitions during the year. It then charges a full year of depreciation in the year of disposal. Other variations charge one-half year's depreciation both in the year of acquisition and in the year of disposal (referred to as the **half-year convention**), or charge a full year in the year of acquisition and none in the year of disposal.

In fact, Steeltex may adopt any one of these several fractional-year policies in allocating cost to the first and last years of an asset's life so long as it applies the method consistently. However, **unless otherwise stipulated, companies normally compute depreciation on the basis of the nearest full month.**

Illustration 11-12 shows depreciation allocated under five different fractional-year policies using the straight-line method on the $45,000 automated drill machine purchased by Steeltex Company on June 10, 2006, discussed earlier.

ILLUSTRATION 11-12
Fractional-Year
Depreciation Policies

Partial Periods

whatever choose must be consistent

Machine Cost = $45,000	Depreciation Allocated per Period Over 5-Year Life*					
Fractional-Year Policy	2006	2007	2008	2009	2010	2011
1. Nearest fraction of a year.	$5,000[a]	$9,000	$9,000	$9,000	$9,000	$4,000[b]
2. Nearest full month.	5,250[c]	9,000	9,000	9,000	9,000	3,750[d]
3. Half year in period of acquisition and disposal.	4,500	9,000	9,000	9,000	9,000	4,500
4. Full year in period of acquisition, none in period of disposal.	9,000	9,000	9,000	9,000	9,000	–0–
5. None in period of acquisition, full year in period of disposal.	–0–	9,000	9,000	9,000	9,000	9,000

[a]6.667/12 ($9,000)   [b]5.333/12 ($9,000)   [c]7/12 ($9,000)   [d]5/12 ($9,000)
*Rounded to nearest dollar.

Depreciation and Replacement of Fixed Assets

A common misconception about depreciation is that it provides funds for the replacement of fixed assets. Depreciation is like other expenses in that it reduces net income. It differs, though, in that **it does not involve a current cash outflow**.

To illustrate why depreciation does not provide funds for replacement of plant assets, assume that a business starts operating with plant assets of $500,000 that have a useful life of five years. The company's balance sheet at the beginning of the period is:

Plant assets	$500,000	Owners' equity	$500,000

If we assume that the company earns no revenue over the five years, the income statements are:

	Year 1	Year 2	Year 3	Year 4	Year 5
Revenue	$ –0–	$ –0–	$ –0–	$ –0–	$ –0–
Depreciation	(100,000)	(100,000)	(100,000)	(100,000)	(100,000)
Loss	$(100,000)	$(100,000)	$(100,000)	$(100,000)	$(100,000)

Total depreciation of the plant assets over the five years is $500,000. The balance sheet at the end of the five years therefore is:

Plant assets	–0–	Owners' equity	–0–

This extreme example illustrates that depreciation **in no way** provides funds for the replacement of assets. **The funds for the replacement of the assets come from the revenues** (generated through use of the asset). Without the revenues, no income materializes and no cash inflow results.

Revision of Depreciation Rates

When purchasing a plant asset, companies carefully determine depreciation rates based on past experience with similar assets and other pertinent information. The provisions for depreciation are only estimates, however. They may need to revise them during the life of the asset. Unexpected physical deterioration or unforeseen obsolescence may decrease the estimated useful life of the asset. Improved maintenance procedures, revision of operating procedures, or similar developments may prolong the life of the asset beyond the expected period.[10]

For example, assume that **International Paper Co.** purchased machinery with an original cost of $90,000. It estimates a 20-year life with no salvage value. However, during year 11, International Paper estimates that it will use the machine for an additional 20 years. Its total life, therefore, will be 30 years instead of 20. Depreciation has been recorded at the rate of 1/20 of $90,000, or $4,500 per year by the straight-line method. On the basis of a 30-year life, International Paper should have recorded depreciation as 1/30 of $90,000, or $3,000 per year. It has therefore overstated depreciation, and understated net income, by $1,500 for each of the past 10 years, or a total amount of $15,000. Illustration 11-13 shows this computation.

	Per Year	For 10 Years
Depreciation charged per books (1/20 × $90,000)	$4,500	$45,000
Depreciation based on a 30-year life (1/30 × $90,000)	3,000	30,000
Excess depreciation charged	$1,500	$15,000

ILLUSTRATION 11-13
Computation of Accumulated Difference Due to Revisions

International Paper should report this change in estimate in the current and prospective periods. It should not make any changes in previously reported results. And it does not adjust opening balances nor attempt to "catch up" for prior periods. The reason? Changes in estimates are a continual and inherent part of any estimation process. Continual restatement of prior periods would occur for revisions of estimates unless handled prospectively. Therefore, no entry is made at the time the change in estimate occurs. Charges for depreciation in subsequent periods (assuming use of the straight-line method) are determined by **dividing the remaining book value less any salvage value by the remaining estimated life.**

Machinery	$90,000
Less: Accumulated depreciation	45,000
Book value of machinery at end of 10th year	$45,000

Depreciation (future periods) = $45,000 book value ÷ 20 years remaining life = $2,250

ILLUSTRATION 11-14
Computing Depreciation after Revision of Estimated Life

The entry to record depreciation for each of the remaining 20 years is:

Depreciation Expense	2,250	
Accumulated Depreciation—Machinery		2,250

---

[10]As an example of a change in operating procedures, **General Motors** (GM) used to write off its tools—such as dies and equipment used to manufacture car bodies—over the life of the body type. Through this procedure, it expensed tools twice as fast as **Ford** and three times as fast as **DaimlerChrysler**. However, it slowed the depreciation process on these tools and lengthened the lives on its plant and equipment. These revisions reduced depreciation and amortization charges by approximately $1.23 billion, or $2.55 per share, in the year of the change. In Chapter 22, we provide a more complete discussion of changes in estimates.

WHAT DO THE NUMBERS MEAN?

The amount of depreciation expense recorded depends on both the depreciation method used and estimates of service lives and salvage values of the assets. Differences in these choices and estimates can significantly impact a company's reported results and can make it difficult to compare the depreciation numbers of different companies.

For example, when **Willamette Industries** extended the estimated service lives of its machinery and equipment by five years, it increased income by nearly $54 million.

An analyst determines the impact of these management choices and judgments on the amount of depreciation expense by examining the notes to financial statements. For example, Willamette Industries provided the following note to its financial statements.

Note 4: Property, Plant, and Equipment (partial)

	Range of Useful Lives
Land	—
Buildings	15–35
Machinery & equipment	5–25
Furniture & fixtures	3–15

During the year, the estimated service lives for most machinery and equipment were extended five years. The change was based upon a study performed by the company's engineering department, comparisons to typical industry practices, and the effect of the company's extensive capital investments which have resulted in a mix of assets with longer productive lives due to technological advances. As a result of the change, net income was increased by $54,000,000.

IMPAIRMENTS

OBJECTIVE 5
Explain the accounting issues related to asset impairment.

The general accounting standard of **lower-of-cost-or-market for inventories does not apply to property, plant, and equipment**. Even when property, plant, and equipment has suffered partial obsolescence, accountants have been reluctant to reduce the asset's carrying amount. Why? Because, unlike inventories, it is difficult to arrive at a fair value for property, plant, and equipment that is not subjective and arbitrary.

For example, **Falconbridge Ltd. Nickel Mines** had to decide whether to write off all or a part of its property, plant, and equipment in a nickel-mining operation in the Dominican Republic. The project had been incurring losses because nickel prices were low and operating costs were high. Only if nickel prices increased by approximately 33 percent would the project be reasonably profitable. Whether a write-off was appropriate depended on the future price of nickel. Even if the company decided to write off the asset, how much should be written off?

Recognizing Impairments

As discussed in the opening story, the FASB and international accounting standard-setters have developed rules for recognizing impairments on long-lived assets.[11] According to these standards, when the carrying amount of an asset is not recoverable, a company records a write-off. This write-off is referred to as an **impairment**.

UNDERLYING CONCEPTS

The *going concern concept* assumes that the company can recover the investment in its assets. Under GAAP companies do not report the fair value of long-lived assets because a going concern does not plan to sell such assets. However, if the assumption of being able to recover the cost of the investment is not valid, then a company should report a reduction in value.

[11] "Accounting for the Impairment or Disposal of Long-lived Assets," *Statement of Financial Accounting Standards No. 144* (Norwalk, Conn.: 2001).

Various events and changes in circumstances might lead to an impairment. Examples are:

a. A significant decrease in the market value of an asset.

b. A significant change in the extent or manner in which an asset is used.

c. A significant adverse change in legal factors or in the business climate that affects the value of an asset.

d. An accumulation of costs significantly in excess of the amount originally expected to acquire or construct an asset.

e. A projection or forecast that demonstrates continuing losses associated with an asset.

These events or changes in circumstances indicate that the company may not be able to recover the carrying amount of the asset. In that case, a **recoverability test** is used to determine whether an impairment has occurred.

To apply the first step of the recoverability test, a company like **UPS** estimates the future net cash flows expected from the **use of that asset and its eventual disposition**. If the sum of the expected future net cash flows (undiscounted) is **less than the carrying amount** of the asset, UPS considers the asset impaired. Conversely, if the sum of the expected future net cash flows (undiscounted) is **equal to or greater than the carrying amount** of the asset, no impairment has occurred.

The recoverability test therefore screens for asset impairment. For example, if the expected future net cash flows from an asset are $400,000 and its carrying amount is $350,000, no impairment has occurred. However, if the expected future net cash flows are $300,000, an impairment has occurred. The rationale for the recoverability test relies on a basic presumption: A balance sheet should report long-lived assets at no more than the carrying amounts that are recoverable.

Measuring Impairments

If the recoverability test indicates an impairment, UPS computes a loss. The **impairment loss** is the amount by which the carrying amount of the asset **exceeds its fair value**. How does UPS determine the fair value of an asset? It is measured based on the market value if an active market for the asset exists. If no active market exists, UPS uses the **present value of expected future net cash flows to determine fair value**.

To summarize, the process of determining an impairment loss is as follows.

1 Review events or changes in circumstances for possible impairment.

2 If the review indicates impairment, apply the recoverability test. If the sum of the expected future net cash flows from the long-lived asset is less than the carrying amount of the asset, an impairment has occurred.

3 Assuming an impairment, the impairment loss is the amount by which the carrying amount of the asset exceeds the fair value of the asset. The fair value is the market value or the present value of expected future net cash flows.

Impairment—Example 1

M. Alou Inc. has an asset that, due to changes in its use, it reviews for possible impairment. The asset's carrying amount is $600,000 ($800,000 cost less $200,000 accumulated depreciation). Alou determines the expected future net cash flows (undiscounted) from the use of the asset and its eventual disposal to be $650,000.

The recoverability test indicates that the $650,000 of expected future net cash flows from the asset's use exceed the carrying amount of $600,000. As a result, no impairment occurred. (Recall that the undiscounted future net cash flows must be less than the carrying amount for Alou to deem an asset to be impaired and to measure the impairment loss.) Therefore, M. Alou Inc. does not recognize an impairment loss in this case.

Impairment—Example 2

Assume the same facts as in Example 1, except that the expected future net cash flows from Alou's asset are $580,000 (instead of $650,000). The recoverability test indicates that the expected future net cash flows of $580,000 from the use of the asset are less than its carrying amount of $600,000. Therefore an impairment has occurred.

The difference between the carrying amount of Alou's asset and its fair value is the impairment loss. Assuming this asset has a market value of $525,000, Illustration 11-15 shows the loss computation.

ILLUSTRATION 11-15
Computation of
Impairment Loss

Carrying amount of the equipment	$600,000
Fair value of equipment (market value)	525,000
Loss on impairment	$ 75,000

M. Alou records the impairment loss as follows.

Loss on Impairment	75,000	
Accumulated Depreciation		75,000

M. Alou Inc. reports the impairment loss as part of income from continuing operations, in the "Other expenses and losses" section. Generally, Alou **should not report this loss as an extraordinary item**. Costs associated with an impairment loss are the same costs that would flow through operations and that it would report as part of continuing operations. Alou will continue to use these assets in operations. Therefore, it should not report the loss below "Income from continuing operations."

A company that recognizes an impairment loss should disclose the asset(s) impaired, the events leading to the impairment, the amount of the loss, and how it determined fair value (disclosing the interest rate used, if appropriate).

Restoration of Impairment Loss

After recording an impairment loss, the reduced carrying amount of an asset held for use becomes its new cost basis. A company does not change the new cost basis except for depreciation or amortization in future periods or for additional impairments.

To illustrate, assume that Damon Company at December 31, 2006, has equipment with a carrying amount of $500,000. Damon determines this asset is impaired and writes it down to its fair value of $400,000. At the end of 2007, Damon determines that the fair value of the asset is $480,000. The carrying amount of the equipment should not change in 2007 except for the depreciation taken in 2007. Damon **may not restore an impairment loss for an asset held for use**. The rationale for not writing the asset up in value is that the new cost basis puts the impaired asset on an equal basis with other assets that are unimpaired.

INTERNATIONAL
INSIGHT

International accounting standards permit write-ups for subsequent recoveries of impairment. U.S. GAAP prohibits those write-ups, except for assets to be disposed of.

Impairment of Assets to Be Disposed of

What happens if a company intends to dispose of the impaired asset, instead of holding it for use? Recently **Kroger** recorded an impairment loss of $54 million on property, plant, and equipment it no longer needs due to store closures. In this case, Kroger reports the impaired asset at the lower of cost or net realizable value (fair value less cost to sell). Because Kroger intends to dispose of the assets in a short period of time, it uses net realizable value in order to provide a better measure of the net cash flows that it will receive from these assets.

Kroger does not depreciate or amortize assets held for disposal during the period it holds them. The rationale is that depreciation is inconsistent with the notion of assets to be disposed of and with the use of the lower of cost or net realizable value. In other words, **assets held for disposal are like inventory; companies should report them at the lower of cost or net realizable value**.

Because Kroger will recover assets held for disposal through sale rather than through operations, it continually revalues them. Each period, the assets are reported at the lower of cost or net realizable value. Thus **Kroger can write up or down an asset held for disposal in future periods, as long as the carrying value after the write-up never exceeds the carrying amount of the asset before the impairment.** Companies should report losses or gains related to these impaired assets as part of **income from continuing operations**.

Illustration 11-16 summarizes the key concepts in accounting for impairments.

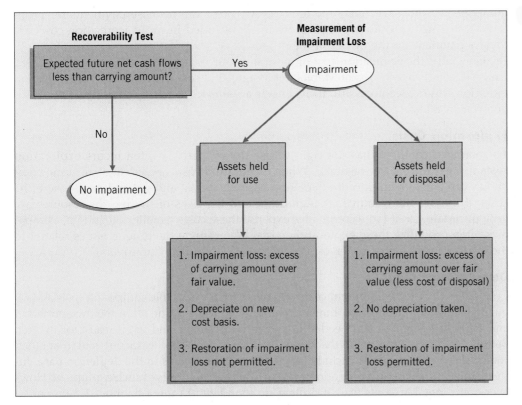

ILLUSTRATION 11-16
Graphic of Accounting for Impairments

DEPLETION

Natural resources, often called wasting assets, include petroleum, minerals, and timber. They have two main features: (1) the complete removal (consumption) of the asset, and (2) replacement of the asset only by an act of nature. Unlike plant and equipment, natural resources are consumed physically over the period of use and do not maintain their physical characteristics. Still, the accounting problems associated with natural resources are similar to those encountered with fixed assets. The questions to be answered are:

OBJECTIVE 6
Explain the accounting procedures for depletion of natural resources.

1 How do companies establish the cost basis for write-off?
2 What pattern of allocation should companies employ?

Recall that the accounting profession uses the term **depletion** for the process of allocating the cost of natural resources.

Establishing a Depletion Base

How do we determine the depletion base for natural resources? For example, a company like **ExxonMobil** makes sizable expenditures to find natural resources, and for every successful discovery there are many failures. Furthermore, it encounters long delays between the time it incurs costs and the time it obtains the benefits from the extracted resources. As a result, a company in the extractive industries, like ExxonMobil, frequently adopts a conservative policy in accounting for the expenditures related to finding and extracting natural resources.

Computation of the depletion base involves four factors: (1) acquisition cost of the deposit, (2) exploration costs, (3) development costs, and (4) restoration costs.

Acquisition Costs

Acquisition cost is the price ExxonMobil pays to obtain the property right to search and find an undiscovered natural resource. It also can be the price paid for an already-discovered resource. A third type of acquisition cost can be lease payments for property containing a productive natural resource; included in these acquisition costs are royalty payments to the owner of the property.

Generally, the acquisition cost of natural resources is recorded in an account titled Undeveloped Property. ExxonMobil later assigns that cost to the natural resource if exploration efforts are successful. If the efforts are unsuccessful, it writes off the acquisition cost as a loss.

Exploration Costs

As soon as a company has the right to use the property, it often incurs **exploration costs** needed to find the resource. When exploration costs are substantial, some companies capitalize them into the depletion base. In the oil and gas industry, where the costs of finding the resource are significant and the risks of finding the resource are very uncertain, most large companies expense these costs. Smaller oil and gas companies often capitalize these exploration costs. We examine the unique issues related to the oil and gas industry on pages 539–541 (see "Continuing Controversy").

Development Costs

Companies divide **development costs** into two parts: (1) tangible equipment costs and (2) intangible development costs. Tangible equipment costs include all of the transportation and other heavy equipment needed to extract the resource and get it ready for market. Because companies can move the heavy equipment from one extracting site to another, companies do not normally include **tangible equipment costs in the depletion base**. Instead, they use separate depreciation charges to allocate the costs of such equipment. However, some tangible assets (e.g., a drilling rig foundation) cannot be moved. Companies depreciate these assets over their useful life or the life of the resource, whichever is shorter.

Intangible development costs, on the other hand, are such items as drilling costs, tunnels, shafts, and wells. These costs have no tangible characteristics but are needed for the production of the natural resource. **Intangible development costs are considered part of the depletion base.**

Restoration Costs

Companies sometimes incur substantial costs to restore property to its natural state after extraction has occurred. These are **restoration costs**. Companies consider **restoration costs part of the depletion base**. The amount included in the depletion base is the fair value of the obligation to restore the property after extraction. A more complete discussion of the accounting for restoration costs and related liabilities (sometimes referred to as asset retirement obligations) is provided in Chapter 13. Similar to other long-lived assets, companies deduct from the depletion base any salvage value to be received on the property.

Write-Off of Resource Cost

Once the company establishes the depletion base, the next problem is determining how to allocate the cost of the natural resource to accounting periods.

Normally, companies compute depletion on a **units-of-production method** (an activity approach). Thus, depletion is a function of the number of units extracted during the period. In this approach, the total cost of the natural resource less salvage value is divided by the number of units estimated to be in the resource deposit, to obtain a **cost**

per unit of product. To compute depletion, the cost per unit is then multiplied by the number of units extracted.

For example, MaClede Co. acquired the right to use 1,000 acres of land in Alaska to mine for gold. The lease cost is $50,000, and the related exploration costs on the property are $100,000. Intangible development costs incurred in opening the mine are $850,000. Total costs related to the mine before the first ounce of gold is extracted are, therefore, $1,000,000. MaClede estimates that the mine will provide approximately 100,000 ounces of gold. Illustration 11-17 shows computation of the depletion cost per unit (depletion rate).

$$\frac{\text{Total cost} - \text{Salvage value}}{\text{Total estimated units available}} = \text{Depletion cost per unit}$$

$$\frac{\$1,000,000}{100,000} = \$10 \text{ per ounce}$$

ILLUSTRATION 11-17
Computation of
Depletion Rate

If MaClede extracts 25,000 ounces in the first year, then the depletion for the year is $250,000 (25,000 ounces × $10). It records the depletion as follows:

Inventory	250,000	
Accumulated Depletion		250,000

MaClede debits Inventory for the total depletion for the year and credits Accumulated Depletion to reduce the carrying value of the natural resource. MaClede credits Inventory when it sells the inventory. The amount not sold remains in inventory and is reported in the current assets section of the balance sheet.

Sometimes companies do not use an Accumulated Depletion account. In that case, the credit goes directly to the natural resources asset account. MaClede's balance sheet would present the cost of the natural resource and the amount of accumulated depletion entered to date as follows:

Gold mine (at cost)	$1,000,000	
Less: Accumulated depletion	250,000	$750,000

ILLUSTRATION 11-18
Balance Sheet
Presentation of Natural
Resource

In the income statement, the depletion cost is part of the cost of goods sold.

MaClede may also depreciate on a units-of-production basis the tangible equipment used in extracting the gold. This approach is appropriate if it can directly assign the estimated lives of the equipment to one given resource deposit. If MaClede uses the equipment on more than one job, other cost allocation methods such as straight-line or accelerated depreciation methods would be more appropriate.

Continuing Controversy

A major controversy relates to the accounting for exploration costs in the oil and gas industry. Conceptually, the question is whether unsuccessful ventures are a cost of those that are successful. Those who hold the **full-cost concept** argue that the cost of drilling a dry hole is a cost needed to find the commercially profitable wells. Others believe that companies should capitalize only the costs of successful projects. This is the **successful-efforts concept**. Its proponents believe that the only relevant measure for a project is the cost directly related to that project, and that companies should report any remaining costs as period charges. In addition, they argue that an unsuccessful company will end up capitalizing many costs that will make it, over a short period of time, show no less income than does one that is successful.[12]

---

[12]Large international oil companies such as **ExxonMobil** use the successful-efforts approach. Most of the smaller, exploration-oriented companies use the full-cost approach. The differences in net income figures under the two methods can be staggering. Analysts estimated that the difference between full-cost and successful efforts for **ChevronTexaco** would be $500 million over a 10-year period (income lower under successful efforts).

The FASB has attempted to narrow the available alternatives, with little success. Here is a brief history of the debate.

1 **1977—The FASB issued *Statement No. 19*, which required oil and gas companies to follow successful efforts accounting.** Small oil and gas producers, voicing strong opposition, lobbied extensively in Congress. Governmental agencies assessed the implications of this standard from a public interest perspective and reacted contrary to the FASB's position.[13]

2 **1978—In response to criticisms of the FASB's actions, the SEC reexamined the issue and found both the successful-efforts and full-cost approaches inadequate. Neither method, said the SEC, reflects the economic substance of oil and gas exploration.** As a substitute, the SEC argued in favor of a yet-to-be developed method, **reserve recognition accounting (RRA)**, which it believed would provide more useful information. Under RRA, as soon as a company discovers oil, it reports the value of the oil on the balance sheet and in the income statement. Thus, RRA is a fair-value approach, in contrast to full-costing and successful-efforts, which are historical cost approaches.[14]

3 **1979–1981—As a result of the SEC's actions, the FASB issued another standard that suspended the requirement that companies follow successful-efforts accounting.** Therefore, full costing was again permissible. In attempting to implement RRA, however, the SEC encountered practical problems in estimating **(1) the amount of the reserves, (2) the future production costs, (3) the periods of expected disposal, (4) the discount rate, and (5) the selling price.** Companies needed an estimate for each of these to arrive at an accurate valuation of existing reserves. Estimating the future selling price, appropriate discount rate, and future extraction and delivery costs of reserves that are years away from realization can be a formidable task.

4 **1981—The SEC abandoned RRA in the primary financial statements of oil and gas producers.** The SEC decided that RRA did not possess the required degree of reliability for use as a primary method of financial reporting. However, it continued to stress the need for some form of fair-value–based disclosure for oil and gas reserves. As a result, the FASB issued *Statement No. 69*, "Disclosure about Oil and Gas Producing Activities," which requires current-value disclosures.

Currently, companies can use either the full-cost approach or the successful-efforts approach. It does seem ironic that Congress directed the FASB to develop one method of accounting for the oil and gas industry, and when the FASB did so, the government chose not to accept it. Subsequently, the SEC attempted to develop a new approach, failed, and then urged the FASB to develop the disclosure requirements in this area. After all these changes, the two alternatives still exist.[15]

---

[13]The Department of Energy indicated that companies using the full-cost method at that time would reduce their exploration activities because of the unfavorable earnings impact associated with successful-efforts accounting. The Justice Department asked the SEC to postpone adoption of one uniform method of accounting in the oil and gas industry until the SEC could determine whether the information reported to investors would be enhanced and competition constrained by adoption of the successful-efforts method.

[14]The use of RRA would make a substantial difference in the balance sheets and income statements of oil companies. For example, **Atlantic Richfield Co.** at one time reported net producing property of $2.6 billion. Under RRA, the same properties would be valued at $11.8 billion. Similarly, **Standard Oil of Ohio**, which reported net producing properties of $1.7 billion, would have reported approximately $10.7 billion in producing properties under RRA.

[15]One requirement of the full-cost approach is that companies can capitalize costs only up to a ceiling, which is the present value of company reserves. Companies must expense costs above that ceiling. When the price of oil fell in the mid-1980s, so did the present value of companies' reserves, thus forcing expensing of costs beyond the ceiling. Companies lobbied for leniency, but the SEC decided that the write-offs had to be taken. **Mesa Limited Partnerships** restated its $31 million profit to a $169 million loss, and **Pacific Lighting** restated its $44.5 million profit to a $70.5 million loss.

This controversy in the oil and gas industry provides a number of lessons. First, it demonstrates the strong influence that the federal government has in financial reporting matters. Second, the concern for economic consequences places pressure on the FASB to weigh the economic effects of any required standard. Third, the experience with RRA highlights the problems that accompany any proposed change from an historical-cost to a fair-value approach. Fourth, this controversy illustrates the difficulty of establishing standards when affected groups have differing viewpoints. Finally, it reinforces the need for a conceptual framework with carefully developed guidelines for recognition, measurement, and reporting, so that interested parties can more easily resolve issues of this nature in the future.

Special Problems in Depletion Accounting

Accounting for natural resources has some interesting problems that are not common to most other types of assets. Four categories of depletion accounting problems exist:

1 Difficulty of estimating recoverable reserves.

2 Problems of discovery value.

3 Tax aspects of natural resources.

4 Accounting for liquidating dividends.

Estimating Recoverable Reserves

Not infrequently companies need to change the estimate of recoverable reserves. They do so either because they have new information or because more sophisticated production processes are available. Natural resources such as oil and gas deposits and some rare metals have recently provided the greatest challenges. Estimates of these reserves are in large measure merely "knowledgeable guesses."

This problem is the **same as accounting for changes in estimates for the useful lives of plant and equipment**. The procedure is to **revise the depletion rate on a prospective basis**: A company divides the remaining cost by the new estimate of the recoverable reserves. This approach has much merit because the required estimates are so shaky.

RAH-RAH SURPRISE

Recent cuts in the estimates of oil and natural gas reserves at Royal Dutch/Shell, El Paso Corporation, and other energy companies highlight the importance of reserve disclosures. Investors appear to believe that these disclosures provide useful information for assessing the future cash flows from a company's oil and gas reserves. For example, when Shell's estimates turned out to be overly optimistic (to the tune of 3.9 billion barrels or 20 percent of reserves), Shell's stock price fell.

The experience at Shell and other companies has led the SEC to look at how companies are estimating their "proved" reserves. *Proved reserves* are quantities of oil and gas that can be shown ". . . with reasonable certainty to be recoverable in future years. . . ." The phrase "reasonable certainty" is crucial to this guidance, but differences in interpretation of what is reasonably certain can result in a wide range of estimates.

In one case, for example, ExxonMobil's estimate was 29 percent higher than an estimate the SEC developed. ExxonMobil was more optimistic about the effects of new technology that enables the industry to retrieve more of the oil and gas it finds. Thus, to ensure the continued usefulness of RRA disclosures, the SEC may have to work on a measurement methodology that keeps up with technology changes in the oil and gas industry.

Source: S. Labaton and J. Gerth, "At Shell, New Accounting and Rosier Outlook," *New York Times* (nytimes.com) (March 12, 2004); and J. Ball, C. Cummins, and B. Bahree, "Big Oil Differs with SEC on Methods to Calculate the Industry's Reserves," *Wall Street Journal* (February 24, 2005), p. C1.

WHAT DO THE NUMBERS MEAN?

Discovery Value

Discovery value accounting is similar to reserve recognition accounting. RRA specifically relates to the oil and gas industry, whereas **discovery value** is a broader term associated with the entire natural resources area. As indicated earlier, current standards do not allow discovery values.

However, if the accounting standard were to change, to allow discovery value to be recorded, companies would debit an asset account and credit an Unrealized Appreciation account. Unrealized Appreciation is part of stockholders' equity. The company then would transfer Unrealized Appreciation to revenue as it sells the natural resources.

A similar issue arises with resources such as growing timber, aging liquor, and maturing livestock that increase in value over time. One method is to record the increase in value as the accretion occurs: to debit the asset account and credit revenue or an unrealized revenue account. These increases can be substantial. **Boise Cascade** at one time valued its timber resources at $1.7 billion, while their book value was approximately $289 million. Accountants have been hesitant to record these increases because of the uncertainty regarding the final sales price and the problem of estimating the costs involved in getting the resources ready for sale.

Tax Aspects of Natural Resources

Some of the most controversial provisions of the Internal Revenue Code relate to the tax aspects of accounting for natural resources. The tax law has long provided a deduction against revenue from oil, gas, and most minerals for the greater of **cost** or **percentage depletion**. The percentage (statutory) depletion allows some companies a write-off ranging from 5 percent to 22 percent (depending on the natural resource) of gross revenue received. As a result of this tax benefit, the amount of depletion may exceed the cost assigned to a given natural resource. An asset's carrying amount may be zero, but the company may take a depletion deduction if it has gross revenue.

The significance of the percentage depletion allowance is now greatly reduced, since Congress repealed it for most oil and gas companies.

Liquidating Dividends

A company often owns as its only major asset a property from which it intends to extract natural resources. If the company does not expect to purchase additional properties, it may gradually distribute to stockholders their capital investments by paying **liquidating dividends**, which are dividends greater than the amount of accumulated net income.

The major accounting problem is to distinguish between dividends that are a return of capital and those that are not. Because the dividend is a return of the investor's original contribution, the company issuing a liquidating dividend should debit Paid-in Capital in Excess of Par for that portion related to the original investment, instead of debiting Retained Earnings.

To illustrate, at year-end, Callahan Mining had a retained earnings balance of $1,650,000, accumulated depletion on mineral properties of $2,100,000, and paid-in capital in excess of par of $5,435,493. Callahan's board declared a dividend of $3 a share on the 1,000,000 shares outstanding. It records the $3,000,000 cash dividend as follows.

Retained Earnings	1,650,000	
Paid-in Capital in Excess of Par	1,350,000	
Cash		3,000,000

Callahan must inform stockholders that the $3 dividend per share represents a $1.65 ($1,650,000 ÷ 1,000,000 shares) per share return on investment and a $1.35 ($1,350,000 ÷ 1,000,000 shares) per share liquidating dividend.

PRESENTATION AND ANALYSIS

Presentation of Property, Plant, Equipment, and Natural Resources

A company should disclose the basis of valuation—usually historical cost—for property, plant, equipment, and natural resources along with pledges, liens, and other commitments related to these assets. It should not offset any liability secured by property, plant, equipment, and natural resources against these assets. Instead, this obligation should be reported in the liabilities section. The company should segregate property, plant, and equipment not currently employed as producing assets in the business (such as idle facilities or land held as an investment) from assets used in operations.

When depreciating assets, a company credits a valuation account normally called Accumulated Depreciation. Using an Accumulated Depreciation account permits the user of the financial statements to see the original cost of the asset and the amount of depreciation that the company charged to expense in past years.

When depleting natural resources, some companies use an Accumulated Depletion account. Many, however, simply credit the natural resource account directly. The rationale for this approach is that the natural resources are physically consumed, making direct reduction of the cost of the natural resources appropriate.

Because of the significant impact on the financial statements of the depreciation method(s) used, companies should disclose the following.

a. Depreciation expense for the period.

b. Balances of major classes of depreciable assets, by nature and function.

c. Accumulated depreciation, either by major classes of depreciable assets or in total.

d. A general description of the method or methods used in computing depreciation with respect to major classes of depreciable assets.[16]

Special disclosure requirements relate to the oil and gas industry. Companies engaged in these activities must disclose the following in their financial statements: (1) the basic method of accounting for those costs incurred in oil and gas producing activities (e.g., full-cost versus successful-efforts), and (2) how the company disposes of costs relating to extractive activities (e.g., dispensing immediately versus depreciation and depletion.)[17]

The 2004 annual report of **International Paper Company** in Illustration 11-19 (page 544) shows an acceptable disclosure. It uses condensed balance sheet data supplemented with details and policies in notes to the financial statements.

> **OBJECTIVE 7**
> **Explain how to report and analyze property, plant, equipment, and natural resources.**

---

[16]"Omnibus Opinion—1967," *Opinions of the Accounting Principles Board No. 12* (New York: AICPA, 1967), par. 5. Some believe that companies should disclose the average useful life of the assets or the range of years of asset life to help users understand the age and life of property, plant, and equipment.

[17]Public companies, in addition to these two required disclosures, must include as supplementary information numerous schedules reporting reserve quantities; capitalized costs; acquisition, exploration, and development activities; and a standardized measure of discounted future net cash flows related to proved oil and gas reserve quantities. See "Disclosures about Oil and Gas Producing Activities," *Statement of Financial Accounting Standards Board No. 69* (Stamford, Conn.: FASB, 1982).

ILLUSTRATION 11-19
Disclosures for
Property, Plant,
Equipment, and Natural
Resources

International Paper Company

Consolidated Balance Sheet (partial)

In millions at December 31	2004	2003
Assets		
Total current assets	$ 9,319	$11,096
Plants, properties and equipment, net	13,432	13,260
Forestlands	3,936	3,979
Investments	679	678
Goodwill	4,994	4,793
Deferred charges and other assets	1,857	1,719
Total assets	$34,217	$35,525

Note 1 (partial)

Plants, Properties and Equipment   Plants, properties and equipment are stated at cost, less accumulated depreciation. Expenditures for betterments are capitalized whereas normal repairs and maintenance are expensed as incurred. The units-of-production method of depreciation is used for major pulp and paper mills and certain wood products facilities and the straight-line method for other plants and equipment. Annual straight-line depreciation rates are, for buildings, 2 1/2% to 8 1/2%, and, for machinery and equipment, 5% to 33%.

Forestlands   At December 31, 2004, International Paper and its subsidiaries owned or controlled about 6.8 million acres of forestlands in the United States, 1.2 million acres in Brazil, 785,000 acres in New Zealand, and had, through licenses and forest management agreements, harvesting rights on government owned forestlands in Russia. Forestlands include owned property as well as certain timber harvesting rights with terms of one or more years, and are stated at cost, less cost of timber harvested (COTH). Costs attributable to timber are charged against income as trees are cut. The rate charged is determined annually based on the relationship of incurred costs to estimated current merchantable volume.

Effective January 1, 2002, International Paper prospectively changed its method of accounting for mid-rotation fertilization expenditures to include such expenditures in the capitalized cost of forestlands. Accordingly, these costs are included as part of the COTH as trees are sold.

Note 11 (partial)

Plants, properties and equipment by major classification were:

In millions at December 31	2004	2003
Pulp, paper and packaging facilities		
Mills	$22,165	$21,234
Packaging plants	5,874	5,826
Wood products facilities	1,411	1,232
Other plants, properties and equipment	1,925	2,091
Gross cost	31,375	30,383
Less: Accumulated depreciation	17,943	17,123
Plants, properties and equipment, net	$13,432	$13,260

Analysis of Property, Plant, Equipment

Analysts evaluate assets relative to activity (turnover) and profitability.

*Additional Property,
Plant, and Equipment
Disclosures*

Asset Turnover Ratio

How efficiently a company uses its assets to generate sales is measured by the **asset turnover ratio**. This ratio divides net sales by average total assets for the period. The resulting number is the dollars of sales produced by each dollar invested in assets. To illustrate, we use the following data from the **Tootsie Roll Industries** 2004 annual report. Illustration 11-20 shows computation of the asset turnover ratio.

Tootsie Roll Industries

	(in millions)
Net sales	$420.1
Total assets, 12/31/04	811.8
Total assets, 12/31/03	665.3
Net income	64.2

$$\text{Asset turnover} = \frac{\text{Net sales}}{\text{Average total assets}}$$
$$= \frac{\$420.1}{(\$811.8 + \$665.3)/2}$$
$$= .569$$

ILLUSTRATION 11-20
Asset Turnover Ratio

The asset turnover ratio shows that Tootsie Roll generated sales of $0.57 per dollar of assets in the year ended December 31, 2004.

Asset turnover ratios vary considerably among industries. For example, a large utility like **Ameren** has a ratio of 0.32 times. A large grocery chain like **Kroger** has a ratio of 2.73 times. Thus, in comparing performance among companies based on the asset turnover ratio, you need to consider the ratio within the context of the industry in which a company operates.

Profit Margin on Sales Ratio

Another measure for analyzing the use of property, plant, and equipment is the **profit margin on sales ratio** (rate of return on sales). Calculated as net income divided by net sales, this profitability ratio does not, by itself, answer the question of how profitably a company uses its assets. But by relating the profit margin on sales to the asset turnover during a period of time, we can ascertain how profitably the company used assets during that period of time in a measure of the rate of return on assets. Using the Tootsie Roll Industries data shown above, we compute the profit margin on sales ratio and the rate of return on assets as follows.

$$\text{Profit margin on sales} = \frac{\text{Net income}}{\text{Net sales}}$$
$$= \frac{\$64.2}{\$420.1}$$
$$= 15.28\%$$
$$\text{Rate of return on assets} = \text{Profit margin on sales} \times \text{Asset turnover}$$
$$= 15.28\% \times .569$$
$$= 8.7\%$$

ILLUSTRATION 11-21
Profit Margin on Sales

Rate of Return on Assets

The rate of return a company achieves through use of its assets is the **rate of return on assets (ROA)**. Rather than using the profit margin on sales, we can compute it directly by dividing net income by average total assets. Using Tootsie Roll's data, we compute the ratio as follows.

$$\text{Rate of return on assets} = \frac{\text{Net income}}{\text{Average total assets}}$$
$$= \frac{\$64.2}{(\$811.8 + \$665.3)/2}$$
$$= 8.7\%$$

ILLUSTRATION 11-22
Rate of Return on Assets

The 8.7 percent rate of return computed in this manner equals (with rounding) the 8.7 percent rate computed by multiplying the profit margin on sales by the asset turnover. The rate of return on assets measures profitability well because it combines the effects of profit margin and asset turnover.

KEY TERMS

accelerated-depreciation methods, *526*

activity method, *525*

amortization, *522*

asset turnover ratio, *544*

composite approach, *528*

composite depreciation rate, *528*

declining-balance method, *527*

decreasing-charge methods, *526*

depletion, *522, 537*

depreciation, *522*

depreciation base, *523*

development costs, *538*

discovery value, *542*

double-declining-balance method, *527*

exploration costs, *538*

full-cost concept, *539*

group method, *528*

impairment, *534*

inadequacy, *523*

liquidating dividends, *542*

natural resources, *537*

obsolescence, *523*

percentage depletion, *542*

profit margin on sales ratio, *545*

rate of return on assets (ROA), *545*

recoverabilty test, *535*

reserve recognition accounting (RRA), *540*

restoration costs, *538*

salvage value, *523*

straight-line method, *526*

successful-efforts concept, *539*

sum-of-the-years'-digits method, *527*

supersession, *523*

SUMMARY OF LEARNING OBJECTIVES

1. Explain the concept of depreciation. Depreciation allocates the cost of tangible assets to expense in a systematic and rational manner to those periods expected to benefit from the use of the asset.

2. Identify the factors involved in the depreciation process. Three factors involved in the depreciation process are: (1) determining the depreciation base for the asset, (2) estimating service lives, and (3) selecting a method of cost apportionment (depreciation).

3. Compare activity, straight-line, and decreasing-charge methods of depreciation. (1) *Activity method:* Assumes that depreciation is a function of use or productivity instead of the passage of time. The life of the asset is considered in terms of either the output it provides, or an input measure such as the number of hours it works. (2) *Straight-line method:* Considers depreciation a function of time instead of a function of usage. The straight-line procedure is often the most conceptually appropriate when the decline in usefulness is constant from period to period. (3) *Decreasing-charge methods:* Provides for a higher depreciation cost in the earlier years and lower charges in later periods. The main justification for this approach is that the asset is the most productive in its early years.

4. Explain special depreciation methods. Two special depreciation methods are: (1) *Group and composite methods*: The group method is frequently used when the assets are fairly similar in nature and have approximately the same useful lives. The composite method may be used when the assets are dissimilar and have different lives. (2) *Hybrid or combination methods*: These methods may combine straight-line/activity approaches.

5. Explain the accounting issues related to asset impairment. The process to determine an impairment loss is as follows: (1) Review events and changes in circumstances for possible impairment. (2) If events or changes suggest impairment, determine if the sum of the expected future net cash flows from the long-lived asset is less than the carrying amount of the asset. If less, measure the impairment loss. (3) The impairment loss is the amount by which the carrying amount of the asset exceeds the fair value of the asset.

After a company records an impairment loss, the reduced carrying amount of the long-lived asset is its new cost basis. Impairment losses may not be restored for assets held for use. If the company expects to dispose of the asset, it should report the impaired asset at the lower of cost or net realizable value. It is not depreciated. It can be continuously revalued, as long as the write-up is never to an amount greater than the carrying amount before impairment.

6. Explain the accounting procedures for depletion of natural resources. To account for depletion of natural resources, companies (1) establish the depletion base and (2) write off resource cost. Four factors are part of establishing the depletion base: (a) acquisition costs, (b) exploration costs, (c) development costs, and (d) restoration costs. To write off resource cost, companies normally compute depletion on the units-of-production method. Thus, depletion is a function of the number of units withdrawn during the period. To obtain a cost per unit of product, the total cost of the natural resource less salvage value is divided by the number of units estimated to be in the resource deposit, to obtain a cost per unit of product. To compute depletion, this cost per unit is multiplied by the number of units withdrawn.

7. Explain how to report and analyze property, plant, equipment, and natural resources. The basis of valuation for property, plant, and equipment and for natural resources should be disclosed along with pledges, liens, and other commitments related to these assets. Companies should not offset any liability secured by property, plant, and equipment or by natural resources against these assets, but should report it in the liabilities section. When depreciating assets, credit a valuation account normally called Accumulated Depreciation. When depleting assets, use an accumulated depletion account, or credit the depletion directly to the natural resource account. Companies engaged in significant oil and gas producing activities must provide additional disclosures about these activities. Analysis may be performed to evaluate the asset turnover ratio, profit margin on sales, and rate of return on assets.

APPENDIX
11A
Income Tax Depreciation

For the most part, a financial accounting course does not address issues related to the computation of income taxes. However, because the concepts of tax depreciation are similar to those of book depreciation, and because tax depreciation methods are sometimes adopted for book purposes, we present an overview of this subject.

> **OBJECTIVE 8**
> Describe income tax methods of depreciation.

Congress passed the Accelerated Cost Recovery System (ACRS) as part of the Economic Recovery Tax Act of 1981. The goal was to stimulate capital investment through faster write-offs and to bring more uniformity to the write-off period. For assets purchased in the years 1981 through 1986, companies use ACRS and its preestablished "cost recovery periods" for various classes of assets.

In the Tax Reform Act of 1986 Congress enacted a **Modified Accelerated Cost Recovery System**, known as **MACRS**. It applies to depreciable assets placed in service in 1987 and later. The following discussion is based on these MACRS rules. Realize that tax depreciation rules are subject to change annually.[1]

MODIFIED ACCELERATED COST RECOVERY SYSTEM

The computation of depreciation under MACRS differs from the computation under GAAP in three respects: (1) a mandated tax life, which is generally shorter than the economic life; (2) cost recovery on an accelerated basis; and (3) an assigned salvage value of zero.

---

[1]For example, in an effort to jump-start the economy following the September 11, 2001, terrorist attacks, Congress passed the Job Creation and Worker Assistance Act of 2002 (the Act). The Act allows a 30 percent first-year bonus depreciation for assets placed into service after September 11, 2001, but before September 11, 2004. A follow-up provision enacted in 2003 extended the tax savings to assets placed in service before January 1, 2005. The law encourages companies to invest in fixed assets because they can front-load depreciation expense, which lowers taxable income and amount of taxes companies pay in the early years of an asset's life. Although the Act may be a good thing for the economy, it can distort cash flow measures—making them look artificially strong when the allowances are in place but reversing once the bonus depreciation expires. See D. Zion and B. Carcache, "Bonus Depreciation Boomerang," *Credit Suisse First Boston Equity Research* (February 19, 2004).

Tax Lives (Recovery Periods)

Each item of depreciable property belongs to a property class. The recovery period (depreciable tax life) of an asset depends on its property class.[2] Illustration 11A-1 presents the MACRS property classes.

ILLUSTRATION 11A-1
MACRS Property Classes

> **3-year property**—includes small tools, horses, and assets used in research and development activities
>
> **5-year property**—includes automobiles, trucks, computers and peripheral equipment, and office machines
>
> **7-year property**—includes office furniture and fixtures, agriculture equipment, oil exploration and development equipment, railroad track, manufacturing equipment, and any property not designated by law as being in any other class
>
> **10-year property**—includes railroad tank cars, mobile homes, boilers, and certain public utility property
>
> **15-year property**—includes roads, shrubbery, and certain low-income housing
>
> **20-year property**—includes waste-water treatment plants and sewer systems
>
> **27.5-year property**—includes residential rental property
>
> **39-year property**—includes nonresidential real property

Tax Depreciation Methods

Companies compute depreciation expense using the tax basis—usually the cost—of the asset. The depreciation method depends on the MACRS property class, as shown below.

ILLUSTRATION 11A-2
Depreciation Method for Various MACRS Property Classes

MACRS Property Class	Depreciation Method
3-, 5-, 7-, and 10-year property	Double-declining-balance
15- and 20-year property	150% declining-balance
27.5- and 39-year property	Straight-line

Depreciation computations for income tax purposes are based on the **half-year convention**. That is, a half year of depreciation is allowable in the year of acquisition and in the year of disposition.[3] A company depreciates an asset to a zero value so that there is no salvage value at the end of its MACRS life.

Use of IRS-published tables, shown in Illustration 11A-3, simplifies application of these depreciation methods.

Example of MACRS System

To illustrate depreciation computations under both the MACRS system and GAAP straight-line accounting, assume the following facts for a computer and peripheral equipment purchased by Denise Rode Company on January 1, 2006.

Acquisition date	January 1, 2006
Cost	$100,000
Estimated useful life	7 years
Estimated salvage value	$16,000
MACRS class life	5 years
MACRS method	200% declining-balance
GAAP method	Straight-line
Disposal proceeds—January 2, 2013	$11,000

---

[2]Tax depreciation changed numerous times in the 1980s and 1990s. For example, since 1980, Congress has enacted six different depreciation requirements. The tax life of certain real property changed from 35 years in 1980 to 15 in 1981, 18 in 1982, 19 in 1984, 31.5 in 1986, and 39 in 1993. As one writer noted, "It appears that the useful life of a depreciation law is 2.2 years."

[3]The tax law requires mid-quarter and mid-month conventions for MACRS purposes in certain circumstances.

			MACRS Depreciation Rates by Class of Property			
Recovery Year	3-year (200% DB)	5-year (200% DB)	7-year (200% DB)	10-year (200% DB)	15-year (150% DB)	20-year (150% DB)
1	33.33	20.00	14.29	10.00	5.00	3.750
2	44.45	32.00	24.49	18.00	9.50	7.219
3	14.81*	19.20	17.49	14.40	8.55	6.677
4	7.41	11.52*	12.49	11.52	7.70	6.177
5		11.52	8.93*	9.22	6.93	5.713
6		5.76	8.92	7.37	6.23	5.285
7			8.93	6.55*	5.90*	4.888
8			4.46	6.55	5.90	4.522
9				6.56	5.91	4.462*
10				6.55	5.90	4.461
11				3.28	5.91	4.462
12					5.90	4.461
13					5.91	4.462
14					5.90	4.461
15					5.91	4.462
16					2.95	4.461
17						4.462
18						4.461
19						4.462
20						4.461
21						2.231

*Switchover to straight-line depreciation.

Using the rates from the MACRS depreciation rate schedule for a 5-year class of property, Rode computes depreciation as follows for tax purposes.

MACRS Depreciation

2006	$100,000 × .20	=	$ 20,000
2007	$100,000 × .32	=	32,000
2008	$100,000 × .192	=	19,200
2009	$100,000 × .1152	=	11,520
2010	$100,000 × .1152	=	11,520
2011	$100,000 × .0576	=	5,760
	Total depreciation		$100,000

Rode computes the depreciation under GAAP straight-line method, with $16,000 of estimated salvage value and an estimated useful life of 7 years, as shown in Illustration 11A-5.

GAAP Depreciation

($100,000 − $16,000) ÷ 7 = $12,000 annual depreciation
× 7 years

1/1/06–1/2/13 $84,000 total depreciation

The MACRS depreciation recovers the total cost of the asset on an accelerated basis. But, a taxable gain of $11,000 results from the sale of the asset at January 2, 2013. Therefore, the net effect on taxable income for the years 2006 through 2013 is $89,000 ($100,000 depreciation − $11,000 gain).

Under GAAP, the company recognizes a loss on disposal of $5,000 ($16,000 book value − $11,000 disposal proceeds). The net effect on income before income taxes for the years 2006 through 2013 is $89,000 ($84,000 depreciation + $5,000 loss), the same as the net effect of MACRS on taxable income.

Even though the net effects are equal in amount, the deferral of income tax payments under MACRS from early in the life of the asset to later in life is desirable. The different amounts of depreciation for income tax reporting and financial GAAP reporting in each year are a matter of timing and result in temporary differences, which require **interperiod tax allocation**. (See Chapter 19 for an extended treatment of this topic.)

Optional Straight-Line Method

INTERNATIONAL INSIGHT

In Switzerland, depreciation in the financial statements conforms to that on the tax returns. As a consequence, companies may depreciate as much as 80% of the cost of assets in the first year.

An alternate MACRS method exists for determining depreciation deductions. Based on the straight-line method, it is referred to as the **optional** (elective) **straight-line method**. This method applies to the six classes of property described earlier. The alternate MACRS applies the straight-line method to the MACRS recovery periods. It ignores salvage value.

Under the optional straight-line method, in the first year in which the property is put in service, the company deducts half of the amount of depreciation that would be permitted for a full year (half-year convention). Use the half-year convention for homework problems.

Tax versus Book Depreciation

GAAP requires that companies allocate the cost of depreciable assets to expense over the expected useful life of the asset in a systematic and rational manner. Some argue that from a cost-benefit perspective it would be better for companies to adopt the MACRS approach in order to eliminate the necessity of maintaining two different sets of records.

However, the tax laws and financial reporting have different objectives: The purpose of taxation is to raise revenue from constituents in an equitable manner. The purpose of financial reporting is to reflect the economic substance of a transaction as closely as possible and to help predict the amounts, timing, and uncertainty of future cash flows. Because these objectives differ, the adoption of one method for both tax and book purposes in all cases would be unfortunate.

KEY TERM

Modified Accelerated
   Cost Recovery System
   (MACRS), 547

SUMMARY OF LEARNING OBJECTIVE FOR APPENDIX 11A

8. Describe income tax methods of depreciation. Congress enacted a Modified Accelerated Cost Recovery System (MACRS) in the Tax Reform Act of 1986. It applies to depreciable assets placed in service in 1987 and later. The computation of depreciation under MACRS differs from the computation under GAAP in three respects: (1) a mandated tax life, which is generally shorter than the economic life; (2) cost recovery on an accelerated basis; and (3) an assigned salvage value of zero.

Note: All **asterisked** Questions, Exercises, Problems, and Concepts for Analysis relate to material contained in the appendix to the chapter.

QUESTIONS

1. Distinguish between depreciation, depletion, and amortization.

2. Identify the factors that are relevant in determining the annual depreciation charge, and explain whether these factors are determined objectively or whether they are based on judgment.

3. Some believe that accounting depreciation measures the decline in the value of fixed assets. Do you agree? Explain.

4. Explain how estimation of service lives can result in unrealistically high valuations of fixed assets.

5. The plant manager of a manufacturing firm suggested in a conference of the company's executives that accountants should speed up depreciation on the machinery in the finishing department because improvements were rapidly making those machines obsolete and a depreciation fund big enough to cover their replacement is needed. Discuss the accounting concept of depreciation and the effect on a business concern of the depreciation recorded for plant assets, paying particular attention to the issues raised by the plant manager.

6. For what reasons are plant assets retired? Define inadequacy, supersession, and obsolescence.

7. What basic questions must be answered before the amount of the depreciation charge can be computed?

8. Elizabeth Ashley Company purchased a machine on January 2, 2006, for $600,000. The machine has an estimated useful life of 5 years and a salvage value of $100,000. Depreciation was computed by the 150% declining-balance method. What is the amount of accumulated depreciation at the end of December 31, 2007?

9. Linda Blair Company purchased machinery for $120,000 on January 1, 2007. It is estimated that the machinery will have a useful life of 20 years, salvage value of $15,000, production of 84,000 units, and working hours of 42,000. During 2007 the company uses the machinery for 14,300 hours, and the machinery produces 20,000 units. Compute depreciation under the straight-line, units-of-output, working hours, sum-of-the-years'-digits, and declining-balance (use 10% as the annual rate) methods.

10. What are the major factors considered in determining what depreciation method to use?

11. Under what conditions is it appropriate for a business to use the composite method of depreciation for its plant assets? What are the advantages and disadvantages of this method?

12. If Brad Pitt, Inc. uses the composite method and its composite rate is 7.5% per year, what entry should it make when plant assets that originally cost $50,000 and have been used for 10 years are sold for $16,000?

13. A building that was purchased December 31, 1982, for $2,400,000 was originally estimated to have a life of 50 years with no salvage value at the end of that time. Depreciation has been recorded through 2006. During 2007 an examination of the building by an engineering firm discloses that its estimated useful life is 15 years after 2006. What should be the amount of depreciation for 2007?

14. Armand Assante, president of Flatbush Company, has recently noted that depreciation increases cash provided by operations and therefore depreciation is a good source of funds. Do you agree? Discuss.

15. Melanie Mayron purchased a computer for $6,000 on July 1, 2007. She intends to depreciate it over 4 years using the double-declining balance method. Salvage value is $1,000. Compute depreciation for 2008.

16. Astaire Inc. is considering the write-down of its long-term plant because of a lack of profitability. Explain to the management of Astaire how to determine whether a write-off is permitted.

17. Last year Wilde Company recorded an impairment on an asset held for use. Recent appraisals indicate that the asset has increased in value. Should Wilde record this recovery in value?

18. Kuga Co. has equipment with a carrying amount of $700,000. The expected future net cash flows from the equipment are $705,000, and its fair value is $590,000. The equipment is expected to be used in operations in the future. What amount (if any) should Kuga report as an impairment to its equipment?

19. Explain how gains or losses on impaired assets should be reported in income.

20. It has been suggested that plant and equipment could be replaced more quickly if depreciation rates for income tax and accounting purposes were substantially increased. As a result, business operations would receive the benefit of more modern and more efficient plant facilities. Discuss the merits of this proposition.

21. Neither depreciation on replacement cost nor depreciation adjusted for changes in the purchasing power of the dollar has been recognized as generally accepted accounting principles for inclusion in the primary financial statements. Briefly present the accounting treatment that might be used to assist in the maintenance of the ability of a company to replace its productive capacity.

22. List (a) the similarities and (b) the differences in the accounting treatments of depreciation and cost depletion.

23. Describe cost depletion and percentage depletion. Why is the percentage depletion method permitted?

24. In what way may the use of percentage depletion violate sound accounting theory?

25. In the extractive industries, businesses may pay dividends in excess of net income. What is the maximum permissible? How can this practice be justified?

26. The following statement appeared in a financial magazine: "RRA—or Rah-Rah, as it's sometimes dubbed—has kicked up quite a storm. Oil companies, for example, are convinced that the approach is misleading. Major accounting firms agree." What is RRA? Why might oil companies believe that this approach is misleading?

27. Adriana Oil uses successful efforts accounting and also provides full-cost results as well. Under full-cost, Adriana Oil would have reported retained earnings of $42 million and net income of $4 million. Under successful efforts, retained earnings were $29 million, and net income was $3 million. Explain the difference between full costing and successful efforts accounting.

28. **Target Corporation** in 2004 reported net income of $3.2 billion, net sales of $45.7 billion, and average total assets of $29.8 billion. What is Target's asset turnover ratio? What is Target's rate of return on assets?

*29. What is a modified accelerated cost recovery system (MACRS)? Speculate as to why this system is now required for tax purposes.

BRIEF EXERCISES

(LO 4) **BE11-1** Castlevania Corporation purchased a truck at the beginning of 2007 for $42,000. The truck is estimated to have a salvage value of $2,000 and a useful life of 160,000 miles. It was driven 23,000 miles in 2007 and 31,000 miles in 2008. Compute depreciation expense for 2007 and 2008.

(LO 2, 3) **BE11-2** Cheetah Company purchased machinery on January 1, 2007, for $60,000. The machinery is estimated to have a salvage value of $6,000 after a useful life of 8 years. (a) Compute 2007 depreciation expense using the straight-line method. (b) Compute 2007 depreciation expense using the straight-line method assuming the machinery was purchased on September 1, 2007.

(LO 2, 3) **BE11-3** Use the information for Cheetah Company given in BE11-2. (a) Compute 2007 depreciation expense using the sum-of-the-years'-digits method. (b) Compute 2007 depreciation expense using the sum-of-the-years'-digits method assuming the machinery was purchased on April 1, 2007.

(LO 2, 3) **BE11-4** Use the information for Cheetah Company given in BE11-2. (a) Compute 2007 depreciation expense using the double-declining balance method. (b) Compute 2007 depreciation expense using the double-declining balance method assuming the machinery was purchased on October 1, 2007.

(LO 2, 3) **BE11-5** Garfield Company purchased a machine on July 1, 2008, for $25,000. Garfield paid $200 in title fees and county property tax of $125 on the machine. In addition, Garfield paid $500 shipping charges for delivery, and $475 was paid to a local contractor to build and wire a platform for the machine on the plant floor. The machine has an estimated useful life of 6 years with a salvage value of $3,000. Determine the depreciation base of Garfield's new machine. Garfield uses straight-line depreciation.

(LO 4) **BE11-6** Battlesport Inc. owns the following assets.

Asset	Cost	Salvage	Estimated Useful Life
A	$70,000	$ 7,000	10 years
B	50,000	10,000	5 years
C	82,000	4,000	12 years

Compute the composite depreciation rate and the composite life of Battlesport's assets.

(LO 2) **BE11-7** Myst Company purchased a computer for $7,000 on January 1, 2006. Straight-line depreciation is used, based on a 5-year life and a $1,000 salvage value. In 2008, the estimates are revised. Myst now feels the computer will be used until December 31, 2009, when it can be sold for $500. Compute the 2008 depreciation.

(LO 5) **BE11-8** Dinoland Company owns machinery that cost $900,000 and has accumulated depreciation of $360,000. The expected future net cash flows from the use of the asset are expected to be $500,000. The fair value of the equipment is $400,000. Prepare the journal entry, if any, to record the impairment loss.

(LO 6) **BE11-9** Genghis Khan Corporation acquires a coal mine at a cost of $400,000. Intangible development costs total $100,000. After extraction has occurred, Khan must restore the property (estimated fair value of the obligation is $75,000), after which it can be sold for $160,000. Khan estimates that 4,000 tons of coal can be extracted. If 700 tons are extracted the first year, prepare the journal entry to record depletion.

(LO 7) **BE11-10** In its 2004 annual report **Campbell Soup Company** reports beginning-of-the-year total assets of $6,205 million, end-of-the-year total assets of $6,675 million, total sales of $7,109 million, and net income of $647 million. (a) Compute Campbell's asset turnover ratio. (b) Compute Campbell's profit margin on sales. (c) Compute Campbell's rate of return on assets (1) using asset turnover and profit margin and (2) using net income.

(LO 8) ***BE11-11** Timecap Corporation purchased an asset at a cost of $40,000 on March 1, 2008. The asset has a useful life of 8 years and a salvage value of $4,000. For tax purposes, the MACRS class life is 5 years. Compute tax depreciation for each year 2008–2013.

EXERCISES

(LO 2, 3) **E11-1** **(Depreciation Computations—SL, SYD, DDB)** Deluxe Ezra Company purchases equipment on January 1, Year 1, at a cost of $469,000. The asset is expected to have a service life of 12 years and a salvage value of $40,000.

Instructions

(a) Compute the amount of depreciation for each of Years 1 through 3 using the straight-line depreciation method.

(b) Compute the amount of depreciation for each of Years 1 through 3 using the sum-of-the-years'-digits method.

(c) Compute the amount of depreciation for each of Years 1 through 3 using the double-declining balance method. (In performing your calculations, round constant percentage to the nearest one-hundredth of a point and round answers to the nearest dollar.)

(LO 2, 3) **E11-2 (Depreciation—Conceptual Understanding)** Rembrandt Company acquired a plant asset at the beginning of Year 1. The asset has an estimated service life of 5 years. An employee has prepared depreciation schedules for this asset using three different methods to compare the results of using one method with the results of using other methods. You are to assume that the following schedules have been correctly prepared for this asset using (1) the straight-line method, (2) the sum-of-the-years'-digits method, and (3) the double-declining balance method.

Year	Straight-Line	Sum-of-the-Years'-Digits	Double-Declining Balance
1	$ 9,000	$15,000	$20,000
2	9,000	12,000	12,000
3	9,000	9,000	7,200
4	9,000	6,000	4,320
5	9,000	3,000	1,480
Total	$45,000	$45,000	$45,000

Instructions

Answer the following questions.

(a) What is the cost of the asset being depreciated?

(b) What amount, if any, was used in the depreciation calculations for the salvage value for this asset?

(c) Which method will produce the highest charge to income in Year 1?

(d) Which method will produce the highest charge to income in Year 4?

(e) Which method will produce the highest book value for the asset at the end of Year 3?

(f) If the asset is sold at the end of Year 3, which method would yield the highest gain (or lowest loss) on disposal of the asset?

(LO 2, 3) **E11-3 (Depreciation Computations—SYD, DDB—Partial Periods)** Judds Company purchased a new plant asset on April 1, 2007, at a cost of $711,000. It was estimated to have a service life of 20 years and a salvage value of $60,000. Judds' accounting period is the calendar year.

Instructions

(a) Compute the depreciation for this asset for 2007 and 2008 using the sum-of-the-years'-digits method.

(b) Compute the depreciation for this asset for 2007 and 2008 using the double-declining balance method.

(LO 2, 3) **E11-4 (Depreciation Computations—Five Methods)** Jon Seceda Furnace Corp. purchased machinery for $315,000 on May 1, 2007. It is estimated that it will have a useful life of 10 years, salvage value of $15,000, production of 240,000 units, and working hours of 25,000. During 2008 Seceda Corp. uses the machinery for 2,650 hours, and the machinery produces 25,500 units.

Instructions

From the information given, compute the depreciation charge for 2008 under each of the following methods. (Round to the nearest dollar.)

(a) Straight-line.

(b) Units-of-output.

(c) Working hours.

(d) Sum-of-the-years'-digits.

(e) Declining-balance (use 20% as the annual rate).

(LO 2, 3) **E11-5 (Depreciation Computations—Four Methods)** Robert Parish Corporation purchased a new machine for its assembly process on August 1, 2007. The cost of this machine was $117,900. The company estimated that the machine would have a salvage value of $12,900 at the end of its service life. Its life is estimated at 5 years and its working hours are estimated at 21,000 hours. Year-end is December 31.

Instructions

Compute the depreciation expense under the following methods. Each of the following should be considered unrelated.

(a) Straight-line depreciation for 2007.

(b) Activity method for 2007, assuming that machine usage was 800 hours.

  (c) Sum-of-the-years'-digits for 2008.
  (d) Double-declining balance for 2008.

(LO 2, 3) **E11-6** **(Depreciation Computations—Five Methods, Partial Periods)** Muggsy Bogues Company purchased equipment for $212,000 on October 1, 2006. It is estimated that the equipment will have a useful life of 8 years and a salvage value of $12,000. Estimated production is 40,000 units and estimated working hours are 20,000. During 2006, Bogues uses the equipment for 525 hours and the equipment produces 1,000 units.

Instructions

Compute depreciation expense under each of the following methods. Bogues is on a calendar-year basis ending December 31.

  (a) Straight-line method for 2006.
  (b) Activity method (units of output) for 2006.
  (c) Activity method (working hours) for 2006.
  (d) Sum-of-the-years'-digits method for 2008.
  (e) Double-declining balance method for 2007.

(LO 2, 3) **E11-7** **(Different Methods of Depreciation)** Jackel Industries presents you with the following information.

Description	Date Purchased	Cost	Salvage Value	Life in Years	Depreciation Method	Accumulated Depreciation to 12/31/07	Depreciation for 2008
Machine A	2/12/06	$142,500	$16,000	10	**(a)**	$33,350	**(b)**
Machine B	8/15/05	**(c)**	21,000	5	SL	29,000	**(d)**
Machine C	7/21/04	75,400	23,500	8	DDB	**(e)**	**(f)**
Machine D	10/12/**(g)**	219,000	69,000	5	SYD	70,000	**(h)**

Instructions

Complete the table for the year ended December 31, 2008. The company depreciates all assets using the half-year convention.

(LO 2, 3) **E11-8** **(Depreciation Computation—Replacement, Nonmonetary Exchange)** George Zidek Corporation bought a machine on June 1, 2005, for $31,000, f.o.b. the place of manufacture. Freight to the point where it was set up was $200, and $500 was expended to install it. The machine's useful life was estimated at 10 years, with a salvage value of $2,500. On June 1, 2006, an essential part of the machine is replaced, at a cost of $1,980, with one designed to reduce the cost of operating the machine. The cost of the old part and related depreciation cannot be determined with any accuracy.

On June 1, 2009, the company buys a new machine of greater capacity for $35,000, delivered, trading in the old machine which has a fair market value and trade-in allowance of $20,000. To prepare the old machine for removal from the plant cost $75, and expenditures to install the new one were $1,500. It is estimated that the new machine has a useful life of 10 years, with a salvage value of $4,000 at the end of that time. (The exchange has commercial substance.)

Instructions

Assuming that depreciation is to be computed on the straight-line basis, compute the annual depreciation on the new equipment that should be provided for the fiscal year beginning June 1, 2009. (Round to the nearest dollar.)

(LO 2, 3) **E11-9** **(Composite Depreciation)** Presented below is information related to LeBron James Manufacturing Corporation.

Asset	Cost	Estimated Salvage	Estimated Life (in years)
A	$40,500	$5,500	10
B	33,600	4,800	9
C	36,000	3,600	9
D	19,000	1,500	7
E	23,500	2,500	6

Instructions

  (a) Compute the rate of depreciation per year to be applied to the plant assets under the composite method.
  (b) Prepare the adjusting entry necessary at the end of the year to record depreciation for the year.
  (c) Prepare the entry to record the sale of asset D for cash of $4,800. It was used for 6 years, and depreciation was entered under the composite method.

(LO 2, 3) **E11-10** **(Depreciation Computations, SYD)** Five Satins Company purchased a piece of equipment at the beginning of 2004. The equipment cost $430,000. It has an estimated service life of 8 years and an expected salvage value of $70,000. The sum-of-the-years'-digits method of depreciation is being used. Someone has already correctly prepared a depreciation schedule for this asset. This schedule shows that $60,000 will be depreciated for a particular calendar year.

Instructions

Show calculations to determine for what particular year the depreciation amount for this asset will be $60,000.

(LO 2, 3) **E11-11 (Depreciation—Change in Estimate)** Machinery purchased for $60,000 by Tom Brady Co. in 2003 was originally estimated to have a life of 8 years with a salvage value of $4,000 at the end of that time. Depreciation has been entered for 5 years on this basis. In 2008, it is determined that the total estimated life should be 10 years with a salvage value of $4,500 at the end of that time. Assume straight-line depreciation.

Instructions

(a) Prepare the entry to correct the prior years' depreciation, if necessary.
(b) Prepare the entry to record depreciation for 2008.

(LO 2, 3) **E11-12 (Depreciation Computation—Addition, Change in Estimate)** In 1980, Herman Moore Company completed the construction of a building at a cost of $2,000,000 and first occupied it in January 1981. It was estimated that the building will have a useful life of 40 years and a salvage value of $60,000 at the end of that time.

Early in 1991, an addition to the building was constructed at a cost of $500,000. At that time it was estimated that the remaining life of the building would be, as originally estimated, an additional 30 years, and that the addition would have a life of 30 years, and a salvage value of $20,000.

In 2009, it is determined that the probable life of the building and addition will extend to the end of 2040 or 20 years beyond the original estimate.

Instructions

(a) Using the straight-line method, compute the annual depreciation that would have been charged from 1981 through 1990.
(b) Compute the annual depreciation that would have been charged from 1991 through 2008.
(c) Prepare the entry, if necessary, to adjust the account balances because of the revision of the estimated life in 2009.
(d) Compute the annual depreciation to be charged beginning with 2009.

(LO 2, 3) **E11-13 (Depreciation—Replacement, Change in Estimate)** Greg Maddox Company constructed a building at a cost of $2,200,000 and occupied it beginning in January 1988. It was estimated at that time that its life would be 40 years, with no salvage value.

In January 2008, a new roof was installed at a cost of $300,000, and it was estimated then that the building would have a useful life of 25 years from that date. The cost of the old roof was $160,000.

Instructions

(a) What amount of depreciation should have been charged annually from the years 1988 to 2007? (Assume straight-line depreciation.)
(b) What entry should be made in 2008 to record the replacement of the roof?
(c) Prepare the entry in January 2008, to record the revision in the estimated life of the building, if necessary.
(d) What amount of depreciation should be charged for the year 2008?

(LO 2, 3) **E11-14 (Error Analysis and Depreciation, SL and SYD)** Mike Devereaux Company shows the following entries in its Equipment account for 2008. All amounts are based on historical cost.

Equipment					
2008			**2008**		
Jan. 1	Balance	134,750	June 30	Cost of equipment sold	
Aug. 10	Purchases	32,000		(purchased prior	
12	Freight on equipment			to 2008)	23,000
	purchased	700			
25	Installation costs	2,700			
Nov. 10	Repairs	500			

Instructions

(a) Prepare any correcting entries necessary.
(b) Assuming that depreciation is to be charged for a full year on the ending balance in the asset account, compute the proper depreciation charge for 2008 under each of the methods listed

below. Assume an estimated life of 10 years, with no salvage value. The machinery included in the January 1, 2008, balance was purchased in 2006.
  (1) Straight-line.
  (2) Sum-of-the-years'-digits.

(LO 2, 3) **E11-15 (Depreciation for Fractional Periods)** On March 10, 2009, Lost World Company sells equipment that it purchased for $192,000 on August 20, 2002. It was originally estimated that the equipment would have a life of 12 years and a salvage value of $16,800 at the end of that time, and depreciation has been computed on that basis. The company uses the straight-line method of depreciation.

Instructions
  (a) Compute the depreciation charge on this equipment for 2002, for 2009, and the total charge for the period from 2003 to 2008, inclusive, under each of the six following assumptions with respect to partial periods.
    (1) Depreciation is computed for the exact period of time during which the asset is owned. (Use 365 days for base.)
    (2) Depreciation is computed for the full year on the January 1 balance in the asset account.
    (3) Depreciation is computed for the full year on the December 31 balance in the asset account.
    (4) Depreciation for one-half year is charged on plant assets acquired or disposed of during the year.
    (5) Depreciation is computed on additions from the beginning of the month following acquisition and on disposals to the beginning of the month following disposal.
    (6) Depreciation is computed for a full period on all assets in use for over one-half year, and no depreciation is charged on assets in use for less than one-half year. (Use 365 days for base.)
  (b) Briefly evaluate the methods above, considering them from the point of view of basic accounting theory as well as simplicity of application.

(LO 5) **E11-16 (Impairment)** Presented below is information related to equipment owned by Suarez Company at December 31, 2007.

Cost	$9,000,000
Accumulated depreciation to date	1,000,000
Expected future net cash flows	7,000,000
Fair value	4,800,000

Assume that Suarez will continue to use this asset in the future. As of December 31, 2007, the equipment has a remaining useful life of 4 years.

Instructions
  (a) Prepare the journal entry (if any) to record the impairment of the asset at December 31, 2007.
  (b) Prepare the journal entry to record depreciation expense for 2008.
  (c) The fair value of the equipment at December 31, 2008, is $5,100,000. Prepare the journal entry (if any) necessary to record this increase in fair value.

(LO 5) **E11-17 (Impairment)** Assume the same information as E11-16, except that Suarez intends to dispose of the equipment in the coming year. It is expected that the cost of disposal will be $20,000.

Instructions
  (a) Prepare the journal entry (if any) to record the impairment of the asset at December 31, 2007.
  (b) Prepare the journal entry (if any) to record depreciation expense for 2008.
  (c) The asset was not sold by December 31, 2008. The fair value of the equipment on that date is $5,300,000. Prepare the journal entry (if any) necessary to record this increase in fair value. It is expected that the cost of disposal is still $20,000.

(LO 5) **E11-18 (Impairment)** The management of Petro Garcia Inc. was discussing whether certain equipment should be written off as a charge to current operations because of obsolescence. This equipment has a cost of $900,000 with depreciation to date of $400,000 as of December 31, 2007. On December 31, 2007, management projected its future net cash flows from this equipment to be $300,000 and its fair value to be $230,000. The company intends to use this equipment in the future.

Instructions
  (a) Prepare the journal entry (if any) to record the impairment at December 31, 2007.
  (b) Where should the gain or loss (if any) on the write-down be reported in the income statement?
  (c) At December 31, 2008, the equipment's fair value increased to $260,000. Prepare the journal entry (if any) to record this increase in fair value.
  (d) What accounting issues did management face in accounting for this impairment?

(LO 6)   **E11-19   (Depletion Computations—Timber)**   Stanislaw Timber Company owns 9,000 acres of timberland purchased in 1996 at a cost of $1,400 per acre. At the time of purchase the land without the timber was valued at $400 per acre. In 1997, Stanislaw built fire lanes and roads, with a life of 30 years, at a cost of $84,000. Every year Stanislaw sprays to prevent disease at a cost of $3,000 per year and spends $7,000 to maintain the fire lanes and roads. During 1998, Stanislaw selectively logged and sold 700,000 board feet of timber, of the estimated 3,500,000 board feet. In 1999, Stanislaw planted new seedlings to replace the trees cut at a cost of $100,000.

Instructions
- (a)   Determine the depreciation expense and the cost of timber sold related to depletion for 1998.
- (b)   Stanislaw has not logged since 1998. If Stanislaw logged and sold 900,000 board feet of timber in 2009, when the timber cruise (appraiser) estimated 5,000,000 board feet, determine the cost of timber sold related to depletion for 2009.

(LO 6)   **E11-20   (Depletion Computations—Oil)**   Diderot Drilling Company has leased property on which oil has been discovered. Wells on this property produced 18,000 barrels of oil during the past year that sold at an average sales price of $55 per barrel. Total oil resources of this property are estimated to be 250,000 barrels.

The lease provided for an outright payment of $500,000 to the lessor (owner) before drilling could be commenced and an annual rental of $31,500. A premium of 5% of the sales price of every barrel of oil removed is to be paid annually to the lessor. In addition, Diderot (lessee) is to clean up all the waste and debris from drilling and to bear the costs of reconditioning the land for farming when the wells are abandoned. The estimated fair value, at the time of the lease, of this clean-up and reconditioning is $30,000.

Instructions
From the provisions of the lease agreement, you are to compute the cost per barrel for the past year, exclusive of operating costs, to Diderot Drilling Company.

(LO 6)   **E11-21   (Depletion Computations—Timber)**   Forda Lumber Company owns a 7,000-acre tract of timber purchased in 2000 at a cost of $1,300 per acre. At the time of purchase the land was estimated to have a value of $300 per acre without the timber. Forda Lumber Company has not logged this tract since it was purchased. In 2007, Forda had the timber cruised. The cruise (appraiser) estimated that each acre contained 8,000 board feet of timber. In 2007, Forda built 10 miles of roads at a cost of $7,840 per mile. After the roads were completed, Forda logged and sold 3,500 trees containing 850,000 board feet.

Instructions
- (a)   Determine the cost of timber sold related to depletion for 2007.
- (b)   If Forda depreciates the logging roads on the basis of timber cut, determine the depreciation expense for 2007.
- (c)   If Forda plants five seedlings at a cost of $4 per seedling for each tree cut, how should Forda treat the reforestation?

(LO 6)   **E11-22   (Depletion Computations—Mining)**   Alcide Mining Company purchased land on February 1, 2007, at a cost of $1,190,000. It estimated that a total of 60,000 tons of mineral was available for mining. After it has removed all the natural resources, the company will be required to restore the property to its previous state because of strict environmental protection laws. It estimates the fair value of this restoration obligation at $90,000. It believes it will be able to sell the property afterwards for $100,000. It incurred developmental costs of $200,000 before it was able to do any mining. In 2007 resources removed totaled 30,000 tons. The company sold 22,000 tons.

Instructions
Compute the following information for 2007.

- (a)   Per unit material cost.
- (b)   Total material cost of December 31, 2007, inventory.
- (c)   Total materials cost in cost of goods sold at December 31, 2007.

(LO 6)   **E11-23   (Depletion Computations—Minerals)**   At the beginning of 2007, Aristotle Company acquired a mine for $970,000. Of this amount, $100,000 was ascribed to the land value and the remaining portion to the minerals in the mine. Surveys conducted by geologists have indicated that approximately 12,000,000 units of the ore appear to be in the mine. Aristotle incurred $170,000 of development costs associated with this mine prior to any extraction of minerals. It also determined that the fair value of its obligation to prepare the land for an alternative use when all of the mineral has been removed was $40,000. During 2007, 2,500,000 units of ore were extracted and 2,100,000 of these units were sold.

Instructions

Compute the following.

(a) The total amount of depletion for 2007.

(b) The amount that is charged as an expense for 2007 for the cost of the minerals sold during 2007.

(LO 7) **E11-24 (Ratio Analysis)** The 2004 Annual Report of **Eastman Kodak** contains the following information.

(in millions)	December 31, 2004	December 31, 2003
Total assets	$14,737	$14,846
Total liabilities	10,926	11,601
Net sales	13,516	12,909
Net income	556	253

Instructions

Compute the following ratios for Eastman Kodak for 2004.

(a) Asset turnover ratio.

(b) Rate of return on assets.

(c) Profit margin on sales.

(d) How can the asset turnover ratio be used to compute the rate of return on assets?

(LO 8) ***E11-25 (Book vs. Tax (MACRS) Depreciation)** Futabatei Enterprises purchased a delivery truck on January 1, 2007, at a cost of $27,000. The truck has a useful life of 7 years with an estimated salvage value of $6,000. The straight-line method is used for book purposes. For tax purposes the truck, having an MACRS class life of 7 years, is classified as 5-year property; the optional MACRS tax rate tables are used to compute depreciation. In addition, assume that for 2007 and 2008 the company has revenues of $200,000 and operating expenses (excluding depreciation) of $130,000.

Instructions

(a) Prepare income statements for 2007 and 2008. (The final amount reported on the income statement should be income before income taxes.)

(b) Compute taxable income for 2007 and 2008.

(c) Determine the total depreciation to be taken over the useful life of the delivery truck for both book and tax purposes.

(d) Explain why depreciation for book and tax purposes will generally be different over the useful life of a depreciable asset.

(LO 8) ***E11-26 (Book vs. Tax (MACRS) Depreciation)** Shimei Inc. purchased computer equipment on March 1, 2007, for $31,000. The computer equipment has a useful life of 10 years and a salvage value of $1,000. For tax purposes, the MACRS class life is 5 years.

Instructions

(a) Assuming that the company uses the straight-line method for book and tax purposes, what is the depreciation expense reported in (1) the financial statements for 2007 and (2) the tax return for 2007?

(b) Assuming that the company uses the double-declining balance method for both book and tax purposes, what is the depreciation expense reported in (1) the financial statements for 2007 and (2) the tax return for 2007?

(c) Why is depreciation for tax purposes different from depreciation for book purposes even if the company uses the same depreciation method to compute them both?

> **See the book's website, www.wiley.com/college/kieso, for Additional Exercises.**

PROBLEMS

(LO 2, 3) **P11-1 (Depreciation for Partial Period—SL, SYD, and DDB)** Onassis Company purchased Machine #201 on May 1, 2007. The following information relating to Machine #201 was gathered at the end of May.

Price	$73,500
Credit terms	2/10, n/30
Freight-in costs	$ 970
Preparation and installation costs	$ 3,800
Labor costs during regular production operations	$10,500

It was expected that the machine could be used for 10 years, after which the salvage value would be zero. Onassis intends to use the machine for only 8 years, however, after which it expects to be able to sell it for $1,200. The invoice for Machine #201 was paid May 5, 2007. Onassis uses the calendar year as the basis for the preparation of financial statements.

Instructions

(a) Compute the depreciation expense for the years indicated using the following methods. (Round to the nearest dollar.)
 (1) Straight-line method for 2007.
 (2) Sum-of-the-years'-digits method for 2008.
 (3) Double-declining balance method for 2007.

(b) Suppose Jackie Ari, the president of Onassis, tells you that because the company is a new organization, she expects it will be several years before production and sales reach optimum levels. She asks you to recommend a depreciation method that will allocate less of the company's depreciation expense to the early years and more to later years of the assets' lives. What method would you recommend?

(LO 2, 3) **P11-2** (**Depreciation for Partial Periods—SL, Act., SYD, and DDB**) The cost of equipment purchased by Boris Becker, Inc., on June 1, 2007 is $67,000. It is estimated that the machine will have a $4,000 salvage value at the end of its service life. Its service life is estimated at 7 years; its total working hours are estimated at 42,000 and its total production is estimated at 525,000 units. During 2007 the machine was operated 6,000 hours and produced 55,000 units. During 2008 the machine was operated 5,500 hours and produced 48,000 units.

Instructions

Compute depreciation expense on the machine for the year ending December 31, 2007, and the year ending December 31, 2008, using the following methods.

(a) Straight-line.
(b) Units-of-output.
(c) Working hours.
(d) Sum-of-the-years'-digits.
(e) Declining balance (twice the straight-line rate).

(LO 2, 3) **P11-3** (**Depreciation—SYD, Act., SL, and DDB**) The following data relate to the Plant Assets account of Arthur Fiedler, Inc. at December 31, 2007.

Plant Assets

	A	B	C	D
Original cost	$35,000	$51,000	$80,000	$80,000
Year purchased	2002	2003	2004	2006
Useful life	10 years	15,000 hours	15 years	10 years
Salvage value	$ 3,100	$ 3,000	$ 5,000	$ 5,000
Depreciation method	Sum-of-the-years'-digits	Activity	Straight-line	Double-declining balance
Accum. Depr. through 2007*	$23,200	$35,200	$15,000	$16,000

*In the year an asset is purchased, Fiedler, Inc. does not record any depreciation expense on the asset. In the year an asset is retired or traded in, Fiedler, Inc. takes a full year's depreciation on the asset.

The following transactions occurred during 2008.

(a) On May 5, Asset A was sold for $13,000 cash. The company's bookkeeper recorded this retirement in the following manner in the cash receipts journal.

Cash	13,000	
Asset A		13,000

(b) On December 31, it was determined that Asset B had been used 2,100 hours during 2008.

(c) On December 31, before computing depreciation expense on Asset C, the management of Fiedler, Inc. decided the useful life remaining from January 1, 2008, was 10 years.

(d) On December 31, it was discovered that a plant asset purchased in 2007 had been expensed completely in that year. This asset cost $22,000 and has a useful life of 10 years and no salvage value. Management has decided to use the double-declining balance method for this asset, which can be referred to as "Asset E."

Instructions

Prepare the necessary correcting entries for the year 2008. Record the appropriate depreciation expense on the above-mentioned assets.

(LO 2, 3) **P11-4 (Depreciation and Error Analysis)** A depreciation schedule for semitrucks of Oglala Manufacturing Company was requested by your auditor soon after December 31, 2008, showing the additions, retirements, depreciation, and other data affecting the income of the company in the 4-year period 2005 to 2008, inclusive. The following data were ascertained.

Balance of Semitrucks account, Jan. 1, 2005	
Truck No. 1 purchased Jan. 1, 2002, cost	$18,000
Truck No. 2 purchased July 1, 2002, cost	22,000
Truck No. 3 purchased Jan. 1, 2004, cost	30,000
Truck No. 4 purchased July 1, 2004, cost	24,000
Balance, Jan. 1, 2005	$94,000

The Semitrucks—Accumulated Depreciation account previously adjusted to January 1, 2005, and duly entered in the ledger, had a balance on that date of $30,200 (depreciation on the four trucks from the respective dates of purchase, based on a 5-year life, no salvage value). No charges had been made against the account before January 1, 2005.

Transactions between January 1, 2005, and December 31, 2008, and their record in the ledger were as follows.

July 1, 2005   Truck No. 3 was traded for a larger one (No. 5), the agreed purchase price of which was $34,000. Oglala Mfg. Co. paid the automobile dealer $15,000 cash on the transaction. The entry was a debit to Semitrucks and a credit to Cash, $15,000. The transaction has commercial substance.

Jan. 1, 2006   Truck No. 1 was sold for $3,500 cash; entry debited Cash and credited Semitrucks, $3,500.

July 1, 2007   A new truck (No. 6) was acquired for $36,000 cash and was charged at that amount to the Semitrucks account. (Assume truck No. 2 was not retired.)

July 1, 2007   Truck No. 4 was damaged in a wreck to such an extent that it was sold as junk for $700 cash. Oglala Mfg. Co. received $2,500 from the insurance company. The entry made by the bookkeeper was a debit to Cash, $3,200, and credits to Miscellaneous Income, $700, and Semitrucks, $2,500.

Entries for depreciation had been made at the close of each year as follows: 2005, $20,300; 2006, $21,100; 2007, $24,450; 2008, $27,800.

Instructions

   (a)   For each of the 4 years compute separately the increase or decrease in net income arising from the company's errors in determining or entering depreciation or in recording transactions affecting trucks, ignoring income tax considerations.

   (b)   Prepare one compound journal entry as of December 31, 2008, for adjustment of the Semitrucks account to reflect the correct balances as revealed by your schedule, assuming that the books have not been closed for 2008.

(LO 3, 6) **P11-5 (Depletion and Depreciation—Mining)** Richard Wright Mining Company has purchased a tract of mineral land for $600,000. It is estimated that this tract will yield 120,000 tons of ore with sufficient mineral content to make mining and processing profitable. It is further estimated that 6,000 tons of ore will be mined the first and last year and 12,000 tons every year in between. The land will have a residual value of $30,000.

The company builds necessary structures and sheds on the site at a cost of $36,000. It is estimated that these structures can serve 15 years but, because they must be dismantled if they are to be moved, they have no salvage value. The company does not intend to use the buildings elsewhere. Mining machinery installed at the mine was purchased second-hand at a cost of $48,000. This machinery cost the former owner $100,000 and was 50% depreciated when purchased. Richard Wright Mining estimates that about half of this machinery will still be useful when the present mineral resources have been exhausted but that dismantling and removal costs will just about offset its value at that time. The company does not intend to use the machinery elsewhere. The remaining machinery will last until about one-half the present estimated mineral ore has been removed and will then be worthless. Cost is to be allocated equally between these two classes of machinery.

Instructions

   (a)   As chief accountant for the company, you are to prepare a schedule showing estimated depletion and depreciation costs for each year of the expected life of the mine.

   (b)   Also compute the depreciation and depletion for the first year assuming actual production of 7,000 tons. Nothing occurred during the year to cause the company engineers to change their estimates of either the mineral resources or the life of the structures and equipment.

(LO 6) **P11-6** **(Depletion, Timber, and Extraordinary Loss)** ~~C~~ Logging and Lumber Company owns 3,000 acres ~~~~ which was purchased in 1968 at a cost of $550 per a ~~~~ g this ~~~~ er tract. In May of 1980, Mount St. Helens erupte ~~~~ foot o ~~~~ All of the timber on the O'Brien tract was downe ~~~~ ost ~~~~ .000, were destroyed, as well as the logging equip ~~~~

At the time of ~~~~ d 500,000 board feet of timber. Prior to the erupt ~~~~ 0 per acre after the timber was harvested. O'Brie ~~~~

O'Brien estima ~~~~ t a cost of $700,000. The timber can be sold for pu ~~~~ e value of the land is unknown, but must be consi ~~~~

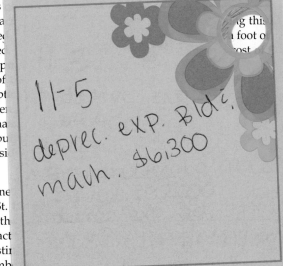

11-5
deprec. exp. Bldʒ.
mach. $61,300

Instructions

(a) Determine ~~~~ vested prior to the eruption of Mount St. ~~~~

(b) Prepare th ~~~~ ption.

(c) If this tract ~~~~ O'Brien, determine the amount of the esti ~~~~ ery, and timber and the salvage of the timb ~~~~ ien for the year ended December 31, 1980.

(LO 6) **P11-7** **(Natural Resources—Timber)** Western Paper Products purchased 10,000 acres of forested timberland in March 2008. The company paid $1,700 per acre for this land, which was above the $800 per acre most farmers were paying for cleared land. During April, May, June, and July 2008, Western cut enough timber to build roads using moveable equipment purchased on April 1, 2008. The cost of the roads was $195,000, and the cost of the equipment was $189,000; this equipment was expected to have a $9,000 salvage value and would be used for the next 15 years. Western selected the straight-line method of depreciation for the moveable equipment. Western began actively harvesting timber in August and by December had harvested and sold 472,500 board feet of timber of the estimated 6,750,000 board feet available for cutting.

In March 2009, Western planted new seedlings in the area harvested during the winter. Cost of planting these seedlings was $120,000. In addition, Western spent $8,000 in road maintenance and $6,000 for pest spraying during calendar-year 2009. The road maintenance and spraying are annual costs. During 2009 Western harvested and sold 774,000 board feet of timber of the estimated 6,450,000 board feet available for cutting.

In March 2010, Western again planted new seedlings at a cost of $150,000, and also spent $15,000 on road maintenance and pest spraying. During 2010, the company harvested and sold 650,000 board feet of timber of the estimated 6,500,000 board feet available for cutting.

Instructions

Compute the amount of depreciation and depletion expense for each of the 3 years (2008, 2009, 2010). Assume that the roads are usable only for logging and therefore are included in the depletion base.

(LO 2, 3) **P11-8** **(Comprehensive Fixed Asset Problem)** Selig Sporting Goods Inc. has been experiencing growth in the demand for its products over the last several years. The last two Olympic Games greatly increased the popularity of basketball around the world. As a result, a European sports retailing consortium entered into an agreement with Selig's Roundball Division to purchase basketballs and other accessories on an increasing basis over the next 5 years.

To be able to meet the quantity commitments of this agreement, Selig had to obtain additional manufacturing capacity. A real estate firm located an available factory in close proximity to Selig's Roundball manufacturing facility, and Selig agreed to purchase the factory and used machinery from Starks Athletic Equipment Company on October 1, 2005. Renovations were necessary to convert the factory for Selig's manufacturing use.

The terms of the agreement required Selig to pay Starks $50,000 when renovations started on January 1, 2006, with the balance to be paid as renovations were completed. The overall purchase price for the factory and machinery was $400,000. The building renovations were contracted to Malone Construction at $100,000. The payments made, as renovations progressed during 2006, are shown below. The factory was placed in service on January 1, 2007.

	1/1	4/1	10/1	12/31
Starks	$50,000	$100,000	$100,000	$150,000
Malone		30,000	30,000	40,000

On January 1, 2006, Selig secured a $500,000 line-of-credit with a 12% interest rate to finance the purchase cost of the factory and machinery, and the renovation costs. Selig drew down on the line-of-credit to meet the payment schedule shown above; this was Selig's only outstanding loan during 2006.

Rob Stewart, Selig's controller, will capitalize the maximum allowable interest costs for this project. Selig's policy regarding purchases of this nature is to use the appraisal value of the land for book purposes and prorate the balance of the purchase price over the remaining items. The building had originally cost Starks $300,000 and had a net book value of $50,000, while the machinery originally cost $125,000 and had a net book value of $40,000 on the date of sale. The land was recorded on Starks' books at $40,000. An appraisal, conducted by independent appraisers at the time of acquisition, valued the land at $280,000, the building at $105,000, and the machinery at $45,000.

Linda Safford, chief engineer, estimated that the renovated plant would be used for 15 years, with an estimated salvage value of $30,000. Safford estimated that the productive machinery would have a remaining useful life of 5 years and a salvage value of $3,000. Selig's depreciation policy specifies the 200% declining-balance method for machinery and the 150% declining-balance method for the plant. One-half year's depreciation is taken in the year the plant is placed in service and one-half year is allowed when the property is disposed of or retired. Selig uses a 360-day year for calculating interest costs.

Instructions

(a) Determine the amounts to be recorded on the books of Selig Sporting Goods Inc. as of December 31, 2006, for each of the following properties acquired from Starks Athletic Equipment Company.
    (1) Land.   **(2)** Building.   **(3)** Machinery.

(b) Calculate Selig Sporting Goods Inc.'s 2007 depreciation expense, for book purposes, for each of the properties acquired from Starks Athletic Equipment Company.

(c) Discuss the arguments for and against the capitalization of interest costs.

(CMA adapted)

(LO 5) **P11-9** **(Impairment)** Olsson Company uses special strapping equipment in its packaging business. The equipment was purchased in January 2007 for $8,000,000 and had an estimated useful life of 8 years with no salvage value. At December 31, 2008, new technology was introduced that would accelerate the obsolescence of Olsson's equipment. Olsson's controller estimates that expected future net cash flows on the equipment will be $5,300,000 and that the fair value of the equipment is $4,400,000. Olsson intends to continue using the equipment, but it is estimated that the remaining useful life is 4 years. Olsson uses straight-line depreciation.

Instructions

(a) Prepare the journal entry (if any) to record the impairment at December 31, 2008.

(b) Prepare any journal entries for the equipment at December 31, 2009. The fair value of the equipment at December 31, 2009, is estimated to be $4,600,000.

(c) Repeat the requirements for (a) and (b), assuming that Olsson intends to dispose of the equipment and that it has not been disposed of as of December 31, 2009.

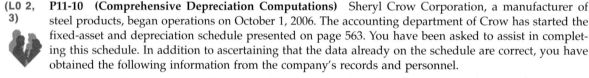

(LO 2, 3) **P11-10** **(Comprehensive Depreciation Computations)** Sheryl Crow Corporation, a manufacturer of steel products, began operations on October 1, 2006. The accounting department of Crow has started the fixed-asset and depreciation schedule presented on page 563. You have been asked to assist in completing this schedule. In addition to ascertaining that the data already on the schedule are correct, you have obtained the following information from the company's records and personnel.

1. Depreciation is computed from the first of the month of acquisition to the first of the month of disposition.

2. Land A and Building A were acquired from a predecessor corporation. Crow paid $820,000 for the land and building together. At the time of acquisition, the land had an appraised value of $90,000, and the building had an appraised value of $810,000.

3. Land B was acquired on October 2, 2006, in exchange for 2,500 newly issued shares of Crow's common stock. At the date of acquisition, the stock had a par value of $5 per share and a fair value of $30 per share. During October 2006, Crow paid $16,000 to demolish an existing building on this land so it could construct a new building.

4. Construction of Building B on the newly acquired land began on October 1, 2007. By September 30, 2008, Crow had paid $320,000 of the estimated total construction costs of $450,000. It is estimated that the building will be completed and occupied by July 2009.

5. Certain equipment was donated to the corporation by a local university. An independent appraisal of the equipment when donated placed the fair market value at $30,000 and the salvage value at $3,000.

6. Machinery A's total cost of $164,900 includes installation expense of $600 and normal repairs and maintenance of $14,900. Salvage value is estimated at $6,000. Machinery A was sold on February 1, 2008.

7. On October 1, 2007, Machinery B was acquired with a down payment of $5,740 and the remaining payments to be made in 11 annual installments of $6,000 each beginning October 1, 2007. The prevailing interest rate was 8%. The following data were abstracted from present-value tables (rounded).

Present value of $1.00 at 8%		Present value of an ordinary annuity of $1.00 at 8%	
10 years	.463	10 years	6.710
11 years	.429	11 years	7.139
15 years	.315	15 years	8.559

SHERYL CROW CORPORATION
Fixed Asset and Depreciation Schedule
For Fiscal Years Ended September 30, 2007, and September 30, 2008

Assets	Acquisition Date	Cost	Salvage	Depreciation Method	Estimated Life in Years	Depreciation Expense Year Ended September 30	
						2007	2008
Land A	October 1, 2006	$ (1)	N/A	N/A	N/A	N/A	N/A
Building A	October 1, 2006	(2)	$40,000	Straight-line	(3)	$17,450	(4)
Land B	October 2, 2006	(5)	N/A	N/A	N/A	N/A	N/A
Building B	Under Construction	$320,000 to date	—	Straight-line	30	—	(6)
Donated Equipment	October 2, 2006	(7)	3,000	150% declining balance	10	(8)	(9)
Machinery A	October 2, 2006	(10)	6,000	Sum-of-the-years'-digits	8	(11)	(12)
Machinery B	October 1, 2007	(13)	—	Straight-line	20	—	(14)

N/A—Not applicable

Instructions

For each numbered item on the schedule above, supply the correct amount. Round each answer to the nearest dollar.

(LO 2, 3) **P11-11 (Depreciation for Partial Periods—SL, Act., SYD, and DDB)** On January 1, 2005, a machine was purchased for $77,000. The machine has an estimated salvage value of $5,000 and an estimated useful life of 5 years. The machine can operate for 100,000 hours before it needs to be replaced. The company closed its books on December 31 and operates the machine as follows: 2005, 20,000 hrs; 2006, 25,000 hrs; 2007, 15,000 hrs; 2008, 30,000 hrs; 2009, 10,000 hrs.

Instructions

(a) Compute the annual depreciation charges over the machine's life assuming a December 31 year-end for each of the following depreciation methods.
  (1) Straight-line method.   (3) Sum-of-the-years'-digits method.
  (2) Activity method.   (4) Double-declining balance method.
(b) Assume a fiscal year-end of September 30. Compute the annual depreciation charges over the asset's life applying each of the following methods.
  (1) Straight-line method.
  (2) Sum-of-the-years'-digits method.
  (3) Double-declining balance method.

(LO 2, 3, 8) ***P11-12 (Depreciation—SL, DDB, SYD, Act., and MACRS)** On January 1, 2005, Begen Company, a small machine-tool manufacturer, acquired for $1,100,000 a piece of new industrial equipment. The new equipment had a useful life of 5 years, and the salvage value was estimated to be $50,000. Begen estimates that the new equipment can produce 12,000 machine tools in its first year. It estimates that production will decline by 1,000 units per year over the remaining useful life of the equipment.

The following depreciation methods may be used: (1) straight-line; (2) double-declining balance; (3) sum-of-the-years'-digits; and (4) units-of-output. For tax purposes, the class life is 7 years. Use the MACRS tables for computing depreciation.

Instructions

(a) Which depreciation method would maximize net income for financial statement reporting for the 3-year period ending December 31, 2007? Prepare a schedule showing the amount of accumulated depreciation at December 31, 2007, under the method selected. Ignore present value, income tax, and deferred income tax considerations.

(b) Which depreciation method (MACRS or optional straight-line) would minimize net income for income tax reporting for the 3-year period ending December 31, 2007? Determine the amount of accumulated depreciation at December 31, 2007. Ignore present value considerations.

(AICPA adapted)

CONCEPTS FOR ANALYSIS

CA11-1 (Depreciation Basic Concepts) Prophet Manufacturing Company was organized January 1, 2007. During 2007, it has used in its reports to management the straight-line method of depreciating its plant assets.

On November 8 you are having a conference with Prophet's officers to discuss the depreciation method to be used for income tax and stockholder reporting. Frank Peretti, president of Prophet, has suggested the use of a new method, which he feels is more suitable than the straight-line method for the needs of the company during the period of rapid expansion of production and capacity that he foresees. Following is an example in which the proposed method is applied to a fixed asset with an original cost of $248,000, an estimated useful life of 5 years, and a salvage value of approximately $8,000.

Year	Years of Life Used	Fraction Rate	Depreciation Expense	Accumulated Depreciation at End of Year	Book Value at End of Year
1	1	1/15	$16,000	$ 16,000	$232,000
2	2	2/15	32,000	48,000	200,000
3	3	3/15	48,000	96,000	152,000
4	4	4/15	64,000	160,000	88,000
5	5	5/15	80,000	240,000	8,000

The president favors the new method because he has heard that:

1. It will increase the funds recovered during the years near the end of the assets' useful lives when maintenance and replacement disbursements are high.
2. It will result in increased write-offs in later years and thereby will reduce taxes.

Instructions

(a) What is the purpose of accounting for depreciation?

(b) Is the president's proposal within the scope of generally accepted accounting principles? In making your decision discuss the circumstances, if any, under which use of the method would be reasonable and those, if any, under which it would not be reasonable.

(c) The president wants your advice on the following issues.

　(1) Do depreciation charges recover or create funds? Explain.

　(2) Assume that the Internal Revenue Service accepts the proposed depreciation method in this case. If the proposed method were used for stockholder and tax reporting purposes, how would it affect the availability of cash flows generated by operations?

 CA11-2 (Unit, Group, and Composite Depreciation) The certified public accountant is frequently called upon by management for advice regarding methods of computing depreciation. Of comparable importance, although it arises less frequently, is the question of whether the depreciation method should be based on consideration of the assets as units, as a group, or as having a composite life.

Instructions

(a) Briefly describe the depreciation methods based on treating assets as (1) units and (2) a group or as having a composite life.

(b) Present the arguments for and against the use of each of the two methods.

(c) Describe how retirements are recorded under each of the two methods.

(AICPA adapted)

CA11-3 (Depreciation—Strike, Units-of-Production, Obsolescence) Presented below are three different and unrelated situations involving depreciation accounting. Answer the question(s) at the end of each situation.

Situation I

Recently, Davenport Company experienced a strike that affected a number of its operating plants. The controller of this company indicated that it was not appropriate to report depreciation expense during this period because the equipment did not depreciate and an improper matching of costs and revenues would result. She based her position on the following points.

1. It is inappropriate to charge the period with costs for which there are no related revenues arising from production.
2. The basic factor of depreciation in this instance is wear and tear, and because equipment was idle, no wear and tear occurred.

Instructions

Comment on the appropriateness of the controller's comments.

Situation II

Sharapova Company manufactures electrical appliances, most of which are used in homes. Company engineers have designed a new type of blender which, through the use of a few attachments, will perform more functions than any blender currently on the market. Demand for the new blender can be projected with reasonable probability. In order to make the blenders, Sharapova needs a specialized machine that is not available from outside sources. It has been decided to make such a machine in Sharapova's own plant.

Instructions

(a) Discuss the effect of projected demand in units for the new blenders (which may be steady, decreasing, or increasing) on the determination of a depreciation method for the machine.

(b) What other matters should be considered in determining the depreciation method? Ignore income tax considerations.

Situation III

Venus Paper Company operates a 300-ton-per-day kraft pulp mill and four sawmills in Wisconsin. The company is in the process of expanding its pulp mill facilities to a capacity of 1,000 tons per day and plans to replace three of its older, less efficient sawmills with an expanded facility. One of the mills to be replaced did not operate for most of 2007 (current year), and there are no plans to reopen it before the new sawmill facility becomes operational.

In reviewing the depreciation rates and in discussing the residual values of the sawmills that were to be replaced, it was noted that if present depreciation rates were not adjusted, substantial amounts of plant costs on these three mills would not be depreciated by the time the new mill came on stream.

Instructions

What is the proper accounting for the four sawmills at the end of 2007?

CA11-4 (Depreciation Concepts) As a cost accountant for San Francisco Cannery, you have been approached by Merton Miller, canning room supervisor, about the 2006 costs charged to his department. In particular, he is concerned about the line item "depreciation." Miller is very proud of the excellent condition of his canning room equipment. He has always been vigilant about keeping all equipment serviced and well oiled. He is sure that the huge charge to depreciation is a mistake; it does not at all reflect the cost of minimal wear and tear that the machines have experienced over the last year. He believes that the charge should be considerably lower.

The machines being depreciated are six automatic canning machines. All were put into use on January 1, 2006. Each cost $469,000, having a salvage value of $40,000 and a useful life of 12 years. San Francisco depreciates this and similar assets using double-declining balance depreciation. Miller has also pointed out that if you used straight-line depreciation the charge to his department would not be so great.

Instructions

Write a memo to Merton Miller to clear up his misunderstanding of the term "depreciation." Also, calculate year-1 depreciation on all machines using both methods. Explain the theoretical justification for double-declining balance and why, in the long run, the aggregate charge to depreciation will be the same under both methods.

CA11-5 (Depreciation Choice) Dusty Baker, Waveland Corporation's controller, is concerned that net income may be lower this year. He is afraid upper-level management might recommend cost reductions by laying off accounting staff, including him.

Baker knows that depreciation is a major expense for Waveland. The company currently uses the double-declining balance method for both financial reporting and tax purposes, and he's thinking of selling equipment that, given its age, is primarily used when there are periodic spikes in demand. The equipment has a carrying value of $2,000,000 and a market value of $2,180,000. The gain on the sale would be reported in the income statement. He doesn't want to highlight this method of increasing income. He thinks, "Why don't I increase the estimated useful lives and the salvage values? That will decrease depreciation expense and require less extensive disclosure, since the changes are accounted for prospectively. I may be able to save my job and those of my staff."

Instructions

Answer the following questions.
- **(a)** Who are the stakeholders in this situation?
- **(b)** What are the ethical issues involved?
- **(c)** What should Baker do?

USING YOUR JUDGMENT

Financial Reporting Problem

The Procter & Gamble Company (P&G)

The financial statements of P&G are presented in Appendix 5B or can be accessed on the KWW website .

Instructions

Refer to P&G's financial statements and the accompanying notes to answer the following questions.
- **(a)** What descriptions are used by P&G in its balance sheet to classify its property, plant, and equipment?
- **(b)** What method or methods of depreciation does P&G use to depreciate its property, plant, and equipment?
- **(c)** Over what estimated useful lives does P&G depreciate its property, plant, and equipment?
- **(d)** What amounts for depreciation and amortization expense did P&G charge to its income statement in 2004, 2003, and 2002?
- **(e)** What were the capital expenditures for property, plant, and equipment made by P&G in 2004, 2003, and 2002?

Financial Statement Analysis Case

McDonald's Corporation

McDonald's is the largest and best-known global food service retailer, with more than 30,000 restaurants in 121 countries. On any day, McDonald's serves approximately 1 percent of the world's population. Presented on the next page is information related to McDonald's property and equipment.

Instructions
- **(a)** What method of depreciation does McDonald's use?
- **(b)** Does depreciation and amortization expense cause cash flow from operations to increase? Explain.
- **(c)** What does the schedule of cash flow measures indicate?

McDonald's Corporation
Summary of Significant Accounting Policies Section

Property and Equipment. Property and equipment are stated at cost, with depreciation and amortization provided on the straight-line method over the following estimated useful lives: buildings—up to 40 years; leasehold improvements—lesser of useful lives of assets or lease terms including option periods; and equipment—3 to 12 years.

[In the notes to the financial statements:]

Property and Equipment
Net property and equipment consisted of:

(in millions)	December 31, 2004	2003
Land	$ 4,661.1	$ 4,483.0
Buildings and improvements on owned land	10,260.3	9,693.4
Buildings and improvements on leased land	10,520.7	9,792.1
Equipment, signs, and seating	4,426.1	4,090.5
Other	639.6	681.2
	30,507.8	28,740.2
Accumulated depreciation and amortization	(9,804.7)	(8,815.5)
Net property and equipment	$20,703.1	$19,924.7

Depreciation and amortization expense was (in millions):
2004–$1,138.3; 2003–$1,113.3; 2002–$971.1.

[In the management discussion and analysis section, McDonald's provides the following schedule.]

Cash Provided by Operations

(dollars in millions)	2004	2003	2002
Cash provided by operations	$3,904	$3,269	$2,890
Cash provided by operations as a percent of capital expenditures	275%	250%	144%

Comparative Analysis Case

The Coca-Cola Company and PepsiCo., Inc.

Instructions
Go to the book's website and use information found there to answer the following questions related to The Coca-Cola Company and PepsiCo, Inc.

(a) What amount is reported in the balance sheets as property, plant, and equipment (net) of Coca-Cola at December 31, 2004, and of PepsiCo at December 25, 2004? What percentage of total assets is invested in property, plant, and equipment by each company?

(b) What depreciation methods are used by Coca-Cola and PepsiCo for property, plant, and equipment? How much depreciation was reported by Coca-Cola and PepsiCo in 2004, 2003, and 2002?

(c) Compute and compare the following ratios for Coca-Cola and PepsiCo for 2004.

    (1) Asset turnover.

    (2) Profit margin on sales.

    (3) Rate of return on assets.

(d) What amount was spent in 2004 for capital expenditures by Coca-Cola and PepsiCo? What amount of interest was capitalized in 2004?

Research Case

An article by Martin Peers and Robin Sidel, entitled "Days May Be Numbered for EBITDA's Role," appeared in the July 5, 2002, issue of the *Wall Street Journal*.

Instructions

Read the article and answer the following questions.

(a) Explain what is meant by EBITDA and why companies are reporting this number.

(b) Why has the WorldCom bankruptcy caused EBITDA to fall into disfavor as a performance metric?

(c) What is wrong with performance metrics such as EBITDA, cash earnings, or other pro-forma income measures?

International Reporting Case

Companies following international accounting standards are permitted to revalue fixed assets above the assets' historical costs. Such revaluations are allowed under various countries' standards and the standards issued by the International Accounting Standards Board (IASB). **Liberty International**, a real estate company, headquartered in United Kingdom (U.K.), follows U.K. standards. In a recent year, Liberty disclosed the following information on revaluations of its tangible fixed assets. The revaluation reserve measures the amount by which tangible fixed assets are recorded above historical cost and is reported in Liberty's stockholders' equity.

Liberty International

Completed Investment Properties

Completed investment properties are professionally valued on a market value basis by external valuers at the balance sheet date. Surpluses and deficits arising during the year are reflected in the revalution reserve.

Liberty reported the following additional data. Amounts for **Kimco Realty** (which follows U.S. GAAP) in the same year are provided for comparison.

	Liberty (pounds sterling, in thousands)	Kimco (dollars, in millions)
Total revenues	£ 741	$ 517
Average total assets	5,577	4,696
Net income	125	297

Instructions

(a) Compute the following ratios for Liberty and Kimco.

(1) Return on assets.

(2) Profit margin.

(3) Asset turnover.

How do these companies compare on these performance measures?

(b) Liberty reports a revaluation reserve of 1,952 pounds. Assume that 1,550 of this amount arose from an increase in the net replacement value of investment properties during the year. Prepare the journal entry to record this increase. (*Hint:* Credit the Revaluation Reserve account.)

(c) Under U.K. (and IASB) standards, are Liberty's assets and equity overstated? If so, why? When comparing Liberty to U.S. companies, like Kimco, what adjustments would you need to make in order to have valid comparisons of ratios such as those computed in (a) above?

Professional Research: Financial Accounting and Reporting

Nomar Garcia recently joined Hamm Company as a staff accountant in the controller's office. Hamm Company provides warehousing services for companies in several midwestern cities.

The location in Dubuque, Iowa, has not been performing well due to increased competition and the loss of several customers that have recently gone out of business. Nomar's department manager suspects that the plant and equipment may be impaired and wonders whether those assets should be written down. Given the company's prior success, this issue has never arisen in the past, and Nomar has been asked to conduct some research on this issue.

Instructions

Using the **Financial Accounting Research System (FARS)**, respond to the following items. (Provide text strings used in your search.)

(a) What accounting standard provides the authoritative guidance for asset impairments? Briefly discuss the scope of the standard (i.e., explain the types of transactions to which the standard applies).

(b) Give several examples of events that would cause an asset to be tested for impairment. Does it appear that Hamm should perform an impairment test? Explain.

(c) What is the best evidence of fair value? Describe alternate methods of estimating fair value.

Professional Simulation

In this simulation you are asked to address questions regarding the accounting for property, plant, and equipment. Prepare responses to all parts.

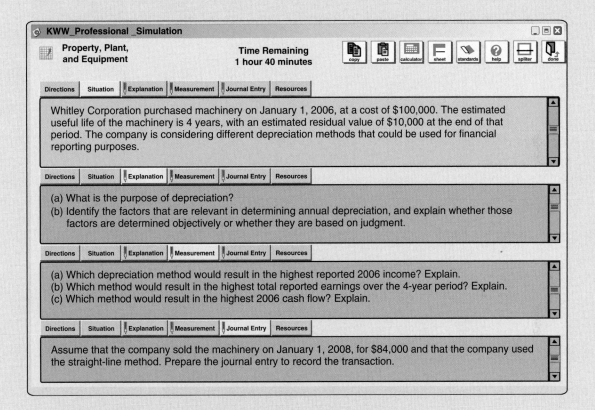

| KWW_Professional _Simulation | | | | | | | | | □ ▣ ☒ |

Property, Plant, and Equipment

Time Remaining 1 hour 40 minutes

copy · paste · calculator · sheet · standards · help · spliter · done

| Directions | Situation | Explanation | Measurement | Journal Entry | Resources |

Whitley Corporation purchased machinery on January 1, 2006, at a cost of $100,000. The estimated useful life of the machinery is 4 years, with an estimated residual value of $10,000 at the end of that period. The company is considering different depreciation methods that could be used for financial reporting purposes.

| Directions | Situation | Explanation | Measurement | Journal Entry | Resources |

(a) What is the purpose of depreciation?
(b) Identify the factors that are relevant in determining annual depreciation, and explain whether those factors are determined objectively or whether they are based on judgment.

| Directions | Situation | Explanation | Measurement | Journal Entry | Resources |

(a) Which depreciation method would result in the highest reported 2006 income? Explain.
(b) Which method would result in the highest total reported earnings over the 4-year period? Explain.
(c) Which method would result in the highest 2006 cash flow? Explain.

| Directions | Situation | Explanation | Measurement | Journal Entry | Resources |

Assume that the company sold the machinery on January 1, 2008, for $84,000 and that the company used the straight-line method. Prepare the journal entry to record the transaction.

Remember to check the book's companion website to find additional resources for this chapter.

INTANGIBLE ASSETS

Untouchable

As shown in the graph below, tangible assets as a percent of all assets have declined dramatically in the last 50 years. Consequently, companies today increasingly derive value from intangible assets—intellectual property, technology, or reputation. Many well-known companies make most of their money from intangible assets: **Microsoft Corp.**'s software, **Pfizer Inc.**'s drug patents, and **Walt Disney Co.**'s film and television productions.

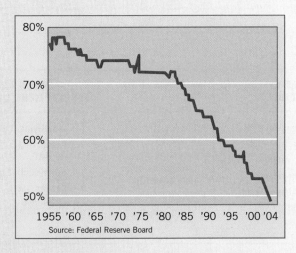

Tangible assets as a percentage of all assets of nonfinancial businesses

Source: Federal Reserve Board

However, the experience at **Winstar Communications** illustrates how quickly the value of intangible assets can erode. Just before Winstar filed for bankruptcy, it listed $5 billion in assets, a large share comprised of questionable intangible assets related to its customer base. Within just a few months, its assets fetched just $42 *million*. Winstar's investors and creditors learned the shocking speed at which the value of such assets can decline.

Perhaps Federal Reserve Chairman Alan Greenspan's remarks are relevant in these turbulent times: ". . . a firm is inherently fragile if its value-added emanates more from conceptual as distinct from physical assets. Trust and reputation can vanish overnight. A factory cannot."[1]

---

[1]Adapted from Greg Ip, "The Rise and Fall of Intangible Assets Leads to Shorter Company Life Spans, *Wall Street Journal Online* (April 4, 2002).

Learning Objectives

After studying this chapter, you should be able to:

1 Describe the characteristics of intangible assets.

2 Identify the costs to include in the initial valuation of intangible assets.

3 Explain the procedure for amortizing intangible assets.

4 Describe the types of intangible assets.

5 Explain the conceptual issues related to goodwill.

6 Describe the accounting procedures for recording goodwill.

7 Explain the accounting issues related to intangible-asset impairments.

8 Identify the conceptual issues related to research and development costs.

9 Describe the accounting for research and development and similar costs.

10 Indicate the presentation of intangible assets and related items.

As our opening story indicates, the accounting and reporting of intangibles is taking on increasing importance in this information age, especially for companies like **Microsoft Corp., Pfizer Inc.,** and **Walt Disney Co.** In this chapter we explain the basic conceptual and reporting issues related to intangible assets. The content and organization of the chapter are as follows.

INTANGIBLE ASSET ISSUES

Characteristics

OBJECTIVE 1
Describe the characteristics of intangible assets.

Gap Inc.'s most important asset is its brand image, not its store fixtures. **Coca-Cola**'s success comes from its secret formula for making Coke, not its plant facilities. **America Online**'s subscriber base provides its most important asset, not its Internet connection equipment. As these examples show, we have an economy dominated today by information and service providers. For these companies, their major assets are often intangible in nature. Accounting for these intangibles is difficult.

What exactly are intangible assets? **Intangible assets** have two main characteristics.[2]

1 **They lack physical existence.** Unlike tangible assets such as property, plant, and equipment, intangible assets derive their value from the rights and privileges granted to the company using them.

2 **They are not financial instruments.** Assets such as bank deposits, accounts receivable, and long-term investments in bonds and stocks also lack physical substance. However, they are not classified as intangibles, because these assets are financial instruments. They derive their value from the right (claim) to receive cash or cash equivalents in the future.

In most cases, intangible assets provide benefits over a period of years. Therefore, companies normally classify them as long-term assets. We discuss the most common types

---

[2]"Goodwill and Other Intangible Assets," *Statement of Financial Accounting Standards No. 142* (Norwalk, Conn.: FASB, 2001).

of intangibles (patents, copyrights, franchises or licenses, trademarks or trade names, and goodwill) later in the chapter.

Valuation

Purchased Intangibles

Intangibles purchased from another party are **recorded at cost**. Cost includes all costs of acquisition and expenditures necessary to make the intangible asset ready for its intended use. Typical costs include purchase price, legal fees, and other incidental expenses.

If a company acquires intangibles for stock or in exchange for other assets, **the cost of the intangible is the fair value of the consideration given or the fair value of the intangible received, whichever is more clearly evident**. When a company buys several intangibles, or a combination of intangibles and tangibles, in a "basket purchase," it should allocate the cost on the basis of fair values. Essentially the accounting treatment for purchased intangibles closely parallels that for purchased tangible assets.

Internally Created Intangibles

Costs incurred internally to create intangibles are generally expensed. Thus, even though a company may incur substantial research and development costs to create an intangible, it expenses these costs.

How do companies justify this approach? Some argue that the costs incurred internally to create intangibles bear no relationship to their real value. Therefore, expensing these costs is appropriate. Others note that it is difficult to associate internal costs with a specific intangible. And others contend that due to the underlying subjectivity related to intangibles, companies should follow a conservative approach—that is, expense as incurred. As a result, **companies only capitalize direct costs** incurred in developing the intangible, such as legal costs.

Amortization of Intangibles

Intangibles have either a **limited (finite) useful life** or an **indefinite useful life**. For example, a company like **Walt Disney** has both types of intangibles. Walt Disney **amortizes** its **limited life** intangible assets. It **does not amortize** intangible assets with an **indefinite life**.

Limited-Life Intangibles

The allocation of the cost of intangible assets in a systematic way is called **amortization**. Walt Disney amortizes its limited-life intangibles by systematic charges to expense over their useful life. The useful life should reflect the periods over which these assets will contribute to cash flows. Walt Disney considers these factors in determining useful life:

1 The expected use of the asset by the company.

2 The expected useful life of another asset or a group of assets to which the useful life of the intangible asset may relate (such as lease rights to a studio lot).

3 Any legal, regulatory, or contractual provisions that may limit the useful life.

4 Any legal, regulatory, or contractual provisions that enable renewal or extension of the asset's legal or contractual life without substantial cost. This factor assumes that there is evidence to support renewal or extension. Disney also must be able to accomplish renewal or extension without material modifications of the existing terms and conditions.

OBJECTIVE 2
Identify the costs to include in the initial valuation of intangible assets.

UNDERLYING CONCEPTS

The basic attributes of intangibles, their uncertainty as to future benefits, and their uniqueness have discouraged valuation in excess of cost.

OBJECTIVE 3
Explain the procedure for amortizing intangible assets.

5   The effects of obsolescence, demand, competition, and other economic factors. Examples include the stability of the industry, known technological advances, legislative action that results in an uncertain or changing regulatory environment, and expected changes in distribution channels.

6   The level of maintenance expenditure required to obtain the expected future cash flows from the asset. For example, a material level of required maintenance in relation to the carrying amount of the asset may suggest a very limited useful life.[3]

The amount of amortization expense for a limited-life intangible asset should reflect the pattern in which the company consumes or uses up the asset, if the company can reliably determine that pattern. For example, assume that Second Wave, Inc. purchases a license to provide a limited quantity of a gene product, called Mega. Second Wave should amortize the cost of the license following the pattern of use of Mega. If it cannot determine the pattern of production or consumption, Second Wave should use the straight-line method of amortization. (*For homework problems, assume the use of the straight-line method unless stated otherwise.*)

When Second Wave amortizes these licenses, it should show the charges as expenses. It should credit either the appropriate asset accounts or separate accumulated amortization accounts.

The amount of an intangible asset to be amortized should be its cost less residual value. The residual value is assumed to be zero unless at the end of its useful life the intangible asset has value to another company. For example, if Hardy Co. commits to purchasing an intangible asset from U2D Co. at the end of the asset's useful life, U2D Co. should reduce the cost of its intangible asset by the residual value. Similarly, U2D Co. should consider market values, if reliably determined, for residual values.

What happens if the life of a limited-life intangible asset changes? In that case the remaining carrying amount should be amortized over the revised remaining useful life. Companies should, on a regular basis, evaluate the limited-life intangibles for impairment. Similar to property, plant, and equipment, an impairment loss should be recognized if the carrying amount of the intangible is not recoverable and its carrying amount exceeds its fair value.

Indefinite-Life Intangibles

If no legal, regulatory, contractual, competitive, or other factors limit the useful life of an intangible asset, a company considers its useful life indefinite. **Indefinite** means that there is no foreseeable limit on the period of time over which the intangible asset is expected to provide cash flows. A company does not amortize an intangible asset with an indefinite life.

To illustrate, assume that Double Clik, Inc. acquired a trademark that it uses to distinguish a leading consumer product. It renews the trademark every 10 years at minimal cost. All evidence indicates that this trademark product will generate cash flows for an indefinite period of time. In this case, the trademark has an indefinite life; Double Clik does not record any amortization.

Companies should test indefinite-life intangibles for impairment at least annually. The **impairment test** for indefinite-life intangibles differs from the one for limited-life intangibles in that only the fair value test is performed. There is no recoverability test related to indefinite-life intangibles. The reason: Indefinite-life intangible assets might never fail the undiscounted cash flows recoverability test because cash flows could extend indefinitely into the future.

Illustration 12-1 summarizes the accounting treatment for intangible assets.

---

[3]Ibid, par. 11.

	Manner Acquired			
Type of Intangible	Purchased	Internally Created	Amortization	Impairment Test
Limited-life intangibles	Capitalize	Expense*	Over useful life	Recoverability test and then fair value test
Indefinite-life intangibles	Capitalize	Expense*	Do not amortize	Fair value test

*Except for direct costs, such as legal costs.

ILLUSTRATION 12-1
Accounting Treatment for Intangibles

TYPES OF INTANGIBLE ASSETS

As indicated, the accounting for intangible assets depends on whether the intangible has a limited or an indefinite life. There are many different types of intangibles, often classified into the following six major categories.[4]

1 Marketing-related intangible assets.

2 Customer-related intangible assets.

3 Artistic-related intangible assets.

4 Contract-related intangible assets.

5 Technology-related intangible assets.

6 Goodwill.

OBJECTIVE 4
Describe the types of intangible assets.

Marketing-Related Intangible Assets

Companies primarily use **marketing-related intangible assets** in the marketing or promotion of products or services. Examples are trademarks or trade names, newspaper mastheads, Internet domain names, and noncompetition agreements.

A common form of a marketing-related intangible asset is a trademark or trade name. A **trademark** or **trade name** is a word, phrase, or symbol that distinguishes or identifies a particular company or product. Under common law, the right to use a trademark or trade name, whether registered or not, rests exclusively with the original user as long as the original user continues to use it. Registration with the U.S. Patent and Trademark Office provides legal protection for an **indefinite number of renewals for periods of 10 years each**. Therefore a company that uses an established trademark or trade name may properly consider it to have an indefinite life. Trade names like Kleenex, Pepsi-Cola, Buick, Excedrin, Wheaties, and Sunkist create immediate product identification in our minds, thereby enhancing marketability.

If a company acquires a trademark or trade name, it capitalizes the cost at the purchase price. If a company develops a trademark or trade name, it capitalizes costs related to securing it, such as attorney fees, registration fees, design costs, consulting fees, and successful legal defense costs. However, it excludes research and development costs. When the total cost of a trademark or trade name is insignificant, a company may simply expense it. In most cases, the life of a trademark or trade name is indefinite. Therefore companies do not amortize its cost.

The value of a marketing-related intangible can be substantial. Consider Internet domain names. The name **Drugs.com** recently sold for $800,000. The bidding for the name **Loans.com** approached $500,000.

---

[4]This classification framework is based on "Business Combinations," *Statement of Financial Accounting Standards No. 141* (Norwalk, Conn.: FASB, 2001).

Company names themselves identify qualities and characteristics that companies work hard and spend much to develop. In a recent year an estimated 1,230 companies took on new names in an attempt to forge new identities, and paid over $250 million to corporate-identity consultants. Among these were **Primerica** (formerly American Can), **Navistar** (formerly International Harvester), and **Nissan** (formerly Datsun).[5]

Customer-Related Intangible Assets

Customer-related intangible assets result from interactions with outside parties. Examples include customer lists, order or production backlogs, and both contractual and noncontractual customer relationships.

To illustrate, assume that We-Market Inc. acquires the customer list of a large newspaper for $6,000,000 on January 1, 2007. This customer database includes name, contact information, order history, and demographic information. We-Market expects to benefit evenly from the information over a three-year period. In this case, the customer list is a limited-life intangible that We-Market should amortize on a straight-line basis over the three-year period.

We-Market records the purchase of the customer list and the amortization of the customer list at the end of each year as follows.

January 1, 2007

Customer List	6,000,000	
Cash		6,000,000
(To record purchase of customer list)		

December 31, 2007, 2008, 2009

Customer List Amortization Expense	2,000,000	
Customer List (or Accumulated Customer		
List Amortization)		2,000,000
(To record amortization expense)		

The preceding example assumed no residual value for the customer list. But what if We-Market determines that it can sell the list for $60,000 to another company at the end of three years? In that case We-Market should subtract this residual value from the cost in order to determine the proper amortization expense for each year. Amortization expense would therefore be $1,980,000, as shown in Illustration 12-2.

ILLUSTRATION 12-2
Calculation of
Amortization Expense
with Residual Value

Cost	$6,000,000
Residual value	60,000
Amortization base	$5,940,000
Amortization expense per period: $1,980,000 ($5,940,000 ÷ 3)	

Companies should assume a zero residual value unless the asset's useful life is less than the economic life and reliable evidence is available concerning the residual value.[6]

---

[5]To illustrate how various intangibles arise from a given product, consider how the creators of the highly successful game Trivial Pursuit protected their creation. First, they copyrighted the 6,000 questions that are at the heart of the game. Then they shielded the Trivial Pursuit name by applying for a registered trademark. As a third mode of protection, they obtained a design patent on the playing board's design as a unique graphic creation.

[6]"Goodwill and Other Intangible Assets," *Statement of Financial Accounting Standards No. 142* (Norwalk, Conn.: FASB, 2001), par. B55.

Artistic-Related Intangible Assets

Artistic-related intangible assets involve ownership rights to plays, literary works, musical works, pictures, photographs, and video and audiovisual material. Copyrights protect these ownership rights.

A **copyright** is a federally granted right that all authors, painters, musicians, sculptors, and other artists have in their creations and expressions. A copyright is granted for the **life of the creator plus 70 years**. It gives the owner, or heirs, the exclusive right to reproduce and sell an artistic or published work. Copyrights are not renewable. Companies may capitalize the costs of acquiring and defending a copyright. However, they must expense the research and development costs involved as incurred.

Copyrights can be valuable. For example, the **Walt Disney Company** faced the loss of its copyright on Mickey Mouse, which could have affected sales of billions of dollars of Mickey-related goods and services (including theme parks). This copyright was so valuable that Disney and many other big entertainment companies fought all the way to the Supreme Court (and won) an extension of copyright lives from 50 to 70 years. Another example of the value of these intangibles is **Really Useful Group**, which owns copyrights on the musicals of Andrew Lloyd Webber—*Cats, Phantom of the Opera, Jesus Christ-Superstar,* and others. It has little hard assets, yet analysts value it at over $300 million.

Generally, the useful life of the copyright is less than its legal life (life of the creator plus 70 years). Thus, Really Useful Group should allocate the costs of its copyrights to the years in which it expects to receive the benefits. The difficulty of determining the number of years over which it will receive benefits normally encourages a company like Really Useful Group to write off these costs over a fairly short period of time.

Contract-Related Intangible Assets

Contract-related intangible assets represent the value of rights that arise from contractual arrangements. Examples are franchise and licensing agreements, construction permits, broadcast rights, and service or supply contracts. A common form of contract-based intangible asset is a franchise.

A **franchise** is a contractual arrangement under which the franchisor grants the franchisee the right to sell certain products or services, to use certain trademarks or trade names, or to perform certain functions, usually within a designated geographical area. We deal with franchises everyday, from driving in an automobile purchased from a **Toyota** dealer, to eating lunch at **McDonald's**, to living in a home purchased through a **Century 21** real estate broker, or to vacationing at a **Marriott** resort.

The franchisor, having developed a unique concept or product, protects its concept or product through a patent, copyright, or trademark or trade name. The franchisee acquires the right to exploit the franchisor's idea or product by signing a franchise agreement.

A municipality (or other governmental body) and a company that uses public property often enter into another type of franchise arrangement. In such cases, a municipality allows a privately owned company to use public property in performing its services. Examples are the use of public waterways for a ferry service, the use of public land for telephone or electric lines, the use of phone lines for cable TV, the use of city streets for a bus line, or the use of the airwaves for radio or TV broadcasting. Such operating rights, obtained through agreements with governmental units or agencies, are frequently referred to as **licenses** or **permits**.

Franchises and licenses may be for a definite period of time, for an indefinite period of time, or perpetual. The company securing the franchise or license carries an intangible asset account entitled Franchise or License on its books, only when it can identify costs (such as a lump-sum payment in advance or legal fees and other expenditures) with the acquisition of the operating right. **A company should amortize the cost of a franchise (or license) with a limited life as operating expense over the life of the franchise.** It should not amortize a franchise with an indefinite life, or a perpetual franchise, but instead should carry it at cost.

Annual payments made under a franchise agreement should be entered as operating expenses in the period in which they are incurred. The payments do not represent an asset since they do not relate to future rights to use public property.

SWEET TO SOUR

WHAT DO THE NUMBERS MEAN?

Krispy Kreme, the doughnut maker once dubbed the "hottest brand in the land," has taken a series of beatings. The latest: a formal inquiry by the Securities and Exchange Commission in October 2004 into its accounting. The problem seems to be with franchises Krispy Kreme reacquired a few years ago from owners who wanted to exit the business. Krispy Kreme decided to book most of the purchase price as an intangible asset called "reacquired franchise rights," which it does not amortize, or write-down, over time.

Management justified the accounting based on its belief that reacquired franchise rights have "indefinite lives." But critics charge that this artificially inflates profits and doesn't reflect the cost of the stores on its balance sheet. To compound its woes, some of the reacquired franchises were purchased from related parties, at prices some allege were too generous.

Accounting experts say it's unclear whether Krispy Kreme's method violates GAAP. One research firm found that all of the companies it follows with reacquired franchise rights amortize the costs over time. Krispy Kreme's methods are "definitely not conservative," according to one analyst.

The SEC probe couldn't have come at a worse time. Krispy Kreme's profits have plunged, and the stock lost about 75 percent of its value in the last year. Given the company's tumbling profits and hyper-aggressive accounting, investors should expect restatements and a big write-down when its auditor performs its annual impairment test. In other words, Krispy Kreme's outlook has gone from sweet to sour.

Source: Adapted from David Stires, "Accounting," *Fortune* (November 1, 2004), p. 42.

Technology-Related Intangible Assets

Technology-related intangible assets relate to innovations or technological advances. Examples are patented technology and trade secrets granted by the U.S. Patent and Trademark Office. A **patent** gives the holder exclusive right to use, manufacture, and sell a product or process **for a period of 20 years** without interference or infringement by others. With this exclusive right, fortunes can be made. For example, companies such as **Merck**, **Polaroid**, and **Xerox** were founded on patents.[7] The two principal kinds of patents are **product patents**, which cover actual physical products, and **process patents**, which govern the process of making products.

If a company like **Qualcomm** purchases a patent from an inventor (or other owner), the purchase price represents its cost. Qualcomm can capitalize other costs incurred in connection with securing a patent, as well as attorneys' fees and other unrecovered costs of a successful legal suit to protect the patent, as part of the patent cost. However, it **must expense as incurred** any research and development costs related to the **development** of the product, process, or idea that it subsequently patents. We discuss accounting for research and development costs in more detail on pages 587–590.

---

[7]Consider the opposite result: Sir Alexander Fleming, who discovered penicillin, decided not to use a patent to protect his discovery. He hoped that companies would produce it more quickly to help save sufferers. Companies, however, refused to develop it because they did not have the patent shield and, therefore, were afraid to make the investment.

Qualcomm should amortize the cost of a patent over its legal life or its useful life (the period benefits are received), whichever is **shorter**. If it owns a patent from the date it is granted, and Qualcomm expects the patent to be useful during its entire legal life, the company should amortize it over 20 years. If it appears that the patent will be useful for a shorter period of time, say, for five years, it should amortize its cost over five years.

Changing demand, new inventions superseding old ones, inadequacy, and other factors often limit the useful life of a patent to less than the legal life. For example, the useful life of patents in the pharmaceutical and drug industry is frequently less than the legal life because of the testing and approval period that follows their issuance. A typical drug patent has 5 to 11 years knocked off its 20-year legal life. Why? Because a drug-maker spends one to four years on animal tests, four to six years on human tests, and two to three years for the Food and Drug Administration to review the tests. All this time occurs after issuing the patent but before the product goes on a pharmacist's shelves.

PATENT BATTLES

WHAT DO THE NUMBERS MEAN?

From bioengineering to software design to the Internet, global competition is bringing battles over patents to the boiling point. For example, **Priceline.com** filed suit against **Microsoft** for launching Hotel Price Matcher, a service that operates much like the name-your-own-price-system Priceline pioneered.

Do you ever wonder who thought of the technology that saves your shipping and credit card information when you shop online? It was **Amazon.com**, which patented "one-click" shopping. To protect its technology, Amazon.com filed a complaint against **Barnesandnoble.com**, its rival in the Web-retailing wars, alleging infringement on its patent for one-click shopping. Even though Amazon.com and Barnesandnoble.com settled their dispute, patent battles continue between online retailers and independent software developers, claiming that companies like Amazon.com are unfairly undercutting its competition through these "business-method" patents.

Source: Adapted from "Battle over Patents Threatens to Damp Web's Innovative Spirit," *Wall Street Journal* (November 8, 1999); and L. Rohde, "Amazon, Barnes and Noble Settle Patent Dispute, *CNN.com* (March 8, 2002).

A company charges all legal fees and other costs incurred in successfully defending a patent suit to Patents, an asset account, because such a suit establishes the legal rights of the holder of the patent. Such costs should be amortized along with acquisition cost, over the remaining useful life of the patent.

Amortization expense should reflect the pattern, if reliably determined, in which a company uses up the patent.[8] A company may credit amortization of patents directly to the Patents account or to an Accumulated Patent Amortization account. To illustrate, assume that Harcott Co. incurs $180,000 in legal costs on January 1, 2007 to successfully defend a patent. The patent's useful life is 20 years, amortized on a straight-line basis. Harcott records the legal fees and the amortization at the end of 2007 as follows.

	January 1, 2007	
Patents	180,000	
Cash		180,000
(To record legal fees related to patent)		

	December 31, 2007	
Patent Amortization Expense	9,000	
Patents (or Accumulated Patent Amortization)		9,000
(To record amortization of patent)		

---

[8]Companies may compute amortization on a units-of-production basis in a manner similar to that described for depreciation on property, plant, and equipment. See Chapter 11, page 525.

We've said that a patent's useful life should not extend beyond its legal life of 20 years. However, companies often make small modifications or additions that lead to a new patent. For example, **Astra Zeneca Plc** filed for additional patents on minor modifications to its heartburn drug, Prilosec. The effect may be to extend the life of the old patent. In that case Astra Zeneca can apply the unamortized costs of the old patent to the new patent if the new patent provides essentially the same benefits.[9] Alternatively, if a patent becomes impaired because demand drops for the product, the asset should be written down or written off immediately to expense.

WHAT DO THE NUMBERS MEAN?

THE VALUE OF A SECRET FORMULA

The nuclear secrets contained within the Los Alamos nuclear lab seem easier to check out than a library book. But **The Coca-Cola Company** has managed to keep the recipe for the world's best-selling soft drink under wraps for more than 100 years. How has it done so?

Coca-Cola offers almost no information about its lifeblood. The only written copy of the formula resides in a bank vault in Atlanta. This handwritten sheet is available to no one except by vote of Coca-Cola's board of directors.

Can't science offer some clues? Coke purportedly contains 17 to 18 ingredients. That includes the usual caramel color and corn syrup, as well as a blend of oils known as 7X (rumored to be a mix of orange, lemon, cinnamon, and others). Distilling natural products like these is complicated, since they're made of thousands of compounds. One ingredient you will not find is cocaine. Although the original formula did contain trace amounts, today's Coke doesn't. When was it removed? That too is a secret.

Some experts indicate that the power of the Coca-Cola formula and related brand image account for almost 95 percent of Coke's $150 billion stock value.

Source: Adapted from Reed Tucker, "How Has Coke's Formula Stayed a Secret?" *Fortune* (July 24, 2000), p. 42.

Goodwill

OBJECTIVE 5
Explain the conceptual issues related to goodwill.

Although companies may capitalize certain costs to develop specifically identifiable assets such as patents and copyrights, the amounts capitalized are generally insignificant. But companies do record material amounts of intangible assets when purchasing intangible assets, particularly in situations involving the purchase of another business (often referred to as a business combination).

In a business combination, a company assigns the cost (purchase price), where possible, to the identifiable tangible and intangible net assets. It records the remainder in an intangible asset account called **Goodwill**. Goodwill is often referred to as the most intangible of intangible assets, because it is only identified with the business as a whole. The only way to sell it is to sell the business.

The problem of determining the proper cost to allocate to intangible assets in a business combination is complex. Many different types of intangibles may be considered, such as those we discussed earlier. It is extremely difficult not only to identify certain types of intangibles but also to assign a value to them in a business combination.

---

[9]Another example is **Eli Lilly**'s drug Prozac (prescribed to treat depression). In 1998 this product accounted for 43 percent of Eli Lilly's sales. The patent on Prozac expired in 2001, and the company was unable to extend its protection with a second-use patent for the use of Prozac to treat appetite disorders. Sales of the product slipped substantially as generic equivalents entered the market.

As a result, companies only record identifiable intangible assets that they can reliably measure. They record all other intangible assets, too difficult to identify or measure, as goodwill.[10]

Recording Goodwill

Internally Created Goodwill. **Goodwill generated internally should not be capitalized in the accounts.** The reason? Measuring the components of goodwill is simply too complex, and associating any costs with future benefits is too difficult. The future benefits of goodwill may have no relationship to the costs incurred in the development of that goodwill. To add to the mystery, goodwill may even exist in the absence of specific costs to develop it. Finally, because no objective transaction with outside parties takes place, a great deal of subjectivity—even misrepresentation—may occur.

OBJECTIVE 6
Describe the accounting procedures for recording goodwill.

Purchased Goodwill. Goodwill is recorded only when an entire business is purchased. Because goodwill is a "going concern" valuation, it cannot be separated from the business as a whole. To record goodwill, a company compares the fair market value of the net tangible and identifiable intangible assets with the purchase price of the acquired business. The difference is considered goodwill. This is why goodwill is sometimes referred to as a "plug," or "gap filler," or "**master valuation**" account. **Goodwill is the residual—the excess of cost over fair value of the identifiable net assets acquired.**

UNDERLYING CONCEPTS

Capitalizing goodwill only when it is purchased in an arm's-length transaction, and not capitalizing any goodwill generated internally, is another example of reliability winning out over relevance.

To illustrate, Multi-Diversified, Inc. decides that it needs a parts division to supplement its existing tractor distributorship. The president of Multi-Diversified is interested in buying a small concern in Chicago (Tractorling Company). Illustration 12-3 presents the balance sheet of Tractorling Company.

ILLUSTRATION 12-3
Tractorling Balance Sheet

TRACTORLING CO.			
BALANCE SHEET			
AS OF DECEMBER 31, 2007			
Assets		**Equities**	
Cash	$ 25,000	Current liabilities	$ 55,000
Receivables	35,000	Capital stock	100,000
Inventories	42,000	Retained earnings	100,000
Property, plant, and equipment, net	153,000		
Total assets	$255,000	Total equities	$255,000

After considerable negotiation, Tractorling Company decides to accept Multi-Diversified's offer of $400,000. What, then, is the value of the goodwill, if any?

The answer is not obvious. Tractorling's historical cost-based balance sheet does not disclose the fair market values of its identifiable assets. Suppose, though, that as the negotiations progress, Multi-Diversified investigates Tractorling's underlying assets to determine their fair market values. Such an investigation may be accomplished

Expanded Discussion—Valuing Goodwill

[10]*SFAS No. 141* provides detailed guidance regarding the recognition of identifiable intangible assets in a business combination. Using this guidance, it was expected that companies would recognize more identifiable intangible assets, and less goodwill, in the financial statements as a result of business combinations. According to *Accounting Trends and Techniques* (AICPA 2004), companies surveyed reported nearly twice as many identifiable intangible assets compared to the survey in 2001. There was little change in the number of survey companies reporting goodwill.

either through a purchase audit undertaken by Multi-Diversified's auditors or by an independent appraisal from some other source. The investigation determines the valuations shown in Illustration 12-4.

ILLUSTRATION 12-4
Fair Market Value of
Tractorling's Net Assets

Fair Market Values	
Cash	$ 25,000
Receivables	35,000
Inventories	122,000
Property, plant, and equipment, net	205,000
Patents	18,000
Liabilities	(55,000)
Fair market value of net assets	$350,000

Normally, differences between current fair market value and book value are more common among long-term assets than in the current assets category. Cash obviously poses no problems as to value. And receivables normally are fairly close to current valuation, although they may at times need certain adjustments due to inadequate bad debt provisions. Liabilities usually are stated at book value. However, if interest rates have changed since the company incurred the liabilities, a different valuation (such as present value based on expected cash flows) might be appropriate. Careful analysis must be made to determine that no unrecorded liabilities are present.

The $80,000 difference in Tractorling's inventories ($122,000 − $42,000) could result from a number of factors, the most likely being that the company uses LIFO. Recall that during periods of inflation, LIFO better matches expenses against revenues. However, it also creates a balance sheet distortion. Ending inventory consists of older layers costed at lower valuations.

In many cases, the values of long-term assets such as property, plant, and equipment, and intangibles may have increased substantially over the years. This difference could be due to inaccurate estimates of useful lives, continual expensing of small expenditures (say, less than $300), inaccurate estimates of salvage values, and the discovery of some unrecorded assets (as in Tractorling's case, where analysis determines Patents have a fair value of $18,000). Or, fair values may have substantially increased.

Since the investigation now determines the fair market value of net assets to be $350,000, why would Multi-Diversified pay $400,000? Undoubtedly, Tractorling points to its established reputation, good credit rating, top management team, well-trained employees, and so on. These factors make the value of the business greater than $350,000. At the same time, Multi-Diversified places a premium on the future earning power of these attributes as well as the basic asset structure of the company today. At this point in the negotiations, price can be a function of many factors. The most important is probably sheer skill at the bargaining table.

Multi-Diversified labels the difference between the purchase price of $400,000 and the fair market value of $350,000 as goodwill. Goodwill is viewed as one or a group of unidentifiable values (intangible assets), the cost of which "is measured by the difference between the cost of the group of assets or enterprise acquired and the sum of the assigned costs of individual tangible and identifiable intangible assets acquired less liabilities assumed."[11] This procedure for valuation, a **master valuation**

---

[11]The FASB expressed concern about measuring goodwill as a residual, but noted that there is no real measurement alternative since goodwill is not separable from the company as a whole. "Business Combinations," *Statement of Financial Accounting Standards No. 141* (Norwalk, Conn.: FASB, 2001), par. B145.

approach, assumes goodwill covers all the values that cannot be specifically identified with any identifiable tangible or intangible asset. Illustration 12-5 shows this approach.

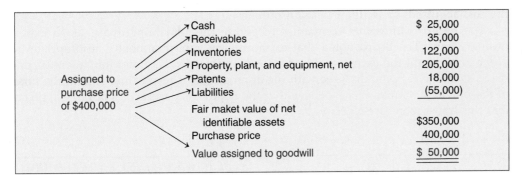

	Cash	$ 25,000
	Receivables	35,000
	Inventories	122,000
Assigned to purchase price of $400,000	Property, plant, and equipment, net	205,000
	Patents	18,000
	Liabilities	(55,000)
	Fair maket value of net identifiable assets	$350,000
	Purchase price	400,000
	Value assigned to goodwill	$ 50,000

ILLUSTRATION 12-5
Determination of Goodwill—Master Valuation Approach

Multi-Diversified records this transaction as follows.

Cash	25,000	
Receivables	35,000	
Inventories	122,000	
Property, Plant, and Equipment	205,000	
Patents	18,000	
Goodwill	50,000	
Liabilities		55,000
Cash		400,000

Companies often identify goodwill on the balance sheet as the **excess of cost over the fair value** of the net assets acquired.

Goodwill Write-off

Companies that recognize goodwill in a business combination **consider it to have an indefinite life and therefore should not amortize it**. The reason: Investors find the amortization charge of little use in evaluating financial performance. In addition, although goodwill may decrease over time, predicting the actual life of goodwill and an appropriate pattern of amortization is extremely difficult.

Furthermore, goodwill often is the largest intangible asset on a company's balance sheet and the investment community wants to know the amount invested in goodwill. Therefore, **companies only adjust its carrying value when goodwill is impaired**. This approach significantly impacts the income statements of some companies. For example, **AOL Time Warner** (now **Time Warner**), **AT&T**, and other companies wrote off $750 billion of goodwill in a recent year. (See "What Do the Numbers Mean?" discussion on page 584.)

Some believe that goodwill's value eventually disappears. Therefore, they argue companies should charge goodwill to expense over the periods affected. Amortizing goodwill better matches expense with revenues. Others note that the accounting treatment for purchased goodwill and goodwill created internally should be consistent. They point out that companies immediately expense goodwill created internally and thus it does not appear as an asset. Companies should follow the same treatment, they argue, for purchased goodwill. Even though these arguments may have some merit, nonamortization of goodwill combined with an adequate impairment test should provide the most useful financial information to the investment community.

Negative Goodwill—Badwill

Negative goodwill (often referred to as a **bargain purchase** or **badwill**) arises when the fair value of the assets acquired exceeds the purchase price of the assets. This situation results from a market imperfection. In this case, the seller would have been better off to sell the assets individually than in total. However, situations do occur (e.g., a forced liquidation or distressed sale due to the death of a company founder), in which the purchase price is less than the value of the net identifiable assets. This results in a credit, which is referred to as **negative goodwill** or, alternatively, as **excess of fair value over the cost acquired**, **badwill**, or **bargain purchase**.

The FASB requires that companies recognize this remaining excess as an extraordinary gain. The Board noted that extraordinary gain treatment is appropriate in order to highlight the excess, and to reflect the unusual nature and infrequent occurrence of the item. Some disagree with the approach, as it results in a gain at the time of the purchase. However, we believe that the Board took a practical approach, given that this transaction rarely occurs.[12]

WHAT DO THE NUMBERS MEAN?

REAL NEWS OR JUST BOOKKEEPING?

Companies used 2002 to take massive write-offs. As Chief Investment Strategist Abby Joseph Cohen of **Goldman Sachs** noted, "Simply stated, many companies are writing off not only the kitchen sink but the bathtub as well." For instance, **AOL Time Warner Inc.** (now **Time Warner**) had a goodwill write-down in the first quarter of that year that—by itself—reduced S&P 500 earnings by $2 to $4 on an after-tax basis, Ms. Cohen said.

In her investment letter, Ms. Cohen attributed companies' massive write-downs to "the air"—that is, a confluence of the impacts from the September 11, 2001, terrorist attacks, the official announcement that the country is in a recession, and new rules for the write-down of goodwill.

Though earnings hits can be tough to swallow in the quarter in which they are taken, they often are not of lasting impact psychologically or operationally. "The quarter in which the write-offs are recorded typically bears the statistical brunt, but may not be reflective of performance in future quarters," according to Ms. Cohen.

Goodwill impairment issues continue to grab their share of business headlines. For example, **Hewlett-Packard** has received a fair amount of criticism for it failure to take goodwill impairment charges on goodwill arising from its merger with **Compaq**. HP's chief financial officer acknowledges the issue, but plays down its significance: "There's no question that if profitability doesn't improve, there will be an impairment charge." He makes the case that it wouldn't matter much, given that it would be just a bookkeeping entry. What do you think? Is an impairment charge just an entry or can it provide some new information about the merits of the merger with Compaq?

Source: Carol J. Loomis, "Why Carly's Big Bet Is Failing," *Fortune* (February 7, 2005), p. 50.

IMPAIRMENT OF INTANGIBLE ASSETS

OBJECTIVE 7
Explain the accounting issues related to intangible-asset impairments.

In some cases, the carrying amount of a long-lived asset (property, plant, and equipment or intangible assets) is not recoverable. Therefore, a company needs a write-off. As discussed in Chapter 11, this write-off is referred to as an impairment.

Impairment of Limited-Life Intangibles

The rules that apply to **impairments of property, plant, and equipment also apply to limited-life intangibles**. As discussed in Chapter 11, a company should review property, plant, and equipment for impairment at certain points—whenever events or

---

[12]"Business Combinations," *Statement of Financial Accounting Standards No. 141* (Norwalk, Conn.: FASB, 2001), pars. B187–B192.

changes in circumstances indicate that the carrying amount of the assets may not be recoverable.

In performing this **recoverability test**, the company estimates the future cash flows expected from use of the assets and its eventual disposal. If the sum of the expected future net cash flows (undiscounted) is less than the carrying amount of the asset, the company would measure and recognize an impairment loss.[13] The company then uses the **fair value test**. This test measures the impairment loss by comparing the asset's fair value with its carrying amount. The impairment loss is the carrying amount of the asset less the fair value of the impaired asset. As with other impairments, the loss on the limited-life intangible is reported as part of income from continuing operations. The entry generally appears in the "Other expenses and losses" section.

To illustrate, assume that Lerch, Inc. has a patent on how to extract oil from shale rock. Unfortunately, reduced oil prices adversely affected the shale oil technology. Thus, the patent has provided little income to date. As a result, Lerch performs a **recoverability test**. It finds that the expected net future cash flows from this patent are $35 million, and Lerch's patent has a carrying amount of $60 million. Because the expected future net cash flows of $35 million are less than the carrying amount of $60 million, Lerch must determine an impairment loss.

Discounting the expected net future cash flows at its market rate of interest, Lerch determines the fair value of its patent to be $20 million. Illustration 12-6 shows the impairment loss computation (based on fair value).

Carrying amount of patent	$60,000,000	
Fair value (based on present value computation)	20,000,000	
Loss on impairment	$40,000,000	

ILLUSTRATION 12-6
Computation of Loss on Impairment of Patent

Lerch records this loss as follows:

Loss on Impairment	40,000,000	
Patents		40,000,000

After recognizing the impairment, the reduced carrying amount of the patents is its new cost basis. Lerch should amortize the patent's new cost over its remaining useful life or legal life, whichever is shorter. Even if oil prices increase in subsequent periods, and the value of the patent increases, Lerch **may not recognize restoration of the previously recognized impairment loss**.

Impairment of Indefinite-Life Intangibles Other Than Goodwill

Indefinite-life intangibles (other than goodwill) should be tested for impairment at least annually. The impairment test for an indefinite-life asset other than goodwill is a **fair value test**. This test compares the fair value of the intangible asset with the asset's carrying amount. If the fair value of the intangible asset is less than the carrying amount, an impairment is recognized. Companies use this one-step test because many indefinite-life assets easily meet the recoverability test (because cash flows may extend many years into the future). **As a result, the recoverability test is not used.**

To illustrate, assume that Arcon Radio purchased a broadcast license for $2,000,000. The license is renewable every 10 years if the company provides appropriate service and does not violate Federal Communications Commission (FCC) rules and procedures. Arcon Radio has renewed the license with the FCC twice, at a minimal cost. Because

---

[13]"Accounting for the Impairment or Disposal of Long-lived Assets," *Statement of Financial Accounting Standards No. 144* (Norwalk, Conn.: 2001).

it expects cash flows to last indefinitely, Arcon Radio reports the license as an indefinite-life intangible asset. Recently the FCC decided to no longer renew broadcast licenses, but to auction these licenses to the highest bidder. Arcon Radio expects cash flows for the remaining two years of its existing license. Arcon Radio performs an impairment test and determines that the fair value of the intangible asset is $1,500,000. It therefore reports an impairment loss of $500,000, computed as follows.

ILLUSTRATION 12-7
Computation of Loss on Impairment of Broadcast License

Carrying amount of broadcast license	$2,000,000
Fair value of broadcast license	1,500,000
Loss on impairment	$ 500,000

Arcon Radio now reports the license at $1,500,000, its fair value. Even if the value of the license increases in the remaining two years, Arcon Radio may not restore the previously recognized impairment loss.

Impairment of Goodwill

The impairment rule for goodwill is a two-step process. First, a company should compare the fair value of the reporting unit to its carrying amount, including goodwill. If the fair value of the reporting unit exceeds the carrying amount, it does not consider goodwill impaired. The company does not have to do anything else.

To illustrate, assume that Kohlbuy Corporation has three divisions in its company. It purchased one division, Pritt Products, four years ago for $2 million. Unfortunately, Pritt experienced operating losses over the last three quarters. Kohlbuy management is now reviewing the division for purposes of recognizing an impairment. Illustration 12-8 lists the Pritt Division's net assets, including the associated goodwill of $900,000 from the purchase.

ILLUSTRATION 12-8
Net Assets of Pritt Division, Including Goodwill

Cash	$ 200,000
Receivables	300,000
Inventory	700,000
Property, plant, and equipment (net)	800,000
Goodwill	900,000
Less: Accounts and notes payable	(500,000)
Net assets	$2,400,000

Kohlbuy determines that the fair value of Pritt Division is $2,800,000. **As a result, it does not recognize any impairment, because the fair value of the division exceeds the carrying amount of the net assets.**

However, if the fair value of Pritt Division is less than the carrying amount of the net assets, then Kohlbuy performs a second step to determine possible impairment. In the second step, Kohlbuy determines the fair value of the goodwill (implied value of goodwill) and compares it to its carrying amount. To illustrate, assume that the fair value of the Pritt Division is $1,900,000 instead of $2,800,000. Illustration 12-9 computes the implied value of the goodwill in this case.[14]

---

[14]Illustration 12-9 assumes that the carrying amount equals the fair value of net identifiable assets (excluding goodwill). If different, companies use the fair value of the net identifiable assets (excluding goodwill) to determine the implied goodwill.

Fair value of Pritt Division	$1,900,000
Net identifiable assets (excluding goodwill) ($2,400,000 − $900,000)	1,500,000
Implied value of goodwill	$ 400,000

ILLUSTRATION 12-9
Determination of Implied Value of Goodwill

Kohlbuy then compares the implied value of the goodwill to the recorded goodwill to determine impairment, as shown in Illustration 12-10.

Carrying amount of goodwill	$900,000
Implied value of goodwill	400,000
Loss on impairment	$500,000

ILLUSTRATION 12-10
Measurement of Goodwill Impairment

Illustration 12-11 summarizes the impairment tests for various intangible assets.

Type of Intangible Asset	Impairment Test
Limited life	Recoverability test, then fair value test
Indefinite life other than goodwill	Fair value test
Goodwill	Fair value test on reporting unit, then fair value test on implied goodwill

ILLUSTRATION 12-11
Summary of Intangible Asset Impairment Tests

RESEARCH AND DEVELOPMENT COSTS

Research and development (R&D) costs are not in themselves intangible assets. We present the accounting for R&D costs here, however, because research and development activities frequently result in the development of something that a company patents or copyrights (such as a new product, process, idea, formula, composition, or literary work).

Many companies spend considerable sums of money on research and development to create new products or processes, to improve present products, and to discover new knowledge that may be valuable at some future date. Illustration 12-12 shows the outlays for R&D made by selected U.S. companies.

OBJECTIVE 8
Identify the conceptual issues related to research and development costs.

Company	R&D ($ million)	R&D/Sales	R&D/Net Income
Caterpillar	$ 928.0	3.07%	45.60%
Deere & Co.	611.6	3.06%	43.50%
Dell	463.0	0.94%	15.22%
General Mills	158.0	1.43%	14.98%
Hewlett-Packard	3,506.0	4.39%	100.26%
Johnson & Johnson	5,203.0	10.99%	61.15%
Kellogg	148.9	1.55%	16.72%
Merck	4,010.2	17.48%	68.98%

ILLUSTRATION 12-12
R&D Outlays, as a Percentage of Sales and Profits

INTERNATIONAL INSIGHT

International accounting standards require the capitalization of appropriate development expenditures. This conflicts with U.S. GAAP.

Two difficulties arise in accounting for these research and development (R&D) expenditures: (1) identifying the costs associated with particular activities, projects, or achievements, and (2) determining the magnitude of the future benefits and length of time over which such benefits may be realized. Because of these latter uncertainties, the accounting practice in this area has been simplified. **Companies must expense all research and development costs when incurred.**[15]

Identifying R&D Activities

Illustration 12-13 shows the definitions for **research activities** and **development activities**. These definitions differentiate research and development costs from similar costs.[16]

ILLUSTRATION 12-13
R&D Activities

Research Activities	**Development Activities**
Planned search or critical investigation aimed at discovery of new knowledge.	Translation of research findings or other knowledge into a plan or design for a new product or process or for a significant improvement to an existing product or process whether intended for sale or use.
Examples	**Examples**
Laboratory research aimed at discovery of new knowledge; searching for applications of new research findings.	Conceptual formulation and design of possible product or process alternatives; construction of prototypes and operation of pilot plants.

Note that R&D activities do not include routine or periodic alterations to existing products, production lines, manufacturing processes, and other ongoing operations, even though these alterations may represent improvements. For example, routine ongoing efforts to refine, enrich, or improve the qualities of an existing product are not considered R&D activities.

Accounting for R&D Activities

OBJECTIVE 9
Describe the accounting for research and development and similar costs.

The costs associated with R&D activities and the accounting treatments accorded them are as follows.

1 *Materials, Equipment, and Facilities.* Expense the entire costs, **unless the items have alternative future uses** (in other R&D projects or otherwise), in which case carry as inventory and allocate as consumed; or capitalize and depreciate as used.
2 *Personnel.* Expense salaries, wages, and other related costs of personnel engaged in R&D as incurred.
3 *Purchased Intangibles.* Expense the entire cost, **unless the items have alternative future uses** (in other R&D projects or otherwise), in which case capitalize and amortize.
4 *Contract Services.* Expense the costs of services performed by others in connection with the R&D as incurred.
5 *Indirect Costs.* Include a reasonable allocation of indirect costs in R&D costs, except for general and administrative cost, which must be clearly related in order to be included in R&D.[17]

---

[15]"Accounting for Research and Development Costs," *Statement of Financial Accounting Standards No. 2* (Stamford, Conn.: FASB, 1974), par. 12.

[16]Ibid., par. 8.

[17]Ibid., par. 11.

Consistent with item 1 above, if a company owns a research facility consisting of buildings, laboratories, and equipment that conducts R&D activities and that has alternative future uses (in other R&D projects or otherwise), it should capitalize the facility as an operational asset. The company accounts for depreciation and other costs related to such research facilities as R&D expenses.[18]

To illustrate, assume that Next Century Incorporated develops, produces, and markets laser machines for medical, industrial, and defense uses.[19] Illustration 12-14 lists the types of expenditures related to its laser machine activities, along with the recommended accounting treatment.

<table>
<tr><td colspan="2" align="center">**Next Century Incorporated**</td></tr>
<tr><td align="center">Type of Expenditure</td><td align="center">Accounting Treatment</td></tr>
<tr><td>1. Construction of long-range research facility for use in current and future projects (three-story, 400,000-square-foot building).</td><td>Capitalize and depreciate as R&D expense.</td></tr>
<tr><td>2. Acquisition of R&D equipment for use on current project only.</td><td>Expense immediately as R&D.</td></tr>
<tr><td>3. Acquisition of machinery to be used on current and future R&D projects.</td><td>Capitalize and depreciate as R&D expense.</td></tr>
<tr><td>4. Purchase of materials to be used on current and future R&D projects.</td><td>Inventory and allocate to R&D projects; expense as consumed.</td></tr>
<tr><td>5. Salaries of research staff designing new laser bone scanner.</td><td>Expense immediately as R&D.</td></tr>
<tr><td>6. Research costs incurred under contract with New Horizon, Inc., and billable monthly.</td><td>Record as a receivable (reimbursable expenses).</td></tr>
<tr><td>7. Material, labor, and overhead costs of prototype laser scanner.</td><td>Expense immediately as R&D.</td></tr>
<tr><td>8. Costs of testing prototype and design modifications.</td><td>Expense immediately as R&D.</td></tr>
<tr><td>9. Legal fees to obtain patent on new laser scanner.</td><td>Capitalize as patent and amortize to overhead as part of cost of goods manufactured.</td></tr>
<tr><td>10. Executive salaries.</td><td>Expense as operating expense (general and administrative).</td></tr>
<tr><td>11. Cost of marketing research to promote new laser scanner.</td><td>Expense as operating expense (selling).</td></tr>
<tr><td>12. Engineering costs incurred to advance the laser scanner to full production stage.</td><td>Expense immediately as R&D.</td></tr>
<tr><td>13. Costs of successfully defending patent on laser scanner.</td><td>Capitalize as patent and amortize to overhead as part of cost of goods manufactured.</td></tr>
<tr><td>14. Commissions to sales staff marketing new laser scanner.</td><td>Expense as operating expense (selling).</td></tr>
</table>

ILLUSTRATION 12-14
Sample R&D Expenditures and Their Accounting Treatment

---

[18]Companies in **the extractive industries** can use the following accounting treatment for the unique costs of research, exploration, and development activities and for those costs that are similar to but not classified as R&D costs: (1) expense as incurred, (2) capitalize and either depreciate or amortize over an appropriate period of time, or (3) accumulate as part of inventoriable costs. Choice of the appropriate accounting treatment for such costs is based on the degree of certainty of future benefits and the principle of matching revenues and expenses.

[19]Sometimes companies conduct R&D activities for other companies under a contractual arrangement. In this case, the contract usually specifies that the company performing the R&D work be reimbursed for all direct costs and certain specific indirect costs, plus a profit element. Because reimbursement is expected, the company doing the R&D work records the R&D costs as a receivable. The company for whom the work has been performed reports these costs as R&D and expenses them as incurred.

For a more complete discussion of how an enterprise should account for funding of its R&D by others, see "Research and Development Arrangements," *Statement of Financial Accounting Standards No. 68* (Stamford, Conn.: FASB, 1982).

Other Costs Similar to R&D Costs

Many costs have characteristics similar to research and development costs. Examples are:

1 Start-up costs for a new operation.
2 Initial operating losses.
3 Advertising costs.
4 Computer software costs.

For the most part, these costs are expensed as incurred, similar to the accounting for R&D costs. We briefly explain these costs in the following sections.

Start-Up Costs

Start-up costs are incurred for one-time activities to start a new operation. Examples include opening a new plant, introducing a new product or service, or conducting business in a new territory or with a new class of customers. Start-up costs include **organizational costs**, such as legal and state fees incurred to organize a new business entity.

The accounting for start-up costs is straightforward: **Expense start-up costs as incurred.** The profession recognizes that companies incur start-up costs with the expectation of future revenues or increased efficiencies. However, to determine the amount and timing of future benefits is so difficult that a conservative approach—expensing these costs as incurred—is required.[20]

To illustrate the type of costs that companies expense as start-up costs, assume that U.S.-based Hilo Beverage Company decides to construct a new plant in Brazil. This represents Hilo's first entry into the Brazilian market. As part of its overall strategy, Hilo plans to introduce the company's major U.S. brands into Brazil, on a locally produced basis. The following costs might be involved:

1 Travel-related costs; costs related to employee salaries; and costs related to feasibility studies, accounting, tax, and government affairs.
2 Training of local employees related to product, maintenance, computer systems, finance, and operations.
3 Recruiting, organizing, and training related to establishing a distribution network.

Hilo Beverage should expense all these start-up costs as incurred.

Start-up activities commonly occur at the same time as activities such as the acquisition of assets. For example, as it is incurring start-up costs for the new plant, Hilo also probably is buying or building property, plant, equipment, and inventory. Hilo should not immediately expense the costs of these assets. Instead, it should charge them to operations and report them on the balance sheet using appropriate GAAP reporting guidelines.

Initial Operating Losses

Some contend that companies should be allowed to capitalize initial operating losses incurred in the start-up of a business. They argue that such operating losses are a cost of starting a business and are unavoidable.

For example, assume that Hilo lost money in its first year of operations and wishes to capitalize this loss. Hilo's CEO argues that as the company becomes profitable, it will offset these losses in future periods. What do *you* think? We believe that this approach is unsound, since losses have no future service potential and therefore cannot be considered an asset.

---

[20]"Reporting on the Costs of Start-up Activities," *Statement of Position 98-5* (New York: AICPA, 1998).

GAAP requires that operating losses during the early years should not be capitalized. In short, **the accounting and reporting standards should be no different for an enterprise trying to establish a new business than they are for other enterprises.**[21]

Advertising Costs

Over the years, **PepsiCo** has hired various pop stars, such as Britney Spears and Beyoncé, to advertise its products. How should it report such advertising costs related to its star spokespeople? Pepsi could expense the costs in various ways:

1 When they have completed their singing assignments.

2 The first time the advertising runs.

3 Over the estimated useful life of the advertising.

4 In an appropriate fashion to each of the three periods identified above.

5 Over the period revenues are expected to result.

For the most part, Pepsi must expense advertising costs as incurred or the first time the advertising takes place. These two alternatives are permitted because whichever approach is followed, the results are essentially the same. On the other hand, companies record as assets any tangible assets used in advertising, such as billboards or blimps. The rationale is that such assets do have alternative future uses. Again the

---

BRANDED

For many companies, developing a strong brand image is as important as developing the products they sell. Now more than ever, companies see the power of a strong brand, enhanced by significant and effective advertising investments.

As the following chart indicates, the value of brand investments is substantial. **Coca-Cola** heads the list with an estimated brand value of nearly $70 billion.

WHAT DO THE NUMBERS MEAN?

The World's 10 Most Valuable Brands
(in billions)

1	Coca-Cola	$67.3	6	Disney	$27.1
2	Microsoft	61.3	7	McDonald's	25.0
3	IBM	53.8	8	Nokia	24.0
4	GE	44.1	9	Toyota	22.7
5	Intel	33.5	10	Marlboro	22.1

Source: 2004 data, from Interbrand Corp. and J. P. Morgan Chase.

Occasionally you may find the value of a brand included in a company's financial statements under goodwill. But generally you won't find the estimated values of brands recorded in companies' balance sheets. The reason? The subjectivity that goes into estimating a brand's value. In some cases, analysts base an estimate of brand value on opinion polls or on some multiple of ad spending. In estimating the brand values shown above, **Interbrand Corp.** estimates the percentage of the overall future revenues the brand will generate and then discounts the net cash flows, to arrive at a present value. Some analysts believe that information on brand values is relevant. Others voice valid concerns about the reliability of brand value estimates due to subjectivity in the estimates for revenues, costs, and the risk component of the discount rate.

Source: Adapted from Gerry Khermouch, "The Best Global Brands," *Businessweek* (August 5, 2002), pp. 93–95; and D. Brady, R. D. Hof, and A. Reinhardt, "Cult Brands," *Businessweek Online* (August 2, 2004).

---

[21]"Accounting and Reporting by Development Stage Enterprises," *Statement of Financial Accounting Standards No. 7* (Stamford, Conn.: FASB, 1975), par. 10. A company is considered to be in the developing stages when it is directing its efforts toward establishing a new business and either the company has not started the principal operations or it has earned no significant revenue.

profession has taken a conservative approach to recording advertising costs because defining and measuring the future benefits can be so difficult.[22]

Computer Software Costs

UNDERLYING CONCEPTS

The requirement that companies expense all R&D costs as incurred is an example of the conflict between relevance and reliability. Here, this requirement leans strongly in support of reliability, as well as conservatism, consistency, and comparability. No attempt is made to match costs and revenues.

A special problem arises in distinguishing R&D costs from selling and administrative activities. The FASB's intent was that companies exclude from the definition of R&D activities the acquisition, development, or improvement of a product or process **for use in their selling or administrative activities**. For example, the costs of software incurred by an airline in improving its computerized reservation system, or the costs incurred in developing a management information system **are not** research and development costs.

Accounting for computer software costs is a specialized and complicated accounting topic that we discuss and illustrate in Appendix 12A (pages 596–599).

Conceptual Questions

The requirement that companies expense immediately all R&D costs (as well as start-up costs) incurred internally is a conservative, practical solution. It ensures consistency in practice and uniformity among companies. But the practice of immediately writing off expenditures made in the expectation of benefiting future periods is conceptually incorrect.

Proponents of immediate expensing contend that from an income statement standpoint, long-run application of this standard frequently makes little difference. They argue that because of the ongoing nature of most companies' R&D activities, the amount of R&D cost charged to expense each accounting period is about the same, whether there is immediate expensing or capitalization and subsequent amortization. Others criticize this practice. They believe that the balance sheet should report an intangible asset related to expenditures that have future benefit. To preclude capitalization of all R&D expenditures removes from the balance sheet what may be a company's most valuable asset. This standard represents one of the many trade-offs made among relevance, reliability, and cost-benefit considerations.[23]

PRESENTATION OF INTANGIBLES AND RELATED ITEMS

Presentation of Intangible Assets

OBJECTIVE **10**
Indicate the presentation of intangible assets and related items.

The reporting of intangible assets differs from the reporting of property, plant, and equipment in that contra accounts are not normally shown for intangibles. (See Illustration 12-15.) On the balance sheet, companies should report all intangible assets other than goodwill as a separate item. If goodwill is present, companies should report it separately. The FASB concluded that since goodwill and other intangible assets differ significantly from other types of assets, this disclosure benefits users of the balance sheet.

---

[22]"Reporting on Advertising Costs," *Statement of Position 93-7* (New York: AICPA, 1993). Note that there are some exceptions for immediate expensing of advertising costs when they relate to direct-response advertising, but this subject is beyond the scope of this book.

[23]Research findings indicate that capitalizing R&D costs may be helpful to investors. For example, one study showed a significant relationship between R&D outlays and subsequent benefits in the form of increased productivity, earnings, and shareholder value for R&D–intensive companies. Baruch Lev and Theodore Sougiannis, "The Capitalization, Amortization, and Value-Relevance of R&D," *Journal of Accounting and Economics* (February 1996).

Another study found that there was a significant decline in earnings usefulness for companies that were forced to switch from capitalizing to expensing R&D costs, and that the decline appears to persist over time. Martha L. Loudder and Bruce K. Behn, "Alternative Income Determination Rules and Earnings Usefulness: The Case of R&D Costs," *Contemporary Accounting Research* (Fall 1995).

On the income statement, companies should present amortization expense and impairment losses for intangible assets other than goodwill as part of continuing operations. Goodwill impairment losses should also be presented as a separate line item in the continuing operations section, unless the goodwill impairment is associated with a discontinued operation.

ILLUSTRATION 12-15
Intangible Asset
Disclosures

HARBAUGH COMPANY
Balance Sheet (partial)
(in thousands)

Intangible Assets (Note C)	$3,840
Goodwill (Note D)	2,575

Income Statement (partial)
(in thousands)
as part of Continuing operations

Amortization expense	$380
Impairment losses (goodwill)	46

Note C: Acquired Intangible Assets

	As of December 31, 2007	
	Gross Carrying Amount	Accumulated Amortization
Amortized intangible assets		
Trademark	$2,000	$(100)
Customer list	500	(310)
Other	60	(10)
Total	$2,560	$(420)
Unamortized intangible assets		
Licenses	$1,300	
Trademark	400	
Total	$1,700	

Aggregate Amortization Expense

For year ended 12/31/07	$380

Estimated Amortization Expense

For year ended 12/31/08	$200
For year ended 12/31/09	90
For year ended 12/31/10	70
For year ended 12/31/11	60
For year ended 12/31/12	50

Note D: Goodwill
The changes in the carrying amount of goodwill for the year ended December 31, 2007, are as follows:

($000s)	Technology Segment	Communications Segment	Total
Balance as of January 1, 2007	$1,413	$904	$2,317
Goodwill acquired during year	189	115	304
Impairment losses	—	(46)	(46)
Balance as of December 31, 2007	$1,602	$973	$2,575

The Communications segment is tested for impairment in the third quarter, after the annual forecasting process. Due to an increase in competition in the Texas and Louisiana cable industry, operating profits and cash flows were lower than expected in the fourth quarter of 2006 and the first and second quarters of 2007. Based on that trend, the earnings forecast for the next 5 years was revised. In September 2007, a goodwill impairment loss of $46 was recognized in the Communications reporting unit. The fair value of that reporting unit was estimated using the expected present value of future cash flows.

The notes to the financial statements should include information about acquired intangible assets, including the aggregate amortization expense for each of the succeeding 5 years. The notes should include information about changes in the carrying amount of goodwill during the period. As noted earlier, Illustration 12-15 shows the type of disclosure made related to intangible assets in the financial statements and related notes for Harbaugh Company.

Presentation of Research and Development Costs

Additional Disclosures of Intangibles and R&D Costs

Acceptable accounting practice requires that companies disclose in the financial statements (generally in the notes) the total R&D costs charged to expense each period for which they present an income statement. **Merck & Co., Inc.,** a global research pharmaceutical company, reported both internal and acquired research and development in its recent income statement, as shown in Illustration 12-16.

ILLUSTRATION 12-16
Income Statement
Disclosure of R&D Costs

Merck & Co., Inc.
(in millions)

	Years Ended December 31		
	2004	2003	2002
Sales	$22,938.6	$22,485.9	$21,445.8
Costs, expenses, and other			
Materials and production	4,959.8	4,436.9	4,004.9
Marketing and administrative	7,346.3	6,394.9	5,652.2
Research and development	4,010.2	3,279.9	2,677.2
Equity income from affiliates	(1,008.2)	(474.2)	(644.7)
Other (income) expense, net	(344.0)	(203.2)	104.5
	$14,964.1	$13,434.3	$11,794.1

In addition, Merck provides a discussion about R&D expenditures in its annual report, as shown in Illustration 12-17.

ILLUSTRATION 12-17
Merck's R&D
Disclosure

Merck & Co., Inc.

Research and development in the pharmaceutical industry is inherently a long-term process. The following data show an unbroken trend of year-to-year increases in the Company's research and development spending. For the period 1995 to 2004, the compounded annual growth rate in research and development was 13%.

KEY TERMS

amortization, 573

copyright, 577

development activities, 588

fair value test, 585

franchise, 577

goodwill, 580

impairment, 584

indefinite-life intangibles, 573

intangible assets, 572

license (permit), 577

limited-life intangibles, 573

master valuation approach, 582–583

negative goodwill (badwill), 583

organizational costs, 590

patent, 578

recoverability test, 585

research activities, 588

research and development (R&D) costs, 587

start-up costs, 590

trademark, trade name, 575

SUMMARY OF LEARNING OBJECTIVES

1. **Describe the characteristics of intangible assets.** Intangible assets have two main characteristics: (1) They lack physical existence, and (2) they are not financial instruments. In most cases, intangible assets provide services over a period of years. As a result, they are normally classified as long-term assets.

2. **Identify the costs to include in the initial valuation of intangible assets.** Intangibles are recorded at cost. Cost includes all costs of acquisition and expenditures necessary to make the intangible asset ready for its intended use. If intangibles are acquired for stock or in exchange for other assets, the cost of the intangible is the fair value of the consideration given or the fair value of the intangible received, whichever is more clearly evident. When a company buys several intangibles, or a combination of intangibles and tangibles, in a "basket purchase," it should allocate the cost on the basis of fair values.

3. **Explain the procedure for amortizing intangible assets.** Intangibles have either a limited useful life or an indefinite useful life. Companies amortize intangible assets with a limited life. They do not amortize intangible assets with indefinite lives. Limited-life intangibles should be amortized by systematic charges to expense over their useful life. The useful life should reflect the period over which these assets will contribute to cash flows. The amount to report for amortization expense should reflect the pattern in which a company consumes or uses up the asset, if it can reliably determine that pattern. Otherwise the company should use a straight-line approach.

4. **Describe the types of intangible assets.** Major types of intangibles are: (1) *marketing-related intangibles,* used in the marketing or promotion of products or services; (2) *customer-related intangibles,* resulting from interactions with outside parties; (3) *artistic-related intangibles,* giving ownership rights to such items as plays and literary works; (4) *contract-related intangibles,* representing the value of rights that arise from contractual arrangements; (5) *technology-related intangibles,* relating to innovations or technological advances; and (6) *goodwill,* arising from business combinations.

5. **Explain the conceptual issues related to goodwill.** Goodwill is unique because unlike receivables, inventories, and patents that a company can sell or exchange individually in the marketplace, goodwill can be identified only with the company as a whole. Goodwill is a "going concern" valuation and is recorded only when an entire business is purchased. A company should not capitalize goodwill generated internally in the accounts, because measuring the components of goodwill is too complex and associating any costs with future benefits too difficult. The future benefits of goodwill may have no relationship to the costs incurred in the development of that goodwill. Goodwill may exist even in the absence of specific costs to develop it.

6. **Describe the accounting procedures for recording goodwill.** To record goodwill, a company compares the fair market value of the net tangible and identifiable intangible assets with the purchase price of the acquired business. The difference is considered goodwill. Goodwill is the residual—the excess of cost over fair value of the identifiable net assets acquired. Goodwill is often identified on the balance sheet as the excess of cost over the fair value of the net assets acquired.

7. **Explain the accounting issues related to intangible-asset impairments.** Impairment occurs when the carrying amount of the intangible asset is not recoverable. Companies use a recoverability test and a fair value test to determine impairments for limited-life intangibles. They use only a fair value test for indefinite-life intangibles. Goodwill impairments require a two-step process: First, test the fair value of the reporting unit, then do the fair value test on implied goodwill.

8. **Identify the conceptual issues related to research and development costs.** R&D costs are not in themselves intangible assets, but R&D activities frequently result in the development of something a company patents or copyrights. The difficulties in accounting for R&D expenditures are: (1) identifying the costs associated with particular activities, projects, or achievements, and (2) determining the magnitude of the future benefits and length of time over which a company may realize such benefits. Because of these latter uncertainties, companies are required to expense all research and development costs when incurred.

9. **Describe the accounting for research and development and similar costs.** Pages 587–589 show the costs associated with R&D activities and the accounting treatment accorded them. Many costs have characteristics similar to R&D costs. Examples are start-up costs, initial operating losses, and advertising costs. For the most part, these costs are expensed as incurred, similar to the accounting for R&D costs.

10. **Indicate the presentation of intangible assets and related items.** The reporting of intangibles differs from the reporting of property, plant, and equipment in that contra accounts are not normally shown. On the balance sheet, companies should report all intangible assets other than goodwill as a separate item. If goodwill is present, it too should be reported as a separate item. On the income statement, companies should report amortization expense and impairment losses in continuing operations. The notes to the financial statements have additional detailed information. Financial statements must disclose the total R&D costs charged to expense each period for which an income statement is presented.

APPENDIX

12A Accounting for Computer Software Costs

OBJECTIVE 11
Understand the accounting treatment for computer software costs.

Our economy is changing from a focus on manufacturing processes (tangible outputs) to a focus on information flow (intangible outputs).[1] As a result, the accounting for computer software products becomes increasingly important. This appendix discusses the basic issues involved in accounting for computer software.

DIVERSITY IN PRACTICE

Companies can either **purchase** computer software or **create** it. They may purchase or create software for **external use** (such as spreadsheet applications like Excel or Lotus 1-2-3) or for **internal use** (e.g., to establish a better internal accounting system).

---

[1] A major contributing factor was **IBM's** decision in 1969 to "unbundle" its hardware and software—to state the cost of the hardware and software separately. Previously, computer companies provided most application software free with the hardware. This unbundling led to the creation of a whole new industry, the software industry, whose members began selling software to hardware users.

How should companies account for the costs of developing software? Should they expense such costs immediately or capitalize and amortize them in the future? At one time, some companies expensed all software costs, and others capitalized such costs. Still others differentiated such costs on the basis of whether the software was purchased or created, or whether it was used for external or internal purposes.

Another major question is whether the costs involved in developing software are research and development costs. If they are actually R&D costs, then companies should expense them as incurred. If they are not R&D costs, then a strong case can be made for capitalization. As one financial executive of a software company, who argues for capitalization, noted, "The key distinction between our spending and R&D is recoverability. We know we are developing something we can sell."

THE PROFESSION'S POSITION

In an attempt to resolve the issue of how to account for software (at least for companies that sell computer software), the FASB issued *Statement of Financial Accounting Standards No. 86*, "Accounting for the Costs of Computer Software to Be Sold, Leased, or Otherwise Marketed."[2] The major recommendations of this pronouncement are:

1 Until a company has established **technological feasibility** for a software product, it should charge to R&D expense the costs incurred in creating the product.

2 Technological feasibility is established when the company has completed a detailed program design or a working model.

In short, the FASB has taken a conservative position in regard to computer software costs. For example, a company like **Microsoft** must expense all costs until it has completed the activities (planning, designing, coding, and testing) necessary to establish that it can produce the product to meet its design specifications. From that point on, Microsoft should capitalize subsequently incurred costs and amortize them to current and future periods.

Two additional points: First, **if Microsoft purchases software and it has alternative future uses, then it may be capitalized.** Second, **this standard applies only to the development of software that is to be sold, leased, or otherwise marketed to third parties** (i.e., for external use).

The profession has also indicated how to account for software to be used internally. Activities performed during the preliminary project stage of development (e.g., conceptual formulation and evaluation of alternatives) are similar to R&D costs. Companies should expense such costs immediately. Once the software is at the application development stage (e.g., at the coding or installation stages), its future economic benefits become probable. At that point, companies must capitalize the software costs. Finally, subsequent to the application development stage, costs related to training and application maintenance should be expensed as incurred.[3]

ACCOUNTING FOR CAPITALIZED SOFTWARE COSTS

If companies are to capitalize software costs, then they must establish a proper amortization pattern for such costs. As **a basis for amortization, one of two amounts is used: (1) the ratio of current revenues to current and anticipated revenues (the percent- of-revenue approach), or (2) the straight-line method over the remaining**

[2]"Accounting for the Cost of Computer Software to Be Sold, Leased, or Otherwise Marketed," *Statement of Financial Accounting Standards No. 86* (Stamford, Conn.: FASB, 1985). Also see Robert W. McGee, *Accounting for Software* (Homewood, Ill.: Dow Jones-Irwin, 1985).

[3]"Accounting for the Costs of Computer Software Developed or Obtained for Internal Use," *Statement of Position 98-1* (New York: AICPA, 1998).

useful life of the asset (straight-line approach). A company must use whichever of those amounts is greater. This rule can result in the use of the percent-of-revenue method one year and the straight-line method in another.[4]

To illustrate, assume that **AT&T** has capitalized software costs of $10 million, and current (first-year) revenues from sales of this product of $4 million. AT&T anticipates earning $16 million in additional future revenues from this product; it estimates that the product has an economic life of 4 years. Using the percent-of-revenue approach, AT&T's current (first) year's amortization is $2 million ($4,000,000/$20,000,000 times the capitalized software costs of $10,000,000). Using the straight-line approach, its amortization is $2.5 million ($10,000,000/4 years). Thus AT&T uses the straight-line approach because it results in the **greater amortization charge**.

REPORTING SOFTWARE COSTS

Much concern exists about the reliability of an asset such as software. Therefore, the FASB indicated that companies should value capitalized software costs at the **lower of unamortized cost (book value) or net realizable value**. If net realizable value is lower, then companies should write down the capitalized software costs to this value. Once companies have written down the costs, **they may not write them back up**.

In addition to the regular disclosures for R&D costs, companies should report in the financial statements the following information relating to software.

1 Unamortized software costs.

2 The total amount charged to expense and the amounts, if any, written down to net realizable value.

Again, these accounting and reporting requirements apply only to software **developed for external purposes**.

Illustration 12A-1 presents an example of software development cost disclosure, taken from the annual report of **Analogic Corporation**.

ILLUSTRATION 12A-1
Disclosure of Software
Development Costs

Analogic Corporation
(in thousands)

	2004	2003
Total current assets	$328,121	$335,903
Property, plant and equipment, net	91,077	83,926
Investments in and advances to affiliated companies	10,967	14,050
Capitalized software, net	9,502	6,339
Goodwill	1,565	2,306
Intangible assets, net	9,223	11,708
Other assets	1,616	3,185
Total assets	$452,071	$457,417

Significant Accounting Policies

Capitalized Software Costs: Software development costs incurred subsequent to establishing technological feasibility through general release of the software products are capitalized in accordance to SFAS No. 86 "Accounting for the Costs of Computer Software to be Sold, Leased, or Otherwise Marketed." Capitalized costs are amortized on a straight-line basis over the economic lives of the related products, generally three years. Amortization expense was $1,801, $1,813 and $1,772 in fiscal 2004, 2003, and 2002, respectively and is included in product cost of sales. The unamortized balance of capitalized software was $9,502 and $6,339 at July 31, 2004, and 2003, respectively.

---

[4]Because there are no revenues associated with software developed for internal use, amortization of these internal use capitalized costs is based on the straight-line approach.

SETTING STANDARDS FOR SOFTWARE ACCOUNTING

"It's unreasonable to expense all software costs, and it's unreasonable to capitalize all software costs," said **IBM**'s director of financial reporting. "If you subscribe to those two statements, then it follows that there is somewhere in between where development ends and capitalization begins. Now you have to define that point."[5] The FASB defined that point as **technological feasibility**, which is established upon completion of a detailed program design or a working model.

The difficulty of applying this criterion to software is that "there is no such thing as a real, specific, baseline design. But you could make it look like you have one as early or as late as you like," says Osman Erlop of **Hambrecht & Quist**.[6] That is, if a company wishes to capitalize, it draws up a detailed program design quickly. If it wants to expense lots of development costs, it simply holds off writing a detailed program design. And, once capitalized, the costs are amortized over the useful life specified by the developer. Because of either constant redesign or supersession, software's useful life is generally quite short (two to four years).

As another example, some companies "manage by the numbers." That is, they are very careful to identify projects that are worthwhile and capitalize the computer software costs associated with them. They believe that good projects must be capitalized and amortized in the future; otherwise, the concept of properly matching expense and revenues is abused. In contrast, other companies choose not to manage by the numbers. They simply expense all development costs. Companies that expense all these costs have no use for a standard that requires capitalization. In their view, it would mean only that they would need a more complex, more expensive cost accounting system, which would provide little if any benefit.

Financial analysts have reacted almost uniformly against any capitalization of software costs. They believe such costs should be expensed because of the rapid obsolescence of software and the potential for abuse that may result from capitalizing costs inappropriately. As Donald Kirk, a former chairman of the FASB, stated, "The Board is now faced with the problem of balancing what it thought was good theory with the costs for some companies of implementing a new accounting system with the concerns of users about the potential for abuse of the standard."[7]

Resolving the software accounting problem again demonstrates the difficulty of establishing reporting standards.

SUMMARY OF LEARNING OBJECTIVE FOR APPENDIX 12A

11. Understand the accounting treatment for computer software costs. Costs incurred in creating a software product should be charged to R&D expense when incurred until technological feasibility has been established for the product. Subsequent costs should be capitalized and amortized to current and future periods. Software that a company purchases for sale or lease to third parties and has alternative future uses may be capitalized and amortized using the greater of the percent-of-revenue approach or the straight-line approach.

Note: All **asterisked** Questions, Brief Exercises, Exercises, Problems, and Concepts for Analysis relate to material contained in the appendix to the chapter.

---

[5]"When Does Life Begin?" *Forbes* (June 16, 1986), pp. 72–74.

[6]Ibid.

[7]Donald J. Kirk, "Growing Temptation & Rising Expectation = Accelerating Regulation," *FASB Viewpoints* (June 12, 1985), p. 7.

QUESTIONS

1. What are the two main characteristics of intangible assets?

2. If intangibles are acquired for stock, how is the cost of the intangible determined?

3. Intangibles have either a limited useful life or an indefinite useful life. How should these two different types of intangibles be amortized?

4. Why does the accounting profession make a distinction between internally created intangibles and purchased intangibles?

5. In 2006 Sheila Wright Corp. spent $420,000 for "goodwill" visits by sales personnel to key customers. The purpose of these visits was to build a solid, friendly relationship for the future and to gain insight into the problems and needs of the companies served. How should this expenditure be reported?

6. What are factors to be considered in estimating the useful life of an intangible asset?

7. What should be the pattern of amortization for a limited-life intangible?

8. **Columbia Sportswear Company** acquired a trademark that is helpful in distinguishing one of its new products. The trademark is renewable every 10 years at minimal cost. All evidence indicates that this trademark product will generate cash flows for an indefinite period of time. How should this trademark be amortized?

9. Michael Redd Company spent $190,000 developing a new process, $45,000 in legal fees to obtain a patent, and $91,000 to market the process that was patented, all in the year 2006. How should these costs be accounted for in 2006?

10. Yellow 3 purchased a patent for $450,000 which has an estimated useful life of 10 years. Its pattern of use or consumption cannot be reliably determined. Prepare the entry to record the amortization of the patent in its first year of use.

11. Explain the difference between artistic-related intangible assets and contract-related intangible assets.

12. What is goodwill? What is negative goodwill?

13. Under what circumstances is it appropriate to record goodwill in the accounts? How should goodwill, properly recorded on the books, be written off in order to conform with generally accepted accounting principles?

14. In examining financial statements, financial analysts often write off goodwill immediately. Evaluate this procedure.

15. Astaire Inc. is considering the write-off of a limited life intangible because of its lack of profitability. Explain to the management of Astaire how to determine whether a write-off is permitted.

16. Last year Blair Company recorded an impairment on an intangible asset held for use. Recent appraisals indicate that the asset has increased in value. Should Blair record this recovery in value?

17. Explain how losses on impaired intangible assets should be reported in income.

18. Mills Company determines that its goodwill is impaired. It finds that its implied goodwill is $380,000 and its recorded goodwill is $400,000. The fair value of its identifiable assets is $1,450,000. What is the amount of goodwill impaired?

19. What is the nature of research and development costs?

20. Research and development activities may include (a) personnel costs, (b) materials and equipment costs, and (c) indirect costs. What is the recommended accounting treatment for these three types of R&D costs?

21. Which of the following activities should be expensed currently as R&D costs?

    (a) Testing in search for or evaluation of product or process alternatives.

    (b) Engineering follow-through in an early phase of commercial production.

    (c) Legal work in connection with patent applications or litigation, and the sale or licensing of patents.

22. Indicate the proper accounting for the following items.

    (a) Organization costs.

    (b) Advertising costs.

    (c) Operating losses.

23. In 2005, Cassie Logan Corporation developed a new product that will be marketed in 2006. In connection with the development of this product, the following costs were incurred in 2005: research and development costs $420,000; materials and supplies consumed $60,000; and compensation paid to research consultants $125,000. It is anticipated that these costs will be recovered in 2008. What is the amount of research and development costs that Cassie Logan should record in 2005 as a charge to expense?

24. Recently, a group of university students decided to incorporate for the purposes of selling a process to recycle the waste product from manufacturing cheese. Some of the initial costs involved were legal fees and office expenses incurred in starting the business, state incorporation fees, and stamp taxes. One student wishes to charge these costs against revenue in the current period. Another wishes to defer these costs and amortize them in the future. Which student is correct?

25. An intangible asset with an estimated useful life of 30 years was acquired on January 1, 1996, for $450,000. On January 1, 2006, a review was made of intangible assets and their expected service lives, and it was determined that this asset had an estimated useful life of 30 more years from the date of the review. What is the amount of amortization for this intangible in 2006?

*26. An article in the financial press stated, "More than half of software maker **Comserve**'s net worth is in a pile of tapes and ring-bound books. That raises some accountants' eyebrows." What is the profession's position regarding the incurrence of costs for computer software that will be sold?

*27. Matt Antonio, Inc. has incurred $6 million in developing a computer software product for sale to third parties. Of the $6 million costs incurred, $4 million is capitalized. The product produced from this development work has generated $2 million of revenue in 2007 and is anticipated to generate another $8 million in future years. The estimated useful life of the project is 4 years. How much of the capitalized costs should be amortized in 2007?

*28. In 2007, U-Learn Software developed a software package for assisting calculus instruction in business colleges, at a cost of $2,000,000. Although there are tens of thousands of calculus students in the market, college instructors seem to change their minds frequently on the use of teaching aids. Not one package has yet been ordered or delivered. Prepare an argument to advocate expensing the development cost in the current year. Offer an argument for capitalizing the development cost over its estimated useful life. Which stakeholders are harmed or benefited by either approach?

BRIEF EXERCISES

(LO 2, 3) **BE12-1** Doom Troopers Corporation purchases a patent from Judge Dredd Company on January 1, 2007, for $64,000. The patent has a remaining legal life of 16 years. Doom Troopers feels the patent will be useful for 10 years. Prepare Doom Troopers' journal entries to record the purchase of the patent and 2007 amortization.

(LO 2, 3) **BE12-2** Use the information provided in BE12-1. Assume that at January 1, 2009, the carrying amount of the patent on Doom Troopers' books is $51,200. In January, Doom Troopers spends $24,000 successfully defending a patent suit. Doom Troopers still feels the patent will be useful until the end of 2016. Prepare the journal entries to record the $24,000 expenditure and 2009 amortization.

(LO 2, 3) **BE12-3** Dr. Robotnik's, Inc., spent $60,000 in attorney fees while developing the trade name of its new product, the Mean Bean Machine. Prepare the journal entries to record the $60,000 expenditure and the first year's amortization, using an 8-year life.

(LO 9) **BE12-4** Incredible Hulk Corporation commenced operations in early 2007. The corporation incurred $70,000 of costs such as fees to underwriters, legal fees, state fees, and promotional expenditures during its formation. Prepare journal entries to record the $70,000 expenditure and 2007 amortization, if any.

(LO 2, 3) **BE12-5** Knuckles Corporation obtained a franchise from Sonic Hedgehog Inc. for a cash payment of $100,000 on April 1, 2007. The franchise grants Knuckles the right to sell certain products and services for a period of 8 years. Prepare Knuckles' April 1 journal entry and December 31 adjusting entry.

(LO 6) **BE12-6** On September 1, 2007, Dungeon Corporation acquired Dragon Enterprises for a cash payment of $750,000. At the time of purchase, Dragon's balance sheet showed assets of $620,000, liabilities of $200,000, and owners' equity of $420,000. The fair value of Dragon's assets is estimated to be $800,000. Compute the amount of goodwill acquired by Dungeon.

(LO 7) **BE12-7** Nobunaga Corporation owns a patent that has a carrying amount of $330,000. Nobunaga expects future net cash flows from this patent to total $190,000. The fair value of the patent is $110,000. Prepare Nobunaga's journal entry, if necessary, to record the loss on impairment.

(LO 7) **BE12-8** Evander Corporation purchased Holyfield Company 3 years ago and at that time recorded goodwill of $400,000. The Holyfield Division's net assets, including the goodwill, have a carrying amount of $800,000. The fair value of the division is estimated to be $1,000,000. Prepare Evander's journal entry, if necessary, to record impairment of the goodwill.

(LO 7) **BE12-9** Use the information provided in BE12-8. Assume that the fair value of the division is estimated to be $750,000 and the implied goodwill is $325,000. Prepare Evander's journal entry, if necessary, to record impairment of the goodwill.

(LO 9) **BE12-10** Dorsett Corporation incurred the following costs in 2007.

Cost of laboratory research aimed at discovery of new knowledge	$140,000
Cost of testing in search for product alternatives	100,000
Cost of engineering activity required to advance the design of a product to the manufacturing stage	210,000
	$450,000

Prepare the necessary 2007 journal entry or entries for Dorsett.

(LO 9) **BE12-11** Indicate whether the following items are capitalized or expensed in the current year.

- **(a)** Purchase cost of a patent from a competitor.
- **(b)** Research and development costs.
- **(c)** Organizational costs.
- **(d)** Costs incurred internally to create goodwill.

(LO 3, 9) **BE12-12** Langer Industries had one patent recorded on its books as of January 1, 2007. This patent had a book value of $240,000 and a remaining useful life of 8 years. During 2007, Langer incurred research and development costs of $96,000 and brought a patent infringement suit against a competitor. On December 1, 2007, Langer received the good news that its patent was valid and that its competitor could not use the process Langer had patented. The company incurred $85,000 to defend this patent. At what amount should patent(s) be reported on the December 31, 2007, balance sheet, assuming monthly amortization of patents?

(LO 3, 10) **BE12-13** Wiggens Industries acquired two copyrights during 2007. One copyright related to a textbook that was developed internally at a cost of $9,900. This textbook is estimated to have a useful life of 3 years from September 1, 2007, the date it was published. The second copyright (a history research textbook) was purchased from University Press on December 1, 2007, for $19,200. This textbook has an indefinite useful life. How should these two copyrights be reported on Wiggens' balance sheet as of December 31, 2007?

(LO 11) ***BE12-14** Earthworm Jim Corporation has capitalized software costs of $700,000, and sales of this product the first year totaled $420,000. Earthworm Jim anticipates earning $980,000 in additional future revenues from this product, which is estimated to have an economic life of 4 years. Compute the amount of software cost amortization for the first year.

EXERCISES

(LO 1, 4) **E12-1** **(Classification Issues—Intangibles)** Presented below is a list of items that could be included in the intangible assets section of the balance sheet.

1. Investment in a subsidiary company.
2. Timberland.
3. Cost of engineering activity required to advance the design of a product to the manufacturing stage.
4. Lease prepayment (6 months' rent paid in advance).
5. Cost of equipment obtained.
6. Cost of searching for applications of new research findings.
7. Costs incurred in the formation of a corporation.
8. Operating losses incurred in the start-up of a business.
9. Training costs incurred in start-up of new operation.
10. Purchase cost of a franchise.
11. Goodwill generated internally.
12. Cost of testing in search for product alternatives.
13. Goodwill acquired in the purchase of a business.
14. Cost of developing a patent.
15. Cost of purchasing a patent from an inventor.
16. Legal costs incurred in securing a patent.
17. Unrecovered costs of a successful legal suit to protect the patent.
18. Cost of conceptual formulation of possible product alternatives.
19. Cost of purchasing a copyright.
20. Research and development costs.
21. Long-term receivables.
22. Cost of developing a trademark.
23. Cost of purchasing a trademark.

Instructions

- **(a)** Indicate which items on the list above would generally be reported as intangible assets in the balance sheet.
- **(b)** Indicate how, if at all, the items not reportable as intangible assets would be reported in the financial statements.

(LO 1, 4) **E12-2 (Classification Issues—Intangibles)** Presented below is selected account information related to Martin Burke Inc. as of December 21, 2007. All these accounts have debit balances.

Cable television franchises
Music copyrights
Research and development costs
Goodwill
Cash
Discount on notes payable
Accounts receivable
Property, plant, and equipment
Internet domain name

Film contract rights
Customer lists
Prepaid expenses
Covenants not to compete
Brand names
Notes receivable
Investments in affiliated companies
Organization costs
Land

Instructions

Identify which items should be classified as an intangible asset. For those items not classified as an intangible asset, indicate where they would be reported in the financial statements.

(LO 1, 4) **E12-3 (Classification Issues—Intangible Asset)** Joni Hyde Inc. has the following amounts included in its general ledger at December 31, 2007.

Organization costs	$24,000
Trademarks	15,000
Discount on bonds payable	35,000
Deposits with advertising agency for ads to promote goodwill of company	10,000
Excess of cost over fair value of net identifiable assets of acquired subsidiary	75,000
Cost of equipment acquired for research and development projects; the equipment has an alternative future use	90,000
Costs of developing a secret formula for a product that is expected to be marketed for at least 20 years	80,000

Instructions

(a) On the basis of the information above, compute the total amount to be reported by Hyde for intangible assets on its balance sheet at December 31, 2007. Equipment has alternative future use.

(b) If an item is not to be included in intangible assets, explain its proper treatment for reporting purposes.

(LO 3, 9) **E12-4 (Intangible Amortization)** Presented below is selected information for Alatorre Company.

1. Alatorre purchased a patent from Vania Co. for $1,000,000 on January 1, 2005. The patent is being amortized over its remaining legal life of 10 years, expiring on January 1, 2015. During 2007, Alatorre determined that the economic benefits of the patent would not last longer than 6 years from the date of acquisition. What amount should be reported in the balance sheet for the patent, net of accumulated amortization, at December 31, 2007?

2. Alatorre bought a franchise from Alexander Co. on January 1, 2006, for $400,000. The carrying amount of the franchise on Alexander's books on January 1, 2006, was $500,000. The franchise agreement had an estimated useful life of 30 years. Because Alatorre must enter a competitive bidding at the end of 2015, it is unlikely that the franchise will be retained beyond 2015. What amount should be amortized for the year ended December 31, 2007?

3. On January 1, 2007, Alatorre incurred organization costs of $275,000. What amount of organization expense should be reported in 2007?

4. Alatorre purchased the license for distribution of a popular consumer product on January 1, 2007, for $150,000. It is expected that this product will generate cash flows for an indefinite period of time. The license has an initial term of 5 years but by paying a nominal fee, Alatorre can renew the license indefinitely for successive 5-year terms. What amount should be amortized for the year ended December 31, 2007?

Instructions

Answer the questions asked about each of the factual situations.

(LO 2, 3, 8) **E12-5 (Correct Intangible Asset Account)** As the recently appointed auditor for William J. Bryan Corporation, you have been asked to examine selected accounts before the 6-month financial statements of June 30, 2007, are prepared. The controller for William J. Bryan Corporation mentions that only one account is kept for Intangible Assets. The account is shown on the next page.

Intangible Assets

		Debit	Credit	Balance
Jan. 4	Research and development costs	940,000		940,000
Jan. 5	Legal costs to obtain patent	75,000		1,015,000
Jan. 31	Payment of 7 months' rent on property leased by Bryan	91,000		1,106,000
Feb. 11	Premium on common stock		250,000	856,000
March 31	Unamortized bond discount on bonds due March 31, 2027	84,000		940,000
April 30	Promotional expenses related to start-up of business	207,000		1,147,000
June 30	Operating losses for first 6 months	241,000		1,388,000

Instructions

Prepare the entry or entries necessary to correct this account. Assume that the patent has a useful life of 10 years.

(LO 3, 9) **E12-6 (Recording and Amortization of Intangibles)** Rolanda Marshall Company, organized in 2006, has set up a single account for all intangible assets. The following summary discloses the debit entries that have been recorded during 2007.

1/2/07	Purchased patent (8-year life)	$ 350,000
4/1/07	Purchased goodwill (indefinite life)	360,000
7/1/07	Purchased franchise with 10-year life; expiration date 7/1/17	450,000
8/1/07	Payment of copyright (5-year life)	156,000
9/1/07	Research and development costs	215,000
		$1,531,000

Instructions

Prepare the necessary entries to clear the Intangible Assets account and to set up separate accounts for distinct types of intangibles. Make the entries as of December 31, 2007, recording any necessary amortization and reflecting all balances accurately as of that date. (Use straight-line amortization.)

(LO 2, 3) **E12-7 (Accounting for Trade Name)** In early January 2006, Outkast Corporation applied for a trade name, incurring legal costs of $16,000. In January of 2007, Outkast incurred $7,800 of legal fees in a successful defense of its trade name.

Instructions

(a) Compute 2006 amortization, 12/31/06 book value, 2007 amortization, and 12/31/07 book value if the company amortizes the trade name over 10 years.

(b) Compute the 2007 amortization and the 12/31/07 book value, assuming that at the beginning of 2007, Outkast determines that the trade name will provide no future benefits beyond December 31, 2010.

(c) Ignoring the response for part (b), compute the 2008 amortization and the 12/31/08 book value, assuming that at the beginning of 2008, based on new market research, Outkast determines that the fair value of the trade name is $15,000. Estimated total future cash flows from the trade name is $16,000 on January 3, 2008.

(LO 9) **E12-8 (Accounting for Organization Costs)** Horace Greeley Corporation was organized in 2006 and began operations at the beginning of 2007. The company is involved in interior design consulting services. The following costs were incurred prior to the start of operations.

Attorney's fees in connection with organization of the company	$15,000
Purchase of drafting and design equipment	10,000
Costs of meetings of incorporators to discuss organizational activities	7,000
State filing fees to incorporate	1,000
	$33,000

Instructions

(a) Compute the total amount of organization costs incurred by Greeley.

(b) Prepare the journal entry to record organization costs for 2007.

(LO 2, 3, 8) **E12-9 (Accounting for Patents, Franchises, and R&D)** Jimmy Carter Company has provided information on intangible assets as follows.

A patent was purchased from Gerald Ford Company for $2,000,000 on January 1, 2006. Carter estimated the remaining useful life of the patent to be 10 years. The patent was carried in Ford's accounting records at a net book value of $2,000,000 when Ford sold it to Carter.

During 2007, a franchise was purchased from Ronald Reagan Company for $480,000. In addition, 5% of revenue from the franchise must be paid to Reagan. Revenue from the franchise for 2007 was $2,500,000. Carter estimates the useful life of the franchise to be 10 years and takes a full year's amortization in the year of purchase.

Carter incurred research and development costs in 2007 as follows.

Materials and equipment	$142,000
Personnel	189,000
Indirect costs	102,000
	$433,000

Carter estimates that these costs will be recouped by December 31, 2010. The materials and equipment purchased have no alternative uses.

On January 1, 2007, because of recent events in the field, Carter estimates that the remaining life of the patent purchased on January 1, 2006, is only 5 years from January 1, 2007.

Instructions

(a) Prepare a schedule showing the intangibles section of Carter's balance sheet at December 31, 2007. Show supporting computations in good form.

(b) Prepare a schedule showing the income statement effect for the year ended December 31, 2007, as a result of the facts above. Show supporting computations in good form.

(AICPA adapted)

(LO 2, 3) **E12-10** **(Accounting for Patents)** During 2003, George Winston Corporation spent $170,000 in research and development costs. As a result, a new product called the New Age Piano was patented. The patent was obtained on October 1, 2003, and had a legal life of 20 years and a useful life of 10 years. Legal costs of $18,000 related to the patent were incurred as of October 1, 2003.

Instructions

(a) Prepare all journal entries required in 2003 and 2004 as a result of the transactions above.

(b) On June 1, 2005, Winston spent $9,480 to successfully prosecute a patent infringement suit. As a result, the estimate of useful life was extended to 12 years from June 1, 2005. Prepare all journal entries required in 2005 and 2006.

(c) In 2007, Winston determined that a competitor's product would make the New Age Piano obsolete and the patent worthless by December 31, 2008. Prepare all journal entries required in 2007 and 2008.

(LO 2, 3) **E12-11** **(Accounting for Patents)** Tones Industries has the following patents on its December 31, 2006, balance sheet.

Patent Item	Initial Cost	Date Acquired	Useful Life at Date Acquired
Patent A	$30,600	3/1/03	17 years
Patent B	$15,000	7/1/04	10 years
Patent C	$14,400	9/1/05	4 years

The following events occurred during the year ended December 31, 2007.

1. Research and development costs of $245,700 were incurred during the year.
2. Patent D was purchased on July 1 for $36,480. This patent has a useful life of 9½ years.
3. As a result of reduced demands for certain products protected by Patent B, a possible impairment of Patent B's value may have occurred at December 31, 2007. The controller for Tones estimates the expected future cash flows from Patent B will be as follows.

Year	Expected Future Cash Flows
2008	$2,000
2009	2,000
2010	2,000

The proper discount rate to be used for these flows is 8%. (Assume that the cash flows occur at the end of the year.)

Instructions

(a) Compute the total carrying amount of Tones' patents on its December 31, 2006, balance sheet.

(b) Compute the total carrying amount of Tones' patents on its December 31, 2007, balance sheet.

(LO 5, 6) **E12-12 (Accounting for Goodwill)** Fred Moss, owner of Moss Interiors, is negotiating for the purchase of Zweifel Galleries. The balance sheet of Zweifel is given in an abbreviated form below.

ZWEIFEL GALLERIES
BALANCE SHEET
AS OF DECEMBER 31, 2007

Assets		**Liabilities and Stockholders' Equity**		
Cash	$100,000	Accounts payable		$ 50,000
Land	70,000	Long-term notes payable		300,000
Building (net)	200,000	Total liabilities		350,000
Equipment (net)	175,000	Common stock	$200,000	
Copyright (net)	30,000	Retained earnings	25,000	225,000
Total assets	$575,000	Total liabilities and stockholders' equity		$575,000

Moss and Zweifel agree that:

1. Land is undervalued by $30,000.
2. Equipment is overvalued by $5,000.

Zweifel agrees to sell the gallery to Moss for $350,000.

Instructions

Prepare the entry to record the purchase of Zweifel Galleries on Moss's books.

(LO 3, 5, 6) **E12-13 (Accounting for Goodwill)** On July 1, 2006, Brigham Corporation purchased Young Company by paying $250,000 cash and issuing a $100,000 note payable to Steve Young. At July 1, 2006, the balance sheet of Young Company was as follows.

Cash	$ 50,000	Accounts payable	$200,000
Receivables	90,000	Stockholders' equity	235,000
Inventory	100,000		$435,000
Land	40,000		
Buildings (net)	75,000		
Equipment (net)	70,000		
Trademarks	10,000		
	$435,000		

The recorded amounts all approximate current values except for land (fair value of $60,000), inventory (fair value of $125,000), and trademarks (fair value of $15,000).

Instructions

(a) Prepare the July 1 entry for Brigham Corporation to record the purchase.
(b) Prepare the December 31 entry for Brigham Corporation to record amortization of intangibles. The trademark has an estimated useful life of 4 years with a residual value of $3,000.

(LO 7) **E12-14 (Copyright Impairment)** Presented below is information related to copyrights owned by Walter de la Mare Company at December 31, 2007.

Cost	$8,600,000
Carrying amount	4,300,000
Expected future net cash flows	4,000,000
Fair value	3,200,000

Assume that Walter de la Mare Company will continue to use this copyright in the future. As of December 31, 2007, the copyright is estimated to have a remaining useful life of 10 years.

Instructions

(a) Prepare the journal entry (if any) to record the impairment of the asset at December 31, 2007. The company does not use accumulated amortization accounts.
(b) Prepare the journal entry to record amortization expense for 2008 related to the copyrights.
(c) The fair value of the copyright at December 31, 2008, is $3,400,000. Prepare the journal entry (if any) necessary to record the increase in fair value.

✶

(LO 6, 7) **E12-15** **(Goodwill Impairment)** Presented below is net asset information related to the Carlos Division of Santana, Inc.

CARLOS DIVISION
NET ASSETS
AS OF DECEMBER 31, 2007
(IN MILLIONS)

Cash	$ 50
Receivables	200
Property, plant, and equipment (net)	2,600
Goodwill	200
Less: Notes payable	(2,700)
Net assets	$ 350

The purpose of the Carlos division is to develop a nuclear-powered aircraft. If successful, traveling delays associated with refueling could be substantially reduced. Many other benefits would also occur. To date, management has not had much success and is deciding whether a write-down at this time is appropriate. Management estimated its future net cash flows from the project to be $400 million. Management has also received an offer to purchase the division for $335 million. All identifiable assets' and liabilities' book and fair value amounts are the same.

Instructions
   (a) Prepare the journal entry (if any) to record the impairment at December 31, 2007.
   (b) At December 31, 2008, it is estimated that the division's fair value increased to $345 million. Prepare the journal entry (if any) to record this increase in fair value.

(LO 9) **E12-16** **(Accounting for R&D Costs)** Leontyne Price Company from time to time embarks on a research program when a special project seems to offer possibilities. In 2006 the company expends $325,000 on a research project, but by the end of 2006 it is impossible to determine whether any benefit will be derived from it.

Instructions
   (a) What account should be charged for the $325,000, and how should it be shown in the financial statements?
   (b) The project is completed in 2007, and a successful patent is obtained. The R&D costs to complete the project are $110,000. The administrative and legal expenses incurred in obtaining patent number 472-1001-84 in 2007 total $16,000. The patent has an expected useful life of 5 years. Record these costs in journal entry form. Also, record patent amortization (full year) in 2007.
   (c) In 2008, the company successfully defends the patent in extended litigation at a cost of $47,200, thereby extending the patent life to December 31, 2015. What is the proper way to account for this cost? Also, record patent amortization (full year) in 2008.
   (d) Additional engineering and consulting costs incurred in 2008 required to advance the design of a product to the manufacturing stage total $60,000. These costs enhance the design of the product considerably. Discuss the proper accounting treatment for this cost.

(LO 9) **E12-17** **(Accounting for R&D Costs)** Thomas More Company incurred the following costs during 2007 in connection with its research and development activities.

Cost of equipment acquired that will have alternative ~capitalize~	
uses in future R&D projects over the next 5 years	
(uses straight-line depreciation)	$280,000 ~÷ 5 = 56000 A year~
Materials consumed in R&D projects ~expense~	59,000
Consulting fees paid to outsiders for R&D projects ~expense~	100,000
Personnel costs of persons involved in R&D projects ~expense~	128,000
Indirect costs reasonably allocable to R&D projects ~expense~	50,000
Materials purchased for future R&D projects ~capitalize~	34,000

Instructions
Compute the amount to be reported as research and development expense by More on its income statement for 2007. Assume equipment is purchased at the beginning of the year.

(LO 11) ***E12-18** **(Accounting for Computer Software Costs)** New Jersey Inc. has capitalized computer software costs of $3,600,000 on its new "Trenton" software package. Revenues from 2007 (first year) sales are $2,000,000. Additional future revenues from "Trenton" for the remainder of its economic life, through 2011, are estimated to be $10,000,000.

Instructions

(a) What method or methods of amortization are to be applied in the write-off of capitalized computer software costs?

(b) Compute the amount of amortization for 2007 for "Trenton."

(LO 11) *E12-19 (Accounting for Computer Software Costs) During 2007, Delaware Enterprises Inc. spent $5,000,000 developing its new "Dover" software package. Of this amount, $2,200,000 was spent before technological feasibility was established for the product, which is to be marketed to third parties. The package was completed at December 31, 2007. Delaware expects a useful life of 8 years for this product with total revenues of $16,000,000. During the first year (2008), Delaware realizes revenues of $3,200,000.

Instructions

(a) Prepare journal entries required in 2007 for the foregoing facts.

(b) Prepare the entry to record amortization at December 31, 2008.

(c) At what amount should the computer software costs be reported in the December 31, 2007, balance sheet? Does the net realizable value of this asset affect your answer?

(d) What disclosures are required in the December 31, 2008, financial statements for the computer software costs?

(e) How would your answers to above be different if the computer software was devel-

[handwritten notes:]
12-3
13. total expenses
2007 $63,028

12-4
B. patent 66,000

12-5
C. impairment loss
300,000

Visit the website www.wiley.com/college/kieso, for Additional Exercises.

PROBLEMS

(LO 2, 3) P12-1 (Correct Intangible Asset Account) Reichenbach Co., organized in 2006, has set up a single account for all intangible assets. The following summary discloses the debit entries that have been recorded during 2006 and 2007.

Intangible Assets

7/1/06	8-year franchise; expiration date 6/30/14	$ 42,000
10/1/06	Advance payment on laboratory space (2-year lease)	28,000
12/31/06	Net loss for 2006 including state incorporation fee, $1,000, and related legal fees of organizing, $5,000 (all fees incurred in 2006)	16,000
1/2/07	Patent purchased (10-year life)	74,000
3/1/07	Cost of developing a secret formula (indefinite life)	75,000
4/1/07	Goodwill purchased (indefinite life)	278,400
6/1/07	Legal fee for successful defense of patent purchased above	12,650
9/1/07	Research and development costs	160,000

Instructions

Prepare the necessary entries to clear the Intangible Assets account and to set up separate accounts for distinct types of intangibles. Make the entries as of December 31, 2007, recording any necessary amortization and reflecting all balances accurately as of that date. (Ignore income tax effects.)

(LO 2, 3) P12-2 (Accounting for Patents) Ankara Laboratories holds a valuable patent (No. 758-6002-1A) on a precipitator that prevents certain types of air pollution. Ankara does not manufacture or sell the products and processes it develops. Instead, it conducts research and develops products and processes which it patents, and then assigns the patents to manufacturers on a royalty basis. Occasionally it sells a patent. The history of Ankara patent number 758-6002-1A is as follows.

Date	Activity	Cost
1997–1998	Research conducted to develop precipitator	$384,000
Jan. 1999	Design and construction of a prototype	87,600
March 1999	Testing of models	42,000
Jan. 2000	Fees paid engineers and lawyers to prepare patent application; patent granted June 30, 2000	62,050
Nov. 2001	Engineering activity necessary to advance the design of the precipitator to the manufacturing stage	81,500

Dec. 2002	Legal fees paid to successfully defend precipitator patent	35,700
April 2003	Research aimed at modifying the design of the patented precipitator	43,000
July 2007	Legal fees paid in unsuccessful patent infringement suit against a competitor	34,000

Ankara assumed a useful life of 17 years when it received the initial precipitator patent. On January 1, 2005, it revised its useful life estimate downward to 5 remaining years. Amortization is computed for a full year if the cost is incurred prior to July 1, and no amortization for the year if the cost is incurred after June 30. The company's year ends December 31.

Instructions

Compute the carrying value of patent No. 758-6002-1A on each of the following dates:

(a) December 31, 2000.

(b) December 31, 2004.

(c) December 31, 2007.

(LO 2, 3) **P12-3** **(Accounting for Franchise, Patents, and Trade Name)** Information concerning Haerhpin Corporation's intangible assets is as follows.

1. On January 1, 2007, Haerhpin signed an agreement to operate as a franchisee of Hsian Copy Service, Inc. for an initial franchise fee of $75,000. Of this amount, $15,000 was paid when the agreement was signed, and the balance is payable in 4 annual payments of $15,000 each, beginning January 1, 2008. The agreement provides that the down payment is not refundable and no future services are required of the franchisor. The present value at January 1, 2007, of the 4 annual payments discounted at 14% (the implicit rate for a loan of this type) is $43,700. The agreement also provides that 5% of the revenue from the franchise must be paid to the franchisor annually. Haerhpin's revenue from the franchise for 2007 was $950,000. Haerhpin estimates the useful life of the franchise to be 10 years. (*Hint:* You may want to refer to Appendix 18A to determine the proper accounting treatment for the franchise fee and payments.) *1,700 Amort.*

2. Haerhpin incurred $65,000 of experimental and development costs in its laboratory to develop a patent that was granted on January 2, 2007. Legal fees and other costs associated with registration of the patent totaled $13,600. Haerhpin estimates that the useful life of the patent will be 8 years.

3. A trademark was purchased from Shanghai Company for $32,000 on July 1, 2004. Expenditures for successful litigation in defense of the trademark totaling $8,160 were paid on July 1, 2007. Haerhpin estimates that the useful life of the trademark will be 20 years from the date of acquisition.

Instructions

(a) Prepare a schedule showing the intangible assets section of Haerhpin's balance sheet at December 31, 2007. Show supporting computations in good form.

(b) Prepare a schedule showing all expenses resulting from the transactions that would appear on Haerhpin's income statement for the year ended December 31, 2007. Show supporting computations in good form.

(AICPA adapted)

land don't depreciate

(LO 9, 10) **P12-4** **(Accounting for R&D Costs)** During 2005, Florence Nightingale Tool Company purchased a building site for its proposed research and development laboratory at a cost of $60,000. Construction of the building was started in 2005. The building was completed on December 31, 2006, at a cost of $280,000 and was placed in service on January 2, 2007. The estimated useful life of the building for depreciation purposes was 20 years. The straight-line method of depreciation was to be employed, and there was no estimated salvage value.

Management estimates that about 50% of the projects of the research and development group will result in long-term benefits (i.e., at least 10 years) to the corporation. The remaining projects either benefit the current period or are abandoned before completion. A summary of the number of projects and the direct costs incurred in conjunction with the research and development activities for 2007 appears below.

Internal don't amortize

	Number of Projects	Salaries and Employee Benefits	Other Expenses (excluding Building Depreciation Charges)
Completed projects with long-term benefits	15	$ 90,000	$50,000
Abandoned projects or projects that benefit the current period	10	65,000	15,000
Projects in process—results indeterminate	5	40,000	12,000
Total	30	$195,000	$77,000

Upon recommendation of the research and development group, Florence Nightingale Tool Company acquired a patent for manufacturing rights at a cost of $80,000. The patent was acquired on April 1, 2006, and has an economic life of 10 years.

Instructions

If generally accepted accounting principles were followed, how would the items above relating to research and development activities be reported on the following financial statements?

(a) The company's income statement for 2007.
(b) The company's balance sheet as of December 31, 2007.

Be sure to give account titles and amounts, and briefly justify your presentation.

(CMA adapted)

(LO 5, 6) **P12-5** **(Goodwill, Impairment)** On July 31, 2007, Postera Company paid $3,000,000 to acquire all of the common stock of Mendota Incorporated, which became a division of Postera. Mendota reported the following balance sheet at the time of the acquisition.

Current assets	$ 800,000	Current liabilities	$ 600,000
Noncurrent assets	2,700,000	Long-term liabilities	500,000
Total assets	$3,500,000	Stockholders' equity	2,400,000
		Total liabilities and	
		stockholders' equity	$3,500,000

It was determined at the date of the purchase that the fair value of the identifiable net assets of Mendota was $2,650,000. Over the next 6 months of operations, the newly purchased division experienced operating losses. In addition, it now appears that it will generate substantial losses for the foreseeable future. At December 31, 2007, Mendota reports the following balance sheet information.

Current assets	$ 450,000
Noncurrent assets (including goodwill recognized in purchase)	2,400,000
Current liabilities	(700,000)
Long-term liabilities	(500,000)
Net assets	$1,650,000

It is determined that the fair value of the Mendota Division is $1,850,000. The recorded amount for Mendota's net assets (excluding goodwill) is the same as fair value, except for property, plant, and equipment, which has a fair value $150,000 above the carrying value.

Instructions

(a) Compute the amount of goodwill recognized, if any, on July 31, 2007.
(b) Determine the impairment loss, if any, to be recorded on December 31, 2007.
(c) Assume that fair value of the Mendota Division is $1,500,000 instead of $1,850,000. Determine the impairment loss, if any, to be recorded on December 31, 2007.
(d) Prepare the journal entry to record the impairment loss, if any, and indicate where the loss would be reported in the income statement.

(LO 2, 3, 6, 7, 10) **P12-6** **(Comprehensive Intangible Assets)** Montana Matt's Golf Inc. was formed on July 1, 2006, when Matt Magilke purchased the Old Master Golf Company. Old Master provides video golf instruction at kiosks in shopping malls. Magilke plans to integrate the instruction business into his golf equipment and accessory stores. Magilke paid $750,000 cash for Old Master. At the time Old Master's balance sheet reported assets of $650,000 and liabilities of $200,000 (thus owners' equity was $450,000). The fair value of Old Master's assets is estimated to be $800,000. Included in the assets is the Old Master trade name with a fair value of $10,000 and a copyright on some instructional books with a fair value of $20,000. The trade name has a remaining life of 5 years and can be renewed at nominal cost indefinitely. The copyright has a remaining life of 40 years.

Instructions

(a) Prepare the intangible assets section of Montana Matt's Golf Inc. at December 31, 2006. How much amortization expense is included in Montana Matt's income for the year ended December 31, 2006? Show all supporting computations.
(b) Prepare the journal entry to record amortization expense for 2007. Prepare the intangible assets section of Montana Matt's Golf Inc. at December 31, 2007. (No impairments are required to be recorded in 2007.)
(c) At the end of 2008, Magilke is evaluating the results of the instructional business. Due to fierce competition from online and television (e.g., the Golf Channel), the Old Master reporting unit has been losing money. Its book value is now $500,000. The fair value of the Old Master reporting

unit is $430,000. The implied value of goodwill is $80,000. Magilke has collected the following information related to the company's intangible assets.

Intangible Asset	Expected Cash Flows (undiscounted)	Fair Values
Trade name	$ 9,000	$ 3,000
Copyright	30,000	25,000

Prepare the journal entries required, if any, to record impairments on Montana Matt's intangible assets. (Assume that any amortization for 2008 has been recorded.) Show supporting computations.

CONCEPTS FOR ANALYSIS

CA12-1 (Accounting for Pollution Expenditure) Phil Mickelson Company operates several plants at which limestone is processed into quicklime and hydrated lime. The Eagle Ridge plant, where most of the equipment was installed many years ago, continually deposits a dusty white substance over the surrounding countryside. Citing the unsanitary condition of the neighboring community of Scales Mound, the pollution of the Galena River, and the high incidence of lung disease among workers at Eagle Ridge, the state's Pollution Control Agency has ordered the installation of air pollution control equipment. Also, the Agency has assessed a substantial penalty, which will be used to clean up Scales Mound.

After considering the costs involved (which could not have been reasonably estimated prior to the Agency's action), Phil Mickelson Company decides to comply with the Agency's orders, the alternative being to cease operations at Eagle Ridge at the end of the current fiscal year. The officers of Mickelson agree that the air pollution control equipment should be capitalized and depreciated over its useful life, but they disagree over the period(s) to which the penalty should be charged.

Instructions

Discuss the conceptual merits and reporting requirements of accounting for the penalty in each of the following ways.

(a) As a charge to the current period.
(b) As a correction of prior periods.
(c) As a capitalizable item to be amortized over future periods.

(AICPA adapted)

CA12-2 (Accounting for Pre-Opening Costs) After securing lease commitments from several major stores, Lobo Shopping Center, Inc. was organized and built a shopping center in a growing suburb.

The shopping center would have opened on schedule on January 1, 2007, if it had not been struck by a severe tornado in December. Instead, it opened for business on October 1, 2007. All of the additional construction costs that were incurred as a result of the tornado were covered by insurance.

In July 2006, in anticipation of the scheduled January opening, a permanent staff had been hired to promote the shopping center, obtain tenants for the uncommitted space, and manage the property.

A summary of some of the costs incurred in 2006 and the first nine months of 2007 follows.

	2006	January 1, 2007 through September 30, 2007
Interest on mortgage bonds	$720,000	$540,000
Cost of obtaining tenants	300,000	360,000
Promotional advertising	540,000	557,000

The promotional advertising campaign was designed to familiarize shoppers with the center. Had it been known in time that the center would not open until October 2007, the 2006 expenditure for promotional advertising would not have been made. The advertising had to be repeated in 2007.

All of the tenants who had leased space in the shopping center at the time of the tornado accepted the October occupancy date on condition that the monthly rental charges for the first 9 months of 2007 be canceled.

Instructions

Explain how each of the costs for 2006 and the first 9 months of 2007 should be treated in the accounts of the shopping center corporation. Give the reasons for each treatment.

(AICPA adapted)

CA12-3 **(Accounting for Patents)** On June 30, 2007, your client, Bearcat Company, was granted two patents covering plastic cartons that it had been producing and marketing profitably for the past 3 years. One patent covers the manufacturing process, and the other covers the related products.

Bearcat executives tell you that these patents represent the most significant breakthrough in the industry in the past 30 years. The products have been marketed under the registered trademarks Evertight, Duratainer, and Sealrite. Licenses under the patents have already been granted by your client to other manufacturers in the United States and abroad and are producing substantial royalties.

On July 1, Bearcat commenced patent infringement actions against several companies whose names you recognize as those of substantial and prominent competitors. Bearcat's management is optimistic that these suits will result in a permanent injunction against the manufacture and sale of the infringing products as well as collection of damages for loss of profits caused by the alleged infringement.

The financial vice-president has suggested that the patents be recorded at the discounted value of expected net royalty receipts.

Instructions
- **(a)** What is the meaning of "discounted value of expected net receipts"? Explain.
- **(b)** How would such a value be calculated for net royalty receipts?
- **(c)** What basis of valuation for Bearcat's patents would be generally accepted in accounting? Give supporting reasons for this basis.
- **(d)** Assuming no practical problems of implementation, and ignoring generally accepted accounting principles, what is the preferable basis of valuation for patents? Explain.
- **(e)** What would be the preferable theoretical basis of amortization? Explain.
- **(f)** What recognition, if any, should be made of the infringement litigation in the financial statements for the year ending September 30, 2007? Discuss.

(AICPA adapted)

 CA12-4 **(Accounting for Research and Development Costs)** Indiana Jones Co. is in the process of developing a revolutionary new product. A new division of the company was formed to develop, manufacture, and market this new product. As of year-end (December 31, 2007), the new product has not been manufactured for resale. However, a prototype unit was built and is in operation.

Throughout 2007 the new division incurred certain costs. These costs include design and engineering studies, prototype manufacturing costs, administrative expenses (including salaries of administrative personnel), and market research costs. In addition, approximately $900,000 in equipment (with an estimated useful life of 10 years) was purchased for use in developing and manufacturing the new product. Approximately $315,000 of this equipment was built specifically for the design development of the new product. The remaining $585,000 of equipment was used to manufacture the pre-production prototype and will be used to manufacture the new product once it is in commercial production.

Instructions
- **(a)** How are "research" and "development" defined in *Statement of Financial Accounting Standards No. 2*?
- **(b)** Briefly indicate the practical and conceptual reasons for the conclusion reached by the Financial Accounting Standards Board on accounting and reporting practices for research and development costs.
- **(c)** In accordance with *Statement of Financial Accounting Standards No. 2*, how should the various costs of Indiana Jones described above be recorded on the financial statements for the year ended December 31, 2007?

(AICPA adapted)

 CA12-5 **(Accounting for Research and Development Costs)** Waveland Corporation's research and development department has an idea for a project it believes will culminate in a new product that would be very profitable for the company. Because the project will be very expensive, the department requests approval from the company's controller, Ron Santo.

Santo recognizes that corporate profits have been down lately and is hesitant to approve a project that will incur significant expenses that cannot be capitalized due to the requirements of *FASB Statement No. 2*. He knows that if they hire an outside firm that does the work and obtains a patent for the process, Waveland Corporation can purchase the patent from the outside firm and record the expenditure as an asset. Santo knows that the company's own R&D department is first-rate, and he is confident they can do the work well.

Instructions
Answer the following questions.
- **(a)** Who are the stakeholders in this situation?
- **(b)** What are the ethical issues involved?
- **(c)** What should Santo do?

USING YOUR JUDGMENT

Financial Reporting Problem

P&G The Procter & Gamble Company (P&G)

The financial statements of **P&G** are presented in Appendix 5B or can be accessed on the KWW website.

Instructions

Refer to P&G's financial statements and the accompanying notes to answer the following questions.

(a) Does P&G report any intangible assets, especially goodwill, in its 2004 financial statements and accompanying notes?

(b) How much research and development (R&D) cost was expensed by P&G in 2004 and 2003? What percentage of sales revenue and net income did P&G spend on R&D in 2004 and 2003?

Financial Statement Analysis Case

Merck and Johnson & Johnson

Merck & Co., Inc. and Johnson & Johnson are two leading producers of health care products. Each has considerable assets, and each expends considerable funds each year toward the development of new products. The development of a new health care product is often very expensive, and risky. New products frequently must undergo considerable testing before approval for distribution to the public. For example, it took Johnson & Johnson 4 years and $200 million to develop its 1-DAY ACUVUE contact lenses. Below are some basic data compiled from the financial statements of these two companies.

(all dollars in millions)	Johnson & Johnson	Merck
Total assets	$53,317	$42,573
Total revenue	47,348	22,939
Net income	8,509	5,813
Research and development expense	5,203	4,010
Intangible assets	11,842	2,765

Instructions

(a) What kinds of intangible assets might a health care products company have? Does the composition of these intangibles matter to investors—that is, would it be perceived differently if all of Merck's intangibles were goodwill, than if all of its intangibles were patents?

(b) Suppose the president of Merck has come to you for advice. He has noted that by eliminating research and development expenditures the company could have reported $1.3 billion more in net income. He is frustrated because much of the research never results in a product, or the products take years to develop. He says shareholders are eager for higher returns, so he is considering eliminating research and development expenditures for at least a couple of years. What would you advise?

(c) The notes to Merck's financial statements note that Merck has goodwill of $1.1 billion. Where does recorded goodwill come from? Is it necessarily a good thing to have a lot of goodwill on your books?

Comparative Analysis Case

The Coca-Cola Company and PepsiCo, Inc.

Instructions

Go to the book's website and use information found there to answer the following questions related to The Coca-Cola Company and PepsiCo, Inc.

(a) (1) What amounts for intangible assets were reported in their respective balance sheets by Coca-Cola and PepsiCo?

(2) What percentage of total assets is each of these reported amounts?

(3) What was the change in the amount of intangibles from 2003 to 2004 for Coca-Cola and PepsiCo?

(b) (1) On what basis and over what periods of time did Coca-Cola and PepsiCo amortize their intangible assets?

(2) What were the amounts of accumulated amortization reported by Coca-Cola and PepsiCo at the end of 2004 and 2003?

(3) What was the composition of the identifiable and unidentifiable intangible assets reported by Coca-Cola and PepsiCo at the end of 2004?

Research Case

The online edition of the March 5, 2002, *Wall Street Journal* includes an article by John Carreyrou titled "Vivendi May Reveal Write-Down of Up to $13 Billion for Goodwill."

Instructions
Read the story and answer the following questions.

(a) **Vivendi** currently prepares its financial statements using French GAAP. As revealed in the story, how do French and U.S. GAAP differ in the accounting for goodwill impairments? Does the story reveal other areas in which U.S. and French GAAP differ? Explain.

(b) Why are some analysts warning against reading too much negativity into Vivendi's expected goodwill write-down? Do you agree? Explain.

(c) What measure of profitability is used in the media business? Explain how, if at all, this measure of profitability might be affected by Vivendi's changes in accounting, as discussed in the story.

International Reporting Case

Bayer, Glaxo SmithKline, and Merck

Presented below are data and accounting policy notes for the goodwill of three international drug companies. **Bayer**, a German company, prepares its statements in accordance with International Financial Reporting Standards (IFRS); **Glaxo SmithKline** follows United Kingdom (U.K.) rules; and **Merck**, a U.S. company, prepares its financial statements in accordance with U.S. GAAP.

Related Information	Bayer (€ millions)	Glaxo SmithKline (£ millions)	Merck ($ millions)
Research and development expense	2,107	2,839	4,010
Amortization expense	0	12	0
Net income	603	4,302	5,813
Accumulated goodwill amortization	0	84	0
Stockholders' equity	12,268	10,091	17,288

Both U.S. GAAP and IFRS do not allow amortization of goodwill. Under U.K. standards, goodwill is amortized over useful lives not to exceed 20 years.

Instructions

(a) Compute the return on equity for each of these companies, and use this analysis to briefly discuss the relative profitability of the three companies.

(b) Assume that each of the companies uses the maximum allowable amortization period for goodwill (if any). Discuss how these companies' goodwill amortization policies affect your ability to compare their amortization expense and income.

(c) Some analysts believe that the only valid way to compare companies that follow different goodwill accounting practices is to treat all goodwill as an asset and record expense only if the goodwill is impaired.* Using the data above, make these adjustments as appropriate, and compare the profitability of the three drug companies, comparing this information to your analysis in (a).

(d) IFRS requires that development costs must be capitalized if technical and commercial feasibility of the resulting product has been established. Assume that Bayer recorded € 1 million of development costs in the year reported above. Discuss briefly how this accounting affects your ability to compare the financial results of Bayer and Merck.

---

*Trevor Harris, *Apples to Apples: Accounting for Value in World Markets* (New York: Morgan Stanley Dean Witter, February 1998).

Professional Research: Financial Accounting and Reporting

Mills Company is contemplating the purchase of a smaller company, which is a distributor of Mills's products. Top management of Mills is convinced that the acquisition will result in significant synergies in its selling and distribution functions. The financial management group (of which you are a part) has been asked to prepare some analysis of the effects of the acquisition on the combined company's financial statements. This is the first acquisition for Mills, and some of the senior staff insist that based on their recollection of goodwill accounting, any goodwill recorded on the acquisition will result in a "drag" on future earnings for goodwill amortization. Other younger members on the staff argue that goodwill accounting has changed. Your supervisor asks you to research this issue.

Instructions

Using the **Financial Accounting Research System (FARS)**, respond to the following items. (Provide text strings used in your search.)

(a) Identify the accounting standard that addresses goodwill and other intangible assets. When was it issued? Might this explain the disagreement among the accounting staff? Explain.

(b) Define goodwill.

(c) Is goodwill subject to amortization? Explain.

(d) When goodwill is recognized by a subsidiary, should it be tested for impairment at the consolidated level or the subsidiary level? Discuss.

Professional Simulation

In this simulation you are asked to address questions related to intangible assets and similar costs. Prepare responses to all parts.

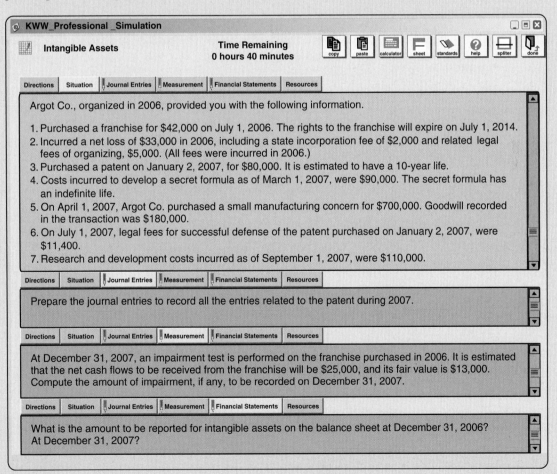

KWW_Professional _Simulation

Intangible Assets

Time Remaining
0 hours 40 minutes

copy | paste | calculator | sheet | standards | help | splitter | done

Directions | Situation | Journal Entries | Measurement | Financial Statements | Resources

Argot Co., organized in 2006, provided you with the following information.

1. Purchased a franchise for $42,000 on July 1, 2006. The rights to the franchise will expire on July 1, 2014.
2. Incurred a net loss of $33,000 in 2006, including a state incorporation fee of $2,000 and related legal fees of organizing, $5,000. (All fees were incurred in 2006.)
3. Purchased a patent on January 2, 2007, for $80,000. It is estimated to have a 10-year life.
4. Costs incurred to develop a secret formula as of March 1, 2007, were $90,000. The secret formula has an indefinite life.
5. On April 1, 2007, Argot Co. purchased a small manufacturing concern for $700,000. Goodwill recorded in the transaction was $180,000.
6. On July 1, 2007, legal fees for successful defense of the patent purchased on January 2, 2007, were $11,400.
7. Research and development costs incurred as of September 1, 2007, were $110,000.

Directions | Situation | Journal Entries | Measurement | Financial Statements | Resources

Prepare the journal entries to record all the entries related to the patent during 2007.

Directions | Situation | Journal Entries | Measurement | Financial Statements | Resources

At December 31, 2007, an impairment test is performed on the franchise purchased in 2006. It is estimated that the net cash flows to be received from the franchise will be $25,000, and its fair value is $13,000. Compute the amount of impairment, if any, to be recorded on December 31, 2007.

Directions | Situation | Journal Entries | Measurement | Financial Statements | Resources

What is the amount to be reported for intangible assets on the balance sheet at December 31, 2006? At December 31, 2007?

Remember to check the book's companion website to find additional resources for this chapter.

CURRENT LIABILITIES AND CONTINGENCIES

Now You See It, Now You Don't

A look at the liabilities side of the balance sheet of the German company **Beru AG Corporation**, dated March 31, 2003, shows how international standards are changing the reporting of financial information. Here is how one liability was shown on this date:

Anticipated losses arising from pending transactions   3,285,000 euros

Do you believe a liability should be reported for such transactions? *Anticipated losses* means the losses have not yet occurred; *pending transactions* mean that the condition that might cause the loss has also not occurred. So where is the liability? To whom does the company owe something? Where is the obligation?

U.S. GAAP provides guidance on this subject. A company can accrue a liability for a contingency only if an obligation has arisen from a past event, if payment is probable, and if the company can reasonably estimate the obligation. In short, under U.S. GAAP, companies cannot accrue anticipated future losses today.

German accounting rules are more permissive. They permit companies to report liabilities for possible future events. In essence, the establishment of this general-purpose "liability" provides a buffer for Beru if losses do materialize. If you take a more skeptical view, you might say the accounting rules let Beru smooth its income by charging expenses in good years and reducing expenses in bad years.

The story has a happy ending, from a U.S. accounting point of view. As we indicated earlier in the text, European companies switched to International Financial Reporting Standards (IFRS) in 2005. Because IFRS are similar to U.S. GAAP, liabilities like "Anticipated losses from pending transactions" disappear. So when we look at Beru's 2005 financial statements, we find a note stating that the company has reported as liabilities only obligations arising from past transactions that can be reasonably estimated.

Learning Objectives

After studying this chapter, you should be able to:

1 Describe the nature, type, and valuation of current liabilities.
2 Explain the classification issues of short-term debt expected to be refinanced.
3 Identify types of employee-related liabilities.
4 Identify the criteria used to account for and disclose gain and loss contingencies.
5 Explain the accounting for different types of loss contingencies.
6 Indicate how to present and analyze liabilities and contingencies.

As our opening story indicates, the convergence of U.S. GAAP with IFRS should lead to improved reporting of liabilities. In this chapter we explain the basic issues related to accounting and reporting for current and contingent liabilities. The content and organization of the chapter are as follows.

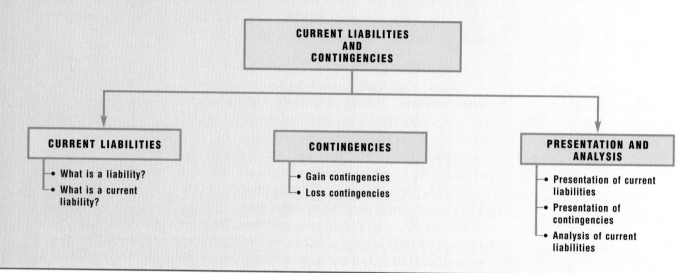

SECTION 1	*CURRENT LIABILITIES*

WHAT IS A LIABILITY?

UNDERLYING CONCEPTS

To determine the appropriate classification of specific financial instruments, companies need proper definitions of assets, liabilities, and equities. They often use the conceptual framework definitions as the basis for resolving controversial classification issues.

The question, "What is a liability?" is not easy to answer. For example, is preferred stock a liability or an ownership claim? The first reaction is to say that preferred stock is in fact an ownership claim, and companies should report it as part of stockholders' equity. In fact, preferred stock has many elements of debt as well.[1] The issuer (and in some cases the holder) often has the right to call the stock within a specific period of time—making it similar to a repayment of principal. The dividend on the preferred stock is in many cases almost guaranteed (the cumulative provision)—making it look like interest. As a result, preferred stock is but one of many financial instruments that are difficult to classify.[2]

To help resolve some of these controversies, the FASB, as part of its conceptual framework study, defined liabilities as **"probable future sacrifices of economic benefits arising from present obligations of a particular entity to transfer assets**

---

[1]This illustration is not just a theoretical exercise. In practice, a number of preferred stock issues have all the characteristics of a debt instrument, except that they are called and legally classified as preferred stock. In some cases, the IRS has even permitted companies to treat the dividend payments as interest expense for tax purposes.

[2]The FASB has issued a new standard for addressing this issue: "Accounting for Certain Financial Instruments with Characteristics of Both Liabilities and Equity," *Statement of Financial Accounting Standards No. 150* (Norwalk, Conn.: FASB, 2003).

or provide services to other entities in the future as a result of past transactions or events."[3] In other words, a liability has three essential characteristics:

1 It is a present obligation that entails settlement by probable future transfer or use of cash, goods, or services.

2 It is an unavoidable obligation.

3 The transaction or other event creating the obligation has already occurred.

Because liabilities involve future disbursements of assets or services, one of their most important features is the date on which they are payable. A company must satisfy currently maturing obligations in the ordinary course of business to continue operating. Liabilities with a more distant due date do not, as a rule, represent a claim on the company's current resources. They are therefore in a slightly different category. This feature gives rise to the basic division of liabilities into (1) current liabilities and (2) long-term debt.

WHAT IS A CURRENT LIABILITY?

Recall that current assets are cash or other assets that companies reasonably expect to convert into cash, sell, or consume in operations within a single operating cycle or within a year (if completing more than one cycle each year). **Current liabilities are "obligations whose liquidation is reasonably expected to require use of existing resources properly classified as current assets, or the creation of other current liabilities."**[4] This definition has gained wide acceptance because it recognizes operating cycles of varying lengths in different industries. This definition also considers the important relationship between current assets and current liabilities.[5]

The **operating cycle** is the period of time elapsing between the acquisition of goods and services involved in the manufacturing process and the final cash realization resulting from sales and subsequent collections. Industries that manufacture products requiring an aging process, and certain capital-intensive industries, have an operating cycle of considerably more than one year. On the other hand, most retail and service establishments have several operating cycles within a year.

Here are some typical current liabilities:

1 Accounts payable.

2 Notes payable.

3 Current maturities of long-term debt.

4 Short-term obligations expected to be refinanced.

5 Dividends payable.

6 Customer advances and deposits.

7 Unearned revenues.

8 Sales taxes payable.

9 Income taxes payable.

10 Employee-related liabilities.

> **OBJECTIVE 1**
> Describe the nature, type, and valuation of current liabilities.

Accounts Payable

Accounts payable, or **trade accounts payable**, are balances owed to others for goods, supplies, or services purchased on open account. Accounts payable arise because of the time lag between the receipt of services or acquisition of title to assets and the payment

---

[3]"Elements of Financial Statements of Business Enterprises," *Statement of Financial Accounting Concepts No. 6* (Stamford, Conn.: FASB, 1980).

[4]Committee on Accounting Procedure, American Institute of Certified Public Accountants, "Accounting Research and Terminology Bulletins," Final Edition (New York: AICPA, 1961), p. 21.

[5]The FASB affirmed this concept of "maturity within one year or the operating cycle whichever is longer" in its definition of short-term obligations in *Statement No. 6*. "Classification of Short-term Obligations Expected to Be Refinanced," *Statement of Financial Accounting Standards No. 6* (Stamford, Conn.: FASB, 1975), par. 2.

for them. The terms of the sale (e.g., 2/10, n/30 or 1/10, E.O.M.) usually state this period of extended credit, commonly 30 to 60 days.

Most companies record liabilities for purchases of goods upon receipt of the goods. If title has passed to the purchaser before receipt of the goods, the company should record the transaction at the time of title passage. A company must pay special attention to transactions occurring near the end of one accounting period and at the beginning of the next. It needs to ascertain that the record of goods received (the inventory) agrees with the liability (accounts payable), and that it records both in the proper period.

Measuring the amount of an account payable poses no particular difficulty. The invoice received from the creditor specifies the due date and the exact outlay in money that is necessary to settle the account. The only calculation that may be necessary concerns the amount of cash discount. See Chapter 8 for illustrations of entries related to accounts payable and purchase discounts.

Notes Payable

Notes payable are written promises to pay a certain sum of money on a specified future date. They may arise from purchases, financing, or other transactions. Some industries require notes (often referred to as **trade notes payable**) as part of the sales/purchases transaction in lieu of the normal extension of open account credit. Notes payable to banks or loan companies generally arise from cash loans. Companies classify notes as short-term or long-term, depending on the payment due date. Notes may also be interest-bearing or zero-interest-bearing.

Interest-Bearing Note Issued

Assume that Castle National Bank agrees to lend $100,000 on March 1, 2007, to Landscape Co. if Landscape signs a $100,000, 6 percent, four-month note. Landscape records the cash received on March 1 as follows:

March 1

Cash	100,000	
Notes Payable		100,000
(To record issuance of 6%, 4-month note to Castle National Bank)		

If Landscape prepares financial statements semiannually, it makes the following adjusting entry to recognize interest expense and interest payable of $2,000 ($100,000 × 6% × 4/12) at June 30:

June 30

Interest Expense	2,000	
Interest Payable		2,000
(To accrue interest for 4 months on Castle National Bank note)		

If Landscape prepares financial statements monthly, its adjusting entry at the end of each month is $500 ($100,000 × 6% × 1/12).

At maturity (July 1), Landscape must pay the face value of the note ($100,000) plus $2,000 interest ($100,000 × 6% × 4/12). Landscape records payment of the note and accrued interest as follows.

July 1

Notes Payable	100,000	
Interest Payable	2,000	
Cash		102,000
(To record payment of Castle National Bank interest-bearing note and accrued interest at maturity)		

Zero-Interest-Bearing Note Issued

A company may issue a zero-interest-bearing note instead of an interest-bearing note. A zero-interest-bearing note does not explicitly state an interest rate on the face of the note. **Interest is still charged**, however. At maturity the borrower must pay back an amount greater than the cash received at the issuance date. In other words, the borrower receives in cash the present value of the note. The present value equals the face value of the note at maturity minus the interest or discount charged by the lender for the term of the note. In essence, the bank takes its fee "up front" rather than on the date the note matures.

To illustrate, assume that Landscape issues a $102,000, four-month, zero-interest-bearing note to Castle National Bank. The present value of the note is $100,000.[6] Landscape records this transaction as follows.

March 1		
Cash	100,000	
Discount on Notes Payable	2,000	
Notes Payable		102,000
(To record issuance of 4-month, zero-interest-bearing		
note to Castle National Bank)		

Landscape credits the Notes Payable account for the face value of the note, which is $2,000 more than the actual cash received. It debits the difference between the cash received and the face value of the note to Discount on Notes Payable. **Discount on Notes Payable is a contra account to Notes Payable, and therefore is subtracted from Notes Payable on the balance sheet.** Illustration 13-1 shows the balance sheet presentation on March 1.

Current liabilities		
Notes payable	102,000	
Less: Discount on notes payable	2,000	100,000

ILLUSTRATION 13-1
Balance Sheet
Presentation of Discount

The amount of the discount, $2,000 in this case, represents the cost of borrowing $100,000 for 4 months. Accordingly, Landscape charges the discount to interest expense over the life of the note. That is, the Discount on Notes Payable balance **represents interest expense chargeable to future periods**. Thus, Landscape should not debit Interest Expense for $2,000 at the time of obtaining the loan. We discuss additional accounting issues related to notes payable in Chapter 14.

Current Maturities of Long-Term Debt

PepsiCo reports as part of its current liabilities the portion of bonds, mortgage notes, and other long-term indebtedness that matures within the next fiscal year. It categorizes this amount as **current maturities of long-term debt**. Companies, like PepsiCo, exclude long-term debts maturing currently as current liabilities if they are to be:

1 retired by assets accumulated for this purpose that properly have not been shown as current assets,

2 refinanced, or retired from the proceeds of a new debt issue, or

3 converted into capital stock.

In these situations, the use of current assets or the creation of other current liabilities does not occur. Therefore, classification as a current liability is inappropriate. A company should disclose the plan for liquidation of such a debt either parenthetically or by a note to the financial statements. When only a part of a long-term debt is to be

---

[6]The bank discount rate used in this example to find the present value is 5.96 percent.

paid within the next 12 months, as in the case of serial bonds that it retires through a series of annual installments, **the company reports the maturing portion of long-term debt as a current liability**, and the remaining portion as a long-term debt.

However, a company should classify as current any liability that is **due on demand** (callable by the creditor) or will be due on demand within a year (or operating cycle, if longer). Liabilities often become callable by the creditor when there is a violation of the debt agreement. For example, most debt agreements specify a given level of equity to debt be maintained, or specify that working capital be of a minimum amount. If the company violates an agreement, it must classify the debt as current because it is a reasonable expectation that existing working capital will be used to satisfy the debt. Only if a company can show that it is **probable** that it will cure (satisfy) the violation within the grace period specified in the agreements can it classify the debt as noncurrent.[7]

Short-Term Obligations Expected to Be Refinanced

OBJECTIVE 2
Explain the classification issues of short-term debt expected to be refinanced.

Short-term obligations are debts scheduled to mature within one year after the date of a company's balance sheet or within its operating cycle, whichever is longer. Some **short-term obligations** are **expected to be refinanced** on a long-term basis. These short-term obligations will not require the use of working capital during the next year (or operating cycle).[8]

At one time, the accounting profession generally supported the exclusion of short-term obligations from current liabilities if they were "expected to be refinanced." But the profession provided no specific guidelines, so companies determined whether a short-term obligation was "expected to be refinanced" based solely on management's **intent** to refinance on a long-term basis. Classification was not clear-cut. For example, a company might obtain a five-year bank loan but handle the actual financing with 90-day notes, which it must keep turning over (renewing). In this case, is the loan a long-term debt or a current liability? Another example was the **Penn Central Railroad** before it went bankrupt. The railroad was deep into short-term debt but classified it as long-term debt. Why? Because the railroad believed it had commitments from lenders to keep refinancing the short-term debt. When those commitments suddenly disappeared, it was "good-bye Pennsy." As the Greek philosopher Epictetus once said, "Some things in this world are not and yet appear to be."

Refinancing Criteria

To resolve these classification problems, the accounting profession has developed authoritative criteria for determining the circumstances under which short-term obligations may be properly excluded from current liabilities. A company is required to exclude a short-term obligation from current liabilities if **both** of the following conditions are met:

1 It must **intend to refinance** the obligation on a long-term basis.

2 It must **demonstrate an ability** to consummate the refinancing.[9]

Intention to refinance on a long-term basis means that the company intends to refinance the short-term obligation so that it will not require the use of working capital during the ensuing fiscal year (or operating cycle, if longer).

---

[7]"Classification of Obligations That Are Callable by the Creditor," *Statement of Financial Accounting Standards No. 78* (Stamford, Conn.: FASB, 1983).

[8]*Refinancing a short-term obligation on a long-term basis* means either replacing it with a long-term obligation or equity securities, or renewing, extending, or replacing it with short-term obligations for an uninterrupted period extending beyond one year (or the operating cycle, if longer) from the date of the enterprise's balance sheet.

[9]"Classification of Short-term Obligations Expected to Be Refinanced," *Statement of Financial Accounting Standards No. 6* (Stamford, Conn.: FASB, 1975), pars. 10 and 11.

The company demonstrates the **ability** to consummate the refinancing by:

(a) Actually refinancing the short-term obligation by issuing a long-term obligation or equity securities after the date of the balance sheet but before it is issued; or

(b) Entering into a **financing agreement** that clearly permits the company to refinance the debt on a long-term basis on terms that are readily determinable.

If an actual refinancing occurs, the portion of the short-term obligation to be excluded from current liabilities may not exceed the proceeds from the new obligation or equity securities used to retire the short-term obligation. For example, **Montavon Winery** had $3,000,000 of short-term debt. Subsequent to the balance sheet date, but before issuing the balance sheet, the company issued 100,000 shares of common stock, intending to use the proceeds to liquidate the short-term debt at its maturity. If Montavon's net proceeds from the sale of the 100,000 shares total $2,000,000, it can exclude from current liabilities only $2,000,000 of the short-term debt.

An additional question is whether a company should exclude from current liabilities a short-term obligation if it is paid off after the balance sheet date and replaced by long-term debt before the balance sheet is issued. To illustrate, Marquardt Company pays off short-term debt of $40,000 on January 17, 2008, and issues long-term debt of $100,000 on February 3, 2008. Marquardt's financial statements, dated December 31, 2007, are to be issued March 1, 2008. Should Marquardt exclude the $40,000 short-term debt from current liabilities? No—here's why: Repayment of the short-term obligation required the use of **existing** current assets **before** the company obtained funds through long-term financing. Therefore, Marquardt must include the short-term obligations in current liabilities at the balance sheet date (see graphical presentation below).

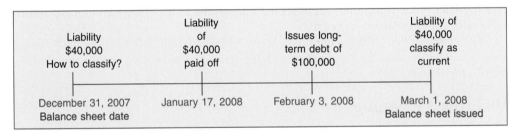

ILLUSTRATION 13-2
Short-Term Debt Paid Off after Balance Sheet Date and Later Replaced by Long-Term Debt

WHAT ABOUT THAT SHORT-TERM DEBT?

WHAT DO THE NUMBERS MEAN?

The evaluation of credit quality involves more than simply assessing a company's ability to repay loans. Credit analysts also evaluate debt management strategies. Analysts and investors will reward what they view as prudent management decisions with lower debt service costs and a higher stock price. The wrong decisions can bring higher debt costs and lower stock prices.

General Electric Capital Corp., a subsidiary of **General Electric**, recently experienced the negative effects of market scrutiny of its debt management policies. Analysts complained that GE had been slow to refinance its mountains of short-term debt. GE had issued these current obligations, with maturities of 270 days or less, when interest rates were low. However, in light of expectations that the Fed would raise interest rates, analysts began to worry about the higher interest costs GE would pay when it refinanced these loans. Some analysts recommended that it was time to reduce dependence on short-term credit. The reasoning goes that a shift to more dependable long-term debt, thereby locking in slightly higher rates for the long-term, is the better way to go.

Thus, scrutiny of GE debt strategies led to analysts' concerns about GE's earnings prospects. Investors took the analysis to heart, and GE experienced a 2-day 6 percent drop in its stock price.

Source: Adapted from Steven Vames, "Credit Quality, Stock Investing Seem to Go Hand in Hand," *Wall Street Journal* (April 1, 2002), p. R4.

Dividends Payable

A **cash dividend payable** is an amount owed by a corporation to its stockholders as a result of board of directors' authorization. At the date of declaration the corporation assumes a liability that places the stockholders in the position of creditors in the amount of dividends declared. Because companies always pay cash dividends within one year of declaration (generally within three months), they classify them as current liabilities.

On the other hand, companies do not recognize accumulated but undeclared dividends on cumulative preferred stock as a liability. Why? Because **preferred dividends in arrears** are not an obligation until the board of directors authorizes the payment. Nevertheless, companies should disclose the amount of cumulative dividends unpaid in a note, or show it parenthetically in the capital stock section.

Dividends payable in the form of additional shares of stock are not recognized as a liability. Such **stock dividends** (as we discuss in Chapter 15) do not require future outlays of assets or services. Companies generally report such undistributed stock dividends in the stockholders' equity section because they represent retained earnings in the process of transfer to paid-in capital.

Customer Advances and Deposits

Current liabilities may include **returnable cash deposits** received from customers and employees. Companies may receive deposits from customers to guarantee performance of a contract or service or as guarantees to cover payment of expected future obligations. For example, a company like **Alltel Corp.** often requires a deposit on equipment that customers use to connect to the Internet or to access its other services. Alltel also may receive deposits from customers as guarantees for possible damage to property. Additionally, some companies require their employees to make deposits for the return of keys or other company property.

The classification of these items as current or noncurrent liabilities depends on the time between the date of the deposit and the termination of the relationship that required the deposit.

Unearned Revenues

A magazine publisher, such as **Golf Digest**, receives payment when a customer subscribes to its magazines. An airline company, such as **American Airlines**, sells tickets for future flights. And software companies, like **Microsoft**, issue coupons that allow customers to upgrade to the next version of their software. How do these companies account for **unearned revenues** that they receive before delivering goods or rendering services?

1 Upon receipt of the advance, debit Cash, and credit a current liability account identifying the source of the unearned revenue.

2 Upon earning the revenue, debit the unearned revenue account, and credit an earned revenue account.

To illustrate, assume that Allstate University sells 10,000 season football tickets at $50 each for its five-game home schedule. Allstate University records the sales of season tickets as follows:

August 6

Cash	500,000	
Unearned Football Ticket Revenue		500,000
(To record sale of 10,000 season tickets)		

After each game, Allstate University makes the following entry.

September 7

Unearned Football Ticket Revenue	100,000	
Football Ticket Revenue		100,000
(To record football ticket revenues earned)		

Unearned Football Ticket Revenue is, therefore, unearned revenue. Allstate University reports it as a current liability in the balance sheet. As revenue is earned, a transfer from unearned revenue to earned revenue occurs. Unearned revenue is material for some companies: In the airline industry, tickets sold for future flights represent almost 50 percent of total current liabilities.

Illustration 13-3 shows specific unearned and earned revenue accounts used in selected types of businesses.

Type of Business	Account Title	
	Unearned Revenue	Earned Revenue
Airline	Unearned Passenger Ticket Revenue	Passenger Revenue
Magazine publisher	Unearned Subscription Revenue	Subscription Revenue
Hotel	Unearned Rental Revenue	Rental Revenue
Auto dealer	Unearned Warranty Revenue	Warranty Revenue
Retailers	Unearned Gift Card Revenue	Sales Revenue

ILLUSTRATION 13-3
Unearned and Earned Revenue Accounts

The balance sheet should report obligations for any commitments that are redeemable in goods and services. The income statement should report revenues earned during the period.

MICROSOFT'S LIABILITIES—GOOD OR BAD?

Users of financial statements generally examine current liabilities to assess a company's liquidity and overall financial flexibility. Companies must pay many current liabilities, such as accounts payable, wages payable, and taxes payable, sooner rather than later. A substantial increase in these liabilities should raise a red flag about a company's financial position.

This is not the case for all current liabilities. For example, **Microsoft** has a current liability entitled "Unearned revenue" that has increased substantially year after year. Unearned revenue is a liability that arises from sales of Microsoft products such as *Windows* and *Office*. At the time of a sale, customers pay not only for the current version of the software but also for future upgrades. Microsoft recognizes sales revenue from the current version of the software and records as a liability (unearned revenue) the value of future upgrades to the software that it "owes" to customers.

Market analysts read such an increase in unearned revenue as a positive signal about Microsoft's sales and profitability. When Microsoft's sales are growing, its unearned revenue account increases. Thus, an *increase* in a liability is good news about Microsoft sales. At the same time, a decline in unearned revenue is bad news. As one analyst noted, a slowdown or reversal of the growth in Microsoft's unearned revenues indicates slowing sales, which is bad news for investors. Thus, increases in current liabilities can sometimes be viewed as good signs instead of bad.

Source: Adapted from David Bank, "Some Fans Cool to Microsoft, Citing Drop in Old Indicator," *Wall Street Journal* (October 28, 1999).

WHAT DO THE NUMBERS MEAN?

Sales Taxes Payable

Retailers like **Wal-Mart**, **Circuit City**, and **Gap** must collect sales taxes from customers on transfers of tangible personal property and on certain services and then must remit these taxes to the proper governmental authority. GAP, for example, sets up a liability to provide for taxes collected from customers but not yet remitted to the tax authority. The Sales Taxes Payable account should reflect the liability for sales taxes due various governments.

The entry below illustrates use of the Sales Taxes Payable account on a sale of $3,000 when a 4 percent sales tax is in effect.

Cash or Accounts Receivable	3,120	
Sales		3,000
Sales Taxes Payable		120

Sometimes the sales tax collections credited to the liability account are not equal to the liability as computed by the governmental formula. In such a case, GAP makes an adjustment of the liability account by recognizing a gain or a loss on sales tax collections.

Many companies do not segregate the sales tax and the amount of the sale at the time of sale. Instead, the company credits both amounts in total in the Sales account. Then, to reflect correctly the actual amount of sales and the liability for sales taxes, the company would debit the Sales account for the amount of the sales taxes due the government on these sales, and would credit the Sales Taxes Payable account for the same amount.

To illustrate, assume that the Sales account balance of $150,000 includes sales taxes of 4 percent. Thus, the amount recorded in the Sales account is comprised of the sales amount plus sales tax of 4 percent of the sales amount. Sales therefore are $144,230.77 ($150,000 ÷ 1.04) and the sales tax liability is $5,769.23 ($144,230.77 × 0.04; or $150,000 − $144,230.77). The following entry would record the amount due the taxing unit.

Sales	5,769.23	
Sales Taxes Payable		5,769.23

Income Taxes Payable

Expanded Discussion of Property Taxes Payable

Any federal or state income tax varies in proportion to the amount of annual income. Using the best information and advice available, a business must prepare an income tax return and compute the income tax payable resulting from the operations of the current period. Corporations should classify as a current liability the taxes payable on net income, as computed per the tax return.[10] Unlike a corporation, proprietorships and partnerships are not taxable entities. Because the individual proprietor and the members of a partnership are subject to personal income taxes on their share of the business's taxable income, income tax liabilities do not appear on the financial statements of proprietorships and partnerships.

Most corporations must make periodic tax payments throughout the year in an authorized bank depository or a Federal Reserve Bank. These payments are based upon estimates of the total annual tax liability. As the estimated total tax liability changes, the periodic contributions also change. If in a later year the taxing authority assesses an additional tax on the income of an earlier year, the company should credit Income Taxes Payable and charge the related debit to current operations.

Differences between taxable income under the tax laws and accounting income under generally accepted accounting principles sometimes occur. Because of these differences, the amount of income tax payable to the government in any given year may differ substantially from income tax expense as reported on the financial statements. Chapter 19 is devoted solely to income tax matters and presents an extensive discussion of this complex topic.

Employee-Related Liabilities

OBJECTIVE 3
Identify types of employee-related liabilities.

Companies also report as a current liability amounts owed to employees for salaries or wages at the end of an accounting period. In addition, they often also report as current liabilities the following items related to employee compensation.

---

[10]Corporate taxes are based on a progressive tax rate structure. Companies with taxable income of $50,000 or less are taxed at a 15 percent rate; higher levels of income are taxed at rates ranging up to 39 percent.

1 Payroll deductions.

2 Compensated absences.

3 Bonuses. (Accounting for bonuses is covered in Appendix 13A.)

Payroll Deductions

The most common types of payroll deductions are taxes, insurance premiums, employee savings, and union dues. **To the extent that a company has not remitted the amounts deducted to the proper authority at the end of the accounting period, it should recognize them as current liabilities.**

Social Security Taxes. Since January 1, 1937, Social Security legislation has provided federal old age, survivor, and disability insurance (O.A.S.D.I.) benefits for certain individuals and their families. Funds for these payments come from taxes levied on both the employer and the employee. Employers collect the employee's share of this tax by deducting it from the employee's gross pay, and remit it to the government along with their share. The government taxes both the employer and the employee at the same rate, currently 6.2 percent based on the employee's gross pay up to a $90,000 annual limit. The O.A.S.D.I. tax is usually referred to as F.I.C.A. (the Federal Insurance Contribution Act).

In 1965 Congress passed the first federal health insurance program for the aged—popularly known as **Medicare**. This two-part program alleviates the high cost of medical care for those over age 65. A separate Hospital Insurance tax, paid by both the employee and the employer at the rate of 1.45 percent on the employee's total compensation, finances the Basic Plan, which provides hospital and other institutional services. The Voluntary Plan covers the major part of doctors' bills and other medical and health services. Monthly payments from all who enroll, plus matching funds from the federal government, finance this plan.

The combination of the O.A.S.D.I. tax (F.I.C.A.) and the federal Hospital Insurance Tax is commonly referred to as the **Social Security tax**. The combined rate for these taxes, 7.65 percent on an employee's wages to $90,000 and 1.45 percent in excess of $90,000, changes intermittently by acts of Congress. **Companies should report the amount of unremitted employee and employer Social Security tax on gross wages paid as a current liability.**

Unemployment Taxes. Another payroll tax levied by the federal government in cooperation with state governments provides a system of unemployment insurance. All employers who meet the following criteria are subject to the Federal Unemployment Tax Act (F.U.T.A.): (1) those who paid wages of $1,500 or more during any calendar quarter in the year or preceding year, or (2) those who employed at least one individual on at least one day in each of 20 weeks during the current or preceding calendar year.

Only employers pay the unemployment tax. The rate of this tax is 6.2 percent on the first $7,000 of compensation paid to each employee during the calendar year. The employer receives a tax credit not to exceed 5.4 percent for contributions paid to a state plan for unemployment compensation. Thus, if an employer is subject to a state unemployment tax of 5.4 percent or more, it pays only 0.8 percent tax to the federal government.

State unemployment compensation laws differ both from the federal law and among various states. Therefore, employers must refer to the unemployment tax laws in each state in which they pay wages and salaries. The normal state tax may range from 3 percent to 7 percent or higher. However, all states provide for some form of **merit rating**, which reduces the state contribution rate. Employers who display by their benefit and contribution experience that they provide steady employment may receive this reduction—if the size of the state fund is adequate. In order not to penalize an employer who has earned a reduction in the state contribution rate, federal law allows a credit of 5.4 percent, even when the effective state contribution rate is less than 5.4 percent.

To illustrate, Appliance Repair Co. has a taxable payroll of $100,000. It is subject to a federal rate of 6.2 percent and a state contribution rate of 5.7 percent. However, its stable employment experience reduces the company's state rate to 1 percent. Appliance Repair computes its federal and state unemployment taxes as shown in Illustration 13-4.

ILLUSTRATION 13-4
Computation of
Unemployment Taxes

State unemployment tax payment (1% × $100,000)	$1,000
Federal unemployment tax [(6.2% − 5.4%) × $100,000]	800
Total federal and state unemployment tax	$1,800

Companies pay federal unemployment tax quarterly, and file a tax form annually. Companies also generally pay state contributions quarterly as well. Because both the federal and the state unemployment taxes accrue on earned compensation, companies should record the amount of accrued but unpaid employer contributions **as an operating expense and as a current liability when preparing financial statements at year-end**.

Income Tax Withholding. Federal and some state income tax laws require employers to withhold from each employee's pay the applicable income tax due on those wages. The employer computes the amount of income tax to withhold according to a government-prescribed formula or withholding tax table. That amount depends on the length of the pay period and each employee's taxable wages, marital status, and claimed dependents. If the income tax withheld plus the employee and the employer Social Security taxes exceeds specified amounts per month, the employer must make remittances to the government during the month. Illustration 13-5 summarizes payroll deductions and liabilities.

ILLUSTRATION 13-5
Summary of Payroll
Liabilities

Item	Who Pays	
Income tax withholding FICA taxes—employee share Union dues	Employee	Employer reports these amounts as liabilities until remitted.
FICA taxes—employer share Federal unemployment State unemployment	Employer	

Payroll Deductions Example. Assume a weekly payroll of $10,000 entirely subject to F.I.C.A. and Medicare (7.65%), federal (0.8%) and state (4%) unemployment taxes, with income tax withholding of $1,320 and union dues of $88 deducted. The company records the wages and salaries paid and the **employee payroll deductions** as follows:

Wages and Salaries Expense	10,000	
Withholding Taxes Payable		1,320
F.I.C.A. Taxes Payable		765
Union Dues Payable to Local No. 257		88
Cash		7,827

It records the **employer payroll taxes** as follows:

Payroll Tax Expense	1,245	
F.I.C.A. Taxes Payable		765
Federal Unemployment Tax Payable		80
State Unemployment Tax Payable		400

The employer must remit to the government its share of F.I.C.A. tax along with the amount of F.I.C.A. tax deducted from each employee's gross compensation. It should record all unremitted employer F.I.C.A. taxes as payroll tax expense and payroll tax payable.[11]

Compensated Absences

Compensated absences are paid absences from employment—such as vacation, illness, and holidays. Companies should accrue a liability for the cost of compensation for future absences if **all of the following conditions** exist.[12]

(a) The employer's obligation relating to employees' rights to receive compensation for future absences is attributable to employees' services **already rendered**.

(b) The obligation relates to the rights that **vest or accumulate**. *→ carry over if not used*

(c) Payment of the compensation is **probable**.

(d) The amount can be **reasonably estimated**.[13]

UNDERLYING CONCEPTS

When these four conditions exist, all elements in the definition of a liability exist. In addition, the matching concept requires that the company report the expense for the services in the same period as the revenue was generated.

Illustration 13-6 shows an example of an accrual for compensated absences, in an excerpt from the balance sheet of **Clarcor Inc.**

Clarcor Inc.

Current liabilities	
Accounts payable	$ 6,308
Accrued salaries, wages and commissions	2,278
Compensated absences	2,271
Accrued pension liabilities	1,023
Other accrued liabilities	4,572
	$16,452

ILLUSTRATION 13-6
Balance Sheet Presentation of Accrual for Compensated Absences

If an employer meets conditions (a), (b), and (c) but does not accrue a liability because of a failure to meet condition (d), it should disclose that fact. Illustration 13-7 (on page 630) shows an example of such a disclosure, in a note from the financial statements of **Gotham Utility Company**.

---

[11]A manufacturing company allocates all of the payroll costs (wages, payroll taxes, and fringe benefits) to appropriate cost accounts such as Direct Labor, Indirect Labor, Sales Salaries, Administrative Salaries, and the like. This abbreviated and somewhat simplified discussion of payroll costs and deductions is not indicative of the volume of records and clerical work that may be involved in maintaining a sound and accurate payroll system.

[12]"Accounting for Compensated Absences," *Statement of Financial Accounting Standards No. 43* (Stamford, Conn.: FASB, 1980), par. 6.

[13]*FASB Statement No. 112*, "Employers' Accounting for Postemployment Benefits," requires that companies apply these same four conditions to **postemployment benefits**. "Employers' Accounting for Postemployment Benefits," *Statement of Financial Accounting Standards No. 112* (Norwalk, Conn.: FASB, November 1992), par. 18. Companies provide **postemployment benefits** to past or inactive employees **after employment but prior to retirement**. Examples include salary continuation, supplemental unemployment benefits, severance pay, job training, and continuation of health and life insurance coverage.

ILLUSTRATION 13-7
Disclosure of Policy
for Compensated
Absences

Gotham Utility Company

Employees of the Company are entitled to paid vacation, personal, and sick days off, depending on job status, length of service, and other factors. Due to numerous differing union contracts and other agreements with nonunion employees, it is impractical to estimate the amount of compensation for future absences, and, accordingly, no liability has been reported in the accompanying financial statements. The Company's policy is to recognize the cost of compensated absences when actually paid to employees; compensated absence payments to employees totaled $2,786,000.

The following considerations are relevant to the accounting for compensated absences.

Vested rights exist when an employer has an obligation to make payment to an employee even after terminating his or her employment. Thus, vested rights are not contingent on an employee's future service. **Accumulated rights** are those that employees can carry forward to future periods if not used in the period in which earned. For example, assume that you earn four days of vacation pay as of December 31, the end of your employer's fiscal year. Company policy is that you will be paid for this vacation time even if you terminate employment. In this situation, your four days of vacation pay are vested, and your employer must accrue the amount.

Now assume that your vacation days are not vested, but that you can carry the four days over into later periods. Although the rights are not vested, they are accumulated rights for which the employer must make an accrual. However, the amount of the accrual is adjusted to allow for estimated forfeitures due to turnover.

A modification of the general rules relates to the issue of **sick pay**. If sick pay benefits vest, a company must accrue them. If sick pay benefits accumulate but do not vest, a company may choose whether to accrue them. Why this distinction? Companies may administer compensation designated as sick pay in one of two ways. In some companies, employees receive sick pay only if illness causes their absence. Therefore, these companies may or may not accrue a liability because its payment depends on future employee illness. Other companies allow employees to accumulate unused sick pay and take compensated time off from work even when not ill. For this type of sick pay, a company must accrue a liability because the company will pay it, regardless of whether employees become ill.

Companies should recognize the expense and related liability for compensated absences in the year earned by employees. For example, if new employees receive rights to two weeks' paid vacation at the beginning of their second year of employment, a company considers the vacation pay to be earned during the first year of employment.

What rate should a company use to accrue the compensated absence cost—the current rate or an estimated future rate? *FASB Statement No. 43* is silent on this subject. Therefore, companies will likely use the current rather than future rate. The future rate is less certain and raises time value of money issues. To illustrate, assume that Amutron Inc. began operations on January 1, 2006. The company employs 10 individuals and pays each $480 per week. Employees earned 20 unused vacation weeks in 2006. In 2007, the employees used the vacation weeks, but now they each earn $540 per week. Amutron accrues the accumulated vacation pay on December 31, 2006, as follows.

Wages Expense	9,600	
Vacation Wages Payable ($480 × 20)		9,600

At December 31, 2006, the company reports on its balance sheet a liability of $9,600. In 2007, it records the payment of vacation pay as follows.

Vacation Wages Payable	9,600	
Wages Expense	1,200	
Cash ($540 × 20)		10,800

In 2007 the use of the vacation weeks extinguishes the liability. Note that Amutron records the difference between the amount of cash paid and the reduction in the liability account as an adjustment to Wages Expense in the period when paid. This difference arises because it accrues the liability account at the rates of pay in effect during the period when employees *earned* the compensated time. The cash paid, however, depends on the rates in effect during the period when employees *used* the compensated time. If Amutron used the future rates of pay to compute the accrual in 2006, then the cash paid in 2007 would equal the liability.[14]

Bonus Agreements

Many companies give a **bonus** to certain or all employees in addition to their regular salaries or wages. Frequently the bonus amount depends on the company's yearly profit. For example, employees at **Ford Motor Company** share in the success of the company's operations on the basis of a complicated formula using net income as its primary basis for computation. A company may consider **bonus payments to employees** as additional wages and should include them as a deduction in determining the net income for the year.

To illustrate the entries for an employee bonus, assume that Palmer Inc. shows income for the year 2007 of $100,000. It will pay out bonuses of $10,700 in January 2008. Palmer makes an adjusting entry dated December 31, 2007, to record the bonuses as follows.

Employees' Bonus Expense	10,700	
Profit-Sharing Bonus Payable		10,700

In January 2008, when Palmer pays the bonus, it makes this journal entry:

Profit-Sharing Bonus Payable	10,700	
Cash		10,700

INTERNATIONAL INSIGHT

In Japan, companies do not treat bonuses to members of the board of directors and to the Commercial Code auditors as expenses. Instead, they consider such bonuses to be a distribution of profits and charge them against retained earnings.

Palmer should show the expense account in the income statement as an operating expense. **The liability, Profit-Sharing Bonus Payable, is usually payable within a short period of time. Companies should include it as a current liability in the balance sheet.** Similar to bonus agreements are contractual agreements for **conditional expenses**. Examples would be agreements covering rents or royalty payments conditional on the amount of revenues earned or the quantity of product produced or extracted. Conditional expenses based on revenues or units produced are usually less difficult to compute than bonus arrangements.

For example, assume that a lease calls for a fixed rent payment of $500 per month and 1 percent of all sales over $300,000 per year. The company's annual rent obligation would amount to $6,000 plus $0.01 of each dollar of revenue over $300,000. Or, a royalty agreement may give to a patent owner $1 for every ton of product resulting from the patented process, or give to a mineral rights owner $0.50 on every barrel of oil extracted. As the company produces or extracts each additional unit of product, it creates an additional obligation, usually a current liability.

CONTINGENCIES	SECTION 2

Companies often are involved in situations where uncertainty exists about whether an obligation to transfer cash or other assets has arisen and/or the amount that will be required to settle the obligation. For example:

- **Merck** may be a defendant in a lawsuit, and any payment is contingent upon the outcome of a settlement or an administrative or court proceeding.

---

[14]Some companies have obligations for benefits paid to employees after they retire. The accounting and reporting standards for postretirement benefit payments are complex. These standards relate to two different types of **postretirement benefits**: (1) pensions, and (2) postretirement health care and life insurance benefits. We discuss these issues extensively in Chapter 20.

- **Ford Motor Co.** provides a warranty for a car it sells, and any payments are contingent on the number of cars that qualify for benefits under the warranty.
- **Briggs & Stratton** acts as a guarantor on a loan for another entity, and any payment is contingent on whether the other entity defaults.

Broadly, these situations are called contingencies. A **contingency** is "an existing condition, situation, or set of circumstances involving uncertainty as to possible gain **(gain contingency)** or loss **(loss contingency)** to an enterprise that will ultimately be resolved when one or more future events occur or fail to occur."[15]

GAIN CONTINGENCIES

OBJECTIVE 4
Identify the criteria used to account for and disclose gain and loss contingencies.

Gain contingencies are claims or rights to receive assets (or have a liability reduced) whose existence is uncertain but which may become valid eventually. The typical gain contingencies are:

1 Possible receipts of monies from gifts, donations, bonuses, and so on.
2 Possible refunds from the government in tax disputes.
3 Pending court cases with a probable favorable outcome.
4 Tax loss carryforwards (discussed in Chapter 19).

Companies follow a conservative policy in this area. Except for tax loss carryforwards, they do not record gain contingencies. A company discloses gain contingencies in the notes only when a high probability exists for realizing them. As a result, it is unusual to find information about contingent gains in the financial statements and the accompanying notes. Illustration 13-8 presents an example of a disclosure gain contingency.

ILLUSTRATION 13-8
Disclosure of Gain
Contingency

BMC Industries, Inc.

Note 13: Legal Matters.   In the first quarter, a U.S. District Court in Miami, Florida, awarded the Company a $5.1 million judgment against **Barth Industries** (Barth) of Cleveland, Ohio and its parent, **Nesco Holdings, Inc.** (Nesco). The judgment relates to an agreement under which Barth and Nesco were to help automate the plastic lens production plant in Fort Lauderdale, Florida. The Company has not recorded any income relating to this judgment because Barth and Nesco have filed an appeal.

LOSS CONTINGENCIES

Loss contingencies involve possible losses. A liability incurred as a result of a loss contingency is by definition a contingent liability. **Contingent liabilities** depend on the occurrence of one or more future events to confirm either the amount payable, the payee, the date payable, or its existence. That is, these factors depend on a contingency.

When a loss contingency exists, the likelihood that the future event or events will confirm the incurrence of a liability can range from probable to remote. The FASB uses the terms **probable**, **reasonably possible**, and **remote** to identify three areas within that range and assigns the following meanings.

Probable. The future event or events are likely to occur.

Reasonably possible. The chance of the future event or events occurring is more than remote but less than likely.

Remote. The chance of the future event or events occurring is slight.

[15]"Accounting for Contingencies," *Statement of Financial Accounting Standards No. 5* (Stamford, Conn.: FASB, 1975), par. 1. According to *Accounting Trends and Techniques—2004*, the most common gain contingencies are related to operating loss carryforwards and other tax credits. The most common loss contingencies are related to litigation, environmental, and insurance losses.

Companies should accrue an estimated loss from a loss contingency by a charge to expense and a liability recorded only if **both** of the following conditions are met.[16]

1 Information available prior to the issuance of the financial statements indicates that it is **probable that a liability has been incurred** at the date of the financial statements.

2 The amount of the loss can be **reasonably estimated**.

To record a liability, a company does not need to know the exact payee nor the exact date payable. **What a company must know is whether it is probable that it incurred a liability.**

To meet the second criterion, a company needs to be able to reasonably determine an amount for the liability. To determine a reasonable estimate of the liability, a company may use its own experience, experience of other companies in the industry, engineering or research studies, legal advice, or educated guesses by qualified personnel. Illustration 13-9 shows an accrual recorded for a loss contingency, from the annual report of **Quaker State Oil Refining Company**.

Quaker State Oil Refining Company

Note 5: Contingencies. During the period from November 13 to December 23, a change in an additive component purchased from one of its suppliers caused certain oil refined and shipped to fail to meet the Company's low-temperature performance requirements. The Company has recalled this product and has arranged for reimbursement to its customers and the ultimate consumers of all costs associated with the product. Estimated cost of the recall program, net of estimated third party reimbursement, in the amount of $3,500,000 has been charged to current operations.

ILLUSTRATION 13-9
Disclosure of Accrual for Loss Contingency

Use of the terms probable, reasonably possible, and remote to classify contingencies involves judgment and subjectivity. Illustration 13-10 lists examples of loss contingencies and the general accounting treatment accorded them.

ILLUSTRATION 13-10
Accounting Treatment of Loss Contingencies

Usually Accrued

  Loss Related to:

  1. Collectibility of receivables
  2. Obligations related to product warranties and product defects
  3. Premiums offered to customers

Not Accrued

  Loss Related to:

  4. Risk of loss or damage of enterprise property by fire, explosion, or other hazards
  5. General or unspecified business risks
  6. Risk of loss from catastrophes assumed by property and casualty insurance companies, including reinsurance companies

May Be Accrued*

  Loss Related to:

  7. Threat of expropriation of assets
  8. Pending or threatened litigation
  9. Actual or possible claims and assessments**
  10. Guarantees of indebtedness of others
  11. Obligations of commercial banks under "standby letters of credit"
  12. Agreements to repurchase receivables (or the related property) that have been sold

  *Should be accrued when both criteria—probable and reasonably estimable—are met.
  **Estimated amounts of losses incurred prior to the balance sheet date but settled subsequently should be accrued as of the balance sheet date.

[16]We discuss loss contingencies that result in the incurrence of a liability in this chapter. We discuss loss contingencies that result in the impairment of an asset (e.g., collectibility of receivables or threat of expropriation of assets) in other sections of this textbook.

Practicing accountants express concern over the diversity that now exists in the interpretation of "probable," "reasonably possible," and "remote." Current practice relies heavily on the exact language used in responses received from lawyers (such language is necessarily biased and protective rather than predictive). As a result, accruals and disclosures of contingencies vary considerably in practice. Some of the more common loss contingencies are:[17]

1 Litigation, claims, and assessments.
2 Guarantee and warranty costs.
3 Premiums and coupons.
4 Environmental liabilities.

As discussed in the opening story, companies do not record or report in the notes to the financial statements general risk contingencies inherent in business operations (e.g., the possibility of war, strike, uninsurable catastrophes, or a business recession).

Litigation, Claims, and Assessments

OBJECTIVE 5
Explain the accounting for different types of loss contingencies.

Companies must consider the following factors, among others, in determining whether to record a liability with respect to **pending or threatened litigation** and actual or possible **claims** and **assessments**.

1 The **time period** in which the underlying cause of action occurred.
2 The **probability** of an unfavorable outcome.
3 The ability to make a **reasonable estimate** of the amount of loss.

To report a loss and a liability in the financial statements, **the cause for litigation must have occurred on or before the date of the financial statements**. It does not matter that the company became aware of the existence or possibility of the lawsuit or claims after the date of the financial statements but before issuing them. To evaluate the probability of an unfavorable outcome, a company considers the following: the nature of the litigation; the progress of the case; the opinion of legal counsel; its own and others' experience in similar cases; and any management response to the lawsuit.

Companies can seldom predict the outcome of pending litigation, however, with any assurance. And, even if evidence available at the balance sheet date does not favor the company, it is hardly reasonable to expect the company to publish in its financial statements a dollar estimate of the probable negative outcome. Such specific disclosures might weaken the company's position in the dispute and encourage the plaintiff to intensify its efforts. A typical example of the wording of such a disclosure is the note to the financial statements of **Apple Computer, Inc.**, relating to its litigation concerning repetitive stress injuries, as shown in Illustration 13-11.

ILLUSTRATION 13-11
Disclosure of Litigation

Apple Computer, Inc.

"Repetitive Stress Injury" Litigation.   The Company is named in numerous lawsuits (fewer than 100) alleging that the plaintiff incurred so-called "repetitive stress injury" to the upper extremities as a result of using keyboards and/or mouse input devices sold by the Company. On October 4, in a trial of one of these cases (*Dorsey v. Apple*) in the United States District Court for the Eastern District of New York, the jury rendered a verdict in favor of the Company, and final judgment in favor of the Company has been entered. The other cases are in various stages of pretrial activity. These suits are similar to those filed against other major suppliers of personal computers. Ultimate resolution of the litigation against the Company may depend on progress in resolving this type of litigation in the industry overall.

---

[17]*Accounting Trends and Techniques—2004* reports that of the 600 companies surveyed, companies report loss contingencies for the following: litigation, 506; environmental, 245; insurance, 122; governmental investigation, 94; possible tax assessments, 76; and others, 47.

With respect to **unfiled suits** and **unasserted claims and assessments**, a company must determine (1) the degree of **probability** that a suit may be filed or a claim or assessment may be asserted, and (2) the **probability** of an unfavorable outcome. For example, assume that the Federal Trade Commission investigates the Nawtee Company for restraint of trade, and institutes enforcement proceedings. Private claims of triple damages for redress often follow such proceedings. In this case, Nawtee must determine the probability of the claims being asserted **and** the probability of triple damages being awarded. If both are probable, if the loss is reasonably estimable, and if the cause for action is dated on or before the date of the financial statements, then Nawtee should accrue the liability.[18]

Guarantee and Warranty Costs

A **warranty (product guarantee)** is a promise made by a seller to a buyer to make good on a deficiency of quantity, quality, or performance in a product. Manufacturers commonly use it as a sales promotion technique. Automakers, for instance, "hyped" their sales by extending their new-car warranty to seven years or 100,000 miles. For a specified period of time following the date of sale to the consumer, the manufacturer may promise to bear all or part of the cost of replacing defective parts, to perform any necessary repairs or servicing without charge, to refund the purchase price, or even to "double your money back."

Warranties and guarantees entail future costs. These additional costs, sometimes called "after costs" or "post-sale costs," frequently are significant. Although the future cost is indefinite as to amount, due date, and even customer, a liability is probable in most cases. Companies should recognize this liability in the accounts if they can reasonably estimate it. The estimated amount of the liability includes all the costs that the company will incur after sale and delivery and that are incident to the correction of defects or deficiencies required under the warranty provisions. Warranty costs are a classic example of a loss contingency.

Companies use two basic methods of accounting for warranty costs: (1) the cash-basis method and (2) the accrual method.

Cash Basis

Under the **cash-basis method**, companies expense warranty costs as incurred. In other words, a **seller or manufacturer charges warranty costs to the period in which it complies with the warranty**. The company does not record a liability for future costs arising from warranties, nor does it charge the period of sale. Companies frequently justify use of this method, the only one recognized for income tax purposes, on the basis of expediency when warranty costs are immaterial or when the warranty period is relatively short. A company must use the cash-basis method when it does not accrue a warranty liability in the year of sale either because:

1 it is not probable that a liability has been incurred, or
2 it cannot reasonably estimate the amount of the liability.

Accrual Basis

If it is probable that customers will make warranty claims and a company can reasonably estimate the costs involved, the company must use the accrual method. Under the **accrual method**, companies charge warranty costs to operating expense **in the year of sale**. The accrual method is the generally accepted method. Companies should use it whenever the warranty is an integral and inseparable part of the sale and is viewed as a loss contingency. We refer to this approach as the **expense warranty approach**.

---

[18]Companies need not disclose contingencies involving an unasserted claim or assessment when no claimant has come forward unless (1) it is considered probable that a claim will be asserted, and (2) there is a reasonable possibility that the outcome will be unfavorable.

Example of Expense Warranty Approach. To illustrate the expense warranty method, assume that Denson Machinery Company begins production on a new machine in July 2006, and sells 100 units at $5,000 each by its year-end, December 31, 2006. Each machine is under warranty for one year. Denson estimates, based on past experience with a similar machine, that the warranty cost will average $200 per unit. Further, as a result of parts replacements and services rendered in compliance with machinery warranties, it incurs $4,000 in warranty costs in 2006 and $16,000 in 2007.

1 Sale of 100 machines at $5,000 each, July through December 2006:

Cash or Accounts Receivable	500,000	
Sales		500,000

2 Recognition of warranty expense, July through December 2006:

Warranty Expense	4,000	
Cash, Inventory, Accrued Payroll		4,000
(Warranty costs incurred)		
Warranty Expense	16,000	
Estimated Liability under Warranties		16,000
(To accrue estimated warranty costs)		

The December 31, 2006, balance sheet reports "Estimated liability under warranties" as a current liability of $16,000, and the income statement for 2006 reports "Warranty expense" of $20,000.

3 Recognition of warranty costs incurred in 2007 (on 2006 machinery sales):

Estimated Liability under Warranties	16,000	
Cash, Inventory, or Accrued Payroll		16,000
(Warranty costs incurred)		

If Denson Machinery applies the cash-basis method, it reports $4,000 as warranty expense in 2006 and $16,000 as warranty expense in 2007. It records all of the sale price as revenue in 2006. In many instances, application of the cash-basis method fails to match the warranty costs relating to the products sold during a given period with the revenues derived from such products. As such, **it violates the matching principle**. Where ongoing warranty policies exist year after year, the differences between the cash and the expense warranty bases probably would not be so great.

Sales-Warranty Approach. A warranty is sometimes **sold separately from the product**. For example, when you purchase a television set or DVD player, you are entitled to the manufacturer's warranty. You also will undoubtedly be offered an extended warranty on the product at an additional cost.[19]

In this case, the seller should recognize separately the sale of the television or DVD player, with the manufacturer's warranty and the sale of the extended warranty.[20] This approach is referred to as the **sales-warranty approach**. **Companies defer revenue on the sale of the extended warranty** and generally recognize it on a straight-line basis over the life of the contract. The seller of the warranty defers revenue because it has an obligation to perform services over the life of the contract. The seller should only defer and amortize costs that vary with and are directly related to the sale of the contracts (mainly commissions). It expenses those costs, such as employees' salaries, advertising, and general and administrative expenses that it would have incurred even if it did not sell a contract.

---

[19]A company separately prices a contract **if the customer has the option to purchase** the services provided under the contract for an expressly stated amount separate from the price of the product. An extended warranty or product maintenance contract usually meets these conditions.

[20]"Accounting for Separately Extended Warranty and Product Maintenance Contracts," *FASB Technical Bulletin No. 90–1* (Stamford, Conn.: FASB, 1990).

To illustrate, assume you purchase a new automobile from Hanlin Auto for $20,000. In addition to the regular warranty on the auto (the manufacturer will pay for all repairs for the first 36,000 miles or three years, whichever comes first), you purchase at a cost of $600 an extended warranty that protects you for an additional three years or 36,000 miles. Hanlin Auto records the sale of the automobile (with the regular warranty) and the sale of the extended warranty on January 2, 2006, as follows:

Cash	20,600	
Sales		20,000
Unearned Warranty Revenue		600

It recognizes revenue at the end of the fourth year (using straight-line amortization) as follows.

Unearned Warranty Revenue	200	
Warranty Revenue		200

Because the extended warranty contract only starts after the regular warranty expires, Hanlin Auto defers revenue recognition until the fourth year. If it incurs the costs of performing services under the extended warranty contract on other than a straight-line basis (as historical evidence might indicate), Hanlin Auto should recognize revenue over the contract period in proportion to the costs it expected to incur in performing services under the contract.[21]

Premiums and Coupons

Numerous companies offer premiums (either on a limited or continuing basis) to customers in return for boxtops, certificates, coupons, labels, or wrappers. The **premium** may be silverware, dishes, a small appliance, a toy, or free transportation. Also, **printed coupons** that can be redeemed for a cash discount on items purchased are extremely popular.[22] A more recent marketing innovation is the **cash rebate**, which the buyer can obtain by returning the store receipt, a rebate coupon, and Universal Product Code (UPC label) or "bar code" to the manufacturer.

Companies offer premiums, coupon offers, and rebates to stimulate sales. Thus companies should charge the **costs of premiums and coupons to expense in the period of the sale** that benefits from the plan. The period that benefits is not necessarily the period in which the company offered the premium. At the end of the accounting period many premium offers may be outstanding and must be redeemed when presented in subsequent periods. In order to reflect the existing current liability and to match costs with revenues, the company estimates the number of outstanding premium offers that customers will present for redemption. The company then charges the cost of premium offers to Premium Expense. It credits the outstanding obligations to an account titled Estimated Liability for Premiums.

The following example illustrates the accounting treatment for a premium offer. Fluffy Cakemix Company offered its customers a large nonbreakable mixing bowl in exchange for 25 cents and 10 boxtops. The mixing bowl costs Fluffy Cakemix Company 75 cents, and the company estimates that customers will redeem 60 percent of

UNDERLYING CONCEPTS

Warranties and coupons are loss contingencies that satisfy the conditions necessary for a liability. Regarding the income statement, the *matching principle* requires that companies report the related expense in the period in which the sale occurs.

---

[21]Ibid, par. 3. The FASB recently issued additional disclosure requirements for warranties. A company must disclose its accounting policy and the method used to determine its warranty liability, and must present a tabular reconciliation of the changes in the product warranty liability. *FASB Interpretation No. 45*, "Guarantor's Accounting and Disclosure Requirements for Guarantees, Including Indirect Guarantees of Indebtedness of Others" (Norwalk, Conn.: FASB, 2002).

[22]Approximately 4 percent of coupons are redeemed. Redeemed coupons eventually make their way to the corporate headquarters of the stores that accept them. From there they are shipped to clearinghouses operated by **A. C. Nielsen Company** (of TV-rating fame) that count them and report back to the manufacturers who, in turn, reimburse the stores.

the boxtops. The premium offer began in June 2007 and resulted in the transactions journalized below. Fluffy Cakemix Company records purchase of 20,000 mixing bowls at 75 cents as follows.

Inventory of Premium Mixing Bowls	15,000	
Cash		15,000

The entry to record sales of 300,000 boxes of cake mix at 80 cents would be:

Cash	240,000	
Sales		240,000

Fluffy records the actual redemption of 60,000 boxtops, the receipt of 25 cents per 10 boxtops, and the delivery of the mixing bowls as follows.

Cash [(60,000 ÷ 10) × $0.25]	1,500	
Premium Expense	3,000	
Inventory of Premium Mixing Bowls		4,500
Computation: (60,000 ÷ 10) × $0.75 = $4,500		

Finally, Fluffy makes an end-of-period adjusting entry for estimated liability for outstanding premium offers (boxtops) as follows.

Premium Expense	6,000	
Estimated Liability for Premiums		6,000
Computation:		
Total boxtops sold in 2007	300,000	
Total estimated redemptions (60%)	180,000	
Boxtops redeemed in 2007	60,000	
Estimated future redemptions	120,000	
Cost of estimated claims outstanding		
(120,000 ÷ 10) × ($0.75 − $0.25) = $6,000		

The December 31, 2007, balance sheet of Fluffy Cakemix Company reports an "Inventory of premium mixing bowls" of $10,500 as a current asset and "Estimated liability for premiums" of $6,000 as a current liability. The 2007 income statement reports a $9,000 "Premium expense" among the selling expenses.

Environmental Liabilities

Estimates to clean up existing toxic waste sites total upward of $752 billion over a 30-year period. In addition, cost estimates of cleaning up our air and preventing future deterioration of the environment run even higher. The average environmental cost per company for various industries at one time was: high-tech companies, $2 million (6.1% of revenues); utilities, $340 million (6.1% of revenues); steel and metals, $50 million (2.9% of revenues), and oil companies, $430 million (1.9% of revenues).

These costs will only grow when considering "Superfund legislation." This federal legislation provides the Environmental Protection Agency (EPA) with the power to clean up waste sites and charge the clean-up costs to parties the EPA deems responsible for contaminating the site. These potentially responsible parties can have a significant liability.

In many industries, the construction and operation of long-lived assets involves obligations for the retirement of those assets. When a mining company opens up a strip mine, it may also commit to restore the land once it completes mining. Similarly, when an oil company erects an offshore drilling platform, it may be legally obligated to dismantle and remove the platform at the end of its useful life.

Accounting Recognition of Asset Retirement Obligations

A company must recognize an **asset retirement obligation (ARO)** when it has an existing legal obligation associated with the retirement of a long-lived asset and when it can reasonably estimate the amount of the liability. Companies should record the ARO at fair value.[23]

Obligating Events. Examples of existing legal obligations, which require recognition of a liability include, but are not limited to:

- decommissioning nuclear facilities,
- dismantling, restoring, and reclamation of oil and gas properties,
- certain closure, reclamation, and removal costs of mining facilities,
- closure and post-closure costs of landfills.

In order to capture the benefits of these long-lived assets, **the company is generally legally obligated for the costs associated with retirement of the asset, whether the company hires another party to perform the retirement activities or performs the activities with its own workforce and equipment**. AROs give rise to various recognition patterns. For example, the obligation may arise at the outset of the asset's use (e.g., erection of an oil-rig), or it may build over time (e.g., a landfill that expands over time).

Measurement. A company initially measures an ARO at fair value, which is defined as the amount that the company would pay in an active market to settle the ARO. While active markets do not exist for many AROs, companies should estimate fair value based on the best information available. Such information could include market prices of similar liabilities, if available. Alternatively, companies may use present value techniques to estimate fair value.

Recognition and Allocation. To record an ARO in the financial statements, a company includes the cost associated with the ARO in the carrying amount of the related long-lived asset, and records a liability for the same amount. It records an asset retirement cost as part of the related asset because these costs are tied to operating the asset and are necessary to prepare the asset for its intended use. Therefore, the specific asset (e.g., mine, drilling platform, nuclear power plant) should be increased because the future economic benefit comes from the use of this productive asset. **Companies should not**

---

[23]"Accounting for Asset Retirement Obligations," *Statement of Financial Accounting Standards No. 143* (Norwalk, Conn.: FASB, 2001).

record the capitalized asset retirement costs in a separate account because there is no future economic benefit that can be associated with these costs alone.

In subsequent periods, companies allocate the cost of the ARO to expense over the period of the related asset's useful life. Companies may use the straight-line method for this allocation, as well as other systematic and rational allocations.

Example of ARO Accounting Provisions. To illustrate the accounting for AROs, assume that on January 1, 2006, Wildcat Oil Company erected an oil platform in the Gulf of Mexico. Wildcat is legally required to dismantle and remove the platform at the end of its useful life, estimated to be five years. Wildcat estimates that dismantling and removal will cost $1,000,000. Based on a 10 percent discount rate, the present value of the asset retirement obligation is $620,920 ($1,000,000 × .62092). Wildcat records this ARO as follows.

January 1, 2006

Drilling Platform	620,920	
Asset Retirement Obligation		620,920

During the life of the asset, Wildcat allocates the asset retirement cost to expense. Using the straight-line method, Wildcat makes the following entries to record this expense.

December 31, 2006, 2007, 2008, 2009, 2010

Depreciation Expense ($620,920 ÷ 5)	124,184	
Accumulated Depreciation		124,184

In addition, Wildcat must accrue interest expense each period. Wildcat records interest expense and the related increase in the asset retirement obligation on December 31, 2006, as follows.

December 31, 2006

Interest Expense ($620,920 × 10%)	62,092	
Asset Retirement Obligation		62,092

On January 10, 2011, Wildcat contracts with Rig Reclaimers, Inc. to dismantle the platform at a contract price of $995,000. Wildcat makes the following journal entry to record settlement of the ARO.

January 10, 2011

Asset Retirement Obligation	1,000,000	
Gain on Settlement of ARO		5,000
Cash		995,000

Companies need to provide more extensive disclosure regarding environmental liabilities. In addition, companies should record more of these liabilities. The SEC believes that companies should not delay recognition of a liability due to significant uncertainty. The SEC argues that if the liability is within a range, and no amount within the range is the best estimate, then management should recognize the minimum amount of the range. That treatment is in accordance with *FASB Interpretation No. 14*, "Reasonable Estimation of the Amount of a Loss." The SEC also believes that companies should report environmental liabilities in the balance sheet independent of recoveries from third parties. Thus, companies may not net possible insurance recoveries against liabilities but must show them separately. Because there is much litigation regarding recovery of insurance proceeds, these "assets" appear to be gain contingencies. Therefore, companies should not be report these on the balance sheet.[24]

---

[24]As we indicated earlier, the FASB requires that, when some amount within the range appears at the time to be a better estimate than any other amount within the range, a company accrues that amount. When no amount within the range is a better estimate than any other amount, the company **accrues** the dollar amount at the low end of the range and **discloses** the dollar amount at the high end of the range. Unfortunately, in many cases, zero may arguably be the low point of the range, resulting in no liability being recognized. See *FASB Interpretation No. 14*, "Reasonable Estimation of the Amount of a Loss" (Stamford, Conn.: FASB, 1976), par. 3, and *FASB Statement No. 5*, "Accounting for Contingencies" (Stamford, Conn.: FASB, 1975).

MORE DISCLOSURE PLEASE

WHAT DO THE NUMBERS MEAN?

On November 19, 2001, Enron filed its third-quarter financial statements and reported on its balance sheet debt of approximately $13 billion. Yet on the same day, at a meeting to discuss its liquidity crisis, Enron informed its bankers that its debt was approximately $38 billion. Company officers described the difference of $25 billion as being either off-balance-sheet or on the balance sheet other than debt.

As a result of the Enron bankruptcy and other financial reporting scandals, Congress passed the Sarbanes-Oxley Act of 2002. One of its provisions mandates that the Securities and Exchange Commission conduct a study to determine the extent of off-balance-sheet transactions occurring in U.S. businesses.

Table 1 below indicates the extent of disclosure and recognition of contingent liabilities. The study classified contingent liabilities into three categories (1) litigation contingent liabilities, (2) environmental liabilities, and (3) guarantees. The statistics provided relate to reports filed by 10,100 companies listed on the U.S. stock exchanges in 2005.

Table 1

Type of Contingency	Companies Disclosing	Companies Recording
Litigation contingent liabilities	46.3%	5.1%
Environmental contingent liabilities	10.2%	5.1%
Guarantees	35.4%	10.2%

As Table 1 indicates, approximately 46 percent of companies disclosed litigation contingent liabilities, but only 5.1 percent recorded any liability related to these contingencies. On the other hand, 35 percent of the companies disclosed guarantees but a third of these companies (10.2 percent) recorded a liability for these contingencies.

Table 2 below shows the dollar amounts of the contingent liabilities companies disclosed and recorded.

Table 2

Type of Contingency	Companies Disclosing ($ millions)	Companies Recording ($ millions)
Litigation contingent liabilities	$52,354	$11,814
Environmental contingent liabilities	$23,414	$18,723
Guarantees	$46,535,399	$123,949

Table 2 indicates that companies disclosed litigation contingent liabilities of approximately $52 billion, but recorded only $11.8 billion as liabilities. Incredibly, companies disclosed more than *$46 trillion* of guarantees, a small fraction of which (just $124 billion) they recorded as liabilities.

The results of this study suggest that the FASB must continue to address the issue of contingencies to ensure that companies provide relevant and reliable information for these types of financial events.

Source: "Report and Recommendations Pursuant to Section 401(c) of the Sarbanes-Oxley Act of 2002 on Arrangements with Off-Balance Sheet Implications, Special Purpose Entities, and Transparency of Filings by Issuers," United States Securities and Exchange Commission, Office of Chief Accountant, Office of Economic Analyses, Division of Corporation Finance (June 2005).

Self-Insurance

As discussed earlier, contingencies are not recorded for general risks (e.g., losses that might arise due to poor expected economic conditions.) Similarly, companies do not record contingencies for more specific future risks such as allowances for repairs. The reason: These items do meet the definition of a liability because they do not arise from a past transaction but instead relate to future events.

Some companies take out insurance policies against the potential losses from fire, flood, storm, and accident. Other companies do not. The reasons: Some risks are not

UNDERLYING CONCEPTS

Even if companies can estimate the amount of losses with a high degree of certainty, the losses are not liabilities because they result from a future event and not from a past event.

insurable, the insurance rates are prohibitive (e.g., earthquakes and riots), or they make a business decision to self-insure. Self-insurance is another item that is not recognized as a contingency.

Despite its name, **self-insurance** is **not insurance, but risk assumption**. Any company that assumes its own risks puts itself in the position of incurring expenses or losses as they occur. There is little theoretical justification for the establishment of a liability based on a hypothetical charge to insurance expense. This is "as if" accounting. The conditions for accrual stated in *FASB Statement No. 5* are not satisfied prior to the occurrence of the event. Until that time there is no diminution in the value of the property. And unlike an insurance company, which has contractual obligations to reimburse policyholders for losses, a company can have no such obligation to itself and, hence, no liability either before or after the occurrence of damage.[25]

The note shown in Illustration 13-12 from the annual report of **Adolph Coors Company** is typical of the self-insurance disclosure.

ILLUSTRATION 13-12
Disclosure of Self-Insurance

Adolph Coors Company

Notes to Financial Statements

Note 4: Commitments and Contingencies. It is generally the policy of the Company to act as a self-insurer for certain insurable risks consisting primarily of physical loss to corporate property, business interruption resulting from such loss, employee health insurance programs, and workers' compensation. Losses and claims are accrued as incurred.

Exposure to **risks of loss resulting from uninsured past injury to others**, however, is an existing condition involving uncertainty about the amount and timing of losses that may develop. In such a case, a contingency exists. A company with a fleet of vehicles for example, would have to accrue uninsured losses resulting from injury to others or damage to the property of others that took place prior to the date of the financial statements (if the experience of the company or other information enables it to make a reasonable estimate of the liability). However, it should not establish a liability for **expected future injury** to others or damage to the property of others, even if it can reasonably estimate the amount of losses.

SECTION 3	*PRESENTATION AND ANALYSIS*

Presentation of Current Liabilities

OBJECTIVE 6
Indicate how to present and analyze liabilities and contingencies.

In practice, current liabilities are usually recorded and reported in financial statements at their full maturity value. Because of the short time periods involved, frequently less than one year, the difference between the present value of a current liability and the maturity value is usually not large. The profession accepts as immaterial any slight overstatement of liabilities that results from carrying current liabilities at maturity value.[26]

---

[25]"Accounting for Contingencies," *FASB Statement No. 5*, op. cit., par. 28. A commentary in *Forbes* (June 15, 1974), p. 42, stated its position on this matter quite succinctly: "The simple and unquestionable fact of life is this: Business is cyclical and full of unexpected surprises. Is it the role of accounting to disguise this unpleasant fact and create a fairyland of smoothly rising earnings? Or, should accounting reflect reality, warts and all—floods, expropriations and all manner of rude shocks?"

[26]"Interest on Receivables and Payables," *Opinions of the Accounting Principles Board No. 21* (New York: AICPA, 1971), par. 3. *APB Opinion No. 21* specifically exempts from present value measurements those payables arising from transactions with suppliers in the normal course of business that do not exceed approximately one year.

The current liabilities accounts are commonly presented as the first classification in the liabilities and stockholders' equity section of the balance sheet. Within the current liabilities section, companies may list the accounts in order of maturity, in descending order of amount, or in order of liquidation preference. Illustration 13-13 presents an excerpt of **Best Buy Company**'s financial statements that is representative of the reports of large corporations.

Best Buy Co. (dollars in thousands)	Feb. 26, 2005	Feb. 28, 2004
Current assets		
Cash and cash equivalents	$ 470	$ 245
Short-term investments	2,878	2,355
Receivables	375	343
Merchandise inventories	2,851	2,607
Other current assets	329	174
Total current assets	$6,903	$5,724
Current liabilities		
Accounts payable	$2,824	$2,460
Unredeemed gift card liabilities	410	300
Accrued compensation and related expenses	234	269
Accrued liabilities	844	724
Accrued income taxes	575	380
Current portion of long-term debt	72	368
Total current liabilities	$4,959	$4,501

ILLUSTRATION 13-13
Balance Sheet
Presentation of Current
Liabilities

Additional Disclosures of Current Liabilities

Detail and supplemental information concerning current liabilities should be sufficient to meet the requirement of full disclosure. Companies should clearly identify secured liabilities, as well as indicate the related assets pledged as collateral. If the due date of any liability can be extended, a company should disclose the details. Companies should not offset current liabilities against assets that it will apply to their liquidation. Finally, current maturities of long-term debt are classified as current liabilities.

A major exception exists when a company will pay a currently maturing obligation from assets classified as long-term. For example, if a company will retire a bond payable using a bond sinking fund that is classified as a long-term asset, it should report the bonds payable in the long-term liabilities section. Presentation of this debt in the current liabilities section would distort the working capital position of the enterprise.

If a company excludes a short-term obligation from current liabilities because of refinancing, it should include the following in the note to the financial statements:

1 A general description of the financing agreement.
2 The terms of any new obligation incurred or to be incurred.
3 The terms of any equity security issued or to be issued.

When a company expects to refinance on a long-term basis by issuing equity securities, it is not appropriate to include the short-term obligation in stockholders' equity. At the date of the balance sheet, the obligation is a liability and not stockholders' equity. Illustration 13-14 (on page 644) shows the disclosure requirements for an actual refinancing situation.

ILLUSTRATION 13-14
Actual Refinancing of
Short-Term Debt

	December 31, 2006
Current liabilities	
Accounts payable	$ 3,600,000
Accrued payables	2,500,000
Income taxes payable	1,100,000
Current portion of long-term debt	1,000,000
Total current liabilities	$ 8,200,000
Long-term debt	
Notes payable refinanced in January 2007 (Note 1)	$ 2,000,000
11% bonds due serially through 2017	15,000,000
Total long-term debt	$17,000,000

Note 1: On January 19, 2007, the Company issued 50,000 shares of common stock and received proceeds totaling $2,385,000, of which $2,000,000 was used to liquidate notes payable that matured on February 1, 2007. Accordingly, such notes payable have been classified as long-term debt at December 31, 2006.

Presentation of Contingencies

Additional Disclosures of Contingencies

A company records a loss contingency and a liability if the loss is both probable and estimable. But, if the loss is **either probable or estimable but not both**, and if there is at least a **reasonable possibility** that a company may have incurred a liability, it must disclose the following in the notes.

1 The nature of the contingency.

2 An estimate of the possible loss or range of loss or a statement that an estimate cannot be made.

Illustration 13-15 presents an extensive litigation disclosure note from the financial statements of **Raymark Corporation**. The note indicates that Raymark charged actual losses to operations and that a further liability may exist, but that the company cannot currently estimate this liability.

ILLUSTRATION 13-15
Disclosure of Loss
Contingency through
Litigation

Raymark Corporation

Note I: Litigation. Raymark is a defendant or co-defendant in a substantial number of lawsuits alleging wrongful injury and/or death from exposure to asbestos fibers in the air. The following table summarizes the activity in these lawsuits:

Claims	
Pending at beginning of year	8,719
Received during year	4,494
Settled or otherwise disposed of	(1,445)
Pending at end of year	11,768
Average indemnification cost	$3,364
Average cost per case, including defense costs	$6,499
Trial activity	
Verdicts for the Company	23
Total trials	36

The following table presents the cost of defending asbestos litigation, together with related insurance and workers' compensation expenses.

Included in operating profit	$ 1,872,000
Nonoperating expense	9,077,000
Total	$10,949,000

The Company is seeking to reasonably determine its liability. However, it is not possible to predict which theory of insurance will apply, the number of lawsuits still to be filed, the cost of settling and defending the existing and unfiled cases, or the ultimate impact of these lawsuits on the Company's consolidated financial statements.

Companies should disclose certain other contingent liabilities, even though the possibility of loss may be remote, as follows.

1 Guarantees of indebtedness of others.

2 Obligations of commercial banks under "stand-by letters of credit."

3 Guarantees to repurchase receivables (or any related property) that have been sold or assigned.

Disclosure should include the nature and amount of the guarantee and, if estimable, the amount that the company can recover from outside parties.[27] **Cities Service Company** disclosed its guarantees of others' indebtedness in the following note.

Cities Service Company

Note 10: Contingent Liabilities. The Company and certain subsidiaries have guaranteed debt obligations of approximately $62 million of companies in which substantial stock investments are held. Also, under long-term agreements with certain pipeline companies in which stock interests are held, the Company and its subsidiaries have agreed to provide minimum revenue for product shipments. The Company has guaranteed mortgage debt ($80 million) incurred by a 50 percent owned tanker affiliate for construction of tankers which are under long-term charter contracts to the Company and others. It is not anticipated that any loss will result from any of the above described agreements.

ILLUSTRATION 13-16
Disclosure of Guarantees of Indebtedness

Analysis of Current Liabilities

The distinction between current liabilities and long-term debt is important. It provides information about the liquidity of the company. Liquidity regarding a liability is the expected time to elapse before its payment. In other words, a liability soon to be paid is a current liability. A liquid company is better able to withstand a financial downturn. Also, it has a better chance of taking advantage of investment opportunities that develop.

Analysts use certain basic ratios such as net cash flow provided by operating activities to current liabilities, and the turnover ratios for receivables and inventory, to assess liquidity. Two other ratios used to examine liquidity are the current ratio and the acid-test ratio.

Current Ratio

The **current ratio** is the ratio of total current assets to total current liabilities. Illustration 13-17 shows its formula.

$$\text{Current ratio} = \frac{\text{Current assets}}{\text{Current liabilities}}$$

ILLUSTRATION 13-17
Formula for Current Ratio

The ratio is frequently expressed as a coverage of so many times. Sometimes it is called the **working capital ratio** because working capital is the excess of current assets over current liabilities.

---

[27]As discussed earlier (footnote 21), the FASB recently issued additional disclosure and recognition requirements for guarantees. The interpretation responds to confusion about the application of *SFAS No. 5* to guarantees used in certain transactions. The new rules expand existing disclosure requirements for most guarantees, including loan guarantees such as standby letters of credit. It also will result in companies recognizing more liabilities at fair value for the obligations assumed under a guarantee (*FASB Interpretation No. 45*, op. cit.).

A satisfactory current ratio does not disclose that a portion of the current assets may be tied up in slow-moving inventories. With inventories, especially raw materials and work in process, there is a question of how long it will take to transform them into the finished product and what ultimately will be realized in the sale of the merchandise. Eliminating the inventories, along with any prepaid expenses, from the amount of current assets might provide better information for short-term creditors. Therefore, some analysts use the acid-test ratio in place of the current ratio.

Acid-Test Ratio

Many analysts favor an **acid-test** or **quick ratio** that relates total current liabilities to cash, marketable securities, and receivables. Illustration 13-18 shows the formula for this ratio. As you can see, the acid-test ratio does not include inventories.

ILLUSTRATION 13-18
Formula for Acid-Test
Ratio

$$\text{Acid-test ratio} = \frac{\text{Cash} + \text{Short-term investments} + \text{Net receivables}}{\text{Current liabilities}}$$

To illustrate the computation of these two ratios, we use the information for **Best Buy Co.** in Illustration 13-13 (on page 643). Illustration 13-19 shows the computation of the current and acid-test ratios for Best Buy.

ILLUSTRATION 13-19
Computation of Current
and Acid-Test Ratios for
Best Buy Co.

$$\text{Current ratio} = \frac{\text{Current assets}}{\text{Current liabilities}} = \frac{\$6,903}{\$4,959} = 1.39 \text{ times}$$

$$\text{Acid-test ratio} = \frac{\text{Cash} + \text{Short-term investments} + \text{Net receivables}}{\text{Current liabilities}} = \frac{\$3,723}{\$4,959} = 0.75 \text{ times}$$

From this information, it appears that Best Buy's current position is adequate. However, the acid-test ratio is well below 1. A comparison to another retailer, **Circuit City**, whose current ratio is 2.13 and whose acid-test ratio is 0.75, indicates that Best Buy is carrying less inventory than its industry counterparts.

KEY TERMS

accumulated rights, 630

acid-test (quick) ratio, 646

assessments, 634

asset retirement
   obligation, 639

bonus, 631

cash dividend payable,
   624

claims, 634

compensated absences,
   629

contingency, 632

contingent liabilities, 632

current liabilities, 619

current maturities of
   long-term debt, 621

current ratio, 645

SUMMARY OF LEARNING OBJECTIVES

1. **Describe the nature, type, and valuation of current liabilities.** Current liabilities are obligations whose liquidation a company reasonably expects to require the use of current assets or the creation of other current liabilities. Theoretically, liabilities should be measured by the present value of the future outlay of cash required to liquidate them. In practice, companies usually record and report current liabilities at their full maturity value.

There are several types of current liabilities, such as: (1) accounts payable, (2) notes payable, (3) current maturities of long-term debt, (4) dividends payable, (5) customer advances and deposits, (6) unearned revenues, (7) taxes payable, and (8) employee-related liabilities.

2. **Explain the classification issues of short-term debt expected to be refinanced.** A short-term obligation is excluded from current liabilities if both of the following conditions are met: (1) the company must intend to refinance the obligation on a long-term basis, *and* (2) it must demonstrate an ability to consummate the refinancing.

3. **Identify types of employee-related liabilities.** The employee-related liabilities are: (1) payroll deductions, (2) compensated absences, and (3) bonus agreements.

4. **Identify the criteria used to account for and disclose gain and loss contingencies.** Gain contingencies are not recorded. Instead, they are disclosed in the notes only when the probabilities are high that a gain contingency will occur. A company should accrue an estimated loss from a loss contingency by charging expense and recording a liability only if *both* of the following conditions are met: (1) Information available prior to the issuance of the financial statements indicates that it is probable that a liability has been incurred at the date of the financial statements, and (2) the amount of the loss can be reasonably estimated.

5. **Explain the accounting for different types of loss contingencies.** The following factors must be considered in determining whether to record a liability with respect to pending or threatened litigation and actual or possible claims and assessments: (1) the time period in which the underlying cause for action occurred; (2) the probability of an unfavorable outcome; and (3) the ability to reasonably estimate the amount of loss.

If it is probable that customers will make claims under warranties relating to goods or services that have been sold and it can reasonably estimate the costs involved, the company uses the accrual method. It charges warranty costs under the accrual basis to operating expense in the year of sale.

Premiums, coupon offers, and rebates are made to stimulate sales. Companies should charge their costs to expense in the period of the sale that benefits from the premium plan.

A company must recognize asset retirement obligations when it has an existing legal obligation related to the retirement of a long-lived asset and it can reasonably estimate the amount.

6. **Indicate how to present and analyze liabilities and contingencies.** The current liability accounts are usually presented as the first classification in the liabilities and stockholders' equity section of the balance sheet. Within the current liabilities section, companies may list the accounts in order of maturity, in descending order of amount, or in order of liquidation preference. Detail and supplemental information concerning current liabilities should be sufficient to meet the requirement of full disclosure. If the loss is either probable or estimable but not both, and if there is at least a reasonable possibility that a company may have incurred a liability, it should disclose in the notes both the nature of the contingency and an estimate of the possible loss. Two ratios used to analyze liquidity are the current and acid-test ratios.

expense warranty approach, *635*
gain contingencies, *632*
liabilities, *618*
litigation, claims, and assessments, *634*
loss contingencies, *632*
notes payable (trade notes payable), *620*
operating cycle, *619*
preferred dividends in arrears, *624*
premiums, *637*
probable (contingency), *632*
reasonably possible (contingency), *632*
remote (contingency), *632*
returnable cash deposits, *624*
sales-warranty approach, *636*
self-insurance, *642*
short-term obligations expected to be refinanced, *622*
Social Security tax, *627*
trade accounts payable, *619*
trade notes payable, *620*
unearned revenues, *624*
vested rights, *630*
warranty, *635*
working capital ratio, *645*

APPENDIX 13A

Computation of Employees' Bonuses

Computing the amount of employee bonus based on income can be complex. For example, assume that Senbet Company has income of $100,000 before considering the bonus expense. According to the terms of the bonus agreement, Senbet is to set aside 20 percent of its income for distribution to employees. If the bonus were not itself an expense to be deducted in determining net income, the amount of the bonus could be computed very simply as 20 percent of the $100,000 income before bonus.

OBJECTIVE 7
Compute employee bonuses under differing arrangements.

However, the bonus itself is an expense that Senbet must deduct to determine the amount of income on which the bonus is to be based. Hence, the figure on which the bonus is to be computed is $100,000 reduced by the bonus. That is, the bonus is equal to 20 percent of $100,000 less the bonus. Stated algebraically:

$$B = 0.20 (\$100,000 - B)$$
$$B = \$20,000 - 0.2B$$
$$1.2B = \$20,000$$
$$B = \$16,666.67$$

A similar problem results from the relationship of bonus payments to income taxes. Again, assume income of $100,000 computed without subtracting either the employees' bonus or income taxes. The bonus is to be based on income **after deducting income taxes but before deducting the bonus**. The rate of income tax is 40 percent, and the 20 percent bonus is a deductible expense for tax purposes. The bonus therefore equals 20 percent of $100,000 minus the tax; the tax equals 40 percent of $100,000 minus the bonus. Thus we have two simultaneous equations. By using B as the symbol for the bonus and T for the tax, we can state the equations algebraically as follows.

$$B = 0.20(\$100,000 - T)$$
$$T = 0.40 (\$100,000 - B)$$

We can solve these equations by substituting the value of T as indicated in the second equation for T in the first equation:

$$B = 0.20[\$100,000 - 0.40(\$100,000 - B)]$$
$$B = 0.20(\$100,000 - \$40,000 + 0.4B)$$
$$B = 0.20(\$60,000 + 0.4B)$$
$$B = \$12,000 + 0.08B$$
$$0.92B = \$12,000$$
$$B = \$13,043.48$$

Substituting this value for B into the second equation allows us to solve for T:

$$T = 0.40 (\$100,000 - \$13,043.48)$$
$$T = 0.40 (\$86,956.52)$$
$$T = \$34,782.61$$

To prove these amounts, we work both back into the original equation:

$$B = 0.20 (\$100,000 - T)$$
$$\$13,043.48 = 0.20 (\$100,000 - \$34,782.61)$$
$$\$13,043.48 = 0.20 (\$65,217.39)$$
$$\$13,043.48 = \$13,043.48$$

If the terms of the agreement provide for deducting both the tax and the bonus to arrive at the income figure on which to compute the bonus, the equations would be:

$$B = 0.20 (\$100,000 - B - T)$$
$$T = 0.40 (\$100,000 - B)$$

Substituting the value of T from the second equation into the first equation enables us to solve for B:

$$B = 0.20 [\$100,000 - B - 0.40 (\$100,000 - B)]$$
$$B = 0.20 (\$100,000 - B - \$40,000 + 0.4B)$$
$$B = 0.20 (\$60,000 - 0.6B)$$
$$B = \$12,000 - 0.12B$$
$$1.12B = \$12,000$$
$$B = \$10,714.29$$

We then substitute the value for B into the second equation above, and solve that equation for T:

$$T = 0.40 (\$100,000 - \$10,714.29)$$
$$T = 0.40 (\$89,285.71)$$
$$T = \$35,714.28$$

If we then substitute these values into the original bonus equation, we prove them as follows.

$$
\begin{aligned}
B &= 0.20\,(\$100{,}000 - B - T) \\
\$10{,}714.29 &= 0.20\,(\$100{,}000 - \$10{,}714.29 - \$35{,}714.28) \\
\$10{,}714.29 &= 0.20\,(\$53{,}571.43) \\
\$10{,}714.29 &= \$10{,}714.29
\end{aligned}
$$

Drawing up a legal document such as a bonus agreement is a task for a lawyer, not an accountant. However, accountants are frequently called on to express an opinion on the agreement's feasibility. In this respect, one should always insist that the agreement state specifically whether income taxes and the bonus itself are expenses deductible in determining income for purposes of the bonus computation.

SUMMARY OF LEARNING OBJECTIVE FOR APPENDIX 13A

7. Compute employee bonuses under differing arrangements. If the bonus is based on net income and is deductible in determining net income, it may have to be determined algebraically. Its computation is made more difficult by the bonus being deductible for tax purposes and the taxes being deductible from the income on which the bonus is based.

Note: All **asterisked** Brief Exercises, Exercises, and Problems relate to material contained in the appendix to the chapter.

QUESTIONS

1. Distinguish between a current liability and a long-term debt.

2. Assume that your friend Greg Jonas, who is a music major, asks you to define and discuss the nature of a liability. Assist him by preparing a definition of a liability and by explaining to him what you believe are the elements or factors inherent in the concept of a liability.

3. Why is the liabilities section of the balance sheet of primary significance to bankers?

4. How are current liabilities related by definition to current assets? How are current liabilities related to a company's operating cycle?

5. Jon Bryant, a newly hired loan analyst, is examining the current liabilities of a corporate loan applicant. He observes that unearned revenues have declined in the current year compared to the prior year. Is this a positive indicator about the client's liquidity? Explain.

6. How is present value related to the concept of a liability?

7. What is the nature of a "discount" on notes payable?

8. How should a debt callable by the creditor be reported in the debtor's financial statements?

9. Under what conditions should a short-term obligation be excluded from current liabilities?

10. What evidence is necessary to demonstrate the ability to consummate the refinancing of short-term debt?

11. Discuss the accounting treatment or disclosure that should be accorded a declared but unpaid cash dividend; an accumulated but undeclared dividend on cumulative preferred stock; a stock dividend distributable.

12. How does unearned revenue arise? Why can it be classified properly as a current liability? Give several examples of business activities that result in unearned revenues.

13. What are compensated absences?

14. Under what conditions must an employer accrue a liability for the cost of compensated absences?

15. Under what conditions is an employer required to accrue a liability for sick pay? Under what conditions is an employer permitted but not required to accrue a liability for sick pay?

16. Caitlin Carter operates a health food store, and she has been the only employee. Her business is growing, and she is considering hiring some additional staff to help her in the store. Explain to her the various payroll deductions that she will have to account for, including their potential impact on her financial statements, if she hires additional staff.

17. Define (a) a contingency and (b) a contingent liability.

18. Under what conditions should a contingent liability be recorded?

19. Distinguish between a current liability and a contingent liability. Give two examples of each type.

20. How are the terms "probable," "reasonably possible," and "remote" related to contingent liabilities?

21. Contrast the cash basis method and the accrual method of accounting for warranty costs.

22. Kren Company has had a record-breaking year in terms of growth in sales and profitability. However, market research indicates that it will experience operating losses in two of its major businesses next year. The controller has proposed that the company record a provision for these future losses this year, since it can afford to take the charge and still show good results. Advise the controller on the appropriateness of this charge.

23. How does the expense warranty approach differ from the sales warranty approach?

24. Zucker-Abrahams Airlines Inc. awards members of its Flightline program a second ticket at half price, valid for 2 years anywhere on its flight system, when a full-price ticket is purchased. How would you account for the full-fare and half-fare tickets?

25. Northeast Airlines Co. awards members of its Frequent Fliers Club one free round-trip ticket, anywhere on its flight system, for every 50,000 miles flown on its planes. How would you account for the free ticket award?

26. When must a company recognize an asset retirement obligation?

27. Should a liability be recorded for risk of loss due to lack of insurance coverage? Discuss.

28. What factors must be considered in determining whether or not to record a liability for pending litigation? For threatened litigation?

29. Within the current liabilities section, how do you believe the accounts should be listed? Defend your position.

30. How does the acid-test ratio differ from the current ratio? How are they similar?

31. When should liabilities for each of the following items be recorded on the books of an ordinary business corporation?

(a) Acquisition of goods by purchase on credit.

(b) Officers' salaries.

(c) Special bonus to employees.

(d) Dividends.

(e) Purchase commitments.

BRIEF EXERCISES

(LO 1) **BE13-1** Congo Corporation uses a periodic inventory system and the gross method of accounting for purchase discounts. On July 1, Congo purchased $40,000 of inventory, terms 2/10, n/30, FOB shipping point. Congo paid freight costs of $1,200. On July 3, Congo returned damaged goods and received credit of $6,000. On July 10, Congo paid for the goods. Prepare all necessary journal entries for Congo.

(LO 1) **BE13-2** Peloton Company borrowed $50,000 on November 1, 2007, by signing a $50,000, 9%, 3-month note. Prepare Peloton's November 1, 2007, entry; the December 31, 2007, annual adjusting entry; and the February 1, 2008, entry.

(LO 1) **BE13-3** Kawasaki Corporation borrowed $50,000 on November 1, 2007, by signing a $51,125, 3-month, zero-interest-bearing note. Prepare Kawasaki's November 1, 2007, entry; the December 31, 2007, annual adjusting entry; and the February 1, 2008, entry.

(LO 1, 2) **BE13-4** At December 31, 2007, Fifa Corporation owes $500,000 on a note payable due February 15, 2008. (a) If Fifa refinances the obligation by issuing a long-term note on February 14 and using the proceeds to pay off the note due February 15, how much of the $500,000 should be reported as a current liability at December 31, 2007? (b) If Fifa pays off the note on February 15, 2008, and then borrows $1,000,000 on a long-term basis on March 1, how much of the $500,000 should be reported as a current liability at December 31, 2007?

(LO 1) **BE13-5** Game Pro Magazine sold 10,000 annual subscriptions on August 1, 2007, for $18 each. Prepare Game Pro's August 1, 2007, journal entry and the December 31, 2007, annual adjusting entry.

(LO 1) **BE13-6** Flintstones Corporation made credit sales of $30,000 which are subject to 6% sales tax. The corporation also made cash sales which totaled $19,610 including the 6% sales tax. (a) Prepare the entry to record Flintstones' credit sales. (b) Prepare the entry to record Flintstones' cash sales.

(LO 3) **BE13-7** Future Zone Corporation's weekly payroll of $23,000 included FICA taxes withheld of $1,426, federal taxes withheld of $2,990, state taxes withheld of $920, and insurance premiums withheld of $250. Prepare the journal entry to record Future Zone's payroll.

(LO 3) **BE13-8** Tale Spin Inc. provides paid vacations to its employees. At December 31, 2007, 30 employees have each earned 2 weeks of vacation time. The employees' average salary is $600 per week. Prepare Tale Spin's December 31, 2007, adjusting entry.

(LO 3)   **BE13-9**   Gargoyle Corporation provides its officers with bonuses based on income. For 2007, the bonuses total $450,000 and are paid on February 15, 2008. Prepare Gargoyle's December 31, 2007, adjusting entry and the February 15, 2008, entry.

(LO 4, 5)   **BE13-10**   Justice League Inc. is involved in a lawsuit at December 31, 2007. (a) Prepare the December 31 entry assuming it is probable that Justice League will be liable for $700,000 as a result of this suit. (b) Prepare the December 31 entry, if any, assuming it is *not* probable that Justice League will be liable for any payment as a result of this suit.

(LO 4, 5)   **BE13-11**   Kohlbeck Company recently was sued by a competitor for patent infringement. Attorneys have determined that it is probable that Kohlbeck will lose the case and that a reasonable estimate of damages to be paid by Kohlbeck is $200,000. In light of this case, Kohlbeck is considering establishing a $100,000 self-insurance allowance. What entry(ies), if any, should Kohlbeck record to recognize this loss contingency?

(LO 4, 5)   **BE13-12**   Darby's Drillers erects and places into service an off-shore oil platform on January 1, 2008, at a cost of $10,000,000. Darby is legally required to dismantle and remove the platform at the end of its useful life in 10 years. Darby estimates it will cost $1,000,000 to dismantle and remove the platform at the end of its useful life in 10 years. (The present value at January 1, 2008, of the dismantle and removal costs is $500,000.) Prepare the entry to record the asset retirement obligation.

(LO 4, 5)   **BE13-13**   Frantic Factory provides a 2-year warranty with one of its products which was first sold in 2007. In that year, Frantic spent $70,000 servicing warranty claims. At year-end, Frantic estimates that an additional $500,000 will be spent in the future to service warranty claims related to 2007 sales. Prepare Frantic's journal entry to record the $70,000 expenditure, and the December 31 adjusting entry.

(LO 4, 5)   **BE13-14**   LaRussa Corporation sells DVD players. The corporation also offers its customers a 2-year warranty contract. During 2007, LaRussa sold 15,000 warranty contracts at $99 each. The corporation spent $180,000 servicing warranties during 2007, and it estimates that an additional $900,000 will be spent in the future to service the warranties. Prepare LaRussa's journal entries for (a) the sale of contracts, (b) the cost of servicing the warranties, and (c) the recognition of warranty revenue.

(LO 4, 5)   **BE13-15**   Klax Company offers a set of building blocks to customers who send in 3 UPC codes from Klax cereal, along with 50¢. The blocks sets cost Klax $1.10 each to purchase and 60¢ each to mail to customers. During 2007, Klax sold 1,000,000 boxes of cereal. The company expects 30% of the UPC codes to be sent in. During 2007, 120,000 UPC codes were redeemed. Prepare Klax's December 31, 2007, adjusting entry.

(LO 7)   ***BE13-16**   Locke Company provides its president, Cyan Garamonde, with a bonus equal to 10% of income after deducting income tax and bonus. Income *before* deducting income tax and bonus is $265,000, and the tax rate is 40%. Compute the amount of Cyan Garamonde's bonus.

EXERCISES

(LO 1)   **E13-1**   **(Balance Sheet Classification of Various Liabilities)**   How would each of the following items be reported on the balance sheet?

(a)   Accrued vacation pay.
(b)   Estimated taxes payable.   *depends*
(c)   Service warranties on appliance sales.
(d)   Bank overdraft.
(e)   Employee payroll deductions unremitted.
(f)   Unpaid bonus to officers.
(g)   Deposit received from customer to guarantee performance of a contract.
(h)   Sales taxes payable.
(i)   Gift certificates sold to customers but not yet redeemed.

(j)   Premium offers outstanding.
(k)   Discount on notes payable.
(l)   Personal injury claim pending.
(m)   Current maturities of long-term debts to be paid from current assets.
(n)   Cash dividends declared but unpaid.
(o)   Dividends in arrears on preferred stock.
(p)   Loans from officers.

(LO 1)   **E13-2**   **(Accounts and Notes Payable)**   The following are selected 2007 transactions of Sean Astin Corporation.

Sept. 1   Purchased inventory from Encino Company on account for $50,000. Astin records purchases gross and uses a periodic inventory system.
Oct. 1   Issued a $50,000, 12-month, 8% note to Encino in payment of account.
Oct. 1   Borrowed $50,000 from the Shore Bank by signing a 12-month, zero-interest-bearing $54,000 note.

Instructions

(a) Prepare journal entries for the selected transactions above.

(b) Prepare adjusting entries at December 31.

(c) Compute the total net liability to be reported on the December 31 balance sheet for:
 (1) the interest-bearing note.
 (2) the zero-interest-bearing note.

(LO 2) **E13-3 (Refinancing of Short-Term Debt)** On December 31, 2007, Hattie McDaniel Company had $1,200,000 of short-term debt in the form of notes payable due February 2, 2008. On January 21, 2008, the company issued 25,000 shares of its common stock for $38 per share, receiving $950,000 proceeds after brokerage fees and other costs of issuance. On February 2, 2008, the proceeds from the stock sale, supplemented by an additional $250,000 cash, are used to liquidate the $1,200,000 debt. The December 31, 2007, balance sheet is issued on February 23, 2008.

Instructions

Show how the $1,200,000 of short-term debt should be presented on the December 31, 2007, balance sheet, including note disclosure.

(LO 2) **E13-4 (Refinancing of Short-Term Debt)** On December 31, 2007, Kate Holmes Company has $7,000,000 of short-term debt in the form of notes payable to Gotham State Bank due in 2008. On January 28, 2008, Holmes enters into a refinancing agreement with Gotham that will permit it to borrow up to 60% of the gross amount of its accounts receivable. Receivables are expected to range between a low of $6,000,000 in May to a high of $8,000,000 in October during the year 2008. The interest cost of the maturing short-term debt is 15%, and the new agreement calls for a fluctuating interest at 1% above the prime rate on notes due in 2012. Holmes's December 31, 2007, balance sheet is issued on February 15, 2008.

Instructions

Prepare a partial balance sheet for Holmes at December 31, 2007, showing how its $7,000,000 of short-term debt should be presented, including footnote disclosure.

(LO 3) **E13-5 (Compensated Absences)** Matt Broderick Company began operations on January 2, 2006. It employs 9 individuals who work 8-hour days and are paid hourly. Each employee earns 10 paid vacation days and 6 paid sick days annually. Vacation days may be taken after January 15 of the year following the year in which they are earned. Sick days may be taken as soon as they are earned; unused sick days accumulate. Additional information is as follows.

Actual Hourly Wage Rate		Vacation Days Used by Each Employee		Sick Days Used by Each Employee	
2006	2007	2006	2007	2006	2007
$10	$11	0	9	4	5

Matt Broderick Company has chosen to accrue the cost of compensated absences at rates of pay in effect during the period when earned and to accrue sick pay when earned.

Instructions

(a) Prepare journal entries to record transactions related to compensated absences during 2006 and 2007.

(b) Compute the amounts of any liability for compensated absences that should be reported on the balance sheet at December 31, 2006 and 2007.

(LO 3) **E13-6 (Compensated Absences)** Assume the facts in the preceding exercise, except that Matt Broderick Company has chosen not to accrue paid sick leave until used, and has chosen to accrue vacation time at expected future rates of pay without discounting. The company used the following projected rates to accrue vacation time.

Year in Which Vacation Time Was Earned	Projected Future Pay Rates Used to Accrue Vacation Pay
2006	$10.75
2007	11.60

Instructions

(a) Prepare journal entries to record transactions related to compensated absences during 2006 and 2007.

(b) Compute the amounts of any liability for compensated absences that should be reported on the balance sheet at December 31, 2006, and 2007.

(LO 1) **E13-7 (Adjusting Entry for Sales Tax)** During the month of June, Rowling Boutique had cash sales of $233,200 and credit sales of $153,700, both of which include the 6% sales tax that must be remitted to the state by July 15.

Instructions
Prepare the adjusting entry that should be recorded to fairly present the June 30 financial statements.

(LO 3) **E13-8 (Payroll Tax Entries)** The payroll of YellowCard Company for September 2006 is as follows.

Total payroll was $480,000, of which $110,000 is exempt from Social Security tax because it represented amounts paid in excess of $90,000 to certain employees. The amount paid to employees in excess of $7,000 was $400,000. Income taxes in the amount of $80,000 were withheld, as was $9,000 in union dues. The state unemployment tax is 3.5%, but YellowCard Company is allowed a credit of 2.3% by the state for its unemployment experience. Also, assume that the current F.I.C.A. tax is 7.65% on an employee's wages to $90,000 and 1.45% in excess of $90,000. No employee for YellowCard makes more than $125,000. The federal unemployment tax rate is 0.8% after state credit.

Instructions
Prepare the necessary journal entries if the wages and salaries paid and the employer payroll taxes are recorded separately.

(LO 3) **E13-9 (Payroll Tax Entries)** Green Day Hardware Company's payroll for November 2007 is summarized below.

			Amount Subject to Payroll Taxes	
			Unemployment Tax	
Payroll	Wages Due	F.I.C.A.	Federal	State
Factory	$120,000	$120,000	$40,000	$40,000
Sales	32,000	32,000	4,000	4,000
Administrative	36,000	36,000	—	—
Total	$188,000	$188,000	$44,000	$44,000

At this point in the year some employees have already received wages in excess of those to which payroll taxes apply. Assume that the state unemployment tax is 2.5%. The F.I.C.A. rate is 7.65% on an employee's wages to $90,000 and 1.45% in excess of $90,000. Of the $188,000 wages subject to F.I.C.A. tax, $20,000 of the sales wages is in excess of $90,000. Federal unemployment tax rate is 0.8% after credits. Income tax withheld amounts to $16,000 for factory, $7,000 for sales, and $6,000 for administrative.

Instructions
 (a) Prepare a schedule showing the employer's total cost of wages for November by function. (Round all computations to nearest dollar.)
 (b) Prepare the journal entries to record the factory, sales, and administrative payrolls including the employer's payroll taxes.

(LO 5) **E13-10 (Warranties)** Soundgarden Company sold 200 color laser copiers in 2007 for $4,000 apiece, together with a one-year warranty. Maintenance on each copier during the warranty period averages $330.

Instructions
 (a) Prepare entries to record the sale of the copiers and the related warranty costs, assuming that the accrual method is used. Actual warranty costs incurred in 2007 were $17,000.
 (b) On the basis of the data above, prepare the appropriate entries, assuming that the cash basis method is used.

(LO 5) **E13-11 (Warranties)** Sheryl Crow Equipment Company sold 500 Rollomatics during 2007 at $6,000 each. During 2007, Crow spent $20,000 servicing the 2-year warranties that accompany the Rollomatic. All applicable transactions are on a cash basis.

Instructions
 (a) Prepare 2007 entries for Crow using the expense warranty approach. Assume that Crow estimates the total cost of servicing the warranties will be $120,000 for 2 years.
 (b) Prepare 2007 entries for Crow assuming that the warranties are not an integral part of the sale. Assume that of the sales total, $150,000 relates to sales of warranty contracts. Crow estimates the total cost of servicing the warranties will be $120,000 for 2 years. Estimate revenues earned on the basis of costs incurred and estimated costs.

(LO 5) **E13-12 (Premium Entries)** No Doubt Company includes 1 coupon in each box of soap powder that it packs, and 10 coupons are redeemable for a premium (a kitchen utensil). In 2007, No Doubt Company purchased 8,800 premiums at 80 cents each and sold 110,000 boxes of soap powder at $3.30 per box; 44,000 coupons were presented for redemption in 2007. It is estimated that 60% of the coupons will eventually be presented for redemption.

Instructions

Prepare all the entries that would be made relative to sales of soap powder and to the premium plan in 2007.

(LO 4, 5) **E13-13 (Contingencies)** Presented below are three independent situations. Answer the question at the end of each situation.

1. During 2007, Salt-n-Pepa Inc. became involved in a tax dispute with the IRS. Salt-n-Pepa's attorneys have indicated that they believe it is probable that Salt-n-Pepa will lose this dispute. They also believe that Salt-n-Pepa will have to pay the IRS between $900,000 and $1,400,000. After the 2007 financial statements were issued, the case was settled with the IRS for $1,200,000. What amount, if any, should be reported as a liability for this contingency as of December 31, 2007?

2. On October 1, 2007, Alan Jackson Chemical was identified as a potentially responsible party by the Environmental Protection Agency. Jackson's management along with its counsel have concluded that it is probable that Jackson will be responsible for damages, and a reasonable estimate of these damages is $5,000,000. Jackson's insurance policy of $9,000,000 has a deductible clause of $500,000. How should Alan Jackson Chemical report this information in its financial statements at December 31, 2007?

3. Melissa Etheridge Inc. had a manufacturing plant in Bosnia, which was destroyed in the civil war. It is not certain who will compensate Etheridge for this destruction, but Etheridge has been assured by governmental officials that it will receive a definite amount for this plant. The amount of the compensation will be less than the fair value of the plant, but more than its book value. How should the contingency be reported in the financial statements of Etheridge Inc.?

(LO 5) **E13-14 (Asset Retirement Obligation)** Oil Products Company purchases an oil tanker depot on January 1, 2007, at a cost of $600,000. Oil Products expects to operate the depot for 10 years, at which time it is legally required to dismantle the depot and remove the underground storage tanks. It is estimated that it will cost $75,000 to dismantle the depot and remove the tanks at the end of the depot's useful life.

Instructions

(a) Prepare the journal entries to record the depot and the asset retirement obligation for the depot on January 1, 2007. Based on an effective interest rate of 6%, the present value of the asset retirement obligation on January 1, 2007, is $41,879.

(b) Prepare any journal entries required for the depot and the asset retirement obligation at December 31, 2007. Oil Products uses straight-line depreciation; the estimated residual value for the depot is zero.

(c) On December 31, 2016, Oil Products pays a demolition firm to dismantle the depot and remove the tanks at a price of $80,000. Prepare the journal entry for the settlement of the asset retirement obligation.

(LO 5) **E13-15 (Premiums)** Presented below are three independent situations.

1. Hairston Stamp Company records stamp service revenue and provides for the cost of redemptions in the year stamps are sold to licensees. Hairston's past experience indicates that only 80% of the stamps sold to licensees will be redeemed. Hairston's liability for stamp redemptions was $13,000,000 at December 31, 2006. Additional information for 2007 is as follows.

Stamp service revenue from stamps sold to licensees	$9,500,000
Cost of redemptions (stamps sold prior to 1/1/07)	6,000,000

If all the stamps sold in 2007 were presented for redemption in 2008, the redemption cost would be $5,200,000. What amount should Hairston report as a liability for stamp redemptions at December 31, 2007?

2. In packages of its products, Burnitz Inc. includes coupons that may be presented at retail stores to obtain discounts on other Burnitz products. Retailers are reimbursed for the face amount of coupons redeemed plus 10% of that amount for handling costs. Burnitz honors requests for coupon redemption by retailers up to 3 months after the consumer expiration date. Burnitz estimates that 60% of all coupons issued will ultimately be redeemed. Information relating to coupons issued by Burnitz during 2007 is as follows.

Consumer expiration date	12/31/07
Total face amount of coupons issued	$800,000
Total payments to retailers as of 12/31/07	330,000

What amount should Burnitz report as a liability for unredeemed coupons at December 31, 2007?

3. Roland Company sold 700,000 boxes of pie mix under a new sales promotional program. Each box contains one coupon, which submitted with $4.00, entitles the customer to a baking pan. Roland pays $6.00 per pan and $0.50 for handling and shipping. Roland estimates that 70% of the coupons will be redeemed, even though only 250,000 coupons had been processed during 2007. What amount should Roland report as a liability for unredeemed coupons at December 31, 2007?

(AICPA adapted)

(LO 6) **E13-16** **(Financial Statement Impact of Liability Transactions)** Presented below is a list of possible transactions.

1. Purchased inventory for $80,000 on account (assume perpetual system is used).
2. Issued an $80,000 note payable in payment on account (see item 1 above).
3. Recorded accrued interest on the note from item 2 above.
4. Borrowed $100,000 from the bank by signing a 6-month, $112,000, zero-interest-bearing note.
5. Recognized 4 months' interest expense on the note from item 4 above.
6. Recorded cash sales of $75,260, which includes 6% sales tax.
7. Recorded wage expense of $35,000. The cash paid was $25,000; the difference was due to various amounts withheld.
8. Recorded employer's payroll taxes.
9. Accrued accumulated vacation pay.
10. Recorded an asset retirement obligation.
11. Recorded bonuses due to employees.
12. Recorded a contingent loss on a lawsuit that the company will probably lose.
13. Accrued warranty expense (assume expense warranty approach).
14. Paid warranty costs that were accrued in item 13 above.
15. Recorded sales of product and related warranties (assume sales warranty approach).
16. Paid warranty costs under contracts from item 15 above.
17. Recognized warranty revenue (see item 15 above).
18. Recorded estimated liability for premium claims outstanding.

Instructions
Set up a table using the format shown below and analyze the effect of the 18 transactions on the financial statement categories indicated.

#	Assets	Liabilities	Owners' Equity	Net Income
1				

Use the following code:
  I: Increase   D: Decrease   NE: No net effect

(LO 6) **E13-17** **(Ratio Computations and Discussion)** Sprague Company has been operating for several years, and on December 31, 2007, presented the following balance sheet.

SPRAGUE COMPANY
BALANCE SHEET
DECEMBER 31, 2007

Cash	$ 40,000	Accounts payable	$ 80,000
Receivables	75,000	Mortgage payable	140,000
Inventories	95,000	Common stock ($1 par)	150,000
Plant assets (net)	220,000	Retained earnings	60,000
	$430,000		$430,000

The net income for 2007 was $25,000. Assume that total assets are the same in 2006 and 2007.

Instructions
Compute each of the following ratios. For each of the four indicate the manner in which it is computed and its significance as a tool in the analysis of the financial soundness of the company.

(a) Current ratio.   (c) Debt to total assets.
(b) Acid-test ratio.   (d) Rate of return on assets.

(LO 6) **E13-18** **(Ratio Computations and Analysis)** Prior Company's condensed financial statements provide the following information.

PRIOR COMPANY
BALANCE SHEET

	Dec. 31, 2007	Dec. 31, 2006
Cash	$ 52,000	$ 60,000
Accounts receivable (net)	198,000	80,000
Short-term investments	80,000	40,000
Inventories	440,000	360,000
Prepaid expenses	3,000	7,000
Total current assets	$ 773,000	$ 547,000
Property, plant, and equipment (net)	857,000	853,000
Total assets	$1,630,000	$1,400,000
Current liabilities	240,000	160,000
Bonds payable	400,000	400,000
Common stockholders' equity	990,000	840,000
Total liabilities and stockholders' equity	$1,630,000	$1,400,000

INCOME STATEMENT
FOR THE YEAR ENDED 2007

Sales	$1,640,000
Cost of goods sold	(800,000)
Gross profit	840,000
Selling and administrative expense	(440,000)
Interest expense	(40,000)
Net income	$ 360,000

Instructions

(a) Determine the following for 2007.
  (1) Current ratio at December 31.
  (2) Acid-test ratio at December 31.
  (3) Accounts receivable turnover.
  (4) Inventory turnover.
  (5) Rate of return on assets.
  (6) Profit margin on sales.
(b) Prepare a brief evaluation of the financial condition of Prior Company and of the adequacy of its profits.

(LO 6) **E13-19** **(Ratio Computations and Effect of Transactions)** Presented below and on page 637 is information related to Carver Inc.

CARVER INC.
BALANCE SHEET
DECEMBER 31, 2007

Cash		$ 45,000	Notes payable (short-term)	$ 50,000
Receivables	$110,000		Accounts payable	32,000
Less: Allowance	15,000	95,000	Accrued liabilities	5,000
Inventories		170,000	Capital stock (par $5)	260,000
Prepaid insurance		8,000	Retained earnings	141,000
Land		20,000		
Equipment (net)		150,000		
		$488,000		$488,000

CARVER INC.
INCOME STATEMENT
FOR THE YEAR ENDED DECEMBER 31, 2007

Sales		$1,400,000
Cost of goods sold		
Inventory, Jan. 1, 2007	$200,000	
Purchases	790,000	
Cost of goods available for sale	990,000	
Inventory, Dec. 31, 2007	170,000	
Cost of goods sold		820,000
Gross profit on sales		580,000
Operating expenses		170,000
Net income		$ 410,000

Instructions

(a) Compute the following ratios or relationships of Carver Inc. Assume that the ending account balances are representative unless the information provided indicates differently.
  (1) Current ratio.
  (2) Inventory turnover.
  (3) Receivables turnover.
  (4) Earnings per share.
  (5) Profit margin on sales.
  (6) Rate of return on assets on December 31, 2007.

(b) Indicate for each of the following transactions whether the transaction would improve, weaken, or have no effect on the current ratio of Carver Inc. at December 31, 2007.
  (1) Write off an uncollectible account receivable, $2,200.
  (2) Purchase additional capital stock for cash.
  (3) Pay $40,000 on notes payable (short-term).
  (4) Collect $23,000 on accounts receivable.
  (5) Buy equipment on account.
  (6) Give an existing creditor a short-term note in settlement of account.

(LO 7) ***E13-20 (Bonus Computation)** Jud Buechler, president of the Supporting Cast Company, has a bonus arrangement with the company under which he receives 15% of the net income (after deducting taxes and bonuses) each year. For the current year, the net income before deducting either the provision for income taxes or the bonus is $299,750. The bonus is deductible for tax purposes, and the effective tax rate may be assumed to be 40%.

Instructions

(a) Compute the amount of Jud Buechler's bonus.
(b) Compute the appropriate provision for federal income taxes for the year.
(c) Prepare the December 31 entry to record the bonus (which will not be paid until next year).

(LO 7) ***E13-21 (Bonus Computation and Income Statement Preparation)** The incomplete income statement of Scottie Pippen Company follows.

SCOTTIE PIPPEN COMPANY
INCOME STATEMENT
FOR THE YEAR 2007

Revenue		$10,000,000
Cost of goods sold		7,000,000
Gross profit		3,000,000
Administrative and selling expenses	$1,000,000	
Profit-sharing bonus to employees	?	?
Income before income taxes		?
Income taxes		?
Net income		$?

The employee profit-sharing plan 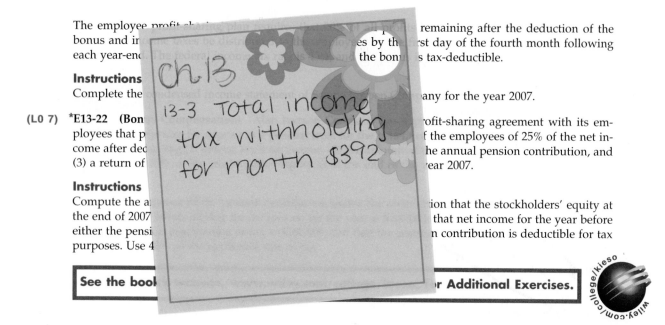 remaining after the deduction of the bonus and in[...] [...]es by th[...] [...]rst day of the fourth month following each year-end[...] the bon[...] s tax-deductible.

Instructions

Complete the [...]redeemed income [...] [...]any for the year 2007.

(LO 7) *E13-22 (Bon[...] [...]ofit-sharing agreement with its employees that p[...] [...] f the employees of 25% of the net income after ded[...] [...]he annual pension contribution, and (3) a return of[...] [...]ear 2007.

Instructions

Compute the a[...] [...]ion that the stockholders' equity at the end of 2007[...] [...]that net income for the year before either the pensi[...] [...]n contribution is deductible for tax purposes. Use 4[...]

Handwritten note: Ch. 13 / 13-3 Total income tax withholding for month $392

See the book[...] [...]r Additional Exercises.

PROBLEMS

(LO 1) **P13-1 (Current Liability Entries and Adjustments)** Described below are certain transactions of James Edwards Corporation.

1. On February 2, the corporation purchased goods from Jack Haley Company for $50,000 subject to cash discount terms of 2/10, n/30. Purchases and accounts payable are recorded by the corporation at net amounts after cash discounts. The invoice was paid on February 26.
2. On April 1, the corporation bought a truck for $40,000 from General Motors Company, paying $4,000 in cash and signing a one-year, 12% note for the balance of the purchase price.
3. On May 1, the corporation borrowed $86,000 from Chicago National Bank by signing a $92,000 zero-interest-bearing note due one year from May 1.
4. On August 1, the board of directors declared a $300,000 cash dividend that was payable on September 10 to stockholders of record on August 31.

Instructions

(a) Make all the journal entries necessary to record the transactions above using appropriate dates.

(b) James Edwards Corporation's year-end is December 31. Assuming that no adjusting entries relative to the transactions above have been recorded, prepare any adjusting journal entries concerning interest that are necessary to present fair financial statements at December 31. Assume straight-line amortization of discounts.

(LO 1, 5) **P13-2 (Liability Entries and Adjustments)** Listed below are selected transactions of Kobe Bryant Department Store for the current year ending December 31.

1. On December 5, the store received $500 from the Phil Jackson Players as a deposit to be returned after certain furniture to be used in stage production was returned on January 15.
2. During December, cash sales totaled $834,750, which includes the 5% sales tax that must be remitted to the state by the fifteenth day of the following month.
3. On December 10, the store purchased for cash three delivery trucks for $99,000. The trucks were purchased in a state that applies a 5% sales tax.
4. The store determined it will cost $100,000 to restore the area surrounding one of its store parking lots, when the store is closed in 2 years. Bryant estimates the fair value of the obligation at December 31 is $84,000.

Instructions

Prepare all the journal entries necessary to record the transactions noted above as they occurred and any adjusting journal entries relative to the transactions that would be required to present fair financial statements at December 31. Date each entry. For simplicity, assume that adjusting entries are recorded only once a year on December 31.

(LO 3) **P13-3 (Payroll Tax Entries)** Star Wars Company pays its office employee payroll weekly. Below is a partial list of employees and their payroll data for August. Because August is their vacation period, vacation pay is also listed.

Employee	Earnings to July 31	Weekly Pay	Vacation Pay to Be Received in August	
Mark Hamill	$4,200	$180	—	180
Carrie Fisher	3,500	150	$300	450
Harrison Ford	2,700	110	220	330
Alec Guinness	7,400	250	—	250
Peter Cushing	8,000	290	580	870

Assume that the federal income tax withheld is 10% of wages. Union dues withheld are 2% of wages. Vacations are taken the second and third weeks of August by Fisher, Ford, and Cushing. The state unemployment tax rate is 2.5% and the federal is 0.8%, both on a $7,000 maximum. The F.I.C.A. rate is 7.65% on employee and employer on a maximum of $90,000 per employee. In addition, a 1.45% rate is charged both employer and employee for an employee's wage in excess of $90,000.

Instructions

Make the journal entries necessary for each of the four August payrolls. The entries for the payroll and for the company's liability are made separately. Also make the entry to record the monthly payment of accrued payroll liabilities.

(LO 3) **P13-4 (Payroll Tax Entries)** Below is a payroll sheet for Jedi Import Company for the month of September 2007. The company is allowed a 1% unemployment compensation rate by the state; the federal unemployment tax rate is 0.8% and the maximum for both is $7,000. Assume a 10% federal income tax rate for all employees and a 7.65% F.I.C.A. tax on employee and employer on a maximum of $90,000. In addition, 1.45% is charged both employer and employee for an employee's wage in excess of $90,000 per employee.

Name	Earnings to Aug. 31	September Earnings	Income Tax Withholding	F.I.C.A.	State U.C.	Federal U.C.
B.D. Williams	$ 6,800	$ 800				
D. Prowse	6,300	700				
K. Baker	7,600	1,100				
F. Oz	13,600	1,900				
A. Daniels	105,000	15,000				
B. Mayhew	112,000	16,000				

Instructions

(a) Complete the payroll sheet and make the necessary entry to record the payment of the payroll.

(b) Make the entry to record the payroll tax expenses of Jedi Import Company.

(c) Make the entry to record the payment of the payroll liabilities created. Assume that the company pays all payroll liabilities at the end of each month.

(LO 5) **P13-5 (Warranties, Accrual, and Cash Basis)** Jeeter Corporation sells computers under a 2-year warranty contract that requires the corporation to replace defective parts and to provide the necessary repair labor. During 2007 the corporation sells for cash 300 computers at a unit price of $3,500. On the basis of past experience, the 2-year warranty costs are estimated to be $155 for parts and $185 for labor per unit. (For simplicity, assume that all sales occurred on December 31, 2007.) The warranty is not sold separately from the computer.

Instructions

(a) Record any necessary journal entries in 2007, applying the cash basis method.

(b) Record any necessary journal entries in 2007, applying the expense warranty accrual method.

(c) What liability relative to these transactions would appear on the December 31, 2007, balance sheet and how would it be classified if the cash basis method is applied?

(d) What liability relative to these transactions would appear on the December 31, 2007, balance sheet and how would it be classified if the expense warranty accrual method is applied?

In 2008 the actual warranty costs to Jeeter Corporation were $21,400 for parts and $24,900 for labor.

(e) Record any necessary journal entries in 2008, applying the cash basis method.

(f) Record any necessary journal entries in 2008, applying the expense warranty accrual method.

(LO 5) **P13-6 (Extended Warranties)** Brett Perriman Company sells televisions at an average price of $750 and also offers to each customer a separate 3-year warranty contract for $75 that requires the company to perform periodic services and to replace defective parts. During 2007, the company sold 300 televisions and 270 warranty contracts for cash. It estimates the 3-year warranty costs as $20 for parts and $40 for labor and accounts for warranties separately. Assume sales occurred on December 31, 2007, income is recognized on the warranties, and straight-line recognition of warranty revenues occurs.

Instructions
  (a) Record any necessary journal entries in 2007.
  (b) What liability relative to these transactions would appear on the December 31, 2007, balance sheet and how would it be classified?

In 2008, Brett Perriman Company incurred actual costs relative to 2007 television warranty sales of $2,000 for parts and $3,000 for labor.

  (c) Record any necessary journal entries in 2008 relative to 2007 television warranties.
  (d) What amounts relative to the 2007 television warranties would appear on the December 31, 2008, balance sheet and how would they be classified?

(LO 4, 5) **P13-7** **(Warranties, Accrual, and Cash Basis)** Albert Pujols Company sells a machine for $7,400 under a 12-month warranty agreement that requires the company to replace all defective parts and to provide the repair labor at no cost to the customers. With sales being made evenly throughout the year, the company sells 650 machines in 2008 (warranty expense is incurred half in 2008 and half in 2009). As a result of product testing, the company estimates that the warranty cost is $370 per machine ($170 parts and $200 labor).

Instructions
Assuming that actual warranty costs are incurred exactly as estimated, what journal entries would be made relative to the following facts?

  (a) Under application of the expense warranty accrual method for:
    (1) Sale of machinery in 2008.
    (2) Warranty costs incurred in 2008.
    (3) Warranty expense charged against 2008 revenues.
    (4) Warranty costs incurred in 2009.
  (b) Under application of the cash basis method for:
    (1) Sale of machinery in 2008.
    (2) Warranty costs incurred in 2008.
    (3) Warranty expense charged against 2008 revenues.
    (4) Warranty costs incurred in 2009.
  (c) What amount, if any, is disclosed in the balance sheet as a liability for future warranty costs as of December 31, 2008, under each method?
  (d) Which method best reflects the income in 2008 and 2009 of Albert Pujols Company? Why?

(LO 5) **P13-8** **(Premium Entries)** To stimulate the sales of its Alladin breakfast cereal, Khamsah Company places 1 coupon in each box. Five coupons are redeemable for a premium consisting of a children's hand puppet. In 2008, the company purchases 40,000 puppets at $1.50 each and sells 440,000 boxes of Alladin at $3.75 a box. From its experience with other similar premium offers, the company estimates that 40% of the coupons issued will be mailed back for redemption. During 2008, 105,000 coupons are presented for redemption.

Instructions
Prepare the journal entries that should be recorded in 2008 relative to the premium plan.

(LO 5, 6) **P13-9** **(Premium Entries and Financial Statement Presentation)** Roberto Hernandez Candy Company offers a CD single as a premium for every five candy bar wrappers presented by customers together with $2.00. The candy bars are sold by the company to distributors for 30 cents each. The purchase price of each CD to the company is $1.80; in addition it costs 30 cents to mail each CD. The results of the premium plan for the years 2007 and 2008 are as follows. (All purchases and sales are for cash.)

	2007	2008
CDs purchased	250,000	330,000
Candy bars sold	2,895,400	2,743,600
Wrappers redeemed	1,200,000	1,500,000
2007 wrappers expected to be redeemed in 2008	290,000	
2008 wrappers expected to be redeemed in 2009		350,000

Instructions
  (a) Prepare the journal entries that should be made in 2007 and 2008 to record the transactions related to the premium plan of the Roberto Hernandez Candy Company.
  (b) Indicate the account names, amounts, and classifications of the items related to the premium plan that would appear on the balance sheet and the income statement at the end of 2007 and 2008.

(LO 4, 5) **P13-10 (Loss Contingencies: Entries and Essay)** On November 24, 2007, 26 passengers on Branson Airlines Flight No. 901 were injured upon landing when the plane skidded off the runway. Personal injury suits for damages totaling $5,000,000 were filed on January 11, 2008, against the airline by 18 injured passengers. The airline carries no insurance. Legal counsel has studied each suit and advised Branson that it can reasonably expect to pay 60% of the damages claimed. The financial statements for the year ended December 31, 2007, were issued February 27, 2008.

Instructions

(a) Prepare any disclosures and journal entries required by the airline in preparation of the December 31, 2007, financial statements.

(b) Ignoring the Nov. 24, 2007, accident, what liability due to the risk of loss from lack of insurance coverage should Branson Airlines record or disclose? During the past decade the company has experienced at least one accident per year and incurred average damages of $3,200,000. Discuss fully.

(LO 4, 5) **P13-11 (Loss Contingencies: Entries and Essays)** Ichiro Corporation, in preparation of its December 31, 2007, financial statements, is attempting to determine the proper accounting treatment for each of the following situations.

1. As a result of uninsured accidents during the year, personal injury suits for $350,000 and $60,000 have been filed against the company. It is the judgment of Ichiro's legal counsel that an unfavorable outcome is unlikely in the $60,000 case but that an unfavorable verdict approximating $225,000 will probably result in the $350,000 case.

2. Ichiro Corporation owns a subsidiary in a foreign country that has a book value of $5,725,000 and an estimated fair value of $8,700,000. The foreign government has communicated to Ichiro its intention to expropriate the assets and business of all foreign investors. On the basis of settlements other firms have received from this same country, Ichiro expects to receive 40% of the fair value of its properties as final settlement.

3. Ichiro's chemical product division consisting of five plants is uninsurable because of the special risk of injury to employees and losses due to fire and explosion. The year 2007 is considered one of the safest (luckiest) in the division's history because no loss due to injury or casualty was suffered. Having suffered an average of three casualties a year during the rest of the past decade (ranging from $60,000 to $700,000), management is certain that next year the company will probably not be so fortunate.

Instructions

(a) Prepare the journal entries that should be recorded as of December 31, 2007, to recognize each of the situations above.

(b) Indicate what should be reported relative to each situation in the financial statements and accompanying notes. Explain why.

(LO 5) **P13-12 (Warranties and Premiums)** Ray Charles Music Emporium carries a wide variety of musical instruments, sound reproduction equipment, recorded music, and sheet music. Charles uses two sales promotion techniques—warranties and premiums—to attract customers.

Musical instruments and sound equipment are sold with a one-year warranty for replacement of parts and labor. The estimated warranty cost, based on past experience, is 2% of sales.

The premium is offered on the recorded and sheet music. Customers receive a coupon for each dollar spent on recorded music or sheet music. Customers may exchange 200 coupons and $20 for a CD player. Charles pays $34 for each CD player and estimates that 60% of the coupons given to customers will be redeemed.

Charles's total sales for 2007 were $7,200,000—$5,400,000 from musical instruments and sound reproduction equipment and $1,800,000 from recorded music and sheet music. Replacement parts and labor for warranty work totaled $164,000 during 2007. A total of 6,500 CD players used in the premium program were purchased during the year and there were 1,200,000 coupons redeemed in 2007.

The accrual method is used by Charles to account for the warranty and premium costs for financial reporting purposes. The balances in the accounts related to warranties and premiums on January 1, 2007, were as shown below.

Inventory of Premium CD Players	$39,950
Estimated Premium Claims Outstanding	44,800
Estimated Liability from Warranties	136,000

Instructions

Ray Charles Music Emporium is preparing its financial statements for the year ended December 31, 2007. Determine the amounts that will be shown on the 2007 financial statements for the following.

(1) Warranty Expense.

(2) Estimated Liability from Warranties.

(3) Premium Expense.

(4) Inventory of Premium CD Players.

(5) Estimated Premium Claims Outstanding.

(CMA adapted)

(LO 4, 5) **P13-13** **(Liability Errors)** You are the independent auditor engaged to audit Christine Agazzi Corporation's December 31, 2007, financial statements. Christine Agazzi manufactures household appliances. During the course of your audit, you discovered the following contingent liabilities.

1. Christine Agazzi began production of a new dishwasher in June 2007 and, by December 31, 2007, sold 100,000 to various retailers for $500 each. Each dishwasher is under a one-year warranty. The company estimates that its warranty expense per dishwasher will amount to $25. At year-end, the company had already paid out $1,000,000 in warranty expenses. Christine Agazzi's income statement shows warranty expenses of $1,000,000 for 2007. Agazzi accounts for warranty costs on the accrual basis.

2. In response to your attorney's letter, Robert Sklodowski, Esq., has informed you that Agazzi has been cited for dumping toxic waste into the Kishwaukee River. Clean-up costs and fines amount to $3,330,000. Although the case is still being contested, Sklodowski is certain that Agazzi will most probably have to pay the fine and clean-up costs. No disclosure of this situation was found in the financial statements.

3. Christine Agazzi is the defendant in a patent infringement lawsuit by Heidi Goldman over Agazzi's use of a hydraulic compressor in several of its products. Sklodowski claims that, if the suit goes against Agazzi, the loss may be as much as $5,000,000; however, Sklodowski believes the loss of this suit to be only reasonably possible. Again, no mention of this suit occurs in the financial statements.

As presented, these contingencies are not reported in accordance with GAAP, which may create problems in issuing a clean audit report. You feel the need to note these problems in the work papers.

Instructions

Heading each page with the name of the company, balance sheet date, and a brief description of the problem, write a brief narrative for each of the above issues in the form of **a memorandum** to be incorporated in the audit work papers. Explain what led to the discovery of each problem, what the problem really is, and what you advised your client to do (along with any appropriate journal entries) in order to bring these contingencies in accordance with GAAP.

(LO 7) ***P13-14** **(Bonus Computation)** Henryk Inc. has a contract with its president, Nathalie Sarraute, to pay her a bonus during each of the years 2006, 2007, 2008, and 2009. The federal income tax rate is 40% during the 4 years. The profit before deductions for bonus and federal income taxes was $250,000 in 2006, $308,000 in 2007, $350,000 in 2008, and $380,000 in 2009. The president's bonus of 12% is deductible for tax purposes in each year and is to be computed as follows.

(a) In 2006 the bonus is to be based on profit before deductions for bonus and income tax.
(b) In 2007 the bonus is to be based on profit after deduction of bonus but before deduction of income tax.
(c) In 2008 the bonus is to be based on profit before deduction of bonus but after deduction of income tax.
(d) In 2009 the bonus is to be based on profit after deductions for bonus and income tax.

Instructions

Compute the amounts of the bonus and the income tax for each of the 4 years.

(LO 5, 7) **P13-15** **(Warranty, Bonus, and Coupon Computation)** Hiaasen Company must make computations and adjusting entries for the following independent situations at December 31, 2007.

1. Its line of amplifiers carries a 3-year warranty against defects. On the basis of past experience the estimated warranty costs related to dollar sales are: first year after sale—2% of sales; second year after sale—3% of sales; and third year after sale—4% of sales. Sales and actual warranty expenditures for the first 3 years of business were:

	Sales	Warranty Expenditures
2005	$ 800,000	$ 6,500
2006	1,100,000	17,200
2007	1,200,000	62,000

Instructions

Compute the amount that Hiaasen Company should report as a liability in its December 31, 2007, balance sheet. Assume that all sales are made evenly throughout each year with warranty expenses also evenly spaced relative to the rates above.

*2. Hiaasen Company's profit-sharing plan provides that the company will contribute to a fund an amount equal to one-fourth of its net income each year. Income before deducting the profit-sharing contribution and taxes for 2007 is $1,035,000. The applicable income tax rate is 40%, and the profit-sharing contribution is deductible for tax purposes.

Instructions

Compute the amount to be contributed to the profit-sharing fund for 2007.

3. With some of its products, Hiaasen Company includes coupons that are redeemable in merchandise. The coupons have no expiration date and, in the company's experience, 40% of them are redeemed. The liability for unredeemed coupons at December 31, 2006, was $9,000. During 2007, coupons worth $25,000 were issued, and merchandise worth $8,000 was distributed in exchange for coupons redeemed.

Instructions

Compute the amount of the liability that should appear on the December 31, 2007, balance sheet.

(AICPA adapted)

CONCEPTS FOR ANALYSIS

CA13-1   (Nature of Liabilities)   Presented below is the current liabilities section of Nomar Corporation.

	($000)	
	2007	2006
Current Liabilities		
Notes payable	$ 68,713	$ 7,700
Accounts payable	179,496	101,379
Compensation to employees	60,312	31,649
Accrued liabilities	158,198	77,621
Income taxes payable	10,486	26,491
Current maturities of long-term debt	16,592	6,649
Total current liabilities	$493,797	$251,489

Instructions

Answer the following questions.

(a) What are the essential characteristics that make an item a liability?

(b) How does one distinguish between a current liability and a long-term liability?

(c) What are accrued liabilities? Give three examples of accrued liabilities that Nomar might have.

(d) What is the theoretically correct way to value liabilities? How are current liabilities usually valued?

(e) Why are notes payable reported first in the current liabilities section?

(f) What might be the items that comprise Nomar's liability for "Compensation to employees"?

CA13-2   (Current versus Noncurrent Classification)   D'Annunzio Corporation includes the following items in its liabilities at December 31, 2007.

1. Notes payable, $25,000,000, due June 30, 2008.
2. Deposits from customers on equipment ordered by them from D'Annunzio, $6,250,000.
3. Salaries payable, $3,750,000, due January 14, 2008.

Instructions

Indicate in what circumstances, if any, each of the three liabilities above would be excluded from current liabilities.

CA13-3   (Refinancing of Short-Term Debt)   Levi Eshkol Corporation reports in the current liability section of its balance sheet at December 31, 2007 (its year-end), short-term obligations of $15,000,000, which includes the current portion of 12% long-term debt in the amount of $11,000,000 (matures in March 2008). Management has stated its intention to refinance the 12% debt whereby no portion of it will mature during 2008. The date of issuance of the financial statements is March 25, 2008.

Instructions

(a) Is management's intent enough to support long-term classification of the obligation in this situation?

(b) Assume that Eshkol Corporation issues $13,000,000 of 10-year debentures to the public in January 2008 and that management intends to use the proceeds to liquidate the $11,000,000 debt maturing in March 2008. Furthermore, assume that the debt maturing in March 2008 is paid from these proceeds prior to the issuance of the financial statements. Will this have any impact on the balance sheet classification at December 31, 2007? Explain your answer.

(c) Assume that Eshkol Corporation issues common stock to the public in January and that management intends to entirely liquidate the $11,000,000 debt maturing in March 2008 with the proceeds of this equity securities issue. In light of these events, should the $11,000,000 debt maturing in March 2008 be included in current liabilities at December 31, 2007?

(d) Assume that Eshkol Corporation, on February 15, 2008, entered into a financing agreement with a commercial bank that permits Eshkol Corporation to borrow at any time through 2009 up to $15,000,000 at the bank's prime rate of interest. Borrowings under the financing agreement mature three years after the date of the loan. The agreement is not cancelable except for violation of a provision with which compliance is objectively determinable. No violation of any provision exists at the date of issuance of the financial statements. Assume further that the current portion of long-term debt does not mature until August 2008. In addition, management intends to refinance the $11,000,000 obligation under the terms of the financial agreement with the bank, which is expected to be financially capable of honoring the agreement.

    (1) Given these facts, should the $11,000,000 be classified as current on the balance sheet at December 31, 2007?

    (2) Is disclosure of the refinancing method required?

CA13-4 (Refinancing of Short-Term Debt) Medvedev Inc. issued $10,000,000 of short-term commercial paper during the year 2006 to finance construction of a plant. At December 31, 2006, the corporation's year-end, Medvedev intends to refinance the commercial paper by issuing long-term debt. However, because the corporation temporarily has excess cash, in January 2007 it liquidates $4,000,000 of the commercial paper as the paper matures. In February 2007, Medvedev completes an $18,000,000 long-term debt offering. Later during the month of February, it issues its December 31, 2006, financial statements. The proceeds of the long-term debt offering are to be used to replenish $4,000,000 in working capital, to pay $6,000,000 of commercial paper as it matures in March 2007, and to pay $8,000,000 of construction costs expected to be incurred later that year to complete the plant.

Instructions

(a) How should the $10,000,000 of commercial paper be classified on the December 31, 2006, January 31, 2007, and February 28, 2007, balance sheets? Give support for your answer and also consider the cash element.

(b) What would your answer be if, instead of a refinancing at the date of issuance of the financial statements, a financing agreement existed at that date?

 CA13-5 (Loss Contingencies) On February 1, 2007, one of the huge storage tanks of Paunee Manufacturing Company exploded. Windows in houses and other buildings within a one-mile radius of the explosion were severely damaged, and a number of people were injured. As of February 15, 2007 (when the December 31, 2006, financial statements were completed and sent to the publisher for printing and public distribution), no suits had been filed or claims asserted against the company as a consequence of the explosion. The company fully anticipates that suits will be filed and claims asserted for injuries and damages. Because the casualty was uninsured and the company considered at fault, Paunee Manufacturing will have to cover the damages from its own resources.

Instructions

Discuss fully the accounting treatment and disclosures that should be accorded the casualty and related contingent losses in the financial statements dated December 31, 2006.

CA13-6 (Loss Contingency) Presented below is a note disclosure for Federer Corporation.

> **Litigation and Environmental:** The Company has been notified, or is a named or a potentially responsible party in a number of governmental (federal, state and local) and private actions associated with environmental matters, such as those relating to hazardous wastes, including certain sites which are on the United States EPA National Priorities List ("Superfund"). These actions seek cleanup costs, penalties and/or damages for personal injury or to property or natural resources.

> In 2007, the Company recorded a pre-tax charge of $56,229,000, included in the "Other expense (income)—net" caption of the Company's consolidated statements of income, as an additional provision for environmental matters. These expenditures are expected to take place over the next several years and are indicative of the Company's commitment to improve and maintain the environment in which it operates. At December 31, 2007, environmental accruals amounted to $69,931,000, of which $61,535,000 are considered noncurrent and are included in the "Deferred credits and other liabilities" caption of the Company's consolidated balance sheets.

> While it is impossible at this time to determine with certainty the ultimate outcome of environmental matters, it is management's opinion, based in part on the advice of independent counsel (after taking into account accruals and insurance coverage applicable to such actions) that when the costs are finally determined they will not have a material adverse effect on the financial position of the Company.

Instructions
Answer the following questions.

(a) What conditions must exist before a loss contingency can be recorded in the accounts?
(b) Suppose that Federer Corporation could not reasonably estimate the amount of the loss, although it could establish with a high degree of probability the minimum and maximum loss possible. How should this information be reported in the financial statements?
(c) If the amount of the loss is uncertain, how would the loss contingency be reported in the financial statements?

CA13-7 (Warranties and Loss Contingencies) The following two independent situations involve loss contingencies.

Part 1
Clarke Company sells two products, John and Henrick. Each carries a one-year warranty.

1. Product John—Product warranty costs, based on past experience, will normally be 1% of sales.
2. Product Henrick—Product warranty costs cannot be reasonably estimated because this is a new product line. However, the chief engineer believes that product warranty costs are likely to be incurred.

Instructions
How should Clarke report the estimated product warranty costs for each of the two types of merchandise above? Discuss the rationale for your answer. Do not discuss disclosures that should be made in Clarke's financial statements or notes.

Part 2
Toni Morrison Company is being sued for $4,000,000 for an injury caused to a child as a result of alleged negligence while the child was visiting the Toni Morrison Company plant in March 2007. The suit was filed in July 2007. Toni Morrison's lawyer states that it is probable that Toni Morrison will lose the suit and be found liable for a judgment costing anywhere from $400,000 to $2,000,000. However, the lawyer states that the most probable judgment is $800,000.

Instructions
How should Toni Morrison report the suit in its 2007 financial statements? Discuss the rationale for your answer. Include in your answer disclosures, if any, that should be made in Toni Morrison's financial statements or notes.

(AICPA adapted)

 CA13-8 (Warranties) The Elwood Company, owner of Bleacher Mall, charges Blue Clothing Store a rental fee of $600 per month plus 5% of yearly profits over $500,000. Jake Blue, the owner of the store, directs his accountant, Cab Callaway, to increase the estimate of bad debt expense and warranty costs in order to keep profits at $475,000.

Instructions
Answer the following questions.

(a) Should Callaway follow his boss's directive?
(b) Who is harmed if the estimates are increased?
(c) Is Jake Blue's directive ethical?

USING YOUR JUDGMENT

Financial Reporting Problem

P&G The Procter & Gamble Company (P&G)
The financial statements of P&G are presented in Appendix 5B or can be accessed on the KWW website.

 Instructions
Refer to these financial statements and the accompanying notes to answer the following questions.

(a) What was P&G's 2004 short-term debt and related weighted average interest rate on this debt?
(b) What was P&G's 2004 working capital, acid-test ratio, and current ratio? Comment on P&G's liquidity.
(c) What types of commitments and contingencies has P&G's reported in its financial statements? What is management's reaction to these contingencies?

Financial Statement Analysis Cases

Case 1 Northland Cranberries

Despite being a publicly traded company only since 1987, Northland Cranberries of Wisconsin Rapids, Wisconsin, is one of the world's largest cranberry growers. Despite its short life as a publicly traded corporation, it has engaged in an aggressive growth strategy. As a consequence, the company has taken on significant amounts of both short-term and long-term debt. The following information is taken from recent annual reports of the company.

Northland Cranberries	Current Year	Prior Year
Current assets	$ 6,745,759	$ 5,598,054
Total assets	107,744,751	83,074,339
Current liabilities	10,168,685	4,484,687
Total liabilities	73,118,204	49,948,787
Stockholders' equity	34,626,547	33,125,552
Net sales	21,783,966	18,051,355
Cost of goods sold	13,057,275	8,751,220
Interest expense	3,654,006	2,393,792
Income tax expense	1,051,000	1,917,000
Net income	1,581,707	2,942,954

Instructions

(a) Evaluate the company's liquidity by calculating and analyzing working capital and the current ratio.

(b) The following discussion of the company's liquidity was provided by the company in the Management Discussion and Analysis section of the company's annual report. Comment on whether you agree with management's statements, and what might be done to remedy the situation.

> The lower comparative current ratio in the current year was due to $3 million of short-term borrowing then outstanding which was incurred to fund the Yellow River Marsh acquisitions last year. As a result of the extreme seasonality of its business, the company does not believe that its current ratio or its underlying stated working capital at the current, fiscal year-end is a meaningful indication of the Company's liquidity. As of March 31 of each fiscal year, the Company has historically carried no significant amounts of inventories and by such date all of the Company's accounts receivable from its crop sold for processing under the supply agreements have been paid in cash, with the resulting cash received from such payments used to reduce indebtedness. The Company utilizes its revolving bank credit facility, together with cash generated from operations, to fund its working capital requirements throughout its growing season.

Case 2 Mohican Company

Presented below is the current liabilities section and related note of Mohican Company.

Mohican Company	(dollars in thousands) Current Year	(dollars in thousands) Prior Year
Current liabilities		
Current portion of long-term debt	$ 15,000	$ 10,000
Short-term debt	2,668	405
Accounts payable	29,495	42,427
Accrued warranty	16,843	16,741
Accrued marketing programs	17,512	16,585
Other accrued liabilities	35,653	33,290
Accrued and deferred income taxes	16,206	17,348
Total current liabilities	$133,377	$136,796

Notes to Consolidated Financial Statements

Note 1 (in part): Summary of Significant Accounting Policies and Related Data
Accrued Warranty The company provides an accrual for future warranty costs based upon the relationship of prior years' sales to actual warranty costs.

Instructions

Answer the following questions.

(a) What is the difference between the cash basis and the accrual basis of accounting for warranty costs?

(b) Under what circumstance, if any, would it be appropriate for Mohican Company to recognize deferred revenue on warranty contracts?

(c) If Mohican Company recognized deferred revenue on warranty contracts, how would it recognize this revenue in subsequent periods?

Comparative Analysis Case

The Coca-Cola Company and PepsiCo, Inc.

Instructions

Go to the book's website and use information found there to answer the following questions related to **The Coca-Cola Company and PepsiCo, Inc.**

(a) How much working capital do each of these companies have at the end of 2004?

(b) Compute both company's (a) current cash debt coverage ratio, (b) cash debt coverage ratio, (c) current ratio, (d) acid-test ratio, (e) receivable turnover ratio and (f) inventory turnover ratio for 2004. Comment on each company's overall liquidity.

(c) In PepsiCo's financial statements, it reports in the long-term debt section "short-term borrowings, reclassified." How can short-term borrowings be classified as long-term debt?

(d) What types of loss or gain contingencies do these two companies have at the end of 2004?

Research Cases

Case 1

Instructions

Obtain the most recent edition of *Accounting Trends and Techniques.* Examine the disclosures included under the section regarding gain contingencies, and answer the following questions.

(a) Determine the nature of each of the disclosed gain contingencies. Are there any common themes?

(b) How many of the footnotes include dollar amounts?

(c) What are the smallest and largest amounts disclosed?

Case 2

The January 25, 2002, edition of the *Wall Street Journal* contained an article by Schad Terhune titled "**Georgia Pacific** Says Asbestos Charge Will Result in Fourth Quarter Net Loss."

Instructions

Read the article and answer the following questions.

(a) Under what conditions does GAAP require firms to take charges for "anticipated claims"? Based on the information in the article, does it appear that Georgia-Pacific (GP) meets those conditions? Why or why not?

(b) Prepare the journal entry to record GP's $221 million charge. How would it be reported in the financial statements?

(c) Estimated losses must be based on a "reasonable" estimate. How did GP arrive at its estimate? Do you think this process would result in a reasonable estimate? Why or why not?

Case 3

As discussed in the chapter, an important consideration in evaluating current liabilities is a company's operating cycle. The operating cycle is the average time required to go from cash-to-cash in generating revenue. To determine the length of the operating cycle, two measures are used: the average days to sell inventory (inventory days) and the average days to collect receivables (receivable days). The inventory-days computation measures the average number of days it takes to move an item from raw materials or purchase to final sale (from the day it comes in the company's door to the point it is converted to cash or an account receivable). The receivable-days computation measures the average number of days it takes to collect an account.

Most businesses must then determine how to finance the period of time when the liquid assets are tied up in inventory and accounts receivable. To determine how much to finance, companies first determine how long it takes to pay their creditors, or *accounts payable days*. Accounts payable days measures the number of days it takes to pay a supplier invoice. Consider the following operating cycle worksheet for BOP Clothing Co. shown below.

	2006	2007
Cash	$ 45,000	$ 30,000
Accounts Receivable	250,000	325,000
Inventory	830,000	800,000
Accounts Payable	720,000	775,000
Purchases	1,100,000	1,425,000
Cost of Goods Sold	1,145,000	1,455,000
Sales	1,750,000	1,950,000
Operating Cycle		
Inventory days[1]	264.6	200.7
Receivable days[2]	52.1	60.8
Operating cycle	316.7	261.5
Less: Accounts payable days[3]	238.9	198.5
Days to be financed	77.8	63.0
Working capital	$405,000	$380,000
Current ratio	1.56	1.49
Acid-test ratio	0.41	0.46

[1]Inventory Days = (Inventory × 365)/Cost of Goods Sold
[2]Receivable Days = (Accounts Receivable × 365)/Sales
[3]Accounts Payable Days = (Accounts Payable × 365)/Purchases
Purchases = Cost of Goods Sold + Ending Inventory − Beginning Inventory. The ratios above assume that other current assets and liabilities are negligible.

These data indicate that BOP has reduced its overall operating cycle (to 261.5 days) as well as the number of days to be financed with sources of funds other than accounts payable (from 78 to 63 days). Most businesses cannot finance the operating cycle with accounts payable financing alone, so working capital financing, usually short-term interest-bearing loans, is needed to cover the shortfall. In this case, BOP would need to borrow less money to finance its operating cycle in 2007 than in 2006.

Instructions

(a) Use the BOP analysis to briefly discuss how the operating cycle data relate to the amount of working capital and the current and acid-test ratios.

(b) Select two other real companies that are in the same industry and complete the operating cycle worksheet above, along with the working capital and ratio analysis. Briefly summarize and interpret the results. To simplify the analysis, you may use ending balances to compute turnover ratios.

[Adapted from Operating Cycle Worksheet at www.entrepreneur.com]

Professional Research: Financial Accounting and Reporting

Hincapie Co. manufactures specialty bike accessories. The company is known for product quality, and it has offered one of the best warranties in the industry on its higher-priced products—a lifetime guarantee, performing all the warranty work in its own shops. The warranty on these products is included in the sales price.

Due to the recent introduction and growth in sales of some products targeted to the low-price market, Hincapie is considering partnering with another company to do the warranty work on this line of products, if customers purchase a service contract at the time of original product purchase. Hincapie has called you to advise the company on the accounting for this new warranty arrangement.

Instructions

Using the **Financial Accounting Research System (FARS)**, respond to the following items. (Provide text strings used in your search.)

(a) Identify the accounting literature that addresses the accounting for the type of separately priced warranty that Hincapie is considering.

(b) When are warranty contracts considered separately priced?

(c) What are incremental direct acquisition costs and how should they be treated?

(d) How many letters of comment were received on this proposed Technical Bulletin? Why did some of the respondents feel that the effective date of this Technical Bulletin should be delayed?

Professional Simulation

In this simulation you are asked to address questions related to the accounting for current liabilities. Prepare responses to all parts.

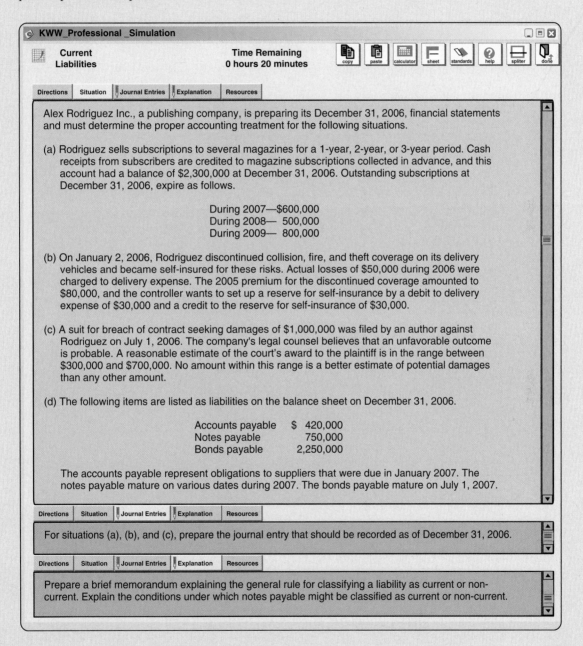

KWW_Professional _Simulation

Current Liabilities   **Time Remaining** 0 hours 20 minutes

copy | paste | calculator | sheet | standards | help | splitter | done

Directions | Situation | Journal Entries | Explanation | Resources

Alex Rodriguez Inc., a publishing company, is preparing its December 31, 2006, financial statements and must determine the proper accounting treatment for the following situations.

(a) Rodriguez sells subscriptions to several magazines for a 1-year, 2-year, or 3-year period. Cash receipts from subscribers are credited to magazine subscriptions collected in advance, and this account had a balance of $2,300,000 at December 31, 2006. Outstanding subscriptions at December 31, 2006, expire as follows.

> During 2007—$600,000
> During 2008— 500,000
> During 2009— 800,000

(b) On January 2, 2006, Rodriguez discontinued collision, fire, and theft coverage on its delivery vehicles and became self-insured for these risks. Actual losses of $50,000 during 2006 were charged to delivery expense. The 2005 premium for the discontinued coverage amounted to $80,000, and the controller wants to set up a reserve for self-insurance by a debit to delivery expense of $30,000 and a credit to the reserve for self-insurance of $30,000.

(c) A suit for breach of contract seeking damages of $1,000,000 was filed by an author against Rodriguez on July 1, 2006. The company's legal counsel believes that an unfavorable outcome is probable. A reasonable estimate of the court's award to the plaintiff is in the range between $300,000 and $700,000. No amount within this range is a better estimate of potential damages than any other amount.

(d) The following items are listed as liabilities on the balance sheet on December 31, 2006.

> Accounts payable $ 420,000
> Notes payable 750,000
> Bonds payable 2,250,000

The accounts payable represent obligations to suppliers that were due in January 2007. The notes payable mature on various dates during 2007. The bonds payable mature on July 1, 2007.

Directions | Situation | Journal Entries | Explanation | Resources

For situations (a), (b), and (c), prepare the journal entry that should be recorded as of December 31, 2006.

Directions | Situation | Journal Entries | Explanation | Resources

Prepare a brief memorandum explaining the general rule for classifying a liability as current or non-current. Explain the conditions under which notes payable might be classified as current or non-current.

> **Remember to check the book's companion website to find additional resources for this chapter.**

LONG-TERM LIABILITIES

Your Debt Is Killing My Stock

Traditionally, investors in the stock and bond markets operate in their own separate worlds. However, in recent volatile markets, even quiet murmurs in the bond market have been amplified into movements (usually negative) in stock prices. At one extreme, these gyrations heralded the demise of a company well before the investors could sniff out the problem.

The swift decline of **Enron** in late 2001 provided the ultimate lesson: A company with no credit is no company at all. As one analyst remarked, "You can no longer have an opinion on a company's stock without having an appreciation for its credit rating." Other energy companies, such as **Calpine**, **NRG Energy**, and **AES Corp.**, also felt the effect of Enron's troubles as lenders tightened or closed down the credit supply and raised interest rates on already-high levels of debt. The result? Stock prices took a hit.

Other industries are not immune from the negative stock price effects of credit problems. For example, analysts at **TheStreet.com** compiled a list of companies with high debt levels and low ability to cover interest costs. Among them is **Goodyear Tire and Rubber**, which reported debt six times greater than its equity. Goodyear is a classic example of how swift and crippling a heavy debt-load can be. Not too long ago, Goodyear had a high debt rating and was paying a good dividend. But with mounting operating losses, Goodyear's debt became a huge burden, its debt rating fell to junk-status, the company cut its dividend, and its stock price dropped 80%. This was yet another example of stock prices taking a hit due to concerns about credit quality. Thus, even if your investment tastes are in stocks, keep an eye on the liabilities.[1]

---

[1]Adapted from Steven Vames, "Credit Quality, Stock Investing Seem to Go Hand in Hand," *Wall Street Journal* (April 1, 2002), p. R4 and Herb Greenberg, "The Hidden Dangers of Debt," *Fortune* (July 21, 2003), p. 153.

Learning Objectives

After studying this chapter, you should be able to:

1 Describe the formal procedures associated with issuing long-term debt.

2 Identify various types of bond issues.

3 Describe the accounting valuation for bonds at date of issuance.

4 Apply the methods of bond discount and premium amortization.

5 Describe the accounting for the extinguishment of debt.

6 Explain the accounting for long-term notes payable.

7 Explain the reporting of off-balance-sheet financing arrangements.

8 Indicate how to present and analyze long-term debt.

As our opening story indicates, investors pay considerable attention to a company's liabilities. The stock market severely punishes companies with high debt levels and the related impact of higher interest costs on income performance. In this chapter we explain the accounting issues related to long-term debt. The content and organization of the chapter are as follows.

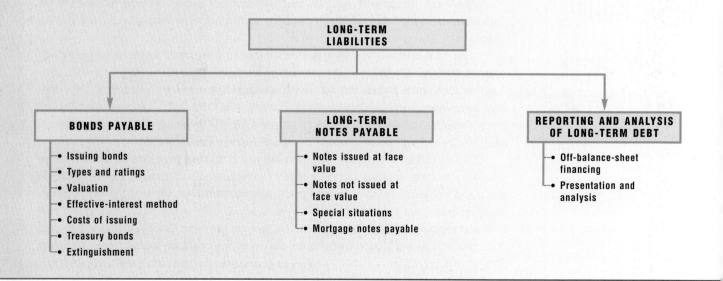

SECTION 1 | *BONDS PAYABLE*

Long-term debt consists of probable future sacrifices of economic benefits arising from present obligations that are not payable within a year or the operating cycle of the company, whichever is longer. Bonds payable, long-term notes payable, mortgages payable, pension liabilities, and lease liabilities are examples of long-term liabilities.

A corporation, per its bylaws, usually requires approval by the board of directors and the stockholders before bonds or notes can be issued. The same holds true for other types of long-term debt arrangements.

OBJECTIVE 1
Describe the formal procedures associated with issuing long-term debt.

Generally, long-term debt has various **covenants** or **restrictions** that protect both lenders and borrowers. The indenture or agreement often includes the amounts authorized to be issued, interest rate, due date(s), call provisions, property pledged as security, sinking fund requirements, working capital and dividend restrictions, and limitations concerning the assumption of additional debt. Companies should describe these features in the body of the financial statements or the notes if important for a complete understanding of the financial position and the results of operations.

Although it would seem that these covenants provide adequate protection to the long-term debtholder, many bondholders suffer considerable losses when companies add more debt to the capital structure. Consider what can happen to bondholders in leveraged buyouts (LBOs), which are usually led by management. In an LBO of **RJR Nabisco**, for example, solidly rated 9⅜ percent bonds due in 2016 plunged 20 percent in value when management announced the leveraged buyout. Such a loss in value occurs because the additional debt added to the capital structure increases the likelihood of default. Although covenants protect bondholders, they can still suffer losses when debt levels get too high.

ISSUING BONDS

A bond arises from a contract known as a **bond indenture**. A bond represents a promise to pay: (1) a sum of money at a designated maturity date, plus (2) periodic interest at a specified rate on the maturity amount (face value). Individual bonds are evidenced by a paper certificate and typically have a $1,000 face value. Companies usually make bond interest payments semiannually, although the interest rate is generally expressed as an annual rate. The main purpose of bonds is to borrow for the long term when the amount of capital needed is too large for one lender to supply. By issuing bonds in $100, $1,000, or $10,000 denominations, a company can divide a large amount of long-term indebtedness into many small investing units, thus enabling more than one lender to participate in the loan.

A company may sell an entire bond issue to an investment bank which acts as a selling agent in the process of marketing the bonds. In such arrangements, investment banks may either underwrite the entire issue by guaranteeing a certain sum to the company, thus taking the risk of selling the bonds for whatever price they can get (firm underwriting). Or they may sell the bond issue for a commission on the proceeds of the sale (best-efforts underwriting). Alternatively, the issuing company may sell the bonds directly to a large institution, financial or otherwise, without the aid of an underwriter (private placement).

TYPES AND RATINGS OF BONDS

Below, we define some of the more common types of bonds found in practice.

OBJECTIVE 2
Identify various types of bond issues.

TYPES OF BONDS

SECURED AND UNSECURED BONDS. **Secured bonds** are backed by a pledge of some sort of collateral. Mortgage bonds are secured by a claim on real estate. Collateral trust bonds are secured by stocks and bonds of other corporations. Bonds not backed by collateral are **unsecured**. A **debenture bond** is unsecured. A "junk bond" is unsecured and also very risky, and therefore pays a high interest rate. Companies often use these bonds to finance leveraged buyouts.

TERM, SERIAL BONDS, AND CALLABLE BONDS. Bond issues that mature on a single date are called **term bonds**; issues that mature in installments are called **serial bonds**. Serially maturing bonds are frequently used by school or sanitary districts, municipalities, or other local taxing bodies that receive money through a special levy. **Callable bonds** give the issuer the right to call and retire the bonds prior to maturity.

CONVERTIBLE, COMMODITY-BACKED, AND DEEP-DISCOUNT BONDS. If bonds are convertible into other securities of the corporation for a specified time after issuance, they are **convertible bonds**.

Two types of bonds have been developed in an attempt to attract capital in a tight money market—commodity-backed bonds and deep-discount bonds. **Commodity-backed bonds** (also called **asset-linked bonds**) are redeemable in measures of a commodity, such as barrels of oil, tons of coal, or ounces of rare metal. To illustrate, Sunshine Mining, a silver-mining company, sold two issues of bonds redeemable with either $1,000 in cash or 50 ounces of silver, whichever is greater at maturity, and that have a stated interest rate of 8½ percent. The accounting problem is one of projecting the maturity value, especially since silver has fluctuated between $4 and $40 an ounce since issuance.

JCPenney Company sold the first publicly marketed long-term debt securities in the United States that do not bear interest. These **deep-discount bonds**, also referred to as **zero-interest debenture bonds**, are sold at a discount that provides the buyer's total interest payoff at maturity.

> **REGISTERED AND BEARER (COUPON) BONDS.** Bonds issued in the name of the owner are **registered bonds** and require surrender of the certificate and issuance of a new certificate to complete a sale. A **bearer** or **coupon bond**, however, is not recorded in the name of the owner and may be transferred from one owner to another by mere delivery.
>
> **INCOME AND REVENUE BONDS. Income bonds** pay no interest unless the issuing company is profitable. **Revenue bonds**, so called because the interest on them is paid from specified revenue sources, are most frequently issued by airports, school districts, counties, toll-road authorities, and governmental bodies.

WHAT DO THE NUMBERS MEAN?

ALL ABOUT BONDS

How do investors monitor their bond investments? Typically, they review the bond listings found in the newspaper or online. Corporate bond listings in the financial press show the coupon or interest rate, maturity date, and last price. However, because corporate bonds are more actively traded by large institutional investors, the listings also indicate the current yield and include the volume traded. Corporate bond listings would look like those below.

Bonds	Cur. Yld.	Vol	Close	Net Chg.
BosCelts 6s38	9.2	22	65 3/8	+1/4
PacBell 6 5/8 34	6.7	5	99 1/8	−1/8

The companies issuing the bonds are listed in the first column—in this case, the professional basketball team the **Boston Celtics**, and the telecommunications company **Pacific Bell**. Immediately after the names, comes the interest rate paid by the bond as a percentage of its par value. The Celtics' bond pays 6 percent; PacBell's pays 6 5/8 percent. (The small "s" in the Celtics' listing simply separates the interest rate from the year the bond matures, 2038.) The PacBell bond matures in 2034.

Reading on, the basketball team's bond has a current yield of 9.2 percent based on its closing price of $653.75 per $1,000. The volume traded on the exchange the day before amounted to $22,000, and the price rose $2.50. Similarly, PacBell had a volume of $5,000 and closed nearer its par value, $991.25, down $1.25 for the day.

Also, as indicated in the chapter, interest rates and the bond's term to maturity have a real effect on bond prices. For example, an increase in interest rates will lead to a decline in bond values; a decrease in interest rates will lead to a rise in bond values. These effects are shown in the data reported below, based on three different bond funds.

Bond Price Changes in Response to Interest Rate Changes	1% Interest Rate Increase	1% Interest Rate Decrease
Short-term fund (2–5 years)	−2.5%	+2.5%
Intermediate-term fund (5 years)	−5%	+5%
Long-term fund (10 years)	−10%	+10%

Source: Data from The Vanguard Group.

Another factor that affects bond prices is the call feature, which decreases the value of the bond. Investors must be rewarded for the risk that the issuer will call the bond if interest rates decline, which forces the investor to reinvest at lower rates.

Source: The Bond Market Association (*www.investinginbonds.com*).

OBJECTIVE 3
Describe the accounting valuation for bonds at date of issuance.

VALUATION OF BONDS PAYABLE—DISCOUNT AND PREMIUM

The issuance and marketing of bonds to the public does not happen overnight. It usually takes weeks or even months. First, the issuing company must arrange for underwriters that will help market and sell the bonds. Then it must obtain the Securities and Exchange

Commission's approval of the bond issue, undergo audits, and issue a prospectus (a document which describes the features of the bond and related financial information). Finally, the company must generally have the bond certificates printed. Frequently the issuing company establishes the terms of a bond indenture well in advance of the sale of the bonds. Between the time the company sets these terms and the time it issues the bonds, the market conditions and the financial position of the issuing corporation may change significantly. Such changes affect the marketability of the bonds and thus their selling price.

The selling price of a bond issue is set by the supply and demand of buyers and sellers, relative risk, market conditions, and the state of the economy. The investment community values a bond at the **present value of its expected future cash flows**, which consist of (1) interest and (2) principal. The rate used to compute the present value of these cash flows is the interest rate that provides an acceptable return on an investment commensurate with the issuer's risk characteristics.

The interest rate written in the terms of the bond indenture (and often printed on the bond certificate) is known as the **stated, coupon,** or **nominal rate.** The issuer of the bonds sets this rate. The stated rate is expressed as a percentage of the **face value** of the bonds (also called the **par value, principal amount,** or **maturity value**).

If the rate employed by the investment community (buyers) differs from the stated rate, the present value of the bonds computed by the buyers (and the current purchase price) will differ from the face value of the bonds. The difference between the face value and the present value of the bonds determines the actual price that buyers pay for the bonds. This difference is either a discount or premium.[2] If the bonds sell for less than face value, they sell at a **discount.** If the bonds sell for more than face value, they sell at a **premium.**

The rate of interest actually earned by the bondholders is called the **effective yield** or **market rate.** If bonds sell at a discount, the effective yield exceeds the stated rate. Conversely, if bonds sell at a premium, the effective yield is lower than the stated rate. Several variables affect the bond's price while it is outstanding, most notably the market rate of interest. There is an inverse relationship between the market interest rate and the price of the bond.

Here we consider an example to illustrate the computation of the **present value of a bond issue.** Assume that ServiceMaster issues $100,000 in bonds, due in five years with 9 percent interest payable annually at year-end. At the time of issue, the market rate for such bonds is 11 percent. The time diagram in Illustration 14-1 depicts both the interest and the principal cash flows.

INTERNATIONAL INSIGHT

IFRS for long-term debt permit valuation of long-term debt and other liabilities at fair value with gains and losses on changes in fair value recorded in income (referred to as the "fair value option").

ILLUSTRATION 14-1
Time Diagram for Bond Cash Flows

---

[2]Until the 1950s, corporations commonly issued bonds with low, even-percentage coupons (such as 4 percent) to demonstrate their financial solidity. Frequently, large discounts resulted. More recently, it has become acceptable to set the stated rate of interest on bonds in rather precise fractions (such as 10 ⅞ percent). Companies usually attempt to align the stated rate as closely as possible with the market or effective rate at the time of issue.

Although discounts and premiums continue to occur, their absolute magnitude tends to be much smaller; many times it is immaterial. A study conducted in the mid-80's documented that of 685 new debt offerings, none were issued at a premium. Approximately 95 percent were issued either with no discount or at a price above 98. Now, however, zero-interest (deep discount) bonds are more popular, and they cause substantial discounts.

The actual principal and interest cash flows are discounted at an 11 percent rate for five periods as shown in Illustration 14-2.

ILLUSTRATION 14-2
Present Value
Computation of Bond
Selling at a Discount

Present value of the principal:	
$100,000 × .59345 (Table 6-2)	$59,345.00
Present value of the interest payments:	
$9,000 × 3.69590 (Table 6-4)	33,263.10
Present value (selling price) of the bonds	$92,608.10

By paying $92,608.10 at the date of issue, investors realize an effective rate or yield of 11 percent over the five-year term of the bonds. These bonds would sell at a discount of $7,391.90 ($100,000 − $92,608.10). The price at which the bonds sell is typically stated as a percentage of the face or par value of the bonds. For example, the ServiceMaster bonds sold for 92.6 (92.6% of par). If ServiceMaster had received $102,000, then the bonds sold for 102 (102% of par).

HOW'S MY RATING?

WHAT DO THE NUMBERS MEAN?

Two major publication companies, **Moody's Investors Service** and **Standard & Poor's Corporation**, issue quality ratings on every public debt issue. The following table summarizes the ratings issued by Standard & Poor's, along with historical default rates on bonds with different ratings. As expected, bonds receiving the highest quality rating of AAA have the lowest historical default rates. Bonds rated below BBB, which are considered below investment grade ("junk bonds"), experience default rates ranging from 20 to 50 percent.

Original Rating	AAA	AA	A	BBB	BB	B	CCC
Default Rate*	0.52%	1.31	2.32	6.64	19.52	35.76	54.38

*Percentage of defaults by issuers recently rated by Standard & Poor's, based on rating they were initially assigned. *Source*: Data from Standard & Poor's Corp.

Debt ratings reflect credit quality. The market closely monitors these ratings when determining the required yield and pricing of bonds at issuance and in periods after issuance, especially if a bond's rating is upgraded or downgraded. Data on recent upgrades and downgrades suggest there are a lot more fallen angels (downgraded debt) than rising stars (upgraded debt).

Whereas the dollar amount of upgrades exceeded downgrades in 1999, the dollar amount of downgrades was more than seven times the rising-star amounts in 2002. It is not surprising, then, that bond investors and companies who issue bonds keep a close watch on debt ratings—both when bonds are issued and while the bonds are outstanding.

Source: A. Borrus, M. McNamee, and H. Timmons, "The Credit Raters: How They Work and How They Might Work Better," *Business Week* (April 8, 2002), pp. 38–40; and the T. Rowe Price Report (Winter 2003).

When bonds sell below face value, it means that investors demand a rate of interest **higher** than the stated rate. Usually this occurs because the investors can earn a greater rate on alternative investments of equal risk. They cannot change the stated rate, so they refuse to pay face value for the bonds. Thus, by changing the amount invested, they alter the effective rate of return. The investors receive interest at the stated rate computed on the face value, but they actually earn at **an effective rate that exceeds the stated rate because they paid less than face value for the bonds.** (Later in the chapter, in Illustrations 14-6 and 14-7, we show an illustration for a bond that sells at a premium.)

Bonds Issued at Par on Interest Date

When a company issues bonds on an interest payment date at par (face value), it accrues no interest. No premium or discount exists. The company simply records the cash proceeds and the face value of the bonds. To illustrate, if Buchanan Company issues at par 10-year term bonds with a par value of $800,000, dated January 1, 2007, and bearing interest at an annual rate of 10 percent payable semiannually on January 1 and July 1, it records the following entry:

Cash	800,000	
Bonds Payable		800,000

Buchanan records the first semiannual interest payment of $40,000 ($800,000 × .10 × 1/2) on July 1, 2007, as follows.

Bond Interest Expense	40,000	
Cash		40,000

It records accrued interest expense at December 31, 2007 (year-end) as follows.

Bond Interest Expense	40,000	
Bond Interest Payable		40,000

Bonds Issued at Discount or Premium on Interest Date

If Buchanan Company issues the $800,000 of bonds on January 1, 2007, at 97 (meaning 97 percent of par), it records the issuance as follows.

Cash ($800,000 × .97)	776,000	
Discount on Bonds Payable	24,000	
Bonds Payable		800,000

> **OBJECTIVE 4**
> Apply the methods of bond discount and premium amortization.

Recall from our earlier discussion that because of its relation to interest, **companies amortize the discount and charge it to interest expense over the period of time that the bonds are outstanding.**

The **straight-line method**[3] amortizes a constant amount each year. For example, using the bond discount of $24,000, Buchanan amortizes $2,400 to interest expense each year for 10 years ($24,000 ÷ 10 years). It records amortization annually as follows.

Bond Interest Expense	2,400	
Discount on Bonds Payable		2,400

At the end of the first year, 2007, following the amortization entry above, the unamortized balance in Discount on Bonds Payable is $21,600 ($24,000 − $2,400).

If Buchanan dates and sells the bonds on October 1, 2007, and if the fiscal year of the corporation ends on December 31, the discount amortized during 2007 would be only 3/12 of 1/10 of $24,000, or $600. Buchanan must also record three months of accrued interest on December 31.

---

[3]Although the effective-interest method is preferred for amortization of discount or premium, to keep these initial illustrations simple, we have chosen to use the straight-line method (which is acceptable if the results obtained are not materially different from those produced by the effective-interest method).

Premium on Bonds Payable is accounted for in a manner similar to that for Discount on Bonds Payable. If Buchanan dates and sells 10-year bonds with a par value of $800,000 on January 1, 2007, at 103, it records the issuance as follows.

Cash ($800,000 × 1.03)	824,000	
Premium on Bonds Payable		24,000
Bonds Payable		800,000

At the end of 2007 and for each year the bonds are outstanding, Buchanan amortizes the premium on a straight-line basis with the following entry.

Premium on Bonds Payable	2,400	
Bond Interest Expense		2,400

Amortization of a discount increases bond interest expense. Amortization of a premium decreases bond interest expense. Later in the chapter we discuss amortization of a discount or premium under the effective-interest method.

The issuer may call some bonds at a stated price after a certain date. This call feature gives the issuing corporation the opportunity to reduce its bonded indebtedness or take advantage of lower interest rates. **Whether callable or not, a company must amortize any premium or discount over the bond's life to maturity because early redemption (call of the bond) is not a certainty.**

Bonds Issued between Interest Dates

Companies usually make bond interest payments semiannually, on dates specified in the bond indenture. When companies issue bonds on other than the interest payment dates, **buyers of the bonds will pay the seller the interest accrued from the last interest payment date to the date of issue.** The purchasers of the bonds, in effect, pay the bond issuer in advance for that portion of the full six-months' interest payment to which they are not entitled because they have not held the bonds for that period. **Then, on the next semiannual interest payment date, purchasers will receive the full six-months' interest payment.**

To illustrate, assume that on March 1, 2007, Taft Corporation issues 10-year bonds, dated January 1, 2007, with a par value of $800,000. These bonds have an annual interest rate of 6 percent, payable semiannually on January 1 and July 1. Because Taft issues the bonds between interest dates, it records the bond issuance at **par plus accrued interest** as follows.

Cash	808,000	
Bonds Payable		800,000
Bond Interest Expense ($800,000 × .06 × 2/12)		8,000
(Interest Payable might be credited instead)		

The purchaser advances two months' interest. On July 1, 2007, four months after the date of purchase, Taft pays the purchaser six months' interest. Taft makes the following entry on July 1, 2007.

Bond Interest Expense	24,000	
Cash		24,000

The Bond Interest Expense account now contains a debit balance of $16,000, which represents the proper amount of interest expense—four months at 6 percent on $800,000.

The illustration above was simplified by having the January 1, 2007, bonds issued on March 1, 2007, **at par**. If, however, Taft issued the 6 percent bonds at 102, its March 1 entry would be:

Cash [($800,000 × 1.02) + ($800,000 × .06 × 2/12)]	824,000	
Bonds Payable		800,000
Premium on Bonds Payable ($800,000 × .02)		16,000
Bond Interest Expense		8,000

Taft would amortize the premium **from the date of sale** (March 1, 2007), not from the date of the bonds (January 1, 2007).

EFFECTIVE-INTEREST METHOD

The preferred procedure for amortization of a discount or premium is the **effective-interest method** (also called **present value amortization**). Under the effective-interest method, companies:

1 Compute bond interest expense first by multiplying the **carrying value** (book value) of the bonds at the beginning of the period by the effective interest rate.[4]

2 Determine the bond discount or premium amortization next by comparing the bond interest expense with the interest (cash) to be paid.

Illustration 14-3 depicts graphically the computation of the amortization.

ILLUSTRATION 14-3
Bond Discount and
Premium Amortization
Computation

The effective-interest method produces a periodic interest expense equal to **a constant percentage of the carrying value of the bonds.** Since the percentage is the effective rate of interest incurred by the borrower at the time of issuance, the effective-interest method matches expenses with revenues better than the straight-line method.

Both the effective-interest and straight-line methods result in the **same total amount of interest expense over the term of the bonds.** However, when the annual amounts are materially different, generally accepted accounting principles require use of the effective-interest method.[5]

Bonds Issued at a Discount

To illustrate amortization of a discount under the effective-interest method, Evermaster Corporation issued $100,000 of 8 percent term bonds on January 1, 2007, due on January 1, 2012, with interest payable each July 1 and January 1. Because the investors required an effective-interest rate of 10 percent, they paid $92,278 for the $100,000 of bonds, creating a $7,722 discount. Evermaster computes the $7,722 discount as follows.[6]

Maturity value of bonds payable		$100,000
Present value of $100,000 due in 5 years at 10%, interest payable semiannually (Table 6-2); *FV*(*PVF*₁₀,₅%); ($100,000 × .61391)	$61,391	
Present value of $4,000 interest payable semiannually for 5 years at 10% annually (Table 6-4); *R*(*PVF-OA*₁₀,₅%); ($4,000 × 7.72173)	30,887	
Proceeds from sale of bonds		92,278
Discount on bonds payable		$ 7,722

ILLUSTRATION 14-4
Computation of Discount
on Bonds Payable

---

[4]The **carrying value** is the face amount minus any unamortized discount or plus any unamortized premium. The term *carrying value* is synonymous with *book value.*

[5]"Interest on Receivables and Payables," *Opinions of the Accounting Principles Board No. 21* (New York: AICPA, 1971), par. 16.

[6]Because companies pay interest semiannually, the interest rate used is 5% (10% × ½). The number of periods is 10 (5 years × 2).

The five-year amortization schedule appears in Illustration 14-5.

ILLUSTRATION 14-5
Bond Discount
Amortization Schedule

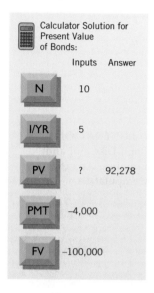

Calculator Solution for
Present Value
of Bonds:

	Inputs	Answer
N	10	
I/YR	5	
PV	?	92,278
PMT	–4,000	
FV	–100,000	

SCHEDULE OF BOND DISCOUNT AMORTIZATION
EFFECTIVE-INTEREST METHOD—SEMIANNUAL INTEREST PAYMENTS
5-YEAR, 8% BONDS SOLD TO YIELD 10%

Date	Cash Paid	Interest Expense	Discount Amortized	Carrying Amount of Bonds
1/1/07				$ 92,278
7/1/07	$ 4,000[a]	$ 4,614[b]	$ 614[c]	92,892[d]
1/1/08	4,000	4,645	645	93,537
7/1/08	4,000	4,677	677	94,214
1/1/09	4,000	4,711	711	94,925
7/1/09	4,000	4,746	746	95,671
1/1/10	4,000	4,783	783	96,454
7/1/10	4,000	4,823	823	97,277
1/1/11	4,000	4,864	864	98,141
7/1/11	4,000	4,907	907	99,048
1/1/12	4,000	4,952	952	100,000
	$40,000	$47,722	$7,722	

[a]$4,000 = $100,000 $\times$.08 $\times$ 6/12
[b]$4,614 = $92,278 $\times$.10 $\times$ 6/12
[c]$614 = $4,614 − $4,000
[d]$92,892 = $92,278 + $614

Evermaster records the issuance of its bonds at a discount on January 1, 2007, as follows:

Cash	92,278	
Discount on Bonds Payable	7,722	
Bonds Payable		100,000

It records the first interest payment on July 1, 2007, and amortization of the discount as follows:

Bond Interest Expense	4,614	
Discount on Bonds Payable		614
Cash		4,000

Evermaster records the interest expense accrued at December 31, 2007 (year-end) and amortization of the discount as follows:

Bond Interest Expense	4,645	
Bond Interest Payable		4,000
Discount on Bonds Payable		645

Bonds Issued at a Premium

Now assume that for the bond issue described above, investors are willing to accept an effective interest rate of 6 percent. In that case, they would pay $108,530 or a premium of $8,530, computed as follows.

ILLUSTRATION 14-6
Computation of Premium
on Bonds Payable

Maturity value of bonds payable		$100,000
Present value of $100,000 due in 5 years at 6%, interest payable semiannually (Table 6-2); $FV(PVF_{10,3\%})$; ($100,000 $\times$ .74409)	$74,409	
Present value of $4,000 interest payable semiannually for 5 years at 6% annually (Table 6-4); $R(PVF\text{-}OA_{10,3\%})$; ($4,000 $\times$ 8.53020)	34,121	
Proceeds from sale of bonds		108,530
Premium on bonds payable		$ 8,530

The five-year amortization schedule appears in Illustration 14-7.

SCHEDULE OF BOND PREMIUM AMORTIZATION
EFFECTIVE-INTEREST METHOD—SEMIANNUAL INTEREST PAYMENTS
5-YEAR, 8% BONDS SOLD TO YIELD 6%

Date	Cash Paid	Interest Expense	Premium Amortized	Carrying Amount of Bonds
1/1/07				$108,530
7/1/07	$ 4,000[a]	$ 3,256[b]	$ 744[c]	107,786[d]
1/1/08	4,000	3,234	766	107,020
7/1/08	4,000	3,211	789	106,231
1/1/09	4,000	3,187	813	105,418
7/1/09	4,000	3,162	838	104,580
1/1/10	4,000	3,137	863	103,717
7/1/10	4,000	3,112	888	102,829
1/1/11	4,000	3,085	915	101,914
7/1/11	4,000	3,057	943	100,971
1/1/12	4,000	3,029	971	100,000
	$40,000	$31,470	$8,530	

[a]$4,000 = $100,000 × .08 × 6/12
[b]$3,256 = $108,530 × .06 × 6/12
[c]$744 = $4,000 − $3,256
[d]$107,786 = $108,530 − $744

ILLUSTRATION 14-7
Bond Premium
Amortization Schedule

Evermaster records the issuance of its bonds at a premium on January 1, 2007, as follows:

Cash	108,530	
Premium on Bonds Payable		8,530
Bonds Payable		100,000

Evermaster records the first interest payment on July 1, 2007, and amortization of the premium as follows:

Bond Interest Expense	3,256	
Premium on Bonds Payable	744	
Cash		4,000

Evermaster should amortize the discount or premium as an adjustment to interest expense over the life of the bond in such a way as to result in a **constant rate of interest** when applied to the carrying amount of debt outstanding at the beginning of any given period.

Accruing Interest

In our previous examples, the interest payment dates and the date the financial statements were issued were the same. For example, when Evermaster sold bonds at a premium (page 680), the two interest payment dates coincided with the financial reporting dates. However, what happens if Evermaster wishes to report financial statements at the end of February 2007? In this case, the company **prorates** the premium by the appropriate number of months, to arrive at the proper interest expense, as follows.

Interest accrual ($4,000 × 2/6)	$1,333.33
Premium amortized ($744 × 2/6)	(248.00)
Interest expense (Jan.–Feb.)	$1,085.33

ILLUSTRATION 14-8
Computation of Interest
Expense

Evermaster records this accrual as follows.

Bond Interest Expense	1,085.33	
Premium on Bonds Payable	248.00	
Bond Interest Payable		1,333.33

If the company prepares financial statements six months later, it follows the same procedure. That is, the premium amortized would be as follows.

ILLUSTRATION 14-9
Computation of Premium Amortization

Premium amortized (March–June) ($744 × $\frac{4}{6}$)	$496.00
Premium amortized (July–August) ($766 × $\frac{2}{6}$)	255.33
Premium amortized (March–August 2004)	$751.33

The interest-accrual computation is much simpler if the company uses the straight-line method. For example, the total premium is $8,530, which Evermaster allocates evenly over the five-year period. Thus, premium amortization per month is $142.17 ($8,530 ÷ 60 months).

Classification of Discount and Premium

Discount on bonds payable is **not an asset**. It does not provide any future economic benefit. In return for the use of borrowed funds, a company must pay interest. A bond discount means that the company borrowed less than the face or maturity value of the bond. It therefore faces an actual (effective) interest rate higher than the stated (nominal) rate. Conceptually, discount on bonds payable is a liability valuation account. That is, it reduces the face or maturity amount of the related liability.[7] This account is referred to as a **contra account**.

Similarly, premium on bonds payable has no existence apart from the related debt. The lower interest cost results because the proceeds of borrowing exceed the face or maturity amount of the debt. Conceptually, premium on bonds payable is a *liability* valuation account. It adds to the face or maturity amount of the related liability.[8] This account is referred to as an **adjunct account**. As a result, **companies report bond discounts and bond premiums as a direct deduction from or addition to the face amount of the bond**.

COSTS OF ISSUING BONDS

The issuance of bonds involves engraving and printing costs, legal and accounting fees, commissions, promotion costs, and other similar charges. Companies are required to charge these costs to an asset account, often referred to as Unamortized Bond Issue Costs. Companies then allocate these Unamortized Bond Issue Costs over the life of the debt, in a manner similar to that used for discount on bonds.[9]

We disagree with this approach. Unamortized bond issue cost in our view is an expense (or a reduction of the related liability.)

Apparently the FASB also disagrees with the current GAAP treatment and notes in *Concepts Statement No. 6* that debt issue cost is not considered an asset because it provides no future economic benefit. The cost of issuing bonds, in effect, reduces the proceeds of the bonds issued and increases the effective interest rate. Companies may thus account for it the same as the unamortized discount.

---

[7]"Elements of Financial Statements of Business Enterprises," *Statement of Financial Accounting Concepts No. 6* (Stamford, Conn.: FASB, 1980).

[8]Ibid., par. 238.

[9]"Interest on Receivables and Payables," op. cit., par. 15.

There is an obvious difference between GAAP and *Concepts Statement No. 6*'s view of debt issue costs. However, until an issued standard supersedes existing GAAP, **unamortized bond issue costs are treated as a deferred charge and amortized over the life of the debt**.

To illustrate the accounting for costs of issuing bonds, assume that Microchip Corporation sold $20,000,000 of 10-year debenture bonds for $20,795,000 on January 1, 2007 (also the date of the bonds). Costs of issuing the bonds were $245,000. Microchip records the issuance of the bonds and amortization of the bond issue costs as follows.

	January 1, 2007		
Cash	20,550,000		
Unamortized Bond Issue Costs	245,000		
Premium on Bonds Payable		795,000	
Bonds Payable		20,000,000	
(To record issuance of bonds)			

	December 31, 2007		
Bond Issue Expense	24,500		
Unamortized Bond Issue Costs		24,500	
(To amortize one year of bond issue costs—straight-line methods)			

Microchip continues to amortize the bond issue costs in the same way over the life of the bonds. Although the effective-interest method is preferred, in practice companies may use the straight-line method to amortize bond issue costs because it is easier and the results are not materially different.

TREASURY BONDS

Bonds payable that have been reacquired by the issuing corporation or its agent or trustee and have not been canceled are known as **treasury bonds**. Similar to treasury stock (discussed in Chapter 15), these bonds are reported on the balance sheet as a deduction from "Bonds payable." When the treasury bonds are later sold or canceled, the company credits the Treasury Bonds account.

EXTINGUISHMENT OF DEBT

How do companies record the payment of debt—often referred to as **extinguishment of debt**? If a company holds the bonds (or any other form of debt security) to maturity, the answer is straightforward: The company does not compute any gains or losses. It will have fully amortized any premium or discount and any issue costs at the date the bonds mature. As a result, the carrying amount will equal the maturity (face) value of the bond. As the maturity or face value will also equal the bond's market value at that time, no gain or loss exists.

In some cases, a company extinguishes debt before its maturity date.[10] The amount paid on extinguishment or redemption before maturity, including any call

> **OBJECTIVE 5**
> Describe the accounting for the extinguishment of debt.

---

[10]Some companies have attempted to extinguish debt through an in-substance defeasance. **In-substance defeasance** is an arrangement whereby a company provides for the future repayment of a long-term debt issue by placing purchased securities in an irrevocable trust. The company pledges the principal and interest of the securities in the trust to pay off the principal and interest of its own debt securities as they mature. However, it is not legally released from its primary obligation for the debt that is still outstanding. In some case, debt holders are not even aware of the transaction and continue to look to the company for repayment. This practice is not considered an extinguishment of debt, and therefore the company does not record a gain or loss.

premium and expense of reacquisition, is called the **reacquisition price**. On any specified date, the **net carrying amount** of the bonds is the amount payable at maturity, adjusted for unamortized premium or discount, and cost of issuance. Any excess of the net carrying amount over the reacquisition price is a **gain from extinguishment**. The excess of the reacquisition price over the net carrying amount is a **loss from extinguishment**. At the time of reacquisition, **the unamortized premium or discount, and any costs of issue applicable to the bonds, must be amortized up to the reacquisition date.**

To illustrate, assume that on January 1, 2000, General Bell Corp. issued at 97 bonds with a par value of $800,000, due in 20 years. It incurred bond issue costs totaling $16,000. Eight years after the issue date, General Bell calls the entire issue at 101 and cancels it.[11] At that time, the unamortized discount balance is $14,400, and the unamortized issue cost balance is $9,600. Illustration 14-10 indicates how General Bell computes the loss on redemption (extinguishment).

ILLUSTRATION 14-10
Computation of Loss on Redemption of Bonds

Reacquisition price ($800,000 × 1.01)		$808,000
Net carrying amount of bonds redeemed:		
Face value	$800,000	
Unamortized discount ($24,000* × 12/20)	(14,400)	
Unamortized issue costs ($16,000 × 12/20)		
(both amortized using straight-line basis)	(9,600)	776,000
Loss on redemption		$ 32,000

*[$800,000 × (1 − .97)]

General Bell records the reacquisition and cancellation of the bonds as follows:

Bonds Payable	800,000	
Loss on Redemption of Bonds	32,000	
Discount on Bonds Payable		14,400
Unamortized Bond Issue Costs		9,600
Cash		808,000

Note that it is often advantageous for the issuer to acquire the **entire** outstanding bond issue and replace it with a new bond issue bearing a lower rate of interest. The replacement of an existing issuance with a new one is called **refunding**. Whether the early redemption or other extinguishment of outstanding bonds is a nonrefunding or a refunding situation, a company should recognize the difference (gain or loss) between the reacquisition price and the net carrying amount of the redeemed bonds in income of the period of redemption.[12]

---

[11]The issuer of callable bonds must generally exercise the call on an interest date. Therefore, the amortization of any discount or premium will be up to date, and there will be no accrued interest. However, early extinguishments through purchases of bonds in the open market are more likely to be on other than an interest date. If the purchase is not made on an interest date, the discount or premium must be amortized, and the interest payable must be accrued from the last interest date to the date of purchase.

[12]Until recently, companies reported gains and losses on extinguishment of debt as extraordinary items. In response to concerns that such gains or losses are neither unusual nor infrequent, the FASB eliminated extraordinary item treatment for extinguishment of debt. "Recission of *FASB Statements No. 4, 44,* and *64* and Technical Corrections," *Statement of Accounting Standards No. 145* (Norwalk, Conn.: FASB, 2002).

DEAD-WEIGHT DEBT

As the opening story in the chapter indicated, high debt levels translate into high interest costs, which are a drag on profitability. The chart below shows that the ratio of interest payments to earnings has been on an upward trend. This is bad news for companies that have a lot of debt on their balance sheet.

WHAT DO THE NUMBERS MEAN?

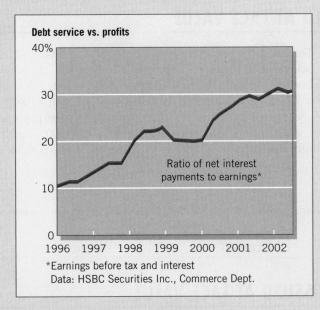

However in a low interest rate environment, as experienced recently, companies with debt-laden balance sheets benefit when interest rates fall. **Exelon Corp.**, a Chicago-based energy company, is a good example. Exelon has been refinancing its long-term debt by retiring bonds with 6.5 percent rates in exchange for newly issued bonds with rates ranging from 3.7 percent to 5.9 percent. This refinancing saved Exelon approximately $30 million dollars in annual interest costs. Exelon was able to get out of its higher cost debt when the getting was good. Other debt-laden companies might not fare so well if interest rates rise before they can refinance.

Source: Adapted from Gregory Zuckerman, "Climb of Corporate Debt Trips Analysts' Alarm," *Wall Street Journal* (December 31, 2001), p. C1; and James Mehring, "The Dead Weight of Debt," *Business Week* (February 24, 2003), p. 60.

LONG-TERM NOTES PAYABLE	SECTION 2

The difference between current notes payable and **long-term notes payable** is the maturity date. As discussed in Chapter 13, short-term notes payable are those that companies expect to pay within a year or the operating cycle—whichever is longer. Long-term notes are similar in substance to bonds in that both have fixed maturity dates and carry either a stated or implicit interest rate. However, notes do not trade as readily as bonds in the organized public securities markets. Noncorporate and small corporate enterprises issue notes as their long-term instruments. Larger corporations issue both long-term notes and bonds.

Accounting for notes and bonds is quite similar. **Like a bond, a note is valued at the present value of its future interest and principal cash flows. The company amortizes any discount or premium over the life of the note**, just as it would the discount

> **OBJECTIVE 6**
> Explain the accounting for long-term notes payable.

or premium on a bond.[13] Companies compute the present value of an **interest-bearing note**, record its issuance, and amortize any discount or premium and accrual of interest in the same way that they do for bonds (as shown on pages 674–682 of this chapter).

As you might expect, accounting for long-term notes payable parallels accounting for long-term notes receivable as was presented in Chapter 7.

NOTES ISSUED AT FACE VALUE

In Chapter 7, we discussed the recognition of a $10,000, three-year note Scandinavian Imports issued at face value to Bigelow Corp. In this transaction, the stated rate and the effective rate were both 10 percent. The time diagram and present value computation on page 327 of Chapter 7 (see Illustration 7-9) for Bigelow Corp. would be the same for the issuer of the note, Scandinavian Imports, in recognizing a note payable. Because the present value of the note and its face value are the same, $10,000, Scandinavian would recognize no premium or discount. It records the issuance of the note as follows.

Cash	10,000	
Notes Payable		10,000

Scandinavian Imports would recognize the interest incurred each year as follows.

Interest Expense	1,000	
Cash		1,000

NOTES NOT ISSUED AT FACE VALUE

Zero-Interest-Bearing Notes

Calculator Solution for Effective Interest on Note:

	Inputs	Answer
N	8	
I/YR	?	15
PV	-327	
PMT	0	
FV	1,000	

If a company issues a zero-interest-bearing (non-interest-bearing) note[14] solely for cash, it measures the note's present value by the cash received. The implicit interest rate is the **rate that equates the cash received with the amounts to be paid in the future.** The issuing company records the difference between the face amount and the present value (cash received) as **a discount and amortizes that amount to interest expense over the life of the note.**

An example of such a transaction is Beneficial Corporation's offering of $150 million of zero-coupon notes (deep-discount bonds) having an eight-year life. With a face value of $1,000 each, these notes sold for $327—a deep discount of $673 each. The present value of each note is the cash proceeds of $327. We can calculate the interest rate by determining the rate that equates the amount the investor currently pays with the amount to be received in the future. Thus, Beneficial amortizes the discount over the eight-year life of the notes using an effective interest rate of 15 percent.[15]

---

[13] According to *APB Opinion No. 21*, all payables that represent commitments to pay money at a determinable future date are subject to present value measurement techniques, except for the following specifically excluded types:

1. Normal accounts payable due within one year.
2. Security deposits, retainages, advances, or progress payments.
3. Transactions between parent and subsidiary.
4. Obligations payable at some indeterminable future date.

[14] Although we use the term "note" throughout this discussion, the basic principles and methodology apply equally to other long-term debt instruments.

[15] $327 = \$1,000(PVF_{8,i})$

$$PVF_{8,i} = \frac{\$327}{\$1,000} = .327$$

.327 = 15% (in Table 6-2 locate .32690).

To illustrate the entries and the amortization schedule, assume that Turtle Cove Company issued the three-year, $10,000, zero-interest-bearing note to Jeremiah Company illustrated on page 328 of Chapter 7 (notes receivable). The implicit rate that equated the total cash to be paid ($10,000 at maturity) to the present value of the future cash flows ($7,721.80 cash proceeds at date of issuance) was 9 percent. (The present value of $1 for 3 periods at 9 percent is $0.77218.) Illustration 14-11 shows the time diagram for the single cash flow.

ILLUSTRATION 14-11
Time Diagram for Zero-Interest Note

Turtle Cove records issuance of the note as follows.

Cash	7,721.80	
Discount on Notes Payable	2,278.20	
Notes Payable		10,000.00

Turtle Cove amortizes the discount and recognizes interest expense annually using the **effective-interest method**. Illustration 14-12 shows the three-year discount amortization and interest expense schedule. (This schedule is similar to the note receivable schedule of Jeremiah Company in Illustration 7-11.)

ILLUSTRATION 14-12
Schedule of Note Discount Amortization

SCHEDULE OF NOTE DISCOUNT AMORTIZATION
EFFECTIVE-INTEREST METHOD
0% NOTE DISCOUNTED AT 9%

	Cash Paid	Interest Expense	Discount Amortized	Carrying Amount of Note
Date of issue				$ 7,721.80
End of year 1	$–0–	$ 694.96[a]	$ 694.96[b]	8,416.76[c]
End of year 2	–0–	757.51	757.51	9,174.27
End of year 3	–0–	825.73[d]	825.73	10,000.00
	$–0–	$2,278.20	$2,278.20	

[a]$7,721.80 × .09 = $694.96
[b]$694.96 − 0 = $694.96
[c]$7,721.80 + $694.96 = $8,416.76
[d]5¢ adjustment to compensate for rounding

Turtle Cove records interest expense at the end of the first year using the effective-interest method as follows.

Interest Expense ($7,721.80 × 9%)	694.96	
Discount on Notes Payable		694.96

The total amount of the discount, $2,278.20 in this case, represents the expense that Turtle Cove Company will incur on the note over the three years.

Interest-Bearing Notes

The zero-interest-bearing note above is an example of the extreme difference between the stated rate and the effective rate. In many cases, the difference between these rates is not so great.

Consider the example from Chapter 7 where Marie Co. issued for cash a $10,000, three-year note bearing interest at 10 percent to Morgan Corp. The market rate of interest for a note of similar risk is 12 percent. Illustration 7-12 (page 329) shows the time diagram depicting the cash flows and the computation of the present value of this note. In this case, because the effective rate of interest (12%) is greater than the stated rate (10%), the present value of the note is less than the face value. That is, the note is exchanged at a **discount**. Marie Co. records the issuance of the note as follows.

Cash	9,520	
Discount on Notes Payable	480	
Notes Payable		10,000

Marie Co. then amortizes the discount and recognizes interest expense annually using the **effective-interest method**. Illustration 14-13 shows the three-year discount amortization and interest expense schedule.

ILLUSTRATION 14-13
Schedule of Note
Discount Amortization

SCHEDULE OF NOTE DISCOUNT AMORTIZATION
EFFECTIVE-INTEREST METHOD
10% NOTE DISCOUNTED AT 12%

	Cash Paid	Interest Expense	Discount Amortized	Carrying Amount of Note
Date of issue				$ 9,520
End of year 1	$1,000[a]	$1,142[b]	$142[c]	9,662[d]
End of year 2	1,000	1,159	159	9,821
End of year 3	1,000	1,179	179	10,000
	$3,000	$3,480	$480	

[a]$10,000 × 10% = $1,000
[b]$9,520 × 12% = $1,142
[c]$1,142 − $1,000 = $142
[d]$9,520 + $142 = $9,662

Marie Co. records payment of the annual interest and amortization of the discount for the first year as follows (amounts per amortization schedule).

Interest Expense	1,142	
Discount on Bonds Payable		142
Cash		1,000

When the present value exceeds the face value, Marie Co. exchanges the note at a premium. It does so by recording the premium as a credit and amortizing it using the effective-interest method over the life of the note as annual reductions in the amount of interest expense recognized.

SPECIAL NOTES PAYABLE SITUATIONS

Notes Issued for Property, Goods, and Services

Sometimes, companies may receive property, goods, or services in exchange for a note payable. When exchanging the debt instrument for property, goods, or services in a bargained transaction entered into at arm's length, the stated interest rate is presumed to be fair unless:

1 No interest rate is stated, or

2 The stated interest rate is unreasonable, or

3 The stated face amount of the debt instrument is materially different from the current cash sales price for the same or similar items or from the current market value of the debt instrument.

In these circumstances the company measures the present value of the debt instrument by the fair value of the property, goods, or services or by an amount that reasonably approximates the market value of the note.[16] If there is **no stated rate of interest, the amount of interest is the difference between the face amount of the note and the fair value of the property**.

For example, assume that Scenic Development Company sells land having a cash sale price of $200,000 to Health Spa, Inc. In exchange for the land, Health Spa gives a five-year, $293,866, zero-interest-bearing note. The $200,000 cash sale price represents the present value of the $293,866 note discounted at 8 percent for five years. Should both parties record the transaction on the sale date at the face amount of the note, which is $293,866? No—if they did, Health Spa's Land account and Scenic's sales would be overstated by $93,866 (the interest for five years at an effective rate of 8 percent). Similarly, interest revenue to Scenic and interest expense to Health Spa for the five-year period would be understated by $93,866.

Because the difference between the cash sale price of $200,000 and the $293,866 face amount of the note represents interest at an effective rate of 8 percent, the companies' transaction is recorded at the exchange date as follows.

Health Spa, Inc. (Buyer)			Scenic Development Company (Seller)		
Land	200,000		Notes Receivable	293,866	
Discount on Notes Payable	93,866		Discount on Notes Rec.		93,866
Notes Payable		293,866	Sales		200,000

ILLUSTRATION 14-14
Entries for Noncash Note Transactions

During the five-year life of the note, Health Spa amortizes annually a portion of the discount of $93,866 as a charge to interest expense. Scenic Development records interest revenue totaling $93,866 over the five-year period by also amortizing the discount. The effective-interest method is required, unless the results obtained from using another method are not materially different from those that result from the effective-interest method.

Choice of Interest Rate

In note transactions, the effective or market interest rate is either evident or determinable by other factors involved in the exchange, such as the fair market value of what is given or received. But, if a company cannot determine the fair value of the property, goods, services, or other rights, and if the note has no ready market, the problem of determining the present value of the note is more difficult. To estimate the present value of a note under such circumstances, a company must approximate an applicable interest rate that may differ from the stated interest rate. This process of interest-rate approximation is called **imputation**, and the resulting interest rate is called an **imputed interest rate**.

The prevailing rates for similar instruments of issuers with similar credit ratings affect the choice of a rate. Other factors such as restrictive covenants, collateral, payment schedule, and the existing prime interest rate also play a part. Companies determine the imputed interest rate when they issue a note; any subsequent changes in prevailing interest rates are ignored.

To illustrate, assume that on December 31, 2007, Wunderlich Company issued a promissory note to Brown Interiors Company for architectural services. The note has a face value of $550,000, a due date of December 31, 2012, and bears a stated interest rate of 2 percent, payable at the end of each year. Wunderlich cannot readily determine the fair value of the architectural services, nor is the note readily marketable. On the basis of Wunderlich's credit rating, the absence of collateral, the prime interest rate at that date, and the prevailing interest on Wunderlich's other outstanding debt, the

---

[16]"Interest on Receivables and Payables," op. cit., par. 12.

company imputes an 8 percent interest rate as appropriate in this circumstance. Illustration 14-15 shows the time diagram depicting both cash flows.

ILLUSTRATION 14-15
Time Diagram for
Interest-Bearing Note

The present value of the note and the imputed fair value of the architectural services are determined as follows.

ILLUSTRATION 14-16
Computation of Imputed
Fair Value and Note
Discount

Face value of the note		$550,000
Present value of $550,000 due in 5 years at 8% interest payable annually (Table 6-2); $FV(PVF_{5,8\%})$; ($550,000 \times .68058$)	$374,319	
Present value of $11,000 interest payable annually for 5 years at 8%; $R(PVF\text{-}OA_{5,8\%})$; ($11,000 \times 3.99271$)	43,920	
Present value of the note		418,239
Discount on notes payable		$131,761

Wunderlich records issuance of the note in payment for the architectural services as follows.

December 31, 2007

Building (or Construction in Process)	418,239	
Discount on Notes Payable	131,761	
Notes Payable		550,000

The five-year amortization schedule appears below.

ILLUSTRATION 14-17
Schedule of Discount
Amortization Using
Imputed Interest Rate

Calculator Solution for
the Fair Value of Services:

	Inputs	Answer
N	5	
I/YR	8	
PV	?	418,241*
PMT	−11,000	
FV	−550,000	

*Difference due to rounding.

SCHEDULE OF NOTE DISCOUNT AMORTIZATION
EFFECTIVE-INTEREST METHOD
2% NOTE DISCOUNTED AT 8% (IMPUTED)

Date	Cash Paid (2%)	Interest Expense (8%)	Discount Amortized	Carrying Amount of Note
12/31/07				$418,239
12/31/08	$11,000[a]	$ 33,459[b]	$ 22,459[c]	440,698[d]
12/31/09	11,000	35,256	24,256	464,954
12/31/10	11,000	37,196	26,196	491,150
12/31/11	11,000	39,292	28,292	519,442
12/31/12	11,000	41,558[e]	30,558	550,000
	$55,000	$186,761	$131,761	

[a]$550,000 \times 2\% = \$11,000$
[b]$418,239 \times 8\% = \$33,459$
[c]$33,459 - \$11,000 = \$22,459$

[d]$418,239 + \$22,459 = \$440,698$
[e]$3 adjustment to compensate for rounding.

Wunderlich records payment of the first year's interest and amortization of the discount as follows.

December 31, 2008

Interest Expense	33,459	
Discount on Notes Payable		22,459
Cash		11,000

MORTGAGE NOTES PAYABLE

The most common form of long-term notes payable is a mortgage note payable. A **mortgage note payable** is a promissory note secured by a document called a mortgage that pledges title to property as security for the loan. Individuals, proprietorships, and partnerships use mortgage notes payable more frequently than do corporations. (Corporations usually find that bond issues offer advantages in obtaining large loans.)

The borrower usually receives cash for the face amount of the mortgage note. In that case, the face amount of the note is the true liability, and no discount or premium is involved. When the lender assesses "points," however, the total amount received by the borrower is less than the face amount of the note.[17] Points raise the effective interest rate above the rate specified in the note. A **point** is 1 percent of the face of the note.

For example, assume that Harrick Co. borrows $1,000,000, signing a 20-year mortgage note with a stated interest rate of 10.75 percent as part of the financing for a new plant. If Associated Savings demands 4 points to close the financing, Harrick will receive 4 percent less than $1,000,000—or $960,000—but it will be obligated to repay the entire $1,000,000 at the rate of $10,150 per month. Because Harrick received only $960,000, and must repay $1,000,000, its effective interest rate is increased to approximately 11.3 percent on the money actually borrowed.

On the balance sheet, Harrick should report the mortgage note payable as a liability using a title such as "Mortgage Notes Payable" or "Notes Payable—Secured," with a brief disclosure of the property pledged in notes to the financial statements.

Mortgages may be payable in full at maturity or in installments over the life of the loan. If payable at maturity, Harrick classifies its mortgage payable as a long-term liability on the balance sheet until such time as the approaching maturity date warrants showing it as a current liability. If it is payable in installments, Harrick shows the current installments due as current liabilities, with the remainder as a long-term liability.

Lenders have partially replaced the traditional **fixed-rate mortgage** with alternative mortgage arrangements. Most lenders offer **variable-rate mortgages** (also called *floating-rate* or *adjustable-rate* mortgages) featuring interest rates tied to changes in the fluctuating market rate. Generally the variable-rate lenders adjust the interest rate at either one- or three-year intervals, pegging the adjustments to changes in the prime rate or the U.S. Treasury bond rate.

REPORTING AND ANALYSIS OF LONG-TERM DEBT	SECTION 3

Reporting of long-term debt is one of the most controversial areas in financial reporting. Because long-term debt has a significant impact on the cash flows of the company, reporting requirements must be substantive and informative. One problem is that the definition of a liability established in *Concepts Statement No. 6* and the recognition criteria established in *Concepts Statement No. 5* are sufficiently imprecise that some continue to argue that certain obligations need not be reported as debt.

OFF-BALANCE-SHEET FINANCING

What do **Krispy Kreme, Cisco, Enron,** and **Adelphia Communications** have in common? They all have been accused of using off-balance-sheet financing to minimize the reporting of debt on their balance sheets. **Off-balance-sheet financing** is an attempt to

OBJECTIVE 7
Explain the reporting of off-balance-sheet financing arrangements.

---

[17]Points, in mortgage financing, are analogous to the original issue discount of bonds.

borrow monies in such a way to prevent recording the obligations. It has become an issue of extreme importance. Many allege that Enron, in one of the largest corporate failures on record, hid a considerable amount of its debt off the balance sheet. As a result, any company that uses off-balance-sheet financing today risks investors dumping their stock. Consequently (as discussed in the opening story), their share price will suffer. Nevertheless, a considerable amount of off-balance-sheet financing continues to exist. As one writer noted, "The basic drives of humans are few: to get enough food, to find shelter, and to keep debt off the balance sheet."

Different Forms

Off-balance-sheet financing can take many different forms:

1   **Non-Consolidated Subsidiary:** Under GAAP, a parent company does not have to consolidate a subsidiary company that is less than 50 percent owned. In such cases, the parent therefore does not report the assets and liabilities of the subsidiary. All the parent reports on its balance sheet is the investment in the subsidiary. As a result, users of the financial statements may not understand that the subsidiary has considerable debt for which the parent may ultimately be liable if the subsidiary runs into financial difficulty.

2   **Special Purpose Entity (SPE):** A company creates a **special purpose entity** to perform a special project. To illustrate, assume that Clarke Company decides to build a new factory. However, management does not want to report the plant or the borrowing used to fund the construction on its balance sheet. It therefore creates an SPE, the purpose of which is to build the plant. (This arrangement is called a **project financing arrangement**.) The SPE finances and builds the plant. In return, Clarke guarantees that it or some outside party will purchase all the products produced by the plant. (Some refer to this as a **take-or-pay contract**). As a result, Clarke might not report the asset or liability on its books. The accounting rules in this area are complex; we discuss the accounting for SPE's in Appendix 17B.

3   **Operating Leases:** Another way that companies keep debt off the balance sheet is by leasing. Instead of owning the assets, companies lease them. Again, by meeting certain conditions, the company has to report only rent expense each period and to provide note disclosure of the transaction. Note that SPEs often use leases to accomplish off-balance-sheet treatment. We discuss accounting for lease transactions extensively in Chapter 21.

Rationale

Why do companies engage in off-balance-sheet financing? A major reason is that many believe that **removing debt enhances the quality of the balance sheet** and permits credit to be obtained more readily and at less cost.

Second, loan covenants often limit the amount of debt a company may have. As a result, the company uses off-balance-sheet financing, because **these types of commitments might not be considered in computing the debt limitation**.

Third, some argue that the asset side of the balance sheet is severely understated. For example, companies that use LIFO costing for inventories and depreciate assets on an accelerated basis will often have carrying amounts for inventories and property, plant, and equipment that are much lower than their current values. As an offset to these lower values, some believe that part of the debt does not have to be reported. In other words, **if companies report assets at current values**, less pressure would undoubtedly exist for off-balance-sheet financing arrangements.

Whether the arguments above have merit is debatable. The general idea of "out of sight, out of mind" may not be true in accounting. Many users of financial statements indicate that they factor these off-balance-sheet financing arrangements into their computations when assessing debt to equity relationships. Similarly, many loan covenants also attempt to account for these complex arrangements. Nevertheless, many companies still believe that benefits will accrue if they omit certain obligations from the balance sheet.

As a response to off-balance-sheet financing arrangements, the FASB has increased disclosure (note) requirements. This response is consistent with an "efficient markets" philosophy: the important question is not whether the presentation is off-balance-sheet or not, but whether the items are disclosed at all. In addition, the SEC, in response to the Sarbanes-Oxley Act of 2002, now requires companies to provide related information in their management discussion and analysis sections. Specifically, companies must disclose (1) all contractual obligations in a tabular format and (2) contingent liabilities and commitments in either a textual or tabular format.[18]

We believe that recording more obligations on the balance sheet will enhance financial reporting. Given the problems with companies such as **Enron, Dynergy, Williams Company, Adelphia Communications**, and **Calpine**, and the new Sarbanes-Oxley requirements, we expect that less off-balance-sheet financing will occur in the future.

OBLIGATED

The off-balance-sheet world is slowly but surely becoming more on-balance-sheet. New interpretations on guarantees (discussed in Chapter 13) and variable interest entities (discussed in Appendix 17B) are doing their part to increase the amount of debt reported on corporate balance sheets.

In addition, the SEC recently issued a rule that requires companies to disclose off-balance-sheet arrangements and contractual obligations that currently have, or are reasonably likely to have, a material future effect on the companies' financial condition. Companies now must include a tabular disclosure (following a prescribed format) in the management discussion and analysis section of the annual report. Presented below is **Best Buy**'s tabular disclosure of its contractual obligations.

WHAT DO THE NUMBERS MEAN?

INTERNATIONAL INSIGHT

There is no comparable institution to the SEC in international securities markets. As a result, many international companies (those not registered with the SEC) are not required to provide disclosures such as those related to contractual obligations.

Best Buy Co.
Contractual Obligations

The following table presents information regarding our contractual obligations by fiscal year ($ in millions):

Contractual Obligations	Total	Payments due by period			
		Less than 1 year	1–3 years	3–5 years	More than 5 years
Long-term debt obligations	$ 425	$ 2	$ 408	$ 12	$ 3
Capital lease obligations	13	5	4	3	1
Master lease obligations	55	55	—	—	—
Financing lease obligations	107	10	17	19	61
Interest payments	218	23	37	32	126
Operating lease obligations	5,850	541	1,065	997	3,247
Purchase obligations	1,514	689	404	259	162
Total	$8,182	$1,325	$1,935	$1,322	$3,600

Note: For more information refer to Note 4, Debt; Note 7, Leases; and Note 11, Contingencies and Commitments, respectively, in the Notes to Consolidated Financial Statements.

Enron's abuse of off-balance-sheet financing to hide debt was shocking and inappropriate. One silver lining in the Enron debacle however is that the standard-setting bodies in the accounting profession are now providing increased guidance on companies' reporting of contractual obligations. We believe the new SEC rule which requires companies to report their obligations over a period of time will be extremely useful to the investment community.

---

[18]It is unlikely that the FASB will be able to stop all types of off-balance-sheet transactions. Financial engineering is the Holy Grail of Wall Street. Developing new financial instruments and arrangements to sell and market to customers is not only profitable, but also adds to the prestige of the investment firms that create them. Thus, new financial products will continue to appear that will test the ability of the FASB to develop appropriate accounting standards for them.

PRESENTATION AND ANALYSIS OF LONG-TERM DEBT

Presentation of Long-Term Debt

OBJECTIVE 8
Indicate how to present and analyze long-term debt.

Companies that have large amounts and numerous issues of long-term debt frequently report only one amount in the balance sheet, supported with comments and schedules in the accompanying notes. Long-term debt that **matures within one year** should be reported as a current liability, unless using noncurrent assets to accomplish retirement.

ILLUSTRATION 14-18
Long-Term Debt
Disclosure

Best Buy Co.
(dollars in millions)

	February 26, 2005	February 28, 2004
Total current assets	$6,903	$5,724
Current liabilities		
Accounts payable	$2,824	$2,460
Unredeemed gift card liabiliities	410	300
Accrued compensation and related expenses	234	269
Accrued liabilities	844	724
Accrued income taxes	575	380
Current portion of long-term debt	72	368
Total current liabilities	4,959	4,501
Long-term liabilities	358	247
Long-term debt	528	482

4. Debt (in part)	February 26, 2005	February 28, 2004
Convertible subordinated debentures, unsecured, due 2022, interest rate 2.25%	$402	$402
Convertible debentures, unsecured, due 2021, interest rate 2.75%	—	353
Master lease obligations, due 2006, interest rate 5.9%	55	58
Capital lease obligations, due 2005, interest rate ranging from 5.9% to 8.0%	13	16
Financing lease obligations, due 2008 to 2022, interest rates ranging from 5.6% to 6.0%	107	—
Mortgage and other debt, interest rates ranging from 1.8% to 8.9%	23	21
Total debt	600	850
Less: Current portion	(72)	(368)
Total long-term debt	$528	$482

The mortgage and other debt are secured by certain property and equipment with a net book value of $98 and $97 at February 26, 2005, and February 28, 2004, respectively.

The future maturities of long-term debt, including master and capitalized leases, consist of the following:

Fiscal Year	
2006	$ 72
2007	415
2008	14
2009	14
2010	20
Thereafter	65
	$600

The fair value of long-term debt approximated $603 and $902 as of February 26, 2005, and February 28, 2004, respectively, based on the ask prices quoted from external sources, compared with carrying values of $600 and $850, respectively.

If the company plans to refinance debt, convert it into stock, or retire it from a bond retirement fund, it should continue to report the debt as noncurrent. However, the company should disclose the method it will use in its liquidation.[19]

Note disclosures generally indicate the nature of the liabilities, maturity dates, interest rates, call provisions, conversion privileges, restrictions imposed by the creditors, and assets designated or pledged as security. Companies should show any assets pledged as security for the debt in the assets section of the balance sheet. The fair value of the long-term debt should also be disclosed if it is practical to estimate fair value. Finally, companies must disclose future payments for sinking fund requirements and maturity amounts of long-term debt during each of the next five years.[20] These disclosures aid financial statement users in evaluating the amounts and timing of future cash flows. Illustration 14-18 (on page 694) shows an example of the type of information provided for **Best Buy Co.** Note that if the company has any off-balance-sheet financing, it must provide extensive note disclosure.[21]

Analysis of Long-Term Debt

Long-term creditors and stockholders are interested in a company's long-run solvency, particularly its ability to pay interest as it comes due and to repay the face value of the debt at maturity. Debt to total assets and times interest earned are two ratios that provide information about debt-paying ability and long-run solvency.

Debt to Total Assets Ratio

The **debt to total assets ratio** measures the percentage of the total assets provided by creditors. To compute it, divide total debt (both current and long-term liabilities) by total assets, as Illustration 14-19 shows.

$$\text{Debt to total assets} = \frac{\text{Total debt}}{\text{Total assets}}$$

ILLUSTRATION 14-19
Computation of Debt to Total Assets Ratio

The higher the percentage of debt to total assets, the greater the risk that the company may be unable to meet its maturing obligations.

Times Interest Earned Ratio

The **times interest earned ratio** indicates the company's ability to meet interest payments as they come due. As shown in Illustration 14-20, it is computed by dividing income before interest expense and income taxes by interest expense.

$$\text{Times interest earned} = \frac{\text{Income before income taxes and interest expense}}{\text{Interest expense}}$$

ILLUSTRATION 14-20
Computation of Times Interest Earned Ratio

To illustrate these ratios, we use data from **Best Buy's** 2005 annual report. Best Buy has total liabilities of $5,845 million, total assets of $10,294 million, interest expense of $44 million, income taxes of $509 million, and net income of $984 million. We

---

[19]"Balance Sheet Classification of Short-Term Obligations Expected to Be Refinanced," *FASB Statement of Financial Accounting Standards No. 6* (Stamford, Conn.: FASB, 1975), par. 15. Also see "Disclosure of Information about Capital Structure," *FASB Statement of Financial Accounting Standards No. 129* (Norwalk, Conn.: 1997), par. 4.

[20]"Disclosure of Long-Term Obligations," *FASB Statement of Financial Accounting Standards No. 47* (Stamford, Conn.: 1981), par. 10.

[21]Ibid.

compute Best Buy's debt to total assets and times interest earned ratios as shown in Illustration 14-21.

ILLUSTRATION 14-21
Computation of Long-
Term Debt Ratios for Best
Buy

$$\text{Debt to total assets} = \frac{\$5,845}{\$10,294} = 56.8\%$$

$$\text{Times interest earned} = \frac{(\$984 + \$44 + \$509)}{\$44} = 35 \text{ times}$$

Even though Best Buy has a relatively high debt to total assets percentage of 56.8 percent, its interest coverage of 35 times indicates it can easily meet its interest payments as they come due.

SUMMARY OF LEARNING OBJECTIVES

KEY TERMS

bearer (coupon) bonds, 674

bond discount, 675

bond indenture, 673

bond premium, 675

callable bonds, 673

carrying value, 679

commodity-backed bonds, 673

convertible bonds, 673

debenture bonds, 673

debt to total assets ratio, 695

deep-discount (zero-interest debenture) bonds, 673

effective-interest method, 679

effective yield, or market rate, 675

extinguishment of debt, 683

face, par, principal or maturity value, 675

imputation, 689

imputed interest rate, 689

income bonds, 674

long-term debt, 672

long-term notes payable, 685

mortgage notes payable, 691

off-balance-sheet financing, 691

refunding, 684

registered bonds, 674

1. Describe the formal procedures associated with issuing long-term debt. Incurring long-term debt is often a formal procedure. The bylaws of corporations usually require approval by the board of directors and the stockholders before corporations can issue bonds or can make other long-term debt arrangements. Generally, long-term debt has various covenants or restrictions. The covenants and other terms of the agreement between the borrower and the lender are stated in the bond indenture or note agreement.

2. Identify various types of bond issues. Various types of bond issues are: (1) Secured and unsecured bonds. (2) Term, serial, and callable bonds. (3) Convertible, commodity-backed, and deep-discount bonds. (4) Registered and bearer (coupon) bonds. (5) Income and revenue bonds. The variety in the types of bonds results from attempts to attract capital from different investors and risk takers and to satisfy the cash flow needs of the issuers.

3. Describe the accounting valuation for bonds at date of issuance. The investment community values a bond at the present value of its future cash flows, which consist of interest and principal. The rate used to compute the present value of these cash flows is the interest rate that provides an acceptable return on an investment commensurate with the issuer's risk characteristics. The interest rate written in the terms of the bond indenture and ordinarily appearing on the bond certificate is the stated, coupon, or nominal rate. The issuer of the bonds sets the rate and expresses it as a percentage of the face value (also called the par value, principal amount, or maturity value) of the bonds. If the rate employed by the buyers differs from the stated rate, the present value of the bonds computed by the buyers will differ from the face value of the bonds. The difference between the face value and the present value of the bonds is either a discount or premium.

4. Apply the methods of bond discount and premium amortization. The discount (premium) is amortized and charged (credited) to interest expense over the life of the bonds. Amortization of a discount increases bond interest expense, and amortization of a premium decreases bond interest expense. The profession's preferred procedure for amortization of a discount or premium is the effective-interest method. Under the effective-interest method, (1) bond interest expense is computed by multiplying the carrying value of the bonds at the beginning of the period by the effective-interest rate; then, (2) the bond discount or premium amortization is determined by comparing the bond interest expense with the interest to be paid.

5. Describe the accounting for the extinguishment of debt. At the time of reacquisition of long-term debt, the unamortized premium or discount and any costs of issue applicable to the debt must be amortized up to the reacquisition date. The reacquisition price is the amount paid on extinguishment or redemption before maturity, including any call premium and expense of reacquisition. On any specified date, the net carrying amount of the debt is the amount payable at maturity, adjusted for unamortized premium or discount and issue costs. Any excess of the net carrying amount over the reacquisition price is a gain from extinguishment. The excess of the reacquisition price over the net carrying amount is a loss from extinguishment. Gains and losses on extinguishments are recognized currently in income.

6. **Explain the accounting for long-term notes payable.** Accounting procedures for notes and bonds are similar. Like a bond, a note is valued at the present value of its expected future interest and principal cash flows, with any discount or premium being similarly amortized over the life of the note. Whenever the face amount of the note does not reasonably represent the present value of the consideration in the exchange, a company must evaluate the entire arrangement in order to properly record the exchange and the subsequent interest.

7. **Explain the reporting of off-balance-sheet financing arrangements.** Off-balance-sheet financing is an attempt to borrow funds in such a way to prevent recording obligations. Examples of off-balance-sheet arrangements are (1) non-consolidated subsidiaries, (2) special purpose entities, and (3) operating leases.

8. **Indicate how to present and analyze long-term debt.** Companies that have large amounts and numerous issues of long-term debt frequently report only one amount in the balance sheet and support this with comments and schedules in the accompanying notes. Any assets pledged as security for the debt should be shown in the assets section of the balance sheet. Long-term debt that matures within one year should be reported as a current liability, unless retirement is to be accomplished with other than current assets. If a company plans to refinance the debt, convert it into stock, or retire it from a bond retirement fund, it should continue to report it as noncurrent, accompanied with a note explaining the method it will use in the debt's liquidation. Disclosure is required of future payments for sinking fund requirements and maturity amounts of long-term debt during each of the next five years. Debt to total assets and times interest earned are two ratios that provide information about debt-paying ability and long-run solvency.

revenue bonds, 674
secured bonds, 673
serial bonds, 673
special purpose entity (SPE), 692
stated, coupon, or nominal rate, 675
straight-line method, 677
term bonds, 673
times interest earned ratio, 695
treasury bonds, 683
zero-interest debenture bonds, 673

Accounting for Troubled Debt

APPENDIX 14A

Practically every day the *Wall Street Journal* runs a story about some company in financial difficulty. For example, recently **Huffy Corp.**, a name that adorned the first bicycle of many American children, declared bankruptcy. Its creditors, Chinese suppliers, ended up taking a 30 percent equity stake in Huffy. Other examples are **Delphi**, **Northwest Airlines**, and **United Airlines**. The purpose of this appendix is to explain how creditors and debtors report information in financial statements related to these troubled debt situations. Two different types of situations result with troubled debt.

1 Impairments.
2 Restructurings:
   a. Settlements.
   b. Modification of terms.

For example, as in the case of Huffy's creditors, the creditor usually recognizes a loss on impairment. Subsequently, the creditor either modifies the terms of the loan, or settles it on terms unfavorable to the creditor. In unusual cases, the creditor forces the debtor into bankruptcy in order to ensure the highest possible collection on the loan.

IMPAIRMENTS

OBJECTIVE 9
Describe the accounting for a loan impairment.

A creditor considers a loan[1] impaired when it is probable,[2] based on current information and events, that it will not collect all amounts due (both principal and interest). Creditors should apply their normal review procedures in making the judgment as to the probability of collection.[3]

If considering a loan impaired, the creditor should measure the loss due to the **impairment** as the difference between the investment in the loan (generally the principal plus accrued interest) and the expected future cash flows discounted at the loan's historical effective interest rate.[4] When using the historical effective loan rate, the value of the investment will change only if some of the legally contracted cash flows are reduced. A company recognizes a loss in this case because the expected future cash flows have changed. The company ignores interest rate changes caused by current economic events that affect the fair value of the loan. In estimating future cash flows, the creditor should use reasonable and supportable assumptions and projections.[5]

Example of Loss on Impairment

On December 31, 2006, Prospect Inc. issued a $500,000, five-year, zero-interest-bearing note to Community Bank. Prospect issued the note to yield 10% annual interest. As a result, Prospect received, and Community Bank paid, $310,460 ($500,000 × .62092) on December 31, 2006.[6] The time diagram in Illustration 14A-1 depicts the factors involved.

ILLUSTRATION 14A-1
Time Diagram for Zero-Interest-Bearing Loan

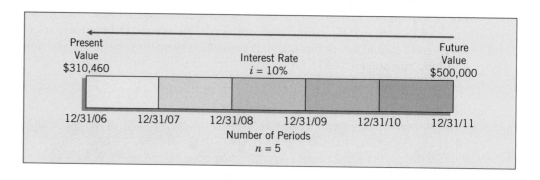

---

[1]*FASB Statement No. 114*, "Accounting by Creditors for Impairment of a Loan," (Norwalk, Conn.: FASB, May 1993), defines a loan as "a contractual right to receive money on demand or on fixed and determinable dates that is recognized as an asset in the creditor's statement of financial position." For example, accounts receivable with terms exceeding one year are considered loans.

[2]Recall the definitions of probable, reasonably possible, and remote with respect to contingencies, as defined in *FASB Statement No. 5*.

[3]Normal review procedures include examination of "watch lists," review of regulatory reports of examination, and examination of management reports of total loan amounts by borrower.

[4]The creditor may also, for the sake of expediency, use the market price of the loan (if such a price is available) or the fair value of collateral if it is a collateralized loan. *FASB Statement No. 114*, par. 13.

[5]*FASB Statement No. 114*, par. 15.

[6]Present value of $500,000 due in five years at 10%, annual compounding (Appendix 6-2) equals $500,000 × .62092.

Illustration 14A-2 shows how Community Bank (creditor) and Prospect (debtor) record these transactions.

December 31, 2006				
Community Bank (Creditor)			**Prospect Inc. (Debtor)**	
Notes Receivable	500,000		Cash	310,460
Discount on Notes			Discount on Notes	
Receivable		189,540	Payable	189,540
Cash		310,460	Notes Payable	500,000

ILLUSTRATION 14A-2
Creditor and Debtor Entries to Record Note

Assuming that Community Bank and Prospect use the effective-interest method to amortize discounts, Illustration 14A-3 shows the amortization of the discount and the increase in the carrying amount of the note over the life of the note.

COMMUNITY BANK				
Date	Cash Received (0%)	Interest Revenue (10%)	Discount Amortized	Carrying Amount of Note
12/31/06				$310,460
12/31/07	$0	$ 31,046[a]	$ 31,046	341,506[b]
12/31/08	0	34,151	34,151	375,657
12/31/09	0	37,566	37,566	413,223
12/31/10	0	41,322	41,322	454,545
12/31/11	0	45,455	45,455	500,000
Total	$0	$189,540	$189,540	

[a]$31,046 = $310,460 \times .10$
[b]$341,506 = $310,460 + $31,046$

ILLUSTRATION 14A-3
Schedule of Interest and Discount Amortization (Before Impairment)

Unfortunately, during 2008 Prospect's business deteriorated due to increased competition and a faltering regional economy. After reviewing all available evidence at December 31, 2008, Community Bank determines that Prospect will probably pay back only $300,000 of the principal at maturity. As a result, Community Bank declares the loan impaired. It now needs to record a loss.

To determine the loss, Community Bank first computes the present value of the expected cash flows, discounted at the historical effective rate of interest (10%). This amount is $225,396. The time diagram in Illustration 14A-4 highlights the factors involved in this computation.

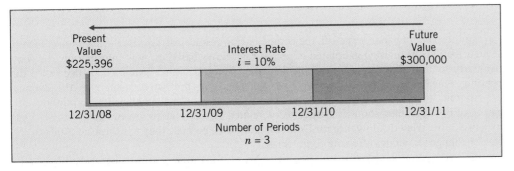

ILLUSTRATION 14A-4
Time Diagram for Impaired Loan

The loss due to impairment is the difference between the present value of the expected future cash flows and the recorded carrying amount of the investment in the loan. Illustration 14A-5 (on page 700) shows the calculation of the loss.

ILLUSTRATION 14A-5
Computation of Loss Due
to Impairment

Carrying amount of investment (12/31/08)—Illustration 14A-3	$375,657
Less: Present value of $300,000 due in 3 years at 10% interest compounded annually (Table 6-2); $FV(PVF_{3,10\%})$; ($300,000 × .75132)	225,396
Loss due to impairment	$150,261

The loss due to the impairment is $150,261, not $200,000 ($500,000 − $300,000). Why? Because Community Bank must measure the loss at a present-value amount, not an undiscounted amount, at the time it records the loss.

Community Bank records the loss as follows.

ILLUSTRATION 14A-6
Creditor and Debtor
Entries to Record Loss on
Note

December 31, 2008		
Community Bank (Creditor)		**Prospect Inc. (Debtor)**
Bad Debt Expense	150,261	No entry
Allowance for Doubtful Accounts	150,261	

Community Bank (creditor) debits Bad Debt Expense for the expected loss. At the same time, it reduces the overall value of its loan receivable by crediting Allowance for Doubtful Accounts.[7] What entry does Prospect (the debtor) make? It makes no entry because it still legally owes $500,000.[8]

TROUBLED DEBT RESTRUCTURINGS

OBJECTIVE 10
Describe the
accounting for a debt
restructuring.

A **troubled debt restructuring** occurs when a creditor "for economic or legal reasons related to the debtor's financial difficulties grants a concession to the debtor that it would not otherwise consider."[9] Thus a troubled debt restructuring does not apply to modifications of a debt obligation that reflect general economic conditions leading to a reduced interest rate. Nor does it apply to the refunding of an old debt with new debt having an effective interest rate approximately equal to that of similar debt issued by nontroubled debtors.

A troubled debt restructuring involves one of two basic types of transactions:

1 Settlement of debt at less than its carrying amount.
2 Continuation of debt with a modification of terms.

---

[7]In the event of a loan write-off, the company charges the loss against the allowance. In subsequent periods, if revising estimated expected cash flows based on new information, the company adjusts the allowance account and bad debt account (either increased or decreased depending whether conditions improved or worsened) in the same fashion as the original impairment. We use the terms "loss" and "bad debt expense" interchangeably throughout this discussion. Companies should charge losses related to receivables transactions to Bad Debt Expense or the related Allowance for Doubtful Accounts, because they use these accounts to recognize changes in values affecting receivables.

[8]Many alternatives are permitted to recognize income by Community Bank in subsequent periods. See *FASB Statement No. 118*, "Accounting by Creditors for Impairment of a Loan—Income Recognition and Disclosures" (Norwalk, Conn.: FASB, October 1994) for appropriate methods.

[9]"Accounting by Debtors and Creditors for Troubled Debt Restructurings," *FASB Statement No. 15* (Norwalk, Conn.: FASB, June, 1977), par. 1.

Settlement of Debt

Settling a debt obligation can involve either a transfer of noncash assets (real estate, receivables, or other assets) or the issuance of the debtor's stock. In these situations, **the creditor should account for the noncash assets or equity interest received at their fair value**.

The debtor must determine the excess of the carrying amount of the payable over the fair value of the assets or equity transferred (gain). Likewise, the creditor must determine the excess of the receivable over the fair value of those same assets or equity interests transferred (loss). The debtor recognizes a gain equal to the amount of the excess. The creditor normally charges the excess (loss) against Allowance for Doubtful Accounts. In addition, the debtor recognizes a gain or loss on disposition of assets to the extent that the fair value of those assets differs from their carrying amount (book value).

Transfer of Assets

Assume that American City Bank loaned $20,000,000 to Union Mortgage Company. Union Mortgage, in turn, invested these monies in residential apartment buildings. However, because of low occupancy rates, it cannot meet its loan obligations. American City Bank agrees to accept from Union Mortgage real estate with a fair market value of $16,000,000 in full settlement of the $20,000,000 loan obligation. The real estate has a carrying value of $21,000,000 on the books of Union Mortgage. American City Bank (creditor) records this transaction as follows.

Real Estate	16,000,000	
Allowance for Doubtful Accounts	4,000,000	
Note Receivable from Union Mortgage		20,000,000

The bank records the real estate at fair market value. Further, it makes a charge to the Allowance for Doubtful Accounts to reflect the bad debt write-off.

Union Mortgage (debtor) records this transaction as follows.

Note Payable to American City Bank	20,000,000	
Loss on Disposition of Real Estate	5,000,000	
Real Estate		21,000,000
Gain on Restructuring of Debt		4,000,000

Union Mortgage has a loss on the disposition of real estate in the amount of $5,000,000 (the difference between the $21,000,000 book value and the $16,000,000 fair market value). It should show this as an ordinary loss on the income statement. In addition, it has a gain on restructuring of debt of $4,000,000 (the difference between the $20,000,000 carrying amount of the note payable and the $16,000,000 fair market value of the real estate).

Granting of Equity Interest

Assume that American City Bank agrees to accept from Union Mortgage 320,000 shares of common stock ($10 par) that has a fair market value of $16,000,000, in full settlement of the $20,000,000 loan obligation. American City Bank (creditor) records this transaction as follows.

Investment	16,000,000	
Allowance for Doubtful Accounts	4,000,000	
Note Receivable from Union Mortgage		20,000,000

It records the stock as an investment at the fair market value at the date of restructure.

Union Mortgage (debtor) records this transaction as follows.

Note Payable to American City Bank	20,000,000	
Common Stock		3,200,000
Additional Paid-in Capital		12,800,000
Gain on Restructuring of Debt		4,000,000

It records the stock issued in the normal manner. It records the difference between the par value and the fair value of the stock as additional paid-in capital.

Modification of Terms

In some cases, a debtor's serious short-run cash flow problems will lead it to request one or a combination of the following modifications:

1 Reduction of the stated interest rate.

2 Extension of the maturity date of the face amount of the debt.

3 Reduction of the face amount of the debt.

4 Reduction or deferral of any accrued interest.

The creditor's loss is based on expected cash flows discounted at the historical effective rate of the loan.[10] The debtor calculates its gain based on **undiscounted amounts**, as required by the previous standard. As a consequence, **the gain recorded by the debtor will not equal the loss recorded by the creditor under many circumstances.**[11]

Two examples demonstrate the accounting for a troubled debt restructuring by debtors and creditors:

1 The debtor does not record a gain.

2 The debtor does record a gain.

In both instances the creditor has a loss.

Example 1—No Gain for Debtor

This example demonstrates a restructuring in which the debtor records no gain.[12] On December 31, 2006, Morgan National Bank enters into a debt restructuring agreement with Resorts Development Company, which is experiencing financial difficulties. The bank restructures a $10,500,000 loan receivable issued at par (interest paid to date) by:

1 Reducing the principal obligation from $10,500,000 to $9,000,000;

2 Extending the maturity date from December 31, 2006, to December 31, 2010; and

3 Reducing the interest rate from 12% to 8%.

Debtor Calculations. The total future cash flow, after restructuring of $11,880,000 ($9,000,000 of principal plus $2,880,000 of interest payments[13]), exceeds the total pre-restructuring carrying amount of the debt of $10,500,000. Consequently, **the debtor**

---

[10]*FASB Statement No. 114,* par. 42.

[11]In response to concerns expressed about this nonsymmetric treatment, the FASB stated that *Statement No. 114* does not address debtor accounting because the FASB was concerned that expansion of the scope of the statement would delay its issuance. By basing the debtor calculation on undiscounted amounts, the amount of gain (if any) recognized by the debtor is reduced at the time the modification of terms occurs. If fair value were used, the gain recognized would be greater. The result of this approach is to spread the unrecognized gain over the life of the new agreement. We believe that this accounting is inappropriate and hopefully will change as more fair value measurements are introduced into the financial statements.

[12]Note that the examples given for restructuring assume the creditor made no previous entries for impairment. In actuality it is likely that, in accordance with *Statement No. 114*, the creditor would have already made an entry when the loan initially became impaired. Restructuring would, therefore, simply require an adjustment of the initial estimated bad debt by the creditor. Recall, however, that the debtor makes no entry upon impairment.

[13]Total interest payments are: $9,000,000 × .08 × 4 years = $2,880,000.

records no gain nor makes any adjustment to the carrying amount of the payable. As a result, Resorts Development (debtor) makes no entry at the date of restructuring.

The debtor must compute a new effective-interest rate in order to record interest expense in future periods. The new effective-interest rate equates the present value of the future cash flows specified by the new terms with the pre-restructuring carrying amount of the debt. In this case, Resorts Development computes the new rate by relating the pre-restructure carrying amount ($10,500,000) to the total future cash flow ($11,880,000). The rate necessary to discount the total future cash flow ($11,880,000), to a present value equal to the remaining balance ($10,500,000), is 3.46613%.[14]

On the basis of the effective rate of 3.46613%, the debtor prepares the schedule shown in Illustration 14A-7.

ILLUSTRATION 14A-7
Schedule Showing
Reduction of Carrying
Amount of Note

		RESORTS DEVELOPMENT CO. (DEBTOR)		
Date	Cash Paid (8%)	Interest Expense (3.46613%)	Reduction of Carrying Amount	Carrying Amount of Note
12/31/06				$10,500,000
12/31/07	$ 720,000[a]	$ 363,944[b]	$ 356,056[c]	10,143,944
12/31/08	720,000	351,602	368,398	9,775,546
12/31/09	720,000	338,833	381,167	9,394,379
12/31/10	720,000	325,621	394,379	9,000,000
	$2,880,000	$1,380,000	$1,500,000	

[a]$720,000 = $9,000,000 × .08
[b]$363,944 = $10,500,000 × 3.46613%
[c]$356,056 = $720,000 − $363,944

Calculator Solution for Interest Rate

	Inputs	Answer
N	4	
I/YR	?	3.466
PV	10,500,000	
PMT	−720,000	
FV	−9,000,000	

Thus, on December 31, 2007 (date of first interest payment after restructure), the debtor makes the following entry.

December 31, 2007

Notes Payable	356,056	
Interest Expense	363,944	
Cash		720,000

The debtor makes a similar entry (except for different amounts for debits to Notes Payable and Interest Expense) each year until maturity. At maturity, Resorts Development makes the following entry.

December 31, 2010

Notes Payable	9,000,000	
Cash		9,000,000

Creditor Calculations. Morgan National Bank (creditor) must calculate its loss based on the expected future cash flows discounted at the historical effective rate of the loan. It calculates this loss as shown in Illustration 14A-8 (on page 704).

---

[14]An accurate interest rate i can be found by using the formulas given at the tops of Tables 6-2 and 6-4 to set up the following equation.

$$\$10,500,000 = \underbrace{\frac{1}{(1+i)^4}}_{\text{(from Table 6-2)}} \times \$9,000,000 + \underbrace{\frac{1 - \dfrac{1}{(1+i)^4}}{i}}_{\text{(from Table 6-4)}} \times \$720,000$$

Solving algebraically for i, we find that $i = 3.46613\%$.

ILLUSTRATION 14A-8
Computation of Loss to
Creditor on Restructuring

Pre-restructure carrying amount	$10,500,000
Present value of restructured cash flows:	
Present value of $9,000,000 due in 4 years	
at 12%, interest payable annually (Table 6-2);	
$FV(PVF_{4,12\%})$; ($9,000,000 × .63552)	$5,719,680
Present value of $720,000 interest payable annually for 4	
years at 12% (Table 6-4); $R(PVF\text{-}OA_{4,12\%})$;	
($720,000 × 3.03735)	2,186,892
Present value of restructured cash flows	7,906,572
Loss on restructuring	$ 2,593,428

As a result, Morgan National Bank records bad debt expense as follows (assuming no establishment of an allowance balance from recognition of an impairment).

Bad Debt Expense	2,593,428	
Allowance for Doubtful Accounts		2,593,428

In subsequent periods, Morgan National Bank reports interest revenue based on the historical effective rate. Illustration 14A-9 provides the following interest and amortization information.

ILLUSTRATION 14A-9
Schedule of Interest and
Amortization after Debt
Restructuring

MORGAN NATIONAL BANK (CREDITOR)				
Date	Cash Received (8%)	Interest Revenue (12%)	Increase of Carrying Amount	Carrying Amount of Note
12/31/06				$7,906,572
12/31/07	$ 720,000[a]	$ 948,789[b]	$ 228,789[c]	8,135,361
12/31/08	720,000	976,243	256,243	8,391,604
12/31/09	720,000	1,006,992	286,992	8,678,596
12/31/10	720,000	1,041,404[d]	321,404[d]	9,000,000
Total	$2,880,000	$3,973,428	$1,093,428	

[a]$720,000 = $9,000,000 × .08
[b]$948,789 = $7,906,572 × .12
[c]$228,789 = $948,789 − $720,000
[d]$28 adjustment to compensate for rounding.

On December 31, 2007, Morgan National Bank makes the following entry.

December 31, 2007

Cash	720,000	
Allowance for Doubtful Accounts	228,789	
Interest Revenue		948,789

The creditor makes a similar entry (except for different amounts debited to Allowance for Doubtful Accounts and credited to Interest Revenue) each year until maturity. At maturity, the company makes the following entry.

December 31, 2010

Cash	9,000,000	
Allowance for Doubtful Accounts	1,500,000	
Notes Receivable		10,500,000

Example 2—Gain for Debtor

If the pre-restructure carrying amount exceeds the total future cash flows as a result of a modification of the terms, the debtor records a gain. To illustrate, assume the facts in the previous example except that Morgan National Bank reduces the principal to $7,000,000 (and extends the maturity date to December 31, 2010, and reduces the interest from 12% to 8%). The total future cash flow is now $9,240,000 ($7,000,000 of principal plus $2,240,000 of interest[15]), which is $1,260,000 ($10,500,000 − $9,240,000) less than the pre-restructure carrying amount of $10,500,000.

Under these circumstances, Resorts Development (debtor) reduces the carrying amount of its payable $1,260,000 and records a gain of $1,260,000. On the other hand, Morgan National Bank (creditor) debits its Bad Debt Expense for $4,350,444. Illustration 14A-10 shows this computation.

Pre-restructure carrying amount		$10,500,000
Present value of restructured cash flows:		
Present value of $7,000,000 due in 4 years at 12%,		
interest payable annually (Table 6-2);		
$FV(PVF_{4,12\%})$; ($7,000,000 × .63552)	$4,448,640	
Present value of $560,000 interest payable annually		
for 4 years at 12% (Table 6-4);		
$R(PVF\text{-}OA_{4,12\%})$; ($560,000 × 3.03735)	1,700,916	6,149,556
Creditor's loss on restructuring		$ 4,350,444

Illustration 14A-11 shows the entries to record the gain and loss on the debtor's and creditor's books at the date of restructure, December 31, 2006.

December 31, 2006 (date of restructure)				
Resorts Development Co. (Debtor)			**Morgan National Bank (Creditor)**	
Notes Payable	1,260,000		Bad Debt Expense	4,350,444	
Gain on Restructuring of			Allowance for Doubtful Accounts		4,350,444
Debt		1,260,000			

For Resorts Development (debtor), because the new carrying value of the note ($10,500,000 − $1,260,000 = $9,240,000) equals the sum of the undiscounted cash flows ($9,240,000), the imputed interest rate is 0 percent. Consequently, all of the future cash flows reduce the principal balance, and the company recognizes no interest expense.

Morgan National reports the interest revenue in the same fashion as the previous example—that is, using the historical effective interest rate applied toward the newly discounted value of the note. Illustration 14A-12 shows interest computations.

	MORGAN NATIONAL BANK (CREDITOR)				
Date	Cash Received (8%)	Interest Revenue (12%)	Increase in Carrying Amount	Carrying Amount of Note	
12/31/06				$6,149,556	
12/31/07	$ 560,000[a]	$ 737,947[b]	$177,947[c]	6,327,503	
12/31/08	560,000	759,300	199,300	6,526,803	
12/31/09	560,000	783,216	223,216	6,750,019	
12/31/10	560,000	809,981[d]	249,981[d]	7,000,000	
Total	$2,240,000	$3,090,444	$850,444		

[a]$560,000 = $7,000,000 × .08
[b]$737,947 = $6,149,556 × .12
[c]$177,947 = $737,947 − $560,000
[d]$21 adjustment to compensate for rounding.

---

[15]Total interest payments are: $7,000,000 × .08 × 4 years = $2,240,000.

The journal entries in Illustration 14A-13 demonstrate the accounting by debtor and creditor for periodic interest payments and final principal payment.

Resorts Development Co. (Debtor)		Morgan National Bank (Creditor)		
December 31, 2007 (date of first interest payment following restructure)				
Notes Payable	560,000	Cash	560,000	
Cash	560,000	Allowance for Doubtful Accounts	177,947	
		Interest Revenue		737,947
December 31, 2008, 2009, and 2010 (dates of 2nd, 3rd, and last interest payments)				
(Debit and credit same accounts as 12/31/07 using applicable amounts from appropriate amortization schedules.)				
December 31, 2010 (date of principal payment)				
Notes Payable	7,000,000	Cash	7,000,000	
Cash	7,000,000	Allowance for Doubtful Accounts	3,500,000	
		Notes Receivable		10,500,000

ILLUSTRATION 14A-13
Debtor and Creditor
Entries to Record Periodic
Interest and Final
Principal Payments

Concluding Remarks

The accounting for troubled debt is complex because the accounting standards allow for use of different measurement standards to determine the loss or gain reported. In addition, the assets and liabilities reported are sometimes not stated at cost or fair value, but at amounts adjusted for certain events but not others. This cumbersome accounting demonstrates the need for adoption of a comprehensive fair-value model for financial instruments that is consistent with finance concepts for pricing these financial instruments.

SUMMARY OF LEARNING OBJECTIVES

KEY TERMS

impairment, *698*
troubled debt
  restructuring, *700*

9. Describe the accounting for a loan impairment. A creditor bases an impairment loan loss on the difference between the present value of the future cash flows (using the historical effective interest rate) and the carrying amount of the note.

10. Describe the accounting for a debt restructuring. There are two types of debt settlements: (1) transfer of noncash assets, and (2) granting of equity interest. Creditors and debtors record losses and gains on settlements based on fair values. For accounting purposes there are also two types of restructurings with continuation of debt with modified terms: (1) the carrying amount of debt is less than the future cash flows, and (2) the carrying amount of debt exceeds the total future cash flows. Creditors record losses on these restructurings based on the expected future cash flows discounted at the historical effective interest rate. The debtor determines its gain based on undiscounted cash flows.

Note: All **asterisked** Questions, Brief Exercises, Exercises, and Problems relate to material contained in the appendix to the chapter.

QUESTIONS

1. (a) From what sources might a corporation obtain funds through long-term debt? (b) What is a bond indenture? What does it contain? (c) What is a mortgage?

2. **Potlatch Corporation** has issued various types of bonds such as term bonds, income bonds, and debentures. Differentiate between term bonds, mortgage bonds, collateral trust bonds, debenture bonds, income bonds, callable bonds, registered bonds, bearer or coupon bonds, convertible bonds, commodity-backed bonds, and deep discount bonds.

3. Distinguish between the following interest rates for bonds payable:

(a) yield rate   (d) market rate

(b) nominal rate   (e) effective rate

(c) stated rate

4. Distinguish between the following values relative to bonds payable:

(a) maturity value   (c) market value

(b) face value   (d) par value

5. Under what conditions of bond issuance does a discount on bonds payable arise? Under what conditions of bond issuance does a premium on bonds payable arise?

6. How should discount on bonds payable be reported on the financial statements? Premium on bonds payable?

7. What are the two methods of amortizing discount and premium on bonds payable? Explain each.

8. Zeno Company sells its bonds at a premium and applies the effective interest method in amortizing the premium. Will the annual interest expense increase or decrease over the life of the bonds? Explain.

9. Briggs and Stratton recently reported unamortized debt issue costs of $5.1 million. How should the costs of issuing these bonds be accounted for and classified in the financial statements?

10. Where should treasury bonds be shown on the balance sheet?

11. What is the "call" feature of a bond issue? How does the call feature affect the amortization of bond premium or discount?

12. Why would a company wish to reduce its bond indebtedness before its bonds reach maturity? Indicate how this can be done and the correct accounting treatment for such a transaction.

13. How are gains and losses from extinguishment of a debt classified in the income statement? What disclosures are required of such transactions?

14. What is done to record properly a transaction involving the issuance of a non-interest-bearing long-term note in exchange for property?

15. How is the present value of a non-interest-bearing note computed?

16. When is the stated interest rate of a debt instrument presumed to be fair?

17. What are the considerations in imputing an appropriate interest rate?

18. Differentiate between a fixed-rate mortgage and a variable-rate mortgage.

19. What disclosures are required relative to long-term debt and sinking fund requirements?

20. What is off-balance-sheet financing? Why might a company be interested in using off-balance-sheet financing?

21. What are some forms of off-balance-sheet financing?

22. What are take-or-pay contracts and through-put contracts?

*23. What are the types of situations that result in troubled debt?

*24. What are the general rules for measuring and recognizing gain or loss by both the debtor and the creditor in an impairment?

*25. What are the general rules for measuring gain or loss by both creditor and debtor in a troubled debt restructuring involving a settlement?

*26. (a) In a troubled debt situation, why might the creditor grant concessions to the debtor?

(b) What type of concessions might a creditor grant the debtor in a troubled debt situation?

(c) What is meant by "impairment" of a loan? Under what circumstances should a creditor or debtor recognize an impaired loan?

*27. What are the general rules for measuring and recognizing gain or loss by both the debtor and the creditor in a troubled debt restructuring involving a modification of terms?

*28. What is meant by "accounting symmetry" between the entries recorded by the debtor and creditor in a troubled debt restructuring involving a modification of terms? In what ways is the accounting for troubled debt restructurings and impairments non-symmetrical?

*29. Under what circumstances would a transaction be recorded as a troubled debt restructuring by only one of the two parties to the transaction?

BRIEF EXERCISES

(LO 3)   **BE14-1**   Ghostbusters Corporation issues $300,000 of 9% bonds, due in 10 years, with interest payable semiannually. At the time of issue, the market rate for such bonds is 10%. Compute the issue price of the bonds.

(LO 3, 4) **BE14-2** The Goofy Company issued $200,000 of 10% bonds on January 1, 2008. The bonds are due January 1, 2013, with interest payable each July 1 and January 1. The bonds are issued at face value. Prepare Goofy's journal entries for (a) the January issuance, (b) the July 1 interest payment, and (c) the December 31 adjusting entry.

(LO 3, 4) **BE14-3** Assume the bonds in BE14-2 were issued at 98. Prepare the journal entries for (a) January 1, (b) July 1, and (c) December 31. Assume The Goofy Company records straight-line amortization annually on December 31.

(LO 3, 4) **BE14-4** Assume the bonds in BE14-2 were issued at 103. Prepare the journal entries for (a) January 1, (b) July 1, and (c) December 31. Assume The Goofy Company records straight-line amortization annually on December 31.

(LO 3, 4) **BE14-5** Toy Story Corporation issued $500,000 of 6% bonds on May 1, 2008. The bonds were dated January 1, 2008, and mature January 1, 2013, with interest payable July 1 and January 1. The bonds were issued at face value plus accrued interest. Prepare Toy Story's journal entries for (a) the May 1 issuance, (b) the July 1 interest payment, and (c) the December 31 adjusting entry.

(LO 3, 4) **BE14-6** On January 1, 2008, Qix Corporation issued $400,000 of 7% bonds, due in 10 years. The bonds were issued for $372,816, and pay interest each July 1 and January 1. Qix uses the effective interest method. Prepare the company's journal entries for (a) the January 1 issuance, (b) the July 1 interest payment, and (c) the December 31 adjusting entry. Assume an effective interest rate of 8%.

(LO 3, 4) **BE14-7** Assume the bonds in BE14-6 were issued for $429,757 and the effective interest rate is 6%. Prepare the company's journal entries for (a) the January 1 issuance, (b) the July 1 interest payment, and (c) the December 31 adjusting entry.

(LO 3, 4) **BE14-8** Izzy Corporation issued $400,000 of 7% bonds on November 1, 2008, for $429,757. The bonds were dated November 1, 2008, and mature in 10 years, with interest payable each May 1 and November 1. Izzy uses the effective interest method with an effective rate of 6%. Prepare Izzy's December 31, 2008, adjusting entry.

(LO 8) **BE14-9** At December 31, 2008, Treasure Land Corporation has the following account balances:

Bonds payable, due January 1, 2016	$2,000,000
Discount on bonds payable	98,000
Bond interest payable	80,000

Show how the above accounts should be presented on the December 31, 2008, balance sheet, including the proper classifications.

(LO 4) **BE14-10** Austin Powers Corporation issued 10-year bonds on January 1, 2008. Costs associated with the bond issuance were $180,000. Powers uses the straight-line method to amortize bond issue costs. Prepare the December 31, 2008, entry to record 2008 bond issue cost amortization.

(LO 5) **BE14-11** On January 1, 2008, Uncharted Waters Corporation retired $600,000 of bonds at 99. At the time of retirement, the unamortized premium was $15,000 and unamortized bond issue costs were $5,250. Prepare the corporation's journal entry to record the reacquisition of the bonds.

(LO 6) **BE14-12** Jennifer Capriati, Inc. issued a $100,000, 4-year, 11% note at face value to Forest Hills Bank on January 1, 2008, and received $100,000 cash. The note requires annual interest payments each December 31. Prepare Capriati's journal entries to record (a) the issuance of the note and (b) the December 31 interest payment.

(LO 6) **BE14-13** McNabb Corporation issued a 4-year, $50,000, zero-interest-bearing note to Reid Company on January 1, 2008, and received cash of $31,776. The implicit interest rate is 12%. Prepare McNabb's journal entries for (a) the January 1 issuance and (b) the December 31 recognition of interest.

(LO 6) **BE14-14** Larry Byrd Corporation issued a 4-year, $50,000, 5% note to Magic Johnson Company on January 1, 2008, and received a computer that normally sells for $39,369. The note requires annual interest payments each December 31. The market rate of interest for a note of similar risk is 12%. Prepare Larry Byrd's journal entries for (a) the January 1 issuance and (b) the December 31 interest.

(LO 6) **BE14-15** King Corporation issued a 4-year, $50,000, zero-interest-bearing note to Salmon Company on January 1, 2008, and received cash of $50,000. In addition, King agreed to sell merchandise to Salmon at an amount less than regular selling price over the 4-year period. The market rate of interest for similar notes is 12%. Prepare King Corporation's January 1 journal entry.

(LO 9) ***BE14-16** Assume that Toni Braxton Company has recently fallen into financial difficulties. By reviewing all available evidence on December 31, 2006, one creditor of Toni Braxton, the National American Bank, determined that Toni Braxton would pay back only 65% of the principal at maturity. As a result, the bank decided that the loan was impaired. If the loss is estimated to be $225,000, what entries should both Toni Braxton and National American Bank make to record this loss?

EXERCISES

(LO 2) **E14-1** **(Classification of Liabilities)** Presented below are various account balances of K.D. Lang Inc.

(a) Unamortized premium on bonds payable, of which $3,000 will be amortized during the next year.
(b) Bank loans payable of a winery, due March 10, 2011. (The product requires aging for 5 years before sale.)
(c) Serial bonds payable, $1,000,000, of which $200,000 are due each July 31.
(d) Amounts withheld from employees' wages for income taxes.
(e) Notes payable due January 15, 2010.
(f) Credit balances in customers' accounts arising from returns and allowances after collection in full of account.
(g) Bonds payable of $2,000,000 maturing June 30, 2009.
(h) Overdraft of $1,000 in a bank account. (No other balances are carried at this bank.)
(i) Deposits made by customers who have ordered goods.

Instructions
Indicate whether each of the items above should be classified on December 31, 2008, as a current liability, a long-term liability, or under some other classification. Consider each one independently from all others; that is, do not assume that all of them relate to one particular business. If the classification of some of the items is doubtful, explain why in each case.

(LO 2) **E14-2** **(Classification)** The following items are found in the financial statements.

(a) Discount on bonds payable
(b) Interest expense (credit balance)
(c) Unamortized bond issue costs
(d) Gain on repurchase of debt
(e) Mortgage payable (payable in equal amounts over next 3 years)
(f) Debenture bonds payable (maturing in 5 years)
(g) Notes payable (due in 4 years)
(h) Premium on bonds payable
(i) Treasury bonds
(j) Income bonds payable (due in 3 years)

Instructions
Indicate how each of these items should be classified in the financial statements.

(LO 3, 4) **E14-3** **(Entries for Bond Transactions)** Presented below are two independent situations.

1. On January 1, 2007, Simon Company issued $200,000 of 9%, 10-year bonds at par. Interest is payable quarterly on April 1, July 1, October 1, and January 1.
2. On June 1, 2007, Garfunkel Company issued $100,000 of 12%, 10-year bonds dated January 1 at par plus accrued interest. Interest is payable semiannually on July 1 and January 1.

Instructions
For each of these two independent situations, prepare journal entries to record the following.

(a) The issuance of the bonds.
(b) The payment of interest on July 1.
(c) The accrual of interest on December 31.

(LO 3, 4) **E14-4** **(Entries for Bond Transactions—Straight-Line)** Celine Dion Company issued $600,000 of 10%, 20-year bonds on January 1, 2008, at 102. Interest is payable semiannually on July 1 and January 1. Dion Company uses the straight-line method of amortization for bond premium or discount.

Instructions

Prepare the journal entries to record the following.

    (a) The issuance of the bonds.
    (b) The payment of interest and the related amortization on July 1, 2008.
    (c) The accrual of interest and the related amortization on December 31, 2008.

(LO 3, 4)
E14-5 (Entries for Bond Transactions—Effective Interest) Assume the same information as in E14-4, except that Celine Dion Company uses the effective interest method of amortization for bond premium or discount. Assume an effective yield of 9.7705%.

Instructions

Prepare the journal entries to record the following. (Round to the nearest dollar.)

    (a) The issuance of the bonds.
    (b) The payment of interest and related amortization on July 1, 2008.
    (c) The accrual of interest and the related amortization on December 31, 2008.

(LO 3, 4)
E14-6 (Amortization Schedules—Straight-line) Devon Harris Company sells 10% bonds having a maturity value of $2,000,000 for $1,855,816. The bonds are dated January 1, 2007, and mature January 1, 2012. Interest is payable annually on January 1.

Instructions

Set up a schedule of interest expense and discount amortization under the straight-line method.

(LO 3, 4)
E14-7 (Amortization Schedule—Effective Interest) Assume the same information as E14-6.

Instructions

Set up a schedule of interest expense and discount amortization under the effective interest method. (*Hint:* The effective interest rate must be computed.)

(LO 3, 4)
E14-8 (Determine Proper Amounts in Account Balances) Presented below are three independent situations.

    (a) CeCe Winans Corporation incurred the following costs in connection with the issuance of bonds: (1) printing and engraving costs, $12,000; (2) legal fees, $49,000, and (3) commissions paid to underwriter, $60,000. What amount should be reported as Unamortized Bond Issue Costs, and where should this amount be reported on the balance sheet?
    (b) George Gershwin Co. sold $2,000,000 of 10%, 10-year bonds at 104 on January 1, 2007. The bonds were dated January 1, 2007, and pay interest on July 1 and January 1. If Gershwin uses the straight-line method to amortize bond premium or discount, determine the amount of interest expense to be reported on July 1, 2007, and December 31, 2007.
    (c) Ron Kenoly Inc. issued $600,000 of 9%, 10-year bonds on June 30, 2007, for $562,500. This price provided a yield of 10% on the bonds. Interest is payable semiannually on December 31 and June 30. If Kenoly uses the effective interest method, determine the amount of interest expense to record if financial statements are issued on October 31, 2007.

(LO 3, 4)
E14-9 (Entries and Questions for Bond Transactions) On June 30, 2008, Mischa Auer Company issued $4,000,000 face value of 13%, 20-year bonds at $4,300,920, a yield of 12%. Auer uses the effective interest method to amortize bond premium or discount. The bonds pay semiannual interest on June 30 and December 31.

Instructions

    (a) Prepare the journal entries to record the following transactions.
        (1) The issuance of the bonds on June 30, 2008.
        (2) The payment of interest and the amortization of the premium on December 31, 2008.
        (3) The payment of interest and the amortization of the premium on June 30, 2009.
        (4) The payment of interest and the amortization of the premium on December 31, 2009.
    (b) Show the proper balance sheet presentation for the liability for bonds payable on the December 31, 2009, balance sheet.
    (c) Provide the answers to the following questions.
        (1) What amount of interest expense is reported for 2009?
        (2) Will the bond interest expense reported in 2009 be the same as, greater than, or less than the amount that would be reported if the straight-line method of amortization were used?
        (3) Determine the total cost of borrowing over the life of the bond.
        (4) Will the total bond interest expense for the life of the bond be greater than, the same as, or less than the total interest expense if the straight-line method of amortization were used?

(LO 3, 4) **E14-10 (Entries for Bond Transactions)** On January 1, 2007, Aumont Company sold 12% bonds having a maturity value of $500,000 for $537,907.37, which provides the bondholders with a 10% yield. The bonds are dated January 1, 2007, and mature January 1, 2012, with interest payable December 31 of each year. Aumont Company allocates interest and unamortized discount or premium on the effective interest basis.

Instructions
(a) Prepare the journal entry at the date of the bond issuance.
(b) Prepare a schedule of interest expense and bond amortization for 2007–2009.
(c) Prepare the journal entry to record the interest payment and the amortization for 2007.
(d) Prepare the journal entry to record the interest payment and the amortization for 2009.

(LO 3) **E14-11 (Information Related to Various Bond Issues)** Karen Austin Inc. has issued three types of debt on January 1, 2007, the start of the company's fiscal year.

(a) $10 million, 10-year, 15% unsecured bonds, interest payable quarterly. Bonds were priced to yield 12%.
(b) $25 million par of 10-year, zero-coupon bonds at a price to yield 12% per year.
(c) $20 million, 10-year, 10% mortgage bonds, interest payable annually to yield 12%.

Instructions
Prepare a schedule that identifies the following items for each bond: (1) maturity value, (2) number of interest periods over life of bond, (3) stated rate per each interest period, (4) effective interest rate per each interest period, (5) payment amount per period, and (6) present value of bonds at date of issue.

(LO 3, 4, 5) **E14-12 (Entry for Retirement of Bond; Bond Issue Costs)** On January 2, 2002, Banno Corporation issued $1,500,000 of 10% bonds at 97 due December 31, 2011. Legal and other costs of $24,000 were incurred in connection with the issue. Interest on the bonds is payable annually each December 31. The $24,000 issue costs are being deferred and amortized on a straight-line basis over the 10-year term of the bonds. The discount on the bonds is also being amortized on a straight-line basis over the 10 years. (Straight-line is not materially different in effect from the preferable "interest method".)

The bonds are callable at 101 (i.e., at 101% of face amount), and on January 2, 2007, Banno called $900,000 face amount of the bonds and retired them.

Instructions
Ignoring income taxes, compute the amount of loss, if any, to be recognized by Banno as a result of retiring the $900,000 of bonds in 2007 and prepare the journal entry to record the retirement.

(AICPA adapted)

(LO 3, 4, 5) **E14-13 (Entries for Retirement and Issuance of Bonds)** Matt Perry, Inc. had outstanding $6,000,000 of 11% bonds (interest payable July 31 and January 31) due in 10 years. On July 1, it issued $9,000,000 of 10%, 15-year bonds (interest payable July 1 and January 1) at 98. A portion of the proceeds was used to call the 11% bonds at 102 on August 1. Unamortized bond discount and issue cost applicable to the 11% bonds were $120,000 and $30,000, respectively.

Instructions
Prepare the journal entries necessary to record issue of the new bonds and the refunding of the bonds.

(LO 3, 4, 5) **E14-14 (Entries for Retirement and Issuance of Bonds)** On June 30, 1999, County Crows Company issued 12% bonds with a par value of $800,000 due in 20 years. They were issued at 98 and were callable at 104 at any date after June 30, 2007. Because of lower interest rates and a significant change in the company's credit rating, it was decided to call the entire issue on June 30, 2008, and to issue new bonds. New 10% bonds were sold in the amount of $1,000,000 at 102; they mature in 20 years. County Crows Company uses straight-line amortization. Interest payment dates are December 31 and June 30.

Instructions
(a) Prepare journal entries to record the retirement of the old issue and the sale of the new issue on June 30, 2008.
(b) Prepare the entry required on December 31, 2008, to record the payment of the first 6 months' interest and the amortization of premium on the bonds.

(LO 3, 4, 5) **E14-15 (Entries for Retirement and Issuance of Bonds)** Linda Day George Company had bonds outstanding with a maturity value of $300,000. On April 30, 2008, when these bonds had an unamortized discount of $10,000, they were called in at 104. To pay for these bonds, George had issued other bonds a month earlier bearing a lower interest rate. The newly issued bonds had a life of 10 years. The new bonds were issued at 103 (face value $300,000). Issue costs related to the new bonds were $3,000.

Instructions

Ignoring interest, compute the gain or loss and record this refunding transaction.

(AICPA adapted)

(LO 6) **E14-16 (Entries for Zero-Interest-Bearing Notes)** On January 1, 2008, Ellen Greene Company makes the two following acquisitions.

1. Purchases land having a fair market value of $200,000 by issuing a 5-year, zero-interest-bearing promissory note in the face amount of $337,012.
2. Purchases equipment by issuing a 6%, 8-year promissory note having a maturity value of $250,000 (interest payable annually).

The company has to pay 11% interest for funds from its bank.

Instructions

(a) Record the two journal entries that should be recorded by Ellen Greene Company for the two purchases on January 1, 2008.
(b) Record the interest at the end of the first year on both notes using the effective interest method.

(LO 6) **E14-17 (Imputation of Interest)** Presented below are two independent situations:

(a) On January 1, 2008, Robin Wright Inc. purchased land that had an assessed value of $350,000 at the time of purchase. A $550,000, zero-interest-bearing note due January 1, 2011, was given in exchange. There was no established exchange price for the land, nor a ready market value for the note. The interest rate charged on a note of this type is 12%. Determine at what amount the land should be recorded at January 1, 2008, and the interest expense to be reported in 2008 related to this transaction.
(b) On January 1, 2008, Sally Field Furniture Co. borrowed $5,000,000 (face value) from Gary Sinise Co., a major customer, through a zero-interest-bearing note due in 4 years. Because the note was zero-interest-bearing, Sally Field Furniture agreed to sell furniture to this customer at lower than market price. A 10% rate of interest is normally charged on this type of loan. Prepare the journal entry to record this transaction and determine the amount of interest expense to report for 2008.

(LO 6) **E14-18 (Imputation of Interest with Right)** On January 1, 2006, Margaret Avery Co. borrowed and received $400,000 from a major customer evidenced by a zero-interest-bearing note due in 3 years. As consideration for the zero-interest-bearing feature, Avery agrees to supply the customer's inventory needs for the loan period at lower than the market price. The appropriate rate at which to impute interest is 8%.

Instructions

(a) Prepare the journal entry to record the initial transaction on January 1, 2006. (Round all computations to the nearest dollar.)
(b) Prepare the journal entry to record any adjusting entries needed at December 31, 2006. Assume that the sales of Avery's product to this customer occur evenly over the 3-year period.

(LO 8) **E14-19 (Long-Term Debt Disclosure)** At December 31, 2006, Helen Reddy Company has outstanding three long-term debt issues. The first is a $2,000,000 note payable which matures June 30, 2009. The second is a $6,000,000 bond issue which matures September 30, 2010. The third is a $17,500,000 sinking fund debenture with annual sinking fund payments of $3,500,000 in each of the years 2008 through 2012.

Instructions

Prepare the note disclosure required by *FASB Statement No. 47*, "Disclosure of Long-term Obligations," for the long-term debt at December 31, 2006.

(LO 10) ***E14-20 (Settlement of Debt)** Larisa Nieland Company owes $200,000 plus $18,000 of accrued interest to First State Bank. The debt is a 10-year, 10% note. During 2007, Larisa Nieland's business deteriorated due to a faltering regional economy. On December 31, 2007, First State Bank agrees to accept an old machine and cancel the entire debt. The machine has a cost of $390,000, accumulated depreciation of $221,000, and a fair market value of $190,000.

Instructions

(a) Prepare journal entries for Larisa Nieland Company and First State Bank to record this debt settlement.
(b) How should Larisa Nieland report the gain or loss on the disposition of machine and on restructuring of debt in its 2007 income statement?
(c) Assume that, instead of transferring the machine, Larisa Nieland decides to grant 15,000 shares of its common stock ($10 par) which has a fair market value of $190,000 in full settlement of the loan obligation. If First State Bank treats Larisa Nieland's stock as a trading investment, prepare the entries to record the transaction for both parties.

(LO 10) **E14-21* **(Term Modification without Gain—Debtor's Entries)** On December 31, 2007, the Firstar Bank enters into a debt restructuring agreement with Nicole Bradtke Company, which is now experiencing financial trouble. The bank agrees to restructure a 12%, issued at par, $2,000,000 note receivable by the following modifications:

1. Reducing the principal obligation from $2,000,000 to $1,600,000.
2. Extending the maturity date from December 31, 2007, to December 31, 2010.
3. Reducing the interest rate from 12% to 10%.

Bradtke pays interest at the end of each year. On January 1, 2011, Bradtke Company pays $1,600,000 in cash to Firstar Bank.

Instructions
(a) Based on *FASB Statement No. 114*, will the gain recorded by Bradtke be equal to the loss recorded by Firstar Bank under the debt restructuring?
(b) Can Bradtke Company record a gain under the term modification mentioned above? Explain.
(c) Assuming that the interest rate Bradtke should use to compute interest expense in future periods is 1.4276%, prepare the interest payment schedule of the note for Bradtke Company after the debt restructuring.
(d) Prepare the interest payment entry for Bradtke Company on December 31, 2009.
(e) What entry should Bradtke make on January 1, 2011?

(LO 10) **E14-22* **(Term Modification without Gain—Creditor's Entries)** Using the same information as in E14-21 above, answer the following questions related to Firstar Bank (creditor).

Instructions
(a) What interest rate should Firstar Bank use to calculate the loss on the debt restructuring?
(b) Compute the loss that Firstar Bank will suffer from the debt restructuring. Prepare the journal entry to record the loss.
(c) Prepare the interest receipt schedule for Firstar Bank after the debt restructuring.
(d) Prepare the interest receipt entry for Firstar Bank on December 31, 2009.
(e) What entry should Firstar Bank make on January 1, 2011?

(LO 10) **E14-23* **(Term Modification with Gain—Debtor's Entries)** Use the same information as in E14-21 above except that Firstar Bank reduced the principal to $1,300,000 rather than $1,600,000. On January 1, 2011, Bradtke pays $1,300,000 in cash to Firstar Bank for the principal.

Instructions
(a) Can Bradtke Company record a gain under this term modification? If yes, compute the gain for Bradtke Company.
(b) Prepare the journal entries to record the gain on Bradtke's books.
(c) What interest rate should Bradtke use to compute its interest expense in future periods? Will your answer be the same as in E14-21 above? Why or why not?
(d) Prepare the interest payment schedule of the note for Bradtke Company after the debt restructuring.
(e) Prepare the interest payment entries for Bradtke Company on December 31, of 2008, 2009, and 2010.
(f) What entry should Bradtke make on January 1, 2011?

(LO 10) **E14-24* **(Term Modification with Gain—Creditor's Entries)** Using the same information as in E14-21 and E14-23 above, answer the following questions related to Firstar Bank (creditor).

Instructions
(a) Compute the loss Firstar Bank will suffer under this new term modification. Prepare the journal entry to record the loss on Firstar's books.
(b) Prepare the interest receipt schedule for Firstar Bank after the debt restructuring.
(c) Prepare the interest receipt entry for Firstar Bank on December 31, 2008, 2009, and 2010.
(d) What entry should Firstar Bank make on January 1, 2011?

(LO 10) **E14-25* **(Debtor/Creditor Entries for Settlement of Troubled Debt)** Petra Langrova Co. owes $199,800 to Mary Joe Fernandez Inc. The debt is a 10-year, 11% note. Because Petra Langrova Co. is in financial trouble, Mary Joe Fernandez Inc. agrees to accept some property and cancel the entire debt. The property has a book value of $80,000 and a fair market value of $120,000.

Instructions
(a) Prepare the journal entry on Langrova's books for debt restructure.
(b) Prepare the journal entry on Fernandez's books for debt restructure.

(LO 10) **E14-26* **(Debtor/Creditor Entries for Modification of Troubled Debt)** Steffi Graf Corp. owes $225,000 to First Trust. The debt is a 10-year, 12% note due December 31, 2007. Because Graf Corp. is in financial trouble, First Trust agrees to extend the maturity date to December 31, 2009, reduce the principal to $200,000, and reduce the interest rate to 5%, payable annually on December 31.

Instructions

(a) Prepare the journal entries on Graf's books on December 31, 2007, 2008, 2009.

(b) Prepare the journal entries on First Trust's books on December 31, 2007, 2008, 2009.

(LO 9) *E14-27 **(Impairments)** On December 31, 2006, Iva Majoli Company borrowed $62,092 from Paris Bank, signing a 5-year, $100,000 zero-interest-bearing note. The note was issued to yield 10% interest. Unfortunately, during 2008, Majoli began to experience financial difficulty. As a result, at December 31, 2008, Paris Bank determined that it was probable that it would receive back only $75,000 at maturity. The market rate of interest on loans of this nature is now 11%.

Instructions

(a) Prepare the entry 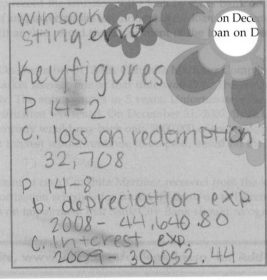 ecember 31, 2006.

(b) Prepare the entry (on Dece er 31, 2008, by Paris Bank.

(c) Prepare the entry an on D mber 31, 2008, by Majoli
Company.

(LO 9) *E14-28 **(Impairments)** signed a $1,000,000 note
to Sauk City Bank. The m interest rate on the note
was 10%, payable annual use of lower sales, Conchita Martinez's financial y Bank determined that
it was probable that the cc at maturity. However, it
was considered likely tha ,000,000 loan.

Handwritten note (keyfigures):
keyfigures
P 14-2
c. loss on redemption
32,708
P 14-8
b. depreciation exp
2008 - 44,640.80
c. Interest exp.
2009 - 30,052.44

Instructions

(a) Determine the am n on December 31, 2006.

(b) Prepare a note am er 31, 2008.

(c) Determine the los e on December 31, 2008.

See the book's websi nal Exercises.

PROBLEMS

(LO 3, 4) **P14-1 (Analysis of Amortization Schedule and Interest Entries)** The following amortization and interest schedule reflects the issuance of 10-year bonds by Terrel Brandon Corporation on January 1, 2000, and the subsequent interest payments and charges. The company's year-end is December 31, and financial statements are prepared once yearly.

Amortization Schedule

Year	Cash	Interest	Amount Unamortized	Book Value
1/1/2000			$5,651	$ 94,349
2000	$11,000	$11,322	5,329	94,671
2001	11,000	11,361	4,968	95,032
2002	11,000	11,404	4,564	95,436
2003	11,000	11,452	4,112	95,888
2004	11,000	11,507	3,605	96,395
2005	11,000	11,567	3,038	96,962
2006	11,000	11,635	2,403	97,597
2007	11,000	11,712	1,691	98,309
2008	11,000	11,797	894	99,106
2009	11,000	11,894		100,000

Instructions

(a) Indicate whether the bonds were issued at a premium or a discount and how you can determine this fact from the schedule.

(b) Indicate whether the amortization schedule is based on the straight-line method or the effective interest method and how you can determine which method is used.

(c) Determine the stated interest rate and the effective interest rate.

(d) On the basis of the schedule above, prepare the journal entry to record the issuance of the bonds on January 1, 2000.

(e) On the basis of the schedule above, prepare the journal entry or entries to reflect the bond transactions and accruals for 2000. (Interest is paid January 1.)

(f) On the basis of the schedule above, prepare the journal entry or entries to reflect the bond transactions and accruals for 2007. Brandon Corporation does not use reversing entries.

(LO 3, 4, 5) **P14-2 (Issuance and Retirement of Bonds)** Palmiero Co. is building a new hockey arena at a cost of $2,000,000. It received a downpayment of $500,000 from local businesses to support the project, and now needs to borrow $1,500,000 to complete the project. It therefore decides to issue $1,500,000 of 10.5%, 10-year bonds. These bonds were issued on January 1, 2005, and pay interest annually on each January 1. The bonds yield 10%. Palmiero paid $50,000 in bond issue costs related to the bond sale.

Instructions

(a) Prepare the journal entry to record the issuance of the bonds and the related bond issue costs incurred on January 1, 2005.

(b) Prepare a bond amortization schedule up to and including January 1, 2009, using the effective interest method.

(c) Assume that on July 1, 2008, Palmiero Co. retires half of the bonds at a cost of $800,000 plus accrued interest. Prepare the journal entry to record this retirement.

(LO 3, 4) **P14-3 (Negative Amortization)** Slippery Sales Inc. developed a new sales gimmick to help sell its inventory of new automobiles. Because many new car buyers need financing, Slippery offered a low downpayment and low car payments for the first year after purchase. It believes that this promotion will bring in some new buyers.

On January 1, 2007, a customer purchased a new $25,000 automobile, making a downpayment of $1,000. The customer signed a note indicating that the annual rate of interest would be 8% and that quarterly payments would be made over 3 years. For the first year, Slippery required a $300 quarterly payment to be made on April 1, July 1, October 1, and January 1, 2008. After this one-year period, the customer was required to make regular quarterly payments that would pay off the loan as of January 1, 2010.

Instructions

(a) Prepare a note amortization schedule for the first year.

(b) Indicate the amount the customer owes on the contract at the end of the first year.

(c) Compute the amount of the new quarterly payments.

(d) Prepare a note amortization schedule for these new payments for the next 2 years.

(e) What do you think of the new sales promotion used by Slippery?

(LO 3, 4, 5, 8) **P14-4 (Issuance and Retirement of Bonds; Income Statement Presentation)** Chris Mills Company issued its 9%, 25-year mortgage bonds in the principal amount of $5,000,000 on January 2, 1993, at a discount of $250,000, which it proceeded to amortize by charges to expense over the life of the issue on a straight-line basis. The indenture securing the issue provided that the bonds could be called for redemption in total but not in part at any time before maturity at 104% of the principal amount, but it did not provide for any sinking fund.

On December 18, 2007, the company issued its 11%, 20-year debenture bonds in the principal amount of $6,000,000 at 102, and the proceeds were used to redeem the 9%, 25-year mortgage bonds on January 2, 2008. The indenture securing the new issue did not provide for any sinking fund or for retirement before maturity.

Instructions

(a) Prepare journal entries to record the issuance of the 11% bonds and the retirement of the 9% bonds.

(b) Indicate the income statement treatment of the gain or loss from retirement and the note disclosure required.

(LO 3, 4, 5) **P14-5 (Comprehensive Bond Problem)** In each of the following independent cases the company closes its books on December 31.

1. Danny Ferry Co. sells $250,000 of 10% bonds on March 1, 2007. The bonds pay interest on September 1 and March 1. The due date of the bonds is September 1, 2010. The bonds yield 12%. Give entries through December 31, 2008.

2. Brad Dougherty Co. sells $600,000 of 12% bonds on June 1, 2007. The bonds pay interest on December 1 and June 1. The due date of the bonds is June 1, 2011. The bonds yield 10%. On October 1, 2008, Dougherty buys back $120,000 worth of bonds for $126,000 (includes accrued interest). Give entries through December 1, 2009.

Instructions

(Round to the nearest dollar.)

For the two cases prepare all of the relevant journal entries from the time of sale until the date indicated. Use the effective interest method for discount and premium amortization (construct amortization tables where applicable). Amortize premium or discount on interest dates and at year-end. (Assume that no reversing entries were made.)

(LO 3, 4, 5) **P14-6 (Issuance of Bonds between Interest Dates, Straight-line, Retirement)** Presented below are selected transactions on the books of Powerglide Corporation.

May 1, 2007   Bonds payable with a par value of $700,000, which are dated January 1, 2007, are sold at 106 plus accrued interest. They are coupon bonds, bear interest at 12% (payable annually at January 1), and mature January 1, 2017. (Use interest expense account for accrued interest.)

Dec. 31   Adjusting entries are made to record the accrued interest on the bonds, and the amortization of the proper amount of premium. (Use straight-line amortization.)

Jan. 1, 2008   Interest on the bonds is paid.

April 1   Bonds of par value of $420,000 are purchased at 102 plus accrued interest, and retired. (Bond premium is to be amortized only at the end of each year.)

Dec. 31   Adjusting entries are made to record the accrued interest on the bonds, and the proper amount of premium amortized.

Instructions

Prepare journal entries for the transactions above.

(LO 3, 4, 5) **P14-7 (Entries for Life Cycle of Bonds)** On April 1, 2007, Fontenot Company sold 12,000 of its 11%, 15-year, $1,000 face value bonds at 97. Interest payment dates are April 1 and October 1, and the company uses the straight-line method of bond discount amortization. On March 1, 2008, Fontenot took advantage of favorable prices of its stock to extinguish 3,000 of the bonds by issuing 100,000 shares of its $10 par value common stock. At this time, the accrued interest was paid in cash. The company's stock was selling for $31 per share on March 1, 2008.

Instructions

Prepare the journal entries needed on the books of Fontenot Company to record the following.

    (a) April 1, 2007: issuance of the bonds.
    (b) October 1, 2007: payment of semiannual interest.
    (c) December 31, 2007: accrual of interest expense.
    (d) March 1, 2008: extinguishment of 3,000 bonds. (No reversing entries made.)

(LO 6) **P14-8 (Entries for Zero-Interest-Bearing Note)** On December 31, 2007, Jose Luis Company acquired a computer from Cuevas Corporation by issuing a $400,000 zero-interest-bearing note, payable in full on December 31, 2011. Jose Luis Company's credit rating permits it to borrow funds from its several lines of credit at 10%. The computer is expected to have a 5-year life and a $50,000 salvage value.

Instructions

    (a) Prepare the journal entry for the purchase on December 31, 2007.
    (b) Prepare any necessary adjusting entries relative to depreciation (use straight-line) and amortization (use effective interest method) on December 31, 2008.
    (c) Prepare any necessary adjusting entries relative to depreciation and amortization on December 31, 2009.

(LO 6) **P14-9 (Entries for Zero-Interest-Bearing Note; Payable in Installments)** Sun Yat-sen Cosmetics Co. purchased machinery on December 31, 2006, paying $40,000 down and agreeing to pay the balance in four equal installments of $30,000 payable each December 31. An assumed interest of 8% is implicit in the purchase price.

Instructions

Prepare the journal entries that would be recorded for the purchase and for the payments and interest on the following dates.

    (a) December 31, 2006.   **(d)** December 31, 2009.
    (b) December 31, 2007.   **(e)** December 31, 2010.
    (c) December 31, 2008.

(LO 3, 4, 5, 8) **P14-10** **(Comprehensive Problem; Issuance, Classification, Reporting)** Presented below are four independent situations.

(a) On March 1, 2008, Heide Co. issued at 103 plus accrued interest $3,000,000, 9% bonds. The bonds are dated January 1, 2008, and pay interest semiannually on July 1 and January 1. In addition, Heide Co. incurred $27,000 of bond issuance costs. Compute the net amount of cash received by Heide Co. as a result of the issuance of these bonds.

(b) On January 1, 2007, Reymont Co. issued 9% bonds with a face value of $500,000 for $469,280 to yield 10%. The bonds are dated January 1, 2007, and pay interest annually. What amount is reported for interest expense in 2007 related to these bonds, assuming that Reymont used the effective interest method for amortizing bond premium and discount?

(c) Czeslaw Building Co. has a number of long-term bonds outstanding at December 31, 2008. These long-term bonds have the following sinking fund requirements and maturities for the next 6 years.

	Sinking Fund	Maturities
2009	$300,000	$100,000
2010	100,000	250,000
2011	100,000	100,000
2012	200,000	—
2013	200,000	150,000
2014	200,000	100,000

Indicate how this information should be reported in the financial statements at December 31, 2008.

(d) In the long-term debt structure of Marie Curie Inc., the following three bonds were reported: mortgage bonds payable $10,000,000; collateral trust bonds $5,000,000; bonds maturing in installments, secured by plant equipment $4,000,000. Determine the total amount, if any, of debenture bonds outstanding.

(LO 4) **P14-11** **(Effective Interest Method)** Mathilda B. Reichenbacher, an intermediate accounting student, is having difficulty amortizing bond premiums and discounts using the effective interest method. Furthermore, she cannot understand why GAAP requires that this method be used instead of the straight-line method. She has come to you with the following problem, looking for help.

On June 30, 2006, Joan Elbert Company issued $3,000,000 face value of 13%, 20-year bonds at $3,225,690, a yield of 12%. Elbert Company uses the effective interest method to amortize bond premiums or discounts. The bonds pay semiannual interest on June 30 and December 31. Compute the amortization schedule for four periods.

Instructions

Using the data above for illustrative purposes, write a short memo (1–1.5 pages double-spaced) to Mathilda, explaining what the effective interest method is, why it is preferable, and how it is computed. (Do not forget to include an amortization schedule, referring to it whenever necessary.)

(LO 9) ***P14-12** **(Loan Impairment Entries)** On January 1, 2007, Botosan Company issued a $1,200,000, 5-year, zero-interest-bearing note to National Organization Bank. The note was issued to yield 8% annual interest. Unfortunately, during 2008, Botosan fell into financial trouble due to increased competition. After reviewing all available evidence on December 31, 2008, National Organization Bank decided that the loan was impaired. Botosan will probably pay back only $800,000 of the principal at maturity.

Instructions

(a) Prepare journal entries for both Botosan Company and National Organization Bank to record the issuance of the note on January 1, 2007. (Round to the nearest $10.)

(b) Assuming that both Botosan Company and National Organization Bank use the effective interest method to amortize the discount, prepare the amortization schedule for the note.

(c) Under what circumstances can National Organization Bank consider Botosan's note to be "impaired"?

(d) Compute the loss National Organization Bank will suffer from Botosan's financial distress on December 31, 2008. What journal entries should be made to record this loss?

(LO 10) ***P14-13** **(De /Creditor Entries for Continuation of Troubled Debt)** Jeremy Hillary is the sole shareholder of Hillary Inc., which is currently under protection of the U.S. bankruptcy court. As a "debtor in possession," he has negotiated the following revised loan agreement with Valley Bank. Hillary Inc.'s $400,000, 12%, 10-year note was refinanced with a $400,000, 5%, 10-year note.

Instructions

(a) What is the accounting nature of this transaction?

(b) Prepare the journal entry to record this refinancing:

  (1) On the books of Hillary Inc.
  (2) On the books of Valley Bank.

 (c) Discuss whether generally accepted accounting principles provide the proper information useful to managers and investors in this situation.

(LO 10) ***P14-14 (Restructure of Note under Different Circumstances)** Sandro Corporation is having financial difficulty and therefore has asked Botticelli National Bank to restructure its $3 million note outstanding. The present note has 3 years remaining and pays a current rate of interest of 10%. The present market rate for a loan of this nature is 12%. The note was issued at its face value.

Instructions

Presented below are four independent situations. Prepare the journal entry that Sandro and Botticelli National Bank would make for each of these restructurings.

 (a) Botticelli National Bank agrees to take an equity interest in Sandro by accepting common stock valued at $2,200,000 in exchange for relinquishing its claim on this note. The common stock has a par value of $1,000,000.
 (b) Botticelli National Bank agrees to accept land in exchange for relinquishing its claim on this note. The land has a book value of $1,950,000 and a fair value of $2,400,000.
 (c) Botticelli National Bank agrees to modify the terms of the note, indicating that Sandro does not have to pay any interest on the note over the 3-year period.
 (d) Botticelli National Bank agrees to reduce the principal balance due to $2,500,000 and require interest only in the second and third year at a rate of 10%.

(LO 10) ***P14-15 (Debtor/Creditor Entries for Continuation of Troubled Debt with New Effective Interest)** Mildred Corp. owes D. Taylor Corp. a 10-year, 10% note in the amount of $110,000 plus $11,000 of accrued interest. The note is due today, December 31, 2007. Because Mildred Corp. is in financial trouble, D. Taylor Corp. agrees to forgive the accrued interest, $10,000 of the principal, and to extend the maturity date to December 31, 2010. Interest at 10% of revised principal will continue to be due on 12/31 each year.

Assume the following present value factors for 3 periods.

	$2\frac{1}{4}\%$	$2\frac{3}{8}\%$	$2\frac{1}{2}\%$	$2\frac{5}{8}\%$	$2\frac{3}{4}\%$	3%
Single sum	.93543	.93201	.92859	.92521	.92184	.91514
Ordinary annuity of 1	2.86989	2.86295	2.85602	2.84913	2.84226	2.82861

Instructions

 (a) Compute the new effective interest rate for Mildred Corp. following restructure. (*Hint:* Find the interest rate that establishes approximately $121,000 as the present value of the total future cash flows.)
 (b) Prepare a schedule of debt reduction and interest expense for the years 2007 through 2010.
 (c) Compute the gain or loss for D. Taylor Corp. and prepare a schedule of receivable reduction and interest revenue for the years 2007 through 2010.
 (d) Prepare all the necessary journal entries on the books of Mildred Corp. for the years 2007, 2008, and 2009.
 (e) Prepare all the necessary journal entries on the books of D. Taylor Corp. for the years 2007, 2008, and 2009.

CONCEPTS FOR ANALYSIS

CA14-1 (Bond Theory: Balance Sheet Presentations, Interest Rate, Premium) On January 1, 2008, Branagh Company issued for $1,075,230 its 20-year, 13% bonds that have a maturity value of $1,000,000 and pay interest semiannually on January 1 and July 1. Bond issue costs were not material in amount. Below are three presentations of the long-term liability section of the balance sheet that might be used for these bonds at the issue date.

1. Bonds payable (maturing January 1, 2028)	$1,000,000
Unamortized premium on bonds payable	75,230
Total bond liability	$1,075,230
2. Bonds payable—principal (face value $1,000,000 maturing	
January 1, 2028)	$ 97,220[a]
Bonds payable—interest (semiannual payment $65,000)	978,010[b]
Total bond liability	$1,075,230

3. Bonds payable—principal (maturing January 1, 2028)	$1,000,000
Bonds payable—interest ($65,000 per period for 40 periods)	2,600,000
Total bond liability	$3,600,000

[a]The present value of $1,000,000 due at the end of 40 (6-month) periods at the yield rate of 6% per period.
[b]The present value of $65,000 per period for 40 (6-month) periods at the yield rate of 6% per period.

Instructions

(a) Discuss the conceptual merit(s) of each of the date-of-issue balance sheet presentations shown above for these bonds.

(b) Explain why investors would pay $1,075,230 for bonds that have a maturity value of only $1,000,000.

(c) Assuming that a discount rate is needed to compute the carrying value of the obligations arising from a bond issue at any date during the life of the bonds, discuss the conceptual merit(s) of using for this purpose:

(1) The coupon or nominal rate.

(2) The effective or yield rate at date of issue.

(d) If the obligations arising from these bonds are to be carried at their present value computed by means of the current market rate of interest, how would the bond valuation at dates subsequent to the date of issue be affected by an increase or a decrease in the market rate of interest?

(AICPA adapted)

CA14-2 **(Various Long-Term Liability Conceptual Issues)** Emma Thompson Company has completed a number of transactions during 2007. In January the company purchased under contract a machine at a total price of $1,200,000, payable over 5 years with installments of $240,000 per year. The seller has considered the transaction as an installment sale with the title transferring to Thompson at the time of the final payment.

On March 1, 2007, Thompson issued $10 million of general revenue bonds priced at 99 with a coupon of 10% payable July 1 and January 1 of each of the next 10 years. The July 1 interest was paid and on December 30 the company transferred $1,000,000 to the trustee, Branaugh Company, for payment of the January 1, 2008, interest.

Due to the depressed market for the company's stock, Thompson purchased $500,000 par value of their 6% convertible bonds for a price of $455,000. It expects to resell the bonds when the price of its stock has recovered.

As the accountant for Emma Thompson Company, you have prepared the balance sheet as of December 31, 2007, and have presented it to the president of the company. You are asked the following questions about it.

1. Why has depreciation been charged on equipment being purchased under contract? Title has not passed to the company as yet and, therefore, they are not our assets. Why should the company not show on the left side of the balance sheet only the amount paid to date instead of showing the full contract price on the left side and the unpaid portion on the right side? After all, the seller considers the transaction an installment sale.

2. What is bond discount? As a debit balance, why is it not classified among the assets?

3. Bond interest is shown as a current liability. Did we not pay our trustee, Branaugh Company, the full amount of interest due this period?

4. Treasury bonds are shown as a deduction from bonds payable issued. Why should they not be shown as an asset, since they can be sold again? Are they the same as bonds of other companies that we hold as investments?

Instructions

Outline your answers to these questions by writing a brief paragraph that will justify your treatment.

CA14-3 **(Bond Theory: Price, Presentation, and Retirement)** On March 1, 2008, Jackie Chan Company sold its 5-year, $1,000 face value, 9% bonds dated March 1, 2008, at an effective annual interest rate (yield) of 11%. Interest is payable semiannually, and the first interest payment date is September 1, 2008. Chan uses the effective interest method of amortization. Bond issue costs were incurred in preparing and selling the bond issue. The bonds can be called by Chan at 101 at any time on or after March 1, 2009.

Instructions

(a) (1) How would the selling price of the bond be determined?

(2) Specify how all items related to the bonds would be presented in a balance sheet prepared immediately after the bond issue was sold.

(b) What items related to the bond issue would be included in Chan's 2008 income statement, and how would each be determined?

(c) Would the amount of bond discount amortization using the effective interest method of amortization be lower in the second or third year of the life of the bond issue? Why?

(d) Assuming that the bonds were called in and retired on March 1, 2009, how should Norris report the retirement of the bonds on the 2009 income statement?

(AICPA adapted)

CA14-4 (Bond Theory: Amortization and Gain or Loss Recognition)
Part I. The appropriate method of amortizing a premium or discount on issuance of bonds is the effective interest method.

Instructions

(a) What is the effective interest method of amortization and how is it different from and similar to the straight-line method of amortization?

(b) How is amortization computed using the effective interest method, and why and how do amounts obtained using the effective interest method differ from amounts computed under the straight-line method?

Part II. Gains or losses from the early extinguishment of debt that is refunded can theoretically be accounted for in three ways:

1. Amortized over remaining life of old debt.
2. Amortized over the life of the new debt issue.
3. Recognized in the period of extinguishment.

Instructions

(a) Develop supporting arguments for each of the three theoretical methods of accounting for gains and losses from the early extinguishment of debt.

(b) Which of the methods above is generally accepted and how should the appropriate amount of gain or loss be shown in a company's financial statements?

(AICPA adapted)

CA14-5 (Off-Balance-Sheet Financing) Brad Pitt Corporation is interested in building its own soda can manufacturing plant adjacent to its existing plant in Partyville, Kansas. The objective would be to ensure a steady supply of cans at a stable price and to minimize transportation costs. However, the company has been experiencing some financial problems and has been reluctant to borrow any additional cash to fund the project. The company is not concerned with the cash flow problems of making payments, but rather with the impact of adding additional long-term debt to its balance sheet.

The president of Pitt, Aidan Quinn, approached the president of the Aluminum Can Company (ACC), their major supplier, to see if some agreement could be reached. ACC was anxious to work out an arrangement, since it seemed inevitable that Pitt would begin their own can production. The Aluminum Can Company could not afford to lose the account.

After some discussion a two part plan was worked out. First ACC was to construct the plant on Pitt's land adjacent to the existing plant. Second, Pitt would sign a 20-year purchase agreement. Under the purchase agreement, Pitt would express its intention to buy all of its cans from ACC, paying a unit price which at normal capacity would cover labor and material, an operating management fee, and the debt service requirements on the plant. The expected unit price, if transportation costs are taken into consideration, is lower than current market. If Pitt did not take enough production in any one year and if the excess cans could not be sold at a high enough price on the open market, Pitt agrees to make up any cash shortfall so that ACC could make the payments on its debt. The bank will be willing to make a 20-year loan for the plant, taking the plant and the purchase agreement as collateral. At the end of 20 years the plant is to become the property of Pitt.

Instructions

(a) What are project financing arrangements using special purpose entities?

(b) What are take-or-pay contracts?

(c) Should Pitt record the plant as an asset together with the related obligation?

(d) If not, should Pitt record an asset relating to the future commitment?

(e) What is meant by off-balance-sheet financing?

CA14-6 (Bond Issue) Roland Carlson is the president, founder, and majority owner of Thebeau Medical Corporation, an emerging medical technology products company. Thebeau is in dire need of additional capital to keep operating and to bring several promising products to final development, testing, and production. Roland, as owner of 51% of the outstanding stock, manages the company's operations. He places heavy emphasis on research and development and long-term growth. The other principal stockholder is Jana Kingston who, as a nonemployee investor, owns 40% of the stock. Jana would like to

deemphasize the R & D functions and emphasize the marketing function to maximize short-run sales and profits from existing products. She believes this strategy would raise the market price of Thebeau's stock.

All of Roland's personal capital and borrowing power is tied up in his 51% stock ownership. He knows that any offering of additional shares of stock will dilute his controlling interest because he won't be able to participate in such an issuance. But, Jana has money and would likely buy enough shares to gain control of Thebeau. She then would dictate the company's future direction, even if it meant replacing Roland as president and CEO.

The company already has considerable debt. Raising additional debt will be costly, will adversely affect Thebeau's credit rating, and will increase the company's reported losses due to the growth in interest expense. Jana and the other minority stockholders express opposition to the assumption of additional debt, fearing the company will be pushed to the brink of bankruptcy. Wanting to maintain his control and to preserve the direction of "his" company, Roland is doing everything to avoid a stock issuance and is contemplating a large issuance of bonds, even if it means the bonds are issued with a high effective-interest rate.

Instructions
(a) Who are the stakeholders in this situation?
(b) What are the ethical issues in this case?
(c) What would you do if you were Roland?

USING YOUR JUDGMENT

Financial Reporting Problem

The Procter & Gamble Company (P&G)

The financial statements of P&G are presented in Appendix 5B or can be accessed on KWW website.

Instructions
Refer to P&G's financial statements and the accompanying notes to answer the following questions.
(a) What cash outflow obligations related to the repayment of long-term debt does P&G have over the next 5 years?
(b) P&G indicates that it believes that it has the ability to meet business requirements in the foreseeable future. Prepare an assessment of its solvency and financial flexibility using ratio analysis.

Financial Statement Analysis Cases

Case 1 Commonwealth Edison Co.
The following article appeared in the *Wall Street Journal*.

> **Bond Markets**
> *Giant Commonwealth Edison Issue Hits Resale Market With $70 Million Left Over*
> NEW YORK—Commonwealth Edison Co.'s slow-selling new 9¼% bonds were tossed onto the resale market at a reduced price with about $70 million still available from the $200 million offered Thursday, dealers said.
> The Chicago utility's bonds, rated double-A by Moody's and double-A-minus by Standard & Poor's, originally had been priced at 99.803, to yield 9.3% in 5 years. They were marked down yesterday the equivalent of about $5.50 for each $1,000 face amount, to about 99.25, where their yield jumped to 9.45%.

Instructions
(a) How will the development above affect the accounting for Commonwealth Edison's bond issue?
(b) Provide several possible explanations for the markdown and the slow sale of Commonwealth Edison's bonds.

Case 2 PepsiCo, Inc.

PepsiCo, Inc. based in Purchase, New York, is a leading company in the beverage industry. Assume that the following events occurred relating to PepsiCo's long-term debt in a recent year.

1 The company decided on February 1 to refinance $500 million in short-term 7.4% debt to make it long-term 6%.

2 $780 million of long-term zero-coupon bonds with an effective interest rate of 10.1% matured July 1 and were paid.

3 On October 1, the company issued $200 million in Australian dollar 6.3% bonds at 102 and $95 million in Italian lira 11.4% bonds at 99.

4 The company holds $100 million in perpetual foreign interest payment bonds that were issued in 1989, and presently have a rate of interest of 5.3%. These bonds are called perpetual because they have no stated due date. Instead, at the end of every 10-year period after the bond's issuance, the bondholders and PepsiCo have the option of redeeming the bonds. If either party desires to redeem the bonds, the bonds must be redeemed. If the bonds are not redeemed, a new interest rate is set, based on the then-prevailing interest rate for 10-year bonds. The company does not intend to cause redemption of the bonds, but will reclassify this debt to current next year, since the bondholders could decide to redeem the bonds.

Instructions

(a) Consider event 1. What are some of the reasons the company may have decided to refinance this short-term debt, besides lowering the interest rate?

(b) What do you think are the benefits to the investor in purchasing zero-coupon bonds, such as those described in event 2? What journal entry would be required to record the payment of these bonds? If financial statements are prepared each December 31, in which year would the bonds have been included in short-term liabilities?

(c) Make the journal entry to record the bond issue described in event 3. Note that the bonds were issued on the same day, yet one was issued at a premium and the other at a discount. What are some of the reasons that this may have happened?

(d) What are the benefits to PepsiCo in having perpetual bonds as described in event 4? Suppose that in the current year the bonds are not redeemed and the interest rate is adjusted to 6% from 7.5%. Make all necessary journal entries to record the renewal of the bonds and the change in rate.

Comparative Analysis Case

The Coca-Cola Company

The Coca-Cola Company and PepsiCo, Inc.

Instructions

Go to the KWW website and use information found there to answer the following questions related to The Coca-Cola Company and PepsiCo, Inc.

(a) Compute the debt to total assets ratio and the times interest earned ratio for these two companies. Comment on the quality of these two ratios for both Coca-Cola and PepsiCo.

(b) What is the difference between the fair value and the historical cost (carrying amount) of each company's debt at year-end 2004? Why might a difference exist in these two amounts?

(c) Both companies have debt issued in foreign countries. Speculate as to why these companies may use foreign debt to finance their operations. What risks are involved in this strategy, and how might they adjust for this risk?

Research Cases

Case 1

Instructions

Use an appropriate source (such as those identified in Chapter 2 Research Case 1) to identify a firm that recently had its bond rating changed. Answer the following questions.

(a) Which rating agency(ies) changed the rating?

(b) What was the bond rating before and after the change?

(c) What reasons did the rating agency give in support of its action? What accounting data was used as support?

(d) Are additional changes possible?

Case 2

The February 2, 2002, edition of the *Wall Street Journal* includes an article by Mark Maremount entitled "**Tyco** May Alter Plan to Buy Back $11 Billion in Bonds with Tenders." (You can access the article at the KWW website.)

Instructions

Read the article and answer the following questions.

(a) Tyco had announced earlier that it intended to "tender" for $11 billion of its bonds. Now it says it may repurchase the bonds in the open market. What's the difference between a "tender" and an open-market purchase?

(b) How would the transaction (tender or repurchase) be reported in the income statement? That is, what amount would be reported, and where would it appear?

(c) Under U.S. GAAP, should Tyco write down its bonds to their current market value? What accounting principle would justify this treatment?

Professional Research: Financial Accounting and Reporting

Wie Company has been operating for just 2 years, producing specialty golf equipment for women golfers. To date, the company has been able to finance its successful operations with investments from its principal owner, Michelle Wie, and cash flows from operations. However, current expansion plans will require some borrowing to expand the company's production line.

As part of the expansion plan, Wie will acquire some used equipment by signing a zero-interest-bearing note. The note has a maturity value of $50,000 and matures in 5 years. A reliable fair value measure for the equipment is not available, given the age and specialty nature of the equipment. As a result, Wie's accounting staff is unable to determine an established exchange price for recording the equipment (nor the interest rate to be used to record interest expense on the long-term note). They have asked you to conduct some accounting research on this topic.

Instructions

Using the **Financial Accounting Research System (FARS)**, respond to the following items. (Provide text strings used in your search.)

(a) Identify the accounting standard that provides guidance on the zero-interest-bearing note. Use some of the examples to explain how the standard applies in this setting.

(b) How is present value determined when an established exchange price is not determinable and a note has no ready market? What is the resulting interest rate often called?

(c) Where should a discount or premium appear in the financial statements? What about issue costs?

Professional Simulation

In this simulation you are asked to address questions related to the accounting for long-term liabilities. Prepare responses to all parts.

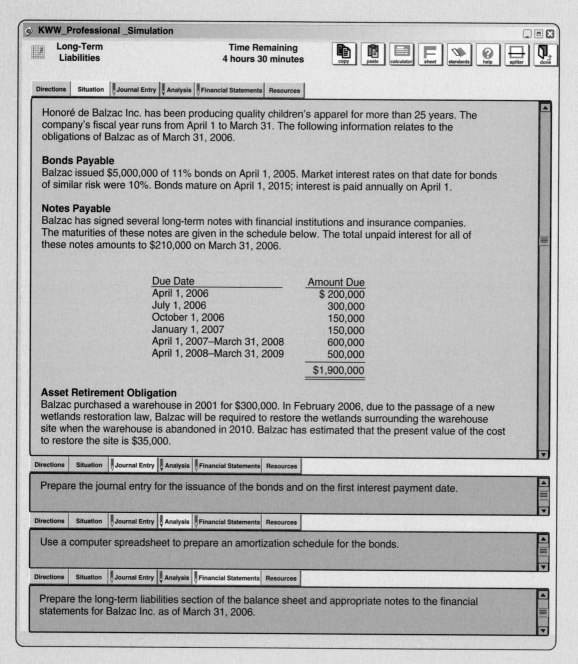

KWW_Professional _Simulation

| Long-Term Liabilities | Time Remaining 4 hours 30 minutes |

copy   paste   calculator   sheet   standards   help   splitter   done

| Directions | Situation | Journal Entry | Analysis | Financial Statements | Resources |

Honoré de Balzac Inc. has been producing quality children's apparel for more than 25 years. The company's fiscal year runs from April 1 to March 31. The following information relates to the obligations of Balzac as of March 31, 2006.

Bonds Payable
Balzac issued $5,000,000 of 11% bonds on April 1, 2005. Market interest rates on that date for bonds of similar risk were 10%. Bonds mature on April 1, 2015; interest is paid annually on April 1.

Notes Payable
Balzac has signed several long-term notes with financial institutions and insurance companies. The maturities of these notes are given in the schedule below. The total unpaid interest for all of these notes amounts to $210,000 on March 31, 2006.

Due Date	Amount Due
April 1, 2006	$ 200,000
July 1, 2006	300,000
October 1, 2006	150,000
January 1, 2007	150,000
April 1, 2007–March 31, 2008	600,000
April 1, 2008–March 31, 2009	500,000
	$1,900,000

Asset Retirement Obligation
Balzac purchased a warehouse in 2001 for $300,000. In February 2006, due to the passage of a new wetlands restoration law, Balzac will be required to restore the wetlands surrounding the warehouse site when the warehouse is abandoned in 2010. Balzac has estimated that the present value of the cost to restore the site is $35,000.

| Directions | Situation | Journal Entry | Analysis | Financial Statements | Resources |

Prepare the journal entry for the issuance of the bonds and on the first interest payment date.

| Directions | Situation | Journal Entry | Analysis | Financial Statements | Resources |

Use a computer spreadsheet to prepare an amortization schedule for the bonds.

| Directions | Situation | Journal Entry | Analysis | Financial Statements | Resources |

Prepare the long-term liabilities section of the balance sheet and appropriate notes to the financial statements for Balzac Inc. as of March 31, 2006.

Remember to check the book's companion website to find additional resources for this chapter.

LOGO CREDITS

The following companies have granted permission for their logos to be included in this text.

Avon Rubber. Reprinted by permission of Avon Rubber.

Caterpillar

The Coca-Cola Company. The world famous COCA-COLA and COCA-COLA Script Logo trademarks are registered trademarks of The Coca-Cola Company.

Eastman Kodak. Used with permission of Eastman Kodak Company.

Hewlett-Packard. Reprinted by permission of Hewlett-Packard.

Intuit Inc. Reprinted by permission of Intuit Inc.

Johnson & Johnson. Reprinted by permission of Johnson & Johnson.

Kellogg Company. © 2006 Kellogg North American Company.

Oracle. Reprinted by permission of Oracle International Corporation.

PepsiCo. All rights reserved. Used with permission.

Procter & Gamble

Southwest Airlines

Tomkins. Reprinted by permission of Tomkins PLC.

Westinghouse. Reprinted by permission of Westinghouse Electric Corporation.

A. C. Nielsen Company, 637*n*.22
Abbott Laboratories, 176
Abnormal shortages, 441
Absences, compensated, 629–631
Accelerated Cost Recovery System (ACRS), 547
Accounting, ethics in, 16–17
Accounting cycle, 67–93; adjusted trial balance, 84; adjusting entries, 75–84; closing, 86–88; journalizing, 69–70; post-closing trial balance, 88–89; posting, 70–74; preparing financial statements, 85–86; reversing entries, 89; steps of, 89; transactions and other events, identifying/recording, 68–69; trial balance, 74–75
Accounting information system, 62–67
Accounting policies: and APB Opinion No. 22, 185; on balance sheets, 184, 185
Accounting principle, changes in, 142
Accounting Principles Board (APB), 8, 21. *See also Opinions of the Accounting Principles Board*
Accounting Research Bulletins, 7, 380*n*.9, 423*n*.1, 431*n*.8
Accounting Research Study No. 13 ("The Accounting Basis of Inventories"), 429*n*.6
Accounting standards: authority of, 13*n*.9; economic consequences of, 15; need for development of, 5–6; politicization of, 21; principle-based vs. rule-based, 13; before SFAS No. 140, 335*n*.21
Accounting Standards Executive Committee (AcSEC), 11, 475*n*.2, 494*n*.17, 529*n*.8
Accounting theory, and cash basis accounting, 94–95
Accounts payable(s), 619–620
Accounts receivable(s), 319; age of, 325*n*.12; and *APB Opinion* No. 21, 321*n*.8; days to collect, 338*n*.23; disposition of, 332–337; recognition of, 320–321; trade, 331; uncollectible, 322–326; valuation of, 321–326
Accounts receivable written off, 326
Accruals: as class of adjusting entries, 75; in reversing entries illustration, 99–100
Accrual basis accounting: cash basis accounting vs., 94–98; conversion to cash basis accounting, 96–98; for warranties, 635
Accrued expenses: adjusting entries for, 81; as class of adjusting entries, 75
Accrued interest, adjusting entries for, 81–82

Accrued revenue(s): adjusting entries for, 80–81; as class of adjusting entries, 75
Accrued salaries, adjusting entries for, 82–83
Accumulated Depreciation account, 543
Accumulated rights, 630
Acid-test ratio, 646
Acquisition costs, 491–495, 538
ACRS (Accelerated Cost Recovery System), 547
AcSEC, *see* Accounting Standards Executive Committee
Activity method for depreciation, 525
Activity ratios, 200
Actually refinancing, 623
Additions, 492
Adelphia, 37, 691, 693
Adjunct account, 682
Adjustable-rate mortgage, 691
Adjusted trial balance, 63, 84, 88, 103
Adjustments, 75–84; for accruals, 80–84; for bad debts, 83–84; defined, 63; for depreciation, 78–79; for insurance, 77–78; for prepayments, 76–80; prior period, 141; for statement presentation, 79; types of, 75–76; for unearned revenues, 79–80; on worksheet, 102–104
Adjustments columns, 102
Administrative expenses, on income statement, 131
Adolph Coors Company, 319, 642
Advertising costs, 591
AES, 138, 671
After-closing trial balance, 63
Age of accounts receivables, 325*n*.12
AICPA, *see* American Institute of Certified Public Accountants
AICPA Task Force on LIFO Inventory Problems, 385*n*.11, 394*n*.21, 426*n*.2, 427*n*.4
AIG, 3, 45
Airline industry, 171, 524*n*.3
Alberto-Culver Company, 188
Albertson's, 418
Allowance method, 322, 323, 426–427
Alltel Corp., 624
Almost Family, Inc., 83
Alterra Healthcare Corp., 174
Altman, E. I., 184
Amazon.com, 125, 171, 180, 247–248, 380, 579
Ameren, 545
American Airlines, 79, 624
American Express, 332
American Institute of Certified Public Accountants (AICPA), 185. *See also* AICPA Task Force on LIFO Inventory

Problems and Accounting Standards Executive Committee, 11; and APB, 8; Code of Professional Conduct, 12; and Committee on Accounting Procedure, 7, 21; and GAAP standards development, 7–8; and government intervention, 24; and SEC, 6
American Maize-Products Company, 385
America Online (AOL), 572
America West, 171
Ames Department Stores, 421
AM International, 377
Amortization: of bonds, 278–279, 677–678; defined, 522; effective-interest method, of bond, 278–279; of intangible assets, 573–575; on units-of-production basis, 579*n*.8
Ampco-Pittsburgh Corporation, 529
Anadarko Petroleum Corporation, 481
Analogic Corporation, 598
Anixter Bros., Inc., 377
Annual interest rate, in compound interest tables, 257
Annual reports, on World Wide Web, 4
Annuity(-ies), 275–276
Annuity due, 267, 275; future value of, 267–270, 286; present value of, 272–275
Ante, S. E., 428
AOL Time Warner, 583, 584
APB, *see* Accounting Principles Board
APB Opinions, *see* Opinions of the Accounting Principles Board
Apple Computer, 436, 634
April-Marcus, Inc., 373
AROs (asset retirement obligations), 639
Artistic-related intangible assets, 577
Assessments, 634–635
Asset(s): on balance sheet, 173; current assets, 173–177; depreciable base for, 523; held for disposal, 536–537; non-current, 177–179; replacement of fixed, 532; transfer of, 701
Asset expenditures, 492
Asset-linked bonds, 673
Asset retirement obligations (AROs), 639
Asset turnover ratio, 544–545
Asset valuation, 490
Astra Zeneca Plc., 580
Atlantic Richfield, 540*n*.14
AT&T, 68, 528, 583, 598
Auditing Standards Board, 12
Auto loan, calculating, 287
Available-for-sale securities, 147*n*.27, 175
Average cost method, 382
Average days to sell inventory, 444
Avon Products, 169
Avon Rubber PLC., 167

Badanhausen, K., 169n.1
Bad debts, adjusting entries for, 83–84
Bad debt expense, 700n.7
Badwill, 583–584
Bahree, B., 541
Balance sheet(s), 63, 170–190; accounting
  policies on, 184; classification in,
  172–184; classified, 172; columns on,
  103; contingencies on, 184, 185; contractual situations on, 184–186; current
  assets on, 173–177; elements of, 173;
  example, 91; fair values on, 184, 186–187;
  format of, 182–184; liabilities on, 173,
  179–181; limitations of, 172; noncurrent
  assets on, 177–179; owner's equity on,
  182; presentation of, 149; stockholders'
  equity on, 66; usefulness of, 170–171
Balance sheet (percentage-of-receivables)
  approach, 323–326
Ball, J., 541
Bank, David, 625
Bank accounts, 340
Bank charges, reconciling, 342
Bank credits, reconciling, 342
Bank errors, reconciling, 342
Bank of America, 61, 344
BankOne, 4, 326
Bank overdrafts, 317
Bank reconciliation, 342–344
Bankruptcies, of retailers, 421
Bankruptcy-prediction model, 184
Bank statements, 342
Barnesandnoble.com, 579
Barrick Gold Corporation, 468
Barth, Mary, 16
Barth Industries, 632
Basket purchase, 430
Bayer, 614
Bearer (coupon) bonds, 674
Beaver, W. H., 127n.3
Beckett, Paul, 344
Behn, Bruce K., 592n.23
Beresford, Dennis R., 166
Bernard, Victor, 367n.3
Beru AG Corporation, 617
Best Buy, 36, 49, 106, 320, 370, 421, 422,
  436–437, 643, 646, 693–696
Biddle, Gary C., 396n.28
Biggs, Stanley F., 433n.10
Black & Decker, 49
Bloomingdale's, 436
Blow-out sales, 367
BLS (Bureau of Labor Statistics), 392n.16
Blumenstein, Rebecca, 491
BMC Industries, Inc., 632
Boeing Company, 78, 172, 368, 472, 491
Boise Cascade, 431, 542
Bonds. See also specific types, e.g.: Dis-
  count bonds: accounting for, 685; cor-
  porate listings, 674; effective-interest
  method for, 679–682; and extinguishment of debt, 683–685; face value of,
  675; and interest date, 677–678; between interest dates, issuance, 678; issuance of, 673, 682–683; monitoring
  investments in, 674; notes vs.,
  685–686; par on interest date, issuance
  at, 677; premium, 675; types of,
  673–674
Bond amortization, effective-interest
  method of, 278–279

Bond indenture, 673
Bonds payable, 672–685; and contra ac-
  counts, 682; discount, 682
Bond premiums, valuation of, 674–678
Bonus agreements, 631, 647–649
Book depreciation, tax depreciation vs.,
  550
Book of original entry, 63
Book value (bonds), 79, 679n.4
BOP Clothing Co., 667–668
Borrowing arrangements, and ASR No.
  148, 316n.4
Borrus, A., 676
Boston Celtics, 674
Bradlees Stores, 421
Brady, D., 591
Brand images, 591
Braniff, 171
Briggs & Stratton, 632, 707
Briston-Myers Squibb Company, 215
Brooker, K., 315n.3
Brown, K. L., 45
Brown, Robert Moren, 395n.26
Brown Shoe Company, 385, 386
Burden, 474
Bureau of Labor Statistics (BLS), 392n.16
Burton, John C., 7n.6
Bush, George W., 17
Business combinations, as present value-
  based measurement, 253
Business-method patents, 579
Buyback agreements, 374

Callable bonds, 673, 684n.11
Calpine, 671, 693
Campbell Soup Company, 552
Cannondale Corporation, 49
CAP, see Committee on Accounting
  Procedure
Capettini, Robert, 488n.13
Capital allocation, 3
Capital expenditures, 492
Capitalization period, 476
Capital maintenance approach, 129n.5
Capital One Financial, 169
Carcache, B., 547n.1
Carreyrou, John, 614
Carrying value (bonds), 679n.4
Cash and cash equivalents, 174–175,
  314–318; alternate terminology for,
  317n.6; on balance sheets, 174; basis of
  valuation of, 173; internal control
  over, 315; management and control of,
  315–316; from operating activities, 193;
  reporting, 316–317; restricted cash vs.,
  316
Cash balances, physical protection of,
  341–342
Cash basis accounting: and accounting
  theory, 94–95; accrual-basis accounting
  vs., 94–98; conversion to accrual basis,
  96–98; financial statements, 94; modified cash basis, 96; theoretical weaknesses of, 98; users of, 96n.1; warranties, 635
Cash controls, 340–344; and bank
  balances reconciliation, 342–344;
  and imprest petty cash system,
  340–341; and physical protection of
  cash balances, 341–342; using bank
  accounts, 340
Cash crunch, 196

Cash debt coverage ratio, 197
Cash deposits, returnable, 624
Cash discounts, 320–321, 379, 481
Cash flows, 5n.3; free, 197–198; net in-
  come vs., 196
Cash flow statement, see Statement of
  cash flows
Cash funds, 315
Cash over account, 341
Cash rebates, 637
Cash-related items, 317–318
Caterpillar, Inc., 78, 369, 394, 587
CDs (certificates of deposits), 315n.1
Ceiling (upper), 423–424
Cendant, 15
Century 21, 577
Certificates of deposits (CDs), 315n.1
Changes in accounting estimate, 141,
  142
Changes in accounting principle, 142
Checks: bouncing, 344; outstanding, 342;
  paper, 342n.1; postdated, 315
Check fraud, 342n.1
Checkfree, 125
Checking accounts, 340
Chesapeake Corporation, 185
ChevronTexaco, 539n.12
ChexSystems, 344
Chrysler Corporation, 395
Ciba-Geigy, 418
Circuit City, 36, 322, 338, 421, 441, 625,
  646
Cisco Systems, 34, 86, 127, 428, 691
Citicorp, 140n.20
Cities Service Company, 645
Citigroup, 140n.20, 322
Citizens Bank, 332n.18
Claims, 634–635
Clarcor Inc., 629
Classified balance sheets, 172
Closing, 86–88
Closing entries, 64, 87–88, 92
Closing prices, 86–88
The Coca-Cola Company, 16, 58, 75, 122,
  166, 248, 365, 469, 567, 572, 580, 591,
  613, 667, 722
"Cockroach theory," 135
Code of Professional Conduct (AICPA),
  12
"The codification," 13n.10, 17
Cohen, Abby Joseph, 584
Collateralized receivables, 332n.18
Collection float, 340
Columbia Sportswear Company, 600
Columbia Tri-Star (Sony), 41
Combination methods for depreciation,
  529–530
Combined statement, 148
Commercial paper, 315n.1
Commercial substance, 484–485
Committee on Accounting Procedure
  (CAP), 7, 21
Commodity-backed bonds, 673
Commonwealth Edison, 260, 721
Company names (intangible asset), 576
Compaq, 584
Compensated absences, 629–631
Compensating balances, 316
Components, 136
Component depreciation, 529n.8
Composite depreciation rate, 528–529
Composite life, 529

Composite methods for depreciation, 528–529
Compounded continuously, 257*n*.5
Compounded daily, 258
Compounding periods, 285
Compound interest, 255–258; future value as variable in, 258; present value as variable in, 258; rate of interest as variable in, 258; and Social Security, 256; tables for, 256–257, 302–311; variables fundamental to, 258–259
Comprehensive dollar-value LIFO method, 389–390
Comprehensive income, 147–149; combined statement of, 148; corrections of errors as, 149*n*.30; display requirements of, 147*n*.29; and SFAS No, 130, 147*n*.28
Computer software, *see under* Software
Comserve, 601
Condensed income statements, 133–134
Conditional expenses, 631
Consigned goods, 373–374
Consignment shipment, 373
Consolidated Natural Gas Company, 300
Consolidated Papers, Inc., 188
ContiFinancial, 336
Continental Airlines, 171
Contingencies, 631–642; on balance sheets, 184, 185; defined, 185; presentation of, 644–645; and SFAS No. 5, 323*n*.9, 630*n*.15, 642
Contingent liabilities, *see* Loss contingencies
Continuously compounded, 257*n*.5
Contra accounts, and bonds payable, 682
Contract-related intangible assets, 577–578
Contractual situations, on balance sheets, 184–186
Contra items, 189
Contributions, accounting for, 489–490
Control device, 437
Convertible bonds, 673
Cookie jar reserves, 128
Coon, William R., 388*n*.14
Copyrights, 577
Corning, 125
Corporate bond listings, 674
Corporate taxes, 626*n*.10. *See also* Income taxes, accounting for
Corrections of errors: as comprehensive income, 149*n*.30; in income statement, 142
Cost, 423
Cost allocation, 381*n*.10, 522–534. *See also* Depreciation
Cost approach, 483*n*.6
Cost flow assumption, 372; and ARB No. 43, 380*n*.9; average cost method for, 382; and first-in, first-out, 382–383; identification, 381; and last-in, first-out, 384–394
Costs included in inventory, 372; period costs, 378–379; product costs, 377–378; and treatment of purchase discounts, 379–380
Cost method, 437
Costs of financing, 378
Cost of goods available for sales or use, 372
Cost of goods sold, 372; example, 92–93; multiple pools contributing to, 388*n*.14; in periodic inventory system, 370; section of income statement, 131

Cost per unit of product, 538–539
Cost-to-retail ratio, 440
Coughlan, J. D., 523*n*.2
Coupons, 637
Coupon bonds, 674
Coupon rate, 675
Coverage ratios, 200
CPC International, 325
Craswell, Julie, 325
Credits (Cr.), 64–65, 171
Credit balance, 64
Credit cards, 333*n*.19
Creditors, 196
Creditor calculations, 703–704
Credit quality, 676
Credit risk, 337*n*.22
Credit risk rate of interest, 280
Credit squeeze, 331
Creswell, J., 138
Cron, William R., 392*n*.17
Cross-reference items, 189
Cummins, C., 541
Current assets, 173–177; on balance sheets, 173–177; cash, 174–175
Current cash debt coverage ratio, 197
Current liability(-ies), 619–631. *See also* specific types, e.g.: Accounts payable(s): analysis of, 645–646; APB Opinions No. 21, 642*n*.26; on balance sheets, 179–180; presentation of, 642–644
Current maturities of long-term debt, 621–622
Current operating performance approach, 135
Current ratios, 386, 645–646
Current receivables, 318
Current-value disclosures, SFAS No. 69 on, 540
Cushing, Barry E., 395*n*.25
Customary form, of balance sheets, 183*n*.13
Customer-related intangible assets, 576
Cycle, accounting, *see* Accounting cycle

Daily compounding, 258
Daimler-Benz, 25
DaimlerChrysler, 25, 36, 126, 395, 533*n*.10
Daley, Clayton C., Jr., 205
Days outstanding, 338*n*.23
Days to collect accounts receivable, 338*n*.23
Dead-weight debt, 685
Debenham, 436
Debenture bonds, 673
Debit balance, 64
Debits (Dr.), 64–65
Debt(s). *See also* Extinguishment of debt: continuation of, 702–706; current maturities of, 621–622; dead-weight, 685; issue cost (SFAS No. 6), 682*n*.7; long-term, *see* Long-term debt; settlement of, 701–702
DebtforSale.com, 326
Debtor accounting, 702*n*.11
Debtor calculations, 702–703
Debt ratings, 676
Debt to total assets ratio, 695
Declining-balance method, 527–528
Decreasing-charge methods for depreciation, 526–528
Deep-discount bonds, 673, 675*n*.2
Deere & Company, 165, 247, 332, 396, 587

Deferred annuities, 275–276
Deferred-payment contracts, 481–482
Dell Computer, 4, 172, 587
Delphi Corp., 697
Delta Airlines, 171
Deluxe Corp., 344
Depletion, 537–542; acquisition costs of, 538; defined, 522; development costs of, 538; and discovery value, 542; exploration costs of, 538; issues in oil and gas industry, 539–542; and liquidating dividends, 542; and recoverable reserves, 541; restoration costs of, 538
Depletion base, 537–538
Deposits: legally restricted, 317; in transit, 342
Depositor errors, reconciling, 342
Depreciable base, for assets, 523
Depreciable tax life, *see* Recovery periods
Depreciation, 522–534; Accumulated Depreciation account, 543; activity method for, 525; adjusting entries for, 78–79; decreasing-charge methods for, 526–528; defined, 522; factors involved in process of, 523; group and composite methods for, 528–529; hybrid or combination methods for, 529–530; issues in airline industry, 524*n*.3; under partial periods, 531–532; post-September 11, 2001 measures, 547*n*.1; rate revision for, 532–533; and replacement of fixed assets, 532; straight-line method for, 526; tax methods for, 547–550
Designated market value, 424
Development costs, 538
Diners Club, 332
Dingell, John, 24
Direct method, 426–427
Direct write-off method, 322, 323
Disclosure(s), 337*n*.22; of interest rates, 254*n*.3; as present value-based measurement, 253; and Sarbanes-Oxley Act of 2002, 641; and SFAS No. 107, 337*n*.22; and *Statement of Position 94–6*, 185; techniques of, 187–190
Discontinued operations, 136–137; on income statement, 131, 142; and SFAS No. 144, 136*n*.14
Discounts, cash, 320–321
Discount bonds, 675, 675*n*.2, 682, 691*n*.17
Discounting, 261
Discount notes, 688
Discover, 332
Discovery value, 542
Dividends, liquidating, 542
Dividends payable, 624
Dollar-value LIFO method, 387–392, 437, 446–449; and AICPA Task Force on LIFO Inventory Problems, 426*n*.2; comprehensive, 389–390; for determining cost of single item, 426*n*.2; example, 388; and price index selection, 390–392; specific-goods pooled approach vs., 387–392
Dollar-value retail method, 388*n*.12
Double-declining-balance method, 527
Double-entry accounting system, 64
Double-extension method, 391
Dr. (debits), 64–65
Dresser Industries, 165

Drugs.com, 575
Drugstore.com, 27, 380
Due process system, 9
Duffy, Wendy A., 478n.5
Dynegy, 196, 693

E. F. Hutton, 317n.5
Eagle Clothes, Inc., 373
Earnings, 126n.2. *See also* Retained earnings
Earnings before interest, taxes, depreciation, and amortization (EBITDA), 524
Earnings management, 128
Earnings per common share, 145
Earnings per share (EPS), 144–146; calculating, 144n.23; on income statement, 131, 133n.9; and SFAS No. 128, 145n.24
Eastman Kodak Company, 50, 140n.20, 324–325, 422, 493, 558
Ebbers, Bernie, 23
EBITDA (earnings before interest, taxes, depreciation, and amortization), 524
Ecolab, 169
Economic consequences, 15n.11, 523–524
Economic Recovery Tax Act of 1981, 547
Effective-interest method, 329, 687, 688; and accruing interest, 681–682; and *APB Opinion* No. 21, 679n.5; of bond amortization, 278–279; for bonds, 679–682; for bonds issued at discount, 679–680; for bonds issued at premium, 680–681
Effective interest rate, 327n.14
Effective rate, calculating, 258n.6
Effective yield, 327n.14, 675
EFund, 344
EITF, *see* Emerging Issues Task Force
EITF Issue No 86-29 ("Nonmonetary Transactions: Magnitude of Boot and the Exception to the Use of Fair Value"), 487n.12
Elective straight-line method, 550
Electronic commerce, 315
Eli Lilly, 580n.9
Elliott, J., 140n.20
El Paso Corporation, 541
Elstrom, P., 380
Emerging Issues Task Force (EITF), 10, 138
Employee bonus agreements, 647–649
Employee discounts, 441
Employee payroll deductions, 628
Employee-related liabilities, 626–627
Employers, payroll taxes paid by, 628
Ending inventory, misstated, 375–376
Enron, 1, 3, 7, 15, 17, 29, 39, 45, 172, 325, 641, 671, 691–693
"Enronitis," 1
Entries: adjusting, *see* Adjustments; reversing, 89
Environmental liabilities, 639–640
Epictetus, 622
EPS, *see* Earnings per share
Equity: on balance sheets, 173; owner's, 182
Equity interest, 701–702
Erlop, Osman, 599
Errors, correction of accounting, 141–142
Estimate, changes in, *see* Changes in accounting estimate
Estimates, judgments and, 172
E-tailers, 380

Ethics, 16–17
Event, defined, 63
Exchange price, 320
Exelon Corp., 685
Expectations gap, 15–16
Expected cash flow approach, 279, 281
Expected inflation rate of interest, 280
Expense(s): conditional, 631; on financial statements, 129; on income statement, 131; prepaid, *see* Prepaid expenses
Expense expenditures, 492
Expense warranty approach, 635, 636
Exploration costs of depletion, 538
Extensible business markup language (XBL), 4
External events, 63, 69
External indexes, 390n.15, 392n.16
Extinguishment of debt, 138n.18, 683–685
Extractive industries, R&D costs of, 589n.18
Extraordinary gains, 143–144
Extraordinary items: and *APB Opinion* No. 30, 137; determining, 138n.19; and extinguishment of debt, 138n.18; frequency of, in 2004 survey, 137n.17; on income statement, 131, 137–139, 142; reporting, after September 11, 2001, 138; and SFAS No. 144, 137; and SFAS No. 145, 138n.18
Extraordinary losses, 144
ExxonMobil, 68, 368, 537–538, 539n.12, 541

Face rate (interest), 258
Face value (bonds), 675
Factors, 333
Factoring arrangement, 333n.19
Factoring receivables, 333
Faircloth, Lauch, 24
Fair value(s): of asset, 489; on balance sheets, 184, 186–187; and EITF Issue No. 86–29, 487n.12
Fair-value tests: for indefinite-life intangible impairment, 585; for limited-life intangible impairment, 585
Falconbridge Ltd, Nickel Mines, 534
Fannie Mae, 17
FASAC (Financial Accounting Standards Advisory Council), 8
FASB, *see* Financial Accounting Standards Board
FASB Concepts, *see* Statements of Financial Accounting Concepts
FASB Interpretations: No. 14 ("Reasonable Estimation of the Amount of a Loss"), 640; No. 30 ("Accounting for Involuntary Conversions of Nonmonetary Assets to Monetary Assets"), 496; No. 45 ("Guarantor's Accounting and Disclosure Requirements for Guarantees, Including Indirect Guarantees of Indebtedness to Others"), 637n.21
FASB Statements, *see* Statements of Financial Accounting Standards
Federal Insurance Contribution Act (F.I.C.A.), 627
Federal Unemployment Tax Act (F.U.T.A.), 627
Federated Department Stores, 421
FedEx Corporation, 49
"Fed Watching," 280

FFO (funds from operations), 530n.9
FFP Marketing, 61
F.I.C.A. (Federal Insurance Contribution Act), 627
FIFO, *see* First-in, first-out
Fifth Third Bancorp., 4, 280
Financial accounting, as discipline, 2, 4
Financial Accounting Foundation, 8, 23
Financial Accounting Standards Advisory Council (FASAC), 8
Financial Accounting Standards Board (FASB), 23; APB vs., 8; and capitalization of interest costs, 379; and cash and cash equivalents, 190n.17; Concepts of, 10. *See also Statements of Financial Accounting Concepts*; due process system of, 9; and Emerging Issues Task Force, 10; and financial engineering, stance on, 693n.18; and financial statements, 172; and GAAP, 8–10; GASB vs., 10; and goodwill measurement, 582n.11; and guarantees, 645n.27; income reporting, 135n.11; Interpretations, *see* FASB *Interpretations*; and irregular items, 134; and loss contingencies, 323, 632; and sales, 336; and SEC, 6–7, 7n.6; and staff positions, 9; Standards of, 9, 10. *See also Statements of Financial Accounting Standards*; Technical Bulletins of, 9–10, 636n.20; and transactions, 68–69
Financial calculators, 284–288
Financial components approach, 335
Financial engineering, 693n.18
Financial flexibility, 171, 192, 197
Financial instruments, 186
Financial liquidity, 197
Financial position, statement of, *see* Balance sheet(s)
Financial reporting, 2; and expectations gap, 15–16; of international accounting standards, 16; objectives of, 4–5; and politically-influenced standard setting, 13–15
Financial statement(s), 2; defined, 63; elements of, 129; example of, 202–228; general-purpose, 5; inventory accounting for, 426n.3; maintaining monthly vs. quarterly, 89; for merchandising company, 89–93; notes to the, *see* Balance sheet(s); and ownership structure, 66–67; preparing, 85–86; worksheet preparation of, 104
Financing activities, 191
Financing agreement, 623
Firm (as concept), 433n.10
Firm purchase commitments, 433n.10
First Chicago, 331
First-in, first-out (FIFO): and cost flow assumption, 382–383; and LIFO, 386
Fixed assets, 472
Fixed percentage of book value method, *see* Declining-balance method
Fixed-rate mortgage, 691
Fleming, Sir Alexander, 578n.7
Flexibility, financial, 171, 192, 197
Flint, J., 367n.1
Float, collection, 340
Floating-rate mortgage, 691
Floor (lower), 423–424
f.o.b. (free on board) destination, 373
Footstar, 138

Ford Motor Company, 3, 15, 33, 36, 126, 169, 187, 248, 318, 367, 368, 399, 533*n*.10, 631, 632

Foreign Corrupt Practices Act, 61

Forgery, 315*n*.3

Fortune Brands, Inc., 442–443, 521

Forward-looking information, 4

Franchise(s), 577

Franecki, David, 280

Fraud: check, 342*n*.1; recorded by ChexSystems, 344; in U.S., 315*n*.3

Free cash flow, 197–198

Free on board (f.o.b.) destination, 373

Freight costs, 440

Frequent-flyer programs, 638

Frito Lay, 31

Full-cost concept, 539

Full-costing approach, 475

Functional expense classification, 131

Funds from operations (FFO), 530*n*.9

Fuqua Industries, 393

F.U.T.A. (Federal Unemployment Tax Act), 627

Future value: of an annuity due, 267–270; of annuity, 268–269; of annuity due, 286; of an ordinary annuity of 1 (table), 256; computing for unknown, 259; of deferred annuity, 275–276; of 1 (table), 256; of ordinary annuity, 285–286; of single sum, 259–260, 284–285; as variable in compound interest, 258

GAAP, *see* Generally accepted accounting principles

Gage. J., 169*n*.1

Gains: on financial statements, 129; on income statements, 131

Gain contingencies, 632

Gap Inc., 441, 572, 625

GASB (Governmental Accounting Standards Board), 10

General checking account, 340

General Dynamics, 45

General Electric (GE), 1, 45, 49, 127, 140, 324–325, 591, 623

General Electric Capital Corp., 623

General expenses, 131

General indexes, 390*n*.15

General journal entry, 70

General ledger, 63, 69

Generally accepted accounting principles (GAAP), 6, 12–13; and actual interest capitalization, 476; codification of, 13*n*.10, 17; hierarchy, 12*n*.7; major sources of, 12; organizations settings standards for, 6–12; pronouncements of, 13*n*.10

General Mills, 83, 587

General Motors (GM), 33, 36, 318, 332, 367, 533*n*.10

General Motors Acceptance Corp. (GMAC), 332

General-purpose financial statements, 5

General Tire and Rubber, 394*n*.22

Georgia-Pacific, 172, 431, 496, 667

Gerth, J., 541

Gibson, R., 45

Glaxo SmithKline, 614

Global Crossing, 1, 45, 489, 518

Gogoi, P., 326

Goldman, Sachs & Co., 584

Golf Digest, 624

Goods in transit, 373

Goodwill, 580–584; economic consequences of, 14; impairment of, 586–587; negative/badwill, 583–584; recording, 581; and SFAS No. 141, 581*n*.10; as write-off, 583

Goodyear Tire and Rubber, 166, 522, 671

Google, 89

Gore, Richard, 530*n*.9

Gotham Utility Company, 629, 630

Governmental Accounting Standards Board (GASB), 10

Granof, Michael H., 394*n*.28, 396*n*.28

The Great Atlantic & Pacific Tea Company, 181

Greenberg, Herb, 524, 671*n*.1

Greenspan, Alan, 280, 571, 572

Gross margin percentage, 434*n*.13

Gross profit method (gross margin method): evaluation of, 435–436; for inventories, 433–436

Gross profit on selling price, 434

Gross profit percentage, 434–435

Group methods for depreciation, 528–529

Guarantees, 635–637, 637*n*.21, 645*n*.27

Gujarathi, Mahendra R., 433*n*.10

Half-year convention, 531, 548–550

Hall, C., 169*n*.1

Halliburton Company, 180

Hambrecht & Quist, 599

Hanna, D., 140*n*.20

Harris, Trevor, 614

Hayes, Randall, 388*n*.14, 392*n*.17

HCA, 313

Healthsouth, 29

Held-to maturity debt securities, 175

Henry, David, 125*n*.1

Hershey Foods, 166, 396

Herz, Bob, 17

Hewlett-Packard Company, 318, 337*n*.22, 584, 587

Hincapie Co., 668

Historical cost, 172

Hof, R. D., 591

The Home Depot, 473

Homer, Sidney, 251

Huffy Corp., 697, 698

Hutchison Whampoa China Ltd., 214

Hybrid methods for depreciation, 529–530

IASB, *see* International Accounting Standards Board

IBM Corporation, 3, 16, 32, 127, 172, 200, 368, 375, 591, 596*n*.1, 599

IFRS, *see* International Financial Reporting Standards

Ijiri, Yuji, 433*n*.10

Immelt, Jeffrey, 1

Impaired note receivable, 331

Impairments, 534–537, 698–700; measuring, 535–536; recognizing, 534–535; recoverability tests for, 535, 585; and SFAS No. 114, 702*n*.12; and SFAS No. 118, 700*n*.8

Impairment charge, 584

Impairment loss, 536

Impairment test, 574

Implicit interest rate, 328

Imprest bank accounts, 340

Imprest petty cash system, 340–341

Imprest system for petty cash disbursements, 341

Imputation, 331, 689

Imputed interest rate, 331, 689

Inadequacy, 523

Income approach, 483*n*.6

Income bonds, 674

Income reporting, 135*n*.11

Income statement(s), 64, 126–129; alternate terminology for, 126*n*.2; columns on, 103; and comprehensive income, 147–149; condensed, 133–134; and earnings per share, 144–146; example, 90; and extraordinary gains, 143–144; and extraordinary losses, 144; format of, 129–134; intermediate components of, 131; and intraperiod tax allocation, 143; irregular items reported on, 134–143; limitations of, 127; and quality of earnings, 127–128; and retained earnings statement, 146; single-step, 130; and unusual gains and losses, 139–140; usefulness of, 126–127

Income statement (percentage-of-sales) approach, 323

Income statement method, *see* Direct method

Income taxes, accounting for: depreciation, 547–550; on income statement, 131; LIFO, 393*n*.19; and withholding, 628

Income taxes payable, 626

Increasing-charge method, of depreciation, 530

Indefinite-life intangibles, 574–575, 585–586

Indexes, computing, 390–391

Indirect method, 426–427

Individual retirement account (IRA), 288

Initial operating-losses, 590–591

Inland Steel, 526

Input, in depreciation, 525

Installment contracts, 253

Instruments, financial, 186

In-substance defeasance, 683*n*.10

Insurance, adjusting entries for, 77–78

Intangible assets, 571–587, 592–594. *See also specific types, e.g.:* Limited-life intangibles: amortization of, 573–575; on balance sheets, 179; characteristics of, 573–574; defined, 573; impairment of, 584–587; presentation of, 592–594; and SFAS No. 141, 581*n*.10; valuation of, 573

Intel, 41, 79, 254, 318, 428, 495, 591

Interbrand Corp., 591

Interest. *See also* Compound interest; accruing with effective-interest method, 681–682; capitalization of, 379*n*.8, 476*n*.3, 478–480; components of, 280; computation of, 254; costs of, 378, 379; as period cost, 378; and time value concepts, 253–254; variables in computation of, 254

Interest-bearing notes, 326, 328–331, 620, 686–688

Interest rate(s), 477–478; choosing, 280–281, 331; computation of, 274; disclosure requirement, 254*n*.3; implicit, 328; imputed, 331; as variable in interest computation, 254

Interest revenue, 321, 480
Interest tables, 256
Internal controls, 15
Internal events, 69
Internal indexes, 390n.15
Internally created goodwill, 581
Internally created intangibles, 573
Internal Revenue Service (IRS), 61; and indexes, 392n.16; and LIFO conformity rule, 395–396; and purchases-only-approach, 449n.2
International accounting standards, 16
International Accounting Standards Board (IASB), 16
International Financial Reporting Standards (IFRS), 16; GAAP comparison to, 617; and gains on exchanges, 484n.9
International Paper Co., 14, 187–188, 521, 533, 543–544
International Thoroughbred Breeders, 316
Intraperiod tax allocation, 143
Intuit Inc., 175
Inventory(-ies), 368–372; alternative method for estimating, 434n.12; analysis of, 443–444; average days to sell, 444; on balance sheets, 176–177; basis of valuation of, 173; control, 370–372; costs included in, 377–380; defined, 368; estimating, using gross profit percentage, 434n.12; example, 92; gross profit method for, 433–436; land as, 474; management of, 421; method selection for, 395–397; misstated, 376–377; at net realizable value, 429; presentation of, 442–443; purchases of, 392n.17; valuation of, 372, 396–397, 429–433
Inventory errors, 375–377
Inventory methods, 371n.4, 395n.24
Inventory turnover ratio, 444
Investing activities, 191
Investment(s): long-term, 177–178; PPE, 474; short-term, 173, 175
I.O.U.s, 315
Ip, Greg, 571n.1
IRA (individual retirement account), 288
Irregular items: analyzing, 135; categories of, 136; and FASB, 134; in income statement, 142; on income statement, 134–143; and SFAS No. 13, 135n.11; summary of, 142–143
IRS (Internal Revenue Service), 61

J. Crew, 4
J. M. Smucker Company, 215
J. P. Morgan, 39, 331, 591
Jack in the Box, 45
JCPenney Company, 395–396, 421, 673
JDS-Uniphase, 125
Jenkins, Edmund L., 125
Jim Walter's Corporation, 481
Job Creation and Worker Assistance Act of 2002, 547n.1
John Deere and Company, 165, 247, 332, 396, 587
John Deere Credit, 332
Johnson, Carrie, 141n.22
Johnson, L. Todd, 166
Johnson Controls, 14
Johnson & Johnson, 517–518, 587, 613
Jones, S. D., 45

Journal(s), 63, 69, 70
Journal entry, general, 70
Journalizing, 69–70
Judgments and estimates, 172
Junk bonds, 676

Kazenski, Paul M., 478n.5
Kellogg Co., 31, 122, 444, 473, 587
Keystone Consolidated Industries, 138
Khermouch, Gerry, 591
Kimco Realty, 530, 568
King, Thomas E., 488n.13
Kirk, Donald, 599
Kmart, 1, 325, 421
Kmart Holding, 378
Knight-Ridder, Inc., 177
Kohls, 322
Krispy Kreme, 3, 17, 169, 578, 691
Kroger, 169, 536–537, 545
Kurzweil Applied Intelligence Inc., 375

Labaton, S., 541
Lafley, A. G., 204, 205
Land: cost of, 473–474; expenditures for, 480
Last-in, first-out (LIFO): advantages of, 392–393; approach comparisons, 392; and cost flow assumption, 384–394; disadvantages of, 393–394; external indexes computations, 392n.16; and FIFO, 386; and future earning hedge, 393; specific-goods, 387; tax benefits, 393, 395
Layers, 386
LCM, see Lower-of-cost-or-market
Leach, Jim, 24
Leases, operating, 692
LeClere, Marc J., 395n.25
Ledger, 63
Legally restricted deposits, 317
Leslie Fay (company), 377
Lev, Baruch, 592n.23
Level 8 Systems, 34
Levitt, A., 128n.4
Liability(-ies), 618–619; on balance sheets, 173, 179–181; contingent, see Loss contingencies; defined, 618–619; employee-related, 626–627; environmental, 640; and FASB Interpretation No. 14, 640; long-term, 181; and SFAS No. 45, 645n.27
Liability valuation account, 682
Liberty International, 568
Licenses, 577–578
Liesman, S., 13, 135
LIFO, see Last-in, first-out
LIFO conformity rule, 395–396
LIFO liquidations, 385–387, 394n.21, 427n.4
LIFO matches, 393
LIFO method, dollar-value, 387–392
LIFO reserve, 384–386
LIFO retail methods, 437, 445–450; changing from conventional retail method to, 449–450; and stable prices, 445–446
Limited-life intangibles, 573–574; accounting treatment for, 575; fair value tests for, 585; impairment of, 584–585
Liquid assets, 316n.4
Liquidity, 171, 192
Liquidity evaluation, 386

Liquidity ratios, 200
Litigation, 634–635
Loan impairment, and SFAS No. 114, 698n.1
Loans, 698n.4
Loans.com, 575
Loan write-offs, 700n.7
Lockbox accounts, 340
Logarhythmics, 257n.5
Long Island Railroad (LIRR), 61
Long-term assets, 253
Long-term bonds, valuation of, 277–278
Long-term borrowing, 317
Long-term debt, 672; analysis of, 695–696; current maturities of, 621–622; on financial statements, 672; off-balance-sheet financing, 691–693; presentation of, 694–695; reporting, 691–696; and Concept Statement No. 5, 691; and Concept Statement No. 6, 691; and SFAS No. 6, 695; and SFAS No. 47, 695; and SFAS No. 78, 622n.7
Long-term investments, 177–178
Long-term liabilities, 671–696; on balance sheets, 181; bonds payable, 672–685; long-term notes payable, 685–691; and reporting and analysis of debt, 691–696
Long-term notes payable, 685–691
Loomis, Carol J., 584
Loss(es), 700n.7; on financial statements, 129; in income statement, 131; and SFAS No. 6, 129n.7
Loss contingencies, 632–652; coupons, 637; environmental liabilities, 639–640; and FASB, 323, 632; guarantee and warranty costs, 635–637; litigations, claims, and assessments, 634–635; premiums, 637–638; self-insurance, 641–642
Loss impairments, 698–700
Loss measurement, 138
Loudder, Martha L., 592n.23
Lower (floor), 423–424
Lower-of-cost-or-market (LCM), 422–429; applying, 425–426; and net realized value, 423–424; in practice, 429n.6; and recording market instead of cost, 426–429
Lower-of-cost-or-market (LCM) rule, 423, 425, 428, 429
Lucent Technologies, 40
Lump-sum price, 482
Lump-sum purchases, 482–483

McDermott, D., 135n.12
McDonald's Corporation, 3, 45, 75, 129, 566–567, 577
McGee, Robert W., 597n.2
Mack Trucks, Inc., 176
McLean, Bethany, 313, 325
McNamee, M., 676
MACRS, see Modified Accelerated Cost Recovery System
McTauge, R., 45
Maher, Kris, 471n.1
Major repair, 493–494
Maker, 326
Managerial accounting, 2
Manufacturers Hanover Trust Co., 315
Manufacturing, 368, 377–378
Maremount, Mark, 723
Markdowns, 436, 437
Markdown cancellations, 437

Marketable securities, 317*n*.6
Market approach, 483*n*.6
Marketing-related intangible assets, 575–576
Market rate, 327*n*.14, 675
Market value, and accounting quality, 128
Markup, 435, 437
Marriott, 577
MasterCard, 332, 333*n*.19
MasterNet, 61
Master valuation approach, 582–583
Mattel, Inc., 178
Maturity value (bonds), 675
Maxwell House, 320
May Department Stores, 421
Means, Grady, 471*n*.1
Means, Kathryn, 478*n*.5
Medicare, 627
Mehring, James, 685
Merchandising concerns, 368
Merck & Co., Inc., 578, 587, 594, 613, 614, 631
Merit rating, 627
Mesa Limited Partnerships, 540*n*.15
Microsoft Corporation, 3, 4, 16, 127, 254, 363, 571, 572, 579, 591, 597, 624, 625
MicroStrategy, 128, 150
Midway, 171
Modified Accelerated Cost Recovery System (MACRS), 547–550; example of, 548–550; optional straight-line method vs., 550; property classes, 548; and tax depreciation methods, 548
Modified cash basis, 96
Modified perpetual inventory system, 371
Mohican Company, 666–667
Monetary assets, 484*n*.7
Monetary exchange, 487*n*.12
Money-market funds, 315*n*.1
Money-market savings certificates, 315*n*.1
Monsanto Chemical Corporation, 324–325
Montavon Winery, 623
Montgomery Ward, 421
Monthly financial statements, 89
Moody's Investors Service, 676
Morgenson, Gretchen, 27*n*.1, 34, 169*n*.1
Mortgages, 691
Mortgage loan amounts, 287–288
Mortgage notes payable, 691
Motorola Inc., 41, 49, 178, 368
Moving-average method, 382
Multiple-step income statements, 130–133
Mumford of Wyoming, 442
Myers, David, 23

Natural expense classification, 131
Natural resources, 542, 543
Navistar, 576
Negative goodwill, 583–584
Nesco Holdings, Inc., 632
Net income, cash flows vs., 196
Net losses, 133*n*.9
Net method, 379
Net of cash discounts, 379
Net realizable value, 429–430
Net realized value (NRV), 423–424
Net working capital, 180
New allowance account, 427
New average unit cost, 382
Newmont Gold Company, 443
News Corp., 41
New York Community Bancorp., 280

Nicholaisen, Don, 45
Nissan (formerly Datsun), 576
Noel, J., 367*n*.3
Nominal accounts, 63
Nominal rate, 258, 675
Noncalculable purchase commitments, 433*n*.10
Non-check payments, in Japan and Europe, 315*n*.3
Non-consolidated subsidiary, 692
Noncurrent assets, 177–179
Noncurrent receivables, 318–319
Nonfinancial measurements, 4
Non-interest bearing notes, *see* Zero-interest-bearing notes
Nonmonetary assets, 484–489, 490*n*.16, 496
Nonreciprocal transfers, 489
Nontrade receivables, 319
Norby, William C., 30*n*.4
Nordstrom, 421, 423
Norfolk Southern Corporation, 50
Normal shortages, 441
Normand, Troy, 23
Nortel, 3, 313, 314, 472
Northern Trust Company, 260
Northland Cranberries, 666
Northrop Grumman Corp., 166
Northwest Airlines, 79, 171, 697
Note(s): accounting for, 685; bonds vs., 685–686; choice of interest rate for, 689–690; discount, 688; interest-bearing, 326, 328–331, 686–688; issuance of, at face value, 327–328, 686; issuance of, for property, goods, and services, 330–331, 688–689; not issued at face value, 328–331, 686–688; as present value-based measurement, 253
Notes payable, 620–621, 686*n*.13, 688–691
Notes receivable, 319; and *APB Opinion* No. 21, 329*n*.15; disposition of, 332–337; impaired, 331; recognition of, 326–331; valuation of, 331
Notes to the financial statements, 181*n*.12, 187–188
Not-sufficient funds (NSF) checks, 342
Noven Pharmaceuticals, Inc., 418
NRG Energy, 671
NRV, *see* Net realized value
NSF (not-sufficient funds) checks, 342

O.A.S.D.I (old age, survivor, and disability insurance), 627
Obsolescence, 523–524
Occidental Petroleum, 363
Off-balance-sheet financing, 691–693; forms of, 692; rationale for, 692–693; and SEC stance on, 693
Oil and gas industry, depletion issues in, 539–542
Old age, survivor, and disability insurance (O.A.S.D.I), 627
Olofson, Roy, 489
On-balance sheet financing, 693
One-time items, 140*n*.20
Operating activities: cash provided by, 193; on statement of cash flows, 191
Operating cycle, 619
Operating expense computation, 97–98
Operating leases, 692
Operations, 126*n*.2
Opinions of the Accounting Principles Board (APB Opinions), 8, 9; No. 21 ("Interest

on Receivables and Payables"), 321*n*.8, 329*n*.15, 642*n*.26, 679*n*.5, 686*n*.13; No. 22 ("Disclosure of Accounting Policies"), 185; No. 29 ("Accounting for Nonmonetary Transactions"), 484*n*.8; No. 30 ("Reporting the Results of Operations"), 137
Optional straight-line method, 550
Oracle Corporation, 50, 364
Ordinary annuity, 275; future value of, 285–286; present value of, 270–272, 286–287
Original entry, book of, 63
Output, in depreciation, 525
Outstanding checks, 342
Overhead, 474
Owens Corning, Inc., 174–175
Owners' equity, *see* Stockholders' equity
Ownership structure, 66–67
Ozanian, Michael K., 169*n*.1, 521*n*.1

Pacific Bell, 674
Pacific Lighting, 540, 540*n*.15
Panera Bread Company, 36
Paper checks, 342*n*.1
Paramount, 41
Parenthetical explanations, 187
Parking transactions, 374
Partial period depreciation, 531–532
Par value (bonds), 675
Passage of title rule, 373
Patents, business-method, 579
Payee, 326
Payroll deductions, 627–629; example of, 628–629; income tax withholding, 628; Social Security taxes, 627; unemployment taxes, 627–628
Payroll taxes, 628
PCAOB (Public Company Accounting Oversight Board), 15
Peers, Martin, 567
Penn Central Railroad, 622
Pensions, 253
The Pepsi Bottling Group (PBG), 14
PepsiCo. Beverages, 31
PepsiCo, Inc., 31, 58, 122, 138, 166, 179, 248, 365, 469, 567, 591, 613, 621, 667, 722
PepsiCo. International, 31
Percentage depletion, 542
Percentage markup, 434*n*.13
Percentage-of-receivables approach, 323–326
Percentage-of-sales approach, 323
Performance approach, current operating, 135
Periods, compounding, 257, 285
Period costs: interest as, 378; in inventory, 378–379; and SFAS No. 151, 378*n*.7
Periodic inventory system, 370–372
Periodic rent, 274–275
Permanent accounts, 63, 88
Permits, 577–578
Perpetual inventory system, 370, 371, 427
Petroleum Equipment Tools Inc., 496
Petty cash disbursements, imprest system for, 341
Petty cash funds, 315, 341
Pfizer Inc., 571, 572
Physical factors, of depreciation, 523–524
Physical goods included in inventory, 372–377; consigned goods, 373–374; goods in transit, 373; and sales agreements, 374–375

Physical inventory count, 371
Pizza Hut, 186
Plant assets, 472; dispositions of, 495–496; and involuntary conversion, 496; problems with, 496; sale of, 495–496
Pledge, 332n.17
PMC-Sierra, 125
PNC, 3
Points (note), 691
Polaroid, 578
Politicization, 21
Pools, 387, 388nn.13–14, 393n.19
Postage stamps on hand, 315
Post-closing trial balance, 63, 88–89
Postdated checks, 315
Postemployment benefits, 629n.13
Posting, 70–74; closing entries, 87–88; defined, 63
Postretirement benefits, 253, 631n.14
Potlatch Corporation, 706–707
PPE, see Property, plant, and equipment
Practice Bulletins, 11
Preferred dividends in arrears, 624
Premier Parks, 524
Premiums, 637–638
Premium amortization, of bonds, 677–678
Premium bonds, 674–678
Prepaid expenses: adjusting entries for, 76–77; on balance sheets, 177; basis of valuation of, 173; as class of adjusting entries, 75
Preparing financial statements, 85–86
Prepayments: adjusting entries for, 76–80; as class of adjusting entries, 75; in reversing entries illustration, 101–102
Present value, 252; of annuity, 273–275; of annuity due, 272–275; of annuity due of 1 (table), 256; of an ordinary annuity, 273–274; of an ordinary annuity of 1 (table), 256; computing for unknown, 259; of deferred annuity, 276–277; measurement, 279–281; of 1 (table), 256; of ordinary annuity, 270–272, 286–287; of single sum, 261–262, 285; solving for, 259; standards for, 253n.2; as variable in compound interest, 258
Present value-based measurements, 253
Price index selection, 390–392
Priceline.com, 27, 579
Prime Motor Inn, 196
Primerica (formerly American Can), 576
Principal, 254
Principal amount (bonds), 675
Principle-based accounting standards, rule-based vs., 13
Prior period adjustments, 141
Probability, degree of, 635
The Procter & Gamble Company, 58, 105, 122, 164, 186, 202–228, 246, 299, 363, 368, 467, 566, 613, 665, 721
Product costs, 377–378
Product guarantees, see Guarantees
Production variable method, 530
Profitability ratios, 200
Profit margin on sales ratio, 545
Pro forma, 125
Project financing arrangement, 692
Promissory note, 326
Promotional payments, 378

Property, goods, or services, 330–331
Property, plant, and equipment (PPE), 472; acquisition and valuation of, 473–481; analysis of, 544–545; and APB Opinion No. 6, 473; on balance sheets, 178; and cost of buildings, 474; and cost of equipment, 474; and cost of land, 473–474; and interest costs during construction, 475–480; observations for, 480; presentation of, 543–544; and self-constructed assets, 474–475; valuation of, 481–490
Pro rata portion, 475
Prorating, 681
Proved reserves, 541
Public Accounting Oversight Board, 12
Public Company Accounting Oversight Board (PCAOB), 15
Pulliam, Susan, 367n.2
Purchases, misstatement/overstatement of, 376–377
Purchase allowances, 440, 440n.15
Purchase commitments, valuation of, 431–433
Purchased goodwill, 581–583
Purchased intangibles, 573
Purchase discounts, 379–380, 440
Purchase returns, 440
Purchases-only-approach, 449n.2
Pure rate of interest, 280
Puwaslki, A. C., 280

Quaker Foods, 31
Quaker State Oil Refining Corp., 633
Qualcomm Inc., 125, 578, 579
Qualifying assets, 476
Quality of earnings, 127–128
Quality ratings (bonds), 676
Quanex Corporation, 182
Quantum Corporation, 337n.22
Quarterly financial statements, 89
Qwest Communications, 489, 518

R. G. Barry & Co., 68
R. J. Reynolds, 33
Rate of gross profit, 434n.13
Rate of interest, 258
Rate(s) of return, 374–375, 375n.6, 545
Rate of return on assets (ROA), 545
Ratios, 200. See also specific ratios, e.g.: Cash debt coverage ratio
Ratio analysis, 200–201
Raw materials inventory, 368
Raymark Corporation, 644
R&D, see Research and development (R&D) costs
Reacquisition price, 684
Real accounts, 63
Real estate investment trusts (REITs), 530n.9
Really Useful Group, 577
Rearrangements, costs of, 493
Receivables, 318–338. See also Accounts receivable(s); analysis of, 338; on balance sheets, 176; basis of valuation of, 173; classifying, 337; defined, 318, 323; presentation of, 337–338; with recourse, 335–336; sales of, 333–336; trade, 319; without recourse, 334
Receivables turnover ratio, 338
Reconciliation method, see Indirect method
Reconciling items, 342

Recourse: defined, 334n.20; receivables with, 335–336; receivables without, 334; and SFAS No. 140, 334n.20
Recoverability tests, 535, 585
Recovery periods, 548
Reeve, James M., 388n.12, 393n.19
Refinancing, 622, 623
Refunding, 684
Registered bonds, 674
Regulation G, 125
Reinhardt, A., 591
Reinstallation costs, 493
Reither, Cheri L., 166
REITs (real estate investment trusts), 530n.9
Relative sales value, 430–431
Rent-Way, Inc., 128
Repairs, 493–494
Replacements, 439n.14, 492
Reporting, See Financial reporting
Research and development (R&D) costs, 587–590, 592; accounting for, 588–589; under contractual arrangements, 589n.19; of extractive industries, 589n.18; identifying, 588; and investors, 592n.23; presentation of, 594
Reserves, cookie jar, 128
Restoration costs, of depletion, 538
Restricted cash, 316–317
Restructuring, 140n.20, 700–706; continuation of debt, 702–706; settlement of debt, 701–702; and SFAS No. 15, 700n.9
Restructuring charge, 139
Retail inventory methods, 436–442; concepts of, 437–438; with conventional method, 438–440; evaluation of, 441–442; special items relating to, 440–441
Retail methods, 449–450
Retained earnings: restrictions of, 146; statement of, 90; on statement of stockholders' equity, 146n.26
Retained earnings statement, 146
Retirement benefits, see Postretirement benefits
Retrospective adjustment, 140
Returnable cash deposits, 624
Revell, Janice, 165
Revenue(s): on financial statements, 129; in income statement, 131
Revenue bonds, 674
Revenue expenditures, 492
Reversing entries, 89; using, 99–104; and worksheet columns, 102
Rhone-Poulenc Rorer (RPR), 418
Risk, 170n.3
Rite-Aid, 15
RJR Nabisco, 672
ROA (rate of return on assets), 545
Rohde, L., 579
Rounding, 285
Royal Ahold, 378
Royal Dutch/Shell, 541
Rule-based accounting standards, 13
Ryder System, 169

S. C. Johnson, 136
Sack, Robert J., 16
Safeway, 436
Sales: with buyback agreement, 374; conditions for, 336; and FASB, 336; with high rates of return, 374–375; on

installment, 375; with recourse, 335–336; secured borrowing vs., 336–337; without recourse, 334
Sales agreements, 374–375
Sales discounts, 320–321, 440
Sales-warranty approach, 636
Sales tax payable, 625–626
Salvage value, 523
Sampling, statistical, 371n.4
Sandberg, Jared, 491
Sarbanes-Oxley Act of 2002: and auditing standards, 12; and disclosure, 641; key provisions of, 15; and SEC, 641; Section 404 of, 15
Sauter, Douglas, 12
Savings certificates, money-market, 315n.1
Schneider, C., 378
Schneider, David, 471n.1
Seaboard Corporation, 319
Sears Holdings, 322, 370, 421, 436
Sears, Roebuck & Co., 322, 421
SEC, *see* Securities and Exchange Commission
Second income statement, 147–148
Secured bonds, 673
Secured borrowing, 332–333, 336–337
Securities, available-for-sale, 147n.27, 175
Securities and Exchange Commission (SEC), 22; and American Institute of Certified Public Accountants, 6; and earnings management, 128; enforcement by, 7; and environmental liabilities, 640; and FASB, 6–7, 7n.6; and GAAP standards development, 6–7; and liquid assets, 316n.4; and off-balance-sheet financing, 693; in private sector, 7; and Regulation G, 125; and Sarbanes-Oxley Act of 2002, 641
Securitization, 272, 334
Self-insurance, 641–642
Sender, Henny, 196, 489, 518
September 11, 2001 terrorist attacks: depreciation measures taken after, 547n.1; effect on airlines, 171; massive write-downs after, 584; reporting extraordinary items after, 138
Serial bonds, 673
Service lives, 523–524
Service revenue, 96–97
Settlement of debt, 701–702
Sharpe, Michael, 25
Sherwin-Williams Company, 247
Short, Daniel G., 394n.28, 396n.28
Short account, 341
Shortages, normal/abnormal, 441
Short-term borrowing, 317
Short-term debt, 622–623
Short-term financial obligations, 619n.5
Short-term financing, 321n.7
Short-term investments, 173, 175
Short-term obligations, 622n.8
Short-term paper, 315n.1
Short-term receivables, 318
Sick pay, 630
Sidel, Robin, 567
Significant noncash activities, 194–195
Simple interest, 254–255
Single-step income statements, 130
Single sum: future value of, 259–260, 284–285; present value of, 261–262, 285
Single-sum problems, 259–264; and future values of an annuity due,

267–270; and present value of annuity due, 272–275; and present value of ordinary annuity, 270–272; solving for unknown in, 263–267
Sinking funds, 253
Smith, Alison, 436
Social Security, 256, 627
Soft assets, 4
Software costs, 592; accounting for, 596–599; capitalized, 597–598; reporting, 598
Software industry, 596n.1
Solectron Corporation, 49
Solomon, Deborah, 491
Solvency, 171, 192
Sonic, Inc., 467–468
Sonic Foundry Corporation, 293
Sony, 41, 42
SOP (Statements of Position), 11
Sotheby's Holdings, 373
Sougiannis, Theodore, 592n.23
Southwest Airlines, 79, 171, 471, 472
Sparks, D., 331
SPEs, *see* Special purpose entities
Special assessments, 473
Special journals, 70
Special purpose entities (SPEs), 692
Specific-goods LIFO approach, 387
Specific-goods pooled approach, 387–392
Specific-goods pooled LIFO approach, 387
Specific indexes, 390n.15
Specific items, 143
Staff positions, 9
Standard account form, 70
Standardized cost system, 429n.5
Standard Oil of Ohio, 540n.14
Standard & Poor's Corporation, 676
Standards setting: government intervention in, 24; in political environment, 13–14
Stanga, Keith G., 388n.12, 393n.19
Staples, 424
Starbucks, 49, 472
Start-up costs, 590
Stated interest rate, 327n.14
Stated rate, 258, 675
Statement of cash flows, 64, 190–198; content and format of, 191–192; purpose of, 190–191; and SFAS No. 95, 190; usefulness of, 195–196
Statement of cash flows preparation, 193–195
Statements of Financial Accounting Concepts, 10; No. 5 ("Recognition and Measurement in Financial Statements of Business Enterprises"), 135n.13, 691; No. 6 ("Elements of Financial Statements of Business Enterprises"), 129n.7, 433, 619n.3, 619n.5, 682n.7, 691; No. 7 ("Using Cash Flow Information and Present Value in Accounting Measurements"), 279
Statement of financial position, 170. *See also* Balance sheet(s)
Statement of Position 94–6 ("Disclosure of Certain Significant Risks and Uncertainties"), 185
Statement of retained earnings, 90
Statement of stockholders' equity, 146n.26, 148–149
Statements of Financial Accounting Standards, 9, 23; FASB Standards Statement, 9;

No. 5 ("Accounting for Contingencies"), 323n.9, 630n.15, 642, 698n.2; No. 6 ("Classification of Short-term Obligations Expected to be Refinanced), 622n.9, 695; No. 7 ("Accounting and Reporting by Development Stage Enterprises"), 591n.21; No. 15 ("Accounting by Debtors and Creditors for Troubled Debt Restructurings"), 700n.9; No. 34 ("Capitalization of Interest Cost"), 379n.8, 476n.3, 478n.5; No. 43 ("Accounting for Compensated Absences"), 629n.12, 630; No. 45, 645n.27; No. 47 ("Disclosure of Long-Term Obligations"), 695; No. 48 ("Revenue Recognition When Right of Return Exists), 375n.6; No. 49 ("Accounting for Product Financing Arrangements"), 374n.5; No. 69 ("Disclosure about Oil and Gas Producing Activities"), 540; No. 78 ("Classification of Obligations That Are Callable by the Creditor"), 622n.7; No. 84 ("Induced Conversions of Convertible Debt"), 78n.5; No. 86 ("Accounting for the Costs of Computer Software to be Sold, Leased, or Otherwise Marked"), 597; No. 106, 253n.2; No. 107 ("Disclosures about Fair Value of Financial Instruments), 253n.2, 337n.22; No. 109, 253n.2; No. 112 ("Employers' Accounting for Postemployment Benefits"), 629n.13; No. 114 ("Accounting by Creditors for Impairment of a Loan"), 253n.2, 698n.1, 698n.4, 698n.5, 702n.10–702n.12; No. 116 ("Accounting for Contributions Received and Contributions Made"), 253n.2, 490n.15, 490n.16; No. 118 ("Accounting by Creditors for Impairment of a Loan—Income Recognition and Disclosures), 700n.8; No. 128 ("Earnings Per Share"), 145n.24; No. 129 ("Disclosure of Information about Capital Structure"), 695n.19; No, 130 ("Reporting Comprehensive Income"), 147n.28; No. 140 ("Accounting for Transfers and Servicing of Financial Assets and Extinguishments of Liabilities"), 334n.20, 335n.21; No. 141, 253n.2, 581n.10; No. 142, 253n.2; No. 143 ("Accounting for Asset Retirement Obligations"), 639n.23; No. 144 ("Accounting for the Impairment or Disposal of Long-Lived Assets"), 136n.14, 137, 253n.2; No. 145 ("Recission of FASB Statements No. 4, 44, and 64, and Technical Corrections"), 138n.18, 684n.12; No. 150 ("Accounting for Certain Financial Instruments with Characteristics of Both Liabilities and Equity," 618n.2; No. 151 ("Inventory Costs: An Amendment of ARB No. 43, Chapter 4"), 378n.7; No. 154 ("Accounting Changes and Error Corrections"), 140n.21
Statements of Position (SOP), 11
Statistical sampling, 371n.4
Statutory depletion, 542
Stauffer Chemical Company, 392
Stires, David, 578
Stock, issuance of, 483
Stock dividends, 624
Stockholders' equity, 66, 182. *See also* Statement of stockholders' equity

Storey, Reed K., 28*n*.2
Storey, Sylvia, 28*n*.2
Stott, David, 530*n*.9
Straight-line method for depreciation, 526
Strand, W. K., 523*n*.2
Strict cash basis, 94
Study Group on Establishment of Accounting Principles, 8
Subsidiary ledger, 63
Substitution approach, 492–493
Successful-efforts concept, 539
Sullivan, Scott, 23
Summary of Significant Accounting, 185
Summers, Lawrence, 16
Sum-of-the-years'-digits method, 527
Sunbeam, 15, 45
Sunder, Shyam, 395*n*.26
Sunshine Mining, 28–29, 673
SunTrust Banks, 4, 15, 326
Superior Bank FSB, 336
Supersession, 523
Supporting schedules, 189

T-account, 69
Taco Bell, 186
Take-or-pay contract, 692
Target Corporation, 50, 322, 370, 421, 423, 436, 445, 472, 551
Taxes. *See also* Income taxes, accounting for; corporate, 626*n*.10; employer payroll, 628; Social Security, 627; unemployment, 627–628
Tax depreciation: in 1980s and 1990s, 548*n*.2; book depreciation vs., 550
Tax Reform Act of 1986, 547
Technological feasibility, 597, 599
Technology-related intangible assets, 578–580
Teco Energy, 169
Temporary accounts, 88
Tenet Healthcare, 313, 314
Terhune, Schad, 667
Term bonds, 673
Texaco, 325
TheStreet.com, 671
Three-column form of account, 71
Timberland, 169
Time diagram, 258–259
Timelines, 4
Times interest earned ratio, 695
Time value concepts, 252–259; applications of, 252–253; and compound interest, 255–258; and interest, 253–254; and simple interest, 254–255; variables fundamental to, 258–259
Time Warner, 583, 584
Timex, 423
Timmons, H., 331, 676
T J International, 417
Tomkins PLC, 249
Tootsie Roll Industries, 166, 544–545
Townsend, Leah, 15*n*.13, 62*n*.1
Toyota, 577

Trade accounts payable, *see* Accounts payable(s)
Trade accounts receivable, 331
Trade discounts, 320
Trademark (trade name), 575
Trade notes payable, *see* Notes payable
Trade receivables, 319
Trading, 175
Traditional LIFO, 385
Transactions, 63, 68–69
Transaction approach, 129
Transfers-in, 441
Transwitch, 428
Travel advances, 315
Treasury bills, 315*n*.1
Treasury bonds, 683
Trial balance, 63, 74–75. *See also specific types, e.g.:* Adjusted trial balance
Trial balance columns, 102
Troubled debt: accounting for, 697–706; impairments, 698–700; restructuring, 700–706
True-Value Hardware, 436
Tucker, Reed, 580
Turner, Lynn, 34
20th Century Fox, 41
Tyco International, 723

Ugly Duckling, 336
Unamortized bond issue costs, 682
Uncollectible accounts receivable, 322–326
Unearned revenues, 624–625; adjusting entries for, 79–80; as class of adjusting entries, 75
Unemployment taxes, 627–628
Unfiled suits, 635
Uniroyal Technology Corporation (UTC), 246
Unit approach, and Accounting Standards Executive Committee (AcSEC), 529*n*.8
United Airlines, 171, 638, 697
United Parcel Service (UPS), 33, 535
Unit LIFO, 385
Units-of-production approach, 538
Unrealized Appreciation, 542
Unsecured bonds, 673
Unusual gains or losses, 139–140, 142
Upper (ceiling), 423–424
Upton, Wayne, Jr., 172*n*.6
US Airways, 171
USX Corp., 325

Valuation: of accounts receivable, 321–326; of inventories, 372, 429–433; at net realizable value, 429–430; of notes receivables, 331; and purchase commitments, 431–433; using relative sales value, 430–431
Vames, Steven, 623, 671*n*.1
The Vanguard Group, 674
Variable-rate mortgage, 691
Vatter, William J., 322*n*.9

Vendor allowances, 378
Vested rights, 630
Viacom, 42
Vincent, Linda, 530*n*.9
VISA, 332, 333*n*.19
Vishay Technologies, 428
Visteon, 15
Vivendi Universal Entertainment, 614

W. R. Grace, 37, 128
W. T. Grant Company, 191, 196
Walgreen Co., 49, 76, 106, 165, 172, 373
Wallman, Steven H., 36*n*.11
Wal-Mart, 58, 226, 368–370, 421, 436, 445, 452, 471, 473, 625
Walt Disney Company, 31, 571–573, 577
Warranties, 635–637. *See also* Guarantees: accrual method for, 635; cash-basis method for, 635; and FASB Technical Bulletin No. 90–1, 636*n*.20
Waste Management, 521
Watch lists, 698*n*.3
Webber, Andrew Lloyd, 577
Weighted-average accumulated expenditures, 477, 478*n*.5
Weighted-average method, 382
Weil, J., 45, 135, 313
Wella AG, 213–214
Weyerhaeuser Company, 137, 176–177, 431
Wheat, Francis, 8
Wheat Committee, 8
WHX Corporation, 530
Willamette Industries, 188, 534
Williams Companies, 1, 693
William Wrigley Jr. (company), 423
Winstar Communications, 571
Wisconsin Electric, 248
Working capital, 180
Working capital ratio, 645
Work in process inventory, 369
Worksheet(s): adjustments entered on, 102–104; preparation of, 104
WorldCom, 1, 15, 23, 196, 325, 491
Write-offs, 135, 521, 700*n*.7
Written off, accounts receivable, 326

XBL (extensible business markup language), 4
Xerox, 1, 15, 17, 331, 578

Yahoo, Inc., 34, 50, 125
Young, S., 40
YUM! Inc., 186–187

Zeff, Stephen A., 15*n*.11
Zero-interest-bearing notes, 326, 328, 621, 686–687
Zero-interest bonds, 675*n*.2
Zero-interest debenture bonds, 673
Zion, David, 547*n*.1
Z-scores, 184
Zuckerman, G., 685

OFFICIAL ACCOUNTING PRONOUNCEMENTS

The following list of official accounting pronouncements constitutes the major part of *generally accepted accounting principles* (GAAP) and represents the authoritative source documents for much of the discussion contained in this book.

Date Issued		No.	Title

Accounting Research Bulletins (ARB's), Committee on Accounting Procedures, AICPA (1953–1959)

June	1953	No. 43	Restatement and Revision of *Accounting Research Bulletins Nos. 1–42*, and *Accounting Terminology Bulletin No. 1* (originally issued 1939–1953)
Oct.	1954	No. 44	Declining-Balance Depreciation; Revised July, 1958 (amended)
Oct.	1955	No. 45	Long-term Construction-type Contracts (unchanged)
Feb.	1956	No. 46	Discontinuance of Dating Earned Surplus (unchanged)
Sept.	1956	No. 47	Accounting for Costs of Pension Plans (superseded)
Jan.	1957	No. 48	Business Combinations (superseded)
April	1958	No. 49	Earnings Per Share (superseded)
Oct.	1958	No. 50	Contingencies (superseded)
Aug.	1959	No. 51	Consolidated Financial Statements (amended and partially superseded)

Accounting Terminology Bulletins, Committee on Terminology, AICPA

Aug.	1953	No. 1	Review and Résumé (of the eight original terminology bulletins) (amended)
Mar.	1955	No. 2	Proceeds, Revenue, Income, Profit, and Earnings (amended)
Aug.	1956	No. 3	Book Value (unchanged)
July	1957	No. 4	Cost, Expense, and Loss (amended)

Accounting Principles Board (APB) Opinions, AICPA (1962–1973)

Nov.	1962	No. 1	New Depreciation Guidelines and Rules (amended)
Dec.	1962	No. 2	Accounting for the "Investment Credit" (amended)
Oct.	1963	No. 3	The Statement of Source and Application of Funds (superseded)
Mar.	1964	No. 4	Accounting for the "Investment Credit" (amending No. 2)
Sept.	1964	No. 5	Reporting of Leases in Financial Statements of Lessee (superseded)
Oct.	1965	No. 6	Status of Accounting Research Bulletins (partially superseded)
May	1966	No. 7	Accounting for Leases in Financial Statements of Lessors (superseded)
Nov.	1966	No. 8	Accounting for the Cost of Pension Plans (superseded)
Dec.	1966	No. 9	Reporting the Results of Operations (amended and partially superseded)
Dec.	1966	No. 10	Omnibus Opinion—1966 (amended and partially superseded)
Dec.	1967	No. 11	Accounting for Income Taxes (superseded)
Dec.	1967	No. 12	Omnibus Opinion—1967 (partially superseded)
Mar.	1969	No. 13	Amending Paragraph 6 of *APB Opinion No. 9*, Application to Commercial Banks (unchanged)
Mar.	1969	No. 14	Accounting for Convertible Debt and Debt Issued with Stock Purchase Warrants (unchanged)
May	1969	No. 15	Earnings per Share (superseded)
Aug.	1970	No. 16	Business Combinations (superseded)
Aug.	1970	No. 17	Intangible Assets (superseded)
Mar.	1971	No. 18	The Equity Method of Accounting for Investments in Common Stock (amended)
Mar.	1971	No. 19	Reporting Changes in Financial Position (amended)
July	1971	No. 20	Accounting Changes (superseded)
Aug.	1971	No. 21	Interest on Receivables and Payables (amended)
April	1972	No. 22	Disclosure of Accounting Policies (amended)
April	1972	No. 23	Accounting for Income Taxes—Special Areas (superseded)
April	1972	No. 24	Accounting for Income Taxes—Equity Method Investments (unchanged)
Oct.	1972	No. 25	Accounting for Stock Issued to Employees (unchanged)
Oct.	1972	No. 26	Early Extinguishment of Debt (amended)
Nov.	1972	No. 27	Accounting for Lease Transactions by Manufacturer or Dealer Lessors (superseded)
May	1973	No. 28	Interim Financial Reporting (amended and partially superseded)
May	1973	No. 29	Accounting for Nonmonetary Transactions (amended)
June	1973	No. 30	Reporting the Results of Operations (amended)
June	1973	No. 31	Disclosure of Lease Commitments by Lessees (superseded)

Financial Accounting Standards Board (FASB), Statements of Financial Accounting Standards (1973–2002)

Dec.	1973	No. 1	Disclosure of Foreign Currency Translation Information (superseded)
Oct.	1974	No. 2	Accounting for Research and Development Costs (amended)
Dec.	1974	No. 3	Reporting Accounting Changes in Interim Financial Statements (superseded)
Mar.	1975	No. 4	Reporting Gains and Losses from Extinguishment of Debt (superseded)
Mar.	1975	No. 5	Accounting for Contingencies (amended)
May	1975	No. 6	Classification of Short-term Obligations Expected to be Refinanced
June	1975	No. 7	Accounting and Reporting by Development Stage Enterprises
Oct.	1975	No. 8	Accounting for the Translation of Foreign Currency Transactions and Foreign Financial Statements (superseded)

Date Issued		No.	Title
Oct.	1975	No. 9	Accounting for Income Taxes—Oil and Gas Producing Companies (superseded)
Oct.	1975	No. 10	Extension of "Grandfather" Provisions for Business Combinations (superseded)
Dec.	1975	No. 11	Accounting for Contingencies—Transition Method
Dec.	1975	No. 12	Accounting for Certain Marketable Securities (superseded)
Nov.	1976	No. 13	Accounting for Leases (amended, interpreted, and partially superseded)
Dec.	1976	No. 14	Financial Reporting for Segments of a Business Enterprise (amended)
June	1977	No. 15	Accounting by Debtors and Creditors for Troubled Debt Restructurings (amended)
June	1977	No. 16	Prior Period Adjustments (amended)
Nov.	1977	No. 17	Accounting for Leases—Initial Direct Costs
Nov.	1977	No. 18	Financial Reporting for Segments of a Business Enterprise—Interim Financial Statements
Dec.	1977	No. 19	Financial Accounting and Reporting by Oil and Gas Producing Companies (amended)
Dec.	1977	No. 20	Accounting for Forward Exchange Contracts (superseded)
April	1978	No. 21	Suspension of the Reporting of Earnings per Share and Segment Information by Nonpublic Enterprises (amended)
June	1978	No. 22	Changes in the Provisions of Lease Agreements Resulting from Refundings of Tax-Exempt Debt (amended)
Aug.	1978	No. 23	Inception of the Lease
Dec.	1978	No. 24	Reporting Segment Information in Financial Statements That Are Presented in Another Enterprise's Financial Report
Feb.	1979	No. 25	Suspension of Certain Accounting Requirements for Oil and Gas Producing Companies
April	1979	No. 26	Profit Recognition on Sales-Type Leases of Real Estate
May	1979	No. 27	Classification of Renewals or Extensions of Existing Sales-Type or Direct Financing Leases
May	1979	No. 28	Accounting for Sales with Leasebacks
June	1979	No. 29	Determining Contingent Rentals
Aug.	1979	No. 30	Disclosure of Information about Major Customers
Sept.	1979	No. 31	Accounting for Tax Benefits Related to U.K. Tax Legislation Concerning Stock Relief
Sept.	1979	No. 32	Specialized Accounting and Reporting Principles and Practices in AICPA Statements of Position and Guides on Accounting and Auditing Matters (amended and partially superseded)
Sept.	1979	No. 33	Financial Reporting and Changing Prices (amended and partially superseded)
Oct.	1979	No. 34	Capitalization of Interest Cost (amended)
Mar.	1980	No. 35	Accounting and Reporting by Defined Benefit Pension Plans (amended)
May	1980	No. 36	Disclosure of Pension Information (superseded)
July	1980	No. 37	Balance Sheet Classification of Deferred Income Taxes (amended)
Sept.	1980	No. 38	Accounting for Preacquisition Contingencies of Purchased Enterprises (superseded)
Oct.	1980	No. 39	Financial Reporting and Changing Prices: Specialized Assets—Mining and Oil and Gas
Nov.	1980	No. 40	Financial Reporting and Changing Prices: Specialized Assets—Timberlands and Growing Timber
Nov.	1980	No. 41	Financial Reporting and Changing Prices: Specialized Assets—Income-Producing Real Estate
Nov.	1980	No. 42	Determining Materiality for Capitalization of Interest Cost
Nov.	1980	No. 43	Accounting for Compensated Absences (amended)
Dec.	1980	No. 44	Accounting for Intangible Assets of Motor Carriers (superseded)
Mar.	1981	No. 45	Accounting for Franchise Fee Revenue (amended)
Mar.	1981	No. 46	Financial Reporting and Changing Prices: Motion Picture Films
Mar.	1981	No. 47	Disclosure of Long-Term Obligations (amended)
June	1981	No. 48	Revenue Recognition When Right of Return Exists
June	1981	No. 49	Accounting for Product Financing Arrangements
Nov.	1981	No. 50	Financial Reporting in the Record and Music Industry
Nov.	1981	No. 51	Financial Reporting by Cable Television Companies (amended)
Dec.	1981	No. 52	Foreign Currency Translation (amended)
Dec.	1981	No. 53	Financial Reporting by Producers and Distributors of Motion Picture Films (superseded)
Jan.	1982	No. 54	Financial Reporting and Changing Prices: Investment Companies (superseded)
Feb.	1982	No. 55	Determining Whether a Convertible Security is a Common Stock Equivalent (superseded)
Feb.	1982	No. 56	Designation of AICPA Guide and SOP 81-1 on Contractor Accounting and SOP 81-2 on Hospital-Related Organizations as Preferable for Applying *APB Opinion 20* (superseded)
Mar.	1982	No. 57	Related Party Disclosures
April	1982	No. 58	Capitalization of Interest Cost in Financial Statements that Include Investments Accounted for by the Equity Method
April	1982	No. 59	Deferral of the Effective Date of Certain Accounting Requirements for Revision Plans of State and Local Governmental Units
June	1982	No. 60	Accounting and Reporting by Insurance Enterprises (amended)
June	1982	No. 61	Accounting for Title Plant (amended)
June	1982	No. 62	Capitalization of Interest Cost in Situations Involving Certain Tax-Exempt Borrowings and Certain Gifts and Grants
June	1982	No. 63	Financial Reporting by Broadcasters (amended)

Date Issued		No.	Title
Sept.	1982	No. 64	Extinguishment of Debt Made to Satisfy Sinking-Fund Requirements (superseded)
Sept.	1982	No. 65	Accounting for Certain Mortgage Bank Activities (amended)
Oct.	1982	No. 66	Accounting for Sales of Real Estate (amended)
Oct.	1982	No. 67	Accounting for Costs and Initial Rental Operations of Real Estate Projects (amended)
Oct.	1982	No. 68	Research and Development Arrangements (amended)
Nov.	1982	No. 69	Disclosures about Oil and Gas Producing Activities
Dec.	1982	No. 70	Financial Reporting and Changing Prices: Foreign Currency Translation
Dec.	1982	No. 71	Accounting for the Effects of Certain Types of Regulation (amended)
Feb.	1983	No. 72	Accounting for Certain Acquisitions of Banking or Thrift Institutions (amended)
Aug.	1983	No. 73	Reporting a Change in Accounting for Railroad Track Structures
Aug.	1983	No. 74	Accounting for Special Termination Benefits Paid to Employees
Nov.	1983	No. 75	Deferral of the Effective Date of Certain Accounting Requirements for Pension Plans of State and Local Governmental Units (superseded)
Nov.	1983	No. 76	Extinguishment of Debt (superseded)
Dec.	1983	No. 77	Reporting by Transferors for Transfers of Receivables with Recourse (superseded)
Dec.	1983	No. 78	Classifications of Obligations that Are Callable by the Creditor
Feb.	1984	No. 79	Elimination of Certain Disclosures for Business Combinations by Nonpublic Enterprises (superseded)
Aug.	1984	No. 80	Accounting for Futures Contracts (superseded)
Nov.	1984	No. 81	Disclosure of Postretirement Health Care and Life Insurance Benefits
Nov.	1984	No. 82	Financial Reporting and Changing Prices: Elimination of Certain Disclosures
Mar.	1985	No. 83	Designation of AICPA Guides and Statement of Position on Accounting by Brokers and Dealers in Securities, by Employee Benefit Plans, and by Banks as Preferable for Purposes of Applying *APB Opinion 20*
Mar.	1985	No. 84	Induced Conversions of Convertible Debt
Mar.	1985	No. 85	Yield Test for Determining Whether a Convertible Security Is a Common Stock Equivalent (superseded)
Aug.	1985	No. 86	Accounting for the Costs of Computer Software to be Sold, Leased, or Otherwise Marketed
Dec.	1985	No. 87	Employers' Accounting for Pensions (amended)
Dec.	1985	No. 88	Employers' Accounting for Settlements and Curtailments of Defined Benefit Pension Plans and for Termination Benefits (amended)
Dec.	1986	No. 89	Financial Reporting and Changing Prices (amended)
Dec.	1986	No. 90	Regulated Enterprises—Accounting for Abandonments and Disallowances of Plant Costs
Dec.	1986	No. 91	Accounting for Nonrefundable Fees and Costs Associated with Originating or Acquiring Loans and Initial Direct Costs of Leases
Aug.	1987	No. 92	Regulated Enterprises—Accounting for Phase-in Plans
Aug.	1987	No. 93	Recognition of Depreciation by Not-for-Profit Organizations
Oct.	1987	No. 94	Consolidation of All Majority-Owned Subsidiaries
Nov.	1987	No. 95	Statement of Cash Flows (amended)
Dec.	1987	No. 96	Accounting for Income Taxes (superseded)
Dec.	1987	No. 97	Accounting and Reporting by Insurance Enterprises for Certain Long-Duration Contracts and for Realized Gains and Losses from the Sale of Investments
June	1988	No. 98	Accounting for Leases; Sale-Leaseback Transactions Involving Real Estate; Sales-Type Leases of Real Estate; Definition of the Lease Term; Initial Direct Costs of Direct Financing Leases
Sept.	1988	No. 99	Deferral of the Effective Date of Recognition of Depreciation by Not-for-Profit Organizations
Dec.	1988	No. 100	Accounting for Income Taxes—Deferral of the Effective Date of *FASB Statement No. 96*
Dec.	1988	No. 101	Regulated Enterprises—Accounting for the Discontinuation of Application of *FASB Statement No. 71* (amended)
Feb.	1989	No. 102	Statement of Cash Flows—Exemption of Certain Enterprises and Classification of Cash Flows from Certain Securities Acquired for Resale (amended)
Dec.	1989	No. 103	Accounting for Income Taxes—Deferral of the Effective Date of *FASB Statement No. 96*
Dec.	1989	No. 104	Statement of Cash Flows—Net Reporting of Certain Cash Receipts and Cash Payments and Classification of Cash Flows from Hedging Transactions
Mar.	1990	No. 105	Disclosure of Information About Financial Instruments with Off-Balance-Sheet Risk and Financial Instruments with Concentrations of Credit Risk (superseded)
Dec.	1990	No. 106	Employers' Accounting for Postretirement Benefits Other Than Pensions (amended)
Dec.	1991	No. 107	Disclosures about Fair Value of Financial Instruments (amended)
Dec.	1991	No. 108	Accounting for Income Taxes—Deferral of the Effective Date of *FASB Statement No. 96*
Feb.	1992	No. 109	Accounting for Income Taxes (amended)
Aug.	1992	No. 110	Reporting by Defined Benefit Pension Plans of Investment Contracts
Nov.	1992	No. 111	Rescission of *FASB Statement No. 32* and Technical Corrections
Nov.	1992	No. 112	Employers' Accounting for Postemployment Benefits
Dec.	1992	No. 113	Accounting and Reporting for Reinsurance of Short-Duration and Long-Duration Contracts
May	1993	No. 114	Accounting by Creditors for Impairment of a Loan (amended)
May	1993	No. 115	Accounting for Certain Investments in Debt and Equity Securities (amended)

Date Issued		No.	Title
June	1993	No. 116	Accounting for Contributions Received and Contributions Made
June	1993	No. 117	Financial Statements of Not-for-Profit Organizations (amended)
Oct.	1994	No. 118	Accounting by Creditors for Impairments of a Loan—Income Recognition and Disclosures
Oct.	1994	No. 119	Disclosure about Derivative Financial Instruments and Fair Value of Financial Instruments (superseded)
Jan.	1995	No. 120	Accounting and Reporting by Mutual Life Insurance Enterprises
Mar.	1995	No. 121	Accounting for the Impairment of Long-Lived Assets (superseded)
May	1995	No. 122	Accounting for Mortgage Servicing Rights (superseded)
Oct.	1995	No. 123	Accounting for Stock-Based Compensation (revised)
Nov.	1995	No. 124	Accounting for Certain Investments Held by Not-for-Profit Organizations
June	1996	No. 125	Accounting for Transfers and Servicing of Financial Assets and Extinguishment of Liabilities (amended)
Dec.	1996	No. 126	Exemption from Certain Required Disclosures about Financial Instruments for Certain Nonpublic Entities
Dec.	1996	No. 127	Deferral of the Effective Date of Certain Provisions of *FASB Statement No. 125*
Feb.	1997	No. 128	Earnings per Share (amended)
Feb.	1997	No. 129	Disclosure of Information about Capital Structure
June	1997	No. 130	Reporting Comprehensive Income
June	1997	No. 131	Reporting Disaggregated Information about a Business Enterprise
Feb.	1998	No. 132	Employers' Disclosures about Pensions and Other Postretirement Benefits – an amendment of *FASB Statements No. 87, 88,* and *106* (revised)
June	1998	No. 133	Accounting for Derivative Instruments and Hedging Activities (amended)
Oct.	1998	No. 134	Accounting for Mortgage-Backed Securities Retained after the Securitization of Mortgage Loans Held for Sale by a Mortgage Banking Enterprise (an amendment of *FASB Statement No. 65*)
Feb.	1999	No. 135	Rescission of *FASB Statement No. 75* and Technical Corrections (amended)
June	1999	No. 136	Transfers of Assets to a Not-for-Profit Organization or Charitable Trust That Raises or Holds Contributions for Others (amended)
June	1999	No. 137	Accounting for Derivative Instruments and Hedging Activities—Deferral of the Effective Date for *FASB Statement No. 133* (an amendment of *Statement No. 133*)
June	2000	No. 138	Accounting for Certain Derivative Instruments and Certain Hedging Activities (an amendment of *FASB Statement No. 133*)
June	2000	No. 139	Rescission of *FASB Statement No. 53* and amendments to *FASB Statements No. 63, 89,* and *121*
Sept.	2000	No. 140	Accounting for Transfers and Servicing of Financial Assets and Extinguishments of Liabilities (a replacement of *FASB Statement 125*)
June	2001	No. 141	Business Combinations (amended)
June	2001	No. 142	Goodwill and Other Intangible Assets (amended)
June	2001	No. 143	Accounting for Asset Retirement Obligations (amended)
Aug.	2001	No. 144	Accounting for the Impairment or Disposal of Long-Lived Assets (amended)
April	2002	No. 145	Rescission of *FASB Statements No. 4, 44,* and *64,* Amendment of *FASB Statement No. 13,* and Technical Corrections
June	2002	No. 146	Accounting for Costs Associated with Exit or Disposal Activities
Oct.	2002	No. 147	Acquisitions of Certain Financial Institutions, an Amendment of *FASB Statements No. 72* and *144* and *FASB Interpretation No. 9*
Dec.	2002	No. 148	Accounting for Stock-Based Compensation—Transition and Disclosure
April	2003	No. 149	Amendment of *Statement 133* on Derivative Instruments and Hedging Activities
May	2003	No. 150	Accounting for Certain Financial Instruments with Characteristics of Both Liabilities and Equity
Nov.	2004	No. 151	Inventory Costs – an amendment of *ARB No. 43*, Chapter 4
Dec.	2004	No. 152	Accounting for Real Estate Time-Sharing Transactions
Dec.	2004	No. 153	Exchanges on Non-Monetary Assets – an amendment of *APB Opinion No. 29*
May	2005	No. 154	Accounting Changes and Error Corrections – a replacement of *APB Opinion No. 20* and *FASB Statement No. 3*

Financial Accounting Standards Board (FASB), Interpretations (1974–2002)

June	1974	No. 1	Accounting Changes Related to the Cost of Inventory (*APB Opinion No. 20*)
June	1974	No. 2	Imputing Interest on Debt Arrangements Made Under the Federal Bankruptcy Act (*APB Opinion No. 21*) (superseded)
Dec.	1974	No. 3	Accounting for the Cost of Pension Plans Subject to the Employee Retirement Income Security Act of 1974 (*APB Opinion No. 8*)
Feb.	1975	No. 4	Applicability of *FASB Statement No. 2* to Purchase Business Combinations (amended)
Feb.	1975	No. 5	Applicability of *FASB Statement No. 2* to Development Stage Enterprises (superseded)
Feb.	1975	No. 6	Applicability of *FASB Statement No. 2* to Computer Software
Oct.	1975	No. 7	Applying *FASB Statement No. 7* in Statements of Established Enterprises
Jan.	1976	No. 8	Classification of a Short-Term Obligation Repaid Prior to Being Replaced by a Long-Term Security (*FASB Statement No. 6*)

Date Issued		No.	Title
Feb.	1976	No. 9	Applying *APB Opinion No. 16* and *17* when a Savings and Loan or Similar Institution is Acquired in a Purchase Business Combination (*APB Op. No. 16 & 17*) (amended)
Sept.	1976	No. 10	Application of *FASB Statement No. 12* to Personal Financial Statements (*FASB Statement No. 12*)
Sept.	1976	No. 11	Changes in Market Value after the Balance Sheet Date (*FASB Statement No. 12*)
Sept.	1976	No. 12	Accounting for Previously Established Allowance Accounts (*FASB Statement No. 12*)
Sept.	1976	No. 13	Consolidation of a Parent and Its Subsidiaries Having Different Balance Sheet Dates (*FASB Statement No. 12*)
Sept.	1976	No. 14	Reasonable Estimation of the Amount of a Loss (*FASB Statement No. 5*)
Sept.	1976	No. 15	Translation of Unamortized Policy Acquisition Costs by Stock Life Insurance Company (*FASB Statement No. 8*) (amended and partially superseded)
Feb.	1977	No. 16	Clarification of Definitions and Accounting for Marketable Equity Securities That Become Nonmarketable (*FASB Statement No. 12*)
Feb.	1977	No. 17	Applying the Lower of Cost or Market Rule in Translated Financial Statements (*FASB Statement No. 8*) (superseded)
Mar.	1977	No. 18	Accounting for Income Taxes in Interim Periods (*APB Op. No. 28*) (amended)
Oct.	1977	No. 19	Lessee Guarantee of the Residual Value of Leased Property (*FASB Statement No. 13*)
Nov.	1977	No. 20	Reporting Accounting Changes under AICPA Statements of Position (*APB Op. No. 20*)
April	1978	No. 21	Accounting for Leases in a Business Combination (*FASB Statement No. 13*) (amended)
April	1978	No. 22	Applicability of Indefinite Reversal Criteria to Timing Differences (*APB Op. No. 11 and 23*)
Aug.	1978	No. 23	Leases of Certain Property Owned by a Governmental Unit or Authority (*FASB Statement No. 13*)
Sept.	1978	No. 24	Leases Involving Only Part of a Building (*FASB Statement No. 13*)
Sept.	1978	No. 25	Accounting for an Unused Investment Tax Credit (*APB Op. No. 2, 4, 11, and 16*)
Sept.	1978	No. 26	Accounting for Purchase of a Leased Asset by the Lessee During the Term of the Lease (*FASB Statement No. 13*)
Nov.	1978	No. 27	Accounting for a Loss on a Sublease (*FASB Statement No. 13* and *APB Op. No. 30*) (amended)
Dec.	1978	No. 28	Accounting for Stock Appreciation Rights and Other Variable Stock Option or Award Plans (*APB Op. No. 15 and 25*) (amended)
Feb.	1979	No. 29	Reporting Tax Benefits Realized on Disposition of Investments in Certain Subsidiaries and Other Investees (*APB Op. No. 23 and 24*)
Sept.	1979	No. 30	Accounting for Involuntary Conversions of Nonmonetary Assets to Monetary Assets (*APB Op. No. 29*)
Feb.	1980	No. 31	Treatment of Stock Compensation Plans in EPS Computations (*APB Op. No. 15* and *Interp. 28*) (superseded)
Mar.	1980	No. 32	Application of Percentage Limitations in Recognizing Investment Tax Credit (*APB Op. No. 2, 4, and 11*)
Aug.	1980	No. 33	Applying FASB Statement No. 34 to Oil and Gas Producing Operations (*FASB Statement No. 34*)
Mar.	1981	No. 34	Disclosure of Indirect Guarantees of Indebtedness of Others (*FASB Statement No. 5*)
May	1981	No. 35	Criteria for Applying the Equity Method of Accounting for Investments in Common Stock (*APB Op. No. 18*)
Oct.	1981	No. 36	Accounting for Exploratory Wells in Progress at the End of a Period
July	1983	No. 37	Accounting for Translation Adjustments upon Sale of Part of an Investment in a Foreign Entity (Interprets *FASB Statement No. 52*)
Aug.	1984	No. 38	Determining the Measurement Date for Stock Option, Purchase, and Award Plans Involving Junior Stock (Interprets *APB Opinion No. 25*)
Mar.	1992	No. 39	Offsetting of Amounts Related to Certain Contracts (Interprets *APB Opinion No. 10* and *FASB Statement No. 105*) (amended)
Apr.	1993	No. 40	Applicability of Generally Accepted Accounting Principles to Mutual Life Insurance and Other Enterprises (Interprets *FASB Statements No. 12, 60, 97, and 113*)
Dec.	1994	No. 41	Offsetting of Amounts Related to Certain Repurchase and Reverse Repurchase Agreements
Sept.	1996	No. 42	Accounting for Transfers of Assets in Which a Not-for-Profit Organization is Granted Variance Power
June	1999	No. 43	Real Estate Sales (Interprets FASB Statement No. 66) (amended)
		No. 44	Accounting for Certain Transactions involving Stock Compensation (an interpretation of *APB Opinion No. 25*) (amended)
Nov.	2002	No. 45	Guarantor's Accounting and Disclosure Requirements for Guarantees, Including Indirect Guarantees of Indebtedness of Others
Jan.	2003	No. 46	Consolidation of Variable Interest Entities (an interpretation of *ARB No. 51*, revised)
March	2005	No. 47	Accounting for Conditional Asset Retirement Obligations – an interpretation of *FASB Statement No. 143*

Date Issued		No.	Title

**Financial Accounting Standards Board (FASB),
Technical Bulletins (1979–2002)**

Date	Year	No.	Title
Dec.	1979	No. 79-1	Purpose and Scope of FASB Technical Bulletins and Procedures for Issuance (revised)
Dec.	1979	No. 79-2	Computer Software Costs
Dec.	1979	No. 79-3	Subjective Acceleration Clauses in Long-Term Debt Agreements
Dec.	1979	No. 79-4	Segment Reporting of Puerto Rican Operations
Dec.	1979	No. 79-5	Meaning of the Term 'Customer' as it Applies to Health Care Facilities under *FASB Statement No. 14*
Dec.	1979	No. 79-6	Valuation Allowances Following Debt Restructuring
Dec.	1979	No. 79-7	Recoveries of a Previous Writedown under a Troubled Debt Restructuring Involving a Modification of Terms
Dec.	1979	No. 79-8	Applicability of *FASB Statements 21* and *33* to Certain Brokers and Dealers in Securities
Dec.	1979	No. 79-9	Accounting in Interim Periods for Changes in Income Tax Rates
Dec.	1979	No. 79-10	Fiscal Funding Clauses in Lease Agreements
Dec.	1979	No. 79-11	Effect of a Penalty on the Term of a Lease
Dec.	1979	No. 79-12	Interest Rate Used in Calculating the Present Value of Minimum Lease Payments
Dec.	1979	No. 79-13	Applicability of *FASB Statement No. 13* to Current Value Financial Statements
Dec.	1979	No. 79-14	Upward Adjustment of Guaranteed Residual Values
Dec.	1979	No. 79-15	Accounting for Loss on a Sublease Not Involving the Disposal of a Segment
Dec.	1979	No. 79-16	Effect on a Change in Income Tax Rate on the Accounting for Leveraged Leases (revised)
Dec.	1979	No. 79-17	Reporting Cumulative Effect Adjustment from Retroactive Application of *FASB No. 13*
Dec.	1979	No. 79-18	Transition Requirements of Certain FASB Amendments and Interpretations of *FASB Statement No. 13*
Dec.	1979	No. 79-19	Investor's Accounting for Unrealized Losses on Marketable Securities Owned by an Equity Method Investee
Dec.	1980	No. 80-1	Early Extinguishment of Debt through Exchange for Common or Preferred Stock (amended)
Dec.	1980	No. 80-2	Classification of Debt Restructuring by Debtors and Creditors
Feb.	1981	No. 81-1	Disclosure of Interest Rate Futures Contracts and Forward and Standby Contracts
Feb.	1981	No. 81-2	Accounting for Unused Investment Tax Credits Acquired in a Business Combination Accounted for by the Purchase Method
Feb.	1981	No. 81-3	Multiemployer Pension Plan Amendments Act of 1980
Feb.	1981	No. 81-4	Classification as Monetary or Nonmonetary Items
Feb.	1981	No. 81-5	Offsetting Interest Cost to be Capitalized with Interest Income
Nov.	1981	No. 81-6	Applicability of Statement 15 to Debtors in Bankruptcy Situations
Jan.	1982	No. 82-1	Disclosure of the Sale or Purchase of Tax Benefits through Tax Leases (amended)
Mar.	1982	No. 82-2	Accounting for the Conversion of Stock Options into Incentive Stock Options as a Result of the Economic Recovery Tax Act of 1981
July	1983	No. 83-1	Accounting for the Reduction in the Tax Basis of an Asset Caused by the Investment Tax Credit (ITC)
Mar.	1984	No. 84-1	Accounting for Stock Issued to Acquire the Results of a Research and Development Arrangement (amended)
Sept.	1984	No. 84-2	Accounting for the Effects of the Tax Reform Act of 1984 on Deferred Income Taxes Relating to Domestic International Sales Corporations
Sept.	1984	No. 84-3	Accounting for the Effects of the Tax Reform Act of 1984 on Deferred Income Taxes of Stock Life Insurance Enterprises
Oct.	1984	No. 84-4	In-Substance Defeasance of Debt
Mar.	1985	No. 85-1	Accounting for the Receipt of Federal Home Loan Mortgage Corporation Participating Preferred Stock
Mar.	1985	No. 85-2	Accounting for Collateralized Mortgage Obligations (CMOs) (superseded)
Nov.	1985	No. 85-3	Accounting for Operating Leases with Scheduled Rent Increases
Nov.	1985	No. 85-4	Accounting for Purchases of Life Insurance (superseded)
Dec.	1985	No. 85-5	Issues Relating to Accounting for Business Combinations (amended)
Dec.	1985	No. 85-6	Accounting for a Purchase of Treasury Shares
Oct.	1986	No. 86-1	Accounting for Certain Effects of the Tax Reform Act of 1986
Dec.	1986	No. 86-2	Accounting for an Interest in the Residual Value of a Leased Asset (amended)
April	1987	No. 87-1	Accounting for a Change in Method of Accounting for Certain Postretirement Benefits
Dec.	1987	No. 87-2	Computation of a Loss on an Abandonment
Dec.	1987	No. 87-3	Accounting for Mortgage Servicing Fees and Rights (amended)
Dec.	1988	No. 88-1	Issues Relating to Accounting for Leases
Dec.	1988	No. 88-2	Definition of a Right of Setoff
Dec.	1990	No. 90-1	Accounting for Separately Priced Extended Warranty and Product Maintenance Contracts
Apr.	1994	No. 94-1	Application of *Statement 115* to Debt Securities Restructured in a Troubled Debt Restructuring
Dec.	1997	No. 97-1	Accounting under *Statement 123* for Certain Employee Stock Purchase Plans with a Look-Back Option
July	2001	No. 01-1	Effective Date for Certain Financial Institutions of Certain Provisions of *Statement No. 140* Related to the Isolation of Transferred Financial Assets

Date Issued		No.		Title

**Financial Accounting Standards Board (FASB),
Statements of Financial Accounting Concepts (1978–2002)**

Nov.	1978	No.	1	Objectives of Financial Reporting by Business Enterprises
May	1980	No.	2	Qualitative Characteristics of Accounting Information
Dec.	1980	No.	3	Elements of Financial Statements of Business Enterprises
Dec.	1980	No.	4	Objectives of Financial Reporting by Nonbusiness Organizations
Dec.	1984	No.	5	Recognition and Measurement in Financial Statements of Business Enterprises
Dec.	1985	No.	6	Elements of Financial Statements
Feb.	2000	No.	7	Using Cash Flow Information and Present Value in Accounting Measurements

NATIONAL ACCOUNTING BOARDS AND ORGANIZATIONS

American Accounting Association (AAA)
5717 Bessie Drive
Sarasota, FL 34233-2399
(941) 921-7747
www.aaahq.org

American Institute of Certified Public Accountants
(AICPA)
1211 Avenue of the Americas
New York, NY 10036-8775
(212) 596-6200
www.aicpa.org

Association of Government Accountants (AGA)
2208 Mount Vernon Ave.
Alexandria, VA 22301-1314
(703) 684-6931
www.agacgfm.org

Financial Accounting Standards Board (FASB)
401 Merritt 7
P.O. Box 5116
Norwalk, CT 06856-5116
(203) 847-0700
www.fasb.org

Financial Executives International (FEI)
200 Campus Drive
Florham Park, NJ 07932-0674
(973) 765-1000
www.fei.org

Governmental Accounting Standards Board (GASB)
401 Merritt 7
P.O. Box 5116
Norwalk, CT 06856-5116
(203) 847-0700
www.gasb.org

International Accounting Standards Board (IASB)
30 Cannon Street
London EC4M 6XH, United Kingdom
Telephone: +44 (0)20 7246 6410
www.iasb.org

Institute of Internal Auditors (IIA)
247 Maitland Avenue
Altamonte Springs, FL 32701-4201
(407) 937-1100
www.theiia.org

Institute of Management Accountants (IMA)
10 Paragon Drive
Montvale, NJ 07645-1718
(201) 573-9000
www.imanet.org

Securities and Exchange Commission (SEC)
100 F Street, NE
Washington, DC 20549
(202) 551-6551
www.sec.gov